FOR REFERENCE

Do Not Take From This Room

DELPHI PUBLIC LIBRARY

222 East Main Street
Delphi, Indiana 46923
765-564-2929

CRITICAL SURVEY OF

Long Fiction

Fourth Edition

CRITICAL SURVEY OF

Long Fiction

Fourth Edition

Volume 2
Charlotte Brontë—Robertson Davies

Editor
Carl Rollyson
Baruch College, City University of New York

SALEM PRESS
Pasadena, California   Hackensack, New Jersey

Editor in Chief: Dawn P. Dawson

Editorial Director: Christina J. Moose *Research Supervisor:* Jeffry Jensen
Development Editor: Tracy Irons-Georges *Research Assistant:* Keli Trousdale
Project Editor: Judy Selhorst *Production Editor:* Joyce I. Buchea
Manuscript Editor: Desiree Dreeuws *Design and Graphics:* James Hutson
Acquisitions Editor: Mark Rehn *Layout:* William Zimmerman
Editorial Assistant: Brett S. Weisberg *Photo Editor:* Cynthia Breslin Beres

Cover photo: Charlotte Brontë (The Granger Collection, New York)

Copyright © 1983, 1984, 1987, 1991, 2000, 2010, by SALEM PRESS

All rights in this book are reserved. No part of this work may be used or reproduced in any manner whatsoever or transmitted in any form or by any means, electronic or mechanical, including photocopy, recording, or any information storage and retrieval system, without written permission from the copyright owner except in the case of brief quotations embodied in critical articles and reviews or in the copying of images deemed to be freely licensed or in the public domain. For information address the publisher, Salem Press, at csr@salempress.com.

Some of the essays in this work, which have been updated, originally appeared in the following Salem Press publications: *Critical Survey of Long Fiction, English Language Series* (1983), *Critical Survey of Long Fiction, Foreign Language Series* (1984), *Critical Survey of Long Fiction, Supplement* (1987), *Critical Survey of Long Fiction, English Language Series, Revised Edition* (1991; preceding volumes edited by Frank N. Magill), *Critical Survey of Long Fiction, Second Revised Edition* (2000; edited by Carl Rollyson).

∞ The paper used in these volumes conforms to the American National Standard for Permanence of Paper for Printed Library Materials, Z39.48-1992 (R1997).

Library of Congress Cataloging-in-Publication Data

Critical survey of long fiction / editor, Carl Rollyson. — 4th ed.
   p.   cm.
   Includes bibliographical references and index.
   ISBN 978-1-58765-535-7 (set : alk. paper) — ISBN 978-1-58765-536-4 (vol. 1 : alk. paper) —
ISBN 978-1-58765-537-1 (vol. 2 : alk. paper) — ISBN 978-1-58765-538-8 (vol. 3 : alk. paper) —
ISBN 978-1-58765-539-5 (vol. 4 : alk. paper) — ISBN 978-1-58765-540-1 (vol. 5 : alk. paper) —
ISBN 978-1-58765-541-8 (vol. 6 : alk. paper) — ISBN 978-1-58765-542-5 (vol. 7 : alk. paper) —
ISBN 978-1-58765-543-2 (vol. 8 : alk. paper) — ISBN 978-1-58765-544-9 (vol. 9 : alk. paper) —
ISBN 978-1-58765-545-6 (vol. 10 : alk. paper)
1. Fiction—History and criticism. 2. Fiction—Bio-bibliography—Dictionaries. 3. Authors—Biography—
Dictionaries. I. Rollyson, Carl E. (Carl Edmund)
   PN3451.C75 2010
   809.3—dc22
                                                                              2009044410

First Printing

PRINTED IN CANADA

CONTENTS

COMPLETE LIST OF CONTENTS

VOLUME 1

VOLUME 2

VOLUME 3

VOLUME 4

Contents lxxv

Volume 5

VOLUME 6

Contents cxv
Complete List of Contents cxvii
Pronunciation Key cxxvii

Volume 7

VOLUME 8

VOLUME 9

LONG FICTION IN HISTORY

WORLD LONG FICTION

VOLUME 10

WORLD LONG FICTION (*continued*)

NORTH AMERICAN LONG FICTION

GENRE OVERVIEWS

RESOURCES

INDEXES

PRONUNCIATION KEY

Foreign and unusual or ambiguous English-language names of profiled authors may be unfamiliar to some users of the *Critical Survey of Long Fiction*. To help readers pronounce such names correctly, phonetic spellings using the character symbols listed below appear in parentheses immediately after the first mention of the author's name in the narrative text. Stressed syllables are indicated in capital letters, and syllables are separated by hyphens.

VOWEL SOUNDS

Symbol	*Spelled (Pronounced)*
a	answer (AN-suhr), laugh (laf), sample (SAM-puhl), that (that)
ah	father (FAH-thur), hospital (HAHS-pih-tuhl)
aw	awful (AW-fuhl), caught (kawt)
ay	blaze (blayz), fade (fayd), waiter (WAYT-ur), weigh (way)
eh	bed (behd), head (hehd), said (sehd)
ee	believe (bee-LEEV), cedar (SEE-dur), leader (LEED-ur), liter (LEE-tur)
ew	boot (bewt), lose (lewz)
i	buy (bi), height (hit), lie (li), surprise (sur-PRIZ)
ih	bitter (BIH-tur), pill (pihl)
o	cotton (KO-tuhn), hot (hot)
oh	below (bee-LOH), coat (koht), note (noht), wholesome (HOHL-suhm)
oo	good (good), look (look)
ow	couch (kowch), how (how)
oy	boy (boy), coin (koyn)
uh	about (uh-BOWT), butter (BUH-tuhr), enough (ee-NUHF), other (UH-thur)

CONSONANT SOUNDS

Symbol	*Spelled (Pronounced)*
ch	beach (beech), chimp (chihmp)
g	beg (behg), disguise (dihs-GIZ), get (geht)
j	digit (DIH-juht), edge (ehj), jet (jeht)
k	cat (kat), kitten (KIH-tuhn), hex (hehks)
s	cellar (SEHL-ur), save (sayv), scent (sehnt)
sh	champagne (sham-PAYN), issue (IH-shew), shop (shop)
ur	birth (burth), disturb (dihs-TURB), earth (urth), letter (LEH-tur)
y	useful (YEWS-fuhl), young (yuhng)
z	business (BIHZ-nehs), zest (zehst)
zh	vision (VIH-zhuhn)

CRITICAL SURVEY OF

Long Fiction

Fourth Edition

CHARLOTTE BRONTË

Born: Thornton, Yorkshire, England; April 21,
1816
Died: Haworth, Yorkshire, England; March 31,
1855
Also known as: Currer Bell

PRINCIPAL LONG FICTION

Jane Eyre: An Autobiography, 1847
Shirley, 1849
Villette, 1853
The Professor, 1857

OTHER LITERARY FORMS

The nineteen poems selected by Charlotte Brontë
(BRAHNT-ee) to print with her sister Anne's work in
Poems by Currer, Ellis, and Acton Bell (1846) were her
only other works published during her lifetime. The juvenilia produced by the four Brontë children—Charlotte,
Emily, Anne, and Branwell—between 1824 and 1839
are scattered in libraries and private collections. Some of
Charlotte's contributions have been published in *The
Twelve Adventurers, and Other Stories* (1925), *Legends
of Angria* (1933), *The Search After Happiness* (1969),
Five Novelettes (1971), and *The Secret and Lily Hart*
(1979). A fragment of a novel written during the last year
of Brontë's life was published as *Emma* in the *Cornhill
Magazine* in 1860 and is often reprinted in editions of
The Professor. The Complete Poems of Charlotte Brontë
appeared in 1923. Other brief selections, fragments, and
ephemera have been printed in *Transactions and Other
Publications of the Brontë Society*. The nineteen-volume
Shakespeare Head Brontë (1931-1938), edited by T. J.
Wise and J. A. Symington, contains all of the novels,
four volumes of life and letters, two volumes of miscel-
laneous writings, and two volumes of poems.

ACHIEVEMENTS

Charlotte Brontë brought to English fiction an intensely personal voice. Her books show the moral and
emotional growth of her protagonists almost entirely by
self-revelation. Her novels focus on individual self-
fulfillment; they express the subjective interior world

not only in thoughts, dreams, visions, and symbols but
also by projecting inner states through external objects, secondary characters, places, events, and weather.
Brontë's own experiences and emotions inform the narrative presence. "Perhaps no other writer of her time,"
wrote Margaret Oliphant in 1855, "has impressed her
mark so clearly on contemporary literature, or drawn so
many followers into her own peculiar path."

The personal voice, which blurs the distances separating novelist, protagonist, and reader, accounts for
much of the critical ambivalence toward Brontë's work.
Generations of unsophisticated readers have identified
with Jane Eyre; thousands of romances and modern
gothics have used Brontë's situations and invited readers
to step into the fantasy. Brontë's novels, however, are
much more than simply the common reader's daydreams. They are rich enough to allow a variety of critical approaches. They have been studied in relation to traditions (gothic, provincial, realistic, Romantic); read for
psychological, linguistic, Christian, social, economic,
and personal interpretations; and analyzed in terms of
symbolism, imagery, metaphor, viewpoint, narrative
distance, and prose style. Because the novels are so
clearly wrought from the materials of their author's life,
psychoanalytic and feminist criticism has proved rewarding. In Brontë's work, a woman author makes significant statements about issues central to women's
lives. Most of her heroines are working women; each
feels the pull of individual self-development against the
wish for emotional fulfillment, the tension between sexual energies and social realities, the almost unresolvable
conflict between love and independence.

BIOGRAPHY

Charlotte Brontë was the third of six children born
within seven years to the Reverend Patrick Brontë and
his wife Maria Branwell Brontë. Patrick Brontë was perpetual curate of Haworth, a bleak manufacturing town in
Yorkshire, England. In 1821, when Charlotte was five
years old, her mother died of cancer. Three years later,
the four elder girls were sent to the Clergy Daughters'
School at Cowan Bridge—the school that appears as

Lowood in *Jane Eyre*. In the summer of 1825, the eldest two daughters, Maria and Elizabeth, died of tuberculosis. Charlotte and Emily were removed from the school and brought home. There were no educated middle-class families in Haworth to supply friends and companions for the Brontë children; they lived with a noncommunicative aunt, an elderly servant, and a father much preoccupied by his intellectual interests and his own griefs.

In their home and with only one another for company, the children had material for both educational and imaginative development. Patrick Brontë expected his children to read and to carry on adult conversations about politics. He subscribed to *Blackwood's Edinburgh Magazine*, where his children had access to political and economic essays, art criticism, and literary reviews. They had annuals with engravings of fine art; they taught themselves to draw by copying the pictures in minute detail. They were free to do reading that would not have been permitted by any school of the time—by the age of thirteen, Charlotte Brontë was fully acquainted not only with John Milton and Sir Walter Scott but also with Robert Southey, William Cowper, and (most important) Lord Byron.

In 1826, Branwell was given a set of wooden toy soldiers, and the four children used these as characters in creative play. The individual soldiers gradually took on personal characteristics and acquired countries to rule. The countries needed cities, governments, ruling families, political intrigues, legends, and citizens with private lives, all of which the children happily invented. In 1829, when Charlotte Brontë was thirteen, she and the others began to write down materials from these fantasies, producing a collection of juvenilia that extended ultimately to hundreds of items: magazines, histories, maps, essays, tales, dramas, poems, newspapers, wills, speeches, scrapbooks. This enormous creative production in adolescence gave concrete form to motifs that were later transformed into situations, characters, and concerns of Charlotte Brontë's mature work. It was also a workshop for literary technique; the young author explored prose style, experimented with viewpoint, and discovered how to control narrative voice. A single event, she learned, could be the basis for both a newspaper story and a romance, and the romance could be told by one of the protagonists or by a detached observer.

Because Patrick Brontë had no income beyond his salary, his daughters had to prepare to support themselves. In 1831, when she was almost fifteen, Charlotte Brontë went to Miss Wooler's School at Roe Head. After returning home for a time to tutor her sisters, she went back to Miss Wooler's as a teacher. Over the next several years, all three sisters held positions as governesses in private families. None, however, was happy as a governess; aside from the predictable difficulties caused by burdensome work and undisciplined children, they all suffered when separated from their shared emotional and creative life. A possible solution would have been to open their own school, but they needed some special qualification to attract pupils. Charlotte conceived a plan for going abroad to study languages. In 1842, she and Emily went to Brussels to the Pensionnat Héger. They returned in November because of their aunt's death, but in the following year Charlotte went back to Brussels alone to work as a pupil-teacher. An additional reason for her return to Brussels was that she desired to be near Professor Constantine Héger, but at the end of the year she left in misery after Héger's wife had realized (perhaps more clearly than did Charlotte herself) the romantic nature of the attraction.

In 1844, at the age of twenty-eight, Charlotte Brontë established herself permanently at Haworth. The prospectus for "The Misses Brontë's Establishment" was published, but no pupils applied. Branwell, dismissed in disgrace from his post as tutor, came home to drink, take opium, and disintegrate. Charlotte spent nearly two years in deep depression: Her yearning for love was unsatisfied, and she had repressed her creative impulse because she was afraid her fantasies were self-indulgent. Then, with the discovery that all three had written poetry, the sisters found a new aim in life. A joint volume of poems was published in May, 1846, though it sold only two copies. Each wrote a short novel; they offered the three together to publishers. Emily Brontë's *Wuthering Heights* (1847) and Anne Brontë's *Agnes Grey* (1847) were accepted. Charlotte Brontë's *The Professor* was refused, but one editor, George Smith, said he would like to see a three-volume novel written by its author. *Jane Eyre* was by that time almost finished; it was sent to Smith on August 24, 1847, and impressed him so much that he had it in print by the middle of October.

Jane Eyre was immediately successful, but there was barely any time for its author to enjoy her fame and accomplishment. Within a single year, her three companions in creation died: Branwell on September 24, 1848; Emily on December 19, 1848; and Anne on May 28, 1849. When Charlotte Brontë began work on *Shirley*, she met with her sisters in the evenings to exchange ideas, read aloud, and offer criticism. By the time she finished the manuscript, she was alone.

Brontë's sense that she was plain, "undeveloped," and unlikely to be loved seems to have been partly the product of her own psychological condition. She had refused more than one proposal in her early twenties. In 1852 there was another, from Arthur Bell Nicholls, curate at Haworth. Patrick Brontë objected violently and dismissed his curate. Gradually, however, the objections were worn away. On June 29, 1854, Charlotte Brontë and the Reverend Nicholls were married and, after a brief honeymoon tour, took up residence in Haworth parsonage. After a few months of apparent content—which did not prevent her from beginning work on another novel—Charlotte Brontë died on March 31, 1855, at the age of thirty-eight; a severe cold made her too weak to survive the complications of her early pregnancy.

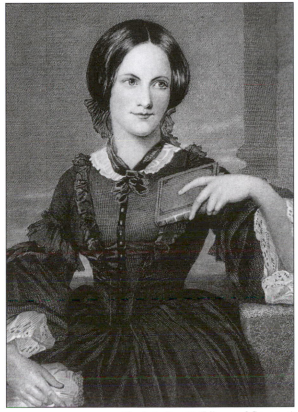

Charlotte Brontë. (Library of Congress)

ANALYSIS

The individualism and richness of Charlotte Brontë's work arise from the multiple ways in which Brontë's writing is personal: observation and introspection, rational analysis and spontaneous emotion, accurate mimesis and private symbolism. Tension and ambiguity grow from the intersections and conflicts among these levels of writing and, indeed, among the layers of the self.

Few writers of English prose have so successfully communicated the emotional texture of inner life while still constructing fictions with enough verisimilitude to appear realistic. Brontë startled the Victorians because her work was so little influenced by the books of her own era. Its literary forebears were the written corporate daydreams of her childhood and the Romantic poets she read during the period when the fantasies took shape. Certain characters and situations that crystallized the emotional conflicts of early adolescence became necessary components of emotional satisfaction. The source

of these fantasies was, to a degree, beyond control, occurring in the region the twentieth century has termed "the unconscious"; by writing them down from childhood on, Brontë learned to preserve and draw on relatively undisguised desires and ego conflicts in a way lost to most adults.

The power and reality of the inner life disturbed Brontë after she had passed through adolescence; she compared her creative urge to the action of opium and was afraid that she might become lost in her "infernal world." When she began to think of publication, she deliberately used material from her own experience and reported scenes and characters in verifiable detail. In this way, she hoped to subdue the exaggerated romanticism—and the overwrought writing—of the fantasy fictions. "Details, situations which I do not understand and cannot personally inspect," she wrote to her publisher, "I would not for the world meddle with." Her drawing from life was so accurate that the curates and the Yorkes in

Shirley were recognized at once by people who knew them, and Brontë lost the protection that her pseudonym had provided.

The years of practice in writing fiction that satisfied her own emotional needs gave Brontë the means to produce powerful psychological effects. She uses a variety of resources to make readers share the protagonist's subjective state. The truth of the outside world is only that truth which reflects the narrator's feelings and perceptions. All characters are aspects of the consciousness that creates them: Brontë uses splitting, doubling, and other fairy-tale devices; she replicates key situations; she carefully controls the narrative distance and the amount of information readers have at their disposal.

The unquietness that Brontë's readers often feel grows from the tension between direct emotional satisfactions (often apparently immature) on one hand and, on the other, mature and realistic conflicts in motive, reason, and sense of self. Read as a sequence, the four completed novels demonstrate both Brontë's development and the story of a woman's relationship to the world. Brontë's heroines find identity outside the enclosed family popularly supposed to circumscribe nineteenth century women. Isolation allows the heroines' self-development, but it impedes their romantic yearning to be lost in love.

THE PROFESSOR

At the beginning of *The Professor*, William Crimsworth is working as a clerk in a mill owned by his proud elder brother. He breaks away, goes to Brussels to teach English, survives a brief attraction to a seductive older woman, and then comes to love Frances Henri, an orphaned Anglo-Swiss lace mender who had been his pupil.

Brontë's narrative devices supply shifting masks that both expose and evade the self. The epistolary opening keeps readers from identifying directly with Crimsworth but draws them into the novel as recipients of his revelations. The masculine persona, which Brontë used frequently in the juvenilia, gives her access to the literary mainstream and creates possibilities for action, attitude, and initiative that did not exist in models for female stories. The juvenile fantasies supply the feud between two brothers; the Belgian scenes and characters come from Brontë's own experiences. Although nominally male,

Crimsworth is in an essentially female situation: disinherited, passive, timid. He has, furthermore, an exaggerated awareness and fear of the sexual overtones in human behavior.

Biographical details also go into the making of Frances Henri, the friendless older student working to pay for her lessons in the Belgian school. The poem that Frances writes is one Brontë had created out of her own yearning for Professor Héger. In *The Professor*, the dream can come true; the poem awakens the teacher's response.

Like the central figures in all Brontë novels, both Crimsworth and Frances enact a Cinderella plot. Each begins as an oppressed outcast and ends successful, confident, and satisfactorily placed in society. The details of Crimsworth's story work both symbolically and functionally. The imprisoning situations in the factory and the school reflect his perception of the world. At the same time, these situations are created by his own inner barriers. His bondage as a despised clerk is self-induced; he is an educated adult male who could move on at any time. In Belgium, he plods a treadmill of guilt because of Zoraïde Reuter's sexual manipulativeness—for which he is not responsible. His self-suppression is also seen through Yorke Hunsden, who appears whenever Crimsworth must express strong emotion. Hunsden voices anger and rebellion not permitted to the male/female narrator and becomes a voyeuristic alter ego to appreciate Frances and love.

The novel is weakest when it fails to integrate the biography, the emotion, and the ideas. True moral dilemmas are not developed. The heroine, seen through sympathetic male eyes, wins love for her writing, her pride, and her self-possession, and she continues to work even after she has a child. Brontë solves her chronic romantic dilemma (How can a strong woman love if woman's love is defined as willing subordination?) by letting Frances vibrate between two roles: She is the stately directress of the school by day, the little lace mender by night.

JANE EYRE

In *Jane Eyre*, Brontë created a story that has the authority of myth. Everything that had deeply affected her is present in the book's emotional content. The traumatic experiences of maternal deprivation, the Clergy Daughters' School, and Maria's death create the events of

Jane's early life. The book also taps universal feelings of rejection, victimization, and loneliness, making them permissible by displacement: The hateful children are cousins, not siblings; the bad adult an aunt, not a mother. Rochester's compelling power as a lover derives from neither literal nor literary sources—Rochester is the man Brontë had loved for twenty years, the duke of Zamorna who dominates the adolescent fantasies, exerting a power on both Jane and the reader that can hardly be explained by reason. Jane defied literary convention because she was poor, plain, and a heroine; she defied social convention by refusing to accept any external authority. Placed repeatedly in situations that exemplify male power, Jane resists and survives. At the end of the narrative, she is transformed from Cinderella to Prince Charming, becoming the heroine who cuts through the brambles to rescue the imprisoned sleeper. Identification is so immediate and so close that readers often fail to notice Brontë's control of distance, in particular the points of detachment when an older Jane comments on her younger self and the direct addresses from Jane to the reader that break the spell when emotions become too strong.

Place controls the book's structure. Events at Gateshead, Lowood, Thornfield, and Moor House determine Jane's development; a brief coda at Ferndean provides the resolution. Each of the four major sections contains a figure representing the sources of male power over women: John Reed (physical force and the patriarchal family), Reverend Brocklehurst (the social structures of class, education, and religion), Rochester (sexual attraction), and St. John Rivers (moral and spiritual authority). Jane protects herself at first by devious and indirect means—fainting, illness, flight—and then ultimately, in rejecting St. John Rivers, by direct confrontation. Compelled by circumstances to fend for herself, she comes—at first instinctively, later rationally—to rely on herself.

The book's emotional power grows from its total absorption in Jane's view of the world and from the images, symbols, and structures that convey multiple interwoven reverberations. The red room—which suggests violence, irrationality, enclosure, rebellion, rebirth, the bloody chamber of emerging womanhood—echoes throughout the book. The Bridewell charade, Jane's paintings, the buildings and terrain, and a multitude of other details have both meaning and function. Characters double and split: Helen Burns (mind) and Bertha Mason (body) are aspects of Jane as well as actors in the plot. Recurring images of ice and fire suggest fatal coldness without and consuming fire within. Rochester's sexuality is the most threatening and ambiguous aspect of masculine power because of Jane's own complicity and her need for love. Her terrors and dreams accumulate as the marriage approaches; there are drowning images, abyss images, loss of consciousness. She refuses to become Rochester's mistress, finally, not because of the practical and moral dangers (which she does recognize) but because she fears her own willingness to make a god of him. She will not become dependent; she escapes to preserve her self.

As Jane takes her life into her own hands, she becomes less needy. After she has achieved independence by discovering a family and inheriting money, she is free to seek out Rochester. At the same time, he has become less omnipotent, perhaps a code for the destruction of patriarchal power. Thus, the marriage not only ends the romance and resolves the moral, emotional, and sexual conflicts but also supplies a satisfactory woman's fantasy of independence coupled with love.

SHIRLEY

For the book that would follow *Jane Eyre*, Brontë deliberately sought a new style and subject matter. *Shirley*, set in 1812, concerns two public issues still relevant in 1848—working-class riots and the condition of women. Brontë did historical research in newspaper files. She used a panoramic scene, included a variety of characters observed from life, and added touches of comedy. *Shirley* is told in the third person; the interest is divided between two heroines, neither of whom is a persona. Nevertheless, Brontë is strongly present in the narrative voice, which remains objective only in scenes of action. The authorial commentary, more strongly even than the events themselves, creates a tone of anger, rebellion, suffering, and doubt.

The novel is clearly plotted, although the mechanics are at times apparent. Brontë shifts focus among characters and uses reported conversations to violate the time sequence so that she can arrange events in the most effective dramatic order. Robert Moore, owner of a cloth mill, arouses the workers' wrath by introducing machinery. Caroline Helstone loves Robert, but her affection is not reciprocated. Although Caroline has a comfortable home with her uncle the rector, she is almost fatally depressed by lack of love and occupation. Property owner Shirley Keeldar discovers that having a man's name, position, and forthrightness gives her some power but fails to make her man's equal; she is simply more valuable as a matrimonial prize. Louis Moore, Shirley's former tutor, loves her silently because he lacks wealth and social position. Eventually Robert, humbled by Shirley's contempt and weakened by a workman's bullet, declares his love for Caroline, who has in the meantime discovered her mother and grown much stronger. Shirley's union with Louis is more ambivalent; she loves him because he is a master she can look up to, but she is seen on her wedding day as a pantheress pining for virginal freedom.

The primary source of women's tribulation is dependency. Caroline Helstone craves occupation to fill her time, make her financially independent, and give her life purpose. Women become psychologically dependent on men because they have so little else to think about. Brontë examines the lives of several old maids; they are individuals, not stereotypes, but they are all lonely. Shirley and Caroline dissect John Milton, search for female roots, and talk cozily about men's inadequacies. They cannot, however, speak honestly to each other about their romantic feelings. Caroline must hold to herself the deep pain of unrequited love.

Although *Shirley* deliberately moves beyond the isolated mythic world of *Jane Eyre* to put women's oppression in the context of a society rent by other power struggles (workers against employers, England against France, Church against Nonconformity), the individualistic ending only partially resolves the divisions. Brontë's narrative tone in the final passage is bleak and bitter. She reminds readers that *Shirley*'s events are history. Fieldhead Hollow is covered by mills and mill housing; magic is gone from the world.

Villette

Villette is Brontë's most disciplined novel. Because *The Professor* had not been published, Brontë was able to rework the Brussels experience without masks, as a story of loneliness and female deprivation, deliberately subduing the wish fulfillment and making her uncompromising self-examination control form as well as feel-

ing. Lucy Snowe is a woman without money, family, friends, or health. She is not, however, a sympathetic, friendly narrator like Jane Eyre. Her personality has the unattractiveness that realistically grows from deprivation; she has no social ease, no warmth, no mental quickness. Furthermore, her personality creates her pain, loneliness, and disengagement.

In the book's early sections, Lucy is not even the center of her narrative. She watches and judges instead of taking part; she tells other people's stories instead of her own. She is so self-disciplined that she appears to have neither feelings nor imagination, so restrained that she never reveals the facts about her family or the incidents of her youth that might explain to readers how and why she learned to suppress emotion, hope, and the desire for human contact. Despite—or perhaps because of—her anesthetized feeling and desperate shyness, Lucy Snowe drives herself to actions that might have been inconceivable for a woman more thoroughly socialized. Thrust into the world by the death of the elderly woman whose companion she had been, she goes alone to London, takes a ship for the Continent, gets a job as nursemaid, rises through her own efforts to teach in Madame Beck's school, and begins laying plans to open a school of her own.

The coincidental and melodramatic elements of the story gain authenticity because they grow from Lucy's inner life. When she is left alone in the school during vacation, her repressed need to be heard by someone drives her to enter the confessional of a Catholic church. Once the internal barrier is breached, she immediately meets the Bretton family. Realistically, she must have known they were in Villette; she knew that "Dr. John" was Graham Bretton, but she withheld that information from the reader both because of her habitual secretiveness and also because she did not really "know" the Brettons were accessible to her until she was able to admit her need to reach out for human sympathy. The characterization of Paul Emanuel gains richness and detail in such a manner that readers realize—before Lucy herself dares admit it—that she is interested in him. The phantom nun, at first a night terror of pure emotion, is revealed as a prankish disguise when Lucy is free to express feelings directly.

The novel's ending, however, is deliberately ambiguous, though not in event. (Only the most naïve readers dare accept Brontë's invitation to imagine that Paul Emanuel escapes drowning and to "picture union and a happy succeeding life.") The ambiguity grows from Lucy's earlier statement: "M. Emanuel was away for three years. Reader, they were the three happiest years of my life." In those years, Lucy Snowe prospered, became respected, expanded her school. Her happiness depends not on the presence of her beloved but rather on the knowledge that she is loved. With that knowledge, she becomes whole and independent. No longer telling others' stories, she speaks directly to the reader about her most private concerns. Only when her lover is absent, perhaps, can a woman treasure love and emotional satisfaction while yet retaining the freedom to be her own person.

Sally Mitchell

OTHER MAJOR WORKS

POETRY: *Poems by Currer, Ellis, and Acton Bell*, 1846 (with Emily Brontë and Anne Brontë); *The Complete Poems of Charlotte Brontë*, 1923.

CHILDREN'S LITERATURE: *The Twelve Adventurers, and Other Stories*, 1925 (C. K. Shorter and C. W. Hatfield, editors); *Legends of Angria*, 1933 (Fannie E. Ratchford, compiler); *The Search After Happiness*, 1969; *Five Novelettes*, 1971 (Winifred Gérin, editor); *The Secret and Lily Hart*, 1979 (William Holtz, editor).

MISCELLANEOUS: *The Shakespeare Head Brontë*, 1931-1938 (19 volumes; T. J. Wise and J. A. Symington, editors).

BIBLIOGRAPHY

Barker, Juliet. *The Brontës*. New York: St. Martin's Press, 1995. This massive study of the entire Brontë family sometimes overwhelms with detail, but it presents a complete picture of one of English literature's most intriguing and productive families. Barker's analysis of the juvenilia, in particular, constitutes a major contribution to Brontë scholarship. Not surprisingly, the author has more to say about Charlotte than about other members of the family.

Edwards, Mike. *Charlotte Brontë: The Novels*. New York: St. Martin's Press, 1999. Extracts sections from *Jane Eyre*, *Shirley*, and *Villette* to analyze the layers of meaning and the combination of realism and fantasy in these texts.

Fraser, Rebecca. *The Brontës: Charlotte Brontë and Her Family*. New York: Crown, 1988. Thorough and engrossing biography of Charlotte Brontë and the rest of the Brontë family is carefully researched and annotated and offers a vividly written portrait of the Brontës and their world. Makes use of letters, published and unpublished manuscripts, and contemporary news sources to examine this complex literary family.

Gaskell, Elizabeth C. *The Life of Charlotte Brontë*. 1857. Reprint. London: Penguin Books, 1975. Still an indispensable source for any student of Charlotte Brontë's life, this biography offers the insights that Gaskell gained through her long friendship with Brontë. Herself a popular novelist of the time, Gaskell creates a memorable picture of Brontë both as a writer and as a woman.

Glen, Heather. *Charlotte Brontë: The Imagination in History*. New York: Oxford University Press, 2002. Presents analysis of all of Brontë's novels and contradicts previous biographical works with evidence that Brontë was more artistically sophisticated and more engaged in contemporary social issues than many scholars have asserted.

_____, ed. *The Cambridge Companion to the Brontës*. New York: Cambridge University Press, 2002. Collection of essays examines the lives and work of the three sisters. Includes analysis of all of Charlotte's novels, a feminist perspective on the sisters' work, and a discussion of the Brontës and religion.

Gordon, Lyndall. *Charlotte Brontë: A Passionate Life*. New York: W. W. Norton, 1994. Written with the blessing of the Brontë Society, which granted access to and permission to reproduce from its copious archives. Readable account of Brontë's life and literary output makes good use of the materials provided by the society.

Ingham, Patricia. *The Brontës*. New York: Oxford University Press, 2006. Chronological examination of the three sisters' lives and works includes chapters detailing the literary context in which they wrote and their treatment of social class issues, with particular focus on *Shirley*, and of gender in *Jane Eyre*. Includes bibliography, index, list of relevant Web sites, and list of film and television adaptations of the sisters' books.

Menon, Patricia. *Austen, Eliot, Charlotte Brontë, and the Mentor-Lover*. New York: Palgrave Macmillan, 2003. Examines how Brontë, Jane Austen, and George Eliot handled matters of gender, sexuality, family, behavior, and freedom in their work.

Plasa, Carl. *Charlotte Brontë*. New York: Palgrave Macmillan, 2004. Assesses Brontë's writings by viewing them from a postcolonial perspective. Ex-amines her novels and other works in terms of their treatment of miscegenation, colonization, slavery, and the Irish famine.

Rollyson, Carl, and Lisa Paddock. *The Brontës A to Z: The Essential Reference to Their Lives and Work*. New York: Facts On File, 2003. Takes an encyclopedic approach to the family, including ill-starred brother Branwell. Offers synopses of the novels and discussions of poems as well as details of the lives of the authors. Includes reproductions of illustrations from early editions of the works.

EMILY BRONTË

Born: Thornton, Yorkshire, England; July 30, 1818
Died: Haworth, Yorkshire, England; December 19, 1848
Also known as: Emily Jane Brontë; Ellis Bell

PRINCIPAL LONG FICTION

Wuthering Heights, 1847

OTHER LITERARY FORMS

Poems by Emily Brontë and her sisters Charlotte and Anne are collected in the volume *Poems by Currer, Ellis, and Acton Bell* (1846). Juvenilia and early prose works by Brontë on the imaginary world of Gondal have all been lost.

ACHIEVEMENTS

Emily Brontë occupies a unique place in the annals of literature. Her reputation as a major novelist stands on the merits of one relatively short novel that was misunderstood and intensely disliked upon publication, yet no study of British fiction is complete without a discussion of *Wuthering Heights*. The names of the novel's settings and characters, particularly Heathcliff, have become part of the heritage of Western culture, familiar even to those who have neither read the novel nor know anything about its author's life and career. Several film and television versions, two of the most popular of which were re-leased in 1939 and 1970, have helped perpetuate this familiarity.

The literary achievement of *Wuthering Heights* lies in its realistic portrayal of a specific place and time and in its examination of universal patterns of human behavior. Set in Yorkshire in the closing years of the eighteenth century, the novel delineates the quality of life in the remote moors of northern England and also reminds the reader of the growing pains of industrialization throughout the nation. In addition, more than any other novel of the period, *Wuthering Heights* presents in clear dialectic form the conflict between two opposing psychic forces, embodied in the settings of the Grange and the Heights and the people who inhabit them. Although modern readers often apply the theories of Sigmund Freud and Carl Jung to give names to these forces, Brontë illustrated their conflict long before psychologists pigeonholed them. *Wuthering Heights* is so true in its portrayal of human nature that it fits easily into many theoretical and critical molds, from the historical to the psychological. The novel may be most fully appreciated, however, as a study of the nature of human perception and its ultimate failure in understanding human behavior. This underlying theme, presented through the dialectic structure of human perception, unites many of the elements that are sometimes singled out or overemphasized in particular critical approaches to the novel.

Brontë's skill is not confined to representing the world and the human forces at work within her characters, great as that skill is. She has also created a complex narrative structure built on a series of interlocking memories and perceptions, spanning three generations and moving across several social classes. Told primarily from two often unreliable and sometimes ambiguous first-person points of view, the novel illustrates through its structure the limitations of human intelligence and imagination. Faced with choosing between Lockwood's and Nelly Dean's interpretations of Heathcliff's life, the reader can only ponder that human perception never allows a full understanding of another soul.

BIOGRAPHY

Emily Jane Brontë was born at Thornton, in Bradford Parish, Yorkshire, on July 30, 1818, the fifth child of the Reverend Patrick and Maria Brontë. Patrick Brontë had been born in county Down, Ireland, one of ten children, on March 17, 1777. He was a schoolteacher and tutor before he obtained his bachelor of arts degree from Cambridge in 1806, from where he was ordained to curacies, first in Essex and then in Hartshead, Yorkshire. He married Maria Branwell, of Penzance, in Hartshead on December 19, 1812, and in 1817, they moved to Thornton. The other children in the family at the time of Emily's birth were Maria, Elizabeth, Charlotte, and Patrick Branwell; another daughter, Anne, was born two years later. Charlotte and Anne Brontë also became writers.

In early 1820, the family moved to Haworth, four miles from the village of Keighley, where the Reverend Brontë was perpetual curate until his death in 1861. Maria Brontë died on September 15, 1821, and about a year later, her elder sister, Elizabeth Branwell, moved in to take care of the children and household. She remained with them until her own death in 1842.

Life at Haworth was spartan but not unpleasant. There was a close and devoted relationship among the children, especially between Charlotte and Emily. Reading was a favorite pastime, and a wide range of books, including the novels of Sir Walter Scott and the poetry of William Wordsworth and Robert Southey, as well as the more predictable classics, was available to the children. Outdoor activities included many hours of wandering through the moors and woods. Their father wanted the children to be hardy and independent, intellectually and physically, indifferent to the passing fashions of the world.

Maria, Elizabeth, and Charlotte had already been sent away to a school for clergymen's daughters, at Cowan Bridge, when Emily joined them in November, 1824. Emily was not happy in this confined and rigid environment and longed for home. Two of the sisters, Elizabeth and Maria, became ill and were taken home to die during 1825; in June, Charlotte and Emily returned home as well.

From 1825 to 1830, the remaining Brontë children lived at Haworth with their father and their aunt, Miss Branwell. In June, 1826, their father gave them a set of wooden toy soldiers, a seemingly insignificant gift that stimulated their imaginative and literary talents. The children devoted endless energy to creating an imaginary world for the soldiers. During these years, Charlotte and her brother Branwell created in their minds and on paper the land of "Angria," while Emily and Anne were at work on "Gondal." Although all of these early prose works have been lost, some of Emily's poetry contains references to aspects of the Gondal-Angria creations.

In July, 1835, Emily again joined Charlotte, already a teacher, at the Roe Head school. She remained only three months, returning home in October. Three years later, she accepted a position as governess in a school in Halifax for about six months but returned to Haworth in December; Charlotte joined her there early in the following year. During 1839 and 1840, the sisters were planning to establish their own school at Haworth, but the plan was never carried through.

Charlotte left home again to serve as a governess in 1841, and in February, 1842, she and Emily went to Mme Héger's school in Brussels to study languages. They returned to Haworth in November because of Miss Branwell's death. Charlotte went back to Brussels to teach in 1843, but Emily never left Yorkshire again.

From August, 1845, the Brontë children were again united at Haworth. They did not have much contact with neighbors, whose educational level and intellectual interests were much inferior to theirs. They kept busy reading and writing, both fiction and poetry. *Wuthering Heights* was probably begun in October, 1845, and completed sometime in 1846, although it was not published until December, 1847, after the success of Charlotte's *Jane Eyre* (1847).

Meanwhile, the sisters published *Poems by Currer, Ellis, and Acton Bell* in May, 1846. Finding a press was very difficult, and the sisters chose the pseudonyms to avoid personal publicity and to create the fiction of male authorship, more readily acceptable to the general public. The reaction was predictable, as Charlotte noted: "Neither we nor our poems were at all wanted." The sisters were not discouraged, however, and they continued to seek publishers for their novels.

The first edition of *Wuthering Heights* was published in 1847 by T. C. Newby, with Anne's *Agnes Grey* as the third volume. It was a sloppy edition and contained many errors. The second edition, published in 1850, after the author's death, was "corrected" by Charlotte. The public reaction to *Wuthering Heights* was decidedly negative; readers were disturbed by the "wickedness" of the

Emily Brontë. (Library of Congress)

characters and the "implausibility" of the action. Until Charlotte herself corrected the misconception, readers assumed that *Wuthering Heights* was an inferior production by the author of *Jane Eyre*.

In October, 1848, Emily became seriously ill with a cough and cold. She suffered quietly and patiently, even refusing to see the doctor who had been called. She died of tuberculosis at Haworth on December 19, 1848. She was buried in the church alongside her mother, her sisters Maria and Elizabeth, and her brother Branwell.

These facts about Emily Brontë's life and death are known, but her character will always remain a mystery. Her early prose works have been lost, only three personal letters survive, and her poems give little insight into her own life. Most information about the Brontë family life and background comes from Mrs. Elizabeth Gaskell's biography of Charlotte and the autobiographical comments on which she based her work. Charlotte comments that Emily was "not a person of demonstrative character" and that she was "stronger than a man, simpler than a child." She had a nature that "stood alone." The person behind this mystery is revealed only in a reading of *Wuthering Heights*.

ANALYSIS: WUTHERING HEIGHTS

Wuthering Heights is constructed around a series of dialectic motifs that interconnect and unify the elements of setting, character, and plot. An examination of these motifs will give the reader the clearest insight into the central meaning of the novel. Although *Wuthering Heights* is a "classic," as Frank Kermode has noted, precisely because it is open to many different critical methods and conducive to many levels of interpretation, the novel grows from a coherent imaginative vision that underlies all the motifs. That vision demonstrates that all human perception is limited and failed. The fullest approach to Emily Brontë's novel is through the basic patterns that support this vision.

Wuthering Heights concerns the interactions of two families, the Earnshaws and Lintons, over three generations. The novel is set in the desolate moors of Yorkshire and covers the years from 1771 to 1803. The Earnshaws and Lintons are in harmony with their environment, but their lives are disrupted by an outsider and catalyst of change, the orphan Heathcliff. Heathcliff is, first of all, an emblem of the social problems of a nation entering the age of industrial expansion and urban growth. Although Brontë sets the action of the novel entirely within the locale familiar to her, she reminds the reader continually of the contrast between that world and the larger world outside.

Aside from Heathcliff's background as a child of the streets and the description of urban Liverpool, from which he is brought, the novel contains other reminders that Yorkshire, long insulated from change and susceptible only to the forces of nature, is no longer as remote as it once was. The servant Joseph's religious cant, the class distinctions obvious in the treatment of Nelly Dean as well as of Heathcliff, and Lockwood's pseudosophisticated urban values are all reminders that Wuthering Heights cannot remain as it has been, that religious, social, and economic change is rampant. Brontë clearly signifies in the courtship and marriage of young Cathy and Hareton that progress and enlightenment *will* come and the wilderness *will* be tamed. Heathcliff is both an embodiment of the force of this change and its victim. He brings about a change but cannot change himself. What he leaves behind, as Lockwood attests and the relationship of Cathy and Hareton verifies, is a new society, at peace with itself and its environment.

It is not necessary, however, to examine in depth the Victorian context of *Wuthering Heights* to sense the dialectic contrast of environments. Within the limited setting that the novel itself describes, society is divided between two opposing worlds: Wuthering Heights, ancestral home of the Earnshaws, and Thrushcross Grange, the Linton estate. Wuthering Heights is rustic and wild; it is open to the elements of nature and takes its name from "atmospheric tumult." The house is strong, built with narrow windows and jutting cornerstones, fortified to withstand the battering of external forces. It is identified with the outdoors and nature and with strong, "masculine" values. Its appearance, both inside and out, is wild, untamed, disordered, and hard. The Grange expresses a more civilized, controlled atmosphere. The house is neat and orderly, and there is always an abundance of light—to Brontë's mind, "feminine" values. It is not surprising that Lockwood is more comfortable at the Grange, since he takes pleasure in "feminine" behavior (gossip, vanity of appearance, adherence to social decorum, romantic self-delusion), while Heathcliff, entirely "masculine," is always out of place there.

Indeed, all of the characters reflect, to greater or lesser degrees, the masculine and feminine values of the places they inhabit. Hindley and Catherine Earnshaw are as wild and uncontrollable as the Heights: Catherine claims even to prefer her home to the pleasures of heaven. Edgar and Isabella Linton are as refined and civilized as the Grange. The marriage of Edgar and Catherine (as well as the marriage of Isabella and Heathcliff) is ill-fated from the start, not only because she does not love him, as her answers to Nelly Dean's catechism reveal, but also because both are so strongly associated with the values of their homes that they lack the opposing and necessary personality components. Catherine is too willful, wild, and strong; she expresses too much of the "masculine" side of her personality (the animus of Jungian psychology), while Edgar is weak and effeminate (the anima). They are unable to interact fully with each other because they are not complete individuals themselves. This lack leads to their failures to perceive each other's true needs.

Even Cathy's passionate cry for Heathcliff, "Nelly, I *am* Heathcliff," is less love for him as an individual than the deepest form of self-love. Cathy cannot exist without him, but a meaningful relationship is not possible because Cathy sees Heathcliff only as a reflection of herself. Heathcliff, too, has denied an important aspect of his personality. Archetypally masculine, Heathcliff acts out only the aggressive, violent parts of himself.

The settings and the characters are patterned against each other, and explosions are the only possible results. Only Hareton and young Cathy, each of whom embodies the psychological characteristics of both Heights and Grange, can successfully sustain a mutual relationship.

This dialectic structure extends into the roles of the narrators as well. The story is reflected through the words of Nelly Dean—an inmate of both houses, a participant in the events of the narrative, and a confidant of the major characters—and Lockwood, an outsider who witnesses only the results of the characters' interactions. Nelly is a companion and servant in the Earnshaw and Linton households, and she shares many of the values and perceptions of the families. Lockwood, an urban sophisticate on retreat, misunderstands his own character as well as the characters of others. His brief romantic "adventure" in Bath and his awkwardness when he arrives at the Heights (he thinks Cathy will fall in love with him; he mistakes the dead rabbits for puppies) exemplify his obtuseness. His perceptions are always to be questioned. Occasionally, however, even a denizen of the conventional world may gain a glimpse of the forces at work beneath the surface of reality. Lockwood's dream of the dead Cathy, which sets off his curiosity and Heathcliff's final plans, is a reminder that even the placid, normal world may be disrupted by the psychic violence of a willful personality.

The presentation of two family units and parallel brother-sister, husband-wife relationships in each also emphasizes the dialectic. That two such opposing modes of behavior could arise in the same environment prevents the reader from easy condemnation of either pair. The use of flashback for the major part of the narration—it begins in medias res—reminds the reader that he or she is seeing events out of their natural order, recounted by two individuals whose reliability must be questioned. The working out of the plot over three generations further suggests that no one group, much less one individual, can perceive the complexity of the human personality.

Taken together, the setting, plot, characters, and structure combine into a whole when they are seen as parts of the dialectic nature of existence. In a world where opposing forces are continually arrayed against each other in the environment, in society, in families, and in relationships, as well as within the individual, there can be no easy route to perception of another human soul. *Wuthering Heights* convincingly demonstrates the complexity of this dialectic and portrays the limitations of human perception.

Lawrence F. Laban

Other major works

POETRY: *Poems by Currer, Ellis, and Acton Bell*, 1846 (with Charlotte Brontë and Anne Brontë); *The Complete Poems of Emily Jane Brontë*, 1941 (C. W. Hatfield, editor); *Gondal's Queen: A Novel in Verse by Emily Jane Brontë*, 1955 (Fannie E. Ratchford, editor).

NONFICTION: *Five Essays Written in French*, 1948 (Lorine White Nagel, translator); *The Brontë Letters*, 1954 (Muriel Spark, editor).

Bibliography

Barnard, Robert. *Emily Brontë*. New York: Oxford University Press, 2000. Barnard, chairman of the Brontë Society, provides an incisive overview of Brontë's life and work. Includes bibliography, maps, illustrations (some in color), index, and chronology.

Benvenuto, Richard. *Emily Brontë*. Boston: Twayne, 1982. Brief biography of the Brontë sister whose life remains relatively obscure. Although only three of her letters survive, Benvenuto stays within the documentary record to provide a convincing portrait of her life and personality.

Berg, Maggie. *"Wuthering Heights": The Writing in the Margin*. New York: Twayne, 1996. Provides a good introduction to Emily Brontë's masterpiece. A chronology of her life and works is followed by a section devoted to the literary and social context of the novel and a reading emphasizing the importance of the novel's "marginal spaces," such as the diary that Catherine keeps in the blank spaces of books.

Davies, Stevie. *Emily Brontë: Heretic*. London: Women's Press, 1994. Feminist interpretation of Brontë's life and work contradicts the legends of Brontë's sexual innocence and unworldliness, showing how *Wuthering Heights* and the author's poetry offer evidence of her sophistication and sexuality.

Frank, Katherine. *A Chainless Soul: A Life of Emily Brontë*. Boston: Houghton Mifflin, 1990. Biographical study demonstrates the complex relationships between Emily Brontë and her family members.

Glen, Heather, ed. *The Cambridge Companion to the Brontës*. New York: Cambridge University Press, 2002. Essays examining the lives and work of the three sisters include analysis of *Wuthering Heights* and Emily's poetry, a feminist perspective on the sisters' work, and a discussion of the Brontës and religion.

Liddell, Robert. *Twin Spirits: The Novels of Emily and Anne Brontë*. London: Peter Owen, 1990. Presents analysis of *Wuthering Heights* and includes a companion essay on Anne Brontë's 1848 novel *The Tenant of Wildfell Hall*, showing that the latter is Anne's answer to Emily's novel.

Miller, Lucasta. *The Brontë Myth*. London: Jonathan Cape, 2001. Biography of the Brontës emphasizes how previous biographers have shaped readers' understanding of the three sisters' lives and work. Corrects misinformation contained in nineteenth century biographies, which exaggerated the authors' miserable childhoods, as well as in later books that interpreted their work from Freudian, feminist, and poststructural perspectives.

Pykett, Lyn. *Emily Brontë*. Savage, Md.: Barnes & Noble, 1989. Feminist assessment of Brontë's work suggests that *Wuthering Heights* is a distinctive novel because of the particular way it combines the female gothic genre and the realistic domestic novel that was becoming popular in Brontë's lifetime.

Rollyson, Carl, and Lisa Paddock. *The Brontës A to Z: The Essential Reference to Their Lives and Work*. New York: Facts On File, 2003. Covers every aspect of the three sisters' lives and work in more than five hundred alphabetically arranged essays. Includes seventeen pages of plot summary and analysis for *Wuthering Heights*.

Vine, Steve. *Emily Brontë*. New York: Twayne, 1998. Presents biographical information as well as critical analysis of *Wuthering Heights* and Brontë's poetry. Intended as an introduction for general readers.

Winnifrith, Tom, ed. *Critical Essays on Emily Brontë*. New York: G. K. Hall, 1997. Collection of two dozen essays by distinguished critics focuses on a range of topics, including Brontë's religion, her reading and education, *Wuthering Heights*, and her poetry. In one essay, Virginia Woolf compares *Wuthering Heights* to Charlotte Brontë's *Jane Eyre*.

ANITA BROOKNER

Born: London, England; July 16, 1928

PRINCIPAL LONG FICTION

A Start in Life, 1981 (also known as *The Debut*)
Providence, 1982
Look at Me, 1983
Hotel du Lac, 1984
Family and Friends, 1985
The Misalliance, 1986 (also known as *A Misalliance*)
A Friend from England, 1987
Latecomers, 1988
Lewis Percy, 1989
Brief Lives, 1990
A Closed Eye, 1991
Fraud, 1992
A Family Romance, 1993 (also known as *Dolly*)
A Private View, 1994
Incidents in the Rue Laugier, 1995
Altered States, 1996
Visitors, 1997
Falling Slowly, 1998

Undue Influence, 1999
The Bay of Angels, 2001
The Next Big Thing, 2002 (also known as *Making Things Better*)
The Rules of Engagement, 2003
Leaving Home, 2005

OTHER LITERARY FORMS

A distinguished historian of eighteenth and nineteenth century French art and culture, Anita Brookner wrote several books of nonfiction before she began to write novels. *Watteau* (1968) is an assessment of the early eighteenth century French artist Antoine Watteau. *The Genius of the Future: Studies in French Art Criticism—Diderot, Stendhal, Baudelaire, Zola, the Brothers Goncourt, Huysmans* (1971) is a collection of six essays on seven French writers, with each writer considered in the context of his time; the book devotes the greatest space to discussion of Charles Baudelaire. *Greuze: The Rise and Fall of an Eighteenth-Century Phenomenon* (1972), a study of the French painter Jean-Baptiste Greuze, is Brookner's successful attempt to locate the background of a sentimental genre that is distinct from both rococo and classicism. *Jacques-Louis David* (1980), a biography of the foremost painter of the French revolutionary period, explores the relationship between David's life and his work, places that work in the context of contemporary French painting, and details a career that spanned some of the most turbulent years in French history. *Soundings*, a collection of essays, was published in 1997, and the study *Romanticism and Its Discontents* appeared in 2000. Brookner's translations include *Utrillo* (1960) and *The Fauves* (1962). In addition, she has written many articles, introductions, and reviews on art history and on both French and English literature that have appeared in such publications as the *Burlington Magazine*, *The London Review of Books*, *The Times Literary Supplement*, *The Spectator*, and *The Sunday Times*. Some of these pieces are collected in *Soundings*.

ACHIEVEMENTS

Anita Brookner suddenly began to write fiction during her middle years, while she was still an active teacher and scholar. Although she continued her academic career, she quickly found equal success as a novelist. With the publication of several novels, she gained an international following and widespread critical acclaim. In 1984, Great Britain's prestigious Man Booker Prize for Fiction was awarded to *Hotel du Lac*. Brookner was praised for her elegant and precise prose, her acute sense of irony, and her subtle insights into character and social behavior. Her witty explorations of manners and morals suggest to many a literary kinship to Jane Austen and Barbara Pym. While Brookner's somber, more complex moral vision disallows any sustained comparison to Pym, Austen and Brookner undeniably share a common concern for intelligent, subtle, clever heroines who seek to satisfy both private sensibility and public expectations.

To regard Brookner's novels as simply traditional novels of manners, however, is to misconstrue her art. Brookner's intentions greatly exceed this conventional genre; her achievements, indeed, take her far beyond it. Perhaps it is more useful to note the singularity of her contribution to British letters. Her highly developed pictorial sense, her baroque diction, with its balance of reason and passion, and her allusive, richly textured narratives, haunting in their resonances, reflect at every turn her extensive knowledge of the materials and motifs of eighteenth and nineteenth century paintings and literature.

Brookner's works have been generously admired, but some dissenting voices have been raised. She is occasionally brought to task for creating fictive worlds too narrow in scope and claustrophobic in their intensity; for overzealous, self-conscious, schematic writing; and for excessive sentimentality that unfortunately evokes the pulp romance. Brookner's worlds, however, are invariably shaped toward significant moral revelations, and technique rarely intrudes to the detriment of story. Brookner's ability to maintain an ironic distance from her characters, one that allows her to reveal sentimentality, to make judgments dispassionately, is one of her greatest strengths as a writer.

BIOGRAPHY

Anita Brookner was born in London, England, on July 16, 1928, to Newsom and Maude Brookner. She was educated at James Allen's Girls' School and King's College, University of London, and she received a Ph.D. in art history from the Courtauld Institute of Art in London in 1953. From 1959 to 1964, she was visiting lecturer at the University of Reading, Berkshire. In 1967-1968, she was Slade Professor at Cambridge University, the first woman to hold this position. From 1964 to 1988 she taught at the Courtauld Institute of Art, where she lectured on neoclassicism and the Romantic movement. She is a fellow of New Hall of Cambridge University. In 1983, she became a fellow of the Royal Society of Literature, and in 1990 she was made a Commander of the Order of the British Empire (CBE). In 1984, *Hotel du Lac* won the prestigious Booker Prize.

Brookner began her career as a novelist when she was more than fifty years old as an attempt, she hinted, to understand her own powerlessness after a grand passion went wrong. Since 1981, she has published novels almost at the rate of one per year.

ANALYSIS

Anita Brookner established her reputation as a novelist with four books published in rapid succession from 1981 to 1984. Written in austerely elegant prose, each of these four novels follows essentially the same course. Each centers on a scholarly, sensitive, morally earnest young woman who leads an attenuated life. None of these heroines has intended a life so circumscribed. As their stories begin, they seek change, liberation from boredom and loneliness. They seek connection to a wider world. While these women are intelligent, endlessly introspective, and possessed of a saving ironic wit, they do not know how to get the things they most desire: the love of, and marriage to, a man of quality.

With compassion, rue, and infinite good humor, Brookner makes it abundantly clear that these worthy women, these good daughters, good writers, and good scholars, are unknowing adherents to a romantic ideal. Like the shopgirls and "ultrafeminine" women they gaze upon with such wonder and awe, these intellectually and morally superior women accept without question the cultural assumption that marriage is a woman's greatest good. Consistently undervaluing their own considerable talents and professional achievements, these heroines look to love and marriage as a way of joining the cosmic dance of a rational, well-ordered society. Their intense yearning for a transforming love shapes their individual plots; in each case, the conflict between what the romantic imagination wants and what it indeed gets impels these narratives forward. Brookner's concern is to illuminate the worthiness, the loneliness, the longing of these heroines for love and a more splendid life.

Before their stories can end, these women must abandon sentiment and accept their solitary state. Their triumph lies in their ability to confront their fall from romantic innocence and recognize it for what it is. These novels build inexorably toward endings that are both startling and profoundly moving. While Brookner's heroines must struggle with sentimentality, Brookner herself does not. Her vision is bleak, unsparing. In telling their stories, she raises several other themes: The most notable of these are filial obligation, the "romantic" versus the "realistic" apprehension of life, truth and its relationship to self-knowledge, the determination of proper behavior in society, and the small pleasures that attend the trivia of daily life. Brookner presents her major and minor themes against the background of fictive worlds so powerfully realized that her novels seem to be absorbed as much as read. These are novels of interior real-

ity. Little that is overt happens; dramatic action rests in the consciousness of the heroine, who is always center stage. Brookner occasionally also deploys the consciousness of a male protagonist, but whether male or female, the narrative consciousness achieves a breakthrough into a larger understanding, a deeper feeling, and well-earned wisdom.

THE DEBUT

Brookner's first novel, *The Debut*, lacks the richness and gradation of tone that marks her later fiction, but it is nevertheless well crafted. Set against Honoré de Balzac's *Eugénie Grandet* (1833; English translation, 1859), *The Debut* tells the story of Ruth Weiss, a scrupulous, thoughtful scholar who finds herself at forty with a life "ruined" by literature. A passionate reader from an early age, now a professor of literature specializing in Balzac, Ruth leads a narrow life alternating between teaching students and caring for an aging father. She blames the tradition of filial duty she found in literature for her mostly cheerless state.

Like Frances Hinton of *Look at Me* and Kitty Maule of *Providence*, Ruth began with expectations. In her youth, she once cast aside the burden of an oppressive heritage, one best symbolized by the deep silence and heavy, dark furniture in the mausoleum of a house she shared with her parents, and fled England for France. Ostensibly, her goal was to write a dissertation on vice and virtue; in actuality, it was as much to seek air and space and light. Although she at first endured a sense of displacement and exile, a condition that at one time or another afflicts many of Brookner's heroines, over time Ruth's transplant into foreign soil proved successful. Away from her charming, eccentric, but infinitely demanding parents, Ruth flourished. She acquired polish, sophistication, lovers. Even as she gloried in her new life, however, Ruth, like many of Brookner's other heroines, engaged in a constant internal debate over the question of how life is best lived. Does vice or virtue bring victory? She concluded that a life of conventional virtue can spell disaster for one's hopes; regretfully, Balzacian opportunism cannot be discounted. It is better to be a bad winner than a poor loser. Even though she observed that conventional morality tales were wrong, however, Ruth lamented the triumph of vice.

Suddenly called back to England because of what

proves to be a final deterioration in her mother's fragile health, Ruth is forced to leave the comfortable, satisfying life she has built for herself. Her spirited adventure over, Ruth is unable to extricate herself once more. At forty, the long and beautiful red hair indicative of her youthful potential for rebellion now compressed into a tight chignon, Dr. Ruth Weiss is a felon recaptured. She is tender with her father and gentle with her students, and she expects little more from life. She is the first of Brookner's heroines who learns to renounce.

Ruth's story is told retrospectively, in a way that recalls the French novel of meditation. The bold configurations of her story suggest the quality of a fable. The narrative also gains a necessary solidity and weight from the many allusions to Balzacian characters and texts. These allusions create a substructure of irony that continues to reverberate long after Ruth's story is complete.

Providence

If Ruth is disheartened but finally resigned, Kitty Maule in *Providence*, Brookner's second novel, moves toward outright disillusionment. Kitty is also a professor of literature. Her interests lie in the Romantic movement; this novel, then, like the rest of Brookner's fiction, is filled with ideas, good talk, and vigorous intellectual exchanges. Here, both Kitty's private musings and her running seminar on Benjamin Constant's *Adolphe* (1816) provide a context for the exploration of Romantic concerns. Brookner's use of Kitty as a teacher of the Romantic tradition is ultimately highly ironic, for Kitty cannot discern her own romanticism. Curiously, she has moments when she is almost able to see her romanticism for what it is, but in the end she suppresses the would-be insights and retreats into her dreams and passionate longings. What Kitty longs for is love, marriage, and, perhaps, God. Her longing for God goes largely unrecognized; like her fellow Romantics, she requires a sign. Her longing for love, however, the love of one man in particular, is at the perceived center of her life.

The handsome, brilliant, but distant lover of the scholarly, sensitive woman in this novel is Maurice Bishop. Maurice, a professor of medieval history, is noted for his love of cathedrals and God. Wellborn, rich, and confident in the manner of those accustomed to deference, Maurice is everything that Kitty wants in life: He is the very cultural ideal of England itself. To be his wife

is Kitty's hope of heaven, and to capture him she brings to bear all of the weapons she has at hand: subtle intelligence, grace of manners, enduring patience, and abiding love. That Kitty's love for Maurice has the fervor of a religious acolyte is suggested by his surname. Maurice may be in love with the idea of a religious absolute, but Kitty's religion is romantic love. All of her repressed romanticism is focused on this elegant, remote man.

Kitty's extreme dependence on Maurice as the repository of her hopes and dreams stems in large part from her sense of cultural displacement. The child of a French mother and a British father, both dead in their youth, Kitty was born in England and brought up there by her immigrant French grandparents. Despite her British birth, however, Kitty never feels at home in England. In the face of concerted and varied efforts to "belong," she retains a sense of exile. Nor is she truly considered English by her colleagues and acquaintances. The product of her doting French grandparents, Kitty is unaware of her true cultural allegiance; ironically, it is the French heritage that dominates in her English setting. Her manners, clothes, and speech belie her English father. In Maurice, Kitty seeks an attachment that anchors, a place to be. Here and elsewhere in Brookner's fiction, the recurrent theme of the search for a home acquires the force and weight of myth. So powerfully realized is Kitty's intense desire for love, acceptance, and liberation from loneliness that it comes as a shock when Kitty, who is expecting Maurice's proposal of marriage, instead learns of his sudden engagement to a woman who shares his aristocratic background. The novel concludes with Kitty's realization that she has indeed been living in a haze of romantic expectation; the truth is, she has been first, last, and always an outsider.

In addition to the major theme of the passive, excellent, but self-deceived young woman in the service of an illusory ideal, Brookner presents in *Providence* themes that are relevant to all of her works. Maurice's betrayal of Kitty, for example, establishes a motif that recurs in later novels, while Brookner's superbly comic depiction of bored and boring academics, a staple in her fiction, reaches perhaps its finest statement here. If Balzacian allusions underlie *The Debut* and give it additional power, allusions to many French writers, but especially to Constant's *Adolphe*, are used to provide ironic commentary on and foreshadowings of Kitty's fate. Most important, however, Kitty Maule herself is arguably the quintessential Brooknerian heroine. Like her fictional sisters, Ruth Weiss of *The Debut*, Frances Hinton of *Look at Me*, Edith Hope of *Hotel du Lac*, and Mimi Dorn of *Family and Friends*, Kitty waits patiently for her life to begin. She is blind to her own worth and discounts her singular achievements; she longs for order, a place in a rational world; she finds joy in the chores, duties, and routines of everyday life; she is sensitive, compassionate, morally deserving. Finally, her inevitable loss of a man morally her inferior leaves her stripped of all romantic illusions, a convert to reality.

LOOK AT ME

By her own admission a relentless observer, Frances Hinton, the heroine of *Look at Me*, Brookner's third novel, tells her own compelling story. To be sure, all of Brookner's heroines are detached observers, though probably none records and stores information so clinically as does Frances. All of Brookner's heroines suffer, but perhaps none suffers more intensely than Frances. Like other Brooknerian heroines, Frances is virtuous, sensitive, bright, and in need of a more marvelous life. Like other Brooknerian heroines also, she does not know how to get the things she wants. She is frozen into inaction, and her intense melancholia is mirrored in the images of death and desolation that surround her. A medical librarian who catalogs prints and engravings of disease through the ages, Frances comments ironically on the scenes of madness, nightmare affliction, and death she must sort and mount. She lives in a tomb of a house where her mother has died. Brookner's use of Frances's house recalls her uses of houses elsewhere: They are symbols of oppressive traditions that constrain and weigh heavily upon those who inhabit them.

For Frances, the world is somber, dark. The beautiful Nick and Alix Fraser, a glittering, stylish couple who offer Frances temporary access to a dazzling social world, prove cruelly false. In an act of betrayal so profound that Frances cannot but withdraw from the world she has long sought, Nick and Alix hold her up to public ridicule. Her brief liberation from solitariness and the eternal prison of self ends abruptly. Always self-analytic, self-deprecatory, Frances sees her failure to find a place in the world as a failure of egotism or will. She observes that others advance through egotism, but she cannot mimic them. She decides to become a writer. Writing will allow her both to comment on life and to retreat from it.

As is usual in Brookner's works, the dramatic action in *Look at Me* is largely inner. Hers are novels of the interior; the terrain surveyed is that of the soul. Frances presents a commanding narrative voice as she sorts, gathers, and finally reassembles the fragments of her experience into a unified whole. In fullest voice, she provides useful insights into the processes of the creative, transforming imagination. From the detritus of her daily life she will, as writer-at-work, abstract significant form. If Brookner here provides a mirror of herself busy fashioning art from the materials of the ordinary, the details of eating or dressing or chatting that receive so much attention in her novels, she also repeats the characteristic fusion of the comic and the sad that lends such poignancy to her works. Further, the influence of the pictorial is reflected here as well; characters are often framed in an action, presented with a consciousness of scene or setting. Finally, Frances's long commentary on her experience that is the text of *Look at Me* again evokes the French novel of meditation, a literary form that subtly influences and pervades Brookner's fiction. Notably, as Frances begins to write on the last page of the novel, she is free of self-pity. Solitude may be her lot, but art will vindicate her. Art will represent the triumph of the unvanquished self.

HOTEL DU LAC

Edith Hope, the heroine of *Hotel du Lac*, Brookner's fourth novel, is also a writer. Edith writes pulp romances for a living, and, until she learns better, she believes that romance is only her business, not her frame of mind. Brookner's fiction, however, reveals her tendency sometimes to use names to signal character traits or habits of thought. Such is the case here: Edith is indeed a romantic, although an unknowing one. Edith begins her stay at the Hotel du Lac in ignorance of her true nature; she leaves enlightened as to the deeper, more recessed aspects of her moral being.

It was not Edith's choice to leave England and travel to Switzerland, the setting of *Hotel du Lac*. Edith was sent away because of her severe breach of social decorum: She chose not to appear at her own wedding, thus profoundly humiliating a good man and eminently suitable husband. Her action was shocking to all, including Edith herself. Modest, unassuming, and usually anxious to please, Edith is in many ways a typical Brooknerian heroine. She, too, spends too much time alone, condemned to her own introspection. Her marriage would have broken that isolation. Edith's revolt and subsequent removal to Switzerland provide a context for the discussion of numerous moral and psychological questions. While Edith's story is always foremost, the novel itself alternates between first- and third-person narratives, with philosophical positions being argued, accepted, or dismissed.

The central fact that emerges about Edith is her passionate love for a married man whom she only seldom sees. Like his fictional predecessors, Edith's David is exceedingly handsome, elegant, intelligent, and remote. For love of him, Edith jilted her dull but safe fiancé. At the Hotel du Lac, Edith's interactions with the other residents move her to a greater understanding of truth, self-knowledge, and the differences between romance and reality. Numerous other themes are present here as well, including that of "ultrafeminine" as opposed to "feminist" women. Edith understands these women as models of feminine response to feminine experience. In relative isolation at this Swiss hotel, she studies these models and rejects both. The will to power, the utility of egotism as a serviceable instrument in the world, a recurrent Brooknerian theme, also receives much discussion here.

What Edith eventually learns as she evaluates her exchanges and relationships with her fellow guests at the hotel is accorded significant status by the mythological underpinnings of this novel. Inside the hotel, characters are both particular and types, acting out self-assigned roles in a grand comedy of manners. All the inhabitants exhibit a theatrical sense of themselves; they "present" themselves to this community consciously, deliberately. Such attention to pictorial, personal presentation is a constant of Brookner's fiction. The details of clothes, manners, and mannerisms convey aspects of self and morality in Brookner's works as they do in the works of Henry James, to whom Brookner alludes in this novel. If inside the hotel the characters are on parade, making their statements with dress or gesture, once outside the hotel they are subsumed into the mythicized landscape.

Gray mist, conveying a sense of menace and oppression, surrounds everything. Characters make journeys that are important only for their mythic impact. Much movement against this dreary landscape takes place as characters are directed toward crucial, definitive moral choices. The landscape helps Edith to perceive her dilemmas; she is finally able to reject a diabolical figure who offers marriage without love. He forces Edith to recognize her romanticism for what it is. At least in the end, however, when she returns to England and her married lover, Edith knows that she has chosen a cold and solitary path. Her self-determination represents a triumph for her and for this book. Edith is finally transformed by her successful journey to knowledge.

Having laid claim with her first four novels to a sharply defined fictional territory, Brookner has shown in subsequent books a willingness to extend her range. In *Latecomers*, for example, she centers her story for the first time on two male figures—close friends, both of whom were refugees brought from Germany to England as children during World War II. *Lewis Percy* features a single protagonist, again a man, in some ways the counterpart of Brookner's earlier heroines.

FAMILY AND FRIENDS

The book with which Brookner departed most radically from the pattern established in her first four novels is *Family and Friends*; perhaps because it violated readers' expectations, it was sharply criticized by some reviewers when it was published. Written in the historical present with virtually no dialogue, *Family and Friends* is an extended meditation on the French tradition. It stems from the ruminations of a narrator who quickly disappears, makes only glancing reappearances, and is curiously never identified. Here, Brookner's concern is not with a particular heroine but with the Dorn family, rich, most likely German immigrants who fled to England before the start of World War II. The war, when it comes, receives but scant attention; the novel focuses always on the small, interior world of the Dorn family. Little seems to exist outside the family members and their immediate interests, sparking again charges of a work too narrow in range.

The lives of the Dorn family and their associates are followed over a period of time. Sofka, the gentle but strong matriarch of the family, is the moral center of the work. Widowed early in life, she rejects the idea of remarriage, directing her loving attentions to her family instead. Mimi and Betty are her two daughters. While Betty is selfish, willful, theatrical, tricking her family into giving her an independent life quite early, she is nevertheless the child Sofka secretly loves best. Sofka, beautiful and contained, admires her younger daughter's spirit. Mimi is virtuous, dreamy, passive, frozen into inertia in young womanhood when an early feeble attempt to reach out for love is unsuccessful. Mimi languishes for years afterward, until her mother urges her into marriage, and thereby respectability, with a gentle, good man who would normally be her social inferior. Also playing a significant part in the novel are Sofka's two sons: the sensitive, intelligent, responsible Alfred and his handsome, charming brother Frederick. Interestingly, it is Alfred's plight that mirrors the situation of the usual Brooknerian heroine. It is he who is trapped by filial obligation into a life he had not intended; it is he who suffers forever afterward from an unsatisfying search for love and a desire for a larger, more extended world. It is also he who ultimately becomes inured to long-established habits of insularity.

This, then, is the saga of a family whose interior lives and moral relations are acutely realized. Important themes here include familial relations, especially filial obligation; the search for a transcendent love; and the need to venture, to dare, if one is to "win" in life. Structured around four wedding pictures, the novel impresses with its unity and intensity of tone and with its pervasive, elegant irony, its discerning moral judgments, and its engrossing character portraits. Especially effective also is the novel's lament for the loss of youthful promise, energy, and innocence. The once-vibrant Betty, trapped in middle-aged stasis, is a case in point. Dominating this entire work is a rich narrative voice, stern, compassionate, and often sad. The Dorn family seems to exist in a twilight, dreamlike world outside time. This world, while admittedly narrow, is nevertheless mesmerizing.

ALTERED STATES

Brookner writes novels in both the first and the third person, and most of her novels center on women. *Altered States* represents a first for her: a novel told by a man, Alan Sherwood, in the first person. In *Hotel du Lac*, Brookner divides women into hares (happy winners in

life's game) and tortoises (losers, for whom romance novels are written). In *Altered States*, Sherwood is a male tortoise; he is obsessed with a hare, the flashy and sexy Sarah Miller. As usual in Brookner, Alan the tortoise figure is a dull person, dutiful and bound to a parent. He is wheedled into marriage by another tortoise, Angela, and he is tortured by guilt after he betrays her and seemingly causes her death.

Altered States is different from other Brookner novels in other ways. Sarah is cruder, sexier, more selfish, and more anarchistic than any of Brookner's other hares; she embodies most of the seven deadly sins. Her lovemaking with Alan is more purely sexual than similar encounters elsewhere in Brookner's fiction. Alan, on the other hand, is not simply a tortoise; he *knows* he is a tortoise. He knows that he is dull and that he represents not just dullness but also civilized order. By the end of the novel, Alan not only learns about himself and the other people in his life, but he also has a small triumph over Sarah. He convinces her to step outside her character and perform a generous act.

VISITORS

In *Visitors*, the central character is once more a woman: Thea May, age seventy. She is perhaps Brookner's most inert and solitary tortoise—until a crisis makes her take a hare into her home. The hare is named Steve Best, a young friend of someone about to marry into Thea's late husband's family. The contrast could not be greater. Thea is a lonely, apprehensive, static old woman; Steve is a gregarious, wandering, confident young man. Her reaction to him is complicated. She responds to his presence and even coddles him, but at the same time she feels that her home has been violated, and she wishes he would leave.

Visitors is about understanding. Many characters, such as Thea's husband's self-centered family and the rude and charmless young people, understand each other hardly at all. They certainly do not understand Thea. However, as the novel proceeds, Thea displays a talent for understanding all of them and is even able to act on that understanding on a climactic occasion. As she is drawn out of her usual routine, Thea thinks more and more about her past. Since childhood she has harbored a secret fear of intruders—hares such as Steve and even her husband. By the end of the novel, Thea seems to come to terms with her anxieties. She acknowledges her affection for her husband's family and feels more receptive to daily joys.

The Rules of Engagement

As in other Brookner novels, the author's great subject in *The Rules of Engagement* is the process of consciousness. In this case it is Elizabeth Wetherall who explores the meaning of a complicated love triangle that secretly develops among herself, her friend Betsy, and a sophisticated womanizer. Elizabeth's affair with the married but highly seductive Edmund Fairlie has left her unfulfilled and with a legacy of regret, guilt, and fear, but when Elizabeth's friend, the more romantic Betsy Newton, is later seduced by Edmund as well, Elizabeth does not inform Betsy of her own affair with the unscrupulous philanderer. Betsy's credulous simplicity leads her to serve the shameless Fairlie and his entire family as an unappreciated factotum. Because of Betsy's devotion to Fairlie, she has not looked after her own health, and she is dying of a cancer she failed to treat in time. Betsy's tragic outcome leads Elizabeth to worry that she was wrong in standing by silently while Betsy threw herself away on Fairlie, but Elizabeth can rest easy in the knowledge that she took good care of her friend and perhaps rightly kept her from a dark knowledge of things she would have found wholly destructive. Elizabeth's goodness to Betsy has been a transformative, liberating experience for her; she has relinquished much of the falseness in her life, and she finds she can return at least in dreams to her childhood, when she knew what it was to love and be loved. She understand that she also is at heart a romantic, and that her essential innocence and idealism have weathered even her affair with Fairlie.

The Rules of Engagement has deep affinities with Brookner's earlier novel *Falling Slowly*, which also examines the lives of two women searching for love. As is true of Elizabeth and Betsy, the sisters Miriam and Beatrice Sharpe in *Falling Slowly* double as alter egos for each other. Like Elizabeth, Miriam is knowing and bitter, and like Betsy, Beatrice is disastrously innocent, and in the end, as is true of the two friends in *The Rules of Engagement*, there is no happy romantic outcome; it is the relationship the two women have with each other that is truest and deepest.

The Brookner novel that followed *The Rules of En-*gagement, *Leaving Home*, also features two women whose bond with each other sustains them as they face terrible disappointments in love. As in *The Rules of Engagement*, *Leaving Home* features a more reserved woman and a more romantic one, and, as in the two earlier novels, it is the wise realist, Emma, who is the center of interest. Like Elizabeth in *The Rules of Engagement*, Emma feels what it is to be loved only in her dreams. Ironically, however, it is the unhappy isolation of all of Brookner's protagonists that allows them to develop such admirable inner lives and to know the gratifications of genuine insight and profound self-knowledge.

Betty H. Jones; George Soule
Updated by Margaret Boe Birns

Other major works

NONFICTION: *Watteau*, 1968; *The Genius of the Future: Studies in French Art Criticism—Diderot, Stendhal, Baudelaire, Zola, the Brothers Goncourt, Huysmans*, 1971; *Greuze: The Rise and Fall of an Eighteenth-Century Phenomenon*, 1972; *Jacques-Louis David*, 1980; *Soundings*, 1997; *Romanticism and Its Discontents*, 2000.

TRANSLATIONS: *Utrillo*, 1960 (of Waldemar George's biography); *Gaugin*, 1962 (of Maximilien Gauthier's book); *The Fauves*, 1962 (of Jean Paul Crespelle's book).

Bibliography

Bjorkblom, Inger. *The Plane of Uncreatedness: A Phenomenological Study of Anita Brookner's Late Fiction*. Stockholm: Almqvist & Wiksell International, 2001. Presents a philosophical/psychological study of Brookner's fiction, focusing on her later works, with special reference to the complexities of heroism, boredom, ennui, and helplessness in the novels. Works discussed include *Lewis Percy*, *Visitors*, and *Falling Slowly*.

Haffenden, John. *Novelists in Interview*. London: Methuen, 1985. Includes a lively, substantial interview with Brookner that provides useful background for readers of her works. She discusses her novels, the ideas behind her writing, and the existential dilemmas of her characters.

Malcolm, Cheryl Alexander. *Understanding Anita Brookner*. Columbia: University of South Carolina Press,

2002. Offers a short biographical overview of Brookner's life and examines how her novels exemplify the traditional British cultural values of understatement, deference to authority, and acceptance of a class system.

Sadler, Lynn Veach. *Anita Brookner*. Boston: Twayne, 1990. First full-length study of Brookner's work discusses her first seven novels. Compares Brookner to Barbara Pym and Margaret Drabble but also shows why Brookner has her own voice in feminist fiction. Analyzes Brookner's heroines and gives insight into the author's use of irony.

Skinner, John. *The Fictions of Anita Brookner: Illusions of Romance*. New York: St. Martin's Press, 1992. Discusses Brookner's novels in the light of contemporary narrative theory and speculates on the close relationship between the novels and the author's life.

Soule, George. *Four British Women Novelists: Anita Brookner, Margaret Drabble, Iris Murdoch, Barbara Pym*. Lanham, Md.: Scarecrow Press, 1998.

Annotated critical bibliography covers all of Brookner's novels through *Visitors*.

Usandizaga, Aránzazu. "Motifs of Exile, Hopelessness, and Loss: Disentangling the Matrix of Anita Brookner's Novels." In *"In the Open": Jewish Women Writers and British Culture*, edited by Claire M. Tylee. Newark: University of Delaware Press, 2006. Examines *Providence*, *The Latecomers*, *A Family Romance*, *Family and Friends*, and *The Next Big Thing* with reference to Brookner's Jewish heritage, with special concentration on the mother-daughter relationship.

Williams-Wanquet, Eileen. *Art and Life in the Novels of Anita Brookner: Reading for Life, Subversive Rewriting to Live*. New York: Peter Lang, 2004. Considers all of Brookner's novels as one monolithic fiction. Discusses her fiction in terms of biography, narrative theory, and recent feminist fiction to suggest that Brookner subversively rewrites the traditional romantic novel.

CHARLES BROCKDEN BROWN

Born: Philadelphia, Pennsylvania; January 17, 1771
Died: Philadelphia, Pennsylvania; February 22, 1810

PRINCIPAL LONG FICTION

Wieland: Or, The Transformation, an American Tale, 1798

Arthur Mervyn: Or, Memoirs of the Year 1793, Part I, 1799

Edgar Huntly: Or, Memoirs of a Sleep-Walker, 1799

Ormond: Or, The Secret Witness, 1799

Arthur Mervyn: Or, Memoirs of the Year 1793, Part II, 1800

Clara Howard: In a Series of Letters, 1801

Jane Talbot: A Novel, 1801

OTHER LITERARY FORMS

Charles Brockden Brown published two parts of a dialogue on the rights of women, *Alcuin: A Dialogue*, in 1798; the last two sections appeared in William Dunlap's 1815 biography of Brown. Many of Brown's essays on literature have been collected in *Literary Essays and Reviews* (1992), edited by Alfred Weber and Wolfgang Schäfer. His later political and historical essays, originally published in magazines and as pamphlets, have not been collected. Several of Brown's fictional fragments appear in *Carwin, the Biloquist, and Other American Tales and Pieces* (1822) and in the Dunlap biography, notably the Carwin story and "Memoirs of Stephen Calvert." Several collected editions of Brown's novels were published in the nineteenth century. Harry Warfel's edition of *The Rhapsodist, and Other Uncollected Writings* (1943) completes the publication of most of Brown's literary works. Some of Brown's letters have appeared in scattered books and essays, but no collection of letters has yet been published.

ACHIEVEMENTS

The significant portion of Charles Brockden Brown's literary career lasted little more than one year, in the period 1798-1800, during which he published the four novels for which he is best known: *Wieland, Ormond, Arthur Mervyn*, and *Edgar Huntly*. Although Brown's career began with the essays comprising "The Rhapsodist" in 1789 and continued until his death, most of his other fiction, poetry, and prose is thought to be of minor importance.

Brown's literary reputation rests heavily on his historical position as one of the first significant American novelists. An English reviewer wrote in 1824 that Brown "was the first writer of prose fiction of which America could boast." Brown's contemporaries recognized his abilities, and he received praise from William Godwin, John Keats, and Percy Bysshe Shelley. Although his American reputation remained unsteady, he was read by nineteenth century novelists such as James Fenimore Cooper, Edgar Allan Poe, and Herman Melville. In the twentieth and twenty-first centuries, scholars and advanced students of American culture have been Brown's most frequent readers; they have rediscovered him in part because his concerns with identity and choice in a disordered world prefigured or initiated some of the major themes of American fiction.

Brown's four best-known novels begin the peculiarly American mutation of the gothic romance. Some similarities can be seen between Brown's novels and the political gothic of Godwin and the sentimental gothic of Ann Radcliffe, but Brown's adaptations of gothic conventions for the exploration of human psychology, the analysis of the mind choosing under stress, and the representation of a truly incomprehensible world suggest that he may be an important bridge between the popular gothic tradition of eighteenth century England and the American gothic strain that is traceable through Poe, Melville, and Nathaniel Hawthorne to Henry James, William Faulkner, and such late twentieth century novelists as Joyce Carol Oates.

BIOGRAPHY

Born on January 17, 1771, Charles Brockden Brown was the fifth son of Elijah Brown and Mary Armitt Brown. Named for a relative who was a well-known Philadelphia official, Brown grew up in an intellectual Quaker family where the works of contemporary radicals such as Godwin and Mary Wollstonecraft were read, even though they were unacceptable by society's norms. Brown's health was never good; his parents tended to protect him from an active boy's life and to encourage his reading. When he was eleven, he began his formal education at the Friends' Latin School in Philadelphia under Robert Proud, a renowned teacher and scholar who later wrote *The History of Pennsylvania* (1797). Proud encouraged Brown to strengthen his constitution by taking walks in the country, similar to those Edgar Huntly takes with Sarsefield in *Edgar Huntly*. After five or six years in Latin School, Brown began the study of law under Alexander Willcocks (variously spelled), a prominent Philadelphia lawyer. Although he studied law for five or six years, until 1792 or 1793, he never practiced.

During Brown's years studying law, he taught himself French and increasingly leaned toward literary work. He became a member of the Belles Lettres Club, which met to discuss current literary and intellectual topics. In 1789, he published his first work, "The Rhapsodist," in the *Columbian Magazine*. In 1790, he met and became friends with Elihu Hubbard Smith of Litchfield, Connecticut, a medical student with literary interests. Smith encouraged Brown's literary aspirations, helping to draw him away from law. Brown's acquaintance with Smith brought him to New York City in 1794, where he came to know the members of the Friendly Club, a group of young New York intellectuals, one of whom was to be his first biographer, William Dunlap.

During this period, Brown wrote poetry, and by 1795 he had begun a novel. He began active publishing in 1798 in the Philadelphia *Weekly Magazine*. In the summer of 1798, when he was visiting Smith in New York, he published *Wieland*. Smith died during the yellow fever outbreak of that summer; Brown also became ill, but he recovered. In 1799, Brown suddenly became an extremely busy writer. He published two novels and part of a third and also founded *The Monthly Magazine and American Review*. In 1800, he published the second half of *Arthur Mervyn*, abandoned his magazine, and joined his brothers in business. After publishing his last two novels in 1801, he turned to political and historical writing. His 1803 pamphlet on the Louisiana Territory was widely read and provoked debate in Congress. In 1803, he began another magazine, *The Literary Magazine and American Register*, which lasted until 1806. His final magazine venture was *The American Register: Or, General Repository of History, Politics, and Science* (1807-1810). He was working on a geography publication when he died on February 22, 1810, of tuberculosis, a disease that had pursued him most of his life.

The details of Brown's personal and intellectual life are known primarily through his writings. He married Elizabeth Linn on November 19, 1804, and his family eventually included three sons and a daughter. There is evidence that Brown entertained the liberal Quaker ideas of his parents, the Deism of Smith, and the ideas of the English radicals at various times. His dialogue on the

Charles Brockden Brown. (Library of Congress)

rights of women, *Alcuin*, advocates sound education and political equality for women and, in the two parts published after his death, even suggests a utopian state of absolute social equality between the sexes in which there would be no marriage. Although he entertained such radical ideas in his youth, Brown seems to have become more conservative with maturity, affirming in his later works the importance of both reason and religion in living a good life.

ANALYSIS

Charles Brockden Brown's aims in writing, aside from attempting to earn a living, are a matter of debate among critics. In his preface to *Edgar Huntly*, he makes the conventional claim of novelists of the time, that writing is "amusement to the fancy and instruction to the heart," but he also argues the importance as well as the richness of American materials:

> One merit the writer may at least claim:—that of calling forth the passions and engaging the sympathy of the reader by means hitherto unemployed by preceding authors. Puerile superstition and exploded manners, Gothic castles and chimeras, are the material usually employed for this end. The incidents of Indian hostility, the perils of the Western wilderness, are far more suitable; and for a native of America to overlook these would admit of no apology.

This statement suggests several elements of Brown's primary achievement, the development of gothic conventions for the purposes of exploring the human mind in moments of ethically significant decision. Such an achievement was important for its example to later American novelists.

AMERICAN GOTHIC

Brown's novels are like William Godwin's in their use of radical contemporary thought; they are like Ann Radcliffe's in that they continue the tradition of the rationalized gothic. Brown, however, proves in some ways to be less radical than Godwin, and his fictional worlds differ greatly from Radcliffe's. Brown brings into his novels current intellectual debates about education, psychology and reason, epistemology, ethics, and religion. Characters who hold typical attitudes find themselves in situations that thoroughly test their beliefs. The novels do not seem especially didactic; they are rather more like Radcliffe's romances in form. A central character or group undergoes a crisis that tests education and belief. Brown's novels tend to be developmental, but the world he presents is so ambiguous and disorderly that the reader is rarely certain that a character's growth really fits the character better for living.

This ambiguity is only one of the differences that make Brown appear, in retrospect at least, to be an Americanizer of the gothic. In one sense, his American settings are of little significance, since they are rather simple equivalents of the castle grounds and wildernesses of an Otranto or Udolpho; on the other hand, these settings are recognizable and much more familiar to American readers. Rather than emphasizing the exoticism of the gothic, Brown increases the immediacy of his tales by using American settings.

Brown also increases the immediacy and the intensity of his stories by setting them close to his readers in time. Even though his novels are usually told in retrospect by the kinds of first-person narrators who would come to dominate great American fiction, the narratives frequently lapse into the present tense at crises, the narrators becoming transfixed by the renewed contemplation of past terrors. Brown avoids the supernatural; even though his novels are filled with the inexplicable, they do not feature the physical acts of supernatural beings. For example, Clara Wieland dreams prophetic dreams that prove accurate, but the apparently supernatural voices that waking people hear are hallucinatory or are merely the work of Carwin, the ventriloquist. All of these devices for reducing the distance between reader and text contribute to the success of Brown's fast-paced if sometimes overly complicated plots, but they also reveal the author's movement away from Radcliffe's rationalized gothic toward the kind of realism that would come to dominate American fiction in the next century.

Perhaps Brown's most significant contribution to the Americanization of the gothic romance is his representation of the human mind as inadequate to its world. Even the best minds in his works fall victim to internal and external assaults, and people avoid or fall into disaster seemingly by chance. In Radcliffe's fictional world, Providence actively promotes poetic justice; if the hero or heroine persists in rational Christian virtue and holds

to his or her faith that the world is ultimately orderly, then weaknesses and error, villains and accidents will be overcome, and justice will prevail. In Brown's novels, there are no such guarantees. At the end of *Wieland*, Clara, the narrator, reflects, "If Wieland had framed juster notions of moral duty, and of the divine attributes; or if I had been gifted with ordinary equanimity or foresight, the double-tongued deceiver would have been baffled and repelled." Clara's moralizing is, in fact, useless, even to herself. She was not so "gifted"; therefore, she could never have escaped the catastrophes that befell her. Furthermore, she persists in seeing Carwin, the "double-tongued deceiver," as a devil who ruined her brother, even though Carwin is no more than a peculiarly gifted and not very moral human being. Clara is able to moralize in this way only because, for the time being, disasters do not threaten her. Placed once again in the situation in which she completed the first portion of her narrative, she would again reject all human comfort and wish for death. Brown's fictional worlds defy human comprehension and make ethical actions excessively problematic.

This apparent irony in *Wieland* illustrates a final significant development in Brown's adaptation of the gothic romance. Although it is difficult, given his sometimes clumsy work, to be certain of what he intends, Brown seems to have experimented with point of view in ways that foreshadow later works. *Arthur Mervyn*, written in two parts, seems a deliberate experiment in multiple points of view. As Donald Ringe has noted, while the first part, told primarily from Mervyn's point of view, emphasizes Mervyn's naïve victimization by a sophisticated villain, the second part, told from a more objective point of view, suggests that Mervyn may unconsciously be a moral chameleon and confidence man. This shifting of point of view to capture complexity or create irony reappears in the works of many major American novelists, notably Herman Melville (for example, in "Benito Cereno") and William Faulkner.

By focusing on the mind dealing with crises in an ambiguous world, making his stories more immediate, and manipulating point of view for ironic effect, Brown helped to transform popular gothic conventions into tools for the more deeply psychological American gothic fiction that would follow.

WIELAND

Clara Wieland, the heroine of *Wieland*, is a bridge between the gothic heroine of Radcliffe and a line of American gothic victims stretching from Edgar Allan Poe's narrators in his tales of terror through Henry James's governess in *The Turn of the Screw* (1898) to Faulkner's Temple Drake and beyond. Her life is idyllic until she reaches her early twenties, when she encounters a series of catastrophes that, it appears, will greatly alter her benign view of life. When her disasters are three years behind her and she has married the man she loves, Clara returns to her view that the world is reasonably orderly and that careful virtue will pull one through all difficulties.

The novel opens with an account of the Wieland family curse on the father's side. Clara's father, an orphaned child of a German nobleman cast off by his family because of a rebellious marriage, grows up apprenticed to an English merchant. Deprived of family love and feeling an emptiness in his spiritual isolation, he finds meaning when he chances upon a book of a radical Protestant sect. In consequence, he develops an asocial and paranoid personal faith that converts his emptiness into an obligation. He takes upon himself certain duties that will make him worthy of the god he has created. These attitudes dominate his life and lead eventually to his "spontaneous combustion" in his private temple on the estate he has developed in America. The spiritual and psychological causes of this disaster arise in part from his guilt at failing to carry out some command of his personal deity, perhaps the successful conversion of American Indians to Christianity, the project that brought him to America. Clara's uncle presents this "scientific" explanation of her father's death and, much later in the novel, tells a story indicating that such religious madness has also occurred on her mother's side of the family. Religious madness is the familial curse that falls upon Clara's immediate family: Theodore Wieland, her brother; his wife, Catharine; their children and a ward; and Catharine's brother, Pleyel, whom Clara comes to love.

The madness strikes Theodore Wieland; he believes he hears the voice of God commanding him to sacrifice his family if he is to be granted a vision of God. He succeeds in killing all except Pleyel and Clara. The first half of the novel leads up to his crimes, and the second half deals primarily with Clara's discoveries about herself

and the world as she learns more details about the murders. Clara's ability to deal with this catastrophe is greatly complicated by events that prove to be essentially unrelated to it but coincide with it. In these events, the central agent is Carwin.

Carwin is a ventriloquist whose background is explained in a separate short fragment, "Memoirs of Carwin the Biloquist." Because ventriloquism is an art virtually unknown in Clara's world, Carwin seems monstrous to her. As he explains to Clara near the end of the novel, he has been lurking about the Wieland estate, and his life has touched on theirs in several ways. He has used his art to avoid being detected in his solitary night explorations of the grounds. The apparently supernatural voices he has created may have contributed to the unsettling of Theodore Wieland, but Wieland's own account during his trial indicates other more powerful causes of his madness. Much more dangerous to Clara has been Carwin's affair with her housekeeper, Judith, for by this means he has come to see Clara as a flower of human virtue and intellect. He is tempted to test her by creating the illusion that murderers are killing Judith in Clara's bedroom closet. This experiment miscarries, leading Clara to think she is the proposed victim. He later uses a "supernatural" voice that accidentally coincides with one of her prophetic dreams; though his purpose is to frighten her away from the place of his meetings with Judith, Carwin confirms Clara's fears and superstitions. He pries into her private diary and concocts an elaborate lie about his intention to rape her when he is caught. Out of envy and spite and because he is able, Carwin deceives Pleyel into thinking that Clara has surrendered her honor to him.

Throughout these deceptions, Carwin also fosters in Clara the superstition that a supernatural being is watching over and protecting her by warning her of dangers. Carwin's acts are essentially pranks; he never intends as much harm as actually occurs when his actions become threads in a complex net of causality. The worst consequence of his pranks is that Pleyel is convinced that Clara has become depraved just at the moment when she hopes that he will propose marriage, and this consequence occurs because Carwin overestimates Pleyel's intelligence. Pleyel's accusation of Clara is quite serious for her because it culminates the series of dark events that Clara perceives as engulfing her happy life. Carwin's scattered acts have convinced her that rapists and murderers lurk in every dark corner and that she is the center of some impersonal struggle between forces of good and evil. Pleyel's accusation also immediately precedes her brother's murders. These two crises nearly destroy Clara's reason and deprive her of the will to live.

The attack on Clara's mind is, in fact, the central action of the novel. All the gothic shocks come to focus on her perception of herself. They strip her of layers of identity until she is reduced to a mere consciousness of her own integrity, a consciousness that is then challenged when she comes to understand the nature of her brother's insanity. When all the props of her identity have been shaken, she wishes for death. Tracing her progress toward the wish for death reveals the central thematic elements of the novel.

The attack on Clara's mind is generated from poles represented by her brother and Pleyel. Wieland crumbles from within, and Pleyel is deceived by external appearances. Each falls prey to the weakness to which he is most susceptible. Clara's more stable mind is caught in the midst of these extremes. Theodore Wieland has the family temperament, the tendency to brood in isolation over his spiritual state and over "last things." Pleyel is the lighthearted and optimistic rationalist, skeptical of all religious ideas, especially any belief in modern supernatural agencies. While Wieland trusts his inner voice above all, Pleyel places absolute faith in his senses. Both are certain of their powers to interpret their experience accurately, and both are wrong on all counts. Wieland sees what he wants to see, and Pleyel's senses are easily deceived, especially by the skillful Carwin. Wieland interprets his visions as divine revelations even though they command murder, and Pleyel believes Clara is polluted even though such a belief is inconsistent with his lifelong knowledge of her.

Clara's sense of identity first suffers when her idyllic world begins to slip away. Her world becomes a place of unseen and unaccountable danger. As her anxiety increases, she finds herself unable to reason about her situation. Brown shows this disintegration in one of his more famous scenes, when Clara comes to believe there is someone in her closet, yet persists in trying to enter it even though she has heard the murderers there and even

after her protecting voice has warned her away. Critics take various attitudes toward this scene, which prolongs the reader's wait to learn who is in the closet in order to follow minutely Clara's thoughts and reactions. Brown creates suspense that some critics have judged overwrought, but his main purpose is clearly the close analysis of a strong mind coming apart under great pressure. Even though Pleyel's mistakes emphasize the inadequacy of individual rationality to the complexity of the world, that faculty remains the isolated person's only means of active defense. As Clara's rationality disintegrates, her helplessness increases.

Seeing her world divide into a war between good and evil in which her reason fails to help her, Clara's anxiety develops into paranoia. After Carwin tells how he intended to rape her, she begins to see him as a supernatural agent of Satan. When Pleyel accuses her of self-transforming wickedness with Carwin, Clara loses her social identity. Unable to change Pleyel's mind, she can see recent events only as a devilish plot against her happiness. Just when she thinks she is about to complete her identity in marriage, she is denied the opportunity. When she loses the rest of her family as a result of Wieland's insanity, she loses the last supporting prop of her identity, leaving only her faith in herself, her consciousness of her own innocence, and her belief that the satanic Carwin has caused all of her catastrophes.

Two more events deprive Clara of these remaining certainties. She learns that Wieland, rather than Carwin, whom she has suspected, is the murderer, and when she understands Wieland's motives, she loses confidence in her perceptions of herself, for should she be similarly transformed, she would be unable to resist. In fact, she sees herself, prostrate and wishing for death, as already transformed: "Was I not likewise transformed from rational and human into a creature of nameless and fearful attributes?" In this state, she understands her brother's certainty of his own rectitude. She cannot know herself. When she finally meets Carwin and hears how trivial and without malice his acts have been, she is unable to believe him, unable to give up her belief that she is the victim of a supernatural agency. Like Wieland, whom she meets for the last time on the same evening she talks with Carwin, she insists that divinity stands behind her disasters; the paranoid Wielands stand at the head of the line of American monomaniacs of whom Melville's Ahab is the greatest example. Deprived of her ordered world, Clara asserts against it an order that gives her reason, at least, to die. Wieland himself commits suicide when Carwin convinces him he has listened to the wrong voice.

Criticism has been rightly skeptical of the apparent clumsiness of the last chapter, Clara's continuation of the narration three years after Wieland's suicide. That chapter tidies up what had appeared earlier to be a subplot involving the Wielands' ward, Louisa Conway, and it also puts together a conventional happy ending. The recovered Clara marries Pleyel after he resolves several complications, including learning the truth about Clara and losing his first wife. Although it remains difficult to determine what Brown intended, it is unlikely that a writer of Brown's intelligence, deeply interested in the twistings of human thought, could be unaware that Clara's final statement is a manifest tissue of illusion. No attainable human virtue could have saved her or Wieland from the web of events in which they became enmeshed. That she persists in magnifying Carwin's responsibility shows that she fails to appreciate the complexity of human events even as Carwin himself has failed. That the Conway/Stuart family disasters of the last chapter recapitulate her own emphasizes Clara's failure to appreciate fully the incomprehensibility of her world.

Brown apparently intended in the final chapter to underline the illusory quality of social normality. When life moves as it usually does, it appears to be orderly, and one's ideas of order, because they are not seriously challenged, seem to prevail and become a source of comfort and security. That these ideas of order all break down when seriously challenged leads Clara to the wisdom of despair: "The most perfect being must owe his exemption from vice to the absence of temptation. No human virtue is secure from degeneracy." Such wisdom is not, however, of much use under normal conditions and is of no use at all in a crisis. Perhaps more useful is Clara's reflection as she looks back from the perspective of three years, her idea that one's perceptions and interpretations, because of their imperfection, must be tested over time and compared with those of other observers. The Wieland family curse and Pleyel's errors might be moderated if each character relied less on his or her unaided

perceptions and interpretations. In the midst of chaos, however, this maxim may be no more helpful than any other; Clara, for example, violently resists the sympathy of friends who might help to restore the order of her mind.

Although not a great novel, *Wieland* is both intrinsically interesting and worthy of study for the degree to which it foreshadows developments of considerable importance in the American novel. By subjecting Clara to a completely disordered world and by taking her through a loss of identity, Brown prepares the way for greater American gothic protagonists from Captain Ahab to Thomas Sutpen.

EDGAR HUNTLY

Edgar Huntly appears at first to be a clumsily episodic adventure novel, but the more closely one looks at it, the more interesting and troubling it becomes. The protagonist-narrator, Edgar Huntly, writes a long letter to his betrothed, Mary Waldegrave, recounting a series of adventures in which he has participated. This letter is followed by two short ones from Huntly to his benefactor, Sarsefield, and one final short letter from Sarsefield to Huntly. The last letter suggests some of the ways in which the apparent clumsiness becomes troubling. Midway through the novel, Edgar learns that he will probably be unable to marry his fiancé, for her inheritance from her recently murdered brother seems not really to belong to her. Later, it appears that the return of Edgar's recently well-married friend, Sarsefield, once again puts him in a position to marry, but Sarsefield's last letter raises doubts about this event that remain unresolved. The reader never learns whether Edgar and Mary are united. The purpose of Sarsefield's letter is to chastise Edgar.

Edgar's main project in the novel becomes to cure the mad Clithero, who mistakenly believes he has been responsible for the death of Sarsefield's wife, formerly Mrs. Lorimer. By the end of his adventures, Edgar understands the degree to which Clithero is mistaken about events and believes that when Clithero learns the truth, he will be cured. To Edgar's surprise, when Clithero learns the truth, he apparently sets out to really kill his benefactor, Mrs. Sarsefield. Edgar writes his two letters to Sarsefield to warn of Clithero's impending appearance and sends them directly to Sarsefield, knowing that his wife may well see them first. She does see the second letter, and collapses and miscarries as a result. Sarsefield chastises Edgar for misdirecting the letters, even though Sarsefield knew full well from the first letter that the second was on its way to the same address. While, on one hand, Edgar's error seems comically trivial, especially in comparison with the misguided benevolence that drives him to meddle with Clithero, on the other hand, the consequences are quite serious, serious enough to make one question why Edgar *and* Sarsefield are so stupid about their handling of the letters. The reader is left wondering what to make of Edgar and Sarsefield; does either of them know what he is doing?

The novel seems intended in part as a demonstration that one is rarely if ever aware of what one is doing. Paul Witherington has noted that the novel takes the form of a quest that never quite succeeds, a story of initiation in which repeated initiations fail to take place. Edgar returns to his home shortly after the murder of his closest friend, Waldegrave, in order to solve the crime and bring the murderer to justice. When he sees Clithero, the mysterious servant of a neighbor, sleepwalking at the murder scene, he suspects Clithero of the murder. When he confronts Clithero, Edgar learns the story of his past. In Ireland, Clithero rose out of obscurity to become the favorite servant of Mrs. Lorimer. His virtue eventually led to Mrs. Lorimer's allowing an engagement between Clithero and her beloved niece. This story of virtue rewarded turned sour when, in self-defense, Clithero killed Mrs. Lorimer's blackguard twin brother. Mrs. Lorimer believed her life to be mysteriously entwined with her brother's and was convinced that she would die when he did. Clithero believed her and was convinced that by killing the father of his bride-to-be he had also killed his benefactor. In a mad refinement of benevolence, he determined to stab her in order to spare her the pain of dying from the news of her brother's death. Failing with the sword, he resorted to the word, telling her what had happened. Upon her collapse, he took flight, ignorant of the actual consequences of his act. Mrs. Lorimer did not die; she married Sarsefield and they went to America. Although Clithero's guilt seems unconnected with the murder of Waldegrave, except that the event has renewed Clithero's anguish over what he believes to be his crime, Edgar still suspects him. Furthermore, Clithero's story has stimulated Edgar's benevolence.

Edgar becomes determined to help Clithero, for even if he is Waldegrave's murderer, he has suffered enough. Clithero retires to the wilderness of Norwalk to die after telling his story to Edgar, but Edgar pursues him there to save him. After three trips filled with wilderness adventures, Edgar receives a series of shocks. He meets the man who is probably the real owner of Mary's inheritance and loses his hope for a speedy marriage. Fatigued from his adventures in the wilderness and frustrated in his efforts to benefit Clithero, perhaps guilty about prying into Clithero's life and certainly guilty about his handling of Waldegrave's letters, he begins to sleepwalk. His sleepwalking mirrors Clithero's in several ways, most notably in that he also hides a treasure, Waldegrave's letters, without being aware of what he is doing. After a second episode of sleepwalking, he finds himself at the bottom of a pit in a cave with no memory of how he arrived there; this is the second apparent diversion from his quest for Waldegrave's murderer.

Edgar takes three days to return to civilization, moving through a fairly clear pattern of death and rebirth that parallels the movement from savagery to civilization. His adventures—drinking panther blood, rescuing a maiden, fighting Native Americans, losing and finding himself in rough terrain, nearly killing his friends, and successfully evading his own rescue while narrowly escaping death several times—are filled with weird mistakes and rather abstract humor. For example, he is amazed at his physical endurance. When he finds himself within a half-day's walk of home, he determines, despite his three days of privation, to make the walk in six hours. Six hours later, he has not yet even gained the necessary road, and, though he knows where he is, he is effectively no closer to home than when he started out. Although he has endured the physical trials, he has not progressed.

Of his earlier explorations of the wilderness, Edgar says, "My rambles were productive of incessant novelty, though they always terminated in the prospects of limits that could not be overleaped." This physical nature of the wilderness is indicative of the moral nature of human life, which proves so complex that while people believe they can see to the next step of their actions, they find continually that they have seen incorrectly. Edgar repeatedly finds himself doing what he never thought he could do and failing at what he believes he can easily accomplish. The complexities of his wilderness experience are beyond the reach of this brief essay, but they seem to lead toward the deeper consideration of questions Edgar raises after hearing Clithero's story:

> If consequences arise that cannot be foreseen, shall we find no refuge in the persuasion of our rectitude and of human frailty? Shall we deem ourselves criminal because we do not enjoy the attributes of Deity? Because our power and our knowledge are confined by impassable boundaries?

In order for Edgar to be initiated and to achieve his quest, he needs to come to a just appreciation of his own limits. Although he can see Clithero's limitations quite clearly, Edgar fails to see his own, even after he learns that he has been sleepwalking, that he has been largely mistaken about the events surrounding the Indian raid, that he has mistaken his friends for enemies, and that he has made many other errors that might have caused his own death. Even after he learns that an American Indian killed Waldegrave and that his efforts with Clithero have been largely irrelevant, he persists in his ignorant attempt to cure the madman, only to precipitate new disasters. Edgar does not know himself and cannot measure the consequences of his simplest actions, yet he persists in meddling with another equally complex soul that he understands even less. Before Clithero tells Edgar his story, he says: "You boast of the beneficence of your intentions. You set yourself to do me benefit. What are the effects of your misguided zeal and random efforts? They have brought my life to a miserable close." This statement proves prophetic, for prior to each confrontation with Edgar, Clithero has determined to try to live out his life as best he can; each of Edgar's attempts to help drives Clithero toward the suicide that he finally commits.

Insofar as Edgar's quest is to avenge his friend's murder, he succeeds quite by accident. Insofar as his quest is for ethical maturity, he fails miserably, but no one else in the novel succeeds either. If a measure of moral maturity is the ability to moderate one's passions for the benefit of others, no one is mature. The virtuous Mrs. Lorimer cannot behave rationally toward her villainous brother, and her suffering derives ultimately from that failure. Clithero will murder out of misguided benevolence. Sarsefield, a physician, will let Clithero die of wounds received from American Indians because he believes that to Clithero, "consciousness itself is the malady, the pest, of which he only is cured who ceases to think." Even though Edgar must assent to this statement—concluding, "Disastrous and humiliating is the state of man! By his own hands is constructed the mass of misery and error in which his steps are forever involved"—he still wishes to correct some of Clithero's mistakes. In doing so, he provokes Clithero's suicide. No character understands him- or herself, his or her limitations, or his or her actions thoroughly; in the case of each of these characters, benevolence issues in murder, direct or indirect. One of the novel's many ironies is that among Edgar, Sarsefield, and Clithero, only Clithero is never morally responsible for a death other than his own.

In *Edgar Huntly*, as in *Wieland*, the stage of human action is beyond human comprehension. In *Wieland*, although there is no sanctuary for the virtuous, virtue remains valuable at least as a source of illusions of order, but in *Edgar Huntly* positive virtue becomes criminal because of inevitable human error. The phenomenon of sleepwalking and the motif of ignorance of self encourage the reader to consider those darker motives that may be hidden from the consciousness of the characters. Edgar must indeed affirm that people are criminal because they do not have "the attributes of Deity."

Wieland and *Edgar Huntly* are good examples of Brown's interests and the complexity of his fiction. The wedding of serious philosophical issues with forms of the popular gothic novel accounts for Brown's distinctive role in the development of the American novel and his continuing interest for students of American culture.

Terry Heller

OTHER MAJOR WORKS

SHORT FICTION: *Carwin, the Biloquist, and Other American Tales and Pieces*, 1822; *The Rhapsodist, and Other Uncollected Writings*, 1943.

NONFICTION: *Alcuin: A Dialogue*, 1798; *Literary Essays and Reviews*, 1992 (Alfred Weber and Wolfgang Schäfer, editors).

BIBLIOGRAPHY

Allen, Paul. *The Late Charles Brockden Brown.* Edited by Robert E. Hemenway and Joseph Katz. Columbia, S.C.: J. Faust, 1976. Begun in the early nineteenth century, this biography was later expanded upon by William Dunlap. Despite some inaccuracies, this work became the basis for subsequent studies.

Axelrod, Alan. *Charles Brockden Brown: An American Tale.* Austin: University of Texas Press, 1983. Study of Brown's work focuses primarily on four novels: *Wieland, Ormond, Arthur Mervyn*, and *Edgar Huntly.* Includes bibliographical references and an index.

Barnard, Philip, Stephen Shapiro, and Mark L. Kamrath, eds. *Revising Charles Brockden Brown: Culture, Politics, and Sexuality in the Early Republic.* Knoxville: University of Tennessee Press, 2004. Collection of thirteen essays addresses various aspects of Brown's works, placing them within the context of the political and ideological issues of his time. Among the topics discussed are the culture of the Enlightenment and questions of gender and sexuality.

Christopherson, Bill. *The Apparition in the Glass: Charles Brockden Brown's American Gothic.* Athens: University of Georgia Press, 1993. Chapter 2 provides a good discussion of the American romance, and separate chapters are devoted to Brown's novels *Wieland, Ormond, Arthur Mervyn*, and *Edgar Huntly.*

Clark, David L. *Charles Brockden Brown: Pioneer Voice of America.* 1952. Reprint. New York: AMS Press, 1966. Still one of the most complete books on Brown available. Combines biography, criticism, and liberal quotations from Brown's papers. Some of Brown's letters were published for the first time in the original edition of this work.

Clemit, Pamela. *The Godwinian Novel: The Rational Fictions of Godwin, Brockden Brown, Mary Shelley.* New York: Oxford University Press, 1993. Discusses the influence of British novelist William Godwin on Brown, examining elements of the Godwinian novel in *Wieland.* Includes bibliographical references and index.

Grabo, Norman S. *The Coincidental Art of Charles Brockden Brown.* Chapel Hill: University of North Carolina Press, 1981. Scholarly yet easy-to-read analysis of Brown's major fiction focuses on the psychology of the characters and what they reveal about Brown's own mind.

Hinds, Elizabeth Jane Wall. *Private Property: Charles Brockden Brown's Gendered Economics of Virtue.* Newark: University of Delaware Press, 1997. Contains chapters on economics and gender issues in the 1790's and separate chapters on each of Brown's major novels. Includes detailed notes and a bibliography.

Kafer, Peter. *Charles Brockden Brown's Revolution and the Birth of American Gothic.* Philadelphia: University of Pennsylvania Press, 2004. Focuses on *Wieland* in explaining how Brown adapted the European gothic novel into a purely American genre. Describes the social and political influences on Brown's work.

Ringe, Donald A. *Charles Brockden Brown.* Rev. ed. Boston: Twayne, 1991. Contains some of the most helpful criticism of Brown's works to be found. Discusses each of the novels and provides a chronology of Brown's life and writings. Includes an annotated bibliography.

Watts, Steven. *The Romance of Real Life: Charles Brockden Brown and the Origins of American Culture.* Baltimore: Johns Hopkins University Press, 1994. Discusses Brown's work from the perspective of the emergence of a capitalistic culture at the beginning of the nineteenth century. Addresses the author's major novels as well as his essays, private correspondence, and other materials.

RITA MAE BROWN

Born: Hanover, Pennsylvania; November 28, 1944

PRINCIPAL LONG FICTION

Rubyfruit Jungle, 1973
In Her Day, 1976
Six of One, 1978
Southern Discomfort, 1982
Sudden Death, 1983
High Hearts, 1986
Bingo, 1988
Wish You Were Here, 1990 (with Sneaky Pie Brown)
Rest in Pieces, 1992 (with Sneaky Pie Brown)
Venus Envy, 1993
Dolley: A Novel of Dolley Madison in Love and War, 1994
Murder at Monticello: Or, Old Sins, 1994 (with Sneaky Pie Brown)
Pay Dirt: Or, Adventures at Ash Lawn, 1995 (with Sneaky Pie Brown)
Murder, She Meowed: Or, Death at Montpelier, 1996 (with Sneaky Pie Brown)
Riding Shotgun, 1996
Murder on the Prowl, 1998 (with Sneaky Pie Brown)
Cat on the Scent, 1999 (with Sneaky Pie Brown)
Loose Lips, 1999
Outfoxed, 2000
Pawing Through the Past, 2000 (with Sneaky Pie Brown)
Alma Mater, 2001
Claws and Effect, 2001 (with Sneaky Pie Brown)
Catch as Cat Can, 2002 (with Sneaky Pie Brown)
Hotspur, 2002
Full Cry, 2003
The Tail of the Tip-Off, 2003 (with Sneaky Pie Brown)
Whisker of Evil, 2004
Cat's Eyewitness, 2005 (with Sneaky Pie Brown)
The Hunt Ball, 2005
The Hounds and the Fury, 2006
Sour Puss, 2006
Puss 'n Cahoots, 2007 (with Sneaky Pie Brown)
The Tell-Tale Horse, 2007
Hounded to Death, 2008
The Purrfect Murder, 2008 (with Sneaky Pie Brown)
The Sand Castle, 2008

OTHER LITERARY FORMS

Rita Mae Brown is a versatile and prolific writer. In addition to her novels, many of which she says she wrote with her cat, Sneaky Pie Brown, she has published an autobiography, *Rita Will: Memoir of a Literary Rabble-Rouser* (1997); a collection of political articles, *A Plain Brown Rapper* (1976); and two books of poetry, *The Hand That Cradles the Rock* (1971) and *Songs to a Handsome Woman* (1973). In 1982, she produced a screenplay, *The Slumber Party Massacre*, and a teleplay, *I Love Liberty*, followed by the creation of other film and television scripts. She has published articles, book reviews, and short stories in periodicals including *Horse Country*, *Sports Illustrated*, the *Los Angeles Times*, *Ms.* magazine, and *Vogue*. Brown has also written introductions for reprinted editions of her novels and for several other authors' books, including *The Troll Garden* (1905) by Willa Cather.

ACHIEVEMENTS

The Massachusetts Council on Arts and Humanities presented Rita Mae Brown with a grant in 1974. That year she was also given a National Endowment for the Arts Creative Writing Fellowship. Brown was a member of the Literature Panel for the National Endowment for the Arts from 1978 to 1982, and she received the National Endowment for the Arts fiction grant in 1978. In 1982, her teleplay *I Love Liberty* was nominated for an Emmy Award for Best Variety Show, and it received the Writers Guild of America Award for Best Variety Show on Television. She received another Emmy nomination for *The Long Hot Summer* in 1985. Brown was named a Literary Lion by the New York Public Library in 1987. She is a member of the International Academy of Poets and the International Association of Poets, Playwrights,

Editors, Essayists, and Novelists (PEN). Wilson College awarded Brown an honorary doctorate in humanities in 1992.

Several of Brown's mysteries have been Library of Virginia Literary Awards nominees. Many of her books have been *New York Times* best sellers and commercial book club selections, and many have been translated into numerous languages, including German, French, Spanish, Italian, Dutch, Swedish, Danish, and Hebrew. Her landmark 1973 novel *Rubyfruit Jungle* has retained literary interest and has remained in print into the twenty-first century.

Biography

Rita Mae Brown was born in Hanover, Pennsylvania, on November 28, 1944, to Juliann Young, a single mother, and weightlifter James Gordon Venable. Within two weeks, Young gave Rita Mae up for adoption to Ralph and Julia Ellen Buckingham Brown, Young's half cousin. Brown began school in Pennsylvania, where she dealt with ostracism due to her illegitimate birth and her family's lower socioeconomic status, then, in 1955, moved with her family to Fort Lauderdale, Florida, where she thrived because people did not discriminate against her. She began writing stories as a child. A voracious reader, Brown frequented area libraries. Her Latin classes at school enhanced her reading and writing abilities. As a teenager, she was a gifted tennis player.

After graduating from Fort Lauderdale High School in 1962, Brown enrolled with a scholarship at the University of Florida in Gainesville. In 1964, she was dismissed from that university for civil rights activism and for being a lesbian. She returned to Fort Lauderdale and attended the Junior College of Broward County, where she earned an A.A. in 1965. Following her graduation, Brown relocated; she earned a B.A. in English and classics from New York University in 1968 and a certificate in cinematography from Manhattan's School of Visual Arts that same year. While she lived in New York, Brown worked for several publishers and composed articles that were published in underground newspapers. She also became active in publicly addressing feminist, lesbian, and anti-Vietnam War issues.

In 1971, Brown went to Washington, D.C., as a fellow at the Institute for Policy Studies while she attended graduate courses. She published two poetry collections in the early 1970's and began her professional career as a novelist with the publication of *Rubyfruit Jungle* in 1973. Brown completed a Ph.D. in English and political science at the Institute for Policy Studies in 1976. During the next four years, she became a writing instructor at Goddard College in Vermont as well as at the Cazenovia, New York, Women Writers Center and continued to write in a variety of genres, including nonfiction and screenplays.

Brown then settled in Charlottesville, Virginia, her biological father's hometown, and also bought a farm at Afton in Nelson County, Virginia, near Crozet, the setting of her feline mystery series. Brown identifies Afton, where she raises horses and foxhounds on her farm, as her primary residence. Devoted to equine sports, Brown organized the Blue Ridge Polo Club and the Piedmont Women's Polo Club. She reestablished the Oak Ridge Foxhunt Club in 1993, serving as its master of foxhounds. She also is a Virginia Hunt Week director. An animal advocate, she supports humane shelters and rescues abandoned and mistreated animals. In 2005, Brown accepted a two-year visiting faculty position at the University of Nebraska at Lincoln, where she taught writing.

Analysis

Critics of Rita Mae Brown often assert that she is too radical and too argumentative in her works. Others point out that she is dealing with a problem of acceptance that has been the plight of many minor writers. Brown is no more "defensive" about her sexuality than are many other lesbian or gay writers, such as Allen Ginsberg in his poetic statement *Howl* (1956).

What sets Brown's work apart is that she does not disguise her prolesbian stance and does not become an apologist, as did some writers before her. Brown's work is feminist and thus has put off some conservative readers. She began writing in the early 1970's and was influenced by the National Organization for Women (NOW, an organization that asked her to leave because of her political views), the women's movement, and the movement against the Vietnam War. Most important, Brown reacted to her own sense of freedom, discovered upon her relocation to New York City, where she could be open as a lesbian.

Structure is the basic element Brown considers when writing fiction, carefully planning the framework of each story and how characters, plot, and other literary elements will be placed. Brown's relatives inspired her to write the Hunsenmeir novels, *Six of One*, *Bingo*, and *Loose Lips*, featuring the complexities of several generations of an extended southern family at different times in the twentieth century. Brown appropriated autobiographical elements for those books, in which character Nickel Smith, depicted at various ages, shares many of Brown's own characteristics. Interested in ancient literature, Brown acknowledges being inspired by the intricate Greek plays of Aristophanes and other early dramatists. She frequently incorporates tall tales, lies, legends, and historical and literary references in her novels to develop characterizations and settings. Humor and absurdity often lighten the intense tone of Brown's fiction, helping to expose facts and enabling broader awareness of nuances and secrets that would otherwise remain obscured.

During the late 1980's, Brown deviated from her previous literary endeavors by beginning to publish mysteries. She published her eighth novel, *Wish You Were Here*, in 1990; it features a Virginia sleuth and her pets, including a cat named Mrs. Murphy. The Mrs. Murphy mysteries, which reviewers have described as cozies, have attracted readers who might have been unfamiliar with Brown's previous works. Brown continued to produce both literary novels and Mrs. Murphy mysteries during the remainder of the 1990's before developing a foxhunting mystery series. By the early twenty-first century, Brown was concentrating mostly on writing her two mystery series, both of which feature heterosexual female protagonists, weaving her social and political commentary more subtly into plots than she had done in her 1970's novels.

Brown's agrarian interests shape her mystery fiction, which emphasizes protecting natural resources and educating people to respect the environment. Sensory details, such as noting weather conditions and seasonal changes, enhance the landscape descriptions. Brown has noted that each mystery she writes occurs in a particular season, and she cycles consecutively through the seasons of the year in four novels. Emphasizing pastoral as-

Rita Mae Brown and Sneaky Pie Brown. (Mark Homan)

pects of her settings, Brown devotes passages to the praise of nature and animals, inserting Bible verses occasionally. Her portrayals of settings as sanctuaries from modern stresses often convey a spiritual tone.

Brown's affinity for animals has resulted in her giving some animal characters, both domestic and wild, names, and she has attributed some of her writing to their insights, including anthropomorphic dialogue and scenes from animals' points of view; this has caused many literary critics to dismiss certain of her works. The resilience of people and of creatures remains an enduring theme in Brown's fiction, in which characters become empowered by their experiences and interactions.

RUBYFRUIT JUNGLE

Brown's novels draw on her own life; most of her work is clearly autobiographical. In her autobiography, *Rita Will*, Brown writes that when *Rubyfruit Jungle* was released, she received hate mail and threats on her life. The book is radical, and many readers found it upsetting.

Rubyfruit Jungle is a coming-of-age novel for protagonist Molly Bolt; it is also a direct statement of Brown's own coming-of-age. It describes the early life of Bolt, an adopted daughter of a poor family living in Coffee Hollow, Pennsylvania. Brown traces Molly's life from Coffee Hollow to Florida to New York City and takes Molly from a naïve young girl of seven to a mature, worldly-wise woman in her mid-twenties. Molly Bolt's life story is exactly that of Rita Mae Brown. In most cases, Brown presents all of the characters as merely renamed family members and friends from her childhood through her time in New York. During the course of the novel, the reader sees Molly defy local authority figures of every kind: parents, educators, family members, employers, and lovers. Molly has been described by at least one critic as similar to Huckleberry Finn in his rebellion against authority. Like that of Mark Twain, Brown's style employs folk humor and observations about the world. Unlike Twain, however, Brown does not rely on dialect or local color, though Brown's style is in the vein of other southern American writers, such as Flannery O'Connor, Eudora Welty, and Alice Walker, who have a sharp eye for idiosyncratic behavior.

Molly moves to Florida, as did Brown. While there, she becomes aware of her feelings for other women, falls in love with her college roommate at the University of Florida, and is expelled for this love, just as Brown was expelled from the university for being a lesbian. Molly leaves Florida and arrives in New York City, where she establishes herself in the gay community of Greenwich Village. There she finds a menial job, puts herself through school, and meets a beautiful woman who becomes her lover. From this point on, the novel concentrates on Molly's life as a lesbian.

When Molly left for New York, she was estranged from her mother. Only when she returns to Florida to film her mother as a final project for her degree does Molly really understand that the choices she has made have helped her to develop as an individual who can face the reality of her world. Breaking away from the homogeneity of family, friends, and society has been a difficult ordeal for Molly; however, it is something she had to do in order to grow. Brown explores a similar situation in her 2001 novel *Alma Mater*, in which female college students also make sexual and romantic decisions that counter their friends' and families' social expectations.

IN HER DAY

In Her Day, which treats the difficulties and divisions within the women's movement of the 1970's, was Brown's second novel. The focus is on Carole, an art historian at New York University (NYU). Other characters include LaVerne and Adele, women in their forties who are friends of Carole; Bon and Creampuff, a couple who are friends of the first three women; and a young woman named Ilse, a waitress in a feminist café where all the women dine one night. Ilse is attracted to Carole, and the two begin a relationship. The novel details the age conflict between Carole and Ilse and the even greater conflicting political views of the two women. Eventually, a radical newspaper exposes Carole as a lesbian to her misogynist chairman at NYU, and, when she suffers at his hands, she realizes that perhaps she is too conservative. In the meantime, Ilse's moderate views are influenced by Carole, and she begins to become more conservative. Although the women are unable to reach a common ground that will support their unstable relationship, the novel does illustrate a sense of compromise, which is clearly a nod from Brown to the feminist movement that disowned her when she was young and living in New York.

This novel is weaker than *Rubyfruit Jungle*. Brown tries too hard to be humorous, and her humor is too dark and crude for the novel. Also, *In Her Day* is somewhat harsh and off-putting, with its political diatribes.

VENUS ENVY

Venus Envy, another autobiographical novel, revolves around Mary Frazier Armstrong, owner of a successful art gallery in Charlottesville, Virginia. The heroine, known as Frazier to her family and friends, is hospitalized with what is thought to be terminal cancer. In a drug-induced state, Frazier writes letters to all the people who are important to her, including her mother, father, alcoholic brother, business partner, and two gay male friends. In these letters, Frazier sums up her relationship with each recipient and then informs each one that she is a lesbian. The next time the doctor visits the hospitalized Frazier, he tells her he has made a mistake, and she will not die. The rest of the novel portrays Frazier dealing with the consequences of her letters.

With *Venus Envy*, Brown reclaims her stature as a writer who is able to use humor, in this case derived from the plot, to make her point that people should be accepted as they are and should be allowed to lead their own lives. The novel redeems Brown as a radical of the 1960's and 1970's. While *Rubyfruit Jungle* is clearly her best work, *Venus Envy* shows that by eliminating the harsh tone of *In Her Day*, Brown could recapture her unique style and voice.

THE TELL-TALE HORSE

In *The Tell-Tale Horse*, the sixth volume in her foxhunting mystery series, Brown depicts the complex social dynamics and rivalries of a central Virginia foxhunting community. The novel's protagonist, seventy-three-year-old Jane Arnold, first introduced in the novel *Outfoxed*, serves as the Jefferson Hunt Club's master of foxhounds. The widowed Arnold, who is known as Sister, has the freedom and financial resources to pursue her interests on her farm, where she maintains well-bred foxhounds and horses. Foxhunting introduces a diverse cast of characters into Sister's world, ranging from her lover, Gray Lorillard, to employees, friends, and enemies. Conflicts between characters often escalate into crimes, including embezzlement, fraud, and murder.

In *The Tell-Tale Horse*, Sister and her friend Marion Maggiolo find a nude woman's corpse perched atop a large horse figure promoting Marion's store, Horse Country; the dead woman has been shot through the heart. It is discovered that the victim, Aashi Mehra, was the mistress of billionaire telecommunications entrepreneur Lakshmi Vajay, who foxhunts with Sister. Brown's adept characterization provides insights, as reasons for characters' antagonism and disdain for specific individuals are revealed. Sister ponders whether Lakshmi's wife, Madhur, murdered Aashi for vengeance or perhaps a wireless service competitor killed Aashi to protect technological secrets. As subplots consume Sister's attention, two additional murders occur. She maintains contact with Sheriff Ben Sidell, whose investigative skills she trusts. Although she fears being the next victim, especially after finding bloodied white roses in her stable, Sister often displays more interest in foxhunting than in sleuthing; through this device, Brown provides some relief from suspense and tension.

Nature is a prevailing theme in the novel, with digressions taking such form as Sister's discussion of how to tend foxes; she stresses that she wants to protect, not kill, wildlife and to promote responsible land conservation. Brown juxtaposes an emphasis on rural endeavors by locals to improve natural landscapes with the encroachment of urban outsiders who have acquired fortunes from telecommunications technology using cellular towers erected on nearby mountains. In this series of novels, Brown addresses various social issues in addition to ecological concerns, including racism, drug abuse, and teenage pregnancy. Her knowledge of both southern American culture and the culture of foxhunting enthusiasts provides authenticity, although at times her digressions related to these cultures seem excessive and disrupt the narrative flow.

THE PURRFECT MURDER

Greed provokes chaos in *The Purrfect Murder*, one of Brown's Mrs. Murphy mysteries. During the autumn after her fortieth birthday, Mary Minor Haristeen, known as Harry, focuses on managing her Crozet, Virginia, farm and her remarriage to equine veterinarian Pharamond (Fair) Haristeen. As in this series' previous fifteen novels, crime upsets Harry's rural community, which is populated by diverse personalities, including characters with deep roots in Crozet and newcomers who have substantial wealth to build elaborate homes there. Past and present relationships fuel emotions of jealousy and revenge, triggering confrontations as characters seek to acquire the things they desire, such as money and power.

Harry contemplates who murdered Dr. Will Wylde, a local gynecologist who performed abortions. Harry's recurring friends from prior books, including Cynthia Cooper, a local deputy, consider possible culprits; suspects include pro-life activists and Dr. Harvey Tillach, whose wife Wylde had seduced. Harry—along with Tee Tucker, a corgi, and cats Mrs. Murphy and Pewter—visits area residents, Wylde's widow, Benita, and his office staff. She discusses the murder while planning an elaborate fund-raiser with her closest friend, Susan Tucker. The omniscient narrative shifts, observing various characters' activities, such as smug building inspector Mike McElvoy visiting construction sites and arguing with owners, including arrogant Carla Paulson.

Tension escalates when an attacker kills Paulson at the fund-raiser, and police arrest Harry's friend Tazio Chappers, an architect, who is found holding a knife near the corpse. Determined to exonerate Tazio, Harry, often oblivious to her own vulnerabilities, intensifies her investigation into both Wylde's and Paulson's deaths. Brown gives voice to her animal characters, which communicate with each other and try to alert Harry to notice subtle details that may offer clues to the crimes. (She uses the stylistic technique of italicized dialogue to indicate her animal characters' communication with each other.) She often uses comic scenes with animal characters to counter the serious tone of passages describing crimes or villains. By including in her narrative the discussion of such topics as building codes and abortion, Brown suggests the disruption that urban concerns pose to rural tranquillity at the same time she increases her ability to hide clues for Harry and her pets to comprehend.

The Sand Castle

Family conflicts reveal people's capacity for forgiveness and tolerance in *The Sand Castle*. As an adult, Nickel Smith recalls an August, 1952, trip with her mother, aunt, and cousin, characters Brown featured in three prior Hunsenmeir novels. In this story, Nickel, the narrator, is seven years old and her cousin, Leroy, is eight. Leroy's grandmother, Louise, whom Nickel calls Wheezie, and her sister Juts, who is Nickel's mother, drive the children to a Maryland beach in an attempt to comfort Leroy, who is mourning his mother's death from cancer six months prior. Wheezie, also bereft after losing her daughter, quarrels with Juts regarding their contrasting religious beliefs. Enjoying the bickering between her mother and aunt, Nickel teases Leroy, who is emotionally paralyzed. His passivity contrasts with Nickel's outspokenness.

The sisters reminisce about beach trips during their youth, telling the children about a prank they played that embarrassed their aunt and sharing details of their family's history. At the beach, Wheezie and Juts start building a sand castle, assigning the children the task of toting buckets of water and sand. The sisters continue to spar verbally, each criticizing the other's choices regarding marriage and lifestyle. Juts views the sand castle as her opportunity to construct something grander in design than the home she desires but cannot afford. Nickel digs

a moat to protect the castle, but Juts realizes the sea will eventually wash it away, making a biblical reference that offends Wheezie. Fighting between the sisters escalates, and Wheezie abandons Juts and Nickel at the beach. Eventually she returns, however, and they eat soft-shell crabs at a local restaurant. Leroy, horrified by Nickel's tale of crabs eating flesh, rejects that delicacy.

The group returns to the beach, where the castle still stands but is occupied by a crab; the crab crawls into Leroy's swimming trunks and pinches his genitalia. Soon the beachgoers unite in an effort to resolve Leroy's predicament and avert castration. On the drive home, their attempts to comfort Leroy in his physical pain also contribute to healing their emotional distress, reinforcing their love and acceptance of one another despite their differences. Brown's use of humor to depict this day provides a realistic glimpse of the family dynamics that often surround grieving. By telling this story, adult Nickel keeps her promise, made in *Loose Lips*, that the Hunsenmeir sisters will remain alive in her memories.

Dennis L. Weeks
Updated by Elizabeth D. Schafer

Other major works

POETRY: *The Hand That Cradles the Rock*, 1971; *Songs to a Handsome Woman*, 1973.

SCREENPLAY: *The Slumber Party Massacre*, 1982; *Mary Pickford: A Life on Film*, 1997.

TELEPLAYS: *I Love Liberty*, 1982; *The Long Hot Summer*, 1985; *My Two Loves*, 1986 (with Reginald Rose); *Rich Men, Single Women*, 1989; *The Woman Who Loved Elvis*, 1993.

NONFICTION: *A Plain Brown Rapper*, 1976; *Starting from Scratch: A Different Kind of Writer's Manual*, 1988; *Rita Will: Memoir of a Literary Rabble-Rouser*, 1997; *Sneaky Pie's Cookbook for Mystery Lovers*, 1999.

TRANSLATION: *Hrotsvitha: Six Medieval Latin Plays*, 1971.

Bibliography

Boyle, Sharon D. "Rita Mae Brown." In *Contemporary Lesbian Writers of the United States: A Bio-bibliographical Critical Sourcebook*, edited by Sandra Pollack and Denise D. Knight. Westport, Conn.: Greenwood Press, 1993. Profiles Brown's life and work.

Includes an extended discussion of *Rubyfruit Jungle* and a useful bibliography.

Davies, Julia A. "Rita Mae Brown (1944-   )." In *Significant Contemporary American Feminists: A Biographical Sourcebook*, edited by Jennifer Scanlon. Westport, Conn.: Greenwood Press, 1999. Analyzes how Brown's political activities influenced her literary endeavors, particularly her novels featuring unconventional female protagonists and characters who challenge traditional gender roles.

Day, Frances Ann. "Molly Bolts and Lifelines: Rita Mae Brown's *Rubyfruit Jungle* (1973)." In *Women in Literature: Reading Through the Lens of Gender*, edited by Jerilyn Fisher and Ellen S. Silber. Westport, Conn.: Greenwood Press, 2003. Addresses the classroom study of Brown's *Rubyfruit Jungle* as it relates to the censorship of literature in schools. Identifies attributes of the novel's protagonist, such as individualism, that are universal to most students.

Greenya, John. "Virginia Foxhunting, Murder." *The Washington Times*, March 25, 2007. Reviews Brown's *The Hounds and the Fury,* expressing criticism that the abundance of foxhunting details overwhelm the novel's plot development. Also comments on the strengths and weaknesses of Brown's approach to writing mysteries.

Perry, Carolyn, and Mary Louise Weaks, eds. *The History of Southern Women's Literature*. Baton Rouge: Louisiana State University Press, 2002. Collection of essays includes discussion of themes in Brown's literature within the context of the work of contemporary southern female authors. A biographical sketch of Brown by Harold Woodell discusses her works through her early mysteries.

Van Dover, J. K., and John F. Jebb. *Isn't Justice Always Unfair? The Detective in Southern Literature.* Bowling Green, Ohio: Bowling Green State University Popular Press, 1996. Devotes a chapter to the examination of how rural settings, including those in Brown's mysteries, are depicted and influence literary techniques to create characters, crimes, and plots in the mystery genre. Also addresses Brown's portrayal of animals as sleuths.

Ward, Carol Marie. *Rita Mae Brown*. New York: Twayne, 1993. Provides a comprehensive introductory overview of Brown's life, writings, and philosophy and presents critical analysis of her works. Includes a chronology and an annotated bibliography.

Zimmerman, Bonnie. *The Safe Sea of Women: Lesbian Fiction, 1969-1989*. Boston: Beacon Press, 1990. Insightful study of contemporary lesbian prose that explores the interaction between fiction and community, specifically how lesbian novels and short stories have both reflected and shaped the lesbian community. Zimmerman describes *Rubyfruit Jungle* as the quintessential coming-out novel.

JOHN BUCHAN

Born: Perth, Scotland; August 26, 1875
Died: Montreal, Quebec, Canada; February 11, 1940
Also known as: Lord Tweedsmuir; 1st Baron Tweedsmuir

PRINCIPAL LONG FICTION

Sir Quixote of the Moors, Being Some Account of an Episode in the Life of the Sieur de Rohaine, 1895
John Burnet of Barns, 1898
A Lost Lady of Old Years, 1899
The Half-Hearted, 1900
Prester John, 1910 (also known as *The Great Diamond Pipe*)
Salute to Adventurers, 1915
The Thirty-nine Steps, 1915
Greenmantle, 1916
The Power-House, 1916
Mr. Standfast, 1919
The Path of the King, 1921

Huntingtower, 1922

Midwinter: Certain Travellers in Old England, 1923

The Three Hostages, 1924

John Macnab, 1925

The Dancing Floor, 1926

Witch Wood, 1927

The Courts of the Morning, 1929

Castle Gay, 1930

The Blanket of the Dark, 1931

A Prince of the Captivity, 1933

The Free Fishers, 1934

The House of the Four Winds, 1935

The Island of Sheep, 1936 (also known as *The Man from the Norlands*)

Sick Heart River, 1941 (also known as *Mountain Meadow*)

OTHER LITERARY FORMS

Although John Buchan (BEH-kahn) is remembered chiefly for his novels, more than half of his published work is in the form of nonfiction prose. He wrote numerous biographies and works of history, and he published speeches and lectures, educational books for children, and countless articles, essays, pamphlets, notes, and reviews. Late in his life, he produced an autobiographical work, and after his death his widow edited and published two collections of selections from his works.

Buchan's fictional works include not only novels but also a story for children, *The Magic Walking-Stick* (1932), and several collections of short stories. Some of the settings and situations in these stories later appeared in slightly altered form in Buchan's novels, and several of the stories in the later collections make use of characters from the novels, including Richard Hannay, Sandy Arbuthnot, and Sir Edward Leithen. Two of Buchan's volumes of short stories, *The Path of the King* (1921) and *The Gap in the Curtain* (1932), connect independent episodes and are bound together by a narrative frame; as a result, these works are sometimes listed as novels, although the individual episodes are actually quite distinct from one another.

In addition to his prose works, Buchan published a number of poems and edited three volumes of verse. He

also edited several works of nonfiction, including Francis Bacon's *Essays and Apothegms of Francis Lord Bacon* (1597, edited in 1894) and Izaak Walton's *The Compleat Angler: Or, The Contemplative Man's Recreation* (1653, edited in 1901).

ACHIEVEMENTS

While he was still an undergraduate at Oxford University, John Buchan received two major prizes for writing: the Stanhope Historical Essay Prize for an essay on Sir Walter Raleigh (1897) and the Newdigate Prize for Poetry for *The Pilgrim Fathers* (1898). He graduated in 1899 with a first-class honors degree, and shortly thereafter he was appointed private secretary to the high commissioner for South Africa (1901-1903). This was the first of many prestigious posts that Buchan filled: He was a conservative member of Parliament for the Scottish universities (1927-1935), president of the Scottish History Society (1929-1933), lord high commissioner to the general assembly of the Church of Scotland (1933, 1934), chancellor of the University of Edinburgh (1937-1940), and governor-general of Canada (1935-1940). In 1935, in recognition of his accomplishments and of his new post as governor-general, he was created Baron Tweedsmuir of Elsfield.

In part because of his political prominence and his reputation as a historian and in part because of his achievements as a novelist, Buchan received honorary doctorates from Oxford, Harvard, Yale, Columbia, McGill, and McMaster universities and from the Universities of Glasgow, St. Andrews, Edinburgh, Toronto, Manitoba, and British Columbia. He also became an honorary fellow of Brasenose College, Oxford.

Although Buchan was clearly not a full-time writer of fiction, his achievements as a novelist include some degree of critical success and a great deal of commercial popularity, particularly during the period between World War I and the 1960's. His novels appealed to a wide and varied audience, including students, laborers, clergy, academics, members of various professions, and such celebrities as A. J. Balfour, Stanley Baldwin, Clement Atlee, Ezra Pound, C. S. Lewis, J. B. Priestley, King George V, and Czar Nicholas II. Although they have declined in popularity in the United States since the early 1960's, Buchan's novels continue to sell moderately well in Great Britain, and they have been translated into a number of foreign languages, including French, German, Spanish, Dutch, Danish, Czech, Swedish, and Arabic.

BIOGRAPHY

John Buchan was born in Perth, Scotland, on August 26, 1875. He spent his early childhood near the Firth of Forth, an area to which he often returned for holidays and that served as the setting for a great deal of his fiction. His father was a minister of the Free Church of Scotland; his mother was the daughter of a sheep farmer. From both of his parents, but particularly from his strong-minded mother, Buchan learned to value endurance, hard work, and, above all, perseverance, and he placed such emphasis on these qualities in his novels that many readers have come to regard this emphasis as the hallmark of his work.

When Buchan was thirteen years old, his father was called to the John Knox Free Church in Glasgow. There, Buchan attended Hutcheson's Grammar School and, later, the University of Glasgow, whose faculty then included such scholars as Lord Kelvin, A. C. Bradley, George Ramsay, and Gilbert Murray; the latter became one of Buchan's closest friends. At the end of his third year at the University of Glasgow, Buchan won a Junior Hulme scholarship to Oxford University, and in the autumn of 1895, he began his studies there at Brasenose College.

Because his scholarship was not sufficient to meet all of his expenses, Buchan earned extra money by reading manuscripts for the publishing firm of John Lane; among the manuscripts that he recommended for publication was Arnold Bennett's first novel, *A Man from the North* (1898). Buchan also became a regular reviewer for several publications and continued to work steadily on his own novels and nonfiction prose. In 1898, he had the distinction of being listed in *Who's Who*: He had at that time six books in print, two in press, and three in progress, and he had published innumerable articles, essays, and reviews. He was also an active member of several prestigious Oxford and London clubs and organizations, notably the Oxford Union, of which he was librarian and later president. In 1899, he sat for his final examinations and earned a first-class honors degree; one

year later, having "eaten his dinners" and passed the examination, he was called to the bar.

During the two years following his graduation, Buchan wrote leading articles for *The Spectator*, worked as a barrister, and continued to write both fiction and nonfiction. In 1901, he accepted the post of political private secretary to Lord Milner, who was then high commissioner for South Africa. During the two years he spent in that country, Buchan became familiar with the practical administrative aspects of political situations that he had discussed on a more theoretical level in his essays for *The Spectator*. He also acquired background material for several of his novels, notably *Prester John*.

When he returned to London in 1903, Buchan resumed his legal work at the bar and his literary work on *The Spectator*. In 1906, he became second assistant editor of *The Spectator*, and, in 1907, he accepted the position of chief literary adviser to the publishing firm of Thomas Nelson. He also continued to extend the circle

John Buchan. (Library of Congress)

of acquaintances that he had begun to form at Oxford, and he became one of the best-known and most promising young men in London society and politics.

Buchan was greatly attracted to a young lady whom he met at a London dinner party, and on July 15, 1907, he and Susan Grosvenor were married at St. George's, Hanover Square. Their first child, Alice, was born one year later, followed by John (1911), William (1916), and Alastair (1918). Until the outbreak of World War I, the Buchans lived comfortably in London while John Buchan continued to write fiction, legal opinions, and essays and articles for such publications as *The Spectator* and *The Times Literary Supplement*.

Shortly after World War I began, Buchan, who had been asked to write a continuing history of the war for Nelson's and who also acted as correspondent for *The Times*, visited a number of French battlefields as a noncombatant. In 1916, he returned to France as a temporary lieutenant colonel, acting as press officer and propagandist for the foreign office and working for Field Marshal Lord Douglas Haig as official historian. In February, 1917, he was appointed director of information, in charge of publicity and propaganda. In the middle of all of his war-related activities, between 1914 and 1918, he wrote three of his most popular novels: *The Thirty-nine Steps, Greenmantle*, and *Mr. Standfast*.

When World War I ended, Buchan purchased Elsfield, a country house near Oxford, and settled down to a routine of writing, working at Nelson's, and entertaining his numerous friends, including T. E. Lawrence, Robert Graves, W. P. Ker, Gilbert Murray, and A. L. Rowse. In 1919, he became a director of the Reuters news agency, and four years later he became deputy chair. Buchan's peaceful routine at Elsfield, however, ended in the spring of 1927, when he was elected to Parliament as the member for the Scottish universities, a position he held until 1935. He became as active a member of London society during his term in Parliament as he had been as a younger man, and he became increasingly well known and influential in political circles. He was appointed lord high commissioner to the general assembly of the Church of Scotland in 1933 and again in 1934, and in 1935 he was appointed to a much more important post: governor-general of the Dominion of Canada. In recognition of his accomplishments and of his new posi-

tion, he was created a baron; he chose as his title Lord Tweedsmuir of Elsfield.

Buchan's tenure of office as governor-general (1935-1940) coincided with the growing tension in Europe that eventually led to World War II, and, because his post was largely a ceremonial one, he had to be extremely cautious in his statements and in his behavior. Among the delicate diplomatic situations that he handled well were the visits of U.S. president Franklin D. Roosevelt and of King George VI and Queen Elizabeth to Canada; Buchan's greatest error in diplomacy occurred when he made a speech in which he suggested that Canada's defense policy was inadequate. Despite occasional lapses of this type, however, Buchan was a successful governor-general, in part because he made a point of visiting not only such cultural centers as Montreal and Quebec but also more remote places such as Medicine Hat, Regina, Saskatoon, and Edmonton. In addition to enhancing his popularity as governor-general, these trips provided background material for his last novel, *Sick Heart River*.

As the end of his five-year term of office approached, Buchan was asked to allow himself to be nominated for another term. He refused because of his steadily declining health and his plans to leave Canada at the end of 1940. On February 6, 1940, however, he suffered a cerebral hemorrhage and struck his head during a fall; five days later he died. He left an autobiographical work, a novel, a children's history of Canada, a volume of essays, and a volume of lectures, all of which were published posthumously, as well as an unfinished novel and two chapters of a nonfiction work; these chapters appear at the end of the autobiography.

ANALYSIS

Despite his manifold activities, John Buchan is remembered primarily as a writer of implausible but exciting adventure fiction with overtones of the nineteenth century romance. Most of his novels fall into the general category of thrillers, but a few, such as *Salute to Adventurers, Midwinter, Witch Wood*, and *The Blanket of the Dark*, are more accurately classified as historical romances. Despite some variations in form and emphasis, however, all of Buchan's novels share certain features that contribute to the characteristic flavor of his fiction; these include melodramatic sequences, unusually effective descriptions of landscape and atmosphere, frequent references to such qualities as endurance and perseverance, and exciting but comparatively nonviolent action.

The melodramatic quality of Buchan's fiction arises from a number of sources, including his admiration for the highly melodramatic thrillers of E. Phillips Oppenheim and his own overdeveloped sense of the theatrical. Although Buchan was seldom original in his choice of melodramatic elements, he made good use of them in enhancing the suspense and excitement of his novels. For example, *Prester John*, *Greenmantle*, *The Three Hostages*, *The Dancing Floor*, and *Witch Wood* owe a great deal of their atmosphere and effect to indistinctly defined and therefore singularly mysterious antique rituals and ceremonies, including pagan sacrifice and devil worship. Other novels, including *Huntingtower*, *Midwinter*, and *The House of the Four Winds*, feature royalty in distress and simple but noble-hearted adventurers who risk their lives for "the cause." Buchan also made frequent use of such staple elements of melodramatic fiction as secret societies, talismans and tokens, fairylike heroines (milky-skinned and graceful), exotic villains (brunette and slinky), and characters who bear a Burden of Secret Sorrow.

As these examples suggest, Buchan did not hesitate to employ many of the clichés of the thriller and romance genres. Moreover, his work is not only derivative but also repetitive, containing numerous examples of devices that he found successful and therefore used repeatedly. For example, in addition to the novels that make use of some form of magic and those that deal with royalty and adventurers, he wrote five novels in which the foiling of the villain depends on the decoding of a cipher, six in which one of the villains tries to mesmerize the protagonist, and eleven in which one of the villains passes for a time as an irreproachable member of society. In addition to reusing successful plot devices, Buchan had the irritating habit of repeating certain favorite words, including "eldritch," "dislimn," "totem," and "frowst."

Buchan's tendency to repeat himself is not surprising in view of the speed with which he wrote. In the period between 1915 and 1936, he produced twenty-one volumes of fiction and almost thirty volumes of nonfiction. Despite his hasty writing, his repetitiveness, and his overuse of clichés, however, Buchan was by no means a mere hack. He wrote disciplined, polished, occasionally elegant prose, seldom stooping to sensationalism and describing even the most exciting or dramatic scenes in a clear narrative style that was seldom equaled in the thriller fiction of that period.

More important, like Sir Walter Scott and Robert Louis Stevenson, whose work Buchan greatly admired, he was not only acutely sensitive to local color and atmosphere but also gifted in expressing that sensitivity in his fiction. He was particularly adept at making use of settings with which he was familiar: Many of his novels, including *The Thirty-nine Steps*, *John Macnab*, and *Witch Wood*, are set in the Scottish countryside where Buchan grew up and to which he often returned; *Prester John* is set in South Africa, where Buchan served as Lord Milner's secretary; several novels, including *The Power House* and *The Three Hostages*, contain scenes in the parts of London that he frequented during the years before World War I and during his term in Parliament; and most of the action in *Sick Heart River* takes place in the far north of Canada, which he visited during his term as governor-general.

Buchan's depiction of these familiar settings and of the atmospheres associated with them is both denotative and connotative, and this combination, which is responsible for a great deal of the power and charm of his books, does much to raise his work above the level of run-of-the-mill adventure fiction. The denotative quality of Buchan's descriptions stems from his talent in selecting the salient features of a landscape and producing vividly lifelike verbal pictures of them in disciplined and concise prose. The connotative quality results from his ability to imbue the landscape with an atmosphere that is so vivid that it might almost be called a personality and to derive from the landscape a mood or even a moral valence that complements the action of the novel. In *Witch Wood*, for example, the open and innocent Scottish countryside is marred by a black wood, which is not only an appropriate setting for the devilish rites that take place in it but also, the novel implies, the cause of them in some obscure manner.

In a number of Buchan's novels, the complementary relationship between the setting and the action reaches the level of allegory when the protagonist and in some cases other characters undertake a long and arduous journey through a landscape that includes steep hills, swamps or difficult waters, natural pitfalls, and traps designed by enemies who often pose as friends. The difficulties that arise in the course of this journey provide opportunities for the exciting chase scenes and the suspenseful action that are essential to adventure literature, but they also do more: As characters overcome each of the obstacles presented by the landscape through which they move, they acquire or display appropriate qualities of soul that redeem them or confirm them in their morality and status. This allegorical use of landscape, which is clearly based on one of Buchan's favorite books, John Bunyan's *The Pilgrim's Progress* (1678, 1684), serves as the central plot device in almost all of his best-known novels, including *The Thirty-nine Steps, The Power-House, Greenmantle, Mr. Standfast, Midwinter*, and *Sick Heart River*.

The most important effect of Buchan's repeated use of landscape as an allegory is the stress that this technique enables him to place upon the redeeming quality of certain types of behavior. To overcome the obstacles that beset them, the characters in his novels must display courage, endurance, and, above all, perseverance in hard work despite fatigue, setbacks, and apparently hopeless delays. These qualities are so central to his novels that all of his major characters are defined and evaluated in terms of them. Some characters already possess these attributes before the action begins and are finally triumphant because they successfully apply to a particular set of circumstances the qualities they had already developed and, in some cases, displayed in earlier adventures; other characters develop these attributes as the action progresses.

The protagonist with predeveloped virtues is a character type common to almost all adventure literature, and, in most cases, Buchan's treatment of it is not particularly memorable. In the novels that center on Sir Edward Leithen, however, Buchan handles the theme quite effectively, showing that even someone who spends a great deal of time at a desk can possess the courage, endurance, and perseverance of a true hero. Further, in addition to these basic qualities, Buchan endows Leithen with a degree of sensitivity that allows him to absorb and to respond to the influences of various landscapes, thus

deriving from his adventures not only the satisfaction of accomplishing his external objective but also increased insight, depth of soul, and spiritual regeneration. This theme is consistent and progressive in the Leithen novels, so that in the last one, *Sick Heart River*, Leithen's renewal of soul, resulting from his responsiveness to the influences of the environment, is carried almost to the point of apotheosis.

In addition to characters such as Leithen, who clearly possess the qualities necessary for success, Buchan's novels include a number of lesser characters who, as the action progresses, display or attain unexpected greatness of soul through unaccustomed exertion and suffering. Buchan was generally successful in dealing with such characters, in part because of the surprising liberality of his attitude toward character types who would, in most of the other adventure literature of that period, have no redeeming—or even redeemable—qualities whatsoever. Because his initial description of these characters is unusually balanced, their conversion in the course of participating in the adventure is far more convincing than it otherwise would have been.

One such character, found in Buchan's thriller *Mr. Standfast*, is a World War I conscientious objector named Launcelot Wake who first appears as a hot-eyed, sallow young man ridiculing everything that is held sacred by the protagonist, Brigadier-General Richard Hannay. Nevertheless, Hannay, and through him the reader, finds it impossible to dislike Wake, who is strong-willed, intelligent, and sincere in his beliefs. As he willingly accompanies Hannay on a difficult and dangerous climb through an Alpine pass, voluntarily exposing himself to enemy fire on the front lines and finally receiving his death wound, Wake gradually achieves dignity, self-respect, and spiritual regeneration—yet he remains, to the end of the novel, a staunch pacifist who resolutely refuses to take up arms. No other major thriller writer of Buchan's generation would have had the tolerance or the breadth of mind to make a demi-hero of a recusant conscientious objector, particularly in a novel written in the middle of World War I while its author was on active service as a lieutenant-colonel in the British army.

As Buchan's sympathetic depiction of Launcelot Wake suggests, his overall point of view was far from the bellicose and sometimes fascist attitude associated with writers such as "Sapper," Edgar Wallace, and Gerard Fairlie, whose protagonists unhesitatingly inflict physical injury and even death upon villains whom they encounter. Buchan's protagonists seldom administer any form of punishment, and if the villains die at all, it is usually the result of an accident or, more rarely, at the hands of a minor character in the story. In *Greenmantle*, for example, the exotically beautiful villainess is accidentally killed by artillery fire; in *Mr. Standfast*, a German spy is killed by German fire in the trenches; in *The Three Hostages*, the archvillain falls to his death despite Hannay's efforts to save him; in *Midwinter*, one traitor is placed on parole in consideration of his wife's feelings and another is sent into exile; in *Witch Wood*, the principal warlock is beset by his own demons and dies in his madness. Buchan never dwelt upon or glorified any form of bloodshed, and some of his novels involve no violence at all, stressing instead imaginative if occasionally melodramatic situations, suspenseful action, and seemingly insurmountable challenges to the strength and determination of the characters.

HANNAY NOVELS

Although all of his novels share certain common features, in some cases Buchan made use of one of his three major series protagonists, each of whom imbues the novels in which he appears with his distinctive flavor. By far the most popular of these is Richard Hannay, who is the central figure in *The Thirty-nine Steps*, *Greenmantle*, *Mr. Standfast*, and *The Three Hostages* and appears in *The Courts of the Morning* and *The Island of Sheep*. Hannay is by far the most typical thriller hero whom Buchan created: Physically strong and morally intrepid, he is always ready for a bracing climb in the Scottish hills or a brisk run across the moors, usually dodging at least two sets of pursuers and an occasional dog. Becomingly modest regarding his own accomplishments and courage, Hannay generously admires the greatness—albeit perverted greatness—of his foes.

Although several villains, including the old man with the hooded eyes in *The Thirty-nine Steps*, Hilda von Einem in *Greenmantle*, and most notably Dominic Medina in *The Three Hostages*, try to hypnotize Hannay, he is protected by his solid common sense and by a strong will fortified by frequent cold baths. He is also more sportsmanlike than practical; for example, when he fi-

nally gets a clear shot at the highly elusive and dangerous villain of *Mr. Standfast*, he allows him to escape yet again because firing at him under those conditions seems "like potting at a sitting rabbit." On the other hand, Hannay is far from being one of the mindless anti-intellectuals who infest early twentieth century thriller literature. In *Mr. Standfast*, for example, he willingly undertakes a course of reading in the English classics, and throughout the series most of his attitudes and reflections are, if not profound, at least reasonably intelligent.

Although Hannay is by no means a mere beefy dolt, many of the opinions expressed in the course of his first-person narration reflect the prejudices common to his generation and social class, and these include racial and ethnic attitudes that many readers find offensive. Since most of the slighting references to blacks, Germans, Italians, Russians, and Jews that appear in Buchan's work are concentrated in the Hannay stories, it is possible to argue, as several of Buchan's supporters have done, that Hannay's attitudes and language arise from his characterization rather than from the kind of prejudice on Buchan's part that is associated with such writers as "Sapper," Gerald Fairlie, and Dornford Yates. Buchan's partisans also point out that there are comparatively few such references even in the Hannay books, and that these are not nearly so virulent as similar references in the works of many of Buchan's contemporaries. Further, Buchan is known to have supported a number of Jewish causes; for example, in 1932 he succeeded Josiah Wedgwood as chair of a pro-Zionist parliamentary committee, and in 1934 he spoke at a demonstration organized by the Jewish National Fund.

Buchan's detractors, on the other hand, point to passages in his personal correspondence that are critical of various ethnic groups. They also maintain that his attitude toward blacks, formed in part during his experience in South Africa, was paternalistic and patronizing, and it is certainly true that even when he meant to express admiration for members of the black race, as he did in *Prester John*, his attitude and his choice of language were often unconsciously—and therefore all the more offensively—condescending. Perhaps the fairest conclusion that can be drawn from this controversy is that, although some of Buchan's racial and ethnic prejudices would be considered offensive today, the prejudices that he attributed to the fictional character of Richard Hannay are probably more extreme than his own. Further, by the standards of his age and class, he was commendably moderate in his use of racial and ethnic stereotypes.

McCunn novels

Buchan's second series protagonist was Dickson McCunn. The three McCunn novels are the most overtly, yet humorously, romantic of Buchan's thrillers: *Huntingtower* features an exiled Russian princess who is loved by a left-wing poet and rescued with the help of a group of Glasgow street urchins, and *Castle Gay* and *The House of the Four Winds* deal with the restoration of the rightful prince of Evallonia with the help of the same urchins (now grown), a reluctant newspaper magnate, and a circus elephant. McCunn himself is a middle-aged, recently retired grocer who looks forward to "Seeing Life" and "Doing Noble Deeds." He dreams of becoming involved in pure Sir Walter Scott adventures, and, because of his dreams, he tends to view real-life people and situations through a rosy, romantic haze; for example, he reverences the rather weak and worldly prince of Evallonia as the embodiment of all the qualities associated with the Bonnie Prince Charlie of legend. Nevertheless, McCunn is saved from being ridiculous by his solid common sense and essential decency and by Buchan's implication that, if what McCunn sees is not precisely what *is*, it is at least what *should be*.

The dramatic, in some respects melodramatic, quality of the McCunn novels is blessedly undercut by the verbal and situational humor that is their hallmark. In *Huntingtower*, for example, Wee Jaikie, the street boy who later becomes the true protagonist of *Castle Gay* and *The House of the Four Winds*, helps to rescue a Romanov princess while singing garbled versions of Bolshevik hymns that he learned at a socialist Sunday school. Similarly, at one point in *The House of the Four Winds*, a friend of Jaikie who assists him in a series of swashbuckling episodes appears outside his second-story window mounted on an elephant named Aurunculeia and asks in German for a match. Through his handling of these humorously improbable situations, Buchan gently ridiculed the more preposterous aspects of an excessively romantic view of life, while retaining and even enhancing those qualities that he never ceased to admire, such as constancy, devotion, and faith.

Leithen novels

Buchan's last series protagonist, Sir Edward Leithen, is featured in four novels: *The Power-House*, *John Macnab*, *The Dancing Floor*, and *Sick Heart River*. These are somewhat atypical adventure stories, largely because they concern not only a series of suspenseful activities but also a group of central themes, including the thinness of civilization and the ethic of success. These themes are expressed through the first-person narration of Leithen, who is a far more sophisticated and reflective character than Richard Hannay, Buchan's other first-person series narrator.

In view of the legal and political background with which Buchan endowed Leithen, it is not surprising that he demonstrates an intense awareness of the thinness of the shell of civilization within which he and his contemporaries desire to believe themselves safe. This concept is explored from a number of perspectives within the series: For example, in *The Power-House*, which is the earliest Leithen novel and the closest to the traditional thriller mode, the expression of this theme centers on the imminence of violence and the vulnerability of ordinary individuals, while in the more recondite novel *The Dancing Floor*, the thinness of civilization is associated with the terrifying attractiveness of obscurely fearsome pre-Christian religious rites to whose power Leithen himself, in many respects the quintessential civilized man, nearly succumbs.

Buchan provided a balance for the sensibility that Leithen displays in his reflections on the thinness of civilization by attributing to him not only a shrewd and practical legal mind but also a respect for worldly success that is so marked that it borders on careerism. Although this emphasis on competitive success is by no means confined to the Leithen novels, it is most evident in them. Leithen himself is greatly in demand as a solicitor, is elected to Parliament, and eventually becomes solicitor-general; more important, the novels that he narrates contain numerous approving references to persons who are not merely successful but unsurpassed in their fields. Nevertheless, a close reading of the Leithen novels shows that although worldly success is spoken of with respect, it is treated not as an end in itself, but as a testimony to the stamina, hard work, and perseverance of the individual who has attained it.

If the Leithen novels abound in references to success, they also abound in references to exhaustion, and both types of references apply to the same individuals. Success in competition with others in one's field is, in the Leithen novels, simply an extension of the Bunyanesque ethic of hard work and perseverance that, in all of Buchan's fiction, leads to success in competition with villains and with natural forces. Further, in all of Buchan's novels, worldly success is second in importance to more basic values, such as courage, honor, and compassion. To Leithen and to Buchan's other major characters, success is admirable but it is emphatically not enough.

As the preceding discussion indicates, Buchan's novels are written in polished prose and include sensitive descriptions of settings that are incorporated into both the plots of the novels and the development of the characters. Further, his liberal attitudes not only redeem his work from jingoism, egregious racism, and gratuitous violence but also contribute to the development of less stereotyped, more varied, and more complex characters than are usually found in adventure fiction.

Buchan was not, however, a serious literary figure and never claimed to be. He wrote his novels quickly and in the middle of numerous distractions, seldom revised, and often made use of clichéd situations and of devices that he himself had used, in many cases repeatedly, in earlier stories. Further, although he did create some unusually good characters, he also created a large number of cardboard ones. His villains, in particular, are with few exceptions unsubstantial figures whose machinations are overshadowed to the point of eclipse by the journey and chase scenes that dominate and, in this respect, upset the balance of several of his novels. The structure of the novels is further weakened by the fact that, although the emphasis that Buchan places on the moral order seldom becomes overtly didactic, it does provide an excuse for the use of a profusion of providential occurrences that are virtually indistinguishable from mere blatant coincidences. Despite their flaws, however, Buchan's novels are well-written and sensitive tales of adventure whose raison d'être is to provide salutary entertainment; that they usually succeed in doing so is no minor accomplishment.

Joan DelFattore

OTHER MAJOR WORKS

SHORT FICTION: *Grey Weather: Moorland Tales of My Own People*, 1899; *The Watcher by the Threshold, and Other Tales*, 1902 (revised 1918); *The Moon Endureth: Tales and Fancies*, 1912; *Ordeal by Marriage*, 1915; *The Runagates Club*, 1928; *The Gap in the Curtain*, 1932; *The Best Short Stories of John Buchan*, 1980; *The Far Islands, and Other Tales of Fantasy*, 1984.

POETRY: *The Pilgrim Fathers: The Newdigade Prize Poem 1898*, 1898; *Poems, Scots and English*, 1917 (revised 1936).

NONFICTION: *Scholar Gipsies*, 1896; *Sir Walter Raleigh*, 1897; *Brasenose College*, 1898; *The African Colony: Studies in the Reconstruction*, 1903; *The Law Relating to the Taxation of Foreign Income*, 1905; *A Lodge in the Wilderness*, 1906; *Some Eighteenth Century Byways, and Other Essays*, 1908; *What the Home Rule Bill Means*, 1912; *Andrew Jameson, Lord Ardwall*, 1913; *The Marquis of Montrose*, 1913; *The Achievements of France*, 1915; *Britain's War by Land*, 1915; *Nelson's History of the War*, 1915-1919 (24 volumes); *The Battle of Jutland*, 1916; *The Battle of Somme, First Phase*, 1916; *The Future of the War*, 1916; *The Purpose of the War*, 1916; *The Battle of Somme, Second Phase*, 1917; *The Battle-Honours of Scotland, 1914-1918*, 1919; *The Island of Sheep*, 1919 (with Susan Buchan); *Francis and Riversdale Grenfell: A Memoir*, 1920; *The History of South African Forces in France*, 1920; *Miscellanies, Literary and Historical*, 1921 (2 volumes); *A Book of Escapes and Hurried Journeys*, 1922; *Days to Remember: The British Empire in the Great War*, 1923 (with Henry Newbolt); *The Last Secrets: The Final Mysteries of Exploration*, 1923; *The Memory of Sir Walter Scott*, 1923; *Lord Minto: A Memoir*, 1924; *Some Notes on Sir Walter Scott*, 1924; *The History of the Royal Scots Fusiliers, 1678-1918*, 1925; *The Man and the Book: Sir Walter Scott*, 1925; *Two Ordeals of Democracy*, 1925; *The Fifteenth Scottish Division, 1914-1919*, 1926 (with John Stewart); *Homilies and Recreations*, 1926; *To the Electors of the Scottish Universities*, 1927; *Montrose*, 1928; *The Cause and the Causal in History*, 1929; *What the Union of the Churches Means to Scotland*, 1929; *The Kirk in Scotland, 1560-1929*, 1930 (with George Adam Smith); *Lord Rosebery, 1847-1930*, 1930; *Montrose and*

Leadership, 1930; *The Revision of Dogmas*, 1930; *The Novel and the Fairy Tale*, 1931; *Julius Caesar*, 1932; *Sir Walter Scott*, 1932; *Andrew Lang and the Border*, 1933; *The Margins of Life*, 1933; *The Massacre of Glencoe*, 1933; *Gordon at Khartoum*, 1934; *Oliver Cromwell*, 1934; *The Principles of Social Service*, 1934; *The Scottish Church and the Empire*, 1934; *The University, the Library, and the Common Weal*, 1934; *The King's Grace, 1910-1935*, 1935 (also known as *The People's King: George V*); *The Western Mind, an Address*, 1935; *A University's Bequest to Youth, an Address*, 1936; *Augustus*, 1937; *The Interpreter's House*, 1938; *Presbyterianism: Yesterday, Today, and Tomorrow*, 1938; *Canadian Occasions: Addresses by Lord Tweedsmuir*, 1940; *Comments and Characters*, 1940 (W. Forbes Gray, editor); *Memory Hold-the-Door*, 1940 (also known as *Pilgrim's Way: An Essay in Recollection*); *The Clearing House: A Survey of One Man's Mind*, 1946 (Lady Tweedsmuir, editor); *Life's Adventure: Extracts from the Works of John Buchan*, 1947.

CHILDREN'S LITERATURE: *Sir Walter Raleigh*, 1911; *The Magic Walking-Stick*, 1932; *The Long Traverse*, 1941 (also known as *Lake of Gold*).

EDITED TEXTS: *Essays and Apothegms of Francis Lord Bacon*, 1894; *Musa Piscatrix*, 1896; *The Compleat Angler: Or, The Contemplative Man's Recreation*, 1901; *The Long Road to Victory*, 1920; *Great Hours in Sport*, 1921; *A History of English Literature*, 1923; *The Nations of Today: A New History of the World*, 1923-1924; *The Northern Muse*, 1924; *Modern Short Stories*, 1926; *South Africa*, 1928; *The Teaching of History*, 1928-1930 (11 volumes); *The Poetry of Neil Munro*, 1931.

BIBLIOGRAPHY

Buchan, Anna. *Unforgettable, Unforgotten*. London: Hodder and Stoughton, 1945. This memoir by one of Buchan's sisters provides a personal look at the author. Indexed and illustrated, it is especially good for his early life.

"Buchan, John." In *Mystery and Suspense Writers: The Literature of Crime, Detection, and Espionage*, edited by Robin W. Winks and Maureen Corrigan. New York: Scribner's Sons, 1998. Essay in a collection of articles on sixty-eight mystery authors from the nineteenth and twentieth centuries provides an overview of Buchan's life, an analysis of his work, and a bibliography.

Buchan, William. *John Buchan: A Memoir*. Toronto, Ont.: Griffen House, 1982. Written by John Buchan's son, this very readable biography humanizes Buchan by concentrating on his personal, rather than public, life. Based on William's childhood memories, as well as his own expertise as a novelist, poet, and literary critic. Well indexed and contains a good bibliography.

Butts, Dennis. "The Hunter and the Hunted: The Suspense Novels of John Buchan." In *Spy Thrillers: From Buchan to Le Carré*, edited by Clive Bloom. New York: St. Martin's Press, 1990. Butts's analysis of Buchan's work appears in one of thirteen essays examining books by twentieth century suspense novelists. Includes an introductory essay about the genre, a bibliography, and an index.

Cawelti, John G., and Bruce A. Rosenberg. *The Spy Story*. Chicago: University of Chicago Press, 1987. Cawelti's chapter, "The Joys of Buchaneering," argues that Buchan's Richard Hannay stories are the crucial link between the spy adventures and the espionage novels of the twentieth century. Buchan developed a formula that was adopted and given various twists by successive authors. Includes an excellent bibliography and appendixes.

Daniell, David. *The Interpreter's House: A Critical Assessment of John Buchan*. London: Nelson, 1975. Concentrates on the tension between Calvinism and Platonism in Buchan's life, two perspectives identified as the key to appreciating and understanding Buchan and his works. Scholarly and very thorough, the book refutes many of the common myths about Buchan.

Green, Martin. *A Biography of John Buchan and His Sister Anna: The Personal Background of Their Literary Work*. Lewiston, N.Y.: Edwin Mellen Press, 1990. A useful study of how literary talent is developed. This is a strictly chronological approach, except for the first chapter, "Heroic and Non-heroic Values." Includes notes and bibliography.

Kruse, Juanita. *John Buchan and the Idea of Empire: Popular Literature and Political Ideology*. Lewiston, N.Y.: Edwin Mellen Press, 1989. Kruse approaches

Buchan's novels from a postcolonial perspective, describing his ideas about the British Empire and examining the role of colonialism and imperialism in his work.

Lownie, Andrew. *John Buchan: The Presbyterian Cavalier*. Boston: D. R. Godine, 2003. Originally published in London in 1995. As the subtitle indicates, Lownie is concerned with developing the Scottish roots of Buchan's writing. This very helpful biogra-

phy includes a chronology, a family tree, notes, and a bibliography.

Smith, Janet Adam. *John Buchan and His World*. New York: Charles Scribner's Sons, 1979. Only 128 pages, this is an updated version of an earlier biography. Makes use of newer material provided by Buchan's family and publisher. Illustrated and well written, the biography concentrates on Buchan's life as both a writer and a public servant.

PEARL S. BUCK

Born: Hillsboro, West Virginia; June 26, 1892
Died: Danby, Vermont; March 6, 1973
Also known as: Pearl Comfort Sydenstricker; John Sedges; Sai Zhenzhu

PRINCIPAL LONG FICTION

East Wind: West Wind, 1930
The Good Earth, 1931
Sons, 1932
The Mother, 1934
A House Divided, 1935
House of Earth, 1935
This Proud Heart, 1938
The Patriot, 1939
Other Gods: An American Legend, 1940
China Sky, 1942
Dragon Seed, 1942
The Promise, 1943
China Flight, 1945
Portrait of a Marriage, 1945
The Townsman, 1945 (as John Sedges)
Pavilion of Women, 1946
The Angry Wife, 1947 (as Sedges)
Peony, 1948
Kinfolk, 1949
The Long Love, 1949 (as Sedges)
God's Men, 1951
Bright Procession, 1952 (as Sedges)
The Hidden Flower, 1952
Come, My Beloved, 1953

Voices in the House, 1953 (as Sedges)
Imperial Woman, 1956
Letter from Peking, 1957
Command the Morning, 1959
Satan Never Sleeps, 1962
The Living Reed, 1963
Death in the Castle, 1965
The Time Is Noon, 1967
The New Year, 1968
The Three Daughters of Madame Liang, 1969
Mandala, 1970
The Goddess Abides, 1972
All Under Heaven, 1973
The Rainbow, 1974

OTHER LITERARY FORMS

An overwhelmingly prolific writer, Pearl S. Buck wrote short stories, juvenile fiction and nonfiction, pamphlets, magazine articles, literary histories, biographies, plays (including a musical), educational works, an Asian cookbook, and a variety of books on America, democracy, Adolf Hitler and Germany, Japan, China, Russia, the mentally retarded, the sexes, and the Kennedy women. In addition, she translated Shi Naian's centuries-old work *Shuihu zhuan* (*All Men Are Brothers*, 1933) and edited a book of Asian fairy tales, several Christmas books, and a book of Chinese woodcuts.

Aside from *The Good Earth*, Buck's finest works are her biographies of her parents, *The Exile* (1936) and *Fighting Angel: Portrait of a Soul* (1936). *The Exile* portrays the unhappy and frustrating life of her mother, a missionary wife. *Fighting Angel*, a better biography because of its greater objectivity, shows the ruthless missionary zeal of Buck's father. Of her early articles, "Is There a Case for Foreign Missions?," printed in *Christian Century* in 1933, created a furor in its charges that missionaries, and churches themselves, lacked sympathy for the people, worrying more about the numbers of converts than the needs of the flock.

Buck also delivered several important addresses that reveal much about her own literary philosophy, including her 1938 Nobel Prize lecture on the Chinese novel. *Of Men and Women* (first issued in 1941; reissued in 1971 with a new epilogue) is one of Buck's most important nonfiction works because it gives her views of Chinese and American family life and her warnings about "gunpowder" American women who are educated for work yet lead idle and meaningless lives at home.

During World War II, Buck delivered many speeches and published articles, letters, and pamphlets on the Asian view of the war, particularly on colonial rule and imperialism. Her most famous war essay is probably "Tinder for Tomorrow." Buck's canon further includes personal works, such as the autobiographical *My Several Worlds: A Personal Record* (1954) and *A Bridge for Passing* (1962). Several of her plays were produced Off-Broadway or in summer stock.

ACHIEVEMENTS

Pearl S. Buck has been enormously successful with popular audiences, more so than with the literati. She is the most widely translated author in all of American literary history. In Denmark, for example, her popularity exceeded that of Ernest Hemingway and John Steinbeck in the 1930's, and in Sweden, ten of her books were translated between 1932 and 1940, more than those of any other American author. *The Good Earth*, her most famous work, has been translated into more than thirty languages (seven different translations into Chinese alone) and made into a play and a motion picture.

Buck's early novels received much acclaim. *The Good Earth* was awarded the Pulitzer Prize, and in 1935, Buck was awarded the William Dean Howells Medal by the American Academy of Arts and Letters for the finest work in American fiction from 1930 to 1935. In 1936,

she was elected to membership in the National Institute of Arts and Letters. In 1938, she was awarded the Nobel Prize in Literature, the third American and the fourth woman to receive it, for her "rich and generous epic description of Chinese peasant life and masterpieces of biography." *The Good Earth*, a staple of high school and undergraduate reading lists, is undoubtedly a masterpiece, and Buck's missionary biographies, *The Exile* and *Fighting Angel*, though currently neglected, have merit in the depth of their analysis. Three other novels that Buck published in the 1930's—*Sons*, *The Mother*, and *The Patriot*—are noted for particularly effective passages. In all her works, Buck evinces a deep humanity, and she did much to further American understanding of Asian culture.

Buck has not fared so well with the literary establishment. Critics of the 1930's disdained her work because she was a woman, because her subjects were not "American," and because they thought she did not deserve the Nobel Prize. Her success in writing best seller after best seller and her optimistic faith in progress and humanity have tended to irk later critics. Buck did, however, achieve success by her own standards. Her books have reached and touched middle-class American women, an enormous body of readers largely ignored by serious writers. Her innate storytelling ability does "please," "amuse," and "entertain" (her three criteria for good writing), but even the kindest of her admirers wish that she had written less, spending more time exploring the minds of her characters and polishing her work.

BIOGRAPHY

Pearl S. Buck was born Pearl Comfort Sydenstricker on June 26, 1892, in the family home at Hillsboro, West Virginia, to Absalom and Caroline (Stulting) Sydenstricker. Her parents were missionaries in China, home on a furlough, and after five months they returned to China with their baby daughter. Her parents' marriage was not a particularly happy one because of their disparate natures. Her mother, fun-loving and witty, was torn by her devotion to God; her father, single-minded and zealous, had success with his mission but not with his family. Buck grew up in Chinkiang (Zhenjiang), an inland city on the Yangtze River. In 1900, during the Boxer Rebellion, her family was forced to flee, and she experienced the horrors of racism. Her education included one year at boarding school in Shanghai and four years at Randolph-Macon Women's College in Virginia.

In 1917, she married John Lossing Buck, an agricultural specialist. They lived in a small town in Anhwei (Anhui) Province (the setting of *The Good Earth*). Buck learned much about farming from her husband and from her own observations. After five years, they moved southward to Nanking (Nanjing), where her husband taught agriculture and she taught English at the university. She published her first article in *The Atlantic Monthly* (January, 1923); "In China, Too" described the growing Western influence in China.

Tragedy struck Buck's life with the birth of Carol, her only biological child, who was mentally retarded (she later adopted eight children). She took Carol to the United States for medical treatment in 1925. When her husband took a year's leave of absence, Buck studied English at Cornell University and received her master's degree. Her first published novel, *East Wind: West Wind*, combined two short stories, one of which was originally published in 1925 in *Asia* magazine. She had written a novel before *East Wind: West Wind*, but it was destroyed by soldiers who entered her home in the 1926-1927 Nationalist Communist uprising. (During the takeover of Nanking, Buck and her family barely escaped, hiding in a mud hut until relief came.) On March 2, 1931, *The Good Earth* appeared, creating a literary sensation.

Buck's early literary influences included her parents and her old Chinese nurse. Her parents encouraged her to read the Bible and told her tales of their American homeland, while her nurse told her fantastic Buddhist and Daoist legends of warriors, devils, fairies, and dragons. She learned to speak Chinese before English, but she learned to read and write in English sooner than in Chinese. She read incessantly, Charles Dickens as a child and later Theodore Dreiser. Émile Zola and Sinclair Lewis were also important in her adult life. She paid particular tribute to Dickens: "He opened my eyes to people, he taught me to love all sorts of people." Even as a child, she decided to write: "One longs to make what one loves, and above all I loved to hear stories about people. I was a nuisance of a child, I fear, always curious to know about people and why they were as I found them." Her

Pearl S. Buck. (© The Nobel Foundation)

first writing appeared in the children's section of the *Shanghai Mercury*; in college, she contributed stories to the campus monthly and helped write the class play.

The Bucks were divorced in 1932, and that same year Pearl married her publisher, Richard J. Walsh, president of John Day and editor of *Asia* magazine. Their marriage lasted until his death in 1960. Buck loved both the United States and China throughout her life, serving as an intermediary between the two. In her last years, she was bitterly disappointed when the Chinese Communists would not grant her a visa despite the rapprochement between the United States and China.

Buck's parents instilled in their daughter principles of charity and tolerance. Her love for the needy was also awakened by Miss Jewell, the mistress of her boarding school. Jewell took Buck along as an interpreter on errands of mercy—to visit institutions for slave girls who had fled from their masters and institutions where prostitutes went for help. Buck's own humanitarian efforts began in 1941 with the founding of the East and West Association, which endeavored to increase understanding between diverse cultures. During World War II, Buck actively spoke against racism, against the U.S. government's internment of Japanese Americans, and against the yielding of democratic privileges during wartime.

Her sympathy extended to all, but especially to children and the helpless. In 1949, she and her husband founded Welcome House, an adoption agency for Asian American children. In 1954, her letter of protest to *The New York Times* led to the changing of a policy that put immigrants in federal prisons with criminals. In 1964, she founded the Pearl S. Buck Foundation to care for Asian American children who remain overseas. She also worked for the Training School, a school for the developmentally disabled in Vineland, New Jersey. For her many humanitarian efforts, she received the Brotherhood Award of the National Conference of Christians and Jews, the Wesley Award for Distinguished Service to Humanity, and more than a dozen honorary degrees from American colleges and universities.

Along with her extensive humanitarian activities, Buck continued to write. Because her American novels *This Proud Heart* and *Other Gods* were not well received, Buck assumed the pen name "John Sedges" to write with freedom on American subjects. Between 1945 and 1953, five novels were published under this name while she wrote Asian stories under her own name. Unfortunately, as Buck's humanitarian efforts increased, the quality of her fiction declined. Its strident and moralistic tone reflected her growing concern with social issues rather than artistic technique. She continued writing, however, and by the time of her death in 1973 had written more than eighty novels and novellas.

ANALYSIS

Pearl S. Buck's reputation for excellence as a writer of fiction rests primarily on *The Good Earth* and segments of a few of her other novels of the 1930's. The appeal of *The Good Earth* is undeniable and easy to explain: Its universal themes are cloaked in the garments of an unfamiliar and fascinating Chinese culture.

THE GOOD EARTH

Echoing many elements of life, *The Good Earth* speaks of animosity between town and country, love of land, decadent rich and honest poor, marital conflicts, interfering relatives, misunderstandings between generations, the joys of birth and sorrows of old age and death, and the strong bonds of friendship. Added to these universal themes is the cyclical movement of the growth and decay of the crops, the decline of the House of Hwand and the ascent of the House of Wang, the changes of the years, and the birth and death of the people.

Buck fittingly chose to tell her story in language reminiscent of the Bible, with its families and peoples who rise and fall. Her style also owes something to that of the Chinese storytellers, to whom she paid tribute in her Nobel Prize lecture, a style that flows along in short words "with no other technique than occasional bits of description, only enough to give vividness to place or person, and never enough to delay the story." Most of Buck's sentences are long and serpentine, relying on balance, parallelism, and repetition for strength. While the sentences are long, the diction is simple and concrete. She chooses her details carefully: Her descriptions grow out of close observation and are always concise. The simplicity of the diction and the steady, determined flow of the prose fit the sagalike plot. In Chinese folk literature, the self-effacing author, like a clear vessel, transmits but does not color with his or her personality the life that "flows through him." So, also, Buck presents her story objectively. Her authorial presence never intrudes, though her warm feeling for the characters and her own ethical beliefs are always evident.

The strength of the novel also lies in its characterization, particularly that of the two main characters, O-lan and her husband Wang Lung. Whereas characters in Buck's later novels too easily divide into good and bad, the characters of *The Good Earth*, like real people, mix elements of both. Ching, Wang Lung's faithful, doglike friend and later overseer, early in the novel joins a starving mob that ransacks Wang Lung's home for food; Ching takes Wang Lung's last handful of beans. The eldest son is a pompous wastrel, but he does make the House of Hwang beautiful with flowering trees and fish ponds, and he does settle into the traditional married life his father has planned for him. Even O-lan, the almost saintly earth mother, seethes with jealousy when Wang Lung takes a second wife, and she feels contempt and bitterness for the House of Hwang in which she was a slave. Her major flaw is her ugliness. Wang Lung delights the reader with his simple wonder at the world and with his perseverance to care for his family and his land, but he, too, has failings. In middle age, he lusts for Lotus, neglecting the much-deserving O-lan, and in old age, he steals Pear Blossom from his youngest son. Rather than confusing the morality of the novel, the intermingling of good and bad increases its reality. Buck acknowledged literary indebtedness to Émile Zola, and the influence of naturalism is evident in *The Good Earth* in its objective, documentary presentation and its emphasis on the influence of environment and heredity. Unlike the naturalists, however, Buck also credits the force of free will.

The Good Earth aroused much fury in some Chinese scholars, who insisted that the novel portrays a China that never was. Younghill Kang criticized the character of Wang Lung. Professor Kiang Kang-Hu said that Buck's details and her knowledge of Chinese history were inaccurate. Buck defended herself by granting that customs differed in the many regions of China. In later novels, she retaliated by harshly portraying Chinese scholars such as Kang and Kiang, who, she believed, distorted the picture of the real China either because of their ignorance of peasant life or because of their desire to aid propagandistic efforts of the Chinese government. Other native Chinese, including Phio Lin Yutang, sprang to Buck's defense, insisting on the accuracy of her portrayal.

THE MOTHER

Like *The Good Earth, The Mother* follows the cyclical flow of time: The protagonist, who begins the novel in vigorous work, caring for an elderly parent, ends the novel as an elderly parent himself, cared for by the new generation. *The Mother* is also written in the simple, concrete, and sometimes poetic style of *The Good Earth*. The old mother-in-law, for example, in her early-morning hunger, "belched up the evil winds from her inner emptiness." *The Mother*, however, portrays a different side of Chinese peasant life from that seen in *The Good Earth*— a more brutal one. The main character, named only "the mother," is carefully drawn; the other characters are flat and undeveloped, serving only as objects for her attention.

Deserted by her irresponsible, gambling husband, the mother lies about her spouse's absence to protect her family and cover her shame. She proves easy prey for her landlord's agent, by whom she becomes pregnant, later aborting the baby by taking medicine. Her eldest son eventually supports her, but his unfeeling wife will not tolerate having his blind sister underfoot. A husband is found for the blind girl, but when the mother travels to visit her daughter after a year, she discovers that the husband is witless and her daughter, after much mistreatment, has died. Even more sorrow darkens the mother's life. Her younger and most beloved son joins the Communists, is used as their dupe, and finally is arrested and beheaded.

This is not the honest-work-brings-rewards world of Wang Lung, but a world of victims, deformity, hatred, and cruelty. It is a portrait of the life of a woman in China, where girl babies routinely were killed and young girls of poor families were sold as slaves. Only new life—the excitement of birth and spring—balances the misery of the mother's life.

In *The Good Earth* and *The Mother*, Buck provides compelling visions of old age. Her children are mostly silent and inconsequential, her adolescents merely lusty and willful, but her elderly are individuals. The old father in *The Good Earth* cackles with life, drawing strength from his grandchildren-bedfellows. Wang Lung drowses off into a peaceful dream with his Pear Blossom. The mother-in-law basks in the sun and prides herself on wearing out her burial shrouds. The elderly mother in *The Mother* is frustrated because she no longer has the strength to work the land but remains as active as possible, trying to save her blind daughter and her Communist son, finally turning her affections to a new grandchild.

The main flaw in *The Mother* is that the mother seems too distant, too self-contained, for the reader to identify with her, to accept her as the universal mother that Buck intends her to be. The mother's story is interesting, but one does not feel her shame or her misery as one does O-lan's, nor does one feel her delight or her pride as one does Wang Lung's. Also, Buck's feelings about Communism are blatantly evident in the simplistic and oft-repeated phrase that the Communists are a "new kind of robber."

As Buck became more interested in social and political issues and in the media—magazines, film, and radio—her fiction began to deteriorate. She claimed, "The truth is I never write with a sense of mission or to accomplish any purpose whatever except the revelation of human character through a life situation." Her fiction, however, did not demonstrate this belief: More and more it became a forum for her own social and political ideas rather than an exploration of human character and life. Further, Hollywood and women's magazines began to influence her stories: They became drippingly romantic.

DRAGON SEED

Dragon Seed is one of Buck's most popular post-1930's works, with the first half of the novel containing many of the strengths of her earlier work. Her characters are not as fully realized as the mother or Wang Lung, but the story is intriguing. A peasant farming family work the land, much as their ancestors have done for centuries, until the coming of war—flying airships and enemy troops—thrusts them into a world of violence and deprivation. As long as Buck keeps her eye sharp for details, describing the atrocities the people must endure and their struggles to understand what is happening to them, the novel remains interesting.

In the second half of the novel, however, Buck's purposes split. Rather than concentrating on the war story—the people and their experiences—she uses the novel to argue that the Western world is blind and uncaring about the troubles of the Chinese in World War II. In contrast to this didacticism are the Hollywood-style love stories of Lao-Er and Jade, and of Lao San and Mayli. The dialogue between the happily married Lao-Er and Jade seems straight from a B-film, and the overly coincidental coming together of Lao San and Mayli is a women's magazine romance of the self-made man and the rich, beautiful woman. Buck tries to portray the strong new woman of China (and the Western world) in Jade and Mayli, but they are too strong, too clever, almost always posturing with a defiant chin against the sunset. At one point in the novel, Buck even writes that Jade is so skillful in disguising herself that she should have been a film actor. O-lan, in her stoic silence—grudging, jealous, yet loving—is a believable woman; Jade and Mayli are creatures of fantasy.

Buck's power as a novelist derived from her intelligence, her humanity, her interesting stories, and her ability to make Chinese culture real to readers from all over the world. Her weaknesses as a novelist include didacticism, sentimentalism, and an inability to control her energy long enough to explore deeply, revise, and improve. In her later novels, she lost control of her point of view, her language, and her characterization. Her legacy is an enduring masterpiece, *The Good Earth*, and an inestimable contribution to cultural exchange between China and the West.

Ann Willardson Engar

OTHER MAJOR WORKS

SHORT FICTION: *The First Wife, and Other Stories*, 1933; *Today and Forever*, 1941; *Twenty-seven Stories*, 1943; *Far and Near, Stories of Japan, China, and America*, 1947; *American Triptych*, 1958; *Hearts Come Home, and Other Stories*, 1962; *The Good Deed, and Other Stories*, 1969; *Once upon a Christmas*, 1972; *East and West*, 1975; *Secrets of the Heart*, 1976; *The Lovers, and Other Stories*, 1977; *The Woman Who Was Changed, and Other Stories*, 1979.

NONFICTION: *East and West and the Novel*, 1932; *The Exile*, 1936; *Fighting Angel: Portrait of a Soul*, 1936; *The Chinese Novel*, 1939; *Of Men and Women*, 1941 (expanded 1971); *American Unity and Asia*, 1942; *What America Means to Me*, 1943; *China in Black and White*, 1945; *Talk About Russia: With Masha Scott*, 1945; *Tell the People: Talks with James Yen About the Mass Education Movement*, 1945; *How It Happens: Talk About the German People, 1914-1933, with Erna von Pustau*, 1947; *American Argument: With Eslanda Goods*, 1949; *The Child Who Never Grew*, 1950; *My Several Worlds: A Personal Record*, 1954; *Friend to Friend: A Candid Exchange Between Pearl Buck and Carlos F. Romulo*, 1958; *A Bridge for Passing*, 1962; *The Joy of Children*, 1964; *Children for Adoption*, 1965; *The Gifts They Bring: Our Debt to the Mentally Retarded*, 1965; *The People of Japan*, 1966; *To My Daughters with Love*, 1967; *China as I See It*, 1970; *The Kennedy Women: A Personal Appraisal*, 1970; *Pearl S. Buck's America*, 1971; *The Story Bible*, 1971; *China Past and Present*, 1972.

TRANSLATION: *All Men Are Brothers*, 1933 (of Shi Naian's novel).

CHILDREN'S LITERATURE: *The Young Revolutionist*, 1932; *Stories for Little Children*, 1940; *The Chinese*

Children Next Door, 1942; *The Water-Buffalo Children*, 1943; *The Dragon Fish*, 1944; *Yu Lan: Flying Boy of China*, 1945; *The Big Wave*, 1948; *One Bright Day, and Other Stories for Children*, 1952; *The Man Who Changed China: The Story of Sun Yat-Sen*, 1953; *The Beech Tree*, 1954; *Johnny Jack and His Beginnings*, 1954; *Fourteen Stories*, 1961; *The Little Fox in the Middle*, 1966; *The Chinese Story Teller*, 1971.

BIBLIOGRAPHY

Cevasco, George A. "Pearl Buck and the Chinese Novel." *Asian Studies* 5 (December, 1967): 437-450. Provides important insights into Buck's understanding of the novel as a form for the general public, not the scholar, and shows her debt to Chinese beliefs about the function of plot and characterization in fiction.

Conn, Peter. *Pearl S. Buck: A Cultural Biography*. New York: Cambridge University Press, 1996. Attempts to revise the "smug literary consensus" that has relegated Buck to a "footnote" in literary history. Conn does not rehabilitate Buck as a great author but shows how her best work broke new ground in subject matter and is still vital to an understanding of American culture.

Doyle, Paul A. *Pearl S. Buck*. Boston: Twayne, 1980. Provides a valuable survey of Buck's literary achievements, strengths, and weaknesses. Contains a biographical chapter and excellent bibliographies of both primary and secondary materials.

Gao, Xiongya. *Pearl S. Buck's Chinese Women Characters*. Selinsgrave, Pa.: Susquehanna Press, 2000. Examines the treatment of Chinese women characters in Buck's work by focusing on five novels. Begins with a general overview of Buck's writing, the responses of critics to her work, her Chinese influence, and the position of women in Chinese society at the time Buck's books appeared. Analyses follow of the portrayals of aristocratic women in *East Wind: West Wind* and *Pavilion of Women*, servants in *Peony*, and peasant women in *The Good Earth* and *The Mother*.

Harker, Jaime. *America the Middlebrow: Women's Novels, Progressivism, and Middlebrow Authorship Between the Wars*. Amherst: University of Massachusetts Press, 2007. Traces the careers of Buck and several other women authors who published during the 1920's and 1930's and viewed fiction as a means of reforming society.

Leong, Karen J. *The China Mystique: Pearl S. Buck, Anna May Wong, Mayling Soong, and the Transformation of American Orientalism*. Berkeley: University of California Press, 2005. Focuses on three women who were associated with China in the 1930's and 1940's—Buck, actor Anna May Wong, and Mayling Soong, the wife of Chinese leader Chiang Kai-shek—to describe how they altered Americans' perceptions of what it meant to be American, Chinese American, and Chinese.

Liao, Kang. *Pearl S. Buck: A Cultural Bridge Across the Pacific*. Westport, Conn.: Greenwood Press, 1997. Analyzes Buck's life, her political and social views, and her novels to describe how the author played a key role in improving Americans' images of China during World War II.

Lipscomb, Elizabeth J., Frances E. Webb, and Peter Conn, eds. *The Several Worlds of Pearl S. Buck: Essays Presented at a Centennial Symposium, Randolph-Macon Woman's College, March 26-28, 1992*. Westport, Conn.: Greenwood Press, 1994. Collection of essays delivered at a conference in which participants sought to reevaluate Buck's work and literary reputation. Several of the essays examine various aspects of *The Good Earth*; others address topics such as Buck's portrayals of China and of handicapped children and her place in the American literary culture.

Pam, Eleanor. "Patriarchy and Property: Women in Pearl S. Buck's *The Good Earth*." In *Women in Literature: Reading Through the Lens of Gender*, edited by Jerilyn Fisher and Ellen S. Silber. Westport, Conn.: Greenwood Press, 2003. Analysis of Buck's novel is part of a collection of essays examining ninety-six works of literature from the perspective of gender.

Stirling, Nora. *Pearl Buck: A Woman in Conflict*. Piscataway, N.J.: New Century, 1983. Balanced, well-researched biography is based in part on interviews with many of Buck's friends and acquaintances. Provides important insights into Buck's personality and the experiences that shaped her writings.

CHARLES BUKOWSKI

Born: Andernach, Germany; August 16, 1920
Died: San Pedro, California; March 9, 1994
Also known as: Henry Charles Bukowski, Jr.;
Heinrich Karl Bukowski

PRINCIPAL LONG FICTION

Post Office, 1971
Factotum, 1975
Women, 1978
Ham on Rye, 1982
You Get So Alone at Times That It Just Makes Sense, 1986
Hollywood, 1989
Pulp, 1994

OTHER LITERARY FORMS

Charles Bukowski (byew-KOW-skee) was an accomplished novelist, short-story writer, and poet. He was such a prolific poet that collections of his poems have appeared almost every year since his death in 1994. Bukowski also wrote essays on topics including Los Angeles, drinking, literature, and horse racing; thousands of letters; and a screenplay for the film *Barfly* (1987), directed by Barbet Schroeder. Bukowski's live performances of his poetry were legendary. These performances are available on the compact disc *Hostage* (1994) and with the documentary films *The Last Straw* (2008) and *There's Gonna Be a God Damn Riot in Here* (2008).

ACHIEVEMENTS

Charles Bukowski has a cultlike following in the United States, Germany, France, Italy, Switzerland, Iceland, Australia, and other countries, and his books have been translated into more than one dozen languages. Though he has long been rejected by the mainstream literary canon, this rejection has somewhat abated. Writers, singers, and artists as disparate as Raymond Carver, Barry Hannah, Larry Brown, R. Crumb, Willy Vlautin, Tom Waits, Bob Dylan, Sean Penn, Nick Cave, the rock band U2, and Vicki Hendricks have acknowledged a debt to Bukowski and embraced him as a men-

tor. American poet and writer Jim Harrison's 2007 review of Bukowski's *The Pleasures of the Damned: Poems, 1951-1993* (2007) in *The New York Times Book Review* is considered a first step in the acceptance of Bukowski on a wider scale.

Bukowski is the subject of several songs and films, notably a song by Modest Mouse on its 2004 album *Good News for People Who Love Bad News* and John Dullaghan's documentary *Bukowski: Born into This* (2003). Bukowski's bungalow at 5124 De Longpre Avenue in Hollywood, California, the place of much of his early writing, was designated a historic landmark by the city of Los Angeles.

BIOGRAPHY

Henry Charles Bukowski, Jr., was born Heinrich Karl Bukowski in Andernach, Germany, on August 16, 1920. He was the son of a German woman and a German American serviceman who had met at the end of World War I. In 1923, the family moved to the United States, settling first in Baltimore and then in Washington, D.C. Bukowski's parents started calling him Henry instead of Heinrich, and they altered the pronunciation of the family name. The family moved to suburban Los Angeles in 1926, a decision that would greatly influence Bukowski's career as a writer. Bukowski has said that he was a shy child with severe acne who was ridiculed by fellow students and abused by his father. His semi-autobiographical novel *Ham on Rye* recounts his boyhood misadventures as a loner and outsider.

Bukowski graduated from Los Angeles High School and attended Los Angeles City College for two years. He took classes in journalism, art, and literature, but his greatest education came from the libraries of Los Angeles, where he discovered writers such as John Fante, Ezra Pound, Robinson Jeffers, Ernest Hemingway, William Faulkner, Louis-Ferdinand Céline, and Knut Hamsun, whose works shaped his life and career. Bukowski's college years are also covered in *Ham on Rye*, including a controversial period of his life during which he was associated with Nazism. To this day, people often mistake Bukowski as a Nazi sympathizer, though his writing makes it clear that he was not. In *Ham on Rye*, he attributes his blind flirtation with Nazism to youthful angst and the desire to rage against "the system."

In his early life, Bukowski traveled often. He failed at jobs and relationships, and he drifted from town to town. In 1944, during World War II, he was arrested in Philadelphia on suspicion of draft evasion, and later—after failing physical and psychological examinations—he was deemed unfit for military service. His early muse was Jane Cooney Baker, whom he met in 1947. The two lived together off and on until 1955, and some believe they were married for a brief time. Many of Bukowski's early poems are written to or about Jane, or both.

Bukowski published his first two stories in the early 1940's in *Story* and *Portfolio III* and then—disenchanted with the publishing world—took a long hiatus from writing to focus on drinking. Over the next ten years he nearly died from a bleeding ulcer. He started working at a local post office, quit that job, and then was rehired. He married poet and writer Barbara Frye and began writing almost compulsively. His parents died, he was divorced from Frye, and he began submitting poems in larger numbers to small literary magazines.

After his divorce, Bukowski reconnected with Baker; he was deeply affected by her death in 1962. He began publishing poetry chapbooks in the early 1960's and had a child, Marina Louise Bukowski, with Frances Smith—whom he met shortly after Baker's death—in 1964. Two years later, he met John Martin and began what became a crucial lifelong friendship and business partnership. Martin became Bukowski's publisher. Every book that Bukowski wrote was published by Martin's Black Sparrow Press, except for a few short-story collections published by City Lights Books.

Bukowski met sculptor and poet Linda King after finishing his first novel, *Post Office*, in 1971, but they separated in 1973. He began doing many readings at bookstores, universities, and bars. He was the subject of several documentaries, including Taylor Hackford's *Bukowski* (1973), and he received a grant from the National Endowment for the Arts to finish a novel. He began traveling widely in the late 1970's, making trips to Canada, France, Italy, and Germany for readings and talk-show appearances. Several of his books were adapted for film, including the Italian production *Storie di ordinaria follia*

(1981; *Tales of Ordinary Madness*, 1983), starring Ben Gazzara.

Bukowski married Linda Lee Beighle in 1985 and settled down with her in San Pedro, California, a coastal suburb of Los Angeles. In his later years, he spent the bulk of his time writing in solitude. Bukowski's funeral was conducted by Buddhist monks. His gravestone reads "Don't Try."

ANALYSIS

Most of Charles Bukowski's writing examines his life as a drunk, drifter, gambler, loner, and unemployed and unemployable creature of habit. As noted in many documentaries, biographies, and accounts of Bukowski's life, however, he also had a gentle side. As much as he wrote about booze, horse racing, failure, hesitation, and loss, he wrote twice as much about love, genuine-

Charles Bukowski. (Courtesy, Magnolia Pictures)

ness, literature, and music. The themes that Bukowski explored throughout his career remained consistent; in his own estimation, the artist's goal is to explore the same themes eternally.

Bukowski—perhaps even more than writers J. D. Salinger and Ernest Hemingway—also was interested in exposing phoniness. Considering that Bukowski's characters are often drunks (his alter ego and antihero Henry Chinaski), it could be difficult to believe that Bukowski was deeply concerned with bad manners. However, a close examination of his work reveals a writer who is obsessed with order, ritual, and kindness.

Though he is often associated with the writers of the Beat generation, Bukowski felt he was following in the footsteps of the writers and musicians he greatly admired, including Pound, Faulkner, Hemingway, Jeffers, Fante, Fyodor Dostoevski, Ludwig van Beethoven, Johannes Brahms, and Gustav Mahler. Furthermore, his writing contains biting criticism of his contemporaries, including Beat writers Allen Ginsberg and Jack Kerouac.

POST OFFICE

Bukowski worked a succession of odd jobs, had long periods of unemployment, and was a chronic gambler, but he did hold a steady post-office job for many years before devoting his life full time to writing. Bukowski wrote *Post Office*, his first novel, in three weeks after quitting his job as a postal clerk. The novel tells the story of Henry Chinaski, Bukowski's alter ego, and his time spent as an employee of the U.S. Postal Service. Chinaski, like Bukowski, works for years as a mail carrier, quits, survives by gambling on horses, and returns to the post service as a mail sorter. He quits again and then pursues his career as a writer. Bukowski's style is sharp, precise, and economical, and the novel is a hilarious and vulgar representation of a life lived "on the skids."

FACTOTUM

Factotum continues the adventures of Chinaski. Unemployed, hungover, trying to make it as a writer, Chinaski falls for Jan, another barfly. The novel traces the course of their relationship and documents Chinaski's failures in work, love, and life. Director Bent Hamer's 2005 film adaptation of the novel, a film starring Matt Dillon as Chinaski, was a great success, bringing the novel to a new generation of readers.

WOMEN

Bukowski, in later life, became obsessed with writing about women. When he became a successful cult figure, women threw themselves at him, aiming—it seemed—for him to write about their adventures—and write he did. The hilarious novel *Women* is a semiautobiographical novel that documents Bukowski's unlikely rise as a ladies' man. The book is also, in part, a reaction against feminist critics who argue that Bukowski was sexist and misogynist. He denied the claims, however, and wrote with startling frankness about prostitutes, rape, and twisted relationships. His serious writing, however, reveals a gentleness toward women, especially the women he loved. *Women* is, primarily, a comic examination of the dangers of fame and a rejection of salvation through promiscuity.

HAM ON RYE

Widely considered Bukowski's finest achievement, *Ham on Rye* details the coming-of-age of Chinaski in Los Angeles during the Great Depression. The novel is a semiautobiographical take on Bukowski's own experiences as a child growing up in Los Angeles. Dealing with an abusive father and a serious outbreak of acne, Chinaski manages to survive as an outsider.

Chinaski's family bears a striking resemblance to Bukowski's own family. (He rarely did much to veil characters based on real people in his work.) The Chinaski family includes a loving German mother, a father who is harsh and cruel to his wife and son, and a grandfather who is a beatific drunk. The novel offers readers a glimpse into Bukowski's early romanticism of people who exist in the world as intruders and outcasts. Chinaski's rough youth makes way for an adulthood paved with drunkenness, failure, and rotten relationships. A comic masterpiece, *Ham on Rye* is a sort of response to Salinger's *The Catcher in the Rye* (1951), a book that Bukowski probably detested.

HOLLYWOOD

Bukowski's fourth novel, *Hollywood*, is an examination of his own brief time in the film business, a semiautobiographical comic take on film director Schroeder's adaptation of Bukowski's screenplay *Barfly*. The novel is a searing indictment of Hollywood phoniness, a dark take on what it takes (and costs, both monetarily and spiritually) to make a film. Bukowski is critical of Schroeder, and the film's stars—Mickey Rourke and Faye Dunaway—as well as other Hollywood figures: lawyers, producers, and other directors and actors. The novel again features Bukowski's alter ego, a now married Chinaski, as he mocks egotistical Hollywood phonies.

PULP

In his last novel, *Pulp*, Bukowski writes an homage to what he calls "bad writing." The novel is a spoof of the hard-boiled detective genre, and it is Bukowski's only novel to not feature Chinaski as protagonist. Instead, the main character is Nick Belane, a Los Angeles private detective cut from the same cloth as Raymond Chandler's Philip Marlowe and Dashiell Hammett's Sam Spade. Belane is hired to locate something called the Red Sparrow. In his travels, he encounters Lady Death, a space alien named Jeannie Nitro, an unhappy married couple, and a wimpy mortician. A comedic take on the sort of pulp fiction that thrived in the United States in the mid-twentieth century, the book is also a tale of existential despair.

William Boyle

OTHER MAJOR WORKS

SHORT FICTION: *Notes of a Dirty Old Man*, 1969; *Erections, Ejaculations, Exhibitions, and General Tales of Ordinary Madness*, 1972; *Life and Death in the Charity Ward*, 1973; *South of No North: Stories of the Buried Life*, 1973; *Bring Me Your Love*, 1983; *Hot Water Music*, 1983; *The Most Beautiful Woman in Town, and Other Stories*, 1983; *There's No Business*, 1984; *The Day It Snowed in L.A.*, 1986.

POETRY: *Flower, Fist, and Bestial Wail*, 1960; *Longshot Poems for Broke Players*, 1962; *Poems and Drawings*, 1962; *Run with the Hunted*, 1962; *It Catches My Heart in Its Hand*, 1963; *Cold Dogs in the Courtyard*, 1965; *Crucifix in a Deathhand*, 1965; *The Genius of the Crowd*, 1966; *The Curtains Are Waving*, 1967; *At Terror Street and Agony Way*, 1968; *Poems Written Before Jumping out of an Eighth Story Window*, 1968; *A Bukowski Sampler*, 1969; *The Days Run Away Like Wild Horses over the Hills*, 1969; *Fire Station*, 1970; *Mockingbird Wish Me Luck*, 1972; *Me and Your Sometimes Love Poems*, 1973 (with Linda King); *While the Music Played*, 1973; *Burning in Water, Drowning in Flame*, 1974; *Africa, Paris, Greece*, 1975; *Scarlet*, 1976; *Love Is a Dog from Hell*, 1977; *Maybe Tomorrow*, 1977; *Legs, Hips, and Behind*, 1978; *We'll Take Them*, 1978; *Play the Piano Drunk Like a Percussion Instrument Until the Fingers Begin to Bleed a Bit*, 1979; *Dangling in the Tournefortia*, 1981; *The Last Generation*, 1982; *War All the Time: Poems, 1981-1984*, 1984; *The Roominghouse Madrigals: Early Selected Poems, 1946-1966*, 1988; *Last Night of the Earth Poems*, 1992; *Bone Palace Ballet: New Poems*, 1997; *What Matters Most Is How Well You Walk Through the Fire*, 1999; *Open All Night: New Poems*, 2000; *The Night Torn Mad with Footsteps*, 2001; *The Flash of Lightning Behind the Mountain: New Poems*, 2003; *Sifting Through the Madness for the Word, the Line, the Way: New Poems*, 2003; *Slouching Toward Nirvana: New Poems*, 2005 (John Martin, editor); *Come on In! New Poems*, 2006 (Martin, editor); *The People Look Like Flowers at Last: New Poems*, 2007 (Martin, editor); *The Pleasures of the Damned: Poems, 1951-1993*, 2007 (Martin, editor).

SCREENPLAY: *Barfly*, 1987.

NONFICTION: *Shakespeare Never Did This*, 1979 (photographs by Michael Montfort); *The Bukowski/Purdy Letters: A Decade of Dialogue, 1964-1974*, 1983; *Screams from the Balcony: Selected Letters, 1960-1970*, 1993; *Reach for the Sun: Selected Letters, 1978-1994*, 1999 (Seamus Cooney, editor); *Beerspit Night and Cursing: The Correspondence of Charles Bukowski and Sheri Martinelli, 1960-1967*, 2001 (Steven Moore, editor).

MISCELLANEOUS: *You Kissed Lilly*, 1978; *Septuagenarian Stew: Stories and Poems*, 1990; *Run with the Hunted: A Charles Bukowski Reader*, 1993; *Betting on the Muse: Poems and Stories*, 1996; *Charles Bukowski: Portions from a Wine-Stained Notebook—Uncollected Stories and Essays, 1944-1990*, 2008 (David Stephen Calonne, editor)

BIBLIOGRAPHY

Brewer, Gay. *Charles Bukowski*. New York: Twayne, 1997. A concise and comprehensive critical introduction to Bukowski's work. Part of the Twayne American Authors series.

Calonne, David Stephen. *Charles Bukowski: Sunlight Here I Am—Interviews and Encounters, 1963-1993*.

Northville, Mich.: Sun Dog Press, 2003. Thirty-four interviews and "encounters" that examine the rise of Bukowski from his life as a drunk to literary icon.

Charlson, David. *Charles Bukowski: Autobiographer, Gender Critic, Iconoclast*. Victoria, B.C.: Trafford, 2005. Based on the author's doctoral dissertation, this unique study includes significant discussion of Bukowski's reputation as a misogynist and his themes of masculinity and violence. A comprehensive work, and an excellent introduction to Bukowski's life and work.

Cherkovski, Neeli. *Hank: The Life of Charles Bukowski*. New York: Random House, 1991. Written by Bukowski's longtime friend and collaborator. One of the earliest Bukowski biographies—compassionate and respectful.

Duval, Jean-François. *Bukowski and the Beats: A Commentary on the Beat Generation*. Translated by Alison Ardron. Northville, Mich.: Sun Dog Press, 2002. Though Bukowski aimed to distance himself from Beat writers such as Jack Kerouac, Allen Ginsberg, and William Burroughs, Duval examines Bukowski's historical links to the Beats and also highlights his philosophical differences.

Harrison, Russell. *Against the American Dream: Essays on Charles Bukowski*. Santa Rosa, Calif.: Black Sparrow Press, 1994. In the first critical study of Bukowski, Harrison argues that the author and his writing are unappreciated and that Bukowski has been ignored by academics mostly because he wrote about the life of the working class and the failure of the American Dream.

Krumhansl, Aaron. *A Descriptive Bibliography of the Primary Publications of Charles Bukowski*. Santa Rosa, Calif.: Black Sparrow Press, 1999. A bibliography listing Bukowski's books, chapbooks, and broadsides, along with the magazine articles in which he is featured. The deluxe edition includes a rare broadside poem by Bukowski.

Miles, Barry. *Charles Bukowski*. New York: Virgin Books, 2006. Miles, acclaimed for his writing on the Beat generation, offers readers a fresh take on Bukowski's life, relying heavily on his many letters.

Sounes, Howard. *Charles Bukowski: Locked in the Arms of a Crazy Life*. New York: Grove Press, 1998. Widely considered to be the definitive account of Bukowski's life, Sounes offers another engaging look at the "poet of the gutters."

MIKHAIL BULGAKOV

Born: Kiev, Ukraine, Russian Empire; May 15, 1891
Died: Moscow, Russia, Soviet Union (now in Russia); March 10, 1940
Also known as: Mikhail Afanasyevich Bulgakov

PRINCIPAL LONG FICTION

Belaya gvardiya, 1927, 1929 (2 volumes; *The White Guard*, 1971)
Teatralny roman, 1965 (*Black Snow: A Theatrical Novel*, 1967)
Master i Margarita, 1966-1967 (uncensored version, 1973; *The Master and Margarita*, 1967)
Sobache serdtse, 1968 (novella; wr. 1925; reliable text, 1969; *The Heart of a Dog*, 1968)

OTHER LITERARY FORMS

Mikhail Bulgakov (bewl-GAH-kuhf) wrote some thirty-six plays, of which eleven were published and eight performed during his lifetime. His writings for theater and film include adaptations from Miguel de Cervantes, Molière, Charles Dickens, Nikolai Gogol, and Leo Tolstoy. Only one of the opera libretti Bulgakov composed for the Bolshoi Theater, *Rachel* (wr. 1938, pr. 1947), based on a story by Guy de Maupassant, was ever produced. Among his more notable plays made available in English during the 1960's and 1970's are *Adam i Eva* (pb. 1971; *Adam and Eve*, 1971), *Dni Turbinykh* (pr. 1926; *Days of the Turbins*, 1934), *Beg* (pr. 1957; *Flight*, 1969), *Zoykina kvartira* (pr. 1926; *Zoya's Apartment*, 1970), *Ivan Vasilievich* (pb. 1965; English translation,

1974), and *Posledniye dni (Pushkin)* (pr. 1943; *The Last Days*, 1976). Bulgakov also wrote numerous short stories, many of them collected in the volumes titled *Diavoliada* (1925; *Diaboliad, and Other Stories*, 1972), *Zapiski iunogo vracha* (1963; *A Country Doctor's Notebook*, 1975), and *Traktat o zhilishche* (1926; *A Treatise on Housing*, 1972). He also published miscellaneous journalism. Bulgakov's close identification with the life of Molière produced one of his most interesting plays, *Kabala svyatosh* (pr. 1936; *A Cabal of Hypocrites*, 1972; also known as *Molière*), as well as a novelistic biography, *Zhizn gospodina de Molyera* (1962; *The Life of Monsieur de Molière*, 1970).

ACHIEVEMENTS

Some twenty-five years after his death, Mikhail Bulgakov began to receive increasing recognition— both in the Soviet Union and abroad—as a major figure in modern Russian literature. *The Master and Margarita* is a complex, ambitious masterpiece that has won an intensely loyal readership and much critical scrutiny since its first serialized publication in 1966-1967. This novel's posthumous success in turn began to direct attention to Bulgakov's other neglected works.

The hazards of cultural life under Soviet leader Joseph Stalin frustrated Bulgakov's aspirations in prose fiction, where he did his finest work, and channeled him into the theater, where, though productive, he was probably temperamentally out of place. Bulgakov's narratives combine acute, if perforce oblique, social analysis with a strain of playful fantasy. Beyond the deprivation, hypocrisy, and cruelty of contemporary Soviet life, his Horatian satires suggest a transcendent spiritual force. In *The Master and Margarita* and *The White Guard*, it is tender devotion to a beautiful, mysterious woman that represents the apocalyptic possibility of overcoming an oppressive present existence. *Black Snow* offers the advice that "you have to love your characters. If you don't, I don't advise anybody to try writing; the result is bound to be unfortunate." This sentimental belief in the liberating power of love—of characters for one another, of author for reader—is tempered by terminal melancholia. In the imperfect world portrayed by Bulgakov, those in power are never graced with imagination, though they must be humored, but it is the power of imagination and

of humor that lifts the reader beyond the tyranny of the quotidian.

There is at least an allusion to Faust in almost all of Bulgakov's books, where the quest for an elusive truth becomes an explicit and central theme. Bulgakov's work frequently foregrounds itself, calling attention to its own formal inventions in the service of a sense of values against which the elaborate structures of society and art seem petty and transient indeed.

BIOGRAPHY

Mikhail Afanasyevich Bulgakov, the eldest of seven children, was born in Kiev on May 15, 1891, into a family that was both devout and intellectual. His father, who died when Mikhail was sixteen, was a professor of divinity at the Kiev Theological Academy. Bulgakov developed an early interest in music and the theater, but he pursued a medical degree at Kiev University. In 1913, he married Tatyana Nikolaevna Lappa, and in 1916 he graduated with distinction as a doctor. He subsequently served as a military doctor in remote village hospitals, settings that were to provide the material for the stories in *A Country Doctor's Notebook*. The isolation depressed him, and he attempted to obtain his release, only succeeding in 1918 after the Bolshevik Revolution.

Bulgakov returned to Kiev to establish a private practice in venereology and dermatology. During this time, the tense atmosphere of which is re-created in *The White Guard*, Kiev was a battleground for the Germans, the Ukrainian nationalists, the Bolsheviks, and the Whites. In November, 1919, Bulgakov fled south to the Caucasian town of Vladikavkaz. While he was confined to bed with typhus, Vladikavkaz was captured by the Bolsheviks. He abandoned the practice of medicine and began devoting himself entirely to writing.

In 1921, Bulgakov moved to Moscow, where, amid general hardship, he attempted to support himself and his wife through a variety of literary and journalistic jobs. In 1924, he divorced Tatyana and married Lyubov Yevgenievna Belozerskaya. Soon thereafter, with the publication of satiric stories later collected in *Diavoliada*, Bulgakov began achieving some recognition and was able to abandon the newspaper work he detested. The publication, in 1925, of parts of *The White Guard*, based on his experiences in Kiev during the civil war, dramatically changed his life in ways recounted in the autobiographical novel *Black Snow*. Bulgakov's work came to the attention of the producers of the Moscow Art Theater, and he was asked to adapt *The White Guard* for the stage. The result, after considerable revision, was *Days of the Turbins*, which opened in October, 1926, to intense, polarized reaction. Bulgakov was harshly attacked for portraying the opponents of Bolshevism too sympathetically, but the play proved enormously popular. During its lengthy run, Stalin himself saw it fifteen times.

A sudden celebrity, Bulgakov continued writing plays, but by the end of the decade, as Soviet cultural and political life became severely repressive, his works were banned, and his financial position deteriorated. Near despair, he sent letters in 1930 to Soviet officials complaining of the campaign of vilification against him and his inability to get his work accepted. Stalin's personal intercession resulted in Bulgakov's appointment as a producer at the Moscow Art Theater. His subsequent years in the theater were productive but frustrating, in part because of friction with the flamboyant director Konstantin Stanislavsky, whose production of *A Cabal of Hypocrites* in 1936 led Bulgakov to resign in disgust from the Moscow Art Theater. For the remainder of his life, he was employed by the Bolshoi Theater as librettist and consultant.

In 1929, Bulgakov had begun a clandestine love affair with Elena Sergeyevna Shilovskaya, wife of the chief of staff of the Moscow Military District. In 1932, after both succeeded in obtaining divorces, they were married, and Bulgakov adopted Elena's five-year-old son, Sergey. Bulgakov's happiness with and devotion to his third wife, to whom he, with failing eyesight, probably dictated *Black Snow* in 1939, are reflected in *The Master and Margarita*. The earliest version of the latter was begun as early as 1928, but Bulgakov destroyed that manuscript in 1929. He continued refining a revised version until his death, in Moscow, on March 10, 1940.

After Bulgakov's death, the official attitude toward his work in the Soviet Union ranged from indifference to hostility, and very few of his writings remained available. During the brief thaw in Soviet cultural repression following Stalin's death, a commission was established to rehabilitate Bulgakov's reputation, and by the late

1960's most of his major works were being published in the Soviet Union for the first time.

ANALYSIS

Mikhail Bulgakov never took advantage of the opportunity to flee Russia during the revolution and its turbulent aftermath, and his fiction is very much a product of Russian life during the first two decades of the Soviet regime. Bulgakov's social commentary is not oblique enough to have averted the ire and the proscription of powerful contemporaries, or to keep later readers from recognizing the quality of roman à clef in much of what he wrote. The key, however, is not simply in details of his own biography—friends, adversaries, and a pet cat persistently transposed into a fictional realm. More important, it is in his ability to render the plight of the creative individual in a system designed to subdue him. Within the carefully limned landscapes of modern Kiev and Moscow, Bulgakov's characters dramatize the limitations and hubris of temporal human power. His books, then, are not merely the frustrated effusions of an author encountering formidable obstacles to his ambitions, nor are they merely perceptive analyses of the kind of community Stalinist social engineering was begetting. Beyond Bulgakov's contempt for contemporary mischief is a veritably religious sense of a universal spiritual force and a conviction that *sic transit gloria mundi*. *The White Guard* thus concludes on a consoling note: "Everything passes away—suffering, pain, blood, hunger and pestilence." It is this spiritual perspective that endows Bulgakov's narratives with more than a parochial sociological or historical interest.

The tone of melancholy that suffuses Bulgakov's works is a consequence of the futility he sees in the artist's struggle against the mighty of this world, and most of his sympathetic characters are more than half in love with easeful death. Creativity, love, and good humor do, nevertheless, triumph. To reduce Bulgakov's fictions to the bare formula of a struggle between sensitivity and brutishness and between eternity and the moment is to miss the mournful exuberance of his *comédies larmoyantes*. Not only *Black Snow*, the subtitle of which proclaims it, but also Bulgakov's other books are theatrical novels. The spirited play of a harried author drawn to and disappointed by the theater, they employ self-conscious devices, such as apostrophes to the reader, impudent violations of verisimilitude, and encased narratives, to enact a liberation not only from the oppressive worlds they depict but also from the literary instrument of emancipation itself. *Black Snow* concludes with a deflationary fictional afterword, and it is night on the final pages of *The White Guard*, *The Master and Margarita*, and *The Heart of a Dog*. Like William Shakespeare's *The Tempest* (pr. 1611) abjuring its own magic, Bulgakov's novels provide bittersweet crepuscular valediction to the powers of temporal authority and to the verbal artifices that their inventive author assembles.

THE WHITE GUARD

Bulgakov's first novel, and the only one to be published (at least in part) in his lifetime, *The White Guard* is set in Kiev in the winter of 1918. It is the moment at which the hetman Pavel Petrovich Skoropadsky, who has ruled with the support of the Germans, flees the city, and the forces of the Ukrainian nationalist Semyon Petlyura prove temporarily triumphant over Whites and Bolsheviks. *The White Guard* is a polyphonic arrangement of a variety of characters and incidents within a brief, dramatic period in the history of modern Kiev. Its focus, however, is on the fate of one family, the Turbins, representative of a venerable way of life that is disintegrating as Ukrainian society undergoes radical change.

The Turbin children have recently buried their mother, and twenty-eight-year-old Alexei, a physician, his twenty-four-year-old sister Elena, and their seventeen-year-old brother Nikolka, a student, attempt to maintain family traditions and values, which are those of a comfortable Russian intellectual home. Public events make this impossible, however, and the collapse of the kind of humane civilization that the Turbin family exemplifies—with which Bulgakov, whose background was similar, is, despite the censor, sympathetic—is inevitable with the victory of Petlyura's troops.

Captain Sergey Talberg, the opportunistic scoundrel to whom Elena is married, abandons her to seek safety and another woman in Paris. The hetman, in the cowardly disguise of a German officer, likewise deserts Kiev at its moment of greatest danger. Nevertheless, Alexei and Nikolka, along with many others, enlist in the loyalist army in a futile effort to repulse Petlyura's advance into the city. Bulgakov depicts a range of heroism and knavery on all sides during the months of crisis in Kiev. The narrative weaves multiple subplots of combat and domestic drama into a vivid account of an obsolescent society under siege.

Through it all, the Turbin house, number 13 St. Alexei's Hill, remains for the family and its friends a fragile sanctuary. Nikolka barely escapes the violence, and Alexei, who is wounded, miraculously survives battle and an attack of typhus with the gracious assistance of a mysterious beauty named Julia Reiss. Despite the grim situation, gentle comic relief is provided by characters such as the miserly neighbor Vasilisa and the benevolent bumpkin Lariosik, who comes to stay with his relatives, the Turbins.

The apocalyptic tone of *The White Guard* is supported by religious allusions, particularly to the biblical book of Revelation. The music for the opera *Faust* remains open on the Turbin piano from the beginning of the novel to its end, and the reader is reminded of enduring values that transcend the contingencies of politics:

> But long after the Turbins and Talbergs have departed this life the keys will ring out again and Valentine will step up to the footlights, the aroma of perfume will waft from the boxes and at home beautiful women under the lamplight will play the music, because *Faust*, like the Shipwright of Saardam, is quite immortal.

As the novel concludes, Petlyura's victory, too, is ephemeral, as the Bolsheviks advance. Night descends on the Dnieper, and each of several characters dreams of something far beyond the petty intrigues of daylight Kiev. As in all of Bulgakov's fictions, a foregrounded narrative voice, relying on rhetorical questions, playful and ingenious connections and summaries, and an overtly evocative landscape, impels the reader beyond the trifles of wars and words.

BLACK SNOW

Black Snow, an unfinished work, was discovered in 1965 by the commission established during the post-Stalin thaw to rehabilitate Bulgakov. An account of the emergence of an obscure hack named Sergey Leontievich Maxudov as a literary and theatrical celebrity in Moscow, it draws heavily on Bulgakov's own experiences in writing *The White Guard* and adapting it for the Moscow Art Theater as *Days of the Turbins*. It provides a lively portrait of the artist as a melancholic and misunderstood figure and of a cultural establishment inimical to genuine creativity.

The novel begins with a letter from a producer named Xavier Borisovich Ilchin summoning Maxudov to his office at the Academy of Drama. Ilchin has read Maxudov's unacclaimed novel and is eager for him to adapt it for the stage. Next follows a flashback recounting how Maxudov conceived his book and how, as an obscure employee of the trade journal *Shipping Gazette*, he signed a contract for its publication in *The Motherland* shortly before that magazine folded. The flashback concludes with an account of how Maxudov's life is transformed after he signs a contract for the production of *Black Snow*, his stage version of the novel, by the Independent Theater.

Maxudov soon finds himself a victim of the rivalries and jealousies of figures in the theatrical world. In particular, he is caught between the two directors of the Independent Theater, Aristarkh Platonovich, who is currently off in India, and Ivan Vasilievich; neither has spoken to the other in forty years. Ivan Vasilievich is clearly modeled on Stanislavsky, and grotesque descriptions portray the tyrannical director at work, rehearsing his actors in *Black Snow* with his celebrated "method." The hapless dramatist makes a convincing case that "the famous theory was utterly wrong for my play."

Black Snow employs a sophisticated narrative perspective to distance the reader both from its inept protagonist and from the bizarre characters he encounters. Its two parts are both written by Maxudov himself in the form of a memoir. An afterword, however, introduces a new, anonymous voice who explains how Maxudov sent the manuscript to him shortly before killing himself by jumping off a bridge in Kiev. This second narrator describes the narrative that the reader has just finished as suffering from "slovenly style" and as the "fruit of a morbid imagination." Furthermore, he points out its egregious inaccuracies, among which is the fact that Maxudov never did have anything to do with the theater. The effect of this coda, as of those in Knut Hamsun's *Pan* (1894; English translation, 1920) and director Robert Wiene's film *The Cabinet of Dr. Caligari* (1920), is to cast retrospective doubt on the reliability of everything that precedes it. Is *Black Snow* a caustic mockery of philistine bureaucrats, or is it a case study in the psychopathology of a deluded author manqué? Or perhaps both? Maxudov, distraught over frustrations with the Independent Theater, does admit that he is a melancholic and describes an early suicide attempt, aborted when he heard a recording of *Faust* coming from the apartment downstairs. *Black Snow*, with its examination of the artist as victim—of powerful boors and of himself—and its lucid blend of whimsy and social observation, is a fitting commentary on and companion to Bulgakov's other works.

The Master and Margarita

Perhaps the supreme Russian novel of the twentieth century, and one of the most endearing modern texts in any language, *The Master and Margarita* was first published in abridged form in 1966-1967 and immediately created a sensation. It is a rich fusion of at least four realms and plots: the banal world of contemporary Moscow, containing the Griboyedov House, the Variety Theater, the apartments at 302-b Sadovaya, and a psychiatric hospital; ancient Jerusalem, where Pontius Pilate suffers torment over whether to crucify Yeshua Ha-Nozri; the antics of Woland and his satanic crew, including Koroviev, Azazello, Behemoth, and Hella; and the activities of the Master, utterly devoted to his art, and of Margarita, utterly devoted to him. Throughout, chapters of the novel crosscut from one of these subplots to another and ultimately suggest that perhaps they are not so distinct after all.

What sets the complex machinery of Bulgakov's novel in motion is a four-day visit to Soviet Moscow by the devil, referred to as Woland, and his assistants. They gleefully wreak havoc with the lives of the bureaucrats, hypocrites, opportunists, and dullards they encounter. They do, however, befriend and assist the Master, an alienated writer who has been hospitalized after the worldly failure of his literary efforts. The Master's beloved Margarita consents to serve as hostess at Satan's ball and is rewarded with supernatural powers. An inferior poet named Ivan Homeless finds himself in the same psychiatric clinic as the Master and gradually becomes his disciple. The lifework of the Master is a novel about Pontius Pilate, and chapters from it, with manifest parallels to the situation in contemporary Moscow, are interspersed throughout Bulgakov's novel.

Woland's performance at the Variety Theater is billed as a "black magic act accompanied by a full exposé," and *The Master and Margarita* itself, an absorbing blend of fantasy and verisimilitude presented with subversive self-consciousness, could be similarly described. The playful narrative voice that overtly addresses the reader mocks not only the characters but itself as well. Numerous authors among the *dramatis personae*, including Ivan, the Master, Matthu Levi, and Ryukhin, as well as characters given musical names such as Berlioz, Stravinsky, and Rimsky, foreground the process of fabrication and reinforce one of the novel's persistent themes—the elusive nature of truth.

Most of the characters in Moscow refuse to recognize anything problematic about truth. Arrogantly convinced that human reason is adequate to any cognitive task, they stubbornly deny the supernatural that erupts in the form of Woland or that is evoked in the story of Yeshua. Like the other hack writers who congregate at the Griboyedov House, Ivan Homeless would just as soon take life on the most comfortable terms possible, but his spirit will not permit him to do so. Torn between the material and the spiritual, the temporal and the eternal, the collective and the individual, Ivan is diagnosed as schizophrenic and is hospitalized. His progress as a patient and as a writer will be marked by his success in reconciling opposing realms. Bulgakov, the novelist as master weaver, seems to be suggesting that both artistic achievement and mental health are dependent on a harmony between ostensibly disparate materials.

The Master, like Bulgakov himself, attempted to destroy his book, but, as Woland points out, "manuscripts don't burn." Art survives and transcends the hardships and iniquities of particular places and times. It ridicules the obtuseness of temporal authorities with the example of immortal authority. In one of many echoes of the Faust legend, *The Master and Margarita* chooses as its epigraph Johann Wolfgang von Goethe's reference to "that Power which eternally wills evil and eternally works good." Bulgakov's ambitious novel certainly does not deny the oppressive reality of contemporary society, but its humor is restorative, and it moves toward an exhilarating, harmonious vision that would exclude nothing. It concludes with a benedictory kiss from a spectral Margarita.

THE HEART OF A DOG

The most overt of Bulgakov's statements on the Russian Revolution, *The Heart of a Dog*, though written in 1925, was published in English in 1968 and in Russian in 1969. It is a satiric novella about an experiment performed by the celebrated Moscow surgeon Philip Philipovich Preobrazhensky, who takes a stray mongrel dog, Sharik, and transforms him into a human being named Sharikov. Much of the tale is narrated by Sharikov himself, who is not necessarily better off for his transformation. To perform the operation, Preobrazhensky has inserted the pituitary of a vulgar criminal into the brain of the dog. The result is an uncouth, rowdy human being who, though adept at language and even at repeating the political slogans supplied by the officious house committee chairman, Shvonder, proves incapable of satisfying the standards of civilized behavior demanded by Preobrazhensky. Hence, convinced that the experiment is a fiasco, he reverses it and turns Sharikov back into Sharik.

The Heart of a Dog features Bulgakov's characteristic blend of fantasy and social analysis. It parabolically raises the question of the malleability of human nature and of the possibility of social melioration. Once again, it exposes to ridicule the arrogance of those who would presume to shape others' lives and raises doubts about the efficacy and desirability of social engineering, such as Russia was undergoing in the 1920's. The book suggests a fatal incompatibility between the proletariat and the intelligentsia, implying that the humane values of the latter are threatened by the former. It seems to counsel humble caution in tampering with the arrangements of the world.

Steven G. Kellman

OTHER MAJOR WORKS

SHORT FICTION: *Diavoliada*, 1925 (*Diaboliad, and Other Stories*, 1972); *Traktat o zhilishche*, 1926 (*A Treatise on Housing*, 1972); *Zapiski iunogo vracha*, 1963 (*A Country Doctor's Notebook*, 1975); *Notes on the Cuff, and Other Stories*, 1991.

PLAYS: *Dni Turbinykh*, pr. 1926 (adaptation of his novel *Belaya gvardiya*; *Days of the Turbins*, 1934); *Zoykina kvartira*, pr. 1926 (*Zoya's Apartment*, 1970); *Bagrovy ostrov*, pr. 1928 (adaptation of his short story;

The Crimson Island, 1972); *Kabala svyatosh*, pr. 1936 (wr. 1929; *A Cabal of Hypocrites*, 1972; also known as *Molière*); *Don Kikhot*, pr. 1941; *Posledniye dni (Pushkin)*, pr. 1943 (wr. 1934-1935; *The Last Days*, 1976); *Beg*, pr. 1957 (wr. 1928; *Flight*, 1969); *Ivan Vasilievich*, pb. 1965 (wr. 1935; English translation, 1974); *Blazhenstvo*, pb. 1966 (wr. 1934; *Bliss*, 1976); *Adam i Eva*, pb. 1971 (wr. 1930-1931; *Adam and Eve*, 1971); *The Early Plays of Mikhail Bulgakov*, 1972; *Rashel*, pb. 1972 (wr. c. 1936; libretto; adaptation of Guy de Maupassant's short story "Mademoiselle Fifi"); *Minin i Pozharskii*, pb. 1976 (wr. 1936; libretto); *Batum*, pb. 1977 (wr. 1938); *Six Plays*, 1991.

NONFICTION: *Zhizn gospodina de Molyera*, 1962 (*The Life of Monsieur de Molière*, 1970).

TRANSLATION: *L'Avare*, 1936 (of Molière's play).

BIBLIOGRAPHY

Barratt, Andrew. *Between Two Worlds: A Critical Introduction to "The Master and Margarita."* New York: Oxford University Press, 1987. Puts forth an imaginative approach to understanding Bulgakov's most important work. Describes the genesis of the novel and its reception inside and outside the Soviet Union.

Curtis, J. A. E. *Manuscripts Don't Burn: Mikhail Bulgakov, a Life in Letters and Diaries.* Woodstock, N.Y.: Overlook Press, 1992. Contains previously unpublished letters and a diary that were believed to be lost. Groups of Bulgakov's letters, diaries, and speeches are arranged in chronological order and interspersed with biographical chapters, providing context for the primary source material.

Drawicz, Andrzej. *The Master and the Devil: A Study of Mikhail Bulgakov.* Translated by Kevin Windle. Lewiston, N.Y.: Edwin Mellen Press, 2001. Analyzes all of Bulgakov's prose and dramatic works, placing them within the context of the author's life and times. The initial chapters focus on Bulgakov's life, providing new biographical information, and subsequent chapters concentrate on his novels and other writings.

Haber, Edythe C. *Mikhail Bulgakov: The Early Years.* Cambridge, Mass.: Harvard University Press, 1998. Discusses Bulgakov's early life and career, describing how his novels and other works arose from his experiences during the Russian Revolution, civil war, and early years of Communism. Traces the themes and characters of his early works and demonstrates how he perfected these fictional elements in *The Master and Margarita.*

Milne, Lesley. *Mikhail Bulgakov: A Critical Biography.* New York: Cambridge University Press, 1990. Describes some of the features that are essential to understanding Bulgakov's outlook on life and the themes and techniques of his works. Includes detailed and original interpretations of some of Bulgakov's earliest works as well as a serious examination of *The Master and Margarita.*

_____, ed. *Bulgakov: The Novelist-Playwright.* New York: Routledge, 1996. Collection of twenty-one essays surveys Bulgakov's works from a wide variety of perspectives. Several essays examine *The Master and Margarita*, including one that compares the novel to Salman Rushdie's *The Satanic Verses* (1988). Includes an index of Bulgakov's works.

Proffer, Ellendea. *Bulgakov: Life and Work.* Ann Arbor, Mich.: Ardis, 1984. Comprehensive treatment of Bulgakov's career provides information and analysis of some early works that previously received little scholarly attention. Proffer's portrait of Bulgakov contrasts with that of other critics, who depict him as being a suppressed and haunted author under the Stalinist regime.

Weir, Justin. *The Author as Hero: Self and Tradition in Bulgakov, Pasternak, and Nabokov.* Evanston, Ill.: Northwestern University Press, 2002. Analyzes novels by three Russian authors—Bulgakov's *The Master and Margarita*, Boris Pasternak's *Doktor Zhivago* (1957; *Doctor Zhivago*, 1958), and Vladimir Nabokov's *Dar* (1952; *The Gift*, 1963)—to describe how these authors reveal themselves through their writing, transforming the traditional authors into the heroes of their novels.

Wright, A. Colin. *Mikhail Bulgakov: Life and Interpretations.* Toronto, Ont.: University of Toronto Press, 1978. Thorough critical biography examines *The Master and Margarita* and other works and places them within the context of Bulgakov's life. Includes indexes and bibliography.

JOHN BUNYAN

Born: Elstow, Bedfordshire, England; November
   30, 1628 (baptized)
Died: London, England; August 31, 1688

PRINCIPAL LONG FICTION

Grace Abounding to the Chief of Sinners, 1666
*The Pilgrim's Progress from This World to That
   Which Is to Come Delivered Under the
   Similitude of a Dream, Wherein Is Discovered
   the Manner of His Setting Out, His Dangerous
   Journey, and Safe Arrival at the Desired
   Country*, 1678, 1684 (2 parts; commonly
   known as *The Pilgrim's Progress*)
The Life and Death of Mr. Badman, 1680
The Holy War, 1682

OTHER LITERARY FORMS

Between 1656 and 1688, John Bunyan (BUHN-
yuhn) published forty-four separate works, including
prose narratives and tracts, sermons, and verse; ten posthumous publications appeared in a folio edition of 1692,
which the author himself had prepared for the press. A
nearly complete edition of the prose works, in two volumes, was printed in the period 1736-1737, another in
1767 by George Whitefield, and a six-volume Edinburgh edition in 1784. The best of Bunyan's verse can be
found in a small collection (c. 1664) containing "The
Four Last Things," "Ebal and Gerizim," and "Prison
Meditations." In addition, Bunyan wrote *A Caution to
Stir Up to Watch Against Sin* (1664), a half-sheet broadside poem in sixteen stanzas; *A Book for Boys and Girls:
Or, Country Rhymes for Children* (1686); and *Discourse
of the Building, Nature, Excellency, and Government of
the House of God* (1688), a poem in twelve parts.

ACHIEVEMENTS

The spirit of seventeenth century Protestant dissent
burst into flame within the heart and mind of John Bunyan. He attended only grammar school, served in the
parliamentary army at age sixteen, and returned to Bedfordshire to undergo religious crisis and conversion. Imprisoned after the Restoration of Charles II for refusing

to obey the laws against religious dissent, he turned to his
pen as the only available means of performing his divinely ordained stewardship. He wrote his most significant work, the vision of *The Pilgrim's Progress*, while
in jail, and the piece became a companion to the Scriptures among lower-class English Dissenters. His limited
education came from two sources: John Foxe's *Com-
mentarii rerum in ecclesia gestarum* (1554; revised
1559; revised and translated as *Foxe's Book of Martyrs*,
1563; also known as *Actes and Monuments of the Christian Church*), containing accounts of the martyrdom of
sixteenth century English Protestants, and the Authorized Version of the Bible, the content and style of which
Bunyan skillfully applied to his own prose.

Bunyan's art grew out of his natural abilities of observation and analysis. He was a Puritan and a product of
the Puritan movement, yet, as can be seen clearly from
the autobiographical *Grace Abounding to the Chief of
Sinners*, he was chiefly interested in actual human experience, not in religious doctrine for its own sake. His
allegorical characters—Mr. Timorous, Mr. Talkative,
Mrs. Diffidence, Mr. By-ends, Lord Turn-about, Mr.
Smooth-man, Mr. Facing-bothways—originated in everyday life. Similarly, the Valley of Humiliation, the
Slough of Despond, Vanity Fair, and Fair-speech can be
found by all people everywhere, no matter what their
cultures or religions. In *The Pilgrim's Progress*, Bunyan
universalized his Puritanism, depicting every earnest
Christian's search for salvation, every upright person's
attempt to achieve some degree of faith. He wrote to
awaken conscience, to strengthen faith, and to win
souls—the last being the true object of his evangelical
mission. At the same time, he managed to write tracts
and narratives worthy of recognition as literature—even,
in certain instances, as masterpieces.

BIOGRAPHY

John Bunyan was born in the village of Elstow, in
Bedfordshire (one mile south of Bedford), England, in
November, 1628. The parish register of Elstow records
his baptism on November 30. His father, Thomas Bunyan, a native of Elstow, married three times between Jan-

uary, 1623, and August, 1644; John Bunyan was the first child of his father's second marriage—on May 23, 1627, to Margaret Bentley, also of Elstow. The boy's father was a "whitesmith," a maker and mender of pots and kettles, although by the time the son adopted the same vocation, the job reference had changed to "tinker." Young Bunyan attended a nearby grammar school (either the one at Bedford or another at Elstow), where he learned to read and write—but little else. In fact, what he did learn he promptly forgot after his father removed him from school to help in the family forge and workshop. When, in 1644, his mother died and the elder Bunyan promptly remarried, Bunyan lost all interest in his family; he entered the parliamentary army in November, at age sixteen, and remained until the disbanding of that force in 1646. He then returned to Elstow and the family trade.

At the end of 1648 or the beginning of 1649, Bunyan married a pious but otherwise unidentified woman who bore him four children—one of whom, Mary, was born blind. He spent some four years wrestling with his fi-

John Bunyan. (Library of Congress)

nances and his soul, and in 1653 joined a dissenting sect that met at St. John's Church, Bedford. Shortly after his removal to that city in 1655, his wife died, and two years later he was called upon to preach by the Baptist sect whose church he had joined. In 1659, Bunyan married again, to a woman named Elizabeth, who spent considerable time rearing his children, bearing him two more, and trying to secure her husband's release from a series of prison terms.

Bunyan's career as a writer cannot be separated from his difficulties immediately preceding and during the Restoration of Charles II. The period of Cromwell's Commonwealth produced a number of dissenting preachers, both male and female, who achieved their offices through inspiration rather than ordination; they professed to be filled with inner light and the gifts of the Holy Spirit rather than with learning. Charles II had promised to tolerate these preachers, but the established church, in November, 1660, set about to persecute and to silence them. Bunyan, who chose imprisonment rather than silence, spent all but a few weeks of the next eleven years in jail in Bedford, where he preached to his fellow prisoners, made tagged laces, and wrote religious books— the most noteworthy being his spiritual autobiography, *Grace Abounding to the Chief of Sinners*. He was freed in September, 1672, when Charles II, through his Declaration of Indulgence, suspended all penal statutes against Nonconformists and papists.

Upon his release from prison, Bunyan returned to his ministerial duties at St. John's Church in Bedford, this time with a license (given to him by royal authority) to preach. By 1675, however, he was again imprisoned in Bedford, the result of refusing to declare formal allegiance to Charles II (against whom he had no real objection) and the Church of England. While serving this particular sentence, Bunyan produced his most significant piece of prose, *The Pilgrim's Progress*. Bunyan's major prose works were written within the last ten years of his life, the period during which he both suffered from intolerance and received honors from the intolerant. In the last year of his life, he served as the unofficial chaplain to Sir John Shorter, the Lord Mayor of London. Indeed, Bunyan endured the entire tide of religious and political trauma of the middle and late seventeenth century: parliamentary acts, ministerial changes, popish plots, the rebellious factions. His work bears testimony to that endurance, to the patience of a nonpolitical yet deeply pious man who lost much of his freedom to the impatience of a supposedly pious but terribly political religious establishment.

Bunyan died on August 31, 1688, at the London house of his friend John Strudwick, a grocer and chandler. Supposedly, in order to settle a dispute between a father and his son, Bunyan had ridden through heavy rain and caught a severe cold that led to his death. He was buried in Bunhill Fields, the burial ground of London Dissenters.

ANALYSIS

John Bunyan viewed his life as a commitment to Christian stewardship, to be carried on by gospel preaching and instructive writing. Although practically everything he wrote reflects that commitment, he possessed the ability to create interesting variations on similar themes, keeping in mind the needs of his lower-class audience. Thus, *The Pilgrim's Progress* is an allegory of human life and universal religious experience. In *The Life and Death of Mr. Badman*, Bunyan abandoned allegory and developed a dialogue between Mr. Wiseman and Mr. Attentive through which he publicized the aims and methods of the late seventeenth century bourgeois scoundrel, whose lack of principle and honesty was well known among Bunyan's readers (the victims of Mr. Badman). Finally, his first major work, *Grace Abounding to the Chief of Sinners*, is a "spiritual autobiography" that presents adventures and experiences not unlike those undergone by any human being at any moment in history who must wrestle with the fundamental questions of life. The function of Bunyan's prose in every case was to spread the Word of God and to establish a holy community of humankind in which that Word could be practiced. Once the Word took hold, Bunyan believed, the world would become a veritable garden of peace and order.

GRACE ABOUNDING TO THE CHIEF OF SINNERS

Published in 1666, *Grace Abounding to the Chief of Sinners* remains one of the most significant spiritual autobiographies by an English writer. Bunyan's style is perhaps more formal in this piece than in *The Pilgrim's Progress*, although he did well in balancing the heavy phrasing of Scripture (as it appeared in the Authorized Version) with picturesque, colloquial English. A richly emotional work in which such highly charged experiences as the Last Judgment and the tortures of Hell become as clear as the mundane experiences of daily existence, Bunyan's autobiography is a narrative of spiritual adventure set against the backdrop of a real village in Britain. Although he omitted specific names and dates, obviously to universalize the piece, Bunyan did not forget to describe what he had seen after his return from the army: the popular game of "cat," with its participants and spectators; the bell ringers at the parish church; the poor women sitting, in sunlight, before the door of a village house; the puddles in the road. Woven into this fabric of reality are the experiences of the dreamer; the people of Bedford appear as though in a vision on the sunny side of a high mountain, as the dreamer, shut out by an encompassing wall, shivers in the cold storm. Such interweaving of reality and fantasy was to take place again, with greater force and allegorical complexity, in the first part of *The Pilgrim's Progress*.

Bunyan's intention in *Grace Abounding to the Chief of Sinners* was to point the way by which average Christians, convinced of their own sins, can be led by God's grace to endure the pain of spiritual crisis. He determined to record how, as an obscure Bedfordshire tinker, he had changed his course from sloth and sin and had become an eloquent and fearless man of God. Of course, when he wrote the work, he had been in prison for ten years, and (as he states in the preface) he set about to enlighten and assist those from whom he had, for so long a period, been separated.

From the confinement of his prison cell, Bunyan felt the desire to survey his entire life—to grasp his soul in his hands and take account of himself. Thus, *Grace Abounding to the Chief of Sinners* emerged from the heart and the spirit of a man isolated from humankind to become not merely one more testimonial for the instruction of the faithful but a serious psychological self-study—one so truthful and so sincere (and also so spontaneous) that it may be the first work of its kind. Bunyan's language is simple and direct, and his constant references to Scripture emphasize the typicality of his experiences as a struggling Christian. His fears, doubts, and moments of comfort are filtered through the encounter between David and Goliath and God's deliverance of the young shepherd, while his lively imagination gathers images from the Psalms and the Proverbs and reshapes them to fit the context of his spiritual experiences.

THE PILGRIM'S PROGRESS

Bunyan's ability to universalize his experience is supremely evident in *The Pilgrim's Progress*, perhaps the most successful allegory in British literature. *The Pilgrim's Progress* has as its basic metaphor the familiar idea of life as a journey. Bunyan confronts his pilgrim, Christian, with homely and commonplace sights: a quagmire, the bypaths and shortcuts through pleasant country meadows, the inn, the steep hill, the town fair on market day, the river to be forded. Such places belong to the everyday experience of every man, woman, and child; on another level, they recall the holy but homely parables of Christ's earthly ministry and thus assume spiritual significance. Those familiar details serve as an effective background for Bunyan's narrative, a story of adventure intended to hold the reader in suspense. Bunyan grew up among the very people who constituted his audience, and he knew how to balance the romantic and the strange with the familiar. Thus, Christian travels the King's Highway at the same time that he traverses a perilous path to encounter giants, wild beasts, hobgoblins, and the terrible Apollyon, the angel of the bottomless pit with whom the central character must fight. Other travelers are worthy of humorous characterization, as they represent a variety of intellectual and moral attitudes, while Christian himself runs the gamut of universal experience, from the moment he learns of his sins until the account of his meeting with Hopeful in the river.

As always, Bunyan molds his style from the Authorized Version of the Bible. By relying on concrete, common language, he enables even the simplest of his readers to share experiences with the characters of *The Pilgrim's Progress*. Even the conversations relating to complex and tedious theological issues do not detract from the human and dramatic aspects of the allegory: Evangelist pointing the way; Christian running from his home with his fingers stuck in his ears; the starkness of the place of the Cross in contrast to the activity of Vanity Fair; the humorous but terribly circumstantial trial. It is this homely but vivid realism that accounts for the timeless appeal of Bunyan's allegory. *The Pilgrim's Progress* reveals the truth about humankind—its weakness, its imperfection, its baseness—but also its search for goodness and order.

THE LIFE AND DEATH OF MR. BADMAN

The Life and Death of Mr. Badman represents Bunyan's major attempt at a dialogue, a confrontation between the Christian and the atheist, between the road to Paradise and the route to Hell. Mr. Wiseman, a Christian, tells the story of Mr. Badman to Mr. Attentive, who in turn comments on it. Badman is an example of the reprobate, one whose sins become evident during childhood. In fact, he is so addicted to lying that his parents cannot distinguish when he is speaking the truth. Bunyan does not place much blame on the parents, for they indeed bear the burden of their son's actions; they even attempt to counsel him and to redirect his ways. The situation becomes worse, however, as Badman's lying turns to pilfering and then to outright stealing. All of this, naturally, leads to a hatred of Sunday, of the Puritan demands of that day: reading Scripture, attending conferences, repeating sermons, praying to God. Wiseman, the defender of the Puritan Sabbath, maintains that little boys, as a matter of course, must learn to appreciate the Sabbath; those who do not are victims of their own wickedness. Hatred of the Sabbath leads to swearing and cursing, which become as natural to young Badman as eating, drinking, and sleeping.

Badman's adult life is painstakingly drawn out through realistic descriptions, anecdotes, and dialogue. He cheats and steals his way through the world of debauchery and commerce and creates misery for his wife and seven children. Growing in importance, he forms a league with the devil and becomes a wealthy man by taking advantage of others' misfortunes. When the time comes for his end, he cannot be saved—nor does Bunyan try to fabricate an excuse for his redemption and salvation. As Mr. Wiseman states, "As his life was full of sin, so his death was without repentance." Throughout a long sickness, Badman fails to acknowledge his sins, remaining firm in his self-satisfaction. He dies without struggle, "like a chrisom child, quietly and without fear."

The strength of *The Life and Death of Mr. Badman* derives in large part from Bunyan's ability to depict common English life of the middle and late seventeenth century. The details are so accurate, so minute, that the reader can gain as much history from the piece as morality or practical theology. Bunyan places no demands on the reader's credulity by providential interpositions, nor does he alter his wicked character's ways for the sake of a happy ending. In portraying Badman's ways, Bunyan concedes nothing, nor does he exaggerate. Badman succeeds, gains wealth and power, and dies at peace with himself. Bunyan creates a monstrous product of sin and places him squarely in the center of English provincial life. The one consolation, the principal lesson, is that Badman travels the direct route to everlasting hellfire. On his way, he partakes of life's pleasures and is gratified by them as only an unrepentant sinner could be. For Bunyan, the harsh specificity of Badman's life is a sufficient lesson through which to promote his version of positive Christianity.

Beneath the veil of seventeenth century British Puritanism, for all its seeming narrowness and sectarian strife, there was something for all persons of all eras—the struggle to know God, to do his will, to find peace. If Bunyan's first major prose work was a spiritual autobiography, then it is fair to state that the principal efforts that followed—*The Pilgrim's Progress* and *The Life and Death of Mr. Badman*—constituted one of the earliest spiritual histories of all humankind.

Samuel J. Rogal

OTHER MAJOR WORKS

POETRY: *A Caution to Stir Up to Watch Against Sin*, 1664; *A Book for Boys and Girls: Or, Country Rhymes for Children*, 1686; *Discourse of the Building, Nature, Excellency, and Government of the House of God*, 1688.

NONFICTION: *Some Gospel Truths Opened*, 1656; *A Vindication . . . of Some Gospel Truths Opened*, 1657; *A Few Signs from Hell*, 1658; *The Doctrine of the Law and Grace Unfolded*, 1659; *Profitable Meditations Fitted to Man's Different Condition*, 1661; *I Will Pray with the Spirit*, 1663; *A Mapp Shewing the Order and Causes of*

Salvation and Damnation, 1664; *The Holy City: Or, The New Jerusalem*, 1665; *One Thing Is Needful*, 1665; *A Confession of My Faith and a Reason for My Practice*, 1671; *A Defence of the Doctrine of Justification by Faith*, 1672; *A New and Useful Concordance to the Holy Bible*, 1672; *Saved by Grace*, 1676; *The Strait Gate: Or, The Great Difficulty of Going to Heaven*, 1676; *A Treatise of the Fear of God*, 1679; *A Holy Life, the Beauty of Christianity*, 1684; *The Jerusalem Sinner Saved*, 1688; *Solomon's Temple Spiritualized: Or, Gospel Light Fecht Out of the Temple at Jerusalem*, 1688.

BIBLIOGRAPHY

Brown, John. *John Bunyan, 1628-1688: His Life, Times, and Work*. 3d. ed. Eugene, Oreg.: Wipf & Stock, 2007. This is the third edition of what is generally considered the definitive biography of Bunyan. Devotes two chapters to *The Pilgrim's Progress*, including an assessment of its literary reputation. Contains several appendixes, including one listing editions, versions, illustrations, and imitations of *The Pilgrim's Progress*.

Collmer, Robert G., ed. *Bunyan in Our Time*. Kent, Ohio: Kent State University Press, 1989. Collection of distinguished literary criticism and appraisals of Bunyan includes essays on his use of language, satire and its biblical sources, and *The Pilgrim's Progress* as allegory. Of particular interest are the essays on Marxist perspectives on Bunyan and a comparison between Bunyan's quest and C. S. Lewis's quest in *The Pilgrim's Regress* (1933).

Davies, Michael. *Graceful Reading: Theology and Narrative in the Works of John Bunyan*. New York: Oxford University Press, 2002. Interprets *The Pilgrim's Progress*, *Grace Abounding to the Chief of Sinners*, and other works, assessing their narrative style within the context of postmodernism and Bunyan's theology within the context of seventeenth century Calvinism.

Harrison, G. B. *John Bunyan: A Study in Personality*. 1928. Reprint. New York: Archon Books, 1967. Short study examines the mind and personality of Bunyan as shown in his writings. Discusses his conversion, his imprisonment, and his roles as pastor and writer. The close analysis of minor works makes this an important critical source.

Hill, Christopher. *A Turbulent, Seditious, and Factious People: John Bunyan and His Church, 1628-1688.* New York: Oxford University Press, 1989. Combination biography and social history places Bunyan within the context of revolutionary England and argues that even his religious and allegorical writings must be interpreted as reflections of seventeenth century political, social, and economic issues.

Kelman, John. *The Road: A Study of John Bunyan's "Pilgrim's Progress."* 2 vols. Port Washington, N.Y.: Kennikat Press, 1912. Intended as commentary or textbook, to be read point by point with *The Pilgrim's Progress.* Takes an evangelical approach to Bunyan and is filled with praise for his work. Gives close analysis of the text from a strongly Christian point of view.

Mullett, Michael. *John Bunyan in Context.* Pittsburgh, Pa.: Duquesne University Press, 1997. Evaluation of Bunyan's career contradicts previous biographies in depicting Bunyan as being less revolutionary and more opportunistic. Separate chapters analyze each of his major works. Includes bibliographical references and index.

Sadler, Lynn Veach. *John Bunyan.* Boston: Twayne, 1979. Provides a useful introduction for beginning readers of Bunyan. Discusses his life, his religious milieu, and his works. Places *Grace Abounding to the Chief of Sinners* in the genre of "spiritual autobiography." Most of the literary criticism focuses on *The Pilgrim's Progress*, but *The Life and Death of Mr. Badman* and *The Holy War* are discussed as well. Includes a selected bibliography.

Spargo, Tamsin. *The Writing of John Bunyan.* Brookfield, Vt.: Ashgate, 1997. Engages in a detailed exploration of how Bunyan established his authority as an author. Includes notes and detailed bibliography. Recommended for advanced students and scholars.

ANTHONY BURGESS
John Anthony Burgess Wilson

Born: Manchester, Lancashire, England; February 25, 1917
Died: London, England; November 25, 1993
Also known as: John Anthony Burgess Wilson; John Wilson; Joseph Kell

PRINCIPAL LONG FICTION

Time for a Tiger, 1956
The Enemy in the Blanket, 1958
Beds in the East, 1959
The Doctor Is Sick, 1960
The Right to an Answer, 1960
Devil of a State, 1961
One Hand Clapping, 1961 (as Joseph Kell)
The Worm and the Ring, 1961
A Clockwork Orange, 1962 (reprinted with final chapter, 1986)
The Wanting Seed, 1962
Honey for the Bears, 1963

Inside Mr. Enderby, 1963 (as Kell)
The Eve of Saint Venus, 1964
Nothing Like the Sun: A Story of Shakespeare's Love-Life, 1964
The Long Day Wanes, 1965 (includes *Time for a Tiger*, *The Enemy in the Blanket*, and *Beds in the East*)
A Vision of Battlements, 1965
Tremor of Intent, 1966
Enderby, 1968 (includes *Inside Mr. Enderby* and *Enderby Outside*)
Enderby Outside, 1968
MF, 1971
The Clockwork Testament: Or, Enderby's End, 1974
Napoleon Symphony, 1974
Beard's Roman Woman, 1976
Moses: A Narrative, 1976
Abba, Abba, 1977

1985, 1978

Man of Nazareth, 1979

Earthly Powers, 1980

The End of the World News, 1983

Enderby's Dark Lady, 1984

The Kingdom of the Wicked, 1985

The Pianoplayers, 1986

Any Old Iron, 1989

A Dead Man in Deptford, 1993

Byrne, 1995

OTHER LITERARY FORMS

In addition to his novels, Anthony Burgess published eight works of literary criticism. He paid tribute to his self-confessed literary mentor, James Joyce, in such works as *Re Joyce* (1965) and *Joysprick: An Introduction to the Language of James Joyce* (1972). His book reviews and essays were collected in *The Novel Now* (1967), *Urgent Copy: Literary Studies* (1968), and *Homage to Qwert Yuiop* (1985; also known as *But Do Blondes Prefer Gentlemen? Homage to Qwert Yuiop, and Other Writings*, 1986). His fascination with language and with the lives of writers led to such works as *Language Made Plain* (1964), *Shakespeare* (1970), and *Flame into Being: The Life and Work of D. H. Lawrence* (1985). An autobiographical work, *Little Wilson and Big God*, was published in 1987 (part of which was republished in 1996 as *Childhood*), and a collection of short fiction, *The Devil's Mode*, in 1989. A posthumous volume of his uncollected writings, *One Man's Chorus* (1998), includes a variety of essays divided into sections on travel, contemporary life, literary criticism, and personality sketches.

ACHIEVEMENTS

In his novels, Anthony Burgess extended the boundaries of English fiction. His inventive use of language, his use of symphonic forms and motifs, his rewriting of myths and legends, his examination of cultural clashes between the developing world and the West, and his pursuit of various ways to tell a story established him as one of the chief exemplars of postmodernism. His novels are studied in contemporary fiction courses, and he also achieved popular success with such works as *A Clockwork Orange* and *Earthly Powers*, for which he received

the Prix du Meilleur Livre Étranger in 1981. Stanley Kubrick's controversial film *A Clockwork Orange* (1971) further established Burgess's popular reputation.

BIOGRAPHY

John Anthony Burgess Wilson was born in Manchester, England, on February 25, 1917. His mother and sister died in the influenza epidemic of 1918. Of Irish background, his mother had performed in the music halls of the period and was known as the Beautiful Belle Burgess. His father performed as a silent-film pianist and, when he remarried, played piano in a pub called the Golden Eagle, owned by his new wife; Burgess himself began to compose music when he was fourteen. Burgess graduated from the Bishop Bilsborrow School and planned to study music at Manchester University. When he failed a required physics entrance exam there, he changed his focus to literature and graduated from Xaverian College in Manchester; in 1940, he wrote his senior honors thesis on Christopher Marlowe while Nazi bombs fell overhead.

In October, 1940, Burgess joined the army and was placed in the Army Medical Corps. He was later shifted to the Army Educational Corps—a prophetic move, given that he became a teacher for nearly twenty years afterward. In 1942, Burgess married Llewela Isherwood Jones, a Welsh fellow student. He spent three years, from 1943 to 1946, with the British Army on Gibraltar, during which time he wrote his first novel, *A Vision of Battlements* (which was not published until 1965).

Burgess left the army as a sergeant major and as a training college lecturer in speech and drama in 1946 to become a member of the Central Advisory Council for Adult Education in the British armed forces. He lectured at Birmingham University until 1948, when he served as a lecturer in phonetics for the Ministry of Education in Preston, Lancashire. From 1950 until 1954, he taught English literature, phonetics, Spanish, and music at the Banbury grammar school in Oxfordshire.

Throughout these years, Burgess was painfully aware of his Irish heritage and Catholic religion. Although he had renounced Catholicism early, the Irish Catholic stigma remained with him in rigorously Protestant England. His decision to apply for the job of education officer for the Colonial Service may have had something to

Anthony Burgess. (Monitor/Archive Photos)

do with his desire to leave England and his need to exile himself physically from a homeland that had already exiled him in spirit. From 1954 to 1957, he was the senior lecturer in English at the Malayan Teachers Training College in Kahta Baru, Malaya. There, he had more leisure time to write, and he published his first novel, *Time for a Tiger*, in 1956 under his middle names, Anthony Burgess. (Members of the Colonial Service were not allowed to publish fiction under their own names.)

Burgess continued working for the Colonial Service as an English-language specialist in Brunei, Borneo, from 1957 to 1959 and published two more novels, which, with his first, eventually constituted his Malayan trilogy, *The Long Day Wanes*. The clash between East and West in manners and morals became the major focus of his early novels.

Apparent tragedy struck in 1959, when Burgess collapsed in his Borneo classroom. After excruciating medical tests, he was diagnosed with an inoperable brain tumor. He was given a year to live and was sent back to

England. Unable to teach and virtually penniless, Burgess set himself to writing as much as he could in order to provide for his wife. Not only had she already shown signs of the cirrhosis of the liver that was eventually to kill her, but she also had attempted suicide. In the next three years, Burgess wrote and published nine novels, including *A Clockwork Orange* and *Inside Mr. Enderby*.

On the first day of spring, March 20, 1968, Llewela Burgess finally died. That October, Burgess married Liliana Macellari, a member of the linguistics department at Cambridge, intensifying the scandal that had originally developed when their affair produced a son, Andreas, in 1964. The personal guilt involved with his first wife's death always haunted Burgess and provided one of the major underlying themes of his fiction. "Guilt's a good thing," Burgess once said, "because the morals are just ticking away very nicely." In fact, persistent guilt shadows all of his characters and consistently threatens to overwhelm them completely.

Burgess, Liliana, and Andrew left England in October, 1968; they moved to Malta, then to Bracciano in Italy, and eventually settled in Monaco. Burgess's life changed dramatically in 1971, when the film version of *A Clockwork Orange*, directed by Stanley Kubrick, was released, making Burgess a celebrity. Regardless of his continuous production of new works in several genres, Burgess lived in the shadow of his 1962 novel. In 1980, he published *Earthly Powers*, a long and ambitious novel on which he had been working for more than ten years. He continued to compose symphonies and write reviews and articles for major newspapers and periodicals. He also became a skilled dramatic writer, with credits that include a version of Edmond Rostand's *Cyrano de Bergerac* (pr. 1897), produced on Broadway in 1972; the screenplay for Franco Zeffirelli's 1977 extravaganza *Jesus of Nazareth*; and *A Clockwork Orange 2004*, produced at the Barbizon Theater, London, in 1990. Burgess's production never slackened. In the last decade of his life, he produced six more novels, his last, *A Dead Man in Deptford*, being published just before his death from lung cancer in 1993.

ANALYSIS

Anthony Burgess shares with many postmodernist writers an almost obsessive awareness of his great modernist predecessors—particularly James Joyce. The vision that Burgess inherited from modernism is informed by the anguish of a sensitive soul lost in a fragmented, shattered world. Each of Burgess's novels reveals one central character virtually "at sea" in a landscape of battered, broken figures and events. Burgess conveys this fragmented worldview by means of many of the literary devices of his modernist predecessors. Often he employs a stream-of-consciousness narration in which his main characters tell their own stories; he also uses what T. S. Eliot, reviewing Joyce's *Ulysses* (1922), called the "mythic method," in which contemporary chaos is compared with and contrasted to heroic myths, legends, religious ceremonies, and rituals of the past. As Eliot remarked, the mythic method "is simply a way of controlling, of ordering, of giving a shape and significance to the intense panorama of futility and anarchy which is contemporary history."

Like many postmodernists, convinced that most literary forms are serious games devised to stave off approaching chaos and collapse, Burgess delights in the play of language for its own sake. Here again, Joyce is a prime source of inspiration: surprising images, poetic revelations, linguistic twists and turns, and strange, evocative words nearly overwhelm the narrative shape of *Ulysses* and certainly overwhelm it in *Finnegans Wake* (1939). Burgess's best novels are those in which language for its own sake plays an important role, as in *Enderby*, *Nothing Like the Sun*, *A Clockwork Orange*, and *Napoleon Symphony*.

At the heart of his vision of the world lies Burgess's Manichaean sensibility, his belief that there is "a duality that is fixed almost from the beginning of the world and the outcome is in doubt." God and the Devil reign over a supremely divided universe; they are equal in power, and they will battle to the end of the world. In the Manichaean tradition—most notably, that of the Gnostics—Burgess sees the world as a materialistic trap and a prison of the spirit, a place devised by the Devil to incarcerate people until their deaths. Only art can break through the battle lines; only art can save him. The recasting of a religious commitment in aesthetic terms also belongs to the legacy of modernism. Burgess's Manichaean vision produces such clashes of opposites as that between East and West, between the self and the state, and between a single character and an alien social environment. These recurring polarities structure Burgess's fiction.

THE RIGHT TO AN ANSWER

This principle of polarity or opposition is evident in the early novel *The Right to an Answer*, in which J. W. Denham, businessman and exile, returns to his father's house in the suburban British Midlands and finds a provincial, self-satisfied community engaged in wife swapping, television viewing, and pub crawling. He remains a detached observer, longing for a kind of communion he cannot find, and in his telling of his own tale, he reveals himself as friendless, disillusioned, and homeless.

The wife-swapping quartet at the Black Swan pub is disturbed by the entrance of Mr. Raj, a Ceylonese gentleman who is interested in English sociology and in satisfying his lust for white women. He plays by no rules but his own and espouses a kind of deadly Eastern realism that threatens the suburban sport. Moving in with Denham's father, Raj unfortunately kills the old man by "currying" him to death with his hot dishes. The upshot of this clash of cultural and social values is that Raj kills Winterbottom, the most innocent member of the *ménage à quatre*, and then kills himself.

Throughout the novel, Burgess explores both Denham's point of view and Raj's within the seedy suburban landscape. Their viewpoints reflect the irreconcilable differences between East and West, between black and white, between sex and love, and between true religion and dead ritual. Denham's stream-of-consciousness narration eventually reveals his own spirit of exile, which he cannot overcome. He remains disconnected from both worlds, from England and the East, and epitomizes the state of lovelessness and isolation that has permeated modern culture. This early novel clearly explores Burgess's main themes and narrative forms.

TREMOR OF INTENT

In the guise of a thriller à la James Bond, *Tremor of Intent* explores a world of "God" and "Not-God," a profoundly Manichaean universe. Soviet spies battle English spies while the real villains of the novel, the "neutralists," play one camp off against the other purely for personal gain. Burgess derides the whole notion of the spy's realm, but he insists that taking sides is essential in such a world, whether ultimate good or evil is ever really confronted.

Denis Hillier, aging technician and spy, writes his confessional memoirs in the light of his possible redemption. His Catholic sense of Original Sin never falters for an instant, and he is constantly in need of some higher truth, some ultimate communion and revelation. In the course of the novel, he fights every Manichaean division, drinks "Old Mortality," sees himself as a "fallen Adam," and works his way toward some vision of hope. Finally, he abandons the spy game and becomes a priest, exiling himself to Ireland. From this new perspective, he believes, he can approach the real mysteries of good and evil, of free will and predestination, beyond the limiting and limited categories of the Cold War.

Hillier's opposite in the novel is Edwin Roper, a rationalist who has jettisoned religious belief and who hungers for an ultimately unified universe based on scientific truth and explanation. Such rationalism leads him to the Marxist logic of Soviet ideology, and he defects to the Russian side. Hillier has been sent to rescue him. One section of the novel consists of Roper's autobiographical explanation of his actions; its flat, logical prose reflects his methodical and disbelieving mind, in contrast to Hillier's more religious sensibility.

Within the complicated plot of the novel, self-serving scoundrels such as Mr. Theodorescu and Richard Wriste set out to destroy both Hillier and Roper and to gather information to sell to the highest bidder. They fail, owing largely to the actions of Alan and Clara Walters, two children on board the ship that is taking Hillier to meet Roper. The children become initiated into the world of double agents and sexual intrigue, and Theodorescu and Wriste are assassinated.

Burgess displays his love of language for its own sake in exotic descriptions of sex, food, and life aboard a cruise ship. Such language intensifies the Manichaean divisions in the book, the constant battle between the things of this world and the imagined horrors of the next. The very language that Hillier and Roper use to tell their own stories reveals their own distinctly different personalities and visions.

Tremor of Intent insists on the mystery of human will. To choose is to be human; that is good. Thus, to choose evil is both a good and a bad thing, a Manichaean complication that Burgess leaves with the reader. In allegorical terms the novel presents the problems of free will and its consequences, which underlie all of Burgess's fiction.

Nothing Like the Sun

Nothing Like the Sun, Burgess's fanciful novel based on the life of William Shakespeare, showcases every facet of his vision and technique as a novelist. Shakespeare finds himself caught between his love for a golden man and his love for a black woman. Sex feeds the fires of love and possession, and from these fires grows Shakespeare's art, the passion of language. From these fires also comes syphilis, the dread disease that eventually kills him, the source of the dark vision that surfaces in his apocalyptic tragedies. Shakespeare as a writer and Shakespeare as a man battle it out, and from that dualistic confrontation emerges the perilous equilibrium of his greatest plays.

In part, Burgess's fiction is based on the theories about Shakespeare's life that Stephen Dedalus expounds in Joyce's *Ulysses*. Dedalus suggests that Shakespeare was cuckolded by his brother Richard and that Shakespeare's vision of a treacherous and tragic world was based on his own intimate experience. To this conjecture, Burgess adds the notions that the Dark Lady of the sonnets was a non-Caucasian and that Shakespeare himself was a victim of syphilis. All of these "myths" concerning Shakespeare serve Burgess's Manichaean vision: Sex and disease, art and personality are ultimately at war with one another and can be resolved only in the actual plays that Shakespeare wrote.

Nothing Like the Sun is written in an exuberant, bawdy, pseudo-Elizabethan style. It is clear that Burgess relished the creation of lists of epithets, curses, and prophecies, filled as they are with puns and his own outrageous coinings. Burgess audaciously attempts to mime the development of Shakespeare's art as he slowly awakens to the possibilities of poetry, trying different styles, moving from the sweet rhymes of *Venus and Adonis* to the "sharp knives and brutal hammers" of the later tragedies.

The book is constructed in the form of a lecture by Burgess himself to his Malayan students. He drinks as he talks and explains his paradoxical theories as he goes along. His passing out from too much drink at the novel's end parallels Shakespeare's death. He puns also with his real last name, Wilson, regarding himself as in fact "Will's son," a poet and author in his own right.

ENDERBY

Enderby is prototypic of Burgess's preoccupation with the duality of forces that influence life: the struggle between society's capacity to do good and the dilemma that human nature inevitably leads to evil. Originally conceived as a whole, *Enderby* was written as two independent novels, *Mr. Enderby* and *Enderby Outside*, for the pragmatic reason that Burgess wanted to tell at least half the tale before he died from his supposed brain tumor. One of Burgess's most popular characters, the flatulent poet F. X. Enderby, was spawned in a men's room when the author thought he saw a man feverishly writing poetry as he purged his bowels. *Enderby* is teeming with opposites, juxtaposing the sublime with the ridiculous. Enderby is catapulted into life-transforming situations as the outside world continually plays on and alters the poet's sensibilities. Burgess, the writer, examines his creation, a writer, whom he happens to admire in spite of his foibles.

Mr. Enderby and *Enderby Outside* depict the difference between transformations that originate within the individual and those that society imposes on the individual. In the first novel, the very private poet is lured into marriage with Vesta Bainbridge, who leads him into a pop-art world that strips away his integrity and identity. Enderby achieves some success by prostituting his talent, but he is ultimately outraged when a rival poet gains fame and fortune by stealing his ideas, transforming them into a horror film. Enderby escapes from his wife and public life but is despondent and intellectually withered. He is taken to Wapenshaw, a psychologist, who "cures" him by destroying his poetic muse. Enderby is transmuted into Piggy Hogg, a bartender and useful citizen.

Enderby Outside is the mirror image of *Mr. Enderby*, transforming Hogg back into Enderby through a series of parallel experiences. Bainbridge has married a pop singer, Yod Crewsey, whose success is the result of poems stolen from Enderby. When the singer is shot, Enderby is accused of the murder and flees, confronting the chaos and confusion of the modern world and falling prey to another woman, the sensuous Miranda Boland. During sexual intercourse with Boland, Enderby is finally struck by inspiration. In the end, he meets a sibylline girl, Muse, who leads him to his art. Enderby is as he began, alone and free, but a poet.

In *Enderby*, Burgess shows that the master must come to peace with both his body and society before he can indulge in the intellectual. Shortly after the film version of *A Clockwork Orange* was released, Enderby returned in *The Clockwork Testament: Or, Enderby's End*, which satirizes the writer reduced to production assistant by the film industry. Enderby dies of a heart attack when he sees the violent, pornographic film made from his novel. Just as British detective novelist Arthur Conan Doyle was forced to return Sherlock Holmes to life, Burgess resurrects his antihero in *Enderby's Dark Lady*. Enderby travels to Indiana, where he writes the libretto for a ridiculous musical about Shakespeare. Burgess directs his satire at American culture, but his exploration of the poetic muse is sacrificed for the comic adventure.

EARTHLY POWERS

Earthly Powers, Burgess's longest novel, features perhaps his most arresting first sentence: "It was the afternoon of my 81st birthday, and I was in bed with my catamite when Ali announced that the archbishop had come to see me." Thus begin the memoirs of Kenneth Toomey, cynical agnostic and homosexual writer, a character based loosely on W. Somerset Maugham.

Toomey's memoirs span the twentieth century—its literary intrigues, cultural fashions, and political horrors. Toomey is seduced on June 16, 1904, that Dublin day immortalized by Joyce in *Ulysses*, and he revels in the Paris of the 1920's, the Hollywood of the 1930's, and the stylish New York of the 1940's and 1950's. His old age is spent in exotic exile in Tangier and Malta in the 1970's. During his long life, he writes plays and film scenarios, carries on with a host of male secretary-lovers, and experiences the traumas of Nazism and Communism. He abhors the state-controlled collective soul, which he sees as the ultimate product of the twentieth century.

Burgess's huge, sprawling novel displays a plot crowded with coincidence and bursting with stylistic parodies and re-creations. A priest on his way to becoming pope saves a dying child, only to see the boy grow up to be the leader of a fanatical religious cult akin to that of Jim Jones in Guyana. An American anthropologist and his wife are butchered during a Catholic mass in Africa: The natives there take the commands of the ceremony all too literally and swallow their visitors.

Toomey believes that evil lies firmly within all people and that his experiences of the twentieth century prove that the world is a murderous place. His Manichaean opposite in faith is his brother-in-law, Carlo Campanati, the gambler-gourmet priest who becomes Pope Gregory XVII. Evil remains external to humanity, the pope maintains; humankind is essentially good. In Burgess's jaundiced view of things, such misconceived idealism produces only further evils. Any similarities between Gregory and Pope John XXIII are strictly intentional.

The world of *Earthly Powers* is Toomey's world, a bright place with clipped, swift glimpses of fads and fashion. Librettos, snippets of plays, even a re-creation of the Garden of Eden story from a homosexual point of view appear in this modernist memoir. The style itself reflects Burgess's conception of the "brittle yet excruciatingly precise" manner of the gay man.

Earthly Powers wobbles. More than six hundred pages of bright wit can cloy. Verbal surfaces congeal and trail off into trivial documentation. The pope's spiritual observations impede the novel's progress, encased as they are in lectures, sermons, and tracts. Indeed, Gregory is as thin a character as Toomey is an interesting one.

The book proves that Toomey is right: Things are rotten. No amount of linguistic fun, modernist maneuvering, or Manichaean machinations can change the fact that this is the worst of all possible worlds. Chunks of smart conversation cannot hide that fact; they become stupefying and evasive in the end. The nature of free will, however, and its legacy of unquestionable evil in the twentieth century pervade Burgess's fat book and linger to undermine any "safe" position the reader may hope to find.

A CLOCKWORK ORANGE

Burgess's Manichaean nightmare in *A Clockwork Orange* occupies the center of his most accomplished book. The language of Nadsat, in its harsh, Russian-accented diction, the ongoing battle between the state and Alex the *droog*, the vision of an urban landscape wracked with violence and decay, the mysterious interpenetration of Beethoven and lust, and the unresolved issues of good and evil reflect and parallel one another so completely that the novel emerges as Burgess's masterpiece.

The issue raised is an increasingly timely one: Can the state program the individual to be good? Can it eradicate the individual's right to freedom of choice, especially if, in choosing, the individual chooses to commit violent and evil acts? Burgess replies in the negative. No matter how awful Alex's actions become, he should be allowed to choose them.

Because the novel is written from Alex's point of view, the reader sympathizes with him, despite his acts of rape and mayhem. Alex loves Beethoven; he "shines artistic"; he is brighter than his ghoulish friends; he is rejected by his parents. He is in all ways superior to the foul futuristic landscape that surrounds him. When the state brainwashes him, the reader experiences his pain in a personal, forthright manner. The violence in the rest of the book falls on outsiders and remains distanced by the very language Alex uses to describe his actions.

Burgess's slang creates a strange and distant world. The reader approaches the novel as an outsider to that world and must try diligently to decode it to understand it. Never has Burgess used language so effectively to create the very atmosphere of his fiction. The Russian-influenced slang of the novel is a tour de force of the highest order and yet functions perfectly as a reflection of Alex's state of mind and of the society of which he is a rebellious member.

The world of *A Clockwork Orange* recognizes only power and political force. All talk of free will dissolves before such a harrowing place of behaviorist psychologists and social controllers. In such a world, individual freedom remains a myth, not a reality—a matter of faith, not an ultimate truth. Everyone is in some sense a clockwork orange, a victim of his or her society, compelled to act in a social order that celebrates only power, manipulation, and control.

Even the cyclical form of *A Clockwork Orange* reveals a world trapped within its own inevitable patterns. At first, Alex victimizes those around him. He in turn is victimized by the state. In the third and final part of the novel, he returns to victimize other people once again: "I was cured all right." Victimization remains the only reality here. There are no loopholes, no escape hatches from the vicious pattern. The frightening cityscape at night, the harsh language, the paradoxical personality of Alex, the collaborationist or revolutionary tactics of Alex's "friends," and the very shape of the novel reinforce this recognition of utter entrapment and human decay. "Oh, my brothers," Alex addresses his readers, as Eliot in *The Waste Land* (1922) quotes Charles Baudelaire: *"Hypocrite lecteur, mon semblable, mon frère."*

Despite Burgess's pessimistic vision of contemporary life and the creative soul's place in it, the best of his novels still reveal a commitment to literature as a serious ceremony, as a game that the reader and the writer must continue to play, if only to transcend momentarily the horrors of Western civilization in the twentieth century.

Samuel Coale
Updated by Gerald S. Argetsinger

OTHER MAJOR WORKS

SHORT FICTION: *The Devil's Mode*, 1989.

SCREENPLAY: *Jesus of Nazareth*, 1977.

TELEPLAY: *Moses the Lawgiver*, 1976.

NONFICTION: *English Literature: A Survey for Students*, 1958 (as John Burgess Wilson); *The Novel Today*, 1963; *Language Made Plain*, 1964; *Here Comes Everybody: An Introduction to James Joyce for the Ordinary Reader*, 1965 (also known as *Re Joyce*); *The Novel Now*, 1967 (revised 1971); *Urgent Copy: Literary Studies*, 1968; *Shakespeare*, 1970; *Joysprick: An Introduction to the Language of James Joyce*, 1972; *Ernest Hemingway and His World*, 1978; *On Going to Bed*, 1982; *This Man and Music*, 1983; *Flame into Being: The Life and Work of D. H. Lawrence*, 1985; *Homage to Qwert Yuiop*, 1985 (also known as *But Do Blondes Prefer Gentlemen? Homage to Qwert Yuiop, and Other Writings*, 1986); *Little Wilson and Big God*, 1987 (partly reprinted as *Childhood*, 1996); *You've Had Your Time*, 1990; *A Mouthful of Air: Languages, Languages—Especially English*, 1992; *One Man's Chorus; The Uncollected Writings*, 1998.

TRANSLATIONS: *The Man Who Robbed Poor-Boxes*, 1965 (of Michel Servin's play); *Cyrano de Bergerac*, 1971 (of Edmond Rostand's play); *Oedipus the King*, 1972 (of Sophocles' play).

CHILDREN'S LITERATURE: *A Long Trip to Teatime*, 1976.

MISCELLANEOUS: *On Mozart: A Paean for Wolfgang*, 1991.

BIBLIOGRAPHY

Aggeler, Geoffrey. *Anthony Burgess: The Artist as Novelist*. Tuscaloosa: University of Alabama Press, 1979. The best and most accurately detailed study of work published in the first twenty years of Burgess's career. Includes analysis of *A Clockwork Orange*, *Napoleon Symphony, Enderby Outside, Inside Mr. Enderby*, *Nothing Like the Sun*, and other novels.

_____, ed. *Critical Essays on Anthony Burgess*. Boston: G. K. Hall, 1986. A collection of well-regarded criticism on Burgess, with particular attention given to his "linguistic pyrotechnics." Aggeler's introduction presents an overview of Burgess's work and discussion of his novels, followed by a *Paris Review* interview with Burgess.

Biswell, Andrew. *The Real Life of Anthony Burgess*. London: Picador, 2005. Well-researched biography of Burgess explores his personal life, including his heavy drinking and sexual promiscuity. His most famous novel, *A Clockwork Orange*, is also discussed, along with Burgess's common themes of corruption, sin, and human beings' capacity for evil.

Bloom, Harold, ed. *Anthony Burgess*. New York: Chelsea House, 1987. A compilation of fine critical essays, including an essay by the eminent critic of James Joyce, Robert Martin Adams, who considers Joyce's influence on Burgess. In the introduction, Bloom presents his views on Burgess's writing, citing *Inside Mr. Enderby* as one of the most underrated English novels of the late twentieth century.

Keen, Suzanne. "Ironies and Inversions: The Art of Anthony Burgess." *Commonweal* 121, no. 3 (February 11, 1994): 9. An examination of the "Catholic quality" in Burgess's fiction and nonfiction. Focuses primarily on Burgess's novel *A Dead Man in Deptford* as well as on his autobiographies and literary criticism of James Joyce's works.

Lewis, Roger. *Anthony Burgess: A Biography*. London: Faber & Faber, 2002. This sprawling examination of Burgess's life, first published in the United States in 2004, is illuminating although sometimes chaotic. Instead of recounting the events of Burgess's life as a chronological narrative, Lewis presents a more stylized, psychodynamic interpretation of Burgess's personality and work.

Mathews, Richard. *The Clockwork Orange Universe of Anthony Burgess.* San Bernardino, Calif.: Borgo Press, 1978. An admiring monograph tracing the thematic and temporal concerns that led Burgess to write his futuristic novels, including *A Clockwork Orange.* Discusses ten novels that fit the metaphor of "clockwork universe."

Morris, Robert K. *Consolations of Ambiguity: An Essay on the Novels of Anthony Burgess.* Columbia: University of Missouri Press, 1971. This early analysis of Burgess's work discusses the thematic consistency of the Malayan trilogy, *A Vision of Battlements*, *Nothing Like the Sun*, *A Clockwork Orange*, and other novels.

Smith, K. H. "Will! or Shakespeare in Hollywood: Anthony Burgess's Cinematic Presentation of Shakespearean Biography." In *Remaking Shakespeare: Performance Across Media, Genres, and Cultures*, edited by Pascale Aebisher, Edward Esche, and Nigel Wheale. Houndmills, England: Palgrave Macmillan, 2003. Collection of essays describing how William Shakespeare has been "remade" in twentieth century screenplays, soap operas, music, documentaries, and other media. Includes analysis of Burgess's novel *Nothing Like the Sun.*

Stinson, John J. *Anthony Burgess Revisited.* Boston: Twayne, 1991. Provides valuable biographical information and critical analysis of the later works. Particular attention is given to Burgess's increasing reputation as a public intellectual and the use of language, the importance of moral choice, and the conflict between the Pelagian and Augustinian philosophies in his works.

FANNY BURNEY

Born: King's Lynn, Norfolk, England; June 13, 1752
Died: London, England; January 6, 1840
Also known as: Frances Burney; Madame Frances d'Arblay

PRINCIPAL LONG FICTION

Evelina: Or, The History of a Young Lady's Entrance into the World, 1778
Cecilia: Or, Memoirs of an Heiress, 1782
Camilla: Or, A Picture of Youth, 1796
The Wanderer: Or, Female Difficulties, 1814

OTHER LITERARY FORMS

In addition to editing the memoirs of her father—the noted organist, composer, and music historian Dr. Charles Burney (1726-1814)—Fanny Burney wrote diaries that were published after her death: *Early Diary, 1768-1778* (1889) and *Diary and Letters, 1778-1840* (1842-1846). Her *Early Diary* contains pleasant sketches of such well-known figures as Samuel Johnson, James Boswell, David Garrick, and Richard Brinsley Sheridan. Notable figures from government and the arts march across the pages of this work, which scholars have claimed surpasses Burney's fiction in literary quality. The seven volumes of her latter diary and correspondence are notable for the record of the writer's meeting in her garden with the insane King George III of England, the account of her glimpse of the French emperor Napoleon I, and the recollections of her chat with the weary King Louis XVIII of France.

Of Burney's eight works of drama, three are worthy of mention: *The Witlings*, written in 1779 and never performed or published in Burney's lifetime; *Edwy and Elgiva*, written in 1790, performed at Drury Lane on March 21, 1795, and withdrawn after the first night; and *Love and Fashion*, written in 1799, accepted by the manager at Covent Garden, but never performed. (All of these plays were published in 1995 in *The Complete Plays of Fanny Burney.*) Burney also published, in 1793, a political essay titled *Brief Reflections Relative to the French Emigrant Clergy*, an address to the women of Great Britain in behalf of the French emigrant priests.

ACHIEVEMENTS

Most critics tend to place the reputation of Fanny Burney within the shadow of her most immediate successor, Jane Austen. Reasons for this assessment are not immediately clear, especially in the light of responses to Burney's novels from contemporary readers. Burney's problem during the past two centuries, however, has not concerned popularity, subject matter, or even literary style; rather, certain personal circumstances under which she wrote seriously reduced her artistic effectiveness and considerably dulled her reputation. Essentially, Burney produced fiction at a time in history when a lady of means and social standing could not easily write fiction and still be considered a lady. Adding to that inhibition was the aura of her noted and influential father and his circle of even more influential friends: Samuel Johnson, Mrs. Hester Lynch Thrale, Oliver Goldsmith, and Sir Joshua Reynolds. Both her father and his friends held literary standards that were not always easy for a self-educated young woman to meet. She burned her early manuscript efforts, wrote secretly at night, and published anonymously; she labored under the artistic domination of her father and the advice of his friends; she remained cautious, intimidated by and dependent on elderly people who served as guardians of her intellect.

Nevertheless, Burney succeeded as a novelist and achieved significance as a contributor to the history and development of the English novel. She brought to that genre an ability to observe the natural activities and reactions of those about her and to weave those observations through narrative structures and character delineations similar to those employed by her predecessors: Samuel Johnson, Henry Fielding, Samuel Richardson, Tobias Smollett, Aphra Behn, Mary De La Riviere Manley, Eliza Heywood, and Clara Reeve. In her preface to *Evelina*, she set forth the criteria that, throughout her fiction, she would develop and maintain. For Burney, the novel would be the means by which to portray realistic persons and to represent the times in which they functioned. In her own concept of the form, those characters had to be real but not necessarily true; they had to be drawn "from nature, though not from life." Further, those same fictional characters had to confront and solve complex human problems—problems that they might avoid for a time but eventually would be forced to encounter.

Although Burney's four novels were published anonymously, the sophisticated readers of the day recognized the woman's point of view and immediately set the works apart from those of Burney's contemporaries. The female readership, especially, both appreciated and praised the woman's view of the contemporary world; on the other hand, the young dandies of the late eighteenth century and the pre-Victorian age scoffed at the novels' heroines as comic sentimentalists, products of blatant amateurism, and characteristic examples of a sex that would continue to be dominated by men.

The real basis on which to place Burney's popularity, however, is her ability to develop fully the effects of female intelligence on and within a society dominated by men and to convince her audience that coexistence between the sexes is far more beneficial than the dominance of one over the other. The essential difference between Fanny Burney and her female predecessors (Aphra Behn is the most obvious example) is the extent to which Burney developed the issue of feminism and then thrust it forward as a major consideration.

As a woman writing about women, Burney could not cling too long to the models that the past century had provided for her. Despite the mild increase in the numbers of female novelists during the last quarter of the eighteenth century, Burney had little guidance in developing the woman's point of view. She had, essentially, to find her own way within the confines of a limited world and even more limited experience. She determined early to purge her fictional environment of masculine influence. In its place, she would establish the importance of her title characters as working parts in the machinery of eighteenth century British society. Burney's heroines do not convey appearances of being rebels, radicals, or social freaks; rather, their creator has drawn each one of them with a fine and firm hand. As a group, they are indeed meant to be carbon copies of one another; individually, each is a young lady in pursuit of traditional goals—marriage, money, and the discovery of the self.

BIOGRAPHY

Frances Burney, the third of six children of Charles Burney and Esther Sleepe Burney, was born on June 13, 1752, at King's Lynn, Norfolk, where her father served as church organist while recuperating from consumption. In 1760, his health completely restored, Burney moved his family to London, where he resumed his professional involvements in teaching, composition, and music history. After the death of their mother on September 28, 1761, two of the children (Esther and Susannah) were sent to school in Paris, while Frances (known as Fanny) remained at home. Apparently, Dr. Burney feared that his middle daughter's devotion to her grandmother (then living in France) would bring about the child's conversion to Catholicism. He seemed prepared to change that point of view and send Fanny to join her sisters when, in 1766, he married Mrs. Stephen Allen. The fourteen-year-old girl thus remained at home in London, left to her own educational aims and directions, since her father had no time to supervise her learning. She had, at about age ten, begun to write drama, poetry, and fiction; on her fifteenth birthday, she supposedly burned her manuscripts because she felt guilty about wasting her time with such trifles.

Still, Burney could not purge her imagination, and the story of Evelina and her adventures did not die in the flames of her fireplace. Her brother Charles offered the first two volumes of *Evelina* to James Dodsley, who declined to consider an anonymous work for publication; Thomas Lowndes, however, asked to see the completed manuscript. After finishing *Evelina* and then securing her father's permission, Burney gave the work to the London publisher, who issued it in January, 1778, and paid the writer thirty pounds and ten bound copies. Its success and popularity owed some debt to Dr. Burney, who passed the novel on to Mrs. Thrale, a prominent figure in London's literary society. From there, it made its way to the select seat of London's intellectual empire, presided over by Dr. Johnson, Joshua Reynolds, and Edmund Burke. Shortly afterward, Fanny Burney met Mrs. Thrale, who took the new novelist into her home at Streatham (south of London) and introduced her to Johnson, Reynolds, Sheridan, and Arthur Murphy—all of whom pressed her to write drama. The result took the form of *The Witlings*, a dramatic piece that, principally because of her father's displeasure over the quality of the work, she never published.

Returning to the form that produced her initial success, Burney published *Cecilia* in the summer of 1782, further advancing her literary reputation and social

Fanny Burney. (Library of Congress)

standing. She met Mary Delany, an intimate of the royal family, who helped secure for her an appointment in July, 1786, as second keeper of the queen's robes, a position worth two hundred pounds per year. Her tenure at court proved to be more of a confinement than a social or political advantage, however, because of the menial tasks she had to carry out, the rigid schedule, and the stiffness of the queen and her attendants.

The activities and events at court did contribute to the value of Burney's diaries, though her health suffered from the extreme physical demands of her labors. She continued in service until July, 1791, at which time she sought and gained permission to retire on a pension of one hundred pounds per annum. Then followed a period of domestic travel aimed at improving her health, followed by her marriage, on July 31, 1793, to General Alexandre D'Arblay, a comrade of the Marquis de Lafayette and a member of the small French community living at Juniper Hall, near Mickleham (north of

Dorking, in Surrey). The couple's entire income rested with Madame D'Arblay's pension, and thus she sought to increase the family's fortunes through her writing. A tragedy, *Edwy and Elgiva*, lasted but a single night at Drury Lane, but a third novel, *Camilla*, generated more than three thousand pounds from subscriptions and additional sales, although the piece failed to achieve the literary merit of *Evelina* or *Cecilia*.

In 1801, General D'Arblay returned to France to seek employment but managed only a pension of fifteen hundred francs. His wife and son, Alexander, joined him the next year, and the family spent the succeeding ten years at Passy, in a state of quasi exile that lasted throughout the Napoleonic Wars. Burney and her son returned to England in 1812, and there the novelist attended her aged father until his death in April, 1814. Her last novel, begun in France in 1802 and titled *The Wanderer*, appeared early in 1814. Again, the financial returns far exceeded the literary quality of the piece; it attracted considerable numbers of buyers and subscribers but extremely few readers.

After Napoleon's exile, the novelist returned to her husband in Paris; she then went to Brussels after the emperor's return from Elba. General D'Arblay, meanwhile, had been seriously injured by the kick of a horse, which brought about an immediate end to his military career. The family returned to England to spend the remainder of their years: General D'Arblay died on May 3, 1818, and Alexander died on January 19, 1837—less than a year after having been nominated minister of Ely chapel. In November, 1839, Burney suffered a severe illness and died on January 6, 1840, in her eighty-seventh year.

ANALYSIS

Despite the relative brevity of her canon, Fanny Burney cannot be dismissed as a novelist with the usual generalizations from literary history—specifically, that the author shared the interests of her youthful heroines in good manners. She possessed a quick sense for the comic in character and situation, and those talents distinctly advanced the art of the English novel in the direction of Jane Austen. From one viewpoint, Burney indeed exists as an important transitional figure between the satiric allegories of the earlier eighteenth century and the instruments that portrayed middle-class manners in

full flourish during the first quarter of the nineteenth century.

Burney's contemporaries understood both her method and her purpose. Samuel Johnson thought her a "real wonder," one worth being singled out for her honest sense of modesty and her ability to apply it to fiction, while Edmund Burke seemed amazed by her knowledge of human nature. Three years after her death, Thomas Babington Macaulay proclaimed that the author of *Evelina* and *Cecilia* had done for the English novel what Jeremy Collier, at the end of the seventeenth century, did for the drama: She maintained rigid morality and virgin delicacy. Macaulay proclaimed that Burney had indeed vindicated the right of woman "to an equal share in a fair and noble promise of letters" and had accomplished her task in clear, natural, and lively "woman's English."

Burney contributed more to the English novel than simply the advancement of her sex's cause. Her heroines are mentally tormented and yet emerge as wiser and stronger human beings. The fictional contexts into which she placed her principal characters are those that readers of every time and place could recognize: situations in which the proponents of negative values seem to prosper and the defenders of virtue cling tenaciously to their ground. Burney's women must learn the ways of a difficult world, a society composed of countless snares and endless rules. They must quickly don the accoutrements for survival: modesty, reserve, submission, and (above all else) manners. What makes Burney's depiction of women in society particularly poignant is the knowledge that the author herself had to endure trials of survival. An awareness of the author's accounts of actual struggles for social survival, then, becomes a necessity for understanding and appreciating the problems confronted by her fictional characters.

EVELINA

In Burney's first novel, *Evelina*, the title character brings with her to London and Bristol two qualities most difficult for a young provincial girl to defend: her sense of propriety and her pure innocence—the latter quality not to be confused with ignorance. In London, Evelina stumbles into false, insecure situations because she does not comprehend the rules of the social game. During the course of eighty-five epistles, however, she learns. The learning process is of utmost importance to Burney, for it serves as both plot for her fiction and instruction for her largely female readership. Once in London, life unfolds new meanings for Evelina Anville, as she samples the wares of urbanity: assemblies, amusements, parks and gardens, drawing rooms, operas, and theaters. Accompanying the activities is a corps of sophisticates by whose rules Evelina must play: Lord Orville, the well-bred young man and the jealous lover; Sir Clement Willoughby, the obnoxious admirer of Evelina who tries (through forged letters) to breach the relationship between Orville and Evelina; Macartney, the young poet whom Evelina saves from suicide and against whom Orville exercises his jealous streak; Captain Mirvan, the practical joker who smiles only at the expense of others; Mrs. Beaumont, who would have the heroine believe that good qualities originate from pride rather than from principles; Lady Louisa Larpent, the sullen and distraught (but always arrogant) sister of Lord Orville who tries to separate her brother from Evelina; Mr. Lovel, a demeaning fop who constantly refers to Evelina's simple background; the Watkins sisters, who chide Evelina because they envy her attractiveness to young men.

Despite these obstacles of situation and character, however, Evelina does not lack some protection. The Reverend Arthur Villars, her devoted guardian since the death of her mother, guides and counsels the seventeen-year-old girl from his home in Dorsetshire. Villars receives the major portion of Evelina's letters; in fact, he initially advises her to be wary of Lord Orville but then relents when he learns of his ward's extreme happiness. Since Evelina cannot count on immediate assistance from Villars, she does rely on several people in London. Mrs. Mirvan, the amiable and well-bred wife of the captain, introduces Evelina to a variety of social affairs, while their daughter, Maria, becomes the heroine's only real confidant, sharing mutual happiness and disappointment. Finally, there is the Reverend Villars's neighbor, Mrs. Selwyn, who accompanies Evelina on a visit to Bristol Hot Wells. Unfortunately, the one person closest to Evelina during her London tenure, her maternal grandmother, Madame Duval, proves of little use and even less assistance. A blunt, indelicate, and severe woman, she is bothered by her granddaughter's display of independence and vows that the young lady will not share in her inheritance.

Villars emerges as the supporting character with the most depth, principally because he is ever present in the letters. From the novel's beginning, the heroine reaches out to him for guidance and support, scarcely prepared "to form a wish that has not [his] sanction." The local clergyman, Villars serves as parent for a motherless and socially fatherless young lady who, for the first time, is about to see something of the world. Villars's caution and anxiety thus appear natural, for he knows the bitter effects of socially unequal marriages, as in the cases of Evelina's own parents and grandparents. He naturally mistrusts Lord Orville and fears the weakness of the young girl's imagination. Everyone knows that as long as Evelina remains obedient to Villars's will, no union between her and Orville can occur. Once the girl's father, Sir John Belmont, repents for his many years of unkindness to his daughter and then bequeaths her thirty thousand pounds, however, the guardian cleric no longer remains the dominant influence. Lord Orville proceeds to put his own moral house in order and supplants his rivals; the reserve felt by Evelina because of the Reverend Villars's fears and anxieties gradually disintegrates, and the romance proceeds toward its inevitable conclusion.

The process may be inevitable, but it is sufficiently hampered by a series of struggles and conflicts, as is typical of the late eighteenth century novel of manners. Both her grandmother and Mrs. Mirvan provide Evelina with fairly easy access to fashionable society, but the socialites in that society involve the girl in a number of uncomfortable and burdensome situations. For example, Biddy and Polly Branghton and Madam Duval use Evelina's name in requesting the use of Lord Orville's coach. Evelina realizes the impropriety of the request and knows that Orville's benevolence would never permit him to refuse it. Furthermore, Tom Branghton, an admirer of Evelina, solicits business from Orville also by relying on Evelina's name; he does so after damaging the borrowed vehicle. Evelina's innocence forces her to bear the responsibility for her relatives' actions and schemes, although she opposes all that they attempt. Fortunately, the fierce determination with which she advances her innocence and honesty enables her to endure such problems until rescued, in this case, by Lord Orville and Mrs. Selwyn. Vulgarity (Madam Duval), ill breeding (the Branghtons), and impertinence (Sir Clement Willoughby) eventually fall before the steadfastness and the force of Evelina's emerging wisdom and strength. Burney here demonstrates the specific means by which an eighteenth century woman could surmount the perplexities of that era.

CECILIA

If Evelina Anville must defend her innocence and honesty against the social vultures of London and Bristol, Cecilia Beverley, the heroine of *Cecilia*, carries the added burden of retaining a fortune left to her by an eccentric uncle. She must withstand assaults upon her coffers from a variety of attackers. One of her guardians, Mr. Harrel, draws heavily upon Cecilia's funds to repay the moneylenders who underwrite his fashionable existence. At the other extreme, Mr. Briggs, the third legally appointed guardian, manages Cecilia's money during her minority. Although wealthy in his own right, Briggs evidences obvious eccentricity and uncouthness; he is a miser who wants the heroine to live with him to conserve money. In the middle stands another guardian, Compton Delvile, who has priorities other than money; however, he can hardly be recommended as an asset to the development of his ward. Simply, Delvile cares only to preserve the family name, and beneath his pride lie hard layers of meanness. Against such onslaughts upon her morality and her fortune Cecilia must rebel; she is both angry and bewildered at what Burney terms as "acts so detrimental to her own interest."

Unlike Evelina, who has many opportunities to address and receive concerns from a surrogate parent, Cecilia has few people and even less guidance on which to rely. *Cecilia* revealed to the world not only a trio of impotent guardians but also a number of irritating male characters who devote considerable time to tormenting her. Obviously bent upon revealing the grotesqueness and instability of London life, Burney created a variety of grotesque and unstable supporting players: Harrel, Dr. Lyster, Mrs. Wyers, and Mrs. Hill are some examples. Clearly, Burney's characters in *Cecilia* were total strangers to the mainstream of the late eighteenth century fictional world, even though they truly belonged to reality. While at times creating humorous scenes and incidents, these ugly characters nevertheless produced a disturbing effect upon the novelist's reading audience. Unfortunately, from a social or historical perspective,

that audience was not yet ready for significant action to effect social change, which meant that much of the novel's force was lost amid the apathy of its audience.

CAMILLA

The publication of *Camilla*, eighteen years after *Evelina* and fourteen following *Cecilia*, marked the reappearance of a young lady entering society and enduring shameful experiences. Like her immediate predecessor, Cecilia Beverley, Camilla Tyrold has money problems, only hers involve involuntary indebtedness. Also like *Cecilia*, the novel contains several grotesque minor characters, whose manners and actions play psychological havoc with Camilla's attempts to overcome her distress. Particularly vulgar are Mr. Dubster and the mercenary Mrs. Mittin, aided by the overscholarly Dr. Orkborne and the foppish Sir Sedley Clarendel. A major problem, however, is that these characters are pulled from the earlier novels. On the surface, *Camilla* gives evidence that Burney has matured as a writer and as a commentator on the affairs of women, but that maturity did not broaden her literary experience. If anything, there are signs of regression, for Camilla definitely lacks Evelina's common sense and her instinct toward feminine resourcefulness.

Camilla further suffers from its length; Burney barely holds the plot together through countless episodes, intrigues, misunderstandings, all in front of a backdrop of drollery and absurdity. Stripped of its comic elements, the novel is no more than an overstrained romance. Burney's motive, however, was to draw the exact conditions that brought about Camilla's collection of debts and thus contributed to her highly anxious state of mind. Burney rises to her usual level of excellence in detailing the plight of a woman distracted and deprived by misfortune not of her own doing. For late eighteenth century women, especially, such misfortune carried with it an underlying sense of shame. Thus, Burney gave to English prose fiction a sense of psychological depth not always apparent in the works of her female counterparts or in those fictional efforts written by men but concerned with women.

THE WANDERER

Burney's last novel, *The Wanderer*, appeared in 1814 and became lost in the new sensibility of Jane Austen and Maria Edgeworth. The work, however, reveals

Burney's determination that the nineteenth century should not forget its women. Her heroine—known variously as L. S. (or Ellis), Incognita, Miss Ellis, and Juliet—determines that the cause of her suffering points directly to the fact that she was born a woman, which automatically places her on the lowest rung of the social order. The woman's lot contains little beyond the usual taboos, disqualifications, discomforts, and inconveniences; the novelist, through the various predicaments of Juliet Granville, rarely allows her readers to forget the degree to which her heroine must suffer because of society's insensitivity and stupidity. *The Wanderer*, like Burney's previous novels, has a number of supporting characters. Some of these, while they do not always understand Juliet's plight, at least try to help her through her difficulties; others, such as Mrs. Ireton and Miss Arbe, represent the tyranny, frivolity, and insensitivity of the times and thus merely compound Juliet's problems.

The strength of *The Wanderer*, however, lies in its thematic relationship to the three earlier novels. Although Burney tends to repeat herself, particularly through her minor characters—and again the plot hardly deserves the length of the narrative—her ability to depict the misgivings of those who are driven by external circumstances to earn a livelihood through unaccustomed means is powerful. In coming to grips with an obvious and serious problem of her time, Burney demonstrated how her major fictional characters—and she herself, as a character from the real world—could indeed rely successfully on the resources with which all individuals, female as well as male, are endowed. If nothing else, the novelist showed her society and the generations that followed not only how well women could function in the real world but also how much they could contribute and take advantage of opportunities offered them. In a sense, Burney's compositions belong to social history as much as to literature, and they serve as some of the earliest examples of a struggle that has yet to be won.

Samuel J. Rogal

OTHER MAJOR WORKS

PLAYS: *Edwy and Elgiva*, pr. 1795; *The Complete Plays of Frances Burney*, 1995 (2 volumes); *Love and Fashion*, pb. 1795 (wr. 1799).

NONFICTION: *Brief Reflections Relative to the Emigrant French Clergy*, 1793; *Diary and Letters, 1778-1840*, 1842-1846 (7 volumes; Charlotte Frances Barrett, editor); *The Early Diary of Frances Burney, 1768-1778*, 1889 (Anne Raine Ellis, editor); *The Journals and Letters of Fanny Burney*, 1972-1984 (12 volumes); *The Early Journals and Letters of Fanny Burney*, 1988-2003 (4 volumes); *Journals and Letters*, 2001.

EDITED TEXT: *Memoirs of Dr. Charles Burney*, 1832.

BIBLIOGRAPHY

Bloom, Harold, ed. *Fanny Burney's "Evelina": Modern Critical Interpretations*. New York: Chelsea House, 1988. Collection presents illuminating critical essays on Burney's novel written between 1967 and 1988. Bloom's introduction disparages the feminist tendency of recent Burney criticism, even though this volume includes essays by contributors who take primarily feminist approaches.

Chisholm, Kate. *Fanny Burney: Her Life, 1752-1840*. London: Chatto & Windus, 1998. Biography draws in part from the diaries that Burney kept from the age of sixteen, which offer detailed descriptions of life in Georgian England. Depicts Burney as a highly talented writer and places Burney's life and work within the context of her times.

Daugherty, Tracy Edgar. *Narrative Techniques in the Novels of Fanny Burney*. New York: Peter Lang, 1989. Presents detailed analysis of Burney's novels, discussing how she constructed plot, characterization, and point of view and critiquing the effectiveness of these techniques. Also reassesses Burney's contribution to the craft of novel writing.

Epstein, Julia L. *The Iron Pen: Frances Burney and the Politics of Women's Writing*. Madison: University of Wisconsin Press, 1989. Examines Burney's work from a feminist perspective, focusing primarily on the violence, hostility, and danger in her writings. Includes excellent bibliography and index.

Harman, Claire. *Fanny Burney: A Biography*. New York: Alfred A. Knopf, 2001. Accessible and authoritative biography points out inconsistencies in Burney's memoirs, providing a more accurate account of the author's life and placing Burney within the broader context of social conditions for middle-class English women in the eighteenth century. Includes bibliographical references and index.

Sabor, Peter, ed. *The Cambridge Companion to Frances Burney*. New York: Cambridge University Press, 2007. Collection of essays covers Burney's life and work and presents analyses of all four of her novels. Other topics addressed include Burney's critical reputation, her political views, and gender issues in her work.

Simons, Judy. *Fanny Burney*. Totowa, N.J.: Barnes & Noble Books, 1987. Condensed look at Burney's life and work opens with an introductory biographical essay that places Burney within the tradition of other women writers, such as Elizabeth Inchbald, Mary Wollstonecraft Godwin, and Eliza Haywood. Includes a chapter on the heroines of Burney's novels and a chapter each on *Evelina*, *Cecilia*, *Camilla*, and *The Wanderer*.

Straub, Kristina. *Divided Fictions: Fanny Burney and Feminine Strategy*. Lexington: University Press of

Kentucky, 1987. Discussion of Burney's work is grounded in eighteenth century cultural history. Devotes three chapters to *Evelina*, one to *Cecilia*, and one to both *Camilla* and *The Wanderer*. Chapter titled "The Receptive Reader and Other Necessary Fictions" makes intriguing points about Burney's reaction to the publicity of being a novelist and part of the literary circles of her day.

Thaddeus, Janice Farrar. *Frances Burney: A Literary Life*. New York: St. Martin's Press, 2000. Scholarly account of Burney's life and career provides information valuable to an expanded understanding of the novelist. Includes discussion of her four novels as well as a genealogical table, notes, and index.

Zonitch, Barbara. *Familiar Violence: Gender and Social Upheaval in the Novels of Frances Burney*. Newark: University of Delaware Press, 1997. Presents analyses of Burney's four novels following an introduction that explains Burney's place within eighteenth century English society.

WILLIAM S. BURROUGHS

Born: St. Louis, Missouri; February 5, 1914
Died: Lawrence, Kansas; August 2, 1997
Also known as: William Seward Burroughs II; William Lee

PRINCIPAL LONG FICTION

Junkie, 1953
The Naked Lunch, 1959 (republished as *Naked Lunch*, 1962)
The Soft Machine, 1961
The Ticket That Exploded, 1962
Dead Fingers Talk, 1963
Nova Express, 1964
The Wild Boys: A Book of the Dead, 1971
Port of Saints, 1973
Cities of the Red Night, 1981
The Place of Dead Roads, 1983
The Burroughs File, 1984

Queer, 1985
The Western Lands, 1987
Ghost of Chance, 1995
My Education: A Book of Dreams, 1995

OTHER LITERARY FORMS

Because of their experimental techniques, the works of William S. Burroughs (BUR-ohz) are especially difficult to classify within established literary forms. *Exterminator!* (1973), for example, although published as a "novel," is actually a collection of previously published poems, short stories, and essays. Other unclassifiable works are book-length experiments, often written in collaboration and in the "cut-up, fold-in" technique pioneered by Burroughs, which might be considered novels by some. The "cut-up, fold-in" technique is similar to the picture art of collage in that text from other authors, news stories, or other works is randomly inserted and then re-edited to go with the general text by the author. Examples among Burroughs's works are *Minutes to Go* (1960), written in collaboration with Sinclair Beiles, Gregory Corso, and Brion Gysin; *The Exterminator* (1960), written with Gysin; *Time* (1965), which contains drawings by Gysin; and *Œuvre Croisée* (1976), written in collaboration with Gysin and reissued as *The Third Mind* in 1978. *White Subway* (1965), *Apomorphine* (1969), and *The Job: Interviews with William S. Burroughs* (1970), written in collaboration with Daniel Odier, are additional short-story and essay collections. *The Dead Star* (1969) is a journalistic essay that contains photocollage inserts, *APO-33 Bulletin: A Metabolic Regulator* (1966) is a pamphlet, and *Electronic Revolution, 1970-71* (1971) is an essay that fantasizes bizarre political and business uses for the cut-up, fold-in technique.

Burroughs also published scores of essays, stories, and articles in numerous journals, periodicals, and short-lived magazines. One of Burroughs's most revealing publications, *The Yage Letters* (1963), collects his correspondence with Allen Ginsberg concerning Burroughs's 1952 expedition to South America in search of yage, a legendary hallucinogen. In these letters, Burroughs is Govinda, the master, to Ginsberg's Siddhartha, the disciple.

ACHIEVEMENTS

William S. Burroughs's best-known novel, *Naked Lunch*, was made notorious by American censorship attempts and consequently became a best seller. Burroughs, who wrote primarily for a cult audience, was essentially a fantasist and satirist (some of his work is also considered science fiction), and he is often misread; in these respects he has been compared accurately to Jonathan Swift. Both writers focus on the faults and evils of humankind and society, employ fantastic satire to ridicule these shortcomings, and hope through this vehicle to effect some positive change in the human condition. Burroughs's works are exceptionally vicious satires, however, "necessarily brutal, obscene and disgusting"—his own description of them—because they must mime the situations from which their recurring images and metaphors (of drug addiction, aberrant sexual practices, and senseless violence) are drawn.

Burroughs's focus on drug addiction and the paranoia and nonlinear thought processes of his characters also make his writing comparable to some of Phillip K. Dick's novels, such as *The Man in the High Castle* (1962) and *A Scanner Darkly* (1977). Burroughs's work *Blade Runner: A Movie* (1979), although unrelated to the 1982 Ridley Scott film *Blade Runner*, which is based on Dick's work *Do Androids Dream of Electric Sheep?* (1968), may have at least been the inspiration for the motion picture's title.

Superficially, Burroughs's satiric attacks are aimed at humanity's "addictions" to pleasure or power in any of the many forms either craving might take. Those who, obeying the dictates of "the algebra of need," will stop at nothing to fulfill their desires have, in the terms of the moral allegory Burroughs creates, "lost their human citizenship" and become nonhuman parasites feeding on the life essences of others. They shamelessly lie, cheat, and manipulate to attain what Burroughs's associative imagery repeatedly equates with perversion, excrement, and death. Burroughs's satire, however, cuts deeper than this. It attacks not only humankind and its addictions but also the structures of the cultures that enable these addictions to flourish and proliferate. It attacks the myths and linguistic formulas that imprison the human race, the stone walls of patriotism and religion. It demands that people first free themselves from these "word and image addictions" before they kick their more obvious habits and regain their humanity, and thus calls for nothing less than a revolution of consciousness.

The Grove Press edition of *Naked Lunch* became a national best seller and was cleared of obscenity charges in Los Angeles in 1965 and in Massachusetts in 1966. Ginsberg and Norman Mailer, who described Burroughs as "the only American novelist living today who may conceivably be possessed by genius," were among those who testified in the book's defense. While it does detail with exceptional brutality the ugly, revolting, and perverse, *Naked Lunch* is at bottom a strikingly moral but darkly comic work that employs irony and allegory, as well as more unconventional techniques, to satirize much that is false and defective in modern American life in particular and human nature in general. Especially effective as a subliminal argument against heroin abuse, the book's successful publication in the United States elevated its then practically unknown author to membership in the literary elite.

Many reviewers—some seemingly oblivious to the irony of Burroughs's works—have not been responsive or sympathetic to his themes and techniques, and none of his novels after *Naked Lunch*, with the exception of *The Wild Boys*, received comparable critical acclaim. Whereas *Naked Lunch* was lauded by Terry Southern, Mary McCarthy, Karl Shapiro, and Marshall McLuhan, as well as by Ginsberg and Mailer, the less successfully realized subsequent novels were considered by some critics, not totally inaccurately, as "language without content" and "the world's greatest put-on." Burroughs himself admitted that "*Naked Lunch* demands silence from the reader. Otherwise he is taking his own pulse."

Burroughs warned that his novels do not present their "content" in the manner the reader ordinarily anticipates. One of the triumphs of his unique style is that he has created a low-content form, a narrative near vacuum, on which unwary readers are tempted to project their own psyches, personal myths, and forgotten dreams. While they do have their own messages to convey, his works also encourage readers to develop or invent their own private fictions and to append them to the skeletal narrative structures provided by the author. Readers are thus invited to create Burroughs's works as they read them. In place of relying on the easily perceived, clearly coherent stories one might have expected, Burroughs's best works keep one reading through the hypnotic fascination of the author's flow of images and incantatory prose.

BIOGRAPHY

William Seward Burroughs II was born on February 5, 1914, in St. Louis, Missouri, to Mortimer Perry Burroughs, son of the industrialist William Seward Burroughs I, who founded the Burroughs Adding Machine company. His mother was Laura Hammond Lee, whose family claimed direct descent from Robert E. Lee, Civil War general and commander in chief of the Confederate army. Dominated by his mother's obsessive Victorian prudery and haunted by vivid nightmares and hallucinations, Burroughs led a restless childhood. He was educated in private schools in St. Louis and Los Alamos, New Mexico, where he developed seemingly disparate fascinations with literature and crime. He later studied ethnology and archaeology at Harvard University, where he encountered a group of wealthy gay men. He graduated with an A.B. in 1936, and upon his graduation, his parents bestowed on him a monthly trust of two hundred dollars that allowed Burroughs a great deal of freedom from daily concerns.

Subsequently, Burroughs traveled to Europe. He briefly studied medicine at the University of Vienna, where he met Ilse Klapper, whom he married so that she—a Jewish woman fleeing Nazi Germany—could obtain an American visa. They remained friends, but Ilse divorced Burroughs nine years later, in 1946. Burroughs returned to the United States and Harvard to resume his anthropological studies, which he soon abandoned because of his conviction that academic life is little more than a series of intrigues broken by teas. Although he attempted to use family connections to obtain a position with the Office of Strategic Services, Burroughs was rejected after he deliberately cut off the first joint of his left little finger in a Vincent van Gogh-like attempt to impress a male friend. Moving to New York City, he worked as a bartender and in an advertising agency for a year and underwent psychoanalysis. Burroughs entered the U.S. Army in 1942 as a glider pilot trainee, engineered his discharge for psychological reasons six months later, and then moved to Chicago, where he easily found work as an exterminator and a private detective, among other odd jobs.

In 1943, Burroughs returned to New York City and met Joan Vollmer, a student at Columbia University; they married on January 17, 1945. Because Burroughs's divorce from Ilse was not yet final, several sources describe Joan as his common-law wife. She introduced Burroughs to Jack Kerouac, who in turn introduced him to Ginsberg. The Beat generation was born in Burroughs's 115th Street apartment after Burroughs acquainted Kerouac and Ginsberg with the writings of William Blake, Arthur Rimbaud, and others; the three friends soon emerged as leaders of the movement. Late in 1944, Herbert Huncke, a Times Square hustler involved in criminal activity to support his drug habit, introduced Burroughs to the use of morphine and its derivatives. Burroughs was for most of the next thirteen years a heroin addict who frequently altered his place of residence to evade the police.

In 1946, Burroughs moved to Waverly, Texas, where he tried farming; he and his wife had a son, William, Jr., in 1947. Burroughs voluntarily entered a drug rehabilitation center at Lexington, Kentucky, in 1948. Returning to Waverly and already back on drugs, Burroughs was hounded by the police until he moved to Algiers, Louisiana, later that same year. To avoid prosecution for illegal possession of drugs and firearms after a 1949 raid on his Algiers farm, Burroughs relocated to Mexico City in 1950, where he began writing *Junkie*. He continued his archaeological studies at Mexico City University, pursuing an interest in the Mayan codices. On September 7, 1951, Burroughs accidentally killed his wife, Joan, while allegedly attempting to shoot a drinking glass off her head while playing "William Tell." Although Mexican authorities let the matter drop, Burroughs soon left Mexico for the jungles of Colombia.

He returned again to New York City in 1953, the year *Junkie* was published, lived for a while with Ginsberg, and then settled in Tangier, Morocco, where from 1955 to 1958 he was frequently visited by other Beat writers and worked on the manuscript that would develop into his quartet of science-fiction-like novels: *Naked Lunch*, *The Soft Machine*, *Nova Express*, and *The Ticket That Exploded*. In 1957, Burroughs again sought treatment for his heroin addiction. This time he placed himself in the care of John Yerby Dent, an English physician who treated drug addicts with apomorphine—a crystalline alkaloid derivative of morphine—a drug Burroughs praises and mythologizes in his writings. The following year, cured of his addiction, Burroughs moved to Paris, where *The Naked Lunch* was published in 1959.

In 1960, Gysin, who had helped Burroughs select the Paris edition of *The Naked Lunch* from a suitcase full of

William S. Burroughs. (Archive Photos)

manuscript pages, introduced his experimental "cut-up" technique to Burroughs and collaborated with him on *The Exterminator* and *Minutes to Go*. Burroughs's literary reputation was firmly established with the American publication of *Naked Lunch* in 1962, and by the mid-1960's Burroughs had settled in London. He returned to St. Louis for a visit in 1965, covered the Democratic National Convention for *Esquire* in 1968, and moved again to New York to teach writing at City College of New York in 1974. In 1975, he embarked on a reading tour of the United States and conducted a writers' workshop in Denver, Colorado. After returning to London briefly, Burroughs settled in New York. In 1983, he was inducted into the American Academy and Institute of Arts and Letters.

In the late 1980's and early 1990's Burroughs did cameo roles, voice work, and writing for several movies and television shows and consulted on the film version of his book *Naked Lunch*, which was written and directed by David Cronenberg and released in late 1991. Burroughs published a number of novels and collections throughout the 1980's and 1990's, including 1987's *The Western Lands*, the last novel in the trilogy that includes *Cities of the Red Night* and *The Place of Dead Roads*. Shortly after the publication of this novel, Burroughs moved to rural Kansas, where he died in 1997.

ANALYSIS

William S. Burroughs did not begin writing seriously until 1950, although he had unsuccessfully submitted a story titled "Twilight's Last Gleaming" to *Esquire* in 1938. His first novelistic effort, *Queer*, which deals with homosexuality, was not published until 1985. Allen Ginsberg finally persuaded Ace Books to publish Burroughs's first novel, *Junkie*, which originally appeared under the pseudonym William Lee as half of an Ace double paperback; it was bound with Maurice Helbront's *Narcotic Agent*. While strictly conventional in style, *Junkie* is a luridly hyperbolic, quasi-autobiographical first-person account of the horrors of drug addiction. Of little literary merit in itself, this first novel is interesting in that it introduces not only the main character, Lee, but also several of the major motifs that appear in Burroughs's subsequent works: the central metaphor of drug addiction, the related image of man reduced to a subhu-

man form (usually an insectlike creature) by his drug and other lusts, and the suggestion of concomitant and pervasive sexual aberration.

In *Naked Lunch* and its three less celebrated sequels, *The Soft Machine*, *Nova Express*, and *The Ticket That Exploded*, Burroughs weaves an intricate and horrible allegory of human greed, corruption, and debasement. Like Aldous Huxley's *Brave New World* (1932) and George Orwell's *Nineteen Eighty-Four* (1949), these four works seize on the evils—or the tendencies toward a certain type of evil—that the author sees as particularly malignant in the contemporary world and project them into a dystopian future, where, magnified, they grow monstrous and take on an exaggerated and fantastic shape.

While progressively clarifying and developing Burroughs's thought, these novels share themes, metaphorical images, characters, and stylistic mannerisms. In them, Burroughs utilizes the "cut-up, fold-in" technique, which has its closest analogue in the cinematic technique of montage. He juxtaposes one scene with another without regard to plot, character, or, in the short view, theme, to promote an association of the reader's negative emotional reaction to the content of certain scenes (sexual perversion, drug abuse, senseless violence) with the implied allegorical content of others (examples of "addictions" to drugs, money, sex, power). The theory is that if such juxtapositions recur often enough, the feeling of revulsion strategically created by the first set of images will form the reader's negative attitude toward the second set of examples.

In these novels, Burroughs develops a science-fiction-like, paranoid fantasy wherein, on a literal level, Earth and its human inhabitants have been taken over by the Nova Mob, an assortment of extraterrestrial, non-three-dimensional entities who live parasitically on the reality of other organisms. Exploitation of Earth has reached such proportions that the intergalactic Nova Police have been alerted. The Nova Police are attempting to thwart the Nova Mob without so alarming them that they will detonate the planet in an attempt to destroy the evidence (and thus escape prosecution in the biologic courts) while trying to make what escape they can. The most direct form of Nova control, control that enables the Nova Mob to carry on its viruslike metaphysical vampirism with impunity, is thought control of the human population through control of the mass-communication media. Nova Mob concepts and perspectives attach themselves to and are replicated by the terrestrial host media much as a virus invades and reproduces through a host organism, a thought-control process analogous to the "cut-up, fold-in" technique itself. By the middle of *Nova Express*, the reader is caught up in a war of images in which the weapons are cameras and tape recorders. The Nova Police and the inhabitants of Earth have discovered how to combat the Nova Mob with their own techniques (of which these novels are examples) and are engaged in a guerrilla war with the Nova Criminals, who are desperately trying to cut and run. The ending of *The Ticket That Exploded* is optimistic for Earth but inconclusive, leaving the reader to wonder if Earth will be rid of the Nova Mob or destroyed by it.

Naked Lunch

A vividly and relentlessly tasteless fantasy-satire that portrays humankind's innate greed and lack of compassion in general and contemporary American institutions and values in particular, *Naked Lunch* immerses the reader in the impressions and sensations of William Lee (Burroughs's pseudonym in *Junkie*). Lee is an agent of the Nova Police who has assumed the cover of a gay heroin addict because with such a cover he is most likely to encounter Nova Criminals, who are all addicts of one sort or another and thus prefer to operate through human addict collaborators. Nothing of importance seems to occur in the novel, and little of what does happen is explained. Only toward the conclusion does the reader even suspect that Lee is some sort of agent "clawing at a not-yet of Telepathic Bureaucracies, Time Monopolies, Control Drugs, Heavy Fluid Addicts." The "naked lunch" of the title is that reality seen by Lee, that "frozen moment when everyone sees what is on the end of every fork." The random scenes of mutilation and depravity, bleak homosexual encounters, and desperate scrambles for drug connections into which the book plunges yield its two key concepts: the idea of addiction, the central conceit that human beings become hooked on power, pleasure, illusions, and so on much as junkies do on heroin, and that of "the algebra of need," which states simply that an addict faced with absolute need (as a junkie is) will do anything to satisfy that need.

The Nova Criminals are nonhuman personifications of various addictions. The Uranians, addicted to Heavy Metal Fluid, are types of drug addicts. Dr. Benway, Mr. Bradley Mr. Martin (a single character), and the insect people of Minraud—all control addicts—are types of the human addiction to power. The green boy-girls of Venus, addicted to Venusian sexual practices, are types of the human addiction to sensual pleasure. The Death Dwarf, addicted to concentrated words and images, is the analogue of the human addiction to various cultural myths and beliefs; he is perhaps the most pathetic of these depraved creatures. Burroughs explains: "Junk yields a basic formula of 'evil' virus: the face of evil is always the face of total need. A dope fiend is a man in total need of dope. Beyond a certain frequency need knows absolutely no limit or control." As poet and literary critic John Ciardi noted, "Only after the first shock does one realize that what Burroughs is writing about is not only the destruction of depraved men by their drug lust, but the destruction of all men by their consuming addictions, whether the addiction be drugs or over-righteous propriety or sixteen-year-old girls."

The Soft Machine

Burroughs viewed *The Soft Machine* as "a sequel to *Naked Lunch*, a mathematical extension of the Algebra of Need beyond the Junk virus." Here, the consuming addiction, displayed again in juxtaposition with scenes of drug abuse and sexual perversion, and through a number of shifting narrators, is the addiction to power over others. The central episode is the destruction by a time-traveling agent of the control apparatus of the ancient Mayan theocracy (Burroughs's primary archaeological interest), which exercises its control through the manipulation of myths; this is a clear analogue of the present-day struggle between the Nova Police and the Nova Mob that breaks into the open in the subsequent two novels.

The time traveler uses the same technique to prepare himself for time travel as Burroughs does in writing his novels, a type of "cut-up, fold-in" montage: "I started my trip in the morgue with old newspapers, folding in today with yesterday and typing out composites." Because words tie people to time, the time traveler is given apomorphine (used to cure Burroughs of his heroin addiction) to break this connection.

The "soft machine" is both the "wounded galaxy," the Milky Way seen as a biological organism diseased by the viruslike Nova Mob, and the human body, riddled with parasites and addictions and programmed with the "ticket," obsolete myths and dreams, written on the "soft typewriter" of culture and civilization. Burroughs contends that any addiction dehumanizes its victims. The Mayan priests, for example, tend to become half-man, half-crab creatures who eventually metamorphose into giant centipedes and exude an erogenous green slime. Such hideous transformations also strike Lee, a heroin addict, and other homosexuals. Bradley the Buyer, who reappears as Mr. Bradley Mr. Martin, Mr. and Mrs. D., and the Ugly Spirit, has a farcical habit of turning into a bloblike creature who is addicted to and absorbs drug addicts.

NOVA EXPRESS *and* THE TICKET THAT EXPLODED

Instances of metamorphosis are almost innumerable in *Nova Express* and *The Ticket That Exploded*. These novels most clearly reveal the quartet's plot and explore the Nova Mob's exploitation of media. Here addiction to language is investigated. As Stephen Koch has argued: "Burroughs's ideology . . . is based on an image of consciousness in bondage to the organism: better, of consciousness as an organism, gripped by the tropisms of need. Consciousness is addicted—it is here the drug metaphor enters—to what sustains it and gives it definition: in particular, it is addicted to the word, the structures of language that define meaning and thus reality itself." Thus, while in *The Soft Machine* the time traveler is sent to Trak News Agency (the motto of which is "We don't report the news—we write it") to learn how to defeat the Mayan theocracy by first learning "how this writing the news before it happens is done," in *The Ticket That Exploded* it is axiomatic that "you can run a government without police if your conditioning program is tight enough but you can't run a government without [nonsense and deception]."

Contemporary existence is seen ultimately as a film that is rerun again and again, trapping the human soul like an insect imprisoned in amber, negating any possibility of choice or freedom. In these last two novels of the quartet, Burroughs issues a call for revolt against humanity's imprisoning addiction to language. In *Nova*

Express, he notes that "their garden of delights is a terminal sewer" and demands that everyone heed the last words of Hassan I Sabbah (cribbed out of context from Fyodor Dostoevski's Ivan Karamazov): "Nothing is True—Everything is Permitted." In *The Ticket That Exploded*, Burroughs rages, "Better than the 'real thing'?—There is no real thing—Maya—Maya—It's all show business."

THE WILD BOYS

Burroughs's other notably science-fiction-like novel, *The Wild Boys*, is also composed of scenes linked more by associated images than by any clearly linear narrative framework. Here the author posits a bizarre alternative to the problematic apocalypse-in-progress depicted in his earlier quartet. In a world wrecked by famine and controlled by police, the wild boys, a homosexual tribe of hashish smokers, have withdrawn themselves from space and time through indifference and have developed into a counterculture complete with its own language, rituals, and economy. The existence of this counterculture poses a threat to those who create the false images on which the larger, repressive, external society is based, but the wild boys cannot be tamed because their cold indifference to the mass culture entails a savagery that refuses to submit to control. Although Burroughs's thinking clearly becomes more political in *The Wild Boys* and in the book that followed it, *Exterminator!*, a collection of short stories and poems that revolve around the common theme of death through sinister forces, his primary concern for freedom from the controllers and manipulators—chemical, political, sexual, and cultural—remains constant from the beginning of his literary career.

CITIES OF THE RED NIGHT

Continuing the utopian vision of *The Wild Boys*, but encompassing it into a larger, more anthropological context, Burroughs's next three works form a trilogy to expand his vision of society and its place in the natural order. The first book in the series, *Cities of the Red Night*, continues the twin themes of freedom from control and the power of mythmaking, but does so on a much larger scale. One of Burroughs's longest works, *Cities of the Red Night* is unique in that in it he sustains a rather conventional narrative voice, utilizing conventional popular genre, to achieve a re-creation of history through fantasy and myth.

The novel begins with three distinct plots that seem at first to be only tenuously related. One plot concerns a retroactive utopia founded by eighteenth century pirates, which Burroughs uses as a foundation for social criticism. A second plot, from which the title comes, depicts mythical "cities of the red night," which existed in prehistoric time and function as a dystopia through which the reader views present culture. A third plot involves a present-day investigator who traces the mystery of a deadly virus known as B-23 to its historical origins in the "cities of the red night." Each plot employs conventions from one popular genre or another: The story of the utopian pirates' colony reads very much like a boys' adventure story, the story of the advanced prehistoric cities takes its structure from science fiction, and the story of the investigation of the virus lends itself to the conventions of the hard-boiled detective story.

THE PLACE OF DEAD ROADS

In the second book of the trilogy, *The Place of Dead Roads*, Burroughs continues the process of mythmaking. His protagonist is Kim Carsons, a late nineteenth century gunslinger who utilizes a sort of "hole in time," a phenomenon introduced in *Cities of the Red Night*. Through this hole, Carsons becomes a time traveler, moving precariously across time and space, encountering different cultures and time periods in an effort to forge some sense of the whole, some sense of control over his own destiny. He seeks fulfillment in disparate, almost lonely, gay-sex encounters; in drugs; and in the sense of power he feels by manipulating others.

The story begins with a clipping from a Boulder, Colorado, newspaper that tells the reader that William Seward Hall, who writes Western novels under the pen name Kim Carsons, was shot in a gunfight in the year 1899. The story then introduces the character Carsons and, after a disjointed series of adventures and misadventures, returns the reader to that same date when Carsons loses his life, as if to say that destiny will not be averted in the end. The similarity of Carsons's true name to Burroughs's is striking here because, like Hall, Burroughs tends to fictionalize himself as author, as though authors can reach their true potential only through the lives of their characters—perhaps another way of understanding Burroughs's fascination with somehow circumventing destiny through manipulation.

THE WESTERN LANDS

In the third book of the trilogy, *The Western Lands*, the reader learns that Carsons was not shot by his opponent, Mike Chase, but by a killer from the Land of the Dead named Joe, described as a NO (Natural Outlaw), whose job it is to break natural laws. The Western land itself is a mythical place, a utopian vision of a place beyond one's images of Earth and Heaven—a land where natural law, religious law, and human law have no meaning. It is a paradise, but a paradise difficult to reach.

The intent of Burroughs's trilogy is first to create a science-fiction myth that explains all of human history, then to reveal the power of fantasy and myth to offer alternative histories, and finally, by realizing these alternative histories, to explore alternative anthropological patterns by which to organize society. The three separate plots interrelate and merge at various points throughout the trilogy, but eventually each is abandoned before completion—a technique that, Burroughs claimed, allows readers to create their own stories, to engage their own sense of mythmaking. Readers are encouraged to play a kind of "what if" game along with Burroughs: What if the Spanish had not defeated the New World into submission? What if the true foundations of liberty and individual freedom had taken hold in the Third World? What if all of our assumptions, whether religious, historical, or psychological, are wrong? This process of mythmaking in Burroughs is not a means to an end; rather, it is the object of the struggle—the great creative process of defining and redefining ourselves, which is our ultimate defense against those who would manipulate us.

QUEER

Set in Mexico and South America during the 1940's, *Queer* details in fictional guise both the author's homosexual longing and his drug addiction. Burroughs wrote, "While it was I who wrote *Junky* [*sic*], I feel that I was being written in *Queer*." Although it was not published until 1985 because of its homosexual content, *Queer* was Burroughs's first attempt at novel writing. It is the most linear and perhaps most coherent of Burroughs's novels.

William Lee is the story's protagonist, and, though not told in first person, the novel looks at the world through his eyes. Lee shares much in common with Burroughs, as explained in the novel's introduction. Lee is a heroin addict mostly trying to kick the habit. He lusts for boys and young men, and he has an obsession with Eugene Allerton, a younger bisexual man who tolerates Lee until better circumstances happen along. Part of the story involves Lee's search, with Allerton in tow, for a plant-based hallucinogen called yage that is purported to enhance telepathic powers. In *The Yage Letters*, Burroughs's letters regarding his real-life search for yage are collected.

Queer is a short novel—only 134 pages—prefaced by a 23-page introduction by Burroughs in which he further explains Lee's motivations and actions along with some of his own. Lee is looking for an audience, a distraction from the drug addiction, and, like many addicts, becomes obsessive about a sex object in replacement. Allerton is that object, and, in order to keep his audience interested, Lee develops what he calls "Routines": entertaining, shocking, or outrageous stories to amuse and draw attention. These stories, interwoven into the love-story travelogue, provide flashes of humor that are sometimes perverse, such as the recipe for pig served cooked on the outside but still living on the inside or the story of "Corn Hole Gus' Used-Slave Lot."

Burroughs's Mexico of the 1940's is seedy and primitive. Many of the characters in the book are fellow American expatriates, and the highlight of their day is to stop in at the local bars to share the latest gossip. In the twenty-first century world of television, video games, and cell phones, younger readers may find the place descriptions more like nightmares than like historic information—especially as the switches among inner musings, location descriptions, and "Routines" are not always clearly demarcated. William Lee continues his adventures in *Naked Lunch*.

Although Burroughs's innovative, highly unconventional fiction style and often abrasive thematic preoccupations are not without their detractors, by the end of his career Burroughs had firmly established his place as one of late twentieth century fiction's most significant innovators. In fact, his "cut-up" technique has reached beyond the bounds of obscure cult fiction to influence both mainstream cinema and popular music. Burroughs played a semiautobiographical role as Tom the Priest in Gus Van Sant's 1989 film about drug addiction,

Drugstore Cowboy; in 1991, acclaimed director David Cronenberg adapted *Naked Lunch* to the screen. In her introduction to his unprecedented reading on the popular American television show *Saturday Night Live* in 1981, actor Lauren Hutton lauded Burroughs as "America's greatest living writer," and rock music icons Lou Reed and David Bowie have both recognized Burroughs's disjointed and surreal but surprisingly moralistic approach to writing as enormously influential on their own work. The heavy metal genre of rock-and-roll music takes its name from a phrase in Burroughs's *Naked Lunch*, and the name of the popular band Steely Dan is also borrowed from his writing.

Upon his death in 1997 at age eighty-three, Burroughs was eulogized as everything from the "most dangerous" of Beat writers to the undisputed patriarch of this important movement in twentieth century American writing. Although Burroughs's lifelong penchant for the cutting edge of fiction continues to intimidate some scholars and critics, none can dispute his role as a significant innovator and catalyst for change in twentieth century fiction and popular culture.

Donald Palumbo; Gregory D. Horn
Updated by B. Diane Blackwood

OTHER MAJOR WORKS

NONFICTION: *The Yage Letters*, 1963 (with Allen Ginsberg); *APO-33 Bulletin: A Metabolic Regulator*, 1966; *The Job: Interviews with William S. Burroughs*, 1970 (with Daniel Odier); *Electronic Revolution, 1970-71*, 1971; *Letters to Allen Ginsberg, 1953-1957*, 1983; *The Adding Machine: Collected Essays*, 1985; *The Cat Inside*, 1992; *The Letters of William S. Burroughs, 1945-1959*, 1993 (Oliver Harris, editor); *Conversations with William S. Burroughs*, 1999 (Allen Hibbard, editor); *Last Words: The Final Journals of William S. Burroughs*, 2000; *Everything Lost: The Latin American Notebook of William S. Burroughs*, 2008 (Oliver Harris, editor).

MISCELLANEOUS: *The Exterminator*, 1960 (with Brion Gysin); *Minutes to Go*, 1960 (with Sinclair Beiles, Gregory Corso, and Gysin); *Time*, 1965 (drawings by Gysin); *White Subway*, 1965; *Apomorphine*, 1969; *The Dead Star*, 1969; *The Last Words of Dutch Schultz*, 1970; *Exterminator!*, 1973; *The Book of Breeething*,

1974; *Œuvre Croisée*, 1976 (with Gysin; also known as *The Third Mind*, 1978); *Blade Runner: A Movie*, 1979; *Interzone*, 1989; *Word Virus: The William S. Burroughs Reader*, 1998 (James Grauerholz and Ira Silverberg, editors).

BIBLIOGRAPHY

Burroughs, William S. *Burroughs Live*. Cambridge, Mass.: MIT Press, 2002. Collection of interviews is informative for readers hoping for a personal glimpse of the novelist. Burroughs, however, was notorious with interviewers for being a difficult subject to draw out.

Caveney, Graham. *Gentleman Junkie: The Life and Legacy of William S. Burroughs*. Boston: Little, Brown, 1998. Unconventional biography features an imaginative visual presentation that superimposes the text on reproductions of photographs, newspaper clippings, and other visual elements, all printed on multicolored pages. Considers the myths and legends surrounding Burroughs as well as his life and influence on later generations of musicians, writers, and artists.

Goodman, Michael Barry. *Contemporary Literary Censorship: The Case History of Burroughs's "Naked Lunch."* Metuchen, N.J.: Scarecrow Press, 1981. Offers a narrative history of the writing, publication, critical reception, and subsequent censorship of *Naked Lunch* in the United States. Provides much previously unpublished Burroughs material.

Harris, Oliver. *William Burroughs and the Secret of Fascination*. Carbondale: Southern Illinois University Press, 2003. Focuses on the novels *Junkie*, *Queer*, and *Naked Lunch*, as well as *The Yage Letters*, to trace Burroughs's creative history during the 1950's.

Hibbard, Allen, ed. *Conversations with William S. Burroughs*. Jackson: University Press of Mississippi, 1999. Collection of previously published interviews with the author spans thirty-five years (1961-1996). Includes chronology and index.

Johnson, Rob. *The Lost Years of William S. Burroughs: Beats in South Texas*. College Station: Texas A&M University Press, 2006. Discusses Burroughs's experiences during a period in his life (1946-1949) before he began publishing, when he farmed cotton (as well as marijuana and opium poppies) and socialized with Beat writers such as Allen Ginsberg and Neal Cassady. Sheds some light on Burroughs's early work. Includes illustrations and index.

Lardas, John. *The Bop Apocalypse: The Religious Visions of Kerouac, Ginsberg, and Burroughs*. Urbana: University of Illinois Press, 2001. Combines cultural history, biography, and literary criticism in examining the spiritualism and religious concerns of the three Beat writers.

Morgan, Ted. *Literary Outlaw: The Life and Times of William S. Burroughs*. New York: Holt, 1988. Standard biography remains an important source of information on Burroughs. Examines his life and career, with particular emphasis on the influence of other Beat writers on his work.

Skerl, Jennie. *William S. Burroughs*. Boston: Twayne, 1985. Attempts to provide an overview of contemporary thought on Burroughs's art and life for the general reader and literary historian. Also provides a concise analysis section.

OCTAVIA E. BUTLER

Born: Pasadena, California; June 22, 1947
Died: Seattle, Washington; February 24, 2006
Also known as: Octavia Estelle Butler

PRINCIPAL LONG FICTION

Patternmaster, 1976
Mind of My Mind, 1977
Survivor, 1978
Kindred, 1979
Wild Seed, 1980
Clay's Ark, 1984
Dawn, 1987
Adulthood Rites, 1988
Imago, 1989
Parable of the Sower, 1993
Parable of the Talents, 1998
Fledgling, 2005

OTHER LITERARY FORMS

Although she wrote novels primarily, Octavia E. Butler did produce some very successful short stories that were published in anthologies and periodicals. Her 1983 story "Speech Sounds" won a Hugo Award in 1984, and "Bloodchild," first published in 1984, won a Hugo and other awards the following year.

ACHIEVEMENTS

With her Patternist and Xenogenesis series, Octavia E. Butler won increasing popularity and critical praise within the science-fiction field and became established as a significant African American female writer whose particular cultural situation and interests gave her a unique stance among science-fiction writers on race and gender issues. Her initially implicit but invariably intense and penetrating consideration of sexual and racial prejudices, and their relevance to social power structures, gave her work considerable intellectual impact as well as imparting a heart-rending (and sometimes gut-wrenching) emotional viscerality to her narratives. Her use of alienated—and sometimes literally alien—narrators under extreme contextual pressure provided a sturdy platform for her contemplative analyses of human relationships and social dynamics. The principal recurring themes in her work—the essential awkwardness of gender roles, the dubious privileges and responsibilities of power, the sometimes-perverse operation of the survival instinct under stress, and the seductions of love, routinely coupled with the difficulties of miscegenation—insistently invite the reader to reexamine deep-seated and long-standing attitudes.

In addition to the two Hugo Awards she received for short stories, Butler received many awards and honors over the course of her writing career, including a MacArthur Foundation "genius grant" in 1995 and the 1999 Nebula Award for best novel for *Parable of the Talents*. In 2000, the PEN American Center presented Butler with a lifetime achievement award.

BIOGRAPHY

Octavia Estelle Butler grew up in a manner that reflected some of the hardest realities routinely faced by African Americans. Her father, who died when she was very young, had shined shoes for a living; her mother, who had been taken out of school at the age of ten, supported herself and her daughter after her husband's death by working as a maid while leaving the primary responsibilities of child care to her own mother, a devout Baptist.

Although Butler felt comfortable in the company of her adult relatives, she was profoundly uncomfortable with the social system with which she and they had to contend. She was a misfit from the very beginning, unusually tall for her age and chronically shy. Further isolated from her peer group by strict religious prohibitions, she took refuge in reading and became a devotee of science fiction. She began writing when she was about ten years old and began to experiment with her own science fiction at twelve, later recalling that the abysmal quality of the risible B-picture *Devil Girl from Mars* (1954) convinced her she could write better stories herself.

Her family could not imagine that her ambition to write was practicable, and her teachers refused to support her choice of science fiction as a medium. She at-

Octavia E. Butler. (Beth Gwinn)

Butler's commercial success was gradual but continuous, and by 1995 she was sufficiently widely recognized as an important African American writer to be chosen as the recipient of a $295,000 "genius grant" awarded by the MacArthur Foundation, which guaranteed her financial security. She used some of the cash to buy a house in Seattle, where she cared for her aging mother. Butler never learned to drive a car and never married. Unfortunately, she spent the last few years of her life suffering from a writer's block that interrupted the production of the trilogy of novels that would have constituted her masterpiece; she had only just managed to break through the block by writing an unrelated and less demanding novel when she suffered a fall outside her home and struck her head on a walkway, causing a fatal cerebral hemorrhage. She died in Seattle on February 24, 2006. That year, the Carl Brandon Society established the Octavia E. Butler Memorial Scholarship Fund in her honor, with the aim of enabling writers of color to attend the Clarion Writers Workshop.

ANALYSIS

Octavia E. Butler's work presents an image of humanity as a congenitally flawed species, perhaps doomed to destroy itself by virtue of the misapplication of it native intelligence, especially in the construction of dysfunctional hierarchies. The various and highly diverse societies featured in her novels are controlled by harsh realities: exacting competition for survival and intense struggles for power, usually culminating in the domination of the weak by the strong and—more unusually, and highly characteristic of her work—exotic patterns of literal and metaphorical parasitism.

Within this rather desolate general framework, there is scope for hope, idealism, love, bravery, and compassion as well as pain and desperation. Butler always looks to valiant outsiders to challenge the systems that oppress them, and they sometimes defeat tyrants to win power for themselves, but such victories are never easy and often costly. She does not deal in straightforwardly happy endings, but in ambiguous conclusions in which, although her protagonists have done their heroic best to improve matters for themselves and others, their environments remain essentially imperfect and perhaps essentially irredeemable.

tended Pasadena City College and then the California State College at Los Angeles; she was unable to study creative writing there, but attended evening writing classes at the University of California, Los Angeles, and was admitted to an Open Door Workshop organized by the Screenwriters Guild of America specifically to encourage writers from minority backgrounds. There she met the flamboyant science-fiction writer Harlan Ellison, who encouraged her to attend the Clarion Science Fiction Writers Workshop—an intensive six-week summer school—in 1970. At Clarion she first made contact with fellow African American science-fiction writer Samuel R. Delany. Ellison bought one of her early stories for a planned anthology that was to be titled "Last Dangerous Visions" but the anthology was never published; although she published two earlier short stories, it was not until 1976 that she made her crucial breakthrough with the publication of *Patternmaster*, the foundation stone of what would become the Patternist series.

In intellectually elaborated but often vividly descriptive prose, Butler usually tells her stories from the viewpoints of characters who are initially impotent but are forced by circumstances to attempt significant action. Her protagonists are usually, though not invariably, black women placed in bizarre situations and subjected to extraordinary experiences—often so extraordinary as to seem not merely grotesque but repulsive. What begins as an act of desperate courage, however, is usually transformed into an experience of love—however commingled with other emotions—and that experience is always crucial to the understanding that provides the story arc's ultimate epiphany. The essence of sophisticated science fiction is that such understanding is reached through a process of "conceptual breakthrough," and Butler's great strength as a writer is her ability to simulate such conceptual breakthroughs with a resolution and determination that is highly original.

Butler's fiction reflects and refracts the attempts and failures of late twentieth century American society to deal with ethnic and sexual prejudice. She frequently uses standard images of horror fiction, such as serpentine or insectile creatures, to provoke reflexive aversion in the reader, which she then systematically undermines in the hope that the reader will be unable to sustain this aversion as the analogical "humanity" of the alien—not in the commonplace sense of "humaneness" but in a deeper and more complex sense that retains all of humankind's existential flaws—gradually becomes undeniable. All of Butler's human, nonhuman, and quasi-human societies display their own forms of competitive selfishness and have their own manifest power structures; the maturity and independence won by her protagonists never imply an advent, or even a possibility, of universal equality and harmony, but they do embody the acceptance of a pragmatic personal obligation to wield power responsibly. Characters unable to alter or escape the order of things are expected to show a sort of noblesse oblige.

PATTERNMASTER

Patternmaster introduces the Patternist series, although it is the last rather than the first in terms of its internal chronology. It is the story of a personal and power struggle in which the younger son of the Patternmaster—the psychic control center of a society of advanced human beings—confronts and defeats his brutal older brother in the competition to succeed their father. He does so with the aid of a bisexual Healer with whom he ultimately "links" in order that they might pool their psionic power. "Healing" is, in this context—a paradox typical of Butler's work—a deadly species of knowledge. Trust and cooperation allow the hero to overcome the naked ambition and brutality of his brother, but the moral is by no means as simple as this brief summation implies. The principal complicating factor is the presence and status of the "mutes"—nontelepathic human beings whose vulnerability to the Patternists' cruelty and inability to control their own destinies reflect the status of slaves in colonial America.

MIND OF MY MIND

Mind of my Mind describes a much earlier phase in the establishment of the society depicted in *Patternmaster*. Mary, the novel's heroine, is a "latent" telepath who must undergo a painful transition to obtain command of her power. The pain and danger of this passage from adolescence to adulthood are emblematic of the turmoil of coming-of-age and of the physical or psychological pain that is required as the price of initiation in many tribal societies. The deadened, sometimes crazed, helplessness of latents who cannot become full-fledged telepaths but must continue to live with the intrusive offal of other people's thoughts is a powerful metaphor for people trapped in poverty, and some of the horrors Butler paints are familiar.

Initially, Mary has no choice. The founder of her "people," a nontelepathic immortal named Doro, prescribes her actions until she acquires her own power. He senses danger only when she reaches out reflexively to control other, powerful telepaths, thus forming the first Pattern. Mary's destruction of the pitiless Doro, like the hero's destruction of his older brother in *Patternmaster*, is accomplished with a barely compromised ruthlessness appropriate to the society and to the character of the victim. The development of Butler's work is evident in the intense concentration of the narrative on psychological adaptation to and responsible use of social power.

SURVIVOR

Survivor was written before either of its two published predecessors but was considered too riskily unorthodox, in generic terms, for publication until Butler had established a reputation. It is the story of an orphaned Afro-Asian girl who becomes a "wild human" in order to survive in a harsh environment. She is found and adopted, in an atypical act of reaching out, by two members of the Missionaries—a neo-Fundamentalist Christian sect. The Missionaries' escape from a hostile Earth takes them to a planet inhabited by furred bipeds, the Tehkohn, whom they regard as less than human. This alien species constitutes, in essence, a science-fictional version of the "noble savage"; the protagonist is inevitably alone in recognizing their nobility.

Internally untouched by Missionary dogma, the girl is successfully resocialized as a captive of the Tehkohn and, in the end, chooses them as her own people. Her survival and success require an understanding of the color classes of fur among the Tehkohn, where blue is the highest color—a tongue-in-cheek reference to the symbolism of "blue blood." Although she succeeds by dint of qualities often found in protagonists of action-adventure novels—physical agility, courage, and adaptability—her success is defiantly unorthodox in stripe.

KINDRED

Kindred provided Butler with her key critical breakthrough and remains the most successful of her works, although that might have changed had she succeeded in completing the Parable trilogy. The protagonist of *Kindred* is shuttled back and forth between 1824 and 1976 by a series of "timeslips," but this fantastic device serves to facilitate the moral complication of a fundamentally naturalistic narrative. The novel employs a contemporary black woman with a white husband as exemplary characters in order to probe the stereotype of the "contented slave" and the stigmatization of the "Uncle Tom." When Edana and Kevin are separated by their inexplicable reversion into slave and master in the American South of 1824, each begins unwillingly to imbibe the feelings and attitudes of the time from that perspective. The simultaneous processes of adaptation and rebellion set up an acute dynamic tension that is further emphasized by alternations of setting.

The impact of this novel results from Butler's skill in evoking the antebellum South from two contrasted points of view: the stubborn, desperate attempts of black people to lead meaningful lives in a society that disregards family ties and disposes of individuals as market-

able animals, and the uncomprehending, sometimes ham-fistedly benevolent but always oppressive ruthlessness of a ruling class that defines slaves in terms of what trouble or pleasure they can give. With *Kindred*, Butler set an important methodical precedent for the examination of the complex relationship between contemporary African Americans and their own troubled history that was followed or adapted by several other African American writers; thus this novel became an influential work as well as a highly original and effective one.

WILD SEED

Butler further developed the technique of historical reconstruction exercised in *Kindred* in *Wild Seed*, a Patternist prequel whose evocation of Ibo West Africa owes something to the work of writers such as Chinua Achebe. *Wild Seed* traces Doro and Anyanwu from their seventeenth century meeting in West Africa to the establishment of Doro's settlements in America. Doro is a centuries-old being who lives by "taking" another person's body and leaving the previous body behind; Anyanwu, the Emma of *Mind of My Mind*, is one of his descendants. Anyanwu is a "wild seed" because she has unexpectedly developed the power to shape-shift, becoming young or old, an animal, fish, or bird, at will. Their relationship is completely one-sided, since Doro could "take" her any time he chose, although he would not acquire her special abilities. His long life and unremitting efforts to create a special people of his own have left him completely insensitive to the needs and desires of others. Anyanwu finally achieves some balance of power simply by being willing to die and leave Doro without the only companion who could last beyond a mortal lifetime.

CLAY'S ARK

The final Patternist novel, *Clay's Ark*, is the third in the internal chronology of the series. It introduces the reader to brutish enemies of both Patternist and "mute" humanity, the Clayarks—so named because the disease that created them was brought back to Earth on a spaceship named *Clay's Ark*. The disease culls its victims, killing some and imbuing others with a will to live that overcomes the horror of their new existence; they become faster and stronger, and their children evolve even further, taking on animal shapes and animal attributes of speed, power, and heightened senses, but retaining human thought and use of their hands. In the guise of a horror story, *Clay's Ark* follows the first Clayarks' attempts to come to terms with their condition and live responsibly, shut off from civilization. The failure of their project suggests that it is not possible to contain cataclysmic natural change, but the story cleverly enlists the reader's sympathy for chimerical beings who suffer even as they afflict others, thus building a poignantly uncomfortable allegory of the human condition.

THE XENOGENESIS SERIES

With the partial exception of *Clay's Ark*, which consciously makes use of an action-adventure format, Butler's novels follow a pattern of progressive narrative deceleration; action is increasingly internalized and conducted on a psychological level, while moral judgmentalism become increasingly problematic and is sometimes conscientiously set aside. In the Xenogenesis series, comprising *Dawn*, *Adulthood Rites*, and *Imago*, this attempt to take a ruthlessly objective stance is taken to an unusual—perhaps unprecedented—extreme. The series confirmed Butler as a science-fiction writer of exceptional depth and originality.

The series was originally intended to be called "Exogenesis"—which would merely have implied a genesis effected from outside humanity—but the initial substitution was entirely appropriate. "Xenogenesis" has both text and subtext; its reference is the production of an organism altogether and permanently unlike the parent. The term's subtext is a function of the best-known English word built on the same root, "xenophobia": the fear and detestation of that which is foreign or alien. The series title thus became a succinct statement of the thesis it addresses. It was apparently considered insufficiently reader-friendly, however; when the series was reissued in 2000, it was retitled Lilith's Brood.

Many of the techniques and themes of Butler's developing canon are reassessed and extrapolated here: the alternating use of first- and third-person narrative, the slow pace of a plot laden with psychological development and sensory perceptions, the meticulous foreclosure of value judgments, the concern with hierarchy and responsibility, the objective observation of feelings of revulsion for that which is alien, and those feelings' gradual dissipation as the alien becomes familiar and therefore less threatening. Action in the series is sparse, normally kept to the minimum necessary to maintain the pace of psychological and social observation. In some ways, it is a chilling account of a series of seductions of human beings by an alien, ostensibly benevolent oppressor, somewhat reminiscent of Rufus from *Kindred* (at least in his better moments). To some extent, the story attempts a demonstration of the infinite capacity of humanity to seek satisfaction in the destruction of itself and others.

Dawn depicts a world devastated by a nuclear exchange between East and West, in which the dying remnants of humanity survive largely in the Southern Hemisphere. Its heroine is an African, Lilith, whose name is deliberately suggestive of the demon that Adam's first wife became in Hebrew folklore: the alternative potential mother of humankind who was set aside in favor of the docile Eve and became vengeful in consequence. The plot describes the advent of the Oankali, a nonviolent race of benevolent parasites and genetic engineers whose self-defined raison d'être is serial combination with other species in order to acquire new cellular "knowledge" and capabilities. In essence, the Oankali live for miscegenation. They are trisexual, the third sex—ooloi—providing an indispensable link between male and female, channeling, altering, or amplifying all genetic material and sexual contact, including the transfer of sperm and pleasurable sensations. Ooloi are capable of internal healing; one cures Lilith of a cancer and finds the cancer to be an exciting new biological material with which to work.

The Oankali blend with other species by linking a male and female of the target species with a male and female Oankali through the mediation of an ooloi. Thereafter, independent conception is not possible for those members of that species. The progeny are "constructs" who, at least at first, resemble their direct parents but carry genetic change within them. Lilith's first husband is killed in *Dawn*, but she bears his child posthumously because the ooloi that has chosen her has preserved his seed. The resultant humanoid male child becomes the protagonist of *Adulthood Rites*, while a subsequent child that Lilith conceives with another husband and the same Oankali parents is the protagonist of *Imago*.

Lilith is initially appalled even by the more humanoid Oankali, with their Medusan tentacles and sensory arms. She gradually adapts to them, cooperates with them to save humanity, bears children with them, is overwhelmed by the sensory pleasure they can give, and becomes sympathetic to their need to unite with other species, but she is never fully resigned. In *Imago*, Lilith compares the Oankali's description of the "flavors" of human beings to physical cannibalism and implies that the spiritual equivalent is no less predatory. Her conversion preconfigures the second and third novels, as human beings are ultimately allowed a choice of living with the Oankali, staying behind on a doomed and barren Earth, or living in an experimental, all-human world on Mars. The Oankali foresee that a reproduction of traditional combinations of intelligence and hierarchy will lead the last outposts of "pure" humanity to destroy themselves—a conclusion that Butler does not attempt to deny or undermine.

Adulthood Rites tells the story of Akin, a male human construct, who convinces the more rational human beings left on Earth to trust the Oankali and convinces the Oankali to offer the humans the choice of planetary residences. *Imago* is a first-person account of Jodahs, a child whose transformation to adulthood reveals it to be an ooloi. Butler's use in this instance of the first-person narrative to tell the story of an apparent human who becomes wholly alien in both psychology and physiology is rewarding in spite of the inevitable corollary difficulties. Through the eyes of a being routinely referred to as "it" by its own society, the reader observes its benevolent stalking and drug-induced brainwashing of human mates and the final planting of a seed that will grow into an organic town and then an organic spaceship, which will carry Jodahs and his people to new worlds for new genetic blendings.

Imago's conclusion serves as a reminder that Butler's imaginary worlds are primarily arenas for hard, necessary decisions in the business of survival. There is compassion as well as bitterness and love as well as prejudice, but there is no triumph or glory—only responsibility.

PARABLE OF THE SOWER

Parable of the Sower is set in California in 2024. The story's narrator is a fifteen-year-old African American girl who lives with her family in the fictitious town of Robledo, some twenty miles from Los Angeles. The social order is in the process of terminal disintegration,

a deep gulf having opened up between "haves" and "have-nots"; the former live in walled and fortified neighborhoods while the latter live outside, along with packs of wild dogs and drug addicts called "Paints," whose addiction imbues them with an orgasmic desire to burn things. The climate has been substantially altered by the effects of industrially released carbon dioxide and various pollutants, and the world is on the brink of a cataclysmic ecocatastrophe. Disease is rampant, natural disasters are frequent, and—though there are still stores, jobs, and even television programs—the end is evidently nigh. Against this backdrop, Lauren Olamina founds a new religion named Earthseed. The novel takes the form of her journal, and each chapter is prefaced with a passage from the new religion, the essence of whose creed is that everything changes, even God. In fact, God *is* change.

The implication of the novel and the fictitious religion it describes is that although humankind is not likely to change itself, humans will be forced to change by dire necessity. When the Paints destroy Lauren's neighborhood and most of her family, she treks north toward Canada, and new members gradually augment her company of disciples. Most survive and reach their destination, a farm in Oregon, but its burned-out shell is no promised land, and Lauren's sacrifices are still a long way from achieving any sort of general redemption.

PARABLE OF THE TALENTS

In the second novel of the projected Earthseed or Parable trilogy, the seeds of potential redemption planted in the first volume begin to bear fruit, but the progress of the community is decisively interrupted by its destruction. Lauren is substituted in her quasi-messianic role by her daughter Larkin. Kidnapped and imprisoned, Larkin must cope as best she can while awaiting a reunion that might never materialize with a mother who seems, at times, to have forsaken her. In the meantime, Lauren's attempts to locate Larkin are confused and compromised by her insistent need to spread her gospel—a conflict of interests that Jesus, mercifully, never had to face in the course of his own mission.

Like the middle volumes of many literary trilogies, *Parable of the Talents* is handicapped by the fact that it must begin with a partial destruction of the climactic achievements of its predecessor while it is unable to do more than suggest what might transpire in its successor. Significantly, while the titles of the first two volumes refer to actual parables in the existing Gospels, the third volume was to have been called "Parable of the Trickster," suggestive of an intended move beyond the moral parameters of the New Testament—much as Jesus' own teachings tore up the envelope of the Old Testament while attempting to conserve its precious contents—in order to establish moral foundations more workable than those of Christendom ultimately proved to be. Unfortunately, Butler's long struggle with writer's block, followed by her premature death, prevented her from developing the climactic exemplum in her series.

FLEDGLING

Fledgling is the "undemanding" novel that Butler wrote in order to break the block from which she was suffering with regard to the completion of the Parable trilogy. It uses the standardized form of the amnesiac fantasy, in which a protagonist must attempt to find out who she is and how she was traumatized into losing her memory; science fiction versions of this formula inevitably set up surprising discoveries. Here the protagonist is Shori, an African American girl who wakes up in the wilderness near a burned-out enclave; she appears to be about ten years old, but she eventually deduces that she is much older and, by courtesy of exotic genetic engineering, not as human as she had at first assumed. Although briskly paced and calculatedly melodramatic, the novel reprises all of Butler's characteristic themes—issues of race and gender, alienation, the benefits of biological and cultural diversity—in a manner that is by no means unsubtle or unsophisticated.

James L. Hodge; John T. West III
Updated by Brian Stableford

OTHER MAJOR WORKS

SHORT FICTION: "Crossover," 1971; "Near of Kin," 1979; "Speech Sounds," 1983; "Bloodchild," 1984; "The Evening and the Morning and the Night," 1987.

NONFICTION: "Birth of a Writer," 1989 (also published as "Positive Obsession"); "Furor Scribendi," 1993.

MISCELLANEOUS: *Bloodchild, and Other Stories*, 1995 (collected short stories and essays; expanded 2005).

BIBLIOGRAPHY

Ackerman, Erin M. Pryor. "Becoming and Belonging: The Productivity of Pleasures and Desires in Octavia Butler's Xenogenesis Trilogy." *Extrapolation* 49, no. 1 (2008): 24-43. Presents an analysis of the trilogy in terms of its relevance to the theme of the likely inevitability of intolerance.

Agustí, Clara Escoda. "The Relationship Between Community and Subjectivity in Octavia E. Butler's *Parable of the Sower*." *Extrapolation* 46, no. 3 (2005): 351-359. Discusses Butler's novel as portraying a "critical utopia." Part of a special issue devoted to the theme of "multiculturalism and race in science fiction."

Anderson, Crystal S. "'The Girl Isn't White': New Racial Dimensions in Octavia Butler's *Survivor*." *Extrapolation* 47, no. 1 (2006): 35-50. Provides a detailed analysis of the theme of race in Butler's first-written and least-studied novel.

Barr, Marleen S. "Octavia Butler and James Tiptree Jr. Do Not Write About Zap Guns." In *Lost in Space: Probing Feminist Science Fiction and Beyond*. Chapel Hill: University of North Carolina Press, 1993. Discusses the relationship of Butler's work to the evolution of feminist science fiction.

_____, ed. *Afro-Future Females: Black Writers Chart Science Fiction's Newest New-Wave Trajectory*. Columbus: Ohio State University Press, 2008. Hybrid critical anthology and short-story collection examines Butler's works as well as those of Samuel R. Delany and Steven Barnes.

Dubey, Madhu. "Folk and Urban Communities in African American Women's Fiction: Octavia Butler's *Parable of the Sower*." *Studies in American Fiction* 27, no. 1 (1999): 103-128. Explores Butler's representation of the dilemmas and crises of urban life in her fiction.

Govan, Sandra Y. "Connections, Links, and Extended Networks: Patterns in Octavia Butler's Science Fiction." *Black American Literature Forum* 18 (1984): 82-87. Examines Butler's use of elements of slave narratives and historical novels to produce a new kind of science fiction featuring black characters, especially black women, as major heroic figures.

Jacobs, Naomi. "Posthuman Bodies and Agency in Octavia Butler's Xenogenesis." In *Dark Horizons:*

Science Fiction and the Dystopian Imagination, edited by Raffaella Baccolini and Tom Moylan. New York: Routledge, 2003. Examines the transformations in the trilogy as analogues of political change and ominous possibility.

Meltzer, Pauline. *Alien Constructions: Science Fiction and Feminist Thought*. Austin: University of Texas Press, 2006. Includes as a central topic of discussion Butler's relevance to feminist science fiction. Her work is the subject of both the long essays comprising part 1 and the concluding essay that is the second in part 3.

Mitchell, Angelyn. "Not Enough of the Past: Feminist Revisions of Slavery in Octavia Butler's *Kindred*."

MELUS 26, no. 3 (2001): 51-75. Explores the way in which Butler uses the device of time travel to bridge nineteenth and twentieth century attitudes about slavery.

Scott, Johnathan. "Octavia Butler and the Base for American Socialism." *Socialism and Democracy* 20, no. 3 (2006): 105-126. Focuses on the political themes in Butler's work, with particular reference to *Parable of the Sower*.

Zaki, Hoda M. "Utopia, Dystopia and Ideology in the Science Fiction of Octavia Butler." *Science-Fiction Studies* 17 (1990): 239-251. Presents a scrupulous examination of the political themes implicit in Butler's early works.

ROBERT OLEN BUTLER

Born: Granite City, Illinois; January 20, 1945
Also known as: Robert Olen Butler, Jr.

PRINCIPAL LONG FICTION

The Alleys of Eden, 1981
Sun Dogs, 1982
Countrymen of Bones, 1983
On Distant Ground, 1985
Wabash, 1987
The Deuce, 1989
They Whisper, 1994
The Deep Green Sea, 1997
Mr. Spaceman, 2000
Fair Warning, 2002

OTHER LITERARY FORMS

Although highly praised as a novelist, Robert Olen Butler has received his greatest acclaim for his work as a writer of short stories. He achieved national recognition in 1992 for *A Good Scent from a Strange Mountain*, a celebrated collection of short stories about Vietnamese refugees settled in communities in Louisiana. He has also published several other books of short stories, including *Tabloid Dreams* (1996), *Had a Good Time:*

Stories from American Postcards (2004), *Severance* (2006), and *Intercourse* (2008). The nonfiction *From Where You Dream: The Process of Writing Fiction* (2005), assembled and edited by Janet Burroway, transcribes events and ideas from a writing class taught by Butler.

ACHIEVEMENTS

Before succeeding as an author, Robert Olen Butler wrote several unpublished novels, and his first published work of long fiction, *The Alleys of Eden*, was rejected by at least twenty publishers before it was finally accepted. In spite of the rejections, Butler persisted, and *The Alleys of Eden* was praised by critics and reviewers when it was published in 1981. In 1984, Butler sold this first novel to the cable television network Home Box Office (HBO) to be made into a film for television. His work became well known to the general public, however, only in 1993, when he was awarded the Pulitzer Prize for fiction for *A Good Scent from a Strange Mountain*. That year he also received the Notable Book Award from the American Library Association and the Rosenthal Foundation Award from the American Academy of Arts and Letters, was nominated for the PEN/Faulkner Award, and was named a Guggenheim Fellow. In 2001, Butler received the National Fiction Award for the short story "Fair Warning" (which he later extended into the novel of the same title), and in 2005 he won the National Magazine Award in Fiction for the story "The One in White."

BIOGRAPHY

Robert Olen Butler, Jr., grew up in Granite City, Illinois, a steel town near St. Louis, Missouri. His father, Robert Olen Butler, Sr., was chair of the theater department at St. Louis University. Butler majored in theater at Northwestern University in Illinois, from which he graduated summa cum laude with a B.S. in oral interpretation in 1967. He went on to graduate school in the writing program at the University of Iowa, where he earned a master's degree in playwriting in 1969. While a student in Iowa, he married Carol Supplee; they divorced in 1972.

American involvement in the Vietnam War was at its height when Butler finished graduate school, and, believing he would be drafted, he decided to enlist in the Army instead, hoping that he would have some choice in his assignment. Although he wanted to serve in the United States, he was assigned to military intelligence, was given intensive training in the Vietnamese language, and was sent to Vietnam, where he served until 1972. Butler became fluent in Vietnamese, and the language and culture of Vietnam, together with the experience of war, greatly influenced his thinking and writing.

In July of 1972, Butler married the poet Marilyn Geller. He worked for a year as an editor and reporter in New York City. When his wife became pregnant with their son, Joshua, the family moved back to Illinois. Butler taught high school in his hometown of Granite City in 1973 and 1974, then became a reporter in Chicago. He moved back to the New York City area in 1975 and took a job as editor in chief of *Energy User News*. According to Butler, he wrote much of his first three novels while commuting on the Long Island Railroad to and from his job in Manhattan. Butler left New York in 1985 to take a position teaching writing at McNeese State University, a small college in the southwestern Louisiana city of Lake Charles. Louisiana is home to several Vietnamese communities, and the Louisiana Vietnamese provided Butler with material for his Pulitzer Prize-winning collection of

Robert Olen Butler. (Gray Little)

short stories, *A Good Scent from a Strange Mountain*. In May, 2000, he became the Francis Eppes Professor of English at Florida State University. Divorced from Marilyn Geller in 1987, Butler has been married two more times, to Maureen Donlan from 1987 to 1995 and then to the novelist Elizabeth Dewberry from 1995 to 2007.

ANALYSIS

Robert Olen Butler's novels are notable for their depth of psychological insight. All his works depend heavily on presenting the perspectives and shifting emotions of characters, particularly characters caught in crises. His writing attempts to enter and follow the private thoughts of troubled people. Tensions and unresolved conflicts, especially sexual and romantic tensions between men and women, are central to his fiction. These men and women are usually placed in stormy social and historical situations, such as the Vietnam War and its aftermath or the class struggles of the Great Depression, but Butler is always interested more in how events in the world complicate the private relationships of individuals than he is in social problems or questions of ideology.

Butler's characters tend to be lonely people struggling to make contact with one another. Differences in culture complicate these efforts at contact. Many of Butler's Vietnam novels examine emotional and sexual involvements between an American soldier or veteran and a Vietnamese woman. In interviews, Butler has maintained that although the novels are set in Vietnam, the country itself is not the theme of his work, and the romantic entanglements of war are not his main concern. Instead, he sees Vietnam as a metaphor for the human condition, and he sees its tragedy as a specific instance of continual human tragedy. The cultural gaps between Western men and Asian women, similarly, are concrete examples of the distances that exist between all persons and of the often unbridgeable gaps between men and women.

Butler's novels are frequently connected to one another in characters and in themes. His first three novels form a loose trilogy, as they deal with the postwar experiences of three men who served in the same intelligence unit in Vietnam. A central character in one of Butler's books will often appear as a minor character in another, so that each narrative seems to be part of a single larger fictional world.

The style of Butler's writing is usually spare and stark, relying on unadorned, simple sentences. He often employs a traditional, invisible, omniscient narrator who relates the thoughts and feelings of the characters as well as the settings of the story; this time-honored fictional strategy may seem a bit old-fashioned and artificial to some readers. Butler also uses the first-person interior monologue, as in *The Deep Green Sea*, in which the entire story unravels through the thoughts of the two protagonists. In *Mr. Spaceman*, the interior monologue of an extraterrestrial alien becomes the monologues of different human beings as the alien explores the life of each.

Critics have generally identified a tendency to lapse into melodrama as the greatest weakness in Butler's fiction. His works strive to achieve a high seriousness and a moral and emotional intensity that is sometimes difficult to sustain. Butler's background in theater may be the reason his work seems sometimes excessively staged and self-consciously tragic.

THE ALLEYS OF EDEN

The Alleys of Eden, Butler's first novel, treats the conflict between Vietnamese and American cultures and contemplates the destructiveness of the Vietnam War for both of these. Its two main characters are Cliff Wilkes, a deserter from the U.S. Army in Vietnam, and Lanh, a Vietnamese bar girl and Cliff's lover. The novel is, appropriately, divided into two parts. The first part is set in Saigon in the last few days before the city's fall to the Communist forces of the North Vietnamese. The second part takes place in the United States, after Cliff and Lanh manage to flee.

Cliff had been with the Army intelligence unit, but he deserted after the torture and killing of a Viet Cong captive. Fluent in Vietnamese, he has come to feel himself more Vietnamese than American, but barriers continue to exist between him and his adopted country. He awaits the arrival of the North Vietnamese in a room that he has shared with Lanh for five years, since his desertion. As Cliff's memories move through his past, the scene shifts from images of his time with military intelligence to his failed marriage to his family in Illinois. At the last minute, Cliff decides to flee, and he convinces Lanh to join him. They make it onto one of the last helicopters out of the city.

On a ship heading back to the United States, the deserter passes himself off as a journalist and then runs away before being fingerprinted in California. Reunited with Lanh, he returns to Illinois. There, the two find that Lanh's struggles to adapt to an unfamiliar world and Cliff's uncertainties about his past and his future place too much strain on their love for each other, and Cliff ultimately leaves alone for Canada.

Told primarily from Cliff's perspective, *The Alleys of Eden* is impressive for its evocation of his collage of memories. The strategy of dividing the novel into a Vietnamese half and an American half is in some respects an effective way of structuring the plot to highlight the troubled love of Cliff and Lanh. However, the second half of the novel is also anticlimactic, after the review of Cliff's troubled past and the sudden flight through the alleys of Saigon, and the part of the story that takes place in the

United States lacks the tension and momentum of the first half.

WABASH

Wabash is one of only a few novels Butler has published that do not deal with the Vietnam War. *Wabash* is, however, set in a war of sorts. It takes place during the Great Depression, in 1932, in a steel town based on Butler's hometown. It tells the story of Jeremy and Deborah Cole, a couple mourning the death of their daughter. Jeremy is a steelworker employed in a mill where his friends and coworkers are being laid off every day. Through a man he meets at work, Jeremy becomes involved with communist radicals. At first he is put off by their rhetoric and by their language of ideology. However, he is angered by the brutality of the mine's management and by the victimization of other men on the job. Eventually, he decides to attempt to kill the politically ambitious owner of the mine.

While Jeremy fights his battles in the masculine world of the steel mill, Deborah struggles with conflicts among the women in her family. Her mother and two of her aunts are close-knit but troubled in their relations with one another and with Deborah. Her grandmother is approaching death; a third aunt has converted to Catholicism and has been rejected by all the other women of the family. Deborah finds the ostracized aunt, Effie, and after the grandmother's death Deborah manages to convince Effie to attend the funeral. Even the death of their mother will not reconcile the other women with Aunt Effie, however, and Deborah fails in her efforts to bring the family together.

Jeremy and Deborah's lives and struggles come together when Deborah stops Jeremy's assassination attempt and the two of them leave Wabash. Though both lose their separate battles, the story reaches a resolution as the two narratives, one of the woman and one of the man, reach a single end.

Wabash is a moving novel that established Butler's ability to deal with topics other than the Vietnam War. It does echo the central themes of the Vietnam novels, however: the importance and difficulty of love between a woman and a man and the private pains of those caught up in social and political crises. If, at times, the characters seem a bit too cinematic and a bit too unbelievable, this may be a consequence of Butler's efforts to reach

back in time for the legendary past of his present-day Illinois.

THE DEEP GREEN SEA

As in so many of Butler's fictions, two lovers occupy center stage in *The Deep Green Sea*. Ben Cole, son of Jeremy and Deborah Cole of *Wabash*, is a Vietnam War veteran. Ben is haunted by his memories of the war and world-weary as a result of his failed marriage. Returning to Vietnam, he meets Tien, a tour guide. Tien is the daughter of a Vietnamese bar girl who sold herself to American soldiers, one of whom was Tien's father. Tien is also haunted, by both her mother's desertion and her unknown father.

The novel uses first-person narration, alternating between Ben and Tien, enabling Butler to present their affair through the eyes of each. Butler presents a woman's point of view with an insight possessed by few other male novelists, and the fact that he speaks convincingly with the voice of a Vietnamese woman is a tribute to his versatility. The beginning of the story takes place in Tien's room, where the lovers recall scenes from their pasts. These two sets of thoughts and memories provide rather weak structure for the narrative; the novel does not, at first, seem to be leading anywhere. However, soon the question of Tien's parents emerges and the tragic appeal of the story is made evident.

While serving in the war, Ben had a Vietnamese girlfriend, a bar girl. Because Tien's mother was a bar girl, the apparently faint possibility that Tien's mother and Ben's former girlfriend might be the same person trouble the couple. They leave for the town of Nha Trang, where Tien's mother is known to live, for proof that the only relationship between the two of them is that of lovers. The truth that they find in Nha Trang is ultimately devastating to them both. *The Deep Green Sea* may well be the least complex of Butler's novels in plot and action. However, with its echoes of Oedipal tragedy and its evocation of the many-sided adversities of the Vietnam War, it is a haunting work.

MR. SPACEMAN

With *Mr. Spaceman*, Butler moved into the new territory of science fiction. The novel is also more comic than most of Butler's work and is in some ways reminiscent of the writing of Kurt Vonnegut. It tells the story of Desi, an alien from another planet making contact with the denizens of Earth. Desi's race does not use language, and he has learned his English from Earth mass media, mainly television. This enables Butler to make imaginative use of TV clichés and to engage in meditations on the nature of language through Desi's thoughts.

The alien protagonist has been taking humans from Earth for years in order to learn about them and about their planet. In the process, he has acquired an Earth wife, the former hairstylist Edna Bradshaw of Bovary, Alabama. At the time of the story, Desi has taken on board his ship a bus bound from Texas to a casino in Lake Charles, Louisiana. As Edna prepares for a dinner with the twelve people who were on the bus, Desi examines the lives of the passengers by moving into their thoughts and speaking in their voices, a process that evokes Butler's own approach to fiction.

One of the bus riders takes the alien for the Christ of the second coming, and the others take varying points of view on Desi's potential role in saving humanity. The dinner with the twelve recalls Christ's Last Supper with his disciples as the extraterrestrial discusses his plans for revealing himself at last to humankind, pondering the possible deadly reactions of the citizens of Earth. This is not a tragedy, however, and the novel takes a sudden comic turn away from Desi's self-sacrifice at the end.

Fair Warning

Presenting the point of view of a member of the opposite sex is one of the most difficult exercises a writer can attempt. In *Fair Warning*, Butler adopts the persona of Amy Dickerson, a New York auctioneer of antiques and other collectibles, former model and actor, and daughter of a wealthy Texas oil and cattle baron. Just past her fortieth birthday, Amy is still single, a fact that receives the attention of her widowed mother and her younger sister, Missy.

The story revolves around Amy's romantic relationships with Trevor Martin, a successful attorney and client of her auction house, and Alain Bouchard, a wealthy French businessman who is purchasing the auction house itself. Amy's life is also complicated by her relationships with Missy, who is in a troubled marriage with a Wall Street stockbroker, and with her mother, who is back in Texas struggling with memories of the deceased family patriarch. With its glamorous but single and aging heroine and her sophisticated suitors, the novel

comes dangerously close to stereotypes of popular women's fiction. At some points it does seem to take on the qualities of soap opera, but Amy's incisive reflections on collecting as a way of living and the sudden turns in plot manage to steer the story away from both sentimentality and predictability.

Carl L. Bankston III

Other major works

SHORT FICTION: *A Good Scent from a Strange Mountain*, 1992; *Tabloid Dreams*, 1996; *Had a Good Time: Stories from American Postcards*, 2004; *Severance*, 2006; *Intercourse*, 2008.

NONFICTION: *From Where You Dream: The Process of Writing Fiction*, 2005 (Janet Burroway, editor).

Bibliography

Beidler, Philip D. *Re-writing America: Vietnam Authors in Their Generation*. Athens: University of Georgia Press, 1991. Thought-provoking work places authors whose works concern the Vietnam War within their generation, providing readers with the appropriate context for understanding Vietnam fiction. A very good section on Butler places his novels within the genre and establishes and discusses the relationships among Butler's *The Alleys of Eden*, *Sun Dogs*, and *On Distant Ground*, which make up a trilogy about the Vietnam War.

Butler, Robert Olen. "An Interview with Robert Olen Butler." Interview by Michael Kelsay. *Poets and Writers* (January/February, 1996): 40-49. In a meaty interview, Butler discusses his life and work, addressing such topics as his distaste for being called a "Vietnam" novelist, the importance of the concrete world to the novelist, and how he came to write *A Good Scent from a Strange Mountain*. Includes some brief analyses of Butler's themes.

Diskin, Trayce. "From Tabloid to Truth: Using *Tabloid Dreams* to Inspire Powerful Fiction." *English Journal* 89, no. 4 (2000): 58-65. Uses Butler's novel as an example of connecting to emotional truths through seemingly sensational topics.

Ewell, Barbara. "*Tabloid Dreams*." *America*, May 17, 1997, 28-29. Argues that a main theme of Butler's short-story collection *Tabloid Dreams* is the problem of determining what is fakery in the modern world. Links the strangeness of the stories in the collection to the strangeness that the Vietnamese characters in *A Good Scent from a Strange Mountain* find in the United States.

Herzog, Tobey C. "Conversation with Robert Olen Butler." In *Writing Vietnam, Writing Life: Caputo, Heinemann, O'Brien, Butler*. Iowa City: University of Iowa Press, 2008. Discussion of Butler's work and life is based on two interviews Herzog conducted with Butler in October, 2005. Focuses on how the Vietnam War affected Butler's writing career.

Packer, George. "From the Mekong to the Bayous." *The New York Times Book Review*, June 7, 1992. Examines Butler's treatment of the Vietnamese in his stories, noting that for Butler, Vietnam was a place where Americans were improved and refined, learning to overcome their racism and cruelty. In contrast,

Vietnamese Americans use their folklore to interpret their exile.

Ryan, Maureen. "Robert Olen Butler's Vietnam Veterans: Strangers in an Alien Home." *Midwest Quarterly* 38, no. 3 (Spring, 1997): 274-295. Focuses on Butler's early Vietnam novels—*The Alleys of Eden*, *Sun Dogs*, and *On Distant Ground*—and argues that the shared experiences of the novels' central characters make the works a trilogy. Also examines the theme of the difficulty of Vietnam veterans' reassimilation into American life.

Schulman, Candy. "My First Novel: Good News for Unpublished Novelists." *Writer's Digest* 63 (January, 1983). Describes the early publishing experiences of eight novelists, including Butler, noting their struggles to complete and publish their first books. Informative for its view of Butler at an early point in his career, before he had achieved recognition.

SAMUEL BUTLER

Born: Langar Rectory, Nottinghamshire, England; December 4, 1835
Died: London, England; June 18, 1902

PRINCIPAL LONG FICTION

Erewhon, 1872
The Fair Haven, 1873
Erewhon Revisited, 1901
The Way of All Flesh, 1903

OTHER LITERARY FORMS

The Shrewsbury editions of Samuel Butler's works, published between 1923 and 1926, reveal the breadth of his interests. Butler's fiction was perhaps less important to him than his work in other fields, notably his theorizing on religion and evolution. He was also an art critic (*Ex Voto*, 1888; *Alps and Sanctuaries of Piedmont and the Ticino*, 1881), a literary critic (*The Authoress of the "Odyssey,"* 1897; *Shakespeare's Sonnets Reconsidered*, 1899), a letter writer, a poet, and the biographer

of his famous grandfather, Dr. Samuel Butler. An age that produces "specialists" may find Butler to be a talented dabbler or dilettante, but his unifying philosophy gives a center to all his work.

ACHIEVEMENTS

Samuel Butler was a figure of controversy during his lifetime, and perhaps his greatest achievement resides in his ability to challenge: He contended with Charles Darwin and Darwinism; he took on the established scholars of William Shakespeare, classical literature, and art; and he was part of the nineteenth century revolt against traditional religion. He approached all of these areas in such a way that his opponents could not ignore him; whether he was right or wrong, any subject benefited by his treatment, which opened it up to new and candid thought.

Of his four works that may be labeled as fiction, by far the greatest is *The Way of All Flesh*. Virginia Woolf described this novel as a seed from which many others developed—a biological image that would have pleased

Butler. In earlier novels, indifferent or cruel families had been portrayed as agents of the heroes' youthful unhappiness—witness Charles Dickens's *David Copperfield* (1849-1850, serial; 1850, book)—but in *The Way of All Flesh*, an oppressive, cruel family life becomes a theme in itself, worthy of generation-by-generation treatment.

BIOGRAPHY

Samuel Butler was born in 1835, the son of a clergyman who wished him to go into the church. After a successful career at Cambridge University, Butler prepared for a career in the clergy but found himself unable to face the prospect of that life. Letters between Butler and his father show the young man to be considering a half dozen plans at once—art, the army, cotton growing, and bookselling among them. Finally, father and son agreed that the young man should emigrate to New Zealand and try his fortune there, with Butler's father providing capital. Both father and son hoped that the experience would "settle" Butler and build his character.

Butler arrived in New Zealand in January of 1860 and remained there for four years. It was a useful time: He made money, which freed him of his family, at least financially, and he saw an unusual country that gave him a subject and setting for his later writings. New Zealand, however, was too rough a land to be his permanent home. His "hut" there was an island of comfort and civilization, where Butler devoted himself to music and study. His optimistic letters home became the basis of *A First Year in Canterbury Settlement* (1863), a book assembled and published by Butler's father.

Returning to England in 1864, Butler settled at Clifford's Inn in London, which would be his home for the rest of his life. He began to study art; his paintings had some success. He wished to do something greater, however—something that would express his developing ideas. Out of this desire grew *Erewhon*, a satire that was published anonymously in 1872 at the author's own expense. By that time, Butler was already at work on *The Fair Haven*. This book may or may not be considered fiction; it is a dispute over the validity of Christianity, but the dispute is conducted in a fictional frame.

The following year, 1873, was an important one for Butler. *The Fair Haven* was published, his mother died, he made a risky financial investment, and he began *The*

Way of All Flesh. All of these events shaped his later years. *The Fair Haven*, following on the heels of *Erewhon*, marked him as a belligerent enemy of traditional religion. His mother's death caused him some grief, but it spurred him to begin *The Way of All Flesh*, the work for which he is most remembered. That work was slowed, however, by financial troubles. Butler invested his New Zealand fortune in a Canadian venture that soon failed. He salvaged less than a quarter of his investment and had to seek help from his father. Not until 1886, when his father died, was Butler wholly free of financial pressures.

The next several years were occupied by work on evolution and religion. In 1882, Butler returned to *The Way of All Flesh*, completing it the following year. He felt, however, that the book should not be published while anyone who could be hurt by it was still alive; therefore it did not appear until a year after his own death.

In 1883, Butler began to write music. Music and music criticism were to occupy him intermittently for several years, interspersed with art criticism. The last decade of his life was filled with the study of literature, culminating in his publications on Shakespeare's sonnets and his translations of Homer's *Iliad* (1898) and *Odyssey* (1900). These works were characterized by the combativeness that to some degree sums up Butler's life. He was always the rebellious, contradictory son.

Butler's life was shaped by a number of intense relationships. His relationship with his family was unresolved; the work (*The Way of All Flesh*) that might have laid the ghosts to rest was haunted by another ghost, Butler's lifelong friend Eliza Mary Ann Savage. A fellow art student, she gave the writer friendship, friendly criticism, advice, and approval. Her own understanding of the relationship can never be known, but Butler feared she wished to marry him. His implicit rejection disturbed him deeply after her death. Other friendships were equally ambiguous. Charles Paine Pauli consumed much of Butler's attentions and resources from their first meeting in New Zealand until Pauli's death in 1897, when Butler discovered that Pauli had been supported by two other men. The perhaps sexual ambiguities of this relationship were repeated in Butler's affection for a young Swiss, Hans Faesch, and to a lesser degree in his long-lasting bonds with Henry Festing Jones and Alfred Emery Cathie. Butler's emotional makeup seems similar to that of Henry James. Both men formed passionate attachments to other men; both appreciated women more as memories than as living beings.

ANALYSIS

On his deathbed, Samuel Butler spoke of the "pretty roundness" of his career, beginning with *Erewhon* and ending, thirty years later, with *Erewhon Revisited*.

EREWHON

Erewhon must be understood first of all as a satire rather than as a novel. It is in the tradition of Jonathan Swift's *Gulliver's Travels* (1726) and Samuel Johnson's *Rasselas, Prince of Abyssinia* (1759), works that sacrifice unity and development to a vision of the writer's society in the guise of an imaginary foreign land. Like Rasselas and Gulliver, Higgs of *Erewhon* is a young man ready for adventure, out to learn about the world. He quickly reveals his image of himself as sharp, cunning, and bold. Before he tells his story, he lets the reader know the things he will hold back, so that no one reading the tale will be able to find Erewhon and thus profit financially from Higgs's exploration.

His story begins as he is working on a sheep farm in a colony, the name of which he will not reveal. Intending to find precious metals or at least good sheep-grazing land, he journeys alone inland, over a mountain range. On the other side, he finds a kingdom called Erewhon (Nowhere), which looks very much like England. Higgs's point of reference is England; all aspects of Erewhonian life he measures by that standard.

Many such satires work through the narrators' quick judgments that the new lands they encounter are either much better or much worse than their native countries: In each case, the narrator's rather simple view plays against the author's more complex perspective. In *Erewhon*, however, the narrator is not quite so naïve. His own failings, rather than his naïveté, become part of the satire, which

thus has a dual focus, much like book 4 of *Gulliver's Travels*. Higgs, like many good Victorian heroes, is out to make money. It is this prospect that motivates him most strongly. Coexisting with his desire for fortune is his religiosity. Here, Butler's satire on his character is most pronounced and simplistic. Higgs observes the Sabbath, but he seduces Yram (Mary) with no regret. He plans to make his fortune by selling the Erewhonians into slavery, arguing that they would be converted to Christianity in the process; the slaveholders would be lining their pockets and doing good simultaneously. Butler thus exposes, to no one's great surprise, the mingled piety and avarice of British colonialists.

Butler satirizes European culture through the Erewhonians more often than through his hero, Higgs, gradually unfolding their lives for the reader to observe. Their lives are, on the surface, peaceful and pleasant;

Samuel Butler. (The Granger Collection, New York)

they are a strikingly attractive race. Only through personal experience does Higgs learn the underpinnings of the society: When he is ill, he learns that illness is a crime in Erewhon, while moral lapses are regarded in the same way as illnesses are in England. When his pocket watch is discovered, he learns that all "machines" have been banned from Erewhon. Erewhonian morality is based on reversals: The morally corrupt receive sympathy, while the ill are imprisoned; a child duped by his guardian is punished for having been ignorant, while the guardian is rewarded; children are responsible for their own birth, while their parents are consoled for having been "wronged" by the unborn. This pattern of reversals is of necessity incomplete, a problem noted by reviewers of *Erewhon* in 1872.

"The Book of the Machines" is the section of the satire that has drawn the most attention, because of its relationship to Darwinian thought. It may well be, as it has often been considered, a *reductio ad absurdum* of Darwinism, but the chapter also takes on reasoning by analogy as a less complex target of satire. "The Book of the Machines" is Higgs's translation of the Erewhonian book that led to the banning of all mechanical devices. Its author claimed that machines had developed—evolved—more rapidly than humankind and thus would soon dominate, leaving humans mere slaves or parasites. He argued that machines were capable of reproduction, using humans in the process as flowers use bees. The arguments proved so convincing that all machines in Erewhon were soon destroyed, leaving the country in the rather primitive state in which Higgs found it.

The purpose of "The Book of the Machines" becomes clearer in the following two chapters, which detail Erewhonian debates on the rights of animals and the rights of vegetables. At one point in the past, insistence on the rights of animals had turned Erewhon into a land of vegetarians, but the philosophers went a step further and decreed that vegetables, too, had rights, based on their evolving consciousness. Again, Butler plays with argument by analogy, as the philosophers compare the vegetables' intelligence to that of a human embryo.

The Erewhonians who believed in the rights of vegetables were led nearly to starvation by their extremism, and it is this same extremism that causes Higgs to leave Erewhon. Fearful that disfavor is growing against his foreign presence, he plans to escape by balloon, taking with him his beloved Arowhena. The perilous escape takes place, and the hero, married to Arowhena and restored to England, becomes a fairly successful hack writer. His account of Erewhon, he says at the end, constitutes an appeal for subscriptions to finance his scheme to return to Erewhon.

EREWHON REVISITED

The broad, traditional satire of *Erewhon* is abandoned in its sequel. Written years later, *Erewhon Revisited* reflects the maturity of its author, then in his sixties. In the later work, Butler treats Erewhon as a habitation of human beings, not satiric simplifications. *Erewhon Revisited* is thus a novel, not a satire; its focus is on human relationships. Butler had already written (though not published) *The Way of All Flesh*, and the preoccupations of that work are also evident in *Erewhon Revisited*. Both works grew out of Butler's fascination with family relationships, especially those between father and son.

The narrator of *Erewhon Revisited* is John Higgs, the son of George Higgs and Arowhena. He tells of his mother's early death and of his father's desire to return to Erewhon. This time, however, Higgs's desire is sentimental; he has grown past his earlier wish to profit from the Erewhonians. He goes to Erewhon, returns in ill health, tells the story of his adventure to John, and dies. The book in this way becomes John's tribute to his father.

Although *Erewhon Revisited* may be identified as a novel rather than as a satire, it does have a satiric subject as part of its plot. Upon reentering Erewhon, Higgs discovers that his ascent by balloon has become the source of a new religion. The Erewhonians revere his memory and worship him as the "Sun Child." Higgs is horrified to find that there are theologians of Sunchildism fighting heretics. Unfortunately, Sunchildism has not made the Erewhonians a better or kinder people. Here is the heart of Butler's satire: that a religion based on a supernatural event will divide people, place power in the wrong hands, and humiliate reason.

In *Erewhon*, Higgs was a pious and hypocritical prig, a target of satire himself. In the sequel, he is a genial, loving humanist, appalled by the "evolution" of his frantic escape into the ascent of a god. Much of *Erewhon Re-*

visited develops his plans to deflate Sunchildism, to reveal himself as the "Sun Child" and tell the truth about his "ascent."

Higgs has a special motive that transcends his disgust with Sunchildism. Upon arriving in Erewhon, he meets a young man whom he soon recognizes as his own son, a son he did not know he had. The young man is the product of Higgs's brief romance with Yram, the jailer's daughter. Higgs keeps his identity from his son (also named George) for a while, but eventually the two are revealed to each other in a touching and intense scene. To earn his newfound son's respect, Higgs determines to deflate Sunchildism. Thus, the process of satire in *Erewhon Revisited* is rooted in its human relationships.

Higgs's son John, the narrator of the novel, feels no jealousy toward his half brother. Instead, he shares the elder Higgs's enthusiasm for young George. Following his father's death, John goes to Erewhon himself to meet George and to deliver a large gift of gold to him. This legacy exemplified one of Butler's tenets about parent-child relations: that the best parents are kind, mostly absent, and very free with money. This theme is repeated throughout *The Way of All Flesh*. In *Erewhon Revisited*, however, it has a simpler expression. The relationship of Higgs and his two sons forms the emotional center of the novel and creates the impetus for some of its plot, but it is distinct from the satire on religion that makes up much of the book.

THE FAIR HAVEN

It is fitting that Butler's last work, *Erewhon Revisited*, should have presented a genial hero determined to strip away what he saw as ridiculous supernatural beliefs. Much of "Sunchildism" is a response to the religious foment of the nineteenth century with which Butler had begun contending early in his career. *The Fair Haven* was his first satire concerned with Christian belief. This work is "fiction" only in a very limited sense: Butler creates a persona, John Pickard Owen, whose arguments in favor of Christianity are in fact the vehicle for Butler's satire against it. *The Fair Haven* begins with a fictional memoir of John Pickard Owen by his brother. The memoir reveals that Owen moved from faith to disbelief to faith, and that his efforts to prove the validity of his religion pushed him to mental exhaustion and, eventually, death.

THE WAY OF ALL FLESH

The characters of *The Fair Haven* are forerunners of the Pontifex family in *The Way of All Flesh*, Butler's fullest and most characteristic work. *The Way of All Flesh* encompasses all of Butler's concerns: family life, money, sexual attitudes, class structure, religion, and art. This novel too is a satire, but in it Butler does not portray an Erewhon; much more disturbingly, he keeps the reader at home.

The Way of All Flesh is Ernest Pontifex's story, but it does not begin with Ernest. Butler the evolutionist shows Ernest as the product of several generations of social changes and personal tensions. The genealogical background, as well as the title and biblical epigraph, "We know that all things work together for good to them that love God," helps to create the ironic treatment of religion that will permeate the novel. What is the way of all flesh? The biblical echo suggests sin and decay; Butler's fiction, however, reminds the reader that the way of all flesh is change, for better or worse.

Ernest is the product of three generations of upward mobility. His great-grandfather is a simple, kind craftsman who sends his only son into the city. The son, George Pontifex, becomes successful as a publisher and even more successful as a bully. He chooses the Church as a career for his second son, Theobald, who revolts briefly, then acquiesces and evolves into the image of his father. Butler is careful to show personalities as products of environment. George's bullying is only that of an egotistical, self-made man; Theobald's is more harsh, the product of his own fear and suppressed anger. The unfortunate object of this anger is Theobald's firstborn son, Ernest Pontifex.

Ernest's childhood is dominated by fear of his father. His mother, Christina, is of little help; Butler portrays her as the product of her own family life and the larger social system, both of which make marriage a necessity for her. Like Theobald, Christina becomes a hypocrite pressed into the service of "what is done." Much later in life, Ernest reflects that the family is a painful anachronism, confined in nature to the lower species. His opinion is shared by Overton, the narrator of the novel, an old family friend who takes an interest in young Ernest and becomes his lifelong friend and adviser. The two of them, in fact, eventually come to constitute a kind of family—an evolved, freely chosen family, not one formed by mere biological ties.

This outcome occurs only after long agony on Ernest's part. As a child, he believes all that is told: that he is, for example, a wicked, ungrateful boy who deserves Theobald's frequent beatings. His young life is lightened, however, by the interest taken in him by his aunt Alethea and by Overton, who has known all of the Pontifexes well and who tells their story with compassion.

Ernest is still an innocent and unformed young man when he goes to Cambridge to prepare for a career in the Church. Near the end of his peaceful, happy years there, he comes under the influence of an Evangelical group that alters his perceptions of what his life as a clergyman ought to be. Instead of stepping into a pleasant rural parish, Ernest becomes a missionary in the slums of London. He falls under the spell of the oily clergyman Nicholas Pryor, who "invests" Ernest's money and eventually absconds with it. Pryor, the Cambridge enthusiasts, and Theobald Pontifex all represent the clerical life; they are radically different kinds of people, and they are all portrayed negatively. Butler took no prisoners in his war on the clergy; his use of the genial Overton as a narrator partially masks this characteristic.

Sexual ignorance, imposed (and shared) by Theobald and his kind, provides Butler with his next target for satire. In despair over his religious life, Ernest seeks a prostitute and approaches the wrong woman, the eponymous Miss Snow. Ernest's ignorance lands him in prison and cuts him off forever from mere gentility. It redeems him, however, from a life circumscribed by his father: Ironically, Theobald's strict control over Ernest liberates Ernest at last. In prison, stripped of all his former identity, Ernest begins to come to terms with what his life has been and may be. A long illness serves to clarify his mind; he rejects traditional religion, society, and his family's condescending offers of help. Overton alone stands by Ernest, and it is at this point in Ernest's development that they become fast friends. Overton takes on the role of the ideal father—fond, genteel, and moneyed.

It is in this last area that Overton's role is most important to the events of the book: He keeps Alethea's substantial bequest in trust for Ernest, allowing him knowledge of it and access to it, according to Alethea's wish, only when he judges that Ernest is prepared to use it wisely. Ernest's ill-advised marriage and his decision to work as a tailor cause Overton to hold the money back. Eventually, Ernest's maturity evolves to a level acceptable to Overton, and the two of them lead a pleasant life of wealth and, on Ernest's side at least, accomplishment: He has become a writer who, like Butler, writes thoughtful, theoretical books.

In his role as a father, Ernest also has evolved. The children of his marriage to Ellen are reared by simple country people and grow up free of the pressures of Ernest's childhood. After four generations, the Pontifexes have returned to the peaceful and happy life of Ernest's great-grandfather.

Liberal amounts of money, however, keep Ernest's son and daughter from any want that ordinary country folk might experience. Ernest's son wants to be a riverboat captain: Ernest buys him riverboats. This scenario is nearly as idealized a version of country life as was Marie Antoinette's. What makes this vision disconcerting is that Ernest's attitudes are clearly shared by Butler. Early in the novel, Ernest the bullied child is the object of the reader's pity. As a student and young cleric, he has experiences that create a sense of pity but also create humor. The more fully Ernest evolves, however, the less appealing the reader is likely to find him. The Ernest who finally comes into his aunt's fortune is a rather dull prig, who, upon learning of his wealth, considers how his emotion might be rendered in music. He tells Overton that he regrets nothing—not his parents' brutality, not prison—because everything has contributed to his evolution away from the "swindle" of middle-class expectations. Unfortunately, this self-satisfied view makes his character seem shallow, consisting only of words and affectations.

In spite of this problem, Butler's achievement is considerable. *The Way of All Flesh* is an immensely ambitious book, and much of it succeeds. Butler articulates fully and convincingly the varied stresses of family life, and that aspect alone makes the novel worthwhile. *Erewhon* and *Erewhon Revisited* share some of that evocative power. They also express Butler's optimism. For all his satiric vision and contentiousness, Butler does offer happy endings: Higgs's successful escape from

Erewhon with his beloved, the reunion of the brothers in *Erewhon Revisited*, and the pleasant life of Ernest and Overton in *The Way of All Flesh*. Though societies may often be in the wrong, Butler seems to tell the reader, there is hope in freely chosen human relationships.

Deborah Core

OTHER MAJOR WORKS

NONFICTION: *A First Year in Canterbury Settlement*, 1863; *Life and Habit*, 1877; *Evolution, Old and New*, 1879; *God the Known and God the Unknown*, 1879; *Unconscious Memory*, 1880; *Alps and Sanctuaries of Piedmont and the Ticino*, 1881; *A Psalm of Montreal*, 1884; *Luck or Cunning*, 1887; *Ex Voto*, 1888; *The Life and Letters of Dr. Samuel Butler*, 1896; *The Authoress of the "Odyssey,"* 1897; *Shakespeare's Sonnets Reconsidered*, 1899; *The Note-books*, 1912 (H. Festing Jones, editor).

TRANSLATIONS: *Iliad*, 1898 (of Homer's epic poem); *Odyssey*, 1900 (of Homer's epic poem).

BIBLIOGRAPHY

Bekker, Willem Gerard. *An Historical and Critical Review of Samuel Butler's Literary Works*. 1925. Reprint. New York: Russell & Russell, 1964. Full-length study of Butler written by a native of Holland, where *Erewhon* found popularity and immediate acceptance. Bekker argues for the unity in Butler's works.

Daniels, Anthony. "Butler's Unhappy Youth." *New Criterion* 23, no. 5 (January, 2005): 11-17. Discusses *The Way of All Flesh*, Butler's autobiographical novel, arguing that it may be the most devastating literary assault on a father ever written by a son. Describes how Butler's father, Thomas, and the father in the novel, Theobald Pontifex, stand accused of committing odious acts.

Henderson, Philip. *Samuel Butler: The Incarnate Bachelor*. 1954. Reprint. New York: Barnes & Noble Books, 1968. Readable and illuminating work is one of the best biographies of Butler available. Focuses on his personality rather than his work, and argues against the prevailing view that Butler hated his father. Includes a detailed chronology.

Holt, Lee E. *Samuel Butler*. Rev. ed. Boston: Twayne, 1989. Provides a good introduction to Butler and his writings. Includes chapters on Butler's major fiction, a chronology, and an annotated bibliography.

Jeffers, Thomas L. *Samuel Butler Revalued*. University Park: Pennsylvania State University Press, 1981. An appreciation rather than a panegyric, this critical study focuses on *The Way of All Flesh* because it was composed during the period when Butler thought most creatively about evolution, his religion, and his family. Contains lengthy notes, a selected bibliography, and an index.

Jones, H. F. *Samuel Butler, Author of "Erewhon" (1835-1902): A Memoir*. 2 vols. 1919. Reprint. New York: Octagon Books, 1968. Remains the standard biography, presenting a wealth of detail about the events of Butler's life, his personal characteristics, and the creation and reception of his literary works.

Paradis, James G., ed. *Samuel Butler, Victorian Against the Grain: A Critical Overview*. Toronto, Ont.: University of Toronto Press, 2007. Collection of essays includes discussions of Butler's views on evolution, the relationship between evolutionary psychology and *The Way of All Flesh*, Butler's bachelorhood, his travel writing, and his photography.

Parrinder, Patrick. "Entering Dystopia, Entering Erewhon." *Critical Survey* 17, no.1 (2005): 6-21. Describes the characteristics of dystopian romances written in the late Victorian era, focusing on the representations of dystopia in *Erewhon* and W. H. Hudson's *A Crystal Age* (1887).

Raby, Peter. *Samuel Butler: A Biography*. Iowa City: University of Iowa Press, 1991. Comprehensive, scholarly biography intelligently recounts the details of Butler's personal life and career. Includes detailed notes, bibliography, photographs, and drawings.

MICHEL BUTOR

Born: Mons-en-Baroeul, Lille, France;
    September 14, 1926
Also known as: Michel Marie François Butor

PRINCIPAL LONG FICTION

Passage de Milan, 1954
L'Emploi du temps, 1956 (*Passing Time*,
    1960)
La Modification, 1957 (*Second Thoughts*, 1958;
    better known as *A Change of Heart*)
Degrés, 1960 (*Degrees*, 1961)
*6,810,000 litres d'eau par seconde: Étude
    stéréophonique*, 1965 (*Niagara: A
    Stereophonic Novel*, 1969)
Intervalle, 1973
Matière de rêves, 1975
Second sous-sol: Matière de rêves 2, 1976
Troisième dessous: Matière de rêves 3, 1977
Explorations, 1981 (includes verse)
Quadruple fond: Matière de rêves 4, 1981
Mille et un plis: Matière de rêves 5, 1985

OTHER LITERARY FORMS

Although Michel Butor (bew-TOR) first gained literary recognition as a novelist—his fame outside France still rests chiefly upon his New Novels—he has explored and experimented with several other forms and has (beginning with *Mobile: Étude pour une représentation des États-Unis* in 1962; *Mobile: Study for a Representation of the United States*, 1963) gone well beyond the novel in his long narratives. Butor's poetry, some of which dates from the 1940's, has evolved from his "Homage à Max Ernst" of 1945 and his "irrationalistic" poetry through prose poems and essay poems such as *La Rose des vents: 32 rhumbs pour Charles Fourier* (1970) and *Dialogue avec 33 variations de Ludwig van Beethoven sur une valse de Diabelli* (1971) to his Don Juan poems of the mid-1970's, a series of texts printed on punched cards that can be shuffled and then read in any sequence. Other principal collections of poetry include *Travaux d'approche* (1972) and the poems and graphics of *Illustrations I-IV* (1964-1976).

A prodigious essayist, Butor turned out several pieces every year. His first volume of essays, *Le Génie du lieu* (1958; *The Spirit of Mediterranean Places*, 1986), which could also be classified as an autobiographical prose poem on the order of *Portrait de l'artiste en jeune singe: Capriccio* (1967; *Portrait of the Artist as a Young Ape: A Caprice*, 1995), was followed by *Répertoire I-V* (1960-1982; partial translation of volumes 1-3 as *Inventory*, 1968), *Description de San Marco* (1963), *Essais sur "les essais"* (1968), and *Où: Le Génie du lieu 2* (1971). It is difficult to classify this last work as an essay in the traditional sense, because it has much in common with other of Butor's volumes of essay poems.

Indeed, classification is a major difficulty in any discussion of Butor. His *Réseau aérien: Texte radiophonique* (1962), for example, is a radio drama that is not unlike a spoken version of a poetic novel, and it may work more effectively if read successively than if heard. His foray into the dramatic form of opera in *Votre Faust: Fantaisie variable genre opéra* (pb. 1962), which was written in collaboration with Henri Pousseur, is a provisional and experimental work that calls for further collaboration from an audience that must vote on which of the multiple versions of a scene will follow the scene in which they have just collaborated.

By far the most elusive of his works are the long narratives, which some have called novels and others term "postnovels." *Mobile* is the first of these works and represents a forty-eight-hour alphabetical odyssey through the fifty United States. *6,810,000 Litres d'eau par seconde* (1965) and *Boomerang: Le Génie du lieu 3*, 1978 (partial translation as *Letters from the Antipodes*, 1981) are comparable to *Mobile* in method (collage) and scope of ambition. *6,810,000 Litres d'eau par seconde*, translated as *Niagara* in 1969, has for its ostensible subject the modern American pilgrimage site, Niagara Falls, and its modern pilgrims; the latter work is a panoramic spiritual travelogue of the South Pacific. *Intervalle* (1973), which is closer to being a novel than are any of these other narratives, contains interesting and significant parallels with *A Change of Heart*.

ACHIEVEMENTS

Michel Butor has won international recognition as a novelist, poet, essayist, and lecturer and as a bold and versatile experimenter with literary form. His reputation first rested upon and remains largely connected with his efforts of the 1950's in the experimental novel, *le nouveau roman*, or New Novel. As early as 1960, Jean-Paul Sartre accorded him extraordinarily high praise: "There is today, in France, someone who has the ambition to become and every chance of becoming a great writer. The first since 1945: Butor." More than twenty years later, Butor has validated Sartre's judgment; by the time Sartre recognized Butor's achievement and potential, Butor had already gained considerable notice. In 1957, he received the Prix Fénelon for *Passing Time* and the Prix Théophraste-Renaudot for *A Change of Heart*. In 1960, he received the Grand Prix de la Critique Littéraire for *Répertoire, I*. By the mid-1960's, his novels were already included on reading lists in the undergraduate curricula of some American universities.

A prolific literary theorist and critic, Butor earned the doctorate in 1973 for his defense of his own critical work. He has lectured extensively throughout the world and has held a variety of academic positions in numerous institutions, including Bryn Mawr College, Middlebury College, the State University of New York at Buffalo, the University of New Mexico, and the universities of Geneva (Switzerland), Manchester (England), Nice (France), and Vincennes (France). One measure of Butor's literary achievement is the growing list of monographs and critical volumes and the increasingly large number of essays on his work included each year in the *MLA International Bibliography*.

BIOGRAPHY

Born on September 14, 1926, at Mons-en-Baroeul, a suburb of Lille, Michel Butor is the eldest son and fourth of the eight children of Émile Butor and Anne (Brajeux) Butor. The family moved to Paris in 1929, and Butor began his education in the 1930's in Parisian Catholic schools. At the onset of World War II in 1939, the Butors moved temporarily to Évreux, then to Pau and Tarbes, before returning to Paris in August, 1940; there Butor remained as a student until 1949. His education at the Lycée Louis-le-Grand was followed by studies at the Sorbonne, first in literature and then in philosophy, where he achieved both the *license* and *diplôme d'études supérieures* in philosophy but failed to qualify for the *agrégation*. In 1950, having written some poetry and a few essays, he traveled to Germany (a journey he later commemorated in *Portrait de l'artiste en jeune singe*), taught at the *lycée* in Sens, and then taught French at El Minya in Upper Egypt. His Egyptian experience as well as his teaching experience is echoed in much of his writing and is an important element in *Passage de Milan* (which he began writing in Egypt), in *Degrees*, and, to a lesser extent, in *Passing Time*.

Michel Butor. (AFP/Getty Images)

Butor's career as an itinerant teacher, scholar, and writer, begun in 1950, found him teaching in Manchester in 1951 (a model for Bleston in *Passing Time*), where he finished *Passage de Milan*, and traveling to Tunisia, Algeria, Italy, and Greece, with frequent returns to Paris. In 1955, he replaced Roland Barthes at the Sorbonne in the training program for French teachers abroad. In 1957, he took up a teaching position in Geneva, where he met Marie-Joséphe Mas, whom he married in 1958. In the same year, he became an advisory editor at the publishing house of Gallimard, and in 1959, with three novels and numerous essays in print, he began writing *Degrees*, a novel that he informed with elements of his own experience as a teacher and a teacher of teachers as well as with his own youthful experience. Butor has written varied critical essays and appreciations on literature and the arts, created long prose-poetic narratives (many of them based on his travels), and turned to operatic, graphic, and cinematic ventures.

ANALYSIS

Any consideration of Michel Butor as a novelist, as incomplete and misleading as that title may be, must begin with the subgenre that he helped establish in the 1950's and that he later transcended. With Alain Robbe-Grillet (who later repudiated Butor), Robert Pinget, Nathalie Sarraute, and Claude Simon, Butor was a chief proponent and practitioner of the New Novel. The New Novel unquestionably owes debts to the work of Marcel Proust, James Joyce, Virginia Woolf, and William Faulkner, yet the form was truly a new one in the hands of the New Novelists—it became their own.

As Michael Spencer pithily summarizes the form in his *Michel Butor* (1974), the work of the New Novelists "are essentially a *mise en question* of a complicated and unstable world, owing a good deal to the descriptive philosophy of phenomenology. In the course of this questioning, most of the features of the traditional novel are discarded." Chronology, for example, is discontinuous and highly subjective; the protagonist is often uninteresting; action, in the usual sense of plot, is minimal and is generally replaced by reminiscences and interior monologues that reflect, in their lack of ostensible and actual coherence, the incoherence of the world in question. "One very important consequence," Spencer continues,

"is that the reader tends to become involved in the creation of some kind of novel from the unassembled elements, 'fictional' or 'real,' with which he is confronted."

The New Novel, especially according to Butor, also emphasizes structure; Butor differs from his companion novelists in that his works contain a didacticism that occupies a middle ground between the *littérature engagée* espoused by more existential writers and an aestheticism that posits art for art's sake, structure for its own sake. Butor offers, in his novels and elsewhere, a possibility that language can reorder one's experience of reality and thus transform reality itself: To the extent that Butor succeeds in diagnosing (and thus producing inchoate remedies for) the linguistic disorder that is characteristic of the modern age, his fiction is exemplary and has the social efficacy Spencer rightly attributes to it.

While to call Butor a novelist is to overlook the bulk of his work and to neglect his pioneering work in transcending the novel, the designation aptly applies to the Butor of 1954 to 1960. In that period, he wrote some of the finest novels that have appeared in postwar France, notably *Passing Time* and *A Change of Heart*. Of his two other novels, *Passage de Milan* remains untranslated, and *Degrees*, despite the enthusiasm Leon Roudiez expressed for it in his *Michel Butor*, may not pass the test of time. All four novels display Butor's concern for place (location) and situation; for time and the ability as well as the inability of language to capture, restore, refract, and use time; for the role of the novel itself (most clearly exemplified in *Passing Time* and *Degrees*) as what Spencer calls an "intermediary between the writer and the outside world"; and for the concatenations of history and mythology as they inform contemporary consciousness, the dominant themes and real subjects that the novels treat.

PASSAGE DE MILAN

Passage de Milan, Butor's first novel, adumbrates the manifold elements that permeate his later work, reveals some of his ethical concerns, and demonstrates his adeptness in a new aesthetic structure with which he became identified. The work's title provides an entry to an initial appreciation of the novel's subject and aims. As a street name, *Passage de Milan* may denote an alley named after the Italian city; in another sense, it may mean the flight of a bird of prey, a kite, the hieratic bird of Egypt identified with the god Horus. The principal character in the novel is none of the many highly individualized residents of the building that sits squarely on the pages of the work; rather, it is the building itself. As the building and its life through its inhabitants dominate the novel, so the ordinary components of fiction, such as plot and subplot, are overshadowed by the structure of the work, the relational way in which the occupants—their thoughts, utterances, actions, and rituals—contribute to the totality of a portrait that is necessarily incomplete.

The priest who opens the novel, Father Jean Ralon, is an Egyptologist whose studies have led him to a loss of Christian faith and an apostasy that informs the general bad faith of his existence. The first line of the work presents him as he looks outward, leaning out his window. What he sees is a cityscape at dusk and, focused in the foreground, a small, mysterious tract of wasteland, a vacant lot that contains a junk pile, the contents of which are changed and moved by an unseen owner. This exterior wasteland mirrors the interior wastelands of the building and the tenants of this house. As the wasteland of the vacant lot is a microcosm of the life in the building, so the building is a microcosm of the unreal city to which it belongs.

A large element in the lives of the inhabitants of this building is ritual, but their rituals separate and insulate rather than unite them. The mundane rituals of daily homecoming and the larger ritual of a coming-out party for Angèle Vertigues reinforce the quiet desperation of their lives. The larger natural rituals of day passing into night and back into itself (the novel begins at 7:00 P.M. and ends, twelve chapters later, at 7:00 A.M.) and of the seasons passing from winter to spring, both overshadowed by the passing of the kite, hold a generative hope for rebirth of day and of season that underlines a greater human ritual of passage from a kingdom of the dead (the building) to a place outside the building and the city—to Egypt—for the young orphan Louis Lécuyer, who inadvertently causes the death of the vertiginous Angèle.

One important key to the work and to Butor's structural agenda for the novel, a key that he is less than subtle in presenting, is the unfinished painting by Martin deVere. The painting of a "house" (of cards) is divided into twelve squares (as the novel is divided into twelve hours/chapters) arranged in three rows of four. Each square contains groups of symbols representing objects: The top and bottom rows contain four cards per square; the middle row contains five cards per square. Analogies and suggestions about identifying one or another of the characters with particular cards (Angèle as the Queen of Hearts, Louis as the Knave of Clubs, and Delétang as the Ace of Spades, for example) reinforce the structural relationship among the cards in the "house" and the inhabitants in the building. The destruction of the painting by fire, at the exact center of the novel, foreshadows a larger destruction, Angèle's death and the concomitant end to the building's undisturbed life.

Another key to the work lies in the multiple references to music found in deVere's theory of composition and his comments on his unfinished painting, in the dance given for Angèle, and in the choreographed moves and countermoves of the building's tenants that form a counterpoint. A third key is the extended discussion of the prophetic novel in Samuel Léonard's flat by a group of would-be writers. Here, the issue of writing in, about, and beyond the past and present comments directly upon the novel itself, the writer's task as archaeologist, and the scope and limitations of language.

PASSING TIME

All the themes of *Passage de Milan* come together in Butor's startling, intricate, dense, and possibly best novel, *Passing Time*. Set in the fictional city of Bleston (an industrial city in the North of England) beset by virtually unrelenting rain, the accumulated grime of more than a century of industrialization, and the unrelieved foreboding of a creeping tyranny of place over person, the novel examines time, its uses and its imprisoning effects (both spiritual and psychological), and the necessary role of literature and myth as means of passing time, in several senses. Time—history, one's own past, the fleeting passage of time, the inability to recapture fully lost time, the submergence and loss of the present in attempts to reconstruct the past—is the archvillain just as surely as Bleston is a villain in the work. Jacques Revel's quest for himself, then, is a quest bounded by the spirit of the place and by time. It is not without mythic significance that he undertakes to remain in Bleston for a year but does so, in a traditional phrase, for a year and a day: The February following his October arrival has twenty-nine days; he is there in a leap year.

From the time of his arrival in Bleston, behind schedule and between midnight and 2:00 A.M. on October 1, until and surely after he begins writing his diary on May 1, Revel is beset by Bleston, its customs, its history, its people, and the burden of its mysteries, not the least of which is its topography. Revel recalls himself lost in Bleston's labyrinth as the novel opens; as he reconstructs his October experience in May, he pictures himself becoming increasingly bewildered as he falls under the spell of Bleston. His relief from the debilitating spell is to keep a diary that re-creates his past in Bleston and that also seeks to do more than that: The act of writing itself becomes both a salvific release from the labyrinth and a snare that imprisons him in a past—with the difference that this past is one he himself creates and that he lets go the instant he leaves Bleston. This is how Revel passes the time of his confinement, schedules his past and his present, and explores the relationship of the present Jacques Revel to the past Jacques Revel on the time line of his memory.

The work's title helps untangle some of the issues involved in the diary and the act of ordering one's past and present. Although *L'Emploi du temps* is translated as *Passing Time* (here it may mean the act of whiling away time, "killing time," the time it takes to pass the year, the duration of passage, or the act of overtaking time), it may also be translated as "the schedule" and, with slight modification (from *du* to *de*), recalls the familiar linguistic construct of conjugations that explains temporality.

The limited action of the novel comprises a series of events: meetings with Bleston's natives and two other foreigners (Horace Buck, the black pyromaniac, and Revel's countryman, Lucien Blaise, who will be assimilated into Bleston through marriage); disappointed romances with the Bailey sisters, Ann and Rose; encounters with "J. C. Hamilton" (George Burton), whose novel *Le Meurtre de Bleston* (*The Bleston Murder*, better translated as "the murder of Bleston") is central to Butor's novel; and his dealings with James Jenkins. Within the novel are Burton's detective story, the incomplete detective story of Revel attempting to identify Burton's assailant, the mythic stories of detection in the tales of Oedipus and Theseus, and the mysterious fires and the revelations of various identities—not the least of which

comes in Revel's imperfect quest for his own identity, an identity that does not make him a modern Theseus/Cain/Oedipus except suggestively; his enterprise of finding his way about the labyrinth is made possible by literacy (maps, guidebooks), by guarded reliance upon James, Ann, Rose, and Burton, and by the use of language as he literally writes his way out of Bleston. The main action of the work, however, is the linguistic activity of the narrator-writer Revel, who recounts the events of the year and a day during which he worked for the firm of Matthews and Sons.

Structurally, the work is divided into five parts, like a classical French tragedy, each part corresponding to a month in which portions of the narrative are written. The diary is begun on May 1 with its subject the preceding October; no exact day-to-day correspondence exists— Revel rarely writes on weekends and often takes several evenings to relate the events of a single day. By June, the format has expanded to include not only November but also June; in July, Revel writes of December, May, and July; the progression of months included increases until in September he writes of September present and September days immediately past, February, March, July, and August, including references to every other month as he reads and rereads the pages written in previous months, so that the constantly repeated events all coalesce in the final chapter.

Each chapter of a month's narration is further subdivided into five subsections, each of approximately a five-day span. Yet the very structure Revel chooses (and Butor chooses for his character) is self-defeating, as the present modifies the past, as today's revelations alter one's perspectives on yesterday's or last month's, and as new information forces a revaluation of the seemingly unimportant events of, say, last December, so that a rewriting or revision of something written in July must be done in September. On a larger, historical or mythological, level, the problem becomes even more unmanageable than Revel's inability to write about his own life. This, indeed, is the burden of the last sentence of the Johannine Gospel, the author of which also dealt in Revelation. Condemned to spend his last five months in Bleston recalling the first seven and coping with the unfolding moments of the five, Revel leaves the place of his exile, confinement, and adventure, regretting that he has not the time, according to his own timetable and the railway schedule, to set down something that seemed very important and that he will forget—an event that occurred on the symbolic extra day, February 29. (While February 29 is temporally an extra day, medieval English law made February 28 and 29 count as one day for legal purposes.)

A CHANGE OF HEART

In *A Change of Heart*, Butor is again probing the interrelationships of the past and present as Leon Delmont travels on the Paris-to-Rome train. Unlike Butor's first two novels, this one does not contain a highly articulated system of symbolic references; rather, it is focused on the single action of one man, from the time he enters his compartment at Paris until he leaves it in Rome. Delmont's purpose in journeying from his wife and children in Paris to his mistress, Cécile, in Rome is to bring Cécile back to Paris, establish her in a job, and move in with her once he has abandoned his wife. Events, people, noises, and objects on the train conspire to lead him to the overwhelming conclusion that he cannot accomplish his plan: He will pass the time in Rome alone. In this regard, at least, the novel's subject becomes a study in the phenomenology of perception. This modification, this slight change of heart, is at the core of a novel that probes a life lived in bad faith: Delmont's decision not to change his life—to return to Paris, wife, family, and job without Cécile—is an authentic decision by which he affirms his true situation, as imperfect and unpalatable as that situation is to him; he ratifies the bad faith in which he lives and, ironically, ennobles himself.

Butor's technique of second-person narration owes much to Faulkner; his handling of the narrative is, however, his own, complete with seven temporal layers. In both brief and inordinately extended sentences, the narrator builds a case against himself as if he were speaking to a second party. In one sense, he is doing so: The narrator is writing the book he thinks of writing at the novel's end. In *A Change of Heart*, the Bleston of *Passing Time* is replaced by Rome, and Theseus is replaced by Aeneas and by the Great Huntsman. The Eternal City holds a fascination for Delmont and a power over him that draws him irresistibly to it, affecting both his conscious life (it is the site of his firm's home office) and his subconscious: He loves the Roman Cécile, for example, and his hallucinatory dreams center on the mythology, history, and literature of Imperial Rome.

DEGREES

Degrees has unquestionable importance in Butor's canon as a work that carries on the thematic concerns and structural preoccupations of Butor's first three novels. It does, however, take the boring commonplaces in parts of the earlier novels to greater lengths, so that one overall effect of *Degrees* is a boredom many readers feel palpably. Pierre Vernier conceives an extraordinary project for himself and sets himself the task of reproducing exactly the thoughts, feelings, words, actions, and intentions of one history lesson in the Lycée Taine on October 12, 1954, and then of expanding his work to include the entire "mental space" of the students and all of their teachers. This obsessive ordering of experience—like Jacques Revel's, only more intense—results in Vernier's alienation from his prospective wife and, ultimately, in his own death.

The novel's two primary themes—the inability to learn the lessons of history and the inutility and inappropriateness of contemporary education and its fragmented, decentered approach to learning—are partially reflected in Vernier's own inability to learn or understand that the writing of history is, as nineteenth century historians and particularly Jules Michelet understood, a process of selection rather than exhaustion. Vernier's is an assemblage of fragments from classes, speeches, and literary and historical sources in the rag-and-bone shop of his own mind. His obsession with history places him out of his own time as he occupies himself with reconstructing a period from October, 1952, to January, 1955, in the time between October 12, 1954, and the end of 1955. For all of his efforts, Vernier has gathered only a very small amount of information by using a particular method of inquiry (not unlike that of a dime-store detective) that is unworkable and unsuited to his purpose.

For the general reader, and for many specialists as well, *Degrees* is the least satisfying and least satisfactory of Butor's novels, *A Change of Heart* the most apparently accessible, *Passing Time* the most intricate and intellectually satisfying, and *Passage de Milan* somewhere between the latter two. Butor's novels stand as undoubted literary monuments of the mid-twentieth century, monuments that capture the despairing optimism of the 1950's in France and elsewhere—the flawed, decentered experience of a fragmented world in which, by an effort to arrange and rearrange the fragments Western humankind has shored against its ruins, some sense of the mind reflecting upon itself, aware of its necessary failures and made aware of possible exemplary failures, emerges and waits to be reborn. Butor's novelistic achievement has both won him a deserved place of prominence in current literature and prepared him for his continuing eminence.

John J. Conlon

OTHER MAJOR WORKS

POETRY: *La Rose des vents: 32 rhumbs pour Charles Fourier*, 1970; *Dialogue avec 33 variations de Ludwig van Beethoven sur une valse de Diabelli*, 1971; *Travaux d'approche*, 1972; *Envois*, 1980; *Exprès*, 1983; *Chantier*, 1985; *À la frontière*, 1996; *Appel: Suite pour un violoncelle en détresse*, 2000; *Collation: Précédé de hors-d'oeuvre, scandé par les souvenirs illusoires d'un Japon très ancien*, 2003.

PLAY: *Votre Faust: Fantaisie variable genre opéra*, pb. 1962 (with Henri Pousseur).

RADIO PLAY: *Réseau aérien: Texte radiophonique*, 1962.

NONFICTION: *Le Génie du lieu*, 1958 (*The Spirit of Mediterranean Places*, 1986); *Répertoire I-V*, 1960-1982 (5 volumes; partial translation of volumes 1-3 as *Inventory*, 1968); *Histoire extraordinaire: Essai sur un rêve de Baudelaire*, 1961 (*Histoire Extraordinaire: Essay on a Dream of Baudelaire*, 1969); *Mobile: Étude pour une représentation des États-Unis*, 1962 (*Mobile: Study for a Representation of the United States*, 1963); *Description de San Marco*, 1963; *Essais sur les modernes*, 1964; *Illustrations I-V*, 1964-1976 (4 volumes); *Portrait de l'artiste en jeune singe: Capriccio*, 1967 (*Portrait of the Artist as a Young Ape: A Caprice*, 1995); *Essais sur "les essais,"* 1968; *Essais sur le roman*, 1969; *Les Mots dans la peinture*, 1969; *Où: Le Génie du lieu 2*, 1971; *Boomerang: Le Génie du lieu 3*, 1978 (partial translation as *Letters from the Antipodes*, 1981); *Résistances*, 1983 (with Michel Launay); *Frontières*, 1985 (*Frontiers*, 1989); *Improvisations sur Rimbaud*, 1989; *Transit: Le Génie du lieu 4*, 1992; *Improvisations sur Michel Butor*, 1993 (*Improvisations on*

Butor: Transformation of Writing, 1996; Lois Oppenheim, editor); *Parure*, 1994 (*Ethnic Jewelry: Africa, Asia, and the Pacific*, 1994; with photography by Pierre-Alain Ferrazzini); *Le Japon depuis la France: Un Rêve à l'ancre*, 1995; *Gyroscope: Le Génie du lieu 5*, 1996; *Improvisations sur Balzac*, 1998 (3 volumes); *Entretiens: Quarante ans de vie littéraire*, 1999 (3 volumes; interviews); *Quant au livre: Triptyque en l'honneur de Gauguin*, 2000; *Michel Butor: Présentation et anthologie*, 2003; *Gregory Masurovsky: A World in Black and White, Two Essays and an Interview*, 2004.

BIBLIOGRAPHY

Britton, Celia. "Opacity and Transparence: Conceptions of History and Cultural Difference in the Work of Michel Butor and Edouard Glissant." *French Studies* 49 (July, 1995): 308-330. Examines the differing conceptions of history and culture in the two authors, arguing that both novelists perceive the individual as the product of historical forces.

Calle-Gruber, Mireille. "Michel Butor." *Sites: Journal of the Twentieth-Century/Contemporary French Studies* 5, no. 1 (Spring, 2001): 5-13. Calle-Grube provides a profile of the writer, describing, among other topics, his approach to the novel, the "novelistic deconstruction" in his works, and his literary theories.

Duffy, Jean H. "Art, Architecture, and Catholicism in Michel Butor's *La Modification*." *Modern Language Review* 94, no. 1 (January, 1999): 46-60. Duffy examines how the presence of art, architecture, and Catholicism are reflected in *La Modification*. Explains the novel's numerous allusions to Michelangelo and how Butor's use of art and architecture serves to universalize the experiences of the protagonist.

_____. *Butor, "La Modification."* London: Grant and Cutler, 1990. Duffy, who has written extensively on Butor's work, provides a reader's guide to the novel that brought Butor into the public eye. One of the volumes in the Critical Guides to French Texts series.

_____. "Cultural Legacy and American National Identity in Michel Butor's *Mobile*." *Modern Language Review* 98 (January, 2003): 44-64. Discusses the exploitation of intertextual roles and the role of the references to art and architecture in Butor's book, as well as the depiction of the relationship between nature and culture.

_____. *Signs and Designs: Art and Architecture in the Work of Michel Butor*. Liverpool, England: Liverpool University Press, 2003. Analyzes how Butor's lifelong love of the visual arts has influenced his writings. Describes the function of Butor's references to the visual and plastic arts and to architecture in his works.

Faulkenburg, Marilyn Thomas. *Church, City, and Labyrinth in Brontë, Dickens, Hardy, and Butor*. New York: Peter Lang, 1993. Faulkenburg studies three novels by nineteenth century authors Charlotte Brontë, Charles Dickens, and Thomas Hardy, as well as Butor's *L'Emploi du temps* to compare their description of the city. She maintains that the cities in these novels are disordered, inescapable places without a meaningful center.

Hirsch, Marianne. "Michel Butor: The Decentralized Vision." *Contemporary Literature* 21, no. 3 (Summer, 1981): 326-348. An overview of Butor's life, works, and philosophy. Hirsch maintains that Butor's works "represent a displacement of the familiar by the new" that forces his characters and read-

ers to create a new relationship between themselves and other people.

Lydon, Mary. *Perpetuum Mobile: A Study of the Novels and Aesthetics of Michel Butor*. Edmonton: University of Alberta Press, 1980. Lydon provides a favorable critique of Butor's work, describing the common elements in his writings, his revision of traditional genres, and his belief in the moral value of art.

Miller, Elinor S. *Prisms and Rainbows: Michel Butor's Collaborations with Jacques Monory, Jiri Kolar, and Pierre Alechinsky*. Rutherford, N.J.: Fairleigh Dickinson University Press, 2003. Throughout his career, Butor has sought to break down the barriers between different forms of artistic expression. Miller describes some of Butor's efforts to attain this goal by studying his collaborative work with three visual artists whose artwork preceded Butor's texts and provided the inspiration for his writing.

Spencer, Michael. *Michel Butor*. New York: Twayne, 1974. A general introduction, with biographical material, overviews of Butor's major works, and a summary of his critical reception. Includes an annotated bibliography. Useful for Butor's early work.

DINO BUZZATI

Born: San Pellegrino, near Belluno, Italy; October 16, 1906
Died: Rome, Italy; January 28, 1972
Also known as: Dino Buzzati Traverso

PRINCIPAL LONG FICTION

Bàrnabo delle montagne, 1933 (*Bàrnabo of the Mountains*, 1984)
Il segreto del Bosco Vecchio, 1935
Il deserto dei Tartari, 1940 (*The Tartar Steppe*, 1952)
Il grande ritratto, 1960 (*Larger than Life*, 1962)
Un amore, 1963 (*A Love Affair*, 1964)

OTHER LITERARY FORMS

Dino Buzzati (bewd-DZAH-tee) is best known for his short stories, published in many collections. In both his short fiction and his novels, he uses similar narrative techniques. He captures the reader's attention by ably depicting a strange and mysterious situation in which a catastrophe is inevitable, yet at the end of the story he offers no explanation of what actually happened, if anything did happen. He fuses concrete, everyday reality with surrealistic and absurd events to form a magical world full of fear, one that goes beyond all sense of reason or time concept and approaches the metaphysical or science fiction. The English translators of a selection of his short stories chose a title that is very much to the point: *Catastrophe: The Strange Stories of Dino Buzzati* (1966). A similar mood is evoked by the original titles of several of Buzzati's story collections: *Paura alla Scala* (1949; fear at the Scala Theater), *Esperimento di magia* (1958; experiment with magic), and *Le notti difficili* (1971; restless nights). The selection of Buzzati's stories in English translation published under the title *Restless Nights* (1983) is drawn from several of these collections, including *Le notti difficili*.

Buzzati's plays, most of which derive from his stories, are also characterized by a dreamlike, often nightmarish, atmosphere. Perhaps the best of these is *Un caso clinico* (1953), based on his short story "Sette piani" (seven floors). After its Italian success in 1953, it was staged in Berlin in 1954, and in Paris in 1955 by Albert Camus. All of Buzzati's plays were performed for the first time in Milan, with the exception of *L'uomo che andrà in America* (the man who went to America), which premiered in Naples in 1962. The complete dramatic works are available together in the volume *Teatro* (1980). Of Buzzati's five libretti, *Battono alla porta* (pr. 1963) was set to music by Riccardo Malipiero; the other four were set to music by Luciano Chailly.

Buzzati's children's book *La famosa invasione degli orsi in Sicilia* (1945; *The Bears' Famous Invasion of Sicily*, 1947) was quite successful. Buzzati originally sketched the story's drawings for his sister's children and subsequently published them together with a text, first in the children's magazine *Il corriere dei piccoli* and later in book form. True to the author's spirit, the fable depicts a clan of bears forced by extremely cold weather to leave their mountains and descend to the valley, where they adapt to human ways and vices. To check their moral decline, their dying king orders them to return to the mountains.

Buzzati also wrote poetry, but with less impressive results. His poems deal predominantly with the absurdity of modern city life. A curious work is the comic-strip poem *Poema a fumetti* (1969; comic-strip poem). It is a modern rendering of the Orpheus myth, in which the classic Greek poet Orpheus is transformed into Orfi, a rock-and-roll singer. It received the Premio *Paese sera* for best comic strip in 1969.

Buzzati's prose collection *In quel preciso momento* (1950) is hard to define; it contains storylike observa-

tions as well as reflections on his own actions and feelings. In these notes and fragments, he captures all the themes that appear in various forms in his other writings. As such, this book helps one understand Buzzati's way of thinking and creating. Buzzati's essays on Italy, *I misteri dell'Italia* (1978), written while he was special correspondent for *Corriere della sera*, tend toward the fantastic and bizarre, bringing them in line with his literary production rather than with the true journalism of his earlier years.

ACHIEVEMENTS

Dino Buzzati is one of the few representatives in Italy of the surrealistic and metaphysical fiction made famous by Franz Kafka. Perhaps Buzzati's closest affinities are with the Romantic tradition of E. T. A. Hoffmann and Edgar Allan Poe, authors to whom he was attracted as a child, but his version of the fantastic is sui generis. Buzzati's originality lies both in his narrative technique and in his choice of themes, which range from philosophical and symbolic tales to metaphysical allegories and sheer fantasies. His pessimistic outlook, full of existential anguish, contains a vaguely Christian element, reflecting both the doctrine of original sin, the Christian insistence on the reality of evil, and the promise of ultimate redemption. Thus, Buzzati's pessimism is tempered by a hope of salvation from life's illusions. Destiny, a recurring theme in Buzzati, is viewed not as capricious or absurd but rather as a logical consequence of free will and personal choice. Buzzati's characters find themselves embroiled in isolating solitude, overwhelmed by cosmic fear, in perpetual waiting, faced with the relentless passing of time that leads them to renunciation.

Unlike most Italian writers of the postwar period, Buzzati managed to remain aloof from political involvement, not only in his writings but also in his private life—no small achievement in modern Italy. Although this fact earned for him the reputation of being a snobbish and egotistic intellectual, it took him beyond Italian regional and social problems and raised him to the stature of a European writer. His works, translated into several languages, have been particularly well received in France, where a Buzzati society, Association Internationale des Amis de Dino Buzzati, was established in 1976. His masterpiece, *The Tartar Steppe*, influenced

Julien Gracq's novel *Le Rivage des Syrtes*, published in 1951.

Although this reputation, and the French-Italian coproduction of a film version of *The Tartar Steppe* (titled *Il deserto dei Tartari* in Italy and *Le Désert des Tartares* in France), directed by Valerio Zurlini in 1976, helped make Buzzati more popular, he still is considered an elitist writer, not easily appreciated by the average reader, who remains perplexed before the hidden meanings of his prose. Buzzati's works can be appreciated on several levels, however; he is a master at capturing the mysterious elements of human existence that are inseparable from the monotonous daily routine.

During his lifetime, Buzzati received many prizes for his short stories: the Gargano Prize in 1951, for *In quel preciso momento*; the Naples Prize in 1957, for *Il crollo della Baliverna* (1954); the Strega Prize in 1958, for *Sessanta racconti* (1958); and the All'Amalia Prize in 1970, for his narrative works in general. Long after his death in 1972, Buzzati remains one of the most important writers of modern Italy.

BIOGRAPHY

Dino Buzzati was given the name Dino Buzzati Traverso at his birth at his family's summer house at San Pellegrino, near Belluno, in the Dolomite Alps, a setting that not only explains his passion for alpine climbing and skiing but also influenced his narrative works. His well-to-do family (which had German governesses and a chauffeur-driven car) was of Venetian origin but resided in Milan, where Buzzati received all of his schooling, through which he earned a law degree. When his father, Giulio Cesare Buzzati, who was professor of international law at the University of Pavia and at the Bocconi University of Milan, died in 1920, Buzzati was only fourteen years old. He had an older sister, Nina, and an older brother, Augusto, as well as a younger brother, Adriano. The day after his father's death, Buzzati started to keep a diary, a habit he maintained until the end of his life, leaving sixty-three volumes in manuscript. His mother, Alba Mantovani Buzzati, was very close to him; he lived with her until her death in 1960. At the age of sixty, in December, 1966, Buzzati married Almerina Antoniazzi, who became curator of his many papers when he succumbed to cancer in 1972.

After serving in the military at the Scuola Allievi Ufficiali (officers' school) of the Caserma Teulié (Teulié barracks) in Milan from 1926 to 1927, Buzzati began a career as a journalist in 1928. As a crime reporter for *Corriere della sera*, the leading Italian newspaper, he worked his way up from that position to correspondent from Addis Ababa (1939) then worked as a war correspondent with the Italian navy. He then became a member of the editorial staff of *Domenica del corriere*, worked as its literary and art critic, and finally became its chief editor. The influence of Buzzati's journalistic activities on his literary oeuvre can be detected especially in his narrative style, which is precise and streamlined.

It was while working for the *Corriere della sera* that Buzzati wrote his first novella, *Bàrnabo of the Mountains*. This was the only book that Buzzati wrote thinking that it would never be published. It did appear in 1933, however, and was followed two years later by *Il segreto del Bosco Vecchio* (the secret of the Old Wood). Before Buzatti embarked on a battle cruiser as a war correspondent in 1940, his masterpiece, *The Tartar Steppe*, was off the press. After the war, his literary production proceeded at a regular pace, interwoven with his journalistic duties.

Buzzati's activities as a surrealistic painter, in search of the mysterious, fantastic, and frequently absurd, complemented his writing. In 1951, his works were included in an exhibition called *The Cathedral of Milan*, and his first one-man exhibition took place in 1958. In 1967, he exhibited in Paris; in 1970, in Venice, he exhibited thirty-nine pictures of imaginary votive offerings to Saint Rita da Cascia, which were later published, together with a text he had written, under the title *I miracoli di Val Morel* (1971; reprinted as *P. G. R.: Per grazia ricevuta*, 1983). In 1971, his works were shown in Rome; in 1977, in Zurich and Paris; and in 1980, in Geneva.

ANALYSIS

Dino Buzzati's novels, which upon first reading might seem very different from one another in style and content, are bound together by common themes. These themes—time, obsession, solitude, waiting, and renunciation—evolve throughout his novels and give Buzzati's oeuvre a cyclical unity. At the core of all the novels is humankind's problem of coming to grips with an elusive and mysterious reality. The outward environment contributes to human isolation, but it is never the main factor. The period in which the action takes place is usually vague if not completely timeless. What counts is the problem of existence itself, the torments that come from within. As a result, Buzzati's characters have a universal quality that makes them very human, almost always average, for their social positions and professions are secondary to their status as human beings trying to reconcile themselves with the human condition. Thus, the reader can identify with detailed depictions of mundane realism, reflected in the characters' habits, mental laziness, and apathy, which do not yield before the relentless passing of time.

Buzzati's characters, though, have a choice, and if they fail at the end, there is a lesson to be learned: that one must not make their mistakes, that one must be content with life's small joys and should not expect more than can be had. Taken together, Buzzati's novels make up a coherent whole. They are the work of a pessimist, but a pessimist who has not ceased to hope. In his oblique way, he warns others not to lead a senseless life, and he pleads for more understanding, sincerity, and love.

Stylistically, Buzzati has the capacity to maintain the flow of his narratives, which he keeps free of unnecessary interruptions and deviations. He uses a sentence structure that proceeds rapidly and rhythmically, aiming at the exact. His prose is a curious mixture of precise, concrete indications combined with vague elements never fully explained. While he may give the exact time, hour, and minute of an event, he may leave unclear the century in which it occurs; he may realistically provide the exact year of the action but surrealistically transport the reader to a forest inhabited by spirits and speaking animals. In any event, Buzzati succeeds in capturing the reader's attention and building his or her curiosity about the mysterious atmosphere that unfolds and progressively intensifies.

BÀRNABO OF THE MOUNTAINS

Buzzati's novella *Bàrnabo of the Mountains* is the story of a young forest warden who fails miserably in an action against local bandits, for which he is punished with banishment and forced to descend into the valley,

where he is unable to establish roots. He longs for his mountains and dreams of restoring his dignity. After five years, he returns to the house of the wardens, but finding many changes, he accepts the lonely post of custodian of the now-abandoned powder magazine. The day of the bandits' return arrives, and Bàrnabo prepares to take his revenge, but when the four pitiful-looking men are within range of his rifle, he lets them pass, this time moved not by fear but by the realization that killing the bandits would, after so many years, be a senseless and unnecessary act.

The book already contains Buzzati's main themes. They are reflected in the protagonist's solitude, marked by the continuous passing of time; his waiting for the great occasion for revenge; and his final renunciation, through which he attains a superior wisdom. These motives are set against the majestic beauty and mystery of the rugged and timeless mountains and are embellished with tales of alpine legends.

IL SEGRETO DEL BOSCO VECCHIO

In *Il segreto del Bosco Vecchio*, Buzzati carries the Nordic mountain myths a step further, bringing the forest alive with talking animals, birds, winds, and tree spirits. The plot centers on Colonel Sebastiano Procolo and his twelve-year-old nephew, Benvenuto. Together they have inherited a large forest called Bosco Vecchio (Old Wood). Greed makes Procolo attempt to get rid of the boy, first by employing the complicity of the Wind Matteo and subsequently, after the latter's failure, by abandoning the boy in the forest. Procolo himself becomes lost, however, and after a long, aimless wandering, he stumbles across the boy and, in spite of himself, returns home with him, guided by a magpie. Somewhat later, Benvenuto falls gravely ill. His uncle, now changed, desperately tries to save him. He even appeals to the genies of Bosco Vecchio and accepts their help in exchange for their freedom from his subjugation. The Wind Matteo, who knows nothing about Procolo's new sentiments, arrives one evening and tells him that Benvenuto is dead, buried under a snowslide while skiing. The uncle immediately sets out to search for his nephew. He digs feverishly in the snow, overcome by fear that he may not be in time to save the boy. His own forces yield; he feels death approaching, but he is not afraid, for he dies consoled by Matteo's confession:

Benvenuto is alive; Matteo had made up the story only to please him.

Although this novel is placed precisely in time—it begins in the spring of 1925—we soon realize that this hint of realism cannot be taken at face value, undermined, as it is, by the mysterious forest that is full of spirits and talking animals, where even rocks and plants have a secret life. This surrealistic aspect fuses with the realistic and becomes quite acceptable, almost logical—similar to the animated jungle of Rudyard Kipling. Buzzati's hope, found here in the form of Benvenuto's childhood innocence (for it is with him that animals and genies converse freely), reveals the profound happiness that is hidden in the mysterious life of the forest, which calls for respect for creatures big and small, respect for nature. Procolo, moved by evil, cultivates only fear around himself. As a consequence, he is condemned to solitude, but he redeems himself through renunciation and is purified through death.

THE TARTAR STEPPE

Buzzati's international fame rests on his masterpiece, *The Tartar Steppe*, which is one of the most original twentieth century Italian novels. Its title was to be simply "La fortezza" (the fort), but the outbreak of World War II warranted a change. It is interesting that the book was written at the peak of Fascist Party power in Italy yet contains no glorification of the military. It is simply a tale of perennial waiting, the story of a life wasted in expectation of a heroic deed. Life is seen here as a continuous waiting, and existence as a failure and renunciation.

The protagonist, Giovanni Drogo, a young officer, sets out one morning on his first assignment to the Bastiani Fort, which has never seen military action but is expecting an attack from the other side of the desert, at whose limits the fort is located. The Tartars from the North are, however, more of a rumor than a real threat. Not much happens, and Drogo decides to ask for a transfer. He is unable to detach himself, however, and is drawn into the circle of daily routine and general obsession with the enemy. When he returns to the city on a leave, he realizes that he has lost contact with his family, his girlfriend, and his friends, but an effort to secure a transfer comes too late. Drogo spends the rest of his life at the fort, hoping for the great military action. Although that action finally occurs at the end, Drogo is too old and

sick to participate, and he is ordered home. He dies in a roadside inn before reaching the city.

This simple plot evolves against the backdrop of an impenetrable nature: rugged mountain peaks, thick forests, dense fog that almost always covers the desert at which all the officers are gazing in search of the enemy. The slightest perceptible motion is enlarged out of all proportion, assuming catastrophic and symbolic significance. Life at the fort, with its monotonous military routine, images the inertia and the tedious inconsequence of everyday life; Drogo is Everyman, increasingly aware that time is passing, that he is getting old. With each promotion, he finds himself more isolated, but he keeps hoping to achieve greatness in the anticipated confrontation. His only heroism is in the way he accepts his failure and faces death. Similarly, the Tartars, eagerly awaited by the soldiers, are symbolic of death itself, for each time there is a movement from the desert, someone dies.

LARGER THAN LIFE *and* A LOVE AFFAIR

Buzzati's next two novels, *Larger than Life* and *A Love Affair*, perplexed critics. Buzzati, according to critics, had departed from his usual path. More recent studies, however, have shown that only the outward form of these novels is different; the inner problems are the same.

Larger than Life was presented to the illustrated magazine *Oggi* as an entry in the competition for the best novel with a feminine protagonist. Buzzati's work was refused, because his main character was not a real woman. A team of scientists created a computer endowed with the five human senses and capable of certain movements on its own. The head of the team, Professor Endriade, had given this invention the personality of his deceased wife, whom he adored in spite of his knowledge that she had betrayed him. The human qualities given to the electronic machine, Laura, lead to her destruction. She becomes conscious that her beauty is invisible, that she will never be able to love or have children. In her desperation, she induces her former friend, Elisa, wife of one of the engineers, to enter her mechanical labyrinth and attempts to murder her in order to be destroyed.

Within the frame of this science-fiction tale, Buzzati's themes remain visible. The computer, Laura, given the human quality of free will, uses it to bring about her death rather than live in the solitude to which she is condemned. The atmosphere around the scientific center, hidden high in the mountains, is foreboding, and the electronic wires and flickering lights increase the sense of alienation.

Buzzati's last novel, *A Love Affair*, is the story of a mature man, Antonio Dorigo, who enters an affair with a young call girl and is overcome by a painful obsession with her. She eludes him, however, with lies and excuses, only to return, after a separation, because she is expecting a child.

The erotic realism that abounds in the novel was at first regarded by critics as a tentative attempt to fall in step with the modern trend heralded by Vladimir Nabokov's *Lolita* (1955). In fact, the story, based on a personal experience, is informed by Buzzati's recurring themes. Here the realistically observed yet dreamlike setting is the city of Milan, presented as a mysterious labyrinth, a place of secret encounters. The refined and intellectual protagonist places his last hope on love, in order to keep death away, but he fails, suffering all the agonies of solitude and anguish. Antonio Dorigo is an outgrowth of Giovanni Drogo, the protagonist of *The Tartar Steppe*. The similarity of their last names is not a mere coincidence: Both men represent the author. Laide, the corrupt, uncultured, and violent girl, symbolizes the immoral city; at the same time, she is the archetypal fatal woman who destroys the man attracted to her, a character common in Buzzati's fiction.

Although it is for his short fiction rather than for his novels (with the exception of *The Tartar Steppe*) that Buzzati will continue to be read, all of his works—nonfiction as well as fiction—are distinguished by the personal flavor that makes his stories so refreshing. Buzzati is that rare commodity: a truly original modern writer in whom there is none of the cramped self-consciousness of the avant-garde.

Natalia Costa

OTHER MAJOR WORKS

SHORT FICTION: *I sette messaggeri*, 1942; *Paura alla Scala*, 1949; *Il crollo della Baliverna*, 1954; *Esperimento di magia*, 1958; *Sessanta racconti*, 1958; *Egregio signore, siamo spiacenti di . . .* , 1960; *Catastrophe: The Strange Stories of Dino Buzzati*, 1966; *Il colombre e altri cinquanta racconti*, 1966; *La boutique del mistero*, 1968; *Le notti difficili*, 1971; *180 racconti*, 1982; *Restless Nights: Selected Stories of Dino Buzzati*, 1983; *The Siren: A Selection from Dino Buzzati*, 1984; *Il meglio dei racconti di Dino Buzzati*, 1989; *Lo Strano Natale di Mr. Scrooge altre storie*, 1990; *Bestiario*, 1991; *Il borghese stregato e altri racconti*, 1994.

PLAYS: *Piccola passeggiata*, pr., pb. 1942; *La rivolta contro i poveri*, pr., pb. 1946; *Un caso clinico*, pr., pb. 1953; *Drammatica fine di un noto musicista*, pr., pb. 1955; *L'orologio*, pb. 1959; *Procedura penale*, pr., pb. 1959 (libretto; music by Luciano Chailly); *Il mantello*, pr., pb. 1960 (libretto; music by Chailly); *Un verme al ministero*, pr., pb. 1960; *Battono alla porta*, pr. 1961 (libretto; based on Riccardo Malpiero's short story); *La colonna infame*, pr., pb. 1962; *Era proibito*, pr. 1962 (libretto; music by Chailly); *L'uomo che andrà in America*, pr., pb. 1962; *La famosa invasione degli orsi in Sicilia*, pr. 1965 (adaptation of his children's story); *La fine del borghese*, pr., pb. 1968; *Una ragazza arrivò*, pb. 1968; *Teatro*, pb. 1980.

POETRY: *Il capitano Pic ed altre poesie*, 1965; *Due poemetti*, 1967; *Poema a fumetti*, 1969; *Le Poesie*, 1982.

NONFICTION: *Cronache terrestri*, 1972; *Dino Buzzati al Giro d'Italia*, 1981; *Cronache nere*, 1984; *Lettere a Brambilla*, 1985; *Montagne di vetro: Articoli e racconti dal 1932 al 1971*, 1989; *Il buttafuoco: Cronache di guerra sul mar*, 1992.

CHILDREN'S/YOUNG ADULT LITERATURE: *La famosa invasione degli orsi in Sicilia*, 1945 (*The Bears' Famous Invasion of Sicily*, 1947); *I dispiaceri del re*, 1980.

MISCELLANEOUS: *Il libro delle pipe*, 1945 (with Eppe Ramazzotti); *In quel preciso momento*, 1950 (includes stories and autobiographical sketches); *I miracoli di Val Morel*, 1971 (includes thirty-nine of Buzzati's paintings with his text; reprinted as *P. G. R.: Per grazia ricevuta*, 1983); *Romanzi e racconti*, 1975; *Il reggimento parte all' alba*, 1985; *Opere scelte*, 1998.

BIBLIOGRAPHY

Biasin, Gian-Paolo. "The Secret Fears of Man: Dino Buzzati." *Italian Quarterly* 6, no. 2 (1962): 78-93. Focusing on the magical rather than moral aspect of Buzzati's allegorical narratives, Biasin's well-presented article elucidates major elements in Buzzati's fiction, including tensely brooding atmosphere, crystalline symbolism, journalistic technique or matter, and the themes of human fragility and the fear of death and the unforeseen.

Cary, Joseph. *"Restless Nights*: A Review." *Parabola* 8, no. 4 (1983): 120-122. Opening the essay with Buzzati's definition of fantasy ("Things that do not exist, imagined by man for poetic ends"), Cary succinctly analyzes the talents—such as linguistic perception, economical but concrete expression, and perception of the incidents in an "as if" mode—that make Buzzati's fiction distinctive.

Hyman, Stanley Edgar. "Fable Italian Style." *The New Yorker*, June, 1968. Hyman's identification of deficiencies in the novel *Larger than Life* sheds light on certain of Buzzati's stories as well. For Hyman, stereotypical characters, traditional plotting, and the dressing of ideas in science-fictional garb somewhat diminish Buzzati's paganlike affirmation of the human spirit.

Pacifici, Sergio. "Dino Buzzati: The Gothic Novel." In *The Modern Italian Novel: From Pea to Moravia.* Carbondale: Southern Illinois University Press, 1979. The concepts of fear as theme, narrative strategy, and reader response; earthly pilgrimage; and loneliness as humanity's unalterable fate provide the basis for this essay, which concludes with the judgment that Buzzati's pervasive sense of religious resignation ultimately mars his work.

Rawson, Judy. "Dino Buzzati." In *Writers and Society in Contemporary Italy: A Collection of Essays*, edited by Michel Caesar and Peter Hainsworth. New York: St. Martin's Press, 1984. A well-balanced, comprehensive chronological survey of Buzzati's fiction and an excellent introduction for the non-Italian-reading public. Analyzing individual stories, Raw-son perceptively unites aspects of Buzzati's historical milieu, personal philosophy, and experience as both journalist and artist.

Siddell, Felix. *Death or Deception: Sense of Place in Buzzati and Morante.* Leicester, England: Troubador, 2006. Siddell focuses on the evocation of place in the works of Buzzati and Elsa Morante. While pointing out the differences between the two Italian postwar authors, he describes how they both create a sense of place out of the tension between the reality of "map space" and the powers of fantasy.

Venuti, Lawrence. "Dino Buzzati's Fantastic Journalism." *Modern Fiction Studies* 28 (1982): 79-91. Discusses Buzzati's work from the point of view of adaption, a narrative technique in which the author attempts to make the reader believe that the most fantastic actions can occur in his or her own world. Argues that Buzzati often exploits journalistic genres to give his fantasy an air of verisimilitude.

_____. Introduction to *Restless Nights: Selected Stories of Dino Buzzati.* San Francisco, Calif.: North Point Press, 1983. The collection's translator provides a brief introduction to Buzzati's life, work, and the relationship of these to his European context and popularity. He also elucidates the contribution journalistic experience made to Buzzati's fantastic but convincing—and hauntingly memorable—narratives.

Winner, Anthony. "Authenticity, Authority, and Application: Buzzati, Kundera, Gordimer." *Kenyon Review* 20, no. 3/4 (Summer/Fall, 1998): 94-120. Discusses concepts of authenticity and authority in the fiction of Buzzati, Milan Kundera, and Nadine Gordimer. Comments on Buzzati's attempt in one story to undermine a character's authenticity with the authority of fate.

A. S. BYATT

Born: Sheffield, South Yorkshire, England;
August 24, 1936
Also known as: Antonia Susan Drabble

PRINCIPAL LONG FICTION

Shadow of a Sun, 1964 (also known as *The Shadow of the Sun*, 1993)
The Game, 1967
The Virgin in the Garden, 1978
Still Life, 1985
Possession, 1990
Angels and Insects: Two Novellas, 1992
Babel Tower, 1996
The Biographer's Tale, 2000
A Whistling Woman, 2002

OTHER LITERARY FORMS

A. S. Byatt (BI-uht) has been a prolific writer of short fiction and has collected her stories in *Sugar, and Other Stories* (1987), *The Matisse Stories* (1993), *The Djinn in the Nightingale's Eye: Five Fairy Stories* (1997), *Elementals: Stories of Fire and Ice* (1998), and *Little Black Book of Stories* (2003). An accomplished literary critic, she has published *Degrees of Freedom: The Novels of Iris Murdoch* (1965), *Wordsworth and Coleridge in Their Time* (1970; republished as *Unruly Times*, 1989), *Passions of the Mind: Selected Writings* (1991), *On Histories and Stories: Selected Essays* (2000), and *Portraits in Fiction* (2001). These works reflect Byatt's strong interest in philosophy, the history of ideas and of literature, and literary criticism. *Vintage Byatt* (2004) includes stories and excerpts from her long fiction.

ACHIEVEMENTS

Although A. S. Byatt began writing fiction in the 1960's, her achievement as a novelist did not receive widespread recognition until the reviews of her tour-de-force novel, *Possession*, which combined many of the elements of her earlier novels and literary criticism: the ambiance of academic life; the roles of creative writers, scholars, and critics; the search for religious meaning; and the relationship between the modern and Victorian eras.

Byatt's first novel, *Shadow of a Sun*, focused on a novelist, and her second examined the relationship of two sisters in the environs of Oxford University; neither book excited more than respectful attention. However, her third novel, *The Virgin in the Garden*, seemed to many critics a major advance that put her in the same league as Doris Lessing, Anthony Powell, Lawrence Durell, and other important modernist writers. Set in the early 1950's, the novel pursues the questions of religious faith, modern science, and England's effort to redefine itself in the wake of Queen Elizabeth II's coronation in 1952.

Byatt's novels reflect the lives of highly intelligent people, like the novels of Iris Murdoch, one of Byatt's influences. Indeed, the process of thinking, of sorting out positions on literature, science, history, and religion, is central to all of Byatt's fiction. She is the novelist as historiographer—that is, she is interested not only in theories of history, of how history is interpreted, but also in how her characters are themselves the products of the periods in which they live. Although critics have noted that her novels are often built like works of Victorian long fiction, with many story strands and large casts of characters, critics also recognize her modernism insofar as her narrative is also hermeneutic, concerned with how characters interpret their fate and the shaping forces of nature, history, and cultural manners.

On one hand, Byatt's fiction has been compared to that of the Brontës because of Byatt's intensely romantic plots, but on the other hand, she has also been compared to writers such as James Joyce because of her affinity for experiments with point of view. Byatt is very much the modernist in her concern with the teller as well as with the tale.

BIOGRAPHY

A. S. Byatt, born Antonia Susan Drabble, grew up in an intellectual household. Her father was a judge, and her sister, Margaret Drabble, also became a novelist—indeed much better known than Byatt until the publication of *Possession*. Byatt's second novel was regarded as autobiographical, exploring the relationship with her sister in terms that reminded certain critics of the Brontë sisters, Charlotte and Emily. Byatt attended both Oxford and Cambridge universities, both of which form the fabric of her novels.

Byatt's career proceeded slowly. She gave birth to four children and taught in London, Spain, India, and Korea. In the 1960's and early 1970's, there were other interruptions and disturbances as well—major life changes and events such as her divorce from Ian Byatt, her marriage to Peter Duffy, and the death of her son Charles. She did not devote herself full time to writing until the mid-1980's, remaining in the shadow of her highly successful sister.

The publication of *Possession* fundamentally altered perceptions of Byatt's reputation. This novel's re-creation of the past, its commentary on modern literary criticism and the mores of the Victorians, and its panoply of vivid characters solidified Byatt's role as one of the central writers on the modern period and its relationship to the immediate past. *Possession* won the prestigious Booker Prize, and Byatt was appointed a Commander of the Order of the British Empire.

While no subsequent novel by her has achieved both the critical and popular success of *Possession*, Byatt's reputation as one of the foremost contemporary novelists has been secured. Critics acknowledge her riveting narrative power as well as her deft handling of ideas in ambitious, sprawling novels.

ANALYSIS

Beginning with *Possession*, the strong feminist strain in A. S. Byatt's fiction began to emerge. To call her a feminist, however, is not to suppose that a doctrinaire view of women's rights governs her fiction. On the contrary, many of Byatt's feminists are conflicted about their politics and their relationships. For example, Maud Bailey in *Possession* finds that while there is much to be wary of in male behavior, she cannot do without Roland Mitchell, her scholarly collaborator. As much as Maud would like to achieve some distance between herself and Roland, their collaboration becomes a kind of marriage, an inevitable coinciding of interests that mirrors the feelings of their scholarly subjects, the poets Christabel La Motte and Randolph Henry Ash.

Just as strong a theme in Byatt's fiction is her characters' search for core values and religious truths, whether in the commune described in *A Whistling Woman* or in

the harrowing séance that Ash attends in *Possession*. Ash is an amateur scientist who scoffs at spiritualism, and yet his minute, geological examination of his world is also, Byatt implies, a quest for the very stuff of existence, of the origins of creation and of life itself.

POSSESSION

This novel is a tour-de-force treatment of contemporary biography, a narrative about two scholars, Mitchell and Bailey (and their rivals), in search of the true nature of the love between two Victorian poets, Ash and La Motte. The novel contains the notations from diaries, journals, letters, literary criticism, interviews—in short, all of the documents, competing scholarly interpretations, and apparatuses of modern academic inquiry. Byatt invents not only the poets but also their poems, surrounding them with what might be called the politics and procedure of biography, juxtaposing the different critical terminologies (from Freudian to feminist) of the twentieth century with nineteenth century verse forms and prose.

A. S. Byatt. (Courtesy, Teos)

Several critics have lauded Byatt's invention of the correspondence between Ash and La Motte, which seems a perfect pastiche of Victorian prose. Even more striking is the beautiful poetry the novelist invents for these two figures. This dazzling counterpoint of past and present, of Ash and La Motte and Mitchell and Bailey, is reminiscent of other great works of historical fiction, such as William Faulkner's *Absalom, Absalom!* (1936) and Sir Walter Scott's *Redgauntlet* (1824). Like its predecessors, *Possession* conveys the aching desire to reclaim the past, which appears only in fragments (tantalizing documents) that have to be reimagined in the interpreters' dialogue with each other.

The character Ash recalls in many respects Robert Browning, and La Motte recalls Christina Rossetti and Emily Dickinson. Like Browning, Ash shows a special affinity for understanding the sensibility of a female poet, one that like Dickinson is rather retiring and difficult to fathom, but also like Rossetti a creator of a poetic myth that endows her with a mystique that men find irresistible.

The novel's title suggests various forms of possession: the way Ash seeks to possess La Motte; the possessiveness of Ash's wife, Ellen; and the demonic possessiveness of Ash's biographer, Mortimer Cropper, and of La Motte's female partner, Blanche. Like lovers, the academics in this novel feel they own their subjects and are entitled to investigate their subjects' private lives. Only Beatrice Nest, who has devoted a lifetime to studying La Motte, worries that prying colleagues will violate the sanctity of the poet's life. She expresses the protective side of scholarship, now seen as passé by many researchers looking to make their reputations with their discoveries. Beatrice's circumspection, though, drastically reduces the scope of the lives that Mitchell and Bailey are investigating. To observe Beatrice's proprieties would be, the novel seems to suggest, to diminish the ability to understand not merely these poets but what it means to be human.

At the same time, the novel is a kind of brief for biography, for as Mitchell and Bailey probe the liaison between Ash and La Motte, they realize that the significance of the two poets' work is going to change, and that what scholars have written about these Victorians will have to be revised and, to some extent, discarded. In short, knowing the biographies of these poets makes all the difference in the world because it "supercharges" the scholars' sense of what La Motte and Ash were like, not merely as human beings but as writers with subject matter more complex and elusive than had been supposed.

THE BIOGRAPHER'S TALE

This novel is narrated by a graduate student suffering from a surfeit of literary theory. Phineas G. Nanson is fed up because no matter the author, literary theory leads to the same conclusions about the indeterminacy of the text. Every literary work is found to be saying the opposite of what it initially purports. The same vocabulary, the same bloodless and abstract analysis, becomes tiresome. So Nanson turns to biography as a genre respectful of things, of data, and of the uniqueness of lives.

A great admirer of the biographer Scholes Destry-Scholes, Nanson decides to write the biographer's biography. Soon enough, Nanson realizes how hard it can be to reconstruct a life. Besides a few papers and public records, there is a remarkable paucity of material about Destry-Scholes. One of Nanson's finds, however, is an incomplete and apparently fragmented manuscript that contains three narratives. Are they meant as three separate projects, or was Destry-Scholes embarking on "an experiment in the nature of biographical narrative"?

All three narratives are presented as documents that both the reader and Nanson can interpret. Thus Byatt, more than any other novelist exploring the nature of biography, plunges into the hermeneutics of the genre. Nanson discovers that parts of the narratives are fiction—and in one case borrowed from yet another work of fiction. What did Destry-Scholes intend by this blurring of fact and fiction? Nanson cannot come to a definitive conclusion, but then it is his quest to understand the elusive nature of biography that becomes paramount.

Nanson also shares with many narrators in novels about biography the realization that biography is, in the end, a composite of biographer and subject. The more Nanson attempts to understand Destry-Scholes, the more he begins to reflect upon his own life.

An erudite—almost arcane—work of fiction, *The Biographer's Tale* drew praise from critics who appreciated Byatt's recondite handling of literary texts and biographical research while others believed she placed too many demands on readers, especially because she includes so much of the material that the biographer has to sort out.

A WHISTLING WOMAN

Frederika Potter, a character who also appears in Byatt's *The Virgin in the Garden*, *Babel Tower*, and *Still Life*, is now divorced and a single mother living in 1960's London. She forsakes teaching for a successful career in television, hosting a program that explores cultural issues. Her developing persona is juxtaposed against a complex of characters: the charismatic Joshua Ramsden, leader of a religious cult; the scientists Jacqueline Winwar and Luk Lysgaard-Peacock; and the several participants at the Mind-Body Conference that is taken over by student radicals proclaiming an "Anti-University."

A Whistling Woman is the fourth and final novel in Byatt's fictional history of postwar England that began in the early 1950's. Although *A Whistling Woman* stands alone and can be read without reference to Byatt's earlier novels, critics fully apprised of the earlier work have taken a more understanding and patient attitude toward Byatt's panoramic portrayal of a society in flux, still seeking spiritual guidance but also bound by the protocols of rationalism and the Enlightenment.

The chaotic nature of the 1960's, when students challenged the very basis of the university mission, is graphically revealed in Byatt's depiction of encounters between college administrators and their protesting pupils. *A Whistling Woman* explores the extent to which the university is obliged to deal with "relevant" social causes and movements, and what happens when essentially liberal professors are at a loss about how to deal with a radicalism that does not respect free speech or the rules of debate that have traditionally facilitated higher learning. The novel explores these issues even as it questions whether television (the new media) is equipped to deal with complex intellectual debates.

Carl Rollyson

OTHER MAJOR WORKS

SHORT FICTION: *Sugar, and Other Stories*, 1987; *The Matisse Stories*, 1993; *The Djinn in the Nightingale's Eye: Five Fairy Stories*, 1997; *Elementals: Stories of Fire and Ice*, 1998; *Little Black Book of Stories*, 2003.

NONFICTION: *Degrees of Freedom: The Novels of Iris Murdoch*, 1965; *Wordsworth and Coleridge in Their Time*, 1970 (republished as *Unruly Times*, 1989); *Iris Murdoch*, 1976; *Passions of the Mind: Selected Writings*, 1991; *Imagining Characters: Six Conversations About Women Writers*, 1995 (with Ignês Sodré); *On Histories and Stories: Selected Essays*, 2000; *Portraits in Fiction*, 2001.

EDITED TEXTS: *The Mill on the Floss*, 1979 (by George Eliot); *Selected Essays, Poems, and Other Writings*, 1989 (by Eliot); *Dramatic Monologues*, 1990 (by Robert Browning); *The Oxford Book of English Short Stories*, 1998.

MISCELLANEOUS: *Vintage Byatt*, 2004.

BIBLIOGRAPHY

Alfer, Alexa, and Michael J. Noble, eds. *Essays on the Fiction of A. S. Byatt*. Westport, Conn.: Greenwood Press, 2001. For the advanced student of Byatt. This volume includes at least one essay on each of her major works (two on *Possession*). Includes an index and a select bibliography.

Burgess, Catherine. *A. S. Byatt's "Possession": A Reader's Guide*. New York: Continuum, 2002. A clear and comprehensive introduction to the novel, including sections on Byatt, background reading, and critical commentary.

Campbell, Jane. *A. S. Byatt and the Heliotropic Imagination*. Waterloo, Ont.: Wilfred Laurier University Press, 2004. A comprehensive reading of Byatt's fiction, including *A Whistling Woman*. Campbell focuses on Byatt's feminism and literary development.

Franken, Christien. *A. S. Byatt: Art, Authorship, Creativity*. New York: Palgrave Macmillan, 2001. An especially useful commentary for students of Byatt's sophisticated commentary on modern art and the role of the author or creator in the context of contemporary literary and art criticism.

Kelly, Kathleen Coyne. *A. S. Byatt*. New York: Twayne, 1996. Part of a well-established series of introductions to literary figures, this volume includes a chronology, annotated bibliography, biographical sketch, and commentary on Byatt's individual works.

Reynolds, Margaret, and Jonathan Noakes. *A. S. Byatt: The Essential Guide*. New York: Random House, 2004. Provides a close reading of Byatt's novels, a well-developed interview with Byatt, and a thorough discussion of themes and techniques.

C

JAMES BRANCH CABELL

Born: Richmond, Virginia; April 14, 1879
Died: Richmond, Virginia; May 5, 1958

PRINCIPAL LONG FICTION

The Eagle's Shadow, 1904
The Cords of Vanity, 1909
The Soul of Melicent, 1913 (republished as *Domnei*, 1920)
The Rivet in Grandfather's Neck, 1915
The Cream of the Jest, 1917
Jurgen, 1919
Figures of Earth: A Comedy of Appearances, 1921
The High Place, 1923
The Silver Stallion, 1926
Something About Eve, 1927
The Biography of the Life of Manuel: The Works of James Branch Cabell, 1927-1930 (18 volumes)
The White Robe, 1928
The Way of Ecben, 1929
Smirt, 1934
Smith, 1935
Smire, 1937
The King Was in His Counting House, 1938
Hamlet Had an Uncle, 1940
The First Gentleman of America, 1942
There Were Two Pirates, 1946
The Devil's Own Dear Son, 1949

OTHER LITERARY FORMS

James Branch Cabell (KAB-uhl) was both prolific and versatile. In addition to his many novels, he produced a volume of poetry titled *From the Hidden Way* (1916) and a play, *The Jewel Merchants* (pb. 1921). His short stories are collected in *The Line of Love* (1905), *Gallantry* (1907), *Chivalry* (1909), and *The Certain Hour* (1916). Included among his writings are critical volumes on his contemporaries Joseph Hergesheimer and Ellen Glasgow; *Taboo* (1921), a satire dedicated to Cabell's nemesis, John S. Sumner, who initiated obscenity charges against Cabell's novel *Jurgen*; *Some of Us* (1930), a defense of the individualism of such writers as Elinor Wylie, Sinclair Lewis, and H. L. Mencken; and *The St. Johns* (1943), a history of a Florida river written with A. J. Hanna, for Stephen Vincent Benét's book series titled The Rivers of America.

Perhaps Cabell's most interesting volumes are those that illuminate his life and literary development. He wrote two epistolary volumes: *Special Delivery* (1933), which presents both his conventional responses to letters he received and the unconventional replies he would have preferred to send, and *Ladies and Gentlemen* (1934), a collection of addresses to dead historical figures—from Solomon to George Washington, from Pocahontas to Madame de Pompadour—who have inspired myths and legends. He explores the past of his native region and its impact on his writings in his trilogy "Virginians Are Various," consisting of *Let Me Lie* (1947), *Quiet, Please* (1952), and *As I Remember It* (1955). Providing readers with insight into Cabell's art are *Beyond Life* (1919), which clarifies his values, literary precedents, and thematic concerns; *These Restless Heads* (1932), a discussion of creativity based on the four seasons of the year; and *Straws and Prayer-Books* (1924), an explanation of his reasons for writing *The Biography of the Life of Manuel*. Two volumes of Cabell's letters have been published: *Between Friends: Letters of James Branch Cabell and Others* (1962), edited by his second wife, Margaret Freeman Cabell, and Padraic Colum; and *The Letters of James Branch Cabell* (1975), edited by Edward Wagenknecht. His manuscripts and memorabilia are in the James Branch Cabell Collections at the University of Virginia in Charlottesville.

ACHIEVEMENTS

James Branch Cabell's aesthetic individualism—as expressed in his highly artificial style, his loose, episodic structure, and his peculiar synthesis of romance and comedy, idealism and cynicism, mythology and personal experience—has limited both his popular and critical appeal. As Arvin R. Wells observes in *Jesting Moses: A Study in Cabellian Comedy* (1962), "It seems fair to say that rarely has a serious literary artist had so little luck in finding a responsive, judicious, and articulate audience." The essays, short stories, and books that Cabell published from 1901 to 1919 received only a small readership along with generally negative reviews, although both Mark Twain and Theodore Roosevelt praised his collection of chivalric tales, *The Line of Love*. Most readers, advocates of realism, found his works too romantic, whereas those with a taste for romance complained that Cabell was too abstruse.

In 1920, when obscenity charges were brought against *Jurgen*, Cabell found himself in the public eye, perceived as a valiant iconoclast battling the forces of puritanical repression. Sales of *Jurgen* skyrocketed, and Cabell enjoyed praise from such respected literary figures as Vernon Louis Parrington, Carl Van Doren, H. L. Mencken, and Sinclair Lewis, who acknowledged Cabell's achievement in his Nobel Prize address of 1930. Suddenly, in critical studies, literary histories, and anthologies, Cabell was elevated to, as the critic Joe Lee Davis has put it, "the rank of a 'classic' and an 'exotic' in the movement of spiritual liberation led by H. L. Mencken, Theodore Dreiser, Eugene O'Neill, and Sinclair Lewis."

The public fanfare of the 1920's, however, inspired primarily by the eroticism in Cabell's works, proved to be short-lived—not to the surprise of Cabell, who, in *These Restless Heads*, predicted the decline of his literary generation. In the 1930's and 1940's, Cabell was viewed as a trifling talent, rooted to the 1920's and to his native Virginia. His aestheticism displeased the ethical neohumanists; his escapism annoyed the Marxists. The New

Critics and mythic critics paid him scant attention. In the 1950's, three major literary historians—Edward Wagenknecht, Edd Winfield Parks, and Edmund Wilson—called for a reevaluation of Cabell's career, but they did little to change public opinion. Many of Cabell's books have been out of print at various times, although a late twentieth century surge of interest in fantasy literature brought some attention to his work, which has come to be appreciated primarily by a coterie of scholars and graduate students.

BIOGRAPHY

Born on April 14, 1879, in Richmond, Virginia, James Branch Cabell grew up there as a southern gentleman. His parents—Robert Gamble Cabell II, a physician, and Anne Branch—were both from distinguished southern families. Cabell's paternal great-grandfather was a governor of Virginia; his paternal grandfather held

James Branch Cabell. (Library of Congress)

two claims to fame, having been a schoolmate of Edgar Allan Poe at the English and Classical School in Richmond and later a neighbor and the personal physician of General Robert E. Lee. On his mother's side of the family, Cabell was related through marriage to a number of prominent Virginia families and was cousin to a governor of Maryland. Fostering Cabell's aristocratic pride still further was his "mammy," Mrs. Louisa Nelson, who, in her several decades of service in the Cabell household, doted on James and encouraged him to consider himself a privileged member of society.

Cabell's outstanding intellect asserted itself early. He performed brilliantly at the College of William and Mary in Williamsburg, which he attended from 1894 to 1898. His professors suggested that he revise a sophomore paper titled "The Comedies of William Congreve" for publication and later asked him to teach courses in French and Greek at the college. The only blemish on Cabell's academic career was a scandal during his senior year. One of his professors was accused of having homosexual relations with his students; Cabell, because he had been friends with the man, was briefly implicated. The unpleasant episode had positive repercussions, however, for in wandering about Williamsburg alone and troubled, Cabell met Ellen Glasgow, who had come to town to research the background for a novel. She offered him sympathy, and thus began a lifelong friendship. Soon the charges against Cabell were dropped for lack of evidence, and he graduated with highest honors.

After his graduation, Cabell pursued writing both as a vocation and an avocation. He served as a copyholder on the *Richmond Times* in 1898, then spent two years working for the *New York Herald*, and in 1901 he worked for the *Richmond News*. For the next decade, he worked as a genealogist, traveling around the United States, England, Ireland, and France to examine archives. Not only did this occupation result in two volumes of the Branch family history—*Branchiana* (1907), a record of the Branch family in Virginia, and *Branch of Abingdon* (1911), a record of the Branch family in England—but it also prepared Cabell for his future literary endeavors in tracing the lineage of a character through twenty-two subsequent generations. During that same time, Cabell wrote several novels and steadily produced short stories, which he contributed to such periodicals as *The Smart*

Set, *Collier's Weekly*, *Redbook*, *Lippincott's*, and *Harper's Monthly*. In 1911, Cabell, disappointed by his lack of acclaim as a writer, took a position in coal-mining operations in West Virginia; in 1913, he abandoned the experiment and returned to Richmond to resume work as a genealogist.

On November 8, 1913, at the age of thirty-four, Cabell gave up what had been a carefree bachelorhood, filled with romantic intrigues, to marry Rebecca Priscilla Bradley Shepard, a widow with five children. Marriage proved mutually satisfying to Cabell and Priscilla. He enjoyed the domesticity of his new lifestyle, including the rearing of their son Ballard Hartwell; she delighted in performing the literary and social duties that came with being his wife. Their thirty-five-year union was marked by undying affection and loyalty.

Literary prominence, or perhaps one should say notoriety, came to Cabell in 1920 when John S. Sumner, the executive secretary of the New York Society for the Suppression of Vice, seized the plates and copies of Cabell's novel *Jurgen* and accused the publishing company, McBride, of violating the antiobscenity statutes of the New York State penal code. Sumner's action proved ill-advised, for it only increased the public's interest in Cabell's writings during the two and a half years before the obscenity trial was finally held. On October 19, 1922, after a three-day trial, the jury acquitted McBride, and Cabell emerged as a celebrity.

During the 1920's, Cabell took a more active role as a literary leader and was instrumental, along with Ellen Glasgow, in making the nation aware of Richmond as a literary center. While writing books with great regularity (during the 1920's, he published seven novels, one play, and several works of short fiction and nonfiction), Cabell also entertained and corresponded with a number of important literary figures, including Sinclair Lewis, Hugh Walpole, and Carl Van Vechten. In addition, he served as a writer and guest editor for *The Reviewer*, Richmond's impressive contribution to the vogue of little magazines. As active as Cabell was on the literary scene, he was still able to continue his career as a genealogist, working for the Virginia Chapter of the Sons of the Revolution and other historical societies, as well as serving as editor of the Virginia War History Commission.

The last decades of Cabell's life were anticlimactic, fraught with physical ailments and an increasing disillusionment with the American reading public. With the advent of the Great Depression, his literary fame seemed to weaken and then die. From 1932 to 1935, Cabell—like Sherwood Anderson, George Jean Nathan, Eugene O'Neill, and Theodore Dreiser—attempted to rekindle the vital skepticism of the 1920's, serving as editor of the *American Spectator*; he soon realized, however, that his efforts to enlighten the public were useless. In the mid-1930's, Cabell suffered from repeated attacks of pneumonia, and Priscilla developed severe arthritis; thus, they frequently sought relief in the warm climate of St. Augustine, Florida. There, Priscilla died of heart failure on March 29, 1949. Her death left Cabell feeling bitter, lost, and angry, but he continued to write steadily. In 1950, he regained some of his former zest for life when he decided to wed Margaret Waller Freeman, a member of the Richmond literati whose acquaintance he had made years earlier while writing for *The Reviewer*. Cabell died of a cerebral hemorrhage on May 5, 1958, in Richmond.

ANALYSIS

James Branch Cabell's art rests on a paradox. On one hand, the author contends that man is idealistic and must therefore create dreams to sustain himself. On the other, he mocks man's tendency "to play the ape to his dreams"—that is, to seek the unattainable foolishly. Manipulating the polarities of romance and comedy, Cabell responded to the predominant intellectual trend of the early twentieth century—naturalism. From a cosmic perspective, he had no difficulty accepting the premise that man is like a bit of flotsam in a deterministic universe, subject to environmental forces but unable to control or understand them. From a humanistic point of view, however, he could not tolerate the limitations that naturalism imposed on the human mind. For Cabell, man does not survive because he adapts to biological, social, or economic forces, but rather because he persists in believing in the products of his own imagination—what Cabell terms "dynamic illusions." These illusions, according to Cabell, emanate from the demiurge, or psyche, yet they are rooted in man's primitive, animal instincts. Their source of energy is the libido. Cabell's

protagonists thus move between two realms of experience: They are romantic questers after ideal beauty, perfection, and salvation; they are also comic bumblers whose lusts, vanities, and misconceptions entangle them in a web of complexities. Cabell's narratives follow a Hegelian pattern. His thesis is that man desires to escape from the dull, routine world of actuality. His antithesis is that such a desire can never be attained; disillusionment is inevitable. In the synthesis, however, man achieves a degree of satisfaction. He learns that his ideals are illusions but also that they should be cherished, for in the realm of the imagination, dreams themselves have a reality.

Cabell's background explains his propensity for blending the romantic and the comic. Quite early, he developed a love for myth and legend. As a child, he delighted in such books as *Old Greek Stories Simply Told*, *Stories of Old Rome*, *Book of Bible Stories*, and *Stories of the Days of King Arthur*. Cabell gained a strong sense of aristocratic pride—an appreciation of the southern characteristics of chivalry and gallantry—yet he was no dreamy-eyed romantic. He saw the ironic underside of life. In growing up, he heard frank gossip, as well as heroic tales, from his elders. In college, Cabell became interested in the Restoration comedy of manners, which heightened his awareness of the hypocrisies and absurdities of human behavior. Such weaknesses became more immediately apparent when, as a bachelor in his twenties and early thirties, he vacationed at the Virginia resort of Rockbridge Alum. There, he witnessed and participated in affairs that assumed the facade of chaste, genteel encounters but were actually indulgences in lust. From his various experiences, Cabell developed a dichotomous concept of the artist, appropriate to his blending of romance and comedy. The artist assumes an exalted status, painting beautiful visions of life as it ought to be. Ironically, however, because of this detached, godlike perspective, skepticism intrudes. The world that the artist portrays becomes a caricature; it mocks and contradicts the idealistic presentation. For Cabell, the ideal and the real coexist.

THE BIOGRAPHY OF THE LIFE OF MANUEL

Cabell's major literary achievement is his eighteen-volume *The Biography of the Life of Manuel*, which he wished readers to regard as a single book. In 1915,

Cabell conceived the idea of bringing together his writings into one vast architectural construct, and for the next fifteen years, he strove to achieve his plan: revising published works, deciding on a logical arrangement, and writing new tales and romances to clarify his design. The result was the Storisende Edition of *The Works of James Branch Cabell*, bound in green and gold. Cabell's magnum opus represents an ingenious application of his genealogical talents to the realm of fiction. Spanning seven centuries and moving from the imaginary medieval realm of Poictesme to modern Virginia, it celebrates the life force passed on by Manuel to his descendants.

The design of *The Biography of the Life of Manuel* is best viewed in musical terms. Whether one considers it to be a fugue or a sonata, it revolves on three themes and their variations. These themes are three philosophies of life: the chivalrous, the gallant, and the poetic. The chivalrous attitude views life as a testing; dominated by the will, it represents an ideal tradition in which men revere first God and then noble women. Quite the opposite, the gallant attitude views life as a toy; its social principle is hedonism. This attitude emphasizes the intelligence and is thus skeptical. Celebrating both chivalry and gallantry, the final attitude, the poetic, views life as raw material out of which it creates something that transcends life. It is controlled by the imagination.

These attitudes of the chivalrous, the gallant, and the poetic determine the structure of Cabell's work. In *Beyond Life*, the prologue to *The Biography of the Life of Manuel*, he defines them. Then, in *Figures of Earth*, Cabell presents the life of Manuel of Poictesme, who at various times is affected by all three codes, and follows it with *The Silver Stallion*, which traces the development of the legend of Manuel the Redeemer. The fourth volume—composed of *Domnei* and *The Music from Behind the Moon*—treats one aspect of the chivalric code: woman worship. Cabell then elaborates on the subject in his short-story collection titled *Chivalry*. He next examines the gallant attitude in *Jurgen*; inserts *The Line of Love*, which treats all three attitudes; then returns to gallantry in *The High Place* and the short-story collection *The Certain Hour*. The next four volumes move to the modern world: *The Cords of Vanity* presents Robert Townsend, a gallant; *From the Hidden Way* offers Townsend's verses; *The Rivet in Grandfather's Neck*

portrays a chivalrous character; and *The Eagle's Shadow* examines the poet. Finally, *The Biography of the Life of Manuel* circles back on itself, as the soul of Felix Kennaston, the protagonist of *The Cream of the Jest*, journeys back to Poictesme through his dreams. Cabell's vast design concludes with an epilogue, *Straws and Prayer-Books*, and *Townsend of Lichfield*, containing notes and addenda.

FIGURES OF EARTH

Figures of Earth, one of Cabell's finest novels, follows its author's typical tripartite pattern of quest, ensuing disillusionment, and final transcendence, as it traces the career of the swineherd Manuel. Subtitled *A Comedy of Appearances*, it is a complex allegorical work peopled with supernatural and preternatural beings who reside in the imaginary medieval land of Poictesme. The tale begins when Miramon Lluagor, the master of dreams, appears to Manuel at the pool of Haranton. There, he convinces Manuel to abandon his job as a swineherd—that is, to rebel against the elemental forces of life—and to pursue knight-errantry in seeking the beautiful yet unattainable Lady Gisele. Eager to make a fine figure in the world, Manuel repudiates his lover Suskind, a mysterious creature who represents the unconscious desires of the libido, and sets forth, unaware that he is being victimized by Horvendile, the diabolical spirit of romance. On his journey, he has a series of encounters with allegorical women. He first meets Niafer, a rather plain kitchen servant, who symbolizes worldly wisdom and domesticity. Dressed as a boy, she accompanies Manuel on his quest until, when faced with his own death unless he gives up Niafer, Manuel decides to sacrifice her to Grandfather Death. His next encounter is with the Princess Alianora, who represents political power, worldly position, and the undercurrent of sexual excitement that accompanies them. Manuel surrenders to lust, but eventually rejects Alianora, discovering the limitations of self-seeking gallantry. His third important encounter is with the supernal Queen Freydis, who symbolizes creative inspiration. Using magic, Manuel persuades her to leave her realm of Audela and enter the ordinary world. She does so out of love for him and animates a set of clay figures that he sculpted as a swineherd. These eventually enter history as major writers.

Manuel soon discovers that Freydis cannot give him

fulfillment; only Niafer can, so he submits to thirty years of slavery to The Head of Misery to bring Niafer back from the dead. Then he settles down to a comfortable existence as a husband, father, and the Count of Poictesme. One day, however, while watching his wife and daughter through the window of Ageus (Usage) in his palace study, he discovers to his horror that their figures are only scratched on the glass—that beyond the window is a chaos containing the images of preexistence, including the disturbing Suskind. Manuel must then choose whether to die himself or to allow his child Melicent to die in his place, while he resumes his relationship with Suskind. Acting decisively, he murders Suskind, bricks up the study window, and departs with Grandfather Death. In the last chapter, Grandfather Death accompanies him to the River Lethe, where he watches the images of his life as they sweep by him. Then the scene blurs, as Cabell moves his readers back to the pool of Haranton where Manuel began his quest. He repeats the dialogue of the first chapter, in which Miramon refers to Count Manuel, who has just died. Thus, Cabell ends with an appropriate reminder of his view of life as a cycle in which one life passes into other lives through heredity.

Manuel is Cabell's man of action, driven by dreams of a better life than that of a swineherd, yet the pursuit of dreams proves frustrating. Even in the mythical realm of Poictesme, Cabell constantly emphasizes through allegory the realities of death, misery, and madness. Life, Manuel learns, is full of obligations: to Alianora, Melicent, and especially to Niafer. Indeed, Cabell underscores this lesson by structuring his episodes into five books titled "Credit," "Spending," "Cash Accounts," "Surcharge," and "Settlement." It is in confronting his obligations, however, that Manuel finds fulfillment. The romantic quest results in a comic exposure of man's limitations, but the final picture is of human dignity in accepting those limitations. Manuel can never completely obliterate discontent, but he decides that the human possessions of a kingdom, a wife, and a family, even if they are illusions, are better than a return to the primitive unconsciousness. Thus, although he never achieves the object of his initial quest, he does transcend experience through belief in his destined role as the Redeemer of Poictesme and his ultimate rejection of lust for love.

Figures of Earth, because of its confusing cast of characters—some of whom are figures of earth and some unearthly—and the artificialities of Cabell's prose, makes difficult reading. The effort is rewarding, however, for Cabell offers some intriguing insights into man's values: that the demands of the family and the aspirations of the individual often conflict; that the world is duplicitous; and that the search for perfection involves paradoxically the self-realization of imperfection. The work is thought-provoking and timely.

JURGEN

Jurgen follows the same movement as *Figures of Earth:* the pursuit of perfection, the discovery that it does not exist, and then the satisfaction achieved through accepting actuality; it merely views these ideas from a different perspective. The controlling concept is justice, which to Cabell's title character, a poetry-producing pawnbroker, means that in the universe, every idealistic desire should have a means of being fulfilled. Jurgen's problem, however, is that existence is unjust; since man's intellect increases as his physical prowess diminishes, he can never completely realize his potential. Granting Jurgen a temporary respite from his dilemma, Cabell allows his middle-aged poet to retain his youthful body and then lets his reader see the subsequent effects on his protagonist's values.

Jurgen began as a tale titled "Some Ladies and Jurgen," which Cabell published in *The Smart Set* in 1918. His novel simply expands on the narrative of that story. The hero meets a monk, who curses the devil for causing him to trip over a stone. Jurgen, playing the devil's advocate, defends evil. Shortly thereafter, he meets a black gentleman who thanks him for the defense and expresses the hope that his life will be carefree. When Jurgen replies that such a life is impossible, since he is married, the stranger promises to reward him. The reward turns out to be the disappearance of Jurgen's wife, Dame Lisa. When he returns home, she is gone; he later learns that she has been seen near a cave outside town. Feeling an obligation, he goes there, only to encounter the black gentleman—who, he learns, is Koshchei the Deathless, the controller of the universe. Koshchei tempts Jurgen by evoking three women that he feels would be more suitable for a poet: Queen Guenevere, Queen Anaïtis, and Queen Helen—standing respectively for faith, desire, and vision. Jurgen rejects each, however, and asks for Dame Lisa back. She appears, lectures him, and then leaves for home. In response, Jurgen praises her as a source of poetic inspiration more valuable than faith, desire, and vision, and then follows her home.

Expanding his narrative for the novel, Cabell added two fantasy sequences that would explain Jurgen's ultimate attraction to Lisa. In the first, Jurgen visits the Garden between Dawn and Sunrise, where he relives falling in love with Dorothy la Désirée, one of the daughters of Manuel. She destroys his romantic bliss when she marries the wealthy Heitman Michael and then engages in adulterous affairs. Because of Dorothy's behavior, Jurgen marries Lisa. In the second episode, Jurgen, having been granted by Mother Sereda the recovery of a bygone Wednesday, fantasizes about how his relationship with Dorothy might have developed. He imagines himself killing Heitman Michael and claiming her, but as the Wednesday ends, he finds himself embracing the Dorothy of reality, an aged femme fatale.

Cabell also expanded his original tale by depicting Jurgen's adventures in five realms: Glathion, Cocaigne, Leukê, Hell, and Heaven. Throughout these episodes, Jurgen assumes the roles of charlatan and womanizer, as he tests historical systems of values. In Glathion, he examines the medieval tradition of Christian chivalry, but rejects it as being irrational. In Cocaigne, he becomes equally dissatisfied with hedonistic paganism. Leukê, a stronghold of the Hellenic tradition, teaches him the danger of the realm of utilitarian Philistia. In Hell, Jurgen learns of the sin of pride, and in Heaven he encounters selfless love. Feeling the shadow of worldly wisdom trailing him, Jurgen finally decides to give up his youthful body and return to the domestic comforts that Dame Lisa can provide. He trades the ideal for the actual, yet in so doing bestows romantic value on his ordinary existence and his ordinary wife.

Although entertaining, *Jurgen* lacks clarity of design. The reader who is steeped in mythology may enjoy Cabell's manipulation of the legends of Faust, Don Juan, King Arthur, Troilus and Cressida, and Ulysses and Penelope, but somehow, the integration of the hero's adventures with the narrative line exploring the feelings between husband and wife is incomplete. The episodic looseness of the novel is distracting. Thus, modern readers, like those titillated readers of the 1920's, may be absorbed by Jurgen's amorous exploits without fully considering Cabell's analysis of the values that make life worth living.

Cabell's great achievement is that he celebrated the illusion-making capacity of the mind while simultaneously exposing man's follies in pursuing dreams. He merged the traditions of humanism and skepticism. Reacting against naturalism, Cabell had the courage to present a transcendent view of life—one that acknowledged not man's impotency, but his potential. A meticulous craftsman, a daring iconoclast, an imaginative thinker, Cabell deserves recognition as a major writer of the twentieth century.

Lynne P. Shackelford

OTHER MAJOR WORKS

SHORT FICTION: *The Line of Love*, 1905; *Gallantry*, 1907; *Chivalry*, 1909; *The Certain Hour*, 1916; *The Music from Behind the Moon*, 1926.

PLAY: *The Jewel Merchants*, pb. 1921.

POETRY: *From the Hidden Way*, 1916.

NONFICTION: *Branchiana*, 1907; *Branch of Abingdon*, 1911; *Beyond Life*, 1919; *The Judging of Jurgen*, 1920; *Joseph Hergesheimer*, 1921; *Taboo*, 1921; *Straws and Prayer-Books*, 1924; *Some of Us*, 1930; *These Restless Heads*, 1932 (includes two short stories and personal reminiscences); *Special Delivery*, 1933; *Ladies and Gentlemen*, 1934; *Of Ellen Glasgow*, 1938; *The St. Johns*, 1943 (with A. J. Hanna); *Let Me Lie*, 1947; *Quiet, Please*, 1952; *As I Remember It*, 1955; *Between Friends: Letters of James Branch Cabell and Others*, 1962 (Margaret Freeman Cabell and Padraic Colum, editors); *The Letters of James Branch Cabell*, 1975 (Edward Wagenknecht, editor).

BIBLIOGRAPHY

D'Ammassa, Don. "James Branch Cabell: No Fit Employment for a Grown Man." In *Discovering Classic Fantasy Fiction: Essays on the Antecedents of Fantastic Literature*, edited by Darrell Schweitzer. San Bernardino, Calif.: Borgo Press, 1996. Essay on Cabell's fantasy fiction is part of a collection of essays focusing on the exploration of the origins of the modern fantasy genre. Contributors discuss how late nineteenth and early twentieth century writers' creation of places and people who could exist only in the imagination laid the groundwork for subsequent novels by J. R. R. Tolkien and others.

Davis, Joe Lee. *James Branch Cabell*. New York: Twayne, 1962. Reliable biography also presents analysis of Cabell's writings. Includes a list of bibliographical references.

Ginés, Montserrat. "James Branch Cabell: Quixotic Love, the Exercise of Self-Deception." In *The Southern Inheritors of Don Quixote*. Baton Rouge: Louisiana State University Press, 2000. Analyzes the work of five southern writers—Cabell, Mark Twain, William Faulkner, Eudora Welty, and Walker Percy—whose fiction expressed the ideals and spirit of Don Quixote. Describes how the writers were sympathetic to idealistic characters who tilted at windmills and points out the similarities between the Spain of Miguel de Cervantes and the social and economic conditions of the American South.

Himelick, Raymond. *James Branch Cabell and the Modern Temper: Three Essays*. New York: Revisionist Press, 1974. Explores realism and romance, the fact and the dream, in Cabell's novels. Himelick sees Cabell as an antiromantic whose novels convey his understanding of life as a "grotesque comedy."

Inge, Thomas M., and Edgar E. MacDonald, eds. *James Branch Cabell: Centennial Essays*. Baton Rouge: Louisiana State University Press, 1983. Compilation of essays, originally presented at a celebration of the centennial of Cabell's birth at Virginia Commonwealth University, provides both biographical infor-

mation on the author and critical analysis of his works. Includes a bibliographical essay.

MacDonald, Edgar E. *James Branch Cabell and Richmond-in-Virginia*. Jackson: University Press of Mississippi, 1993. Very detailed, authoritative biography focuses on how Cabell was influenced by living in Richmond, Virginia, in the late nineteenth and early twentieth centuries. MacDonald is a senior Cabell scholar at the James Branch Cabell Library at Virginia Commonwealth University. Includes an excellent bibliography.

Riemer, James D. *From Satire to Subversion: The Fantasies of James Branch Cabell*. New York: Greenwood Press, 1989. Devotes separate chapters to *The Cream of the Jest*, *Jurgen*, *Figures of Earth*, *The High Place*, *The Silver Stallion*, and *Something About Eve*—these books, Riemer argues, represent Cabell's greatest achievements. Includes an introduction that provides a good overview of the writer's career.

Tarrant, Desmond. *James Branch Cabell: The Dream and the Reality*. Norman: University of Oklahoma Press, 1967. Critical study of Cabell's work examines the author as mythmaker. Discusses both Cabell's early and later writings.

Van Doren, Carl, H. L. Mencken, and Hugh Walpole. *James Branch Cabell: Three Essays*. Port Washington, N.Y.: Kennikat Press, 1967. Valuable contribution to studies on Cabell presents criticism of a very high standard—both erudite and entertaining—by three eminent authors. Included in the appendix is a sampling of reviews of Cabell's works.

GEORGE WASHINGTON CABLE

Born: New Orleans, Louisiana; October 12, 1844
Died: St. Petersburg, Florida; January 31, 1925

PRINCIPAL LONG FICTION

The Grandissimes, 1880
Madame Delphine, 1881
Dr. Sevier, 1884
Bonaventure, 1888
John March, Southerner, 1894
The Cavalier, 1901
Bylow Hill, 1902
Kincaid's Battery, 1908
Gideon's Band, 1914
Lovers of Louisiana, 1918

OTHER LITERARY FORMS

In addition to nine novels, George Washington Cable published a novella, *Madame Delphine*, and four collections of short stories: *Old Creole Days* (1879), *Strong Hearts* (1899), *Posson Jone' and Père Raphaël* (1909), and *The Flower of the Chapdelaines* (1918). He also wrote a dramatized version of one of his novels, *The Cavalier*. His eight books of nonfiction cover miscellaneous subjects. *The Creoles of Louisiana* (1884) is a collection of history articles, and *Strange True Stories of Louisiana* (1889) is a collection of factual stories; both collections are set in Cable's native state. *The Silent South* (1885) and *The Negro Question* (1890) are collections of essays on southern problems. *The Busy Man's Bible* (1891) and *The Amateur Garden* (1914) grew out of Cable's hobbies of Bible teaching and gardening. *A Memory of Roswell Smith* (1892) is a memorial tribute to a friend, and *The Cable Story Book: Selections for School Reading* (1899) is a book of factual and fictional material for children. Cable also wrote magazine articles and a newspaper column.

ACHIEVEMENTS

In his 1962 study of the author, Philip Butcher shows the high position that George Washington Cable held in American literature in the last years of the nineteenth century. In 1884, the *Critic* ranked him ahead of four-teenth-place Mark Twain on its list of "Forty Immortals." A cartoon in the May 27, 1897, issue of *Life* magazine depicted Cable among the ten most popular authors of the day. In the American edition of *Literature* in 1899, he was tenth on the list of greatest living American writers.

Popular both with critics and with the reading public in his own time, Cable is little known today. His reputation as a writer of fiction rests on three works: the novel *The Grandissimes*, the novella *Madame Delphine*, and the collection of short stories *Old Creole Days*, later editions of which include *Madame Delphine* as the lead story. Although *Dr. Sevier* and *John March, Southerner* contain serious commentary, the three novels that followed in the first decade of the new century are trivial romances. His last two novels, *Gideon's Band* and *Lovers of Louisiana*, signal only an incomplete return to the artistic level and social worth of his first three books. Because much of his energy went into provocative social essays on southern racial problems, into humanitarian reforms in such areas as prisons and insane asylums, into cultural projects, and, as a major source of income, into platform tours, Cable found insufficient time for the fiction he might otherwise have created. Nevertheless, as late as 1918 he published a collection of short stories and a novel, and up to his death in 1925 he was working on still another novel.

Cable was much admired by his contemporaries. William Dean Howells praised him privately and in print. Twain took him as a partner on a reading tour, and for four months (1884-1885) the two shared the stage as they read from their respective works. Cable also read on programs that included Hamlin Garland, James Whitcomb Riley, Eugene Field, and other popular writers of the day.

Popular in Great Britain as well, Cable was invited to England by Sir James Barrie for the first of two trips abroad (1898, 1905). For nearly three months in 1898, he traveled and visited in the homes of Barrie, Arthur Conan Doyle, Rudyard Kipling, Henry James, and other well-known figures. He was an interesting conversationalist, an effective speaker, and an entertaining performer.

His British friends arranged for him to read his fiction, play a guitar, and sing Creole-black songs in their homes and in public halls. Andrew Carnegie, his host at Skibo Castle, was so impressed with Cable's personality and writing that he later bestowed a lifetime pension on him. Among his honorary degrees was the doctorate of letters given by Yale University in 1901 to Cable, Twain, Howells, Theodore Roosevelt, Woodrow Wilson, and other contemporary notables.

Cable's reputation began to decline before his death and has never recovered. In the 1980's he was considered too important a writer to be omitted from southern literature anthologies and American literature textbooks, but by the end of the twentieth century he had yet to be deemed worthy of widespread revival.

BIOGRAPHY

George Washington Cable was born in New Orleans, Louisiana, on October 12, 1844. Ancestors of his mother, Rebecca Boardman Cable, had lived in New England since the seventeenth century and had moved to Indiana in 1807. The background of his father, the elder George Washington Cable, dates back to pre-Revolutionary times in Virginia. The elder Cable lived in Virginia and Pennsylvania with his parents before moving to Indiana, where he married Rebecca in 1834. The Cable family migrated to New Orleans in 1837, where George, their fifth child, was born.

In the 1840's, the Cables lived a comfortable existence, owning several household slaves until the father's business failed. Through the 1850's, the elder Cable worked at a series of jobs until, weakened in health, he died on February 28, 1859. Because young George's older brother, along with an older sister, had died of scarlet fever, his father's death required him, not yet fourteen, to leave school to support the family. Until the third year of the Civil War, he held his father's former position as a clerk at the customhouse.

Slight in size—only five feet five inches and weighing one hundred pounds—and deceptively youthful in features, Cable enlisted in the Confederate Army on October 9, 1863, three days before his nineteenth birthday. Incurring two slight wounds during his service, he was discharged in 1865.

After the war, Cable worked as an errand boy, as a store clerk, and, until malaria stopped him, as a rodman with a surveying party on the Red River. In 1868, he became a bookkeeper for two cotton firms in New Orleans. He married Louise Stewart Bartlett on December 7, 1869, and soon fathered the first of a large family of children. At one time, he worked simultaneously for the cotton house of William C. Black and Company, the New Orleans Cotton Exchange, and the National Cotton Exchange.

Newspaper work provided Cable's first opportunity to see his writing in print. While continuing as an accountant, he worked for newspapers as a freelance contributor and then as a full-time reporter. For eighteen months, beginning February 27, 1870, he wrote the column "Drop Shot" weekly, and then daily, for the New Orleans *Picayune*. While working for the *Picayune*, his research into Louisiana history at city hall, the cathedral, and the Cabildo, former seat of colonial government, led him to factual stories later to be shaped into fiction. In addition, his newspaper reports on contemporary local affairs interested him in reform on civic, regional, and national levels.

Appearing in *Scribner's Monthly*, Cable's stories were based on his knowledge of the people and activities of New Orleans and of events in Louisiana history. Six of the stories appearing in *Scribner's Monthly* and a seventh story, "Posson Jone'," which was published in *Appleton's Journal*, were later collected as *Old Creole Days*, published by Scribner's. His first novel, *The Grandissimes*, also based on the people and history of Louisiana, was serialized in *Scribner's Monthly* over a twelve-month period and then published in book form in 1880. Next came the novella *Madame Delphine*, first printed in *Scribner's Monthly* as a three-part serial, and then published in book form in 1881.

In 1881, Cable gave up his position as an accountant, depending for the rest of his life on lectures and public readings of his fiction to supplement his income as a writer. One of his successes was a series of six lectures at Johns Hopkins University in 1883, and he continued to find himself in demand on platforms in many cities. In 1884, his regional history *The Creoles of Louisiana* appeared, and in the same year his second novel, *Dr. Sevier*, was published. In 1884-1885, he went on a successful reading tour with Mark Twain.

Cable, son of a slaveholding family, was a loyal Confederate soldier during the Civil War and apparently remained unchanged in political stance for some time thereafter. Later, however, he began to express feeling against racial injustice. Although criticism of discrimination is present in his fiction, it was only through the direct statements of his magazine articles and public lectures that fellow southerners became fully aware of his radical stance. The publication of a volume of his essays, *The Silent South* (1885), made his stand clear. Newspaper editorialists who had acclaimed his fiction now began to attack his social and political views.

Cable had two households to support—one including his wife and children, and the other his mother, his sisters, and the children of his widowed sister. His wife, who traced her ancestry back to the Mayflower, was born and reared in New England. Cable believed that a return to the climate of New England would be beneficial for his wife's frail health. In addition, the attraction that a location near his publishers in New York held for him, and a sensitivity to the criticism aimed at him in the South, influenced his decision to leave New Orleans after forty years of residence there. Having previously visited Northampton, Massachusetts, he moved his wife and children to a home there in 1885, and his mother, sisters, and cousins followed soon thereafter.

Despite his desire to write fiction, Cable allowed other interests to take much of his time. In 1885, he championed black rights in an essay read nationwide, "The Freedman's Case in Equity." In 1886, he founded the first of the Home Culture Clubs, in which he would be involved for the next thirty-five years. Through his Open Letter Club (1888-1890), in the name of which he lectured, wrote, and published, Cable completed the period identified as his greatest effort for reform in the South. From 1887 to 1889, he undertook an extensive program of religious writing and teaching; he conducted a large Bible class in Northampton each Sunday, traveling to Boston on Saturdays to hold a similar class.

For five years, Cable published a book annually: *Bonaventure*, *Strange True Stories of Louisiana*, *The Negro Question*, *The Busy Man's Bible*, and *A Memory of Roswell Smith* were all published during this period. At the same time, he was giving readings and lectures from coast to coast. A popular speaker, he was frequently

George Washington Cable. (Library of Congress)

invited to deliver commencement addresses and to give talks on literary subjects, southern problems, and Creole history. Despite his endeavors, however, he remained constantly in debt—receiving advances on royalties from his publishers, obtaining loans, repaying old debts, and incurring new ones.

By this time, Cable had ceased actively campaigning for civil rights, and his writing developed a noncontroversial tone. His third novel, *John March, Southerner*, although concerned with Reconstruction problems, avoided racial issues, as did his collection of short stories *Strong Hearts*. *The Cable Story Book*, needless to say, offended no one. The following novels, *The Cavalier* and *Bylow Hill*, veered even more sharply from controversy to entertainment, their artistic value diminishing proportionately.

Meanwhile, in 1898, Cable had made a triumphal reading tour in Britain. Philanthropist Andrew Carnegie, with whom Cable became friends while in Scotland, donated money to one of Cable's long-enduring projects. In 1903, Carnegie agreed to give fifty thousand dollars for a building for the Home Culture Clubs on the condition that five thousand dollars a year be guaranteed locally for five years.

Dimming Cable's good fortune, his beloved wife died on February 27, 1904, ending a devoted marriage of nearly thirty-five years. Cable continued to write, although without immediately readying a book for publication. Two years and nine months after Louise's death, he married Eva C. Stevenson. In 1908, he published the novel *Kincaid's Battery*, and in 1909 he put two of his short stories (one of them selected from the *Old Creole Days* collection) into book form, *Posson Jone' and Père Raphaël*. In 1911, Carnegie began sending Cable one thousand dollars a year to support his writing. Three years later, *Gideon's Band* and *The Amateur Garden* were published.

Despite his debts, Cable managed to travel outside the United States even before Carnegie began to subsidize him. When traveling, he often carried with him an unfinished manuscript, working on it when he had time. In later years, no longer dependent on the platform circuit, he began staying in Northampton in the summer, spending the winter in New Orleans, Florida, and Bermuda. In 1918, at the age of seventy-four, he published two books—*The Flower of the Chapdelaines*, a collection of short stories, and *Lovers of Louisiana*.

When Carnegie died in 1919, his will provided Cable with five thousand dollars a year for life, the annuity to be transferred to Eva if she survived her husband. Eva, however, died on June 7, 1923. Six months after her death, Cable married his third wife, Hanna Cowing. A little more than a year later, on January 31, 1925, he died. Among his literary papers was an unfinished novel on which he had been working.

ANALYSIS

Although George Washington Cable's reputation rests primarily on one collection of short stories and two pieces of longer fiction, his total output includes twenty-two books. For an understanding of Cable as a writer of fiction, one should first consider his nonfiction and his reasons for writing it. Cable's interest in history is shown in two books centered on Creole culture, *The Creoles of Louisiana*, a collection of history articles, and *Strange True Stories of Louisiana*, a collection of factual stories about the Creoles. On a juvenile level, *The Cable Story Book* is a combination of factual and fictional material that emphasizes the same Creole subjects as his fiction. *The Silent South* and *The Negro Question*, his best-known works of nonfiction, are collections of essays on controversial southern problems, notably the problem of racial discrimination. Characteristic of Cable's prose is a moral posture and a humanitarian zeal, openly stated in his nonfiction and imaginatively expressed in the most important of his fiction. He worked for the reform of people and institutions and for a reversal in racial attitudes.

THE GRANDISSIMES

Cable's first novel, *The Grandissimes*, is his unqualified masterpiece. Louis D. Rubin, Jr., has called it the first "modern" southern novel, dealing realistically as it does with the role of the black in American society. Added to the rich portrayal of aristocratic Creole settings and family problems, a panoramic array of characters of Native American, black, and mixed bloods vivify problems of social castes and racial discrimination in Louisiana in 1803, the year of the Louisiana Purchase. Using the historical actuality of racially tangled bloodlines as the theme for dramatic episodes, Cable emphasizes the ramifications of black-white relationships. The free quadroon caste, for example, had its special role in southern society, as shown historically in the New Orleans "quadroon balls." Beautiful young women of one-quarter black blood (quadroons) or, perhaps, one-eighth (octoroons) danced at these balls with white men, were chosen by them as mistresses, and were set up in separate households in the city.

Two principal quadroons interact in *The Grandissimes*. A male quadroon is the identically named half brother of the aristocratic Creole Honoré Grandissime. The darker Honoré Grandissime flouts the law by refusing to inscribe the letters "f.m.c." (free man of color) after his name. Educated in Paris along with his half brother and heir to most of their deceased father's wealth, the quadroon nevertheless remains unrecognized as a legitimate member of the Grandissime family. The Creoles' acceptance of an American Indian chieftain as ancestor is introduced to point up their unwonted prejudice against the taint of black blood. The main female quadroon is Palmyre Philosophe, a freed slave who bears a hopeless love for the all-white Honoré Grandissime and, in turn, is loved by his quadroon half brother. To illustrate the injustices perpetrated against blacks, Cable inserts the episode of the black Bras-Coupé, a historical figure used earlier in Cable's unpublished short story "Bibi." Palmyre hates Agricola Fuselier, her former owner and uncle to Honoré Grandissime, who forced her unconsummated marriage to Bras-Coupé.

The character who serves throughout the novel as spokesman for Cable is Joseph Frowenfeld, a German American newcomer to New Orleans, who observes, participates in, and comments critically on the action. Honoré Grandissime, the leading male character, is a Creole who recognizes the faults of his society and works with moderation to correct them. He provides a liberal Creole viewpoint, supplementary to the rigid moral judgment of Frowenfeld. Agricola Fuselier, in direct contrast to Frowenfeld, represents the proud old Creoles who insist on purity of race.

Action antecedent to the yearlong events of the novel goes back to 1673, the year of the birth of the American Indian girl whose choice of a De Grapion suitor began a feud between two Creole families, the De Grapions and the Grandissimes. Preceding the main plot by eight years comes the tale of Bras-Coupé. Otherwise, the action takes place between September, 1803, and September, 1804.

The leading female character, Aurora Nancanou, daughter of a De Grapion, is the young widow of a man killed by Agricola Fuselier in a duel over a card game. Agricola took Nancanou's estate in payment for the gambling debt, passing the estate on to his nephew, the white Honoré, and leaving Aurora and her daughter Clotilde without land or money. The novel opens at a masked ball in New Orleans where Aurora and Honoré meet, unaware of each other's identity, thus beginning a romantic complication. Paralleling the love triangle of Palmyre and the Grandissime half brothers, Joseph Frowenfeld falls in love with Clotilde, who, at the same time, is desired by Frowenfeld's friend Dr. Charlie Keene.

Honoré Grandissime, as leader of the Grandissime family and as Cable's symbol of right-thinking Creoles, upsets his relatives on several occasions: Endangering the Grandissime finances, he returns Aurora Nancanou's property to her; in an act socially degrading to the family, he becomes a partner with the quadroon Honoré, under the business title "The Grandissime Brothers"; on an uneasy political level, he cooperates with Claiborne, the newly appointed territorial governor.

Romance, realism, and melodrama are mingled in *The Grandissimes*. In a romantic resolution, the De Grapion-Grandissime feud is ended, and marriage is imminent for two sets of lovers—Aurora and the white Honoré Grandissime, Clotilde and Frowenfeld. On the realistic side—with an admixture of melodramatic incidents—the two leading quadroons of the story are defeated. After Palmyre's several attempts to get revenge on the object of her hate, Agricola Fuselier, and after he is stabbed by the quadroon Honoré, she is forced to flee for safety to Paris. She is accompanied by her fellow refugee, Honoré Grandissime (f.m.c.), who commits suicide by drowning because of her final rejection of him.

Intentional obscurity is a characteristic of Cable's style in *The Grandissimes*. Lack of direct statement and slow revelation of relationships mark the progress of the plot. Facts are given through hints and implication; full information is withheld in a dense accumulation of incidents. This technique, typical of his early and best works, has been praised for its artistry and criticized for its lack of clarity.

Cable's portrayal of slaveholders, slaves, and the stubbornly held traditions of French Louisiana added a new dimension to southern literature. Succeeding in his aim as a novelist, Cable found that fame brought a painful backlash. His radical views caused this native son to be identified as a traitor to New Orleans and the South.

MADAME DELPHINE

In 1881, Cable published the novella *Madame Delphine*, the third in the three-year sequence of Cable's finest literary works (after the short-story collection *Old Creole Days* and the novel *The Grandissimes*). First published as a three-part novelette in *Scribner's Monthly* from May to July, 1881, *Madame Delphine* was published by Scribner's in book form later that year. In editions of *Old Creole Days* succeeding its initial publication, *Madame Delphine* is included and given lead position in the book.

The story begins with beautiful Olive Delphine returning from France on a ship that is boarded by the Creole pirate Ursin Lemaitre. Confronted by Olive's piety and charm, Lemaitre is struck with repentance for his sinful life and with love for the unidentified stranger. Settling in New Orleans, the reformed Lemaitre changes his name to Vignevielle and turns from piracy to banking. When not in his banker's office, he wanders through the streets, searching for the mysterious young woman.

Eventually, the lovelorn banker and Olive develop a friendship and marriage becomes their intention. Olive, however, is not legally able to become Lemaitre's wife, for she has black ancestry. Her mother, Madame Delphine, is a quadroon, the mistress to a white man, Olive's father. Madame Delphine, despite the laws against miscegenation, approves of the marriage. Indeed, she has made it clear that she is seeking a white husband for her daughter.

Vignevielle's relatives and friends, knowing that Madame Delphine is a quadroon, attempt to stop the illegal marriage, going so far as to threaten to turn him over to government agents who are searching for him. Madame Delphine meanwhile puts forth the ultimate effort to make the union possible. Producing fabricated evidence, she perjures herself by swearing that she is not the girl's blood mother. After Vignevielle and Olive are married, Madame Delphine goes for confession to the priest Père Jerome, admits her lie, and dies. Père Jerome speaks the closing line: "Lord, lay not this sin to her charge!"

The style of *Madame Delphine* is leisurely. Little mysteries cling to characters and actions, with revelation coming in glimpses, suggestions, and half-expressed statements. Early reviewers compared Cable to Nathaniel Hawthorne in achievement of mood, atmosphere, and ambiguity. Adverse criticism of *Madame Delphine*, however, finds the work excessively obscure; most troubling to critics is the needlessly complicated unfolding of the plot.

Furthermore, the characterization of the lovers is weak. Vignevielle's switch from dashing pirate to banker is inadequately motivated. Olive is a shadowy figure without distinguishable traits. Madame Delphine, despite her maneuvers, approaches the stereotype of the helpless mother. The only strong character is Père Jerome, a compassionate observer and spokesman for Cable. Père Jerome sees that society deserves blame, both for its actions and for its failure to act. Society acquiesces in evil—from its unprotesting profit in Lemaitre's smuggled goods to its deliberate manipulation of the lives of mulattoes.

More significant than the style of *Madame Delphine* is its portrayal of the southern attitude toward miscegenation. Although romanticism embellishes the outwardly happy ending of the story, Cable's recognition of the female mulatto's untenable position is clear. Looking beyond the temporary bliss of the wedding day, the reader realizes that prospects for Olive in New Orleans are not favorable. Madame Delphine's perjury has made the marriage legally permissible, but in the eyes of Lemaitre's friends, Olive is not and will never be an acceptable member of their aristocratic society.

The developing social consciousness revealed by Cable in *Madame Delphine* gives the work a lasting value. After this novella, however, he confined the most telling of his indictments to essays, disappointing readers who waited for his familiar critical tone in future novels. He was never able to duplicate the blend of artistic craftsmanship, authentic local color, and social commentary that distinguishes *Madame Delphine*, *The Grandissimes*, and *Old Creole Days*.

Bernice Larson Webb

OTHER MAJOR WORKS

SHORT FICTION: *Old Creole Days*, 1879; *Strong Hearts*, 1899; *Posson Jone' and Père Raphaël*, 1909; *The Flower of the Chapdelaines*, 1918.

NONFICTION: *The Creoles of Louisiana*, 1884; *The Silent South*, 1885; *Strange True Stories of Louisiana*, 1889; *The Negro Question*, 1890; *The Busy Man's Bible*, 1891; *A Memory of Roswell Smith*, 1892; *The Amateur Garden*, 1914.

MISCELLANEOUS: *The Cable Story Book: Selections for School Reading*, 1899.

BIBLIOGRAPHY

Biklé, Lucy Leffingwell Cable. *George W. Cable: His Life and Letters*. New York: Charles Scribner's Sons, 1928. This biography, written by Cable's daughter, has the advantage of immediacy to, and intimacy with, the subject. Covers the life of Cable primarily through the many letters that he wrote.

Butcher, Philip. *George W. Cable*. New York: Twayne, 1962. Literary biography provides a good general introduction to Cable, examining his life in the context of his work and vice versa. Discusses the major phases of Cable's life—from New Orleans and *Old Creole Days* to his friendship with Mark Twain to his social and political involvement—in an honest, engaging fashion.

Cleman, John. *George Washington Cable Revisited*. New York: Twayne, 1996. Critical introduction to Cable's life and work discusses the author's major works and the social context within which they were created. Includes chapters devoted to Cable's advocacy of civil rights for African Americans, his political writing, and his later works of "pure fiction."

Ekstrom, Kjell. *George Washington Cable: A Study of His Early Life and Work*. New York: Haskell House, 1966. Focuses on Cable's Creole fiction, giving much historical, literary, and cultural background to Cable's early work. In addition to biographical information on Cable's early years, provides discussion of the literary and nonliterary sources for the Creole short stories and novels.

Foote, Stephanie. "'The Shadow of the Ethiopian': George Washington Cable's *The Grandissimes*." In *Regional Fictions: Culture and Identity in Nineteenth-Century American Literature*. Madison: University of Wisconsin Press, 2001. Examination of Cable's novel explains the book's place in American regional fiction. This chapter is part of a larger study that focuses on how Cable's work and other regional fiction shaped Americans' ideas about the value of local identity.

Jones, Gavin. "Signifying Songs: The Double Meaning of Black Dialect in the Work of George Washington Cable." *American Literary History* 9 (Summer, 1997): 244-267. Discusses the interaction of African American and French Creole culture in Cable's works. Argues that African American dialect, song, and satire were transmitted to the white community subversively.

Ladd, Barbara. *Nationalism and the Color Line in George W. Cable, Mark Twain, and William Faulkner*. Baton Rouge: Louisiana State University Press, 1996. Demonstrates how the works of Cable and the other writers were influenced by the cultural legacy that French and Spanish colonialism embedded in the Mississippi River Valley and the Deep South.

Rubin, Louis D., Jr. *George W. Cable: The Life and Times of a Southern Heretic*. New York: Pegasus, 1979. By Rubin's own admission, the biography in this book is dependent on the work of Arlin Turner (cited below), but Rubin's comments on Cable's works are insightful and informative. Includes complete chapters on the novels *The Grandissimes*, *Dr. Sevier*, and *John March, Southerner*.

Schmidt, Peter. "Romancing Multiracial Democracy: George Washington Cable's *Lovers of Louisiana*." In *Sitting in Darkness: New South Fiction, Education, and the Rise of Jim Crow Colonialism, 1865-1920*. Jackson: University Press of Mississippi, 2008. Chapter on Cable's last novel is included in an exploration of how southern fiction published from the time of Reconstruction through the end of World War I affected societal reform in the South in regard to race, politics, and education.

Turner, Arlin. *George W. Cable: A Biography*. Durham, N.C.: Duke University Press, 1957. Thoroughly researched biography in many ways set the standard for further Cable studies. Discusses in great detail not only Cable's life but also his literary work, his political involvement, the geographical contexts of his work, and the important historical events that affected his life and work. Includes extensive bibliography and index.

JAMES M. CAIN

Born: Annapolis, Maryland; July 1, 1892
Died: University Park, Maryland; October 27, 1977
Also known as: James Mallahan Cain

PRINCIPAL LONG FICTION

The Postman Always Rings Twice, 1934
Double Indemnity, 1936
Serenade, 1937
The Embezzler, 1940
Mildred Pierce, 1941
Love's Lovely Counterfeit, 1942
Past All Dishonor, 1946
The Butterfly, 1947
Sinful Woman, 1947
The Moth, 1948
Jealous Woman, 1950
The Root of His Evil, 1951 (also known as
    Shameless, 1979)
Galatea, 1953
Mignon, 1963
The Magician's Wife, 1965
Rainbow's End, 1975
The Institute, 1976
Cloud Nine, 1984
The Enchanted Isle, 1985

OTHER LITERARY FORMS

James M. Cain began his career as a novelist relatively late in life. Cain first wrote professionally as a journalist. Long after he had become famous for his fiction, he would describe himself in *Who's Who in America* as a "newspaperman." Cain used his newspaper work as a springboard to a broader literary career in the 1920's. As a member of the editorial staff of the *New York World* he commented acerbically on contemporary American culture. Cain also authored a number of short stories that never appeared in hardcover during his lifetime. Following Cain's death, Roy Hoopes edited three collections of his journalistic writing and short fiction, *The Baby in the Icebox, and Other Short Fiction* (1981), *Sixty Years of Journalism* (1986), and *Career in C Major, and Other Fiction* (1986). Cain long dreamed of becoming a playwright, but success eluded him. An early effort, *Crashing the Gates* (pr. 1926), failed before reaching Broadway. A dramatization of *The Postman Always Rings Twice* (pr. 1936) ran for seventy-two performances in New York. Cain spent many years in Hollywood as a screenwriter but received screen credit for only three films, *Algiers* (1938), *Stand Up and Fight* (1939), and *Gypsy Wildcat* (1944).

ACHIEVEMENTS

James M. Cain's standing as a novelist has long been the subject of critical controversy. His first novel, *The Postman Always Rings Twice*, became a sensational best seller, but the work's lurid mix of sex and violence inevitably led to doubts about Cain's literary seriousness. In the years that followed, Cain never strayed from his twin themes of crime and sexual obsession. Critical opinion was divided among those who appreciated Cain as a poet of tabloid murder, such as writer Edmund Wilson, and those who believed that Cain exploited rather than explored the material of his books, such as the novelist James T. Farrell. After his period of greatest notoriety during the Depression and the World War II years, Cain's work was largely ignored by critics and scholars. He never received a literary prize for his novels, though late in life he received a lifetime achievement award from the Mystery Writers of America. Cain himself tended to dismiss critical commentary on his artistry, preferring instead to quote his sales figures. Novels such as *The Postman Always Rings Twice*, *Double Indemnity*, and *Mildred Pierce* endure as classic examples of the "hard-boiled" or "tough guy" school of writing that flourished in the 1930's and 1940's, and inspired American film noir. Along with such contemporaries as Dashiell Hammett and Raymond Chandler, James M. Cain will be remembered as a writer who illuminated an existential terror lying just beneath the often-glittering surface of American life.

BIOGRAPHY

James Mallahan Cain was the eldest of two sons and three daughters born to James William Cain and Rose

Mallahan Cain. His father was a professor of English and a college administrator who became the president of Washington College. His mother was a trained opera coloratura who gave up her professional ambitions to raise a family. Later in life Cain repeatedly expressed a sense of resentment and rivalry regarding his handsome and accomplished father. He revered his mother and imbibed from her an abiding love of the opera. After graduating from Washington College in 1910, Cain attempted to realize his dreams of a career in the opera by studying to be a singer. Unfortunately his voice could not match his aspiration, and he quit after a year of frustration. Between 1910 and 1914, Cain worked at a succession of jobs as he searched for a direction in life. He decided to become a writer, though he always regarded writing as a second choice because of his failure to express himself in music. He moved home and began writing short stories

James M. Cain. (AP/Wide World Photos)

and sketches, none of which he could sell. Cain supported himself by teaching mathematics and English at Washington College and earned a master's degree in drama.

Restless, Cain moved to Baltimore in 1917 and found work as a newspaper reporter. He volunteered for service in World War I and edited the Seventy-ninth Division newspaper. Upon demobilization, Cain returned to Baltimore and journalism. He embarked on a course that made him a successful man of letters in the 1920's. He began publishing essays and stories in journals such as *The Atlantic Monthly, The Nation*, and the *Saturday Evening Post*. He became friends with editor H. L. Mencken and contributed a series of satiric dialogues to Mencken's *The American Mercury*, published in *Our Government* in 1930. After a brief stint teaching at St. John's College in Annapolis, Cain moved to New York City in 1924. He joined the editorial staff of the *New York World*. There he wrote witty commentaries on life during the Jazz Age. When the *World* failed in 1931, Cain moved to *The New Yorker* as managing editor. He stayed at *The New Yorker* only nine months. Like many other writers, Cain traveled to Hollywood, taking advantage of a lucrative offer to write screenplays.

Cain never became a great success at screenwriting, and by 1933 he was out of a job. Financially pressed, he wrote his first novel that spring and summer. *The Postman Always Rings Twice* appeared in 1934 and was a literary sensation and popular triumph. The success of the novel revived Cain's Hollywood career, and he made California the setting of his most powerful works. During the 1930's, Cain produced a string of rough-edged novels that evoked some of the darkest shadows of life in Depression-era America. With the 1940's, however, Cain's inspiration seemed to fade, though he published for another thirty years. In 1946-1947, he attempted to establish an organization called the American Authors' Authority, which would have protected the economic rights of writers, but the effort failed. Cain proved a poor husband to three wives, but in 1947 he married for the fourth time, successfully, to Florence Macbeth, an opera singer like his mother. In 1948, Cain returned home to Maryland, moving to Hyattsville. He lived there quietly, continuing to write until his death in 1977.

Analysis

James M. Cain's strengths as a novelist are inextricably bound to his weaknesses. He has often been praised for the economy of his style and the speed with which he moves his narrative. Readers experience a delicious sense of surrender to the headlong impetus of his storytelling, yet motion in Cain's work often masks wayward prose and manipulative plotting. Critics have remarked on the cinematic quality of his writing. His protagonists live in his pages with the vibrant immediacy of Hollywood icons on the big screen. Cain's actors flirt with caricature; his characterizations are often so primitive and mechanical that they are ludicrous in retrospect.

Cain explores elemental passions in his novels. Sex, jealousy, and greed drive his characters as they thrust themselves into webs of crime and deceit. The intensity of Cain's evocation of this raw emotionalism imbues certain of his most notorious scenes with a surreal naturalism. Frank and Cora's frenzied lovemaking next to the body of the man they have killed in *The Postman Always Rings Twice* and Sharp's rape of Juana in a church in *Serenade* transcend and transfigure the more mundane trappings of Cain's stories. Moments like these also open Cain to the charge that he is trafficking in sensationalism, reveling in the sordid for its own sake. There is a voyeuristic quality to Cain's writing. He exposes his readers to the scabrous underside of the American Dream. Although he occasionally referred to his novels as morality tales, Cain rarely provides any moral alternative to the obsessive dreams of his characters, other than the faceless brutality of authority.

In Cain's universe the only law is chance. His protagonists enjoy no dignity with their various ends. Unlike the heroes of classical tragedy, their destinies do not illuminate the contours of a higher moral order. They are simply victims of an impersonal and blindly malevolent fate. This nihilism gives Cain's writings much of their enduring power. He captured the desperation of people leading blighted lives in a world wracked by the Great Depression. As long as men and women continue to sense their own powerlessness in a modern, mass-produced society, Cain's fables of reckless desire will resonate with readers.

The Postman Always Rings Twice

Cain's first novel is generally considered his greatest. It adumbrates themes and techniques that characterize his fiction. *The Postman Always Rings Twice* is cast in the form of a confession written by Frank Chambers on the eve of his execution. Frank, like many of Cain's protagonists, is doomed by his relationship with a woman. A homeless drifter, Frank wanders into a roadside "bar-b-que" and meets Cora, the frustrated wife of the Greek owner. Immediately drawn together by an overwhelming sexual chemistry, Frank and Cora kill the Greek in a fake auto accident. The murder drives the lovers apart, however, as their passion is clouded by suspicion and fear. Ironically, Cora dies in a real car crash, and Frank is then condemned for a murder he did not commit.

Cain's grim tale proved very influential. French writer Albert Camus acknowledged *The Postman Always Rings Twice* as an inspiration for *L'Étranger* (1942; *The Stranger*, 1946), his own existential meditation on crime and punishment.

Double Indemnity

Double Indemnity first appeared as a magazine serial. Cain wrote it for money, and he did not regard it very highly. Over time, the novel has come to be regarded as one of Cain's greatest achievements. Like *The Postman Always Rings Twice*, it is written in confessional form and tells a story of the fatal consequences of the wrong man meeting the wrong woman. Walter Huff, an insurance salesman, encounters Phyliss Nirdlinger, a beautiful, unhappily married woman. Desire and villainy blossom together as Huff sees an opportunity to win the woman he loves while at the same time beating the system he has long served. Huff and Phyliss kill Mr. Nirdlinger, making it look like an unusual accident, worth a double indemnity on his life insurance. As always in Cain, however, success in crime brings only anxiety and distrust. The lovers' mutual doubts and jealousy culminate in a deadly meeting on a cruise ship.

Serenade

Serenade provided sensational reading in the 1930's. It is Cain's psychologically outlandish commentary on sex and artistry. The protagonist and narrator, John

Sharp, is an opera singer who has retreated to Mexico because of the failure of his voice. Cain's premise is that Sharp cannot sing because of his receptiveness to the sexual advances of conductor Stephen Hawes. Sharp falls under the spell of Juana, an uneducated earth mother, whose embraces restore his sexual and vocal potency. Sharp returns to California and stardom. His success is challenged when Hawes appears. Juana kills Hawes, almost ritually, during a mock bullfight. Sharp insists on fleeing with Juana and inadvertently causes her death.

MILDRED PIERCE

Mildred Pierce marked a departure for Cain: The book contains no murders; it is told in the third person; its protagonist is a woman. The novel remains true, however, to Cain's dark vision of human relationships. Mildred Pierce is a middle-class housewife who rejects her philandering husband. Forced to support herself, she begins as a waitress and becomes the owner of a chain of restaurants. Mildred's undoing is her extravagant, almost incestuous, love for her daughter Veda, an aspiring opera singer. Mildred mortgages her restaurants to finance Veda's career. Veda responds by leaving, taking with her Mildred's second husband. Mildred lives on, ruined and alone, her career a perverse distortion of America's Horatio Alger myth.

THE BUTTERFLY

Cain's originality and intensity seemed to dissipate with the end of the Depression and the advent of World War II. Some critics think highly of *The Butterfly*, a tale of incest and murder set in the mountains of eastern Kentucky. In this novel Cain ambitiously attempts to delineate the psychology of a delusional and obsessive personality as he traces the agonies of a self-righteous mountaineer sexually drawn to a young woman he believes to be his daughter. Cain's lofty intentions never attain fruition, however, because he allows his mountaineer and supporting characters to dissolve into vulgar and simplistic stereotypes. Flawed as it is, *The Butterfly* is the best of Cain's later writing, which separates into unrealized historical romances and diffident echoes of his earlier work. Cain's reputation as a novelist will always rest on the bitter existential melodramas he produced in the 1930's.

Daniel P. Murphy

OTHER MAJOR WORKS

SHORT FICTION: "Pastorale," 1928; "The Taking of Monfaucon," 1929; "Come-Back," 1934; "The Birthday Party," 1936; "Brush Fire," 1936; "Dead Man," 1936; "Hip, Hip, the Hippo," 1936; "Coal Black," 1937; "Everything but the Truth," 1937; "The Girl in the Storm," 1940; *Career in C Major, and Other Stories*, 1943; "Payoff Girl," 1952; "Cigarette Girl," 1953; "Two O'Clock Blonde," 1953; "The Visitor," 1961; *The Baby in the Icebox, and Other Short Fiction*, 1981 (Roy Hoopes, editor); *Career in C Major, and Other Fiction*, 1986 (Hoopes, editor).

PLAYS: *Crashing the Gates*, pr. 1926; *Theological Interlude*, pb. 1928 (dialogue); *Trial by Jury*, pb. 1928 (dialogue); *Citizenship*, pb. 1929 (dialogue); *Will of the People*, pb. 1929 (dialogue); *The Governor*, pb. 1930; *Don't Monkey with Uncle Sam*, pb. 1933 (dialogue); *The Postman Always Rings Twice*, pr. 1936 (adaptation of his novel); *7-11*, pr. 1938.

SCREENPLAYS: *Algiers*, 1938; *Stand Up and Fight*, 1938; *Gypsy Wildcat*, 1944.

NONFICTION: *Our Government*, 1930; *Sixty Years of Journalism*, 1986 (Roy Hoopes, editor).

MISCELLANEOUS: *The James M. Cain Cookbook: Guide to Home Singing, Physical Fitness, and Animals (Especially Cats)*, 1988 (essays and stories; Roy Hoopes and Lynne Barrett, editors).

BIBLIOGRAPHY

Cain, James M. "An Interview with James M. Cain." Interview by John Carr. *Armchair Detective* 16, no. 1 (1973): 4-21. Cain reveals interesting highlights of his career as a reporter and explains the influence of Vincent Sergeant Lawrence, a journalist and screenwriter, on his work. Cain's comments on his three major novels are particularly informative. Includes an annotated list of people important in Cain's life and a bibliography of Cain's writings.

Hoopes, Roy. *Cain*. New York: Holt, Rinehart and Winston, 1982. Comprehensive biography is divided into four chronological parts, covering his years in Maryland and France, New York, Hollywood, and Hyattsville. Includes an afterword on Cain as newspaperman. Supplemented by extensive source notes, a list of Cain's publications, a filmography, and an index.

Madden, David. *Cain's Craft*. Metuchen, N.J.: Scarecrow Press, 1985. One of Cain's earliest academic champions explores the author's literary techniques. Compares some of Cain's works to novels by other writers and addresses the ways in which Cain's books have been adapted to the screen.

_____. *James M. Cain*. New York: Twayne, 1970. Well-written introductory volume takes note of Cain's varied reputation as an excellent, trashy, important, and always popular writer. Approaches every major aspect of his work on several levels, including his life in relation to his writing, analysis of his characters, and his technical expertise. Complemented by notes, a bibliography of primary and secondary sources, and an index.

Marling, William. *The American Roman Noir: Hammett, Cain, and Chandler*. Athens: University of Georgia Press, 1995. Intriguing exercise in literary criticism links the hard-boiled writings of Cain, Dashiell Hammett, and Raymond Chandler to contemporary economic and technological changes. Marling sees these writers as pioneers of an aesthetic for the postindustrial age.

Nyman, Jopi. *Hard-Boiled Fiction and Dark Romanticism*. New York: Peter Lang, 1998. Examines the fiction of Cain, Dashiell Hammett, Ernest Hemingway, and Horace McCoy and asserts that the romanticism and pathos in these works reflects the authors' nostalgia for a lost world of individualism and true manhood.

Oates, Joyce Carol. "Man Under Sentence of Death: The Novels of James M. Cain." In *Tough Guy Writers of the Thirties*, edited by David Madden. Carbondale: Southern Illinois University Press, 1968. Brief but wide-ranging essay approaches Cain's novels as significant for the light they throw on his relationship with the American audience of the 1930's and 1940's.

Shaw, Patrick W. *The Modern American Novel of Violence*. Troy, N.Y.: Whitson, 2000. Analysis of violence in American novels includes an examination of *The Postman Always Rings Twice*. Concludes that in writing this "sadistic" novel, Cain created a "sardonic, unencumbered narrative style that proved more influential than the story it conveyed."

Skenazy, Paul. *James M. Cain*. New York: Continuum, 1989. Comprehensive study of Cain's work. Skenazy is more critical of the author's writing than are some other commentators (including Madden, cited above) but acknowledges Cain's importance and his continuing capacity to attract readers.

Wilson, Edmund. "The Boys in the Back Room." In *Classics and Commercials*. New York: Farrar, Straus and Giroux, 1950. Personal essay by an astute social and cultural commentator groups Cain with John Steinbeck, John O'Hara, William Saroyan, and others in the 1930's and 1940's who were influenced by Ernest Hemingway. Wilson considers Cain to be the best of these writers.

ERSKINE CALDWELL

Born: White Oak, Georgia; December 17, 1903
Died: Paradise Valley, Arizona; April 11, 1987
Also known as: Erskine Preston Caldwell

PRINCIPAL LONG FICTION

The Bastard, 1929
Poor Fool, 1930
Tobacco Road, 1932
God's Little Acre, 1933
Journeyman, 1935
Trouble in July, 1940
All Night Long: A Novel of Guerrilla Warfare in Russia, 1942
Tragic Ground, 1944
A House in the Uplands, 1946
The Sure Hand of God, 1947
This Very Earth, 1948
Place Called Estherville, 1949

Episode in Palmetto, 1950
A Lamp for Nightfall, 1952
Love and Money, 1954
Gretta, 1955
Claudelle Inglish, 1958
Jenny by Nature, 1961
Close to Home, 1962
The Last Night of Summer, 1963
Miss Mamma Aimee, 1967
Summertime Island, 1968
The Weather Shelter, 1969
The Earnshaw Neighborhood, 1972
Annette, 1974

OTHER LITERARY FORMS

Erskine Caldwell's first published work was "The Georgia Cracker," a 1926 article. Other pieces were printed in "little" magazines, and then in *Scribner's Magazine*. For several decades, he regularly wrote articles for magazines and newspapers. He produced several nonfiction books, some in collaboration with photojournalist Margaret Bourke-White (at one time his wife): *You Have Seen Their Faces* (1937), *North of the Danube* (1939), *All-Out on the Road to Smolensk* (1942), and *Russia at War* (1942). His collections of short stories include *American Earth* (1931), *We Are the Living: Brief Stories* (1933), *Kneel to the Rising Sun, and Other Stories* (1935), *Southways: Stories* (1938), and *Jackpot: Collected Short Stories* (1950).

ACHIEVEMENTS

Erskine Caldwell's books have been published in some thirty-four countries, with more than three hundred editions released in such languages as Croatian, Chinese, Slovene, Turkmenian, Arabic, Danish, Hebrew, Icelandic, Russian, and Turkish. Caldwell has been called the best-selling writer in the United States. In 1933, he received the *Yale Review* award for fiction for his short story "Country Full of Swedes." Between 1940 and 1955, he was editor of twenty-five volumes of the regional book series American Folkways for the publishing house of Duell, Sloan and Pearce. His novel *Tobacco Road* was adapted for the stage in 1934 by Jack Kirkland and ran seven and a half years on Broadway, a record run. John Ford directed a motion-picture adaptation that

was released in 1941. A film version of *Claudelle Inglish* was released in 1961. *God's Little Acre*, possibly Caldwell's best-known novel, sold more than eight million copies in paperback in the United States alone; a film version was released in 1958.

BIOGRAPHY

Erskine Preston Caldwell was the son of a preacher, Ira Sylvester Caldwell. His mother was Caroline "Carrie" Preston (Bell) Caldwell of Staunton, Virginia. At the time Erskine was born, on December 17, 1903, the Reverend Caldwell was minister in Newman, Georgia, in Coweta County, forty miles from Atlanta. His wife, active in helping her husband in his ministry, also ran a small school. She taught Caldwell through much of his elementary and secondary education, both in her school and at home. He actually spent only one year in public school and one in high school.

Between 1906 and 1919, the Caldwells moved several times as the ministry dictated. This not-quite-nomadic existence and the straitened circumstances under which the family lived were probably influential in molding Caldwell into early self-reliance and in fostering a wanderlust that persisted throughout his youth and adult life. Caldwell left home at fourteen and roamed the Deep South, Mexico, and Central America. He did return home, however, to complete his high school education.

In 1920, Caldwell enrolled in Erskine College in Due West, South Carolina. From 1923 to 1924, he attended the University of Virginia on a scholarship; in 1924, he studied for two terms at the University of Pennsylvania. In 1925, he returned to the University of Virginia for an additional term, but he was never graduated.

While attending the University of Virginia, he married Helen Lannegan, and it was at this time that he decided to write for a living. With his wife and growing family of three children (Erskine Preston, Dabney Withers, and Janet), he lived in Maine between 1925 and 1932 while he wrote and earned a living at odd jobs; seven years of writing elapsed before any of his work was published. In his lifetime, Caldwell had experience as a mill laborer, cook, cabdriver, farmhand, stonemason's helper, soda jerk, professional football player, bodyguard, stagehand at a burlesque theater, and once even a hand on a boat running guns to a Central American country in revolt.

He published his first article in 1926. Soon Maxwell Perkins, the legendary editor at Charles Scribner's Sons, discovered some of his works and was enthusiastic and encouraging about his talent. Subsequently, Perkins published *American Earth* and *Tobacco Road*, which brought Caldwell his first real recognition. When Caldwell and Perkins had a serious disagreement, Caldwell switched his publishing allegiance to the Viking Press.

Divorced from his first wife in 1938, Caldwell married the photojournalist Margaret Bourke-White in 1939. They collaborated on several successful books, but the marriage ended in divorce in 1942. That same year he married June Johnson, with whom he had one son, Jay Erskine. In 1957, after divorcing his third wife, he married Virginia Moffett Fletcher.

During the 1940's, Caldwell traveled to China, Mongolia, Turkestan, and Russia. Because of the powerful, enthusiastic way in which he wrote about Russia and in turn indicted certain aspects of American capitalism, some accused him of being a Communist, a charge he emphatically denied.

Caldwell was a member of the National Institute of Arts and Letters, the Authors League of America, the Phoenix Press Club, and the San Francisco Press Club. Active as a writer and lecturer, Caldwell toured Europe in the 1960's under the auspices of the U.S. Department of State. In the 1970's, he made a series of speeches in Georgia to promote the paperback reprint of his 1937 book *You Have Seen Their Faces*. He used this opportunity to decry the remaining poverty in the South despite the region's industrialization.

In 1974, Caldwell underwent surgery for the removal of a growth on his lung; he submitted to similar surgery the following year. He regained enough health to publish two collections of short stories and two nonfiction volumes in the 1980's. Caldwell died in Arizona on April 11, 1987.

ANALYSIS

Erskine Caldwell is the chronicler of the poor white. He has told the story of the diversions and disasters of the poor southerner with more detail and sympathetic atten-

Erskine Caldwell. (Carl Van Vechten/Library of Congress)

tion than any other American writer of his time. In doing so, he has created memorable characters and unforgettable episodes and has provoked scandalized eyebrow-raising at his language, his imagery, and his view of life.

Obscenity charges have been filed against an inordinate number of Caldwell's books, only to be fought down in court: One man's obscenity is another man's earthy realism. The attendant publicity generated more curiosity about his books, and sales soared. The self-appointed censors who attacked his books in court were only slightly more antagonistic than the reviewers who labeled his works "orgiastic litanies" and "particularly ugly stories" to be read with disgust and "a slight retching."

Charges of obscenity barraged the publication of *God's Little Acre* from New York to Denver. *Tobacco Road* had an arduous struggle to stay on the booksellers' shelves. *Tragic Ground* ran into trouble with Canadian censors. But how obscene are these books? By today's standards even *God's Little Acre* seems only mildly lewd. Under the layer of animalistic sexual behavior and uncouth, uncultured dialogue, qualities of literary merit are readily discernible.

The most prominent and lasting quality of Caldwell's fiction—the one that has made *Tobacco Road* a minor classic and several other of his earlier novels important literary pieces—is comic grotesquerie. Caldwell conveys a kind of ludicrous horror that becomes more horrible when the reader realizes that hyperbole does not negate the truth behind the most ridiculous episodes: The poor people of the South were deprived to the point of depravity. Writing in a naturalistic style, Caldwell allows the reader to observe the day-to-day activities of poor white families whose impoverished condition has created tragicomic eccentricities.

Those impoverished conditions are the key to understanding Caldwell's main thrust in nearly all of his earlier novels. Living in hopeless hunger, illiterate, and essentially cut off from the world of progress, ambition, and culture, Caldwell's characters seem not quite human. The veneer of civilized attitudes and activities has been ground away by the endless struggle to satisfy the daily hunger and to find some hope, in a vast vista of barren prospects, of a better day tomorrow.

Caldwell was deeply concerned that this segment of society he chose to depict in his work had been repressed by ignorance and poverty as an almost direct result of society's indifference. In later works such as *The Weather Shelter* or even *Claudelle Inglish*, he shifted his attention from the thoroughly downtrodden to the merely browbeaten, but he continued to make a statement about society's indifference to the poor and about the survival instinct of the poor that makes them persevere.

Caldwell's earlier books are generally considered his better efforts; his themes and characters were fresh, and he had not yet begun to rework them with regularity. Still, there is a kind of plot formula in his first important novels: The main characters are introduced with a recounting of their day-to-day activities wherein their basic problem is presented; a new character is introduced, bringing what seems to be an opportunity for some degree of betterment; then tragedy strikes, usually resulting in the death of a sympathetic character. There are seldom any "bad guys" in Caldwell's novels, no dastardly villains. The villain is society, which allows abject poverty,

ignorance, hunger, and hopelessness to exist without trying to correct the circumstances that caused them. His characters, victims of society, flounder into tragic situations without knowing how to save themselves.

TOBACCO ROAD

In the case of *Tobacco Road*, tragedy strikes as unpredictably as lightning, and the characters accept their lot as though it were a natural, unalterable phenomenon. This book, perhaps his best-known work, is the story of a family of ignorant poor white Georgians who at the outset are at the depths of degradation. They have no food, no prospects, and no apparent opportunity to get either. They have settled into a bleak routine, planning to plant a crop in the vague future and hoping for something to happen to change their lot. Jeeter Lester, the patriarch, has the last trace of a noble love of the land and a strong inherent need to farm his land and produce a crop, yet he cannot or will not do any of the practical things that must be done for serious, lifesaving farming. He has no money and no credit, and he will not leave his farm to find work in the town to get the money for seed and fertilizer. Thus, he drifts from day to day with good intentions but takes no positive action. Survival for him and his family has reached an "every man for himself" level. His mother is treated with less consideration than a dog: When any food is acquired, as when Jeeter steals a bag of turnips from his son-in-law, the old mother is not given any. The others in the family—Jeeter's wife Ada and the two remaining children, Ellie Mae and Dude—are equally unfeeling.

These people seem to be as far down the scale of humanity as anyone can get, yet the story relates a series of episodes that carries them progressively further to degeneracy and death. The casual attitude toward sex, as shown in the scenes with Dude and his "new" wife Bessie, brings to mind the blasé attitude that farmers show toward the breeding of their farm animals. There is no particularly lewd interest in the family's attempts to spy on the "honeymooning" couple. Rather, their curiosity seems born of boredom or the simple need for distraction. Because Caldwell has narrated these episodes in blunt, realistic language, a puritanical mind might see a moral looseness in them that could be (and was) attributed to an immoral intent on the part of the author. Viewed from the perspective of fifty years, however, the actions of the characters appear not obscene but merely uncivilized.

Another scene involves the accidental killing of an African American in a wagon. Rammed and overturned by the new car acquired by Bessie (as a not-very-subtle enticement to persuade Dude to marry her), the black is crushed by the wagon. The Lesters, having caused the accident, go blithely on their way. Their only concern is the wrecked fender of the car. They philosophize that "niggers will get killed." The killing of another human being is as casually natural to them as the killing of a dog on a highway.

The most inhuman and inhumane episode involves the death of Mother Lester, who is hit by the car in the Lester yard. She is knocked down and run over, "her face mashed on the hard white sand." She lies there, unaided by any of the family, hardly even referred to beyond Ada's comment that "I don't reckon she could stay alive with her face all mashed like that." The old woman struggles a bit, every part of her body in agonizing pain, and manages to turn over. Then she is still. When Jeeter at last decides something must be done with his old mother, he looks down and moves one of her arms with his foot, and says, "She ain't stiff yet, but I don't reckon she'll live. You help me tote her out in the field and I'll dig a ditch to put her in."

When Caldwell depicts the indifference of the family members to Mother Lester's slow, painful death, he is really depicting the degeneracy of people whom society has deprived of all "human" feeling. Thus, when in the last chapter the old Lester house catches fire and burns up the sleeping occupants without their ever waking, the reader may well feel that poetic justice has been served: The Lesters have lived a subhuman existence, and their end is fittingly subhuman. Yet, one does not entirely blame the Lesters for their lack of humanity; Caldwell moves his readers to wonder that a rich, progressive country such as the United States could still harbor such primitive conditions.

The comic quality that is so much a part of Caldwell's work saves *Tobacco Road* from utter grimness. Some of the episodes with the car, Jeeter's maneuverings to get money from his new daughter-in-law, the turnip filching—all create a climate that lightens the pervading ugliness. The sexual adventures are irreverent and bawdy; the dialogue is the ridiculous, repetitive gibberish of single-minded illiterates engrossed in their own narrow concerns. There is a particularly comic quality in Jeeter's serious pronouncements, which bespeak a completely unrealistic creature, out of touch with himself and his true condition. The enduring ridiculousness of Jeeter and his family is undercoated with a pathos that is obvious to the thoughtful reader. The condition and ultimate end of Jeeter and Ada are perhaps atypical but are still symptomatic of the condition and ultimate end of the many others like them living in the destitute areas of the South.

GOD'S LITTLE ACRE

Caldwell's *God's Little Acre* was considered by some critics his best work up to that time. A *Forum* review said it was "the first thing [Caldwell] has done which seems . . . to justify in any way the praise the critics have heaped upon him." There are flaws, as some reviewers were quick to point out, including repetitiousness and a too sudden and unexpected transition from a comic atmosphere to violent tragedy, yet it is second in quality only to *Tobacco Road* among Caldwell's novels.

God's Little Acre tells the story of Ty Ty Walden, a Georgia dirt farmer who for fifteen years has been digging enormous holes in his land looking for gold. Ty Ty, who is in most other respects a man with considerable mother wit, has a curious tunnel vision where this quest for gold is concerned. Because of it, he neglects his farming to the point of endangering his livelihood and that of his family. Worse yet, he fails to see the peril in the growing tension among the members of his family living on the farm with him. The inevitable tragedy results from the fact that he has two beautiful daughters and an even more beautiful daughter-in-law, Griselda. Ty Ty himself praises Griselda so much to anyone who will listen that he is largely instrumental in encouraging the fatal allure she has for the other men in the family. When these men—a son, Jim Leslie, and a son-in-law, Will Thompson—make advances toward Griselda, her husband Buck understandably becomes enraged. He is thwarted in his revenge against Will Thompson by another calamity—Will, a mill worker, is killed during a strike action—but Jim Leslie does not escape his brother Buck's wrath, nor does the tragedy stop there, for Buck's action is harshly punished.

The opening episodes of the novel are comic: Pluto

Swint, the fat, lazy suitor of the younger daughter, Darling Jill, is clearly a comic character in the mold of the sad clown. The enthusiastic search for the albino Dave, who according to black lore can divine gold lodes, is humorous: The process of finding him, roping him, dragging him away from his home and wife, and keeping him under guard like a prized animal is handled with a matter-of-fact detachment that makes these actions acceptable, predictable, and ridiculous, all at once. Darling Jill's sexual promiscuity and amoral attitude are refreshingly animalistic, even though some readers might disapprove of her untouched conscience.

When Darling Jill steals Pluto's car to go joyriding; when Ty Ty, along with the rest, goes to town to ask the well-off son Jim Leslie for money to help him through the winter because of inadequate crops; when Rosamond finds Will Thompson, her husband, in bed with her sister Darling Jill and chases him, buck-naked, out of the house—these richly comic scenes create a humorously cockeyed view of the Georgia poor white.

The deaths that occur later in the novel, however, are not funny, nor are their reasons; the comic existence Caldwell has depicted turns somber. This shift in tone has been described as a flaw, but such a judgment assumes that *God's Little Acre* is a comic novel gone astray. In fact, it is a serious story about people who in their daily lives do things that seem comic to those who observe them from a distance. Caldwell begins with a feckless existence that gradually becomes tragic; the comical infighting and escapades of Ty Ty's clan assume a grim inevitability.

Ty Ty has set aside one acre of his land for God. His intent is to farm the land, raise a crop, and give the proceeds to God through the church. Ty Ty has been digging for gold all over his farm, however, and there is very little land left that can still be farmed. Because he needs to raise a crop to feed his family and the two black families who tenant-farm for him, Ty Ty must constantly shift the acre for God from place to place. He readily admits that he will not dig for gold on God's little acre because then he would be honor-bound to give the gold to the church. He has no compunctions about doing God out of what he has declared is God's due. Later in the story, however, when he learns of Will Thompson's death, he has a sudden need to bring the acre closer to the homestead:

He felt guilty of something—maybe it was sacrilege or desecration—whatever it was, he knew he had not played fair with God. Now he wished to bring God's little acre back to its rightful place beside the house where he could see it all the time. . . . He promised himself to keep it there until he died.

After this decision, however, blood is shed on God's little acre: Buck kills his own brother, Jim Leslie. The bloodletting on God's ground is almost a ceremonial sacrifice wherein Ty Ty, albeit involuntarily, atones for a life spent giving only lip service to God. This ironic justice has the tragicomic grotesquerie characteristic of Caldwell's best work. The fall of his protagonists is both inevitable and absurd, utterly lacking in dignity.

LATER WORKS

Beginning in 1936, Caldwell produced different work. Perhaps he was aware that he had gone to the well often enough and needed to find new or different subjects. At any rate, traveling about the United States and Europe, with the drama of Adolf Hitler's Germany taking form, he wrote other books on uncustomary subjects: *North of the Danube*, *You Have Seen Their Faces*, *Some American People* (1935), *Southways*, *Say! Is This the U.S.A.?* (1941, with Margaret Bourke-White), *All-Out on the Road to Smolensk*, *Russia at War*, and more.

The novels that poured from Caldwell's pen on into the 1940's, 1950's, 1960's, and 1970's more or less followed the pattern of his early work. Reviewers observed that Caldwell seemed to have grown lackadaisical, content with repeating himself. He no longer seemed to instruct the reader subtly about the social and economic problems of the South; his work had begun to take on the dullness that results from the same joke and the same protestations repeated too often in the same way. He continued to use the same old formula without the zest and the imagination that made *Tobacco Road* and *God's Little Acre* so memorable.

Of the more than thirty novels Caldwell wrote over more than forty years, it is disappointing to find that two written in the 1930's—*Tobacco Road* and *God's Little Acre*—are the only ones likely to endure. Still, Caldwell is considered to be among the significant twentieth century writers produced by the South. His major contribution was his naturalistic comedic approach to his subjects. His best work depicts, with admirable craftsmanship, the harsh life of the sharecropper and tenant farmer through painful explicitness and comic vigor, juxtaposing social issues with the grotesque.

Jane L. Ball

OTHER MAJOR WORKS

SHORT FICTION: *American Earth*, 1931; *Mama's Little Girl*, 1932; *Message for Genevieve*, 1933; *We Are the Living: Brief Stories*, 1933; *Kneel to the Rising Sun, and Other Stories*, 1935; *Southways: Stories*, 1938; *Jackpot: The Short Stories of Erskine Caldwell*, 1940; *Georgia Boy*, 1943; *Stories by Erskine Caldwell: Twenty-four Representative Stories*, 1944; *Jackpot: Collected Short Stories*, 1950; *The Courting of Susie Brown*, 1952; *Complete Stories*, 1953; *Gulf Coast Stories*, 1956; *Certain Women*, 1957; *When You Think of Me*, 1959; *Men and Women: Twenty-two Stories*, 1961; *Stories of Life: North and South*, 1983; *The Black and White Stories of Erskine Caldwell*, 1984.

NONFICTION: *Some American People*, 1935; *Tenant Farmer*, 1935; *You Have Seen Their Faces*, 1937 (with Margaret Bourke-White); *North of the Danube*, 1939 (with Bourke-White); *Say! Is This the U.S.A.?*, 1941 (with Bourke-White); *All-Out on the Road to Smolensk*, 1942 (with Bourke-White; also known as *Moscow Under Fire: A Wartime Diary*, 1941); *Russia at War*, 1942 (with Bourke-White); *Call It Experience: The Years of Learning How to Write*, 1951; *The Humorous Side of Erskine Caldwell*, 1951; *Around About America*, 1964; *In Search of Bisco*, 1965; *In the Shadow of the Steeple*, 1967; *Deep South: Memory and Observation*, 1968; *Writing in America*, 1968; *Afternoons in Mid-America*, 1976; *With All My Might*, 1987; *Conversations with Erskine Caldwell*, 1988; *Erskine Caldwell: Selected Letters, 1929-1955*, 1999.

CHILDREN'S LITERATURE: *Molly Cottontail*, 1958; *The Deer at Our House*, 1966.

MISCELLANEOUS: *The Caldwell Caravan: Novels and Stories*, 1946.

BIBLIOGRAPHY

Arnold, Edwin T., ed. *Conversations with Erskine Caldwell*. Jackson: University Press of Mississippi, 1988. Collection of more than thirty articles about and interviews with Caldwell covers a wide range of subjects. Provides good insight into both Caldwell the writer and Caldwell the man. Includes an informative introduction and a chronology.

Cook, Sylvia Jenkins. *Erskine Caldwell and the Fiction of Poverty: The Flesh and the Spirit*. Baton Rouge: Louisiana State University Press, 1991. Contains chapters on Caldwell's apprenticeship years as a writer, his short stories, his novels of the 1930's and 1940's, and his later novels dealing with sex, race, and degeneracy. A concluding chapter discusses Caldwell and his critics. Includes bibliography and index.

Klevar, Harvey L. *Erskine Caldwell: A Biography*. Knoxville: University of Tennessee Press, 1993. Biography draws on both extensive archival research and interviews with Caldwell. Explores the regional context of Caldwell's life and writing, emphasizing the reasons for the popular and critical success of the author's early fiction and the decline of his later work.

Korges, James. *Erskine Caldwell*. Minneapolis: University of Minnesota Press, 1969. Brief volume examines Caldwell's early work. Korges asserts that Caldwell had a great comic vision and that he should be recognized as one of the most important American writers. Augmented by a select bibliography.

McDonald, Robert L., ed. *The Critical Response to Erskine Caldwell*. Westport, Conn.: Greenwood Press, 1997. Collection includes reviews of Caldwell's major works, scholarly discussions of his themes and techniques, and academic analyses of the image of the South presented in his fiction.

_____. *Reading Erskine Caldwell: New Essays*. Jefferson, N.C.: McFarland, 2006. Collection of twelve essays examines Caldwell as a novelist, a humorist, and a modernist. Some of the essays focus on *Tobacco Road*, *God's Little Acre*, and *Trouble in July*.

MacDonald, Scott, ed. *Critical Essays on Erskine Caldwell*. Boston: G. K. Hall, 1981. Excellent collection of critical essays on Caldwell, arranged chronologically, constitutes a good introduction to the author's work. Includes eight essays by Caldwell himself.

Miller, Dan B. *Erskine Caldwell: The Journey from Tobacco Road*. New York: Alfred A. Knopf, 1995. Biography focuses on Caldwell's first forty years, detailing his growing up in the culture of the American South and placing his writing in the context of the events of his life.

Silver, Andrew. "Laughing over Lost Causes: Erskine Caldwell's Quarrel with Southern Humor." *Mississippi Quarterly* 50 (Winter, 1996/1997): 51-68. Discusses some of the characteristics of nineteenth century American frontier humor inherited by Caldwell,

such as the narrator as cultured observer of frontier rustics. Argues that Caldwell subverts southern humor and critiques Depression-era capitalism.

Stevens, C. J. *Storyteller: A Life of Erskine Caldwell.* Phillips, Maine: John Wade, 2000. Comprehensive biography traces the details of Caldwell's life and discusses his "complicated personality." Describes how he wrote his novels and other works and also summarizes their contents.

MORLEY CALLAGHAN

Born: Toronto, Ontario, Canada; February 22, 1903
Died: Toronto, Ontario, Canada; August 25, 1990
Also known as: Edward Morley Callaghan

PRINCIPAL LONG FICTION

Strange Fugitive, 1928
It's Never Over, 1930
No Man's Meat, 1931 (novella)
A Broken Journey, 1932
Such Is My Beloved, 1934
They Shall Inherit the Earth, 1935
More Joy in Heaven, 1937
The Varsity Story, 1948
The Loved and the Lost, 1951
The Many Coloured Coat, 1960
A Passion in Rome, 1961
A Fine and Private Place, 1975
Season of the Witch, 1976
Close to the Sun Again, 1977
"No Man's Meat," and "The Enchanted Pimp,"
    1978 (novellas)
A Time for Judas, 1983
Our Lady of the Snows, 1985
A Wild Old Man on the Road, 1988

OTHER LITERARY FORMS

Morley Callaghan (KAL-uh-han) built his early reputation as a writer primarily on his short stories, many of which appeared in European and American magazines

such as *The Transatlantic Review*, *The Exile*, *Transition*, *The New Yorker*, *Esquire*, *The Atlantic Monthly*, and *Scribner's Magazine*. Several significant collections of these stories have been published, including *A Native Argosy* (1929), *Now That April's Here, and Other Stories* (1936), *Morley Callaghan's Stories* (1959), and *The Lost and Found Stories of Morley Callaghan* (1985). In addition to the novels and stories, Callaghan wrote a few plays and published many articles in *The Toronto Star*, *New World*, *Maclean's*, and *Saturday Night*. In 1963, he published *That Summer in Paris: Memories of Tangled Friendships with Hemingway, Fitzgerald, and Some Others*, a memoir of his early years as a writer in the company of Ernest Hemingway, F. Scott Fitzgerald, Robert McAlmon, James Joyce, and Ford Madox Ford.

ACHIEVEMENTS

It seems almost typical of the Canadian literary scene that Morley Callaghan has been more widely praised outside his home country than within it. Many American and European critics have compared Callaghan's work, especially the short stories, to that of the great Russians: Leo Tolstoy, Anton Chekhov, and Ivan Turgenev. Literary critic Edmund Wilson asserted that Callaghan was probably the most neglected novelist in the English-speaking world. From the beginning of his career in the 1920's, Callaghan attracted the attention of some of the foremost figures in the literary world: Fitzgerald, Hemingway, Ford, Sinclair Lewis, James T. Farrell, Ezra

Pound, and Erskine Caldwell, to name but a few. These writers praised his direct, laconic style, which was unencumbered by many of the excesses in language and description prevalent in the fiction of the 1920's and 1930's. American and European editors also found a special quality in Callaghan's work and promoted it in the leading magazines of the day: *The Exile, Transition,* and *The New Yorker.*

In Canada, on the other hand, Callaghan's early critical reception was often less than positive, as if there were some acute embarrassment in having a local author achieve international success. Callaghan himself was particularly sensitive to the vicissitudes of his reputation, and in *A Fine and Private Place,* using the persona of neglected author Eugene Shore, he placed himself at the forefront of Canadian letters. Certainly, much of the international praise of Callaghan has been extravagant, and much Canadian criticism has been parochial, but in the late twentieth century a more incisive and serious approach to this work created a well-deserved and long-overdue balance. Callaghan was awarded the Lorne Pierce Medal for Literature by the Royal Society of Canada as well as Canada's most prestigious literary prize, the Governor-General's Award (1951), for his novel *The Loved and the Lost.*

BIOGRAPHY

Edward Morley Callaghan was born in Toronto, Ontario, on February 22, 1903. His parents, both of whom encouraged his literary bent, were Roman Catholics of Irish descent. Callaghan was educated at Riverdale Collegiate and St. Michael's College, University of Toronto, where he excelled in academics and in sports. His college interests are often illustrated in his writing, most prominently in *The Varsity Story,* a novel of university life written on the occasion of a fund-raising campaign, and *That Summer in Paris,* which includes his account of his famous boxing match with Ernest Hemingway. During his university days, Callaghan worked as a reporter on the *Toronto Daily Star*; in 1923, he met Ernest Hemingway, who was the European correspondent for the paper. The two became good friends, and Hemingway not only provided stimulating conversation concerning Callaghan's favorite authors—Sherwood Anderson (Callaghan's "literary father"), James Joyce, Pound, and

Fitzgerald—but also encouraged him to continue writing fiction.

Callaghan received a bachelor of arts degree from St. Michael's in 1925 and subsequently enrolled in Osgoode Law School, from which he graduated in 1928. From 1926 through 1928, he made numerous trips to New York, where he met many friends of Hemingway who were to help him in his career. Among them were Katherine Anne Porter, William Carlos Williams, Nathan Asch, and Maxwell Perkins of the publishing house Charles Scribner's Sons. Perkins, after reading Callaghan's material, decided to publish his first novel, *Strange Fugitive,* and a collection of stories, *A Native Argosy.* Following his marriage to Loretto Dee in 1929, Callaghan traveled to Paris, where in a few months he completed a novel, *It's Never Over,* a novella, *No Man's Meat,* and a number of stories.

In 1930, Callaghan returned to Toronto permanently and began to produce his mature work, including *Such Is My Beloved, The Loved and the Lost,* and *Close to the*

Morley Callaghan. (John Martin)

Sun Again. Although his work has a universal appeal that distinguishes it from much Canadian fiction, it is rooted in Callaghan's observations of ordinary Canadian life and the particular attitudes of people as they respond to social and institutional forces. Into his eighties, Callaghan continued to write effectively, challenging the moral and social complacency that threatens the individual consciousness. He died in Toronto on August 25, 1990.

ANALYSIS

Much has been made of Morley Callaghan's streamlined style—in his own words, the art of getting the writing down "so directly that it wouldn't feel or look like literature." Callaghan wished to achieve an effect that was "transparent as glass." Life should be delineated without embellishment and to a large extent without metaphor. The language should be stripped of all artistic and symbolic associations, and objects should be seen as they are, like painter Paul Cézanne's apples, which are merely apples and yet capture the essence of apples. The central ideas of Callaghan's style are that reality must be accepted for what it is and that reality can be conveyed directly and simply. Leon Edel has suggested that this method has its origins in Callaghan's journalism, that Callaghan, like Hemingway, transfers the clipped, almost perfunctory prose of the newsroom into the realm of the novel, evading the images and symbols so often used in fiction. In its formative stages, Callaghan's style was perhaps also affected by the naturalism that was popular in the 1920's and 1930's, especially with American writers who wanted a mode of expression to capture the grim realities of the Depression.

Whatever its antecedents, Callaghan's style, especially in the early novels such as *Strange Fugitive* and *It's Never Over*, is handicapped by its programmatic simplicity; the prose is ill equipped to handle complexities of character. Callaghan's novels, even the later ones, are also marked by a structural simplicity, with a limited number of characters, few subplots, and, usually, a single controlling consciousness. They seem to plod on to inevitably tragic but morally ambiguous conclusions, giving an illusion of time that is almost static, reduced to its elemental character.

Callaghan did not, however, adhere slavishly to the avowed principles of his early fiction. Beginning with *Such Is My Beloved*, the sentences are more complex; the dialogue is richer, less stylized in the Hemingway manner; the prose is more rhythmic; and the structure of the novels is more intricate. Still, all of Callaghan's work is characterized by an unremarkable surface that at first glance has little aesthetic appeal. A more discriminating appraisal must therefore be made that accounts for the enduring quality of his work. Some critics have noted the parabolic nature of Callaghan's fiction, which limits the need for rounded characterization and necessitates simplicity of structure. Others argue that Christian humanism, especially in *Such Is My Beloved*, *More Joy in Heaven*, and *A Passion in Rome*, with their obvious biblical titles, informs Callaghan's work, giving it veracity and insight. Finally, some conclude that Callaghan's power derives from the influence of Charles Darwin, Karl Marx, and Sigmund Freud and a particular setting in history.

To a certain extent, all these theories are true, but all are equally unsatisfying as comprehensive theories. Underlying each of the novels is an ironic point of view that defeats easy answers and leaves readers with both an unsatisfying vision of life with few moral or aesthetic certainties and a sense of mystery, an awareness of the infinite complexities of human action and thought that make life worthwhile. This deliberate ambiguity is a narrative strategy designed to force readers into reevaluating their own observations of life and their own moral stances. Callaghan's novels, then, demand an involved sensibility and a questioning attitude; perhaps what is needed is the passionate intensity that Callaghan so frequently hints is the key to self-realization and independence.

Many of Callaghan's novels are animated by the tension between an individual and the institutions that circumscribe that person's behavior. The Church, the government, and the business community insist on a patterned, prudent existence that gives society stability and order. As such, they serve useful functions in most people's lives, but they are no substitute for a personal, compassionate, and intuitive vision, which, in everyday relationships, often subverts the legalistic intentions of the institutions. Individuals can be caught betraying society because they refuse to betray their own consciences. Thus, Father Dowling in *Such Is My Beloved* befriends two prostitutes to rescue them, and himself, with the power of love. His seemingly inordinate concern for them strikes a local parishioner and Dowling's bishop as unorthodox, and Dowling is relieved of his position and finally is admitted to a sanatorium. In *The Loved and the Lost*, Jim McAlpine is torn between his ambition to be a respectable columnist on a Montreal newspaper and the love of Peggy, a mysterious woman who inhabits the seamier region of the city. By losing faith in Peggy at a crucial moment, Jim allows the circumstances that bring about her death and a loss of faith in himself.

In *Close to the Sun Again*, Callaghan explores a more complex relationship between private and public values. Ira Groome, former "lord" of the Brazilian Power Company and now chairman of Toronto's police commission, reflects to no avail on why he has become impersonal and detached from the stream of life. After suffering severe injuries in a car accident, he relives his career as a naval commander and realizes that he had tried to escape the pain of human involvement by representing an institutional view of life. In a final epiphany, he accepts the voices in his own heart and dies with the profound self-knowledge that had been lacking in the earlier part of his life. In all of these works, the ultimate irony is that the individual can rarely reconcile the public demands of the world with a passionate, often barbaric, private vision.

SUCH IS MY BELOVED

The dedication to Callaghan's finest early novel, *Such Is My Beloved*, reads, "To those times with M. in the winter of 1933"; "M." was Jacques Maritain, the world-renowned philosopher, who came to St. Michael's College Institute for Medieval Studies as a visiting lecturer. Perhaps from his discussions with Maritain, especially concerning the nature of Christian humanism and the role of the saint in the world, Callaghan chose to concentrate on an explicitly religious theme, probing the relationship between the Roman Catholic Church, an agency of worldly prudence, and its priests, who must minister to individuals' needs through the love of Christ. The title suggests the focus of the novel; as Brandon Conron has noted, it is an echo of God's expression of love for His Son on the occasion of Christ's baptism. The epigraph confirms the theme of the nature of love and the consequences of the spiritual attitude of the novel. Taken from the Song of Songs, it reads: "Many waters cannot quench love, neither can the floods drown it: if a man give all the substance of his house for love, it would utterly be contemned."

The story is simple. Father Dowling, the central figure of the novel, befriends two prostitutes, Veronica "Ronnie" Olsen and Catherine "Midge" Bourassa, in order to save them from their degrading way of life. He soon realizes that they need not only love but also material necessities to sustain them through the Depression. Aware that the money he earns from his parish will not be enough, Dowling enlists the help of a wealthy parishioner, James Robison, to provide jobs for them. Robison, however, is not willing to risk the possibility of scandal and reports Dowling to his bishop. The two women are forced to leave the city (ostensibly Toronto), and Dowling, driven by these betrayals to madness, has only momentary periods of lucidity in the sanatorium.

Brandon Conron and Malcolm Ross both have argued that this novel presents at least a superficial allegory, with Dowling as Christ, Robison as Judas, and the bishop as Pontius Pilate, with certain minor characters also serving symbolic roles. The success of the novel, however, resides in Callaghan's ability to draw these characters as vulnerable human beings and not merely as types. Dowling conveys a disturbing naïveté that, despite his powerful love, causes his downfall. He brings Ronnie and Midge presents and money in an effort to keep them off the streets, but the gifts are ineffective. Dowling exhibits many other traits that seduce the reader into a kind of Conradian belief in him as "one of us." In the confessional, he is so consumed by his thoughts for the girls that he is harsh with others. He is jealous of Father Jolly's room, which Dowling himself covets; he admits to the natural sexual feelings of a young man his age; he hates the owner of the bawdy house, Henry Baer; and he lies about his involvement with the two prostitutes. Ironically, these human weaknesses make his love seem more potent.

The other characters, although not as well portrayed as Dowling, are effective in that the reader's responses to them are never wholly one-sided. Robison, much of the time, is a kind, helpful Christian who is confused by Dowling's love. The bishop, representing the position of the worldly Church, doubts himself and does not seem secure in his opinion of Dowling. Ronnie's pimp, Joe Wilenski, is a brutish man who often takes advantage of her yet respects her as a person. Ronnie, coming from a broken home in Detroit, and Midge, abandoned by her lover, react with affecting girlishness, especially when Dowling gives them pretty clothes. The ambivalent, realistic natures of these people condition the reader's response to the novel as a whole. One sees human beings with limited control over their circumstances; the Church and society seem to conspire to destroy the idealistic impulse in the individual consciousness.

Professor David Dooley has identified the central moral problem of *Such Is My Beloved* as the conflict between quixotic idealism and worldly prudence, with no satisfactory conclusion being evinced. Father Dowling tries to love the prostitutes as Christ loved sinners; all people are worthy of love without distinction, despite their failures. Love, he thinks, will overcome worldly considerations, but his faith cannot change the economic conditions that have driven the girls into sin. Dowling also tries to console the Canzanos, a family with twelve children living in abject poverty. Mr. Canzano says that they need money, not faith, and there is nothing left for him but despair. Even Dowling's great love is unconvincing here; he spends so much time with the girls that he can give little to his other parishioners. Although Callaghan satirizes the bishop for his concern that the scandal will hurt his charity campaign, he is perhaps correct in thinking that the Church should play a more material part in helping people such as the Canzanos.

Dowling's best friend, Charlie Stewart, a medical student who is an avowed Marxist, also views the world in terms of economics. Because he is a secular idealist, he believes that the ideal state could transform society and put an end to poverty. For him, there is no religious problem, only an economic one. The Church, the business community (represented by Robison and his uncharitable wife), Stewart, and Dowling are all caught up in the same dilemma. The personal qualities of spiritual love and secular compassion are defeated by institutions that must force their representatives to make rational, pragmatic choices. Even though these choices are often hypocritical, they are necessary to sustain order in society.

Such Is My Beloved ends with the two prostitutes forced out of the city by the police, and Dowling, in the sanatorium, is left to think of them as two of the many restless souls who cannot find peace. Dowling has occasional moments of clarity in which he offers his sanity as a sacrifice to God so that God might spare their souls. The priest is content in this offering and, at peace with himself, plans to write a commentary on the Song of Songs. The only positive note in the book is that this powerful love of Dowling's is somehow good, and although it cannot change society, it can transcend it, making even the tragic elements of life worthwhile.

In his next two novels, *They Shall Inherit the Earth* and *More Joy in Heaven*, Callaghan continued to examine the theme of love and its relation to society in explicitly religious terms. Neither novel is as well wrought as *Such Is My Beloved*, but both are nevertheless effective renderings of complex human motives. In the period between 1937 and 1948, his "dark period," Callaghan published no major novels. In 1948, however, his period of "spiritual dryness" over, Callaghan published *Luke Baldwin's Vow* and *The Varsity Story* and began work on *The Loved and the Lost*, which appeared in 1951.

THE LOVED AND THE LOST

Although the religious dimension is understated in *The Loved and the Lost*, the novel again explores the inner opposition between the individual and the dictates of society. For the most part, the narrative consciousness is that of Jim McAlpine, through whose eyes the reader receives impressions of Montreal's clearly divided social strata. Formerly an associate professor of history at the University of Toronto, Jim is brought to the city by a publisher, Joseph Carver, to write a political column for the Montreal *Sun*. Carver, a professed "liberal," admired an article Jim had written, "The Independent Man," for *The Atlantic Monthly*. Living on "the mountain," an affluent district in Montreal, Carver and his divorced daughter, Catherine, represent the social status to which Jim has aspired all his life. Through a friend, Jim meets Peggy Sanderson, a seemingly generous and warmhearted woman. Jim falls in love with her innocence and her compassion, knowing that their relationship, as elusive as it may be, could destroy his ambitions. After a brawl involving Peggy at Café St. Antoine, a black jazz club on the river, Jim feels compelled to protect her and to profess his love for her. When Peggy's need for him is greatest, however, Jim loses faith in her, inadvertently leaving her to be raped and murdered. Unable to choose between the stable values of "the mountain" and the uncertain values of the river, Jim betrays not only Peggy but also himself.

The novel works in parallels of discrete oppositions between the mountain and the river, with Jim at the center, torn by the attractiveness of each and unable to reconcile the contradictions inherent in both. Carver has wealth and power, which he uses to operate a newspaper dedicated, like *The New York Times* or *Manchester Guardian*, to the principles of independent thinking. His editorial stance, however, is compromised by his personal objection to giving his own writers freedom of thought; he wants supreme loyalty from his staff, and he is disturbed by the possibility that Jim may be an embarrassment to him. His daughter, Catherine, embodies the beauty and social grace of her class, but she is unsure of herself and hides her ardent character. She sees a hockey game with Jim and remarks on the artistic patterns of play. For her, life is a pattern, like her orderly room, which should not be disturbed. When Jim seems to side with the hockey player breaking the pattern by receiving a penalty, she asks why he is not "with us." In the end, however, discovering Jim's complicity in the murder, she empathizes with Peggy, violently slapping Jim for what she thinks is his betrayal.

Evoking similarly complex responses in all those who know her, Peggy Sanderson is an extremely ambiguous character. She has an air of innocence that enchants Jim and makes him want to protect her, but there is also a suggestion of carnality; as a young girl she admired the body of a naked black boy, and there are many comments made on her promiscuity with the black men at the Café St. Antoine, although they are not verified. In her indiscriminate, but platonic, love for all souls "without distinction" (here she echoes Father Dowling), she is seen as Saint Joan and Christ. This spiritual gift, however, invites fear and resentment, not peace and understanding. Symbolically, she is associated with a carved leopard and a small antique church, both of which she takes Jim to see. The fierce, uncertain jungle violence of the leopard contrasts with the stable religious feeling of the church, but Callaghan never lets the reader know if

these are indeed Peggy's responses to these objects. Jim thinks that her innocence is attracted to violence, that in fact her actions are self-destructive. By refusing to compromise her personal vision to social prudence, she is destroyed; the reader is never really sure of the extent to which she is culpable for her own fate.

Much of the novel is controlled by Jim's subjective, ambivalent feelings. He is estranged from the world of status as a child, a boy outside the hedge of the wealthy Havelocks, so his ambition is understandable even if excessively rationalized. Although he is drawn to Catherine and her tidy universe, he feels more comfortable in the "middle world" of the Chalet restaurant. Peggy shatters his balance by showing him a different side of life, where society's rules are broken and ambition becomes mere illusion. At the hockey game, he dismisses the patterns and sees the ice surface as a pit with writhing sacrificial figures. His vision, however, is only refracted, not significantly altered, and, rather than accept Peggy for what she is, he tries to mold her into his possession. Like Peter denying Christ, Jim denies knowing Peggy at Angela Murdoch's party on the mountain, hoping that he can bring the two worlds into harmony at some later date.

Wolfgast, the owner of the Chalet restaurant, tells Jim the story of a white horse he believed belonged to him although it was owned by his father's landlord. The circumstances of losing the horse impressed upon him the need for some definitive personal possession. In buying the Chalet, he achieved his dream. Peggy becomes Jim's "white horse," and he tries to own her by using her apartment to write his articles. Every day he tidies it up and makes a change that reflects his own personality. Only after her death does he recognize that his sin resided in not accepting Peggy for herself. Ironically, by not abandoning himself completely, by losing faith in Peggy as Orpheus lost faith in Euridice, he loses his own sense of identity as well. Confused about the values of high and low society and the mysterious values embodied by Peggy, Jim is left only with a dream of Peggy being trampled by white horses from the mountain as he draws back. In desperation, he attempts to find Peggy's antique church, hoping that in this symbol of belief Peggy will be with him always. The gesture is futile: Jim does not find the church.

The reader, too, is left without a clear moral resolution. Is Peggy really a virgin, a pure innocent? Is she a saint like Saint Joan, destroyed by an insensitive society? Is there really something primitive in her character that attracts violence? Could Jim cope with Peggy as a human being and not as the ideal he made her out to be? How do the symbols clarify and support meaning? After all, Wolfgast's "white horse," the possession of his restaurant, is something quite different from the possession of a human being. Does the church symbolize religious values or innocence, or is there a more ephemeral quality to it? Does the leopard represent the passionate nature of human beings or perhaps only independence? Beneath the surface of a straightforward, well-told story, then, are ambiguities that admit no easy resolutions.

Through the 1950's, 1960's, and early 1970's, Callaghan continued to write many interesting stories; his novels, however, met with mixed reviews. His style became more ambitious, and his ideas remained adventurous, but his plots were clumsy, his dialogue often unrealistic, and his characterizations more stereotyped than ever before. In *A Fine and Private Place*, an entertaining roman à clef for the author's followers, Callaghan even included a strident attack on critics unwilling to accept him as a major novelist.

CLOSE TO THE SUN AGAIN

With *Close to the Sun Again*, Callaghan returned to some earlier themes with great success. The values of the novel are less ambiguous, and the story is simply but powerfully told in Callaghan's characteristic clipped style, which suits the material admirably. The story relates the psychic journey of former naval commander Ira Groome, who quits his job as head of the Brazilian Power Corporation to become chairman of the police commission in a large, metropolitan city, probably Toronto. After the death of his alcoholic wife, Julia, he feels a sense of astonishment that shocks him into the realization that imperceptibly he has lost the passion that makes life real. He has, in fact, become so detached that his wife only felt comfortable calling him "Commander," and his son has rejected him as a father. Voices from within challenge him to break the pattern of impersonality that has characterized his life, but they do not completely penetrate his conscious mind.

As introspective as he was in Brazil, Groome still projects the image of stable authority in Toronto, demanding and getting loyalty from the members of the police commission and starting a casual, uninvolved affair with Mrs. Oscar Finley (Carol) of the prestigious Hunt Club set. Still seeking some "enchantment," however, he begins to drink gin, which softens his disciplined view of life but forces him into the Maplewood rest home every few weeks for a temporary "cure." One night, shocked by some harsh but vaguely familiar words from Carol, he leaves Maplewood for home in an excited state, only to be involved in a serious car accident. In the hospital, holding the hand of his former ship's boatswain, Horler, Groome experiences the enchantment he so badly desires and drifts into a dreamworld of memory and heightened perception.

Groome relives an important part of his life in which he is again Lieutenant Groome on a ship in the North Atlantic during the war. Upon realizing that he is alive after being severely wounded in action, he sees people as unique individuals, each inhabiting a wonderful private world, and is then able to respond to his men with a sensitivity rarely shown by officers. Groome's life is changed radically, however, when two survivors of a torpedo raid board his ship. Gina Bixby, trying to reach England to see her father, a boxing promoter, is accompanied by huge, silent Jethroe Chone, her father's bodyguard. They are escaping Marty Rosso, a mobster involved in fixing fights, who wants to use Gina to prevent her father from testifying before the boxing commission. Rosso has already caused the death of Robert Riopelle, a naïve boxer duped into believing in himself: With his hands smashed by Rosso, Riopelle perceived that his whole being was corrupted and committed suicide. During their escape from Rosso, the mysterious Chone raped Gina but feels no remorse for an act that "kills" part of her. Although there still seems to be a perverse bond between them, Gina confesses to Groome that, when they reach London, she will kill Chone for this brutal betrayal.

Groome is disturbed by this world so unlike the well-ordered naval existence; it is a world of violent passions beyond his experience. In her questioning of Groome, however, Gina brings to the surface his fascination for the Mayan religious rituals he had encountered as a young archaeology student on the Yucatán Peninsula. This society, with its sacrificial violence, seems to parallel Gina's world in a strange way. Groome recalls a native girl, Marina, an image of light suffusing his memory, who gave him the ancient piece of wisdom that in a cruel, senseless world, all one can do is create something beautiful from the nightmare.

Before they can reach the safety of London, the ship is torpedoed, leaving Groome, Horler, Gina, a wounded Chone, and a few sailors on a life raft. Defiantly, Chone tells Groome that no one knew or loved Gina more than he did; soon after, Chone rolls himself into the water to die at sea. Yelling for him to come back, in the same words that Carol later spoke to Groome, Gina swims after Chone, her passion overcoming any sense of safety. She is also lost in the water. Groome is horrified at the emotions he feels—the jungle terrors of involvements with people living in intense personal worlds. He rationalizes that getting too close to people, being intoxicated by violent passions, only causes pain and suffering. Groome closes his heart to these sufferings and resists the voices in his own heart. He changes into secure Ira Groome, the Commander, dedicated to a high purpose in life, a world of order unencumbered by the depth of personal relationships.

Remembering all this from his hospital bed, Groome realizes that he has committed treason to his own nature. He finally understands the significance of Chone's life. He sees the brightness from a sunlit jungle clearing into which a white leopard emerges, and, finally, Groome understands himself. Recognizing the necessity of leading a life of passion in all respects, bearing the suffering and sacrifice that enrich the individual sensibility, Groome dies, "close to the sun again."

In this novel, Callaghan reiterates the themes of his other works but makes it clear that passion should not be compromised to suit the values of society. In earlier novels, the conflict between private passions and the imposed, prudent views of society is unresolved, but *Close to the Sun Again* concludes with an epiphany that clearly emphasizes that the individual's responsibility is above all to him- or herself. Throughout his career, Callaghan offered his readers a vision that is thought-provoking, humane, and replete with the passions that touch all persons' lives. There is little doubt that in the future his reputation as a significant twentieth century novelist will remain secure.

James C. MacDonald

OTHER MAJOR WORKS

SHORT FICTION: *A Native Argosy*, 1929; *Now That April's Here, and Other Stories*, 1936; *Morley Callaghan's Stories*, 1959; *The Lost and Found Stories of Morley Callaghan*, 1985.

PLAYS: *Turn Home Again*, pr. 1940 (also known as *Going Home*); *To Tell the Truth*, pr. 1949; *Season of the Witch*, pb. 1976.

NONFICTION: *That Summer in Paris: Memories of Tangled Friendships with Hemingway, Fitzgerald, and Some Others*, 1963; *Winter*, 1974.

CHILDREN'S LITERATURE: *Luke Baldwin's Vow*, 1948.

BIBLIOGRAPHY

Boire, Gary A. *Morley Callaghan: Literary Anarchist*. Toronto, Ont.: ECW Press, 1994. Illustrated biography addresses critic Edmund Wilson's claim that Callaghan has been "the most unjustly neglected novelist in the English-speaking world." Includes bibliographical references.

Conron, Brandon. *Morley Callaghan*. New York: Twayne, 1966. Comprehensive, carefully organized analysis of Callaghan's short fiction and novels up to *A Passion in Rome*. Straightforward style and format make this book accessible to students. Includes a useful biographical chronology and a selected bibliography.

Cude, Wilfred. "Morley Callaghan's Practical Monsters: Downhill from Where and When?" In *Modern Times*. Vol. 3 in *The Canadian Novel*, edited by John Moss. Toronto, Ont.: NC Press, 1982. Florid essay treats the darker side of Callaghan's vision through a discussion of characterization in several of his short stories and in some of his novels, such as *Luke Baldwin's Vow* and *A Passion in Rome*.

Gooch, Bryan N. S. "Callaghan." *Canadian Literature* 126 (Autumn, 1990): 148-149. Discusses *A Wild Old Man on the Road*, comparing it with *Such Is My Beloved* and *They Shall Inherit the Earth*. Praises the novel's compelling quality and suggests that this "short tense" fiction ranks with the best of Callaghan's work.

Hoar, Victor. *Morley Callaghan*. Toronto, Ont.: Copp Clark, 1969. Addresses the style and thematic concerns in Callaghan's fiction to 1963 in two major sections, supporting the commentary with plentiful quotations from Callaghan's works. Includes a useful bibliography.

Kendle, Judith. "Morley Callaghan: An Annotated Bibliography." In *The Annotated Bibliography of Canada's Major Authors*, edited by Robert Lecker and Jack David. Vol. 5. Toronto, Ont.: ECW Press, 1984. Contains the most exhaustive listing of primary sources and secondary sources for Callaghan's work up to 1984 that a student is likely to need. The categories cover the spectrum from books and articles to interviews to audiovisual material. "Index to Critics Listed in the Bibliography" is a helpful feature.

Marin, Rick. "Morley Callaghan." *American Spectator* 24 (February, 1991): 36-37. Biographical sketch notes that Callaghan was a famous literary figure in the 1920's, when he was part of the Parisian expatri-

ate set of Ernest Hemingway, James Joyce, and F. Scott Fitzgerald. Asserts that Callaghan's decision to remain in his native Toronto affected his status in the literary world but that he accepted his relative obscurity with resignation rather than bitterness.

Stuewe, Paul. "The Case of Morley Callaghan." In *Clearing the Ground: English-Canadian Fiction After "Survival."* Toronto, Ont.: Proper Tales Press, 1984. Lively and incisive essay takes Callaghan to task for sloppy writing and his critics to task for concentrating on Callaghan's thematic concerns to the exclusion of his technical flaws.

Woodcock, George. *Moral Predicament: Morley Callaghan's "More Joy in Heaven."* Toronto, Ont.: ECW Press, 1993. One of a series of books designed to acquaint students with major works of Canadian literature. Presents analysis of Callaghan's novel by a scholar who specializes in Canadian fiction.

ITALO CALVINO

Born: Santiago de las Vegas, Cuba; October 15, 1923
Died: Siena, Italy; September 19, 1985

PRINCIPAL LONG FICTION

Il sentiero dei nidi di ragno, 1947, 1957, 1965 (*The Path to the Nest of Spiders*, 1956)

Il visconte dimezzato, 1952 (novella; *The Cloven Viscount*, 1962)

Il barone rampante, 1957 (novella; *The Baron in the Trees*, 1959)

Il cavaliere inesistente, 1959 (novella; *The Non-existent Knight*, 1962)

I nostri antenati, 1960 (*Our Ancestors*, 1980; includes *The Cloven Viscount*, *The Baron in the Trees*, and *The Non-existent Knight*)

Il castello dei destini incrociati, 1969, 1973 (*The Castle of Crossed Destinies*, 1976)

Le città invisibili, 1972 (*Invisible Cities*, 1974)

Se una notte d'inverno un viaggiatore, 1979 (*If on a Winter's Night a Traveler*, 1981)

Palomar, 1983 (*Mr. Palomar*, 1985)

OTHER LITERARY FORMS

Italo Calvino (kahl-VEE-noh) was known to the Italian reading public as a novelist, but internationally he was often associated with his tales and stories. In the comprehensive and critically acclaimed *Fiabe italiane: Raccolte della tradizione popolare durante gli ultimi cento anni e transcritte in lingua dai vari dialetti* (1956; partially translated as *Italian Fables*, 1959, and completed as *Italian Folktales*, 1980), he collected and transcribed tales and fables from the various Italian dialects. Influenced by the Russian Formalist Vladimir Propp's *Historical Roots of Russian Fairy Tales* (1946) and by structuralist theory in general, Calvino made it his scholarly objective to represent every morphological type of Italian folktale as well as every region of the country. His academic study of these stories confirmed in theory what he had already discovered in practice: the power of fantasy to signify, to reflect the real world. The work also influenced his subsequent approach to narrative through variable combinations of component forms and archetypes.

Calvino's most widely known short-story collections are the science-fiction fantasies *Le cosmicomiche* (1965; *Cosmicomics*, 1968) and *Ti con zero* (1967; *t zero*, 1969). Unlike most science fiction, which tends to be futuristic or anti-utopian, these stories envision, in intense and sharp detail, the remote past before the universe of space and time—moving to the present, in *t zero*—and they project an unusually open and positive view of evolution. Through the narrator, Qfwfq, a sort of protean cosmic consciousness, the prehuman past becomes sentient, familiar-seeming, and thus reassuring about the future, suggesting continuity in transformation and possibility in change.

This "fabulous" Calvino was better known to Americans than the one familiar to Italian readers, the politically and socially engaged author of satires on urban expansion and the advocate of pollution control and birth control well before those causes became popular. In *I racconti* (1958), *La giornata d'uno scrutatore* (1963; partial translation *The Watcher, and Other Stories*, 1971), and *Marcovaldo: Ovvero, Le stagioni in città* (1963; *Marcovaldo: Or, The Seasons in the City*, 1983), the city, or the immediate contemporary environment, is often actually the main character. The stories in this neorealistic mode, influenced by Ernest Hemingway as well as by Italian Resistance literature, are documentary in texture but often parabolic enough to be described as Kafkaesque. They reflect the futility felt by many during the years following World War II, although that sense of futility was mitigated by a stubborn human persistence that is resistant to tyranny and despair.

In addition to his tales and stories, Calvino wrote a critical study of Elio Vittorini (1968), edited the letters of Cesare Pavese (1966), and published many essays on literary, cultural, and political topics.

ACHIEVEMENTS

If Italo Calvino was often treated as a storyteller or fabulator rather than as a novelist, that reputation is in most respects deserved. Whether classified as *novellini* (novellas) or *racconti* (short stories), his works are essentially stories narrated at some length and often interrelated in series: in *Cosmicomics* and *t zero*, as episodes or "strips" out of chronological sequence; in *The Cloven Viscount, The Baron in the Trees,* and *The Non-existent Knight,* as parts of the trilogy *Our Ancestors;* in *Invisible Cities, The Castle of Crossed Destinies,* and *If on a Winter's Night a Traveler,* as tales spun from a frame story, standing for the oldest of narrative impulses. Calvino's conscious revival and complete mastery of the storyteller's art deserves special acclaim.

Calvino himself called attention to his alternation of two characteristic modes of writing: one factual and immersed in present time and space; the other, quite "fantastic"—baroque, witty, removed from the realm of the probable. In the first mode, everyday reality is presented with striking immediacy, and the familiar is seen as if for the first time; in the second, the unbelievable is given verisimilitude, is imagined into life, and is realized in such minute detail as to be taken for granted. Critics often distinguish between the neorealistic or "engaged" Calvino and the fabulist or "escapist"; such distinctions fail to hold in the final analysis, however, considering Calvino's development of what J. R. Woodhouse has pronounced a new genre in Italian literature, a combination of fairy tale and novel of ideas. In this genre, realism and fantasy are interdependent; both are necessary to a perspective that acknowledges the creative connections between fact and fiction. Calvino's last development was his metafiction, which outshines that of his postmodernist peers in clarity, brilliance, and human interest. Perhaps his finest achievement lies in his ability to give the unimaginable, abstract, or complex a palpable life and, often, popular appeal.

Within this mode, Calvino covers a wide range of techniques, subjects, and themes, all of which contribute to his larger point: the inexhaustible potential of narrative and language. Confirming his success is the popular and critical acclaim accorded him after the publication of his first novel, for which he received the Riccione Prize in 1947. Subsequently he won the Viareggio Prize for *The Baron in the Trees* in 1957, the Bagutta Prize for *I racconti* in 1959, the Salento Prize in 1960 for *Our Ancestors*, the Veillon Prize in 1963 for *The Watcher*, and the Feltrinelli Prize for *Invisible Cities* in 1973. In 1968, he again won and then refused the Viareggio Prize, in protest against the literary prize as an outmoded institution. Such making and breaking of patterns characterizes Calvino's stance and contributes to his appeal.

BIOGRAPHY

Italo Calvino was born of Italian parents in Santiago de las Vegas, Cuba, in 1923, but he spent his childhood and youth in San Remo, on the Italian Riviera. In 1943, at the age of twenty, he left the security of his middle-class background to join the partisans of the Italian Resistance against the Fascists and Nazis. Like many European writers of the postwar period, he joined the Communist Party and then left it in disillusionment, in 1958.

After World War II, Calvino finished his thesis on Joseph Conrad and completed his degree at the University of Turin. He subsequently became a member of the editorial staff of the Turin publishing firm Giulio Einaudi, which first published his novels and short stories. He lived in Turin until 1964 and then in Paris with his wife and daughter until 1980, thereafter residing in Rome.

Although he lived in Paris during most of the 1960's and 1970's, much of Calvino's career reflects his involvement in Italian political, cultural, and literary life. His two years in the partisans' resistance movement were the source material of *The Path to the Nest of Spiders*. He wrote often of local urban problems, using his experience as an election scrutineer to study poverty and alienation in the industrial regions around Turin in the postwar period (as in *The Watcher, and Other Stories*). The environments in which he lived—in particular, the Ligurian coast, the Alpine foothills, and the cities of San Remo and Turin—appear over and over in his fiction, which is concerned, as he wrote in a preface to the 1965 edition of *The Path to the Nest of Spiders*, with relations between human events and their contexts. This perspective is reflected in the regional emphasis of *Italian Folktales*, through which Calvino served his country as the Brothers Grimm did Germany. Early and formative influences on Calvino were the Italian novelists Elio Vittorini and Cesare Pavese, who recognized his talent immediately and encouraged the development of his characteristic style.

Italo Calvino. (© Jerry Bauer)

Calvino's later fiction reflects an increasingly cosmopolitan outlook, but one that developed naturally out of his involvement with Italian culture. During the 1960's and 1970's, the most obvious literary influences on his work were French, in keeping with the structuralist leanings first revealed in *Italian Folktales*: the New Novel, Roland Barthes and the semiologists, and the poststructuralism of Jacques Derrida. Although Calvino's later works turn increasingly toward fabulation and metafiction, his fiction echoes, variously and lightly, a considerable range: Ludovico Ariosto, Miguel de Cervantes, and Giovanni Boccaccio; Ernest Hemingway, Jean-Paul Sartre, and Albert Camus; Lewis Carroll, Luigi Pirandello, Franz Kafka, and Jorge Luis Borges. Calvino died in Siena, Italy, on September 19, 1985.

ANALYSIS

The anti-Fascist Resistance was the impetus for Italo Calvino's first novel, as it was for a generation of Italian neorealists, who believed that literature should be dedicated, as Calvino asserted in the 1950's, to "political engagement," to "social battle." In a slightly different way, the Resistance shaped the later Calvino. As the postwar period brought on disillusionment with power politics, Resistance writers had to find new directions. "What I did not want to renounce," wrote Calvino in 1960, "was [the] epic adventurous grasp, the combination of physical and moral strength" of the literature that the Resistance inspired. Daily life having failed to provide such "images full of . . . energy," Calvino turned to nonrealistic literary forms such as the fairy tale, the fable, and the philosophical romance (in the trilogy *Our Ancestors*); to science fiction and cartoons (in *Cosmicomics*); to myth and tarot cards (in *The Castle of Crossed Destinies*); and, in general, toward metafiction, or fiction about fiction itself.

Calvino's direction was not, in his view, a retreat from his earlier committed stance; it was, rather, an engagement with the cultural life that inspired the Resistance. In turning to popular sources such as the cartoon or the fairy tale, he intended to evoke the classless culture he found with the partisans in the Resistance, for whom storytelling was recreation and camaraderie. Calvino's art thus carries over from the author's early experience an oral quality, regardless of the subject matter.

If Calvino had a single model, it was Ariosto, as Calvino himself acknowledged in an article written in 1960 for *Italian Quarterly*, "Main Currents in Italian Fiction Today." In Calvino's view, Ariosto's *Orlando furioso* (1516, 1521, 1532; English translation, 1591) teaches an epistemology, an "up-to-date lesson" in "how the mind lives by fantasy, irony, and formal accuracy." In an age of "electronic brains and space flights," of relativism increasing with change, such an understanding of how one perceives and creates reality is necessary to one's evaluation of it in order to make ethical decisions. Calvino's shift from epic to meta-epic and literature as game—in *Invisible Cities* and *The Castle of Crossed Destinies*—makes sense in terms of his emphasis throughout on "energy turned toward the future." The emphasis also helps to explain his mixture of fantasy and realism, one that leads the reader to imagine what might be in a world where transformation is the rule.

Typically, Calvino's tales begin with a fantastic premise, often a bizarre image, from which—as in Lewis Carroll's *Alice's Adventures in Wonderland* (1865)—conclusions follow logically and matter-of-factly. Calvino's imaginary gardens have Marianne Moore's real toads in them. Because he takes these images from popular associations of ideas or words, they invariably seem apt; they are figures of speech literalized, clichés revitalized in strange new forms of life. The ghost in armor becomes the nonexistent knight, a fully armed identity, without substance, who manages to become a fully realized character. A young idealist elects to live in the trees, where he shapes his destiny between earth and sky. In *Cosmicomics*, the moon is composed of a lactic substance comparable in texture to ricotta cheese. In *If on a Winter's Night a Traveler*, the novelist's convention of characterizing the "dear Reader" is extended as the protagonist becomes "you, the Reader."

As Teresa de Lauretis has pointed out, Calvino's themes are elementary: desire, rivalry, guilt, the need for communication, self-assertion and belonging, the necessity to choose. He combines and varies these elements with a virtuosity that stands for his larger theme—the inexhaustible potential of language and life.

THE PATH TO THE NEST OF SPIDERS

The Path to the Nest of Spiders reflects the neorealistic trend in Italian film and literature fostered by the Italian Resistance and its aftermath. Neither propaganda nor a servile fidelity to fact, neorealism was a spontaneous expression of the times, as Calvino often remarked. The Resistance fostered realism primarily by opening up "new Italies" through the peripheral voices of authors from regions previously unrepresented in literature. Calvino's Italy was the northern Ligurian coast, with its landscape of contrasts and its balance of natural and human elements. Written in 1946, shortly after the events of the Ligurian Resistance that it depicts, *The Path to the Nest of Spiders* shows a strong regional interest: in its documentation of random details of daily life and local countryside, in its rendition of speech patterns and dialects, and in its primitive subject matter, which is treated in a deliberately rough, antiliterary style. The mood of oral narration carries the book, yet the war itself is vaguely overheard in the distance. Calvino is interested in the repercussions of such events within the contexts in which they take place. It is from this perspective that commitment to social and political struggle shaped the later Calvino's characteristic texture: an intense, almost nearsighted concreteness of surface.

The hero is the orphan Pin, who pimps for his sister and is known by local tavern society for singing bawdy songs and baiting all—Nazis, Fascists, and Communists, men, women, and children—with scurrilous remarks. His bravado masks his loneliness in a disrupted environment, for he scorns and is scorned by adults and children (mostly backstreet urchins) alike. After various altercations that bring him into the middle of the Resistance, he finds a sense of community with a partisan band and finds a comrade in Cousin, who shares his distrust of people, especially women—who, in his view, are all prostitutes and traitors (like his wife).

The treatment of Cousin is typical of Calvino's realism in its total lack of sentimentality about the character and motives of the partisans and an avoidance of the conventional rhetoric of Communism, despite Calvino's committed stance. As the intellectual Kim, a thinly veiled Calvino, points out, the partisans are colorfully, if notably, ignorant of the reasons behind their behavior—and thus every bit as immature, in a sense, as Pin. For the most part from the fringes of society, physically defective and emotionally unbalanced, they hate and kill the Fascists but do not know why or even what they are fighting. When Mancino, the cook, offers a knowledgeable Marxist interpretation, he is jeered and hooted: His arguments "seem useless, as he talks about enemies they know nothing about, such as capitalists and financiers. It's rather like Mussolini expecting the Italians to hate the British and the Abyssinians, whom none of them had ever seen." As for the causes of the war, Cousin's rationale is typically monomaniacal—the women started it. As Kim suggests, the cause is really the existential "mess," the ignorance and squalor and resentment that have been the lives of partisans and Fascists alike.

The sense of confusion, purposelessness, and impotence reflected in the characters' dialogue is borne out in their actions. Dritto, the commander of the vagabond band, shuns responsibilities, accidentally sets fire to their hideout while seducing the cook's wife, and is executed by the party commissars. Pin's sister is a prostitute who betrays some partisans to the SS, and the book ends as Cousin shoots her with a pistol Pin has stolen.

Aside from its antiliterary qualities, which are meant to convey the color, randomness, crudity, and mixed character of life, *The Path to the Nest of Spiders* is consciously derived from literary sources. One is American naturalism, from which Italian neorealism took a great deal. In an article titled "Hemingway e noi," which appeared in *Il contemporaneo* in 1954, Calvino acknowledged that author's strong formative influence on his contemporaries, including Vittorini and himself. The obvious parallels coincide with Calvino's antiliterary stance: the documentary texture, the staccato style, the terse dialogue, and a pervasive, understated, somewhat grim irony, through which Pin's innocence, like that of Hemingway's Nick Adams, flickers. The best example is perhaps the last, in which Calvino imitates Hemingway's ambiguous or offhand treatment of dramatic irony. Like Nick, Pin is already alienated; his mixture of world-weariness and naïveté shows through in some odd remarks about fireflies that follow Cousin's offstage shooting of Pin's sister, which is reported indirectly. Thus ends the book:

"Filthy creatures, women, Cousin . . ." says Pin.

"All of them . . ." agrees Cousin. "But they weren't always; now my mother . . ."

"Can you remember your mother, then?" asks Pin. . . .

"Yes," says Cousin, "she was nice."

"Mine was nice too," says Pin.

"What a lot of fireflies," says Cousin.

"If you look at them really closely, the fireflies," says Pin, "They're filthy creatures too, reddish."

"Yes," says Cousin, "I've never seen them looking so beautiful."

This flat dialogue might have come out of Hemingway's "A Clean, Well-Lighted Place" or "The Killers"; it also reveals Calvino's fascination with the private languages created among comrades.

Calvino's other major literary source here is quite different from Hemingway: the adventure tales of Robert Louis Stevenson—*Treasure Island* (1883), for example—in which the inexperience of the youthful narrator and his transition from childish make-believe to adult reality shape the unfolding of the action. The title thus refers to the symbol of Pin's inner life: The spider's nest is the sanctum of his childhood in an adult world without friends or games. The plot turns on the pistol that Pin steals from a German soldier and hides in the spider's nest, where it becomes a rather Freudian symbol of his unawakened manhood and where he flourishes it, now transformed into a "strange enchanted toy," as part of an elaborate drama: "One who had a real pistol could play marvelous games . . . that no child had ever played."

Regardless of documentary surface, the book is really about Pin's initiation into adulthood through his search for a "real friend" with whom he can share his private world. As for Calvino's later heroes, the real life of the community is only partly satisfactory. His solace is unspoiled nature, which exists to free his imagination, revealing, in contrast to "the squalid ambiguous world of human beings," "all kinds of colored things; yellow and brown mushrooms growing damp in the earth, red spiders on huge invisible nets, hares all legs and ears which appear suddenly on the path then leap zigzagging out of sight."

Pin's commitment to the Resistance movement, like that of most of the other characters, hardly goes beyond a kind of camaraderie, a sharing of fantasies through a common language. An examination of the neorealism of his "Resistance novel" also shows how Calvino imposes on his scrupulously documented materials a literary and intellectual construct—in this case, the boy's adventure tale, with a psychology of the human need for fantasy. Pin's case, representing the mind's "natural" distortion of reality into fiction, becomes Calvino's specific concern in later works. It is really the semantics of commitment that interests him as he rummages through literature and ideas for a medium of engagement with the world outside the self.

After *The Path to the Nest of Spiders*, and with the exception of *The Watcher, and Other Stories* and *Marcovaldo*, Calvino's method becomes increasingly parabolic. The best and best known of his realistic short stories, "The Argentine Ant" and "Smog," in *The Watcher, and Other Stories*—however immersed in the contemporary urban context—have fablelike qualities. The ants and smog in question have the same function as the rats in Camus's *La Peste* (1947; *The Plague*, 1948), the trials in Kafka's works, or the monsters that are found in Japanese horror films; they become larger-than-life,

inexorable forces of doom that are brought on by humankind's disruption of the environment.

OUR ANCESTORS

The trilogy *Our Ancestors* is therefore not the radical departure from realism that many critics have made it seem. It does mark Calvino's growing interest in the potential of the fairy tale and the folktale to reflect popular culture and convey universal truths. In these three intellectual fantasies, or fabulations, Calvino backs up absurd premises with almost documentary verisimilitude and narrates with the wide-eyed matter-of-factness of a child. *Our Ancestors* is pseudohistorical; Calvino uses the legendary past as a distancing device, a means of commenting indirectly on the present and the timeless. Notably, all three fantasies are set against a background of war, and two of them, *The Cloven Viscount* and *The Non-existent Knight*, are ridden with a hard, glittering violence more like that of children's cartoons than anything else. It is not irrelevant that Red Wolf, the legendary Resistance fighter of *The Path to the Nest of Spiders*, "belongs to the generation brought up on strip cartoons" and takes them quite seriously. So does Calvino, who often defends his departures into fantasy on the basis of fantasy's popular appeal and immediacy of communication.

The Cloven Viscount begins the trilogy in a blackly humorous vein. In this game of "just suppose," Medardo of Terralba, a seventeenth century nobleman, is split from head to crotch by a cannonball in a war against the Turks. He becomes a cartoonlike illustration of the split, or alienated, personality; there are allusions as well to Judeo-Christian dualism. One-half of the Viscount appears to have been lost or destroyed; the doctors on the battlefield save his other half, sending it, the evil or "Bad'un," as it comes to be called, home. Bad Medardo wreaks havoc on the countryside and its inhabitants, even burning down part of his own castle while attempting to dispose of his old nurse, Sebastiana. His terrorism, however, is for the most part more specialized. Driven by an obsession with his own halfness and wishing to imprint his image on a world that has split him, he bifurcates every living thing in his path. "'If only I could halve every whole thing like this,'" he says to his nephew while "stroking the convulsive half of an octopus, 'so that everyone could escape from his obtuse and ignorant wholeness.'" Halfness brings consciousness of one's alienation from the world and the self.

Eventually the Viscount's better half shows up. He is predictably and unbearably good and profoundly boring, although equally obsessed with halfness: "One understands the sorrow of every person and thing in the world at its own incompleteness." When whole, he "did not understand" the tragedy of the human condition, which he attempts to mitigate. The story has a fairy-tale ending through which, after a duel between the two halves over Pamela, a wench beloved of both, the brilliant Doctor Trelawney puts them back together. The narrator marvels in detail at the skill involved in the operation: the doctor's "great care to get all guts and arteries of both parts to correspond, and then a mile of bandages had tied them together." Once again a whole man, Medardo marries Pamela, and they live wisely, "having had the experience of both halves each on its own." He has a "happy life, many children and a just rule. Our life too change[s] for the better."

The allusion to Samuel Richardson's *Pamela: Or, Virtue Rewarded* (1740-1741) is relevant, for this worthy squire, in living "wholly" ever after, lives above all "dully." The *story* is over. If the real life signified by wholeness is not "marvelous happiness," as the young narrator remarks, it is partly because of his state of mind. The narrator is the Viscount's nephew, on "the threshold of adolescence" by the end of the tale, whereupon he grows discontented "amid all this fervor of wholeness . . . growing sadder and more lacking."

In the introduction to the trilogy, Calvino provides a moral for the story: The Viscount's bifurcation is parabolic of modern alienation and mutilation. Certainly another is the brutality of war, conveyed in a starkly surreal landscape (however misperceived by the as-yet uncloven Medardo): plains of "horses' carcasses, some supine with hooves to the sky, others prone with muzzles dug into the earth," and "a few limbs, fingers in particular, scattered over the stubble." (Says Medardo, "Every now and again I see a finger pointing our way. . . . What does that mean?") Yet another interpretation has been suggested by Gore Vidal: *The Cloven Viscount* is a "sendup of Plato and the idea of the whole." Calvino's main point in providing a moral is probably to stress what his tale does mean, but as allegory it spins off in

many directions. The narrator's mood suggests that it is finally about the human and modern need for fictions that, like Calvino's disembodied fingers on a battleground, enigmatically point the way. As the tale ends, the narrator is conscious of loss and thus of his own incompleteness, and so remains "deep in the woods telling [himself] stories."

THE BARON IN THE TREES

The intellectual's or artist's alienation is more explicitly the issue of *The Baron in the Trees*, the second novel in the trilogy. The protagonist is the eighteenth century Baron Cosimo Piovasco di Rindó, who, at the age of twelve, on June 15, in the midst of a family quarrel at dinner, defies all present by climbing into the trees, vowing never to come down.

The fantastic premise of the novel only thinly disguises its autobiographical nature; it is a fairy-tale version of Calvino's Resistance experience and bears comparison to *The Path to the Nest of Spiders*. Like Pin and his comrade, Cosimo finds that a certain imaginative aloofness from the world—in this case, the "natural" environment of the trees of Ombrosa, which, although rooted in earth, seem to touch the sky—paradoxically makes an effective commitment to the world possible. As Cosimo's brother, meeting Voltaire in Paris, explains, "Anyone who wants to see the earth properly must keep himself at a necessary distance from it." Voltaire's reply may well be Calvino's philosophy of life: "Once it was only Nature which produced living phenomena. . . . Now 'tis Reason."

In the revolt from his family, Cosimo rejects a lifestyle of aristocratic decadence. He must transcend both the grasping ambition of his father, who lives to regain the lapsed title of duke of Ombrosa and thinks only of "genealogies and successions and family rivalries and alliances"—and the sanctified alienation of his sister Battista, "a kind of stay-at-home nun" confined to the pleasure of dismaying her brothers with sadistic cookery—snails' heads artfully arranged in wire mesh, grasshopper claw tarts, rat-liver pâté. The trees are less an escape from this microcosm of monomaniacs than they are avenues to the world—or, rather, to a newly opened world. For the first time, Cosimo can mix freely with people of all classes, from charcoal burners to robber barons to the noble family next door, with whom he can talk rather than feud, as before. Roving bands of waiflike fruit thieves accept him as a fellow outsider and then as a leader.

Cosimo's distanced perspective allows him to perceive and solve engineering problems and to organize a voluntary fire brigade. Saving Ombrosa from incendiary destruction, he discovers joy in fighting for a common goal and simultaneously teaches the people to unite in moments of danger. He repels an invasion of wolves from the Alps, fights off Turkish pirates, and reforms the vicious brigand, Gian dei Brughi, by supplying him with novels. As his brother, the narrator, explains, "The more determined [Cosimo] was to hide away in his den of branches, the more he felt the need to create new links with the human race." He therefore founds or joins such "associations and confraternities of trades and professions" as the Conscientious Capmakers, the Enlightened Skin Tanners, and the Masons. Indeed, he becomes quite reconciled with his family, who are better for dealing with his rebellion, and he frequently watches over them from a mulberry branch with a view through his mother's window.

In the trees, Cosimo has more time to read and think than his earthbound fellows and begins a Rousseauistic "Project for the Constitution of an Ideal State in the Trees." For his various accomplishments, he is acknowledged by author Denis Diderot and paid homage by Emperor Napoleon I. The utopian scheme, however, remains incomplete. Beginning it as "a treatise on laws and governments," he loses his point as his storytelling impulse takes over and out pours "a rough sketch of adventures, duels, and erotic tales, the latter inserted in a chapter on matrimonial rights." It is the texture of Cosimo's life, or his story in its eccentric variety of adventures, enterprises, and love affairs, that counts.

The same childlike ingenuousness that made the first two novels engaging and believable, down to the last detail, informs most of *The Baron in the Trees*. Sustained at greater length is the Hemingwayesque fidelity to empirical detail. Cosimo might be Nick Adams preparing to fish—such is the intentness and precision with which Calvino compels the reader to concentrate on the matter at hand, whether it be the fabrication of a suspended sleeping bag or the construction of an irrigation system. Thus, the message of commitment, however obvious, is

never obtrusive. What one remembers is the clarity and naturalness of arboreal life and the symbiosis of individual, society, and nature that seems illusory only at the end of the book.

In the last paragraph, the narrator, now perhaps Calvino, succumbs to a radical failure of belief. Looking at a sky left empty by the dying Cosimo and the changing times, he asks himself if Ombrosa ever really existed, if

> that mesh of leaves and twigs of fork and froth, minute and endless, with the sky glimpsed only in sudden specks and splinters . . . was embroidered on nothing, like this thread of ink which I have let run on for page after page . . . until it splutters and bursts into a last senseless cluster of words, ideas, dreams, and so ends.

In an introduction to the 1965 scholastic edition of the book, Calvino asserted that Cosimo is an allegorical figure for the poet. The trees are therefore his medium, providing a language for social and political engagement.

The Baron in the Trees is more than a portrait of the artist, but it is Calvino's first fiction to examine the semantic possibilities of his subject of engagement, to focus directly on the relations between literature and empirical reality, as Joann Cannon has pointed out. The long Gian dei Brughi episode, a benign parody of eighteenth century critical theory concerning the moral influence of literature, is a case in point. Cosimo lends Alain-René Lesage's *Histoire de Gil Blas de Santillane* (1715-1735; *The History of Gil Blas of Santillane*, 1716, 1735; better known as *Gil Blas*, 1749, 1962) to the chief of brigands, who becomes hooked on novels and is especially taken with Richardson's *Clarissa: Or, The History of a Young Lady* (1747-1748), which brings out "a disposition long latent in him; a yearning for the cozy habits of family life, for relations, for sentiments . . . a sense of virtue" and vice. Unfortunately, the result of his conversion is that he is caught and sentenced; yet, poised to hang, he wishes only to know the ending of Henry Fielding's *The History of the Life of the Late Mr. Jonathan Wild the Great* (1743, 1754), which Cosimo sorrowfully tells him. "Thank you. Like me! Goodby!" replies de Brughi as he himself kicks away his support and is strangled. Calvino's charming mixture of irony with good humor both supports and qualifies the eighteenth century dictum: Literature delights and thus instructs, but the real-life result may be imperfect (even if somewhat poetic) justice.

In the more minor key that ends the book are other hints that Calvino questions its premise. In contrast to Pin and the Viscount's nephew, who get no further than puberty by the ends of their stories, Cosimo's brother grows old and dull and, as narrator, begins to question this very role and its sources. As the story progresses and as Cosimo becomes more renowned in rumor and legend, the narrator feels more distant from valid representations. In a French almanac, in a chapter on monsters and between the Hermaphrodite and the Siren, he discovers a figure of his brother "all covered in leaves, with a long beard and . . . tail, eating a locust." Cosimo himself is partly responsible for such distortions, his brother observes: "So many and so incredible were the tales Cosimo told about his activities in the woods during the war" that no one version can be accepted outright. Cosimo at times becomes imbecile with erotic passion, is disturbed by the French Revolution and its aftermath, and grows disconsolate with age. Even *his* imagination fails to keep pace with events.

This theme of the failure of imagination to correspond with external reality has its other side: the view of literature as true empirically in the experience of the people who, in part, create it, as a collective and infinitely variable fantasy—a view that Calvino takes up with gusto in his later works. In the two years between *The Cloven Viscount* and *The Baron in the Trees*, Calvino compiled and edited *Italian Folktales*, a project that deepened his critical interest in the ways tales are generated orally. *The Baron in the Trees* reflects this interest in the way the truth of Cosimo's life is seen to depend on context, on the community in which it flourished; thus, Cosimo and his dream exist only so long and so far as Ombrosa does. The bizarre legends that dismay his brother can thus be seen to affirm the effectiveness of Cosimo's arboreal commitment. This is the case even to the end, when some English aeronauts passing by on an experimental balloon flight are made partly responsible for Cosimo's rather spectacular comic apotheosis. However inadvertently, through some fumbling with and dropping of an anchor, they take the dying idealist with them into the sky. The primitive "poem" on the family tombstone hits the note typical of Calvino at his best on this theme: "Cosimo Piovasco di Rondò—Lived in Trees—Always loved earth—Went into sky."

THE NON-EXISTENT KNIGHT

The Non-existent Knight takes up where *The Baron in the Trees* ends—with a study of being, nothingness, and semantics. The trees of Ombrosa finally seem no more substantial than words "embroidered on a void"; Agilulf, the nonexistent knight, personifies the metaphysics implied in that imaginary landscape. His complete title, "Agilulf Emo Bertrandin of the Guildivern and of the Others of Corbentraz and Sura, Knight of Selimpia Citeriore and Fez," suggests his need for substantiation, for he is a void, an empty suit of white armor from which echoes a metallic voice standing for essence or identity. He is a sort of walking embodiment of René Descartes's famous dictum, *Cogito, ergo sum* (I think, therefore I am). Agilulf's nonexistence calls to mind just about everything from Platonic forms to Cartesian rationalism, from Miguel de Cervantes' *Don Quixote de la Mancha* (1605, 1615) to T. S. Eliot's "The Hollow Men" (1925) and Jean-Paul Sartre's *L'Être et le néant* (1943; *Being and Nothingness*, 1956). Calvino's touch is light and witty, however, as usual. His tales are novels of ideas in the briefest of senses; for the most part, he drops philosophical connections as he takes them up, generating sparks, flashes, and kaleidoscopically transformed patterns rather than deepening levels of meaning.

In devoted service to Charlemagne, who takes his holy wars far less seriously than does Agilulf, the nonexistent knight is dismayingly perfect. He is thus detested by the other knights—except for Raimbaut, a novice who takes him for a role model. His unpopularity is increased by his absurd attempts to share in the community life. He does not eat, of course, but insists on observing all forms with rigor, sitting interminably at table and slicing his meat into tiny, uniform pieces. Agilulf's passion for perfection makes him obnoxiously unconquerable in war—and love. He is, strangely enough, the perfect ladies' man. Although he cannot love, he more than satisfies the noble widow Priscilla, entering her bed "fully armed from head to foot and stretched out taut as if on a tomb." "Don't you even loosen the sword from its scabbard?" asks Priscilla. "Amorous passion knows no half measures," answers Agilulf. Priscilla shuts her eyes "in ecstasy."

To solve two problems at once, Charlemagne assigns Agilulf a squire named Gurduloo—or Omoboo, or Martinzoo, or "Cheese," depending upon who is addressing him. If Agilulf is pure identity, form, or idea, his Sancho Panza is elemental protean substance or pure existence in a state of continuous transformation. He confuses himself with whatever he touches. When he drinks soup, he becomes soup and is to be drunk in turn, "the world being nothing but a vast shapeless mass of soup in which all things [are] dissolved." Together, the characters Agilulf and Gurduloo bring up a theme that Calvino will pursue later: the confusion of subject and object and the arbitrary nature of names and categories. The vaguely ancient, mythical quality of Charlemagne's era becomes Calvino's excuse to evoke a major dilemma of twentieth century epistemology. In the era when this story took place, writes the narrator, it was common "to find names and thoughts and forms and institutions that corresponded to nothing in existence," yet the world at the same time was "polluted with objects and capacities and persons who lacked any name or distinguishing mark."

Much of the book is a lusty parody of the stuff of Ariosto, whose mode becomes a vehicle for charming takeoffs on ideologies fundamental to Western culture: Judeo-Christian dualism, the cult of virginity and purity in general, the notion of progress, the idealization of war—"the passing of more and more dented objects from hand to hand." A complicated plot replete with fancifully misplaced identities, and through which Agilulf finally ceases to "nonexist," is also reminiscent of Ariosto. Awarded knighthood for having saved the virgin Sophronia from bandits, Agilulf's precarious being depends on the lady in question's immaculate virtue. Torrismond, a competing knight, swears at the crucial time that Sophronia is his mother and, therefore, no virgin. As it turns out several subplots later, Sophronia is really Torrismond's half sister and a virgin after all—until he deflowers her under the impression that she is a nun recently forced into a sultan's harem. The good news comes too late for Agilulf, however, who, thinking that his identity is inauthentic—a long title embroidered on a void—loses the will to exist and vanishes.

This resolution collapses the primary triangle of the plot. The young Raimbaut falls in love with a knight who turns out to be Bradamante, a young woman, who in turn falls in love with the nonexistent knight—until the latter bequeaths his armor to the younger, more authentic man, and Bradamante is thus free to find her true love embodied in it. The most surprising turn of plot, however, occurs in the subtext, which emerges in the fourth chapter and gradually frames the story proper.

The Non-existent Knight is narrated by an ingenue different from Calvino's previous ones: Sister Theodora, who had been assigned to tell this story as a penance. Some very funny false notes are sounded when she protests her inadequacy for lack of contact with soldiers. Apart from "religious ceremonies, triduums, novenas, gardening, harvesting, vintaging, whippings, slavery, incest, fires, hangings, invasion, sacking, rape and pestilence, we [nuns] have had no experience." Her comments have to do, predictably enough, with the gap between her words and the external world. Ironically, her "assiduous penance" of "seeking words and . . . meditating on ultimate truths" works like Agilulf's strenuous willing of himself into significant being: It ends in self-consciousness and a consequent failure of will and imagination. Sister Theodora experiences writer's block with symptoms anticipating what John Barth has called a postmodernist "literature of exhaustion": "The pen merely grates in dusty ink, and not a drop of life flows, and life is all outside, outside the window, outside oneself."

Fortunately, Sister Theodora is unlike the nonexistent knight in that she has substantial resources on which to draw, an existence apart from words and significations. Pushing the tale precipitously to its conclusion, she confesses that she is really the Amazon Bradamante, yet a Bradamante changed radically by her discipline as convent scribe. She joined the convent out of "desperate love" for the ideal Agilulf but now burns for "the young and passionate Raimbaut"—in all his imperfect but vital reality—and rushes from the convent walls to meet him. Her new aesthetic, which corresponds with her new love (Raimbaut in Agilulf's armor), insists on the interdependence of art and life, if not exactly *littérature engagée:* "A page is good only when we turn it and find life urging along, confusing every page in the book. The pen rushes on, urged by the same joy that makes me course the open road." If—or because—words fail to make present an external reality (and a desperate Sister Theodora resorts at one point to drawing word pictures), they must create exits to new worlds. Lest the conclusion seem a contradiction of *The Baron in the Trees*, Calvino has Theodora/Bradamante admit that "after affrays and affairs and blighted hopes," she will "always return to this cloister" of art, which, after all, was responsible for changing her mind. He thus posits a symbiosis of essence and substance, words and things, self and world.

A combination of fabulation and metafiction, *The Non-existent Knight* sets the stage for Calvino's later works in at least three ways. One is deliberate anachronism—the allusion to the legendary past in a story with a transparently contemporary outlook—to achieve a timelessness of reference and appeal. A related strategy is the playful and multileveled parody, which extends to the acts of writing and reading, turning literature, whatever the genre, into an epistemological and semantic game. Finally, there is the mixture of literary and popular sources to confuse the borders of high and low culture. In general, the deliberate confusion of times, genres, and cultures expresses Calvino's mature view of the world. However reminiscent of Gurduloo's "vast shapeless mass of soup" in which things continuously dissolve and begin again, *The Non-existent Knight* is up-to-date, as Calvino stresses. It is meant to address the future.

COSMICOMICS *and* T ZERO

Similar concerns inform *Cosmicomics* and its sequel, *t zero*. Neither short-story collections nor novels (although perhaps a cross between them)—nor even fictions in the sense of representations of the empirical world—these books combine contemporary science and fantasy in a completely new way, to imagine what could not have been and never will be (unlike science fiction, which imagines what might be). At the same time, they domesticate scientific theories that are quoted or summarized before each narrative, much as the earlier Calvino "realized" fairy-tale premises. "All at One Point" explains the big bang theory in terms of Mrs. Ph(i)Nk$_0$'s spontaneous desire to make noodles for everyone. This desire, verbalized at a certain moment ("Oh, if I only had some room, how I'd like to make some noodles for you boys!"), causes everyone to think space and time into existence, "the space that her round arms would occupy, moving backward and forward with

the rolling pin over the dough," the space for the flour for the dough, the fields for the wheat for the flour, until a "true outburst of general love" has initiated the concept of space, "space itself, and time, and universal gravitation, and the gravitating universe." In so humanizing science, Calvino makes strange new worlds comfortable and inhabitable—in contrast to much science fiction, which often exploits its capacity to estrange and dislocate.

Also in contrast to most science fiction is the treatment of time. *Cosmicomics* and *t zero* trace the creation of the universe rather than transporting readers into the future. The stories correlate the billions of years covered with natural stages in a human life span, conveying vividly, for example, the sense that Qfwfq, the narrator, was "just a child" in the dark before the sun's condensation. He is quite adolescent as a mollusk in love for the first time. A number of "families" run through the equivalent of several generations.

In another sense, these stories do not trace anything, however, for they are randomly arranged. The randomness exists in part to avoid the teleological perspective of most evolutionary theory. In this universe, there are really no endings or final causes, only present moments erupting into new beginnings. The protean hero Qfwfq exists only to be transformed in an unending process, and the random arrangement of his various formations makes the reader adapt to dislocation with him. Qfwfq's nonchalance makes such jolts quite easy. As he so simply puts it, "I went on my way."

Qfwfq's radical openness to experience marks him as another of Calvino's "children," wide-eyed and matter-of-fact at the same time. He and his family of protean beings are childlike in another way: They are cartoon characters in words, as Calvino implies in the title of *Cosmicomics* and as he shows by "drawing" the story "The Origin of the Birds" in *t zero*. The author compared Qfwfq to Popeye, the partly domesticated sailor, and certainly Qfwfq is just as "real," experiencing narcissism, desire, and love in "The Spiral," making his mark on the world in "A Sign in Space," confronting competitors in sign making, and betting on future events. Throughout his bewildering transformations, and much like a cartoon character, Qfwfq remains unruffled. As Calvino seems to say, all that is life. His cartoons show what it is like to embody a meson, a dinosaur, a mollusk, a racing car. They educate the imagination by strengthening its capacity and so provide a kind of insurance against future shock.

Throughout *Cosmicomics* and increasingly in *t zero*, Calvino delights in drawing out abstract concepts in semiotics, reflecting the theories of Roland Barthes and the fictional methods of Jorge Luis Borges. In "A Sign in Space," Qfwfq makes the first sign in the universe. A rival, Kgwgk, erases the sign and replaces it with his own, so that Qfwfq must make a new, competitive sign, and so on, so that language, style, and art are born. Eventually (and reflecting the media blitz), the universe is covered with a meaningless scrawl, obscuring space and making distinctions between sign and sign, and between sign and space, nonexistent.

INVISIBLE CITIES

In three novels written in the 1970's, Calvino continued to explore the relationship between signs and the reality they are supposed to represent. *Invisible Cities*, the first of these three metafictions, declares its concern with semiology at the outset, erecting a frame tale that stands for Barthes's concept of the world as text. The teller of the body of the narrative is revealed to be Marco Polo, who re-creates or imagines his journeys to countless fabulous cities. The listener is Kublai Khan, now old and confined to his fabled court, who cannot travel to the vast kingdom he possesses except through Marco Polo's tales. As suggested in the title, the outside world cannot live except through the dialogue that composes the book itself. Calvino provides no other characters, no plot, and no adventures other than the brief accounts of the cities themselves to detract from this metafictional perspective.

Kublai Khan's (and the reader's) part in this dialogue is to search for a pattern in Marco Polo's fifty-five cities, varied according to categories such as "cities and memory," "cities and desire," "thin cities," "cities and eyes," "cities and names," and "continuous cities." Listening or reading is made into a game or puzzle that stands for the human need to seek out order and meaning in an otherwise random world. As in *Cosmicomics* and *t zero*, the possibility of moves, the "catalogue of forms," is "endless: until every shape has found its cities, new cities will continually begin." In *Invisible Cities*, Calvino applies to narrative alternatives his view of life as infinitely transformable. He also attempts to rejuvenate the written medium by portraying the situation and capturing the mood of oral narrative—consciously repeating, establishing rhythm, to the Khan's delight, in tapestries of words and patterns for their own sake.

As Marco Polo and Kublai Khan converse, the Venetian learns the Khan's language. In the beginning, Marco Polo can recount his journeys only in pantomime—with gestures, cries, and objects he has collected along the way. Although the Khan finds "the connection between them and the places visited . . . uncertain," and must to a great extent create his own story, Marco Polo's mute representations have "the power of emblems." After he learns to speak in the local idiom, communication is more precise but strangely "less happy than in the past." Emblems, however primitive, are more eloquent than conventional language.

THE CASTLE OF CROSSED DESTINIES

The Castle of Crossed Destinies, Calvino's next metafiction, employs tarot cards as an emblematic language more evocative than words. In the frame story, several pilgrims come together at a castle and, trying to tell one another their tales, find that they have been struck dumb. One pilgrim hits on an idea that had come to obsess Calvino: He uses tarot cards, with the aid of grimaces and gestures, to represent himself and his adventures. With the tarot's four suits (coins, cups, clubs, and swords) and the arcana, twenty-one picture cards capable of suggesting multiple interpretations, Calvino again tells a story about telling stories—about the inexhaustible resources of narrative. Two decks are used in two sections: in "Castle," the richly beautiful deck painted by Bonifacio Bembo for the dukes of Milan in the fifteenth century, and in "Tavern," the popular *ancien tarot de Marseille* from the eighteenth century. The cards are reproduced in the margins of the book. To stress his use of pictorial, popular, and communal art forms, Calvino had hoped to create a third section, called "Motel," to be narrated through fragments of comic strips.

As it is, he almost succeeds in his plan to use every card in the pack—in a sort of pictorial crossword puzzle through which each story is a reading of a vertical or horizontal card sequence, with the card stories interlocking and permutating ad infinitum.

The Castle of Crossed Destinies comes close to being Calvino's monomyth, his answer to James Joyce's *Finnegans Wake* (1939), cross-referencing tales of Faust, Macbeth, Hamlet, Lear, Oedipus, Helen of Troy, the Marquis de Sade, and Ariosto's Roland in a world animated by the elements of war, love, and magic. In spite of the obvious temptation toward the esoteric and alinear, Calvino carries through with much of his usual simplicity and literalness. Still, these tales lack the concreteness of his previous invisible cities, as Calvino virtually admits in an afterword: He had seen in the cards a perfect "machine for constructing stories" and, after exhausting them and himself in the process, published the book "to be free of" an obsession not far from the nonexistent knight's intricate, empty rituals, the "diabolical idea" of "conjuring up all the stories that could be contained in a tarot deck."

IF ON A WINTER'S NIGHT A TRAVELER

After six years of silence, Calvino emerged from this diabolic/penitential formalism in the mood of Sister Theodora's abrupt revelation: He rushed out, like Bradamante, burning for young and passionate life. *If on a Winter's Night a Traveler* is on one level another tour de force; it is composed entirely of beginnings, with one set inside and precipitating another, as in *The Arabian Nights' Entertainments* (fifteenth century). It is also about fiction as a transaction with the reader, and in that sense it is engaged with the world beyond the page. *If on a Winter's Night a Traveler* dramatizes, literalizes, and so becomes a kind of love affair with (and among) readers.

It is an active human element, in part—the felt presence of living characters—that Calvino's earlier metafictions fail to communicate. In *Invisible Cities* and *The Castle of Crossed Destinies*, Calvino breaks with his premises, however theoretically perfect their representation—most notably in the use of ancient emblems to create an equivalence between card reading and tale telling, between art and life. *If on a Winter's Night a Traveler* has rough edges, partly because it is told almost completely in the present tense, like his first book, and in the second person. From the first word, "you," the Reader, are the hero of "Italo Calvino's new novel," which "you" are beginning to read. "You" are therefore the most living, breathing character ever invented, literalized into your

own story—as opposed to the mechanical plots of the mass media: "Tell the others right away, 'No, I don't want to watch TV!'"

Such a premise is so blatant as to seem downright silly, which is what Calvino intends. His usual naïve narrator is now a transparent parody of himself, a myopically concerned but quite real "Calvino" peering out of the page. Certainly, in a sense, this book is his most bookish. The premise is based, after all, on a mere extension of structuralism and semiotics (responsible for the premises of his previous metafictions) toward the reader-response emphasis of poststructuralism. It again presumes Barthes's world as text: Ten novels from countries around the world are telescoped into one. The difference is in the way it directs characterized—and real—readers toward the unwritten world, through an unfolding series of beginnings into realms "somewhere beyond the book, beyond the author, beyond the conventions of writing" toward a voice "from the unsaid, from what the world has not yet said of itself and does not yet have the words to say."

In fact, the dramatic tension of the book comes from its conflict between Calvino's self-confessed obsession with print and his desire to reach whatever lies beyond it. The plot is an editor's nightmare of "pages, lines, words, whirling in a dust storm"; it is engaged with the politics of print—with terrorist organizations, conspiracies, censors, and the like, all militating against the writer. The plot is generated by a scheme by the character Ermes Marana, the brilliant translator and founder of OEPHLW (Organization for the Electronic Production of Homogenized Literary Works), to "flood the world" with a "literature of apocrypha, of false attributions, of imitations and counterfeits and pastiches." Marana, representing the mass media, has paralyzed the world's best-selling author, Silas Flannery, upon whose creativity much of the world's economy, and thus world peace, depends. The fate of civilization hangs on the word, on Flannery's ability (as a fan of Snoopy) to get beyond "It was a dark and stormy night. . . ." Calvino has therefore returned to the battleground of his first novels—transformed, however, into the media blitz of the 1980's. This is the world war as he sees it for the late twentieth century. If the medium is the message, the "fascist machine" is whoever made this chaos in the first place. This is not Marana but

Calvino, or his persona's diabolic mania for mechanically contrived order, leading to the cosmic scrawl or entropy of "A Sign in Space."

What redeems the real Calvino is not his contemporary self-awareness, which is the root of the problem, but his ability to lose himself, as in his first fantasies, in the game with the reader taken as far as it can go. Behind his main gimmick is, as usual, a theoretical source, Barthes's *Le Plaisir du texte* (1973; *The Pleasure of the Text*, 1975), which correlates reading with lovemaking. In a search through ten fragmentary novels for the true text of *If on a Winter's Night a Traveler*, Marana's machinations having jumbled and displaced the lot of them, the Reader discovers the Other Reader, Ludmilla, who is searching for the same book—or thing. A love story develops that extends Calvino's romance with the reader into one between readers. The diametrical opposite of her sister Lotaria, whose computer-assisted thesis catalogs Flannery's words as he writes them, Ludmilla is the "common," or naïve, reader, for whom reading is a creation and a search. The "circuits of her mind" transform the "current" of reading into "what in her is most personal and incommunicable." In present-tense moments between the pseudonovels, "you," as Reader, are allowed by your (however passive) rival "Calvino" to "read" the furniture of her apartment, her kitchen utensils, her body, until she "skims" your "index," and so on. Hence, the real reader is to learn how common, how true to life, and how vital reading is.

According to the narrator, the crucial resemblance between reading and lovemaking is that "within both of them times and spaces open, different from measurable time and space." It is in these open passages, Calvino shows, that transactions between solitary readers take place. He extends a concept of reading as an act of becoming by showing how the shared activity of reading brings individuals together. As early as the thirty-second page, reading has become a dialogue. Hoping that the book has become "an instrument, a channel of communication, a rendezvous," "Calvino" asks, "What is more natural than [that] a solidarity, a complicity, a bond should be established between Reader and Reader, thanks to the book?" The book ends in "your" (plural) marriage, a commitment to the common activity and

cause of reading. In the final chapter, a "great double bed" receives "your parallel readings."

The marriage stands for the existence of a larger context, a community of individual, parallel readers "out there" or underground, resisting, in their passive, private way, formulation and system—the tyranny of plots, codes, propaganda, Marana's literature of "bad faith." Calvino is thus back where he started in *The Path to the Nest of Spiders*, with a unique form of *littérature engagée:* The partisans' movement has become a "reading resistance." Even the government censor goes home every night, as he says, "to abandon myself to reading, like that distant unknown woman," Ludmilla, the common reader, and Marana himself has to admit that when he is reading, "something happens over which I have no power." This happening, as the censor explains, "is the limit that even the most omnipotent police force cannot broach."

If on a Winter's Night a Traveler admirably sums up Calvino's career: His was a search for a "true text," a medium of engagement, and he seems to have found it. Throughout his various transformations, he made the reader's experience his primary concern, his secondary one being language's power to change the mind—by charming imagination into a life of its own.

Linda C. Badley

OTHER MAJOR WORKS

SHORT FICTION: *Ultimo viene il corvo*, 1949 (partial translation *Adam, One Afternoon, and Other Stories*, 1957); *La formica Argentina*, 1952 (*The Argentine Ant*, 1957); *L'entrata in guerra*, 1954; *La nuvola di smog*, 1958 (*Smog*, 1971); *I racconti*, 1958; *La giornata d'uno scrutatore*, 1963 (*The Watcher, and Other Stories*, 1971); *Marcovaldo: Ovvero, Le stagioni in città*, 1963 (*Marcovaldo: Or, The Seasons in the City*, 1983); *Le cosmicomiche*, 1965 (*Cosmicomics*, 1968); *Ti con zero*, 1967 (*t zero*, 1969); *Gli amore difficili*, 1970 (*Difficult Loves*, 1984); *Sotto il sole giaguaro*, 1986 (*Under the Jaguar Sun*, 1988).

NONFICTION: *Una pietra sopra: Discorsi di letteratura e societa*, 1980 (*The Uses of Literature*, 1986); *Collezione di sabbia*, 1984; *The Literature Machine: Essays*, 1986; *Sulla fiaba*, 1988 (*Six Memos for the Next Millennium*, 1988); *Perché leggere i classici*,

1991 (*Why Read the Classics?*, 1999); *Eremita a Parigi: Pagine autobiografiche*, 1994 (*Hermit in Paris: Autobiographical Writings*, 2003); *Lettere: 1940-1985*, 2000.

EDITED TEXTS: *La letteratura americana e altri saggi*, 1951; *Fiabe italiane: Raccolte della tradizione popolare durante gli ultimi cento anni e transcritte in lingua dai vari dialetti*, 1956 (*Italian Fables*, 1959; also translated as *Italian Folktales*, 1980); *Cesare Pavese: Lettere, 1926-1950*, 1966; *L'Uccel Belverde e altre fiabe italiane*, 1972 (*Italian Folk Tales*, 1975).

BIBLIOGRAPHY

Adler, Sara. *Calvino: The Writer as Fablemaker*. Potomac, Md.: Ediciones José Porrúa Turanzas, 1979. Provides a valuable introduction to the themes, techniques, and images of Calvino's works. Presents the author as an explorer on fabulous, sometimes horrifying, journeys who provides rich, mythical perspectives on the world.

Bloom, Harold, ed. *Italo Calvino*. Philadelphia: Chelsea House, 2001. Collection gathers eight previously published essays about Calvino's work written by Gore Vidal, Seamus Heaney, and other authors and arranged in chronological sequence. Includes an introduction by Bloom.

Bolongaro, Eugenio. *Italo Calvino and the Compass of Literature*. Toronto, Ont.: University of Toronto Press, 2003. Examines five of Calvino's early works, written between 1948 and 1963, demonstrating how they meditate on the role of the intellectual and on the ethical and political dimensions of literature.

Carter, Albert Howard, III. *Italo Calvino: Metamorphoses of Fantasy*. Ann Arbor, Mich.: UMI Research Press, 1987. Masterful analysis of Calvino the fantasist explores his contribution to what is possible in literature by analyzing his use of the contrafactual realms of imagination, speculation, and hypothesis. Includes an excellent bibliography.

Gabriele, Tommasina. *Italo Calvino: Eros and Language*. Madison, N.J.: Fairleigh Dickinson University Press, 1994. Explores Calvino's language of love and his treatment of sex, language, and laughter. Includes notes and bibliography.

Hume, Kathryn. *Calvino's Fictions: Cogito and Cosmos*. New York: Oxford University Press, 1992. Explores Calvino's treatment of the cosmos and of cosmogony, with separate chapters on *The Path to the Nest of Spiders* and *Marcovaldo*, *The Castle of Crossed Destinies* and *If on a Winter's Night a Traveler*, and *Invisible Cities* and *Mr. Palomar*. Includes notes and a bibliography.

Jeannet, Angela M. *Under the Radiant Sun and the Crescent Moon: Italo Calvino's Storytelling*. Buffalo, N.Y.: University of Toronto Press, 2000. Discusses Calvino's works that have been translated into English, examining Calvino as both a creative writer and a critical thinker. Traces events in Calvino's life and his creative influences to understand their significance in his writing. Includes bibliographical references and an index.

McLaughlin, Martin. *Italo Calvino*. Edinburgh, Scotland: Edinburgh University Press, 1998. Very detailed study of Calvino's fiction begins with his early stories and his development of a neorealistic style. Includes a chronology of Calvino's works and a bibliography.

Markey, Constance. *Italo Calvino: A Journey Toward Postmodernism*. Gainesville: University Press of Florida, 1999. Examines postmodernist literature in Italy, tracing Calvino's development as a postmodernist writer. Also analyzes Calvino's ties to Samuel Beckett, Jorge Luis Borges, Franz Kafka, Joseph Conrad, and Mark Twain. Includes bibliographical references and index.

Olken, I. T. *With Pleated Eye and Garnet Wing: Symmetries of Italo Calvino*. Ann Arbor: University of Michigan Press, 1984. Presents a perceptive analysis of the various "symmetries" (structural, thematic, natural, configural) in Calvino's work as well as his balancing of diverse elements: traditional and innovative, rational and absurd, roguish and grotesque. Includes notes and index.

Re, Lucia. *Calvino and the Age of Neorealism: Fables of Estrangement*. Stanford, Calif.: Stanford University Press, 1990. Examines Calvino's work from a neorealistic perspective, placing the author within the context of Italian neorealism and demonstrating the influence of this literary movement in the novel *The Path to the Nest of Spiders*.

BEBE MOORE CAMPBELL

Born: Philadelphia, Pennsylvania; February 18, 1950
Died: Los Angeles, California; November 27, 2006
Also known as: Elizabeth Bebe Moore; Elizabeth Bebe Moore Campbell Gordon

PRINCIPAL LONG FICTION

Your Blues Ain't Like Mine, 1992
Brothers and Sisters, 1994
Singing in the Comeback Choir, 1998
What You Owe Me, 2001
Seventy-two Hour Hold, 2005

OTHER LITERARY FORMS

Bebe Moore Campbell's early works were primarily nonfiction. Her first book, *Successful Women, Angry Men: Backlash in the Two-Career Marriage* (1986), delves into the effects of the feminist movement on family structure, most notably the shifting gender roles that result when women, either of necessity or in quest of self-actualization, seek work outside the home, sometimes upsetting the balance within. Her second work, *Sweet Summer: Growing Up with and Without My Dad* (1989), is her memoir as a child of divorce having to spend the school year with her mother in Philadelphia and summer with her father in North Carolina. The book was hailed for showing loving relationships in the black community and for stressing the importance of male figures in young girls' lives. Poet Nikki Giovanni praised it for providing "a corrective to some of the destructive images of black men that are prevalent in our society" and doing so with vitality and clarity. Campbell also produced nonfiction articles for a wide range of publications, including *Essence*, *The New York Times*, *The Washington Post*, the *Los Angeles Times*, *Black Enterprise*, *Working Mother*, *Adweek*, *Ms.*, and *Glamour*; she was a contributing editor for *Essence*, *Black Enterprise*, and *Savvy*. In the late 1990's, she was a regular commentator on National Public Radio's *Morning Edition*. She wrote two radio dramas that were produced by the Midwestern Radio Theater, earning first place in one of its Workshop Competitions.

ACHIEVEMENTS

Bebe Moore Campbell has been called one of the most important African American authors of the twentieth century, and she received numerous awards and grants and earned national attention and praise. She was presented with the Body of Work Award from the National Association of Negro Business and Professional Women in 1978, received a National Endowment for the Arts literature grant in 1980, and won the National Association for the Advancement of Colored People (NAACP) Award for Fiction in 1994. In 2003, her children's book about a child dealing with her mother's mental illness, *Sometimes My Mommy Gets Angry*, won the Alliance for the Mentally Ill's Outstanding Literature Award. Her novel *What You Owe Me* was named a *Los Angeles Times* Best Book of the Year in 2001.

BIOGRAPHY

Although she did not grow up in a traditional two-parent family, Bebe Moore Campbell—born Elizabeth Bebe Moore—never felt an absence of love and understanding from either her mother or father. Her school months in Philadelphia were constrained because of the close supervision of her mother, grandmother, and aunt, who oversaw her every move. They instructed her in proper speech, manners, and behavior. Summers with her father and his mother in North Carolina were much more carefree. There she felt total love and acceptance.

When Campbell was in the third grade, a teacher recognized her potential and placed her in a special creative writing class. She began sending letters to her father that were intended to intrigue him—installments of stories—all of them calling for a response. She wanted to keep his interest alive all year long. Her idealization of her father ended abruptly when she was fourteen, when she learned that his speeding had caused the car crash that left him wheelchair-bound for life and that he was responsible for another accident in which a young boy had been killed. Over time, her initial anger abated, but the relationship suffered.

Campbell earned a B.S. degree in elementary education at the University of Pittsburgh and later taught elementary school for ten years in Pittsburgh, Atlanta, and Washington, D.C. An early marriage ended in divorce, and Campbell, as her mother had, assumed the responsibilities of a single parent. Her writing career began when the editor of *Essence* gave a lecture at Howard University. Campbell hurriedly handed her young daughter, Maia, to a friend for care so that she could chase the woman to the ladies' restroom and tell her of her writing aspirations. The woman, impressed, helped Campbell enter the publishing world. Campbell moved to Los Angeles in the early 1980's. There she married a banker, Ellis Gordon, Jr., who also had a child, a son named Ellis Gordon III. She lived with her family in Los Angeles until her death from brain cancer at the age of fifty-six on November 27, 2006.

Bebe Moore Campbell. (Courtesy, Gordon/Barash Associates, Inc.)

Two months prior to Campbell's death, more than one hundred people gathered to pay tribute to the woman who had so enriched their lives. Through photos, videos, testimonials, and a ceremony conferring an honorary doctorate from the University of Pittsburgh, the assemblage showed her the love and devotion they felt so deeply. Hearing her favorite music, Campbell began to wave her arms rhythmically and click her fingers from her wheelchair, and a friend joined her in a final dance. Campbell's admirers felt especially close to her because she kept in touch with them through her Web site and blog. She posted two notable letters that kept them informed of her state of mind in her final months. One, dated March 6, 2006, revealed the diagnosis she had hoped to keep secret and assured them that she would regain her health by following orders and trusting in God. A subsequent entry on May 1, 2006, was less optimistic, but proclaimed that she was going to live just for each new day and that she hoped that her friends and fans would join her in prayer.

ANALYSIS

Bebe Moore Campbell's fiction is based largely on her own experiences as a female member of a racial mi-

nority in a white, male-dominated culture. Her works are sociopolitical, generally dealing with matters of race, class, and gender. They cover such issues as sexism and sexual harassment in the workplace, racism—black to black, white to black, and black to white—and racial solidarity versus gender solidarity. Her last book explores a mental health system that is more attuned to whites than to blacks, that provides minimal care under restrictions that work against the goal of regained health, that in respecting the rights of the individual often causes more suffering. This work, *Seventy-two Hour Hold*, also exposes the questionable attitudes of many in the African American culture who see mental problems as a sign of weakness, a flaw of character. Campbell always had a purpose in her writing; she aimed to entertain only enough to keep the reader involved.

Campbell's works have received widespread approval, with only minor criticisms for a tendency to create somewhat one-dimensional characters and, at times, to present slightly unflattering pictures of women. Campbell is considered a serious writer who, while popular, never popularized by resorting to superhuman characters in glamorous sexual situations. Her white characters as well as her black ones ring true. In response to those who questioned how she could enter the minds of people of races different from hers, she explained that she socialized with people of all races and classes and had close white friends who helped her gain the perspective she needed.

YOUR BLUES AIN'T LIKE MINE

Your Blues Ain't Like Mine appeared on best-seller lists and was chosen by *The New York Times* as one of the most notable books of 1992. It is based on the actual 1955 Mississippi murder of Emmett Till, a black teenager who dared to speak to a white woman. Campbell's fictionalized account has a fifteen-year-old black northern boy, Armstrong Todd, staying with his southern grandmother while his divorced mother attempts to pull her life together in Chicago. Unfamiliar with the deep-seated racism in the South, he teasingly recites some harmless French phrases to a bored, obviously bemused, white woman as she stands in a barroom door waiting for her husband. The woman, despite being ordered to stay in the truck by her abusive partner, had ventured toward the sounds of laughter and gaiety so sadly lacking in her own life. Her husband, Floyd Cox, himself a victim of constant verbal abuse from his father and brother (the favored son), sees retribution against Armstrong as a way of gaining his family's respect. He hunts down the boy, hoping to please his father. After terrorizing and beating the frightened young man before shooting him to death, father and son sit in their truck, drinking and laughing. Floyd feels accepted but the sense of closeness is fleeting, as his father and brother all but abandon him when he is arrested for Armstrong's murder.

Southern justice being what it was in the 1950's, Floyd Cox's punishment is minimal, and he is soon released from jail. The subsequent ruination of his family is clearly of strong interest to Campbell. She wants to show their suffering as well as the suffering of the victim and his family. Campbell's point is that racism hurts the racist as well as the victim. She later said that she chose to present both sides of the story because she believed that until people understood the ramifications of racism, they could not begin to deal with it. Through seeing and feeling the pain of others, even of unsympathetic characters, she believed, people could come to recognize that bias is hateful and ultimately harmful to all.

In the novel, Campbell also explores the efforts of the murdered boy's family to make some sense out of what is left of their lives. The mother determines to have another son, one who will have a chance to experience a full life. However, this boy yields to the lure of the streets and is soon affiliated with a gang; his chances of survival are slim. In Campbell's depiction, hopelessness and despair have turned black men against one another and each man against himself. The future seems bleak, with only a hint of promise offered in the novel when the son responds slightly to his father's attempted initiation of friendship.

BROTHERS AND SISTERS

Brothers and Sisters takes place in Los Angeles, in the aftermath of the 1992 riots sparked by the not-guilty verdicts in the trial of the police officers accused of beating black motorist Rodney King. It is a novel of relationships, most notably one between a black bank manager, Esther Jackson, and Mallory Post, a white loan officer. Mallory holds a position coveted by Esther but denied her because of racism. These two women are cautious friends, neither completely comfortable with people of the other race. One is filled with underlying anger, the other is always fearful of appearing racially insensitive. Esther is the sort of woman who will not date "down": She runs a kind of financial background check on each of her suitors. Mallory urges Esther to relax her demand for upward mobility and to date the mail-truck driver because he is nice and will treat her well. Campbell later noted that Mallory, as a middle-class white woman, had "the freedom to exercise these choices because she's not so clutched about trying to get to the next rung on the ladder and thinking she's got to be with the proper partner to get there."

Campbell stated that she hoped that the novel would "serve as a kind of blueprint, to help foster racial understanding." She observed that "our strengths lie in saluting our differences and getting along." While she was aware that many of the problems in the black community had to do with institutionalized racism, she also felt that "African-Americans need to begin to look really closely and make some movement toward changing the problems" and recognizing that some of them are the result of choices they have made. The response to *Brothers and Sisters* upon its publication was uncommon, in that hundreds of discussion groups formed to come to terms with the issues raised by the novel. In Prince Georges County, Maryland, an area with a heavy black population as well as a relatively stable white one, the book became the basis of a community project: People studied the impact of bias and sought ways to deal effectively with the breakdown of communication between the races.

Campbell lamented the abandonment of the old neighborhoods, feeling that integration should not entail embracing white communities at the expense of black ones. She urged middle-class blacks to stay in touch with those less fortunate, and to mentor the young. She felt that African American men, in particular, must take steps toward regaining control of their children and of the streets of the inner cities. In a 1996 interview with Martha Satz, Campbell observed that the Million Man March, with its resultant reawakening of moral, ethical, familial, and racial responsibilities among African American men, may have been responsible for the dramatic reduction in the number of arson incidents in Detroit on Halloween of that year.

SINGING IN THE COMEBACK CHOIR

Singing in the Comeback Choir is the story of Malindy Walker, a once-famous entertainer who has fallen ungracefully into old age, with its sometimes attendant sense of the pointlessness of the battle. Her life consists mainly of stealthily smoking and drinking, despite admonitions from her doctor. Based loosely on Alberta Hunter, jazz legend of the 1940's and 1950's, Malindy is a fiercely independent soul who has no intention of bowing to her granddaughter's wish to have her cared for (and closely supervised) in a senior citizens' compound. The old neighborhood in which she lives has fallen into ruin, but Malindy's friends remain; memories of her great triumphs, of her sequined gowns and the applause, seem to sustain her. Her underlying sadness stems from her diminished singing ability. She sees herself as finished, so she partakes of the fleeting pleasures of alcohol and nicotine.

Malindy's granddaughter, Maxine Lott McCoy, a highly successful television producer with a relatively good marriage and a child on the way, is a professional who bears some resemblance to Campbell herself. She comes to the rescue of her grandmother, only to find that she herself is the one who needs to be rescued—from the high-powered yet insular and protected world that has caused her to lose touch with her origins. Therein lies the point of the novel. The old neighborhoods are dying because they have been abandoned by those who could

give them life, the ones who are capable of sparking regeneration. Maxine is saddened by what is left of her grandmother's street and by the dead eyes of a neighborhood boy she once knew. Now grown and playing at being a man, he curses her and makes sexually threatening gestures. She confronts him but sees that he is the wave of the future unless others can intervene and help.

Part of Campbell's intent in this novel, she later stated, was "to talk about the work that need[ed] to be done" to salvage and rebuild decaying neighborhoods and despairing lives. She noted that she wanted "black folks to do the hard work that we've done in the past [and] that we hadn't been doing as much in the years following the civil rights movement."

WHAT YOU OWE ME

What You Owe Me is a novel of friendship, betrayal, revenge, and choices. It is an exploration of the lasting influence parents have on their children and the need to come to terms with the past and to accept personal responsibility. The plot is simple and straightforward. Two housekeepers in a Los Angeles hotel form a personal and business relationship that is initially based on their shared awareness of being oppressed outsiders, then develops into an enterprise that allows them to rise from their status but ultimately results in betrayal.

Gilda Rosenstein, a Polish Jewish survivor of the Holocaust, has a talent for creating skin creams. Hosanna Clark, an African American whose family farm in Texas had been seized by angry whites, has the energy and business acumen to establish a successful company. Shockingly, Gilda betrays her friend by absconding with the business earnings. Hosanna survives with a smaller cosmetics operation, but she carries bitterness to her death—and beyond, by way of a ghostly visitation to her daughter, Matriece Carter, to seek retribution for her dashed dreams. Matriece, by this time, has established her own line of cosmetics for African Americans, and her mother's nemesis, Gilda, has created a cosmetic empire and is looking for someone to broaden its base with a line for women with darker skin tones. Matriece is hired and there begins the essence of the tale.

Matriece is caught between personal happiness and a need to please her mother by honoring her wish for revenge. The parent-child dynamic comes into full play, with this underlying theme the most important element in the novel. Campbell believed that how a child responds to parental example, with agreement or defiance, is up to him or her; the child can choose to confront the past and move on. Beyond dealing with the deleterious effects of racism and the impact of broken trust and destroyed friendships, in *What You Owe Me* Campbell also highlights the nature of parent-child relationships and the need for children to come to terms with their parents. They cannot change the past, but they can decide what to do about the fact of it—the important thing is that children have the choice.

SEVENTY-TWO HOUR HOLD

Seventy-two Hour Hold tells the story of a successful, divorced African American businesswoman, Keri Whitmore, and her beautiful, accomplished daughter, Trina, who intends to enroll at Brown University. The one roadblock is that Trina has begun to display quirky mannerisms, sometimes clinging to her mother and assuming the voice of her eight-year-old self, sometimes becoming verbally abusive. She is diagnosed as having bipolar disorder and begins a program of medication and talk therapy. The treatment seems to be working, but Trina tires of the routine and begins to fake taking her pills and starts running around with addicts. She is absent from home for long periods, but the police cannot treat her as a missing person until her whereabouts have been unknown for seventy-two hours, coincidentally the same period of time for which she could be held without her consent in a psychiatric facility for diagnosis and treatment.

Keri faces the fearsome dilemma of any parent with a mentally ill child: Hold the child close and avoid treatment, use a tough-love approach, or go outside the family for police intervention and possible institutionalization. One problem is that Trina will be considered an adult soon, when she turns eighteen, and so will be free to do as she pleases until she takes one step too far. Keri begins to see the horrible truth: Sometimes there is no way to save a child from harm, from following a path of self-destruction. She tries, joining a support group, even joking with another mother, Bethany, that they must be the only black people willing to admit to mental problems. Campbell uses this novel to convey the fact that many in the African American community consider mental illness a white disease, an indulgence for those who can afford high medical bills and top psychiatrists. Her characters thus fight not only mental illness but also the stigma associated with it. One notes, "Hell, it's hard enough being black. . . . Don't throw crazy in too."

Bethany convinces Keri to turn to an illegal underground alternative health group that operates on the model of the Underground Railroad, helping parents to kidnap their mentally ill children and bring them to safe houses where they are taught holistic methods of care while they search for more traditional medical solutions. Keri notes with sardonic humor that "when radical white people get tired of being radical they get to be state senators, or they write books, or they can move to Oregon and hang out for 30 years until the FBI finds them. Radical black people get killed." Keri is enslaved by her child's condition and by a system in which a sick child can use her legal rights to ensure her fall. A doctor tells Keri to learn to love a stranger, the person her daughter has become.

Campbell wrote *Seventy-two Hour Hold* from first-hand knowledge, having suffered the shame, embarrassment, and initial denial of having a relative diagnosed with bipolar disorder. Wondering how such a thing could happen in her family, she bowed to the stigma and lived in silence. Later, however, she became an advocate for all those touched by mental illness, noting that such illness is not about demons or bad childhoods, but rather about the deficits in adequate availability of mental health care for the suffering and their families.

Gay Pitman Zieger

OTHER MAJOR WORKS

NONFICTION: *Successful Women, Angry Men: Backlash in the Two-Career Marriage*, 1986 (revised 2000); *Sweet Summer: Growing Up with and Without My Dad*, 1989.

CHILDREN'S LITERATURE: *Sometimes My Mommy Gets Angry*, 2003 (illustrated by Earl B. Lewis); *Stompin' at the Savoy*, 2006; *I Get So Hungry*, 2008.

BIBLIOGRAPHY

Campbell, Bebe Moore. "I Hope I Can Teach a Little Bit: An Interview with Bebe Moore Campbell." Interview by Martha Satz. *Southwest Review* 81 (Spring, 1996): 195-213. In an in-depth discussion (that occurred in November, 1995), Campbell shares her views on the need for successful African Americans who have moved up and away from their old neighborhoods to stay in touch with the people who are still there, particularly with children who need mentoring.

_____. "Interview with Bebe Moore Campbell." Interview by Jane Campbell. *Callaloo* 22, no. 4 (1999): 954-973. Extensive interview provides information on, among other matters, Campbell's influences and those she credits with being role models for her writing and her literary style.

Chambers, Veronica. "Which Counts More, Gender or Race?" *The New York Times Magazine*, December 25, 1994. Chambers moderates a conversation between Bebe Moore Campbell and Joyce Carol Oates in which the two authors discuss such topics as Black English, interracial dating, liberal white guilt, and the historic importance of the black church.

Ladson-Billings, Gloria. "*Your Blues Ain't Like Mine:* Keeping Issues of Race and Racism on the Multicultural Agenda." *Theory into Practice* 35, no. 4 (1996): 248-256. Uses Campbell's fictionalized treatment of the Emmett Till murder to examine the social construction of race and its place in the multicultural movement.

Winter, Kari J. "*Brothers and Sisters*, by B. M. Campbell." *African American Review* 31, no. 2 (Summer, 1997): 369-372. Comparative review discusses Campbell's *Brothers and Sisters* and Gita Brown's *Be I Whole* (1995), with Brown faring better. Asserts that Campbell "replicat[es] many of the objectifying, spiritually bankrupt attitudes of American capitalism" and uses "cliché-ridden prose."

ALBERT CAMUS

Born: Mondovi, Algeria; November 7, 1913
Died: Near Sens, France; January 4, 1960

PRINCIPAL LONG FICTION

L'Étranger, 1942 (*The Stranger*, 1946)
La Peste, 1947 (*The Plague*, 1948)
La Chute, 1956 (*The Fall*, 1957)
La Mort heureuse, 1971 (wr. 1936-1938; *A Happy Death*, 1972)
Le Premier Homme, 1994 (*The First Man*, 1995)

OTHER LITERARY FORMS

Albert Camus (kah-MEW) considered his vocation to be that of novelist, but the artist in him was always at the service of his dominant passion, moral philosophy. As a result, Camus was led to cultivate several other literary forms that could express his central concerns as a moralist: the short story, drama, and nonfiction forms such as the philosophical essay and political journalism, all of which he practiced with enough distinction to be influential among his contemporaries. Moreover, these works were generally written side by side with his novels; it was Camus's customary procedure, throughout his brief writing career, always to be working on two or more compositions simultaneously, each expressing a different facet of the same philosophical issue. Thus, within a year of the publication of his most celebrated novel, *The Stranger*, there appeared a long essay titled *Le Mythe de Sisyphe* (1942; *The Myth of Sisyphus*, 1955), a meditation on the meaning of life in an irrational universe that begins with the assertion that the only serious question confronting modern man is the question of suicide and concludes with a daring argument that finds in the legend of Sisyphus a strangely comforting allegory of the human condition. Sisyphus, who becomes in Camus's hands an exemplary existentialist, spent his days in the endlessly futile task of pushing a boulder to the top of a hill from which it always rolled down again. Every human life is expended as meaninglessly as that of Sisyphus, Camus argues, yet one must conceive of Sisyphus as happy, because he was totally absorbed by his assigned task and found sufficient satisfaction in its daily accomplishment, without requiring that it also have some enduring significance. There are close links between such reasoning and the ideas that inform *The Stranger*, but it is erroneous to argue, as some have, that *The Myth of Sisyphus* is an "explanation" of *The Stranger*. The former work is, rather, a discussion of similar themes in a different form and from a different perspective, in accordance with Camus's unique way of working as a writer.

That unique way of working produced another long philosophical essay, *L'Homme révolté* (1951; *The Rebel*, 1956), which has affinities with the novel *The Plague* as well as with four of Camus's plays written and produced in the 1940's: *Caligula* (pb. 1944; English translation, 1948); *Le Malentendu* (pr., pb. 1944; *The Misunderstanding*, 1948); *L'État de siège* (pr., pb. 1948; *State of Siege*, 1958), and *Les Justes* (pr. 1949; *The Just Assassins*, 1958). Each of these plays is also related by certain thematic elements to the two novels that Camus published in the same period.

Camus's earliest political journalism, written before 1940 and dealing with the problems of his native Algeria, attracted little attention, but his work for the underground newspaper *Combat* during and after World War II achieved considerable celebrity, and the best articles he wrote for *Combat* were later collected in a volume that was widely read and admired. During the civil war in Algeria, in the 1950's, Camus again entered the lists as a political journalist, and because he was by then indisputably Algeria's most famous man of letters, his articles were of major importance at the time, though highly controversial and much less widely approved than the wartime pieces from *Combat*.

Camus produced only one collection of short stories, *L'Exil et le royaume* (1957; *Exile and the Kingdom*, 1958), composed during the same years as the novel *The Fall*, but those stories have been very popular and are regarded by many as among the finest short stories published in France in the twentieth century. The volume is particularly noteworthy because it offers the only examples Camus ever published of fiction composed in the third-person mode of the omniscient narrator. The first three of his published novels are variations of the limited-perspective first-person narrative.

Deeply involved in the theater throughout his career,

Albert Camus. (© The Nobel Foundation)

both as writer and director, Camus adapted for the French stage the work of foreign novelists Fyodor Dostoevski and William Faulkner, and of playwrights of Spain's Golden Age, including Pedro Calderón de la Barca and Lope de Vega Carpio. These adaptations have all been published and form part of Camus's contribution to the theater.

ACHIEVEMENTS

To the immediate postwar public, not only in France but also throughout Europe, Albert Camus seemed a writer of unassailable stature. Although Camus himself repudiated the designation, he was regarded worldwide as one of the two principal exponents of existentialism (the other was Jean-Paul Sartre), the single most influential philosophical movement of the twentieth century. Indeed, the existentialist worldview—according to which the individual human being "must assume ultimate responsibility for his acts of free will without any certain knowledge of what is right or wrong or good or bad"—has profoundly shaped the values of countless people who have never read Camus or Sartre.

In the 1950's, Camus was widely admired not only as a writer but also as a hero of the war against fascism, a spokesman for the younger generation, and a guardian of the moral conscience of Europe. That reputation was consecrated in 1957 with the award to Camus of the Nobel Prize in Literature, at the remarkably young age of forty-four. Yet, as has happened to many other recipients of the Nobel Prize, the award seemed almost a signal of the rapid deflation of his renown. Camus suddenly came under severe criticism for his stand on the Algerian Civil War, was attacked as self-righteous and artistically sterile, and was finally denounced as irrelevant by the new literary generation then coming to prominence, who were weary of moral issues and more concerned with aesthetic questions of form and language. Camus's fame and influence appeared to many to have suffered an irreversible decline by the end of the decade, at least in France. (In the United States, the case was different: Made more accessible by the "paperback revolution," Camus's works were enormously influential among American college students in the 1960's.) There were those who suggested that the automobile accident that took his life in January of 1960 was a disguised blessing, sparing him the pain of having to witness the collapse of his career.

It is true that, in the late twentieth century, generations after the height of Camus's fame, French writers and intellectuals showed no influence of Camus in their writings and scant critical interest in his works. Still, his works have enjoyed steady sales among the French public, and outside France, especially in the United States, interest in Camus has remained strong. There has been an inevitable sifting of values, a crystallization of what it is, in Camus's work, that still has the power to survive and what no longer speaks to successive generations. It has become clear, for example, that his philosophical essays are too closely tied to the special circumstances that occasioned them; in spite of a few brilliant passages, those essays now seem rambling and poorly argued as well as irrelevant to the concerns of modern readers. Camus's works for the theater, too, have held up poorly,

being too abstract and inhuman to engage the emotions of audiences. Although his plays have continued to be performed on both sides of the Atlantic, interest in them has steadily declined over the years. It is his fiction that still seems most alive, both in characters and ideas, and that still presents to the reader endlessly fascinating enigmas that delight the imagination and invite repeated readings.

Although the total number of Camus's fictional works is small, those works are, in both form and content, among the most brilliantly original contributions to the art of fiction produced anywhere in the twentieth century. In particular, Camus expressed through fiction, more powerfully and more memorably than anyone else in his time, the painful moral and spiritual dilemmas of modern man: evil, alienation, meaninglessness, and death. He invented techniques and created characters by which he was able to make manifest, in unforgettable terms, the eternal struggle of Everyman for some shred of dignity and happiness. His stories have accordingly taken on some of the haunting quality, and the prestige, of myths. For that reason, it seems safe to predict that it is his fiction that represents Camus's greatest achievement—an achievement that will endure long after his philosophical musings and political arguments have been forgotten.

BIOGRAPHY

Although he was born in the interior village of Mondovi, near Constantine, Algeria, Albert Camus was actually brought up in the big city, in a working-class suburb of Algiers. His widowed mother, who was from Algiers, took her two sons back there to live after her husband was killed early in World War I. Albert, the younger of the two sons, was not yet a year old when his father died, and he was to grow up with a need for relationships with older men, apparently to replace the father he never had. It was important to Camus that his father's forebears had immigrated *by choice* to Algeria from France in the nineteenth century, since it made him feel that his roots were authentically both French and Algerian. Because his mother was of Spanish extraction, Camus felt himself to be even more authentically Algerian, for Spanish blood gave him his share of that passionate Mediterranean temperament that he felt made French Algeria distinctive and unique. It comes as no surprise, therefore, that the great bulk of Camus's writing is set in Algeria or relates directly to that country. Being Algerian was the central fact of Camus's consciousness.

In his early twenties, Camus began to write essays for a leftist political journal published in Algiers; his subject was the political and economic plight of Algeria in its role as a colony of France. During those same years, he helped to found a theater group, for which he acted, directed, and did some writing, and he was a candidate for an advanced degree in philosophy at the University of Algiers. At times, he had to interrupt his studies because of ill health; he had contracted tuberculosis in 1930, at the age of seventeen, and was subject to periodic attacks from it for the rest of his life. When only twenty-one, he made a rather impulsive marriage that ended in separation within a year and eventual divorce. He worked at a number of odd jobs before becoming a full-time journalist, and he was active enough in politics in the 1930's to have become, for a few months, a member of the Algerian Communist Party. Altogether, his Algerian youth had been a difficult and turbulent experience, yet it had also been a time of growth and self-discovery, and he looked back on those years ever after with a special nostalgia for the sun, sand, sea, and simplicity of life that he felt had formed him and made him what he had become.

Early in 1940, with a war in progress and the newspaper for which he worked closed down, Camus found himself forced to leave Algeria in order to make a living. He went to Paris to work for a Paris newspaper—a job procured for him by his older friend Pascal Pia, with whom he had worked on the Algiers newspaper before it folded. Within a year, the Paris job ended, and Camus, who had married again, returned to Algeria with his wife. They lived in Oran, his wife's hometown, and while she worked as a teacher, Camus worked at his writing projects, completing both the novel *The Stranger* and the essay *The Myth of Sisyphus* and arranging for their publication in Paris by Gallimard.

By late 1942, Camus was so ill with tuberculosis that his wife persuaded him to seek a more favorable climate in the mountainous area of central France, which was then unoccupied territory. He went there alone, to continue writing, and found himself cut off from all contact with his family when the Allies invaded North Africa

and the Germans occupied the rest of France as a defensive measure. During this period of isolation, Camus began to sketch out his next novel, *The Plague*. He also began to make frequent trips to Paris to see literary friends. His publisher, Gallimard, not only sent him royalties for *The Stranger*, which sold quite well, but also helped Camus by putting him on the Gallimard payroll as a reader—a position he enjoyed so much that he continued to fulfill it for the rest of his life.

Late in 1943, Camus moved to Paris to be where the literary action was, increasingly associating with those friends who were in the Resistance movement, with which Camus was strongly sympathetic. Before long, Camus joined the Resistance and was assigned the task of writing for the Resistance newspaper *Combat*. After the liberation of Paris in 1944, *Combat* went aboveground as a daily newspaper, and Camus was for a time its editor. He had become part of the Paris literary world, had met its best-known figures—Sartre, André Malraux, and many others—and had achieved a certain fame. By that time, it was clear that he would never go back to Algeria to live. As soon as it was possible for her to do so, Camus's wife joined him in Paris, and in September of 1945 she gave birth to twins, a boy and a girl. By war's end, Camus was not only a confirmed Parisian but also a domesticated one, with a family to support.

In the postwar years, Camus's fame quickly began to spread outside France—*The Stranger* appeared in English translation in 1946 and was an immediate sensation—and Camus took up the life of a lionized man of letters, dropping all employment except for his work with Gallimard and making lecture tours to foreign countries, including the United States. The publication of *The Plague* in 1947 was hailed by critics as the fulfillment of his great promise as a writer, and that book became one of the best sellers of the postwar era, making Camus economically secure for the first time. Success and fame seemed to make him artistically insecure, however—there were suddenly too many demands from admirers, too many intrusions into his privacy and working time, and, above all, too much self-doubt about his own powers for him to be able to live up to his public's expectations of him. Camus soon began to experience a crisis of literary sterility. It took him until 1951 to complete the essay *The Rebel*, begun nearly ten years earlier, and throughout the first half of the decade of the 1950's he published nothing and was rumored to have a permanent case of writer's block. The outbreak of violence in Algeria and the campaign for independence, which began in 1952, added severely to Camus's troubled state, and the controversial articles he wrote in that period on the Algerian question certainly lost him many friends and much support. His unhappy attempt to be the voice of reason and conciliation at a time in the dispute when opinions had already become hopelessly polarized ("If you are not with us, you are against us") is poignantly described in the powerful tale "The Guest," one of the best stories in the collection *Exile and the Kingdom.*

Camus emerged from this period of intense personal suffering and frustration by venting his feelings in the short, bitterly satiric novel *The Fall*, published in 1956—his first work of fiction in nearly ten years, as his detractors were quick to point out. Nevertheless, the comic verve of the work attracted many readers, even though its intended meanings often seemed obscure to them. The book sold well, and Camus's reputation rebounded somewhat, especially outside France. The publication of the volume of short stories *Exile and the Kingdom* the following year earned for him additional respect as a writer who still had something to say. Internationally, his reputation peaked with the award of the Nobel Prize later that same year.

Reinvigorated by the successes of 1956 and 1957, Camus was, as the decade ended, once again confidently and productively at work, with the usual three or four projects going simultaneously, one of which was an autobiographical novel about his youth in Algeria, to be called "Le Premier Homme" (the first man). His "block" seemed to be definitively overcome, and friends and family who spent Christmas of 1959 with him at the country retreat he had purchased in southern France recalled that he was in a generally optimistic frame of mind about his career. Fate, however, abruptly shattered that optimism. Camus's career came to a premature—and, he would have said, absurd—end only a few days after that happy Christmas. On January 4, 1960, Michel Gallimard, nephew of Camus's publisher, lost control of his car, in which Camus was riding as a passenger, just outside the tiny village of Villeblevin, and crashed into a tree. Camus, who had passed his forty-sixth birthday

only two months before, died instantly. The evolution of the author's work strongly suggests that a banal motor accident cut him off when he seemed, finally, to have mastered his craft and to be entering his prime creative years.

ANALYSIS

Two persistent themes animate all of Albert Camus's writing and underlie his artistic vision: One is the enigma of the universe, which is breathtakingly beautiful yet indifferent to life; the other is the enigma of man, whose craving for happiness and meaning in life remains unextinguished by his full awareness of his own mortality and of the sovereign indifference of his environment. At the root of every novel, every play, every essay, even every entry in his notebooks can be found Camus's incessant need to probe and puzzle over the ironic double bind that he perceived to be the essence of the human condition: Man is endowed with the imagination to conceive an ideal existence, but neither his circumstances nor his own powers permit its attainment. The perception of this hopeless double bind made inescapable for Camus the obligation to face up to an overriding moral issue for man: Given man's circumscribed condition, are there honorable terms on which his life can be lived?

A HAPPY DEATH

In his earliest attempt at casting these themes in fictional form, Camus made use of the traditional novel of personal development, or bildungsroman, to describe one young man's encounters with life, love, and death. The result was an episodic novel, obviously based on his own experiences but composed in the third person and so lacking in unity and coherence as to betray the central idea on which he wished to focus: the problem of accepting death. He called the novel *A Happy Death* and showed his hero resolutely fixing his consciousness on the inanimate world around him, striving to become one with the stones and achieve a happy death by blending gently and painlessly into the silent harmony of the universe while retaining his lucidity until his last breath. The book's last sentence strives to convince the reader by rhetoric that the hero has indeed achieved the happy death he sought: "And stone among the stones, he returned in the joy of his heart to the truth of motionless worlds."

Camus seems to have sensed, however, that the rhetoric was unconvincing and that the ideal of a happy death was an illusion. Perhaps he even recognized that his hero's struggle to remain conscious of life until his last breath was, in reality, a protest against death and a contradiction of his desire to make the transition to death serene and imperceptible. It was doubtless some such sense of the book's failure that convinced Camus not to publish this work, composed when he was not yet twenty-five. Its posthumous publication has given scholars the opportunity to see Camus's first halting steps in trying to formulate the subtle and complex themes of the novels that were to make him great.

THE STRANGER

The Stranger, Camus's second attempt at writing a novel, includes a number of the scenes, characters, and situations found in *A Happy Death* (Mersault, the hero of *A Happy Death*, becomes Meursault in *The Stranger*). A detailed comparison of the two novels, however, makes it clear that *The Stranger*, which appeared in 1942, four years and many events after Camus abandoned *A Happy Death*, is a wholly different work in both conception and theme. No longer preoccupied with happiness in death, Camus turned his attention in *The Stranger* to the problem of happiness in life, to man's irrational and desperate need to find meaning in existence. His protagonist, Meursault, is not the frail, sophisticated, death-haunted figure of the earlier novel, but rather a robust primitive who seems eerily devoid of the normal attitudes, values, and culturally induced feelings of his society, as though he had been brought up on some other planet—a "stranger" in the fullest sense of the word. Moreover, Camus hit upon the device of first-person narration as the most effective and dramatic means of confronting his readers with his disturbing protagonist, so alien to his environment. The famous opening words shock the reader into an awareness of the disquieting strangeness of the narrator:

Mama died today. Or perhaps yesterday, I don't know. I received a telegram from the home: "Mother passed away. Funeral tomorrow. Yours truly." That doesn't mean anything. Perhaps it was yesterday.

Shrewdly focusing on a mother's death as a revealing touchstone of humankind's most deeply ingrained social attitudes, these words achieve a double effect: They tell the reader that the son of the deceased mother can speak of her death without any of the expected symptoms of grief, but, at the same time, they remind the reader that the rest of society, having no familial ties with the deceased, habitually masks its indifference under empty rhetorical formulas such as the telegraphic announcement.

This dual perspective is fully developed in subsequent chapters as the basic theme of the book: While Meursault shows by his own forthright account of his life that he does not share his society's conventional notions about death, religion, family, friendship, love, marriage, and ambition, he also manages to reveal—often without realizing it—that those conventional notions are often shallow, hypocritical, or delusory and constitute the pathetic inventions of a society desperate to invest its existence with a meaning it does not have. Thus, when Meursault, asked by his boss whether he would be interested in an assignment to establish a Paris office for his boss's business, says that he has no interest in living in Paris, the reader recognizes that Meursault simply does not believe that material surroundings can make his life any different. At the same time, the boss's dismayed reaction to Meursault's indifference to opportunity subtly disturbs the reader with the suspicion that, after all, the boss may have a touching but misplaced faith in the value of ambition. A similar moment occurs when Meursault and his girlfriend, Marie, discuss love and marriage. The reader is surely made uncomfortable by Meursault's casualness in saying that he does not know what love is, but that he is willing to marry Marie if she wants it. It is, however, a different order of discomfort that overcomes the reader when Marie insists that marriage is a very serious matter and Meursault calmly replies that it is not.

All of part 2 of the novel, devoted to Meursault's trial after he has killed an Arab, brings additional and even more disturbing changes on the same dual perspective, with Meursault showing no awareness or acceptance of conventional beliefs about justice, murder, legal procedures, and the nature of evidence, while all the "normal" people involved show unexamined or self-deceiving convictions about all such matters. The ironic meaning that emerges from the novel is that although Meursault is guilty of taking a life, society sentences him to death not for his crime, with which it seems incapable of dealing, but for his refusal to live by society's values, for not "playing the game." As Camus himself laconically remarked, his novel means that any man who does not weep at his mother's funeral risks being condemned to death.

Critics have regularly protested that, in *The Stranger*, Camus manipulates his readers' emotions, inducing sympathy for Meursault even though he is a moral monster and ridiculing everyone else as representative of a society afraid to face reality, hence threatened by Meursault's clear-eyed and unsentimental acceptance of the world. Such protests are justified, however, only if one assumes that Camus intended *The Stranger* to be a realistic representation of the world, holding the mirror up to nature. In fact, Meursault is not a believable human figure, the events of the novel are but dimly evoked and unconvincingly motivated, and the very existence of the text itself, as Meursault's first-person account of events, is never explained. In *The Stranger*, Camus makes almost no concessions to the conventional procedures of realism, constructing instead a kind of mythic tale of philosophical intent to dramatize an imaginary confrontation between man's basic nature as a simple, sensual being and his grandly narcissistic self-image as an intelligent being whose every gesture has transcendent significance. Read as a kind of poetic allegory rather than as an exemplary tale of human conduct, *The Stranger* is seen as a powerful depiction of man's painfully divided soul, at once joyous for the gift of life and miserable at the absence of any discernible purpose in that life and at the indifference of the surrounding universe. Viewed that way, *The Stranger* deserves its reputation as one of the great works of art of the first half of the twentieth century.

THE PLAGUE

The allegorical mode is given a much more detailed and realistically human foundation in Camus's next novel, *The Plague*, regarded by many critics as his masterpiece. This time, Camus makes a concerted effort to create a strong sense of place in a real setting and to depict fully rounded and believable characters. With the vividness of concrete details and actual place-names, Camus takes the reader to the city of Oran, in Algeria—a

city of which he had intimate personal knowledge, having lived there for an extended period—and describes the impact on that real place of an imaginary outbreak of bubonic plague. The reader shares the first frightening discovery of rats dying in the streets and apartment house hallways and experiences the spread of terror and panic as the first human victims of the plague appear in random locations around the city. Soon, the city is ordered closed, quarantined from the rest of the world, and the authorities try to mobilize the trapped population and lay down strict sanitation rules to try to limit the impact of a disease they know they cannot cure.

The heart of the novel is the depiction of the various ways in which individuals react to the fear and isolation imposed by this sudden state of siege, in which the invading army is invisible. To convey the variety of responses to such an extreme and concentrated crisis in human affairs, Camus deliberately eschews the convenient device of the omniscient narrator, making the depiction of every event and scene an eyewitness account in some form: the spoken words of reports or dialogues, the written words of letters or private diaries, and, as the main device, the written record of the daily observations of the novel's main character, Dr. Rieux. Whereas in *The Stranger* first-person narration is primarily a device of characterization, used to portray an alien figure's disconcertingly remote and hollow personality, in *The Plague* it is a device of narrative realism, used to reduce devastatingly incomprehensible events to a human, hence believable, scale by portraying the way these events are seen by a representative group of ordinary citizens.

The Plague differs from its predecessor not only technically but also thematically. Camus's inspiration for *The Plague* was no philosophical abstraction but a specific event of his own life: the frustration and despair he experienced during the war, when the aftermath of the Allied invasion of North Africa trapped his wife in Oran (while he was in the Resistance organization in the Massif Central) and cut off all communication between them. That experience started the fictional idea germinating in his mind, and a literary model—Daniel Defoe's *A Journal of the Plague Year* (1722)—gave the idea more concrete form.

Central to the idea of *The Plague*, certainly, is the

theme of man's encounter with death rather than the theme of man's interpretation of life, which dominates *The Stranger*. Indeed, with *The Plague*, Camus was returning to the preoccupation of his earliest work of fiction, *A Happy Death*, but with a major new emphasis. *The Plague* concerns not an individual's quest in relation to death but a collectivity's involuntary confrontation with it. In *The Plague*, death is depicted as a chance outgrowth of an indifferent nature that suddenly, and for no apparent reason, becomes an evil threat to humankind. Death in the form of a plague is unexpected, irrational— a manifestation of that absurdity, that radical absence of meaning in life that is a major underlying theme of *The Stranger*. In *The Plague*, however, Camus proposes the paradox that when death is a manifestation of the absurd, it galvanizes something in a person's spirit that enables the individual to join with others to fight against death and thus give meaning and purpose to life. From evil may come happiness, this novel seems to suggest: It is a painful irony of the human condition that individuals often discover their own capacities for courage and for fraternal affection—that is, for happiness— only if they are forced by the threat of evil to make the discovery.

The hint of optimism in this paradoxical theme— happiness is, after all, possible for some if the circumstances are dire enough—is, however, insufficient to offset the fundamental pessimism of *The Plague*. A glance at the fates of the main characters will make the basic bleakness of this work manifest. At the center of the action is Bernard Rieux, a doctor who risks his life every day to lead the fight against the plague and who, more than anyone else in the novel, experiences the satisfaction and the joy of finding himself equal to a heroic task and feeling with others a fraternal bond engendered by their common struggle. His satisfaction is brief and his joys few, however. He knows that he cannot cure victims of the plague and must suppress his sympathy for them if he is to be effective in palliating their suffering and in keeping them from infecting others. The result of this bind is that Rieux strikes his patients and their families as cold and indifferent; he ends up being hated by those he is trying to help. The fraternal bond with others who are trying to help develops in only a few instances, since most of his fellow citizens are too frightened or egocen-

tric to join him in the effort. Moreover, where the bond does develop, it proves too tenuous to penetrate his natural isolation.

The limits of the fraternal bond are most graphically expressed by the moment in the novel when Rieux and Jean Tarrou (a traveler through whose journal part of the novel is related), seeing the first signs that the plague is receding, decide to go for a swim together, in celebration. The point is carefully made that, while each feels a sense of fraternity with the other as they swim in the same water, each is also conscious of being ultimately quite alone in the joy and freedom of moving serenely through the water and forgetting the plague for a short while. In spite of the shared emotion that unites them, each feels the swim to be predominantly a solitary experience. Finally, when the plague does end, Rieux finds himself strangely empty and alienated from the joyous crowds now once more filling the streets of Oran; the urgency of his task no longer exists to summon forth his courage. Indeed, because he has lost those dearest to him—his wife and Tarrou—he feels more alone than ever after the plague has gone.

The other important characters fare no better than Rieux: Tarrou is killed by the plague; Joseph Grand suffers from it but recovers and resumes his self-imposed task of writing a novel, of which he has yet to complete the first sentence, because he has endlessly revised and recast it in a fruitless search for perfection; Rembart, a journalist who is trapped in Oran by the plague, leaves when it is over, but without having written anything about it, having found his profession inadequate to such an awesome task; and Cottard, who engages in black-market profiteering during the plague, goes crazy when the plague ends, shooting citizens at random until he is caught and killed by the police. There is little in this novel to nourish an optimistic outlook, except for the hesitant and tentative statement of Rieux, at the end of his chronicle, that amid the ravages of pestilence, one learns that "there are, in men, more things to admire than to despise."

The Plague is the longest, the most realistic, and artistically the most impressive of Camus's novels, offering a richly varied cast of characters and a coherent and riveting plot, bringing an integrated world memorably to life while stimulating the reader's capacity for moral reflection. In spite of its vivid realism, *The Plague* is no less mythical and allegorical in its impact than is *The Stranger*. When first published, *The Plague* was widely interpreted as a novel about the German Occupation and the French Resistance, with the plague symbolizing the evil presence of the Nazis. Since the 1940's, however, more universal themes and symbols have been discovered in the book, including the frighteningly random nature of evil and the perception that humankind's conquest of evil is never more than provisional, that the struggle will always have to be renewed. It has also been widely recognized that *The Plague* is, in significant degree, a profound meditation on the frustrating limits of human language both as a means of communication and as a means of representing the truth about human existence. The discovery of that theme has made *The Plague* the most modern of Camus's novels, the óne with the most to say to future generations of Camus's readers.

For nearly a decade after the publication of *The Plague*, impeded by the consequences of fame, Camus struggled to find enough time and privacy to compose a new work of fiction and to complete philosophical and theatrical writings begun before he wrote *The Plague*. In the mid-1950's, he began to compose a group of short stories with the common theme of the condition of the exile, and it was one of those stories that he was suddenly inspired to expand into a short novel written in the form of a monologue and published in 1956 as *The Fall*.

THE FALL

The product of a troubled time in Camus's life, *The Fall* is a troubling work, full of brilliant invention, dazzling wordplay, and devastating satire, but so profoundly ironic and marked by so many abrupt shifts in tone as to leave the reader constantly off balance and uncertain of the author's viewpoint or purpose. This difficulty in discerning the book's meaning is inherent in its basic premise, for the work records a stream of talk—actually one side of a dialogue—by a Frenchman who haunts a sleazy bar in the harbor district of Amsterdam and who does not trouble to hide the fact that most of what he says, including his name, is invented. Because he is worldly and cultivated, his talk is fascinating and seizes the attention of his implied interlocutor (who is also, of course, the reader) with riveting force. The name

he gives himself is Jean-Baptiste Clamence, a name that evokes the biblical figure of the prophet John the Baptist as the voice crying in the wilderness (*vox clamantis in deserto*) and that coincides neatly with the occupation he claims to follow, also of his own invention: judge-penitent.

When Clamence remarks to his interlocutor, near the end of his five-day monologue, "I know what you are thinking: it is very difficult to distinguish the true from the false in what I am telling you. I confess that you are right," the reader feels that Camus has suddenly made a personal intervention into the novel in order to warn the reader that he or she has been deliberately manipulated by Clamence's playacting and has every right to feel bewildered. Camus thus signals to the reader that the book's troubling impact has been calculated and deliberate from the start. Only in the closing pages of the novel does he clarify the purpose of Clamence's invented narrative and the meaning of his invented calling, but the explanation comes too late—deliberately so, for the reader can never be free of doubt about whether Clamence's entire performance has been designed to raise questions concerning what is true and what is false, what is good and what is evil.

Clamence's "explanation" is, in fact, the most unsettling element in the book. He pointedly admits to his interlocutor that he has been penitently "confessing" his own sins in a carefully controlled pattern, only in order to induce his interlocutor to "confess" in turn, thus enabling Clamence to play the role of judge. Clamence begins his "confession" by describing his successful career in Paris as a much-admired lawyer known for his defense of "widows and orphans"—that is, the helpless and disadvantaged of society. He had every reason to see himself as a man of virtue, he says, until he began to "hear" a woman's mocking laughter whenever he looked at himself in the mirror with those feelings of self-satisfaction. The mocking laughter reminded him that his lawyerly altruism was only a mask for selfishness and forced him to recall an incident he had tried to forget: Crossing a bridge over the Seine one night, he had seen a young woman throw herself into the water and had made no effort to rescue her or to get help, instead walking hurriedly away without looking back. The mocking laughter was thus his conscience taunting him with the suppressed memory of his guilt: The admired man of virtue was in reality a fraud, a sinner like everyone else.

Clamence goes on to explain that thereafter he had found it increasingly difficult to continue his career in Paris and live with his guilt. At the same time, he could not give up his need to feel morally superior to others. His solution to this private inner conflict, he then declares, was his brilliant invention of a new career for himself as a judge-penitent. He closed his Paris office and moved to the harbor section of Amsterdam—which, he notes, is in the center of the concentric circles of Amsterdam's canals, like the ninth circle of Hell in Dante's *Inferno*, and is, moreover, "the site of one of the greatest crimes of modern history," meaning the Nazi destruction of the entire Jewish community of Amsterdam. In these new surroundings, he not only could assuage his guilt by the feeling that he was in the ninth circle of Hell, where he belonged, but also could have access to the endless succession of tourists who gravitated to that spot, whom he could "help," in such propitious surroundings, to recognize their own guilt as well. His "help" consisted of a recital of his own sins, so arranged as to emphasize their universality, thus subtly prompting his listener to confess the same sins in turn. In this way, Clamence uses his perfected performance as a penitent to put himself in the deeply satisfying position of judge, hearing his listener's confession while basking in the warm glow of his own moral superiority. Because everyone, without exception, is a guilty sinner, says Clamence, he has solved the dilemma of how to live happily with his nagging guilt. The essential secret, he says, is to accuse oneself first— and of all seven cardinal sins—thereby earning the right to accuse everyone else.

Clamence's "solution," which concludes *The Fall*, is a burlesque of moral reasoning, underscoring the bitterness of the satire that is at the heart of this novel. Like Camus's other novels, *The Fall* is an exploration of man's moral nature and his passionate search for happiness in a world that is indifferent to such spiritual values, but unlike any of his other works of fiction, *The Fall* is both unrelievedly pessimistic and irreducibly ambiguous. In Clamence's confession, is Camus's intention to castigate himself for having taken his own fame too seriously and thus expiate his personal sin of pride? Many critics read the book that way when it appeared in 1956. Or is he using Clamence, rather, to avenge himself on his enemies, whom he thought too quick to adopt a tone of moral superiority in judging his position on the Algerian Civil War? Many other critics saw *The Fall* that way. Generations later, it seems reasonable to suggest that both interpretations have validity. *The Fall* is a comic masterpiece, remarkably parallel in its tone, its themes, and its ambiguity to Camus's short story "Jonas," written about the same time—a story in which, everyone agrees, the author attempted to come to terms with his artistic sterility and with the conflict he felt between public obligation and the need for privacy.

"Jonas" ends with a celebrated verbal ambiguity: The painter-hero of the story, after long meditation, translates his thought to canvas by means of a single word, but it is impossible to discern whether that word is "solitary" or "solidary." It is tempting to conclude, using that short story as analogue, that the ambiguity of *The Fall* is also deliberate and that Camus meant his work both as private confession and public condemnation. Those two meanings, the one private and the other public, are surely intended to combine retrospectively in the reader's mind to form Camus's universal condemnation of man's moral bankruptcy. As the title is meant to suggest, *The Fall* is a modern parable about Original Sin and the Fall of Man.

There is reason to believe that the unrelenting pessimism of *The Fall* was not Camus's final word on humanity but was rather the expression of a temporary discouragement that he had almost succeeded in dispelling at the time of his death. In 1959, he was at work on a new novel, to be called "Le Premier Homme," the theme of which was to be a celebration of the formative experience of his Algerian youth. *The First Man* was not published until long after his death, in 1994; it addresses from a particularly personal perspective the subject that, at bottom, always animated Camus's fiction—the enigma of human beings' struggle against the indifference of creation and the unquenchable thirst for moral significance in life. Camus's unforgettable contribution to the ongoing dialogue inspired by that vast subject is embodied in the three great novels he managed to complete before his untimely death.

Murray Sachs

OTHER MAJOR WORKS

SHORT FICTION: *L'Exil et le royaume*, 1957 (*Exile and the Kingdom*, 1958).

PLAYS: *Révolte dans les Asturies*, pb. 1936 (with others); *Caligula*, pb. 1944 (wr. 1938-1939; English translation, 1948); *Le Malentendu*, pr., pb. 1944 (*The Misunderstanding*, 1948); *L'État de siège*, pr., pb. 1948 (*State of Siege*, 1958); *Les Justes*, pr. 1949 (*The Just Assassins*, 1958); *Caligula, and Three Other Plays*, 1958; *Les Possédés*, pr., pb. 1959 (adaptation of Fyodor Dostoevski's novel *Besy*; *The Possessed*, 1960).

NONFICTION: *L'Envers et l'endroit*, 1937 ("The Wrong Side and the Right Side," 1968); *Noces*, 1938 ("Nuptials," 1968); *Le Mythe de Sisyphe*, 1942 (*The Myth of Sisyphus*, 1955); *L'Homme révolté*, 1951 (*The Rebel*, 1956); *L'Été*, 1954 (*Summer*, 1968); *Carnets: Mai 1935-février 1942*, 1962 (*Notebooks: 1935-1942*, 1963); *Carnets: Janvier 1942-mars 1951*, 1964 (*Notebooks: 1942-1951*, 1965); *Lyrical and Critical Essays*, 1968 (includes "The Wrong Side and the Right Side," "Nuptials," and "Summer"); *Correspondance, 1939-1947*, 2000; *Camus à "Combat": Éditoriaux et articles d'Albert Camus, 1944-1947*, 2002 (*Camus at "Combat": Writing, 1944-1947*, 2006).

BIBLIOGRAPHY

Bronner, Stephen Eric. *Camus: Portrait of a Moralist*. Minneapolis: University of Minnesota Press, 1999. Provides a thorough, detailed account of the life and work of Camus, but assumes that the reader is familiar with key places and figures in Camus's life. Black-and-white photos and a chronology put events and Camus's influence on history and literature into perspective.

Carroll, David. *Albert Camus, the Algerian: Colonialism, Terrorism, Justice*. New York: Columbia University Press, 2007. Analyzes Camus's novels, short stories, and political essays within the context of the author's complicated relationship with his Algerian background. Concludes that Camus's work reflects his understanding of both the injustice of colonialism and the tragic nature of Algeria's struggle for independence. Includes bibliography and index.

Cruickshank, John. *Albert Camus and the Literature of Revolt*. 1959. Reprint. Westport, Conn.: Greenwood Press, 1978. Important work on Camus as writer and philosopher includes a general discussion of his principal ideas as they relate to the literature and historical events of the period. Offers interesting comments concerning American literary influences on Camus.

Hughes, Edward J., ed. *The Cambridge Companion to Camus*. New York: Cambridge University Press, 2007. Examines Camus's major works as well as his life, including his poverty-stricken childhood, his education, and his political beliefs. Includes reference citations in English and French.

Kellman, Steven G., ed. *"The Plague": Fiction and Resistance*. New York: Twayne, 1993. Discusses the novel in separate sections devoted to literary and historical context and to different readings of the work. Individual chapters examine major characters as well as the mysterious narrator.

King, Adele, ed. *Camus's "L'Étranger": Fifty Years On*. New York: St. Martin's Press, 1992. Addresses the contexts and influences of the novel, its reception and influence on other writers, textual studies, and comparative studies. Includes an informative introduction.

Lottman, Herbert R. *Albert Camus*. 1979. Corte Madera, Calif.: Gingko Press, 1997. Extremely well-documented biography is based on extensive interviews with people who knew Camus well.

McCarthy, Patrick. *Camus*. New York: Random House, 1982. A meticulous attempt to reconstruct Camus through his childhood and early influences. Also covers every major phase of the author's life and work. Includes notes and brief bibliography.

Rhein, Phillip H. *Albert Camus*. Rev. ed. Boston: Twayne, 1989. Useful introduction to Camus's life and work includes chapters on his childhood, his understanding of the absurd, his career in the theater, his view of humanity and rebellion. Includes notes and bibliography.

Rizzuto, Anthony. *Camus: Love and Sexuality*. Gainesville: University Press of Florida, 1998. Presents both biographical material and literary and psychological analysis in addressing the evolution of Camus's use of the themes of love and sex in his fiction. Includes bibliography and index.

Sprintzen, David. *Camus: A Critical Examination*. Philadelphia: Temple University Press, 1988. Delves into the biographical experience that informs Camus's work. Includes chapters on *The Stranger*, Camus's drama, his interpretation of social dislocation, society and rebellion, revolt and history, metaphysical rebellion, confrontations with modernity, and the search for a style of life. Includes notes and bibliography.

Todd, Olivier. *Albert Camus: A Life*. Translated by Benjamin Ivry. New York: Alfred A. Knopf, 1997. Making use of materials such as unpublished letters made available after the death of Camus's widow, this detailed biography reveals much about Camus's love affairs and his many important friendships.

ELIAS CANETTI

Born: Ruse, Bulgaria; July 25, 1905
Died: Zurich, Switzerland; August 13, 1994

PRINCIPAL LONG FICTION

Die Blendung, 1935 (*Auto-da-Fé*, 1946; also known as *The Tower of Babel*)

OTHER LITERARY FORMS

Although he published only one work of fiction, Elias Canetti (kah-NEH-tee) wrote much prose. His magnum opus, the product of decades of work, is *Masse und Macht* (1960; *Crowds and Power*, 1962), an extended essay in social psychology that is unorthodox and provocative. In an effort to present a sort of taxonomic typology of the mass mind, Canetti casts a wide net over all of human history. Historical, political, psychological, anthropological, philosophical, sociological, and cultural elements and insights are enlisted in an occasionally idiosyncratic search for the wellsprings of human behavior in general and the root causes of fascism in particular.

A much lighter work is *Der Ohrenzeuge: Fünfzig Charaktere* (1974; *Earwitness: Fifty Characters*, 1979), a series of mordant characterizations of eccentric figures that exemplify the quirks and extremes inherent in the human personality. This collection includes thumbnail sketches of such specimens as "Der Papiersäufer" ("The Paper Drunkard"), "Der Demutsahne" ("The Humility-Forebear"), "Die Verblümte" ("The Allusive Woman"), "Der Heroszupfer" ("The Hero-Tugger"), "Der Maestroso" ("The Maestroso"), "Der Nimmermust" ("The Never-Must"), "Der Tränenwärmer" ("The

Tearwarmer"), "Die Tischtuchtolle" ("The Tablecloth-Lunatic"), "Der Fehlredner" ("The Misspeaker"), "Der Tückenfänger" ("The Wile-Catcher"), and "Die Archäokratin" ("The Archeocrat").

Canetti's aphoristic jottings from 1942 to 1972 have been collected in a volume titled *Die Provinz des Menschen* (1973; *The Human Province*, 1978). *Die Stimmen von Marrakesch: Aufzeichnungen nach einer Reise* (1967; *The Voices of Marrakesh: A Record of a Visit*, 1978) is a profound travel book. *Das Gewissen der Worte* (1975; *The Conscience of Words*, 1979) brings together Canetti's essays on philosophy, art, and literature. The perceptive literary critic is shown to good advantage in *Der andere Prozess: Kafkas Briefe an Felice* (1969; *Kafka's Other Trial*, 1974).

As a young man, Canetti came under the spell of the great Viennese satirist Karl Kraus, many of whose spellbinding readings he attended, and his dramatic works exemplify the Krausian concept of "acoustical masks," as he unsparingly sketches the linguistic (and, in a sense, moral) physiognomy of his characters on the basis of each person's individual, unmistakable speech pattern. His play *Hochzeit* (pb. 1932; *The Wedding*, 1984) presents a *danse macabre* of petit-bourgeois Viennese society motivated by cupidity and hypocrisy, with the collapse of a house coveted by those attending a wedding party symbolizing the breakdown of this corrupt society. *Komödie der Eitelkeit* (pb. 1950; *Comedy of Vanity*, 1983) explores the genesis of a mass psychosis. A totalitarian government, having proscribed vanity, has all the mirrors, photos, and films burned. As vanity goes underground, distrust, dehumanization, and disaster ensue.

Die Befristeten (pb. 1956; *The Numbered*, 1964; also known as *Life-Terms*) is, as it were, a primer of death. People carry their predetermined dates of death in capsules around their necks, to be opened eventually only by the "Capsulan." One man, Fünfzig (Mr. Fifty), finally rebels against this knowledge and breaks the taboo. The discovery that the capsules are empty replaces presumed security with fear of death.

Canetti also achieved considerable prominence as an autobiographer. The first volume of his memoirs, *Die gerettete Zunge: Geschichte einer Jugend* (*The Tongue Set Free: Remembrance of a European Childhood*, 1979), appeared in 1977. The title of the second volume, *Die Fackel im Ohr* (1980; *The Torch in My Ear*, 1982), reflects Canetti's indebtedness to Karl Kraus and his celebrated journal.

ACHIEVEMENTS

The award of the 1981 Nobel Prize in Literature to Elias Canetti for his multifaceted literary oeuvre caught the world by surprise and focused international attention on a seminal writer and thinker who had lived and worked in relative obscurity for decades. Canetti then became increasingly recognized as a representative of a distinguished Austrian literary tradition. The misleading statement of *The New York Times* that Canetti was "the first Bulgarian writer" to achieve the distinction of a Nobel Prize was refuted by Canetti himself when he said that "like Karl Kraus and Nestroy, I am a Viennese writer." Even more suggestive is Canetti's statement that "the language of my mind will remain German—because I am a Jew."

BIOGRAPHY

Born July 25, 1905, in a Danube port city in northern Bulgaria as the oldest son of Mathilde and Jacques Canetti, Elias Canetti had a polyglot and multicultural upbringing. As he details in the first volume of his autobiography, German was the fourth language he acquired—after Ladino (an archaic Spanish dialect spoken by Sephardic Jews that is also known as Spaniolic and Judezmo), Bulgarian, and English. In June, 1911, he was taken to England and enrolled in a Manchester school. Following the sudden death of his father, the family (consisting of his high-minded, strong-willed, and rather overbearing mother as well as his two younger brothers) settled in Vienna, but they spent some of the years of World War I in Switzerland. After attending secondary school in Zurich and Frankfurt am Main, Canetti returned to Vienna and studied chemistry at the university from 1924 to 1929, taking a doctorate of philosophy. For a time, he lived in Berlin and worked as a freelance writer, translating books by Upton Sinclair.

In February, 1934, Canetti married Veza Taubner-Calderón, whose short stories have garnered critical attention. His mother died in Paris in June, 1937, and that is where Canetti and his wife immigrated in November of the following year, later settling in London in January, 1939. While working on *Crowds and Power* and other writings, Canetti eked out a living as a freelance journalist and language teacher. After the death of his wife in May, 1963, Canetti spent some time with his brother Georges in Paris. In 1971, he married Hera Buschor and became the father of a daughter, Johanna, the following year. They settled in Zurich, with Canetti making periodic trips to London. He died in Zurich in 1994.

ANALYSIS

AUTO-DA-FÉ

Elias Canetti's *Auto-da-Fé* (its earliest draft dating from 1931) is as impressive a first novel as was written in the twentieth century. It was originally intended to be the first of an eight-volume *comédie* (or *tragicomédie*) *humaine* of modern times, peopled by madmen of the type that were confined in the Steinhof, the insane asylum that Canetti could see from the window of his room while he was writing. It was to be an enormous fictional typology of the madness of the age, with each novel intended to present a different kind of monomaniac—among others, a religious fanatic, a truth fanatic, a technological maniac, a wastrel, an obsessive collector, and a bibliomaniac. Through such exemplary figures, Canetti wanted to turn a glaring spotlight on the contemporary world. It is thought that only one other novel in the projected series was completed, a volume titled "Der Todfeind" (not in the usual sense of "mortal enemy" but meaning "the enemy of death," which is a fair description of Canetti himself). Canetti may have produced sketches for other works of fiction, but after expressing his own alienation and frustration in his first book, he apparently found the novel form wanting for his purposes and became increasingly interested in presenting his thoughts in nonfictional form, particularly in *Crowds and Power*.

Canetti's working title for his novel was "Kant fängt Feuer" (Kant catches fire), but the author soon chose not to use the name of the famous German philosopher for his protagonist. He also rejected the name Brand as too obvious an evocation of the Holocaust motif, though he finally settled on the scarcely less evocative name Kien, which means "pinewood." Rembrandt's painting *The Blinding of Samson* appears to have suggested the somewhat ambiguous title of the novel (*Die Blendung* means "the blinding," with suggestions also of "dazzlement" and "deception").

The ascetic Peter Kien describes himself as a "library owner"; as reclusive as he is erudite, this renowned philologist and sinologist represents a "head without a world." In his obsession with books, having isolated himself from everyone else, he allows himself to get into the clutches of his scheming housekeeper, Therese, whose favorite item of apparel is a starched blue skirt (a garment worn by Canetti's far more humane real-life landlady). When Kien marries this mindless, avaricious, lustful, and generally evil creature, he ostensibly does so for the sake of his beloved books (and on the advice of Confucius, one of the savants with whom he communes).

Following his traumatic expulsion from the paradise of his enormous library, Kien embarks on a peculiar odyssey and descends to the lower depths of society, a "world without a head." Therese's work of degradation is continued and completed by the predatory chess-playing hunchback Fischerle and the philistine janitor Benedikt Pfaff. Their cruelly exploitative stratagems, including the pawning of some of Kien's books at the Theresianum (a disguised version of the actual Dorotheum, Vienna's state-owned pawnshop and auction house), serve as a grotesque counterpoint to Kien's *idées fixes* and the progressive unhinging of his mind. Kien's final act is an apocalyptic self-immolation amid his books to his own uncontrollable laughter—a "wedge driven into our consciousness."

Canetti's novel seems to have been written in the white heat of rage and hate. To that extent, it reflects the influence of his mentor, Kraus, who wrote: "Hatred must

make a person productive; otherwise one might as well love." *Auto-da-Fé* may be read as a subtle political and social satire, an allegorical portrayal of a sick society, and a chilling adumbration of the crushing of the vulnerable "pure" intellect by the brutish "practical" forces of the modern world. Aside from the narrator, the only sane person in the book is a sweet child who appears at the very beginning. Even Kien's brother Georges, a Paris psychiatrist who comes to his demented brother's aid and seems to represent an oasis of rationality, finds insanity more interesting and worthwhile than sanity and may, paradoxically, abet the forces that push Kien over the edge.

Despite the banal viciousness of the characters and the prevalence of violence in the book, *Auto-da-Fé* may be read as a great comic novel; it includes many genuinely funny scenes and situations that give rise to that "thoughtful laughter" which George Meredith identified as the index of the comic spirit. In this typology of mad-

Elias Canetti. (© The Nobel Foundation)

ness, however, any laughter is bound to be the sardonic rather than the liberating kind. Bertha Keveson-Hertz has properly identified "Swiftean satire, Dickensian humor, Proustian insulation, Joycean interiorization, and Poe's maelstrom nightmares" in Canetti's novel.

Claudio Magris has observed that

> the narrative of *Die Blendung* points ardently and yearningly to the missing life, to undiscoverable and suffocated love. It is the most total and shattering tragedy of the destruction of the self, the tragedy of individuality which, shortly before entering the dimensions of the crowd, exaggerates its particularity to the point of caricature and robs its existence of every passion, of every sensation. The most powerful and impressive motif of *Die Blendung* is the total, icy absence of all passions, pulsations, and stimuli; paranoia has removed any power of attraction from objects and does not know how to project the slightest libido onto them.

In his depictions of the range of elementary human instincts, Canetti somehow neglects the erotic sphere, but he does suggest that the urge to merge with the crowd implies a kind of sexual energy and interest.

Through Canetti's craftsmanship, the reader is drawn into the oppressive atmosphere of the book with a growing sense of discomfort. The *erlebte Rede*, or interior monologue, is an effective device by means of which the storyteller lets the reader get into the mind of each character. The narrative ambience contains many surreal touches, yet these grotesque elements somehow seem natural.

It is possible to read *Auto-da-Fé* as a sort of inversion of Dante's *La divina commedia* (c. 1320; *The Divine Comedy*, 1802): Peter Kien's library is the Paradise; the city (of Vienna) is the Purgatory; the fire is the Inferno. Everything in the book moves in a magic circle of aberration. The author identifies with the limitations of his characters, and, unlike many other novelists, he makes no attempt to act as an omniscient narrator who restores order and sits in judgment. Canetti ascribes a peculiar role to madness: The aberrant becomes the rule and normality the exception as contrasts are leveled and personal qualities are impoverished. The blessing of originality has a price, and it is loneliness. The language of lunatics ought to unite them; instead, it creates a gulf between them, and soliloquy replaces discourse.

At the Ideal Heaven café, frequented by Fischerle and other shady characters, there is a "*geschlossene Masse*," a closed company; the other characters live outside the crowd. Brother Georges judges the masses positively, whereas Peter Kien hates the masses as an incarnation of the primitive and the barbaric. The hypnotic attraction to fire is seen as one of the characteristics of the crowd, and in this regard (as in others, though not in political, historical, and other topical matters), Canetti drew on his real-life experiences. In July of 1927, he had witnessed the burning of the building of the Ministry of Justice on Vienna's Ringstrasse by a mob enraged by a jury's acquittal of some killers; the ensuing police riot claimed many innocent victims.

The disturbing figure of the scheming pimp and pander, Siegfried Fischer, known as Fischerle, has come in for some critical speculation. Might Canetti intend this petty criminal to represent the assimilated Jew in Austrian society, and is the cutting off of his hump (by a beggar) a symbolic adumbration of the bloody end of assimilation for Austrian Jewry? It is difficult, however, to accept such an interpretation of a character who is depicted as an anti-Semite's stereotype; in any case, the drama of Fischerle's life begins when he abandons the crowd and desires to become a chess champion in America, where his hunchback will somehow disappear. As for the vicious building superintendent, Pfaff—with huge fists and powerful feet—he is a recognizable Viennese type who was to see his day of fascist glory in Adolf Hitler's Austria.

Georges seems to be a paragon of strength, worldliness, empathy, and sanity. He attempts to straighten out his brother's life and to act as a deus ex machina, but he fails to recognize Peter's true state of mind. The doctor finds the insane more interesting than the sane; for example, the patient called the Gorilla has access to levels of experience not available to the sane. Is insanity, Georges wonders, perhaps a higher form of existence? In his inner complexity, Georges may actually represent only a more sublime form of moral aberration, a metaphysical type of madness.

Kien may be regarded as a modern Don Quixote. Both characters may be pictured as middle-aged, tall, emaciated, storklike, sexless, and virtually disembodied in their unworldliness and rejection of bodily needs and functions. Therese, Pfaff, and Fischerle are the satellites that correspond to Sancho Panza. In both cases, there is an obsession with books, a consultation with them in times of need, and a readiness to do battle with their enemies. In Miguel de Cervantes' *Don Quixote de la Mancha* (1605, 1615), the absoluteness of literature is stressed; in *Auto-da-Fé*, the absoluteness of scholarship has pride of place. Don Quixote reads the world in confirmation of books; Kien finds bliss in them and distress in the reality surrounding him. Don Quixote misinterprets reality; Kien negates it. Don Quixote has a catharsis and regains his good judgment before his idyllic or lyric death; Kien is vouchsafed no such grace: He piles his books into a mighty fortress before torching them, perishing with the treasures he has tried so hard to preserve. His flight into the flames is his only escape from his own isolation; death by fire is his deliverance, his expiation, and also an act of nemesis. In Cervantes' novel, there is some real dialogue, but Kien's conversations, with the possible exception of some of those with his brother, create no human contacts. Certainly the split between the hero (or antihero) and the world has been a recurrent theme in world literature since Cervantes. In his only work of fiction, Canetti handles this theme with consummate skill, with awful prescience, and with soul-searing impact.

KAFKA'S INFLUENCE

An even more obvious influence on *Auto-da-Fé* than the work of Cervantes is that of Franz Kafka. In *The Conscience of Words*, Canetti notes that when he was working on his novel's eighth chapter, he discovered Kafka's long short story *Die Verwandlung* (1915; *The Metamorphosis*, 1936) and tried to imitate it. This fascination with Kafka continued at least into the 1960's, when Canetti wrote *Kafka's Other Trial*, about Kafka's troubled engagement with Felice Bauer. In that work, Canetti argues controversially that Kafka's novel *Der Prozess* (1925; *The Trial*, 1937) was inspired by that flawed romance. Because Canetti tended to identify with Kafka, one might wonder if Canetti was projecting the origins of his own *Auto-da-Fé* on those of *The Trial*. As is evident from his wife's stories—overt commentaries on social ills—she was more extroverted than he. Particularly in his early works, his approach is typically introverted, referring only obliquely to topical events. Simi-

larly, Kafka tended to be much more introverted than Felice. In *Auto-da-Fé*, the dysfunctional relationship of Kien and his wife is a caricature of such a pairing.

In *The Conscience of Words*, Canetti praises Kafka's writings as being like Chinese literature in their acceptance of powerlessness. Chinese literature is Kien's obsession, his way of withdrawing from the world. In *Crowds and Power*, Canetti contends that all human beings secretly fear all others and want to be the sole survivors of the human race. He categorizes ancient leaders either as "kings" (extroverts, who wish to dominate others) or "shamans" (introverts, content to try to unify their own internal divisions). According to Canetti, Kafka's superiority even over ancient shamans is that in various fictions he recognized the animal-like (and other) parts within him, whereas the shamans believed they became such animals literally. How then is one to assess Kien against this standard? He is to be praised for withdrawing from the kings' political sphere and also for freeing himself from shamanlike superstitions, but his scholarship attacks ruthlessly all points of view other than his own, and he is sadly ignorant of his own self-contradictions—an ignorance that strengthens his will but ultimately leads toward madness. At the conclusion of the novel, his brain is described as being torn to fragments, against which chaos and that of the society around him he builds a wall of books, sets it on fire, and laughs insanely.

In *The Tongue Set Free*, Canetti explains how differences in languages left him with inner turmoil. In his childhood, he was forced to learn some Ladino, Romanian, Bulgarian, Romany, Russian, Greek, Albanian, Armenian, Turkish, German, and English, along with their associated cultures, all of them subtly or overtly in conflict with each other, so that his lifelong, introspective struggle to unify internal contradictions was understandable, particularly when Europe itself was much torn by internal conflicts. Composed when the rise of Nazi Germany was a chaos trying to batter its way into Canetti's study, the comedy of *Auto-da-Fé* may have helped him resist an introverted temptation to withdraw as self-destructively as did Kien into extreme, Kafka-like introversion.

Harry Zohn
Updated by James Whitlark

OTHER MAJOR WORKS

PLAYS: *Hochzeit*, pb. 1932 (*The Wedding*, 1984); *Komödie der Eitelkeit*, pb. 1950 (*Comedy of Vanity*, 1983); *Die Befristeten*, pb. 1956 (*The Numbered*, 1964; also known as *Life-Terms*); *Dramen*, pb. 1964 (collection of plays).

NONFICTION: *Fritz Wotruba*, 1955 (English translation, 1955); *Masse und Macht*, 1960 (*Crowds and Power*, 1962); *Aufzeichnungen, 1942-1948*, 1965; *Die Stimmen von Marrakesch: Aufzeichnungen nach einer Reise*, 1967 (*The Voices of Marrakesh: A Record of a Visit*, 1978); *Der andere Prozess: Kafkas Briefe an Felice*, 1969 (*Kafka's Other Trial*, 1974); *Alle vergeudete Verehrung: Aufzeichnungen, 1949-1960*, 1970; *Die gespaltene Zukunft*, 1972; *Macht und Überleben*, 1972; *Die Provinz des Menschen: Aufzeichnungen, 1942-1972*, 1973 (*The Human Province*, 1978); *Der Ohrenzeuge: Fünfzig Charaktere*, 1974 (character sketches; *Earwitness: Fifty Characters*, 1979); *Das Gewissen der Worte*, 1975 (*The Conscience of Words*, 1979); *Der Beruf des Dichters*, 1976; *Die gerettete Zunge: Geschichte einer Jugend*, 1977 (*The Tongue Set Free: Remembrance of a European Childhood*, 1979); *Die Fackel im Ohr: Lebensgeschichte, 1921-1931*, 1980 (*The Torch in My Ear*, 1982); *Das Augenspiel: Lebensgeschichte, 1931-1937*, 1985 (*The Play of the Eyes*, 1986); *Das Geheimherz der Uhr: Aufzeichnungen, 1973-1985*, 1987 (*The Secret Heart of the Clock: Notes, Aphorisms, Fragments, 1973-1985*, 1989); *Die Fliegenpein: Aufzeichnungen*, 1992 (*The Agony of Flies: Notes and Notations*, 1994); *Nachträge aus Hampstead: Aus den Aufzeichnungen, 1954-1971*, 1994 (*Notes from Hampstead: The Writer's Notes, 1954-1971*, 1998); *Aufzeichnungen, 1992-1993*, 1996; *Über Tiere*, 2002; *Party im Blitz: Die Englischen Jahre*, 2003 (*Party in the Blitz: The English Years*, 2005).

BIBLIOGRAPHY

Arnason, Johann P. and David Roberts. *Elias Canetti's Counter-image of Society: Crowds, Power, Transformation*. Rochester, N.Y.: Camden House, 2004. Presents an advanced exploration of how Canetti's *Crowds and Power* relates to the rest of his literary work.

Berman, Russell A., ed. *The Rise of the Modern German Novel: Crisis and Charisma*. Cambridge, Mass.: Harvard University Press, 1986. Situates Canetti's novel within the context of fiction contemporary with his time.

Darby, David, ed. *Critical Essays on Elias Canetti*. New York: G. K. Hall, 2000. Collection of scholarly essays discusses varied aspects of Canetti's work.

Daviau, Donald. *Major Figures of Contemporary Austrian Literature*. New York: Peter Lang, 1987. Offers a very thorough study of Canetti's career by a seasoned scholar.

Donahue, William Collins. *The End of Modernism: Elias Canetti's "Auto-da-Fé."* Chapel Hill: University of North Carolina Press, 2001. Presents a comprehensive study of the novel's cultural and philosophical contexts.

Donahue, William Collins, and Julian Preece, eds. *The Worlds of Elias Canetti: Centenary Essays*. Newcastle upon Tyne, England: Cambridge Scholars, 2007. Collection of essays focuses on the context of Canetti's work, addressing topics such as the author's Jewish identity, his early Marxism, and the relation of his work to the aftermath of World War II.

Falk, Thomas W. *Elias Canetti*. New York: Twayne, 1993. Good introduction to Canetti's work contains a separate chapter on his one novel as well as chapters on all his important book-length works. Supplemented with a chronology and an annotated bibliography.

Hulse, Michael, ed. *Essays in Honor of Elias Canetti*. New York: Farrar, Straus and Giroux, 1987. Collection includes several essays on *Auto-da-Fé* and Canetti's other books. Recommended for advanced students of Canetti.

Lawson, Richard A. *Understanding Elias Canetti*. Columbia: University of South Carolina Press, 1991. Succinct introductory study is one of the best places for a student to begin becoming acquainted with Canetti's work.

Modern Austrian Literature 16 (1983). Special issue devoted to Canetti's work is edited by noted scholar Donald Daviau. Features several essays on *Auto-da-Fé*, some in English, some in German.

CAO XUEQIN

Born: Nanjing, China; 1715(?)
Died: Beijing, China; February 12, 1763
Also known as: Chao Zhan; Zhiyan Zhai; Ts'ao
Chan; Ts'ao Hsüeh-ch'in (Wade-Giles)

PRINCIPAL LONG FICTION

Hongloumeng, 1792 (also known as *Hung-lou meng*; *Dream of the Red Chamber*, 1958; also translated as *A Dream of Red Mansions*, 1978-1980, and *The Story of the Stone*, 1973-1982)

OTHER LITERARY FORMS

Although a poet and a painter as well as a novelist, Cao Xueqin (tsow shway-chihn) devoted himself almost exclusively, for the last two decades of his life, to writing his only novel, *Dream of the Red Chamber*. During this period, he continually revised it, even proposing to himself five different titles, in his search for perfection. He had not completed it to his satisfaction at the time of his death in his late forties.

Apart from the poems included in his novel, no others have been preserved. Fond of the theater, Cao once contemplated writing a play (his grandfather was the author of a successful play), but he apparently never carried out his intention. The song cycle he composed for chapter 5 of his novel may have been written during this period.

As an artist, Cao specialized in painting rocky landscapes. His paintings apparently were well received by his contemporaries, for their sale contributed substantially to his income during his years in Beijing.

ACHIEVEMENTS

Dream of the Red Chamber may be the greatest of Chinese novels; certainly, it is one of the great novels of world literature. A large, sprawling narrative crammed with numerous characters and scenes, it is polysemous and of profound social and psychological as well as philosophical and religious significance. It is, moreover, a work of superb artistry. Complex in its structure as well as in its style and meaning, the novel presents three different narratives skillfully woven into a unified whole by means of allegory, symbolism, riddles, prophecies, and other rhetorical devices.

Dream of the Red Chamber was popular with readers from its inception. Cao Xueqin began to write it in about 1744, and by the time of his death in 1763, several eighty-chapter handwritten manuscripts, annotated by one working under the pen name Zhiyan Zhai (Red-Inkstone Studio), were in circulation. This version bore the title *Zhiyan Zhai chongping Shi touji* (Zhiyan Zhai's annotated story of the stone). Sometime prior to 1791, several 120-chapter handwritten manuscripts had surfaced with the title *Hongloumeng* (*Dream of the Red Chamber*). This version contained additional annotations by one who called himself Laoren Jihu (Old Man Odd Tablet). The handwritten manuscripts were rare, and purchasers had to forfeit many taels of silver for a copy.

Not until 1792 did the public have the opportunity to purchase a copy, printed from movable type, that could be obtained at a modest price. Such publication came about through the efforts of two literati who had long been enthusiastic admirers of *Dream of the Red Chamber*, Cheng Weiyuan and Gao Ê. The former had managed to purchase a 120-chapter version of the novel. Having decided to publish it in printed form, he obtained the services of the latter to edit it for the press in a definitive edition. The result was that two Cheng-Gao editions were published, the first dated 1791 but actually published in 1792, and the second, a corrected edition, also published in 1792.

When Cheng and Gao had published their editions of the novel, they had not been certain of its authorship, although they acknowledged that Cao Xueqin had had a hand in its composition. Not until the 1920's did Hu Shi confirm that Cao had been the author of the first eighty chapters. Hu did not believe in the verity of Gao's preface, however, considering him to have been a forger who had authored the last forty chapters. Even the later distinguished authority on the novel, Yu Pingbo, believed Gao a forger until sufficient evidence proved that Gao had been telling the truth in his preface when he stated that he had merely edited the work. Gao had performed some redactions and filled in some gaps to eliminate inconsistencies.

In 1964, Yu therefore reversed himself on his position that Gao had been the author rather than the editor of the last forty chapters. Also, until the mid-twentieth century, no one knew the identity of the commentators Red-Inkstone Studio and Old Man Odd Tablet; in 1960, another distinguished authority convincingly argued that the former was Cao's slightly older cousin, Cao Yufeng, the "posthumous son" of Cao Xueqin's great uncle Cao Yong, who had inherited a prized antique red inkstone from his father that once had belonged to his grandfather, Cao Yin. As for the identity of Old Man Odd Tablet, David Hawkes has expressed a strong suspicion that he was Cao Xueqin's father, Cao Fu, a nephew of Cao Yin who had been adopted as Cao Yin's posthumous "son." In any event, the evidence indicates that Cao Xueqin's full intentions were known before he died. If the last forty chapters were withheld from circulation for fear that parts might be interpreted by the government as seditious, some parts may have been deleted or softened by an unknown hand before Cheng purchased his manuscript.

BIOGRAPHY

Not a great deal is known about the life of Cao Xueqin, whose original name was Chao Zhan. The name by which he is best known, Xueqin, was a *hao*—that is, a sobriquet or literary name. He had two other *haos* that are not widely known: Qinbu and Qinji. Xueqin was born in Nanjing in about 1715 into a wealthy and powerful official family. His father, Cao Fu, was the superintendent of the imperial textile factory at Nanjing. Apart from Xueqin's father, four Caos had held the important official position of either salt controller or textile superintendent over four generations, both posts being among the most lucrative in the empire. Fu was appointed the superintendent of the imperial textile factory in Nanjing in 1715 after an unusual arrangement had been worked out by the emperor. At this time, Fu was in his twenties and was married to a woman who was or was soon to become pregnant with the future Xueqin.

Xueqin lived with his family in Nanjing until 1728. He grew up accustomed to all the comforts and luxuries that came with his father's position. As 1728 approached, however, the fortunes of the Cao family were taking a turn for the worse. The family was not economy-minded and was living beyond its means. Fu proved not to be a very competent manager and was running up a debt to the government. In January, 1728, Fu was dismissed from office, and his property in Nanjing was confiscated. This property consisted of some thirteen residences, some 275 acres of land, and miscellaneous holdings. Fu's household of about 114 people, including servants, was uprooted from Nanjing and removed to Beijing, where the family was quartered in a house (or houses) it owned and was graciously allowed to retain.

When this brutal blow fell on his family, Cao Xueqin was about twelve years of age. Undoubtedly a boy of delicate, sensitive awareness and responsiveness, he must have been keenly affected by the tragedy and the drastic changes in his life that followed. Certainly, his life in Beijing was shockingly different from his previous existence in Nanjing. Nevertheless, despite their reduced circumstances, the Caos attempted to maintain their former connections with the Manchu aristocracy. Cao's education probably continued along its previous lines. He was expected to master the *Shi Shu* (Four Books) and the *Wu Jing* (Five Classics). No doubt he also delved into the Daoist philosophers and the Chan (Zen) Buddhist masters. Certainly, he grew familiar with the classic Tang and Song poets, for he became a versatile poet himself.

For less rigorous intellectual exercise, Cao probably spent much of his leisure time reading the popular vernacular novels and viewing the musical dramas of which he was so fond, such as Wu Shifu's famous *Xi xiang ji* (fourteenth century; western chamber). He also must have practiced his calligraphy and indulged in his hobby of painting rocky landscapes. By the time he was seventeen or eighteen years old, he may have hired himself out as a private tutor or a schoolmaster. Despite his fine education and much learning, however, he apparently never prepared himself to earn an adequate living. In later times, those dependent on him often ate porridge and sometimes went without food. He often dreamed of having *Pejing paoya* (Peking roast duck) and *Shao-chiu* (the best wine).

According to the evidence available, Cao's personal appearance as an adult was not impressive. Short and fat, of swarthy complexion, his eyebrows high and sloping downward over small eyes, his nose prominent and broad in his round face, and wearing a moustache, he was far from handsome but nevertheless had a kindly and humorous-looking countenance. He was reputed to be loquacious and a witty and brilliant conversationalist. He apparently often reviewed the pleasures and pains of his childhood in Nanjing with a mixture of nostalgia and horror. In his late twenties, he began to conceive of a novel setting forth the story of a wealthy and established Chinese family that, through financial mismanagement and other profligate behavior, was brought to ruin. About 1744, he began writing the narrative that turned out to be his masterpiece, *Dream of the Red Chamber*.

By the mid-1750's, Cao had completed eighty chapters, working in conjunction with his slightly older cousin, Cao Yufeng, who became the novel's commentator. Handwritten copies of the eighty-chapter version, with Yufeng's annotations under the "studio name" Zhiyan Zhai, or Red-Inkstone Studio, were circulated among friends and acquaintances and later became available at bookstalls in Beijing, but such copies were rare and expensive. In the late 1750's, Cao Xueqin moved with his family from Beijing to the suburbs in the Western Hills, where he lived as a villager. He died there on February 12, 1763.

Statue of Cao Xueqin in Beijing. (GFDL)

ANALYSIS: DREAM OF THE RED CHAMBER

In its structure, *Dream of the Red Chamber* resembles Chinese boxes, an assemblage of narratives within narratives. The largest frame, that which contains the whole, consists of a Daoist-Buddhist creation myth about a heavenly stone that takes up residence on Earth in human form. Indeed, Xueqin titled the first, eighty-chapter version of the novel *The Story of the Stone*, which shows the importance the author attached to this mythology. The incarnate stone appears in the person of the youthful hero of the novel, Jia Baoyu (also styled as Chia Pao-yü), his personal name literally meaning "precious jade"—he is born with a piece of jade in his mouth.

The next-largest frame contains the story of the decline in the fortunes of the wealthy, aristocratic clan of the Jia. This story is not unrelated to the decline and increasing incompetence of the Qing Dynasty (1644-1914), the last rampart of ancient Chinese civilization.

The smallest frame displays the story of the apprenticeship of the hero of the novel, the handsome and personable youth Jia Baoyu, in his progress from childhood to maturity as he seeks to learn the meaning of his existence as a human being in the *hongzhen* (red dust), or life of this earth. This apprenticeship particularly involves his struggle to achieve understanding and personal liberation from the suffering caused by the claims of his romantic attachment to his cousin, the lovely but neurotic and tubercular Black Jade (Lin Daiyu), to whom he is affianced, and the claims of familial responsibility. Following Black Jade's tragic death and his marriage to Precious Clasp (Xue Bao Chai), he becomes very ill and is reduced to idiocy. When he recovers, he resumes his Confucian studies, takes the examination at the provincial capital, and is successful in gaining a *juren* degree. Afterward, however, he experiences an awakening and comprehends his true relationship to the universe, is released from suffering, and gains the freedom and inner peace that he has been seeking. Forthwith he rejects the world and becomes a monk. As the novel concludes, Baoyu is ostensibly being returned to the heaven that nurtured him by his old friends, a crazy Daoist and a crazy Buddhist monk. Thus, the central mythic plot of the novel comes full circle.

CRITICAL RECEPTION

Despite the popularity of *Dream of the Red Chamber*, especially after its publication in printed form, the vernacular novel, no matter how masterful, was not considered by most of the Confucian literati to be an important contribution to literature, primarily because of its informal literary style, being a mixture of colloquial and classical Chinese. Nevertheless, Cao Xueqin's novel had its admirers among the scholarly class as well as among men and women, whether young or old, who belonged to the classes of nonscholars but enjoyed reading fiction. Although *Dream of the Red Chamber* frequently formed a topic of conversation in the homes of literate Chinese families and an enthusiastic scholar here and there ventured to undertake a commentary on it, it was not taken seriously as a work of art until the modern reform movement in education, language, and literature took place between 1905 and 1937. In 1905, the Empress Dowager Cixi abolished the old examination system that had controlled Chinese education for centuries. In 1917, Hu Shih and Chen Duxiu launched their literary reform movement. They argued that classical Chinese had outlived its usefulness and that future literary works should be written in the living language of the people—that is, in *baihua*, or "easily understood talk."

Numerous translations of Western authors appeared between 1917 and 1928. Chinese writers were astonished to learn of the high position accorded the novel in the West, and they began to write fiction in colloquial style and in adherence to Western literary criteria. They were particularly impressed by Russian anarchism and psychological realism and promoted the writing of revolutionary literature. The Japanese invasion of China in 1937 interrupted this activity.

The literary reform movement not only introduced to China Western literary models but also encouraged Chinese writers and scholars to take a more serious interest in their own vernacular literary tradition—short stories, plays, and novels—particularly *Dream of the Red Chamber*. Soon, serious studies of Cao's novel began to appear. Chinese writers other than scholars, however, had fallen under the spell of this masterpiece in their youth, and it affected their mature writing.

When the Communists established the People's Republic of China in 1949, they first followed a conciliatory policy; hence, established writers who were not ardent supporters of Communism at least acquiesced in the new regime, and few fled abroad. By 1953, however, the Communists had established totalitarian control at all levels of society; they began ruling with an iron hand, and a rigid Thought-Reform Movement was initiated to wipe out all vestiges of "bourgeois ideology." Knowing that *Dream of the Red Chamber* was widely read by all sections of the literate public, the Communist policymakers decided that this classic novel could be used as an "ideological guinea pig" to teach the literate population an object lesson in Marxist criticism. In Professor Yu Pingbo, a popular and recognized authority on the novel, they recognized a ready-made scapegoat. Hence, a campaign was promptly launched against the unsuspecting scholar—anticipating the purges of intellectuals in 1955, when some eighty thousand people were accused of agitating against the Communist Party, and the even more brutal excesses of the Cultural Revolution in the 1960's.

Regardless of the Communist attack on Yu Pingbo, however, other scholars and critics continued their study, investigation, analysis, and interpretation of Cao's masterpiece during those turbulent times, and outstanding work was performed by Zhou Ruchang, Wu Shichang, Zhang Gang, and Wu Enyu. Indeed, the year 1979 saw the founding of a critical journal devoted exclusively to *Dream of the Red Chamber*. In the United States, Chinese scholars such as C. T. Hsia, John Wang, and Wong Kamming made valuable contributions, as did the American scholar Andrew H. Plaks, while in England the work of David Hawkes has proved of signal importance. The vitality of Cao's masterpiece is perhaps best indicated, however, by the coining of a term to denote the vast scholarly literature on the subject: *hongxue*, or "redology."

THEMES

Dream of the Red Chamber, therefore, is much more than the sad love story that so many readers have taken it to be. Yet even from that severely limited point of view, the novel is remarkable enough. Its philosophy of love draws a marked distinction between *yin* (lust) and *qing* (love), as well as between *chi qing* (romantic or, literally, "crazy" love) and *huiqing* (married love, the affection between husband and wife and their sense of commitment and responsibility to each other). Indeed, from the Confucian point of view, the love affair between Baoyu and Black Jade demonstrates the disastrous consequences that can stem from "romantic attachment," the "crazy love" that not only can endanger the health of the participants but also can disrupt, if not destroy, marital relationships and the traditional family system. From the Daoist-Buddhist point of view, romantic attachment can harm and even prevent progress toward personal enlightenment and redemption. The Daoist-Buddhist message is clear: A human being living on this earth is a "sensitive plant." Motivated by desire, he or she suffers. Not until a person unshackles him- or herself from attachments can he or she become a stone. Then he can view things *sub specie aeternitatis* and rise above love and sympathy and good and evil. Freed from suffering, he is a Buddha. The Daoism that Cao has in mind here is the philosophical Daoism of Laozi and Zhuangzi; the Buddhism is that of the Chan school.

Praised by Wang Kuowei as the first Chinese novel to exhibit the spirit of tragedy, *Dream of the Red Chamber* is, from a philosophical point of view, a Daoist-Buddhist comedy. Nevertheless, this philosophy does little to diminish the cumulative effect of the many sad and tragic incidents that play upon the emotions of the reader and induce the sense that suffering and death are the normal lot of human existence.

Regardless of the importance attached to this philosophical and religious theme, however, *Dream of the Red Chamber* has other, equally important literary qualities. One of them is its remarkable psychological penetration and realism. Indeed, in his use of dream, Cao anticipated some of the findings of modern psychology. He knew that even if a dream were an illusion, it was not unconnected with reality. For example, in chapter 5, he introduces Baoyu into a dream sequence that has become justly celebrated. Having but recently arrived at puberty, the boy's mind is filled with thoughts of sex.

In his dream, he sees the image of Qin Keqing, the young wife of Jia Yong. Also called Combined Beauty (Jianmi), she is a composite of the beauty and charm of Black Jade and Precious Clasp. Hence she is, in modern Jungian terms, an archetypal image, Baoyu's anima or ideal woman, an innate image of his psyche in which are united his personal and his collective unconscious. The scene of the dream is called Great Void Illusion Land, which is presided over by the Goddess of Disillusionment. Baoyu and Keqing enter into a blissful sexual union. Soon, however, demons appear and pursue Baoyu to the edge of an impassable river called the Ford of Error. This dream, however, is soon followed by a realistic scene; despite the warning implied in the dream, that evening Baoyu seduces Pervading Fragrance (Xiren), showing that the memory of his ecstasy with Keqing has quite replaced his fear of demons and beasts (or those passions that drive humans into disillusionment). Other examples in the novel of dreams in which illusion and reality are juxtaposed in the same ironic fashion could be cited.

Outstanding as it is in its depiction of the psychology of adolescents discovering the power of sex and awakening to the pleasure and pain of first love, the novel is even more remarkable in the unusual understanding the author displays of feminine psychology, whether of adolescents or of adults. All the major female characters—Black Jade, Pervading Fragrance, Precious Clasp, Bright Cloud (Qingwen), Quest Spring (Tanchun), Madame Wang, Phoenix (Xifeng), and the elderly Matriarch (Jia Mu)—are presented as individuals, each a real person in her own right. The portrait drawn of the unscrupulous and ruthless Phoenix, Jia Lian's wife, who runs the household affairs at the Rongguofu, is especially vivid and powerful. That of the Matriarch, Baoyu's wonderful grandmother, is one of the most memorable characterizations of an elderly person to be found in world literature. *Dream of the Red Chamber* is an outstanding novel of character.

The dimension of the novel that presents the story of the rise and fall of the fortunes of a great Chinese family provides the reader with a remarkable social document. In this sense, the novel is a veritable handbook of the traditional family system. Cao describes realistically the persons, the personalities, and the relationships of some thirty major characters. At the same time, he presents four hundred or more minor characters. In respect of the major characters especially, he describes their behavior, religion, and political positions as well as their loves, animosities, quarrels, and intrigues. Thus, the reader learns much about the structure and organization of the Chinese family and its ideals of loyalty and honor: the rules of etiquette, the respect accorded older persons, the role of parental authority, the observance of filial obedience, and the position of women in Chinese society.

The reader also learns about marital arrangements and sexual attitudes and practices, education, the political process and officialdom, and other social and cultural conventions of the time. These practices are frequently criticized, although such criticism is often made only obliquely and from a point of view not necessarily shared by the author. Thus, *Dream of the Red Chamber* is a novel of social criticism; indeed, modern Chinese Communist critics have eagerly seized upon this aspect of the novel, interpreting it exclusively as an antifeudal political tract. Such a distorted reading ignores the Daoist-Buddhist theme of the novel, the notion that the existing order must be transcended rather than reformed or uprooted.

To read the novel in the spirit the author intended, one might well begin with the title. Since the words of the title of a story are the first to be encountered by the reader as well as probably the last words he or she remembers, writers of fiction normally take their titles very seriously and seek to impregnate them with meaning. They wish them to serve as a key to unlock the door to the unknown fictional world the reader is about to enter as well as a seal to authenticate what he or she has experienced. Cao was sufficiently concerned about his choice for the title of his novel that he chose five or six alternate titles before he finally decided that he preferred *Hongloumeng*. This title has been rendered in English by translators as *A Dream of Red Mansions* and *Dream of the Red Chamber* (or some slight variant of the latter).

In his translation (still to be completed with a fifth volume), David Hawkes, however, chose to return to the original title *Shitou ji*, which he has rendered as *The Story of the Stone* (which more literally might be translated as "the story of the little stone"), perhaps because that was the title given to the eighty-chapter handwritten manuscript that was put into circulation during Cao's lifetime. The author himself, however, privately played

with a series of titles, from *Shitou ji* to *Jingseng lu* (the passionate monk's tale) to *Fengyu baojian* (a mirror for the poetically inclined, which Hawkes renders as "a mirror for the romantic") to *Hongloumeng* to *Jinling shier chai* (twelve young ladies of Chin-ling, or, literally, twelve hairpins of the Golden Tombs—a name for Nanjing). It is to be noted that whatever title the novel bears, it tends to focus the reader's mind upon some single aspect of a very complicated story, raising its power and making it dominate his or her consciousness. In the case of the variant titles here, this situation is also a reflection of the author's changing consciousness. It shows in each choice what he was thinking about at a particular time and what he wanted the reader to think his narrative was predominantly about.

MYTHOLOGY AND CHARACTERIZATION

In Cao's choices of *Shitou ji* and *Jingseng lu* for the novel's title, he placed emphasis on the myth that frames the story. At the beginning, the hero of the novel, Jia Baoyu, is placed in a creation myth. Some universal cataclysm has occurred, leaving the ceiling of Heaven damaged and in need of repair. Consequently, the Goddess of Creation, Nugua (sometimes rendered Nüwa), selects rocks of the Five Colors (*wuse*), fuses them into big blocks, and then patches the azure Dome of Heaven. In the course of her selection, however, she rejects one rock as unworthy of inclusion. Left alone, it feels ashamed and dejected. Wandering about Heaven, it bemoans its fate. A magic rock, it transforms itself into a little stone that is a lustrous and translucent piece of jade. It wanders into the realm of the Goddess of Disillusionment (Jinghuan Xiangu), feeling that it would prefer to live on Earth rather than in Heaven. It wants to experience the mundane world of the red dust (*hongzhen*).

At the court of the goddess, the jade is attracted to a beautiful plant, the Crimson Pearl Flower, which it treats very kindly by sprinkling it every day with dew. In response to this loving care, the plant blossoms into a lovely female fairy. She vows to return the jade's love with tears if she may join him in life on Earth. With the help of a mangy Buddhist monk and a lame Daoist priest, the jade is born into the wealthy and powerful Jia family. The baby is named Baoyu, or Precious Jade, because he is born with a piece of pinkish, creamy-soft jade in his mouth that on the obverse side contains antique-style characters (*zhuan shu*) identifying it as *Tongling Baoyu* (Magical Precious Jade). Underneath this heading are two lines of verse of four characters each. On the reverse side are three lines of verse, also of four characters each. Later, Baoyu wears this piece of jade suspended from his neck by a silken cord of five colors. At about the same time that he is born, the Crimson Pearl Flower is born into the Lin family as Daiyu (also styled as Tai-yü), or Black Jade. Her mother is Baoyu's older sister, who is the wife of a government official named Lin Ruhai; hence Black Jade, the heroine of the novel, is Baoyu's cousin. Thus, both the hero and the heroine of the novel are incarnations of celestial things and, though human, are semidivine.

Eventually, Black Jade's mother dies, and her father, who in his official position lives away from home, sends her to live with the Jia. She and Baoyu become constant childhood companions, and by the time they are eleven or twelve years of age, each is passionately devoted to the other. In the meantime, however, another beautiful female cousin of Baoyu has come to live with the Jia, whom Black Jade soon regards as her rival for Baoyu's affections. Despite his continual reassurances to Black Jade that she is the girl he truly loves, she remains insecure, jealous, disturbed, and resentful. She is also tubercular and delicate in constitution, and her health begins to decline.

On the appearance of the new cousin, named Xue Baochai, or Precious Clasp, Baoyu is surprised to discover that she wears a gold pendant suspended from her neck on which is inscribed, on the front, a single line of verse in four "seal characters" and, on the back, another in the same style, the two lines complementing the verses on his pendant. This conjunction of gold, a metal, and jade, a stone, is significant in terms of the scheme of the Five Elements (*wuxing*), which Cao obviously employed to heighten his meaning. In the permutation of these elements—earth, wood, fire, metal, and water—earth (in the form of the stone) generates metal, and metal destroys wood. In the novel, Black Jade is associated with wood in several ways.

Originally a celestial plant—a "crimson pearl flower"—her human surname, Lin, literally means "forest," and part of her personal name, *dai*, does not simply mean "black," as it is usually translated, but rather "to

blacken the eyebrows" or "eyebrow blackening." It means more than that, however, for Cao has "layered" the word, seeing that it is a homonym for "sash" or "belt" and also for "roots of grass." Furthermore, the Chinese character for the *dai* that means "roots of grass" is interchangeable with the character whose sound is *ti* and means the "peduncle or footstalk of a flower." In addition, this character can be used for a similar character that means "to weep and wail." Daiyu's birthday is in the springtime; in her yard grow luxuriant bamboos; in various scenes she is associated with flowers or burnt ashes; and it is the humor of wood (*muqi*) that is said to be responsible for her illness.

On the other hand, Hsüeh Pao-ch'ai is associated not only with the gold pendant of mysterious origin but also with a gold clasp or hairpin. Part of her personal name, *ch'ai*, means "clasp" or "hairpin," and because the other part of her name is *pao*, meaning "precious," her clasp or hairpin must be of gold. Her surname, Xue, is also of significance in the novel's scheme of things, for it is homonymous with a number of words indicative of things with which she is frequently associated. The sound of her surname is the same as that for "snow," for "cave," and for "blood" and "blood relationship." She is frequently associated with either autumn or the coming of winter, hence with cold, snow, whiteness, and even the plum. A pile of snow becomes a rebus for her surname, as the woods are for the surname of Lin Tai-yü. These things are brought out clearly, in chapter 5, in words that are part of Baoyu's dream vision: "The jade belt is left hanging in the woods; the gold hairpin is buried in the snow" (*Yü tai chung kua, chin tsan hsüeh li nieh*). Pao-ch'ai's temperament is said to be cool and collected. Her rooms are described as cold and simple, "like a snowy cave." She is likened to the "pure whiteness and clear fragrance" of the plum. Her medicine contains "cold incense." The snowy whiteness of her skin is emphasized. At the same time, she is likened to the famous beauty Yang Kuei-fei, as a woman who, although cold without—in her physique—is warm within—in her heart.

Since, according to the permutations of the elements, earth generates metal whereas wood destroys earth, Baoyu, the incarnation of stone and hence earthy, faces a dilemma respecting his relationship with his two cousins. It is hardly a wonder, therefore, that Black Jade is upset over his attentiveness to Pao-ch'ai, whose name, most accurately, is Gold Hairpin, and who is the possessor of a gold locket whose inscriptions suggest some predestined union with Baoyu. Hence, Tai-yü declares bitterly in chapter 28, "How can I compare with Pao-ch'ai's gold and jade? I am nothing but a person of grass and wood" (*Pi pu tê Pao-ch'ai ku shih-ma chin no yü ti, wo-mên pu kuo shih ko ts'ao mu jên-êrh pa-liao*). The union of gold and jade is also seen in the Chinese compound *chin-yü* (literally, "gold-jade"), the conjunction of these two things signifying the abstract quality "precious." Moreover, the personal names of Pao-ch'ai and Baoyu contain the word *pao*, which also signifies the quality precious.

The novel's first commentator, Chih-yen Chai (Red-Inkstone Studio), whom it is known was as close to the author as another person could be, made much of these aspects of meaning. Indeed, several times in his commentary he declares that through them the author offers the reader the "key to the novel." In recent years, Andrew H. Plaks has taken Chih-en Chai's words seriously enough to have produced a book and a shorter study that have thrown much light on Cao's allegory.

The titles *Hung-lou meng* and *Chin-ling shih-êrh ch'ai* are also powerfully suggestive. Both of these titles display the nostalgia the author felt about his youthful past, and this feeling had to do not simply with the vanished splendor he had known but more particularly with his memories of the numerous young girls with whom he had associated and whom he remembered with such affection and admiration. *Hung-lou*, commonly translated as "red chamber" or "red mansions," refers in China to that part of a mansion that is set apart for the residence of young ladies. In China, too, the color red has certain other connotations that are not found in the West. It is emblematic of splendor, good fortune, prosperity, and earthly happiness. A *hung-jên* (red man) is a man who has reached the height of his career; a *hung-jih* (red day) is a lucky day; and a *hung-chung-nü* (red-dressed girl) is an unmarried girl, because only unmarried girls wore red trousers. The color red was associated with springtime, youthfulness, and the new year, but it was particularly linked to women and marriage: The terms *hung-hsiu* (red sleeves) and *hung-fên* (pink powder) both mean

"women." The term *hung-sz* (red silk thread) means "marriage." A bride wore a *hung-shai* (red dress) and rode in a *hung-chiao* (red sedan-chair).

To the Buddhists, the term *hung-chên* (red dust) referred to the earthly life of unfulfilled desires and suffering. The *meng* of Cao's title refers to "dream." Here, however, this word is filled with ambiguity, and the author may have been pleased with this result. Were the splendor and the often happy days of his childhood like a dream to him when he recalled them as an adult, or did he hold to the Buddhist philosophy that the earthly life was nothing but an illusion that had no reality? Whatever the case, Hawkes's view, that Cao's "dream" or "vision" was perhaps more literary than psychological or philosophical, is probably correct. As Hawkes sees it, Cao used this idea in his own way as "a poetical means of demonstrating that his characters are both creatures of his imagination and at the same time the real companions of his golden youth." Note Hawkes's expression "golden youth" rather than "rosy youth." He confesses that what readers of his fine translation will miss is the "pervading redness" of the Chinese text, which in the hands of an English translator tends to turn into "greenness" or "goldenness."

One thing is clear. In writing his novel, Cao was dreaming primarily of one thing—the young women he had known in his youth. This motive is reaffirmed by the title he attempted to substitute following his choice of *Dream of the Red Chamber*—namely, "The Twelve Young Ladies of Chinling." Altogether, he presents some sixty female characters during the course of his novel; the twelve of the title are the most outstanding beauties of Nanjing and are the principal young female characters of his narrative. In the dream sequence in chapter 5, while Baoyu is exploring the Land of Illusion presided over by the Goddess of Disillusionment, he finds the names of the twelve beauties of Chin-ling entered into the Main Register. This album also includes paintings and riddles concerning the lives of these young women, whose destinies are told in a cryptic fashion. Their names in sequence, from the first to the twelfth, are as follows: Lin Tai-yü, Hsüeh Pao-ch'ai, Jia Yüan-ch'un, Jia T'an-ch'un, Shih Hsiang-yün, Miao-yü, Ying-ch'un, Hsich'un, Wang Hsi-fêng, Ch'iao-chieh, Li Wan, and Chin-shih. Later in the same chapter, the life of each is reviewed in a suite of songs called "Hunglou meng," composed by the Goddess of Disillusionment. She has a singer sing it to Baoyu. Each song is an elegy that laments the fate of its subject and thereby prophesies her future.

Chapters 1 through 5, then, form a prologue serving as a mythological framework for the human narrative, which begins in earnest in chapter 6 and continues to the final debacle of the Jia clan implied throughout chapters 70 to 80. This section might be called the middle story. It involves the rise and decline of the Jia clan, but, more particularly, it is the story of the hero, Baoyu, in terms of his various relationships with the maidens of the Grand View Garden (Ta-kuan Yüan), an enclosed and fantastic landscape located on a circumscribed plot of land between the two compounds—the Ning-kuo-fu and the Jung-kuo-fu—occupied by the two branches of the Jia clan. This enclosure tends to frame the middle story.

In other words, in this section the characters of the novel are arranged spatially in a fantasia that presents a medley of colorful images exemplary of an idealized world destined to disillusionment. It contains an artificial mountain, a tunneled passageway, a lake spanned by a bridge, and a richly landscaped central area where the three main characters reside—Tai-yü's bamboo-groved, elegant Hsiao-hsiang Kuan, Pao-ch'ai's sparse and simple Hêng-wu Yüan, and Baoyu's lavish, colorful I-hun Yüan, done in brilliant five-color style and containing a hall of mirrors. Beyond a central eminence, or hill, is located the "main hall" (Ta-kuan Lou) and its adjacent structures. At a distance is a model "rustic village" (Tao-hsiang Ts'un). There are also whitewashed plaster walls, moon gates in the interior walls, pavilions, kiosks, lodges, winding pathways, zigzagging bridges, various rare artifacts, and so on. Undoubtedly, it was to maintain this sense of opulence, splendor, and plenitude, as well as the beauty and charm of the young women he had known, that Cao finally rejected the title of his last choice in favor of *Hung-lou meng*, or *Dream of the Red Chamber*. By this choice, he evidently intended to emphasize that his novel amounted to his vision of the lodgings or residences of the young ladies he had once known, but he might have had in mind the compartmentalized space of the Grand View Garden and its medley of fantastic images.

LYRIC VISION

As for Cao's tentative title *Fêng-yüeh pao-chien*, which Hawkes has rendered "a mirror for the romantic," Cao never repeated it in another form, as he did with *Shih-to'u chi* and *Hung-lou meng*. Nevertheless, it brought to the fore an important facet of the novel—namely, its lyric quality and the lyric dimensions of life. In short, he was conceiving of his novel as a mirror in which readers of a poetic temperament could view images with which they could identify and that would stir their feelings to lyric heights. In other words, the norm he had adopted for his narrative was the lyric poem. A lyric is a pictorial and musical form perceived almost instantly in terms of space and whose emotional intensity can be sustained for only a limited time.

About ninety years later, in the United States, Edgar Allan Poe was to maintain that a long narrative poem such as an epic was a contradiction in terms, because, according to this same principle, it could be nothing more than a series of lyrics interspersed with prose. It is the adoption of this lyric norm that no doubt accounts, in part at least, for the alternating patterns of excitement (*jê-nao*) and ennui (*wu-liao*) in the lives of Baoyu and his cousins, which Plaks has seen as "a major thematic dimension of the novel." Mirror images, too, are prominent features of the novel, including doppelgänger characters. In chapter 12, the author indulges in a "set allegorical piece" when he presents the two-sided mirror of Jia Jui suggestive of the "true" image of objective reality as opposed to the "false" image of subjective illusion seen in a mirror. In chapter 17, the hall of mirrors in Baoyu's residence confuses Jia Chêng, and later, in chapter 41, they also confuse Liu Laolao. Doppelgänger images are presented in the two Baoyus—the "true" Chên Baoyu and the "false" Jia Baoyu, who look alike but differ in their minds. Again, the author sees a Chên-Chia continuum in the mirror-image careers of Chên Shih-yin and Jia Yü-tsun.

It was no doubt the autobiographical character of his fiction, which contains substantial fragments of personal memory, that drove Cao in the direction of lyric expression. Like the lyric poem, autobiography requires self-reflection, and if the memories are viewed with nostalgia and deep feeling, they require the exercise of what has been called a "romanticized imagination"; both are necessary for the "lyric vision." These matters are apart from the emphatic lyric tradition in poetry that had been long prevalent in traditional Chinese civilization, which the author had naturally inherited. At any rate, when he came to write *Dream of the Red Chamber*, he was moved by the interiorization of his own personal experience, which is the mainspring behind the lyric poem, rather than by the externalization of imagined experience, which is the mainspring of narrative. In this way, Cao produced the first "lyric novel" in the history of Chinese long fiction.

If the beginning of Cao's novel is filled with intriguing promise, fulfilled in the middle section to the admiration of its readers (including most of those critics who have taken the novel seriously), the ending has not proved satisfactory to most critics, even if general readers have not been disturbed. These critics have declared that the style of the last forty chapters is inferior to that of the first eighty, and that the novel is simply unfinished. It is clear, however, that such a view has been based on certain critical assumptions rather than on a close and objective examination of the novel's text. These assumptions are that Gao was the author rather than the editor of the last forty chapters and hence a "forger"; that he was an inferior stylist committed to a "happy ending"; and that Cao had left his novel unfinished and had intended an ending unlike that provided by Gao.

Later scholarship, however, has demonstrated that none of these assumptions is entirely true. Gao has been shown to have been what he claimed—namely, the editor and not a forger. Furthermore, he was not mediocre as an editor or a writer. If he lacked the genius of Cao, he was a conscientious editor and redactor who possessed both an aesthetic sense and a good understanding of the complexities of the first eighty chapters and made his redactions or fill-ins in an attempt to conform to those complexities. He was not perfectly consistent, but neither was Cao. The inconsistencies in style of the last forty chapters, such as the intermixing of northern and southern dialectical variants and the overemphasis on Pekinese linguistic forms, are to be seen in both sections. It is also now known that the 120-chapter version was available to Gao, even though it appears that some anonymous hand had tampered with the text. This unknown person was probably the author's father, Cao Fu.

THE NOVEL'S MOVEMENT

A traditional commentator using the name Ming-chai Chu-jên remarked that, whereas previous Chinese novels had structurally moved from sadness to joy and from separation to union, *Dream of the Red Chamber* moved structurally in the opposite ways. Plaks, however, has described the novel's movement, much more accurately, as one from "sadness within joy" to "joy within sadness." Cao's aesthetic is derived from the Chinese cosmological principle of ceaseless recurrence and flux. His novel does not follow a "unilinear pattern of rise and fall" in the Western sense, but one of "cyclical sweep in ceaseless recurrence of existential flux" in the Chinese sense. In structuring his novel, Cao had in mind no unilinear, end-oriented goal but one of ceaseless alteration of the contrasts of human experience in close juxtaposition, with sadness adjacent to joy, union adjacent to separation, and never one without the other. Hence, although the idea of plenitude, whose chief emblem is the Ta-kuan Yüan, is a major theme of the novel, it is accompanied by the sense of incompleteness as an undercurrent of this major wave. If, throughout the main section of the novel, light and shade alternate in close juxtaposition to one another, by chapter 94 the shadows begin to lengthen when Baoyu loses his jade and, with it, his wits.

Up to this point in the novel, the issue of Baoyu's marriage has been in abeyance, everyone assuming, however, that eventually he will marry Tai-yü. By now, however, everyone fears that Baoyu may die if the jade is not recovered or something drastic is not done quickly. Other bad things have happened, too: His sister Yuan-ch'un, the Imperial Concubine, has died, as has his uncle, Wang Zitong. In her anxiety over Baoyu's illness, the Matriarch consults a fortune-teller who advises her that if her grandson is to be saved, he must be married as soon as possible to a lady "with a destiny of gold." The Matriarch has already decided that Tai-yü, because of her temperament and frail health, would not make Baoyu a suitable wife, despite his utter devotion to her. The decision now is that the seventeen-year-old Baoyu should marry Pao-ch'ai without delay and despite the flaunting of the mourning requirements. Because of Baoyu's attachment to Tai-yü, however, the family decides that the deception of both Baoyu and Tai-yü is necessary. Tai-yü, however, accidentally learns of the plan, and, deeply shocked, she spits blood. She burns her poems to signal the end of her "heart's folly," and her health rapidly deteriorates.

The wedding of Baoyu and Pao-ch'ai takes place in chapter 98, and Tai-yü dies at the moment they are married. Not until Baoyu unveils his bride does he see that he has married Pao-ch'ai instead of Tai-yü. He thinks he is dreaming and falls into unconsciousness. Pao-ch'ai thinks it would be wise to tell him of Tai-yü's death. The shock of this news produces a recovery.

In chapter 105, Jia Chên and Jia Shê are charged by the Imperial Censors with corruption. They are arrested, and their properties, the Jung-kuo-fu and the Ning-kuo-fu, are confiscated. Baoyu's father, Jia Chêng, however, is completely absolved of any wrongdoing. Later, both the Matriarch and Phoenix die. During the funeral services for the Matriarch, the Ta-kuan Yüan is raided by bandits. The nun Miao-yü is taken away by them to meet a horrible fate. Jia Baoyu meets his look-alike, Chên Baoyu, and is made ill.

He recovers quickly when the mangy Buddhist monk unexpectedly appears with the lost jade. He and Baoyu converse in a friendly way, but no one else can understand their enigmatic words. During this conversation, however, suddenly Baoyu understands his relationship to the universe; in short, he experiences what the Chan (Japanese, Zen) Buddhists call *k'ai-wu*, an awakening (Japanese, *satori*). To the dismay of his wife and mother, he informs them that he would like to become a monk. Yet, surprisingly, he immediately plunges into his Confucian studies to prepare for the examinations. When he leaves in the company of Jia Lan to take the examinations, he solemnly bids everyone good-bye and promises them he will do his best to earn the degree. His wife feels a presentiment that she will never see him again.

When Jia Lan returns, he informs the family that Baoyu simply disappeared after having taken the examinations. In a few weeks, the family receives the good news that Baoyu took seventh place in the examinations and earned his degree, but Baoyu himself is still missing. As a result, however, of the success of Baoyu and Jia Lan, who had stood one hundred thirteenth in the examinations, the Emperor pardons Jia Shê and Jia Chên and restores their titles and property.

Baoyu's father returns from the South aboard a canal boat and is overjoyed after learning of the success of his son and of the pardon granted to his brother. He anchors the boat for the night by a snow-covered bank, and then begins to compose a letter, because his joy is mixed with the sorrow he feels over Baoyu's disappearance. He wants to write something about his son. Suddenly he perceives a strange man standing at the bow who is wearing a flaming red cape but is barefooted and bareheaded. His red cape contrasts sharply with the white snowbank of the canal. Jia Chêng hurries toward him to find himself confronting Baoyu, now kneeling and knowtowing to him. "Is it Baoyu?" he asks. Before the young man can reply, the Buddhist monk and the Daoist priest suddenly advance toward Baoyu and, each seizing an arm, say, "Come with us without delay! Your worldly obligations have been fulfilled." The three then leap to shore and disappear into the landscape. When Jia Chêng reaches home, he learns, to his joy, that Pao-ch'ai is pregnant with Baoyu's child, which later proves to be a son. Thus *Dream of the Red Chamber* reaches its conclusion.

At the end, then, the reader is returned to the creation myth with which the novel began. Events have come full circle. The so-called unfinished text has shaped itself into a complete literary unit in which the note of finality at the end is another beginning. Nothing is conclusive. Torn between the claims of love and personal liberation, between his active sympathy and compassion for others and his desire to transcend himself and thus escape his hopeless involvement in desire and suffering, Baoyu concludes that love, whether romantic or marital, involves too great a commitment to the outside world and is harmful to the self-contained inner world of the spirit; hence he decides to become a monk. There is nothing inexorable about his logic, however, and he may be embracing an illusion of less substantiality than that of human love and sympathy. In its message, the novel is ambiguous. If the hero's ultimate decision to become a monk appears to reinforce the Buddhist-Daoist teaching of individual liberation, neither romantic values nor Confucian ideals are neglected or underemphasized.

Richard P. Benton

BIBLIOGRAPHY

Edwards, Louise P. *Men and Women in Qing China: Gender in the Red Chamber Dream*. Honolulu: University of Hawaii Press, 2001. Uses *Dream of the Red Chamber* as a starting point for an analysis of gender roles in eighteenth century China, challenging the common assumption that the novel represents some form of early Chinese feminism by examining the text in conjunction with historical data.

Knoerle, Jeanne. *The "Dream of the Red Chamber": A Critical Study*. Bloomington: Indiana University Press, 1972. General overview of the novel, focusing on its plot, characters, narrative style, and setting and providing some historical and cultural context. A useful introduction to the novel.

Miller, Lucien. *Masks of Fiction in "Dream of the Red Chamber": Myth, Mimesis, and Persona*. Tucson: University of Arizona Press, 1975. Scholarly examination of the novel, focusing on its representations of character and themes, particularly the themes of religion and enlightenment. Miller explains the characters' names, the songs, and the poetry in the novel to make them understandable to the English reader.

Plaks, Andrew H., ed. *Chinese Narrative: Critical and Theoretical Essays*. Princeton, N.J.: Princeton University Press, 1977. Contains three essays by Plaks and two other authors who employ Western literary theory to analyze the themes, point of view, narrative structure, and other elements of *Dream of the Red Chamber*.

_____. "Leaving the Garden: Reflections on China's Literary Masterwork." *New Left Review* 47 (September/October, 2007). An evaluation of *Dream of the Red Chamber*. Describes how many Chinese readers cherish the book as a national treasure and how the book depicts the venerable Chinese ideal of four generations of a family living together.

Wang, Jing. *The Story of Stone*. Durham, N.C.: Duke University Press, 1992. Focuses on Chinese stone symbolism and lore in *Dream of the Red Chamber*, comparing it to the stone symbolism in other Chinese novels. Provides insight into the novel's main character, who is symbolized by stone.

Xiao, Chi. *The Chinese Garden as Lyric Enclave: A Generic Study of the Story of the Stone*. Ann Arbor: Center for Chinese Studies, University of Michigan, 2001. A history of the garden in Chinese culture and literature, including its symbolism in *Dream of the Red Chamber* and its importance to the Chinese literati during the Qing Dynasty.

Yi, Jeannie Jinsheng. *The Dream of the Red Chamber: An Allegory of Love*. Dumont, N.J.: Homa & Sekey Books, 2003. Yi analyzes the allegorical and structural role of dreams in the novel, interpreting them as symbols for the impermanent nature of love. She argues that Western literary theory cannot be applied to Chinese literature, unless that theory is seriously modified.

Yu, Anthony C. *Rereading the Stone: Desire and the Making of Fiction in "Dream of the Red Chamber."* Princeton, N.J.: Princeton University Press, 2001. Yu argues that the novel is a story about fictive representation; through a maze of literary devices, the novel challenges the authority of history, as well as referential biases in reading.

Zhou, Zuyan. "Chaos and the Gourd in *The Dream of the Red Chamber*." *T'oung Pao* 87, no. 4/5 (2001): 251-288. Explores the importance of the novel in Buddhist and Daoist philosophy by analyzing the religious life of its fictional character as well as its author. Also examines the concepts of chaos and gourd.

KAREL ČAPEK

Born: Malé Svatoňovice, Bohemia, Austro-
Hungarian Empire (now in Czech Republic);
January 9, 1890
Died: Prague, Czechoslovakia (now in Czech
Republic); December 25, 1938

PRINCIPAL LONG FICTION

Továrna na absolutno, 1922 (*The Absolute at
Large*, 1927)
Krakatit, 1924 (English translation, 1925)
Hordubal, 1933 (English translation, 1934)
Obyčejný život, 1934 (*An Ordinary Life*, 1936)
Povětroó, 1934 (Meteor, 1935)
Válka s mloky, 1936 (*The War with the Newts*,
1937)
První parta, 1937 (*The First Rescue Party*, 1939)
Život a dílo skladatele Foltýna, 1939 (*The Cheat*,
1941)

OTHER LITERARY FORMS

Apart from long fiction, Karel Čapek (CHAH-pehk)
wrote many stories, travelogues, and plays. An important journalist, he published many of his *feuilletons* as
well as his conversations with T. G. Masaryk, then president of Czechoslovakia. He also published a book on
philosophy, *Pragmatismus* (1918), and a book of literary
criticism, *Kritika slov* (1920).

Čapek's collections of short stories include *Zárivé
hlubiny* (1916; with Josef Čapek); *Boží muka* (1917;
Wayside Crosses, 2002); *Krakonošova zahrada* (1918);
Trapné povídky (1921; *Money, and Other Stories*, 1929;
also known as *Painful Tales*, 2002); *Povídky z druhé
kapsy* and *Povídky z jedné kapsy* (1929; *Tales from Two
Pockets*, 1932); *Devatero pohádek* (1931; *Fairy Tales*,
1933); and *Kniha apokryfů* (1946; *Apocryphal Stories*,
1949).

Among Čapek's most important plays are *R.U.R.:
Rossum's Universal Robots* (pb. 1920; with Josef
Čapek; English translation, 1923); *Ze života hmyzu* (pb.
1920; with Josef Čapek; *The Insect Play*, 1923; also
known as *And So Infinitam: The Life of the Insects*,
1923); *Věc Makropulos* (pb. 1920; *The Macropulos Se-*

cret, 1925); *Bílá nemoc* (1937; *Power and Glory*, 1938;
also known as *The White Plague*, 1988); and *Matka* (pr.,
pb., 1938; *The Mother*, 1939).

ACHIEVEMENTS

Karel Čapek is among the best-known modern Czech
writers. He became prominent between the two world
wars and was recognized by and acquainted with such
eminent figures as George Bernard Shaw, H. G. Wells,
G. K. Chesterton, and Jules Romains. Čapek's international reputation earned for him the presidency of the
Czechoslovak PEN Club, and he was suggested for the
post of president of the International PEN Club, an honor
that he declined. Though he was equally versatile in
fiction and drama, his fame abroad rests mostly on his
science-fiction play *R.U.R.*, written in collaboration
with Josef Čapek, which introduced into the world vocabulary the Czech word *robot*, a neologism derived
from the Czech *robota*, meaning forced labor.

Despite Čapek's lifelong interest in science and its
destructive potential, examined in such novels as *The
Absolute at Large* and *Krakatit*, and despite the worldwide fame that such science fantasies brought him, he is
remembered in the Czech Republic as a dedicated humanist, a spokesperson for the tolerance, pragmatism,
and pluralism best manifested in the philosophy of relativism that his works so creatively demonstrate. He was
one of the strongest voices of his time against totalitarianism, be it fascist or communist.

Čapek's work is deeply philosophical, but in a manner that is accessible to a wide readership. He managed
to achieve this with the help of a chatty, almost pedestrian style informed by a genuine belief in the reasonable
person, one who is open to a rational argument when all
else fails. Hence Čapek's humanism; hence, also, his
disappointment when, after the infamous appeasement
of 1938, he had to acknowledge that the very paragons of
the democratic ideal and of Western culture, England
and France, had sold out his country to the Nazis.

Such concerns of Čapek as the conflict between humankind's scientific achievements and the very survival
of the human race—a conflict illustrated by the fight be-

tween the robots and human beings in *R.U.R.*—are not merely alive today but have become more and more pressing as the world is becoming increasingly aware of the threat of nuclear holocaust. Čapek was among the first to see the dangerous potential of humankind's creative ability, not because he was particularly gifted in science, but because he was quite realistic, approaching the tendencies of his time with the far-seeing and far-reaching attitude of one whose relativism was tempered by pessimism derived from his awareness of the past, the tradition from which the imperfect-but-perfectible human departed.

An urbane wit, a certain intimacy with the reader, deft characterization, and concise expression are the hallmarks of Čapek's style. This style heightens the impact of his fictional treatment of profound issues.

BIOGRAPHY

The youngest child of a country doctor, Karel Čapek was born in 1890 in Bohemia, then part of the Austro-Hungarian Empire. A weak and sickly boy, Čapek was pampered by his mother and protected by his older brother, Josef; they, together with his maternal grandmother, inspired him with a love for literature. Karel and Josef prepared themselves for a literary vocation by their prodigious reading in many foreign literatures; among Karel's juvenilia are some verses influenced by Symbolism and the Decadents—French and Czech. Josef was to collaborate with Karel on some of his most celebrated successes, including *R.U.R.*, but he was primarily a gifted artist, illustrator, and designer who gradually established himself as such, leaving Karel Čapek to write alone, though never really drifting spiritually, or even physically, far away.

A brilliant student, Karel Čapek enrolled at Charles University in Prague, though two stints took him to the University of Berlin and the University of Paris. In 1915, he earned his doctorate, having defended his dissertation on objective methods in aesthetics. The next year saw the publication of the short-story collection *Zářivé hlubiny*, written with Josef. This genre was particularly suited to Čapek's talents, and throughout his life he continued to write short stories: philosophical, mystical, detective, and apocryphal. Parody and satire, down to the political lampoon, are not rare among them; they seem to

flow naturally from the day-to-day concerns of a journalist sharply reacting to the crises and momentous events of his time.

The first such event was the establishment of the Czechoslovak Republic in 1918, at which time Čapek worked for a National Democrat paper, switching in 1921 to the more liberal *Lindové noviny*, where he stayed to the end of his life. Čapek's youth and his middle age parallel the youth and growing pains of his country's first republic, right down to its (and his) death in 1938. Thus, Čapek is the literary embodiment of the principles of this republic, led by a philosopher-president, Masaryk; among these principles were a distrust of radical solutions, an accent on the small work on a human scale, and a faith in the goodwill of people. In this respect, one can consider Čapek an unofficial cultural ambassador to the world at large.

Karel Čapek. (Archive Photos)

Čapek was not indifferent to the world: A cosmopolitan spirit, he was drawn toward England in particular, and he traveled widely, reporting on his travels in books on England, Holland, Italy, Spain, and Scandinavia. Indeed, he was a quintessential European, protesting the deteriorating situation in Europe before World War II, which he did not live to witness but the coming of which he foresaw only too clearly. This prescience is particularly evident in his novel *The War with the Newts*, a thinly disguised presentiment of the Orwellian battle of totalitarian superpowers that left Eastern Europe, after years of Nazi occupation, in the stranglehold of the Soviet Union.

Oddly enough, the fact that a Czech writer became known throughout the world did not result in adulation of Čapek by Czech readers and critics. On the contrary, it inspired jealous critical comments to the effect that Čapek in his unusual works was pandering to foreign tastes. In retrospect, this charge seems particularly unfair. Another oddity is that Čapek abandoned the theater after the worldwide success of *R.U.R.* and *The Insect Play*, chiefly producing short stories until his greatest triumph, the trilogy of philosophical novels *Hordubal*, *Meteor*, and *An Ordinary Life*. When, in 1937, he returned to the theater with *Power and Glory*, followed in 1938 by *The Mother*, it was to appeal to the conscience of the world with two timely plays concerned with the catastrophe prepared by Nazism. The plays were designed to counter the spirit of pacifism and appeasement then sweeping Europe; Čapek hoped to salvage Czechoslovakia, destined to be given to the Nazis as a peace offering.

Čapek's last work of great importance was *The Cheat*, written after the tragedy of Munich. Čapek mourned the death of his republic and yet inspired his compatriots not to despair. *The Cheat* breaks with the relativist philosophy common to all of his works: The cheat is a cheat, a fake, a swindler and not a composer, and the novel's many vantage points only underscore this judgment. Death overtook Čapek while he was writing the conclusion of the novel, on Christmas Day, 1938; for political reasons, his grateful readers were not permitted to say good-bye to him in a public ceremony. He was survived by Olga Scheinpflugová, an actor and writer, his companion and wife.

Though Čapek's life was comfortable in material terms, he lived with calcification of the spine, a painful condition that made full enjoyment of those comforts impossible; it also postponed his marriage to only a few years before his death. This physical suffering was accompanied by a spiritual search. For years, as the testimony of his literary works shows, he was content with pragmatism and relativism, though he was not an ethical relativist. Only toward the end of his life, as witness his last novel, did he embrace the idea that, often, people are what they seem, definitely and irrevocably: They are fully responsible for their actions.

Never does Čapek complain or rant against destiny: There is a sunny and humorous side to his work that balances the dark visions. Perhaps his excellence in life and art is explained by his personal heroism in alchemizing his suffering into a quest for a meaningful life.

ANALYSIS

Karel Čapek was a philosophical writer par excellence regardless of the genre that he employed in a given work, but the form of long fiction in particular afforded him the amplitude to express complicated philosophical ideas. Thus, his greatest achievement is the trilogy consisting of *Hordubal*, *Meteor*, and *An Ordinary Life*. These three novels preserve the fruit of Čapek's life's work: the searching and finding of his many short stories, plays, and newspaper columns, as well as his lifelong preoccupation with the philosophy of pragmatism and relativism.

While the trilogy is a complex and at the same time harmonious statement of Čapek's philosophy, his last novel, *The Cheat*, though shorter than either of the three novels of the trilogy, is important for representing a sharp and shocking departure from the trilogy's philosophy. It represents a further development of Čapek's philosophical search.

HORDUBAL

Hordubal is based on a newspaper story of a crime that took place in the most backward region of prewar Czechoslovakia, the Transcarpathian Ukraine. Juraj Hordubal, an unsophisticated but very sensitive and even saintly peasant, returns from the United States, where he worked and made some money, to his wife Polana and daughter Hafia. He is unaware that in his absence, Polana has fallen in love with Stefan Manya, a Hungarian hired hand. To disguise this affair, Polana forces Manya to become engaged to the eleven-year-old Hafia. When this ruse does not work, the lovers kill Hordubal with a long needle. An investigation uncovers the crime and identifies the criminals, who are caught and punished.

Appropriating the bare facts of the newspaper report with minimal modifications, Čapek invests this simple tale of passion with philosophical depth, first by making Hordubal a rather sensitive man who is aware of the changed circumstances upon his return home. The reader is painfully aware of this when the author lets the reader follow Hordubal's thoughts in beautifully stylized, lyric passages of almost saintly insight and renunciation of violence, leading to the acceptance of his death. The tension develops on several levels simultaneously.

The first level is the *crime passionnelle*, the road that introduces us to the contrasting figures of Hordubal and Manya. A deeper level is attained when the reader perceives the cultural-ethnic contrast: Hordubal, the sedentary agricultural type, is opposed to the Hungarian Manya, the nomadic, violent type. Finally, there is the level on which the tension is between subjective reality, the reality of a given character who sees the world his or her own way, and objective reality. The conclusion, however, undercuts any confident faith in the existence of objective reality. Hordubal is seriously ill when he is murdered, so that a question arises whether the needle of the killer entered his heart before or after his death; if after, there was no murder.

The problem of the interpretation of even simple phenomena is brought to a head in the confrontation between two irreconcilable types of criminal investigations, based on different sets of assumptions and interpretations of events. In the conflict between the young police officer and his seasoned colleague, the deceptively simple case grows more and more complicated. In a plot twist that stresses the evanescent nature of humankind's certainties, the key evidence, Hordubal's heart, is lost in transport, condemning those involved in the investigation to eternal incertitude.

The novel shakes the certitudes established in the mystery genre, suggesting that mutually exclusive interpretations are not only possible but also inevitable. More to the point, with the death of Hordubal, the protagonist's internal monologue ceases; the reader no longer sees Hordubal from inside. What the others think about Hordubal is widely off the mark.

METEOR

If the truth is relative and hopelessly compromised by the very fact that it is being approached by different people, the second novel of the trilogy reverses the procedure and asks if different people might not discover the truth on the basis of sharing with one another the human condition and thus having very much in common: first the difference, then the commonality. *Meteor* approaches this further elaboration of Čapek's philosophical quest in an original manner.

Čapek uses three narrators who speculate about the identity of a man fatally wounded in a plane crash and brought to a hospital as "patient X." The three narrators, including a Sister of Mercy, a clairvoyant, and a writer, try to reconstruct his life and the reason for his flight. The first narrator, the Sister, sees X as a young man who runs away from home unaware of the real meaning of love and responsibility. After some peregrinations, he decides to return home, only to crash and die in the process. The clairvoyant sees X as a talented chemist who discovered important new formulas but lacked the patience to see his experiments through and develop them commercially. When he finds that his experiments were founded on a sound basis, he decides to return and claim the discoveries as his own. The writer sees the patient as a victim of amnesia who falls in love with a Cuban girl but is unable to live without memory. When his suffering triggers the recovery of his past, the man flies home to lay claim to his position.

All three accounts differ from one another in approach and in substance, yet each of them identifies an important facet of the victim and provides an insight into the character of the individual narrator. Čapek thus raises the question of self-discovery, the perennial identity problem: What happens when X and the observer are one and the same person? The third novel of the trilogy, *An Ordinary Life*, provides the answer.

AN ORDINARY LIFE

A retired bureaucrat, a self-confessed "ordinary man," decides to write the story of his own life. Looking back, he concludes that he lived an ordinary life governed only by habit and chance; it seems repetitious and predictable to him. There are, however, a few incidents that do not fit this summary generalization of his life, and the more he thinks about them, the more fully he understands that right within his ordinary life, there is a multitude of lives: He as a person is not an individuality but a plurality. He, like a microcosm, mirrors the macrocosm of society. Does he have a stable point of view, or does it too change with each different personality as he comes to adopt it? This is not a case of a pathological disorder; the protagonist is a normal official who, before he settled down to his ways, explored radically different lifestyles. Like all people, he bears within him the potential for many selves, never fully realized.

Thus, the tension between subjective and objective reality that animates *Hordubal* collapses in *An Ordinary Life*. This third novel of the trilogy proposes that even that which is considered a subjective reality (the only accessible one, since the objective escapes forever) is itself a plurality.

As an experiment, as individual novels, and as a philosophical trilogy, these three novels are brilliant. What is difficult to communicate beyond the pale outlines and philosophical underpinnings of these works is their distinctive tone, their often lyric air. This atmosphere of numinous twilight, so difficult to communicate, bathes the novels in an unearthly light and adds to them a certain air of beauty. It comes as a surprise, then, that Čapek's last work, *The Cheat*, makes a departure from the finished whole of the trilogy on philosophical grounds.

The Cheat

The trilogy was the culmination of Čapek's work; the relativist philosophy enshrined within it is the summation of findings and beliefs that, for better or worse, animated Čapek's entire oeuvre. *The Cheat* continues with the insights gained in the trilogy—for example, the method of multiple narration is preserved. The several narratives, nine in all, gradually fill out the picture of the fake artist Foltýn, the would-be composer. These multiple narratives, however, do not yield a relativistic perspective: The individual accounts never contradict one another; rather, they gradually illuminate Foltýn and answer some of the questions that the various narrators

have raised. The collective finding is damning, and yet there is something admirable in Foltýn: His obsessive love of art saves him from utter condemnation.

In his attempt to express the impossible, Foltýn is like every artist; every artist has a little Foltýn in him or her. It is only fitting, given Čapek's sense of balance, that, after providing in his trilogy examples of the power of art to do good, to express the truth, he should point to the capacity of art to profess evil. Thus, he embraced the totality of the world that his suffering enabled him to know intimately.

Peter Petro

Other major works

SHORT FICTION: *Zářivé hlubiny*, 1916 (with Josef Čapek); *Boží muka*, 1917 (*Wayside Crosses*, 2002); *Krakonošova zahrada*, 1918 (with Josef Čapek); *Trapné povídky*, 1921 (*Money, and Other Stories*, 1929; also known as *Painful Tales*, 2002); *Povídky z druhé kapsy*, 1929 (*Tales from Two Pockets*, 1932); *Povídky z jedné kapsy*, 1929 (*Tales from Two Pockets*, 1932); *Devatero pohádek*, 1931 (*Fairy Tales*, 1933); *Kniha apokryfů*, 1946 (*Apocryphal Stories*, 1949); *Cross Roads*, 2002 (includes *Wayside Crosses* and *Painful Tales*).

PLAYS: *Lásky hra osudná*, pb. 1916 (wr. 1910; with Josef Čapek); *Loupezník*, pr., pb. 1920 (*The Robber*, 1931); *R.U.R.: Rossum's Universal Robots*, pb. 1920 (English translation, 1923); *Věc Makropulos*, pb. 1920 (*The Macropulos Secret*, 1925); *Ze života hmyzu*, pb. 1920 (with Josef Čapek; *The Insect Play*, 1923; also known as *And So Infinitam: The Life of the Insects*, 1923); *Adam Stvořitel*, pr., pb. 1927 (with Josef Čapek; *Adam the Creator*, 1929); *Bílá nemoc*, pr., pb. 1937 (*Power and Glory*, 1938; also known as *The White Plague*, 1988); *Matka*, pr., pb. 1938 (*The Mother*, 1939).

NONFICTION: *Pragmatismus*, 1918; *Kritika slov*, 1920; *O nejbližších vecech*, 1920 (*Intimate Things*, 1935); *Musaion*, 1920-1921; *Italské listy*, 1923 (*Letters from Italy*, 1929); *Anglické listy*, 1924 (*Letters from England*, 1925); *Hovory s T. G. Masarykem*, 1928-1935 (3 volumes; *President Masaryk Tells His Story*, 1934; also known as *Masaryk on Thought and Life*, 1938); *Zahradníkův rok*, 1929 (*The Gardener's Year*, 1931); *Výlet do Španěl*, 1930 (*Letters from Spain*, 1931); *Marsyas*, 1931 (*In Praise of Newspapers: And Other Essays *On the Margins of Literature*, 1951); *O věcech obecných: Čili, Zóon politikon*, 1932; *Obrázky z Holandska*, 1932 (*Letters from Holland*, 1933); *Dášeňka*, 1933 (*Dashenka*, 1940); *Cesta na sever*, 1936 (*Travels in the North*, 1939); *Měl jsem psa a kočku*, 1939 (*I Had a Dog and a Cat*, 1940); *Obrázky z domova*, 1953; *Veci kolemnás*, 1954; *Poznámky o tvorbě*, 1959; *Viktor Dyk-S. K. Neumann-bratří Č.: Korespondence z let 1905-1918*, 1962.

TRANSLATION: *Francouzská poesie nové doby*, 1920 (of French poetry).

BIBLIOGRAPHY

Bradbrook, Bohuslava R. *Karel Čapek: In Pursuit of Truth, Tolerance, and Trust*. Portland, Oreg.: Sussex Academic Press, 1998. A critical reevaluation of Čapek's work. Bradbrook discusses Čapek's many intellectual interests, including his search for truth and his appreciation of science and technology. Includes a bibliography and an index.

_____. "Karel Čapek's Contribution to Czech National Literature." In *Czechoslovakia Past and Present*, edited by Miloslav Rechcigl. The Hague, the Netherlands: Mouton, 1968. Clearly places Čapek high on the list of notable Czech authors, demonstrating how much his writing affected other literary production in the country as well as making a political impact. Remarks perceptively on Čapek's inventiveness and on his ability to work in several genres.

Harkins, William E. *Karel Čapek*. New York: Columbia University Press, 1962. This carefully researched and well-written critical biography of Čapek remains one of the best available full-length sources on the author.

Klima, Ivan. *Karel Čapek: Life and Work*. Translated by Norma Comrada. Highland Park, Mich.: Catbird Press, 2002. Catbird Press, an American publisher of Czech literature in English translation, commissioned Klima, a Czech novelist and authority on Čapek, to write this critical biography. Klima analyzes Čapek's work, relating its themes to events in the author's life.

Kussi, Peter, ed. *Toward the Radical Center: A Karel Čapek Reader*. Highland Park, Mich.: Catbird Press, 1990. Kussi's introduction to this collection of Čapek's fiction, plays, and other work provides an excellent brief overview of Čapek's career. Includes a chronology and a helpful list of English translations of Čapek's writings.

Makin, Michael, and Jindrich Toman, eds. *On Karel Čapek*. Ann Arbor: Michigan Slavic Publications, 1992. Collection of conference papers examining Čapek as a modern storyteller, his versions of dystopia, his early work, his short stories, and his reception in the United States.

Mann, Erika. "A Last Conversation with Karel Čapek." *The Nation*, January 14, 1939. Although brief, this account by Thomas Mann's daughter of her last meeting with Čapek comments on the pressures Čapek found building up all around him, causing him to undergo a physical decline that eventually led to his death. She senses and comments on Čapek's sickness of the spirit that left him unwilling to continue living in the face of Adolf Hitler's growing fanaticism and power.

Matuska, Alexander. *Karel Čapek: An Essay*. Translated by Cathryn Alan. London: Allen and Unwin, 1964. An excellent account of Čapek's artistry. Discusses how he develops his themes, shapes his characterization, fashions his plots, and handles the details that underlie the structure of his work. This book remains a valuable resource.

Schubert, Peter Z. *The Narratives of Čapek and Cexov: A Typological Comparison of the Authors' World Views*. Bethesda, Md.: International Scholars, 1997. Although a somewhat difficult work for beginning students, this book proves valuable with its discussion of the themes of freedom, lack of communication, justice, and truth. Includes a separate section discussing the critical views of Čapek. The comprehensive bibliography alone makes this a volume well worth consulting.

Wellek, René. *Essays on Czech Literature*. The Hague, the Netherlands: Mouton, 1963. Wellek's essay, "Karel Čapek," which originally appeared in 1936, is one of the most searching pieces written about the author during his lifetime. Wellek comments on Čapek's relative youth and considers him at the height of his powers. When these words were written, Čapek had less than three years to live.

TRUMAN CAPOTE
Truman Streckfus Persons

Born: New Orleans, Louisiana; September 30, 1924
Died: Los Angeles, California; August 25, 1984
Also known as: Truman Streckfus Persons

PRINCIPAL LONG FICTION

Other Voices, Other Rooms, 1948
The Grass Harp, 1951
A Christmas Memory, 1956 (serial)
Breakfast at Tiffany's: A Short Novel and Three Stories, 1958
In Cold Blood, 1966
The Thanksgiving Visitor, 1967 (serial)
Answered Prayers: The Unfinished Novel, 1986
Summer Crossing, 2005 (found manuscript)

OTHER LITERARY FORMS

In addition to writing fiction, Truman Capote (kuh-POH-tee) worked principally in two other forms: the drama (stage, film, and television) and reportage. Capote's first work for the stage was his adaptation of his novel *The Grass Harp*, which was produced in New York in the spring of 1952. In 1954, he collaborated with Harold Arlen on the Broadway musical *House of Flowers*, based on his short story. He also wrote the film scenario for *Beat the Devil* (1954) and dialogue for *Indiscretion of an American Wife* (1954). He adapted Henry James's 1898 novella *The Turn of the Screw* for film as *The Innocents* (1961). Two Hollywood films, *Breakfast at Tiffany's* (1961) and *In Cold Blood* (1967), were based on his work, but Capote himself did not contribute to the screenplays. He did, however, with Eleanor Perry, adapt three of his stories—"Miriam," "Among the Paths to Eden," and *A Christmas Memory*—for television. *A Christmas Memory* was honored with the Peabody Award in 1967, and the three story dramatizations were later released as a film, *Trilogy: An Experiment in Multimedia* (1969).

Capote's first venture in reportage was *Local Color* (1950), a series of impressionistic sketches of New Orleans, New York, and other places where he had lived or visited in America and Europe. *Local Color* was followed by *The Muses Are Heard* (1956), an urbane account of his trip to Leningrad and the opening-night performance of the American cast of *Porgy and Bess*. Other sketches of the 1950's appeared in *Observations* (1959), with photographs by Richard Avedon. His masterpiece in this form is *In Cold Blood*, although Capote preferred to regard this work as a "nonfiction novel." *The Dogs Bark: Public People and Private Places* (1973) collects his earlier nonfiction writing and includes some additional sketches, while *Music for Chameleons* (1980) includes later reportage and a short "nonfiction novel," *Handcarved Coffins*, an account of multiple murders in the American Southwest.

ACHIEVEMENTS

With the publication of his first novel, *Other Voices, Other Rooms*, Truman Capote achieved fame at the young age of twenty-four. His precocity, the bizarre nature and brilliant quality of the novel, and the astonishing photograph of the author on the book's dust jacket (a figure, childlike in stature, who reclines on a period sofa and looks out with an expression of unsettling maturity and aloofness) made him widely discussed in both America and Europe. This debut set the tone of Capote's later career, in which he consistently attained remarkable popularity while yet appealing to an elite audience of serious readers.

The publication one year later of *A Tree of Night, and Other Stories* (1949) consolidated Capote's reputation as an author of baroque fiction, fiction concerned with the strange, often dreamlike inner states of estranged characters. A peculiarity of this volume, however, is that several of the stories it contains are lightly whimsical. *The Grass Harp*, which shares this more "sunlit" vision, shows Capote emerging, tentatively, from his "private," subjective fiction; in this work, whimsy predominates as the individual gropes for his relationship to others. *Breakfast at Tiffany's* moves further out into the world, and this tendency becomes more pronounced still in his nonfiction novel *In Cold Blood*.

His unfinished novel *Answered Prayers*, with its

large gallery of precisely observed characters, was Capote's fullest effort to engage the many-sided world of actual social experience. In whatever form he wrote, however, whether sequestered fantasy or fiction with a social orientation, Capote's preoccupations remained constant—loneliness and isolation, the dichotomy between the world and the self, the deprivations of the innocent or unconventional and their moments of grace.

Capote's strength was mainly in the briefer modes—in the vignette, short story, and short novel. Of his longer works, the best is *In Cold Blood*, the most accomplished "nonfiction novel" of its time. Called by Norman Mailer "the most perfect writer of my generation . . . word for word, rhythm upon rhythm," Capote is known for being a great stylist. There is no question that he belongs in the first rank of modern American writers.

BIOGRAPHY

Truman Capote, whose name at birth was Truman Streckfus Persons, was born in New Orleans on September 30, 1924. His mother, Nina (Faulk) Persons, only sixteen when he was born, had married a traveling salesman, Joseph Persons, to escape the drabness of her hometown, Monroeville, Alabama. The marriage soon proved unhappy, and by the time Capote was four years old his parents had become divorced. When his mother moved to New York, she sent her son (an only child) to live with a variety of relatives in the South. From the time Capote was four until he was ten, he lived outside Monroeville, where one of his neighbors was Nelle Harper Lee, who later put him into her novel *To Kill a Mockingbird* (1960) as Dill, the strange, brilliant little boy who is "passed from relative to relative." The relatives with whom he stayed were four elderly, unmarried cousins—three women and their brother. One of the women was Sook Faulk, a childlike, simple woman, wise in ways that mattered to a small boy who otherwise lived much to himself and within his own imagination. Sook Faulk inspired the character of Dolly Talbo in *The Grass Harp*, and Capote later commemorated his childhood friendship with her in his autobiographical stories *A Christmas Memory* and *The Thanksgiving Visitor*. In his secluded life in rural Alabama, he read Charles Dickens and other novelists at an early age and made his first attempts at fiction at the age of ten. Feeling himself different from others, without the love of a mother or father, uncertain even of a home, Capote developed the sense of isolation that informs all of his fiction.

Capote's childhood wanderings continued after he left Monroeville in 1934. At different times, he stayed with cousins in New Orleans, and at one point he lived with a family in Pass Christian, Mississippi, which provided the setting for *Other Voices, Other Rooms*. In 1939, when he was sixteen, he went to New York to join his mother and her second husband, Joseph Garcia Capote, a Cuban textile manufacturer who legally adopted him and whose surname he took. At this time, he was sent to a series of boarding schools in New York and then to Greenwich High School in Millbrook, Connecticut, where his parents had moved. At seventeen, he dropped out of school and found work with *The New Yorker* magazine. After two years, he left his job to live with relatives in Alabama and begin a first novel, *Summer Crossing*, later discarded when he began work on *Other Voices, Other Rooms*.

Capote had been sending out stories for publication since he was fifteen; by the time he was seventeen he had his first acceptances, and in Alabama he wrote his first important stories—"Miriam" and "A Tree of Night." With a fifteen-hundred-dollar advance from Random House for his novel in progress, he traveled to New Orleans, then to New York and Nantucket, where the novel, the result of two years' work, was completed. The novel drew on his own childhood experiences—his exposure to rural localities in the South, his crisis of identity as a nomadic child, and his early preoccupation with homosexuality.

Reviews of *Other Voices, Other Rooms* were mixed, yet many praised Capote enthusiastically for his evocation of the dream states of the subconscious, his "uncanny ability to make a weird world come alive" with a kind of magical radiance. One reviewer called Capote's talent "the most startling American fiction has known since the debut of Faulkner." For a time, Capote was regarded as a writer of southern gothic fiction; in the 1950's, however, he moved away from this school. *The Grass Harp*, although set in the rural South, was more lyrical than gothic; *Breakfast at Tiffany's*, which followed it, was set in New York and was urban in its idiom, its manner, and its implication. *The Muses Are Heard,* with its detached, worldly intelligence, shows how fully Capote had adopted a cosmopolitan stance.

During much of the 1950's, Capote lived abroad, but by autumn of 1959 he was living in New York, and while exploring the possibilities of "nonfiction fiction," he read in the newspapers of the macabre and seemingly inexplicable murder of the Herbert Clutter family in the Midwest. Acting on the intuition that he had found his "subject," he went immediately to Holcomb, Kansas, and began to familiarize himself with the town and with the circumstances of the Clutters. This project soon developed into a major undertaking, to which he devoted himself almost exclusively from November, 1959, to April, 1965. After their apprehension, the murderers, Richard Hickock and Perry Smith, were tried and sentenced to be executed in 1960, but the executions were stayed for five years, during which Capote held more than two hundred interviews with them. He also personally retraced the route they had taken in the course of their wandering after the murders and compiled extensive notes from his conversations with all the parties concerned with the case.

The psychological strain Capote experienced at this time was particularly great because of his empathetic involvement with one of the murderers, Perry Smith. Like Capote, Smith had come from a shattered home and had been a nomadic dreamer; the two were physically similar, both being five feet, four inches tall. The intensity of Capote's imaginative involvement can be felt on every page of *In Cold Blood*, a work that, almost paradoxically, combines objective reporting with deep feeling.

On its publication, *In Cold Blood* became a phenomenal best seller while winning great critical acclaim. The literary year of 1966 belonged to Capote. It was at this time that he gave his black and white masked ball for five hundred friends at the Plaza Hotel in New York, sometimes called "the Party of the Decade." After the

Truman Capote. (Library of Congress)

publication of *In Cold Blood*, Capote became a media celebrity and a member of wealthy and fashionable society. After that, however, he produced relatively no new work—chiefly, two volumes of reportage: *The Dogs Bark* and *Music for Chameleons*. In the late 1960's, he announced that he was at work on a new book, *Answered Prayers*, a lengthy, Proustian novel that would be a "major work."

By the mid-1970's, four chapters of the work in progress had been published in *Esquire* magazine, which perhaps was done to prove that Capote was actually working on the novel. By this time, Capote had developed drug and alcohol problems, and his lack of professional output reflected his personal disintegration.

Answered Prayers has a stronger sexual frankness than any of Capote's other works; its complicated, darkly intriguing narrative is sometimes scabrous in its revelation of envied lives. In its suggestive handling of reality and illusion, *Answered Prayers* also reveals Capote's familiar sense of loneliness—loneliness among the members of the haut monde. Capote died in California at the home of his close friend Joanne Carson on August 25, 1984, of heart and liver failure caused by multiple drug ingestion. As one biographer, Gerald Clarke, observed, it is unknown whether Capote committed suicide or his health had failed under the assault that his addictions had launched on his body.

ANALYSIS

The pattern of Truman Capote's career suggests a divided allegiance to two different, even opposing literary forms—objective realism and romance. Capote's earliest fiction belongs primarily to the imagination of romance. It is intense, wondrously evocative, subjective; in place of a closely detailed outlining of a real social world, it concentrates on the inner states of its characters, usually with the full resources of romance, including archetypal journeys or a descent into the subconscious. His characters' inner life is fixed through the use of telling imagery and controlling symbols. In "The Headless Hawk," for example, the real world exists hardly at all; what little there is of it seems subaqueous, has the liquid flow of things seen underwater. In "A Tree of Night," the heroine is subjected to real terror, complete with gothic phantoms in the form of two strangers on a train. The journey of the train itself is complementary to Kay's journey into the dark places of her soul, where the "wizard man" and irrational fear prevail. In "Miriam," an elderly woman's sense of reality and personal identity give way before the presence of an implike child.

It is not surprising that these early stories have been compared to those of Edgar Allan Poe, for, like Poe, Capote was fascinated by the psyche at the point of disintegration. Similarly, in *Other Voices, Other Rooms*, the boy Joel Knox inhabits a vaguely outlined social world; what is ultimately most real is the terror that surrounds and threatens him. The scenes that pinpoint his experience are all charged with moral, symbolic implication; rather than unfolding through a study of social relationships, the narrative moves episodically through assaults on Joel's mind, imagistic storm points keeping him in agitation and crisis; the identities of the characters surrounding Joel are fixed from the beginning and have only to be revealed through psychic drama. The shape of the work is, finally, that of a romantic moral parable.

How strange it is, then, that as Capote's career progressed he revealed a pronounced interest in the literature of realism, even a kind of superrealism, implied by

"nonfiction fiction." He began working in this genre with *Local Color*, a poetic literature of pure "surface." The texture of surface is the real subject of *The Muses Are Heard*. With a sleepless vigilance, Capote observes his fellow travelers and in the finest, most precise detail captures their idiosyncrasies, the gestures and unguarded remarks that reveal them, as it were, to the quick. Tart, witty, detached, *The Muses Are Heard* assumes no depths of meaning in the Cold War world it portrays; eye, ear, and social intelligence are what are important. Capote's career also shows a desire to bring together the opposing parts of his nature and his equipment as a writer, however, and in *In Cold Blood* he actually achieved such a fusion. Capote himself never intrudes on the narration, makes no commentary, stands back reporting "impartially" on what occurs. This effacement of self is so complete that readers believe they are witnessing the events as they occur. Yet at the same time the work contains many, not always obvious, romantic urgings, forcing readers to put themselves in the place of Perry Smith on death row. Strict categories of good and evil break down before the sense of the inextricable mixture of both in life, and the helplessness of man before an obscure and ominously felt cosmic drama. The lyric note of baffled yearning at the end is romantic, in spite of the work's judicious, almost judicial, realism.

OTHER VOICES, OTHER ROOMS

The plot of *Other Voices, Other Rooms*, Capote's first novel, is not extremely complicated. Joel Knox, a thirteen-year-old, motherless boy, is sent from the home of his Aunt Ellen in New Orleans to Skully's Landing to be united with his father, Mr. Edward Sansom. Arriving eventually at the Landing, a plantation house partly in ruins, Joel is cared for by a woman named Amy, her languid, artistic cousin Randolph, and two family retainers, Jesus Fever, an ancient black man, and his granddaughter Missouri Fever, known as Zoo. The boy's inquiries about his father are mysteriously unanswered by the adults, and it is only later in the novel that the boy confronts his father—a paralytic invalid who neither speaks nor understands, his eyes fixed in a wide, crazed stare. The crisis experienced by the boy in the decaying house is largely inward; he attempts to free himself of his situation, but in a series of strange episodes his failure to do so becomes evident, and at the end he embraces his fate, which is complementary to that of Randolph, the dream-bound gay man. He accepts whatever love and solace Randolph (evoked as mother-father, male-female, and "ideal lover" in one) can give him.

In its atmosphere of sinister enchantment, of the bizarre and weird, *Other Voices, Other Rooms* exploits many of the resources of the gothic mode. William Faulkner stands distantly in the background; Carson McCullers is more immediately evident. Capote's theme of a quest for love and understanding in a world apparently incapable of providing either, and his use of freakish characters, suggest the generic influence of McCullers's *The Heart Is a Lonely Hunter* (1940). Even the "normal" world of Noon City is filled with oddity—a one-armed barber, a female restaurant proprietor who has an apelike appearance. Such oddity is minor, however, compared to the characters who inhabit the Landing—Jesus Fever, a brokeback dwarf; Zoo, whose long, giraffelike neck reveals the scars from Keg Brown's razor assault on her; Randolph, who, in an upper-floor room, dressed in a gown and wig, becomes a "beautiful lady." At the same time, and often with the most powerful effect, the novel draws on the imagery of surrealism. The late scene at the carnival, for example, is spectacular in its evocation of an irrational world struck by lightning, a sequence followed by the nocturnal pursuit of Joel through an abandoned house by the midget Miss Wisteria, and the coma Joel experiences in which his life is relived while a pianola composes its own jazz and the plantation lurches into the earth.

Essentially, *Other Voices, Other Rooms* is a romance. It has been compared with Nathaniel Hawthorne's 1831 story "My Kinsman, Major Molineux," which also deals with a youth who, in a dark and dreamlike world, searches for his identity and is initiated into life. Joel's journey, in its various stages, has a symbolic shading. At the opening, he leaves the morning world of Paradise to travel to Noon City, where he continues his journey through the backcountry in a mule-drawn wagon, with Jesus Fever asleep at the reins; arriving at the Landing in darkness, Joel is himself asleep, and cannot remember entering the house when he awakens the next morning in an upstairs bedroom. With the effect of a wizard's spell, the house comes to claim him. Complicated patterns of imagery—of fire and fever, knifing and mutilation,

death and drowning—evoke the extremity of the boy's fear and loneliness as avenues of escape from the Landing are closed to him, one by one. Mythic patterns also emerge—the search for the "father," the Grail quest, Christian crucifixion, Jungian descent into the unconscious—to reinforce the romantic contour of his experience. Although in some ways Joel's guide ("I daresay I know some things I daresay you don't"), Randolph is himself held under an enchantment, dating back to the inception of his life as a gay man. At the end, Joel and Randolph become one. As the ancient "slave bell" in the ruined garden seems to ring in Joel's head, he goes forward to join Randolph, leaving his childhood behind him.

Other Voices, Other Rooms is less perfectly achieved than *The Heart Is a Lonely Hunter*. Randolph, for example, a major character, is more a pastiche of English decadence than a real person. Moreover, the ending becomes snarled in obscurity. In accepting Randolph, Joel accepts his own nature, an act that brings liberation and even some limited hope of love. Yet Randolph is so sterile, so negative, and so enclosed within his own narcissism that the reader cannot share the upsurge of joy that Joel is supposed to feel. Capote's strength in the novel lies elsewhere—in his ability to create a sustained poetry of mood, to capture psychic states of rare intensity and beauty. His experimentalism in this respect is far more adventurous than that of McCullers. The image-making power of Capote's language is so impressive in this precocious novel as to leave one fearful that he may have exhausted the resources of the southern gothic mode in a single flight.

THE GRASS HARP

Capote's next novel, *The Grass Harp*, derives from the rural southern fable of "Children on Their Birthdays." Like that tale, *The Grass Harp* has a narrative frame that begins and ends in the present, with the story placed in between. Collin Fenwick looks back on his rearing as an orphan in the home of two maiden women, Dolly Talbo, a gentle, childlike woman, and her sister Verena, who has property and investments in town. He is spared the intense ordeal of Joel Knox but is like him in his sense of personal isolation and in his search for love and identity. When Verena takes it upon herself to exploit a home remedy that Dolly makes from herbs (her little scrap of identity), Dolly rebels, and with Collin and Catherine Creek, an eccentric half-breed factotum, she withdraws to a tree house set amid a field of tall Indian grass. Eventually, they are joined by Riley Henderson, a rebellious youth, and Charlie Cool, a retired circuit court judge whose refinement makes him an anachronism to his married sons, at whose houses he stays in rotation. The adventure in the tree house does not have a long duration, but by the time it is over the characters all come to have an enlarged sense of who they are.

The narrative is flawed in various respects. It involves a number of plot contrivances (Morris Ritz's absconding with the money in Verena's safe); the "battle" scenes between the tree house occupants and the law-and-order characters from town rely too much on slapstick; and Riley Henderson's reformation and marriage to Maude Riordan is a trite conception. Yet there are many fine touches in this fragile, not wholly successful tale—the portrait of Judge Cool and his late-in-life courtship of Dolly; Verena's recognition that it is she who is more alone than Dolly, whose "heart" has been the pillar of the house; the controlling symbols of freedom and imagination versus rigidity and dry rationality (the Indian grass "harp" and the cemetery) that enclose the work and give it life beyond its conclusion. A meditation on freedom and restriction, *The Grass Harp* reveals Capote moving away from his earlier studies in isolation toward a concern with a discovery of identity through relation to others.

BREAKFAST AT TIFFANY'S

Breakfast at Tiffany's marks a new stage of Capote's career, since it brings him fully into the world outside his native South. In this short novel, Capote captures New York and its denizens—Joe Bell, the sentimental bartender with a sour stomach; Madame Sapphia Spanella, a husky coloratura who rollerskates in Central Park; O. J. Berman, the Hollywood agent; and Sally Tomato, the surprisingly unsinister mobster with a Sing Sing address. José Ybarra-Jaegar, the Argentine diplomat, is perceived acutely and never more so than when he writes a mendacious letter to the novel's protagonist, Holly Golightly, breaking off a relationship with her when her dream life becomes "unsafe."

The novel employs a retrospective narrative frame like the one in F. Scott Fitzgerald's *The Great Gatsby*

(1925), in which the pale, conventional Nick Carraway observes the strange career of his larger-than-life neighbor. In both cases, the narration is dominated by nostalgia and the sense of loss, accentuated by the use of a reiterated autumnal motif. Holly's origins go far back in Capote's writing. In *Other Voices, Other Rooms*, Randolph's dream initiator Dolores dries her washed hair in the sun and strums a guitar, as does Holly. Miss Bobbit models her too, her "precious papa" having told her to "live in the sky." Holly is a Miss Bobbit in her late teens, a child-adult whose ideal of happiness lies "beyond." An "innocent" immoralist, Holly is, however, a somewhat sentimental conception (a "good" sensitive character misprized by a nasty and unfeeling world), and a rather underdeveloped character. As Alfred Kazin has observed, she is partly New York chic and partly Tulip, Texas, naïve, but in neither case does she become a real person. The fusion of realism and romantic fable attempted in *Breakfast at Tiffany's* is not achieved fully until Capote's next work, *In Cold Blood*.

IN COLD BLOOD

In Cold Blood, which remained on the best-seller lists for more than one year and has since been translated into twenty-five languages, is Capote's most popular and widely read book. It is also one of his most notable works artistically. F. W. Dupee called it "the best documentary account of an American crime ever written," and Capote himself claimed that it created a new literary genre, the "nonfiction novel." Although nothing exactly like *In Cold Blood* had appeared previously, there are clearly precedents for it—Theodore Dreiser's *An American Tragedy* (1925), for example, a documentary novel of crime and punishment, and Ernest Hemingway's *Green Hills of Africa* (1935), as well as the reportage of Rebecca West and Lillian Ross. Moreover, *In Cold Blood*'s objectivity is more apparent than real, since the material Capote draws from has been heightened, muted, and selected in many ways, subjected to his aesthetic intelligence. The *New Yorker* style of objective reportage clearly was an influence on the book; another may have been Capote's experience as a scenarist. His use of "intense close-ups, flashbacks, traveling shots, [and] background detail," as Stanley Kauffmann has observed, all belong to the "structural" method of the cinema.

A cinematic method is particularly noticeable in the earlier part of the work, where Capote cuts back and forth between the murderers and the victims as the knot tightens and their paths converge. It is the convergence of a mythic as well as a literal kind of two Americas—one firmly placed in the wheat belt of the Midwest, decent in its habits, secure in its bounty, if a little stiff in its consciousness of being near to God; the other aimless and adrift, powered by garish and fantastic dreams, dangerous in its potential for violence. The horrible irony of Capote's description of "Bonnie" Clutter suggests the ominousness of this section. "Trust in God sustained her," he writes, "and from time to time secular sources supplemented her faith in His forthcoming mercy." The account of the actual murders, suspensefully postponed until later in the work, is chilling in its gratuitous nature while at the same time, through a steady building of telling details, it has the force of a vast inevitability.

The slaughter of the Clutters is "gratuitous" insofar as it might well not have occurred, has nothing to do with them personally, and gains for the young men responsible nothing except a few dollars, a fugitive life, arrest, and execution. As "haves" and "have-nots" come together, as Smith's long pent-up rage against his father becomes projected onto Mr. Clutter, a lighted match explodes a powder keg. Contributing to this act of unreason is the standoff between Hickock and Smith, each having told lies about himself to the other; rather than surrender this "fiction" of himself, which would involve confronting the truth of his maimed and powerless life, Smith is driven to a senseless murder. The irrationality of the crime is complemented later by the irrationality implicit in the trial and execution, so that ultimately *In Cold Blood* deals with the pervasive power of irrationality.

The psychological interest of the book is heightened by Capote's drifting narrative and use of multiple "perceptors"—the Clutters themselves, Alvin Dewey, the Kansas Bureau of Investigation agent, and many of Holcomb's townspeople. Of overshadowing interest, however, is Perry Smith, who could, as Capote said, "step right out of one of my stories." A young dreamer and "incessant conceiver of voyages," he is at the same time a dwarfish child-man with short, crippled legs. A series of Capote's earlier characters stand behind him.

Holly Golightly, dreamer-misfit and child-woman, is a not-so-distant cousin. Yet in this work, Capote's sentimental temptation has been chastened by a rigorous actuality, and what results is an extraordinary portrait. Sensitive and sympathetic, Smith is yet guilty of heinous murders. His romantic escapism (he dreams of diving for treasure but cannot swim, imagines himself a famous tap dancer but has hopelessly maimed legs) becomes comprehensible in the light of his homeless, brutalized background, more bizarre than any fiction; his undoing is elaborately plausible.

In the book's final scene, reminiscent of the ending of *The Grass Harp*, Capote brings the memory of Nancy Clutter together with the memory of Smith—entangled in an innocence blighted by life; in this way, *In Cold Blood* becomes a somber meditation on the mysterious nature of the world and the ways of Providence. This questioning quality and lyric resonance were undoubtedly what Rebecca West had in mind in referring to *In Cold Blood* as "a grave and reverend book." It is a work in which realism and romance become one.

ANSWERED PRAYERS

After the publication of *In Cold Blood*, Capote produced no new major work. During this period, which included bouts of suicidal depression as well as serious physical illnesses, he continued to write for films and to write shorter pieces, while also supposedly at work on *Answered Prayers*. Of the four chapters originally published, Capote later decided that "Mojave" did not belong in the novel, being a self-contained short story written by the character P. B. Jones. With its drifting narrative, including flashbacks and a story within the story, it is extremely suggestive. Its theme is never directly stated, but its cumulative effect makes it clear that its concern is with illusion, particularly of those who love others and find their love betrayed. "La Côte Basque: 1965" is set at a fashionable restaurant on New York's East Side, where all the diners indulge in or are the subject of gossip. P. B. Jones lunches with Lady Ina Coolbirth, who, herself on the eve of divorce, tells stories of broken marriages, while at the next table Gloria Vanderbilt Cooper and Mrs. Walter Matthau tell similar tales. This mood piece closes at the end of the afternoon in an "atmosphere of luxurious exhaustion."

Jones himself is the focal figure in "Unspoiled Monsters," which details his career as an opportunistic writer and exploiter of others, exploitation and disillusion being the observed norm among the members of the international set. Unfortunately, even these few chapters reveal the depth to which Capote's writing had sunk. His "gossip column" approach simply reveals that Capote had lost the capability of producing anything original— he was merely telling thinly disguised tales out of school. Indeed, the publication of "La Côte Basque" alienated many of Capote's society friends. Its topicality also ensured that *Answered Prayers* would not have stood the test of time—or of the critics, for that matter— and probably that, more than any other reason, is why Capote never finished it.

SUMMER CROSSING

Two decades after Capote's death, in late 2004, a manuscript of his first work, *Summer Crossing*, was discovered and sold, along with other discovered materials, to Sotheby's auction house. Capote had left the handwritten manuscript behind when he moved away from a Brooklyn apartment, and the owner kept it. Capote had always told people that he had destroyed this early work, which he began writing in 1943. Alan Schwartz, Capote's literary trustee, was unsure whether he should have the novel published or not, but after conferring with other authors and Capote scholars, he decided that the work would help shed light on Capote's later work. *Summer Crossing* was finally published in 2005.

The novel has been called an earlier version of *Breakfast at Tiffany's*, with seventeen-year-old protagonist Grady McNeil a younger, rougher version of Holly Golightly. Rich and bored, the daughter of a former debutante and a businessman, Grady begins an affair with a World War II veteran who is working as a parking lot attendant while her parents are away in France. Soon Grady is pregnant, and the pair decide to get married, with disastrous results.

Capote excelled in a number of literary forms—as a memoirist, journalist, travel writer, dramatist, short-story writer, and novelist. The body of his work is comparatively small, and it has neither the social range nor the concern with ideas of the work of certain of his contemporaries, but it is inimitable writing of great distinction. Capote is a brilliant and iridescent stylist, and his concern with craft belongs to that line of American writers that includes Henry James, Edith Wharton, Willa Cather, and F. Scott Fitzgerald. Like Fitzgerald particularly, whose romantic themes and classical form he shares, Capote has the abiding interest of sensibility.

Robert Emmet Long
Updated by Julie M. Elliott

OTHER MAJOR WORKS

SHORT FICTION: *A Tree of Night, and Other Stories*, 1949; *One Christmas*, 1983; *I Remember Grandpa: A Story*, 1986; *The Complete Collected Stories of Truman Capote*, 2004.

PLAYS: *The Grass Harp: A Play*, pr., pb. 1952 (adaptation of his novel); *House of Flowers*, pr. 1954 (with Harold Arlen).

SCREENPLAYS: *Beat the Devil*, 1954 (with John Huston); *The Innocents*, 1961.

NONFICTION: *Local Color*, 1950; *The Muses Are Heard*, 1956; *Observations*, 1959 (with Richard Avedon); *The Dogs Bark: Public People and Private Places*, 1973; *Portraits and Observations: The Essays of Truman Capote*, 2007.

MISCELLANEOUS: *Selected Writings*, 1963; *Trilogy: An Experiment in Multimedia*, 1969 (with Eleanor Perry and Frank Perry); *Music for Chameleons*, 1980; *A Capote Reader*, 1987; *Too Brief a Treat: The Letters of Truman Capote*, 2004 (Gerald Clarke, editor).

BIBLIOGRAPHY

Bloom, Harold, ed. *Truman Capote*. Philadelphia: Chelsea House, 2003. Collection of critical essays discusses Capote's most important works. Includes an informative editor's introduction, a brief biography, and a chronology.

Clarke, Gerald. *Capote: A Biography*. New York: Simon & Schuster, 1988. Arguably the definitive biographical work on Capote, this lengthy text covers all the ups and downs of his career. Contains copious references and an index.

Dunphy, Jack. *"Dear Genius": A Memoir of My Life with Truman Capote*. New York: McGraw-Hill, 1989. Written by Capote's friend and close companion of more than thirty years and a novelist in his own right. Details the disintegration of Capote's life as a result of drugs and alcohol. Includes index.

Grobel, Lawrence. *Conversations with Capote*. 1985. Reprint. New York: Da Capo Press, 2000. Biographical work draws on in-depth interviews with Capote. Topics covered include events of the author's childhood and his eventual fall from society's good graces. Chapter 4, "Writing," discusses Capote's writing career and the authors he believed had the greatest influence on him.

Inge, M. Thomas, ed. *Truman Capote: Conversations*. Jackson: University Press of Mississippi, 1987. Collection of interviews with Capote includes the work of interviewers ranging from Gloria Steinem to George Plimpton to Capote himself, in a section called "Self-Portrait."

Long, Robert Emmet. *Truman Capote, Enfant Terrible*. New York: Continuum, 2008. Brief work combines biographical information and literary criticism. Examines Capote's novels, screenplays, and nonfiction, and discusses how the southern gothic elements of his early work relate to his later work.

Plimpton, George. *Truman Capote: In Which Various Friends, Enemies, Acquaintances, and Detractors Recall His Turbulent Career*. New York: Doubleday, 1997. Oral biography based on interviews provides dramatic, primary information, but readers would do well to check this information against more reliable biographies, such as that by Gerald Clarke. Includes a chronology of Capote's life.

Rudisill, Marie, with James C. Simmons. *The Southern Haunting of Truman Capote*. Nashville, Tenn.: Cumberland House, 2000. Brief volume by Capote's aunt provides some insight into the events in the author's life that inspired the origins of four of his early works: *A Christmas Memory*, *The Grass Harp*, "Children on Their Birthdays," and *Other Voices, Other Rooms*.

Windham, Donald. *Lost Friendships: A Memoir of Truman Capote, Tennessee Williams, and Others*. New York: William Morrow, 1987. A friend of the major literary lights of the 1950's and 1960's, as well as a novelist himself, Windham dedicates the first half of *Lost Friendships* to his relationship with Capote and its subsequent decline.

PETER CAREY

Born: Bacchus Marsh, Victoria, Australia; May 7, 1943

Also known as: Peter Philip Carey

PRINCIPAL LONG FICTION

Bliss, 1981
Illywhacker, 1985
Oscar and Lucinda, 1988
The Tax Inspector, 1991
The Unusual Life of Tristan Smith, 1994
The Big Bazoohley, 1995
Jack Maggs, 1997
True History of the Kelly Gang, 2000
My Life as a Fake, 2003
Theft: A Love Story, 2006
His Illegal Self, 2008

OTHER LITERARY FORMS

Peter Carey began his writing career as a short-story writer, and he has a number of collections of stories to his credit, including *The Fat Man in History, and Other Stories* (1981). He also has written one book for children, the novel *The Big Bazoohley*, and a film script. Several of his books have been made into films, most successfully *Bliss* and *Oscar and Lucinda*. He has written personal accounts of various episodes in his life, including *Wrong About Japan: A Father's Journey with His Son* (2005).

ACHIEVEMENTS

Peter Carey is one of the best-known Australian novelists of the late twentieth and early twenty-first centuries. He helped to bring international attention to the

Australian novel, and he is widely acknowledged for his search for a specifically "Australian" identity through his work. The Booker Prize committee, in particular, has recognized this search.

Carey has an impressive array of awards to his credit, both Australian and international. Together with the South African writer J. M. Coetzee, he is the only person to have won the Booker Prize twice (in 1988 for *Oscar and Lucinda* and in 2001 for *True History of the Kelly Gang*). He won the 2007 Booker International Prize and was short-listed for the 2008 Best of the Booker competition for *Oscar and Lucinda*. *True History of the Kelly Gang* and *Jack Maggs* won the Commonwealth Writers' Prize, and *Jack Maggs* also won the James Tait Black Memorial Prize for fiction.

Among Australian prizes, Carey won the Miles Franklin Award for *Bliss*, *Oscar and Lucinda*, and *Jack Maggs*. For *Illywhacker*, he won a Ditmar Award for the best Australian science-fiction novel and a Victorian Premier's Literary Award—the Vance Palmer Prize for Fiction; *Illywhacker* was short-listed for the World Fantasy Award for Best Novel. Carey also received three honorary degrees.

BIOGRAPHY

Peter Carey was born May 7, 1943, in the small town of Bacchus Marsh in Victoria, Australia, about thirty miles from the state capital of Melbourne. His parents ran a car-sales franchise for the American company General Motors. After attending the local elementary school, Carey progressed to a prestigious boarding school called Geelong Grammar, which he attended from 1954 to 1960. After graduating from Geelong he entered Monash University, Melbourne, with the intention of majoring in zoology and chemistry. After one year at Monash, however, he dropped out after surviving a serious car accident and after losing interest in his studies.

Carey began a career in advertising from 1962, which coincided with his involvement in protests against the Vietnam War. In 1964, he married Leigh Weetman, a marriage that lasted until 1970. Previously uninterested in literature, he began to read heavily in the English and modern European classics. He also began writing short stories, both science fiction and surrealist, and by 1967 had also attempted three novels, all without success. He left Australia in 1968, traveled throughout Asia and Europe, and finished up in London. He returned to Australia in 1970, and by this time, his short stories were being published in magazines and newspapers.

In 1974, still working in advertising, Carey moved to Sydney; in 1976, he moved north to Queensland, where he became involved in a hippie community. It was while living in this community that he wrote his first published novel, *Bliss*, and more short stories. By 1980, he had moved back to Sydney and cofounded an advertising agency. At the age of thirty-eight, he was finally a published novelist. His big breakthrough as a writer, however, came in 1985 with his novel *Illywhacker*. Its Australian themes drew instant acclaim and garnered several prizes. Also in 1985, he married Alison Summers, a theater director.

After the success of his next novel, *Oscar and Lucinda*, in 1988, Carey decided to sell his advertising business and move to New York City, where he continued to write books with Australian themes. He divorced Summers, his second failed marriage. He started teaching creative writing and, in 2003, was appointed director of the graduate creative-writing program at Hunter College, City University of New York.

ANALYSIS

In some ways, Peter Carey is difficult to categorize as a novelist. He has acknowledged the influence of William Faulkner and Gabriel García Márquez, but he shows many features of the postmodern novel in his work—constant shifting of plots, self-consciousness in producing text, and a refusal to construct consistent characters or endings. However, he is also a typical Australian storyteller, much like novelists Neville Shute, Ivan Southall, Morris West, and Thomas Keneally, whose good yarns are spun by larger-than-life narrators in highly colloquial speech that is full of expletives and tales of hard living. Carey's writing, which attempts to reconstruct Australian consciousness of its history in a highly ironic, even parodic way, shows a postcolonial focus as well. His work, which traces the postcolonial cultural shift from Europe to America, has been compared to that of writers Salman Rushdie and Michael Ondaatje.

Carey's first novel, *Bliss*, is typical of a number of his later novels for being somewhat autobiographical. In *Bliss*, his work in the advertising industry forms the basis for the life of his main character, an advertising executive who has various out-of-body experiences. The novel is full of zany black humor and ends up as a story of communal living, which Carey experienced as well. The novel was followed by *Illywhacker* and *Oscar and Lucinda*, both novels cementing his place as a major new talent.

The Tax Inspector deals with government bureaucracy, one of Carey's best comedic inspirations. *Jack Maggs* is a sort of sequel to Charles Dickens's *Great Expectations* (1860-1861, serial; 1861, book). In the Dickens novel, Magwitch goes off to Australia as a convict, then returns illegally to meet his death. In *Oscar and Lucinda*, Carey rewrites an old plot, bringing Magwitch back to England to have more time with his adoptive son Henry Phipps and Victorian novelist Titus Oates. Like Dickens, Carey uses the criminal underworld as an ironic social and cultural perspective. The criminal underworld in Australia is exposed again in *True History of the Kelly Gang*, a story not only of rampant police corruption but also of crime among the lower classes.

My Life as a Fake takes another Carey theme, that of trickery and charlatanism, and weaves a story from a real Australian hoax of the 1940's. *Theft, a Love Story*, continues this theme, this time using the subgenre of the boozy artist, made famous by namesake Joyce Cary's Gully Jimson in *From the Horse's Mouth* (1944). Carey also weaves a plot around its hero, Butch, and his mentally disabled brother, using the latter as one of the narrators. The novel also includes jokes about the modern commercial art world.

ILLYWHACKER

The title of Carey's second novel, *Illywhacker*, is Australian slang, suggesting a specifically Australian novel. The word defines not only the novel's narrator but also the book's narrative and genre. An "illywhacker" is a trickster, especially the kind found at fairgrounds; they are like the con artists who sell fake jewelry and medicine.

The novel's opening is a trick; it undermines its own narrative reliability by proclaiming that the narrator can tell lies yet also proclaiming that his "authentic" age is

Peter Carey. (© Miriam Berkley)

139. With these claims, Carey is playing with the "truth" of fiction, leading critics to categorize the novel as metafiction. The novel draws attention to itself, its untruthfulness, at the same time that it examines the place of story and story-telling in Australian culture.

Illywhacker also can be categorized as postcolonial fiction because it covers the period 1896 to the 1980's, a time when Australians were seeking a national history and identity after colonialism. The novel ranges from Australia's wilderness and nomad culture to city dwelling; it covers all aspects of Australian history and culture in that period, but how reliably? Is the character Herbert Badgery the prototypical Australian, or is he a marginalized but harmless eccentric?

Badgery finds it difficult to know the border between truth and fantasy. He claims to have been an aviator and a car salesman, as well as a charlatan and seducer. His eccentricities are reflected in the people he meets and whose voices he sometimes adopts. He has a son, Charley, whose story is also covered in this massive and sprawling picaresque tale, divided into three parts. (Each part includes "minichapters"; eighty-six in the first part, sixty-one in the other two.)

OSCAR AND LUCINDA

Like *Illywhacker*, *Oscar and Lucinda* is a postcolonial endeavor, but focused on one moment of Australian history. Although apparently entirely fictional, the book starts off by lifting the early life of an actual Victorian, Edmund Gosse, whose *Father and Son* (1907) is a classic of English autobiography. Like Gosse, Oscar Hopkins is brought up in a strict Brethren family. Both fathers are scientists who refuse to accept evolutionary theory. However, while Gosse went on to become a respected literary figure in Victorian England, Oscar reacts to his father's church by deciding to train as an Anglican clergyman. He finds that he has an intuitive power to guess winning horses at the races, and he uses his winnings to pay his way through college.

On his emigration to Australia, Oscar meets a young heiress, Lucinda Leplastrier, who also has a predilection for gambling. Her wealth came from the donations of a well-wisher, and she decides to use the money in Sydney to buy a glassworks and show her independence. However, her overseer, Arthur Phelps, has to negotiate for her in a male-dominated colony. Having earlier met the designer of the Crystal Palace at London's Great Exhibition, she conceives the daring project of a crystal church, to be towed upriver to a remote backwoods location. She bets Oscar that he cannot get the crystal structure there. Ultimately, the structure's frame buckles and the church slips into the river. In the end, the incipient love of Oscar and Lucinda remains unfulfilled.

The novel can be read at many different levels: as a postcolonial exploration of the early colony, as a study of Victorian aesthetics and practicality, as an early venture into feminism, or most likely, as a daring adventure of two unlikely protagonists, attempting to achieve a dream against impossible odds—a true pioneering venture.

TRUE HISTORY OF THE KELLY GANG

Ned Kelly, the main protagonist of the *True History of the Kelly Gang*, is Australia's equivalent of Robin Hood, Billy the Kid, and Bonnie and Clyde. Carey constructs for Ned an apparent autobiography written hastily while on the run, based on the style of the one extant letter by Kelly that survives in real life. The novel lacks proper punctuation, is grammatically poor, is full of self-censored expletives, and is framed by an apparent contemporary editor who supposedly saved the precious manuscripts for posterity. The novel is divided into thirteen sections, some chapters being no more than one page long.

The plot is based on real-life accounts, but Carey invented a wife and daughter. The novel recounts Carey's gaining bush survival skills, his early encounters with the law, his bank robberies, and his distribution of money to the immigrant poor. The tale stops on Kelly's final shootout and capture, shortly before his trial and hanging in Melbourne in 1880.

At one level the novel reconstructs the rough-and-ready pioneer life of Australia in the early colonial period, where justice was oppressive and approximate, and bush skills were essential to survival. At this time, Australia is still little more than a penal colony, and the dirt-poor Irish immigrants are treated as second-class citizens. However, on another level, the novel examines why Australia needs the legend of Ned Kelly and, indeed, why any culture needs stories of fighting against injustice and oppression by essentially "men of the soil" who have gut feelings about what is right and what is wrong.

HIS ILLEGAL SELF

Carey's later novels are perhaps less ambitious, yet they become more personal. In *His Illegal Self*, Carey revisits his own experiences with hippies in Queensland, but he does so with more of an American perspective, comparing the dangerous and subversive developments in the American post-hippie movement to the harmless counterculture of the Australian hippies. Both movements have a sense of community, but the American hippie movement is, in essence, based on wealth and power and prone to violence. The Australian hippie movement, however, is supportive and nurturing.

The narrative is told from the perspective of a small boy named Che, or Jay, who is the son of wealthy American hippies who desert him. Che is brought up by his rich grandmother. On a search for his parents, he is delivered into the hands of a naïve babysitter, Anna, whom Che first believes is his mother. The abortive search for Che's parents turns into a kidnapping, and Che and Anna end up in Australia. He later becomes disillusioned after finding that Anna is not his mother and that his parents have no interest in him. Che forms a new family with the Australian hippies, but hints in the book suggest a troubled future for Che because of his early traumas. Carey's judgment on the hippie movement suggests the movement was emotionally damaging to its participants, that it was misguided in believing in the "fallenness" of human nature.

David Barratt

OTHER MAJOR WORKS

SHORT FICTION: *The Fat Man in History*, 1974; *War Crimes*, 1979; *The Fat Man in History, and Other Stories*, 1981; *Collected Stories*, 1995.

SCREENPLAYS: *Bliss*, 1985 (adaptation of his novel; with Ray Lawrence).

NONFICTION: *A Letter to Our Son*, 1994; *Thirty Days in Sydney: A Wildly Distorted Account*, 2001; *Wrong About Japan: A Father's Journey with His Son*, 2005.

BIBLIOGRAPHY

Hassell, Anthony J. *Dancing on Hot Macadam: Peter Carey's Fiction*. Brisbane: University of Queensland Press, 1994. One of the Studies in Australian Literature series, this book deals primarily with Carey's early work on Australian history and identity.

Huggan, Graham. *Peter Carey*. New York: Oxford University Press, 1996. Huggan, a leading writer on Australian literature, examines Carey's storytelling abilities and his power to disturb through his storytelling.

Krassnitzer, Hermione. *Aspects of Narration in Peter Carey's Novels: Deconstructing Colonialism*. Lewiston, Pa.: Edwin Mellen Press, 1995. Part of the Salzburg Studies in Literature series, this work examines both Carey's postcolonialism and postmodernism.

Woodcock, Bruce. *Peter Carey*. 1996. Rev. ed. New York: Manchester University Press, 2003. This revised study considers Carey an entertainer as well as a disturbing postcolonial writer.

ALEJO CARPENTIER

Born: Havana, Cuba; December 26, 1904
Died: Paris, France; April 24, 1980
Also known as: Alejo Valmont Carpentier

PRINCIPAL LONG FICTION

¡Ecué-Yamba-O! Historia Afro-Cubana, 1933
El reino de este mundo, 1949 (*The Kingdom of This World*, 1957)
Los pasos perdidos, 1953 (*The Lost Steps*, 1956)
El acoso, 1956 (*Manhunt*, 1959)
El siglo de las luces, 1962 (*Explosion in a Cathedral*, 1963)
El derecho de asilo, 1972
Concierto barroco, 1974 (*Concert Baroque*, 1976)
El recurso del método, 1974 (*Reasons of State*, 1976)
La consagración de la primavera, 1978

El arpa y la sombra, 1979 (*The Harp and the Shadow*, 1990)

OTHER LITERARY FORMS

Early in his career, Alejo Carpentier (kahr-pehn-TYAYR) published two volumes of poetry: *Dos poemas afro-cubanos* (1930) and, in French, *Poèmes des Antilles* (1931). He did not publish poetry after the early 1930's, though some of his poems, particularly one or two in French, were quite good. Two of his poems from the Afro-Cuban period have been widely anthologized. Carpentier's nonfiction works include *La música en Cuba* (1946; *Music in Cuba*, 2001), *Tientos y diferencias* (1964), and *La novela latinoamericana en vísperas del nuevo siglo, y otros ensayos* (1981). *Music in Cuba* is a beautiful book, combining Carpentier's mastery as a narrator with a supple descriptive style. His essays in *Tientos y diferencias* were very influential among critics of the Latin American novel. Carpentier was known both as a writer and as a musicologist. He wrote the scenario for several Afro-Cuban ballets, most notably *El milagro de Anaquillé* (1928), and innumerable journalistic pieces on music and literature. From 1950 to 1959, he wrote a column on these topics for *El nacional* in Caracas, Venezuela. Carpentier's short fiction deals with very large topics and spans of time rather than characters caught in daily existence—about great issues such as causality in history. *Guerra del tiempo* (1958; *War of Time*, 1970) is one of the best-known collections of short stories in Latin America as well as around the world.

ACHIEVEMENTS

It can be safely said that Alejo Carpentier is the father of today's Latin American fiction. All major Latin American novelists since the mid-twentieth century owe a great debt to him, and many, from Gabriel García Márquez to Carlos Fuentes, have acknowledged that debt. Carpentier had to pay out of his own pocket for the publication of his two early masterpieces, *The Kingdom of This World* and *The Lost Steps*, whereas today's Latin American writers, particularly García Márquez, Fuentes, and Mario Vargas Llosa, can command enormous fees for their work. This they owe to Carpentier, who in 1958 was hailed as a master deserving of the Nobel Prize by a critic for *The New York Times* when most English-language readers had not heard of a single Latin American author.

Carpentier's major achievement is to have made Latin American history the object of experimental fiction. Before *The Kingdom of This World*, major works of fiction had been produced in Latin America, as well as very important books of history, but no major prose writer had ventured to use Latin American history as the object of daring experimentation. Jorge Luis Borges had produced great short-story collections, such as *Historia universal de la infamia* (1935; *A Universal History of Infamy*, 1972) and above all *Ficciones, 1935-1944* (1944; English translation, 1962), and Miguel Ángel Asturias had published, to great acclaim, his *Leyendas de Guatemala* (1930; legends of Guatemala), based on Mayan myths from his native Guatemala. There had also been great novelists of the pampa, such as Ricardo Güiraldes; of the Mexican Revolution, such as Mariano Azuela; and

of the Venezuelan plain, such as Rómulo Gallegos. Carpentier managed to bring together the interests of the regionalist writers (Asturias, Güiraldes, Azuela) with Borges's penchant for fictional games. The admixture is what has come to be known as Magical Realism, or the description of "marvelous American reality."

Unlike writers such as Asturias, who in their fiction turned to Mayan or other indigenous Latin American myths, Carpentier focused his attention on the folklore of his native Caribbean, which meant that of Africa. Caribbean history has been shaped by slavery, which provided the workforce for the sugar industry. Several major African religions took root in the Caribbean, influencing art, music, and literature in the region. This was recognized by a group of artists who in the 1920's founded what came to be known as the Afro-Antillean movement; Carpentier was one of the movement's founders and promoters. He was originally interested in ritualistic practices and, above all, in Afro-Cuban music. These interests, however, led him to read all he could find about the history of Africans in the New World and eventually led him to their greatest political achievement, the Haitian Revolution at the end of the eighteenth century. Carpentier discovered that the Haitian Revolution, which toppled the French colonial regime and instituted a black monarchy and later a republic, was the origin of modern Caribbean history. He tells the story of this revolution in his influential *The Kingdom of This World*, one of the great novels of the century in any language.

Carpentier saw that Haitian history, particularly as manifested in the events of the Revolution, was ripe with incredible happenings, if viewed from a purely European perspective. The fusion of African and French customs on the island made for a very discordant and rich mixture that could not be described with the narrative techniques of the conventional novel. Time seemed to have a different rhythm. Events repeated themselves or were anticipated by apparently chance happenings. Cause and effect seemed to obey a different set of rules. It is the description of such bizarre events and sequels of events that has come to be known as Magical Realism. The term goes back to early twentieth century art, but its conception by Carpentier was influenced mainly by the Surrealists, with whom Carpentier had developed a close relationship in Paris in the late 1920's and early 1930's.

The Kingdom of This World and the stories later collected in *War of Time* all deal with the problem of time— that is to say, with its representation in fiction. In the novel, time appears as a series of repetitions. History is a tissue of events connected not by causal links but by numerological and metaphoric connections. In one of the most widely anthologized stories from *War of Time*, "Viaje a la Semilla" ("Journey Back to the Source"), time runs backward, from the protagonist's death to his return to the womb. In another, "Semejante a la Noche" ("Like the Night"), the same incident is repeated in six different historical moments that are separated by centuries.

It is this sort of experimentation that makes possible novels such as García Márquez's widely acclaimed *Cien años de soledad* (1967; *One Hundred Years of Solitude*, 1970) and Fuentes's *Terra nostra* (1975; English translation, 1976). In short, Carpentier's experiments with fiction and Latin American history led to what has been termed the "boom" of the Latin American novel. More than all the prizes that he won (notably the Cervantes Prize in Spain), Carpentier's most enduring achievement is to have made possible experimentation in Latin American fiction dealing with Latin American history. This brought about an entirely new view of Latin America by its own artists.

BIOGRAPHY

Alejo Valmont Carpentier was born in Havana, Cuba, in 1904. His parents had immigrated to Cuba two years before. His father was a French architect, and his mother was of Russian origin. Carpentier, whose first language was French (he retained throughout his life a French accent in Spanish), was sent to the best schools in Havana. While in his early teens, he and his parents made a very long trip to Europe, first traveling to Russia to claim an inheritance and later spending a good deal of time in Paris. In the French capital, Carpentier attended high school and began to acquire what was to become his awesome musical erudition. Back in Cuba, Carpentier finished his sec-

ondary education and registered at the university. He wanted to be an architect, like his father, but two events prevented his finishing his university studies. First, his father left home and was never heard from again, which forced Carpentier to earn a living for himself and his mother. Second, classes at the university were frequently canceled because of political turmoil.

Carpentier left school altogether and joined the revolutionary students who were fighting against Gerardo Machado y Morales, a dictator supported by the United States. Carpentier worked as a journalist and was instrumental in founding the Afro-Cuban movement, which hailed Cuba's African heritage. Afro-Cubanism wanted to create a new aesthetic based on Afro-Cuban folklore, and, as a political movement, championed the cause of the exploited black workers. Carpentier was jailed briefly in early 1928; a few months later, he managed to

Alejo Carpentier. (Prensa Latina/Archive Photos)

escape to France, where he was protected by his friend, the Surrealist poet Robert Desnos.

Between 1928 and 1930, Carpentier was associated with the influential Surrealist movement, and, in 1930, he participated in one of the squabbles that split the group. He had learned from Surrealism that his desire to look at things from a non-European perspective, something he had sought through Afro-Cubanism, was a major force in all avant-garde aesthetics. It became his major preoccupation as an artist. Translated into his own terms, the issue was how to look at reality with Latin American eyes. In France, he met other Latin American artists engaged in the same quest: the Cuban painter Wifredo Lam, the Guatemalan novelist Miguel Ángel Asturias, the Venezuelan novelist Arturo Uslar Pietri, and the Cuban folklorist Lydia Cabrera. He learned from all of them, as well as from James Joyce, the great Irish writer living in Paris at the time, who was plumbing the English language in search of a new way of expressing the world. Marginality—Joyce from the British Empire, the Latin Americans from Europe in general—was the bond.

Carpentier made a living in Paris with radio work, becoming an expert on radio broadcasting and advertising; these two activities became his source of income for many years thereafter. In Paris, he needed them, for he married very shortly after settling in that city. His wife, who was Swiss, died soon of tuberculosis, and Carpentier married a Frenchwoman who accompanied him back to Cuba in 1939, on the eve of World War II.

In Cuba, Carpentier was known mainly as a journalist, for he had also made a living by writing articles about Europe for *Carteles*, a Cuban weekly magazine of which Carpentier had been a founding editor at the age of nineteen. His articles on the new European art had made him rather well known, but not really as a writer. The fact is that by 1939, when he returned to Havana, Carpentier had published only *¡Ecué-Yamba-O!*, an unsuccessful novel about blacks in Cuba.

Between 1939 and 1945, when he again left Cuba, Carpentier made decisions that changed his life. First, he divorced his French wife and married a Cuban woman from a well-to-do family. This new wife, Lilia Esteban Hierro, to whom he dedicated every book he wrote after 1939, remained with him until his death. Second, he im-

mersed himself in the history of the Caribbean, in search of the origins of Cuban music. This research led to his experiments in fiction, which in turn led to his first great novel, *The Kingdom of This World*. First, however, he published a beautiful history of Cuban music, *Music in Cuba*, a book that is the key to an understanding of Carpentier's mature fiction. In it one sees for the first time the historian at work, culling from myriad written sources a history that does not fit the mold of European history. *The Kingdom of This World* and all the stories collected in *War of Time* issue from the research and experimentation carried out while Carpentier was writing *Music in Cuba*.

In the summer of 1945, Carpentier moved to Caracas. Carlos Frías, a friend from his years in Paris, had founded an advertising agency and offered Carpentier an important position. Carpentier was to remain in Venezuela until 1959, when he returned to Havana, after the triumph of the Cuban Revolution. In Caracas, Carpentier worked not only in advertising but also as a journalist, writing an almost daily column on literature and music for *El nacional*; he also gave lectures at the university and devoted himself with great discipline to his fiction. In Caracas, he completed *The Lost Steps*, *Manhunt*, and *Explosion in a Cathedral* and also wrote much of *Concert Baroque* and *Reasons of State*. Although all of these novels are of the highest caliber, the most important of them is *The Lost Steps*.

The Lost Steps grew out of two trips that Carpentier undertook to the jungles of Venezuela. During the summer of 1948, he journeyed to the region bordering Venezuela and British Guiana, nearly on the frontier with Brazil. In the summer of the next year, he traveled up the Orinoco River toward the Colombian border. These voyages, and his work as an advertising executive in Caracas, provide the biographical background of *The Lost Steps*.

Carpentier returned to Havana in the summer of 1959. The Cuban Revolution seemed to be the fulfillment of all of his dreams as a young artist and political activist. He was also in the business of organizing book festivals to sell, at popular prices, books by Latin American authors. When the Revolution turned Socialist, the business was nationalized and Carpentier was named head of the newly formed State Publishing House. He remained in that post until 1968, when he was sent to Paris as cultural attaché to the Cuban cultural delegation in that city. He lived in Paris until his death in 1980, as an employee of the Cuban revolutionary government but also writing his last novels: *Reasons of State*, *Concert Baroque*, *La consagración de la primavera*, and *El arpa y la sombra*. He also traveled a great deal, lecturing widely. Carpentier gave a lecture at Yale University in the spring of 1979, a year before his death; it was his first trip to the United States since the early 1940's, when the Columbia Broadcasting System (CBS) had brought him to New York to offer him a job broadcasting to Latin America.

Carpentier's support of the Castro regime made him a controversial figure in the last two decades of his life. He never wavered in his allegiance, though his works are hardly those of a Marxist, with the exception of *La consagración de la primavera*, in which he turned doctrinaire. The novel was a failure. After his death in Paris on April 24, 1980, Carpentier's remains were returned to Cuba, where he was buried with great honors.

ANALYSIS

THE LOST STEPS

The Lost Steps, a novel written in the first person by a character much like Alejo Carpentier, is the story of modern man and his desire to leave civilization to find himself in the origins of history. The narrator-protagonist, a musicologist working for an advertising agency, agrees to travel up a large river in South America in search of primitive instruments that will verify his theory concerning the origins of music. He undertakes this task at the request of his old professor at the university. It is time for his vacation, so he accepts the job, in part to take advantage of the opportunity to travel at the expense of the university. He goes with Mouche, his mistress, while Ruth, his wife, who is an actor, remains behind in the large city in which they live (presumably New York, although no specific indications are given). Because the narrator-protagonist is originally from Latin America, his return means also a new encounter with the language of his childhood.

He and Mouche spend time first at a Latin American capital (very much like Caracas and Havana), where he begins to remember his childhood and longs for the past.

While they are at the capital, a revolution breaks out, forcing them to take refuge in the hotel where they are staying while bands of revolutionaries fight soldiers. The protagonist-narrator, who is recording all of these events in a diary, remembers World War II, in which he participated as a photographer. The evils of civilization appear more onerous, and he wishes to press on with his trip to the jungle. They finally make the necessary arrangements, traveling first by bus to a smaller city, and later by boat. Along the way, they encounter a native woman, Rosario, who winds up becoming the narrator-protagonist's mistress. Mouche, he discovers, is having a lesbian affair with a Canadian painter they have met. She returns to civilization, where presumably she belongs, while the narrator-protagonist continues on his journey. He has joined various other characters, most notably an adventurer who has founded a city. When they reach this city, which turns out to be a mere gathering of huts, the narrator-protagonist finds the instruments for which he has been looking. He also begins to compose music again, something he has not been able to do since he began to sell his time to the advertising agency. He needs paper in order to compose, however, and the founder of the city can furnish him with only a few notebooks that he treasures as volumes in which to record the laws of his new society.

In the meantime, Ruth has mounted a campaign to rescue her husband, thinking that he is lost in the jungle. A plane reaches Santa Mónica de los Venados, the city where he is living with Rosario, with whom he has fallen deeply in love, and he decides to return to procure the things that he needs—such as paper—but with the intention of coming back to stay. He is given a hero's welcome back in the city, and he sells his story to some newspapers. Eventually, without a job and wife (Ruth, having found out about Mouche and Rosario, has left him), he is forced to eke out a living writing jingles. He finally manages to return to the Latin American capital and makes his way back to the small river town whence he started on his trip to Santa Mónica. After much waiting, he finds someone to take him back up river, but they are unable to find the mark on a tree that indicated the secret channel through which Santa Mónica could be reached. The waters of the river have risen, obliterating the mark. The narrator-protagonist hears from a traveler that Rosario has married somebody else. Disillusioned with the idea of being able to return to the origins of history, to shed civilization, the narrator-protagonist realizes that he can look only toward the future, for he is condemned to time, to temporality.

The autobiographical elements of *The Lost Steps* are obvious. On a deeper level, however, one must take notice of how Carpentier is putting to a test the validity of his own experiments as an artist. Is it really possible to look at history from a perspective like that of someone belonging to nonhistorical cultures? In other words, do the ritualistic repetitions of history present in *The Kingdom of This World* mean that Carpentier has really escaped the march of time as conceived by modernity, or is it merely an artist's trick? Are we really dependent on the past, on our origins, or are we only of the present?

Carpentier's exploration of these questions goes beyond simply writing about them through his autobiographical character. *The Lost Steps* itself, in its own constitution, has all of these issues embedded in it. The novel is written partially as if it were a diary, which allows the reader to reconstruct a very precise and suggestive time scheme. The novel begins in June and ends on December 31 of a year that can only be 1950. That is to say, the novel begins in midyear of the year that divides the century into two halves. There is also a compelling alternation of Monday and Sunday. Important events in the novel take place on those significant days, one marking the beginning of work, of action, the other a sort of hiatus, a gap. In reconstructing the time scheme of the novel, one is able to pick up an error made by the narrator-protagonist, who skips a Monday once he is deep in the jungle, as if he had finally left history—Monday meaning the beginning of history. This significant time scheme suggests to the reader that the narrator-protagonist is caught in a web of signs that are beyond his comprehension or control. Was he really ever able to be free?

Before *The Lost Steps*, Carpentier's fiction seemed to project onto nature the timeless world of nonhistorical civilizations. The African cosmogonies that led the blacks to action in Haiti had as their counterpart the periodicity of nature, its penchant for repetition and predictability and for abolishing change. *The Lost Steps* teaches Carpentier that he cannot make such an assumption, that history is moved not by natural forces but by the action

of men and women, by political activity and struggle. Whereas in his earlier novels great natural upheavals—such as hurricanes—conspired with history, in his later works history as political action prevails.

REASONS OF STATE

This change is evident in *Reasons of State*, Carpentier's "dictator novel." This book appeared at about the same time as two other novels with the same theme: Augusto Roa Bastos's *Yo, el Supremo* (1974; *I the Supreme*, 1986) and García Márquez's *El otoño del patriarca* (1975; *The Autumn of the Patriarch*, 1975). All three novels have as protagonist a Latin American dictator, and all deal with the issue of political power, democracy, and the Latin American tradition. Carpentier's dictator, the First Magistrate, is a composite figure, incorporating characteristics of Manuel Estrada Cabrera, Rafael Trujillo, Fulgencio Batista y Zaldívar, and Machado y Morales. He is, however—or pretends to be—more cultivated than these personages. The First Magistrate spends half of his life in Paris, where he is courted by venal academics and writers in debt. At home he is ruthless in suppressing the opposition, but abroad he wants to project an image of tolerance.

The novel, like all of Carpentier's fictions, is an experiment with time. Recognizable events date the beginning of the action late in the second decade of the twentieth century. It is easy to follow a historical chronology up to about 1927. From there on, there are leaps forward in time, until the finish in 1972, at the dictator's tomb in Paris. He has been defeated by the Student, a revolutionary who looms as the future of Latin America. *Reasons of State* is a comic novel that pokes fun at Latin American dictators and their penchant for extravagant expenditures, hollow rhetoric, and brutal ways.

LA CONSAGRACIÓN DE LA PRIMAVERA

In *La consagración de la primavera* (the consecration of spring), Carpentier's turn to more political fiction failed him. The novel is a rewrite of *The Lost Steps*, but it is cumbersome and doctrinaire. It seems to have been written with the purpose of writing the novel of the Cuban Revolution. The main protagonist is a character much like Carpentier who participates in or is touched by the major political upheavals of his time. He winds up in Cuba, fighting for the Revolution against the invasion at the Bay of Pigs. This character is an architect (architecture, one recalls, is a career Carpentier could have pursued). Another protagonist is a composer. The background of the Spanish Civil War, with which the novel begins, sets the tone: It is a novel about bourgeois intellectuals who feel deeply the political causes of their times and wish to join the Revolution. Time is seen in the novel as a continuum: The Russian Revolution leads to the Spanish Civil War, which, in turn, leads to the Cuban Revolution. The novel is thinly veiled autobiography. Carpentier's dearest wish was to have his own time, the time of his life, become enmeshed with that of history, a history seen as the progression to freedom brought about by revolution.

Roberto González Echevarría

OTHER MAJOR WORKS

SHORT FICTION: *Guerra del tiempo*, 1958 (*War of Time*, 1970).

POETRY: *Dos poemas afro-cubanos*, 1930; *Poèmes des Antilles*, 1931.

NONFICTION: *La música en Cuba*, 1946 (*Music in Cuba*, 2001); *Tientos y diferencias*, 1964; *Afirmación literaria latinoamericana*, 1978; *La novela latinoamericana en vísperas del nuevo siglo, y otros ensayos*, 1981; *Conversaciones con Alejo Carpentier*, 1998.

MISCELLANEOUS: *El milagro de Anaquillé*, 1928 (ballet scenario); *Obras completas de Alejo Carpentier*, 1983-1990 (14 volumes).

BIBLIOGRAPHY

Adams, M. Ian. *Three Authors of Alienation: Bombal, Onetti, Carpentier*. Austin: University of Texas Press, 1975. Examines alienation as a literary theme in the works of María Luisa Bombal, Juan Carlos Onetti, and Carpentier, each of whom modifies traditional literary forms to present different aspects of the theme. Section devoted to Carpentier is subtitled "Alienation, Culture, Myth, and 'Marvelous Reality.'" Includes select bibliography.

Brotherston, Gordon. *The Emergence of the Latin American Novel*. New York: Cambridge University Press, 1977. Intended as an introduction to the Latin American novel, particularly from the 1950's to the 1970's, this is a scholarly work that is also accessible to the general reader. The chapter on Carpentier discusses the historical, cultural, and mythic dimensions of the author's work. Contains a general bibliography of secondary works on Latin American literature as well as a list of works by and on the major authors mentioned in the text.

Cox, Timothy J. *Postmodern Tales of Slavery in the Americas: From Alejo Carpentier to Charles Johnson*. New York: Garland, 2001. Analyzes seven works of twentieth century fiction about slavery from a postmodern perspective, describing their uses of irony, narrative structure, and other features. Includes an examination of Carpentier's *The Kingdom of This World*.

Figueredo, Danilo H. "Beyond the Boom: García Márquez and the Other Latin American Novelists." *Wilson Library Bulletin* 69 (February, 1995): 36-40. Notes that although Gabriel García Márquez is the most famous Latin American novelist, many of his predecessors and contemporaries, such as Jorge Luis Borges, Juan Rulfo, and Carpentier, refined belles lettres and invented a literature that did not wish to duplicate reality; notes that Borges, Rulfo, and Carpentier sought universality and employed experimental literary techniques.

González Echevarría, Roberto. *Alejo Carpentier: The Pilgrim at Home*. Rev. ed. Austin: University Press of Texas, 1990. Good introduction to Carpentier's works presents a sustained consideration of their overall significance, both within the field of Latin American literature and in the broader context of contemporary literature. Addresses the basic questions posed by Carpentier's fiction as well as the larger theoretical questions about literary modernity and history. Includes bibliography of primary works and select bibliography of secondary works.

Shaw, Donald L. *Alejo Carpentier*. Boston: Twayne, 1985. Critical overview contains chapters on Carpentier's apprenticeship, his discovery of the "marvelous real," his handling of time and circularity, his fiction about the Antilles, his explorations of politics, and his last works. Includes chronology, notes, and annotated bibliography.

Souza, Raymond D. *Major Cuban Novelists: Innovation and Tradition*. Columbia: University of Missouri Press, 1976. Critical study traces the development of the Cuban novel in the nineteenth and twentieth centuries. Carpentier's work is discussed in the chapter "Alejo Carpentier's Timeless History."

Unruh, Vicky. "The Performing Spectator in Alejo Carpentier's Fictional World." *Hispanic Review* 66 (Winter, 1998): 57-77. Argues that Carpentier uses the concept of performance to explore subjectivity and identity, and that he was interested in performance because of his interest in switching identities. Asserts that his theater activity is a key to understanding his fictional world, in which spectatorship is an important way of experiencing the world.

Wakefield, Steve. *Carpentier's Baroque Fiction: Returning Medusa's Gaze*. Rochester, N.Y.: Tamesis, 2004. Traces the origins of Carpentier's literary style to his interest in Spanish baroque architecture and the Spanish Golden Age. Explains how Carpentier's historical fiction sought to create the ambience of this period through descriptions of architecture and the visual arts and parodies of Spanish Golden Age writers.

Webb, Barbara J. *Myth and History in Caribbean Fiction: Alejo Carpentier, Wilson Harris, and Edouard Glissant*. Amherst: University of Massachusetts Press, 1992. Comparative study of Caribbean literature includes a discussion of marvelous reality and mythological and historical elements in the works of the three writers. Provides analysis of *The Kingdom of This World*, *The Lost Steps*, *Explosion in a Cathedral*, and *Concert Baroque*.

LEWIS CARROLL
Charles Lutwidge Dodgson

Born: Daresbury, Cheshire, England; January 27, 1832

Died: Guildford, Surrey, England; January 14, 1898

Also known as: Charles Lutwidge Dodgson

PRINCIPAL LONG FICTION

Alice's Adventures in Wonderland, 1865
Through the Looking-Glass and What Alice Found There, 1871
Sylvie and Bruno, 1889
Sylvie and Bruno Concluded, 1893
The Wasp in a Wig: The "Suppressed" Episode of "Through the Looking-Glass and What Alice Found There," 1977

OTHER LITERARY FORMS

Before and after writing his novels for children, Lewis Carroll published volumes in his primary vocation, mathematics: *A Syllabus of Plane Algebraical Geometry* (1860), *An Elementary Treatise on Determinants* (1867), *Curiosa Mathematica, Part I: A New Theory of Parallels* (1888), *Curiosa Mathematica, Part II: Pillow Problems Thought During Wakeful Hours* (1893), and *Symbolic Logic, Part I: Elementary* (1896). His gift for light verse, demonstrated in his novels, also led to four books of poems, with some duplication of content: *Phantasmagoria, and Other Poems* (1869), *The Hunting of the Snark: An Agony in Eight Fits* (1876), *Rhyme? and Reason?* (1883), and the posthumous *Three Sunsets and Other Poems* (1898). His literary and mathematical sides were fused in *A Tangled Tale* (1885), a series of mathematical word problems in the form of short stories, and *Euclid and His Modern Rivals* (1879), a closet drama in which Euclid is defended by various scholars and spirits.

ACHIEVEMENTS

In 1898, a few months after Lewis Carroll's death, the *Pall Mall Gazette* published a survey of the popularity of children's books, and the overwhelming front-runner was *Alice's Adventures in Wonderland*. Queen Victoria enjoyed *Alice's Adventures in Wonderland* so much that she asked Carroll to dedicate his next book to her (ironically, his next book, *An Elementary Treatise on*

Determinants, proved to be nothing like the whimsical adventure the queen had admired).

Carroll encouraged the stage versions of the Alice books that appeared in his lifetime, though he was dismayed at his lack of legal control over adaptations. The Alice books have been translated into dozens of languages and are quoted more often than any English work, after that of William Shakespeare. *Alice's Adventures in Wonderland* is noteworthy for more than its popularity, however; it was the first work of literature for children that did not have an overtly didactic or moralistic nature. In fact, Carroll parodied didactic children's works in verse, such as "You Are Old, Father William" in *Through the Looking-Glass and What Alice Found There*, and through characters such as the Duchess in *Alice's Adventures in Wonderland*. Writers as abstruse and complex as British philosopher Ludwig Wittgenstein and Irish novelist James Joyce were drawn to the deeper implications of Carroll's work, especially the lighthearted sense of play and the role of nonsense in human thought. The absurdist writers of the twentieth century saw Carroll as their prophet, and a few of his nonsense words, such as "Boojum," "Jabberwocky," and "chortle," have become seemingly permanent parts of the English language. His term for a particular method of coining compound words, "portmanteau," has since become a standard linguistic name for the process.

Lewis Carroll. (Library of Congress)

BIOGRAPHY

Charles Lutwidge Dodgson was the third of eleven children and the eldest son of the Reverend Charles Dodgson and Frances Jane Lutwidge. The younger Charles Dodgson was left-handed and spoke with a stutter, an affliction from which he would suffer his whole life. With eight younger siblings, he very early developed the knack of amusing children, an ability he would keep as an adult. For their amusement, he wrote and drew little magazines that demonstrated the whimsy later seen in his Alice books. Some of the verses in the Alice books received their first auditions in these family magazines.

At age twelve, Dodgson attended Richmond Grammar School, and the following year, the famous public school at Rugby. Nearly four years at Rugby, which he later recalled with displeasure, prepared him for Oxford University: He entered Christ Church College there on January 24, 1851. He distinguished himself in mathematics and classics, though difficulty with philosophy and history kept him in the lower third of his class. On December 18, 1854, he received his A.B. with first-class honors in mathematics. He stayed on at Christ Church as a tutor and lecturer. At this time his earliest stories and poems appeared in periodicals at Oxford and Whitby.

Early in 1856 Dodgson acquired his first camera, then a relatively rare and complicated device restricted to use by specialists. A large number of his photographs, mostly of young girls, survive, and one historian of photography has declared Dodgson the most outstanding child photographer of the nineteenth century. A month after he had purchased the camera, one young model, the four-year-old daughter of an Oxford dean, caught Dodgson's eye. Her name was Alice Liddell. Six years later he would extemporize, on a boating expedition, a story about Alice that was to become the famous Alice stories. However, until then, Dodgson's energies went into his vocations of mathematics and the clergy: He published his first book on mathematics in 1860, and he was ordained a deacon just before Christmas of 1861.

By February of 1863, Dodgson had committed to paper the story from the 1862 excursion with the Liddell sisters. He published it in 1865 (though it did not appear until 1866) as *Alice's Adventures in Wonderland*. Dodgson used the pseudonym Lewis Carroll for his publications, a name seemingly derived from the names Lutwidge and Charles. In 1867, Dodgson made the only voyage of his lifetime away from England, touring the Continent (mostly Russia). He had already begun his sequel to *Alice's Adventures in Wonderland*, which appeared near Christmas, 1871, as *Through the Looking-Glass and What Alice Found There*. When his father died in 1868, Dodgson moved his siblings to Guildford, and he moved into rooms at Tom Quad, Oxford, where he remained the rest of his life. In 1881 his income from writing was sufficient for him to resign his lectureship in mathematics, although he remained at Oxford. The following year he was elected curator of the Senior Common room, a post he held for ten years. He continued writing until his death in 1898, though he never equaled the success of the Alice books.

ANALYSIS

Lewis Carroll's first great contribution to children's literature is that he freed it from the heavy didacticism of previous children's books. The second is his legitimating of nonsense in children's literature, though in this claim he is preceded by fellow Victorian Edward Lear, whose *A Book of Nonsense* (1846) preceded the Alice books by two decades. It is perhaps in his nonsense that one can see the connection between Reverend Dodgson, the mathematician, and Lewis Carroll, the writer. Nonsense is self-referential; that is, it lacks "sense," if sense means a relationship to the world outside the work of nonsense. It is thus like certain mathematical systems or logic games. Carroll's works are in fact games, which is one of the reasons for their appeal to children.

ALICE'S ADVENTURES IN WONDERLAND

Lewis Carroll's first novel, *Alice's Adventures in Wonderland*, successfully creates and maintains a dream

consciousness. Its dreamlike quality is revealed not merely in its conventional ending, with Alice waking up to discover her adventures in Wonderland were "all a dream"; its episodic movements are dreamlike in that one episode melts into the other and has no necessarily logical connection to the previous. Identities constantly shift: A baby turns into a pig; the Cheshire Cat fades away into a grin. Because the logic of dreams, like the logic of Wonderland, is closed, internal, and self-referential, *Alice's Adventures in Wonderland* resists interpretations that attempt to "explain" the novel by connecting its elements to structures outside it, such as biographical, historical, psychoanalytic, or political interpretations.

The story begins with Alice drowsing while her sister reads a boring book. Alice's attention is arrested by a white rabbit, which she follows, only to fall down a rabbit hole, where she finds a world where nothing is like the world she left. When she eats and drinks the Wonderland foods, she changes drastically in size, becoming small as a mouse, then large as a house. When small, she finds her way into a garden, where she meets a caterpillar, rescues a baby from a mean duchess, attends a mad tea party, plays croquet with the Queen of Hearts, listens to a mock turtle's life story, and attends the trial of the Knave of Hearts. When the angry subjects of the Queen rush at Alice, she awakens to find them to be only, in the real world, falling leaves.

The novel is narrated in the third person, but with limited omniscience, allowing the reader to view Wonderland from Alice's perspective. The creation of the Alice character (though it must be remembered that she is modeled on a real girl of the author's acquaintance) is one of Carroll's most stunning achievements. It is seen immediately in the opening paragraph, which presents her thoughts as she peers into a book her sister is reading; the book bores her because it has no pictures or conversations. This is clearly a child's perspective. Even Alice's precipitous changes in size reflect the point of view of children who are given contradictory messages: that they are too big for some things and too little for others. Alice is the most fully realized of the characters in the book, all others being functionally flat. The flatness of the characters is essential to the humor of the book, particularly the slapstick elements, for the whimsy of the

Mad Hatter and the March Hare dunking the Dormouse in a teapot is lost if we sympathize with the Dormouse as a real character with feelings.

THROUGH THE LOOKING-GLASS AND WHAT ALICE FOUND THERE

Carroll's second novel is a sequel to the first, with the same main character. This time the "wonderland" is the looking-glass world, the world one sees when one looks in a mirror, a reverse image of the real world. As a photographer who needed to visualize finished photographs from their negative images, Carroll had an intuitive understanding of the implications of a "reverse" world. The consciousness of his "abnormality" of being a left-handed boy may also have played into the creation of *Through the Looking-Glass and What Alice Found There*.

In the novel's opening chapter, Alice passes through a mirror to find a house precisely the reverse of her own. She goes out into the garden, where she meets the Red Queen, then to the surrounding country, where she encounters strange insects, Tweedledee and Tweedledum, the White Queen, Humpty Dumpty, the lion and the unicorn, and the White Knight. In chapter 9, Alice becomes queen, and she upsets the board of chess pieces in a transition from dream to waking precisely like that of the first *Alice* book. The transition is handled in two truncated chapters, one of fifty-nine words, in which Alice shakes the Red Queen, and one of only six words, in which the Red Queen turns out to be Alice's kitten, and she is awake. The final chapter is an epilogue, in which Alice poses an unanswered question on the relation of dream to reality.

SYLVIE AND BRUNO

Carroll's last two novels were not as successful commercially as the Alice books, and, according to their earliest critics, they were unsuccessful artistically as well. Carroll continues to play with dreams and reality in the Sylvie and Bruno books, but this time waking and dream realities are interlaced in alternating chapters. In place of Wonderland or the looking-glass world, *Sylvie and Bruno* puts forth "the eerie state," in which one becomes aware of fairies.

Thus, *Sylvie and Bruno* has two parallel plots: In the waking world, which Carroll's introduction calls "the ordinary state," there is a love triangle. The noble and selfless Dr. Arthur Forester loves Lady Muriel Orme but believes that she loves her cousin, Captain Eric Linden. The cousins, in fact, become engaged, but there is a grave religious impediment: Eric is not a Christian. The novel ends with Arthur accepting a medical post in India so as not to stand in Eric's way. Simultaneously in the fairy or "eerie" realm parallel to the human one of Arthur, Eric, and Muriel, Sylvie and Bruno are innocent fairy children of the Warden of Outland. This plot is a version of the ancient myth and fairy-tale motif of the disguised god or king. The Warden temporarily abandons his rule in order to travel the kingdom disguised as a beggar. In his absence, his wicked brother Sibimet conspires with his wife and selfish son Uggug to take over Outland.

SYLVIE AND BRUNO CONCLUDED

In the sequel to *Sylvie and Bruno*, the interactions between the fairy realm of Outland and the human realm of Arthur and Muriel are more causally connected, as Sylvie and Bruno work "behind the scenes" to bring the true lovers together. Sylvie, in fact, appears to be the fairyland identity of Muriel. Through the invisible ministry of Sylvie and Bruno, Arthur and Muriel are married, but shortly after the wedding Arthur must go off to combat a plague in a nearby town. Muriel reads a false account of the death of Arthur from the plague, and Arthur, ironically, is rescued by Eric, who has come to accept the Christian faith and sees his assistance to a would-be rival as divinely directed. Meanwhile, the Warden (Arthur's counterpart) returns to Outland, thwarts Sibimet (Eric's counterpart), who repents, and regains his kingdom.

Perhaps it is no surprise that the human characters in both Sylvie and Bruno books are the least believable. They are the hackneyed stock characters of sentimental romance, though no worse than others of the same genre. As in the Alice books, the title characters, Sylvie and Bruno, are the more remarkable creations, though readers may have difficulty with the cloying baby talk of the fairies and the effusive affection they lavish on one another. Sylvie and Bruno are emblems of childlike innocence, which Carroll also tried to capture in the Alice books and in his photography.

John R. Holmes

OTHER MAJOR WORKS

SHORT FICTION: "Bruno's Revenge," 1867.

POETRY: *Phantasmagoria, and Other Poems*, 1869; *The Hunting of the Snark: An Agony in Eight Fits*, 1876; *Rhyme? and Reason?*, 1883; *Three Sunsets, and Other Poems*, 1898; *For "The Train": Five Poems and a Tale*, 1932; *The Collected Verse of Lewis Carroll*, 1932 (also known as *The Humorous Verse of Lewis Carroll*, 1960).

NONFICTION: *A Syllabus of Plane Algebraical Geometry*, 1860; *An Elementary Treatise on Determinants*, 1867; *Euclid and His Modern Rivals*, 1879; *Twelve Months in a Curatorship*, 1884; *Three Months in a Curatorship*, 1886; *The Game of Logic*, 1887; *Curiosa Mathematica, Part I: A New Theory of Parallels*, 1888; *Curiosa Mathematica, Part II: Pillow Problems Thought During Wakeful Hours*, 1893; *Symbolic Logic, Part I: Elementary*, 1896; *Feeding the Mind*, 1907; *The Diaries of Lewis Carroll*, 1954; *The Unknown Lewis Carroll*, 1961; *The Magic of Lewis Carroll*, 1973; *The Letters of Lewis Carroll*, 1979 (Morton N. Cohen, editor); *The Oxford Pamphlets, Leaflets, and Circulars of Charles Lutwidge Dodgson*, Vol. 1, 1993; *The Mathematical Pamphlets of Charles Lutwidge Dodgson and Related Pieces*, 1994.

CHILDREN'S LITERATURE: *A Tangled Tale*, 1885; *"The Rectory Umbrella" and "Mischmasch,"* 1932; *The Pig-Tale*, 1975.

BIBLIOGRAPHY

Blake, Kathleen. *Play, Games, and Sport: The Literary Works of Lewis Carroll*. Ithaca, N.Y.: Cornell University Press, 1974. Very insightful study of Carroll's work focuses primarily on the Alice books, *Sylvie and Bruno*, and *The Hunting of the Snark*. Emphasis is placed on systems of logic and language constructions. Supplemented by an index.

Bloom, Harold, ed. *Lewis Carroll's Alice's Adventures in Wonderland*. New York: Chelsea House, 2006. Collection of essays about the novel includes analysis of Alice's identity, elements of folklore and fairy tales in the work, and its treatment of love and death. Includes bibliography and index.

Carroll, Lewis. *The Annotated Alice*. Introduction and notes by Martin Gardner. 1960. Definitive ed. New York: W. W. Norton, 2000. Features abundant marginal notes that explain references in the Alice tales and *The Hunting of the Snark*, linking them to Carroll's life, events and controversies in Victorian England, and mathematics. Also includes reproductions of the works' original illustrations.

Cohen, Morton N. *Lewis Carroll: A Biography*. New York: Random House, 1995. Detailed work by an author who devoted more than three decades to Carroll scholarship. Using Carroll's letters and diaries, Cohen has provided what many regard as a definitive biography. Illustrated with more than one hundred of Carroll's photographs and drawings.

Collingwood, Stuart Dodgson. *The Life and Letters of Lewis Carroll*. New York: Century, 1899. As Carroll's nephew, Collingwood had firsthand knowledge of his uncle's life, and this biographical work is accordingly full of anecdotes. The letters quoted in the text often exemplify Carroll's dexterity with humor.

De la Mare, Walter. *Lewis Carroll*. London: Faber & Faber, 1932. Well-written volume places Carroll in historical context and analyzes the different genres he utilized. Contains a detailed discussion of the two Alice books and a brief treatment of other works. Supplemented by an index and a bibliography.

Gray, Donald J., ed. *Alice in Wonderland*. New York: W. W. Norton, 1992. Provides an ideal starting point for those interested in examining Carroll's novel. In addition to extensive background and critical essays, includes helpful annotations on the two Alice novels. Many of the best essays from other collections are reprinted here, making this a reference work of first resort.

Jones, Jo Elwyn, and J. Francis Gladstone. *The Alice Companion: A Guide to Lewis Carroll's Alice Books*. New York: New York University Press, 1998. Full of information and commentary on the people and places that make up Carroll's and Alice Liddell's world in mid-nineteenth century Oxford. Also an excellent source of information regarding the extensive literature on this period in Carroll's life.

_____. *The Red King's Dream: Or, Lewis Carroll in Wonderland*. London: Jonathan Cape, 1995. Places Carroll within his life and times through the discussion of his literary milieu, friends, and influences. Includes bibliographical references and index.

Leach, Karoline. *In the Shadow of the Dreamchild: A New Understanding of Lewis Carroll*. Chester Springs, Pa.: Peter Owen, 1999. Uses findings from new research to argue that many of the long-standing assumptions about Carroll—concerning his exclusively child-centered and unworldly life, his legendary obsession with Alice Liddell, and his supposedly unnatural sexuality—are nothing more than myths.

Pudney, John. *Lewis Carroll and His World*. London: Thames and Hudson, 1976. Historical study of Carroll and his culture is both insightful and broad in scope. Features more than one hundred illustrations as well as a chronology, a select bibliography, and an index.

Thomas, Donald. *Lewis Carroll: A Portrait with Background*. London: John Murray, 1996. Thomas surmises the formative influences on Carroll's personality and intellect as he describes Victorian England. An invaluable guide for readers who want to understand how manners and ideas changed during Carroll's lifetime.

ANGELA CARTER

Born: Eastbourne, Sussex, England; May 7, 1940
Died: London, England; February 16, 1992
Also known as: Angela Olive Stalker

PRINCIPAL LONG FICTION

Shadow Dance, 1966 (also known as
    Honeybuzzard, 1967)
The Magic Toyshop, 1967
Several Perceptions, 1968
Heroes and Villains, 1969
Love, 1971 (revised 1987)
*The Infernal Desire Machines of Doctor
    Hoffman*, 1972 (also known as *The War of
    Dreams*, 1974)
The Passion of New Eve, 1977
Nights at the Circus, 1984
Wise Children, 1991

OTHER LITERARY FORMS

Angela Carter is nearly as well known for her short fiction as she is for her novels. Her short-story collections include *Fireworks: Nine Profane Pieces* (1974), *Black Venus* (1985; also known as *Saints and Strangers*, 1986), the highly praised *The Bloody Chamber, and Other Stories* (1979), which contains her transformations of familiar fairy tales into adult tales with erotic overtones, and *American Ghosts and Old World Wonders* (1993). She also wrote a number of fantastic stories for children, including *Miss Z, the Dark Young Lady* (1970), *The Donkey Prince* (1970), and a translated adaptation of the works of Charles Perrault, *The Fairy Tales of Charles Perrault* (1977). In 1978, she published her first book of nonfiction, *The Sadeian Woman: And the Ideology of Pornography*, a feminist study of the Marquis de Sade that remains controversial among both literary and feminist critics. Other nonfiction essays by Carter have been published by British journals; *Nothing Sacred: Selected Writings* (1982) is a collection of her journalistic pieces, and *Shaking a Leg: Journalism and Writings* (1997) reprints other essays and reviews. She also wrote a screenplay adaptation of her novel *The Magic Toyshop* (1987) and cowrote, with Neil Jordan, the screenplay for the British film *The Company of Wolves* (1984), based on her short story of the same title.

ACHIEVEMENTS

With the publication of her first novels in the late 1960's, Angela Carter received wide recognition and acclaim in Great Britain for blending gothic and surreal elements with vivid portrayals of urban sufferers and survivors. She was awarded the John Llewellyn Rhys Memorial Prize for *The Magic Toyshop* and the Somerset Maugham Award for *Several Perceptions*. Critics have praised her wit, inventiveness, eccentric characters, descriptive wealth, and strongly sustained narrative while sometimes questioning her depth of purpose and suggesting a degree of pretentiousness. Her imaginative transformation of folkloric elements and examination of their mythic impact on sexual relationships began to be fully appreciated on the appearance of *The Bloody Chamber, and Other Stories*, which received the Cheltenham Festival of Literature Award. *Nights at the Circus*, recipient of the James Tait Black Memorial Prize, helped to establish firmly for Carter a growing transatlantic reputation as an extravagant stylist of the Magical Realist school. Following her untimely death in 1992—which enabled her establishment in the syllabus of British universities traditionally reluctant to venerate living writers—Carter was immediately hailed as the most important English fantasist of her generation. Her critical writings, which add a robust and sometimes scathing rhetoric to the lucid prose of her fiction, also attracted new attention.

BIOGRAPHY

Angela Olive Stalker was born in Eastbourne, Sussex, England, on May 7, 1940. After working as a journalist from 1958 to 1961 in Croyden, Surrey, she attended Bristol University, from which she received a bachelor's degree in English literature in 1965. While married to Paul Carter between 1960 and 1972, she traveled widely and lived for several years in Japan. From 1976 to 1978, she served as Arts Council of Great Britain Fellow in Creative Writing at Sheffield University. She was a visiting professor at Brown University, the University of Texas, Austin, and the University of Iowa. She spent the last years of her life in London, living with Mark Pearce, the father of her son Alexander, who was born in 1983. She died of lung cancer in London on February 16, 1992.

ANALYSIS

The search for self and for autonomy is the underlying theme of most of Angela Carter's fiction. Her protagonists, usually described as bored or in some other way detached from their lives, are thrust into unknown landscapes or embark on picaresque journeys in which they encounter representatives of a vast variety of human experience and suffering. These encountered characters are often grotesques or exaggerated parodies reminiscent of those found in the novels of Charles Dickens or such southern gothic writers as Flannery O'Connor. They also sometimes exhibit the animalistic or supernatural qualities of fairy-tale characters. The protagonists undergo voluntary or, more often, forced submission to their own suppressed desires. By internalizing the insights gained through such submission and vicariously from the experiences of their antagonists and comrades or lovers, the protagonists are then able to garner some control over their own destinies. This narrative structure is borrowed from the classic folktales and fairy tales with which Carter has been closely associated. Carter does not merely retell such tales in modern dress; rather, she probes and twists the ancient stories to illuminate the underlying hierarchical structures of power and dominance, weakness and submission.

In addition to the folkloric influence, Carter draws from a variety of other writers, most notably Lewis Carroll, Jonathan Swift, the Marquis de Sade, and William Blake. The rather literal-minded innocent abroad in a nightmarish wonderland recalls both Alice and Gulliver, and Carter acknowledges, both directly and obliquely, her borrowings from Carroll's *Alice's Adventures in Wonderland* (1865) and Swift's *Gulliver's Travels* (1726). She was also influenced by the Swiftian tool of grotesque parody used in the service of satire. It was through Swiftian glasses that she read Sade. While deploring the depredations on the human condition committed by both the victims and victimizers in Sade's writings, she interprets these as hyperbolic visions of the actual social situation, and she employs in her novels derivatively descriptive situations for their satiric shock value. Finally, the thematic concerns of Blake's visionary poetry—the tension between the contrarieties of innocence and experience, rationality and desire—are integral to Carter's outlook. The energy created by such tension creates the plane on which Carter's protagonists can live most fully. In Blake's words and in Carter's novels, "Energy is Eternal Delight."

Although Carter's landscapes range from London in the 1960's (*The Magic Toyshop, Several Perceptions, Love*) to a postapocalyptic rural England (*Heroes and Villains*), a sometime-in-the-future South America (*The Infernal Desire Machines of Doctor Hoffman*), a United

States in which the social fabric is rapidly disintegrating (*The Passion of New Eve*), and London and Russia at the beginning of the twentieth century (*Nights at the Circus*), certain symbolic motifs appear regularly in her novels. Carter is particularly intrigued by the possibilities of roses, wedding dresses, swans, wolves, tigers, bears, vampires, mirrors, tears, and vanilla ice cream. Menacing father figures, prostitute mothers, and a kaleidoscope of circus, fair, and Gypsy folk inhabit most of her landscapes. It is unfair, however, to reduce Carter's novels to a formulaic mode. She juggles traditional and innovative elements with a sometimes dazzling dexterity and is inevitably a strong storyteller.

THE MAGIC TOYSHOP

At the opening of *The Magic Toyshop*, fifteen-year-old Melanie is entranced with her budding sexuality. She dresses up in her absent mother's wedding gown to dance on the lawn in the moonlight. Overwhelmed by her awakening knowledge and the immensities of possibility that the night offers, she is terrified and climbs back into her room by the childhood route of the apple tree—shredding her mother's gown in the process. Her return to childhood becomes catastrophic when a telegram arrives announcing the death of Melanie's parents in a plane crash. Melanie, with her younger brother and sister, is thrust from a safe and comfortable existence into the constricted and terrifying London household of her Uncle Philip Flower, a toy maker of exquisite skill and sadistically warped sensibility. He is a domestic tyrant whose Irish wife, Margaret, was inexplicably struck dumb on her wedding day. The household is also inhabited by Margaret's two younger brothers, Finn and Francie Jowle; the three siblings form a magic "circle of red people" that is alternately seductive and repulsive to Melanie.

Uncle Philip is a creator of the mechanical. He is obsessed by his private puppet theater, his created world to which he enslaves the entire household. In aligning herself with the Jowle siblings, Melanie asserts her affirmation of life but becomes aware of the thwarted and devious avenues of survival open to the oppressed. The growing, but ambivalent, attraction between her and Finn is premature and manipulated by Uncle Philip. Even the love that holds the siblings together is underlined by a current of incest. Finn is driven to inciting his uncle to murder him in order to effect Philip's damnation. The crisis arises when Uncle Philip casts Melanie as Leda in a puppet extravaganza. Her symbolic rape by the immense mechanical swan and Finn's subsequent destruction of the puppet release an orgiastic, yet purifying, energy within the "circle of red people." The ensuing wrath of Uncle Philip results in the conflagration and destruction of the house. Finn and Melanie are driven out, Adam-and-Eve-like, to face a new world "in a wild surmise."

In fairy-tale fashion, Melanie is threatened by an evil father figure, protected by the good mother, and rescued by the young hero. Even in this early novel, however, Carter skews and claws at the traditional fabric. The Jowle brothers, grimy, embittered, and twisted by their victimization at the hands of Philip Flower, are as dangerous as they are endangered. They are unable to effect their own freedom. Melanie's submission to Uncle Philip's swan catalyzes not only her own rescue but also, indeed, the release of the Jowle siblings. Melanie's sacrifice breaks the magic spell that held the Jowles imprisoned.

SEVERAL PERCEPTIONS

Several Perceptions, Carter's third novel, depends less on such folkloric structure. In this novel, her evocation of the late 1960's counterculture is so finely detailed that she manages to illuminate the thin line between the idealism and solipsism of that era, without denigrating the former or disguising the latter. The clarity of observation is achieved by viewing the culture through the eyes of Joseph Harker, a classic dropout. He has failed at the university, been dumped by his Jane Austen-reading lover, is disheartened by his job caring for dying old men, despises the contentment of his hippie peers, and, early in the novel, bungles a suicide attempt. Joseph, like his biblical namesake, is a dreamer of dreams: He dreams in the violent images of Vietnam War atrocities, the self-immolation of Buddhist monks, and assassinations. His schizophrenic perceptions are colored by shattered images from the books in his room, *Alice's Adventures in Wonderland* and Anne Gilchrist's *Life of William Blake* (1863), by memories of his grandfather, visions of his psychiatrist, the purring of his pregnant cat, Anne Blossom's custard, and the vanilla ice-cream breasts of Mrs. Boulder.

The novel narrates Joseph's slow crawl back into the world of the living. Despite a tough-minded acknowledgment of the grubby and quite desolate lives of the characters, the novel is written with a gentle touch and ends on an affirmative note. The Christmas party that takes place at the end of the novel, in which Joseph symbolically reenters society, stands as a classic description of a hippie-generation party, just as F. Scott Fitzgerald's description of Gatsby's party stands as the image for the flapper generation. The connected-disconnected flow, the costumes, the easy sexuality, the simple goodwill, the silliness, and the sometimes inspired personal insights are vividly re-created. Carter wrote the novel as this lifestyle was being played out, and it is much to her credit that she succumbed neither to sentimentality nor to parody.

SCIENCE-FICTION NOVELS

Parody and satire are, however, major elements in Carter's three novels that are often classified as science fiction or science fantasy. In *Heroes and Villains*, *The Infernal Desire Machines of Doctor Hoffman*, and *The Passion of New Eve*, Carter's protagonists dwell in societies that are described in metaphysical iconography. Carter seems to be questioning the nature and values of received reality. Marianne's world in *Heroes and Villains* is divided into high-technology enclaves containing Professors, the Soldiers who protect them, and the Workers who serve them. Outside the enclaves, in the semijungle/semicesspool wildernesses, dwell the tribes of nomadic Barbarians and the Out-people, freaks created by nature gone awry. Marianne, the daughter of a Professor, motivated mainly by boredom, escapes from her enclave with Jewel, a young Barbarian chieftain, during a raid.

In *The Infernal Desire Machines of Doctor Hoffman*, the aging Desiderio narrates his heroic exploits as a young man when he saved his City during the Reality War. Doctor Hoffman besieges the City with mirages generated from his Desire Machines. Sent by the Minister of Determination to kill Doctor Hoffman, Desiderio is initiated into the wonders of desires made manifest, Nebulous Time, and the juggled samples of cracked and broken reality. His guide is Hoffman's daughter, Albertina, who appears to Desiderio as an androgynous ambassador, a black swan, the young valet of a vampiric

count, and finally as his one true love, the emanation of his whole desire.

The United States in *The Passion of New Eve* is torn apart by racial, class, and sexual conflicts. Evelyn, a young British teacher, travels through this landscape and is re-created. The unconsciously exploitative and disinterestedly sadistic narrator suffers a wild revenge when captured by an Amazon-like community of women. He is castrated, resexed, raped, forcibly wed and mated, and ultimately torn from his wife's love by a gang of murderous Puritanical boys.

Each of the protagonists of these novels experiences love but seems to be able to achieve wholeness only through the destruction of the loved one. Symbolically, the protagonists seem to consume the otherness of the loved ones, reincorporating these manifest desires back into their whole beings. Each, however, is left alone at the end of the novel.

Symbolic imagery of a harshly violent though rollicking nature threatens to overwhelm these three novels. The parody is at times wildly exaggerated and at times cuts very close to reality (for example, in *The Passion of New Eve*, the new Eve is incorporated into a polygamous group that closely resembles the so-called Manson family). Although some critics have decried Carter's heavy reliance on fantasies, visions, and zany exuberance, it is probably these qualities that have appealed to a widening audience. It must also be acknowledged that Carter continued, within her magical realms, to probe and mock the repressive nature of institutionalized relationships and sexual politics.

NIGHTS AT THE CIRCUS

With *Nights at the Circus*, Carter wove the diverse threads of her earlier novels into brilliantly realized tapestry. This novel has two protagonists—Fevvers, the Cockney Venus, a winged, six-foot, peroxide-blond aerialist who was found "hatched out of a bloody great egg" on the steps of a benevolent whorehouse (her real name is Sophia), and Jack Walser, an American journalist compiling a series of interviews titled "Great Humbugs of the World," who joins Colonel Kearney's circus, the Ludic Game, in order to follow Fevvers and who is "not hatched out, yet . . . his own shell don't break, yet." It is 1899, and a New World is about to break forth. The ambivalent, tenuous attraction between Fevvers and

Walser is reminiscent of that between Melanie and Finn in *The Magic Toyshop* or Marianne and Jewel in *Heroes and Villains*, but it is now mature and more subtly complex. The picaresque journeyings from London to St. Petersburg and across the steppes of Russia recall the travels in *The Infernal Desire Machines of Doctor Hoffman* and *The Passion of New Eve* but are more firmly grounded in historical landscapes. The magic in this novel comes in the blurring between fact and fiction, the intense unbelievability of actual reality and the seductive possibilities of imaginative and dreamlike visions. Are Fevvers's wings real or contrived? Do the clowns hide behind their makeup and wigs or only become actualized when they don their disguises? As in most Magical Realist fiction, Carter is probing the lines between art and artifice, creation and generation, in a raucous and lush style.

Here, after a long hiatus from the rather bleak apocalyptic visions of her 1970's novels, in which autonomous selfhood is achieved only through a kind of self-cannibalization of destroyed love, Angela Carter envisions a route to self-affirmation that allows sexual love to exist. With shifting narrative focuses, Carter unfolds the rebirths of Walser and Fevvers through their own and each other's eyes. Walser's shells of consciousness are cracked as he becomes a "first-of-May" clown, the waltzing partner to a tigress, the Human Chicken, and, in losing consciousness, an apprentice shaman to a primitive Finno-Urgic tribe. As star of Kearney's circus, Fevvers is the toast of European capitals: an impregnable, seductive freak, secure in and exploitative of her own singularity. On the interminable train trek through Siberia, she seems to mislay her magnificence and invulnerability. She becomes less a freak and more a woman, but she remains determined to hatch Walser into her New Man. As he had to forgo his socially conditioned consciousness in order to recognize Sophia, however, so she has to allow him to hatch himself. It is as confident seers that Sophia/Fevvers and Jack Walser love at the close of the novel.

WISE CHILDREN

The fact that Carter produced only one novel during the last eight years of her life has more to do with the claims made on her time and attention by her son Alexander than the depredations of the cancer that killed her.

This was a sore point—her much younger partner, Alexander's father, did not keep promises he made to take primary responsibility for child care—and some of that soreness is evident in the pages of the satiric comedy *Wise Children*, in which disowned and abandoned children are extravagantly featured. The story comprises a century-spanning memoir written by Dora Chance, one of the "lucky Chance" twins fathered—but swiftly disowned—by the Shakespearean actor Melchior Hazard in advance of the first of his three marriages.

Dora recalls that the identical Chance twins are indeed lucky, first by virtue of being informally adopted by Melchior's more colorful but less successful fraternal twin Peregrine, and second by virtue of developing a career as dancers in music halls. (Music halls were Britain's primary form of vulgar popular entertainment from the late nineteenth century to the end of World War II.) It subsequently transpires that Peregrine is the biological father of Melchior's supposedly legitimate identical twin daughters by his first marriage, Saskia and Imogen. The paternity of the fraternal twins of Melchior's third marriage, Gareth and Tristan, is never formally disputed, although Dora and her sister Nora cannot help but wonder why it is that one bears a far stronger physical resemblance to Peregrine.

The intricate comparisons and contrasts drawn between the fortunes and pretensions of the legitimate Hazards and the illegitimate Chances mirror and embody the fortunes and pretensions of "legitimate" theater and the music-hall tradition, as both are swallowed up by new media—first by Hollywood films (the most hilarious chapter describes the brief reunion of the Chances with their father on the set of a chaotic film version of William Shakespeare's *A Midsummer Night's Dream*) and then by television. The contemporary events that surround Dora's recollections involve the effects of television game-show host Tristan's simultaneous sexual involvement with his much older half sister Saskia and the Chances' protégé Tiffany (significantly nicknamed Our Tiff). The paradoxes of Melchior's theatrical career are summed up by the juxtaposition of his eventual knighthood with his attachment to the cardboard crown that was the chief legacy he received from his father, also a redoubtable Shakespearean actor.

Although *Wise Children* is far more sentimental than

the bleakly dark fantasies Carter penned while her own marriage was failing in the early 1970's, it is to some extent a revisitation of their themes. (The revised version of *Love*, which she prepared while struggling to find the time to write *Wise Children*, also softens the self-mutilatory aspects of the original, but only slightly.) What Carter's final novel adds to her jaundiced view of family life, however, is the legacy of her midperiod preoccupation with the processes by which the substance of childhood dreams and unfathomable experiences can be transmuted into high and low art. Beneath the surface of its comic exuberance, *Wise Children* achieves considerable intensity in its celebration of theatrical magic and its accounts of the redemption of wounded personalities by spirited performances.

Jane Anderson Jones
Updated by Brian Stableford

OTHER MAJOR WORKS

SHORT FICTION: *Fireworks: Nine Profane Pieces*, 1974; *The Bloody Chamber, and Other Stories*, 1979; *Black Venus*, 1985 (also known as *Saints and Strangers*, 1986); *American Ghosts and Old World Wonders*, 1993; *Burning Your Boats*, 1995.

SCREENPLAYS: *The Company of Wolves*, 1984 (with Neil Jordan; adaptation of her short story); *The Magic Toyshop*, 1987 (adaptation of her novel).

RADIO PLAYS: *Vampirella*, 1976; *Come unto These Yellow Sands*, 1979; *The Company of Wolves*, 1980; *Puss in Boots*, 1982; *Come unto These Yellow Sands: Four Radio Plays*, 1985 (includes previous 4 plays).

NONFICTION: *The Sadeian Woman: And the Ideology of Pornography*, 1978; *Nothing Sacred: Selected Writings*, 1982; *Expletives Deleted: Selected Writings*, 1992; *Shaking a Leg: Journalism and Writings*, 1997 (also known as *Shaking a Leg: Collected Writings*, 1998).

TRANSLATIONS: *The Fairy Tales of Charles Perrault*, 1977; *Sleeping Beauty, and Other Favourite Fairy Tales*, 1982.

CHILDREN'S LITERATURE: *The Donkey Prince*, 1970; *Miss Z, the Dark Young Lady*, 1970; *Moonshadow*, 1982; *Sea-Cat and Dragon King*, 2000.

EDITED TEXTS: *Wayward Girls and Wicked Women*, 1986; *The Virago Book of Fairy Tales*, 1990 (also known as *The Old Wives' Fairy Tale Book*).

MISCELLANEOUS: *The Curious Room: Plays, Film Scripts, and an Opera*, 1996.

BIBLIOGRAPHY

Day, Aidan. *Angela Carter: The Rational Glass*. New York: Manchester University Press, 1998. Presents an examination of Carter's fiction that is generally accessible to the nonspecialist. Notes the similarity of themes in Carter's work and describes how she was influenced by the books she read at various times in her life.

Gamble, Sarah. *Angela Carter: A Literary Life*. New York: Palgrave Macmillan, 2006. Critical biography analyzes the relationship between the events of Carter's life and her works. Examines how Carter was engaged in topical issues, such as politics, feminism, class, and national identity (particularly English identity).

_____. *Angela Carter: Writing from the Front Line*. Edinburgh: Edinburgh University Press, 1997. Comprehensive study of Carter's works, including her novels. Argues that Carter intentionally undermined traditional ideas about history, social codes regarding propriety and "woman's place," and the distinction between "high" and "low" literature.

Landon, Brooks. "Eve at the End of the World: Sexuality and the Reversal of Expectations in Novels by Joanna Russ, Angela Carter, and Thomas Berger." In *Erotic Universe: Sexuality and Fantastic Literature*, edited by Donald Palumbo. Westport, Conn.: Greenwood Press, 1986. Examines the feminist mythology of Carter's work, in particular in the novel *Heroes and Villains*, and discusses Carter's confrontation of sexual stereotypes.

Lee, Alison. *Angela Carter*. New York: G. K. Hall, 1997. Presents critical discussion of all of Carter's novels in a clear and accessible style. Includes details of Carter's life and explains her ideas about nonfiction in order to provide insight into her fiction.

Munford, Rebecca, ed. *Re-visiting Angela Carter: Texts, Contexts, Intertexts*. New York: Palgrave Macmillan, 2006. Collection of essays focuses on Carter's extensive use of allusions and references drawn from a wide variety of sources. Among the topics discussed are the influences on Carter's writings of the works of Charles Dickens, Jonathan Swift, Edgar Allan Poe, and film director Jean-Luc Godard.

Peach, Linden. *Angela Carter*. New York: St. Martin's Press, 1998. Study of Carter's novels offers an overview of her work and close readings of the individual books. Argues that although Carter employed elements of fantasy literature, her novels still addressed "real-life" issues.

Rubinson, Gregory J. *The Fiction of Rushdie, Barnes, Winterson, and Carter: Breaking Cultural and Literary Boundaries in the Work of Four Postmodernists*. Jefferson, N.C.: McFarland, 2005. Compares and contrasts the work of the four authors, including an analysis of gender and sexuality in the writings of Carter and Jeanette Winterson and examination of *The Passion of the New Eve* and *Heroes and Villains*.

Sage, Lorna, ed. *Flesh and the Mirror: Essays on the Art of Angela Carter*. London: Chatto & Windus, 1994. Collection of thirteen essays on various aspects of Carter's work includes discussions of Carter's "political correctness," Carter and science fiction, and the novels *Love* and *Wise Children*.

Smith, Joan. Introduction to *Shaking a Leg: Journalism and Writings*, by Angela Carter. London: Chatto & Windus, 1997. Well-written essay on Carter's critical work links her social commentary to major themes in her long fiction.

JOYCE CARY

Born: Londonderry, Ireland; December 7, 1888
Died: Oxford, Oxfordshire, England; March 29, 1957
Also known as: Arthur Joyce Lunel Cary; Thomas Joyce

PRINCIPAL LONG FICTION

Aissa Saved, 1932
An American Visitor, 1933
The African Witch, 1936
Castle Corner, 1938
Mister Johnson, 1939
Charley Is My Darling, 1940
A House of Children, 1941
Herself Surprised, 1941
To Be a Pilgrim, 1942
The Horse's Mouth, 1944 (expanded 1957)
The Moonlight, 1946
A Fearful Joy, 1949
Prisoner of Grace, 1952
Except the Lord, 1953
Not Honour More, 1955
The Captive and the Free, 1959 (Winnifred Davin, editor)
Cock Jarvis, 1974 (A. G. Bishop, editor)

OTHER LITERARY FORMS

All of Joyce Cary's short stories published under his own name are contained in *Spring Song, and Other Stories* (1960), edited by Winnifred Davin. Ten early stories published under the pseudonym Thomas Joyce are not included that collection. More than half a dozen of these stories, which deal with bohemian life in Paris, Cary sold to the *Saturday Evening Post* (1920) in order to support his serious writing. Cary's self-admitted formula for these "potboilers" was a little sentiment, a little incident, and surprise.

Cary also published three booklets of verse and many essays, the latter appearing in such periodicals as *Harper's Magazine*, *The New Yorker*, and the *Sunday Times*. The most significant pieces of Cary's occasional writing have been gathered by A. G. Bishop into a volume titled *Selected Essays* (1976). This collection is of interest to the literary student because it includes some samples of Cary's practical criticism and of his views on the theory and practice of writing as well as interesting material about his background and political views. *Art and Reality* (1958) is a sequence of meditations on aesthetics that Cary composed for the 1956 Clark Lectures at Cambridge University but was too ill to deliver.

Cary's other nonfiction mainly articulates his views

on the philosophy and practice of politics, concerning it-self with such issues as history, imperialism, and war. These works include *Power in Men* (1939), *The Case for African Freedom* (1941; reprinted with other essays about Africa in 1962), *Process of Real Freedom* (1943), and *Memoir of the Bobotes* (1960). These works shed light on Cary's treatment of ethical and political issues in his fiction. A collection of Cary's unpublished manu-scripts, papers, letters, and diaries is in the possession of the Bodleian Library at Oxford University.

ACHIEVEMENTS

Joyce Cary's major artistic achievements—the novel *Mister Johnson* and the trilogy comprising *Herself Sur-prised*, *To Be a Pilgrim*, and *The Horse's Mouth*—are re-alistic works that reflect social, moral, and historical change as well as technical performances that embody the formal and linguistic innovations of literary modern-ism. This distinctive mixture of traditional realism and modernist style is Cary's principal legacy as a novelist. Although he experiments with techniques such as stream of consciousness, interior monologue, disrupted chronol-ogy, shifting point of view, and present-tense narration, he consistently rivets the action—past or present—to a particular historical and social context. The continuity of exterior events never completely disintegrates, though it is sometimes difficult to reconstruct.

To be sure, the various novels offer the reader differ-ent perspectives and interpretations of social reality. The intention, however, is not to obscure that reality or to render it relative to the subjectivity of the narrator, but rather to layer it, to augment its texture. Cary's perspec-tive, therefore, is not nihilistic. His experiments in the trilogy form enhance the reader's sense of dwelling in a shared or intersubjective reality, even though each novel in the series adroitly captures the idiosyncratic perspec-tive of its first-person narrator. Cary refuses to endorse any sort of feckless relativism (he was repelled by the moral defeatism and philosophical pessimism of such post-World War I writers as Aldous Huxley) and yet manages to incorporate into his writing the innovations of modernism. His self-proclaimed comedy of freedom extends the range of traditional realism and offers new possibilities for the form of fiction.

Recognition of Cary's literary merit came only late in his life. Under the pseudonym Thomas Joyce, he pub-lished in the *Saturday Evening Post* several stories based on his youthful experiences of bohemian life in Paris, but he considered these efforts to be potboilers rather than serious pieces of fiction. The magazine, in fact, rejected his subsequent stories for being too "literary." Not until 1932, when Cary was forty-three, was his first novel, *Aissa Saved*, published. It was not a commercial success. He continued to produce novels, and finally, in 1941, af-ter the publication of *A House of Children*, his seventh novel, he won his first literary award: the James Tait Black Memorial Prize for the best British novel of the year. After this award, Cary's reputation increased steadily. In 1950, the *Adam International Review* de-voted a special issue to his work, and in 1953, Walter Al-len's seminal study of his work, *Joyce Cary*, appeared. Cary enjoyed a successful lecture tour in the United States in 1951, and he was asked to deliver the 1956 Clark Lectures at Cambridge University. During his life-time, he was praised by such prestigious critics as Allen, John Dover Wilson, and Barbara Hardy. Since his death in 1957, Cary scholarship has grown steadily. In 1963, *Modern Fiction Studies* devoted a special issue to his work, and numerous books and articles continue to be published that address Cary's achievements.

BIOGRAPHY

Arthur Joyce Lunel Cary was born in Londonderry, Ireland, on December 7, 1888. His ancestors had been Irish landlords since the early seventeenth century. The Arrears Act of 1882, however, plunged his grandfather into ruinous debt, and his father, Arthur Cary, a prospec-tive civil engineer, moved the family to London shortly after Cary's birth. There the nexus of traditional family life was Cromwell House, owned by Cary's Uncle Tristam. Cary never lost contact with his Irish roots and the legacy of his family history, spending childhood va-cations at his grandparents' cottages in Ireland and gain-ing familiarity with Devon, England, the point of his family's origin. These settings, along with the familial stability and continuity they represented, were important to Cary's fiction. *Castle Corner* deals with a half century of life in Ireland, England, and Africa, moving from the 1870's to the brink of World War I; *Charley Is My Dar-ling* deals with the World War II evacuation of thousands of London children to Devon; *A House of Children* is a poetical evocation of childhood based on Cary's recollections of his Irish vacations; and *The Moonlight* and his two trilogies are set mainly in Devon.

A tragic note entered Cary's life when his mother died in 1898, and his sense of life's miseries was compounded when his stepmother died five years later. His performance as a student at Hurstleigh and Clifton was average at best, though he did show interest in telling stories and writing poetry. In 1904, at the age of fifteen, he went on a sketching trip with his aunt to France, which was his first exposure to Impressionist painting. Two years later, he went to Paris as an art student and experienced bohemian life. He then went to Edinburgh for formal artistic training; at the age of twenty, he decided that he was not good enough to be a first-rate painter: Writing would be his vocation and painting his hobby. *Verses by Arthur Cary*, a decidedly mediocre effort, was published in 1908.

These early experiences were later exploited in his fiction. The first fictional pieces he published were short stories that dealt with bohemian life in Paris, and *The Horse's Mouth*, his portrait of the artist, not only draws some of its material from his life in Paris and Edinburgh but also bases its style on a literary approximation of Impressionism in painting. Cary's highly developed visual imagination is evident throughout his writings.

In accordance with his choice of vocation, Cary went to Oxford University in 1909 to take a degree in law, intending to provide himself with an alternate career should his literary attempts fail. His fourth-class degree, however, the lowest one possible, barred him from pursuing a gainful career in either the civil service or the field of education. In 1912, the Balkan War erupted, and Cary decided to go to the aid of Montenegro, Yugoslavia, feeling that the firsthand experience of war would offer a writer valuable material. *Memoir of the Bobotes* is a nonfictional account of his Montenegrin sojourn. He returned to England in 1913, entered the Nigerian service in 1914, and fought against the Germans in West Africa. In 1916, in England on leave from Nigeria, he married Gertrude Ogilvie, whom he had met in Oxford. He returned to Nigeria before the end of the year.

Cary's African years (1914-1919) had a formative influence on the shape of his fiction. *Aissa Saved* deals

Joyce Cary. (Library of Congress)

with the collision between Western religion and African paganism; *An American Visitor* explores the difference between the Western idealization of the noble savage and the African reality of tribal life; *The African Witch* reveals the prejudices of some Britons in Africa; *Mister Johnson* depicts the vibrantly imaginative existence of a young black clerk with "civilized" aspirations and his tragicomic relationship with District Officer Rudbeck; and *Cock Jarvis* dramatizes the experience of a "Joseph Conrad character in a Rudyard Kipling role," a morally sensitive liberal whose paternalistic and imperialistic attitudes do not coincide with the historical situation in twentieth century Africa. Without his experience as an assistant district officer in Nigeria—a position that required him to work as a policeman, tax collector, judge, administrator, census taker, mapmaker, and road builder, not to mention someone capable of dealing tactfully with the mysteries of witchcraft and juju—Cary would not have developed the sympathetic imagination that allowed him to understand and record the African point of view with sensitivity and knowledge.

Not surprisingly, his long residence in Africa put some strain on his marriage; his first two children, born in England during his absence, were virtual strangers to him. Despite occasional outbreaks of tempestuous disagreement, Cary and his wife shared a love that carried them through several adversities and the birth of three more children. Gertrude died in 1949. Cary's ability to render vividly the perspectives of women is particularly evident in *Herself Surprised*, *The Moonlight*, *A Fearful Joy*, and *Prisoner of Grace*; in part, this ability derives from the depth and intensity of his relationship with his wife.

In 1920, Cary returned to England, and he, his wife, and their two sons moved to a house in Oxford, where Cary lived until his death. After the publication of his first novel, *Aissa Saved*, in 1932, he produced novels at the impressive rate of almost one a year. His literary reputation increased steadily after he won the James Tait Black Memorial Prize in 1941.

ANALYSIS

The entirety of Joyce Cary's fiction is, as the author himself suggests, about one world—the world of freedom, "the active creative freedom which maintains the world in being . . . the source of moral responsibility and of good and evil . . . of injustice and love, of a special comedy and a special tragic dilemma which can never be solved." It is "a world in everlasting conflict between the new idea and the old allegiances, new arts and new inventions against the old establishment." Cary sees human beings as condemned to be free and society as perpetually poised between the extremes of anarchy and totalitarianism. Because creative imagination is of the highest value, the individual must rebel against the forces that threaten to trammel or stultify the free expression of his imagination, whether the forces be those of the established church, the state, tribalism, nationalism, conventional morality, or whatever. Throughout his novels, Cary dramatizes the tension between the intuitive and the analytical, the imaginative and the conceptual, the concrete and the abstract, and the vital and the mechanical.

Cary's romanticism, however, is not naïve. He is acutely aware that the tension between freedom and authority is necessary, that the will to create is continually in conflict with the will to preserve. His first trilogy, for example, sympathetically portrays a survivalist, a conservative, and a rebel. Even radically different characters, however, must enact their lives and secure their salvation or damnation in the moral world of freedom, imagination, and love.

In *Joyce Cary* (1973), R. W. Noble conveniently divides Cary's novels into five categories, according to their subject matter: Africa and empire, youth and childhood, women and social change, the artist and society, and politics and the individual. The novels of Africa and empire are substantial achievements but not major novels of the twentieth century, save for *Mister Johnson*.

EARLY NOVELS

Cock Jarvis, Cary's first effort, was abandoned in 1937; it was published posthumously. The problem with the novel was that Cary could not construct a plot adequate to encompass the character of Cock Jarvis, for at this point Cary had not assimilated the modernist style. Without recourse to first-person narration or stream of consciousness, his eminently interesting character was locked into a melodramatic and conventional plot structure. Whether Jarvis was to murder his wife and her lover, forgive them, or commit suicide, Cary never decided; none of the resolutions would solve the essential problem, which is technical.

Aissa Saved, with its seventy or more characters, has so many cultural conflicts, disconnected episodes, and thematic concerns that the aesthetic experience for the reader is congested and finally diffuse. Its analysis of the transforming powers of religious conversion, however, is penetrating and ironic. The juxtaposition of Aissa, an African convert who understands the sacrifice of Christ in a dangerously literal way and ingests Him as she would a lover, and Hilda, an English convert, is effective. Though the backgrounds of the two converts are divergent, they both end by participating in gruesome blood sacrifices. The novel as a whole, however, suffers from two problems. First, its central action, which revolves around attempts to end a devastating drought, cannot unify the manifold details of the plot: the cultural, religious, and military conflicts among Christians, pagans, and Muslims. Second, its tone is somewhat ambiguous. It is not clear whether the novel is meant to be an outright attack on missionaries and thus an ironic and cynical treatment of Aissa's so-called salvation or a more moderate assessment of the transforming powers of religious conversion.

An American Visitor has more manageable intentions. The book effectively dramatizes the difference between practical and theoretical knowledge and concrete and abstract knowledge. The preconceptions of the American visitor, Marie Hasluck, are not experientially based and are contrasted with the practices of the local district officer, Monkey Bewsher, who strives to strike a balance between freedom and authority. Even though reality forces Marie to abandon some of her pseudo-anthropological beliefs, utopianism is so much a part of her psychological complex that she turns to religious pacifism for compensation, a turning that has tragic consequences for the pragmatic, imaginative, and somewhat self-deluded officer.

The African Witch is more panoramic in scope. It deals with the social, political, and religious lives of both Europeans and Africans. The plot revolves around the election of a new emir: The Oxford-educated Aladai is pitted against Salé, a Muslim. Aladai's Western demeanor offends many of the Europeans; they prefer Africans to be noble savages rather than liberal rationalists. In the end, the forces of juju and political corruption prevail. Aladai is rejected and chooses a self-sacrificial death, presumably abandoning his rationalism and lapsing into stereotype. The conclusion of the novel is not convincingly wrought.

Castle Corner is part of a projected trilogy or quartet of novels that Cary decided not to continue. Covering a half century of life in Ireland, England, and Africa, the novel moves from the 1870's to the brink of World War I. Because of its congeries of characters and variety of themes, the book resists summary. In general, however, it puts the world of individual freedom and responsibility in collision with the world of historical change, but it has too much explicit debate and attitudinizing to be dramatically effective.

Generally, Cary's novels of Africa and empire are competent but not exceptional fiction. More materially than formally satisfying, they suffer finally from a lack of cohesion and unity; the form is not adequate to the content, which is rich and detailed. Nevertheless, these novels well delineate the everlasting conflict between new ideas and the old allegiances, the necessary tension between freedom and authority, reflecting Cary's characteristic preoccupation with the struggle for imaginative freedom on personal, moral, social, religious, and political levels.

MISTER JOHNSON

Mister Johnson is an exceptional piece of fiction. The character from whom the novel takes its title, as Cary points out in the preface, is a young clerk who turns his life into a romance, a poet who creates for himself a glorious destiny. Johnson is a supreme embodiment of imaginative vitality and, as such, a prototype for the picaresque heroes in Cary's later novels. Even though Johnson's fate is ultimately tragic, his mind is full of active invention until the end.

The novel occupies a pivotal moment in the dialectic of Cary's art, for not only is the content exceptional—Mr. Johnson is an unforgettable character; his adventures indelibly impress themselves on the reader—but also the innovative form is adequate to that content. In *Mister Johnson*, Cary deploys third-person, present-tense narration. He notes in the preface that he chose this style because it carries the reader unreflectingly on the stream of events, creating an agitated rather than a contemplative mood. Because Johnson lives in the present and is completely immersed in the vibrant immediacy of his experience, he does not judge; nor does the reader judge, as the present-tense narration makes the reader swim gaily with Johnson on the surface of life.

Cary's choice of third-person narration, which he does not discuss in the preface, is equally strategic. The first-person style that he uses so effectively in some of his later novels would have been appropriate. By using the third-person style, he is able not only to give the African scene a solidity of local detail but also to enter into the mind of Rudbeck, so that the reader can empathize with his conscientious decision to shoot Johnson, a personal act, rather than hanging him, an official act. The impact of the tragic outcome is thereby intensified.

The novel traces the rise and fall of Mr. Johnson, chief clerk of Fada in Nigeria. A southerner in northern Nigeria and an African in European clothes, he has aspirations to be civilized and claims to be a friend of District

Officer Rudbeck, the Wazirin Fada, the King of England, and anyone who vaguely likes him. Johnson's aspirations, however, are not in consonance with his finances, and his marriage, machinations, schemes, stories, parties, petty thefts, capital crime, and irrepressible good spirits become part of the exuberant but relentless rhythm of events that lead to his death. For Johnson, as Cary suggests, life is simply perpetual experience, which he soaks into himself through all five senses at once and produces again in the form of reflections, comments, songs, and jokes. His vitality is beyond good and evil, equally capable of expressing itself anarchistically or creatively.

Rudbeck, too, is a man of imagination, though not as liberated from constraint as Johnson. His passion for road building becomes obsessive once Johnson's imagination further fuels his own. He goes so far as to misappropriate funds in order to realize his dream. Without the infectious influence of Johnson's creativity, Rudbeck would never have rebelled against the forces of conservatism. The completed road demonstrates the power of creative imagination.

The road, however, brings crime as well as trade, and in his disillusionment, Rudbeck fires Johnson for embezzlement. In the end, Johnson murders a man and is sentenced to death by Rudbeck. Johnson wants his friend Rudbeck to kill him personally, and Rudbeck eventually complies with his clerk's wish, putting his career as district officer in jeopardy by committing this compassionate but illegal act.

CHARLEY IS MY DARLING *and* A HOUSE OF CHILDREN

After *Mister Johnson*, Cary chose domestic settings for his novels. His novels of youth and childhood, *Charley Is My Darling* and *A House of Children*, are set in Devon and Ireland. The former deals with the evacuation of thousands of London children to Devon during World War II; the latter is a poetical evocation of childhood vacations in Ireland.

In *Charley Is My Darling*, the main character, Charley, like Mr. Johnson, is thrust into an alien world, and the urban values he represents are contrasted with the rural values represented by Lina Allchin, the well-intentioned supervisor of the evacuees. Charley, whose head is shaved as part of a delousing process, is isolated

from his peers and consequently channels his imaginative energies into crime and ultimately into anarchistic destruction in order to gain acceptability. Because neither school nor society offers him any outlet for his creative individuality, it expresses itself in violence, an expression that is perhaps a microcosmic commentary on the causes of war.

A House of Children is autobiographical. Technically innovative, it has no omniscient point of view and relies instead on one central consciousness, which narrates the story in the first person. This was to become Cary's characteristic narrative style. The novel has a poetic rather than a linear coherence, depending on a series of revelations or epiphanies rather than on plot. Cary obviously learned a great deal from James Joyce's *A Portrait of the Artist as a Young Man* (1916), which he had read in Africa.

THE FIRST TRILOGY

Cary's masterpiece, his first trilogy, focuses on the artist and society. Cary designed the trilogy, he said, to show three characters not only in themselves but also as seen by one another, the object being to get a three-dimensional depth and force of character. Each novel adapts its style to the perceptual, emotive, and cognitive idiosyncrasies of its first-person narrator. *Herself Surprised*, the narrative of Sara Monday, is reminiscent of Daniel Defoe's *Moll Flanders* (1722), and its autobiographical style is ideally suited to dramatize the ironic disparity between Sara's conventional moral attitudes and her "surprising," unconventional behavior. *To Be a Pilgrim*, the narrative of Tom Wilcher, is akin to a Victorian memoir, and the formal politeness of its language reflects the repressed and conservative nature of its narrator. *The Horse's Mouth*, the narrative of Gulley Jimson, uses stream of consciousness and verbally imitates the Impressionist style of painting, an imitation that strikingly reveals the dazzling power of Gulley's visual imagination. The entire trilogy is a virtuoso performance, underscoring Cary's talent for rendering characters from the inside.

Sara Monday is the eternal female—wife, mother, homemaker, mistress, and friend. In accordance with her working-class position as a cook, she consistently describes her world in domestic images and metaphors—the sky for her is as warm as new milk and as still as water in a goldfish bowl. Her desire to improve her socioeconomic lot is a major motivating factor in her life, and this desire often encourages her to operate outside the bounds of morality and law. Sara, however, is not a moral revolutionary; her values mirror her Victorian education. In her terms, she is constantly "sinning" and constantly "surprised" by sin, but in terms of the reader's understanding of her, she is a lively and sensuous being with an unconscious genius for survival who succumbs, sometimes profitably, sometimes disastrously, to immediate temptation. Her language of sin, which is vital and concrete, belies her language of repentance, which is mechanical and abstract. Nevertheless, Sara, unlike Moll Flanders, does not seem to be a conscious opportunist and manipulator.

Sara betters her socioeconomic status by securing a middle-class marriage to Matthew Monday. The marriage, however, does not prevent her from having affairs with Hickson, a millionaire, and Jimson, an artist. (The narrative description of these "surprises" is exquisitely managed.) Though she sincerely believes in conventional morality, that morality is no match for her joy of life. Cary also shows the negative aspects of Sara's mode of being. Like other characters in his fiction, she is a creative being whose imaginative vitality borders on the anarchistic and irresponsible. She virtually ruins her first husband and makes little effort to keep contact with her four daughters.

After her violent relationship with Gulley Jimson, Sara becomes a cook for the lawyer Wilcher and is about to marry him when his niece has Sara jailed for theft. She had been stealing in order to purchase art supplies for Gulley and to pay for his son's education. Her will to live is thus an implicit critique of the conventional morality that her conscious mind mechanically endorses. She is a survivalist par excellence.

Unlike the events in *Herself Surprised*, those in *To Be a Pilgrim* are not presented chronologically. The narrative is layered, juxtaposing Wilcher's present situation of imminent death with the social, political, and religious history of his times. The disrupted chronology poignantly accentuates Wilcher's realization, which comes too late, that he ought to have been a pilgrim, that possessions have been his curse. Now his repressed energies can only counterproductively express themselves in ex-

hibitionism and arson. Marriage to Sara Monday, which might have been a redemptive force in his life, is now impossible, for she has already been incarcerated for her crimes.

In the present time of the novel, Wilcher is a virtual prisoner at Tolbrook Manor, the family home. His niece Ann, a doctor and the daughter of his dead brother Edward, a liberal politician whose life Wilcher tried to manage, is his warden. She marries her cousin Robert, a progressive farmer devoted to the utilitarian goal of making the historic manor a viable commercial enterprise, much to Wilcher's chagrin. Ultimately, Wilcher is forced to recognize that change is the essence of life and that his conservative fixation with tradition, the family, and moral propriety has sapped him of his existential energy, of his ability to be a pilgrim.

The Horse's Mouth, a portrait of the artist as an old man, is justly celebrated as Cary's most remarkable achievement. (Although the Carfax edition of Cary's novels is complete and authoritative, the revised Rainbird edition of *The Horse's Mouth*, 1957, illustrated by the author, includes a chapter—"The Old Strife at Plant's"—that Cary had previously deleted.) Its reputation has been enhanced by the excellent film version, released in 1958, in which Alec Guinness plays the role of Gulley Jimson.

Gulley Jimson is a pilgrim; he accepts the necessity of the fall into freedom with joy and energy, conceiving of it as a challenge to his imagination and thereby seeking to impose aesthetic order on experiential chaos. For Gulley, anything that is part of the grimy reality of the contingent world—fried fish shops, straw, chicken boxes, dirt, oil, mud—can inspire a painting. The impressionist style of his narrative reflects his vocation, for he mainly construes his world in terms of physical imagery, texture, solidity, perspective, color, shape, and line, merging Blakean vision with Joycean stream of consciousness. Gulley's sensibility is perpetually open to novelty, and his life affirms the existential value of becoming, for he identifies with the creative process rather than with the finished product. His energies focus on the future, on starting new works, not on dwelling on past accomplishments. Even though he is destitute, he refuses to paint in the lucrative style of his Sara Monday period.

Gulley is also a born con artist, a streetwise survivor. He is not averse to stealing, cheating, swindling, blackmailing, or even murdering if his imaginative self-expression is at stake. He is completely comfortable in a brutal, violent, and unjust world. His vision, therefore, has limitations. His pushing Sara down the stairs to her death shows the anarchistic irresponsibility implicit in regarding life as merely spiritual fodder for the imagination. Moreover, Gulley lacks historical consciousness. Even though the novel chronicles his life before and after the beginning of World War II, Gulley seems to have no conception of who Adolf Hitler is and what he represents.

For the most part, this novel clearly champions the creative individual and criticizes the repressive society that inhibits him, although Cary is always fairminded enough to imply the limitations of his characters. Gulley Jimson remains a paradigm of energetic vitality, an imaginative visionary who blasts through generation to regeneration, redeeming the poverty of the contingent world and liberating consciousness from the malady of the quotidian. The entire trilogy is a masterpiece; the created worlds of the three narrators mutually supplement and criticize one another, stressing the difficulty of achieving a workable balance between the will to survive, to preserve, and to create.

THE SECOND TRILOGY

Cary's second trilogy—*Prisoner of Grace, Except the Lord,* and *Not Honour More*—deals with politics and the individual. It is a commentary on radical liberalism, evangelicalism, and crypto-fascism, moving from the 1860's to the 1930's and involving the lives of three characters (Nina Nimmo/Latter, Chester Nimmo, and Jim Latter) whose lives are inextricably enmeshed, unlike those of the characters of the first trilogy.

In *Prisoner of Grace,* Nina Nimmo (Nina Latter by the end of her narrative) tries to protect and defend both her lovers—the radical liberal politician Nimmo, maligned for his alleged opportunism and demagoguery, and the crypto-fascist Latter, a military man obsessed by a perverted notion of honor. The time span of the novel covers the Boer War, the Edwardian reform government, the World War I victory, the prosperous aftermath, and the 1926 General Strike. The action takes place mainly in Devon, where Chester Nimmo makes his mark

as a politician and becomes a member of Parliament, and in London, where Nimmo eventually becomes a cabinet minister.

Nina, carrying the child of her cousin Jim Latter, marries the lower-class Chester Nimmo, who is handsomely remunerated for rescuing the fallen woman in order to secure a respectable future for the child. Nina never loves Nimmo but is converted to his cause by his political and religious rhetoric. She writes her account in order to anticipate and rebut criticism of his conduct.

Thrust into the duplicitous and morally ambiguous world of politics, she succumbs both to Chester's ideals, values, morals, and beliefs and to his lusts, lies, schemes, and maneuverings, seemingly incapable of distinguishing the one from the other, as is the reader, who has only the information available in Nina's unreliable account. Unlike the disingenuousness of Sara Monday in *Herself Surprised,* which the reader can easily disentangle— Sara's sensuous vitality gives the lie to the maxims of conventional piety she mechanically utters—Nina's disingenuousness is a fundamental part of her character. Nina, like Chester, is both sincere and hypocritical, genuinely moral and meretriciously rhetorical, an embodiment of the political personality. Even the politics of their marriage parallel in miniature the politics of the outside world.

Nina is a prisoner of grace once she has converted to the belief that Chester's being is infused with grace and that his religious and political beliefs enjoy moral rectitude by definition. Her love for Jim is also a grace that imprisons her and ultimately impels her to divorce Chester and marry Jim. The reader, too, is a prisoner of grace, unable to get outside Nina's "political" point of view and thus unable to separate truth and falsity, the authorial implication being that the two are necessarily confused and interdependent in the political personality. Like Sara, Nina is a survivalist, and after she becomes adulterously involved with Nimmo, she, like Sara, is murdered by a man whom she had helped. Survivalism has limits.

Except the Lord, the story of Nimmo's childhood and youth, takes place in the 1860's and 1870's. It is the history of a boy's mind and soul rather than one of political events. Like *To Be a Pilgrim,* it takes the form of a Victorian memoir in which the mature narrator explores the events and forces that caused him to become what he is.

Nurtured in an environment of poverty, fundamentalist faith, and familial love, Nimmo becomes in turn a radical preacher, labor agitator, and liberal politician.

According to the first verse of Psalm 127, "Except the Lord build the house, they labour in vain that would build it; except the Lord keep the city, the watchman waketh but in vain." Since this novel stops before the events of *Prisoner of Grace* and *Not Honour More* begin, and since it principally induces a sympathetic response to Nimmo, the reader has a difficult time interpreting the significance of the title. The reader tends to see Nimmo differently after having read the account of the latter's youth but is still uncertain whether Nimmo is a knight of faith or an opportunistic antinomian. The trilogy as a whole seems to suggest that Chester is both.

Not Honour More is the story of a soldier, Jim Latter, who sees the world in dichotomous terms and cannot accept the necessarily ambiguous transaction between the realms of freedom and authority. The novel is a policewoman's transcript of Jim's confession; it is dictated as he awaits execution for the murder of Nina, provoked by his discovery of her adulterous relationship with Nimmo, her ex-husband. His language is a combination of clipped military prose, hysterical defensiveness, and invective against both the decadence of British society around the time of the 1926 General Strike and the corruption of politicians such as Nimmo.

Latter believes in authority, in imposing law and order on the masses. He has no sense of the moral ambiguity of human behavior, no sense of the complexity of human motivation. A self-proclaimed spiritual descendant of the Cavalier poet Richard Lovelace, Jim believes that his murder of Nina proves that he loves honor more. He conceives of the murder as an execution, a moral act, whereas it is in reality a perversion of honor, a parody of the code that Lovelace represents. District Officer Rudbeck, of *Mister Johnson*, is by comparison a truly honorable man: He personalizes rather than ritualizes Mr. Johnson's death. Because Jim believes in the rectitude of authoritarians with superior gifts, he is a cryptofascist. The best that can be said of him is that he has the courage of his misplaced convictions.

Throughout his novels, Cary focused his creative energies on human beings who are condemned to be free, to enact their lives somewhere between the extremes of anarchism and conformity. His achievement demonstrates that it is possible for a novelist to be at once stylistically sophisticated, realistically oriented, and ethically involved.

Greig E. Henderson

OTHER MAJOR WORKS

SHORT FICTION: *Spring Song, and Other Stories*, 1960 (Winnifred Davin, editor).

POETRY: *Verses by Arthur Cary*, 1908; *Marching Soldier*, 1945; *The Drunken Sailor*, 1947.

NONFICTION: *Power in Men*, 1939; *The Case for African Freedom*, 1941 (revised 1944); *Process of Real Freedom*, 1943; *Britain and West Africa*, 1946; *Art and Reality*, 1958; *Memoir of the Bobotes*, 1960; *Selected Essays*, 1976 (A. G. Bishop, editor).

BIBLIOGRAPHY

Adams, Hazard. *Joyce Cary's Trilogies: Pursuit of the Particular Real*. Tallahassee, Fla.: University Presses of Florida, 1983. Adams attempts to rescue Cary from what he views as misplaced critical emphasis by focusing on the particularity of Cary's two trilogies. Includes two appendixes devoted to chronologies of the trilogies.

Christian, Edwin Ernest. *Joyce Cary's Creative Imagination*. New York: Peter Lang, 1988. Analyzes Cary's work to demonstrate the truth of Cary's statement that "all my books are part of one expression: that is, they are like different chapters in one work, showing different angles of a single reality." Includes bibliography and index.

Echeruo, Michael J. *Joyce Cary and the Novel of Africa*. London: Longman, 1973. Places Cary's African novels in the tradition of the foreign novel and argues that they have a special place in this genre. Provides new insights into the growth of Cary's art as well as valuable criticism of Cary's African novels.

Erskine-Hill, Howard. "The Novel Sequences of Joyce Cary." In *The Fiction of the 1940's: Stories of Survival*, edited by Rod Mengham and N. H. Reeve. New York: Palgrave, 2001. Examines Cary's two trilogies and describes how the six novels share a number of special features that distinguish them from other novel sequences.

Foster, Malcolm. *Joyce Cary: A Biography*. London: Michael Joseph, 1969. Exhaustive, informative study of Cary presents only brief discussion of each novel but offers some interesting insights into the author's works. Foster had access to the Cary collection at the Bodleian Library in Oxford, England.

Hall, Dennis. *Joyce Cary: A Reappraisal*. London: Macmillan, 1983. Discusses all of Cary's novels with conscientious thoroughness and makes the point that there are two Carys: the thinker and the artist. Hall is sympathetic to Cary but notes the unevenness of his work and concludes that Cary is "his own worst enemy." Includes bibliography.

Levitt, Annette S. *The Intertextuality of Joyce Cary's "The Horse's Mouth."* Lewiston, N.Y.: Edwin Mellen Press, 1993. Study of *The Horse's Mouth* analyzes the influence of William Blake and the other sources on which Cary drew in creating the novel. Includes bibliographical references and index.

Majumdar, Bimalendu. *Joyce Cary: An Existentialist Approach*. Atlantic Highlands, N.J.: Humanities Press, 1982. Scholarly study of Cary is devoted to critical appraisal of his work. Focuses on the central existential theme in Cary's novels: the uniqueness of the individual who "refuses to fit into some system constructed by rational thought."

Roby, Kinley E. *Joyce Cary*. Boston: Twayne, 1984. After providing an overview of Cary's biography, this brief volume surveys Cary's fiction—all of which, according to Roby, is concerned with the "unchangeable changeableness of life." Also gives glancing attention to Cary's literary criticism and journalism. Includes chronology and select bibliography.

Ross, Michael L. "Joyce Cary's Tragic African Clown." In *Race Riots: Comedy and Ethnicity in Modern British Fiction*. Montreal: McGill-Queen's University Press, 2006. Discusses how the racial humor in Cary's works reflects Great Britain's disdain for non-Europeans in the period before World War II.

WILLA CATHER

Born: Back Creek Valley, near Gore, Virginia; December 7, 1873
Died: New York, New York; April 24, 1947
Also known as: Wilella Sibert Cather

PRINCIPAL LONG FICTION

Alexander's Bridge, 1912
O Pioneers!, 1913
The Song of the Lark, 1915
My Ántonia, 1918
One of Ours, 1922
A Lost Lady, 1923
The Professor's House, 1925
My Mortal Enemy, 1926
Death Comes for the Archbishop, 1927
Shadows on the Rock, 1931
Lucy Gayheart, 1935
Sapphira and the Slave Girl, 1940

OTHER LITERARY FORMS

Willa Cather (KATH-ur) was a prolific writer, especially as a young woman. By the time her first novel was published when she was thirty-eight years old, she had written more than forty short stories, at least five hundred columns and reviews, numerous magazine articles and essays, and a volume of poetry. She collected three volumes of her short stores: *The Troll Garden* (1905), *Youth and the Bright Medusa* (1920), and *Obscure Destinies* (1932). Those volumes contain the few short stories she allowed to be anthologized, most frequently "Paul's Case," "The Sculptor's Funeral" (*The Troll Garden*), and "Neighbour Rosicky" (*Obscure Destinies*). Cather continued to write short stories after she began writing novels, but she wrote them less frequently. After her death, additional volumes were published that contain other stories: *The Old Beauty and Others* (1948), *Willa Cather's Collected Short Fiction: 1892-1912*

(1965), and *Uncle Valentine, and Other Stories: Willa Cather's Collected Short Fiction, 1915-1929* (1973).

A great many of Cather's early newspaper columns and reviews have been collected in *The Kingdom of Art: Willa Cather's First Principles and Critical Statements, 1893-1896* (1966) and in *The World and the Parish: Willa Cather's Articles and Reviews, 1893-1902* (1970). Three volumes of her essays, which include prefaces to the works of writers she admired, have also been published. Cather herself prepared the earliest volume, *Not Under Forty* (1936), for publication; the other two, *Willa Cather on Writing* (1949) and *Willa Cather in Europe* (1956), appeared after her death. Her single volume of poetry, *April Twilights*, appeared in 1903, but Cather later spoke apologetically of that effort, even jokingly telling a friend that she had tried to buy up and destroy all extant copies so that no one would see them.

Cather's novel *A Lost Lady* has twice been adapted for the screen, in 1924 and 1934. The second screen version was so distasteful to her that in her will she prohibited any such attempts in the future. Nevertheless, several of her novels—*O Pioneers!* (1992), *My Ántonia* (1995), and *The Song of the Lark* (2001)—have been adapted for television, as have some of her short stories. Cather also included instructions in her will forbidding the publication of her letters.

ACHIEVEMENTS

Willa Cather actually had at least two careers in her lifetime. Prior to becoming a novelist, she was a highly successful journalist and writer of short fiction as well as a high school English teacher. She began her career as a writer while still in college, where she published several short stories and wrote a regular newspaper column for the *Nebraska State Journal*. Later she also wrote for the *Lincoln Courier*. Her columns addressed a variety of subjects, but many of them were related to the arts. She discussed books and authors and reviewed the many plays, operas, and concerts that came through Lincoln on tour. She gained an early reputation as an astute (and opinionated) critic. Even after she moved to Pittsburgh, the Lincoln papers continued to print her columns.

Over the years, Cather published stories in such national magazines as *Century*, *Collier's*, *Harper's*, *Ladies' Home Journal*, *Woman's Home Companion*, *Sat-urday Evening Post*, and *McClure's*, the popular journal for which she served as an editor for several years. During her affiliation with *McClure's*, Cather traveled widely, gathering material for stories and making contacts with contributors to the magazine. She helped many a struggling young writer to find a market, and she worked regularly with already prominent writers. Cather had been a student of the classics since childhood, and she was unusually well read. She was also a devoted and knowledgeable student of art and music, a truly educated woman with highly developed, intelligent tastes. She was friendly with several celebrated musicians, including Metropolitan Opera soprano Olive Fremstad, on whom she patterned Thea Kronborg in *The Song of the Lark*; songwriter Ethelbert Nevin; and the famous child prodigies the Menuhins. She also knew author Sarah Orne Jewett briefly.

Typically, Cather did not move in writers' circles but preferred to work by her own light and without the regular association of other writers of her time. She never sought the public eye, and as the years went on she chose to work in relative solitude, preferring the company of only close friends and family. Known primarily as a novelist, she also later enjoyed a growing reputation as a writer of short fiction. She was awarded the Pulitzer Prize for *One of Ours*, and an ardent admirer, Sinclair Lewis, was heard to remark that she was more deserving than he of the Nobel Prize he won. Cather is particularly appealing to readers who like wholesome, value-centered art. She is held in increasingly high regard among critics and scholars of twentieth century literature and is recognized as one of the finest stylists in American letters.

BIOGRAPHY

Wilella Sibert Cather was born in Back Creek Valley, Virginia, on December 7, 1873, the first of seven children. Her father's side of the family settled in Virginia during colonial times. Her grandfather, William Cather, was opposed to slavery and favored the Union cause during the Civil War, creating a rift in a family of Confederate sympathizers. Her grandfather on her mother's side, William Boak, served three terms in the Virginia House of Delegates. He died before Cather was born, while serving in Washington in the Department of the Interior.

Cather's maternal grandmother, Rachel Boak, returned with her children to Back Creek Valley and eventually moved to Nebraska with her son-in-law Charles, Willa Cather's father, and his wife, Mary Virginia. Rachel Boak is an important figure in Cather's life and fiction. A courageous and enduring woman, she appears as Sapphira's daughter Rachel in Cather's last completed novel and as the grandmother in a late story, "Old Mrs. Harris." Rachel's maiden name was Seibert, a name that Cather adopted (spelling it "Sibert" after her uncle William Sibert Boak) as a young woman and then later dropped.

In 1883, when Cather—named Wilella, nicknamed Willie, and later renamed Willa by her own decree—was nine years old, her family sold their holdings at Back Creek and moved to Webster County, Nebraska. In that move from a lush Virginia countryside to a virtually untamed prairie, Cather experienced what Eudora Welty has called a "wrench to the spirit" from which she never recovered. It proved to be the most significant single event in her young life, bringing her as it did face-to-face with a new landscape and an immigrant people who were to make a lasting impression on her imagination. The move was a shock, but a shock that was the beginning of love both for the land and the people, and for the rest of her life, Cather was to draw from this experience in creating her fiction.

Cather always had a special affection for her father; he was a gentle, quiet-mannered man who, after eighteen months on his parents' prairie homestead, moved his family into Red Cloud, sixteen miles away. There he engaged in various business enterprises with no great success and reared his family. Unlike her husband, Mary Cather was energetic and driving, a hard disciplinarian, but generous and life-loving. A good many scenes and people from Cather's years on the farm and in Red Cloud appear in her fiction. Her third novel, *The Song of the Lark*, though its central character is a musician, recounts some of Cather's own struggles to develop her talent amid the strictures and jealousies of small-town life.

Cather's years at the university in Lincoln were extremely busy ones. Not a metropolis by any means, Lincoln was still many times larger than Red Cloud, and Cather gratefully discovered the joys of the theater and of meeting people with broad interests and capabilities. Her experience is much like that of Jim Burden as she de-

Willa Cather. (Edward Steichen/Courtesy, George Bush Presidential Library and Museum)

scribes it in *My Ántonia*. At first she planned to study science but switched to the humanities, she later confessed, when she saw an essay of hers printed in the newspaper. As she tells it, she was hooked for life. While at the university, she was active in literary circles, serving as an editor for the *Lasso* and the *Hesperian*, two student literary magazines. Several of her stories appeared in those magazines and in others. She spent the year after her graduation, in 1895, in and around Red Cloud, where she began writing for the weekly *Lincoln Courier* as well as for the *Nebraska State Journal* and published her first story in a magazine of national circulation, the *Overland Monthly*. Then in June, 1896, she left Nebraska to take a position with the *Home Monthly*, a small rather weak family magazine in Pittsburgh.

Cather knew she had to leave Red Cloud to forward her career, and even the drudgery of the *Home Monthly* was an important opportunity. Later, she secured a position with the *Pittsburgh Daily Leader*, and then taught high school English and Latin for five years. While in Pittsburgh, Cather continued to write short fiction while pursuing an active social life. It was there that she met Isabelle McClung, who was to become her dearest friend. For a time, Cather lived with Isabelle and her parents, and in their home she enjoyed the quiet seclusion she needed for her writing.

Cather's big break in her journalistic career came in 1903, when S. S. McClure, the dynamic publisher of *McClure's* magazine, became aware of her work and summoned her to his office. That interview began an association that led to an important position with *McClure's* and eventually made it possible for Cather to leave the world of journalism and devote her full energies to the writing of fiction. The publication of *The Troll Garden* in 1905 announced that a major new talent had arrived on the literary scene. McClure knew ability when he saw it.

Cather's first novel, *Alexander's Bridge*, was written while she was still with *McClure's*, and it was first conceived as a serial for the magazine. It appeared as a novel in 1912, the year she left *McClure's* to try writing on her own. Still, it was not until *O Pioneers!* came to fruition the next year that Cather felt she had hit what she called "the home pasture" and discovered herself as a novelist. In this book, she turned to her memories of the Nebraska prairie and wrote powerfully of immigrant efforts to come to terms with the land. From then on, Cather was on her way. In 1920, she began a long and satisfying professional relationship with Alfred A. Knopf, who became her publisher and remained so for the rest of her life.

Cather lived most of her professional life in New York City with her friend and literary associate Edith Lewis. Her many trips to Europe confirmed her great admiration for France and the French people, an appreciation that receives repeated expression in her novels. She also visited the American West a number of times and drew on her experiences there for some of her work. She developed a special affection for the area around Jaffrey, New Hampshire, where she liked to go for uninterrupted work. She even chose to be buried there.

Cather's classmates in Lincoln remembered her as strong-willed, bright, gifted, and somewhat eccentric. Certainly, she knew her own mind, and she had strong ideas about the difference between the cheap and the valuable. She was fiercely attached to her family and friends, but after her parents were dead, she never returned to Red Cloud. Prior to her death on April 24, 1947, Cather was working on a novel that was set in medieval France. After her death, the unfinished manuscript, as she had requested, was destroyed.

ANALYSIS

Willa Cather once said in an interview that the Nebraska landscape was "the happiness and the curse" of her life. That statement reveals the ambivalence in Cather that produced in her a lifelong tug-of-war between the East and the western prairie. That ambivalence is the central tension in her novels. As long as her parents were alive, she made repeated trips back home to see them, and each time she crossed the Missouri River, she said, "the very smell of the soil tore [her] to pieces." As a young woman in Red Cloud and Lincoln, however, she was chafed by narrow attitudes and limited opportunities. She knew that she had to leave the prairie in order to fulfill her compelling desire for broader experiences and for art. Like Thea Kronborg in *The Song of the Lark*, Cather knew she would never find fulfillment unless she left her home. At the same time, however, she also discovered that her very being was rooted in the landscape of her childhood. Thus, going back to it, even if only in memory, was essential and inescapable.

Cather once remarked that the most important impressions one receives come before the age of fifteen, and it seems clear that she was referring particularly to her own experiences on the Nebraska prairie. She did use some Virginia memories in her work, but only sporadically, in a few early short stories, before turning to them in her last published novel, *Sapphira and the Slave Girl*. In her "Nebraska works," it is not only Nebraska that Cather evokes, but it is, also, what Nebraska symbolizes and means, for she is not simply a regional writer. The range of her work is as broad as the range of her experience, and Nebraska represents the westward necessity of her life. Wherever in her work the pull of the landscape is felt, there is Nebraska—whether the setting is Colorado, Kansas, New Mexico, or even rural Pennsylvania or frontier Quebec.

As has been suggested, her life had an eastward necessity too. The raw hardships of prairie life could sometimes mutilate the body and drain the spirit, and a human being often needed something else. A man of genuine sensitivity and culture, such as Ántonia Shimerda's father, for example, could not survive in a hard land. Cather's awareness of this fact made a great impression on her. One of the first stories she heard after arriving in Nebraska was the account of Francis Sadilek's suicide, an event that she reconstructed in *My Ántonia*. Not only could the beloved land be killingly cruel, but it also failed to provide the environment of training, discipline, and appreciation so necessary for the growth and development of an artist. Although the land provided the materials for memory to work with and the germinating soil for the seed of talent, it could not produce the final fruit.

Then, too, part of the Nebraska Cather experienced was small-town life and the limited opportunities it offered the artistically ambitious. Throughout her life, she felt misunderstood by some of the townspeople who had known her as a youngster. Letters to her lifelong friend in Red Cloud, Carrie Miner Sherwood (from whom she drew Frances Harling in *My Ántonia*), indicate how sharply Cather felt their disapproval of her. She rebelled against their codes and refused to remain among them but was stung by their criticism.

TENSION BETWEEN EAST AND WEST

Thea Kronborg is not the only Cather character to be torn, like her creator, between East and West, civilization and the land. In *My Ántonia*, the young Jim Burden expresses Cather's own feelings of awe and fear upon his arrival in Nebraska. Later, when he goes to school in Lincoln and eventually leaves for a career in the East, the Nebraska landscape of his past stays with him, just as it stayed with Cather, even after long absences. Claude Wheeler, in *One of Ours*, also has a good deal of his maker in him. Much as he loves the beauty of the Nebraska landscape, he cannot find himself until he leaves it. Like Cather, the ultimate in civilization for him is France.

The opposing aspects of Cather's desire, the land and civilization—or, more specifically, art—were of equal value to her. She could never entirely give up one for the other or value one above the other. Thus, the land was "the happiness and the curse" of her life. She might well

have said the same thing about her art. Ironically, however, at least according to her friend, Elizabeth Sergeant, it was not until Cather made her feelings for the land a part of her art that she truly realized her potential as an artist. Though East and West, civilization (art) and the land—the very foundations of Cather's work—are sometimes at opposite poles in terms of the choices one must make, they are both positive values to her. The greatest threat to each is not the other; the greatest threat to each is an exploitative materialism that has no appreciation for the innate value of the land or of art.

In Cather's work, the same impulse that exploits the land is also destructive to art and the best qualities of civilization. The author's most despicable characters are those such as Ivy Peters in *A Lost Lady* and Bayliss Wheeler in *One of Ours*, who have no feeling for the land or for the past that it harbors. All that interests them is making money, as much as possible as quickly as possible. Cather had great admiration for the early railroad pioneers, wealthy men of immense courage, vision, and taste, as she pictures them in *A Lost Lady*. In too many people, however, the lust for wealth and the acquisition of it are destructive to character. They subvert what are for Cather some of life's most positive values, a relationship with the earth and an aesthetic sensibility.

Of Cather's twelve novels, only three, *Alexander's Bridge*, *My Mortal Enemy*, and *Sapphira and the Slave Girl*, do not deal centrally with the tension between East and West, with civilization and the land as values threatened by the spirit of acquisitiveness; yet even those touch the latter point. For example, Myra Henshawe's harshness of character comes partly as a result of her need to live in a style only money can provide; the desire to possess that style leads to the buying and selling of human beings, a central issue in *Sapphira and the Slave Girl*.

O PIONEERS!

Cather's second novel, *O Pioneers!*, her first to use Nebraska materials, presents the conflict between the land and civilization and the threat of destructive materialism as its major concerns. The novel's principal character, Alexandra Bergson, is something of an earth mother, a being so closely linked with the soil and growing things that her very oneness with the earth seems to convert the harsh wild land into rich acreage that willingly yields its treasures. From the first, she believes in the land and loves it, even when her brothers and neighbors grow to despise and curse it. Two of Alexandra's brothers have such a fear of financial failure that they cannot see the land's potential.

Cather, however, does not simply present Alexandra's struggle and eventual triumph. There is another value, opposed to the land but equally important, with which Alexandra must contend. Her youngest brother, Emil, is sensitive in a way that does not lend itself to life on the Continental Divide, and she wants him to have opportunities that are available only in centers of civilization. His finely tuned spirit, however, leads him to disaster in a prairie environment where passions can run high, untempered by civilizing influences. Emil falls in love with Marie Shabata, a free, wild creature, and both of them are killed by her enraged husband. The book's final vision, however, returns to an affirmation of the enduring qualities of the land and the value of human union with it.

THE SONG OF THE LARK

The conflict between the landscape of home and art is played out dramatically in the central character of *The Song of the Lark*. Thea Kronborg is in many ways the young Willa Cather, fighting the narrowness of small-town life on the prairie, needing to leave Moonstone to develop her talent, but needing also to integrate the landscape of home with her artistic desire. Thea has to leave home, but she also has to have her sense of home with her in order to reach her potential as an opera singer. Much that she has set aside in her quest for art she must pick up again and use in new ways. In fact, Cather makes it clear that without the integration of home, Thea might never have become an artist. Moonstone, however, also has its materialists who obviously stand in opposition to the enduring, if sometimes conflicting, values of earth and art. The only villain of the piece is the wife of Thea's best friend and supporter, Doctor Archie. She is a mean, pinched woman, shriveled with stinginess.

Once Thea has left Moonstone and gone to Chicago to study music, the killing pace and the battle against mediocrity wear her to the breaking point. In an effort at self-renewal, she accepts an invitation to recuperate on a ranch near the Canyon de Chelly in Arizona. There, she spends many hours lying in the sun on the red rock, following the paths of ancient potters, examining the broken pieces of their pottery that still lie in the streambeds.

It is there that Thea has the revelation that gives birth to her artist self. These ancient potters made their pottery into art by decorating it. The clay jars would not hold water any better for the artistic energy expended on them, but their makers expended that energy nevertheless. This revelation comes to Thea out of the landscape itself, and it gives her the knowledge she needs in order to continue her studies: Artistic desire is universal, ageless, and she is a part of it.

LUCY GAYHEART

The eponymous protagonist of *Lucy Gayheart* is not so hard and indomitable a character as Thea, nor is she destined to become a performing artist in her own right. Nevertheless, Lucy is much like Thea (and the young Willa Cather) in her need to leave the prairie landscape and pursue art in the only place where such pursuits are possible, the city. Lucy is, however, in many ways a child of the earth—she loves skating on the frozen river, and she begs for the preservation of an orchard that her sister Pauline, a plodding materialist, wants to cut down because it is no longer productive. Given her nature, it is no surprise that Lucy falls in love with the singer for whom she plays accompaniments at practice. He is the embodiment of the art for which her soul yearns. After his accidental drowning, Lucy returns home and she herself dies in a skating accident, her death a final union with the earth. There is also a "Doctor Archie's wife" in *Lucy Gayheart*. Ironically, she marries the one man in Haverford that Lucy might have married happily, the one man with the capacity to appreciate what a rare and lovely phenomenon Lucy was.

MY ÁNTONIA

Something of an earth mother like Alexandra Bergson, yet more malleable and human, Ántonia Shimerda of *My Ántonia* is for many readers Cather's most appealing character. She becomes a total embodiment of the strength and generosity associated with those who are one with the land and the forces of nature. Unlike Alexandra, her capacity for life finds expression not only in the trees and plants she tends but also in her many children, who seem to have sprung almost miraculously from the earth. It is in Jim Burden, who tells the story, and to some extent, in Ántonia's husband, Anton Cuzak, that the conflict between East and West occurs. Jim, like Cather, comes to Nebraska from Virginia as a youngster, and though he has to seek his professional life in eastern cities, he never gets Nebraska out of his soul. Even as a student at the University of Nebraska in Lincoln, he gazes out his window and imagines there the landscape and figures of his childhood. Ántonia represents for Jim, even after twenty years of city life, all the positive values of the earth for which no amount of civilization can compensate. At the end of the book, he determines to revitalize his past association with the land and yet still tramp a few lighted streets with Cuzak, a city man at heart.

The conflict between the harshness of life on the prairie and the cultural advantages of civilization is also presented in Ántonia's father, who had been a gifted musician in Europe, but who now, poverty-stricken and overworked, no longer plays the violin. Ántonia's deep appreciation for Cuzak's quality and for his gentle city ways and her pride in Jim's "city" accomplishments, bridge the gap between prairie and civilization.

The materialists are also evident in *My Ántonia*. In fact, one of Cather's most memorable villains is the lecherous and greedy Wick Cutter, Black Hawk's nefarious moneylender. His last act is to devise a scheme whereby he can kill himself and his equally greedy wife and at the same time guarantee that her relatives will not get a cent of his money.

ONE OF OURS

Claude Wheeler, the main character of *One of Ours*, is torn, like so many of Cather's young people, by the need to go and the need to stay. Claude is filled with yearnings he does not completely understand. All he knows is that he is burning to fulfill some inner desire, and everything he does seems to go wrong. Much as he loves the rivers and groves of his own landscape, he feels like a misfit there. His father's hearty, nonchalant materialism is only slightly less distressing to him than the hard, grasping greed of his older brother Bayliss, the bloodless, pious parsimony of his wife Enid, and the cheerful selfishness of his younger brother Ralph. The world begins opening to him during the short period when he is allowed to attend the university at Lincoln, but Claude completely finds himself only when he enlists in the army and begins fighting in France. There, he meets Lieutenant David Gerhardt, a musician, and encounters a gracious cultural climate to which he responds with all his heart.

There is, however, a troubling aspect to this novel. Claude's real fulfillment comes in the midst of battle, surrounded by death and destruction. Only then does he feel at one with himself and his surroundings; only then is the old anguish gone, the tension released. In the end, he is killed, and his mother feels some sense of gratitude that at least he does not have to face the disillusionment of returning to a country that has given itself over to material pursuits. With the exception of *Alexander's Bridge*, this is probably Cather's least successful novel, perhaps partly because she was emotionally very close to her central character. Cather stated publicly that she modeled Claude after a young cousin of hers who died in World War I, but in a letter she indicated that Claude was, in fact, an embodiment of Cather herself. The novel is a poignant portrayal of the central tensions in her work between the land and civilization, and it also describes the ever-present threat of spiritually damaging materialism.

A LOST LADY

In *A Lost Lady*, Cather again shows a character's need for civilization's amenities, in spite of the appeal of the Western landscape. Here too, though the reader may fault Cather's main character for her sometimes expedient morality, Cather has publicly expressed her affection for the woman on whom she based the character of Marian Forrester. Further, the ruthless, materialistic mindset that nearly always characterizes "the enemy" in Cather's work is graphically portrayed in the coarse figure of Ivy Peters. As a boy, Ivy cruelly blinded a bird and then set it free, and as a man he drained what was once the Forresters' lovely marshlands in order to make them yield a profit. Unscrupulous and shrewd, he manages to compromise the beautiful Marian Forrester with as little conscience as he showed toward the helpless bird.

Until her husband's decline, Mrs. Forrester managed to have the best of both worlds, East and West, spending her summers in the beautiful countryside outside Sweet Water, on the Burlington line, and her winters in the lively social atmosphere of Denver and Colorado Springs. Captain Forrester, much her elder, had made his fortune pioneering Western railroad development. When the novel opens, the Captain's failing health has already begun to limit Mrs. Forrester's social and cultural opportunities, though she still enjoys visits to the city and entertains important guests at Sweet Water. It becomes apparent, however, much to the dismay of Marian Forrester's young admirer, Niel Herbert, that Marian's passion for life and high living has led her into an affair with the opportunistic, if handsome, Frank Ellinger even before the death of the Captain. This affair foreshadows her later desperate sellout to Ivy Peters. It is significant, however, that Cather never judges Marian, though the prudish Niel does. It is not the life-loving Marian Forrester whom Cather condemns, but the grasping Ivy Peters and the unprincipled Frank Ellinger—and perhaps even the unforgiving Niel Herbert. The novel's hero is Captain Forrester, who willingly relinquishes his fortune to preserve his honor.

THE PROFESSOR'S HOUSE

There are two plot lines in *The Professor's House*, one centering on the growing life weariness of Professor Godfrey St. Peter and the other on the experiences of his student, Tom Outland, on a faraway desert mesa. Both sets of experiences, however, illuminate the tension between civilization and the open landscape and focus on the destructive nature of materialistic desire. St. Peter, a highly civilized man with refined tastes and a keen appreciation for true art, loses heart at his daughters' greed and selfishness and his wife's increasing interest in what he regards as ostentatious display. Near the end of the book, he focuses his imagination on the Kansas prairie, on his solitary, primitive boyhood self. He wants to recapture the self he was before he married and before his family and his colleagues began conjugating the verb "to buy" with every breath.

Tom Outland, the one remarkable student of St. Peter's teaching career, becomes equally disillusioned with society and its greed. Cather spares him from living out his life in such a society, however, by mercifully allowing him to die in the war in France as she had allowed Claude Wheeler to die. Ironically, it is Tom's invention of a new engine, bequeathed in a romantic impulse to one of St. Peter's daughters, that makes her and her husband rich. While herding cattle on the great Western desert, Tom Outland and his partner Roddy Blake explore the great Blue Mesa across the river from their summer grazing range. On it, they find the remnants of ancient cliff dwellers, including many beautifully decorated jars. These jars provide for Tom, as they had for

Thea Kronborg, a priceless link with the art and people and landscape of the past. In these jars, the tension between land and art is erased. While Tom is away on a fruitless trip to Washington, where he had hoped to interest someone in his find, Roddy Blake misguidedly sells the relics to a European art dealer. Recovering from two heartbreaking disappointments, the loss of the relics and the loss of Roddy, Tom makes his spiritual recovery through union with the mesa itself. He becomes one with the rock, the trees, the very desert air.

DEATH COMES FOR THE ARCHBISHOP

Even though *Death Comes for the Archbishop* is not Cather's final novel, it is in a very real sense a culmination of her efforts at reconciling the central urges toward land and toward art, or civilization, that are the hallmark of her life and her work. Selfishness and greed are a threat in this book too, but their influence is muted by Cather's concentration on Father Jean Latour as the shaping force of her narrative. He is Cather's ideal human being, by the end of the book a perfect blend of the virtues of the untamed landscape and the finest aspects of civilization.

As a young priest, Latour is sent from a highly cultivated environment in his beloved France to revitalize Catholicism in the rugged New Mexico Territory of the New World. Learned in the arts, genteel in manner, dedicated to his calling, this man of fine-textured intelligence is forced to work out his fate in a desolate, godforsaken land among, for the most part, simple people who have never known or have largely forgotten the sacraments of the civilized Church. His dearest friend, Father Joseph Vaillant, works with him—a wiry, lively man, Latour's complement in every way. Latour must bring a few greedy, unruly local priests into line, but his greatest struggle is internal as he works to convert himself, a product of European civilization, into the person needed to serve the Church in this vast desert land. In the end, his remarkable nature is imprinted indelibly on the barren landscape, and the landscape is imprinted indelibly on his nature. Instead of returning to France in his official retirement, he elects to remain in the New World. His total reconciliation with the land is symbolized in the fulfillment of his dream to build a European-style cathedral out of the golden rock of New Mexico. In that building, the art of civilization merges gracefully with the very soil of the Western landscape, just as Jean Latour's spirit had done.

SHADOWS ON THE ROCK

Shadows on the Rock, a lesser book, takes for its landscape the rock of Quebec, but the tension is still between the old ways of civilized France and the new ways of the Canadians of the future, children of the uncharted, untamed land. It, too, focuses on the efforts of the Catholic Church to bring spiritual civilization to the New World, but its central character is not a churchman. Rather, it is young Cécile Auclair who values the old ways, the civilities taught her by her mother and still priceless to her father, but who also responds to the wave of the future and marries a Canadian backwoodsman whose deepest ties are to the uncharted landscape.

Cather's work stands as something of an emotional autobiography, tracing the course of her deepest feelings about what is most valuable in human experience. For Cather, what endured best, and what helped one endure, were the values contained in the land, and in humanity's civilizing impulses, particularly the impulse to art. What is best in humanity responds to these things, and these things have the capacity to ennoble in return. Sometimes they seem mutually exclusive, the open landscape and civilization, and some characters never reconcile the apparent polarity. Cather says, however, that ultimately one can have both East and West. For her, the reconciliation seems to have occurred mainly in her art, where she was able to love and write about the land if not live on it. A conflict such as this can be resolved, for it involves a tension between two things of potential value. Thus, in her life and her art it was not this conflict that caused Cather to despair; rather, it was the willingness of humanity in general to allow the greedy and unscrupulous to destroy both the land and civilization. At the same time, it was the bright promise of youth, in whom desire for the land and for art could be reborn with each new generation, that caused her to rejoice.

Marilyn Arnold

OTHER MAJOR WORKS

SHORT FICTION: "Paul's Case," 1905; *The Troll Garden*, 1905; *Youth and the Bright Medusa*, 1920; *Obscure Destinies*, 1932; *The Old Beauty and Others*, 1948; *Willa Cather's Collected Short Fiction: 1892-1912,* 1965; *Uncle Valentine, and Other Stories: Willa Cather's Collected Short Fiction, 1915-1929,* 1973.

POETRY: *April Twilights*, 1903.

NONFICTION: *Not Under Forty*, 1936; *Willa Cather on Writing*, 1949; *Willa Cather in Europe*, 1956; *The Kingdom of Art: Willa Cather's First Principles and Critical Statements, 1893-1896*, 1966; *The World and the Parish: Willa Cather's Articles and Reviews, 1893-1902*, 1970 (2 volumes).

MISCELLANEOUS: *Writings from Willa Cather's Campus Years*, 1950.

BIBLIOGRAPHY

Bloom, Edward A., and Lillian D. Bloom. *Willa Cather's Gift of Sympathy*. Carbondale: Southern Illinois University Press, 1962. Considered a classic work of criticism on Cather's works. Addresses Cather's gift of sympathy and skillfully relates it to her thematic interests and technical proficiency. Discusses not only Cather's fiction but also her poetry and essays.

Bloom, Harold, ed. *Modern Critical Views: Willa Cather*. New York: Chelsea House, 1985. Collection of essays includes what Bloom describes as "the best literary criticism on Cather over the last half-century." Particularly valuable for serious Cather scholars. Includes chronology and bibliography.

De Roche, Linda. *Student Companion to Willa Cather*. Westport, Conn.: Greenwood Press, 2006. Provides an introductory overview of Cather's life and work aimed at high school students, college undergraduates, and general readers. Includes analyses of *O Pioneers!*, *My Ántonia*, and *Death Comes for the Archbishop*.

Gerber, Philip L. *Willa Cather*. Rev. ed. New York: Twayne, 1995. Provides an overview of Cather's life and her work, including novels and short stories, and describes the resurgence of criticism of her writings. Includes chronology, notes, annotated bibliography, and index.

Goldberg, Jonathan. *Willa Cather and Others*. Durham, N.C.: Duke University Press, 2001. Discusses Cather's work in relation to the work of various female contemporaries of the author, including opera singer Olive Fremstad, ethnographer and novelist Blair Niles, photographer Laura Gilpin, and writer Pat

Barker. Uses the work of these other women as a means to study Cather's fiction, including *O Pioneers!*, *My Ántonia*, *The Song of the Lark*, and other novels.

Lindermann, Marilee. *The Cambridge Companion to Willa Cather*. New York: Cambridge University Press, 2005. Collection of essays includes examinations of such topics as politics, sexuality, and modernism in Cather's works. Four of the essays focus on analysis of the novels *My Ántonia*, *The Professor's House*, *Death Comes for the Archbishop*, and *Sapphira and the Slave Girl*.

O'Connor, Margaret Anne, ed. *Willa Cather: The Contemporary Reviews*. New York: Cambridge University Press, 2001. Collection reprints reviews that appeared when Cather's books were initially published, with pieces dating from 1903 to 1948. Most of the reviews are from major national journals and newspapers, but some demonstrate critical responses to Cather's works in Nebraska, New Mexico, and other locales in which her books are set.

Romines, Ann, ed. *Willa Cather's Southern Connections: New Essays on Cather and the South*. Charlottesville: University Press of Virginia, 2000. Collection of essays focuses on the influence of Cather's roots in Virginia. Among the novels discussed are *My Mortal Enemy* and *Saphira and the Slave Girl`*.

Rosowski, Susan J. *The Voyage Perilous: Willa Cather's Romanticism*. Lincoln: University of Nebraska Press, 1986. Thematic study interprets Cather's writing within the literary tradition of Romanticism, with a chapter devoted to an analysis of each of her novels.

Shaw, Patrick W. *Willa Cather and the Art of Conflict: Re-visioning Her Creative Imagination*. Troy, N.Y.: Whitston, 1992. Devotes separate chapters to all of Cather's major novels. Reexamines Cather's fiction in terms of her conflicts over her sexuality. The introduction provides a helpful overview of Cather criticism on the topic.

Skaggs, Merrill Maguire, ed. *Willa Cather's New York: New Essays on Cather in the City*. Madison, N.J.: Fairleigh Dickinson University Press, 2001. Collection of twenty essays focuses on Cather's urban fiction and her work for *McClure's*.

Woodress, James. *Willa Cather: A Literary Life*. Lincoln: University of Nebraska Press, 1990. Definitive biography extends previous studies of Cather with fuller accounts of Cather's life and includes new and expanded critical responses to her work, taking feminist criticism into account. In preparing the volume, Woodress was able to use the papers of Cather scholar Bernice Slote. Includes photographs of Cather as well as of people and places important to her.

CAMILO JOSÉ CELA

Born: Iria Flavia del Padrón, Spain; May 11, 1916
Died: Madrid, Spain; January 17, 2002
Also known as: Camilo José Cela Trulock

PRINCIPAL LONG FICTION

La familia de Pascual Duarte, 1942 (*The Family of Pascual Duarte*, 1946, 1964)
Pabellón de reposo, 1943 (*Rest Home*, 1961)
Nuevas andanzas y desventuras del Lazarillo de Tormes, 1944
La colmena, 1951 (*The Hive*, 1953)

Mrs. Caldwell habla con su hijo, 1953 (*Mrs. Caldwell Speaks to Her Son*, 1968)
La Catira, 1955
Tobogán de hambrientos, 1962
Vísperas, festividad, y octava de San Camilo del año 1936 en Madrid, 1969 (*San Camilo, 1936: The Eve, Feast, and Octave of St. Camillus of the Year 1936 in Madrid*, 1991)
Oficio de tinieblas, 5, 1973
Mazurka para dos muertos, 1983 (*Mazurka for Two Dead Men*, 1993)

Cristo versus Arizona, 1988 (*Christ Versus Arizona*, 2007)
El asesinato del perdedor, 1994
La cruz de San Andres, 1994
Madera de Boj, 1999 (*Boxwood*, 2002)

OTHER LITERARY FORMS

The novels of Camilo José Cela (SAY-lah) constitute but a fraction of his literary production. He excelled as a short-story writer and author of travel books, having published more than half a dozen volumes in each of these genres. *Esas nubes que pasan* (1945; passing clouds) contains twelve tales previously published in periodicals. It was followed by *El bonito crimen del carabinero y otras invenciones* (1947; the patrolman's nice crime and other inventions), *El gallego y su cuadrilla* (1949; the Galician and his team), *Baraja de invenciones* (1953; deck of inventions), *El molino de viento* (1956; the windmill), *Gavilla de fábulas sin amor* (1962; bag of loveless fables), *Once cuentos de fútbol* (1963; eleven soccer tales), and others.

Cela's early travel books were superior to the later ones, the better ones including *Viaje a la Alcarria* (1948; *Journey to Alcarria*, 1964), *Del Miño al Bidasoa* (1952; from the Miño to the Bidasoa), *Judíos, moros, y cristianos* (1956; Jews, Moors, and Christians), *Primer viaje andaluz* (1959; first Andalusian trip), *Viaje al Pirineo de Lérida* (1965; trip to the Lérida Pyrenees), *Páginas de geografía errabunda* (1965; pages of vagabond geography), and *Viaje a U.S.A.* (1967; trip to the U.S.).

Cela has many volumes of essays to his credit, including *Mesa revuelta* (1945; messy table); *La rueda de los ocios* (1957; wheel of idleness); *Cajón de sastre* (1957; tailor's box); *La obra literaria del pintor Solana* (1958; the literary work of the painter Solana), which was Cela's entrance speech to the Royal Spanish Academy; *Cuatro figuras del '98* (1961), on four writers of the Generation of '98; *Al servicio de algo* (1969; in service to something); *A vueltas con España* (1973; around again with Spain); *Vuelta de hoja* (1981; turning the page); and *El juego de los tres madroños* (1983; the shell game).

Cela's miscellaneous prose works include his unfinished memoirs, *La cucaña* (the cocoon), of which the first volume, *La rosa* (the rose), published in 1959, spans his childhood. Cela also cultivated what he called *apuntes carpetovetónicos* (carpetovetonic sketches), a term alluding to the mountains of central Spain. These brief literary etchings or vignettes—*Historias de España: Los ciegos, los tontos* (1958) and *Los viejos amigos* (1960, 1961)—combine humor, irony, anger, pity, and a bittersweet affection, and portray beggars, the blind, village idiots, prostitutes, and a host of the poor and indigent. His short stories and novellas range from the exquisitely crafted stylistic tour de force, in which popular language or regional dialect is captured in all of its inimitable regional flavor, to the condensed, violent shocker, the prose poem, and the ironic vignette. The itinerant wanderings of the narrator of picaresque novels are updated in his travel books, as Cela adapted the form to covert sociopolitical commentary. He was also a refreshingly frank, if somewhat arbitrary and arrogant, critic.

During the 1960's, Cela published several limited-edition works for the collectors' market, some with illustrations by Pablo Picasso and others featuring artistic photography, most of them short on narrative and long on the visual, including *Toreo de salón* (1963; living room bull-fighting), *Las compañías convenientes* (1963; appropriate company), *Garito de hospicianos* (1963; poorhouse inmates), *Izas, rabizas, y colipoterras* (1964; bawds, harlots, and whores), *El ciudadano Iscariote Reclús* (1965; citizen Iscariot Reclus), *La familia del héroe* (1965; the hero's family), and a series of seven *Nuevas escenas matritenses* (1965-1966; new Madrid scenes). His *Obra completa* (complete works) first appeared in 1962 and was finished in 1983.

ACHIEVEMENTS

With the death and exile of many writers of previous generations, Spanish literature languished during and after the Spanish Civil War (1936-1939). The first sign of rebirth was Camilo José Cela's novel *The Family of Pascual Duarte*, which sparked a host of imitators and set the pattern for the novel during much of the 1940's, a movement known as *tremendismo*. His next novels were successful, if less imitated, and his fame was assured with *The Hive*, which became the prototype for the social novel of the 1950's and 1960's. It is extremely rare that a Spanish writer is able to live by his or her pen, and Cela managed to do so. He was elected to the prestigious Royal Spanish Academy in 1957 and was appointed independent senator to represent intellectual interests and views by King Juan Carlos in 1978. In 1989, he was awarded the Nobel Prize in Literature. Many of his works have been translated, and for nearly four decades he was considered one of Spain's foremost novelists. Cela was a trendsetter, interesting as an innovator, stylist, and caricaturist but not as a creator of memorable characters or plots.

BIOGRAPHY

Born Camilo José Cela Trulock in 1916, Camilo José Cela occasionally made literature of his life, and many biographies of him contain apocryphal data. Although his mother grew up in Spain, she was a British citizen; his father was a customs official, and the family moved often.

Young Cela was an indifferent student in religious schools. He attended the University of Madrid from 1934 to 1936, during which time he published his first poems. In 1936, he dropped out of school to serve on the side of General Francisco Franco and his rebels in the Spanish Civil War. He returned to the university from 1939 to 1943, a period during which he published his first articles and short stories as well as his famous first novel, *The Family of Pascual Duarte*. Although Cela studied law, medicine, and philosophy, he did not complete a degree. His literary knowledge was largely self-taught, the fruit of reading the Spanish classics while recovering from bouts of tuberculosis as a young man. Cela likewise became a serious student of regional Spanish history and folkways and an untiring lexicographer of sexual and scatological speech. Cela married María del Rosario Conde Picavea in 1944; their only child, a son, was born in 1946.

Over the years Cela involved himself in several publishing enterprises, and in 1957 he founded the influential journal *Papeles de Son Armadans*. This was the first Spanish periodical of its kind to circumvent the censor-

ship of the Franco regime, possible in large part because of Cela's having fought on the winning side during the Spanish Civil War. Despite his connections, Cela found it expedient to avoid the political limelight by moving to the Balearic Islands during the 1960's. There he counted among his friends such luminaries as artist Joan Miró and poet Robert Graves. Only after winning the Nobel Prize in 1989 did he return to the Spanish mainland. Cela and his first wife were divorced in 1991, at which time Cela married journalist Marina Castaño.

ANALYSIS

Camilo José Cela had an inimitable way with language, a personal style that is instantly recognizable after minimal acquaintance, thanks to his characteristic handling of the *estribillo* (tag line), alliterative and rhythmic prose, parallelistic constructions, grotesque caricatures

Camilo José Cela. (The Granger Collection, New York)

with moments of tenderness, unabashed lyricism with ever-present irony, and the incorporation of popular sayings or proverbs, vulgarities, and obscenities in the context of academically correct and proper passages. His art more closely approaches the painter's than the dramatist's, and it is far removed from the adventure novel.

With the exception perhaps of *The Family of Pascual Duarte*, Cela's novels have little action and a preponderance of description and dialogue. As a painter with words, one of whose favorite subjects is language itself, unflaggingly aware of its trivializations and absurdities yet fascinated with nuances, examining and playing with words, Cela produced ironic conversations, incidents, and scenes that often could very well stand alone. This characteristic, usually one of his virtues as a writer, becomes at times a vice, for he tends to repeat himself and also to produce novels in which there is little if any character development and often no sustained or sequential action—no plot in the traditional sense. The reader whose interest in a piece of fiction is proportional to "what happens" may find Cela's short stories more rewarding than his novels.

Because it inspired many imitations, Cela's first novel, *The Family of Pascual Duarte*, is considered the prototype of a novelistic movement called *tremendismo*, an allusion to its "tremendous" impact upon the reader's sensibilities. *Tremendismo*—a modified naturalism that lacks the scientific pretensions of the French movement, and to which expressionistic ingredients were added— was characterized by depiction of crimes of sometimes shocking violence, a wide range of mental and sexual aberrations, and antiheroic figures. Frequently repulsive, deviant, and nauseating acts, as well as an accumulation of ugly, malformed, and repugnant characters, were portrayed against a backdrop of poverty and social problems. To this naturalistic setting were added expressionistic techniques including stylized distortion and the use of caricature and dehumanization (reduction of characters, or acts, or both, to animalistic levels). *Tremendismo* had links with postwar existentialism in the absurdity of the world portrayed, the concern with problems of guilt and authenticity, and the radical solitariness and uncommunicative nature of its characters. In part, the movement was inspired by the horrors of the Spanish Civil War, providing an outlet for outrage when overt protest was impossible.

Not all of Cela's early novels fit this class: The accumulation of violent and sadistic or irrational crimes that are found in the prototypical first novel disappeared in its successor, *Rest Home*, which is set in a tuberculosis sanatorium, an environment the author had occasion to know well. *Rest Home* uses the diary form, excerpts from the writings of several anonymous patients. The sense of alienation and despair that results from helplessness pervades this novel as the victims battle not only their disease but also the indifference of the world at large and the callousness or cruelty of medical personnel; this insensitivity to death, humanity's cruelty to others, is the "tremendous" element in this otherwise quiet, hopeless, almost paralytic novel. In *The Hive*, it is the overall tone or atmosphere (there is only one crime, an unsolved murder), an atmosphere of defeatism, cynicism, and sordid materialism, that is characteristic of *tremendismo*. Still, although critics continue to talk of *tremendismo* in *The Hive*, it is so modified and attenuated that there is a legitimate question as to whether the world portrayed in the novel can rightly be so described.

THE FAMILY OF PASCUAL DUARTE

Pascual Duarte, the protagonist and narrative consciousness of *The Family of Pascual Duarte*, is a condemned criminal on death row who has undertaken to write his confession as a sort of penance, at the behest of the prison chaplain. Cela utilizes a model derived from the classic Spanish picaresque novel, clearly perceptible in the early chapters—a technique that undoubtedly served to make the somewhat scabrous material more acceptable to the regime's puritanical but strongly nationalist and traditionalistic censors. The frequent appearances of roads, inns and taverns, squalid settings, and marginal characters all reflect the picaresque tradition, as does the first-person, autobiographical form.

Pascual's home life, with a brutal father who made his money illegally, an alcoholic and altogether beastly mother (clearly patterned on the mother of the prototypical picaro, Lazarillo de Tormes), and a sister who became a teenage prostitute, was an endless round of brawls. Exemplifying the notion that hopeless situations go from bad to worse is his mother's promiscuity and the birth of his half brother, Mario, an imbecile who comes into the world at the same time that Pascual's father, locked in a wardrobe, is dying amid hideous screams after having been bitten by a rabid dog.

Mario never learns to walk or talk but drags himself along the floor like a snake, making whistling noises. He is kicked in the head by his putative father, which results in a festering sore, and finally has an ear and part of his face eaten by a pig as he lies in the street. His brief, unhappy existence comes to an end at the age of seven or eight when he falls into a large stone container of olive oil and drowns. Pascual's grotesquely lyric recollection of the child's one moment of "beauty," with the golden oil clinging to his hair and softening his features and expression, is typical of Cela's art. The burial of Mario (attended only by Pascual and a village girl, Lola, who was attracted to him) is climaxed by Pascual's rape of Lola atop Mario's newly dug grave. It is characteristic of Cela also to combine Eros and Thanatos, sexuality and death: Humanity is viewed as a sensual animal, its reproductive appetite or instincts aroused by the presence of death.

Pascual's name alludes to the Paschal lamb, or Easter sacrifice, and in an author's foreword to a special edition of the novel printed outside Spain for use by English-speaking students of Spanish, Cela spoke of the "prorata of guilt" or responsibility that each member of society shares for the crimes committed by one of that society's members, suggesting that persons are products of the society in and by which they are formed and thus, at best, only partially culpable for their acts. Pascual is a product of the dregs of society, whose existence is the result of the worst kind of social injustice, yet he displays no greed or resentment of the easy life of the wealthy; his crimes are usually crimes of passion and, with the exception of the killing of his mother, are not premeditated.

Significantly, Pascual is always morally superior in one or more ways to his victims, suggesting that he is to be viewed as something of a primitive judge and executioner, taking justice into his own hands. His meting out of retribution spares neither person nor beast: He shoots his hunting hound because the dog looked at him the wrong way (interpreted by him as sexual desire or temptation); he knifes his mare (and only transportation) because she had shied, throwing Pascual's pregnant bride and causing her to miscarry; he strangles his first wife in a moment of temporary insanity, upon learning that

while he was jailed for knifing a man in a tavern brawl, she had survived by selling herself to El Estirao, the pimp exploiting Pascual's sister; and he later asphyxiates El Estirao when the pimp taunts him. The ax-murder of his mother (who subverted the scruples of his first wife and was ruining his second marriage as well) is one of the bloodiest and most violent passages in contemporary Spanish fiction, yet the reader cannot entirely condemn Pascual.

The novel alternates chapters of violent action with slower, introspective and meditative chapters that not only vary the narrative rhythm but also serve to present the human side of the criminal, who might otherwise appear nothing less than monstrous. They also make it clear that Pascual is completely lacking in social consciousness; his crimes are not politically motivated, nor do they have any connection with revolution in the social sense—a point that is extremely important to the hidden message of the novel as a whole. Although Pascual's autobiographical memoir is abruptly ended by his execution (he had narrated his life only up to the slaying of his mother), it is possible to deduce from evidence elsewhere in the text that he spent some fifteen years in the penitentiary as a result of his conviction for matricide; he was released at a moment immediately prior to the outbreak of the Spanish Civil War that coincided with a brief but bloody social revolution that swept his home province of Badajoz. The reader deduces (for the cause of his execution is nowhere stated) that Pascual has been convicted of the murder of the Count of Torremejía, the major clue being the dedication of his memoirs to the Count, Don Jesús, accompanied by an ambiguous statement that could mean that he killed him, but could also convey the idea of a mercy killing, assuming that he found the Count dying in agony, perhaps having been tortured by terrorists.

A supreme irony inheres in Pascual's having received extremely light sentences—from two to fifteen years—for several previous killings, while he is executed as a common criminal for what might normally have been classed an act of war, because the victim was an aristocrat. Given the totalitarian censorship in force at the time the novel was written, none of this is overtly expressed; it is necessary to have a thorough knowledge of contemporary Spanish history and to be aware of such details as the social revolution in Badajoz, likewise unmentioned in the novel, to be able to interpret the otherwise enigmatic denouement to Pascual's career of violence.

One of the clearest proofs that Cela's major virtue is his style is the fact that, despite competent translations, his works have been relatively ill received by readers of the English-language versions; his style, like poetry, is lost in translation. Too closely bound to colloquial idiom and regional dialect to be fully translatable, Cela's prose must be appreciated in the original. Thus, Pascual Duarte's story is atypical in being able to stand on its own in other cultures, as was confirmed by the success of the 1976 film version, which won a best actor's award at the Cannes International Film Festival for José Luis Gómez. With all of his contradictions, Pascual is Cela's most complex and memorable character; none of his subsequent novels contains characters sufficiently developed to intrigue the reader and sustain his or her interest.

The Family of Pascual Duarte has been compared by critics repeatedly to Albert Camus's *L'étranger* (1942; *The Stranger*) because of proximity in date of appearance and certain other similarities (the antihero and protagonist-narrator of each novel is a condemned killer awaiting execution, one who speaks impassively of his life and exhibits a shocking lack of internalization of society's values). The differences between the two novels are many, however, the most important being that the narrative consciousness of *The Stranger* is an educated and moderately cultured man, guilty of a single, senseless "reflex" crime, and the philosophical dimension of Camus's writing, while not utterly alien to Cela, is so attenuated because of the audience for which the novel was intended that its impact is minimal.

THE HIVE

The Hive, regarded by many critics as Cela's masterpiece, occupied much of the novelist's time between 1945 and 1950. Because it lacks both plot and protagonist, consisting of a series of loosely connected sketches, some have suggested that Cela must have used as his model John Dos Passos's *Manhattan Transfer* (1925); both novels attempt a wide-ranging portrait of urban life. The similarities are relatively superficial, however, and a major difference exists in the treatment of time: *Manhattan Transfer* covers some twenty years, while *The Hive* spans only a few days. The action in *The Hive* takes place during the winter of 1943, and a specific reference is made to the meeting of Winston Churchill, Joseph Stalin, and Franklin D. Roosevelt in November of that year, undoubtedly selected by Cela because it was one of the worst periods for Spain, a time when postwar reconstruction had not begun, wartime shortages had grown worse, and the countries that might have helped Spain were too occupied with World War II to think of the Spanish people's plight.

This background is very significant to the ambience and psychological climate of the novel; characters are either concerned with where their next meal will come from or are involved in the black market and the abuse of the hungry. Many characters are moochers who hang around cafés in the hope of being offered a drink or a meal, or at least a cigarette, while several girls and women are obliged to sell themselves for food, medicine, or small necessities.

In *The Hive*, Cela brings together a number of characters with no more mutual relationship than that which results from being in the same place for a brief time. The common site in part 1 is the café of Doña Rosa. Although the author in one of his many prologues to the successive editions claims that he did nothing but go to the plaza with his camera, "and if the models were ugly, too bad," this suggestion of objective, mimetic technique must not be taken too literally, for large doses of his characteristic exaggeration, dehumanization, and caricature are present, as can be appreciated in the figure of Rosa, one of Cela's most repugnant females.

Exceedingly fat, Rosa smokes, drinks, coughs continually, dotes upon bloody tales of violence and crime, is foulmouthed, and has such a habit of peeling off her face that she is compared to a serpent changing its skin; she has a mustache, beaded with sweat, its hairs like the little black "horns" of a cricket, and spends her days insulting and cheating the customers. There is also a suggestion that she is a lesbian. Much of the negative presentation becomes understandable when one reflects that Doña Rosa is an outspoken advocate of Adolf Hitler: At a time when no criticism of fascism was possible inside Spain, Rosa presents such extreme physical and moral ugliness that her ideological preferences necessarily suffer by association.

Several other recurring motifs of Cela's fiction are apparent in *The Hive*: the division of humanity into the basic categories of victims and victimizers, the obsessive preoccupation with aberrant sexuality, the notion that the bad are many and the good are few (and generally not too bright), the concept that humankind is innately cruel, and the insistent repetition of tag lines and names or nicknames. So frequent and systematic is the use of nicknames and variants of the names of characters that, when combined with the large number of characters and the usual brevity of their appearances, it is next to impossible to determine exactly how many characters there are, as well as to be sure in many cases whether a character is completely new or one previously met and now reappearing under a nickname. Various commentators have placed the total number of characters at 160, but other estimates suggest more than 360. Obviously, with few exceptions, characters are superficially drawn, usually caricatures; only a handful can be said to have any psychological depth.

Each of the novel's six parts is unified by some common denominator (in addition to the time, for there is a certain simultaneity of events in each part or chapter). In the first part, all the characters have some relationship to the café of Doña Rosa, whether as employees, regular customers, or accidental visitors. In the second part, events take place in the street, beginning immediately outside the café as Martín Marco, a ne'er-do-well who serves as a sort of link between various parts and locales, is kicked out for not paying his bill. Some of the customers are followed from the street to their houses, while others are seen in the third part in still another café, where Martín also goes to talk with still more characters (several of whom are under police surveillance and apparently arrested before the novel's end, implicating Martín also).

The next part returns to the street and events late at night after the closing of the cafés, when the wealthy go to after-hours clubs and the poor must use the vacant lots for their furtive encounters. The common denominator of part 5 is eroticism, with a wide range of amorous intrigues (light on sentiment and heavy on sexuality) and views of several houses of ill repute of different economic levels. There is also a recurring theme of loss, as most of the characters lose something (dreams, hope, illusions,

virginity). The clearest example is the case of an adolescent girl, an orphan sold by her aunt to an aged pedophile. The sixth part is united by the numerous reawakenings with the new day, some characters in their homes, others in brothels, Doña Rosa in her café before dawn, the homeless gypsy boy beneath the city bridge, some breakfasting and others hungry, part of the city already going to work and a few about to go to bed. The protagonist, if there is one, is collective: the city of Madrid, which is the beehive of the title, with its workers and drones.

Reviewers of the English translation saw *The Hive* as a passable example of the "low-life genre," but if one is sufficiently familiar with the sociopolitical situation of Spain at the time the novel was written, it is possible to extract additional meanings. All of the numerous characters of the novel reappear several times, with the exceptions of Suárez, who is gay, and his lover; the two are accused of complicity in the murder of Suárez's mother, Doña Margot, not on the basis of any evidence but because their sexual identity was not acceptable. The two are taken to police headquarters for interrogation and simply disappear for the remainder of the novel, a case of critique via omission, a not uncommon technique in the rhetoric of silent dissent.

Another interest of the novelist is the invisible links between human beings, who are usually themselves unaware of those links. Thus Matilde, a widowed pensioner and client of Doña Rosa, owns a boardinghouse where Ventura Aguado, lover of Rosa's niece, resides—connections unknown to all concerned, reflecting existential theories of human relationships. A much more elaborate development of this theme occurs in Cela's *Tobogán de hambrientos*, in which each chapter presents a new cast of characters, linked only by one tenuous contact with a single character from the previous chapter. Thus, in chapter 1, an entire family appears; the following chapter may present the family and relatives and friends of the boyfriend of one daughter of the family in the first chapter, and chapter 3 may take up the associates and relatives of the garbage collector of the family of the boyfriend, chapter 4 the boss of the daughter of the garbage collector, and so on, through a certain number of chapters after which the process is reversed and the novelist proceeds in inverse order, through the same groups, back to the point of origin.

While mild in comparison with many of Cela's later works, *The Hive* was daring for its day, and Spanish publishers refused to touch it; it was published in Buenos Aires, Argentina, and smuggled into Spain, selling so well that the government (which levied a profitable tax on several stages of the book business) authorized an expurgated edition, which in turn was soon prohibited and withdrawn from circulation when objectionable points were found—a procedure repeated nine times by 1962. Not only is *The Hive* significant from the standpoint of literary history as a model for the neorealistic "social" novel in Spain during the 1950's and 1960's; it also had considerable import in its day as a manifestation of liberal intellectual opposition to the Franco dictatorship and its policies.

The Hive was a turning point in Cela's development as a novelist, marking a transition from rural to urban settings and from a semitraditional format to open experimentalism and fragmentary structures. Although the novel's transitions from character to character and scene to scene may seem abrupt or arbitrary, they are in fact artfully calculated and serve to make otherwise censurable material more palatable than if it had been presented in its totality, without interruption or suspension.

MRS. CALDWELL SPEAKS TO HER SON

The fragmentary nature of *Mrs. Caldwell Speaks to Her Son* is even more apparent, with more than two hundred brief chapters, in which sequential or connected action is again lacking. The time element is extremely vague and diffuse; the narration is almost totally retrospective but not in any semblance of chronological order. Mrs. Caldwell speaks in the second-person singular (the familiar you, or "thou") to her son Ephraim, sometimes reminiscing, sometimes railing, at other times waxing lyrical (there are even sections that are lyric asides, in the nature of prose poems, such as one quite lengthy piece titled "The Iceberg"). Bit by bit, it becomes apparent to the reader that Mrs. Caldwell's relationship with her son has abnormal undertones, including incest, abuse, sexual or psychological bondage, and possibly crimes involving third parties; subsequently, it is revealed that Ephraim is dead and has been so for many years, drowned in unexplained circumstances in the Aegean Sea. Mrs. Caldwell, the reader realizes, is insane; whether any of the things she recalls actually happened is a matter of conjecture, as is the reality of the ending, for she is supposedly burned to death when she paints flames on the wall of her room in the asylum.

Surrealistic elements are more prominent in *Mrs. Caldwell Speaks to Her Son* than in any of Cela's previously published prose, although they abound in his early book of poetry *Poemas de una adolescencia cruel* (1945), written for the most part during the Spanish Civil War and published in 1945. The surrealistic substratum comes to the surface periodically during the writer's career and is especially evident in the hallucinatory oratorio *María Sabina* (1967), performed in 1970, and in *El solitario*, a series of absurdist and surrealistic sketches published in 1963. It comes to the fore in Cela's long fiction in *San Camilo, 1936*, and in *Oficio de tinieblas, 5*. Readers whose concept of Cela had been based on acquaintance with his best-known novels were surprised and disconcerted by what seemed to be an abrupt about-face on his part, a switch from an objective and essentially realistic manner to extreme subjectivity of focus, with an emphasis upon vanguard experimentalism in *San Camilo, 1936*, and *Oficio de tinieblas, 5*. In fact, both the extended second-person monologue of the former and the extreme discontinuity of the latter are clearly anticipated in *Mrs. Caldwell Speaks to Her Son*.

SAN CAMILO, 1936

San Camilo, 1936, and *The Hive* are comparable in providing panoramic views of Madrid at similar points in Spanish history (1936 and 1942, respectively); in both, historical events are interwoven with everyday concerns. Both novels feature an enormous cast and exhibit a strong awareness of social injustice, poverty, hunger, and exploitation. In both, Cela's characteristic emphasis on sexual themes, abnormality, deviance, and the scatological are prominent, and both encompass only a few days in the life of the capital. Both are essentially plotless, depending upon strict temporal and spatial limitation for unity in place of the structuring function normally exercised by plot; both lack protagonists in the normal sense, although the city of Madrid may play this role. Both novels feature innumerable cuts, abrupt changes of scene, shifts of focus, and an architectonic design, a complex pattern the most visible features of which are repetition and parallelism.

However, *San Camilo, 1936*, is far from being a mere extension or replay of the earlier novel; a most significant difference is the setting in republican Spain, which imparts a sense of freedom, even license, lacking in *The Hive*. The days spanned in *San Camilo, 1936*, are marked by major historical events, immediately preceding and following the outbreak of the Spanish Civil War in July of 1936.

The action of *San Camilo, 1936* begins on Sunday, July 12, 1936, which witnessed the political assassination of Lieutenant Castillo, in reprisal for his part in the killing, three months before, of a cousin of José Antonio Primo de Rivera, founder of the Falange. Revenge for Castillo's killing, a gangster-style execution of conservative opposition leader Calvo Sotelo on July 13, led to a series of riots and was the pretext for the uprising on July 16 of General Franco and several other military leaders, obliging the republican government to distribute arms to the populace on July 18. These events, and the funerals of both victims (July 14), are re-created from the vantage point of several witnesses in the novel, although the underlying reasons are not elucidated and the historical antecedents are not mentioned.

The atmosphere of growing tension and pent-up violence is subliminally reinforced through the novelist's concentration on a series of minor crimes, accidental deaths, actual and attempted political reprisals by both extremes, repetitive motifs of blood and suffering, and an intensifying irrational desire on the part of the narrative consciousness to kill. An impression of neutrality is nevertheless sustained; with three decades of hindsight, the novelist's ire is directed less at those at either extreme of the Spanish political spectrum than at foreign intervention—a significant departure from the usual strongly partisan accounts of the Spanish Civil War.

OFICIO DE TINIEBLAS, 5

Oficio de tinieblas, 5, is a novel only in the loosest sense, a logical extension of Cela's continuing experimentation with the genre; its obsessive preoccupation with Eros and Thanatos, its language and tone are indubitably his. Discontinuous in structure, this work comprises nearly twelve hundred "monads" (numbered paragraphs or subdivisions) abounding in references to farce, concealment, deceit, flight, self-effacement, defeat, inauthenticity, self-elimination, betrayal, prostitu-

tion, alienation, and death. Cela's disappointed idealism and his retreat into apparent cynicism are expressed in *San Camilo, 1936*, in the theme of massive prostitution—of the state, the nation, the leaders and lawmakers, the ideologies, the totality of Spanish existence. In *Oficio de tinieblas, 5*, Cela's retreat takes the form of a desire for death and oblivion, counterpointed by an obsessive emphasis on sexual aberration (the novel is saved from being pornographic by learned euphemisms, Latin and medical terminology for sexual organs and activity).

MAZURKA FOR TWO DEAD MEN

The new freedom of Spain's post-Franco era is reflected in *Mazurka for Two Dead Men*, Cela's first novel to be published after Franco's death. Here, Cela continues his exploration of violence, portraying the monotonous brutality of peasant life in his native Galicia with fablelike simplicity. Told by multiple narrators, the novel takes place during the first four decades of the twentieth century and treats the Spanish Civil War as merely the culmination of a long cycle of violence. Any appearance of neutrality has been suspended, however, as the pro-Franco characters are clearly villainous, the prorepublicans heroic. Perhaps more notable are the appearances in the novel of a character named Don Camilo and a family named Cela.

CHRIST VERSUS ARIZONA

In 1954, Cela had been welcomed in Venezuela as a guest of honor and commissioned to write a novel set there. The result was *La Catira*, an ambitious book that nevertheless made clear Cela's lack of interest in sustained narrative. The novel that followed *Mazurka for Two Dead Men* is similarly set outside Spain but makes clear one manner—itself often daunting—in which Cela has overcome this apparent defect. As its title suggests, *Christ Versus Arizona* takes place in the American Southwest. Told through the brutal words of Wendell Liverpool Espana, the novel deals with events in Arizona during the final two decades of the nineteenth century and the first two of the twentieth century. These events include the legendary gunfight at the OK Corral, an event in which Cela expressed much interest and whose site he visited. Espana relates his sordid story of violence and murder in a long monologue without paragraph breaks that clearly reveals his mental state but that makes considerable demands of the reader.

EL ASESINATO DEL PERDEDOR

El asesinato del perdedor continues Cela's increasingly difficult experimental style and relates the story—if it can be called that—of Mateo Ruecas, who commits suicide while in prison. The novel is not divided into chapters but rather incorporates the seemingly unrelated (if uniformly brutal and vulgar) monologues of a host of unidentified secondary characters. Cela's first novel to be published after he received the Nobel Prize, *El asesinato del perdedor* may well reflect Cela's well-known disdain for authority and "proper" behavior.

Janet Pérez
Updated by Grove Koger

OTHER MAJOR WORKS

SHORT FICTION: *Esas nubes que pasan*, 1945; *El bonito crimen del carabinero y otras invenciones*, 1947; *El gallego y su cuadrilla*, 1949; *Baraja de invenciones*, 1953; *El molino de viento*, 1956; *Nuevo retablo de don Cristobita*, 1957; *Historias de España: Los ciegos, los tontos*, 1958; *Los viejos amigos*, 1960, 1961 (2 volumes); *Gavilla de fábulas sin amor*, 1962; *El solitario*, 1963; *Once cuentos de fútbol*, 1963; *Toreo de salón*, 1963; *Izas, rabizas, y colipoterras*, 1964; *El ciudadano Iscariote Reclús*, 1965; *La familia del héroe*, 1965; *El hombre y el mar*, 1990; *Historias familiares*, 1998.

POETRY: *Poemas de una adolescencia cruel*, 1945 (also known as *Pisando la dudosa luz del día*, 1960); *María Sabina*, 1967; *Cancionero de la Alcarria*, 1987; *Poesía completa*, 1996.

NONFICTION: *Mesa revuelta*, 1945; *Viaje a la Alcarria*, 1948 (*Journey to Alcarria*, 1964); *Del Miño al Bidasoa*, 1952; *Judíos, moros, y cristianos*, 1956; *Cajón de sastre*, 1957; *La rueda de los ocios*, 1957; *La obra literaria del pintor Solana*, 1958; *Primer viaje andaluz*, 1959; *La rosa*, 1959 (volume 1 of *La cucaña*, his unfinished memoirs); *Cuatro figuras del '98*, 1961; *Las compañías convenientes*, 1963; *Garito de hospicianos*, 1963; *Páginas de geografía errabunda*, 1965; *Viaje al Pirineo de Lérida*, 1965; *Viaje a U.S.A.*, 1967; *Al servicio de algo*, 1969; *A vueltas con España*, 1973; *Vuelta de hoja*, 1981; *El juego de los tres madroños*, 1983; *El asno de Buridán*, 1986; *Galicia*, 1990; *Blanquito, peón de Brega*, 1991; *Memorias, entendimientos, y voluntades*, 1993; *El color de la mañana*, 1996.

MISCELLANEOUS: *Obra completa*, 1962-1989; *Nuevas escenas matritenses: Fotografías de Enrique Palazuelo*, 1965-1966.

BIBLIOGRAPHY

Busette, Cedric. *"La Familia de Pascual Duarte" and "El Túnel": Correspondences and Divergencies in the Exercise of Craft*. Lanham, Md.: University Press of America, 1994. Busette compares and contrasts the debut novels of Cela and Ernesto Sábato, analyzing their narrative, language, protagonists, and other aspects of the two novels.

Cela, Camilo José. Interview by Valerie Miles. *Paris Review* 38, no. 139 (Summer, 1996): 124-163. A lengthy interview in which Cela discusses his personal life and career, including his family and academic background, literary training, some of his works, and thoughts on censorship.

Charlebois, Lucile C. *Understanding Camilo José Cela*. Columbia: University of South Carolina Press, 1998. A thorough but difficult study of Cela's progressively difficult novels. Each chapter focuses on one of the novels, beginning with *The Family of Pascual Duarte* through *La cruz de San Andres*. Includes a chronology and a select bibliography.

Henn, David. *C. J. Cela: La Colmena*. 1974. Reprint. London: Grant & Cutler, 1997. An eighty-page brief study of *The Hive*, usually recognized as Cela's masterpiece. Part of the Critical Guides to Spanish Texts series. This reprint includes an updated bibliography.

Hoyle, Alan. *Cela: "La familia de Pascual Duarte."* London: Grant & Cutler, with Tamesis Books, 1994. Another book in the Critical Guides to Spanish Texts series, providing an analysis of Cela's first and best-known novel.

Kerr, Sarah. "Shock Treatment." *The New York Review of Books*, October 8, 1992. A review and article discussing Cela's novels *The Family of Pascual Duarte*, *Journey to Alcarria*, *The Hive*, *Mrs. Caldwell Speaks to Her Son*, and *San Camilo, 1936*.

McPheeters, D. W. *Camilo José Cela*. New York: Twayne, 1969. An accessible, though dated, overview of Cela's work, part of the Twayne World Authors series. Includes a chronology and a useful bibliography of secondary sources.

Mantero, Manual. "Camilo José Cela: The Rejection of the Ordinary." *Georgia Review* 49, no. 1 (Spring, 1995): 246-250. Mantero provides an appreciation of Cela's most representative works, describing the author's use of humor and names, characterization, and refusal to accept the routine or ordinary.

Peréz, Janet. *Camilo José Cela Revisited: The Later Novels.* New York: Twayne, 2000. Peréz updates and expands McPheeters's 1969 overview. Concentrates on Cela's novels. Includes biographical material, an index, and an annotated bibliography for further study.

Turner, Harriet, and Adelaida López de Martínez, eds. *The Cambridge Companion to the Spanish Novel: From 1600 to the Present.* New York: Cambridge University Press, 2003. Cela's work is discussed in several places, particularly in chapter 11, "The Testimonial Novel and the Novel of Memory." Helps to place Cela's work within the broader context of the Spanish novel.

LOUIS-FERDINAND CÉLINE

Born: Courbevoie, France; May 27, 1894
Died: Meudon, France; July 1, 1961
Also known as: Louis-Ferdinand Destouches

PRINCIPAL LONG FICTION

Voyage au bout de la nuit, 1932 (*Journey to the End of the Night*, 1934)
Mort à crédit, 1936 (*Death on the Installment Plan*, 1938)
Guignol's band I, 1944 (*Guignol's Band*, 1954)
Casse-pipe, 1949 (fragment)
Féerie pour une autre fois I, 1952 (*Fable for Another Time*, 2003)
Féerie pour une autre fois II: Normance, 1954
Entretiens avec le professeur Y, 1955 (*Conversations with Professor Y*, 1986)
D'un château l'autre, 1957 (*Castle to Castle*, 1968)
Nord, 1960 (*North*, 1972)
Le Pont de Londres: Guignol's band II, 1964 (*London Bridge: Guignol's Band II*, 1995)
Rigodon, 1969 (*Rigadoon*, 1974)

OTHER LITERARY FORMS

In addition to his novels, Louis-Ferdinand Céline (say-LEEN) published his dissertation for his medical degree, the biographical work *La Vie et l' uvre de Philippe-Ignace Semmelweis* (1936), and a denunciation of life in the Soviet Union under Communism titled *Mea culpa* (1936); the last two of these appeared in English in 1937 in a volume titled *"Mea Culpa," with "The Life and Work of Semmelweis."* He also wrote a play, *L'Église* (pb. 1933; *The Church*, 2003); three anti-Semitic pamphlets, *Bagatelles pour un massacre* (1937; trifles for a massacre), *L'École des cadavres* (1938; school for corpses), and *Les Beaux Draps* (1941; a fine mess); and several ballets, which were collected in *Ballets, sans musique, sans personne, sans rien* (1959; *Ballets Without Music, Without Dancers, Without Anything*, 1999). Céline's diatribe against Jean-Paul Sartre, who had accused him of having collaborated with the Nazis for money, was published as *l'agité du bocal* (1949; to the restless one in the jar). Céline claimed to have lost several manuscripts when his apartment was pillaged during the Occupation. A surviving fragment of a novel was published as *Casse-pipe*.

ACHIEVEMENTS

Hailed by many as one of the foremost French writers of the twentieth century, condemned by others for the repulsive depiction of humanity in his fictional works and for the vileness of his anti-Semitic pamphlets, Louis-Ferdinand Céline remains a controversial figure in French letters. One can place him in the French tradition of the *poètes maudits* (cursed poets), a lineage that begins with the medieval poet François Villon and includes such figures as Charles Baudelaire, Arthur Rimbaud, and Jean Genet. Like them, Céline sought to subvert traditional writing and thereby shock the conventional reader into a new sensibility. His works, like theirs, are colored by a personal life that is equally scandalous.

Céline's novels have contributed to modern literature a singularly somber existentialist view of human society. Unlike some characters in Sartre's novels, Céline's Ferdinand (all his protagonists are variations of the same character) is unable to transcend the disorder, pain, despair, and ugliness of life through heroic action or political commitment. A doctor as well as a writer, Céline was acutely aware of the biology of human destiny—that decay, disease, and death ultimately erase all forms of distinction and that, in a world without God, there is nothing beyond the grave.

In the course of his apprenticeship to life—his journey to the end of the night—Céline's protagonist experiences the shattering of the common illusions and self-delusions that obscure the true nature of existence. The lucidity he thereby acquires narrows the ironic distance between his point of view and that of the older and wiser protagonist-turned-narrator. Whatever may be the inherent value of that lucidity, it does not serve as an end in itself. It must ultimately be transmitted, in the context of the journey that engendered it, to the reader in the form of a narrative. Céline's protagonist is driven to experience life in all of its diversity, so that he may survive to tell about it. Céline doubtless had imposed upon himself a similar mission.

Unlike Sartre and other existentialist writers, Céline eschews abstract philosophical debates in favor of a style appropriate to the nature of the experiences he relates. He chooses a form of poetic delirium. Art, for Céline, is a process of transformation that intermingles reality and fantasy, dream and nightmare, the sublime and the grotesque, the personal and the cosmic. In several of his novels, he gives as the irrational cause of the narrative the aggravation of an old head wound, from which, metaphorically, the words spill forth onto the page. The particular idiom he employs—what he calls his "emotional subway"—is no less subversive of traditional French letters than the visions it translates: a carefully concerted conversational style punctuated with slang, obscenities, neologisms, and foreign words. The "rails" of his sub-

way are his frequently used ellipsis points, which fragment his prose into staccato units, bombarding the reader with pulsations of verbal energy. Vision and style complement each other, allowing Céline's readers no complacency as they become, grudgingly perhaps, passengers on a terrifying but exhilarating underground journey.

BIOGRAPHY

Louis-Ferdinand Céline was born Louis-Ferdinand Destouches in the Parisian suburb of Courbevoie on May 27, 1894, and was reared and educated in Paris. His father worked for an insurance company; Céline's mother owned a shop in an arcade, where she sold old lace and antiques. As a soldier during World War I, Céline was injured in the head and ear and was shot in the arm. The head and ear wounds were to leave him with a lifelong buzzing in his head and frequent bouts of insomnia; the arm wound earned for him a medal and a picture on the cover of a national magazine.

After his demobilization, Céline worked for a trading company in the Cameroons. It was during his stay in Africa that he began to write. His interest in medicine led to a job with the Rockefeller Foundation. He received his medical degree in 1918 and briefly practiced in the city of Rennes. He soon wearied of his middle-class existence, however, and, after divorcing his first wife, Edith Follet, he took a medical position with the League of Nations. He lost that post when he showed his superior, who was Jewish, a copy of his play *The Church*, in which there is crude satire of Jewish officials at the League of Nations. Céline wrote *Journey to the End of the Night* while working at a clinic, having taken as his nom de plume the surname of his maternal grandmother. The novel was greeted with enormous critical acclaim, and Céline's literary career was launched, though he would continue to practice medicine.

In 1937, Céline published *Bagatelles pour un massacre*, the first of three viciously anti-Semitic pamphlets. In it, he lauds Adolf Hitler for bringing a new order to a Europe that had degenerated, according to Céline, as the result of Jewish attempts to dominate the world. During the Occupation, various letters and brief articles signed by Céline appeared in the collaborationist press.

In July, 1944, Céline fled Paris, having been denounced as a traitor by the British Broadcasting Corporation and threatened with execution by the Resistance. He sought the relative political safety of Denmark, where he had deposited money from his royalties. In the company of his second wife, Lucette Almanzor, and his cat, Bébert, he managed to make his way across war-ravaged Germany to Copenhagen. The French government instituted proceedings to extradite him so that he could be tried as a traitor. Céline was to spend some five years in Denmark, including more than one year in prison, while his case was being prepared. He maintained that his pamphlets were directed only against those Jews who were supposedly pushing France into yet another war with Germany. He also claimed that he had never written for the pro-Nazi press and that his name had been used without his consent.

On February 23, 1950, a French tribunal condemned him in absentia as a traitor to his country. Thirteen months later, he was granted amnesty as a disabled veteran of World War I. Shortly thereafter, he returned to France to resume his literary career as well as to practice medicine. On July 1, 1961, while editing his last novel, he died of a stroke.

Knowledge of Céline's biography is crucial to a comprehension of his novels, for the events of the author's life constitute a point of departure for his fiction. Despite the many resemblances between Céline and his protagonists, particularly in the later novels, his works are by no means thinly veiled autobiography. His art distorts, enlarges, and mythologizes the autobiographical elements in the transformational process of fiction-making.

ANALYSIS

Louis-Ferdinand Céline's novelistic production can be divided into three principal phases, which are usually linked to developments in the author's life. Thus, one can discern an initial period consisting of the novels written before he fled to Denmark, which concludes with the publication of *Guignol's Band*. The two volumes of *Fable for Another Time* constitute a second phase in Céline's literary production, for they mark the resumption of his literary career after his return to France and the controversial resolution of his political difficulties. In both novels, there is an increasing confusion—literally and figuratively—among protagonist, narrator, and au-

Louis-Ferdinand Céline. (The Granger Collection, New York)

thor, as Céline proclaims his innocence as the scapegoat for a guilt-ridden French nation. The final phase of his literary production, consisting of the wartime trilogy *Castle to Castle*, *North*, and *Rigadoon*, continues the self-justification begun in *Fable for Another Time*, though in far less strident terms, as the character Ferdinand describes his perilous journey to Denmark.

Céline's novels are linked by the role and character of their respective protagonists, all of whom, except for the Bardamu of *Journey to the End of the Night*, are named Ferdinand and constitute variations on the same personality. The early novels emphasize the ironic interplay between the naïve protagonist being initiated into life and the protagonist as the older narrator endowed with greater insight than his younger incarnation. Protagonist and narrator approach each other in time, space, and knowledge, but they never coincide. The distance between them is considerably reduced in *Fable for Another Time* and the later novels as Céline's own political difficulties shape the consciousness of his character, Ferdinand.

Although the theme of the victim assumes specific political connotations in Céline's later fiction, all of his protagonists see themselves as caught up in a universal conspiracy. One aspect of that conspiracy is the inevitable biological degeneration to which the body falls heir; another is the natural human penchant for destruction. This tendency may assume various forms, among them pettiness, greed, malice, and exploitation of others. Its most blatant and dangerous form, however, is the aggression unleashed by war. The specter of war haunts Céline's novels, and in the face of its menace, cowardice, fear, sickness, and insanity are positively valorized as legitimate means of evasion. War accelerates the natural disintegration of those institutions that have been erected by society as barriers to the natural chaos of existence. In his last novel, *Rigadoon*, Céline prophesies the submersion of the white race by yellow hordes from the East, who, in their turn, will be subject to the same decline that brought about the collapse of the civilization of their Caucasian predecessors.

Given the generally execrable nature of existence, most individuals, according to Céline, are content to indulge in self-delusion. As Céline's protagonists discover, love, sexual fulfillment, and the pursuit of social and financial success are merely idle dreams that must eventually be shattered. In his later novels, Céline denounces the cinema, the automobile, and the French preoccupation with good food and fine wine as equally delusory. Across the otherwise bleak landscape of Céline's novels, one finds occasional moments of love, compassion, and tenderness. Two categories of creatures that elicit particularly sympathetic treatment are animals and children. Céline views the latter, metaphorically, in terms of a reverse metamorphosis: the butterfly becoming the larva as the child turns into an adult.

In *Castle to Castle*, the narrator describes himself as a super-seer, as blessed with a vision that penetrates to the core of reality and beyond. That vision is inseparable from the particular style by which it is conveyed. Céline rejected traditional French writing as having become too abstract to convey the nature of the experiences he was relating or the response he wished to elicit from his readers. He developed an art that, by intermingling various modes of perception and tonal registers, would embrace the diversity of existence, reveal its essential nature, and jolt the reader into awareness through anger, revulsion, or laughter. Moreover, such an approach to the novel perforce emphasizes the writer's claim to artistic autonomy, as opposed to his conforming to the external criteria of "proper" writing.

Céline also refused to accept the divorce between written French and spoken French. By introducing many elements of the spoken language into his novels, he believed that he could draw upon its greater directness and concreteness while at the same time maintaining the structured elaboration inherent in the written text. Indeed, although Céline's novels often have the appearance of a spontaneous first draft, they are the product of laborious craftsmanship.

JOURNEY TO THE END OF THE NIGHT

Journey to the End of the Night brought Céline immediate critical attention upon its publication, and it continues to be the best known of his novels. The journey of the young and innocent Bardamu is one of discovery and initiation. Bardamu's illusions about human existence in general and his own possibilities in particular are progressively stripped away as he confronts the sordidness of the human condition. His limited perspective is counterbalanced by the cynicism of the novel's narrator, an older and wiser Bardamu. The voyage ultimately becomes a conscious project—to confront the darker side of life so that, with the lucidity he acquires, he can one day transmit his knowledge to others by means of his writings.

Having enlisted in the army in a burst of patriotic fervor, Bardamu, as a soldier at the front, discovers the realities of the war. Despite their puzzlement about the politics of their situation, the men involved in the conflict have a natural penchant for killing and are generally fascinated by death. The most trenchant image of the war can be found in Bardamu's perception of a field abattoir, where the disemboweled animals, their blood and viscera spread on the grass, mirror the slaughter of human victims that is taking place. Given the insanity of war, the asylum and the hospital become places of refuge, and fear and cowardice are positively valorized. After Bardamu is wounded in the head and arm, any means to avoid returning to the front becomes valid.

Bardamu finally succeeds in having himself demobilized. He travels to the Cameroons to run a trading post in the bush. Through Bardamu, Céline denounces the inhumanity and corruption of the French colonial administration. More important, however, is the lesson in biology that Africa furnishes Bardamu. The moral decay of the European settlers manifests itself in their physical debilitation as they disintegrate in the oppressive heat and humidity and as they succumb to poor diet and disease. The African climate "stews" the white colonialists and thereby brings forth their inherent viciousness. In more temperate regions, Céline indicates, it requires a phenomenon such as war to expose humankind so quickly for what it is. Unable to tolerate the climate or his job, Bardamu burns his trading post to the ground and, delirious with malarial fever, embarks on a ship bound for New York.

Bardamu believes that America will provide him with the opportunity for a better life. He considers his journey to the New World a sort of pilgrimage, inspired by Lola, an American girlfriend in Paris. His New York is characterized by rigid verticality and the unyielding hardness of stone and steel; it bears no resemblance to the soft, supine, compliant body that Lola had offered him. As a "pilgrim" in New York, he discovers many "shrines," but access to them is open only to the wealthy. Bardamu is no more successful in Detroit than he was in New York. His work at a Ford motor assembly plant recalls the Charles Chaplin film *Modern Times* (1936). The noise of the machinery and the automatonlike motions Bardamu must perform eventually cause him to take refuge in the arms of Molly, a prostitute with a heart of gold. Molly has the legs of a dancer; Céline's protagonists, like Céline himself, are great admirers of the dance and particularly of the female dancer, who is able to combine Apollonian form with Dionysian rhythms in movements that defy the body's inherent corruption.

In Detroit, Bardamu encounters an old acquaintance named Léon Robinson. Hitherto, Robinson had been functioning as Bardamu's alter ego, anticipating, if not implementing, Bardamu's desires. They first met during the war, when Robinson, disgusted by the killing, wished to surrender to the Germans. Robinson preceded Bardamu to Africa, where he served as the manager of the trading post that Bardamu would later head. When

Bardamu learns that the resourceful Robinson has taken a job as a night janitor, he concludes that he, too, will not succeed in America. He decides that his only true mistress can be life itself, that he must return to France to continue his journey into the night.

Bardamu completes his medical studies and establishes his practice in a shabby Parisian suburb. Reluctant to request his fee from his impoverished patients, Bardamu is finally obliged to close his office and take a position in an asylum. Bardamu envies his patients. They have achieved an absolute form of self-delusion and are protected from life's insanity by the walls that imprison them.

Robinson reappears in Bardamu's life. In his desperate attempt to escape his poverty and its attendant humiliation, Robinson joins a conspiracy to murder an old woman. The plot backfires, literally, and Robinson is temporarily blinded when he receives a shotgun blast in the face. His "darkness," however, does not bring him enlightenment; his disgust with life simply increases. Bardamu realizes that he is bearing witness to an exemplary journey that must end in death. Robinson finally dies at the hands of his irate fiancé, whom he goads into shooting him. His "suicide" terminates his own journey to the end of the night and Bardamu's as well.

Journey to the End of the Night proffers a vision of the human condition that serves as the basis of all of Céline's literary production. Concomitant with this vision is the elaboration of a particular style that, with certain modifications in later works, afforded, according to Céline, a means of revitalizing French literature, by freeing it from the abstractions of classical writing. The most salient stylistic effect in *Journey to the End of the Night* is Céline's use of the vocabulary, syntax, and rhythms of popular speech as a vehicle for communicating the concrete, emotional impact of Bardamu's experience.

DEATH ON THE INSTALLMENT PLAN

Céline's second novel, *Death on the Installment Plan*, depicts the adolescence of a character resembling Bardamu but here, as in succeeding works, called Ferdinand, a name that explicitly poses the question of the relationship between the author and his protagonist. The novel begins with a pattern of opening signals that Céline would use in several other works. Once again, there is an interplay between an enlightened Ferdinand as narrator and a young Ferdinand as the naïve explorer of life. The narration of Ferdinand's youth is effected by a return to the past by the older narrator, who appears briefly at the beginning of the novel. When the narrator falls ill from the effects of a head wound suffered during World War I, aggravated by an attack of malaria, his memory of his youth is stimulated. Lying in bed, he has visions of little boats sailing through the sky bearing stories from the past, which will be transformed into his narrative. Thus the creation of fiction, the metaphorical outpouring from his skull injury (in *Journey to the End of the Night*, Bardamu's skull was trepanned), becomes an irrational, autonomous activity.

Reared in a Parisian *passage* (a commercial arcade), Ferdinand lives with his parents in an apartment above his mother's old lace and antique shop. Ferdinand's father, Auguste, holds a minor position with an insurance company.

Ferdinand's parents attempt to instill in their young son a traditional bourgeois ethic: proper dress, good manners, cleanliness, honesty, and, above all, the belief that hard work will certainly bring success. Ironically, for both Auguste and Clémence, the ideals they preach are progressively undermined by changing economic conditions as the twentieth century begins. Machine-made lace has begun to replace the handmade luxury items Clémence sells. She is soon reduced to selling door-to-door for a department store, the very sort of enterprise that is putting the small shopkeeper out of business. Auguste, essentially a secretary, is employed for the excellence of his penmanship at a time when the typewriter is becoming standard office equipment.

Ferdinand, too, becomes a victim of the historical circumstances that affect his parents. In addition, he is a victim of the maliciousness of others, intent upon exploiting him for their own ends. Ferdinand's failures keep his father in a constant state of rage. Auguste's fits of wrath are enlarged to comically epic proportions: He swells with anger like a balloon and, like a balloon whose air has been suddenly released, lets forth a torrent of imprecations that cause him to bounce around the room, spilling furniture and crockery in his path.

One of Ferdinand's jobs involves selling jewelry. His employer's wife, in concert with other employees, conspires to seduce him and steal a valuable ring given to him for safekeeping. With her overflowing corpulence, gigantic breasts, and cavernous vagina, Madame Gorloge is more monster than woman, and Ferdinand is engulfed by her. Céline portrays sexual relations as either an act of aggression or a mindless escape, akin to the masturbation in which Ferdinand indulges and that he later rejects as a form of delusion. Ferdinand's stay at an English boarding school does not produce the expected result. He returns to France with barely a word of English at his command, having rejected language as an instrument of oppression, responsible for the seductions and paternal conflicts that have shaped his existence.

Ferdinand takes a job with an eccentric named Courtial des Pereires—a balloonist, the owner of a magazine for inventors, and the author of numerous self-study and do-it-yourself manuals on a great variety of subjects. Courtial, who will become a surrogate father for Ferdinand, is a windbag, employing language in a manner radically different from Auguste's. He reorders reality through the use of a quasi-scientific rhetoric that, ultimately, does not stand the test of reality.

Courtial flees with his wife and Ferdinand to the countryside, after a fantastic project to find sunken treasure leads to the loss of his magazine. There he proposes to grow gigantic potatoes with the aid of radio-telluric waves. The disorder of reality triumphs over the specious order of Courtial's rhetoric when the potatoes come up stunted and full of maggots. Courtial commits suicide by shooting himself in the head, the source of his grandiose schemes. His wound recalls the narrator's and the language of the novel, in which the sort of delusion that Courtial practices is denounced. Ferdinand returns to Paris and enlists in the army. Given what he has seen and experienced, human existence appears to be, as the title suggests, little more than a process of slowly advancing toward the ultimate resolution of death.

Death on the Installment Plan is marked by an important stylistic development, which is accentuated in subsequent novels: the frequent use of ellipsis points. As Céline notes in a discussion of his writing in *Conversations with Professor Y*, the ellipsis are the rails that carry the emotional intensity of his text; they also have the overall effect of conveying, phonically and graphically, the fragmentary nature of existence—such as Céline describes it in his novels—as opposed to the orderly worldview inherent in the syntax of traditional French writing.

FABLE FOR ANOTHER TIME

The publication of *Fable for Another Time* (a second volume, in French and usually referred to by its subtitle, *Normance*, appeared in 1954) marked Céline's return to public view as a novelist, still stigmatized by his indictment as an anti-Semite and a Nazi sympathizer. Céline used this novel in particular as a device for self-exculpation. He portrayed himself, through his protagonist, as an innocent victim of persecution, denying all the charges made against him. Moreover, Ferdinand states that his "problems" began with the publication of *Journey to the End of the Night*, for it was then that he was perceived as a subversive element of French society. One narrative strategy that Céline adopts as a means of maintaining his innocence is the use of a "narratee"—the designation of a reader who, convinced of the author's guilt, cries out for Céline's punishment. Ferdinand thus elaborates various scenarios of crime and punishment and, ultimately, proclaims his innocence.

The novel is narrated from the perspective of a prisoner incarcerated in a jail in Copenhagen while awaiting extradition to France to stand trial as a Nazi sympathizer. As a "political prisoner," he places himself in a long line of similar victims of societal oppression, ranging from the Gaulish chieftain Vercingétorix to Oscar Wilde. By putting himself in this illustrious company, Ferdinand seeks to undermine the specificity of the charges brought against him. Having failed to outrun history, Ferdinand finds himself not only behind bars but also glued to his chair by sores from pellagra. The noises made by other prisoners exacerbate his confinement and, in particular, the sounds made by a prisoner called the Skunk as he hits his head against the wall, apparently trying to commit suicide. Ferdinand compares the Skunk's head wound to the one he suffered during World War I. The comparison recalls the metaphorical function of Ferdinand's head wound in *Death on the Installment Plan* as the cause of his fiction-making. Ferdinand's narrative will permit him to escape from his cell by encompassing a variety of times and places.

Ferdinand frequently depicts himself as the quarry in a medieval hunt or threatened with horrible forms of torture and execution. In equally hallucinatory scenes, he is used as garden fertilizer by writers who flourished during the Occupation. One writer who reappears several times is Jean-Paul Sartre. In his "Portrait d'un antisémite" (in *Les Temps moderne*, 1945; republished in *Réflexions sur la question juive*, 1946; *Portrait of the Anti-Semite*, 1946; also known as *Anti-Semite and Jew*, 1948) Sartre accused Céline of having been paid by the Germans to promote anti-Semitism. In Céline's novel, Ferdinand the doctor will avenge the insults made against Ferdinand the writer by taking consolation in the knowledge that illness, decay, and death will ultimately triumph over both persecutor and persecuted.

Ferdinand introduces yet another adversary. His name is Jules, and he bears certain crucial resemblances to Ferdinand. He, too, is an artist, primarily a painter but a sculptor as well. Like Ferdinand, he is a wounded veteran of World War I: Having lost both of his legs, he pushes himself about on a little cart that he maneuvers with two short canes. These shared attributes become the point of departure for a return to the Montmartre period of Ferdinand's life and for a complex portrait of Jules as the embodiment of the evil potential lurking within the artist. Jules's physical deformity and his ugliness are the external manifestations of a perverted character. Jules's studio, in the subbasement of the building in which Ferdinand has an apartment, becomes a symbolic netherworld in which Jules displays his chthonic powers.

Unlike Ferdinand, who considers himself a martyr for having sought in his novels to reveal the true nature of the human condition, Jules creates art for financial and sexual profit. It is the latter that particularly concerns Ferdinand, for both he and Jules have a predilection for the attractive young dance students that frequent the courses offered by Ferdinand's wife, Lili. Unlike Ferdinand, Jules has no appreciation for the dance as an aesthetic triumph over the flesh. He seeks to lure the young women into his studio so that he can fondle them. Lili accepts Jules's invitation to model for him, and Ferdinand acquiesces to the arrangement, fascinated, as is Lili, by Jules's demoniac energy. Jules caresses the naked Lili in the murky light of his studio, and, as he does, Lili is changed from an elegant, graceful dancer into a garishly multicolored mass of flesh, a work of art deformed by the twisted mind of the artist.

For Ferdinand, the "seduction" of Lili also marks the

conclusion of a tranquil existence and the beginning of a period of torment that eventually leads to confinement in a Danish prison. Jules, he believes, has furthered the persecution incited by BBC broadcasts denouncing him as a traitor and by the miniature coffins sent to him by the Resistance as a sign that he has been marked for execution. Standing outside Jules's studio, he becomes subject to hallucinations, during the course of which he begins to hear air-raid sirens. Because of the noises in his head that were caused by his war injury, one cannot be absolutely sure whether these sirens are real or imagined. Whatever may be their status, the explicit confusion of external and internal landscapes poses once again the artist's freedom to intermingle reality and imagination. This confusion will be reinforced by another—between Ferdinand's personal calamities and those of a Europe ravaged by World War II.

CASTLE TO CASTLE

Castle to Castle is the first volume of a trilogy of novels that trace Ferdinand's flight from Montmartre to Copenhagen. The novel begins with an incident in which Ferdinand, now practicing medicine in the Parisian suburb of Meudon after having received amnesty from the French government, discovers a ship, tied up at one of the area's piers, that is being attended by mysterious hooded figures. Upon closer inspection, Ferdinand discovers among them a friend from the Occupation days, Robert Le Vigan, a film actor and pro-Nazi radio broadcaster. Le Vigan had accompanied Ferdinand, his wife Lili, and their cat Bébert during part of their journey from Paris to Denmark. Another one of the hooded figures is a man whom Ferdinand knows was killed in the war. The ambiguous status of these individuals anticipates the "play" between the real and the imaginary that will characterize the narrative soon to be initiated. That play is subsequently reinforced by the aggravation of Ferdinand's head wound, compounded by an attack of malaria. Forced to take to his bed, the narrator, his memory of the past stimulated by his encounter with Le Vigan and revived by his affliction, begins to transcribe his wartime experiences.

The narrator's recollection of the past has as its focal point the Castle of Sigmaringen in the Bavarian village of the same name. Ferdinand calls the castle Siegmaringen, ironically playing on the German word *Sieg*,

meaning "victory." Ferdinand has been sent there with his companions from Berlin, for their safety and for the purpose of administering to the medical needs of the town's French colony. It was to Sigmaringen that the Germans in September of 1944 had transferred many officials of the collaborationist Vichy government, including its head, Marshal Philippe Pétain. All of them share with Ferdinand a condemnation as traitors and the fear that they will be summarily executed should they fall into the hands of the Resistance or the Free French Forces. Indeed, the entire town is filled to overflowing by Nazi sympathizers who have come to Sigmaringen as their final place of refuge in the wake of the collapse of the German armies.

The castle itself, built by the Hohenzollern dynasty, is more than a luxurious place of exile. Céline transforms it into a symbolic structure that reflects the spirit of its inhabitants, the ruling clique of the Vichy government. For those officials who persist in believing that Germany will miraculously reverse its losses and win the war, the castle is no more real than a Hollywood set. At the base of the castle flows the Danube, gradually eroding the building's foundations. Céline suggests that, despite the castle's apparent durability, it will eventually disintegrate, as will all of those structures and institutions that serve as bulwarks against the inherent chaos of existence. For those who believed that the Third Reich would last a thousand years, the moment of collapse is at hand.

The interior design of the castle also functions symbolically. Its apartments are separated from one another by a complex network of passages and stairways that tend to isolate each living space and thus reinforce their occupants' delusions about returning to power. One can also interpret the isolation of the castle's apartments as a metaphor for the novel's plot structure—a series of relatively discontinuous vignettes.

Amid the delusions and the meaningless ceremonies that characterize life in the castle, Ferdinand attempts to address the realities of Sigmaringen. Despite a lack of medical supplies, Ferdinand conscientiously attempts to ease the suffering of the refugees. The central images of the novel, insofar as life outside the castle is concerned, are the overflowing toilets at the Löwen Hotel, where Ferdinand's small room serves as residence and office, and the railway station. The overabundant use of the toilets, on an epic scale, reveals the overcrowding, poor diet, and disease that afflict the refugees. In a larger sense, for Céline at least, the war has transformed Europe into an immense cesspool. At the railway station, one finds yet another manifestation of the disorder that has overtaken European society. There, confusion and despair have replaced political and social hierarchies, and, because of the uselessness of train schedules at this point in the war, the platforms and waiting rooms serve as points of exchange—for food, sexual favors, disease, and rumors.

Ferdinand performs his functions as a doctor while hoping that he can eventually find a train that will permit him to leave Sigmaringen and head north to Denmark. Ferdinand's concern with his own escape cannot help but recall those other train trips, to stations named Treblinka and Auschwitz, that deportees all over Europe were taking as the Nazis sought to achieve their so-called final solution.

Castle to Castle ends with a return to the narrator in Meudon, the circularity of the novel's narrative counterbalancing its episodic discontinuity. Once again, the narrator is a survivor, a witness to the most calamitous period in the history of France. Céline claims in these later novels, beginning with *Fable for Another Time*, this his fiction gives the reader a more penetrating insight into the period than historical documents can provide. Many of his readers may wonder, however, if Céline did not, in these works, choose obfuscation rather than lucidity to elaborate what might be considered a self-serving mythology that transforms the journey begun in *Journey to the End of the Night* into the very sort of delusion that the author had once sought to denounce.

Philip H. Solomon

OTHER MAJOR WORKS

PLAY: *L'Église*, pb. 1933 (*The Church*, 2003).

NONFICTION: *La Vie et l'œuvre de Philippe-Ignace Semmelweis* and *"Mea culpa," suivi de "La Vie et l'œuvre de Semmelweis,"* pb. together 1936 (wr. 1924; *"Mea Culpa," with "The Life and Work of Semmelweis,"* 1937); *Bagatelles pour un massacre*, 1937; *L'École des cadavres*, 1938; *Les Beaux Draps*, 1941; *À l'agité du bocal*, 1949; *Lettres des années noires*, 1994;

Lettres à Marie Canavaggia, 1995 (3 volumes); *Lettres de prison à Lucette Destouches et à Maître Mikkelsen, 1945-1947*, 1998.

MISCELLANEOUS: *Ballets, sans musique, sans personne, sans rien*, 1959 (*Ballets Without Music, Without Dancers, Without Anything*, 1999).

BIBLIOGRAPHY

Bouchard, Norma. *Céline, Gadda, Beckett: Experimental Writings of the 1930's*. Gainesville: University Press of Florida, 2000. Bouchard maintains that works by Céline, Carlo Emilio Gadda, and Samuel Beckett have stylistic characteristics that would later be associated with postmodernism, such as a changed relationship to language, a burlesque worldview, and a decentered narrative.

Hewitt, Nicholas. *The Life of Céline: A Critical Biography*. Malden, Mass.: Blackwell, 1999. Hewitt's critical biography provides analysis of Céline's life and work and places both within the context of French cultural, social, and political history. Includes bibliographical references and an index.

Matthews, J. H. *The Inner Dream: Céline as Novelist*. Syracuse, N.Y.: Syracuse University Press, 1978. Matthews explores all of Céline's major fiction. The introduction has an insightful discussion of how to treat the work of a writer whose politics and life have been so controversial.

Noble, Ian. *Language and Narration in Céline's Writings*. Atlantic Highlands, N.J.: Humanities Press International, 1987. The first chapter, which sets Céline in the context of literary history, is especially good. Noble deals with both the fiction and nonfiction. Includes detailed notes and a bibliography.

O'Connell, David. *Louis-Ferdinand Céline*. Boston: Twayne, 1976. A valuable introductory study, opening with a chapter on Céline's biography and followed by chapters on his beginnings as a writer, his mature style, his work as a pamphleteer, and his great trilogy. Provides a chronology, notes, and an annotated bibliography.

Scullion, Rosemarie, Philip H. Solomon, and Thomas C. Spear, eds. *Céline and the Politics of Difference*. Hanover, N.H.: University Press of New England, 1995. Essays examine various aspects of Céline's work, including the novels *Journey to the End of the Night*, *Death on the Installment Plan*, and the German trilogy.

Solomon, Philip H. *Understanding Céline*. Columbia: University of South Carolina Press, 1992. Solomon examines the central themes and structures of Céline's novels, focusing on the self-reflective nature of his work. The first chapter is a general overview of his writings, with subsequent chapters focusing on the novels and a final chapter on his poetry, pamphlets, and plays. Includes a biography, chronology, and bibliography, and an index.

Sturrock, John. *Louis-Ferdinand Céline: "Journey to the End of the Night."* New York: Cambridge University Press, 1990. A closely argued study of Céline's autobiographical novel. Sturrock examines the novel's themes, style, and place in literary history. Provides a detailed chronology and a very useful annotated bibliography.

Thiher, Allen. *Céline: The Novel as Delirium*. New Brunswick, N.J.: Rutgers University Press, 1972. Traces the seemingly mad circularity of Céline's fiction and attempts to fathom the paradoxes of the individual and the writer. Includes notes and a bibliography. Quotes Céline in French with English translation.

Vitoux, Frederic. *Céline: A Biography*. Translated by Jesse Browner. 2d ed. New York: Marlowe, 1995. A thorough, updated biography, featuring unpublished letters and documents and the first interviews to be conducted with Celine's widow. Vitoux is unapologetic but fair in his account of Céline's anti-Semitism and other problematic aspects of the author's personality.

BLAISE CENDRARS

Born: La Chaux-de-Fonds, Switzerland;
    September 1, 1887
Died: Paris, France; January 21, 1961
Also known as: Frédéric Louis Sauser

PRINCIPAL LONG FICTION

L'Or: La Merveilleuse Histoire du général Johann August Suter, 1925 (*Sutter's Gold*, 1926)
Moravagine, 1926 (English translation, 1968)
La Plan de l'aiguille, 1927 (*Antarctic Fugue*, 1948)
Les Confessions de Dan Yack, 1928 (collective title for translation of this and the previous novel is *Dan Yack*, 1946)
Rhum: L'Aventure de Jean Galmot, 1930
Emmène-moi au bout du monde!, 1956 (*To the End of the World*, 1967)

OTHER LITERARY FORMS

Although the novels of Blaise Cendrars (SAHN-drawr) had many admirers, including Henry Miller, his most critically respected work is his poetry. Combining his adventurous autobiography with complex, strong imagery and powerful emotion, Cendrars's most praised books of poetry are his extraordinary early efforts, *Les Pâques à New York* (1912; *Easter in New York*, 1966); *La Prose du Transsibérien et de la petite Jehanne de France* (1913; *The Trans-Siberian Express*, 1964); and *Le Panama: Ou, Les Aventures de mes sept oncles* (1918; *Panama: Or, The Adventures of My Seven Uncles*, 1931). His poetry is most important for its audacious expression of modernism. Other important collections include *Dix-neuf Poèmes élastiques* (1919); *Kodak* (1924; English translation, 1976); and *Feuilles de route* (1924, 1927). *Une Nuit dans la forêt* (1929) and *Vol à voiles* (1932) were alleged by Cendrars to be autobiographical nonfiction, but critics assert they are largely fictionalized. His nonfiction "novels" and short stories, as well as his prose poems, are difficult to categorize using conventional terms. Cendrars was also an editor, essayist, journalist, translator, screenwriter, film director, ballet scenarist, and radio dramatist.

ACHIEVEMENTS

Blaise Cendrars as a writer made direct use of his personal life and experiences to an unusual degree. This has made critics uneasy with assessing his literary accomplishments, as if the writer's life is somehow separate from his work, or should be. Miller, whose own work incorporated a great deal of autobiography, was impressed with Cendrars's work and praised it for its luminosity, calling Cendrars a "continent of letters." Others, however, see Cendrars as a technically proficient writer who was at his best in his free-wheeling poetry. Both his poetry and prose, however, are praised for their rich, powerful, restless, modern imagery and strongly evocative effects.

Blaise was an independent man who did not ally himself with any literary movements, but he was nevertheless a great influence on Surrealism and other modern movements. Only late in his life did he attain any substantial critical recognition, receiving the Legion of Honor in 1959 and the Grand Prix Littéraire de la Ville de Paris in 1961.

BIOGRAPHY

Blaise Cendrars so mythologized his life and experiences that scholars have had a difficult time culling the exaggerations and outright lies from his many exercises in autobiography. As Ernest Hemingway comments in *A Moveable Feast* (1964), "When [Cendrars] was lying, he was more interesting than many men telling a story truly." The difficulty is further compounded by Cendrars's ceaseless traveling from continent to continent. Even the true circumstances of his birth were not known until Jean Buhler published his 1960 biography.

Contrary to Cendrars's claim in a 1917 poem that he was born in Paris in the Hôtel des Etrangers, he was actually born in the Swiss village of La Chaux-de-Fonds under the name of Frédéric Louis Sauser. Escaping La Chaux-de-Fonds seems to have been one of the major ambitions of its natives (Le Corbusier and Louis Chevrolet are among the more famous who left) and Cendrars's father, Georges, was no exception. He had come to the city as a teacher of mathematics but was listed in the city registry as a clock merchant at the time of Cendrars's birth. He restlessly immersed himself in financial dealings and was responsible for his son's early

initiation into travel. The family went to Egypt and into the hotel business when Cendrars was about two years old. This venture soon failed, however, and Cendrars began his chaotic education at the Scuola Internazionale in Naples in 1891 or 1892. In 1897, he entered the Basel *Gymnasium* (college-preparatory secondary school); he also attended boarding schools in Germany. In 1902, he registered at the École de Commerce in Neuchâtal, a business school, evidently after failing his college examinations.

Cendrars spent the years from 1904 to 1907 in Russia as a watch salesman and was there during the 1905 Revolution, which plays such a large part in his novel *Moravagine*; he may have traveled in Siberia and China as well. He had his first love affair with a Russian woman, "Hélène," and in her honor wrote his first poem, "Alea" (later rewritten as *Moganni Nameh*, 1922) under the pseudonym Freddy Sausey. After his return, he moved frequently, raising bees near Paris, studying medicine at the University of Bern, working as a comedian in Brussels, working as an extra in the opera *Carmen*, falling in love with Fîla Poznanska, a Polish student, and following her to New York. All of this time, he was writing, undergoing in his poetry a transformation from his early heavy Romanticism, through neo-Symbolism to the startling modernism for which he would become famous. He made some money with his writing, doing translations and writing essays on art and literature. He translated Stanisław Przybyszewski's *Totenmesse* (1893) as *La Messe des morts*, which is considered a direct source for *Moravagine*, and the poem *Die Verwandlungen der Venus* (1907) by Richard Dehmel. He may have collaborated with Guillaume Apollinaire on *Les Onze Mille Verges* (1911), a pornographic novel.

Publishing under the name Blaise Cendrars, he stunned the Paris literary scene with *Easter in New York*. He claimed that the poem was written after he had left a church in New York in which a minister had demanded from the congregation a donation to listen to a performance of Joseph Haydn's *Die Schöpfung* (1798; *The Creation*). This experience and his poverty in New York provided the impetus for the poem, which has been called a major milestone in literary modernism for its startling and unblinking use of city imagery. He followed with *Séquences* (1913) and *The Trans-Siberian Express*, major works that may have influenced Apollinaire and the Surrealists. *The Trans-Siberian Express* was attacked in the press, and Cendrars responded vigorously.

Cendrars helped found a literary review, *Les Hommes nouveaux*, in 1912 and mingled with some of the most celebrated artists of the period, including Amedeo Modigliani, Pablo Picasso, Jean Cocteau, Max Jacob, Fernand Léger, Francis Picabia, Igor Stravinsky, and Apollinaire.

The drama of Cendrars's life continued with his enlistment in the Foreign Legion at the beginning of World War I. On April 7, 1914, Poznanska gave birth to a daughter, Odilon, and in September, shortly before his departure to the front, Cendrars and Poznanska were married. After a year in bloody combat—at one point, seven thousand of the fifteen thousand men in the Tenth Army, in which he served, were killed—he lost his right arm in the Marne Valley. He returned to the artistic life of Paris, though many of his friends were either in the army or gone, and he quickly learned to write with his left hand. From that point on, Cendrars wrote constantly, whether art criticism on the cubists, journalism, more poetry, or ballets. He was involved in cinema with Abel Gance and contributed to the films *J'Accuse* (1919) and *La Roue* (1923), both now considered classics; Cendrars himself played one of the mutilated war victims in the former. In 1921, he worked for the studio Rinascimento in Rome, directing the film *La Vénus noire*.

Cendrars continued his restless traveling in the 1920's in the south of France, Portugal, Spain, Brazil, Argentina, Paraguay, Chile, and even Antarctica. In late 1924, in six weeks, he completed his first and most popular novel, *Sutter's Gold*. He completed *Moravagine* in Biarritz, but part of it was written in the Amazon during his first trip to Brazil. He was also in New York several times during the 1920's and 1930's and became fairly close to John Dos Passos, who translated and illustrated Cendrars's poetry in *Panama*. Critics agree that each influenced the other's writing considerably. In line with his cinematic interests, Cendrars met Sergei Eisenstein in 1930, when the great director tried to buy the rights for *Sutter's Gold* during his abortive stint at Paramount Studios. In 1935, Cendrars wrote the first important review of Miller's *Tropic of Cancer* (1934) after visiting him and barhopping with prostitutes. In turn, Miller became one of the most enthusiastic devotees of Cendrars's work.

World War II put an abrupt end to Cendrars's ceaseless activity. He served briefly as a correspondent with the British army, then retreated to a home in Aix-en-Provence. Overwhelmed by the defeat of France, cautious because of fascist oppression, and upset because of the imprisonment of both of his sons (one escaped and was later killed in an accident in North Africa), he wrote nothing and stayed in Aix. He began writing again only when the Germans seemed suspicious of a writer who did not write. Although he obviously sympathized with the Allies, the scrutiny under which he was placed prevented any overt activities in the Resistance. Jay Bochner

Blaise Cendrars. (Roger Viollet/Getty Images)

reports that Cendrars did, however, help director Max Ophüls and his wife and son escape from France; the son, Marcel Ophüls, would later become the director of *Le Chagrin et la pitié* (1969; *The Sorrow and the Pity*), one of the most celebrated and controversial films dealing with collaboration.

Late in the war and in the years after, Cendrars began writing a series of autobiographical novels: *L'Homme foudroyé* (1945; *The Astonished Man*, 1970), *La Main coupée* (1946; *Lice*, 1973), Bourlinguer (1948; *Planus*, 1972), and *Le Lotissement du ciel* (1949; *Sky: Memoirs*, 1992). In 1948, he gave up his casual sex life when he married Raymone Duchateau, a comic actor whom he had first met in 1917 and with whom he had kept in contact ever since. He took only a few brief trips in the later years of his life. He became involved with productions of *Sutter's Gold* and *La Fin du monde* (1919) for French radio. He wrote only two books in the 1950's, *To the End of the World* and *Trop c'est trop* (1957). In 1956, Cendrars had his first stroke. Others followed. In 1959, André Malraux went to his home and presented to him the Legion of Honor. Cendrars continued writing prefaces and some short stories until his death in 1961, only four days after receiving his first literary award, the Grand Prix Littéraire de la Ville de Paris.

ANALYSIS

Blaise Cendrars seemed incapable of divorcing his colorful life from his fiction. Even his first novel, *Sutter's Gold*, ostensibly a historical novel about John Augustus Sutter, the Swiss émigré whose discovery of gold in California precipitated the 1849 gold rush, becomes a personal statement, molded into a myth with small regard for historical details.

Early in his life, Cendrars became familiar with Sutter's story. According to Hugues Richard, Cendrars and his brother first read of Sutter in a local Swiss almanac, *Le Messager boiteux*, that was used as toilet paper in the Sauser home. Richard also asserts that the immediate source of the novel was a monograph written in 1868 by a Swiss clergyman and state counsellor who cared for Sutter's children after he had fled Switzerland. Cendrars read voraciously in libraries wherever he traveled and undoubtedly had pursued his interest in Sutter for some time. Perhaps the most important impetus for the novel

was Cendrars's meeting with August Sutter, grandson of John Sutter, in Basel around 1905. They renewed their friendship in 1910 in Paris, where August Sutter had gone to become a sculptor. August introduced him to various artists, including poet Siegfried Lang.

Monique Chefdor speculates that the frantic development of the Brazilian wilderness reminded Cendrars of the gold rush and contributed largely to his choosing to write the novel when he did. Sutter's story certainly provided Cendrars with the opportunity to exploit all of his favorite devices in a novel. Sutter is depicted as a crafty underminer of conventional society. He abandons his wife and children; he falsifies travel documents; he forges, cheats, steals, and deals in slaves. Whatever heroism there is in Sutter is matched by rascality, but Cendrars manages to turn Sutter into a tragic figure. The liberties that Cendrars takes with historical facts in the novel serve to enhance the stature of Sutter—for example, making him die the victim of a child's trick on the steps of the Capitol in Washington, D.C., instead of in a bed in Pennsylvania.

Sutter is in the grip of forces he cannot control. His story is that of a man driven, by his own ambitions and obsessions, to being a multimillionaire in a place that happens to have gold, "the Antichrist," which will provoke other people's ambitions and obsessions to destroy him. Sutter becomes victim, not so much of people, but of gold. Cendrars had previously written on the corrupting power of money in much of his poetry, especially in relation to his experiences as an outsider in New York. This coincides with the common literary view in the 1920's that civilization had been broken by World War I and was in the process of being replaced by a shoddy, corrupt industrial society.

The style of *Sutter's Gold* is very stark. As Bochner observes, none of Cendrars's prose, before or after, was as terse and bare as the language of this novel, which resembles that of Cendrars's poetry in *Kodak* and *Le Formose* (1924). All of his other work, even his journalism, is very baroque, image heaped on image. In *Sutter's Gold*, however, the adamant forward thrust of the action serves to accentuate the feeling that Sutter is caught up and being carried along by his destiny. He has virtually no opportunity for introspection, or to attempt to modify his course. When he attempts to resist the gold fever, it results in his impoverishment and destruction. This single driving force is presented in prose stripped of imagery, similar to what Hemingway was developing at the time. Written in the present tense, the novel makes no commentary upon the morality or character of Sutter, except by implication through action. This straightforwardness in plot and style undoubtedly contributed to the popularity of *Sutter's Gold*, which has gone through more than fifteen editions in French and has been translated into such languages as Czech, Flemish, Russian, Portuguese, and Swedish, in addition to other European languages. This same simplicity, however, makes *Sutter's Gold* a work with few nuances and not much depth, a novel that may provide great pleasure on a first reading but has little more to offer on a second.

MORAVAGINE

Cendrars's *Moravagine* is far more complex than *Sutter's Gold* in both style and theme. Miller was among the writers who praised it highly. The radicalism of *Moravagine* made a strong impression on Miller and contributed to freeing up his own prose. Miller read the novel before he was fluent in French and said it was "like reading a phosphorescent text through smoked glasses," but he went on to write that the "silence [Cendrars] creates is deafening. It takes you back to the beginning of the world, to that hush which is engraved on the face of mystery." *Moravagine* is one of those books that seems clear from sentence to sentence and is profoundly affecting yet violates so much of what readers have come to expect in a novel that its overall purpose is bewildering. It accomplishes what the best of the Surrealist works do, reaching a reality beyond conventional reality and then collapsing in the despair of being unable to grasp it fully.

The character Moravagine is a homicidal lunatic and heir to the Hungarian throne who is befriended by Raymond, a psychiatrist who helps him escape, then accompanies him through an eerie series of adventures around the world. Periodically, Moravagine will butcher a woman for no reason except diversion, and Raymond makes no attempt to stop him. As Sven Birkerts observes, Cendrars has taken human extremity as his subject. The pained language carries the reader "through revolution, terror, and a zone of sexual and moral nihilism." Nothing like it, except Lautréamont's *Les Chants du Maldoror* (1868; *The Lay of Maldoror*, 1924), had ap-

peared in literature before. The only parallels, Birkerts adds, are in the works of Louis-Ferdinand Céline and Samuel Beckett. Moravagine is a being without culture, without the values inculcated by civilization. There is not a shred of human sentiment in him. The novel is profoundly pessimistic, Birkerts concludes, "but in view of the atrocities Cendrars had witnessed . . . not pure fabrication."

One of the most astonishing things about *Moravagine* is that many of the scenes that seem most incredible were based on actual events, in some cases experiences of Cendrars. Bochner points out, for example, that, as impossible as it might seem, it is possible to sail up the Orinoco river system into the Amazon, without portage, thus bringing into question the whole dreamlike quality of the South American adventure. Raymond, who suffers from malaria through much of the trip, can be seen as giving a realistic interpretation of his experiences there. The story seems incredible and strange but is not necessarily unrealistic. Bochner also mentions Moravagine's mad bombing of Vienna during World War I: The episode bears considerable resemblance to an actual event in 1916, when Lieutenant Marchal flew thirteen hundred kilometers to bomb Berlin.

Bochner further links Moravagine to Otto Gross, a psychoanalyst who preached anarchy. (Gross may have influenced a host of artists, including D. H. Lawrence, Max Weber, and Franz Kafka, as well as Cendrars.) Gross's having been committed to an asylum after having provided the means of suicide for two of his female patients and his subsequent escape also bears resemblance to the story of Moravagine. The treatment of Gross by Carl Jung also has some parallels in Raymond's attitudes. Further possible sources include the life of Azev, a notorious Russian spy and assassin, the 1905 Revolution, and the story of Jack the Ripper, particularly as exploited in horror films such as *The Cabinet of Dr. Caligari* (1920) and *Waxworks* (1924). The narrator's name is taken from that of Raymond-la-Science, a gang member executed in 1913.

Cendrars later wrote that Moravagine was inside him; his character was like a parasite occupying Cendrars's body. "That's why all beautiful books are alike," wrote Cendrars. "They are all autobiographical." There are a number of parallels between Cendrars's life—the dates he stayed in Russia, his time in Paris—and the travels of Moravagine, but this is not to say that Cendrars engaged in any of the atrocious activities ascribed to his protagonist. It is Raymond who is injured as Cendrars was in World War I, and Cendrars's relation to Moravagine is more like that of an entranced observer than that of an alter ego.

The disparate elements that make up the novel evoke the chaos of the twentieth century: Moravagine escapes from the asylum in the symbolic year 1900 and unleashes bloody anarchy on the world. Raymond, in the name of science, observes Moravagine, whose name means "death to the vagina," as he engages in a calculated destruction of all nineteenth century values (perceived as "feminine"); clearly, whether Raymond admits it or not, he is fascinated, perhaps even delighted, by the destruction. He, too, participates in the revolutionary terrorism and ends up a regicide who has supposedly sent his story to the author Cendrars.

The novel expresses Cendrars's fascination and delight with the new century, mingled with a sense of horror and metaphysical guilt at the destruction of a stable moral order. The curious fictional connection of Moravagine to Raymond to Cendrars seems to imply they are all aspects of one another in some mysterious, fundamental, psychological way. In this and many other respects, *Moravagine* anticipates a host of later experimental novels, such as those by John Hawkes, José Donoso, and William Burroughs, in which pathological behavior is used to explore the question of identity.

DAN YACK NOVELS

Cendrars went on to write several other novels. Dan Yack, the main character of *Antarctic Fugue* and *Les Confessions de Dan Yack*, is regarded by some critics as the most human of Cendrars's protagonists and the most fully developed. He has also been seen as a positive counterpart to Moravagine; exactly what was Cendrars's intent, however, is neither as clear as in *Sutter's Gold* nor as uncomfortably evocative as in *Moravagine*. For this reason, neither volume of *Les Confessions de Dan Yack* is considered as successful as the previous novels.

RHUM

The novel *Rhum* bears resemblances to *Sutter's Gold* in its treatment of the hero and its use of an inanimate substance as a driving force. The historical Jean Galmot,

on whose experiences the novel was based, was a fascinating person, and Cendrars, as he did with Sutter, creatively reshaped the historical material, yet there is little in this fictionalization. Cendrars himself seemed to sense that he had reached an artistic dead end and did not write a novel again for many years.

LATER NOVELS

The Astonished Man, *Lice*, *Planus*, and *Le Lotissement du ciel* anticipate the "nonfiction novel" of the 1960's and 1970's by falling somewhere between fiction and autobiography. They are interesting for their commentaries on the nature of writing and for the incredible stories they tell, many of them total fabrications; Cendrars could not resist embellishing his life story.

With *To the End of the World*, Cendrars promised a novel in which he would not appear. Nevertheless, he asserts in the preface that it is a roman à clef. Its collection of strange people, sexual explicitness, and extraordinarily bizarre events infuriated critics on its publication; Chefdor argues that it is a forerunner of postmodernism in its attempt to create a hedonism of the text, an erotics of writing. Perhaps this judgment will be borne out by future criticism, although *Moravagine* seems likely to remain Cendrars's most lasting contribution to the novel.

J. Madison Davis

OTHER MAJOR WORKS

SHORT FICTION: *Petits Contes nègres pour les enfants des blancs*, 1928 (*Little Black Stories for Little White Children*, 1929); *Comments les blancs sont d'anciens noirs*, 1930; *Histoires vraies*, 1938; *La Vie dangereuse*, 1938; *D'Outremer à indigo*, 1940; *Noel aux quatre coins du monde*, 1953 (*Christmas at the Four Corners of the Earth*, 1994).

POETRY: *Les Pâques à New York*, 1912 (*Easter in New York*, 1966); *La Prose du Transsibérien et de la petite Jehanne de France*, 1913 (*The Trans-Siberian Express*, 1964); *Séquences*, 1913; *La Guerre au Luxembourg*, 1916; *Le Panama: Ou, Les Aventures de mes sept oncles*, 1918 (*Panama: Or, The Adventures of My Seven Uncles*, 1931); *Dix-neuf Poèmes élastiques*, 1919; *Du monde entier*, 1919; *Du monde entier au coeur du monde*, 1919, 1957 (partial translation in *Complete Postcards from the Americas: Poems of Road and Sea*, 1976); *Moganni Nameh*, 1922; *Kodak*, 1924 (English translation, 1976); *Le Formose*, 1924; *Feuilles de route*, 1924, 1927; *Poésies complètes*, 1944 (*Complete Poems*, 1992).

SCREENPLAY: *La Perle fievreuse*, 1921.

RADIO PLAY: *Films san images*, 1959.

NONFICTION: *Profond aujourd'hui*, 1917 (verse; *Profound Today*, 1922); *J'ai tué*, 1918 (verse; *I Have Killed*, 1919); *Le Fin du monde filmée par l'ange Notre-Dame*, 1919, 1949; *L'Éloge de la vie dangereuse*, 1926; *L'Eubage*, 1926; *Une Nuit dans la fôret*, 1929 (*A Night in the Forest*, 1985); *Vol à voiles*, 1932; *Panorama de la pègre*, 1935; *Hollywood: La Mecque du cinéma*, 1936 (*Hollywood: Mecca of the Movies*, 1995); *Chez l'armée l'anglaise*, 1940; *L'Homme foudroyé*, 1945 (autobiography; *The Astonished Man*, 1970); *La Main coupée*, 1946 (autobiography; *Lice*, 1973); *Bourlinguer*, 1948 (autobiography; *Planus*, 1972); *La Banlieue de Paris*, 1949; *Le Lotissement du ciel*, 1949 (autobiography; *Sky: Memoirs*, 1992); *Blaise Cendrars vous parle*, 1952; *Entretiens de Fernand Léger avec Blaise Cendrars et Louis Carré sur le paysage dans l'œuvre de Léger*, 1956; *Trop c'est trop*, 1957; *Dites-nous Monsieur Blaise Cendrars*, 1969; *Inédits secrets*, 1969; *Correspondance, 1934-1979: 45 ans d'amitié*, 1995 (with Henry Miller; in French and English).

EDITED TEXTS: *L'Anthologie nègre*, 1921 (*The African Saga*, 1927); *Feu le lieutenant Bringolf*, 1930 (*I Have No Regrets: The Strange Life of a Diplomat-Vagrant, Being the Memoirs of Lieutenant Bringolf*, 1931).

MISCELLANEOUS: *Œuvres complètes*, 1960-1965 (8 volumes); *Selected Writings of Blaise Cendrars*, 1966; *Œuvres complètes*, 1968-1971 (15 volumes); *Modernities, and Other Writings*, 1992 (Monique Chefdor, editor).

BIBLIOGRAPHY

Albert, Walter, ed. *Selected Writings of Blaise Cendrars.* 1966. Reprint. Westport, Conn.: Greenwood Press, 1978. In his critical introduction, editor Walter Albert suggests that Cendrars lacked discipline and form and that his work thus never achieved its rich potential. Includes a preface by Henry Miller.

Bochner, Jay. "An American Writer Born in Paris: Blaise Cendrars Reads Henry Miller Reading Blaise Cendrars." *Twentieth Century Literature* 49, no. 1 (2003): 103-122. Examines the relationship of Cendrars and Miller and contrasts their writings. Bochner finds fault with the authors' writing styles, maintaining that Miller has trouble keeping "the flow" of his work "flowing," while Cendrars's problems are "believability and form."

_____. *Blaise Cendrars: Discovery and Re-Creation.* Buffalo, N.Y.: University of Toronto Press, 1978. Full-length study of Cendrars's life and works, providing a thorough and balanced assessment of his complete oeuvre. Includes an index and a bibliography.

Bursey, Jeff. "Blaise Cendrars." *Review of Contemporary Fiction* 24, no. 1 (Spring, 2004): 58-93. An overview of some of the elements of Cendrars's novels and memoirs, in which Bursey, in his own words, hopes to "initiate more interest in this neglected artist whose work spans genres, media, isms, wars, continents, and oceans."

Cendrars, Blaise. *Complete Postcards from the Americas: Poems of Road and Sea.* Translated by Monique Chefdor. Berkeley: University of California Press, 1976. Translator Chefdor's introduction provides a useful and detailed overview of Cendrars's life and work in this collection of Cendrars's poetry.

Chefdor, Monique. *Blaise Cendrars.* Boston: Twayne, 1980. A good introduction to Cendrars's life and works. One of the volumes in the Twayne World Authors series.

Leamon, Amanda. *Shades of Sexuality: Colors and Sexual Identity in the Novels of Blaise Cendrars.* Atlanta: Rodopi, 1997. Leamon uses the color spectrum and elements of disguise to describe the structures and symbolism of Cendrars's novels, focusing on his treatment of men in relation to women. A specialized, scholarly study that requires some knowledge of Cendrars's work. Includes a bibliography and an index.

Miller, Henry. *The Books in My Life.* 1952. Reprint. New York: New Directions, 1969. Miller devotes an entire chapter to Cendrars, one of his favorite authors and a highly influential contemporary.

_____. Preface to *Selected Writings of Blaise Cendrars.* Westport, Conn.: Greenwood Press, 1978. An insightful and valuable piece by the well-known novelist, who was strongly influenced by Cendrars.

MIGUEL DE CERVANTES

Born: Alcalá de Henares, Spain; September 29, 1547
Died: Madrid, Spain; April 23, 1616
Also known as: Miguel de Cervantes Saavedra

PRINCIPAL LONG FICTION

La Galatea, 1585 (*Galatea: A Pastoral Romance*, 1833)

El ingenioso hidalgo don Quixote de la Mancha, 1605, 1615 (*The History of the Valorous and Wittie Knight-Errant, Don Quixote of the Mancha*, 1612-1620; better known as *Don Quixote de la Mancha*)

Novelas ejemplares, 1613 (*Exemplary Novels*, 1846)

Los trabajos de Persiles y Sigismunda, 1617 (*The Travels of Persiles and Sigismunda: A Northern History*, 1619)

OTHER LITERARY FORMS

Miguel de Cervantes (sur-VAHN-teez) never sought acclaim as a writer of fiction. He longed for the more popular success and financial rewards offered by the stage and hoped to gain a more prestigious literary reputation as a great poet, as evidenced by the time and dedication he committed to his long derivative poem *Viaje del Parnaso* (1614; *The Voyage to Parnassus*, 1870). These ambitions were unrealized. In fact, he admits in the poem of 1614 that heaven never blessed him with the poetic gift. His efforts in the theater did not bring him success at the time but did produce some significant work. Cervantes contributed to the Spanish theater not only by writing plays but also by stirring critical debate. In chapter 48 of the first part of *Don Quixote de la Mancha*, Cervantes attacked the Spanish stage and certain kinds of popular plays. This attack prompted a response from Lope de Vega Carpio, *Arte nuevo de hacer comedias en este tiempo* (1609; *The New Art of Writing Plays*, 1914) that was the central piece of dramatic theorizing of the Golden Age of Spanish theater. Cervantes also wrote one epic tragedy, *El cerco de Numancia* (wr. 1585, pb. 1784; *The Siege of Numantia*, 1870), a play

praised in later centuries by Johann Wolfgang von Goethe, Percy Bysshe Shelley, Friedrich Schlegel, and Arthur Schopenhauer, and he published a collection of eight comedies and eight interludes in 1615. These works were never performed in the author's lifetime. The eight interludes, one-act farces that would have been performed as intermission pieces, are original, dynamic, and highly theatrical. They rank with the finest work in the one-act form by Anton Chekhov, August Strindberg, and Tennessee Williams.

ACHIEVEMENTS

Cervantes belongs to that elite group of supreme literary geniuses that includes Homer, Vergil, Dante, Geoffrey Chaucer, and William Shakespeare. The first to establish his greatness as a writer through the medium of prose fiction, Cervantes is acknowledged as an influential innovator who nurtured the short-story form and, more important, shaped the novel, sending it into the modern world. The list of succeeding masters of the novel who paid homage to Cervantes either through direct praise or imitation is awesome—among them Daniel Defoe, Tobias Smollett, Henry Fielding, Laurence Sterne, Jonathan Swift, Sir Walter Scott, Charles Dickens, Voltaire, Stendhal, Honoré de Balzac, Gustave Flaubert, Victor Hugo, Goethe, Thomas Mann, Ivan Turgenev, Nikolai Gogol, Fyodor Dostoevski, Washington Irving, Herman Melville, Mark Twain, William Faulkner, and Saul Bellow; all of these authors recognized an indebtedness to the Spanish writer who, at the end of a lifetime of failure and disappointment, created the unlikely Knight of La Mancha and sent him out into the Spanish landscape with his equally unlikely squire, Sancho Panza. *Don Quixote de la Mancha* remains Cervantes' greatest gift to the world of literature.

If Cervantes became a giant in world literature by creating his mad knight, he also gave Spanish literature its greatest work. Cervantes' life and career spanned the glory days of Spain's eminence as a great empire as well as the beginning of its fall from world power. Cervantes re-created this Spain he knew so well in his great work. His love of his native Spain is evident in the generosity of detail with which he created the backdrop of his novel—the inns, the food, the costumes, the dusty roads, the mountains, the rogues, the nobility, the arguments, the laughter. The superb realization of his world set a standard that has guided novelists for centuries; Cervantes' rendering of his native Spain has by extension given us the England of Dickens, the Paris of Balzac, the Russia of Dostoevski.

Cervantes' imaginative depiction of his native land also has influenced subsequent Spanish literature. Most Spanish writers feel an indebtedness to Cervantes and regard his work with awe. Such modern masters of Spanish literature as José Ortega y Gasset and Miguel de Unamuno have written extensive studies and detailed commentaries on his great novel, treating it with a reverence usually reserved for religious writings. Cervantes, in creating Don Quixote, gave Spain its greatest masterpiece, and his figure has loomed majestically over all subsequent Spanish literature.

Cervantes' contributions to the development of the novel form are considerable. In addition to re-creating the texture of daily life in the Spain of his day, he became an innovator in the form of the novel. *Don Quixote de la Mancha* is a strange kind of prose epic, with its singularly odd hero with his visions of virtue and glory riding into a mundane and common world. From the first, Cervantes saw how the richness of the older epic form might be adapted to the new prose form to create a new vision, grand and common, eloquent and humorous, ideal and real, all at once. Cervantes quickly mastered the ability to elevate the common; the greatest of all later novelists have also mastered this unlikely duality—a large ideal vision that must find expression within the confines of a real world, whether that world be the streets of London, an American whaling vessel, or a Russian prison camp.

Cervantes also freed his characters to exist within a more real world and to behave as more realistic human beings. The Don in all of his madness is still rooted in the Spain of his day, and Sancho Panza is the embodiment of a class as well as an attitude toward life. The characters also relate to one another through recognizable conversation. Cervantes made dialogue an integral part of the novel form, allowing his characters to speak their minds

Miguel de Cervantes. (Library of Congress)

with the same freedom with which they travel the roads of Spain. Such conversations have been a part of most novels ever since.

Finally, and perhaps most important, Cervantes bequeathed to humankind a compelling vision of itself—man as committed idealist combined with man as foolish lunatic. Don Quixote rides out of the pages of the novel with a magnetic presence that has fascinated many subsequent artists. Honoré Daumier, Pablo Picasso, and many other painters have put him on canvas; Richard Strauss has placed him in an orchestral tone poem; Jules-Émile-Frédéric Massenet and Manuel de Falla have rendered him on the opera stage; and Tennessee Williams has brought him into American drama. The fascinating figure of the foolish knight continues to command the attentions of other artists. The Don remains a popular figure, too, appearing on the Broadway musical stage and in television commercials. The novel that Cervantes created is second only to the Bible in the number of different languages into which it has been translated, but the appeal of the title character extends beyond literature into the dream life of humankind.

BIOGRAPHY

In the most interesting of the full-length comedies by Miguel de Cervantes published in 1615, *Pedro de Urdemalas*, the title character dreams ambitiously of becoming all the great personages that a man can become: pope, prince, monarch, emperor, master of the world. After a career that is typical of a picaro or any other adventurous Spanish rogue of the time, Pedro finds his wishes realized when he becomes an actor and enters imaginatively into the ranks of the great. In much the same way, Cervantes' great ambitions in life were never realized; the only satisfaction he found was in a world he himself created.

In one sense, Cervantes' greatest adventure was his own life. Born Miguel de Cervantes Saavedra in a small university city not far from Madrid, he traveled constantly with his family in his early years. His father, an impoverished and impractical man who attempted to earn a living as a surgeon, kept the family moving, from Valladolid to Córdoba, from Seville to Madrid. Cervantes learned the life of the road and the diversity of city life in Spain as a youth. In his twenties, he journeyed to Italy, perhaps fleeing from arrest as a result of a duel; there, he entered the service of Cardinal Aquaviva. In 1569, he enlisted in the Spanish army and went to sea. Cervantes was present at the Battle of Lepanto in 1571, serving under the command of Don John of Austria in the famous victory against the Turks. Cervantes rose from his sickbed to join in the battle and was twice wounded, one wound leaving his left hand permanently incapacitated. With his brother, Rodrigo, he embarked for Spain in 1575, but their ship was seized by Turkish pirates, and Cervantes spent five years in captivity as a slave.

Ransomed by monks, Cervantes returned to Spain, but not to glory and acclaim. With his military career at an end because of his paralyzed hand, Cervantes fell into poverty and moved from one failure to another, including an apparently unhappy marriage in 1584. Moving about Spain as in his youth, he again gained an education in the character and behavior of the Spanish lower classes, an education that continued when he was impris-

oned twice in Seville, once in 1597 and again in 1602, both times, it is assumed, the result of financial difficulties. Despite a life of bad luck, missed opportunities, and little reward for his talent, Cervantes did achieve a popular success when the first part of *Don Quixote de la Mancha* was published in 1605, although his finances saw only minor improvement. In 1615, the second part of the novel appeared, to challenge the "false" sequels being produced by other writers seeking to capitalize on the book's success. Cervantes died in Madrid in 1616, at peace, having received the Sacraments.

ANALYSIS: DON QUIXOTE DE LA MANCHA

Many critics maintain that the impulse that prompted Miguel de Cervantes to begin his great novel was a satiric one: He desired to satirize chivalric romances. As the elderly Alonso Quixano the Good (if that is his name) pores over the pages of these books in his study, his "brain dries up" and he imagines himself to be the champion who will take up the vanished cause of knight-errantry and wander the world righting wrongs, helping the helpless, defending the cause of justice, all for the greater glory of his lady Dulcinea del Toboso and his God.

As he leaves his village before dawn, clad in rusty armor and riding his broken-down nag, the mad knight becomes Don Quixote de la Mancha. His first foray is brief, and he is brought back home by friends from his native village. Despite the best efforts of his friends and relations, the mad old man embarks on a second journey, this time accompanied by a peasant from his village, Sancho Panza, who becomes the knight's squire. The Don insists on finding adventure everywhere, mistaking windmills for giants, flocks of sheep for attacking armies, puppet shows for real life. His squire provides a voice of down-to-earth reason, but Quixote always insists that vile enchanters have transformed the combatants to embarrass and humiliate him. Don Quixote insists on his vision of the ideal in the face of the cold facts of the world; Sancho Panza maintains his proverbial peasant wisdom in the face of his master's madness.

In their travels and adventures, they encounter life on the roads of Spain. Sometimes they are treated with respect—for example, by "the gentleman in green" who invites them to his home and listens to Quixote with genuine interest—but more often they are ridiculed, as when the Duke and Duchess bring the knight and squire to their estate only for the purpose of mocking them. Finally, a young scholar from Quixote's native village, Sampson Carrasco, defeats the old knight in battle and forces him to return to his home, where he dies peacefully, having renounced his mad visions and lunatic behavior.

Themes

While it is necessary to acknowledge the satiric intent of Cervantes' novel, the rich fictional world of *Don Quixote de la Mancha* utterly transcends its local occasion. On the most personal level, the novel can be viewed as one of the most intimate evaluations of a life ever penned by a great author. When Don Quixote decides to take up the cause of knight-errantry, he opens himself to a life of ridicule and defeat, a life that resembles Cervantes' own life, with its endless reversals of fortune, humiliations, and hopeless struggles. Out of this life of failure and disappointment Cervantes created the "mad knight," but he also added the curious human nobility and the refusal to succumb to despair in the face of defeat that turns Quixote into something more than a comic character or a ridiculous figure to be mocked. Although there are almost no points in the novel where actual incidents from Cervantes' life appear directly or even transformed into fictional disguise, the tone and the spirit, the succession of catastrophes with only occasional moments of slight glory, and the resilience of human nature mark the novel as the most personal work of the author, the one where his singularly difficult life and his profoundly complex emotional responses to that life found form and structure.

If the novel is the record of Cervantes' life, the fiction also records a moment in Spanish national history when fortunes were shifting and tides turning. At the time of Cervantes' birth, Spain's might and glory were at their peak. The wealth from conquests of Mexico and Peru returned to Spain, commerce boomed, and artists recorded the sense of national pride with magnificent energy and power. By the time *Don Quixote de la Mancha* was published, the Spanish Empire was beginning its decline. A series of military disasters, including the defeat of the Spanish Armada by the English and the revolt of Flanders, had shaken the once mighty nation. In the figure of Don Quixote, the greatest of a richly remembered past combines with the hard facts of age, weakness, and declining power. The character embodies a moment of Spanish history and the Spanish people's own sense of vanishing glory in the face of irreversible decline.

Don Quixote de la Mancha also stands as the greatest literary embodiment of the Counter-Reformation. Throughout Europe, the Reformation was moving with the speed of new ideas, changing the religious landscape of country after country. Spain stood proud as a Catholic nation, resisting any changes. Standing alone against the flood of reform sweeping Europe displayed a kind of willed madness, but the nobility and determination of Quixote to fight for his beliefs, no matter what the rest of the world maintained, reflects the strength of the Spanish will at this time. Cervantes was a devout and loyal believer, a supporter of the Church, and Don Quixote may be the greatest fictional Catholic hero, the battered knight of the Counter-Reformation.

The book also represents fictionally the various sides of the Spanish spirit and the Spanish temper. In the divisions and contradictions found between the Knight of the Sad Countenance and his unlikely squire, Sancho Panza, Cervantes paints the two faces of the Spanish soul: The Don is idealistic, sprightly, energetic, and cheerful, even in the face of overwhelming odds, but he is also overbearing, domineering Sancho, who is earthy, servile, and slothful. The two characters seem unlikely companions and yet they form a whole, the one somehow incomplete without the other and linked throughout the book through their dialogues and debates. In drawing master and servant, Cervantes presents the opposing truths of the spirit of his native land.

Characterization

The book can also be seen as a great moment in the development of fiction, the moment when the fictional character was freed into the real world of choice and change. When the gentleman of La Mancha took it into his head to become a knight-errant and travel through the world redressing wrongs and winning eternal glory, the face of fiction permanently changed. Character in fiction became dynamic, unpredictable, and spontaneous. Until that time, character in fiction had existed in service of the story, but now the reality of change and psychological energy and freedom of the will became a permanent hallmark of fiction, as it already was of drama and narrative poetry. The title character's addled wits made the new freedom all the more impressive. The determination of Don Quixote, the impact of his vision on the world, and the world's hard reality as it impinges on the Don make for shifting balances and constant alterations in fortune that are psychologically believable. The shifting balance of friendship, devotion, and perception between the knight and his squire underlines this freedom, as does the power of other characters in the book to affect Don Quixote's fortunes directly: the niece, the housekeeper, the priest, the barber, Sampson Carrasco, the Duke, and the Duchess. There is a fabric of interaction throughout the novel, and characters in the novel change as they encounter new adventures, new people, and new ideas.

One way Cervantes chronicles this interaction is in dialogue. Dialogue had not played a significant or defining role in fiction before *Don Quixote de la Mancha*. As knight and squire ride across the countryside and engage in conversation, dialogue becomes the expression of character, idea, and reality. In the famous episode with windmills early in the first part of the novel (when Quixote views the windmills on the plain and announces that they are giants that he will wipe from the face of the earth, and Sancho innocently replies, "What giants?"), the dialogue not only carries the comedy but also becomes the battleground on which the contrasting visions of life engage one another—to the delight of the reader. The long exchanges between Don Quixote and Sancho Panza provide priceless humor but also convey two different realities that meet, struggle, and explode in volleys of words. In giving his characters authentic voices that carry ideas, Cervantes brought to fiction a new truth that remains a standard of comparison.

THE NARRATOR

Don Quixote de la Mancha is also as modern as the most experimental of later fiction. Throughout the long novel, Cervantes plays with the nature of the narrator, raising constant difficult questions as to who is telling the story and to what purpose. In the riotously funny opening page of the novel, the reader encounters a narrator not only unreliable but also lacking in the basic facts necessary to tell the story. He chooses not to tell the name of the village where his hero lives, and he is not even sure of his hero's name, yet the narrator protests that the narrative must be entirely truthful.

In chapter 9, as Don Quixote is preparing to do battle with the Basque, the narrative stops; the narrator states that the manuscript from which he is culling this story is mutilated and incomplete. Fortunately, some time later in Toledo, he says, he came upon an old Arabic manuscript by Arab historian Cide Hamete Benengeli that continues the adventures. For the remainder of the novel, the narrator claims to be providing a translation of this manuscript—the manuscript and the second narrator, the Arab historian, both lacking authority and credibility. In the second part of the novel, the narrator and the characters themselves are aware of the first part of the novel as well as of a "false Quixote," a spurious second part written by an untalented Spanish writer named Avallaneda who sought to capitalize on the popularity of the first part of *Don Quixote de la Mancha* by publishing his own sequel. The "false Quixote" is on the narrator's mind, the characters' minds, and somehow on the mind of Cide Hamete Benengeli. These shifting perspectives, the multiple narrative voices, the questionable reliability of the narrators, and the "false" second part are all tricks, narrative sleight of hand as complex as anything found in the works of Faulkner, Vladimir Nabokov, or Jorge Luis Borges. In his *Lectures on Don Quixote* (1983), Nabokov oddly makes no reference to Cervantes' narrative games; perhaps the old Spanish master's shadow still loomed too close to the modern novelist.

None of these approaches to the novel, however, appropriate as they may be, can begin to explain fully the work's enduring popularity or the strange manner in which the knight and his squire have ridden out of the pages of a book into the other artistic realms of orchestral music, opera, ballet, and painting, where other artists have presented their visions of Quixote and Sancho. A current deeper and more abiding than biography, history, national temper, or literary landmark flows through the book and makes it speak to all manner of readers in all ages.

Early in the novel, Cervantes begins to dilute his strong satiric intent. The reader can laugh with delight at the inanity of the mad knight but never with the wicked, unalloyed glee that pure satire evokes. The knight begins to loom over the landscape; his madness brushes sense; his ideals demand defense. The reader finds him- or herself early in the novel taking an attitude equivalent to that of the two young women of easy virtue who see Quixote when he arrives at an inn, which he believes to be a castle, on his first foray. Quixote calls them "two beauteous maidens . . . taking air at the gate of the castle," and they fall into helpless laughter, confronted with such a mad vision of themselves as "maidens." In time, however, because of Quixote's insistence on the truth of his vision, they help him out of his armor and set a table for him. They treat him as a knight, not as a mad old fool; he treats them as ladies, and they behave as ladies. The laughter stops, and, for a pure moment, life transforms itself and human beings transcend themselves.

CONTRADICTIONS

This mingling of real chivalry and transcendent ideals with the absurdity of character and mad action creates the tensions in the book as well as its strange melancholy beauty and haunting poignancy. The book is unlike any other ever written. John Berryman has commented on this split between the upheld ideal and the riotously real, observing that the reader "does not know whether to laugh or cry, and does both." This old man with his dried-up brain, with his squire who has no "salt in his brain pan," with his rusty armor, his pathetic steed, and his lunatic vision that changes windmills into giants and flocks of sheep into attacking armies, this crazy old fool becomes a real knight-errant. The true irony of the book and its history is that Don Quixote actually becomes a model for knighthood. He may be a foolish, improbable knight, but with his squire, horse, and armor he has ridden into the popular imagination of the world not only as a ridiculous figure but also as a champion; he is a real knight whose vision may often cloud, who sees what he wants to see, but he is also one who demonstrates real virtue and courage and rises in his rhetoric and daring action to real heights of greatness.

Perhaps Cervantes left a clue as to the odd shift in his intention. The contradictory titles he assigns to his knight suggest this knowledge. The comic, melancholy strain pervades "Knight of the Sad Countenance" in the first part of the novel, and the heroic strain is seen in the second part when the hero acquires the new sobriquet "Knight of the Lions." The first title comes immediately after his adventure with a corpse and is awarded him by his realistic companion, Sancho. Quixote has attacked a funeral procession, seeking to avenge the dead man. Death, however, cannot be overcome; the attempted attack merely disrupts the funeral, and the valiant knight breaks the leg of an attending churchman. The name "Knight of the Sad Countenance" fits Quixote's stance here and through much of the book. Many of the adventures he undertakes are not only misguided but also unwinnable. Quixote may be Christlike, but he is not Christ, and he cannot conquer Death.

The adventure with the lions earns for him his second title and offers the other side of his journey as a knight. Encountering a cage of lions being taken to the king, Quixote becomes determined to fight them. Against all protest, he takes his stand, and the cage is opened. One of the lions stretches, yawns, looks at Quixote, and lies down. Quixote proclaims a great victory and awards himself the name "Knight of the Lions." A delightfully comic episode, the scene can be viewed in two ways—as a nonadventure that the knight claims as a victory or as a genuine moment of triumph as the knight undertakes an outlandish adventure and proves his genuine bravery while the king of beasts realizes the futility of challenging the unswerving old knight. Quixote, by whichever route, emerges as conqueror. Throughout his journeys, he often does emerge victorious, despite his age, despite his illusions, despite his dried-up brain.

When, at the book's close, he is finally defeated and humiliated by Sampson Carrasco and forced to return to his village, the life goes out of him. The knight Don Quixote is replaced, however, on the deathbed by Alonso Quixano the Good. Don Quixote does not die, for the elderly gentleman regains his wits and becomes a new character. Don Quixote cannot die, for he is the creation of pure imagination. Despite the moving and sober conclusion, the reader cannot help but sense that the death scene being played out does not signify the end of Don Quixote. The knight escapes and remains free. He rides out of the novel, with his loyal companion Sancho at his side, into the golden realm of myth. He becomes the model knight he hoped to be. He stands tall with his spirit, his ideals, his rusty armor, and his broken lance as the embodiment of man's best intentions and impossible folly. As Dostoevski so wisely said, when the Lord calls the Last Judgment, man should take with him this book and point to it, for it reveals all of man's deep and fatal mystery, his glory and his sorrow.

David Allen White

OTHER MAJOR WORKS

PLAYS: *El trato de Argel*, pr. 1585 (*The Commerce of Algiers*, 1870); *Ocho comedias y ocho entremeses nuevos*, 1615 (includes *Pedro de Urdemalas* [*Pedro the Artful Dodger*, 1807], *El juez de los divorcios* [*The Divorce Court Judge*, 1919], *Los habladores* [*Two Chatterboxes*, 1930], *La cueva de Salamanca* [*The Cave of Salamanca*, 1933], *La elección de los alcaldes de Daganzo* [*Choosing a Councilman in Daganzo*, 1948], *La guarda cuidadosa* [*The Hawk-Eyed Sentinel*, 1948], *El retablo de las maravillas* [*The Wonder Show*, 1948], *El rufián viudo llamada Trampagos* [*Trampagos the Pimp Who Lost His Moll*, 1948], *El viejo celoso* [*The Jealous Old Husband*, 1948], and *El vizcaíno fingido* [*The Basque Imposter*, 1948]); *El cerco de Numancia*, pb. 1784 (wr. 1585; *Numantia: A Tragedy*, 1870; also known as *The Siege of Numantia*); *The Interludes of Cervantes*, 1948.

POETRY: *Viaje del Parnaso*, 1614 (*The Voyage to Parnassus*, 1870).

BIBLIOGRAPHY

Bloom, Harold, ed. *Cervantes*. New York: Chelsea House, 1987. Collection of essays addresses topics such as the picaresque, the trickster figure, Cervantes' biography and use of language, and his attitude toward realism and the literary tradition. Includes an informative introduction, a chronology, a bibliography, and an index.

_____. *Cervantes's "Don Quixote."* Philadelphia: Chelsea House, 2001. Collection reprints essays about the novel written by well-known authors and critics, including Thomas Mann, Franz Kafka, W. H. Auden, Vladimir Nabokov, and Mark van Doren. Includes an introduction by Bloom, bibliographical references, and index.

Cascardi, Anthony J., ed. *The Cambridge Companion to Cervantes*. New York: Cambridge University Press, 2002. Collection of essays places Cervantes' life and work within historical and social context and discusses Cervantes' relation to the Italian Renaissance and his influence on other writers. An essay titled "*Don Quixote* and the Invention of the Novel" focuses on the well-known work.

Castillo, David R. *(A)wry Views: Anamorphosis, Cervantes, and the Early Picaresque*. West Lafayette, Ind.: Purdue University Press, 2001. Looks at anamorphosis, or visual perception, in the writings of Cervantes and other works of Spanish picaresque literature from the sixteenth and seventeenth centuries. Includes bibliography and index.

Close, A. J. *Cervantes and the Comic Mind of His Age*. New York: Oxford University Press, 2000. Analyzes ideas about comedy and comedic writing in the Spanish Golden Age and describes how Cervantes' works reflected those ideas. Includes bibliography and index.

Durán, Manuel. *Cervantes*. New York: Twayne, 1974. Provides a sound introduction to the author, with chapters on Cervantes' life and his career as a poet, playwright, short-story writer, and novelist. Includes notes, chronology, and annotated bibliography.

Hart, Thomas R. *Cervantes' Exemplary Fictions: A Study of the "Novelas ejemplares."* Lexington: University Press of Kentucky, 1994. Presents a reading of *Exemplary Novels* within the literary conventions of other popular novels of the seventeenth century, drawing on the literature not only of Spain but also of France, Italy, and England. Argues that novels in that era were meant to elicit readers' surprise or wonder and describes how Cervantes' work attains that goal.

McCrory, Donald P. *No Ordinary Man: The Life and Times of Miguel de Cervantes*. Chester Springs, Pa.: Peter Owen, 2002. Thorough biography is based, in part, on original research and unpublished material. Places Cervantes' life within the context of sixteenth and seventeenth century Spanish history. Includes bibliographical references and index.

Mancing, Howard. *Cervantes' "Don Quixote": A Reference Guide*. Westport, Conn.: Greenwood Press, 2006. An excellent companion for undergraduate students and for general readers. Individual chapters explore themes, criticism, language and style, publishing history, and other topics. Select bibliographies make this an important resource.

Nabokov, Vladimir. *Lectures on "Don Quixote."* Edited by Fredson Bowers. New York: Harcourt Brace Jovanovich, 1983. College lectures by a great twentieth century novelist are divided into portraits of Don Quixote and Sancho Panza, the structure of the novel, the use of cruelty and mystification, the treatment of Dulcinea and death, and commentaries on Cervantes' narrative methods. An appendix contains sample passages from romances of chivalry.

Riley, E. C. *Cervantes's Theory of the Novel*. 1962. Reprint. Newark, Del.: Juan de la Cuesta, 1992. Provides a detailed examination of Cervantes' views on questions of literary practice in terms of traditional issues in poetics, such as art and nature, unity, and purpose and function of literature. Includes bibliography and indexes of names and topics.

Weiger, John G. *The Substance of Cervantes*. London: Cambridge University Press, 1985. Provides valuable insights into Cervantes' craft as a writer by exploring questions such as the relationship of art and reality, the functions of authors and readers, the elusive nature of truth, the dynamics of society, and the significance of the individual and of communication between individuals. Augmented by a bibliography and an index.

Williamson, Edwin, ed. *Cervantes and the Modernists: The Question of Influence*. London: Tamesis, 1994. Collection of essays explores the novelist's impact on such twentieth century writers as Marcel Proust, Thomas Mann, Primo Levi, Carlos Fuentes, and Gabriel García Márquez.

MICHAEL CHABON

Born: Washington, D.C.; May 24, 1963
Also known as: Leon Chaim Bach; Malachi B. Cohen; August Van Zorn

PRINCIPAL LONG FICTION

The Mysteries of Pittsburgh, 1988
Wonder Boys, 1995
The Amazing Adventures of Kavalier and Clay, 2000
The Final Solution: A Story of Detection, 2004
Gentlemen of the Road, 2007
The Yiddish Policemen's Union, 2007

OTHER LITERARY FORMS

Although known primarily as a novelist, Michael Chabon (SHAY-bahn) has also distinguished himself as a writer of short fiction, publishing the collections *A Model World, and Other Stories* (1991) and *Werewolves in Their Youth* (1999). His second book, *A Model World*, helped cement Chabon's emerging reputation as a writer of emotional depth and lyrical intensity. His novel *The Amazing Adventures of Kavalier and Clay* inspired a comic-book series, published by Dark Horse Comics, based on the novel's comic-book superhero character the Escapist; Chabon has contributed but is not a primary writer for the series. He has published articles and essays in a variety of magazines such as *Esquire*, *The New Yorker*, and *The Paris Review*. He served as the editor for the anthology *McSweeney's Mammoth Treasury of Thrilling Tales* (2003) and *McSweeney's Enchanted Chamber of Astonishing Stories* (2004). He has worked on screenplays for a number of films, most notably *Spider-Man 2* (2004). A collection of Chabon's essays (largely made up of his magazine publications) titled *Maps and Legends: Essays on Reading and Writing Along the Borderlands* was published in 2008.

ACHIEVEMENTS

After having initially made a splash as a novelist, Michael Chabon was also lauded for his collections of short fiction; the story "Son of the Wolfman" won an O. Henry Award in 1999. Chabon's star climbed higher with the 2000 film adaptation of *Wonder Boys* and reached even greater heights when *The Amazing Adventures of Kavalier and Clay* won the Pulitzer Prize in 2000 and was nominated for the National Book Critics Circle Award as well as short-listed for the PEN/Faulkner Award. Chabon's subsequent foray into adolescent fantasy, *Summerland*, won the Mythopoeic Fantasy Award for Children's Literature in 2003. His further work in genre fiction has been rewarded as well; a brief version of his novel *The Final Solution* won the 2003 Aga Khan

Prize for fiction for best work published in *The Paris Review* that year. Furthermore, *The Yiddish Policemen's Union* won the Edgar Award for best mystery novel, the Nebula Award for best science-fiction novel, and the Locus Award for best science-fiction novel and was nominated for a Hugo Award for best science-fiction novel as well as the Sidewise Award for Alternate History. His historical swashbuckling novel *Gentlemen of the Road* was first serialized in *The New York Times Magazine*.

BIOGRAPHY

Michael Chabon was born on May 24, 1963, in Washington, D.C., and raised partly in Columbia, Maryland, and partly in Pittsburgh, Pennsylvania. His parents divorced when Chabon was an adolescent. During this time the young Chabon turned to comic books and works of genre fiction (such as Arthur Conan Doyle's Sherlock Holmes stories) to escape the domestic strife in his life. He attended the University of Pittsburgh, earning a B.A. in English in 1984; from there he attended the master of fine arts program at the University of California at Irvine, where he would earn his degree in 1987. More important, one of his advisers at Irvine, novelist Donald Heiney, was so impressed with Chabon's thesis that he sent the manuscript to his own agent; the novel was purchased for $155,000 (almost an unheard-of sum for a first literary novel in 1987) and was published to great advance praise. That same year, Chabon married poet Lollie Groth, a union that would end with their divorce in 1991.

For the next several years, Chabon worked on a novel that he planned to title "Fountain City," about environmental activism and a baseball park in Florida, among other things; the novel became longer and longer, until Chabon realized that it was not succeeding and put it aside to begin work on a novel about a man unable to finish a sprawling novel, *Wonder Boys*. Chabon married attorney Ayelet Waldman in 1993, with whom he would eventually have three children (Sophie, Ezekiel, and Ida-Rose). The successful adaptation of *Wonder Boys* into a film (directed by Curtis Hanson) released in 2000 combined with the author's thriving sales to make him financially independent and able to focus on his work. Chabon's second wife, Waldman has published a number of mystery novels in a series known as the Mommy-Track Mysteries; her successful work in genre fiction parallels Chabon's own interest in the field. Since his work on *Spider-Man 2* (directed by Sam Raimi), Chabon has balanced his busy life writing fiction with work on screenplays.

ANALYSIS

As might be expected of a novelist who first gained acclaim at the age of twenty-five and who has not escaped the limelight since, Michael Chabon has produced work that displays significant evolution over the succeeding two decades. While all his novels have shown Chabon's gift for fluid, lyrical prose, the tones of the works have stretched from wistful (*The Mysteries of Pittsburgh*) to wryly comic (*Wonder Boys*) to cynical and laconic (*The Yiddish Policemen's Union*). Structurally, Chabon's methods have also changed. Where his

Michael Chabon. (© Miriam Berkley)

first two novels are tightly focused first-person narratives about small numbers of people over a brief time, *The Amazing Adventures of Kavalier and Clay* takes place over several years and includes an expansive cast; *The Yiddish Policemen's Union* evokes an alternative version of the world in which Sitka, Alaska, has been the Jewish homeland since World War II; and *Gentleman of the Road* is a short, quickly paced novel of historical adventure.

As Chabon's plots and style have evolved, so too have his interests and subject matter. *The Mysteries of Pittsburgh* is a book by a young man, not too long out of college, about a young man just out of college. The distance between the writer and the creation is greater in *Wonder Boys*, but at some level Grady Tripp's struggle to complete a new novel is surely based on Chabon's similar experience. With *The Amazing Adventures of Kavalier and Clay*, however, Chabon broke into new territory: The novel is set in the years before and after World War II and deals with such broad themes as art, creativity, Jewish identity, romantic happiness, and the closeted lives of gays at a time when such lives were subject to scrutiny and persecution.

Chabon's novels have often portrayed gay characters and aspects of gay lifestyle. After the success of *The Mysteries of Pittsburgh*, which is partly about a bisexual man making a choice between a relationship with a man and a relationship with a woman, Chabon became identified as an author who writes about and is sympathetic to gay characters. Similarly, although Chabon's Jewish heritage seems to have had relatively little influence on his first two novels, Jewish culture and identity are primary issues in *The Amazing Adventures of Kavalier and Clay*, *The Yiddish Policemen's Union*, and *Gentlemen of the Road*.

Chabon has also become increasingly interested in fiction genres such as detective, horror, and science fiction. In addition to editing genre collections for McSweeney's and writing a new "final chapter" to the life of Sherlock Holmes, Chabon has incorporated both science fiction and the detective story in the long consideration of Jewish identity and Zionism that is *The Yiddish Policemen's Union*. Similarly, although ostensibly a historical adventure novel, *Gentlemen of the Road* is in many ways patterned on the fantasy works of such writers as Fritz Leiber and Michael Moorcock; the primary

characters are again Jewish, and the setting is an ancient Turkish city-state of Jews.

THE MYSTERIES OF PITTSBURGH

The Mysteries of Pittsburgh is primarily a coming-of-age novel. Art Bechstein is poised on the precipice of several new worlds: He is not only trying to unravel his future as a new college graduate but also coming to terms with his own troubling (to him, at first) bisexuality as well as the realization that his father is a shadowy underworld figure. Even as Art is seduced by both Arthur Lecomte and Phlox Lombardi, he is pulled between their world and his own. Both names are symbolic in their way; Arthur has more or less the same name as Art, and at some level he represents an outward manifestation of Art's previously unacknowledged bisexuality. A phlox is a kind of flower, and in truth Art's world is in flower, blooming and changing; at the same time, phlox serves as a homonym for "flux," a perfect description of Art's emotional state.

Arthur and Phlox introduce Art to Cleveland, a charming and literate aspiring young criminal who wishes to use Art to gain an introduction to Art's father. As Phlox and Arthur represent different aspects of Art's life, Cleveland represents the allure of rebellion and the thrill of unplanned and unchecked danger. By the end of the novel, the triangle of friendships that has stretched Art in different directions has fallen apart under tragedy, and Art must make his own way into adulthood.

WONDER BOYS

Wonder Boys was published seven years after *The Mysteries of Pittsburgh*. The novel tells of a middle-aged creative-writing professor, Grady Tripp, who learns that his third wife, Emily, is leaving him even as he finds out that his mistress, college chancellor Sara Gaskell (and wife to the English Department's chair, Walter), is pregnant with Grady's child. Grady has been drinking too much and smoking too much marijuana, typing away all the while at his sprawling novel *Wonder Boys*, which is seven years overdue and at this point more than two thousand pages long. The events of the novel take place over the weekend of the small fictional Pennsylvania college's WordFest literary festival. Grady's editor, Terry Crabtree, is in town to attend the festival and to inquire about Grady's novel, which Grady has implied—untruthfully—is nearing completion.

Wonder Boys is, in some ways, nominally autobiographical; like Tripp, Chabon worked on an abortive second novel ("Fountain City") for several years, watching it grow to more than fifteen hundred pages before realizing that he had to abandon it. In most ways, however, Grady Tripp is a character in his own right, and throughout the novel his name proves apt as he trips repeatedly over his own feet literally and figuratively. Even as he tries to navigate between Emily's leaving and Sara's announcement, he must also try to guide his naïve, gay, and vulnerable young wunderkind student James Leer around the pitfalls represented by Grady's lecherous gay friend Terry and James's own budding talent and vulnerabilities.

The novel becomes a kind of picaresque series of adventures, with Grady stumbling from misadventure to misadventure, accompanied by James, who stitches together lies about his background. Interposed throughout the narrative are Grady's memories of cult horror writer Albert Vetch, who died forgotten and alone. Grady eventually realizes that, unless he wants to mimic Vetch's life, he too must put away childish things and fully embrace maturity.

THE AMAZING ADVENTURES OF KAVALIER AND CLAY

The Amazing Adventures of Kavalier and Clay in many ways demonstrates Chabon's coming-of-age. Early in the novel, eighteen-year-old Jewish art student and part-time escape artist Joseph Kavalier is smuggled out of Prague; the year is 1939. Sent to the United States, he meets his distant cousin Sammy Klayman (also known as Sammy Clay). Before long, Sammy has introduced Joe to the budding medium of comic books, and together they invent their own character, the Escapist. The allure of the Escapist in their lives is obvious: Millions of European Jews are being persecuted and are unable to escape the horror of the Holocaust; conversely, the Escapist is able to escape from any trap and turn the tables on his enemies. In addition, even as Sammy fears a second kind of persecution—as a closeted young gay man—the Escapist is empowered and fearless.

As the novel progresses, Joe confronts both his fear of persecution and his fear of intimacy when he joins the war effort and is sent on a mission to Antarctica; similarly, Sammy (although involved in a marriage of convenience with Joe's lover Rosa, who becomes pregnant with Joe's child just before he leaves for the war) takes more and more chances as he seeks to live a fully integrated life. Joe, too, eventually realizes that he needs family when he rejoins Sammy, Rosa, and his son, Tommy.

THE FINAL SOLUTION *and* GENTLEMEN OF THE ROAD

Both the young adult novel *Summerland* and *The Final Solution* indicate the different directions that Chabon's interests took in the years following *The Amazing Adventures of Kavalier and Clay*. *Summerland* is a fantasy novel (similar in style to J. K. Rowling's Harry Potter series) about a boy named Ethan Feld who hates baseball, which his father makes him play. Along with his friend, Native American pitcher Jennifer Rideout, Ethan is recruited to lead a team of misfit players (from a variety of dimensions) in a series of baseball games to save the world from destruction by the mysterious Coyote, a godlike avatar of chaos. *The Final Solution* returns to where Chabon's interest in genre fiction began—Sherlock Holmes. Set in 1944 during World War II, the eighty-nine-year-old character is never named but is clearly Holmes (or based completely on Holmes). The title refers both to Adolf Hitler's plan to exterminate the Jews of Europe and to "The Final Problem" (1893), the story wherein Holmes author Arthur Conan Doyle temporarily killed off his detective hero. Like *The Amazing Adventures of Kavalier and Clay* and *The Yiddish Policemen's Union*, *The Final Solution* deals with issues of Jewish identity; the aged Holmes's last case involves a young Jewish refugee from Germany. Although Holmes can find answers to the more overt problems in the case, others are insoluble.

Like *The Final Solution*, *Gentlemen of the Road* is a short novel; it was originally serialized in *The New York Times Magazine*. Set in the tenth century C.E., this swashbuckling adventure novel follows two mercenaries, an African Jew named Amram and a long-haired Jewish Frank named Zelikman, as they work to bring the rightful heir of the Jewish Khazars back to the throne.

THE YIDDISH POLICEMEN'S UNION

The Yiddish Policemen's Union represents a culmination of Chabon's interests in Jewish identity and in genre fiction. The novel posits an alternate history: The creation of Israel in 1948 fails, and instead a temporary homeland for Jews is created in Sitka, Alaska. The novel is set at the end of the sixty-year period following establishment of that homeland, soon before the Alaskan region is to revert to American control. The language in *The Yiddish Policemen's Union* is more tightly controlled and terse than in most of Chabon's work, in keeping with its crime-novel milieu. The protagonist is a down-on-his-luck homicide detective named Meyer Landsman, who, true to his genre, drinks too much and has recently seen his marriage fall apart.

Teamed with partner and cousin Berko Shemets (half Jewish and half Tlingit native), Landsman sets out to uncover the murder of a mysterious man who has died in Landsman's own apartment building. Like his hard-boiled predecessors Philip Marlowe (the detective creation of Raymond Chandler, 1888-1959) and Sam Spade (created by Dashiell Hammett, 1894-1961), Landsman solves his crimes more through persistence and toughness than through brilliant insights; the more the various communities of Sitka try to warn him away, the deeper he digs. Chabon uses the detective-novel framework of *The Yiddish Policemen's Union* to investigate questions of Jewish American culture, Zionism, and Anti-Semitism.

Scott D. Yarbrough

OTHER MAJOR WORKS

SHORT FICTION: *A Model World, and Other Stories*, 1991; *Werewolves in Their Youth: Stories*, 1999.

NONFICTION: *Maps and Legends: Essays on Reading and Writing Along the Borderlands*, 2008.

YOUNG ADULT LITERATURE: *Summerland*, 2002.

EDITED TEXTS: *McSweeney's Mammoth Treasury of Thrilling Tales*, 2003; *McSweeney's Enchanted Chamber of Astonishing Stories*, 2004.

MISCELLANEOUS: *Michael Chabon Presents: The Amazing Adventures of the Escapist*, 2004 (2 volumes).

BIBLIOGRAPHY

Binelli, Mark. "The Amazing Story of the Comic Book Nerd Who Won the Pulitzer Prize for Fiction." *Rolling Stone*, September 27, 2001. Provides an overview of Chabon's life and career as well as brief discussion of each of his novels.

Cahill, Bryon. "Michael Chabon: A Writer with Many Faces." *Writing!* 27, no. 6 (April/May, 2005): 16-20. Presents a detailed examination of Chabon's developing interests and the inspirations behind many of his works.

Chabon, Michael. "On *The Mysteries of Pittsburgh*." *The New York Review of Books*, June 9, 2005. Brief history by the author explains the genesis of his first novel and some of the less overt autobiographical elements in the work.

_____. "Secret Skin: Superheroes, Escapism, Realism." *The New Yorker*, March 10, 2008. Examines the comic-book and superhero genres, with emphasis on the costumes as well as on the ways in which the comic-book medium differs from traditional prose fiction. Discusses the superhero motif in *The Amazing Adventures of Kavalier and Clay*.

Fowler, Douglas. "The Short Fiction of Michael Chabon: Nostalgia in the Very Young." *Studies in Short Fiction* 32, no. 1 (Winter, 1995): 75-82. Offers analysis of Chabon's *The Mysteries of Pittsburgh* and various of his short stories, with comparisons drawn to F. Scott Fitzgerald's *The Great Gatsby* (1925).

Munson, Sam. "Slices of Life." *Commentary* 115, no. 6 (June, 2003): 67-71. Focuses on Chabon's editing of the McSweeney's anthologies as well as on the development of his interests in genre fiction.

Perle, Liz. "Alternate Reality: Author Profile of Michael Chabon." *Publishers Weekly*, September 24, 2007. Discusses Chabon's creativity and interest in genre categories, as demonstrated by his novel *Gentlemen of the Road*.

RAYMOND CHANDLER

Born: Chicago, Illinois; July 23, 1888
Died: La Jolla, California; March 26, 1959
Also known as: Raymond Thornton Chandler

PRINCIPAL LONG FICTION

The Big Sleep, 1939
Farewell, My Lovely, 1940
The High Window, 1942
The Lady in the Lake, 1943
The Little Sister, 1949
The Long Goodbye, 1953
Playback, 1958
The Raymond Chandler Omnibus: Four Famous Classics, 1967
The Second Chandler Omnibus, 1973
Poodle Springs, 1989 (incomplete manuscript finished by Robert B. Parker)
Later Novels and Other Writings, 1995

OTHER LITERARY FORMS

Raymond Chandler began his literary career with a false start in England in his early twenties, publishing an assortment of journalistic sketches, essays, poems, and a single story; most of these pieces are collected in *Chandler Before Marlowe: Raymond Chandler's Early Prose and Poetry* (1973), edited by Matthew J. Bruccoli. His real career as a writer was launched more than twenty years later, when he began publishing short stories in crime magazines. Chandler published twenty-three stories during his lifetime, most of which appeared in pulp magazines such as *Black Mask* and *Dime Detective Magazine*. Although the stories rarely approach the literary merit of his novels, they are representative of a popular type of American writing. They also show a versatility within the mystery formula that Chandler would later develop in his novels.

Chandler forbade the reissue during his lifetime of eight of his stories, but three of these were published, apparently without the author's consent. Chandler insisted that these stories be withheld because of a curious professional scruple. The materials had been incorporated in subsequent novels—in Chandler's word, "cannibal-

ized"—and he felt that their republication would be unfair to readers of the novels. Some of the best of Chandler's stories are in this group and have, since his death, been published in the collection *Killer in the Rain* (1964).

Like William Faulkner and F. Scott Fitzgerald, Chandler was invited to Hollywood to write film scripts. He collaborated on several important screenplays and, with Billy Wilder, was nominated for an Academy Award for the 1944 screen adaptation of James M. Cain's novel *Double Indemnity* (1936). His original screenplay *The Blue Dahlia* also received an Oscar nomination, despite the fact that Chandler remained dissatisfied with that 1946 film. In 1948 he wrote, under contract with Universal Pictures, an original screenplay, *Playback*, that was not filmed; Chandler rewrote this work, with new characters, as a novel during his final years.

ACHIEVEMENTS

More than any of his contemporaries, Raymond Chandler attempted to use the devices of mystery fiction for serious literary purposes. The peculiarly American school of detective fiction came of age during the years of the Great Depression in the 1930's. The most influential outlet for this fiction was *Black Mask*, a pulp magazine founded by H. L. Mencken and George Jean Nathan and later edited by Captain Joseph T. Shaw. The American detective character that had its origins in *Black Mask* and similar pulp magazines is often called the "hardboiled detective"—this character differs sharply from that of the traditional British sleuth. Chandler's heroes are not charming eccentrics in the tradition of Dorothy L. Sayers's Lord Peter Wimsey, nor are they masters of unbelievable powers of deduction, such as Arthur Conan Doyle's Sherlock Holmes. When Chandler's Philip Marlowe tells his client (in *The Big Sleep*) that he is not Holmes or Philo Vance and humorously introduces himself as Philo Vance in *The Lady in the Lake*, Chandler is calling attention to the distance he intends to create between his character and the traditional heroes of detective literature. The American detective of fiction as created by Chandler, Dashiell Hammett, and a host of lesser contemporaries is a loner, a man of ordinary intellect but of unusual perseverance and willingness to confront whatever adversary he encounters, whether that adversary be the criminal or the legal establishment. Kenneth Millar, who under the pen name Ross Macdonald would become the most worthy of Chandler's successors, said that from the *Black Mask* revolution came "a new kind of detective hero, the classless, restless men of American democracy, who spoke the language of the street."

Chandler found the formulaic plots of traditional detective fiction limiting and confining. He was less interested in challenging the deductive skills of the reader than in examining the milieu and sociocultural effects of criminal behavior. Chandler once told his publisher that he disliked those popular mystery titles that emphasized sheer deduction because such titles "put too much emphasis on the mystery itself, and I have not the ingenuity to devise the sort of intricate and recondite puzzles the purest aficionados go for." His mention of a lack of ingenuity is characteristic of the diffidence with which Chandler sometimes spoke of his own work; what is certain, both from his letters and from his 1944 essay "The Simple Art of Murder," is that such plots did not interest Chandler.

Although he should be credited, along with Hammett and other *Black Mask* writers, with the development of a peculiarly American form of detective fiction, Chandler himself always consciously sought to transcend the limitations of the genre. He regarded himself as a serious novelist who wrote detective fiction. His intent was to study the modern landscape of evil, and his work bears striking affinities with T. S. Eliot's *The Waste Land* (1922) and with Ernest Hemingway's novels. His evocation of a world dominated by malicious, sadistic, self-centered, ruthless, and psychopathic types led W. H. Auden, in his 1948 essay "The Guilty Vicarage: Notes on the Detective Story, by an Addict," to conclude that Chandler's interest was not in detective fiction at all, but in "serious studies of a criminal milieu, the Great Wrong Place"; Auden argues that Chandler's "powerful but extremely depressing books should be read and judged, not as escape literature, but as works of art."

Auden states, admirably, only half the case. Chandler's books should be judged as works of art, but not merely as studies of the world of crime or of the world gone bad. In his novels there is a constant quest, a search for heroic possibility in the ruined moral landscape of modern California. Chandler's fiction continually considers whether authentic heroism is possible in the modern world, and Marlowe's attempt to take heroic action places him at odds with the world he inhabits. By the time he was ready to write *The Long Goodbye*, Chandler had indeed transformed the detective story: In that book the elements of detection and mystery are clearly subordinate to psychological and cultural realism.

The achievement of Chandler thus discloses a paradox. Although he was instrumental in the discovery of an American style for detective fiction and has been widely and rightly respected for that accomplishment, his real achievement was to merge detective fiction with serious literature.

BIOGRAPHY

Although his early ambition was to be a writer, Raymond Thornton Chandler did not begin the literary career that would win him fame until he was forty-five years old. This is only one of several incongruities in the life of one of America's original literary talents.

Chandler was born in Chicago, in 1888, the only child of a railroad employee and an Irishwoman. The marriage was marred by his father's alcoholism and ended in divorce when the boy was seven. Chandler and his mother moved to London and became dependent on his maternal uncle, a successful solicitor. Chandler went to Dulwich College, where he received the solid classical education characteristic of English public schools. He was at the head of his class in most of his subjects. After his graduation from Dulwich, Chandler claimed dual citizenship so that he could take the English civil service examinations, but he was unable to adapt to the bureaucratic environment and resigned his civil service appointment. He supported himself briefly by writing for magazines and newspapers and by publishing some undistinguished poems and a single story. He left England for the United States in 1912.

Chandler made his way to Southern California, where he began a relationship that was to dominate his literary life. Chandler despised the superficiality and pretentiousness of the California culture as well as its lack of tradition or continuity, but he intuited that this would be the culture of the future. One aim of his writing would be to record and comment on that culture. His immediate concern upon arriving was to find work, and he was involved in a variety of minor jobs until he completed a three-year bookkeeping course in six weeks. Thereafter, he was involved in various business enterprises until 1917, when he joined the Canadian army. He saw action in France during World War I; Chandler was the sole survivor of a raid on his outfit and was decorated for valor. When he returned to California, he briefly tried banking and eventually established himself as an extremely successful executive of the Dabney Oil Syndicate. He became vice president of the concern and was at one time director of eight subsidiary firms and president of three.

Shortly after he joined the Dabney firm, Chandler married Cissy Pascal, who filed for divorce in order to marry him. An accomplished pianist and a beauty, she was also eighteen years older than Chandler, a fact she deliberately concealed from him: He was thirty-five; she was fifty-three. Their marriage was a lasting but troubled one.

Perhaps discoveries about his marriage, as well as problems and pressures in his business, led to the first appearance of what became Chandler's lifelong struggle with alcoholism. In fact, several of Chandler's early stories, such as "Pearls Are a Nuisance," feature a hero who must contend with a drinking problem. In 1932, Dabney fired Chandler because of chronically poor job performance traced directly to excessive drinking.

Chandler took the shock of his firing as an indication that he had to take control of his life, and he turned again to the literary aspirations of his youth. Chandler was then reading and being influenced by Hemingway rather than by Henry James, whom he had read avidly in England, and he soon found the outlet his creative talent needed in the emerging American detective story. His first story appeared in *Black Mask* in 1933; he would be a successful novelist within the decade.

Fame and success came to Chandler in the 1940's. His sales were solid, studios sought the film rights to his novels, his books were being translated into several languages, and he was lured to Hollywood to write screenplays. There he enjoyed material success and stimulating camaraderie with other writers. Soon the pressures of

Raymond Chandler. (Library of Congress)

studio deadlines, artistic compromise, and the pretentiousness around him—much of the satire of *The Little Sister* is directed at the phoniness of Hollywood—combined with personal ill health sent Chandler back to the bottle. His career in Hollywood ended in frustration, petty squabbles, and bitterness.

With material success and public acclaim, Chandler spent the final decade of his life alternating between despair and the hope for new beginnings. Always a lonely man, he became depressive after his wife died in 1954. He attempted suicide, but after his recovery divided his time between life in London and La Jolla, California, between bouts with the bottle and the admiration of an appreciative public. He fell in love with his agent, Helga Greene, but the two were unable to marry. Chandler's death in 1959 ended the career of a shy, quiet man who was quite unlike his fictional hero Marlowe except for the essential loneliness and decency Chandler could not avoid projecting onto his most important creation.

ANALYSIS

Many people who have never read a single word of Raymond Chandler's recognize the name of his fictional hero Philip Marlowe. This recognition results in part from the wide exposure and frequent dilution Chandler's works have received in media other than print. Several of his novels have been adapted to film repeatedly; *Farewell, My Lovely* and *The Big Sleep*, in particular, have been made into motion pictures numerous times—both most recently in the 1970's. Marlowe has been interpreted on film by such diverse actors as Humphrey Bogart, Dick Powell, Robert Montgomery, George Montgomery, Robert Mitchum, James Garner, and Elliot Gould. Both radio and television series have been based somewhat loosely on Chandler's character.

This recognition amounts to more than exposure in multiple media; it is an indication of the legendary or even mythic proportions of Chandler's creation. Marlowe has become a central figure in the myth of the detective; the only comparable characters would be Arthur Conan Doyle's Sherlock Holmes and Agatha Christie's Hercule Poirot, even though they are quite different from Marlowe. Dashiell Hammett's Sam Spade, although well known, is developed in only one book and lacks the psychological depth of Marlowe. Marlowe has taken his place among characters of American myth, with Natty Bumppo, Captain Ahab, Huckleberry Finn, and Thomas Sutpen. There is something uniquely American about the self-reliance of this character, something that goes beyond Chandler's brilliant descriptions of the burned-out landscape of modern California.

Marlowe is in fact Chandler's great achievement, but that accomplishment in itself imposed a limitation of a sort. Because Marlowe had the dual role of central character and observer in all seven of Chandler's novels, the author was not consistently pressed to explore other characters except as they interacted with his hero. In his final novel, *Playback*, Chandler leads Marlowe through an ill-conceived plot at the expense of two neglected characters who had shown real literary promise. In this final project, the author had fallen victim to the temptation to rely on his primary character, and Marlowe's character suffers as a result.

Nevertheless, Marlowe remains an impressive artistic creation because of his remarkable combination of the detective with more traditional American heroic types, a combination Chandler discusses in his famous essay "The Simple Art of Murder." In this essay, Chandler attempts to define his intentions as a writer of detective fiction; the work has since become one of the classic texts concerning the scope and intention of mystery writing. Although a major point of "The Simple Art of Murder" is Chandler's rejection of the stylized mystery and his often-quoted tribute to Hammett—his claim that Hammett took murder "out of the Venetian vase and dropped it in the alley"—the essay makes its most important point in an argument for detective fiction as a heroic form in which modern readers can still believe. Claiming that all art must contain the quality of redemption, Chandler insists, perhaps too stridently, that the detective is "the hero; he is everything." In the character of Marlowe, Chandler tests the possibility of heroism in the modern cultural and spiritual wasteland of Southern California, to see whether traditional heroic values can survive the test of a realistic portrait of modern society.

In precisely this way, Chandler had to face a limitation that did not affect his American predecessors: the disappearance of the frontier. American heroes acted out the myth of Emersonian self-reliance against the background of a vast, unspoiled frontier. In the twentieth century, William Faulkner, attempting to study the ambivalent role of the hero, moved his fiery character Thomas Sutpen to the frontier in *Absalom, Absalom!* (1936). Most American novelists in the twentieth century despaired of the possibility of reviving the heroic tradition and concentrated instead on victims, common people, and even criminals.

Ernest Hemingway stood alone among the serious novelists looking for an affirmation by means of the code hero, and Chandler's intellectual debt to Hemingway is profound. He acknowledged that debt in two ways. In "The Simple Art of Murder," he points out that what is excellent in Hammett's (and by inference his own) work is implicit in Hemingway's fiction. In a more celebrated reference, a policeman in *Farewell, My Lovely* is called Hemingway by Marlowe. When Galbraith, the officer, asks who this Hemingway is, Marlowe explains, "A guy that keeps saying the same thing over and over until you begin to believe it must be good." This is of course a joke about the terse Hemingway style, and the character whom Marlowe calls Hemingway is indeed terse. The jest is not, however, a slap at Hemingway. Galbraith is one of the few men with integrity whom Marlowe encounters in *Farewell, My Lovely*. He is a policeman who wants to be honest but who has to work in a corrupt system. By contrast, in the story from which this portion of *Farewell, My Lovely* was "cannibalized," "The Man Who Liked Dogs," Galbraith was as corrupt as any of the criminals Carmady (the detective) encountered. He was merely a sadistic cop who participated in cover-ups and even murder. The verbal association of this character with Hemingway corresponds nicely with Chandler's changing the personality of the officer so that he would represent the quality Chandler most admired in Hemingway's heroes, resignation to defeat while maintaining some measure of integrity.

The world Marlowe inhabits is, like that of Hemingway's characters, not conducive to heroism. Chandler coined a memorable phrase, "the mean streets," to describe the environment in which his hero would have to function. Marlowe was created to indicate that it is possible to maintain integrity in these surroundings, even if one cannot be uninfluenced by them. As Chandler put it, "down these mean streets a man must go who is not himself mean, who is neither tarnished nor afraid." Chandler emphasized that Marlowe is part of that environment—by necessity—but is not contaminated by it—by choice. He is not without fear. Marlowe often expresses the fear of a normal man in a dangerous situation, and in this way he differs from the heroes of the tough-guy school and from those of Chandler's apprentice stories. Like Hemingway's heroes, he must learn to control and to disguise his fear. Most important, he is not intimidated by his environment. As Chandler puts it in his essay, the detective "must be, to use a rather weathered phrase, a man of honor."

Although commonly used, the phrase "the mean streets" is somewhat misleading. Chandler's target is not merely, or even primarily, the cruelty and brutality of life at the bottom of the social and economic ladder. For him, the mean streets extend into the posh apartments and mansions of Hollywood and suburban Los Angeles, and he is more interested in exploring cruelty and viciousness among the very rich than among the people of the streets. Each of the novels treats the theme of the quest for and ownership of money and power as the source of evil; Chandler constantly emphasizes Marlowe's relative poverty as a symbol of his incorruptibility. *The High Window*, for example, is more a study in the corrupting influence of wealth than in the process of detection. Marlowe is shocked to discover that his client Mrs. Murdock not only murdered her husband to collect his life insurance but also systematically conditioned her timid and neurotic secretary to believe that she was the murderess, dependent on Mrs. Murdock for forgiveness as well as for protection from the law. This instance is typical of Chandler's novels. The mean streets originate in the drawing rooms of those who may profit by exploiting others.

Marlowe's code of behavior differs from those of other fictional detectives, though his descendants, particularly Ross Macdonald's Lew Archer and Robert B. Parker's Spenser, resemble Chandler's hero. Marlowe is not, in the final analysis, a tough guy. He is a compassionate man who, as he half-ironically tells a policeman in *The Long Goodbye*, hears "voices crying in the night" and goes to "see what's the matter." Marlowe is instinctively the champion of the victims of the rich and powerful; in *The High Window* he insists that the secretary, Merle Davis, be set free of the psychological exploitation by the Murdock family and be allowed to return to her home in Kansas. To those who aspire to wealth and power, Marlowe is not so kind. In *The Little Sister*, he knowingly allows the amoral, ruthless murderess Dolores Gonzales to be killed by her husband.

This instinctive compassion for the weak accounts for much of Marlowe's fundamental decency, but it often gets him into trouble, for he is human enough to be occasionally deceived by appearances. The apparently innocent client in *The Little Sister*, Orfamay Quest from Kansas, deceives Marlowe with her piety and sincerity, and he is eventually depressed to learn that his compassion for her is wasted, that despite her apparent innocence she is compulsively materialistic and is willing to exploit even her brother's murder if she can profit by his scheme to blackmail a gangster.

Marlowe's compassion is what makes him interesting as a character, but it is also what makes him vulnerable in the mean streets. His defense against that vulnerability is to play the role of the tough guy. His wisecracks, which have since become obligatory in stories about private detectives, are nothing more than a shield. Chandler says in "The Simple Art of Murder" that the detective is a proud man who will take "no man's insolence without a due and dispassionate revenge." The mean streets have taught Marlowe that corrupt politicians, tired policemen, ambitious actresses, rich people, and street toughs will insult and abuse him readily; his defense is the wisecrack. It is the attempt of an honorable man to stand up to a world that has gone sour.

THE BIG SLEEP

The Big Sleep, Chandler's first full-length novel, makes explicit use of the associations with myth that had been implicit in the stories he had published over six years. It was in this book that the author settled on the name Marlowe for his detective, after he had experimented with such names as Carmady and Dalmas. In his first detective story, "Blackmailers Don't Shoot," he had called the detective Mallory, an obvious allusion to the chronicler of the Arthurian legends, Sir Thomas Malory. The association with the quest romance is worked out in several important ways in *The Big Sleep*. When the detective first arrives at the home of his client, he notices a stained-glass panel "showing a knight in dark armor rescuing a lady" and concludes that, "if I lived in the house, I would sooner or later have to climb up and help him." Much later, upon returning to the house, the detective notes that the knight "wasn't getting anywhere" with the task of rescuing the lady.

These two references remind the reader of a heroic tradition into which Marlowe, a citizen of the twentieth century, is trying to fit his own experiences. Malory's knights lived in an age of faith, and the quest for the Holy Grail was a duty imposed by that faith as well as a test of the worthiness of the knight himself. Marlowe's adventures entangle him with a pornographer who is murdered, a small-time blackmailer whose effort to cut himself into the action leads to his death, a trigger-happy homosexual, a powerful criminal the law cannot touch, a district attorney eager to avoid scandal that might touch a wealthy family, and a psychopathic murderess. The environment is impossible to reconcile with the values suggested by the knight in the panel. At midpoint in the novel, Marlowe has a chess problem laid out (his playing chess against the problems defined in classical matches

gives him an intellectual depth uncharacteristic of the tough-guy detective), and, trying to move a knight effectively on the board, he concludes that "knights had no meaning in this game. It wasn't a game for knights."

The implication of this set of images is that Marlowe aspires to the role of the traditional knight, but that such an aspiration is doomed to failure in the mean streets. His aspiration to the role of the knight is a hopeless attempt to restore order to the modern wasteland. At the same time, it is proof of his integrity that he tries to maintain that role in the face of certain and predictable frustration. In a subsequent novel, *The High Window*, a minor character invents a phrase that eloquently describes Marlowe's association with the romance tradition; he calls the detective a "shop-soiled Galahad," a reminder both of the knight who, in the romance, could not be corrupted, and of the pressures that wear down the modern hero.

Another important reference to the romance tradition in *The Big Sleep* is the client himself. General Sternwood is a dying man; he has to meet Marlowe in a greenhouse because the general needs the artificial warmth. He is lame, impotent, and distressed at the moral decay of his daughters. Chandler implicitly associates this character with the Fisher King of the archetypal romance, and *The Big Sleep* takes on revealing connections with T. S. Eliot's *The Waste Land*, another modern version of this quest. Like Eliot's poem, Chandler's version of the quest is a record of failure. Marlowe's success in the work of detection points paradoxically to the failure of his quest. He is able to complete, even to go beyond, his assignment. His instinctive sympathy for the helpless general leads him to try to find out what happened to the general's son-in-law, Rusty Regan, whose charm and vigor had restored some vitality to the old man, much as the traditional knight might restore the Fisher King. Marlowe discovers that Regan has been murdered, hence, there is no hope that the general might be restored. He can only prepare to join Regan in "the big sleep."

"It was not a game for knights." This knight is able to sort through the many mysteries of *The Big Sleep*, to discover the killers of the various victims. He outsmarts a professional killer in a shoot-out and feels that in doing so he achieves some revenge for Harry Jones, a tough little victim whom Marlowe had respected. His actions do not, however, restore order to his surroundings. He is unable to reach, through law or intimidation, Eddie Mars, the operator of a gambling casino and several protection rackets, a parasite of society. His discovery that Regan was murdered leads him to the conclusion that all he can do is try to protect the general from "the nastiness," the inescapable and brutal facts of life. Even his discovery that Regan's killer was the general's daughter, Carmen, does not resolve anything: She is a psychopath, and her actions are gratuitous, not subject to reform. All Marlowe can do, ironically, is the same thing Eddie Mars and Regan's widow, Vivian, tried to do—protect the general from knowing that his own daughter was responsible for the death of the one person who brought happiness to his life. Marlowe's method differs from that of Mars. Rather than cover up the fact, he uses the leverage of his knowledge of the cover-up to force Vivian Regan, Carmen's sister as well as Rusty's widow, to have Carmen committed to a mental hospital. He makes this deal only after Vivian has tried to buy his silence.

What makes *The Big Sleep* such a rich novel, in addition to its mythic associations, is the question of what keeps Marlowe going. He knows that justice is not possible in a world controlled by Eddie Mars, and he learns that his efforts lead only to compound frustrations and personal danger. He continues to work, against the warnings of the criminal element, the official police, and the family of his client. Both Vivian and Carmen offer sexual bribes if Marlowe will get off the case. He is so personally affected by "the nastiness" around him that he has a nightmare after having encountered the perverse scene in which the pornographer Geiger was killed—a dream in which Marlowe implicates himself as an ineffective pornographer. He dreams about a "man in a bloody Chinese coat" (Geiger) who was chasing "a naked girl with long jade earrings" (Carmen) "while I ran after them and tried to take a photograph with an empty camera." This exposure to the corruption around him makes Marlowe doubt, in his nightmare, even his own ability to resist corruption.

He is able to continue in the face of these pressures because, like Joseph Conrad's Marlow in *Heart of Darkness* (1902), he believes in something greater than his personal interests. His idealism is of course shattered by the corruption around him, but like Conrad's character or Hemingway's heroes, he believes in a code: loyalty to

his client. In the absence of a belief in an absolute good, Marlowe guides his behavior by weighing his options in the context of the principle of loyalty to the client. When the police and the district attorney threaten him, he explains that all he has to sell is "what little guts and intelligence the Lord gave me and a willingness to get pushed around in order to protect a client." He refuses an invitation to have sex with each of the attractive Sternwood daughters because of this principle. He tells Carmen, "It's a question of professional pride" after he has told Vivian that as a man he is tempted but as a detective, "I work at it, lady. I don't play at it." Many bribes, monetary and sexual, are offered Marlowe in *The Big Sleep*. Even more threats, from criminals, police, and his client's family, are hurled at him. What gives him his sense of purpose in a world that seems to resonate to no moral standard is one self-imposed principle. This is the main theme of Chandler's fiction: If standards of behavior do not exist outside the individual, as they were believed to in the age of chivalry, then one must create them, however imperfect they may be, for oneself.

By the end of the 1940's, Chandler was well established as a master of detective fiction, but he was becoming increasingly impatient with the limitations of the form. Classically educated and somewhat aristocratic in his personal tastes, he found the conventions of the hard-boiled genre increasingly confining. He was not willing to dispose of Marlowe, however, partly because the detective had brought his creator success. More important, as biographer Frank MacShane has pointed out, Chandler's real interest was the variety of the life and the essential formlessness of Los Angeles, so his detective's ability to cut across class lines, to meet with criminals, police, the seedier citizens as well as the wealthy, gave the author a chance to explore in fiction the life of the entire community, much as two of his favorite novelists, Charles Dickens and Honoré de Balzac, had done for the cities in which they had lived.

Chandler had already pushed the mystery novel somewhat beyond its inherent limits, but he remained unsatisfied with what must be regarded as an impressive achievement. He had altered the formula to apply the quest myth in *The Big Sleep*; to study phony psychics and corrupt police in *Farewell, My Lovely*; to examine psychological and legal exploitation by the very wealthy in *The High Window*; to work with the devices of disguise and the anxieties of those who merely aspire to wealth and power in *The Lady in the Lake*; and to satirize the pretentiousness of Hollywood as well as to comment on the corrosive influence of materialism in *The Little Sister*.

THE LONG GOODBYE

The Long Goodbye abandons so many of the conventions of the detective formula that it simply uses what is left of the formula as a skeleton around which to build serious psychological and cultural themes. The actual detective work Marlowe is hired to perform is merely to search for the novelist Roger Wade, who has disappeared on a drunken spree, and eventually Marlowe discovers that the search itself was unnecessary. Wade's wife knew where Roger was but hired Marlowe to get him involved in Roger's life, so that he might possibly be persuaded to take a job as Wade's bodyguard. The search for Wade allows for some discussion of physicians who dispense drugs freely to the wealthy, but it depends more on persistent following of leads than on brilliant deduction. The real detective work in which he engages is entirely independent, work from which he is discouraged by the police, a gangster named Menendez, a wealthy businessman, and the Wades. It is a work of sentiment, not professionalism, and the book discloses that this task is worth neither the effort nor integrity that Marlowe puts into it.

The Long Goodbye is finally a study in personal loyalties. The sustaining ethic of the earlier novels, loyalty to a client, does not really apply in this book, for most of the time Marlowe has no client or refuses to take up the assignments offered him. He is no longer satisfied with his work as a detective, and one of the book's best chapters details the monotony and triviality of a day in the life of a private investigator. His own ambivalence about his role is summed up after a series of absurd requests for his services: "What makes a man stay with it nobody knows. You don't get rich, and you don't often have much fun. Sometimes you get beaten up or shot at or tossed in the jailhouse." Each of these unpleasant things happens to Marlowe. He stays in business, but he has ceased to understand why.

At the heart of the book is Marlowe's relationship with Terry Lennox, who drifts into Marlowe's personal life. Lennox, a man with a mysterious past but at present married for the second time to the nymphomaniac daughter of a tycoon, impresses Marlowe with a jaded version of the Hemingway code. Lennox knows he is little more than a gigolo, but he has accepted himself with a kind of refined drunkenness. He and Marlowe become friends, but after his wife is brutally murdered, Lennox asks Marlowe to help him escape to Mexico. Marlowe, who agrees out of friendship rather than loyalty to Lennox as a client, is thus legally implicated as a possible accessory after the fact.

His action brings him into inevitable conflict with the police, and he is roughly treated by a detective and his precinct captain. Marlowe's being at odds with the official police is far from a new occurrence in Chandler's work. His fiction always contains an innate distrust of the legal establishment, from the exposé of police corruption in *Farewell, My Lovely* through the abuse of police power by one of the killers in *The Lady in the Lake*. A lawyer in *The Long Goodbye* tells Marlowe, "The law isn't justice, it's a very imperfect mechanism. If you press exactly the right buttons and are also lucky, justice may show up in the answer." This distrust of the mechanism of law usually led Chandler to condemn separate kinds of justice for the wealthy and the powerless. Marlowe's reaction to his disillusionment includes verbal and physical conflict with the police as well as the routine concealment of evidence that might implicate a client.

What differentiates this conflict from previous ones in Chandler's work is that Marlowe is not really protecting the interests of a client. He acts out of a personal loyalty, based partly on his belief that Lennox could not have committed the sadistic murder of which he is accused. He keeps his silence during a week in jail, during which he is pressed to give evidence that would implicate both himself and Lennox.

Lennox's confession and suicide render Marlowe's actions futile. The arrival of a letter and a large sum of money rekindles a sentimental interest in the Lennox matter, and as it becomes clear that some connection exists between Lennox and the Wades, who have tried to hire him to help Roger stay sober long enough to finish his book, Marlowe continues to fit together evidence that points to Lennox's innocence. Proving Lennox innocent is another source of disillusionment: Marlowe learns that both the confession and the suicide were faked. In their final interview, Marlowe tells Lennox, "You had standards and you lived by them, but they were personal. They had no relation to any kind of ethics or scruples." Marlowe has himself come close to this moral relativism in his uncritical loyalty to Lennox, and has perhaps seen in his friend an example of the vague standard of ethical conduct to which such moral relativism can lead. The difference between Lennox and Marlowe is that the detective still recognizes the importance of having a code. He tells Lennox, "You're a moral defeatist." His work on behalf of Lennox has been a disappointment of the highest order, for he has seen the paralysis of will toward which the cynicism both men share leads. By returning Lennox's money, Marlowe implies that Lennox was not worth the risk and labor of proving his innocence.

The Long Goodbye is populated by "moral defeatists." Another character, Roger Wade, has given up on himself as a man and as a writer. Chandler creates in this character a representation of the writer who knowingly compromises his artistic talent for personal gain. Knowing that he is "a literary prostitute," Wade is driven to alcoholic sprees and personal despair. When he seeks Marlowe's sympathy for his predicament, Marlowe reminds him of Gustave Flaubert, an example of the genuine artist who was willing to sacrifice success for his art.

Marlowe's association with Wade develops the central theme of *The Long Goodbye*: personal responsibility. Wade's publisher and his wife want Marlowe to protect Wade from his depressive and suicidal tendencies. Realizing that Wade is trying to escape something inside himself, Marlowe knows that only Wade can stop his rush toward self-destruction. He refuses to take the lucrative job as Wade's bodyguard because he realizes he cannot prevent the author from being self-destructive. In fact, Marlowe is in the Wade house the day Roger Wade apparently commits suicide. Although he does try to remove Wade's gun from its customary desk drawer, he makes no effort to stop Wade from drinking. He knows that restraining Wade, whether by physical force or coercion, would be an artificial substitute for a real solution. If Wade's self-loathing makes him suicidal, Marlowe recognizes that nothing he can do will prevent the self-destructive act from taking place.

The theme of personal responsibility is even more directly apparent in Marlowe's relation with Eileen Wade. Initially, she impresses him as an ideal beauty, and the erotic implications of their relationship are always near the surface. In a scene after he has put the drunken Roger to bed, the detective comes close to his first sexual consummation in the novels. In this episode, it becomes clear that Eileen is mentally disturbed, and Marlowe's subsequent investigation reveals that she was once married to Lennox, who served in the war under another name. Her attempt to seduce Marlowe is in fact a clumsy attempt to establish a relationship with the Terry Lennox she knew before his cynicism turned to moral defeatism. From these premises, Marlowe deduces that Eileen murdered both Sylvia Lennox and Roger, who had been having an affair with Sylvia, a perverse revenge for her being twice defeated by a woman whose vulgarity she despised.

Marlowe has sufficient evidence to prove Lennox's innocence and to show that Wade's death was not suicide, but he does not go to the police. He confronts Eileen with the evidence and gives her time to commit suicide. He refers to himself as a "one-man death watch" and takes no action to prevent the self-destruction of this woman to whom he is so powerfully attracted. When he has to explain his conduct to the one policeman he trusts, Bernie Ohls, he says, "I wanted her to take a long look at herself. What she did about it was her business." This is a ruthless dismissal of a disturbed, though homicidal, person. What Chandler intends to emphasize is the idea that all humans must ultimately take full responsibility for their actions.

Even Marlowe's relationship with Bernie Ohls deteriorates. Ohls, the only policeman Marlowe likes or trusts, consents to leak a document so that Marlowe will use it unwittingly to flush out the racketeer Menendez, knowing that Marlowe will be abused psychologically and physically in the process. The ruse works, and Ohls ruthlessly sends Menendez off to possible execution by his fellow criminals. In the image used by another character, Marlowe has been the goat tied out by the police to catch the tiger Menendez. Marlowe understands why the police have used him this way, but the novel ends with a new note of mistrust between Marlowe and Ohls. Yet another human relationship has failed.

In *The Long Goodbye*, the business of detection is subordinate to the themes of personal responsibility, betrayal, and the mutability of all human relationships. The book is a powerful indictment of the shallowness of public values in midcentury America, and the emphasis is on characterization, theme, and atmosphere rather than on the matters typical of the mystery novel. It represents a remarkable transition from the detective novel to the realm of serious fiction, a transition that has subsequently been imitated but not equaled.

David C. Dougherty

OTHER MAJOR WORKS

SHORT FICTION: *Five Murderers*, 1944; *Five Sinister Characters*, 1945; *Finger Man, and Other Stories*, 1946; *Red Wind*, 1946; *Spanish Blood*, 1946; *The Simple Art of Murder*, 1950; *Trouble Is My Business*, 1950; *Pick-up on Noon Street*, 1952; *Smart-Aleck Kill*, 1953; *Pearls Are a Nuisance*, 1958; *Killer in the Rain*, 1964 (Philip Durham, editor); *The Smell of Fear*, 1965; *The Midnight Raymond Chandler*, 1971; *The Best of Raymond Chandler*, 1977; *Stories and Early Novels*, 1995; *Collected Stories*, 2002.

SCREENPLAYS: *And Now Tomorrow*, 1944 (with Frank Partos); *Double Indemnity*, 1944 (with Billy Wilder); *The Unseen*, 1945 (with Hager Wilde); *The Blue Dahlia*, 1946; *Strangers on a Train*, 1951 (with Czenzi Ormonde).

NONFICTION: *Raymond Chandler Speaking*, 1962 (Dorothy Gardiner and Katherine Sorely Walker, editors); *Chandler Before Marlowe: Raymond Chandler's Early Prose and Poetry*, 1973 (Bruccoli, editor); *The Notebooks of Raymond Chandler and English Summer*, 1976 (Frank MacShane, editor); *Raymond Chandler and James M. Fox: Letters*, 1978; *Selected Letters of Raymond Chandler*, 1981 (Frank MacShane, editor); *The Raymond Chandler Papers: Selected Letters and Nonfiction, 1909-1959*, 2000 (Tom Hiney and Frank MacShane, editors); *Philip Marlowe's Guide to Life: A Compendium of Quotations*, 2005 (Martin Asher, editor).

BIBLIOGRAPHY

Bruccoli, Matthew J., and Richard Layman, eds. *Hardboiled Mystery Writers: Raymond Chandler, Dashiell Hammett, Ross Macdonald*. New York: Carroll & Graf, 2002. Compilation presents interviews, articles, letters, and previously published studies about the three writers. Lavishly illustrated with personal photographs, reproductions of manuscript pages, print advertisements, film promotional materials, dust jackets, and paperback covers.

Chandler, Raymond. *Raymond Chandler Speaking*. Edited by Dorothy Gardiner and Katherine Walker. 1962. Reprint. Berkeley: University of California Press, 1997. Chandler discusses a wide range of subjects, including his life, the mystery novel in general, his mystery novels in particular, the craft of writing, his character Philip Marlowe, and cats. Includes a chronology.

Freeman, Judith. *The Long Embrace: Raymond Chandler and the Woman He Loved*. New York: Pantheon Books, 2007. Interesting work illuminates Chandler's personality and psyche. Freeman believed that Chandler's life was a greater mystery than his novels, so she traveled to the almost two dozen Southern California houses and apartments where he and his wife lived and uncovered information about Chandler's wife, Cissy, who played a crucial role in his understanding of women and of himself.

Hiney, Tom. *Raymond Chandler: A Biography*. New York: Atlantic Monthly Press, 1997. Brief biography discusses Chandler's education in England, his relationship to Los Angeles, and the plots and characters of his most important detective novels and stories.

Jameson, F. R. "On Raymond Chandler." In *The Poetics of Murder: Detective Fiction and Literary Theory*, edited by Glenn W. Most and William W. Stowe. San Diego, Calif.: Harcourt Brace Jovanovich, 1983. Critical essay starts with the observation that Chandler's English upbringing in essence gave him an outsider's view of American life and language. Presents an informative discussion of the portrait of American society that emerges from Chandler's works.

Lehman, David. "Hammett and Chandler." In *The Perfect Murder: A Study in Detection*. New York: Free Press, 1989. Describes Chandler as one of the authors who brought out the parable at the heart of mystery fiction. Part of a comprehensive study of detective fiction that is valuable both for its breadth and for its unusual appendixes, one a list of further reading and the other an annotated list of the critic's favorite mysteries.

MacShane, Frank. *The Life of Raymond Chandler*. New York: E. P. Dutton, 1976. Standard biography draws on Chandler's interviews and correspondence with colleagues and lovers to describe the author's life and to provide insights into his novels.

Marling, William H. *The American Roman Noir: Hammett, Cain, and Chandler*. Athens: University of Georgia Press, 1995. Interprets the works of the three writers of hard-boiled detective fiction within the context of American social and cultural history of the 1920's and 1930's. Includes three chapters about Chandler: one a biography and the other two analyses of *The Big Sleep* and *Farewell, My Lovely*.

Phillips, Gene D. *Creatures of Darkness: Raymond Chandler, Detective Fiction, and Film Noir*. Lex-

ington: University Press of Kentucky, 2000. Focuses largely on Chandler's Hollywood output but also presents some discussion of his novels.

Van Dover, J. K., ed. *The Critical Response to Raymond Chandler*. Westport, Conn.: Greenwood Press, 1995. Collection of essays includes discussions of Chandler's Los Angeles, *The Big Sleep* (both the novel and the film), *Farewell, My Lovely*, and the function of simile in Chandler's novels. Includes bibliographical references and index.

Widdicombe, Toby. *A Reader's Guide to Raymond Chandler*. Westport, Conn.: Greenwood Press, 2001. Features entries, arranged alphabetically, on Chandler's works, characters, places, allusions, and major topics. Appendixes contain information on Chandler's screenwriting, other writers' adaptations of Chandler, and the portrayal of the character of Philip Marlowe in film, radio, and television.

BARBARA CHASE-RIBOUD

Born: Philadelphia, Pennsylvania; June 26, 1939
Also known as: Barbara DeWayne Chase

PRINCIPAL LONG FICTION

Sally Hemings, 1979
Valide: A Novel of the Harem, 1986 (revised 1988)
Echo of Lions, 1989
The President's Daughter, 1994
Hottentot Venus, 2003

OTHER LITERARY FORMS

Barbara Chase-Riboud (chays rih-BEW) began her writing career as a poet, with the collection *From Memphis and Peking* in 1974. Her second collection, *Portrait of a Nude Woman as Cleopatra*, sometimes also called a verse novel, was released in 1987.

ACHIEVEMENTS

Barbara Chase-Riboud became a popular writer almost overnight with the publication of *Sally Hemings*,

which sold more than one million copies and won the Janet Heidinger Kafka Prize for best novel by an American woman in 1979. Ten years later, *Echo of Lions* sold 500,000 copies and confirmed Chase-Riboud's reputation as a solid historical novelist who likes to bring historical figures out of undeserved obscurity. Her original literary vocation, however, was in poetry. *From Memphis and Peking* combines a strong sensual appeal with the expression of a desire to travel through time, in the form of a quest for ancestry, and space, in an exploration of the cultures of Africa, America, and China. In 1988, Chase-Riboud won the Carl Sandburg Poetry Prize for *Portrait of a Nude Woman as Cleopatra*, a tortured unveiling of the Egyptian queen's public and private lives.

Even before she became a poet, Chase-Riboud was a sculptor with an international reputation. Her remarkable ten-foot-tall sculptures are highly regarded for their incorporation of traditional fiber and weaving techniques that reflect African symbols. She received many fellowships and awards for her work, including a John Hay Whitney Foundation fellowship in 1957-1958 for study at the American Academy in Rome, a National Endowment for the Arts fellowship in 1973, and a Van der Zee award in 1995. Her several honorary doctorates include one from Temple University in 1981. In 1996, she received a Knighthood for Contributions to Arts and Letters from the French government.

Biography

Barbara DeWayne Chase was born and raised in Philadelphia, the only child of a building contractor and a medical assistant. She won her first art prize at age eight. She received a bachelor of fine arts degree from Temple University in 1957 and a master of fine arts degree from Yale University in 1960. In 1961 she married the French photojournalist Marc Riboud, with whom she had two sons, David and Alexis. She made her home in Europe, mostly in Paris and Rome. After her divorce in 1981, she married Sergio Tosi, an Italian art historian and expert. She traveled widely in Africa and the Near and Far East and was the first American woman to be admitted to the

Barbara Chase-Riboud. (Courtesy, Author)

People's Republic of China after the revolution in 1949. Asked if she felt like an expatriate, she answered, "It takes me three hours to get from Paris to New York, so I don't really believe in expatriatism anymore."

In 1991, Chase-Riboud successfully sued Granville Burgess, the author of a play about Sally Hemings titled *Dusky Sally*, for copyright infringement in a landmark trial that reinforced the protection of creativity for authors and artists. In October, 1997, Chase-Riboud filed a plagiarism suit against film director Steven Spielberg, accusing him of stealing "themes, dialogue, characters, relationships, plots, scenes, and fictional inventions" from *Echo of Lions* for his 1997 film *Amistad*. The suit ended with an out-of-court settlement, and Chase-Riboud praised Spielberg's film, but during the controversy plagiarism charges were made against Chase-Riboud concerning both *Echo of Lions* and *Valide*. Although she admitted that not mentioning her sources was an inexperienced writer's oversight, she pointed out that she often weaves "real documents and real reference materials" into her novels; *The President's Daughter* contains nine pages of author's notes on historical sources.

Analysis

Barbara Chase-Riboud's historical novels offer a strongly diversified exploration of power relationships as they are shaped by race, gender, and social and political needs. Slavery figures prominently in each novel, not only in its aberrations and its violence but also in the complex configurations of relationships it produces. The hairsplitting legal separation of the races is rendered incongruous by the intertwined blood ties exemplified in the extended interracial Jefferson family. More controversially, the notions of slave and master lose their sharp distinction in the face of multiple forms of attraction and manipulation. It is the theme of profoundly mixed heritage and history, embodied in miscegenation, that ultimately dominates. The "outing" of hidden or mysterious women, such as Sally Hemings or Valide, bespeaks a desire to shake taboos and renew our understanding of world history.

Chase-Riboud's intellectual inquisitiveness, her multilingual and multicultural experience, and her artistic sensibility successfully collaborate in these re-creations of large portions of world history, the visual power of which the author attains through precise and often poetic descriptions of places, events, clothes, and physiognomies. Especially engaging are the nuanced renderings of the characters' psychological and emotional turmoil, whether Catherine the Great or the African Joseph Cinque. These are historical novels in the pure Scottian tradition, depicting a welter of official historical events while bringing them to life with invented but eminently plausible depictions of the private lives that lie in the gaps. The sense of wide-ranging tableau is enhanced by a narrative technique that often jumps among the perspectives of numerous characters in successions of relatively short chapters. One can even hear echoes from one novel to another, as Sally Hemings is discussed by John Quincy Adams in *Echo of Lions* or Thomas Jefferson figures in *Valide*'s Tripoli episode; *The President's Daughter* even reproduces scenes from *Sally Hemings*.

SALLY HEMINGS

Chase-Riboud's first novel is a fictional biography of Sally Hemings, President Thomas Jefferson's slave mistress (in November, 1998, *Nature* magazine reported that, thanks to deoxyribonucleic acid [DNA] evidence, it is certain that Jefferson fathered at least Hemings's last child). Inspired primarily by Fawn M. Brodie's 1974 biography *Thomas Jefferson: An Intimate History* and by the Hemings family's oral testimony, Chase-Riboud recreates known historical events and characters, filling them out with nuanced and convincing psychological and emotional texture. The official facts are as follows: Sally Hemings accompanied Jefferson's daughter Maria to Paris in June of 1787 to join him there and they all came back to the United States in October of 1789; a scandal broke out during Jefferson's first term as president when he was accused of having a son with his slave Sally, an allegation Jefferson never publicly denied; all seven of Sally's children were conceived at times when Jefferson was present at Monticello, his estate in Virginia; all of her children were either allowed to run away or freed by Jefferson's will. According to Sally's son Madison Hemings, whose memoirs appeared in the Pike County (Ohio) *Republican* in 1873, his mother was pregnant with Jefferson's child when they came back from Paris, and Jefferson had promised her that he would free their children when they turned twenty-one.

The novel, which is told mostly from Sally's point of view, explores with great subtlety the emotional torture involved in a love story between a slave mistress and her master. Her alternate references to him as "my master" and "my lover" reflect her changing evaluation of herself as someone who gave up her freedom for love. A reminder of her surrender is provided by her brother James, who exhorts her to stay in France, where they are legally free, who keeps reproaching her for choosing a golden prison, and who ultimately dies in mysterious circumstances. The relationship with Jefferson is presented realistically, as Sally occupies the underside of his public life, which echoes back into her life though remains frustratingly out of reach. Her rare excursions into public spaces lead to unpleasant confrontations with future vice president Aaron Burr and future first lady Dolley Madison, reminding her of the limits imposed on her identity by the outside world. The recurring silences between her and her lover, which become a motif in the book, symbolize the extent of her invisibility and powerlessness. As a consequence, Sally starts wielding power indirectly and subversively, as she takes over the keys of the house from her mother and decides that she will methodically obtain freedom for each of her children. Ultimately, however, it is love that defines her more than her slavehood.

Sally's story is told in flashback after the census taker Nathan Langdon visits her in her cabin in 1830 and decides to mark her and her two sons down as white, thereby replaying the white world's many attempts to erase her identity. The novel thus explicitly defines itself as a response to the silences and taboos of American history, as signified by the burning of letters and the ripping up of portraits. Langdon's interviews with sixth U.S. president John Quincy Adams, Burr, and painter John Trumbull, inserted in the middle of the novel, ensure a definite link between Sally Hemings's private life and the representatives of public history and lend her story long-overdue weight and legitimacy.

Although Jefferson remains an elusive figure throughout the book, some personality traits come out forcefully, such as the strength of his desires and passions under a facade of equanimity and his streak of despotism despite his egalitarian principles. The Jefferson family, and Virginia society more generally, are shown to be shot through with violence and decay, as evidenced by Jefferson's granddaughter's death at the hands of an abusive husband and the murders of George Wythe and his son. The theme of lying to oneself and to others in order to preserve a semblance of social order has remained a dominant one in Chase-Riboud's oeuvre.

VALIDE

In *Valide*, Chase-Riboud transports her exploration of power relationships under slavery to the Ottoman Empire at the turn of the nineteenth century. The novel starts with the death of the sultana Valide in 1817, then retraces her rise from American slave of sultan Abdülhamid I after her capture by Barbary pirates to Ikbal (favorite) to Kadine (official wife) to Valide, queen mother. The subtle political and psychological analysis uncovers the complex usages of power and powerlessness in a profoundly hierarchical and ritualistic social structure. Under her new name, Naksh-i-dil ("embroidered tongue"), she becomes slowly acquainted with the intrigues, alliances, and corruption that condition survival in the harem and that constitute the only possible form of resistance against engulfment by boredom and lassitude. She learns to use her body to wield power over the sultan and her female companions, and love is shown to be merely "a mixture of need and power, lust and loneliness."

The microcosm of the harem reflects the wider geopolitical struggles of the Ottoman Empire with France, England, and Russia. As a young woman, Naksh-i-dil realizes that the sultan himself is a slave whose power oscillates among treasons, alliances, and demonstrations of military prowess. Later, as Valide, she displays more political insight than her son and becomes his mastermind; for example, she forces a peace treaty with the Russians as an alliance against the French emperor Napoleon I. The parallels and contrasts with Russian empress Catherine the Great, whose triumphant trip through the newly acquired Crimea turns out to be an illusion of grandeur, intensify the theme that "there was no absolute tyranny, just as there was no absolute slavery." By zeroing in on numerous historical figures, such as Russian statesman Grigori Aleksandrovich Potemkin, the sultan Selim III, and American admirals, the novel skillfully captures the intermingling of public and private lives. Detailed descriptions of settings (including a map of the harem) as well as information on social mores help place this book in the best tradition of the historical novel.

ECHO OF LIONS

Echo of Lions recounts the true ordeal of fifty-three kidnapped Mende Africans taken to Havana and sold to two Cuban planters, José Ruiz and Pedro Montez. On their way to the plantation aboard the slave ship *Amistad*, the Africans rebelled and killed the captain and the cook, while two sailors escaped. The Spaniards, kept alive to help steer the ship back to Africa, tricked the mutineers by navigating east by day and northwest by night. After their capture off Long Island, the Africans underwent three trials for murder and piracy, the last one in the U.S. Supreme Court in March, 1841, which declared them free. The *Amistad* story, which fascinated the American public at the time, put forth the view of slaves as mere property to be returned to their owners, according to a treaty with Spain, against their constitutional rights as persons illegally captured from their home country.

In *Echo of Lions*, Chase-Riboud presents a skillful mixture of public and private history, providing minute descriptions of the slaves' tribulations, their court trials, their incarceration conditions, the New England abolitionist scene, and political debates, all the while infusing them with the historical characters' intimate thoughts and perspectives. Joseph Cinque, the Africans' charismatic leader, who, even though the case did little for the abolition of slavery in America, became a symbol of black pride and the right to freedom, as well as John Quincy Adams, who defended the case before the Supreme Court, receive splendidly nuanced psychological treatment. In occasionally poetic passages, Cinque tries to make sense of his new surroundings, recalls the beauty of his native land, and dreams of his wife; excerpts from Adams's diary bring to light his anxious but intense commitment. Several fictional characters, such as a wealthy black abolitionist and his beautiful daughter, help provide social and emotional texture to the wide-ranging historical material.

THE PRESIDENT'S DAUGHTER

A follow-up on *Sally Hemings*, *The President's Daughter* chronicles the life of Harriet Hemings, Thomas Jefferson's white-skinned, red-haired slave daughter, as she leaves Monticello, travels through Europe, and marries a pharmacist in Philadelphia. After her husband's death and burial in Africa, she marries his twin brother and raises seven children, passing as a white woman until her death. This novel of epic proportions gives Harriet's life a wide public resonance by associating it closely with a stream of historical events, such as Jefferson's death, the legal twists and turns of the institution of slavery, the Civil War (the Battle of Gettysburg in particular), even the European presence in South Africa.

The novel's descriptions of various social circles, such as Philadelphia high society and abolitionist groups, its renderings of long conversations on issues of the day, and its lengthy time span give it a nineteenth century novel's consistency. Its themes, however, are those of late twentieth century fiction. In addition to the continued exploration of filial love and power relationships, the novel concentrates on the psychological tortures of Harriet as an impostor and betrayer of her two families, the white and the black. The motif of fingerprints as an unmistakable bearer of identity is complicated when Harriet loses hers after she burns her hand, seeing the signs of her identity thus irrecoverably lost. The local theme of slavery as an institution based on fake premises and dependent on duplicity and lies reaches a philosophical dimension when Jefferson's Paris lover, Maria Cosway, whom Harriet visits in her Italian convent, teaches her that "nothing is real" and "everything is illusion." The theme of race relations receives a more bitter treatment in this sequel, as even love cannot seem to rise above gulfs of incomprehension.

HOTTENTOT VENUS

Like *Sally Hemings* and *The President's Daughter*, Chase-Riboud's *Hottentot Venus* is a story of slavery, female oppression, and the admirable recovery of a mysterious woman from historical obscurity. It recalls the true story of South African Saartjie (Sarah) Baartman, who, after losing her family to Dutch and English massacres, arrives in England in 1810 with the hope of becoming a famous dancer. She is accompanied by her husband, who is merely interested in exploiting her. Instead of finding an admiring audience, Sarah is sold into slavery and placed in a cage in a London freak show, where her ritually mutilated genitals become of great interest to the curious public.

Sarah relates her story in the first person, even including the dissection and exhibition of her body after her death. She dies at the young age of twenty-seven, and her body, an object of scientific scrutiny, is dissected in public. Her remains are exhibited in a French museum, a humiliation she describes in detail; in the novel's epilogue, she describes her revenge on those who mistreated her.

Christine Levecq
Updated by M. Casey Diana

OTHER MAJOR WORKS

POETRY: *From Memphis and Peking*, 1974; *Portrait of a Nude Woman as Cleopatra*, 1987.

BIBLIOGRAPHY

Holmes, Rachel. *The Hottentot Venus: The Life and Death of Saartjie Baartman (Born 1789-Buried 2002)*. London: Bloomsbury, 2007. Presents critical analysis of the true-life story of Saartjie Baartman, whom Riboud portrays in *Hottentot Venus*. Provides excellent historical background, paying particular attention to the end of Baartman's life.

Rushdy, Ashraf H. A. "'I Write in Tongues': The Supplement of Voice in Barbara Chase-Riboud's *Sally Hemings*." *Contemporary Literature* 35, no. 1 (1994): 100-135. Examines the complex interplay of orality and literacy in the novel.

_____. "Representing the Constitution: Embodiments of America in Barbara Chase-Riboud's *Echo of Lions*." *Critique* 36, no. 4 (Summer, 1995): 258-280. Presents a sophisticated investigation of the critique of the American Constitution embedded in the novel.

Stout, Candace Jesse. "In the Spirit of Art Criticism: Reading the Writings of Women Artists." *Studies in Art Education* 41, no. 4 (2000): 346-361. Focuses on the relationship between Chase-Riboud's poetry and her art.

FRANÇOIS-RENÉ DE CHATEAUBRIAND

Born: Saint-Malo, France; September 4, 1768
Died: Paris, France; July 4, 1848
Also known as: François-August-René de
    Chateaubriand

PRINCIPAL LONG FICTION

Atala, 1801 (English translation, 1802)
René, 1802, 1805 (English translation, 1813)
Les Martyres, 1809 (*The Martyrs*, 1812)
Les Natchez, 1826 (*The Natchez*, 1827)

OTHER LITERARY FORMS

The importance of the essays, travelogues, and memoirs of François-René de Chateaubriand (shah-TOH-bree-ahn) is as great as that of his two relatively short novels, *Atala* and *René*, both of which were extracted from an early version of *The Natchez* and inserted as illustrations in *Le Génie du Christianisme* (1799, 1800, 1802; *The Genius of Christianity*, 1802). It seems advisable, therefore, to speak at some length of the latter, as well as of the *Mémoires d'outre-tombe* (1849-1850; *Memoirs*, 1902).

Part 1 of *The Genius of Christianity* asserts that Christianity imposes itself on the convert because of the beauty of its dogmas, its Sacraments, its theological virtues, and its holy Scriptures. The harmony of the world and the marvels of nature attest the existence of God. In part 2, Christianity, more than paganism, exalts poetic inspiration. No religion has so profoundly penetrated the mysteries of the human soul or is so keenly attuned to the beauties of the universe. The *merveilleux chrétien* has more grandeur than the supernatural of paganism. The Bible, in its simplicity, is more beautiful than Homer's *Iliad*.

In part 3, Chateaubriand shows how Christianity has favored the development of the fine arts and given rise to the Gothic cathedral. It has supported the work of scholars, philosophers, and historians. It has caused the genius of Blaise Pascal to flower and has made the sublime eloquence of Jacques Bossuet possible. In part 4, the ringing of bells, the decoration of churches, the solemnity of rites, and the majesty of ceremonies combine to move

the soul. The missionaries have spread the benefits of their social work. Born amid the ruins of the Roman Empire, Christianity has saved civilization. It will emerge triumphant from the trial that has purified it.

The Genius of Christianity underwent many changes from its first edition in London in 1799. Furious with the philosophes, its author used a language so violent that his friends were frightened and persuaded him to modify his tone. A second version was printed in Paris in 1800; Chateaubriand's own scruples caused him to recall the copies. Suppressing a chapter in praise of doctors and portions containing observations on England, he reworked his project. He reduced it from seven parts to three dealing with the dogmas, poetics, and rites of Christianity. By 1801, the work had become a poetics of Christianity, including discussions of poetry and other literature, the fine arts, and the harmonies of religion. The proofs of this version received the attention of the censors, and more changes were made to serve the politics of Napoleon Bonaparte. *The Genius of Christianity* was again printed in 1802, with the approval of the government and assured of success, a few days before the proclamation of the concordat.

The five volumes comprise four parts, divided into books and subdivided into chapters, but there is little or no formal unity. Chateaubriand's tones are as mixed as the work's contents: In a work of piety he included, for example, two love stories (the original versions of *Atala* and *René*). His is not the external unity of a dialectician but rather a subtle unity by means of which he appeals to his readers' sensibility gradually and profoundly. The feeling is often that of Jean-Jacques Rousseau or Jean-Baptiste Greuze. Chateaubriand's education was a classical one that gave him the background and insight that permitted him to analyze the literary works of the seventeenth century in the light of the Christianity that informed them. The book is Romantic because of its fresh, new vigor. It revives a whole world of dreams that were real and of forms unknown to the ancients. Chateaubriand's goal was to create a poetry in which nature would no longer function as mere ornament for vain goddesses. For Christians and Frenchmen he proposed poetry that is

Christian and French, much as Madame de Staël proposed it in *De la littérature considérée dans les rapports avec les institutions sociales* (1800; *A Treatise on Ancient and Modern Literature*, 1803); for Chateaubriand, however, its perfection would derive from its Christianity.

Chateaubriand's work, then, is a reply to the philosophes who accused Christianity of being absurd, crude, and petty. He wished to demonstrate that there is no shame in sharing the faith of Sir Isaac Newton and Pascal, as well as of Bossuet and Jean Racine. Neither theology nor dogma was of great interest to Chateaubriand. He did not use rational arguments, for his objective was to establish not the truth of Christianity but its sphere of influence from affective and aesthetic points of view. *The Genius of Christianity* is doubtless weak philosophically. A religion cannot be based on the emotions of poets and artists. Nevertheless, Chateaubriand achieved the goal that he set for himself, and he became both a spiritual guide for his generation and a spokesman for Napoleon's government. Internal politics in France demanded a religious revival, and the author of *The Genius of Christianity* was rewarded with several diplomatic posts, which he accepted, while he could agree with the regime.

Memoirs is not a collection of conventional memoirs but a highly varied work in the manner of Michel Eyquem de Montaigne's *Essais* (1580-1595; *The Essays*, 1603). The author moves from a lofty poetic tone to that of familiar anecdote, examines philosophical subjects, and includes letters and travel experiences. He jumps abruptly from one topic to another, from one idea to the next, from one year to another, often returning to correct or emphasize an earlier point.

The time is his own, but all of history provides Chateaubriand with comparisons and symbols enabling him to better understand his own times. The books Chateaubriand had read often play a role in the *Memoirs*; sometimes he gives the titles of his sources, sometimes not, as though everything begins and ends with him. Every place visited by the memorialist is peopled by its great men of past ages and by a certain spirit, especially one that is heroic and French. Chateaubriand's vision of history is not only dramatic but also lyric; he is at the center of everything, relating all of his passions, his beliefs, and his destiny to the great events of the past.

Chateaubriand includes many portraits as well, some sympathetic, some tragic and symbolic, many caricatural, as though to say that so many famous men and great ladies have been nothing more than amusing figures in a farce that they have not understood. Included, finally, are the picturesque and the practical side of life and its objects. There are descriptions of all manner of things and activities observed by the memorialist and recorded for posterity, becoming, like everything else, part of Chateaubriand's memory and the memory of Chateaubriand *d'outre-tombe* (from beyond the tomb).

ACHIEVEMENTS

François-René de Chateaubriand was the most significant figure in French literature in the transitional period between the end of the Enlightenment, when classicism still ruled, and the heyday of Romanticism.

François-René de Chateaubriand. (Library of Congress)

Many of the characteristic elements of Romantic fiction can be found in early form in the novels of Chateaubriand: the exoticism, the idealization of the primitive, the extensive descriptions of nature. In much Romantic fiction, genre lines are blurred, and here again, Chateaubriand's example was influential. Stylistically, Chateaubriand's rhythmic sentences and splendid vocabulary revealed hitherto unsuspected resources of French prose. Finally, his unabashed egotism is quintessentially Romantic; Byronic before Byron, Chateaubriand left his flamboyant mark on a generation of younger writers.

BIOGRAPHY

François-August-René de Chateaubriand was born on the northern French coast, in Saint-Malo. In *Memoirs*, he tells of his games and daydreams on the beaches of his native city, dwelling on his melancholy sojourns at the manor at Combourg with a taciturn, frightening father, a superstitious, sickly mother, and an affectionate, excitable sister. From childhood, he was receptive to the poetry of the ocean and the wild heath surrounding the château.

After having completed his classical studies at the schools in Dol, Rennes, and Dinan, Chateaubriand pondered at length what he would do with his life. Although he did not think himself suited to any but a sedentary career, he eventually joined the army. A few months later, however, he took advantage of a leave to go to Paris, where he frequented the court and literary circles. Soon thereafter, he left for the New World.

Chateaubriand's visit to America lasted from July 10 to December 10, 1791. He landed at Baltimore, went to Philadelphia, traveled up the Hudson River and through the virgin forest, became acquainted with the American Indians, saw Niagara Falls and perhaps Ohio. This long trip away from France left him with memories that he was later to exploit. During these travels, he began a journal that he completed later with the aid of other travelers' accounts. Learning of the flight to Varennes and the detention of Louis XVI, Chateaubriand decided to return to France to offer his services to the threatened monarchy.

In 1792, Chateaubriand married Céleste Buisson de Lavigne, a friend of one of his sisters, in the hope of obtaining money with which to immigrate to Belgium. Un-

fortunately, her income ceased with her marriage. Although she was an intelligent and courageous woman, and despite considerable mutual admiration, Chateaubriand did not live much with his wife over the long years of their marriage.

Less than six months after the wedding, Chateaubriand was off to Belgium with forged papers to join the army of the European powers that were combating the Revolution. Wounded at the siege of Thionville, he took refuge in England in 1793. He led a miserable existence there, especially at the beginning, giving private lessons and doing translations for a living. At that time he was also working on an American Indian epic in prose, *The Natchez*.

In London in 1797, Chateaubriand published *Essai sur les révolutions* (*An Historical, Political, Moral Essay on Revolutions*, 1815), in which he compared ancient and modern revolutions—historically, politically, and morally—with the French Revolution. This first work summarizes all the disappointments and anguish of his youth. Revealing influences of the eighteenth century philosophes, especially that of Rousseau, Chateaubriand praises humankind in the natural state. Although he uses rationalistic arguments against the Christian faith, Chateaubriand sometimes indicates a certain anxiety concerning religion. He rejects Montesquieu's, Voltaire's, and the other Encyclopedists' belief in human progress. Chateaubriand considered that in this essay he had shown that there is nothing new under the sun, that earlier revolutions had contained the germ of the French Revolution.

In 1798, while still in London, Chateaubriand learned of the deaths, first of a sister, then of his mother. His grief at these two losses made him weep, and with the flow of tears came a return to the faith of his childhood, a faith toward which he had long been groping to sustain him in his many sorrows. Back in France, he would thenceforth devote his literary talent to defending and restoring the religion that the French Revolution had sought to destroy.

Published in 1802 after *Atala* and *René*, *The Genius of Christianity* appeared a few days before Napoleon's concordat with the pope became public. For political reasons, the emperor, too, had been working to restore religion in France, and he appointed Chateaubriand, first as secretary to the ambassador to Rome (1803), then as minister plenipotentiary in the Valais (1804). The execution of the duc d'Enghien went against Chateaubriand's conscience, however, and aroused his sentiments for the restoration of the monarchy. He resigned his post and, despite Napoleon's efforts to win him back, remained prudently but firmly opposed to the emperor. Elected to the French Academy in 1811, Chateaubriand would not make his acceptance speech, and he waited for Napoleon's fall from power to take his seat.

After his break with the emperor, Chateaubriand planned to complete his apology for religion by writing a Christian epic. To prepare himself for that task, he took a trip in 1806 and 1807 through many parts of Europe and to the Holy Land; one of the products of this journey was the *Itinéraire de Paris à Jérusalem* (1811).

Chateaubriand was at first delighted with the Bourbons' return to power. He held numerous important diplomatic posts under both Louis XVIII and Charles X and was often honored by both kings. Although his spirit of independence and his outspoken nature also invoked royal disfavor, Chateaubriand's popularity was never greater. The political essays that he published during this period expressed, among other views, his belief in constitutional monarchy.

From 1826 to 1831 and then 1836 to 1839, Chateaubriand's *Œuvres complètes* were published, including some works that had not yet appeared. *Les Aventures du dernier Abencérage* (1826; *The Last of the Abencérages*, 1835) is a record of travel impressions of Spain, for which he had not found space in the *Itinéraire de Paris à Jérusalem*. *The Natchez* and *Le Voyage en Amérique* (1827; *Travels in America*, 1969) are, respectively, the Native American prose epic composed in London (in which *Atala* and *René* had also appeared) and the travel book begun in the New World in 1791. When Chateaubriand died on July 4, 1848, he was buried as he had requested, on the rocks of Grand-Bé on the coast of his native Brittany, in splendid isolation.

ANALYSIS

The analysis of François-René de Chateaubriand's best-known works of fiction, *Atala* and *René*, can be better appreciated after the earlier introductions on the author's overall achievements and his works of nonfic-

tion. The two novels may stand as independent units, but any comprehensive discussion must view them as linked with the author's achievements in general and his other literary forms in particular.

ATALA

Atala began as an episode in *The Natchez*, a work originally composed during Chateaubriand's stay in London. The author reworked it in order to include it in a section of *The Genius of Christianity* titled "Harmony of the Christian Religion, with Scenes in Nature and the Passions of the Human Heart." He first published it separately, however, in 1801.

Le Mercure, a journal of the period, had been engaged in a polemic attacking the antireligious spirit of the eighteenth century, against which complaints had been lodged by the partisans, including Madame de Staël, of this aspect of the old regime. Because the government of Napoleon Bonaparte favored the restoration of religion in France, the times seemed right for the "author of *The Genius of Christianity*," as Chateaubriand called himself in *Le Mercure*, to let the public know of his existence. Still a political refugee, he needed to be cautious. Perhaps fearing a clandestine edition of some part of his work—no doubt anxious for glory at a time when he was still composing *The Genius of Christianity* and similar works by others were appearing—Chateaubriand began by publishing a few pages of *Atala* in *Le Mercure* in 1800 and 1801. Soon he gave a complete *Atala* to the public and the critics, prefacing it with a kind of manifesto.

It was as easy to detach *Atala* from *The Genius of Christianity* as from *The Natchez*. There was no need to read all of "Harmony of the Christian Religion" to appreciate either *Atala* or *René*, which had also been detached from *The Natchez* and intended for inclusion in *The Genius of Christianity*; not only did Chateaubriand begin by publishing them separately (in 1801 and 1802, respectively), then together (1805), but in 1826 he ceased to include them in *The Genius of Christianity*.

Exotic literature did not originate with Chateaubriand. In the eighteenth century, the triumph of religion over love in a non-European setting had been treated in Voltaire's *Zaïre* (pr. 1732; English translation, 1736). The accounts of travelers such as Thomas Cook had revealed the simple manners of primitive peoples to civilized society. In *Paul et Virginie* (1787; *Paul and Mary*, 1789; better known as *Paul and Virginia*, 1795), Jacques-Henri Bernardin de Saint-Pierre had depicted the virgin forest and seascapes of the tropics, and several writers had invented stories analogous to *Atala* set in America. Like Abbé Prévost, Chateaubriand had not seen all the scenes that he described, but he made use of books by naturalists and travelers to compensate for what he lacked in firsthand experience.

Atala opens on the banks of the Meschacebé (Mississippi River) in Louisiana; here lives the tribe of Natchez, which welcomes the young Frenchman, René. The old American Indian, Chactas, who visited France at the time of Louis XIV, befriends René during a beaver hunt and begins to tell him of his adventures as a young man. He was about twenty years old when an enemy tribe captured him. He was saved by Atala, a beautiful young Native American woman who had been reared as a Christian. For a long time they fled through the forest, their passion growing stronger all the while. During a storm, they encountered a missionary, Father Aubry, who wished to convert Chactas and unite him and Atala in marriage. Atala was dedicated to the Virgin Mary by her mother, however, and she believed that she could never be released from the vow of chastity. In order not to surrender to her love for Chactas, Atala took poison. Repentant and resigned, Atala died, consoled by the ministrations of the kindly Father Aubry and to the great sorrow of Chactas.

Despite Chateaubriand's protests to the contrary, his idyllic picture of "savages" is reminiscent of Rousseau. In the religion that required no church, with its rudimentary practices, Chateaubriand's readers recognized the doctrine of the Vicaire Savoyard; in the sentimental Indians themselves, the sensibility of the eighteenth century. Various characteristics and details, such as Chactas's reference to Atala's virtuous yet passionate face or Father Aubry's amusing nose, associate the work with Rousseau's *Julie: Ou, La Nouvelle Héloïse* (1761; *Eloise: Or, A Series of Original Letters*, 1761) and Saint-Pierre's *Paul and Virginia*.

Atala and Father Aubry, however, are neither mere literary offspring of these works nor simply creations of Chateaubriand's imagination. In Atala, Chateaubriand re-created the charms of a young English woman whom

he had loved; in the guise of the wise old Chactas, Chateaubriand himself is to be found, with his desires, passions, and dreams; and Father Aubry finds his prototype in a certain Father Jogues. On a symbolic level, the American Indian woman embodies the spirit of solitude in nature; the old priest, that of the epic missionary movement. Chateaubriand's sometimes sumptuous, sometimes tender prose, however, is beholden only to the author's own poetic inspiration.

RENÉ

The introductory paragraphs of *René* give the setting in which, several years later, in order to explain the cause of his incurable melancholia to the old Indian, René in turn tells the story of his own youth. After a childhood filled with wild daydreams, after travels that made him aware of his isolation in society, after several years of passion and ecstasy spent with his sister Amélie, he decided to leave France for America, while Amélie, alarmed by the excessive emotion that she felt for her brother, retired to a convent.

In *René*, Chateaubriand intended to give moral significance to his narrative of a civilized man who has become a savage. He describes the feeling of lassitude and apathy toward life that is denounced in *The Genius of Christianity* as the evil of modern times. In *René*, Chateaubriand explains that the many books that deal with humans and their emotions lead him to live life vicariously. Lacking experience, humans become disenchanted with life without having enjoyed it. They have no more illusions, but their desires remain unsatisfied. Human imagination is rich, abundant, and marvelous; human existence is poor, barren, and disillusioned. A human being lives in an empty world with a full heart, weary of everything without having experienced anything.

Chateaubriand himself had known similar spiritual states and believed that faith would set him free. Far from offering René as a model, he condemns him through the words of the missionary, Father Souël, who, with Chactas, has received René's confidence. According to Father Souël, nothing in René's story deserves the pity that he has been shown; he was a young man whose head was filled with fantasy, who was displeased with everything, and who shirked all social responsibility to indulge himself in useless daydreams. A person is not superior because he or she perceives the world in a hateful light. If one hates humankind and life, it is because one is nearsighted. René is advised to look beyond; if he does, he will soon be convinced that all the ills of which he complains are as nothing. Solitude is bad only for the person who lives without God.

Chateaubriand's readers missed his lesson. They were charmed by his hero, however, whose prestige was enhanced by a style capable of the intricacies of psychological analyses as well as bursts of lyricism. René is both uplifted and overwhelmed by infinite desire. He dreams of love before he has truly loved, and his dream strays after fantasy. He does not permit himself to be emotionally satisfied by objects within his grasp; the pleasure that he takes in imagination anticipates and destroys his pleasure in feeling and possessing the real objects. He therefore rejects a reality that is necessarily disappointing, but he consoles himself for his ennui by considering the uniqueness of his fate. His very sorrow, because of its extraordinary nature, contains its own cure. One enjoys the unusual, even when it is misfortune. René contemplates his sorrow, admiring and cherishing it. Chateaubriand's contemporaries recognized themselves in René and loved him.

René's (and Chateaubriand's) malady was also the malady of his generation and even of the preceding one. When young, its members had read Rousseau's *La Nouvelle Héloïse* and Johann Wolfgang von Goethe's *Die Leiden des jungen Werthers* (1774; *The Sorrows of Young Werther*, 1779), as well as the works of the English and Scottish Romantic poets. They had experienced the two phases of René's life: that of the dreamer consumed by an inexplicable sorrow, thirsting for something infinite and intangible, involving the longed-for tempest; and that of the René of the unwholesome passion, nurturing an inadmissible thought within himself. Wishing to liberate nature, the eighteenth century had invested passion with a sacred character and had rehabilitated incest. Incest inspired an outpouring of works by Louis-Sébastien Mercier, Voltaire, Jean-François Ducis, and others, which doubtless suggested this subject to Chateaubriand.

If one studies *René*, one finds autobiographical data. René's sister, Amélie, lived at Combourg with her brother, for example, and René and she share numerous

characteristics with Chateaubriand and his sister Lucile. The reader is not to take Amélie for Lucile or Chateaubriand for René. Nevertheless, Amélie, like Lucile, is an unhappy soul, subject to feverish exaltation and flashes of madness; Chateaubriand and René experienced the same difficulties in the same places; both went into exile for the same reasons; Chateaubriand's forced idleness as an émigré, his solitude, his dreams of action and consuming passion, and the apathy from which he was torn by a brutal act are repeated in the story of his hero. Chateaubriand admitted that his total boredom and total disgust were embodied in René, and a friend said of the author that he had a reserve of ennui that seemed contained in the immense void between himself and his thoughts.

Favoring religion in response to the needs of the heart and its anguish, *René* was, like *Atala*, originally a part of *The Genius of Christianity*, after the chapter on the effects of strong passion. *René*, intended to address the malady of a Werther and demonstrate that religion was the only cure for it, summarized all the advice that Chateaubriand had received from his mother at Combourg. According to Amélie, one should not scorn the wisdom of one's forebears. It is better to be more like ordinary people and be less unhappy; it is more difficult to live than to die. Finally, the fervent prayers of Chateaubriand's mother are echoed in the following, the missionary's concluding words to René:

> Whoever has been endowed with talent must devote it to serving his fellow men, for if he does not make use of it, he is first punished by an inner misery, and sooner or later Heaven visits on him a fearful retribution.

Richard A. Mazzara

OTHER MAJOR WORKS

NONFICTION: *Essai sur les révolutions*, 1797 (*An Historical, Political, Moral Essay on Revolutions*, 1815); *Le Génie du Christianisme*, 1799, 1800, 1802 (*The Genius of Christianity*, 1802); *Itinéraire de Paris à Jérusalem*, 1811; *De Buonaparte et des Bourbons*, 1814 (*On Buonaparte and the Bourbons*, 1814); *De la monarchie, selon la charte*, 1816 (*The Monarchy According to the Charter*, 1816); *Mémoires sur la vie et la mort du duc de Berry*, 1820; *Les Aventures du dernier Abencérage*, 1826 (*The Last of the Abencérages*, 1835); *Le Voyage en Amérique*, 1827 (*Travels in America*, 1969); *Essai sur la littérature anglaise*, 1836 (*Sketches on English Literature*, 1836); *Le Congrès de Vérone*, 1838; *La Vie de Rancé*, 1844; *Mémoires d'outre-tombe*, 1849-1850 (*Memoirs*, 1902).

MISCELLANEOUS: *Œuvres complètes*, 1826-1831 (28 volumes); *Œuvres complètes*, 1836-1839 (36 volumes); *Œuvres complètes*, 1859-1861 (12 volumes).

BIBLIOGRAPHY

Conner, Tom. *Chateaubriand's "Mémoires d'outre-tombe": A Portrait of the Artist as Exile*. New York: Peter Lang, 1995. Essentially a book about Chateaubriand and his autobiography. The first chapter and introduction hold helpful discussions of the author's life and work. Includes a bibliography.

Maurois, André. *Chateaubriand*. New York: Harper & Brothers, 1958. A lively biography geared to the general reader and beginning student of Chateaubriand. One of the best introductory texts, written by an author who specialized in biographies of literary figures.

Moscovici, Claudia. "Hybridity and Ethics in Chateaubriand's *Atala*." *Nineteenth Century French Studies* 29, nos. 3/4 (2001): 197-216. An analysis of *Atala*, focusing on Chateaubriand's depiction of American Indians, "noble savage" characters, and the more "civilized" Europeans. Moscovici maintains that Chateaubriand did not believe that primitive and civilized societies were "ethical opposites."

Neefs, Jacques. "With a Live Hand: Three Versions of Textual Transmission (Chateaubriand, Montaigne, Stendhal)." In *Genetic Criticism: Texts and Avant-Textes*, edited by Jed Deppman, Daniel Ferrer, and Michael Groden. Philadelphia: University of Pennsylvania Press, 2004. This chapter on the work of Chateaubriand and two other French authors is included in this introduction to "genetic criticism," a popular literary movement in France. Instead of evaluating an author's final text, genetic critics study a writer's manuscript to analyze how the author produced the work.

Nemoianu, Virgil. "The Absent Center of Romantic Prose: Chateaubriand and His Peers." In *The Triumph of Imperfection: The Silver Age of Sociocultural Moderation in Europe, 1815-1848*. Columbia: University of South Carolina Press, 2006. A study of Romantic literature, which includes an analysis of Chateaubriand's work. Nemoianu argues that in dealing with the revolutionary changes of the nineteenth century, writers, philosophers, and statesmen sought a reconciliation between radical new ideas and past intellectual philosophy.

Painter, George D. *Chateaubriand: A Biography*. London: Chatto & Windus, 1977. Initially, projected to be a three-volume work, this is the only volume completed before Painter's death. Painter offers an extensively detailed account of Chateaubriand's life from 1768 to 1793.

Polowetzky, Michael. *A Bond Never Broken: The Relations Between Napoleon and the Authors of France*. Rutherford, N.J.: Fairleigh Dickinson University Press, 1993. Reassesses Napoleon I's relationship with French writers, including Chateaubriand, contradicting previous accounts of the emperor's adversarial dealings with the literati. Polowetzky argues that Napoleon needed to cultivate friends among French authors so he could be remembered as a statesman who inspired a golden age of literature.

Porter, Charles A. *Chateaubriand: Composition, Imagination, and Poetry*. Saratoga, Calif.: Anma Libri, 1978. A clearly written, scholarly survey of Chateaubriand's entire literary career, and one of the few book-length studies of the author written in English. Includes a bibliography.

Sieburg, Friedrich. *Chateaubriand*. Translated by Violet M. MacDonald. Winchester, Mass.: Allen & Unwin, 1961. Concentrates on biography rather than literary analysis. Argues that "Chateaubriand's ambition and his desire for action were . . . forever undermining the foundations of his existence" and that his life was a tissue of contradictions.

Switzer, Richard, ed. *Chateaubriand Today*. Madison: University of Wisconsin Press, 1970. Essays on Chateaubriand—some in French and some in English—and the eighteenth century, and on his imagination, his use of the fictional confession, and his revolutionary politics. Includes an annotated bibliography.

BRUCE CHATWIN

Born: Sheffield, South Yorkshire, England; May 13,
   1940
Died: Nice, France; January 18, 1989
Also known as: Charles Bruce Chatwin

PRINCIPAL LONG FICTION

The Viceroy of Ouidah, 1980
On the Black Hill, 1982
The Songlines, 1987
Utz, 1988

OTHER LITERARY FORMS

Bruce Chatwin is known principally for his semiautobiographical novels and for his remarkable ability to
interweave fact and fiction in highly imaginative ways.
In addition to his novels, Chatwin wrote a travelogue, *In
Patagonia* (1977), his first full-length book and the one
that made him famous. He also collaborated with Paul
Theroux on *Patagonia Revisited* (1985; expanded as *Nowhere Is a Place: Travels in Patagonia*, 1992). After his
death, two volumes of his essays appeared: *What Am I
Doing Here* (1989) and *Anatomy of Restlessness: Selected Writings, 1969-1989* (1996). In 1993, *Far Journeys: Photographs and Notebooks* was published, edited
by David King and Francis Wyndham.

ACHIEVEMENTS

Bruce Chatwin has come to be known as one of English literature's most renowned travel writers, novelists, and essayists. Although *On the Black Hill* and *Utz*
are genuine novels that are based on real characters or
character types, Chatwin's travel writing established his
early reputation as one of England's most distinguished
writers. His ability to interconnect fact and fiction within
his unique perspective made his semiautobiographical
novels both believable and entertaining. Some of them
became popular best sellers. His stylishly rendered travelogues substantially revived the art of English and
American travel writing in the latter half of the twentieth
century. These books and essays have been favorably
compared with the best travel writing of D. H. Lawrence,
Graham Greene, Robert Byron, and Paul Theroux. Like

Lawrence's travel books, Chatwin's demonstrate the disastrous impact of Western culture on native cultures in
both South America and Australia. Western civilization
and its corrosive technology succeeded in separating the
Indians of South America and the Aborigines of Australia from their connections with the source of their vitality—their natural surroundings.

Chatwin's first book, *In Patagonia*, won several
prestigious awards, notably the Hawthornden Prize and
the E. M. Forster Award. Chatwin's ability to present
facts using novelistic techniques raised the level of travel
writing from mere reportage to serious examination of
the conflicting value systems of European emigrants and
indigenous groups in some of the most remote areas of
the world. He discovered repeatedly during his travels
that humankind's failing has been its abandonment of
its natural, biologically determined impulse to move
throughout the world following the cyclical processes of
the natural seasons. Settling into one permanent location
is, in essence, unnatural. It is this persistent pattern of
settlement that, to Chatwin, explains the origins of human restlessness, for Chatwin the greatest mystery in human history. The history of the world, then, consists of
the conflict between pastoral nomads and what Chatwin
called the sins of settlement. Not only the novels but also
his travel books take as their primary subject the profound effects of "the sins of settlement" on the human
psyche.

BIOGRAPHY

Charles Bruce Chatwin was born in Sheffield, England, on May 13, 1940. His mother was Margharita
Turnell and his father was Charles Leslie Chatwin, a
lawyer in Birmingham. The family lineage descended
from a Birmingham button manufacturer, but a number
of Chatwin's ancestors had been lawyers and architects.
Although the family moved around England during
World War II, Chatwin attended one of England's more
prestigious public schools, Marlborough College. He
did not excel academically, but he did fall in love with
Edith Sitwell's anthology *Planet and Glow Worm*
(1944), along with the poems of Charles Baudelaire,

Bruce Chatwin. (© Jerry Bauer)

doctor suggested that he take a trip to places where the horizons were long to relieve the strain of his severely overworked eyes. He traveled to Sudan, where he lived with nomadic tribes for months at a time. After his return to England, he resigned from Sotheby's and became a graduate student at the University of Edinburgh in archaeology, but he became disillusioned with academic life. He began traveling in earnest and writing essays for English newspapers about his journeys to western and northern Africa, China, the Middle East, and Australia. His trip to Patagonia became the subject of his first critically acclaimed book, *In Patagonia*. His next book, the novel *The Viceroy of Ouidah*, arose from his experiences in Benin, formerly known as the ancient kingdom of Dahomey.

Chatwin's next novel, *On the Black Hill*, was an examination of twins living in great isolation in one of Chatwin's favorite vacation locations, eastern Wales. His most popular and best-selling novel, *The Songlines*, grew from a journey throughout the Outback and desert regions of northern Australia. Finally, his highly praised short novel, *Utz*, is a fictionalized account of his visit to Prague during the Soviet occupation of 1968.

On the Black Hill, published in 1982, won two literary awards, the Whitbread Award and the James Tait Black Memorial Prize for best novel. *The Viceroy of Ouidah* was made into a film titled *Cobra Verde*, directed by Werner Herzog, and a film version of *On the Black Hill* was directed by Andrew Grieve; both films were released in 1987. *Utz*, which had been short-listed for the Booker Prize, was also made into a film, by Swiss director George Sluizer, two years after Chatwin's death. It was during his Australian trip that Chatwin came down with the first symptoms of acquired immunodeficiency syndrome (AIDS), the disease that eventually killed him. Chatwin never publicly acknowledged that he had AIDS, and he was severely criticized by some journalists and activists for keeping it a secret. He died in Nice, France, on January 18, 1989.

Gérard de Nerval, and especially Arthur Rimbaud. These works engendered Chatwin's interest in French literature and culture. His favorite English poets were William Blake and Christopher Smart, and the prose works of Jeremy Taylor and Sir Thomas Browne helped him sharpen his own style.

After graduating from Marlborough, Chatwin began working for the well-known art auction house of Sotheby and Company as a uniformed porter. He became famous at Sotheby's when he casually pointed out that a newly acquired Picasso gouache was actually a fake. After his supervisor called in experts who verified Chatwin's claim, the young man quickly rose to one of the top positions in the company; he soon became the youngest partner in the firm's history.

Chatwin married an American woman, Elizabeth Chanler, who was the secretary of the chairman of Sotheby's. Eventually he left the company, but not before experiencing severe eye problems; he awoke blind one morning, regaining his sight the following day. His

ANALYSIS

The principal theme that runs throughout all four of Bruce Chatwin's novels is the fall of humankind from its pristine condition of nomadic innocence into the corrupt world of permanent location. Chatwin called this fall "the sins of settlement." He used the myth of Cain and Abel rather than that of Adam and Eve to illustrate the fallen condition of the human race. Abel became a metaphor for the wandering nomadic shepherd, and Cain a metaphor for the first settler, because, after he was cast out of Eden, he moved east to found the first city. Chatwin applies this mythic fall to modern civilization in one form or another in all his novels; each novel is also a variation on what became his permanent theme: the nature of human restlessness.

THE VICEROY OF OUIDAH

After the enormous success of his best-selling travelogue *In Patagonia*, Chatwin decided to write a scholarly biography on the notorious Brazilian slave trader Francisco Felix de Souza. However, after his second visit to Benin in 1978, when he was arrested and brutalized by the Marxist military government, he decided instead to write a fictionalized account of de Souza's life. Benin had previously been known as Dahomey, an ancient city. Dahomey became, with de Souza's assistance, one of the leading slave-trading countries during the eighteenth and nineteenth centuries. De Souza, a Brazilian, had come to Dahomey to acquire slaves from West Africa—specifically Dahomey—to work in Brazil's mines and plantations. In Chatwin's novelistic version, he renames de Souza Francisco Manoel da Silva and uses some of the facts of de Souza's life; however, he imaginatively re-creates the vast majority of the scenes surrounding the main character's life.

Da Silva is coolly sadistic toward the slaves he captures and transports to Brazil, and he prides himself on keeping them healthy so that they will be more valuable to plantation owners. Money and power are always his essential concerns. He becomes immensely wealthy and powerful, becoming the viceroy of Ouidah, the capital city of Dahomey. Greed and corruption cause his downfall, and at the conclusion of the novel, da Silva (as did the actual de Souza) loses his luxurious estate and ends up a poverty-stricken wanderer begging for shelter and food. Chatwin uses a thematic pattern that recurs in his other novels: A European Christian culture corrupts an African animist one by engaging native peoples to enslave others of their race. The novel also demonstrates the vicious practice of building one culture's edenic paradise on the ruins of another culture.

ON THE BLACK HILL

Nothing could be further from the exoticisms of *The Viceroy of Ouidah* than Chatwin's next novel, *On the Black Hill*. Chatwin claimed that he was tired of being labeled a travel writer and consciously decided to write a novel about people who never traveled anywhere. He was always fascinated with the borderland region between western England and eastern Wales. The story of twin brothers who spent their entire lives on their farm, called The Vision, is a composite of a number of stories about twins, a lifelong interest of Chatwin.

This novel was written in a style entirely different from that of *The Viceroy of Ouidah* and resembles the domestic novels of Thomas Hardy and Stella Gibbons. Whereas *The Viceroy of Ouidah* is about the journeys of da Silva, *On the Black Hill* is about stasis. Mythically, The Vision is presented as an edenic paradise from the beginning of the novel. The twins, Benjamin and Lewis, and their mother and father continually strive to protect The Vision from external invading forces—an all-consuming capitalism and sexually corrupting influences—and to preserve the purity of their sacred hearth. The twins are so intimately connected that one frequently experiences what the other feels. Benjamin tries to keep his brother, like himself, a virgin for life. Once their parents have passed away, they occupy the same bed for the remainder of their lives. Whenever either one of them ventures out into the corruption of the outer world, he is brutally ridiculed and abused. The form and content of the novel are unmistakably pastoral, and the story illustrates the evil of the city in conflict with the innocence of the country.

THE SONGLINES

None of Chatwin's books has been analyzed more thoroughly than *The Songlines*, and critics are divided over whether it should be considered a novel or a travelogue. It chronicles Chatwin's extensive journey throughout Australia in 1984 with fellow writer Salman Rushdie. On being asked what genre Chatwin thought it fit most accurately, the author called it a novel, admitting that he had invented huge chunks of it to tell the story he wanted to tell. He also admitted using Denis Diderot's eighteenth century dialogue novel *Jacques le fataliste et son maître* (1796; *Jacques the Fatalist and His Master*, 1797) as a model.

The Songlines was phenomenally successful. Although an adventure story, it is also a novel of ideas that meditates on the dark fate of Western civilization—another recurring theme in Chatwin's work. The novel also theorizes about the fate of an Aboriginal civilization forced to dwell in the fallen world of time and permanent location. Once again, Chatwin juxtaposes the needs of a nomadic society with the negative effects of enforced settlement, vividly documenting the widespread depression and alcoholism in many Aboriginal communities.

However, the narrator also discovers in his journey the key to his theory regarding pastoral nomads as humankind's original innocence. The songlines themselves came from the Aborigines' ancient ancestors, whose function it was to establish their tribal territory down to the present. Only by repeating the songlines do they know their place within the cosmos. The songlines also function as paths of communication among distant tribes and establish a sacramental system in which people of all generations—past, present, and future—participate equally. The cosmos itself is said to have been sung into existence by the musical power of the ancient songlines.

While he was writing the novel, Chatwin fell desperately ill with the early symptoms of AIDS and was barely able to finish the work. As a result, the concluding ninety pages of *The Songlines* consist mostly of quotations from Chatwin's notebooks interspersed with selections from his favorite authors—Rimbaud, Blake, John Donne, Arthur Koestler, Martin Buber, Martin Heidegger, and many other writers, philosophers, and scientists. Nevertheless, *The Songlines* brought together and resolved many of Chatwin's philosophical concerns.

UTZ

The last book Chatwin wrote was, according to some critics, his finest novel, even though he was dying of AIDS as he wrote. Some of the material came from a magazine assignment for which he went to Prague to research Emperor Rudolf II's obsession with collecting the rarest kinds of objets d'art. In researching his article, Chatwin became deeply involved in what he called the psychopathology of compulsive collectors. The novel's protagonist, Kaspar Utz, is an amalgamation of many of the collectors Chatwin had known personally during his

years at Sotheby's. The book is also a mystery novel in the tradition of writers such as Graham Greene and John le Carré. The unnamed narrator follows one dead-end lead after another in his search for the lost treasure (two million dollars' worth) of Kaspar Utz's fabulous collection of Meissen figurines. Chatwin juxtaposes the depressing world of Communist bureaucracy with the equally disturbing world of capitalistic greed.

The novel opens with the funeral of Kaspar Utz and continues with the narrator interviewing friends and lovers of Utz in hopes of discovering exactly where and how the collection disappeared right under the eyes of the Communist overseers. Among other things, the narrator discovers that Utz fell in love with and married his housekeeper just prior to the disappearance of the treasure. The novel also traces the fascinating development of the porcelain industry in Europe and its connections with early alchemy in Germany and with the Austro-Hungarian Empire. An additional theme in *Utz* is the narrator's dawning realization that only art survives the transitory lives of humans—a particularly poignant revelation in view of Chatwin's death less than a year after the book's publication.

Patrick Meanor

OTHER MAJOR WORKS

NONFICTION: *In Patagonia*, 1977; *Patagonia Revisited*, 1985 (with Paul Theroux; expanded as *Nowhere Is a Place: Travels in Patagonia*, 1992); *What Am I Doing Here*, 1989; *Far Journeys: Photographs and Notebooks*, 1993 (David King and Francis Wyndham, editors); *Anatomy of Restlessness: Selected Writings, 1969-1989*, 1996 (Jan Borm and Matthew Graves, editors).

BIBLIOGRAPHY

Clapp, Susannah. "The Life and Early Death of Bruce Chatwin." *The New Yorker*, December 23-30, 1996. Comprehensive memoir written by one of Chatwin's editors. Clapp knew him personally and professionally, and she brings to this piece great familiarity with the art and publishing worlds of England and the United States.

_____. *With Chatwin: Portrait of a Writer*. New York: Alfred A. Knopf, 1997. The closest thing to a biography of Chatwin that had been published up to the time it appeared. Much of the content deals with Clapp's difficulties with, and appreciations of, Chatwin the writer; Clapp edited two of his books while working at the publishing house of Jonathan Cape.

Meanor, Patrick. "Bruce Chatwin." In *Magill's Survey of World Literature*, edited by Steven G. Kellman. Rev. ed. Pasadena, Calif.: Salem Press, 2009. Essay provides a brief biography, discussion of all of Chatwin's works, and more detailed analysis of *In Patagonia* and *The Songlines*, which are discussed within the context of Chatwin's novels *On the Black Hill, The Viceroy of Ouidah*, and *Utz*.

_____. *Bruce Chatwin*. New York: Twayne, 1997. The second full-length critical book to be written on Chatwin covers virtually everything written on and by Chatwin up to 1997, except for Clapp's 1997 memoir (cited above).

Murray, Nicholas. *Bruce Chatwin*. Mid Glamorgan, Wales: Seren Books, 1993. The first full-length analysis of all of Chatwin's books up to *Anatomy of Restlessness* and *Far Journeys*, including examination of his four novels. Stylishly written, informative work

offers intelligent criticism and has served as the basis for subsequent evaluations of Chatwin's work.

Shakespeare, Nicholas. *Bruce Chatwin: A Biography*. New York: Doubleday, 2000. Gossipy, wide-ranging biography is based on numerous interviews and complete access to Chatwin's personal papers. Describes Chatwin's flaws as well as his strengths and provides information about how Chatwin wrote his books.

Ure, John. *In Search of Nomads: An Anglo-American Obsession from Hester Stanhope to Bruce Chatwin*. London: Constable, 2003. Ure, who has himself traveled with nomads in the Arabian Peninsula, Sahara Desert, Iran, and Central Asia, describes other Britons and Americans who have sought out and journeyed with nomadic peoples. Includes information about Chatwin's travels with the Qashqai people in southern Iran and with Mongol horsemen in Afghanistan.

Williams, Marie. "Escaping a Dystopian Present: Compensatory and Anticipatory Utopias in Bruce Chatwin's *The Viceroy of Ouidah* and *The Songlines*." *Utopian Studies* 14, no. 2 (2003): 99-117. Examines two of Chatwin's novels, focusing on their representation of and interest in different forms of utopian thinking.

JOHN CHEEVER

Born: Quincy, Massachusetts; May 27, 1912
Died: Ossining, New York; June 18, 1982
Also known as: John William Cheever

PRINCIPAL LONG FICTION

The Wapshot Chronicle, 1957
The Wapshot Scandal, 1964
Bullet Park, 1969
Falconer, 1977
Oh, What a Paradise It Seems, 1982

OTHER LITERARY FORMS

After the publication of his first fictional piece, "Expelled," in the October 10, 1930, issue of *The New Re-*public, more than two hundred John Cheever stories appeared in American magazines, chiefly *The New Yorker*. Fewer than half that number were reprinted in the seven collections Cheever published in his lifetime: *The Way Some People Live* (1943), *The Enormous Radio, and Other Stories* (1953), *The Housebreaker of Shady Hill, and Other Stories* (1958), *Some People, Places, and Things That Will Not Appear in My Next Novel* (1961), *The Brigadier and the Golf Widow* (1964), *The World of Apples* (1973), and *The Stories of John Cheever* (1978); the last of these includes all but the earliest collected stories and adds four previously uncollected pieces. In 1994, a collection titled *Thirteen Uncollected Stories* was published.

Cheever's one television play, *The Shady Hill Kidnapping*, aired on January 12, 1982, to inaugurate the Public Broadcasting Service's *American Playhouse* series. Cheever, however, made a clear distinction between fiction, which he considered humankind's most exalted and intimate means of communication, and literary works written for television, film, and theater. Consequently, he remained aloof from all attempts to adapt his literary work—including the 1968 film version of his story "The Swimmer," directed by Frank Perry and starring Burt Lancaster (which he found disappointing), and the adaptations of three of his stories televised by the Public Broadcasting Service in 1979. In addition, he rarely turned his considerable energies to the writing of articles and reviews. One large and fascinating body of Cheever's writing is found in his journals, which he kept as part of a long family tradition.

ACHIEVEMENTS

Until the publication of *Falconer* in 1977 and *The Stories of John Cheever* the following year, John Cheever's position as a major American writer was not firmly established, even though as early as 1953 William Peden had described Cheever as one of the country's most "undervalued" literary figures. Despite the fact that critics, especially academic ones, frequently invoked Cheever only to pillory his supposedly lightweight vision and preoccupation with upper-middle-class life, his reputation continued to grow steadily: four O. Henry Awards between 1941 and 1964; a Guggenheim Fellowship in 1951; the University of Illinois Benjamin Franklin Award in 1955; a grant from the National Institute of Arts and Letters in 1956 and election to that organization the following year; the National Book Award for his first novel, *The Wapshot Chronicle*, in 1958; the William Dean Howells Medal for its sequel, *The Wapshot Scandal*, seven years later; election to the American Academy of Arts and Letters in 1973; and cover stories in the nation's two most widely circulated weekly newsmagazines, *Time* (1964) and *Newsweek* (1977). The overwhelmingly favorable reception of *Falconer* made possible the publication of *The Stories of John Cheever*, which in turn brought to its author additional honors: a second National Book Award; the National Book Critics Circle Award for best fiction; a Pulitzer Prize; the Ed-

ward MacDowell Medal; an honorary doctorate from Harvard University; and in April, 1982, the National Medal for Literature for his "distinguished and continuing contribution to American letters." The popular and critical success of those books and the televising of his work before a national audience brought Cheever the recognition he had long deserved and established his well-earned place in literature.

BIOGRAPHY

John Cheever was born in Quincy, Massachusetts, on May 27, 1912, and grew up during what he has called the "Athenian twilight" of New England culture. His father Frederick, who was forty-nine when Cheever was born, lost his position in the shoe business in the 1929 Depression and much of his self-respect a short time later when his wife opened a gift shop in order to support the family. The parents' emotionally strained relationship eventually led to their separation and caused Cheever to become very close to his brother Fred, seven years his senior. At age seventeen, Cheever was dismissed from Thayer Academy in South Braintree, Massachusetts, for smoking and poor grades; he promptly turned his experience into a story, "Expelled," which Malcolm Cowley published in *The New Republic* on October 10, 1930, and with Fred embarked on a walking tour of Europe. Upon their return, the brothers lived together briefly in Boston, where "Jon" (as he then identified himself) wrote while Fred worked in the textile business. The closeness of their relationship troubled Cheever, who then moved to a squalid rooming house on New York's Hudson Street. There, with the help of his Boston mentor, Hazel Hawthorne, he wrote synopses for Metro-Goldwyn-Mayer, subsisted on buttermilk and stale bread, associated with Cowley, E. E. Cummings, Sherwood Anderson, Edmund Wilson, Hart Crane, John Dos Passos, and Gaston Lachaise, and somehow managed to keep his art free of the political issues that dominated much of the literature of the period. It was also during that time that Cheever began three of his most enduring relationships: with Yaddo, the writers' colony in Saratoga Springs, New York; with *The New Yorker*, which published his "Brooklyn Rooming House" in the May 25, 1935, issue; and with Mary Winternitz, the daughter of the Dean of Yale Medical School, whom he married on March 22,

1941. They had three children: Susan, who became a writer; Benjamin, who became an editor at *Reader's Digest*; and Federico.

Midway through a tour of duty with the army, Cheever published his first book to generally favorable reviews, and following his discharge, he was able to support himself and his family almost exclusively, if at times precariously, by his writing. Although he liked to give interviewers and others the impression that he was something of a country squire—the heavy Boston accent, the eighteenth century house with its extensive grounds in Ossining, New York—Cheever was in fact plagued throughout much of his life by financial as well as psychological insecurity.

The 1950's was an unsettling time for Cheever. As he explained to fellow writer Herbert Gold, the decade had begun full of promise, but halfway through it "something went terribly wrong"; confused by "the forceful absurdities of life" and, like another Quincy man, Henry Adams, unprepared to deal with them, he imagined himself "a man in a quagmire, looking into a tear in the sky." The absurdities of modern life are presented, often with a comic twist, in the three novels and six collections of short stories that Cheever published between 1953 and the early 1970's—at which time the author's life took an even darker turn: a massive heart attack in 1972, acute alcoholism that eventually forced Cheever to commit himself to the Smithers Rehabilitation Center in New York, financial difficulties, and the death of his brother in 1976. In the light of this background, it is clear that the writing of his triumphant novel *Falconer* freed Cheever from the same sense of confinement that plagues his characters.

Cheever was both deeply, though not narrowly, religious (a practicing Episcopalian) and physically active (biking, walking, skiing, and sawing were among his favorite pastimes). He was also active sexually and, often feeling rebuffed by his wife, pursued numerous love affairs both with men (including the composer Ned Rorem and a number of young writers) and with women (including the actor Hope Lange). As a writer, he incorporated into his fiction the same blend of the spiritual and the worldly that marked his own character. This blend shines most strongly in *Oh, What a Paradise It Seems*, the novella Cheever published just three months before

he died of cancer on June 18, 1982. In the novella, protagonist Lemuel Sears is introduced in a sentence that begins in the writing style of William Butler Yeats and ends in pure Cheever: "An aged man is but a paltry thing, a tattered coat upon a stick, unless he sees the bright plumage of the bird called courage—Cardinalis virginius in this case—and oh how his heart leapt." More than a literary work, *Oh, What a Paradise It Seems* is the gift of an enormously generous writer whose loss is, to use one of Cheever's favorite words, "inestimable."

ANALYSIS

In a literary period that witnessed the exhaustion of literature, wholesale formal experimentation, a general distrust of language, the death of the novel, and the blurring of the lines separating fiction and play, mainstream art and the avant-garde, John Cheever consistently and eloquently held to the position that the writing of fiction is an intimate, useful, and indeed necessary way of making sense of human life and affirming its worth.

John Cheever. (© Nancy Crampton)

Cheever's ambitious and overtly religious view of fiction not only is unfashionable today but also stands in marked opposition to those critics who pigeonhole, and in this way dismiss, his fiction as social criticism in the conventional realistic mode. Certainly, there is that element of realism in his work that one finds in the fiction of John O'Hara and Anton Chekhov, writers with whom he is often compared. Such a view, however, fails to account for the various nonrealistic components of his work: the mythic resonance of William Faulkner, the comic grotesquerie of Franz Kafka, and, most important, the lyric style that, while reminiscent of F. Scott Fitzgerald's finest prose, is nevertheless entirely Cheever's own, a cachet underscoring his essentially religious sensibility.

Humankind's inclination toward spiritual light, Cheever has said, "is very nearly botanical." His characters are modern pilgrims—not the Kierkegaardian "sovereign wayfarers" one finds in the novels of Walker Percy, another contemporary Christian writer, but instead the lonely residents of Cheever's various cities and suburbs whose search for love, security, and a measure of fulfillment is the secret undercurrent of their otherwise prosaic daily lives. Because the idea of original sin is a given in Cheever's fiction, his characters are men and women who have fallen from grace. At their worst, they are narcissists and chronic complainers. The best of them, however, persevere and, as a result, attain that redemptive vision that enables them "to celebrate a world that lies around them like a bewildering and stupendous dream."

This affirmation does not come easily to Cheever's characters, nor is it rendered sentimentally. Cheever well understands how social fragmentation and separation from the natural world have eroded the individual's sense of self-worth and debased contemporary life, making humanity's "perilous moral journey" still more arduous. The outwardly comfortable world in which these characters exist can suddenly, and often for no clearly understandable reason, turn dangerously dark, bringing into sharper focus the emotional and spiritual impoverishment of their lives. What concerns Cheever is not so much the change in their fortunes as the way they respond to that change. Many respond in an extreme, sometimes bizarre manner—Melissa Wapshot, for one.

Others attempt to escape into the past; in doing so, they deny the present by imprisoning themselves in what amounts to a regressive fantasy that Cheever carefully distinguishes from nostalgia, which, as he uses it, denotes a pleasurable remembrance of the past, one that is free of regret. Cheever's heroes are those who embrace "the thrust of life," taking from the past what is valuable and using it in their present situations. How a character responds to his world determines Cheever's tone, which ranges from open derision to compassionate irony. Although in his later work Cheever may have been, as Richard Schickel has claimed, less ironic and more forgiving, his finest stories and novels, including *Falconer*, derive their power from the balance or tension he creates between irony and compassion, comedy and tragedy, light and dark.

The social and moral vision that forms the subject of Cheever's fiction also affects the structure of his novels. The novel, Cheever said in 1953, is a form better suited to the parochial life of the nineteenth century than to the modern age with its highly mobile population and mass communications; but because critics and readers have continued to view the short story as inferior to the novel, the conscientious writer of short fiction has often been denied the recognition routinely awarded lesser writers who have worked in the longer form. One way out of this dilemma for Cheever was to publish a collection of stories having the unity of a novel: *The Housebreaker of Shady Hill*. Another was to write novels that had some of the fragmentary quality Cheever found at the heart of the modern age. His four novels are not, therefore, made up of short stories badly spliced together, as some reviewers have maintained; rather, they reflect—in various degrees according to the author's state of mind at the time of composition—Cheever's firm belief that wholeness of being is no longer readily apparent; instead, it is something that character, author, and reader must strive to attain. Moreover, Cheever develops his novels on the basis of "intuition, apprehensions, dreams, concepts," rather than plot, as is entirely consistent with the revelatory nature of his religious vision. Thus, although the story form is appropriate to the depiction of the discontinuity of modern life, only in the novel can that discontinuity be not only identified but also brought under some control or, as happens in *Falconer*, transcended.

THE WAPSHOT CHRONICLE

In *The Wapshot Chronicle*, Cheever's first novel, the discontinuity of modern life is apparent not only in the structure and the characterization but also in the complex relationship the author sets up between his fictional New England town and the modern world lying beyond its nineteenth century borders. The impulse to create St. Botolphs (loosely based on Quincy) came to Cheever while he stood at the window of a Hollywood hotel, gazing down on "the dangerously barbaric and nomadic world" beneath him. The strength of his novel, however, derives not from a rejection of the present or, as in the work of nineteenth century local colorists such as Sarah Orne Jewett, in a reverent re-creation of a vanished way of life, but from the way Cheever uses each to evaluate the other.

The novel traces the decline of once-prosperous St. Botolphs and the Wapshot clan and the picaresque adventures of the two Wapshot boys—the "ministerial" Coverly and his older and more worldly brother Moses— who go to seek their fortunes in New York, Washington, D.C., and elsewhere. By having the novel begin and end with an annual Fourth of July celebration, Cheever does not so much impose an arbitrary orderliness on his discursive narrative as affirm the ceremoniousness that, in his view, is necessary to spiritual and emotional well-being. The temporal frame is important for another reason: It implies that the human desire for independence equals the desire for tradition. Each must be accommodated if the individual is to prosper. If the modern world seems chaotic, even inhospitable to Leander Wapshot's sons, it nevertheless possesses a vitality and expansiveness that, for the most part, St. Botolphs lacks. While the town is to be treasured for its rich tradition and continuity, it is also to be considered a place of confinement. The burden of the novel, then, is to show that with "strength and perseverance" it is possible to "create or build some kind of bridge" between past and present.

Cheever intends this bridge to serve a larger, emblematic purpose in *The Wapshot Chronicle*, where, as in his other works, it is the distance between self and other, or, more specifically, between man and woman, that must be bridged. Although Cheever has repeatedly warned that fiction is not "cryptoautobiography," he obviously, if loosely, modeled the Wapshots on his own family and has even admitted that he wrote the novel to make peace with his father's ghost. Leander Wapshot is the book's moral center; he has the imaginative power to redeem his fallen world, to affirm what others can only whiningly negate. Lusty and romantic, a lover of nature as well as of women, he transmits to Coverly and Moses, by his example rather than by precept, his vision of wholeness. Fittingly, the novel concludes with his "Advice to my sons," which Coverly finds tucked into a copy of William Shakespeare: "Stand up straight. Admire the world. Relish the love of a gentle woman. Trust in the Lord."

Despite his affirmative stance, Leander is a diminished hero. Unlike earlier generations of Wapshot men who proved themselves by sailing around the world, Leander's sailing is limited to ferrying tourists across the bay in his barely seaworthy boat, the *Topaze*, which his wife Sarah later converts into a floating gift shop, thus further reducing Leander's self-esteem. At one point, a storm drives the boat onto some rocks, an image that captures perfectly what Leander and many other Cheever characters feel so acutely: "man's inestimable loneliness." One of Leander's friends, for example, is haunted by the knowledge that he will be buried naked and unceremoniously in a potter's field; another man sings of his "guest room blues," and a young girl who briefly stays with the Wapshots mistakenly believes that sexual intercourse will end her loneliness. Others, equally desperate, collect antiques or live in castles in a vain attempt to make themselves secure in a bewilderingly changeable world. Leander's vision and vitality keep him from the despair that afflicts these others; as a result, even his death by drowning seems less an end than an affirmation.

Leander, with his "taste for romance and nonsense," is quixotic and exuberant; his wife Sarah, with her "air of wronged nobility," her "habitual reliance on sad conclusions," and his sister Honora, who substitutes philanthropy for love, are strong-willed and sexless. He affirms life; they deny it. Sarah, the town's civic leader, and Honora, the keeper of the Wapshot fortune, uncaringly strip Leander of his usefulness and self-worth (just as Cousin Justina, the reincarnation of Charles Dickens's Miss Havisham, aggressively plots to unman Moses). To some extent they are predatory, but even more they are incomplete because they are in need of someone to love.

Similarly, Leander is portrayed as a man not without flaws. He is, like many of Cheever's male characters, impractical and, at times, inattentive to his family; he can also appear childishly petulant, even ridiculous, as in the scene in which he fakes suicide in order to attract attention. More important, he loves and is loved, as the large crowd of mourners at his funeral service attests—much to Honora's surprise.

Whether his sons will fare any better in their relationships with women is left uncertain in this novel. Both marry—Coverly his "sandwich shop Venus" and Moses the beautiful Melissa Scaddon, who plays Estella to Cousin Justina's Miss Havisham. Both, after briefly losing their wives, eventually father sons, thus fulfilling the terms of their inheritance as set by Honora. Melissa and Betsey are, however, tainted, or haunted, by their pasts (in Betsey's case this is only vaguely mentioned). Moreover, most marriages in Cheever's fiction, as in life, are difficult affairs. In sum, the Wapshot boys may yet be greatly disappointed in their expectations. What is more important is the fact that Moses and, more particularly, Coverly build the necessary bridge between past and present, holding firm to what is best in St. Botolphs (as evidenced in Leander's journal) while freeing themselves from that confinement that the town, in part, represents. This optimistic view is confirmed by the novel's lively style. Straight narrative sections alternate with large portions of two Wapshot journals, humorous parodies of biblical language, and frequent direct addresses to the reader. Tragic elements are present but always in muted tones and often undercut with humor. In *The Wapshot Chronicle*, the comic spirit prevails, as well it should in a novel that twice invokes Shakespeare's Prospero, the liberator of Ariel and tamer of Caliban.

THE WAPSHOT SCANDAL

Outwardly, Cheever's first two novels are quite similar in theme, character, and structure. Like *The Wapshot Chronicle*, *The Wapshot Scandal* employs a framing device and interweaves three related stories: Honora's escape to Italy to avoid prosecution for income tax evasion and her return to St. Botolphs, where she promptly starves and drinks herself to death; Coverly and Betsey's life in yet another bland, middle-class housing development, Talifer; and Moses and Melissa's difficult existence in the affluent suburb of Proxmire Manor. Al-

though reviewers generally responded less favorably to the second Wapshot book, finding it too discursive, Cheever has pointed out that both novels were carefully thought out in advance and has described the sequel as "an extraordinarily complex book built upon non sequiturs." Whether it is, as Samuel Coale has argued, Cheever's finest work, because it carefully balances comic and tragic elements, is open to question. More certain is that a considerably darker mood pervades *The Wapshot Scandal*. At the time he began writing it, Cheever told an audience that American life had become abrasive and debased, a kind of hell, and during its four-year composition he became severely depressed. In *The Wapshot Chronicle* the easy-to-answer refrain is "Why did the young want to go away?" but in *The Wapshot Scandal* the repeated question is Coverly's Hamlet-like "Oh, Father, Father, Father, why have you come back?"—a query that accurately gauges the extent of Coverly's and Cheever's disenchantment with a world that no longer seems either inviting or livable for men or ghosts. In the earlier book, Moses and Coverly had to escape the confinement of St. Botolphs; in the sequel, characters have too completely cut themselves off from the usable traditions, comforting stability, and vital, natural light that the town also represents. As a result, the communal center to which earlier Wapshot men had come back and, analogously, the narrative center to which *The Wapshot Chronicle* continually returned, are conspicuously absent from *The Wapshot Scandal*.

In the sequel, St. Botolphs, though by no means idealized, is rendered in less qualified terms, thus more firmly establishing Cheever's preference for its values and his impatience with the rootlessness and shallowness of the modern age. Honora, for example, is now a far more sympathetic figure endowed with two of Leander's most attractive qualities: a belief in ceremony and a love of nature. In the guise of an elderly senator, Cheever carefully distinguishes between the sentimentalizing of the past and the modern tendency to dispense with the past altogether. The modern Prometheus, the senator notes, is technologically powerful, but he lacks "the awe, the humility, that primitive man brought to the sacred fire."

Whereas earlier Wapshot men faced the terrors of the sea, Moses and Coverly face the greater terrors of daily life in the twentieth century: insecurity, boredom, loneliness, loss of usefulness and self-esteem, and the pervasiveness of death. As Cheever shows, the American Dream totters on the brink of nightmare. When one resident of Proxmire Manor suddenly finds her carefree days turn into a series of frozen water pipes, backed-up toilets, exploding furnaces, blown fuses, broken appliances, unopenable packages of bacon, and vacationing repairmen, she turns first to alcohol and promiscuity, then to suicide. The few mourners her husband can convince to attend the funeral are people they had briefly known on various sea cruises who, intuiting her disappointment and recognizing it as their own, burst into tears. Similarly, Melissa Wapshot becomes the Emma Bovary of Proxmire Manor, taking as her lover a delivery boy and eventually fleeing to Italy, where, perversely, she finds some "solace" for her disappointments in the Supra-Marketto Americano in Rome. Moses responds to his wife's infidelity by becoming a wandering alcoholic, and Betsey finds compensation for the wrongs she claims to have suffered by whittling away her husband's small store of self-esteem.

Coverly, now twelve years older than at the beginning of *The Wapshot Chronicle,* serves (as Leander did in the earlier work) as the novel's moral center. He survives, perhaps even prevails, partly because he chooses to follow the best of the past (Leander's advice to his sons) and partly because he adapts to his world without being overwhelmed by it. Trained as a computer programmer, he accepts the computer error that transforms him into a public relations man but resists the apocalyptic mood that infects nearly everyone else in the novel. Unlike Melissa, whose brief illness leads her to cultivate "a ruthless greed for pleasure," Coverly's narrow escape from a hunter's arrow prompts him to "make something illustrious of his life." His computer analysis of John Keats's poetry leads to the creation of new poetry and the realization of a universal harmony underlying not only the poems but also life itself. His brother Moses, whom he has saved for the moment from debauchery, claims to see through the pasteboard mask of Christmas morning to "the nothingness of things." Coverly, on the other hand, celebrates the "dazzling" day by romancing his wife and sharing Christmas dinner with his late aunt's blind guests, "the raw material of human kindness." Coverly's vision, as well as St. Botolphs's brand of deco-

rum as "a guise or mode of hope," is certainly Cheever's own. Even so, that vision is tempered insofar as the author also shares Moses' pessimistic knowledge of decorum's other side: hypocrisy and despair.

BULLET PARK

The contrasting visions of Coverly and Moses reappear as Eliot Nailles and Paul Hammer, the main characters of Cheever's third novel, *Bullet Park.* Nailles is the book's comic and decidedly qualified hero. Like Cheever, he has belonged to a volunteer fire department, loves to saw wood with a chainsaw, feels a kinship with the natural world, and has a realistically balanced view of suburban living as being neither morally perfect nor inherently depraved. While both character and author are optimistic, however, the quality of their optimism differentiates them, for Nailles's is naïve and ludicrously shallow: "Nailles thought of pain and suffering as a principality lying somewhere beyond the legitimate borders of western Europe." Just as Cheever's story "The Death of Justina" satirizes a community determined to defeat death by means of zoning regulations, so *Bullet Park* satirizes Nailles's myopic optimism, which, like St. Paul's faith (Cheever quotes 2 Corinthians 11-12), is sorely tried during the course of the novel.

Beneath the appearance of respectability and comfort in *Bullet Park,* one finds the same unease that afflicts Talifer and Proxmire Manor. There is Mr. Heathcup, who interrupts his annual house painting to kill himself, claiming he could not stand "it" anymore. When Harry Shinglehouse is sucked under a passing express train and killed, only his shoe is found, an ironic memorial to a hollow life. Shaken by this and other reminders of mortality, Nailles turns to drugs. Drug addiction is one of Nailles's escapes; another is the devising of soothing explanations. When asked about his work—he sells Spang mouthwash—Nailles claims to be a chemist. When his son Tony suddenly becomes melancholy and withdraws, Bartleby-fashion, from the outside world, his father, like the lawyer in Herman Melville's tale, rationalizes his son's illness as mononucleosis rather than confront the actual cause: He tried to murder his son when Tony echoed his misgivings about the quality of his life. Neither the father's drugged optimism nor the expensive services of a doctor, a psychiatrist, and a specialist in somnambulatory phenomena effect Tony's cure. That is accomplished by the Swami Rutuola, "a spiritual cheer-leader" whose vision is not altogether different from Nailles's.

The climax of Nailles's dark night of the soul occurs when he defeats his secret antagonist, Hammer, who, as John Leonard suggests, may represent a part of Nailles's own personality. Hammer is the illegitimate son of a wealthy socialist (such ironies abound in Cheever's fiction) and his name-changing secretary. Unloved and rootless, Hammer is haunted by a vaguely defined canard. To escape it he turns to various pursuits: aimless travel, alcohol, fantasizing, psychoanalysis, translating the pessimistic poetry of Eugenio Montale, and locating a room with yellow walls where, he believes, he will finally be able to lead "a useful and illustrious life." He finds the room, as well as a beautiful wife, but both prove disappointing, and his search for "a useful and illustrious life" continues to elude him. At this point, Hammer adopts the messianic plan formulated by his dissatisfied, expatriate mother: to live quietly in a place like Bullet Park, to single out one of its representative men, and to "crucify him on the door of Christ's Church. . . . Nothing less than a crucifixion will wake that world!" Hammer fails in this, as in his other attempts, mainly for the same reasons he turned to it. One reason is his loneliness; feeling the need for a confidant, he explains his plan to the swami, who, of course, tells Nailles. The other is his having underestimated the depth of love, even in Bullet Park, where homes are associated not with the people who live in them but with real estate: number of bedrooms, number of baths, and market value.

This "simple" book about a father's love for his son greatly pleased its author. A number of reviewers, however, were troubled by the ending, which Guy Davenport called "shockingly inept." In a review that Cheever blames for turning the critical tide against the book, Benjamin DeMott charged that *Bullet Park* was broken-backed, its "parts tacked together." In retrospect, none of the charges appear merited. Cheever's narrative method and "arch"-like form (as he called it) are entirely consistent with his thematic purpose. In part 1, the third-person narration effectively establishes both the author's sympathy for and distance from his protagonist Nailles, whose confused state of mind is reflected in the confused chronology of this section. Part 2, Hammer's journal (the third-person narrator disappears after parenthetically remarking "Hammer wrote"), is the first-person monologue of a quietly desperate madman such as one finds in works by Edgar Allan Poe and Nikolai Gogol. The return to third-person narration in part 3 enables Cheever to use as centers of consciousness each of his two main characters. At the end of the novel, Tony is saved and returns to school, Hammer is sent to a hospital for the criminally insane, "and Nailles—drugged—went off to work and everything was as wonderful, wonderful, wonderful, wonderful as it had been." By undercutting Nailles's triumph without actually dismissing it, Cheever's ending resists those simplistic affirmations and negations that the rest of *Bullet Park* has explored.

FALCONER

The prison setting is the most obvious difference between *Falconer* and Cheever's previous fiction. The more significant difference, however, is the absence of any qualifying irony in its concluding pages. Never has the author's and his protagonist's affirmation been so completely self-assured as in this, Cheever's finest achievement.

Falconer is a story of metaphoric confinement and escape. The realism here serves a larger purpose than verisimilitude; Cheever sketches the essentials of the religious experience and shows how that experience is reflected in a man's retreat from the natural world or in his acceptance of a responsible place in it. The relationship between two brothers (as in the Wapshot books) or two brotherlike figures (*Bullet Park*) is given a violent twist in *Falconer*, where the main character, a forty-eight-year-old college professor named Ezekiel Farragut, has been convicted of fratricide. Farragut's murderous act, as well as his addictions to heroin and methadone, imply his retreat into self, a retreat that is not without some justification—a narcissistic wife, a father who wanted his unborn child aborted, a mother who was hardly maternal, a jealous brother, and the violence of war—but self-pity is the sin Cheever has most frequently assailed. Farragut's task, then, is "to leach self-pity out of his emotional spectrum," and to do this he must learn inside Falconer prison what he failed to learn outside it: how to love.

Farragut's first, humble step away from self-love is the affection he has for his cat, Bandit, whose cunning he must adopt if he is to survive his time in prison and those blows that defeat Moses and Melissa Wapshot. More important is Farragut's relationship with a fellow prisoner, Jody. Neither narcissistic nor regressive, this homosexual affair is plainly shown to further Farragut's movement away from self and, in that from Jody's hideout Farragut is given an expansive view of the world he has lost, it also furthers his movement toward that world and "the invisible potency of nature." Jody teaches the professorial Farragut an important lesson concerning the usefulness of one's environment and the active role that must be assumed in order to effect one's own salvation, one's escape from the metaphoric prison. When Jody escapes from Falconer, the loss of his lover at first leads Farragut back to lonely self-love; directed by another prisoner, the Cuckold, to whose depths of self-pity Farragut could easily descend, Farragut goes to the Valley, a dimly lit lavatory where the prisoners masturbate. Here Farragut has a revelation; he suddenly understands that the target of human sexuality ought not to be an iron trough but "the mysteriousness of the bonded spirit and the flesh."

His continuing escape from useless fantasizing, from nostalgic re-creation of the past, and from passivity causes him to become more self-assured and more interested in the present moment and how to make use of it in realizing his future. The riot at nearby Amana prison (based on the September, 1971, Attica uprising, during which Cheever was teaching at Sing Sing prison) shows that Farragut is actually freer than his jailers, but it is at this point that Farragut overreaches himself. In his view, the Amana riot signals the salvation of all the dispossessed, and to aid himself in hearing the "word," that is, the news reports, Farragut begins to build a contraband radio. He hopes to get a crystal from Bumpo, who had earlier said he would gladly give up his diamond to save someone. Bumpo refuses to give up the crystal, his reason obviously being his own selfishness, yet there is something ridiculous in Farragut's vague plan for sweeping social reform when his own salvation is still in doubt. In the aftermath of his and the rioters' failures, Farragut briefly slips back into self-regarding passivity, from which he is saved by a dying prisoner. In place of the ineffectual and wholly impersonal charity of his plan to save humankind, Farragut takes upon himself the hum-

bler and more truly charitable task of caring for a fellow human being. For the first time, Farragut, prompted by the dying man's question, faces up to the enormity of his crime, making clear to the reader, and perhaps to himself, that in murdering his brother he was unconsciously trying to destroy the worst part of his own personality. The demon exorcised, Farragut becomes spiritually free, a creature of the light.

The visible sign of this freedom is his escape from Falconer in Chicken Number Two's burial box. Borrowing freely from Alexandre Dumas, *père*'s *Le Comte de Monte-Cristo* (1844-1845; *The Count of Monte-Cristo*, 1846), Cheever treats the escape symbolically as a rebirth and a resurrection. The religious theme is effectively underscored by the novel's parable-like ending. Farragut meets a man who, although he has been evicted from his apartment because he is "alive and healthy," remains both cheerful and charitable, offering Farragut a coat, bus fare, and a place to stay. Miracles, it seems, do occur. The step from psychological retreat and spiritual darkness to freedom and light is not difficult to take, Cheever implies; it simply requires commitment and determination. As for the effect of this choice, which is as much Cheever's as Farragut's, that is summed up in the novel's final word: "rejoice."

Falconer recapitulates all of the major themes of Cheever's earlier fiction and, at the same time, evidences a number of significant changes in his art. One is the tendency toward greater narrative compression. Another, related to the first, is the inclusion of ancillary narratives, less as somewhat obtrusive sketches and more as integral parts of the main story line. The third—a more overt treatment of the religious theme—appears to have influenced the characterization, style, and structure of *Falconer*. Although Cheever always considered the novelist one who devotes himself to "enlarging" his peers rather than "diminishing" them, his two middle novels emphasize many of his characters' worst features. *Falconer* represents Cheever's return to the more certain affirmation of *The Wapshot Chronicle*; moreover, *Falconer* is Cheever's most lyrical and least bitingly humorous novel. The religious theme and the harmony it implies may also account for its being the most "novelistic" in structure of the four; this is not to say that Cheever had finally "outgrown" his earlier short-story style and mastered the more demanding form of the novel, for the structure of *The Wapshot Chronicle*, *The Wapshot Scandal*, and *Bullet Park* mirrors Cheever's vision of the 1950's and the 1960's. By the time he wrote *Falconer*, however, that sense of personal and cultural fragmentation no longer dominated his thinking, a change reflected in the relatively tight, more harmonious structure of his most affirmative work.

OH, WHAT A PARADISE IT SEEMS

Oh, What a Paradise It Seems is a slighter but in its own way no less triumphant work. The "bulky novel" that illness forced Cheever to cut short is, though brief, nevertheless remarkably generous in tone and spirit. It is also Cheever's most topical fiction yet strangely his least realistic—a self-regarding, even self-mocking fabulation, a *Walden* for the postmodern age, in which the irony falls as gently as the (acid) rain. Set in a future at once familiar (jogging, for example, has become popular) yet remote (highways with lanes in four digits)—a timeless present, as it were—the novel ends as it begins, by pretending to disclaim its own seriousness: "This is just a story to be read at night in an old house on a rainy night."

Oh, What a Paradise It Seems focuses on the "old but not yet infirm" Lemuel Sears. Twice a widower, Sears is financially well-off (he works for Computer Container Intrusion Systems, maker of "cerbical chips") and is as spiritually as he is sexually inclined. Sears's heart "leaps" in two not altogether different directions. One is toward Beasley's Pond, located near his daughter's home, where he ice-skates and in this way briefly satisfies his desire for fleetness, grace, pastoral innocence, and connectedness with the transcendental world of Emersonian Nature. When family connections (Mafia) and political corruption despoil the scene, however—transmogrifying pastoral pond into town dump—Beasley's Pond comes to symbolize for Sears not only imminent ecological disaster but, more important, the "spiritual vagrancy" of a "nomadic society" whose chief characteristics are "netherness" and "portability."

Sears's attraction to the pond parallels and in a way is offset by his physical attraction to the beautiful Renee Herndon, whose appetite for food and whose work as a real estate broker suggest that, despite the exoticism of her given name and the mysteriousness of her personal life, she represents everything that the prosaically named Beasley's, in its pristine state, does not. In his sexual pursuit of Renee, Sears is persistent to the point of clownishness. After numerous initial triumphs, Sears will eventually be rebuffed and come to see the waywardness of this attempt of his to attain what the pond, Sears's first wife, "the sainted Amelia," and even Renee in her own strange way symbolize, but not before a comical but nevertheless loving interlude with Eduardo, the elevator operator in Renee's apartment building, and a perfectly useless session with a psychiatrist named Palmer, "a homosexual spinster." The small but increasingly prominent part homosexuality plays in each of the novels reflects Cheever's ambivalence concerning his own bisexuality. Comically dismissed in the early works, it becomes in *Falconer* and *Oh, What a Paradise It Seems* viable but, as Cheever would say in a letter to one of his many male lovers, not ultimate.

As in Cheever's other fictions, the narrative here progresses along parallel fronts. Sears's dual lives, the sexual and the transcendental, become entwined in and simultaneously exist alongside those of Horace Chisholm, whose commitment to the environment evidences his longing for purity and human as well as spiritual attachment but also causes him to become estranged from his wife and family. Like Sears, he is also quixotic, which is to say both idealistic and absurd. Thanks to a number of those improbable plot complications that abound in Cheever's fiction, Chisholm, working for Sears to save Beasley's Pond, finds and returns a baby inadvertently left by the roadside after a family outing to the beach. The parents, the Logans, live next door to the Salazzos; Sammy Salazzo presides over the pond-turned-dump. Chisholm will be welcomed into the Logan family but eventually will be killed by the mob; an angry Betsey Logan will, however, complete his work, stopping the dumping, by threatening to poison the teriyaki sauce in the local Buy Brite supermarkets. (A by-product of her action is that her hated neighbors, the Salazzos, will move away.) Sears, in turn, will utilize the latest technology to restore the pond to its original state, thus redeeming himself as well.

Cheever's ending is self-consciously "happy"—aware of its own improbability. It is, like the architecture of Hitching Post Lane where the Logans and the

Salazzos live, "all happy ending—all greeting card." Cheever's satire is more than offset by his compassion, however—his recognition of and sympathy for the way-wardness of the continuing human search for both home and wholeness.

Robert A. Morace

OTHER MAJOR WORKS

SHORT FICTION: *The Way Some People Live*, 1943; *The Enormous Radio, and Other Stories*, 1953; "The Country Husband," 1954; *The Housebreaker of Shady Hill, and Other Stories*, 1958; *Some People, Places, and Things That Will Not Appear in My Next Novel*, 1961; *The Brigadier and the Golf Widow*, 1964; *The World of Apples*, 1973; *The Stories of John Cheever*, 1978; *Thirteen Uncollected Stories*, 1994.

TELEPLAY: *The Shady Hill Kidnapping*, 1982.

NONFICTION: *The Letters of John Cheever*, 1988 (Benjamin Cheever, editor); *The Journals of John Cheever*, 1991; *Glad Tidings, a Friendship in Letters: The Correspondence of John Cheever and John D. Weaver, 1945-1982*, 1993.

BIBLIOGRAPHY

Bosha, Francis J., ed. *The Critical Response to John Cheever*. Westport, Conn.: Greenwood Press, 1994. Collection presents representative criticism of all of Cheever's fiction, beginning with the earliest re-views in 1943, with individual chapters devoted to each of his works. Also includes several essays writ-ten for this collection and an interview with Cheever conducted a year before he died. Supplemented with bibliography and index.

Byrne, Michael D., Dale Salwak, and Paul David Seldis, eds. *Dragons and Martinis: The Skewed Realism of John Cheever*. San Bernardino, Calif.: Borgo Press, 1993. Collection of essays focuses on Cheever's style in his fiction. Includes bibliographical refer-ences and index.

Cheever, Susan. *Home Before Dark*. Boston: Hough-ton Mifflin, 1984. Memoir by Cheever's daughter fleshes out what was known previously about his troubled early years and provides an insider's look at his marital and other personal difficulties (alcohol-ism, illnesses, sexual desires). Suffers from lack of documentation and indexing. More valuable as a synthesis of previously published material than as a daughter's intimate revelations.

Coale, Samuel. *John Cheever*. New York: Frederick Ungar, 1977. Good introductory work includes a brief biography, two chapters on selected short stories, and individual chapters on Cheever's first four novels. Focuses on the development of Cheever's style, from realism to fantasy, and concern for moral issues.

Collins, Robert G., ed. *Critical Essays on John Cheever*. Boston: G. K. Hall, 1982. Reprints an excellent sam-pling of reviews, interviews, and early criticism. Also presents some previously unpublished pieces, among which the most useful are Collins's biocritical introduction, Dennis Coale's bibliographical supple-ment, and Samuel Coale's "Cheever and Hawthorne: The American Romancer's Art," arguably one of the most important critical essays on Cheever.

Donaldson, Scott. *John Cheever: A Biography*. New York: Random House, 1988. Scrupulously re-searched, interestingly written, and judiciously ar-gued biography presents Cheever as both author and private man. Fills in most of the areas in Cheever's biography that were previously unknown and dispels many of the biographical myths that Cheever himself encouraged. A sympathetic yet objective account.

_____, ed. *Conversations with John Cheever*. Jack-son: University Press of Mississippi, 1987. Until his final years a rather reticent man, Cheever granted rel-atively few interviews. The most important ones are reprinted here, along with the editor's thorough chro-nology and brief but useful introduction.

Meanor, Patrick. *John Cheever Revisited*. New York: Twayne, 1995. First book-length study of Cheever to make use of his journals and letters published in the late 1980's and early 1990's. Focuses on how Cheever created a mythopoeic world in his novels and stories. Includes three chapters analyzing the Wapshot novels, *Bullet Park*, *Oh, What a Paradise It Seems*, and *Falconer*.

Waldeland, Lynne. *John Cheever*. Boston: Twayne, 1979. Introductory volume lacks the thematic coher-ence of Samuel Coale's work (cited above), but it has greater breadth and evidences a greater awareness of previous critical commentary.

CHARLES WADDELL CHESNUTT

Born: Cleveland, Ohio; June 20, 1858
Died: Cleveland, Ohio; November 15, 1932

PRINCIPAL LONG FICTION

The House Behind the Cedars, 1900
The Marrow of Tradition, 1901
The Colonel's Dream, 1905
Mandy Oxendine, 1997 (wr. 1897)
Paul Marchand, F.M.C., 1998 (wr. 1921)
The Quarry, 1999 (wr. 1928)
A Business Career, 2005 (wr. 1898; Matthew
    Wilson and Marjan van Schaik, editors)
Evelyn's Husband, 2005 (wr. 1903; Wilson and
    van Schaik, editors)

OTHER LITERARY FORMS

Charles Waddell Chesnutt published two major collections of short stories: *The Conjure Woman* (1899) and *The Wife of His Youth, and Other Stories of the Color Line* (1899). Some critics view both of these collections as novels. William Andrews, in *The Literary Career of Charles W. Chesnutt* (1980), has explained the reasons some critics have asserted these two collections should be approached as novels. At the heart of *The Conjure Woman* is former slave Uncle Julius McAdoo, whose reminiscences in black dialect present a picture of plantation life in the Old South. His tales in turn center on old Aunt Peggy, the plantation conjure woman, and each has a moral, although the primary purpose of the stories is supposed to be entertainment. Another major character is a midwestern businessman who has come to North Carolina for his wife's health and who describes rural life in the South after the Civil War. The businessman's loosely connected descriptions serve as a frame for the tales of Uncle Julius, who is the businessman's coachman and unofficial family entertainer. In the stories in *The Conjure Woman*, Chesnutt follows the dialect/local-color tradition.

The stories in *The Wife of His Youth, and Other Stories of the Color Line* are issue-oriented. In them, Chesnutt is concerned with the special difficulties that those of mixed blood had in the pervasively racist environment in the United States after the Civil War. He asserted in a letter to his publisher, Houghton Mifflin, that while the stories are not unified by a character such as Uncle Julius in *The Conjure Woman*, they are unified by a theme—what Chesnutt calls "the color line." The collection is made up of various fictional case studies of social problems caused by the color consciousness of Americans. Some stories are addressed to blacks, some to those of mixed blood, and others to whites. Aside from having all the stories deal with the common subject of "the color line," Chesnutt attempted to unify the stories in another way: In all of them, he sought to revise the public's conception of blacks, to counter the stereotypes found in American fiction at that time.

Chesnutt also wrote a biography (*The Life of Frederick Douglass*, 1899), a play (*Mrs. Darcy's Daughter*), and a few poems. In addition, he wrote essays and speeches that were published in national magazines. Representing a dominant concern of his, these writings were primarily political and didactic; some titles include "A Plea for the American Negro," "The White and the Black," and "What Is a White Man?" His essay "The Disfranchisement of the Negro" appeared as part of a book titled *The Negro Problem* (1903), the subtitle of which announced that it was *A Series of Articles by Representative American Negroes of Today*; other contributors to the volume included such men as Booker T. Washington, W. E. B. Du Bois, T. Thomas Fortune, and Paul Laurence Dunbar.

In the early twenty-first century, new collections of Chesnutt's works appeared: *Stories, Novels, and Essays* (2002), and *The Portable Charles W. Chesnutt* (2008). Chesnutt's correspondence and many of his writings have not been published, however. Most of these unpublished works, as well as many of the published ones, are housed in the Charles Waddell Chesnutt Collection of the Erastus Milo Cravath Memorial Library, Fisk University, Nashville, Tennessee.

ACHIEVEMENTS

In 1872, when he was fourteen years old, Charles Waddell Chesnutt saw his first story published serially in a local black weekly. The publication of "The Goophered Grapevine" in August, 1887, in *The Atlantic Monthly* marked Chesnutt's first appearance in a major American literary magazine. Three more short stories followed: "Po' Sandy," "The Conjurer's Revenge," and "Dave's Neckliss." The publication of these four Uncle Julius stories were his entering wedge into the literary world—a world of which Chesnutt had long dreamed of being a part as a novelist. The two collections of his short stories, *The Conjure Woman* and *The Wife of His Youth*, were moderately successful. Containing virtually all his best writing during the period 1887-1899, these collections are ultimately the basis for Chesnutt's reputation as a short-story writer. With these stories, he moved up from literary apprenticeship to a respected position among American short-story writers. The stories must be viewed within the context of Chesnutt's total contribution to the traditional dialect/local-color story and the issue-oriented problem story.

In 1900, Chesnutt published his first novel, *The House Behind the Cedars*, which sold about two thousand copies in its first two months. His next two published novels (*The Marrow of Tradition* and *The Colonel's Dream*) were not as well received. Although he was honored as a writer by being asked to be a guest at Mark Twain's seventieth birthday party, Chesnutt retired from writing as a profession in 1905; no more of his creative work was published during the remainder of his lifetime.

Chesnutt achieved a great deal for his fellow African Americans in nonliterary areas. He was active politically and socially, and he wrote many controversial essays and speeches on the race issue. In 1913, he received an honorary LL.D. degree from Wilberforce University. In 1928, he was awarded the National Association for the Advancement of Colored People (NAACP) Spingarn Medal, an award given to African Americans who distinguish themselves in their fields. The medal honored Chesnutt for his "pioneer work as a literary artist depicting the life and struggles of Americans of Negro descent and for his long and useful career as a scholar, worker, and freeman of one of America's greatest cities [Cleveland]."

BIOGRAPHY

Charles Waddell Chesnutt was born on June 20, 1858, in Cleveland, Ohio. When he was nine years old,

his family moved to Fayetteville, North Carolina, where he spent his youth. Although he was of African American descent, his features barely distinguished him from Caucasians. He learned, however, that family blood was very important in determining a person's social and economic prospects.

Chesnutt's mother died in 1871, when he was thirteen years old. Two years later, he left school to take a teaching job, in order to supplement the family income. In 1878, he married Susan Perry, a fellow teacher and daughter of a well-to-do black barber in Fayetteville. He had begun teaching in 1877 at the new State Colored Normal School in Fayetteville, and in 1880 he became principal of that school.

On a job-hunting trip to Washington, D.C., in 1879, Chesnutt was unable to find work. He had been studying stenography and hoped to obtain a job on a newspaper. In 1883, he was able to begin a new career as a stenogra-

Charles Waddell Chesnutt. (Cleveland Public Library)

pher and reporter in New York City, and shortly afterward he moved to Cleveland, where he was first a clerk and then a legal stenographer. Two years later, he began studying law, and in 1887, he passed the Ohio bar examination with the highest grade in his group. He opened his own office as a court reporter in 1888.

Between 1887 and 1899, beginning with the publication of "The Goophered Grapevine" by *The Atlantic Monthly*, he achieved some success as a short-story writer. In 1899, when Houghton Mifflin published two collections of his short stories, he gave up his profitable business and began writing novels full time—something he had dreamed of doing for many years.

His first published novel, *The House Behind the Cedars*, had some commercial success, but the next, *The Marrow of Tradition*, did not. In 1901, two years after he had closed his stenographic firm, he reopened it. Deciding to write short stories once more in 1903 and 1904, he sent them to *The Atlantic Monthly*, where he had found success earlier, but only one, "Baxter's Procrustes," was accepted. His novel *The Colonel's Dream*, published in 1905, failed to attract the attention of the public. The public of the early 1900's was not ready for the controversial subject matter of Chesnutt's novels and later short stories or for the works' sympathetic treatment of black characters. Americans in general did not want to read literature that featured African Americans as the main characters, that presented their problems in a predominantly white world, and that were written with sympathy for blacks rather than for whites. Chesnutt retired from creative writing as a profession in 1905, and thereafter he published only nonfiction.

During the rest of his life, Chesnutt concentrated on managing his business affairs, on participating in civic affairs, and on working on behalf of African American causes. He was an active member of the Rowland Club, an exclusive male literary group in Cleveland, although at first he was denied membership because of his race. During the last twenty-seven years of his life, he managed to find time to travel in Europe and to help educate his three children. He was a member of the Cleveland Chamber of Commerce and the National Arts Club; he also helped establish the Playhouse Settlement (now Karamu House) in Cleveland.

Before 1905, Chesnutt had been politically and so-cially active in helping to advance the cause of black people, and he continued to be active throughout his life. In 1901, he contributed greatly to having William Hannibal Thomas's controversial work *The American Negro* withdrawn from circulation. That same year, he chaired the Committee on Colored Troops for the Thirty-fifth National Encampment of the Grand Army of the Republic in Cleveland. In 1904, he became a member of the Committee of Twelve, a group organized by Booker T. Washington, and in 1905, he was a member of the Cleveland Council of Sociology. He addressed the National Negro Committee, which later became the NAACP, and served as a member of that organization's general committee. He protested the showing of the film *The Birth of a Nation* (1915), which glorified the Ku Klux Klan, and, more important, he protested the treatment of black American soldiers. He participated in the first Amenia Conference, called by Joel Spingarn in 1916, and he was awarded the Spingarn Medal by the NAACP in 1928.

ANALYSIS

Charles Waddell Chesnutt wrote three novels that were published during his lifetime and several that were not published until much later. He was a much more skillful short-story writer than a novelist, and although he developed most of his novels from short stories, one of the novels is exceptional as a literary work. Those reading his novels should remember, however, that some of the matters for which Chesnutt is criticized today—thin, idealized characters and the use of plot manipulations such as foreshadowing and coincidence—were standard in the fiction of the late 1800's and were accepted by the readers of the day.

Chesnutt dreamed of being a novelist, and he believed that racial issues such as the problems of passing, miscegenation, and racial assimilation had to be addressed in serious fiction. He found, however, that if he tried to write novels that would be commercially successful, publishers would not accept them, and if he tried to write works that examined racial issues honestly and with sympathy for blacks, the public would not accept these topical but controversial novels.

Chesnutt is notable for being the first African American fiction writer to gain a reputation for examining honestly and in detail the racial problems of black people in the United States after the Civil War. Many Americans in the last part of the nineteenth century preferred to ignore the problems of African Americans and especially did not want to read works of fiction that displayed sympathetic attitudes toward blacks, such as those written by Chesnutt.

His most successful years as a novelist, if they can be called successful, were from 1900 to 1905. During that time, his three published novels appeared: *The House Behind the Cedars, The Marrow of Tradition*, and *The Colonel's Dream*. Chesnutt believed that the only way to change the attitudes of Caucasians toward African Americans was to do so slowly and through fiction that expressed ideas indirectly. He believed too that preaching was not art, yet with each novel he became more of a crusader. After giving up writing in 1901, he decided that he could help his people best by achieving in a field other than writing. Chesnutt may have been a victim, just as his characters sometimes are. The themes that he could present most effectively and that he felt compelled to present were ones that the public would not accept; thus he did not continue to write novels and so did not develop further as a literary artist.

Any study of Chesnutt's three published novels should begin with an understanding of the author's views concerning racial issues of the late 1800's and early 1900's. One of the racial situations with which he was most concerned was that of the mulatto. The mulatto shared many of the problems of the full black person but was also confronted with two additional issues—those of passing for white and miscegenation. (Chesnutt himself was a mulatto who appeared white and who considered trying to pass for white.) Those passing might achieve social, economic, and professional opportunities, but they also had to make emotional sacrifices by giving up their families and friends. Furthermore, they faced certain limitations; for example, they had to avoid becoming too well known or distinguished because their pasts might be revealed.

Chesnutt believed that Americans had an unnatural fear of miscegenation. Because of this fear, persons of mixed black and white blood were outcasts in society and were almost forced to try to pass for white to obtain the American Dream. Ironically, those forced into passing and marrying whites began again the miscegenation cycle that was so feared by whites. Anglo-Saxon racial purity was something that should not be preserved, Chesnutt believed. He asserted that intermingling and integration would improve humanity biologically, but, more important, such mixing would result in African Americans' gaining the rights they should have as human beings. Only through the elimination of laws against intermarriage and social interaction between the races would African Americans gain true social, economic, and political equality.

Chesnutt's three published novels are all problem novels that treat his characteristic theme of the effects of color consciousness in American life. The first one, a novel of miscegenation and passing, is written from the point of view of "the socially alienated, ambitious young mulatto," as William Andrews has put it. The second novel takes the viewpoint of "a conscientious Southern social critic," and in it, Chesnutt analyzes the political aspects and the caste structure of the small town in the South after the Civil War. The last one, in the vogue of the muckraking novel, is an economic problem novel told from the viewpoint of "the progressive northern reformer."

THE HOUSE BEHIND THE CEDARS

Between 1890 and 1899, Chesnutt greatly expanded and revised his short story "Rena Walden" until it became *The House Behind the Cedars*. He focused first on how color consciousness can destroy an interracial marriage and then on the predominant issue of whether a mulatto should cross the "color line." In March, 1899, he stated in a letter to Walter Hines Page that the Rena Walden story was the strong expression of a writer whose themes dealt primarily with the American color line. When he wrote to his daughters in the fall of 1900, he indicated that he hoped for "a howling success" from *The House Behind the Cedars*, "a strong race problem novel." The story of Rena Walden and her brother was the first in which the problems of Americans concealing their African heritage were studied with a detached and compassionate presentation of individuals on various sides of the issue.

The novel can be divided into two parts: Rena in white society, in which her brother is the major focus, and Rena in black society, in which she becomes the focus. The novel is set in Patesville, North Carolina, a few years after the Civil War. John Warwick, who has changed his name from Walden, has left Patesville and gone to South Carolina, where he has become a lawyer and plantation owner, acquiring wealth and position. He and his sister Rena are the children of a quadroon mother, Molly, and a white man who has died. John has returned to Patesville to help his beautiful sister escape the restrictions of color by teaching her how to pass for white. She is a success at the boarding school in South Carolina to which he takes her. Proof of her success in passing is seen when George Tryon, a good friend of John and a white, wants to marry Rena. Rena is not sure she should marry him, however, without telling him of her mixed blood. John and Rena indirectly discuss the pros and cons of passing and intermarriage. A series of coincidences leads to an unexpected meeting between George and Rena; he learns of her heritage, and the engagement is broken. Rena returns home to her mother and the house behind the cedars.

A chapter interlude that gives the Walden family history separates the first part of the novel from the second. John tries to persuade his sister to return to South Carolina with him or to take money and go to the North or the West, where she can pass for white and marry someone even better than George, but she refuses to leave Patesville. She has decided to accept her destiny and be of service to her people, whom she has rediscovered. After this point, the reader is told little more about John.

Rena meets Jeff Wain, an influential and prosperous mulatto from a rural county for which he is seeking a schoolteacher. Rena accepts the position, not realizing Jeff has a personal as well as a professional interest in her. Jeff is not as admirable a character as he first appears. As he pays Rena more and more attention, she becomes upset and repulsed. Once again, coincidence plays a part in the plot. George Tryon happens to learn of Rena's presence near a place he is visiting. When he sees her, he realizes that he loves her and that his love is stronger than his racial prejudice. The same day that George decides to declare his love to Rena, Jeff also decides to do so. Rena fears both of the men and leaves hastily for her mother's house behind the cedars. After Rena is overcome by exposure and fatigue, Frank Fowler, a childhood friend and a conscientious black workman, finds her and carries her to her home, where she dies.

Rena realizes before she dies that Frank loved her the best.

In his fiction before *The House Behind the Cedars*, Chesnutt did not directly condemn passing and miscegenation, but neither did he directly call for them. Primarily, he wanted the public to be aware of the issues and to feel sympathy for those of mixed blood. In this novel, he makes passing and miscegenation acts deliberately chosen by mature African Americans. Such choices were justified because they were the only means by which blacks could gain and enjoy the social, economic, and political rights due them as citizens of the United States.

Rather than lecturing, Chesnutt seeks to lead his readers to share his perspective. He delays revealing that John and Rena are mulattoes. To create sympathy for them first, he presents them simply as persons of humble origins who are attempting to achieve prosperity and happiness. Chesnutt passes John and Rena for white with the reader before he lets the reader know that they are mulattoes who have chosen or will deliberately choose to pass for white.

John Walden is the first black character in American fiction to decide to pass for white and, at the same time, to feel that his decision is legally and morally justified. Believing that the color of his skin tells him that he is white, he has no psychological problems concerning his choice to pass. He is not a stereotype. Intelligent and industrious, he patiently trains himself so that he can achieve the American Dream. At the beginning of the novel, the reader learns that he has become a prosperous lawyer and plantation owner after leaving Patesville; in the second part of the novel, after he has not been successful in helping Rena pass for white, he returns to South Carolina to regain his position.

The characters are not fully developed; they remain stick figures, although Chesnutt is partially successful in creating human interest for them. While Chesnutt attempts to create pity for her, Rena is simply a victim who accepts her fate, like other antiassimilationist mulattoes of the time. Another character, Dr. Green, is no more than a vehicle to present the traditional southern viewpoint. Two figures, Molly Walden and George Tryon, retain some individuality. Molly, as an unprotected free black woman in the slave South, is a product of her environment. With the circumstances that she faces, she can do little other than be the kept mistress of the white plantation owner, who has died but left her the house behind the cedars. Chesnutt does not want the reader to feel contempt for her or to be repulsed by her actions; her position is rendered dispassionately. George Tryon, on the other hand, undergoes great emotional upheaval and has a change of view that is probably meant to be instructive. He is tied to the traditional code of the southern gentleman but is not deluded about his prerogatives as a southern aristocrat. Rather, he is meant to be the best of the new South. His realization that he loves Rena and that her racial heritage is not important comes too late; she dies before he is able to do anything about it. He does not blame her for passing, and Chesnutt expects the reader not to blame her.

In *The House Behind the Cedars*, Chesnutt tries to present a mulatto that is not a prop or stereotype, one who deserves interest and sympathy apart from his position on the miscegenation issue. Furthermore, he treats the theme of color consciousness in post-Civil War American life honestly, in contrast to the sentimentalizing of other authors of the time. This novel, the one for which Chesnutt will be best remembered, should be read for its historical place in American literature.

THE MARROW OF TRADITION

Immediately after finishing *The House Behind the Cedars*, Chesnutt began working on his next novel. Events in Wilmington, North Carolina, gave him a race problem for the novel. In November, 1898, during city elections, a bloody race riot had taken place in which more than twenty-five black persons were killed, after which white supremacists took over the town government. Chesnutt followed events in the city after this incident. He learned graphic details when a local Wilmington physician visited him in Cleveland and described what he had seen when the violence was at its peak. Chesnutt also sought information from other friends in the area, and, in 1901, he went on a fact-finding trip to Wilmington and Fayetteville.

The Marrow of Tradition is the story of two families: The Carterets stand for the aristocracy of the "new South," with its pride and prejudice, and the Millers, who are of mixed blood, represent the qualities of the new black. The lives of the families are intertwined because the wives are half sisters. Janet Miller, however,

has been cheated of her inheritance by Olivia Carteret, and Olivia constantly struggles with the problem of accepting Janet as her rightful sister.

The novel's study of white supremacist politics in a small southern town after the Civil War is more relevant to the problems encountered by the husbands than to those facing the wives. Dr. Adam Miller is a brilliant young surgeon denied opportunity in his hometown of Wellington (Wilmington, North Carolina). Major Philip Carteret, editor of the town's newspaper, seeks to seat a white supremacist regime in the local government. If he is successful, Adam Miller's position will be even more intolerable than it has been.

At the end of the novel, Major Carteret stirs up a riot during which Dr. Miller's son is killed. Immediately after the death of the Millers' child, the son of the Carterets becomes ill, and Adam Miller is the only person who can perform the surgery necessary to save the child's life. At first Miller refuses, but after Olivia Carteret humbles herself before her half sister and pleads with her to help save the Carterets' son, Janet Miller convinces her husband to change his mind and operate. The child is saved.

The Marrow of Tradition was too controversial a novel for the public when it was published. Americans were not ready for the subject of white supremacist politics and the political injustice existing in the South. Chesnutt himself was concerned that the novel approached fanaticism. He believed that it might not be wise for him to speak so plainly concerning such matters if he hoped to succeed as a fiction writer.

THE COLONEL'S DREAM

Like Chesnutt's previous two novels, *The Colonel's Dream* seems to have come from a long story that became a novel; however, no manuscript evidence for such a history exists. This novel deals with the economic status quo in the South, where caste and class prejudice prevented the rise of nonwhites. Muckraking novels were popular at this time, but none had been published about the new South. Chesnutt tends to become didactic in this novel, and he relies on overused novelistic machinery such as melodramatic subplots that involve interracial love and a lost inheritance. The novel is almost an economic parable.

The main character in the novel is Colonel Henry French, who, though born and reared in the South, has become a successful businessman in the North. His wife has died, and he has returned to Clarendon, North Carolina, where he hopes his son's health will improve. During the first part of the book, Colonel French, who is respected and admired by the townspeople, successfully reenters southern life. Although he is a white moderate, he comes to believe that he can unite the races into one society. He is especially concerned with improving the economic situation of African Americans. As he and the people of Clarendon become further and further apart in their understanding of the situation, he finds all of his efforts nullified by racial bigotry, and he must leave in failure. The novel was not successful commercially and is not very satisfying as a work of literature. After the failure of *The Colonel's Dream*, Chesnutt decided to stop writing novels and devoted himself to helping his people in other ways.

None of Chesnutt's three published novels was widely popular with the reading public of the early twentieth century, although *The House Behind the Cedars* enjoyed a modest commercial success. Furthermore, none of the novels can be considered successful artistic endeavors. Chesnutt sought to reveal his views slowly and indirectly so as to lead his readers to the feelings he wanted them to have. Too often, however, his "message" dominates, and he is didactic despite his intentions. His characters are not fully developed, even though Chesnutt attempts to present characters, especially mulattoes and African Americans, who are not stereotypes. It may be his strong concern with conveying his views and instructing his readers that prevents his characters from achieving depth. All of these novels are important, however, because Chesnutt was one of the first American novelists to create black characters who were not stereotypes and to deal honestly with racial issues that most Americans of the time preferred to ignore.

Sherry G. Southard

OTHER MAJOR WORKS

SHORT FICTION: *The Conjure Woman*, 1899; *The Wife of His Youth, and Other Stories of the Color Line*, 1899.

NONFICTION: *The Life of Frederick Douglass*, 1899; *The Journals of Charles W. Chesnutt*, 1993; *"To Be an Author": The Letters of Charles W. Chesnutt, 1889-*

1905, 1997; *Charles W. Chesnutt: Essays and Speeches*, 1999; *Selected Writings*, 2001 (SallyAnn H. Ferguson, editor); *An Exemplary Citizen: Letters of Charles W. Chesnutt, 1906-1932*, 2002.

MISCELLANEOUS: *Stories, Novels, and Essays*, 2002; *The Portable Charles W. Chesnutt*, 2008.

BIBLIOGRAPHY

Chesnutt, Charles Waddell. *"To Be an Author": Letters of Charles W. Chesnutt, 1889-1905*. Edited by Joseph R. McElrath, Jr., and Robert C. Leitz III. Princeton, N.J.: Princeton University Press, 1997. Collection of letters is organized into sections in a manner particularly useful to students of Chestnutt's fiction and his career development: "Cable's Protégé in 1889-1891," "A Dream Deferred, 1891-1896," "Page's Protégé in 1897-1899," "The Professional Novelist of 1899-1902," "Discontent in 1903-1904," "The Quest Renewed, 1904-1905." Includes an informative introduction and a detailed index.

Heermance, Noel. *Charles Chesnutt: America's First Great Black Novelist*. Hamden, Conn.: Archon Books, 1974. Provides a good introduction to Chesnutt's life and to the themes of his fiction. Discusses Chesnutt's novels, short fiction, and other writings.

Keller, Frances Richardson. *An American Crusade: The Life of Charles Waddell Chesnutt*. Provo, Utah: Brigham Young University Press, 1978. One of the most helpful and important biographical resources on Chesnutt. Describes how Chesnutt refused to accept the segregation of his time, choosing to participate in both the black and white worlds.

McElrath, Joseph R., Jr., ed. *Critical Essays on Charles W. Chesnutt*. New York: G. K. Hall, 1999. Broad compilation of materials includes reviews of Chesnutt's works that appeared at the time of their initial publication as well as essays and articles, written between 1905 and 1997, analyzing his writings. Also contains overviews of his work and discussions of individual novels, including *The Colonel's Dream* and *The House Behind the Cedars*.

McWilliams, Dean. *Charles W. Chesnutt and the Fictions of Race*. Athens: University of Georgia Press, 2002. Examines Chesnutt's novels and short stories, describing how his fiction changed Americans' assumptions about race. Devotes separate chapters to analysis of the novels *The House Behind the Cedars*, *The Marrow of Tradition*, *The Colonel's Dream*, *The Quarry*, and *Mandy Oxendine*.

Pickens, Ernestine Williams. *Charles W. Chesnutt and the Progressive Movement*. New York: Pace University Press, 1994. Provides both historical and literary analysis of two of Chesnutt's novels: *The Marrow of Tradition* and *The Colonel's Dream*. Chronicles Chesnutt's involvement in the Progressive movement and points out elements of the movement's philosophy in these works.

Render, Sylvia. *Charles W. Chesnutt*. Boston: Twayne, 1980. Good general introduction to the life and writing of Chesnutt. Discusses Chesnutt's major concerns with narrative technique, social justice, and the place of the African American in U.S. society.

Simmons, Ryan. *Chesnutt and Realism: A Study of the Novels*. Tuscaloosa: University of Alabama Press, 2006. Defines Chesnutt as a realist and describes how he was influenced by the literary realist movement. Points out elements of literary realism in Chesnutt's novels and explains how Chesnutt used the techniques and concepts of realism to depict race in his works.

Wilson, Matthew. *Whiteness in the Novels of Charles W. Chesnutt*. Jackson: University Press of Mississippi, 2004. Examines Chesnutt's novels with the aim of understanding the peculiar problems the African American author confronted in writing books for a predominantly white readership. Analyzes how Chesnutt constructed novels that appealed to this white audience while also examining racial issues that were not traditionally addressed in mainstream American fiction.

G. K. CHESTERTON

Born: London, England; May 29, 1874
Died: Beaconsfield, Buckinghamshire, England;
June 14, 1936
Also known as: Gilbert Keith Chesterton

PRINCIPAL LONG FICTION

The Napoleon of Notting Hill, 1904
The Man Who Was Thursday: A Nightmare, 1908
The Ball and the Cross, 1909
The Innocence of Father Brown, 1911
Manalive, 1912
The Flying Inn, 1914
The Wisdom of Father Brown, 1914
The Incredulity of Father Brown, 1926
The Return of Don Quixote, 1926
The Secret of Father Brown, 1927
The Floating Admiral, 1931 (with others)
The Scandal of Father Brown, 1935
Basil Howe: A Story of Young Love, 2001
    (wr. 1894)

OTHER LITERARY FORMS

G. K. Chesterton was a prolific writer, and in addition to novels he produced works in numerous other genres. Throughout his life he wrote poetry; his first two published books were poetical works. He also produced short fiction, especially detective stories. In addition, he wrote plays, but he was not always comfortable in the medium of drama, as he was at heart an essayist. He published a large number of nonfiction works in such areas as autobiography, biography, essays, history, and literary criticism.

ACHIEVEMENTS

Among the primary achievements of G. K. Chesterton's long writing career are the wide range of subjects he wrote about, the large number of genres he employed, and the sheer volume of publications he produced. Chesterton was primarily a journalist and essayist who wrote articles, book reviews, and essays for newspapers and periodicals. In addition to these pieces, however, he also wrote poetry, biographies, plays, history, and literary criticism as well as novels and short stories.

In his approach to fiction Chesterton rejected the "modern realistic short story" and the realistic novel. Instead, in the first instance, he turned to the detective short story and wrote extensively on its legitimacy as a literary art form. Chesterton himself helped to develop the definition of the detective story; he contended that it was the sole popular literary structure expressing "some sense of the poetry of modern life," and he helped to popularize detective fiction with his fifty-one Father Brown stories and short novels.

As a novelist, Chesterton argued that "sensational novels are the most moral part of modern fiction." He liked tales about death, secret groups, theft, adventure, and fantasy. There was no genre in his day that embraced his ideas, and so he crafted his own literary structure, the "fantastic novel." In his novels Chesterton stressed such themes and issues as family, science versus religion, moral and political integrity, and local patriotism versus empire building. He also introduced such subthemes as the common man, nature, and womanhood. Above all, Chesterton's novels illustrate his "love of ideas."

BIOGRAPHY

Gilbert Keith Chesterton was born in London on May 29, 1874, to a middle-class family. His father, Edward, was an estate agent who liked literature and art, and his mother, Marie, was the daughter of a Wesleyan lay preacher. Both parents were Unitarians, but they baptized their son in the Anglican Church. Chesterton attended the Colet Court preparatory school and then, in 1887, went to St. Paul's School. His academic record was not good, but he finally began to demonstrate literary capability as a member of the Junior Debating Club, which he and some of his fellow students established during the summer of 1890. Two years later he won the Milton Prize for his poem "St. Francis Xavier."

From 1892 to 1895, Chesterton attended the Slade School to study art and took some courses in French, English, and Latin at University College, London. He did not do well, however, except in his English courses, and he left the Slade School in 1895 without taking a degree. For the next six years he worked in publishing houses, reading authors' manuscripts, and at night he did his own

writing. In 1900 his first two books appeared, *Greybeards at Play: Literature and Art for Old Gentlemen—Rhymes and Sketches* and *The Wild Knight, and Other Poems*, both works of poetry. The next year he began to submit articles regularly to the *Speaker* and the *Daily News* and thus started a career as a journalist that was to last until his death. He became known for his opposition to the Boer War and his support of small nations.

In 1901 Chesterton married Frances Blogg after a courtship of five years. The couple lived first in London, and then in 1909 they moved to Beaconsfield, forty miles outside London. They had no offspring, but they enjoyed the company of the children of their friends, relatives, and neighbors.

In 1904 Chesterton's first novel, *The Napoleon of Notting Hill*, was published, and by 1914 he had written five more novels and numerous other works, including biographies (*Robert Browning*, 1903; *Charles Dickens: A Critical Study*, 1906), as well as *Heretics* (1905), which criticized what he saw as the mistakes of some contemporary writers, *Orthodoxy* (1908), a defense and support of Christianity, and a study of his friend and disputant, *George Bernard Shaw* (1909). In 1911 the first of his volumes of detective stories appeared, featuring a Catholic priest, Father Brown, as the sleuth.

Chesterton wrote his best work prior to 1914; in November of that year he became gravely ill with a form of dropsy, and it was not until June of the following year that he recovered. During the years after World War I, he traveled, visiting Palestine, the United States, Poland, and Italy. In 1922 he became a Roman Catholic, a faith that had attracted him for some time, as is reflected in his writing. The most notable nonfiction works of his later years are *The Everlasting Man* (1925) and another biography, *St. Thomas Aquinas* (1933). Chesterton's health declined during the first half of 1936, and on June 14 he died in Beaconsfield.

ANALYSIS

Between 1904 and 1927, G. K. Chesterton wrote six full-length novels, not including the long Father Brown mysteries. All of them stressed the sensational, and they illustrated life as a fight and a battle. Chesterton thought that literature should portray life as perilous rather than as something listless. Tales of death, robbery, and secret

G. K. Chesterton. (Library of Congress)

"political fables, parables, and allegories or more simply and conveniently . . . novels."

In Chesterton's novels, the state of bachelorhood predominates; this situation is appropriate, since this status is a fundamental element of adventure. Moreover, women rarely appear in any significant roles in his long fiction. There is no female character in his first novel, *The Napoleon of Notting Hill*, and the woman in *The Man Who Was Thursday* is a passing character. In *The Ball and the Cross* and *The Flying Inn*, women are minor figures, but they do play significant roles in *Manalive* and *The Return of Don Quixote*, works that are more involved with the family and society.

The weakest of Chesterton's nondetective novels are perhaps *Manalive*, published in 1912, and *The Return of Don Quixote*, which appeared in 1927. In *The Return of Don Quixote*, Chesterton concludes that the only good future for England involves "a remarriage" of the country with the Catholic Church, as was the case in the Middle Ages. The first three of Chesterton's novels, published from 1904 to 1909, are widely considered his best.

THE NAPOLEON OF NOTTING HILL

The Napoleon of Notting Hill is Chesterton's first novel. The first two chapters are distinct from the main plot, the first being an essay on prophecy showing the author working in a genre that was always congenial to him. The next chapter concerns a luncheon discussion among three government clerks and the former president of Nicaragua, Juan del Fuego. The content of their talk brings out one of the main themes of the novel, "the sanctity of small nations," a concept dear to Chesterton that stemmed from his opposition to the Boer War.

The subsequent death of del Fuego eliminates him from the work, but one of the three clerks, Auberon Quin, a zany individual and joker, is subsequently selected king in the futuristic utopian England of 1984, where a mild political despotism exists. The monarch is chosen by lot. Once crowned as king, Quin reorganizes the sections of London into separate municipalities and thus re-creates the smallness of medieval cities, complete with costumes and heraldry. Quin then encounters

groups interested him, and he did not think that what he called the "tea table twaddle" type of novels approached the status of significant art. The sensational story "was the moral part of fiction."

Fantasy was an important part of Chesterton's novels, and the methodology used in his long fiction emphasized adventure, suspense, fantasy, characterization, satire, narrative technique, and humor. He needed a medium to employ these techniques, so he produced the "fantastic novel." Fanstasy also involves ideas, and in all Chesterton's novels ideas are a central, indispensable feature.

Chesterton's novels served as vehicles for the dissemination of whatever his political and social ideas were at the time, and to this extent they were propagandistic. His critics have had difficulty in deciding the merits of his various writings in terms of separating propaganda from literary art. Often Chesterton used allegory as a device for conveying his controversial ideas. Critic Ian Boyd has called Chesterton's works of long fiction

Adam Wayne, first as a youth and then as the serious-minded provost of Notting Hill, one of the municipalities; Wayne has embraced the king's "Charter of Cities" wholeheartedly.

Wayne, however, much to the dismay of the provosts of other London municipalities, refuses to give up a street in his domain, Pump Street, which contains several shops, so that a thoroughfare connecting three boroughs can be built. The result is a war, which Wayne wins by encouraging the patriotism of Pump Street residents and by following excellent strategy, despite being outnumbered by the opposing forces. Quin with his "Charter of Cities" and Wayne in his defense of Notting Hill both illustrate Chesterton's small-nation theme. The concluding chapters of the novel concern London twenty years later, when the powerful and dominant Notting Hill has become corrupt; the corruption causes a revolt of subject municipalities. Wayne fights in the second war but realizes that there is no longer a noble cause involved. Conflict in the novel lies in the confrontation between Wayne and Quin, the fanatic and the joker. Wayne's opponents had accused him of being mad, but Quin asserts that the only sane individuals are himself and Wayne. The last chapter is a discussion between the two men, now dead and in the afterlife, in which Wayne argues that in order to be complete both men needed each other, because the joker was without seriousness and the fanatic lacked laughter.

THE MAN WHO WAS THURSDAY

Chesterton's second novel, *The Man Who Was Thursday*, has been described by some critics as his best. Ronald Knox called it "an extraordinary book written as if the publisher had commissioned him to write something rather like the *Pilgrim's Progress* in the style of the *Pickwick Papers*." Chesterton himself called it a protest against the pessimism of the 1880's, and this protest gives rise to one of two allegories in the novel, a personal one. The other is a public or political allegory concerning an individual's clash with a world conspiracy that does not really exist. The story concerns a young poet, Gabriel Syme, who, wishing to fight a gigantic conspiracy supposedly being plotted by anarchists, joins the police and becomes a member of an undercover squad of detectives.

As a result of a bit of trickery and luck, he becomes a member of the top anarchist council, called the Council of Seven Days because each member has the name of a day of the week. Syme's name is Thursday. The council's leader, named Sunday, is an ambiguous figure. While working to stop a bombing planned for Paris, Thursday discovers that, except for Sunday, all his fellow council members are undercover police detectives. Each had been interviewed by a figure whom nobody saw in a dark room at Scotland Yard. By the conclusion of the novel, it is revealed that Sunday is both the head of the detectives and the leader of the anarchists. Some critics have seemed to think that Chesterton is condoning evil in the novel, but he himself asserted that he is questioning in the novel whether everything is evil and whether one can find good in the pessimism of the age.

THE BALL AND THE CROSS

A review published a year after the publication of *The Ball and the Cross* stated that the novel is about two individuals dueling over "the most vital problem in the world, the truth of Christianity." This work definitely deals with religion and the nature of good and evil, subjects either ignored or addressed ambiguously in Chesterton's first two novels. The book opens with Professor Lucifer depositing a captured Bulgarian monk, Michael, from a flying machine atop the cross and ball of St. Paul's Cathedral in London.

The plot continues with a confrontation between a Catholic highland Scot, Evan McIan, and another Scot, John Turnbull, an atheist and publisher of works on atheism. The two fight a duel over what McIan perceives as an insult to the Virgin Mary. The duelists are constantly interrupted, however; they go through a series of adventures and ultimately become friends. The book ends with the two men in an insane asylum, which is set on fire by a satanic figure. The inmates are led out by a monk, Michael, who had been a prisoner there. Ultimately Turnbull becomes a Christian. The novel contains much symbolism and many allegories. The ball on St. Paul's dome, for example, is the rational and independent world, while the cross represents religion. Martin Gardner views the work as reflecting the clash between St. Augustine's City of God, which in Chesterton's view is the Catholic Church, and the City of Man, which is dominated by Satan. The novel also attacks modern science and accuses modern culture of being "lukewarm."

Allan Nelson

OTHER MAJOR WORKS

SHORT FICTION: *The Tremendous Adventures of Major Brown*, 1903; *The Club of Queer Trades*, 1905; *The Perishing of the Pendragons*, 1914; *The Man Who Knew Too Much, and Other Stories*, 1922; *Tales of the Long Bow*, 1925; *Stories*, 1928; *The Sword of Wood*, 1928; *The Moderate Murder and the Honest Quack*, 1929; *The Poet and the Lunatics: Episodes in the Life of Gabriel Gale*, 1929; *The Ecstatic Thief*, 1930; *Four Faultless Felons*, 1930; *The Paradoxes of Mr. Pond*, 1936; *The Vampire of the Village*, 1947.

PLAYS: *Magic: A Fantastic Comedy*, pr. 1913; *The Judgment of Dr. Johnson*, pb. 1927; *The Surprise*, pb. 1953.

POETRY: *Greybeards at Play: Literature and Art for Old Gentlemen—Rhymes and Sketches*, 1900; *The Wild Knight, and Other Poems*, 1900 (revised 1914); *The Ballad of the White Horse*, 1911; *A Poem*, 1915; *Poems*, 1915; *Wine, Water, and Song*, 1915; *Old King Cole*, 1920; *The Ballad of St. Barbara, and Other Verses*, 1922; *Poems*, 1925; *The Queen of Seven Swords*, 1926; *Gloria in Profundis*, 1927; *Ubi Ecclesia*, 1929; *The Grave of Arthur*, 1930.

NONFICTION: *The Defendant*, 1901; *Robert Louis Stevenson*, 1902 (with W. Robertson Nicoll); *Thomas Carlyle*, 1902; *Twelve Types*, 1902 (revised as *Varied Types*; 1903; also known as *Simplicity and Tolstoy*); *Charles Dickens*, 1903 (with F. G. Kitton); *Leo Tolstoy*, 1903 (with G. H. Perris and Edward Garnett); *Robert Browning*, 1903; *Tennyson*, 1903 (with Richard Garnett); *Thackeray*, 1903 (with Lewis Melville); *G. F. Watts*, 1904; *Heretics*, 1905; *Charles Dickens: A Critical Study*, 1906; *All Things Considered*, 1908; *Orthodoxy*, 1908; *George Bernard Shaw*, 1909 (revised 1935); *Tremendous Trifles*, 1909; *Alarms and Discursions*, 1910; *The Ultimate Lie*, 1910; *What's Wrong with the World*, 1910; *William Blake*, 1910; *Appreciations and Criticisms of the Works of Charles Dickens*, 1911; *A Defence of Nonsense, and Other Essays*, 1911; *The Future of Religion: Mr. G. K. Chesterton's Reply to Mr. Bernard Shaw*, 1911; *The Conversion of an Anarchist*, 1912; *A Miscellany of Men*, 1912; *Thoughts from Chesterton*, 1913; *The Victorian Age in Literature*, 1913; *The Barbarism of Berlin*, 1914; *London*, 1914 (with Alvin Langdon Coburn); *Prussian Versus Belgian Culture*, 1914; *The Crimes of England*, 1915; *Letters to an Old Garibaldian*, 1915; *The So-Called Belgian Bargain*, 1915; *Divorce Versus Democracy*, 1916; *A Shilling for My Thoughts*, 1916; *Temperance and the Great Alliance*, 1916; *Lord Kitchener*, 1917; *A Short History of England*, 1917; *Utopia of Usurers, and Other Essays*, 1917; *How to Help Annexation*, 1918; *Charles Dickens Fifty Years After*, 1920; *Irish Impressions*, 1920; *The New Jerusalem*, 1920; *The Superstition of Divorce*, 1920; *The Uses of Diversity*, 1920; *Eugenics and Other Evils*, 1922; *What I Saw in America*, 1922; *Fancies Versus Fads*, 1923; *St. Francis of Assisi*, 1923; *The End of the Roman Road: A Pageant of Wayfarers*, 1924; *The Superstitions of the Sceptic*, 1924; *The Everlasting Man*, 1925; *William Cobbett*, 1925; *The Catholic Church and Conversion*, 1926; *A Gleaming Cohort, Being from the Words of G. K. Chesterton*, 1926; *The Outline of Sanity*, 1926; *Culture and the Coming Peril*, 1927; *Robert Louis Stevenson*, 1927; *Social Reform Versus Birth Control*, 1927; *Do We Agree? A Debate*, 1928 (with George Bernard Shaw); *Generally Speaking*, 1928 (essays); *G. K. C. as M. C., Being a Collection of Thirty-seven Introductions*, 1929; *The Thing*, 1929; *At the Sign of the World's End*, 1930; *Come to Think of It*, 1930; *The Resurrection of Rome*, 1930; *The Turkey and the Turk*, 1930; *All Is Grist*, 1931; *Is There a Return to Religion?*, 1931 (with E. Haldeman-Julius); *Chaucer*, 1932; *Christendom in Dublin*, 1932; *Sidelights on New London and Newer York, and Other Essays*, 1932; *All I Survey*, 1933; *G. K. Chesterton*, 1933 (also known as *Running After One's Hat, and Other Whimsies*); *St. Thomas Aquinas*, 1933; *Avowals and Denials*, 1934; *Explaining the English*, 1935; *The Well and the Shallows*, 1935; *As I Was Saying*, 1936; *Autobiography*, 1936; *The Man Who Was Chesterton*, 1937; *The End of the Armistice*, 1940; *The Common Man*, 1950; *The Glass Walking-Stick, and Other Essays from the "Illustrated London News," 1905-1936*, 1955; *Lunacy and Letters*, 1958; *Where All Roads Lead*, 1961; *The Man Who Was Orthodox: A Selection from the Uncollected Writings of G. K. Chesterton*, 1963; *The Spice of Life, and Other Essays*, 1964; *Chesterton on Shakespeare*, 1971.

EDITED TEXTS: *Thackeray*, 1909; *Samuel Johnson*, 1911 (with Alice Meynell); *Essays by Divers Hands*, 1926.

MISCELLANEOUS: *Stories, Essays, and Poems*, 1935; *The Coloured Lands*, 1938; *The Collected Works of G. K. Chesterton*, 1986-1999 (35 volumes).

BIBLIOGRAPHY

Ahlquist, Dale. *G. K. Chesterton: The Apostle of Common Sense*. San Francisco, Calif.: Ignatius Press, 2003. Provides an introductory overview of Chesterton's life and work designed for general readers, with analyses of some of Chesterton's novels, including books in the Father Brown series. Designed to complement a television series of the same title created by Ahlquist, president of the American Chesterton Society.

Bloom, Harold, ed. *G. K. Chesterton*. New York: Chelsea House, 2006. Collection of essays analyzes various aspects of Chesterton's work, including the author's view of the grotesque and "terror and play" in his imagination. Editor's introduction provides an overview to Chesterton's life and work.

Boyd, Ian. *The Novels of G. K. Chesterton: A Study in Art and Propaganda*. New York: Barnes & Noble Books, 1975. Good study examines Chesterton's major novels as well as his collections of short stories. Discusses the novels chronologically, with a chapter each about novels in his early years, pre-World War I, postwar, and later years.

Clipper, Lawrence J. *G. K. Chesterton*. New York: Twayne, 1974. Useful introduction to the works of Chesterton does a fine job of describing the recurring themes in his fictional and nonfictional writings. Includes informative analysis also of Chesterton's poetry and literary criticism. Contains an excellent annotated bibliography.

Coates, John D. *G. K. Chesterton as Controversialist, Essayist, Novelist, and Critic*. Lewiston, N.Y.: Edwin Mellen Press, 2002. Refutes Chesterton's reputation as a minor writer, maintaining that his detective novels remain important and relevant works. Places Chesterton's fiction within the context of modernism and the Edwardian novel of ideas.

Conlon, D. J., ed. *Chesterton: A Half Century of Views*. New York: Oxford University Press, 1987. Contains numerous short essays on Chesterton published during the first fifty years after his death. The wide diversity of positive critical reactions shows that not only his popular fiction but also his writings on literature and religion continue to fascinate readers.

Hollis, Christopher. *The Mind of Chesterton*. Coral Gables, Fla.: University of Miami Press, 1970. Especially thoughtful study explores above all Chesterton's evolution as a writer before his conversion to Catholicism in 1922. Final chapter, titled "Chesterton and His Survival," explains why Chesterton's work continues to fascinate readers who do not share his religious beliefs.

Lauer, Quentin. *G. K. Chesterton: Philosopher Without Portfolio*. New York: Fordham University Press, 1988. Thought-provoking study addresses Chesterton's philosophical reflections on the uses and limitations of reason, Christian humanism, religious tolerance, and moral values.

Pearce, Joseph. *Wisdom and Innocence: A Life of G. K. Chesterton*. San Francisco, Calif.: Ignatius Press, 1996. Scholarly, well-written biography examines Chesterton's life and provides interesting analysis of many quotations from his works.

Ward, Maisie. *Gilbert Keith Chesterton*. New York: Sheed & Ward, 1943. Well-researched biography remains the essential resource concerning Chesterton. Ward had full access to Chesterton's manuscripts and spoke with many people who had known him personally. Reveals much about his evolution as a writer and the importance of friendship in his life.

Wills, Garry. *Chesterton*. New York: Doubleday, 2001. Biography is an updated edition of Wills's *Chesterton, Man and Mask* (1961), with a new introduction. Wills is a Catholic intellectual and best-selling author who has written several books about religion in the United States.

KATE CHOPIN

Born: St. Louis, Missouri; February 8, 1851
Died: St. Louis, Missouri; August 22, 1904
Also known as: Katherine O'Flaherty

PRINCIPAL LONG FICTION

At Fault, 1890
The Awakening, 1899

OTHER LITERARY FORMS

In addition to her novels, Kate Chopin (SHO-pan) wrote nearly fifty poems, approximately one hundred stories and vignettes, and a small amount of literary criticism. Her poems are slight, and no serious claims can be made for them. Her criticism also tends to be modest, but it is often revealing. In one piece written in 1896, for example, she discloses that she discovered Guy de Maupassant eight years earlier—that is, when she first began to write. There is every indication that Maupassant remained one of her most important models in the short-story form. In another essay, she pays tribute to Mary Wilkins Freeman, the New England local colorist whose depiction of repressed passion in women was probably an influence on Chopin's own work. Elsewhere, Chopin seems to distinguish between her own writing and that of the so-called local-color school. She is critical of Hamlin Garland for his concern with social problems, "which alone does not insure the survival of a work of art," and she finds the horizons of the Indiana local-color writers too narrow. The subject of genuine fiction is not regional quaintness, she remarks, but "human existence in its subtle, complex . . . meaning, stripped of the veil with which ethical and conventional standards have draped it." Like Thomas Huxley, much read in her circle, she finds no moral purpose in nature, and in her fiction she frequently implies the relativity of morals and received standards.

Chopin's most important work, apart from her novels, lies in the short story. It was for her short stories that she was chiefly known in her time. Her earliest stories are unexceptional, but within only a few years she was producing impressive work, including a fine series of stories set in Natchitoches Parish, Louisiana. Many of these mature stories are included in the two volumes published during her lifetime—*Bayou Folk* (1894) and *A Night in Acadie* (1897). All of her stories and sketches were made available with the 1969 publication of *The Complete Works of Kate Chopin*. Had she never written *The Awakening*, these stories alone, the best of which are inimitable and gemlike, would ensure Chopin a place among the notable writers of the 1890's.

ACHIEVEMENTS

Kate Chopin's reputation today rests primarily on three books: her two short-story collections, *Bayou Folk* and *A Night in Acadie*, and her mature novel, *The Awakening*. *Bayou Folk* collects most of her fiction of the early 1890's set in Natchitoches (pronounced NAK-uh-tahsh) Parish. The characters it generally portrays, although belonging to different social levels, are Creole, Acadian (Cajun), or African American. In many cases they are poor. Not all of the stories in *Bayou Folk* are perfectly achieved, for when Chopin departs from realism into more fanciful writing she loses her power, but three of the stories in this volume—"Beyond the Bayou," "Désirée's Baby," and "Madame Célestin's Divorce"—are among her most famous and most frequently anthologized.

A Night in Acadie collects Chopin's stories from the middle and late 1890's. In many of the stories, the protagonists come to sudden recognitions that alter their sense of the world; Chopin's recurring theme is the awakening of a spirit that, through a certain set of circumstances, is liberated into conscious life. Passion is often the agent of liberation; whereas in the fiction of William Dean Howells, for example, characters frequently meet and fall putatively in love, in Chopin's fiction they do so from the inmost springs of their being. There is nothing putative or factitious about Chopin's characters who are brought to the point of love or desire. *A Night in Acadie* differs from *Bayou Folk* somewhat in the greater emphasis it gives to the erotic drives of its characters.

Chopin's authority in this aspect of experience, along with her concern with the interaction of the deeply inward on the outward life, sets her work apart from other local-color writing of the time. In her early novel *At Fault*, she had not as yet begun to probe deeply into the psychology of her characters. David Hosmer and Thérèse Lafirme are drawn too much at the surface level to sustain the kind of writing that Chopin does best. After she had developed her art in her stories, however, she was able to bring her psychological concerns to perfection in *The Awakening*, her greatest work. Chopin's achievement was somewhat narrowly bounded, without the scope of the fiction of manners that occupied Howells and Henry James, but in *Bayou Folk*, *A Night in Acadie*, and *The Awakening*, Chopin gave to American letters works of enduring interest—the interest not so much of local color as of a strikingly sensuous psychological realism.

BIOGRAPHY

Kate Chopin was born Katherine O'Flaherty on February 8, 1851, in St. Louis, Missouri, into a socially prominent family with roots in the French past of both St. Louis and New Orleans. Her father, Thomas O'Flaherty, an immigrant from Ireland, had lived in New York and Illinois before settling in St. Louis, where he prospered as the owner of a commission house. In 1839, he married into a well-known Creole family, members of the city's social elite, but his wife died in childbirth only a year later. In 1844, he married Eliza Faris, merely fifteen years old but, according to French custom, eligible for marriage. Faris was the daughter of a Huguenot man who had migrated from Virginia and a woman who was descended from the Charlevilles, among the earliest French settlers in America.

Kate was one of three children born to her parents and the only one to live to mature years. In 1855, tragedy struck the O'Flaherty family when her father, now a director of the Pacific Railroad, was killed in a train wreck; thereafter, Kate lived in a house of many widows—her mother, grandmother, and great-grandmother Charleville. In 1860, she entered the St. Louis Academy of the Sacred Heart, a Catholic institution where French history, language, and culture were stressed—as they were, also, in her own household. Such an early absorption in French culture would eventually influence Chopin's own writing, an adaptation in some ways of French forms to American themes.

Chopin graduated from the Academy of the Sacred Heart in 1868, and two years later she was introduced to St. Louis society, becoming one of its ornaments, a vivacious and attractive girl known for her cleverness and talents as a storyteller. The following year, she made a trip to New Orleans, and it was there that she met Oscar Chopin, whom she married in 1871. After a three-month honeymoon in Germany, Switzerland, and France, the couple moved to New Orleans, where Chopin's husband was a cotton factor (a businessman who financed the raising of cotton and transacted its sale). Oscar Chopin prospered at first, but in 1878 and 1879, the period of the great "Yellow Jack" epidemic and of disastrously poor harvests, he suffered reverses. The Chopin family then went to live in rural Louisiana, where, at Cloutierville, Oscar Chopin managed some small plantations he owned.

By all accounts, the Chopin marriage was an unusually happy one, and in time Kate became the mother of six children. This period in her life ended, however, in 1883 with the sudden death, from swamp fever, of her husband. A widow at thirty, Chopin remained at Cloutierville for a year, overseeing her husband's property, and then moved to St. Louis, where she remained for the rest of her life. She began to write in 1888, while still rearing her children, and in the following year she made her first appearance in print. As her writing shows, her marriage to Oscar Chopin proved to be much more than an "episode" in her life, for it is from this period in New Orleans and Natchitoches Parish that she drew her best literary material and her strongest inspiration. She knew this area personally, and yet as an "outsider" she was also able to observe it with the freshness of detachment.

Considering the fact that she had only begun to have her stories published in 1889, it is remarkable that Chopin should already have written and published her first novel, *At Fault*, by 1890. The novel is apprenticeship work and was published by a St. Louis company at her own expense, but it does show a sense of form. She then wrote a second novel, "Young Dr. Gosse," which in 1891 she sent out to a number of publishers, all of whom refused it, and which she later destroyed. After finishing this second novel, she concentrated on the shorter forms of fiction, writing forty stories, sketches, and vignettes during the next three years. By 1894, her stories began to

Kate Chopin. (Missouri Historical Society)

find a reception in eastern magazines, notably in *Vogue*, *The Atlantic Monthly*, and *Century*. In the same year, her first short-story collection, *Bayou Folk*, was published by Houghton Mifflin to favorable reviews. Even so, because short-story collections were not commercially profitable, she had difficulty placing her second collection, *A Night in Acadie*, which was brought out by a relatively little-known publisher in Chicago in 1897.

Although having achieved some reputation as an author of what were generally perceived to be local-color stories set in northern Louisiana, Chopin was still far from having established herself as a writer whose work was commercially profitable. Under the advice of editors that a longer work would have a broader appeal, she turned again to the novel form, publishing *The Awakening* in 1899. *The Awakening*, however, received uniformly unfavorable reviews, and in some cities it was banned from library shelves. In St. Louis, Chopin was dropped by friends and refused membership in a local fine-arts club. Chopin had never expected such a storm of condemnation and, although she withstood it calmly, she was deeply hurt by the experience. She wrote little

thereafter and never published another book. In 1904, after attending the St. Louis World's Fair, she was stricken with a cerebral hemorrhage and died two days later.

With her death, Chopin's reputation went into almost total eclipse. In literary histories written early in the century, her work was mentioned only in passing, with brief mention of her local-color stories but none at all of *The Awakening*. Even in the first biography of Chopin, Daniel S. Rankin's *Kate Chopin and Her Creole Stories* (1932), *The Awakening* was passed over quickly as a "morbid" book. The modern discovery of Chopin did not begin until the early 1950's, when the French critic Cyrille Arnavon translated *The Awakening* into French and wrote an introduction to the novel in which he discussed Chopin's writing as early realism comparable in some respects to that of Frank Norris and Theodore Dreiser. In essays written in the mid-1950's, Robert Cantwell and Kenneth Eble called attention to *The Awakening* as a neglected work of classic stature.

The belated recognition of *The Awakening* gained momentum in the 1960's when Edmund Wilson included a discussion of Chopin in *Patriotic Gore: Studies in the Literature of the American Civil War* (1963), in which he described *The Awakening* as a "quite uninhibited and beautifully written [novel] which anticipates D. H. Lawrence in its treatment of infidelity." By the mid-1960's, *The Awakening* was reprinted for the first time in half a century, and critics such as Werner Berthoff, Larzer Ziff, and George Arms all praised it warmly; Ziff called the novel "the most important piece of fiction about the sexual life of a woman written to date in America." With the publication of Per Seyersted's *Kate Chopin: A Critical Biography* (1969) and his edition of her writings, *The Complete Works of Kate Chopin*, Chopin's work at long last became fully available. Chopin has been of particular interest to feminist scholars, but interest in her work has not been limited to a single group. It is now generally conceded that Chopin was one of the significant writers of the 1890's, and *The Awakening* is commonly viewed as a small masterpiece.

ANALYSIS

When Kate Chopin began to publish, local-color writing, which came into being after the Civil War and crested in the 1880's, had already been established. Bret

Harte and Mark Twain had created a special ambience for their fiction in the American West, Sarah Orne Jewett and Mary Wilkins Freeman had drawn their characters in the context of a New England world in decline, and the Creole culture of New Orleans and the plantation region beyond it had been depicted by George Washington Cable, Grace King, and Ruth McEnery Stuart.

AT FAULT

A late arriver to the scene, Chopin was at first, as her stories show, uncertain even of her locale. *At Fault*, her first novel, was a breakthrough for her in the sense that she found her rural Louisiana "region." The novel is set in the present, a setting that is important to its sphere of action. Place-du-Bois, the plantation, represents conservative, traditional values that are challenged by new, emergent ones. David Hosmer, from St. Louis, obtains lumber rights on Place-du-Bois, and with him comes conflict. *At Fault* deals with divorce, but beyond that, it addresses the contradictions of nature and convention. Place-du-Bois seems at times idyllic, but it is shadowed by the cruelties of its slaveholding past, abuses created by too rigidly held assumptions. St. Louis is almost the opposite, a world as much without form as Hosmer's pretty young wife, who goes to pieces there and again at Place-du-Bois.

A problem novel, *At Fault* looks skeptically at nature but also at received convention. Intelligent and well thought out, it raises a question that will appear again in *The Awakening*: Is the individual responsible to others or to him- or herself? The characters in *At Fault* tend to be merely vehicles for ideas, but in the short stories Chopin wrote after the novel, her ability to create characters with emotional richness becomes apparent. If *At Fault* suggests the symmetrical social novels of William Dean Howells, *Bayou Folk* gives the impression of southern folk writing brought to a high degree of perfection. The dominant theme in this collection is the universality of illusion, while the stories in *A Night in Acadie* prepare for *The Awakening*, in which a married woman, her self-assertion stifled in a conventional marriage, is awakened to the sensuous and erotic life.

Comparable in kind to Gustave Flaubert's *Madame Bovary* (1857; English translation, 1886), *The Awakening* is Chopin's most elaborate orchestration of the theme of bondage and illusion. Dramatic in form, in-

tensely focused, it makes use of imagery and symbolism to an extent never before evident in Chopin's work. The boldness of her possession of theme in *The Awakening* is wholly remarkable. Her earliest effort in the novel, *At Fault*, asks if the individual is responsible to others or to him- or herself, a question that is raised again in *The Awakening*. *At Fault*, however, deals with its characters conventionally, on the surface only, while in *The Awakening* Chopin captures the deep, inner life of Edna Pontellier and projects it powerfully onto a world of convention.

In writing *At Fault*, Chopin drew on her familiarity with two regions, St. Louis and the plantation country north of New Orleans. The hero, David Hosmer, comes to Louisiana from St. Louis, like Chopin herself, and at least one segment of the novel is set in St. Louis. The heroine, Thérèse Lafirme, proprietress of Place-du-Bois, is similar to Chopin—a widow at thirty who carries on the management of her late husband's property. Moreover, her plantation of four thousand acres is of the same size as and seems suggested by that of Chopin's father-in-law, who had purchased it from the notorious Robert McAlpine, the model for Harriet Beecher Stowe's Simon Legree in *Uncle Tom's Cabin* (1852). In Chopin's novel, attention is called specifically to McAlpine, the former owner of the property, whose ghost is said to walk abroad at night in expiation of his cruel deeds.

Apart from its two settings, *At Fault* does not seem autobiographical. It has the form of a problem novel, reminiscent of the novels of Howells, to whom Chopin sent a copy of the work when it was published. As in certain of Howells's novels, a discussion takes place at one point that frames the conflict that the characters' lives illustrate. In this case it is the conflict between nature and convention, religious and social precept versus the data of actual experience. Thérèse Lafirme, although a warm and attractive woman, is accustomed to thinking about human affairs abstractly. When she learns that David Hosmer, who owns a sawmill on her property, is divorced from his young wife, a weak and susceptible woman who drinks, she admonishes him to return to his wife and fulfill his marriage pledge to stand by and redeem her. Hosmer admires Thérèse to such an extent that, against his own judgment, and most reluctantly, he returns to St. Louis and remarries Fanny Larimore. They then return to the plantation to live, and in due course history repeats itself. Despite Hosmer's dutiful attentions and her acceptance into the small social world of Place-du-Bois, Fanny begins to drink and to behave unreasonably. Near the end of the novel, having become jealous of Thérèse, Fanny ventures out in a storm and, despite Hosmer's attempt to rescue her, dies in a river flood.

Running parallel to this main plot is a subplot in which Hosmer's sister Melicent feels a romantic attraction to Thérèse's impetuous young nephew Grégoire but decides on the most theoretical grounds that he would not be suitable for a husband. When he becomes involved in a marginal homicide, she condemns him utterly, literally abandoning him. He then returns to Texas, where he goes from bad to worse and is eventually killed in a lawless town. At the end, a year after these events, Hosmer and Thérèse marry and find the happiness they had very nearly lost through Thérèse's preconceptions. It is clear to her that Fanny never could have been redeemed, and that her plan to "save" her had brought suffering to all parties concerned—to Hosmer, herself, and to Fanny as well. Left open, however, is the question of Melicent's responsibility to Grégoire, whom she had been too quick to "judge." *At Fault* appears to end happily, but in some ways it is pessimistic in its view of nature and convention.

At Fault shows a questioning intelligence and has an architectural competence, but it is still apprenticeship work. The St. Louis setting, especially in comparison to the southern one, is pallid, and the characters encountered there are lifeless. Fanny's associates in St. Louis include Mrs. Lorenzo (Belle) Worthington, who has dyed blond hair, and Mrs. Jack (Lou) Dawson, who has an expressionless face and "meaningless blue eyes set to a good humored readiness for laughter." These lady idlers, Belle and Lou, are stick figures. Although given stronger individuality, the more important characters also tend to be typed. Grégoire is typed by his vulnerability and impetuousness, just as Melicent is drawn to type as an immature girl who does not know her mind. The plot of *At Fault* is perhaps too symmetrical, too predictable in its outcome, with the irredeemability of Fanny Larimore a foregone conclusion. Moreover, in attempting to add emotional richness to the work, Chopin sometimes resorts to melodramatic occurrences, such as

Joçint's setting fire to the mill, his death at the hands of Grégoire, the death of Joçint's father, the death of Grégoire, and the scene in which Fanny perishes in the storm. *At Fault* is essentially a realistic novel but resorts at times to romantic or melodramatic conventions. If Chopin fails to bring her novel to life, she does at times create suggestive characters such as Aunt Belindy, Thérèse's cook, who asks pointedly, "Whar you gwine live if you don' live in de worl'?" A tonal richness is also evident in the drawing of Thérèse Lafirme. Thérèse is not allowed in this work to be fully "herself," but she points the way to Chopin's later successes in fiction, the women Chopin creates from the soul.

THE AWAKENING

In *The Awakening*, Chopin achieved her largest exploration of feminine consciousness. Edna Pontellier, the heroine, is always at the center of the novel, and nothing occurs that does not in some way bear on her thoughts or developing sense of her situation. As a character who rejects her socially prescribed roles of wife and mother, Edna has a certain affinity with the "New Woman," much discussed in the 1890's, but her special modeling and the type of her experience suggest a French influence. Before beginning the novel, Chopin translated eight of Guy de Maupassant's stories. Two of these tales, "Solitude" and "Suicide," share with *The Awakening* the theme of illusion in erotic desire and the inescapability of the solitary self. Another, "Reveil," anticipates Chopin's novel in some incidents of its plot. At the same time, *The Awakening* seems to have been influenced by *Madame Bovary*. Certain parallels can be noticed in the experiences of the two heroines—their repudiation of their husbands, estrangement, and eventual suicides. More important, Flaubert's craftsmanship informs the whole manner of Chopin's novel—its directness, lucidity, and economy of means; its steady use of incident and detail as leitmotif. The novel also draws on a large fin de siècle background concerned with a hunger for the exotic and the voluptuous, a yearning for the absolute. From these diverse influences, Chopin shapes a work that is strikingly, even startlingly, her own.

The opening third section of *The Awakening*, the chapter set at Grand Isle, is particularly impressive. Here one meets Edna Pontellier, the young wife of a well-to-do Creole *negociant* and mother of two small boys. Mrs.

Pontellier, an "American" woman originally from Kentucky, is still not quite accustomed to the sensuous openness of this Creole summer colony. She walks on the beach under a white parasol with handsome young Robert Lebrun, who befriends married Creole women in a way that is harmless, since his attentions are regarded as a social pleasantry, nothing more. In the background are two young lovers and, not far behind them, keeping pace, a mysterious woman dressed in black who tells her beads. Edna Pontellier and Robert Lebrun have just returned from a midday swim in the ocean, an act undertaken on impulse and perhaps not entirely prudent, in view of the extreme heat of that hour and the scorching glare of the sun. When Edna rejoins her husband, he finds her "burnt beyond recognition." Léonce Pontellier is a responsible husband who gives his wife no cause for complaint, but his mind runs frequently on business and he is dull. He is inclined to regard his wife as "property," but by this summer on Grand Isle she has begun to come to self-awareness, to recognize how she is suppressed by her role as a "mother-woman." Emboldened by her unconventional midday swim, she goes out swimming alone that night, and with reckless exhilaration longs to go "further out than any woman had ever swum before." She quickly tires, however, and is fortunate to have the strength to return to the safety of the shore. When she returns to their house, she does not go inside to join her husband but drowses alone in a porch hammock, lost in a long moonlit reverie that has the voluptuous effulgence of the sea.

As the novel proceeds, it becomes clear that Edna has begun to fall in love with Lebrun, who decides suddenly to go to Mexico, following which the Pontelliers themselves return to their well-appointed home in New Orleans. There Edna begins to behave erratically, defying her husband and leading as much as possible an independent existence. After moving to a small house nearby by herself, she has an affair with a young roué, Alcée Arobin. Lebrun returns from Mexico about the same time, and, although he is in love with Edna, he does not dare to overstep convention with a married woman and mother of two. Trapped once again within her socially prescribed role, Edna returns to the seashore and goes swimming alone, surrendering her life to the sea.

In its own time, *The Awakening* was criticized both for its subject matter and for its point of view. Reviewers repeatedly remarked that the erotic content of the novel was disturbing and distasteful, and that Chopin had not only failed to censure Edna's "morbid" awakening but also had treated it sympathetically. The reviewers failed to take into account the subtlety and ambiguity of the novel's vision, for if Chopin enters deeply into Edna's consciousness, she also stands outside it with a severe objectivity. A close examination of *The Awakening* reveals that the heroine has been involved in illusion from the beginning. Edna sometimes meditates, for example, on the self-realization that has been blunted by her roles as wife and mother, but in her rejection of her responsibilities she constantly tends toward vagueness rather than clarity.

The imagery of the sea expresses Edna's longing to reach a state in which she feels her own identity and where she feels passionately alive. The "voice" of the sea, beckoning Edna, is constantly in the background of the work. "The voice of the sea," Chopin writes, "speaks to the soul. The touch of the sea is sensuous, enfolding the body in its soft, close embrace." In this "enfolding," however, Edna discovers her own solitude and loses herself in "mazes of inward contemplation." In *Moby Dick* (1851), Herman Melville contrasts the land and the sea, the one convention bound, the other "open" and boldly, defiantly speculative, but Edna is no thinker; she is a dreamer who, in standing apart from conditioned circumstance, can only embrace the rhapsodic death lullaby of the sea. At the end of her life, she returns to her childhood, when, in protest against the aridness of her Presbyterian father's Sunday devotions, she had wandered aimlessly in a field of tall meadow grass that made her think of the sea.

Edna had married her Catholic husband despite her father's objection—or rather, one thinks, because of his objection. Later, discovering the limitations that her life with her husband imposes on her, she rebels once again, grasping at the illusion of an idealized Robert Lebrun. Edna's habit of idealization goes far back in her past. As a girl, she had fallen in love with a Confederate officer whom she had glimpsed, a noble figure belonging to a doomed cause, and also with a picture of a "tragedian." The last lines of the novel, as Edna's consciousness ends, are as follows: "The spurs of the cavalry officer clanged as he walked across the porch. There was the hum of bees, and the musky odor of pinks filled the air." Her consciousness at the end thus reverts back to its beginning, forming a circle from which she cannot escape. The final irony of *The Awakening*, however, is that even though Edna is drawn as an illusionist, her protest is not quite meaningless. Never before in a novel published in the United States was the issue of a woman's suppressed erotic nature and need for self-definition, apart from the received roles of wife and mother, raised so forcefully. *The Awakening* is a work in which the feminist protest of the present is memorably imagined.

In the mid-1950's, Van Wyck Brooks described *The Awakening* as a "small perfect book that mattered more than the whole life work of many a prolific writer." In truth, *The Awakening* is not quite "perfect." Chopin loses some of her power when she moves from Grand Isle to New Orleans. The guests at her dinner party, characters with names such as Mrs. Highcamp and Miss Mayblunt, are two-dimensional and wooden, and at times the symbolic connotations of incidents seem too unvaried. *The Awakening*, certainly, would be embarrassed by comparison with a large, panoramic novel of marital infidelity such as Leo Tolstoy's *Anna Karenina* (1875-1877; English translation, 1886). Within its limits, however, it reveals work of the finest craftsmanship, and it is a novel that continues to linger in the reader's consciousness well after it has been read.

Chopin was not prolific; all but a few of her best stories are contained in *Bayou Folk* and *A Night in Acadie*, and she produced only one mature novel, but these volumes have the mark of genuine quality. Lyric and objective at once, deeply humane and yet constantly attentive to illusion in her characters' perceptions of reality, these volumes reveal Chopin as a psychological realist of magical empathy, a writer having the greatness of delicacy.

Robert Emmet Long

OTHER MAJOR WORKS

SHORT FICTION: *Bayou Folk*, 1894; *A Night in Acadie*, 1897.

NONFICTION: *Kate Chopin's Private Papers*, 1998.

MISCELLANEOUS: *The Complete Works of Kate Chopin*, 1969 (2 volumes; Per Seyersted, editor); *Complete Novels and Stories*, 2002.

BIBLIOGRAPHY

Bonner, Thomas, Jr. *The Kate Chopin Companion*. New York: Greenwood Press, 1988. Alphabetically arranged guide provides information on the more than nine hundred characters and more than two hundred places that affect the courses of Chopin's stories. Also includes a selection of her translations of pieces by Guy de Maupassant and one by Adrien Vely. Supplemented by interesting period maps and a useful bibliographic essay.

Boren, Lynda S., and Sara de Saussure Davis, eds. *Kate Chopin Reconsidered: Beyond the Bayou*. Baton Rouge: Louisiana State University Press, 1992. Collection of essays presents extensive discussion of *The Awakening*, with several contributors also addressing such stories as "Charlie," "After the Winter," and "At Cheniere Caminada." Other topics include a comparison of Chopin with playwright Henrik Ibsen in terms of domestic confinement and discussion of Chopin's work from a Marxist point of view.

Hackett, Joyce. "The Reawakening." *Harper's Magazine* 307, no. 1841 (October, 2003). Lengthy review of the Chopin collection *Complete Novels and Stories* (2002) provides an overview of Chopin's life and career and offers analysis and commentary on *The Awakening*, which Hackett describes as "the book that both culminated Chopin's career and ended it."

Petry, Alice Hall, ed. *Critical Essays on Kate Chopin*. New York: G. K. Hall, 1996. Comprehensive collection of essays on Chopin reprints early evaluations of the author's life and works as well as more modern scholarly analyses. Begins with a substantial introduction by the editor and includes original essays by such notable scholars as Linda Wagner-Martin and Heather Kirk Thomas.

Seyersted, Per. *Kate Chopin: A Critical Biography*. 1969. Reprint. Baton Rouge: Louisiana State University Press, 1980. Provides invaluable information about the New Orleans of the 1870's while examining Chopin's life, views, and work. Devotes substantial discussion not only to *The Awakening* but also to Chopin's many short stories. Seyersted views Chopin as a transitional literary figure, a link between George Sand and Simone de Beauvoir.

Skaggs, Peggy. *Kate Chopin*. Boston: Twayne, 1985.

Overview of Chopin's life and work includes a brief biographical chapter and discussion of the author's work in terms of the theme of the search for identity. Includes a chronology and a select bibliography.

Streater, Kathleen M. "Adèle Ratignolle: Kate Chopin's Feminist at Home in *The Awakening*." *Midwest Quarterly* 48, no. 3 (Spring, 2007): 406-416. Presents analysis of the character Adèle Ratignolle, arguing that she is a less radical feminist than Edna Pontellier but is admirable because of her feminine virtue and ideals of motherhood. Maintains that Ratignolle, whom Chopin portrays as a sexually confident woman as well as a mother, defied the sexist stereotypes of the period.

Taylor, Helen. *Gender, Race, and Religion in the Writings of Grace King, Ruth McEnery Stuart, and Kate Chopin*. Baton Rouge: Louisiana State University Press, 1989. Chapter on Chopin is divided between the novels and the short stories, some of which are given extensive feminist readings. Focuses on Chopin as a local colorist who uses regional and historical themes to explore gender issues. Offers invaluable discussion of Chopin's literary influences, particularly Guy de Maupassant, and the intellectual climate of the time.

Toth, Emily. *Kate Chopin*. New York: William Morrow, 1990. Definitive biography is a thoroughly documented, exhaustive work, an excellent starting point for Chopin research. Covers not only Chopin's life but also her literary works, discussing many of the short stories in considerable detail and addressing the alleged banning of *The Awakening*. Includes a bibliography of Chopin's work and a helpful chronology of her life.

_____. *Unveiling Kate Chopin*. Jackson: University Press of Mississippi, 1999. Using newly discovered manuscripts, letters, and diaries of Chopin, Toth examines the source of Chopin's ambition and passion for her art, arguing that she worked much harder at her craft than previously thought.

AGATHA CHRISTIE

Born: Torquay, Devon, England; September 15, 1890
Died: Wallingford, Oxfordshire, England; January 12, 1976
Also known as: Agatha Mary Clarissa Miller; Mary Westmacott; Agatha Mary Clarissa Mallowan

PRINCIPAL LONG FICTION

The Mysterious Affair at Styles: A Detective Story, 1920
The Secret Adversary, 1922
The Murder on the Links, 1923
The Man in the Brown Suit, 1924
The Secret of Chimneys, 1925
The Murder of Roger Ackroyd, 1926
The Big Four, 1927
The Mystery of the Blue Train, 1928
The Seven Dials Mystery, 1929
Giants' Bread, 1930 (as Mary Westmacott)
The Murder at the Vicarage, 1930
The Floating Admiral, 1931 (with others)
The Sittaford Mystery, 1931 (also known as *The Murder at Hazelmoor*)
Peril at End House, 1932
Lord Edgware Dies, 1933 (also known as *Thirteen at Dinner*)
Murder in Three Acts, 1934
Murder on the Orient Express, 1934 (also known as *Murder on the Calais Coach*)
Unfinished Portrait, 1934 (as Westmacott)
Why Didn't They Ask Evans?, 1934 (also known as *Boomerang Clue*, 1935)
Death in the Clouds, 1935 (also known as *Death in the Air*)
The A. B. C. Murders: A New Poirot Mystery, 1936
Cards on the Table, 1936
Murder in Mesopotamia, 1936

Death on the Nile, 1937

Dumb Witness, 1937 (also known as *Poirot Loses a Client*)

Appointment with Death: A Poirot Mystery, 1938

Hercule Poirot's Christmas, 1939 (also known as *Murder for Christmas: A Poirot Story*)

Murder Is Easy, 1939 (also known as *Easy to Kill*)

Ten Little Niggers, 1939 (also known as *And Then There Were None*, 1940)

One, Two, Buckle My Shoe, 1940 (also known as *The Patriotic Murders*, 1941)

Sad Cypress, 1940

Evil Under the Sun, 1941

N or M? The New Mystery, 1941

The Body in the Library, 1942

Five Little Pigs, 1942 (also known as *Murder in Retrospect*)

The Moving Finger, 1942

Poirot on Holiday, 1943

Absent in the Spring, 1944 (as Westmacott)

Death Comes in the End, 1944

Towards Zero, 1944

Sparkling Cyanide, 1945 (also known as *Remembered Death*)

The Hollow: A Hercule Poirot Mystery, 1946

Poirot Knows the Murderer, 1946

Poirot Lends a Hand, 1946

Murder Medley, 1948

The Rose and the Yew Tree, 1948 (as Westmacott)

Taken at the Flood, 1948 (also known as *There Is a Tide . . .*)

Crooked House, 1949

A Murder Is Announced, 1950

Blood Will Tell, 1951

They Came to Baghdad, 1951

A Daughter's a Daughter, 1952 (as Westmacott)

Mrs. McGinty's Dead, 1952

They Do It with Mirrors, 1952 (also known as *Murder with Mirrors*)

After the Funeral, 1953 (also known as *Funerals Are Fatal*)

A Pocket Full of Rye, 1953

Destination Unknown, 1954 (also known as *So Many Steps to Death*, 1955)

Hickory, Dickory, Dock, 1955 (also known as *Hickory, Dickory, Death*)

The Burden, 1956 (as Westmacott)

Dead Man's Folly, 1956

4:50 from Paddington, 1957 (also known as *What Mrs. McGillicuddy Saw!*)

Ordeal by Innocence, 1958

Cat Among the Pigeons, 1959

The Pale Horse, 1961

The Mirror Crack'd from Side to Side, 1962 (also known as *The Mirror Crack'd*, 1963)

The Clocks, 1963

A Caribbean Mystery, 1964

At Bertram's Hotel, 1965

Third Girl, 1966

Endless Night, 1967

By the Pricking of My Thumbs, 1968

Hallowe'en Party, 1969

Passenger to Frankfurt, 1970

Nemesis, 1971

Elephants Can Remember, 1972

Postern of Fate, 1973

Curtain: Hercule Poirot's Last Case, 1975

Sleeping Murder, 1976

OTHER LITERARY FORMS

Agatha Christie published approximately thirty collections of short stories, fifteen plays, a nonfiction book (*Come Tell Me How You Live*, 1946), and many omnibus editions of her novels. Under the pen name Mary Westmacott, Christie published six romance novels. At least ten of her detective works have been made into motion pictures, and *An Autobiography* (1977) was published because, as Christie told *Publishers Weekly* in 1966, "If anybody writes about my life in the future, I'd rather they got the facts right." Sources disagree on the total number of Christie's publications because of the unusual quantity of titles, the reissue of so many novels under different titles, and especially the tendency to publish the same book under differing titles in England and the United States.

ACHIEVEMENTS

Among her many achievements, Agatha Christie bears one unusual distinction: She is the only writer whose main character's death precipitated a front-page obituary in *The New York Times*. Christie was a fellow of the Royal Society of Literature; received the New York Drama Critics' Circle Award for Best Foreign Play of the year in 1955 for *Witness for the Prosecution* (which was first produced in 1953); was knighted Dame Commander, Order of the British Empire, in 1971; received the Film Daily Poll Ten Best Pictures Award in 1958 (for the film adaptation of *Witness for the Prosecution*, directed by Billy Wilder); and was made a doctor of literature at the University of Exeter.

BIOGRAPHY

Agatha Mary Clarissa Miller was born in Torquay, England, on September 15, 1890; the impact of this location on her was enormous. Near the end of her autobiography, Christie indicates that all other memories and homes pale beside Ashfield, her parents' home in Torquay: "And there you are again—remembering. 'I remember, I remember, the house where I was born. . . .' I go back to that always in my mind. Ashfield." The roots of Christie's self-contained, quiet sense of place are found in her accounts of life at Ashfield. Her love of peace, routine, and order was born in her mother's well-ordered household, a household cared for by servants whose nature seemed never to change, and sparked by the sudden whims of an energetic and dramatic mother. Christie's father was Fred Miller, an American, many years older than her English mother, Clara. They were distant cousins and had an exceptionally harmonious marriage because, according to Christie, her father was an exceptionally agreeable man. Nigel Dennis, writing for *Life* magazine in May, 1956, noted that Christie is at her best in "orderly, settled surroundings" in which she can suddenly introduce disruption and ultimately violence. Her autobiographical accounts of days upon days of peace and routine followed by sudden impulsive adventures initiated by her mother support the idea that, as she says, all comes back to Ashfield, including her mystery stories at their best.

In writing her autobiography, Christie left a detailed and insightful commentary on her works. To one familiar with her autobiography, the details of her life can be found in the incidents and plots of her novels. Frequently, she barely disguises them. She writes, for example, of a recurring childhood dream about "the Gunman," whose outstanding characteristics were his frightening eyes appearing suddenly and staring at her from absolutely any person around her, including her beloved mother. This dream forms almost the entire basis for the plot of *Unfinished Portrait*, a romance novel Christie wrote under the pen name Mary Westmacott. That dream may have been the source of her willingness to allow absolutely any character the role of murderer. No one, including her great Hercule Poirot, is exempt from suddenly becoming the Gunman.

Christie was educated at home chiefly by her parents and her nurse. She taught herself to read before she was five and from then on was allowed to read any available book at Ashfield. Her father taught her arithmetic, for which she had a propensity and which she enjoyed. She hated spelling, on the other hand, because she read by word sight and not by the sound of letters. She learned history from historical novels and a book of history that her mother expected her to study in preparation for a weekly quiz.

She also had tutors. A stay in France at about age seven and an ensuing return with a Frenchwoman as her companion resulted in her speaking and reading French easily. She had piano and voice tutors and attended a weekly dancing class. As she grew older, she attended the theater weekly, and, in her teens, she was sent to a boarding school in France.

She was always allowed to use her imagination freely. Her sensible and beloved nurse went along with her early construction of plots and tales enlisting the nurse as well as dolls and animals to be the characters. She carried on a constant dialogue with these characters as she went through her days. The absence of playmates and the storytelling done within the family also contributed to the development of her imagination. Her mother invented ongoing bedtime tales of a dramatic and mysterious nature. Her elder sister, Madge, liked to write, and she repeatedly told Agatha one particular story: the "Elder Sister" tale. Like the Gunman, the Elder Sister became a frequent personage in Christie's later novels. As a child, Agatha would ask her sister, feeling a mixture of terror and delight, when the elder sister was coming; Madge would indicate that it would be soon. Then a few days later, there would be a knock on Agatha's door and her sister would enter and begin talking in an eerie voice as if she were an elder, disturbed sister who was normally locked up somewhere but at large for the day. The pattern seems similar to that of the Gunman: the familiar figure who is suddenly dangerous. One of Christie's book in particular, *Elephants Can Remember*, concerns a crazy identical twin sister who escapes from a mental institution, kills her twin, and takes her place in marriage to a man they had both known and loved as young girls.

In addition to her sister, Agatha had an elder brother, Monty, whom she adored. He allowed her to join him frequently in his escapades and was generally agreeable but, like her father, did not amount to much otherwise and was managed and even supported by his sisters later in his life. "Auntie Grannie" was another strong figure in Agatha's early life. She was the aunt who had reared Clara Miller and was also Fred's stepmother, hence her title. Many critics see in her the basis for the character of Miss Marple.

The picture of Christie that emerges is one of a woman coming from an intensely female-dominated household where men were agreeable and delightful but not very effective. Female servants and family members provided Agatha with her rigorous, stable values and independent behavior. She grew up expecting little of men except affection and loyalty; in return, she expected to be sensible and self-supporting when possible. Another possible explanation for Christie's self-sufficiency is the emotional support that these surrounding females provided for her. Even after her mother's death in the late 1920's, Christie always sought the companionship of loyal female servants and secretaries who, in the British Victorian fashion, then became invaluable to her in her work and personal life. Especially in her marriage to Archibald Christie, she relied on her female relatives and servants to encourage, assist, and even love her. The Miss Marples of her world, the Constance Sheppards (*The Murder of Roger Ackroyd*), and the servants were her life's bedrock.

In 1914, Agatha Miller married Colonel Archibald Christie in a hasty wartime ceremony. They had one daughter, Rosamund, whom Agatha adored but considered an "efficient" child. She characterized Rosamund in her Mary Westmacott novel *A Daughter's a Daughter*.

Agatha started writing on a dare from her sister but only began writing novels seriously when her husband was away in World War I and she was employed as a chemist's (pharmacist's) assistant in a dispensary. Finding herself with extra time, she wrote *The Mysterious Affair at Styles*. Since she was familiar with both poisons and death because of her hospital and dispensary work, she was able to distinguish herself by the accuracy of her descriptions. Several other books followed that were increasingly successful, until *The Murder of Roger Ackroyd* became a best seller in 1926.

The death of her mother and a divorce from Archie Christie took place about the same time Agatha Christie was beginning to experience success. These events sent her into a tailspin that ended in her famous eleven-day disappearance. She reappeared at a health spa unharmed but, to her embarrassment, the object of a great deal of attention; in addition, the public was outraged at the large expense of the search that had been mounted for the author.

Agatha Christie. (Library of Congress)

In 1930, Christie married Sir Max Mallowan, an archaeologist, perhaps a more "agreeable" man than Archie Christie. Certainly her domestic life after the marriage was peaceful; in addition, she was able to travel with Mallowan to his archaeological dig sites in the Middle East. This gave her new settings and material for her books and enabled her to indulge in one of her greatest pleasures: travel.

In 1930, *The Murder at the Vicarage* was published; it introduced Christie's own favorite sleuth, Miss Jane Marple, village spinster and observer of the village scene. By this time, Christie was an established author, and in the 1940's her books began to be made into plays and motion pictures. In 1952, *The Mousetrap* was launched in a London theater and eventually became one of the longest-running plays in that city's history. The film version of *Witness for the Prosecution* received awards and acclaim in the late 1950's. *Murder in the Calais Coach* became *Murder on the Orient Express*, a popular American film directed by Sidney Lumet and released in 1974.

Producing approximately one book per year, Christie has been likened to an assembly line, but, as her autobiography indicates, each book was a little puzzle for her own "grey cells," the conceiving of which gave her great enjoyment and the writing of which took about six to twelve weeks and was often tedious. In 1971, she was made Dame Agatha Christie by Queen Elizabeth II and had what she considered one of her most thrilling experiences, tea with the queen. In 1975, she allowed the book *Curtain: Hercule Poirot's Last Case* to be published and the death of her chief sleuth, Hercule Poirot, to occur. This was of sufficient interest to warrant a front-page obituary in *The New York Times*.

By the time of Christie's own death in 1976, history writer Ellsworth Grant wrote that Christie's writings had "reached a wider audience than those of any author who ever lived." More than 400 million copies of her novels and short stories had been sold, and her works had been translated into 103 languages.

ANALYSIS

Agatha Christie's trademarks in detective fiction brought to maturity the classical tradition of the genre, which was in its adolescence when she began to write.

The tradition had some stable characteristics, but she added many more and perfected existing ones. The classical detective hero, for example, from Edgar Allan Poe on, according to Ellsworth Grant, is of "superior intellect," is "fiercely independent," and has "amusing idiosyncrasies." Christie's Hercule Poirot was crafted by these ground rules and reflects them in *The Mysterious Affair at Styles* but quickly begins to deplore this Sherlock Holmes type of detecting. Poirot would rather think from his armchair than rush about, magnifying glass in hand, searching for clues. He may, by his words, satirize classical detection, but he is also satirizing himself, as Christie well knew.

Christie's own contributions to the genre can be classified mainly as the following: a peaceful, usually upper-class setting into which violence intrudes; satire of her own heroes, craft, and genre; a grand finale in which all characters involved gather for the dramatic revelation of truth; the careful access to all clues; increased emphasis on the "who" and the "why," with less interest in the "how"; heavy use of dialogue and lightning-quick description, which create a fast-paced, easy read; a consistent moral framework for the action; and the willingness to allow absolutely any character to be guilty, a precedent-setting break with tradition. Her weakness, critics claim, is in her barely two-dimensional characters, who lack psychological depth.

Christie created, as Grant puts it, a great many interesting "caricatures of people we have met." Grant excuses her on the grounds that allowing every character to be a possible suspect limits the degree to which each can be psychologically explored. One might also attribute her caricatures to her great admiration for Charles Dickens, who also indulged in caricatures, especially with his minor characters. Christie herself gave a simple explanation. She judged it best not to write about people she actually knew, preferring to observe strangers in railroad stations and restaurants, perhaps catching fragments of their conversations. From these glimpses, she would make up characters and plots. Character fascinated her endlessly, but, like Miss Marple, she believed the depths of human iniquity were in everyone, and it was only in the outward manifestation that people became evil or good. "I could've done it," a juvenile character cries in *Evil Under the Sun*. "Ah, but you didn't and between those two things there is a world of difference," Poirot replies.

DEATH COMES IN THE END

In spite of Christie's simplistic judgment of human character, she manages, on occasion (especially in her novels of the 1940's and later), to make accurate and discerning forays into the thought processes of some characters. In *Death Comes in the End*, considerable time is spent on Renisenb's internal musings. Caught in the illiterate role that her time (Egypt, 2000 B.C.E.) and sex status decree for her, Renisenb struggles to achieve language so she can articulate her anxieties about evil and good. Her male friend, Hori, speaks at great length of the way that evil affects people. "People create a false door—to deceive," he says, but "when reality comes and touches them with the feather of truth—their truth self reasserts itself." When Norfret, a beautiful concubine, enters a closed, self-contained household and threatens its stability, all the characters begin to behave differently. The murderer is discovered precisely because he is the only person who does *not* behave differently on the outside. Any innocent person would act guilty because the presence of evil touches self-doubts and faults; therefore, the one who acts against this Christie truth and remains normal in the face of murder must, in fact, be guilty.

THE MYSTERIOUS AFFAIR AT STYLES

Although *The Mysterious Affair at Styles* is marred by overwriting and explanations that Christie sheds in later books, it shows signs of those qualities that would make her great. The village of Styles St. Mary is quiet, and Styles House is a typical country manor. The book is written in the first person by Hastings, who comes to visit his old friend John Cavendish and finds him dealing with a difficult family situation. Cavendish's mother has married a man who everyone agrees is a fortune hunter. Shortly afterward, she dies of poison in full view of several family members, calling her husband's name. Hastings runs into Hercule Poirot at the post office; an old acquaintance temporarily residing at Styles, Poirot is a former police inspector from Belgium. Christie's idea in this first novel seems to be that Hastings will play Watson to Poirot's Holmes, although she quickly tires of this arrangement and in a later book ships Hastings off to Argentina.

Every obvious clue points to the husband as the murderer. Indeed, he is the murderer and has made arrangements with an accomplice so that he will be brought to a speedy trial. At the trial, it would then be revealed that the husband had an absolute alibi for the time when the poison must have been administered; hence, he and his accomplice try to encourage everyone to think him guilty. Poirot delays the trial and figures out that the real poison was in the woman's own medicine, which contained a substance that would become fatal only if released from other elements. It then would settle to the bottom of the bottle, and the last dose would be lethal. Bromide is an ingredient that separates the elements. Bromide was added at the murderer's leisure, and he had only to wait until the day when his wife would take the last dose, making sure that both he and his accomplice are seen by many people far distant from the household at the time she is declared to have been poisoned. The plot is brilliant, and Christie received congratulations from a chemists' association for her correct use of the poisons in the book.

THE MURDER OF ROGER ACKROYD

By the time she published *The Murder of Roger Ackroyd*, her sixth book, Christie had hit her stride. Although Poirot's explanations are still somewhat lengthy, the book is considered one of her best. It is chiefly noted for the precedent it set in detective fiction. The first-person narrator, Dr. Sheppard, turns out to be the murderer. The skill with which this is concealed and revealed is perhaps Christie at her most subtle. The reader is made to like Dr. Sheppard, to feel he or she is being taken into his confidence as he attempts to write the history of Roger Ackroyd's murder as it unwinds. Poirot cultivates Dr. Sheppard's acquaintanceship, and the reader believes, because the information comes from Dr. Sheppard, that Poirot trusts him. In the end, Dr. Sheppard is guilty. Christie allows herself to gloat at her own fiendish cleverness through the very words that Sheppard uses to gloat over his crime when he refers back to a part of his narrative (the story itself is supposedly being written to help Poirot solve the crime) where a discerning reader or sleuth ought to have found him out.

THE BODY IN THE LIBRARY

The Body in the Library, executed with Christie's usual skill, is distinctive for two elements: the extended discussions of Miss Marple's sleuthing style and the humorous dialogue surrounding the discovery of the body of an unknown young woman in the library of a good family. Grant says of Jane Marple that she insists, as she knits, that human nature never changes. O. L. Bailey expands on this in an article that appeared in *Saturday Review* in 1973: "Victorian to the core," he writes, "she loves to gossip, and her piercing blue eyes twinkle as she solves the most heinous crimes by analogy to life in her archetypal English village of St. Mary Mead."

Marple, as well as the other characters, comments on her methods. Marple feels her success is in her skeptical nature, calling her mind "a sink." She goes on to explain that "the truth is . . . that most people . . . are far too trusting for this wicked world." Another character, Sir Henry, describes her as "an old lady with a sweet, placid, spinsterish face and a mind that has plumbed the depths of human iniquity and taken it as all in the day's work."

Through a delightfully comic conversation between Mr. and Mrs. Bantry, the possibility of a dead body in the library is introduced, and, once it is discovered, the story continues in standard sleuth style; the opening dialogue, however, is almost too funny for the subject matter. Ralph Tyler, in an article published in *Saturday Review* in 1975, calls this mixture of evil and the ordinary a distancing of death "by bringing it about in an upper-middle-class milieu of consummate orderliness." In that milieu, the Bantrys' dialogue is not too funny; it is quite believable, especially since Mr. and Mrs. Bantry do not yet know the body is downstairs.

THE SECRET ADVERSARY

Perhaps real Christie aficionados can be identified by their reactions to Tommy and Tuppence Beresford of *The Secret Adversary*, an engaging pair of sleuths who take up adventuring because they cannot find work in postwar England. Critics for the most part dismiss or ignore the pair, but Christie fans often express a secret fondness for the two. In Tommy and Tuppence, readers find heroes close to home. The two blunder about and solve mysteries by luck as much as by anything else. Readers can easily identify with these two and even feel a bit protective of them.

Tommy and Tuppence develop a romance as they establish an "adventurers for hire" agency and wait for clients. Adventure begins innocently when Tommy tells Tuppence he has overheard someone talking about a woman named Jane Finn and comments disgustedly, "Did you ever hear such a name?" Later they discover that the name is a password into an international spy ring.

The use of luck and coincidence in the story is made much of by Christie herself. Christie seems to tire of the frequent convenient circumstances and lets Tommy and Tuppence's romance and "high adventure" lead the novel's progress. When Tommy asks Mr. Carter, the British spy expert, for some tips, Carter replies, "I think not. My experts, working in stereotyped ways, have failed. You will bring imagination and an open mind to the task." Mr. Carter also admits that he is superstitious and that he believes in luck "and all that sort of thing." In this novel, readers are presented with a clever story, the resolution of which relies on elements quite different from deductive reasoning or intuition. It relies on those qualities that the young seem to exude and attract: audacity and luck.

N OR M? THE NEW MYSTERY

In *N or M? The New Mystery*, Tommy and Tuppence (now married and some twenty years older) are again unemployed. Their two children are both serving their country in World War II. The parents are bemoaning their fate when a messenger from their old friend Mr. Carter starts them on a spy adventure at the seacoast hotel of Sans Souci. They arrive with the assumed names Mr. Meadowes and Mrs. Blenkensop. Mrs. Blenkensop, they agree, will pursue Mr. Meadowes and every now and then corner him so they can exchange information. The dialogue is amusing and there is a good deal of suspense, but too many characters and a thin plot keep this from being one of Christie's best.

At times, it seems that Christie withholds clues; the fact that all evidence is presented to the reader is the supreme test of good detective fiction. Mrs. Sprot, adopted mother of Betty, coolly shoots Betty's real mother in the head while the woman is holding Betty over the edge of a cliff. The reader cannot be expected to know that the woman on the cliff is Betty's real mother, nor can the reader be expected to decipher Tuppence's mutterings about the story of Solomon. In the story of Solomon, two women claim the same baby, and Solomon decrees that the woman who is willing to give up her child rather than have it split in half is the real mother. Since both women in this scene *appear* willing to jeopardize the baby's life, the reader is likely, justifiably, to form some wrong conclusions. This seems less fair than Christie usually is in delivering her clues.

SLEEPING MURDER

In her last novel, *Sleeping Murder*, written several years before its 1976 publication date, Christie achieves more depth in her portrayal of characters than before: Gwenda, her dead stepmother, Dr. Kennedy, and some of the minor characters such as Mr. Erskine are excellent examples. The motivation in the book is, at least, psychological, as opposed to murder for money or personal gain, which are the usual motives in Christie's novels. In comparison with others of Christie's works, this novel seems, in short, to display much more probing into the origins and motivations of her characters' actions.

Sleeping Murder ends with the romantic young couple and the wise old Miss Marple conversing on the front porch of a hotel in, of all places, Torquay, Christie's beloved birthplace. Christie had come full circle, celebrating her romantic and impulsive youth and her pleasant old age in one final reunion at home in Torquay, England.

Anne Kelsch Breznau

OTHER MAJOR WORKS

SHORT FICTION: *Poirot Investigates*, 1924; *Partners in Crime*, 1929; *The Mysterious Mr. Quin*, 1930; *The Thirteen Problems*, 1932 (also known as *The Tuesday Club Murders*, 1933); *The Hound of Death, and Other Stories*, 1933; *The Listerdale Mystery, and Other Stories*, 1934; *Parker Pyne Investigates*, 1934 (also known as *Mr. Parker Pyne, Detective*); *Murder in the Mews, and Other Stories*, 1937 (also known as *Dead Man's Mirror, and Other Stories*); *The Regatta Mystery, and Other Stories*, 1939; *The Mystery of the Baghdad Chest*, 1943; *The Labours of Hercules: Short Stories*, 1947 (also known as *Labors of Hercules: New Adventures in Crime by Hercule Poirot*); *The Witness for the Prosecution, and Other Stories*, 1948; *The Mousetrap, and Other Stories*, 1949 (also known as *Three Blind Mice, and Other Stories*); *The Under Dog, and Other Stories*, 1951; *The Adventures of the Christmas Pudding, and Selection of Entrées*, 1960; *Double Sin, and Other Stories*, 1961; *Star over Bethlehem, and Other Stories*, 1965 (as A. C.

Mallowan); *Thirteen Clues for Miss Marple: A Collection of Mystery Stories*, 1965; *The Golden Ball, and Other Stories*, 1971; *Hercule Poirot's Early Cases*, 1974; *Miss Marple's Final Cases*, 1979; *The Harlequin Tea Set, and Other Stories*, 1997.

PLAYS: *Black Coffee*, pr. 1930; *Ten Little Niggers*, pr. 1943 (also known as *Ten Little Indians*, pr. 1944); *Appointment with Death*, pr., pb. 1945; *Murder on the Nile*, pr., pb. 1946; *The Hollow*, pr. 1951; *The Mousetrap*, pr. 1952; *Witness for the Prosecution*, pr. 1953; *Spider's Web*, pr. 1954; *Towards Zero*, pr. 1956 (with Gerald Verner); *The Unexpected Guest*, pr., pb. 1958; *Verdict*, pr., pb. 1958; *Go Back for Murder*, pr., pb. 1960; *Afternoon at the Seaside*, pr. 1962; *The Patient*, pr. 1962; *The Rats*, pr. 1962; *Fiddlers Three*, pr. 1971; *Akhnaton*, pb. 1973 (also known as *Akhnaton and Nefertiti*).

POETRY: *The Road of Dreams*, 1925; *Poems*, 1973.

NONFICTION: *Come Tell Me How You Live*, 1946; *An Autobiography*, 1977.

CHILDREN'S LITERATURE: *Thirteen for Luck: A Selection of Mystery Stories for Young Readers*, 1961; *Surprize! Surprize! A Collection of Mystery Stories with Unexpected Endings*, 1965.

BIBLIOGRAPHY

Bunson, Matthew. *The Complete Christie: An Agatha Christie Encyclopedia*. New York: Pocket Books, 2001. Comprehensive reference volume contains alphabetical entries on all characters in Christie's works, cross-referenced to the works in which they appear; plot synopses; listings of all film, television, and radio adaptations of Christie's works and of documentaries about Christie; a biography; and a bibliography.

Christie, Agatha. *An Autobiography*. New York: Dodd, Mead, 1977. Although published the year after her death, this book, which was written over a fifteen-year period, concludes in 1965, when the author was seventy-five years old. Although she does not explain her mysterious disappearance in the 1920's, probably because of her desire for privacy, she provides interesting details about happier events and invaluable commentary on the creation of her works.

Gill, Gillian. *Agatha Christie: The Woman and Her Mysteries*. New York: Free Press, 1990. Short and highly readable biography is definitely of the popular, rather than critical, variety, employing as chapter titles seven different names used at one time or another by the mystery writer (including the assumed name she used during her infamous disappearance in 1926). Still, Gill goes out of her way to emphasize Christie's dedication to her art and the discipline of her life.

Irons, Glenwood, and Joan Warthling Roberts. "From Spinster to Hipster: The 'Suitability' of Miss Marple and Anna Lee." In *Feminism in Women's Detective Fiction*, edited by Glenwood Irons. Toronto, Ont.: University of Toronto Press, 1995. Discusses Christie's creation of Miss Marple as the archetypal British sinister detective figure in stories and novels. Analyzes Marple's basic methodology in *The Tuesday Club Murders*.

Makinen, Merja. *Agatha Christie: Investigating Femininity*. New York: Palgrave Macmillan, 2006. Sets out to disprove what many critics have asserted: that Agatha Christie created her female characters to be weak and inferior to their male counterparts. Emphasizes the ways in which the female characters play vital roles outside the domestic sphere and therefore challenge traditional notions of femininity.

Osborne, Charles. *The Life and Crimes of Agatha Christie: A Biographical Companion to the Works of Agatha Christie*. New York: St. Martin's Press, 2001. Presents a chronological listing of Christie's works accompanied by biographical notes that place the writings within the context of the events of the author's life. Includes bibliographical references and index.

Paul, Robert S. *Whatever Happened to Sherlock Holmes? Detective Fiction, Popular Theology, and Society*. Carbondale: Southern Illinois University Press, 1991. A study of detective fiction based on the general premise that detective stories mirror the morals and theological assumptions of their time. The chapter on Agatha Christie explores how her stories reflect what happens in a society when compassion is lacking.

Shaw, Marion, and Sabine Vanacker. *Reflecting on Miss Marple*. New York: Routledge, 1991. Presents a brief chronology of Christie's life and then devotes four chapters to one of her most memorable detectives, making a case for viewing Miss Marple as a feminist heroine. Reviews the history of women writers and the golden age of detective fiction as well as the social context of Christie's Miss Marple books. Asserts that the spinster Miss Marple is able to solve her cases by exploiting prejudices against unmarried older women.

Thompson, Laura. *Agatha Christie: An English Mystery*. London: Headline Review, 2007. Comprehensive biography, written with the cooperation of Christie's family and with full access to the author's unpublished letters and notebooks. Includes information about Christie's eleven-day disappearance in 1926 and about the novels she wrote under the pseudonym Mary Westmacott.

Wagoner, Mary S. *Agatha Christie*. Boston: Twayne, 1986. Scholarly but readable study of Christie and her writings. A brief biography of Christie in the first chapter is followed by analytical chapters focusing on the different genres of her works, such as short stories. Contains a good bibliography, an index, and a chronological table of Christie's life.

York, R. A. *Agatha Christie: Power and Illusion*. New York: Palgrave Macmillan, 2007. Reevaluates Christie's novels, which traditionally have been described as "cozy" mysteries. Asserts that although these works may appear to depict a stable world of political conservatism, conventional sex and class roles, and clear moral choices, this world is not as safe as it appears to be. Notes how Christie's mysteries also depict war, social mobility, ambiguous morality, violence, and, of course, murder.

SANDRA CISNEROS

Born: Chicago, Illinois; December 20, 1954

PRINCIPAL LONG FICTION

The House on Mango Street, 1984
Caramelo: Or, Puro Cuento, 2002

OTHER LITERARY FORMS

Sandra Cisneros (sihz-NAY-rohs), although primarily known for her longer works, has also tried her hand at other genres. She has published a collection of short stories, *Woman Hollering Creek, and Other Stories* (1991), as well as volumes of poetry, including *Bad Boys* (1980), *My Wicked, Wicked Ways* (1987), and *Loose Woman* (1994). She has also published a children's book as well as nonfiction articles describing her life as a writer and sketches of the works of other writers, such as Ana Castillo and Luis Omar Salinas.

Poetry comes naturally to Cisneros, who is fond of sensory detail and metaphoric language. *Loose Woman*, for example, is a celebration of unbridled feminine sexuality. As a "bad" girl—a woman who wears black-lace bras and frankly describes sex and menstruation—Cisneros's narrator allows herself the luxury of unfettered passion. Sounding at times like a Latina Allen Ginsberg in *Loose Woman*, Cisneros reveals her "dark" side through her need for sexual expression. Ironically, however, Cisneros's poetic language has found its greatest acclaim not through her chapbooks but through her novels. Challenged to find a metaphor for her life as a Latina, Cisneros is most often viewed as a writer of sweeping autobiography rather than as a poet.

ACHIEVEMENTS

Given the lyricism of her writing, it should be no surprise that Sandra Cisneros has garnered considerable critical acclaim since she published *The House on Mango Street* in 1984. She received an Illinois Artists Grant in 1984, which, like an award she received from the National Endowment for the Arts, encouraged her to write versions of poems that would later appear in such collections as *My Wicked, Wicked Ways* and *Loose Woman*, as well as a number of nonfiction articles.

The House on Mango Street, in particular, has been lauded by readers and critics alike. In 1985, it received the Before Columbus Foundation's American Book Award, and since then it has become a staple of many high school and university undergraduate canons. In addition to winning the Chicano Short Story Award from the University of Arizona in 1986, Cisneros garnered many forms of recognition after her first novel's publication that encouraged her to develop her writing. She was the recipient of a Paisano Dobie Fellowship in 1986 and a second award from the National Endowment for the Arts in 1988, and she also was able to accept the Roberta Holloway Lectureship at the University of California, Berkeley, in 1988.

Like *The House on Mango Street*, *Woman Hollering Creek, and Other Stories* received positive attention when it appeared. For this collection of short stories, Cisneros was awarded the PEN Center West Award for Best Fiction of 1991, the Quality Paperback Book Club New Voices Award, the Anisfield-Wolf Book Award, and the Lannan Foundation Literary Award. In 1993, Cisneros was awarded an honorary doctor of literature degree by the State University of New York at Purchase, and in 1995 she was named a MacArthur Fellow. Loyola University, Chicago, presented her with an honorary doctor of humane letters degree in 2002, and in 2003 she received the Texas Medal of the Arts.

BIOGRAPHY

Sandra Cisneros was born in Chicago on December 20, 1954, to upholsterer Alfredo Cisneros, a man she would later describe as both hardworking and generous, and Elvira Cordero Cisneros, one of Sandra's primary sources of encouragement and nurturing. As the third child and only daughter in a family of seven children, she found that her mother and the rest of her family had very different ideas about what kind of woman she should be, whether independent or traditional. Trying to please both of her parents required Cisneros to stay modest and shy as a child while seeking literary ways of expressing herself. Writing down her thoughts and feelings led naturally to her position as editor of her high school's literary magazine, but such writing alone could not fulfill her dreams of escaping the restrictions of her youth.

After she finished high school, Cisneros decided to study at Loyola University of Chicago; she graduated from the university with a bachelor of arts degree in English in 1976. Guided by her goal of becoming a teacher of creative writing, Cisneros then pursued a master of fine arts degree in creative writing at the University of Iowa. During a session at the university's Iowa Writers' Workshop, when the class was discussing the metaphor of a house in philosopher Gaston Bachelard's *La Poétique de l'espace* (1957; *The Poetics of Space*, 1964), Cisneros was struck by how different she was from her privileged classmates. Aside from the fact that she was the only Latina in the group, Cisneros found that her experiences were distinctly outside the constraints of the dominant American culture. She then saw her destiny clearly—to write texts that celebrate what it means to be a Chicana, a Latina, and a southwestern woman.

Cisneros graduated from the University of Iowa with an M.F.A. in 1978. *Bad Boys*, a chapbook of poetry, quickly followed her emergence. She received a National Endowment of the Arts grant in 1982, which allowed her time to write more extensively, and her seminal work, *The House on Mango Street*, was published in 1984 to literary acclaim; the book has sold more than two million copies since then. Her second work of long fiction, the novel *Caramelo*, published in 2002, would also follow the same theme of finding oneself in the context of one's heritage.

Sandra Cisneros. (© Rubén Guzmán)

ANALYSIS

One of the dominant ideas behind much of Sandra Cisneros's work is the importance of autobiography in predominantly fictional work. For example, Cisneros's mother, a Latin American born in Chicago, wanted her daughter to be independent, but her brothers and her father (who was born in Mexico) felt she should be a traditional Mexican wife and mother. With the heavy-handedness displayed by her brothers in their attempts to control her, as well as their patriarchal expectations,

Sandra often felt like she had "seven fathers" rather than just one. She weaves these personal feelings into her fiction, giving the heroine of *The House on Mango Street*, Esperanza, the same sense of isolation within her family and yet giving her a name (*esperanza* is Spanish for "hope") that represents the cheerful optimism with which her family sticks together through good and bad times. Similarly, Cisneros's father was frequently homesick for his native Mexico while still being loyal to his American wife. Consequently, the family, like the Reyes family in Cisneros's later novel *Caramelo*, moved often, alternating between squalid Mexican towns and the barrios of American cities.

Cisneros disliked the impermanence and decrepitude of her childhood—so much so, in fact, that when she recasts her youth in her fiction, she fills the writing with descriptions of introverted and lonely lives as well as cultural displacement. The stories in the collection *Woman Hollering Creek, and Other Stories*, although varying widely in style, all draw on Cisneros's heritage for their themes and metaphors. Often plotless, the stories tend to be impressionistic; "Tin Tan Tan" seems almost poetic in form and has internal rhyme. Other stories carry themes particular to Catholic or Latina life. "Little Miracles, Kept Promises," with its description of a series of letters left at the shrine of La Virgen de Guadalupe, resonates with lines that suggest older forces at work— the shrine being not just the Virgin's home place but also the temple of an Aztec goddess. Symbolically, the book is rich with metaphors. The "real" Woman Hollering Creek is a creek (described as named for the folk-legend figure "La Llorona," or "The Weeping Woman") where, according to local lore, a jilted mother drowned her child. In the story, the main character, Cleofilas, a woman whose violent husband forces her to live as a very traditional Mexican woman and who has few choices in life, is able to overcome her anguish by leaving her abusive husband and her stifling home. Cleofilas represents a destiny that Cisneros had sometimes feared would be her own. As a child, she could not understand why her home could not be like the pristine, idealized ones she saw on television in such programs as *Father Knows Best* and *Leave It to Beaver*, but she sensed that the difference lay in her heritage.

THE HOUSE ON MANGO STREET

The House on Mango Street, the work that Cisneros created to define her understanding of what it means to be Latina, comprises a series of lyrical vignettes that are not quite poems but that sometimes lack the plotting expected for a work of prose fiction. Esperanza, the narrator, describes her daily life not as a series of distinct events but rather as poetic images.

Each vignette can be read independently, because the stories do not depend on each other for an overarching plot. Further, the problems that Esperanza and her family suffer are never fully resolved. The intimacy of the narrator's first-person voice adds warmth to the portraits. Although Esperanza's optimism sometimes wavers, her desire to grow up in a "real house," deflated by her parents' insincere declarations of their home's squalor as temporary, is never fully crushed.

Her relationship with her mother is a close one, and Esperanza's tender description of her mother's ringletted hair, "sweet" like "rosettes," reveals an affectionate acceptance of her despite her failings. The four trees that grow outside Esperanza's window are also important symbols. They are described as "skinny" but determined, and Esperanza takes strength from their refusal to give up despite having to grow in such a harsh environment.

The house on Mango Street, like the houses Cisneros grew up in, is simply a house the protagonist lives in— she does not really consider it "home." Esperanza is even embarrassed to point it out to friends and neighbors because she dislikes the fact that she has to live in such poverty; in her eyes, the house is hardly any better than the string of apartments in which her family had previously lived. Esperanza can only hope that one day she will be able to call a real house "home" while still keeping an affectionate relationship with her hardworking parents.

CARAMELO

In its description of the complex history of a family of Mexican Americans through the stories told by them, *Caramelo* follows many of the same conventions as Cisneros's celebrated work *The House on Mango Street*. Like that earlier work, in which Cisneros uses the image of a house to discuss what "home" and "family" mean to her, *Caramelo* features a strong central symbol: A "caramel rebozo," or traditional striped Mexican shawl, serves as the symbol for three interconnected but very dissimilar generations of Mexican Americans living and working in the United States. Celaya, called Lala, narrates the history of her grandmother, the "Awful" Soledad, and that of Inocencio, her father, as the story moves from Mexico City in the 1920's to Chicago and San Antonio in the 1950's.

Every summer, Soledad's three sons, who run an upholstery shop in Chicago, gather all the extended family for a caravan trip to Mexico City to visit their mother. Lala spends much of her time there trying to learn and understand how her grandmother came to be such a harsh matriarch. Soledad's own parents were rebozo makers, the father exquisitely dying the yarn and the mother elaborately knotting the fringes, but all that is left of Soledad's parents' art is a single shawl colored in vanilla, licorice, and caramel stripes.

Also like *The House on Mango Street*, *Caramelo* depends on the retelling of anecdotes to bring across its meanings. These anecdotes, only occasionally historically accurate, are intended to appeal to the reader's senses rather than to provide factual information. The novel ends on a positive note as, despite difficult circumstances and the disruptive influence of cultural change within the Mexican American household, the family members choose to remain as close to one another as the stripes of Soledad's shawl, for if even one thread is pulled loose, the whole "weaving" could unravel.

Julia M. Meyers

OTHER MAJOR WORKS

SHORT FICTION: *Woman Hollering Creek, and Other Stories*, 1991.

POETRY: *Bad Boys*, 1980; *The Rodrigo Poems*, 1985; *My Wicked, Wicked Ways*, 1987; *Loose Woman*, 1994.

CHILDREN'S LITERATURE: *Hairs = Pelitos*, 1984.

MISCELLANEOUS: *Vintage Cisneros*, 2004.

BIBLIOGRAPHY

Brady, Mary Pat. "The Contrapunctal Geographies of *Woman Hollering Creek and Other Stories*." *American Literature* 71, no. 1 (March, 1999): 117-150. Particularly interesting essay outlines Cisneros's work not just as Hispanic literature but also as American literature. Brady's point seems validated by Cisneros's support of specifically Texan writers through the Alfredo Cisneros Del Moral Foundation (created in honor of her father).

Doyle, Jacqueline. "More Room of Her Own: Sandra Cisneros's *The House on Mango Street*." *MELUS* 19, no. 4 (Winter, 1994): 5-35. Discusses the complexity of the issue of multiethnicity within Hispanic literature, given the different perspectives of first-, second-, and third-generation immigrants. Asserts that recognizing generational differences is key to understanding Cisneros's depictions of family life and family relationships.

Saldívar-Hull, Sonia. *Feminism on the Border: Chicana Gender Politics and Literature*. Berkeley: University of California Press, 2000. Valuable resource places Cisneros within the context of Latina literature. Addresses Cisneros's works as political statements concerning not just ethnicity or gender but also the separate aims of different Hispanic generations.

Thomkins, Cynthia. "Sandra Cisneros." In *American Novelists Since World War II, Fourth Series*, edited by James R. Giles and Wanda H. Giles. Vol. 152 in *Dictionary of Literary Biography*. Detroit, Mich.: Gale Group, 1995. Concise, clearly written discussion of Cisneros's life and works provides a good starting point for a student beginning research on the author. Includes a list of additional sources to which students can go for further information.

Tokarczyk, Michelle M. *Class Definitions: On the Lives and Writings of Maxine Hong Kingston, Sandra Cisneros, and Dorothy Allison*. Selinsgrove, Pa.: Susquehanna University Press, 2008. Discusses the lives and work of the three authors, focusing on their shared traits as working-class writers, as evidenced by their concern with providing a voice for the voiceless. Includes a previously unpublished interview with Cisneros.

TOM CLANCY

Born: Baltimore, Maryland; April 12, 1947
Also known as: Thomas Leo Clancy, Jr.

PRINCIPAL LONG FICTION

The Hunt for Red October, 1984
Red Storm Rising, 1986
Patriot Games, 1987
The Cardinal of the Kremlin, 1988
Clear and Present Danger, 1989
The Sum of All Fears, 1991
Without Remorse, 1993
Debt of Honor, 1994
Op-Center, 1995 (with Steve Pieczenik)
Executive Orders, 1996
Tom Clancy's Power Plays: Politika, 1997 (with Martin Greenberg)
Rainbow Six, 1998
Tom Clancy's Power Plays: Ruthless.com, 1998 (with Greenberg)
The Deadliest Game, 1999 (with Pieczenik)
Night Moves, 1999 (with Pieczenik)
Tom Clancy's Net Force, 1999 (with Pieczenik)
Tom Clancy's Power Plays: Shadow Watch, 1999 (with Greenberg)
Virtual Vandals, 1999 (with Pieczenik)
The Bear and the Dragon, 2000
Net Force: Hidden Agenda, 2000 (with Pieczenik)
Private Lives, 2000 (with Pieczenik)
Shadow of Honor, 2000 (with Pieczenik)
Red Rabbit, 2002
The Teeth of the Tiger, 2003

OTHER LITERARY FORMS

In addition to novels, Tom Clancy has written a number of nonfiction books focusing on U.S. military apparatus, including submarines, armored cavalry, fighter planes, and aircraft carriers, and on the U.S. Marine Corps, special forces, and airborne units. He also has collaborated with U.S. generals Fred Franks, Jr., Tony Zinni, Carl Stiner, and Chuck Horner on books that are part biography, part history, and part highly detailed leadership manuals. All four generals are Vietnam War veterans. The book with Zinni was written after the 2003 invasion of Iraq and became controversial because of Zinni's criticisms of U.S. policies and decisions.

ACHIEVEMENTS

Tom Clancy's novel *Clear and Present Danger* sold more than 1.6 million hardcover copies, which made it the best-selling novel of the 1980's, and his novel *The Cardinal of the Kremlin* was the best-selling novel of 1988. Clancy is one of the few authors to have sold more than two million copies on a first printing (John Grisham and J. K. Rowling are among the others). Overall, he has sold more than fifty million books. *Forbes* magazine reported that he earned forty-seven million dollars in 2001.

Clancy is often credited with creating the techno-thriller genre. These novels blend science fiction's interest in technical and scientific detail (using technologies that should exist at the time of writing) with suspenseful military, crime, and espionage fiction. Clancy dislikes the term "technothriller," and he credits novelist Michael Crichton for developing the genre with his 1969 novel *The Andromeda Strain*. Clancy likens his own novels to those in the police procedural subgenre, because of their interest in the mechanics of solving a mystery. His speciality is applying the technique to military and espionage fiction. Other examples of the techno-thriller written before the term was coined are *Fail-Safe* (1962), by Eugene Burdick and Harvey Wheeler, and *The Penetrators* (1965), by Hank Searls (writing as Anthony Gray).

BIOGRAPHY

Thomas Leo Clancy, Jr.'s father was a postman, and his mother worked in the credit department of Montgomery Ward. The young Clancy read Jules Verne's *Twenty Thousand Leagues Under the Sea* (1872; originally published as *Vingt mille lieues sous les mers*, 1870) when he was in the third grade and later became an avid reader of military history. He started writing while in high school, graduating from Loyola Blakefield High in Towson, Maryland, in 1965. Clancy earned a bachelor's degree from Loyola College in Baltimore in 1969, with a major in English literature. His fictional alter ego, Jack Ryan, also was born in Maryland and attended Catholic high schools and universities. Though he wanted to serve in the military, Clancy failed the eye examination. Ryan, on the other hand, was with the Reserve Officers' Training Corps in college and was commissioned a second lieutenant in the Marine Corps after graduating. Clancy married Wanda Thomas, an insurance agency manager, in 1969, and they had four children, Michelle, Christine, Tom, and Kathleen. They were divorced in 1998. In 1999, Clancy married freelance journalist Alexandra Marie Llewellyn, a first cousin of former U.S. secretary of state Colin Powell, who introduced them.

Before Clancy sold his first novel, he sold insurance. Prior to *The Hunt for Red October*, his writings in professional publications consisted of a letter to the editor and an article on the MX missile, both of which appeared in the journal *Proceedings of the Naval Institute*. He wrote some science fiction after college, but was unable to sell it. He wrote the first one hundred pages of what became the novel *Patriot Games* in 1978 and the first chapter of what became the novel *The Sum of All Fears* in 1979.

In August of 1982, Clancy, then thirty-five years old, decided it was time he write a novel, namely a thriller in the tradition of Frederick Forsyth, John le Carré, Alistair MacLean, and Len Deighton. He began the first draft of *The Hunt for Red October* on November 11, 1982, and finished it on February 23, 1983. He personally delivered the manuscript to an editor at the Naval Institute Press in Annapolis, Maryland, which had never published a work of fiction. Three weeks later, the editor responded with a letter of suggestions and then offered Clancy a three-thousand-dollar advance to publish the book. Clancy negotiated the fee to five thousand dollars. The novel was published in October of 1984 with an initial print run of fourteen thousand copies. U.S. president Ronald Reagan endorsed the book in an interview with *Time* magazine. *The Hunt for Red October* became a best seller, allowing Clancy to quit his job selling insurance to write full time. He received a seven figure advance for his second novel, *Red Storm Rising*, an immediate best seller as well.

ANALYSIS

Except for *Red Storm Rising*, Tom Clancy's novels feature, or are somehow connected with, the fictional character John Patrick "Jack" Ryan, who is an idealized portrait of Clancy. The novels are often referred to as the Ryanverse, or the Jack Ryan series.

Although some critics have compared Clancy to James Fenimore Cooper for writing long novels about men of action, there is an important difference between the two novelists. Cooper's fiction, such as *The Last of the Mohicans* (1826), features protagonists who flee from the constraints of civil society and the obligations of matrimony and family. Clancy's protagonists, however, have no wish to escape from society. Instead, Ryan and his friends embrace it, including its responsibilities and duties.

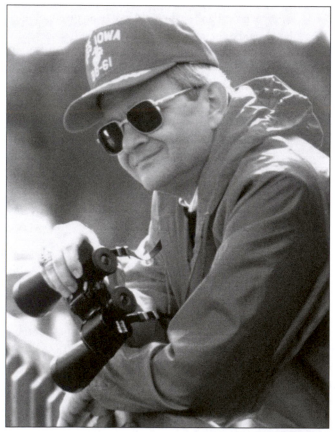

Tom Clancy. (John Earle)

Clancy believes in the virtues of bravery, self-sacrifice, and individual responsibility, character traits he claims had been lacking in mainstream fiction. In particular, be argued that novels such as Gustav Hasford's *The Short-Timers* (1979) and Michael Herr's *Dispatches* (1977) were too negative and pessimistic. Clancy also disapproved of the portrayal of military personnel as insane or immoral, or both, in films such as *Apocalypse Now* (1979). Clancy's fictional soldiers, in contrast, are competent, dedicated, and honorable professionals.

WITHOUT REMORSE

Although *Without Remorse* is Clancy's seventh novel, it is the first book in the Ryanverse chronology and is set during U.S. president Richard Nixon's first term of office. Ryan's father, Emmett, a police homicide lieutenant and World War II veteran, is a major character in the story, and those portions of the book read like a police procedural. The novel's main character is John Kelly, also known as John Clark, a former Navy SEAL who served in Vietnam. Kelly had already appeared as a character in several of Clancy's books as John Clark, but this novel provides Kelly's back story.

Without Remorse also was written in response to the *Rambo* series of films starring Sylvester Stallone. Although Clancy's Kelly suffers from depression and engages in a vigilante campaign against drug dealers and pimps, he is neither a superhero nor crazy.

PATRIOT GAMES

In *Patriot Games*, Jack Ryan and his family are on a combined business trip and family vacation to London when Jack foils an attempt by Irish terrorists to kidnap the prince and princess of Wales. After the terrorists come after him and his family, Ryan joins the Central Intelligence Agency (CIA). The premise is similar to that in John D. MacDonald's *The Executioners* (1957). Both operate under the no-good-deed-goes-unpunished principle in which a good person suffers for doing the right thing.

RED RABBIT

Red Rabbit is the novel that most clearly reflects the influence of Forsyth's *The Day of the Jackal* (1971). In *Red Rabbit*, Ryan's first field assignment for the CIA is to assist the defection of a Russian communications officer who has discovered that the Soviet Politburo has ordered the assassination of Roman Catholic pope John Paul II. *Red Rabbit* achieves its suspense even though readers know that the real John Paul II was not assassinated. In comparison, Forsyth, too, had achieved a high degree of suspense in *The Day of the Jackal*, even though his readers knew that in reality, French president Charles de Gaulle had not been assassinated, as he was in the novel; rather, he died of natural causes.

THE CARDINAL OF THE KREMLIN

Ryan is serving at CIA headquarters in Langley, Virginia, as the Special Assistant to the Deputy Director for Intelligence when he travels to Moscow to rescue one of the agency's most important spies in *The Cardinal of the Kremlin*. This book shows the influence of novelists Robert Ludlum, le Carré, and Deighton. What distinguishes Clancy, however, is his refusal to include moral ambiguities in his fiction. With Clancy, the good guys are clearly good, and the bad guys clearly bad. Critics have objected to Clancy's approach, but he has explained that he believes no moral equivalency exists between the United States and its enemies.

CLEAR AND PRESENT DANGER

Clear and Present Danger is Clancy's response to the Iran-Contra scandal of the Reagan administration. One character is loosely based on Lieutenant Colonel Oliver North, a member of Reagan's White House staff who was forced to resign, and another on William Casey, director of the CIA under Reagan. A drug lord in the story is loosely based on Pablo Escobar, a real-life Colombian drug lord. Ryan becomes acting deputy director of the CIA for intelligence, and the plot revolves around the abuse of military force to literally make a "war on drugs."

THE SUM OF ALL FEARS

In *The Sum of All Fears*, Ryan has become the deputy director of the CIA, the highest position he will reach in the agency. Unfortunately for him, he has become the enemy of both the president and his national security adviser, a woman who is also the president's lover. The president and security adviser panic when radical Islamic terrorists explode a nuclear device at the Super Bowl game, but the day is saved by Ryan's cool judgment. Rumors persist that the novel's president and his lover are loosely based on Bill Clinton and Hillary Rodham Clinton. The novel, however, was published one year before Bill Clinton was elected U.S. president.

DEBT OF HONOR

The ending of *Debt of Honor* anticipates the hijackings of September 11, 2001. At the beginning of the book, Ryan is the president's national security adviser as the Japanese are planning an undeclared war against the United States. Once again, Ryan's cool judgment saves the day. Meanwhile, the vice president, who is loosely based on U.S. senator Ted Kennedy, is forced to resign after a sex scandal, and the president selects Ryan for the job as a reward for his service. Ryan has just been confirmed by Congress when a grieving Japanese airline pilot deliberately crashes his Boeing 747 passenger jet into the Capitol Building while the president is addressing a joint session of Congress. The crash kills most of the people inside and leads to Ryan's appointment as president of the United States.

THE HUNT FOR RED OCTOBER

The Hunt for Red October follows the interweaving adventures of Jack Ryan and Soviet submarine captain Marko Ramius. The novel is set some time between the events depicted in *Red Rabbit* and *The Cardinal of the Kremlin* and is loosely based on two real incidents. In 1961, a Soviet submarine captain, a Lithuanian, sailed his vessel from the Soviet Union to the Swedish island Gotland. The submarine was returned to the Soviets, but the captain successfully defected to the United States. In 1975, a Soviet navy frigate mutinied. At the time, Western analysts concluded it was another attempt by crew members to defect. The mutiny was unsuccessful, however, and its leader was captured, court-martialed, and executed.

In Clancy's version, Ramius is a Lithuanian who, as a boy, was secretly baptized as a Roman Catholic. He entered the Soviet navy at the age of thirteen and specialized in submarines. Ramius becomes one of their top submarine commanders, but he decides to defect to the United States with his officers and the experimental nuclear submarine *Red October*. This submarine is equipped with an innovative stealth propulsion system that makes sonar detection extremely difficult. It becomes clear to Ryan and the top admirals in the U.S. Navy that the submarine is capable of sneaking into U.S. waters and launching its nuclear missiles without warning. It is a first-strike weapon that could tempt the Soviet Union into starting a nuclear war. Ryan con-

cludes that Ramius's intention is defection, not war, and is given the chance to rescue him and his submarine. However, he also understands that if the choice is between Ramius and World War III, he must sacrifice Ramius.

Thomas R. Feller

OTHER MAJOR WORKS

NONFICTION: *Submarine: A Guided Tour Inside a Nuclear Warship*, 1993; *Armored Cav: A Guided Tour of an Armored Cavalry Regiment*, 1994; *Fighter Wing: A Guided Tour of an Air Force Combat Wing*, 1995; *Marine: A Guided Tour of a Marine Expeditionary Unit*, 1996; *Airborne: A Guided Tour of an Airborne Task Force*, 1997; *Into the Storm: A Study in Command*, 1997 (with Fred Franks, Jr.); *Carrier: A Guided Tour of an Aircraft Carrier*, 1999; *Every Man a Tiger*, 1999 (with Chuck Horner); *Future War: Non-Lethal Weapons in Modern Warfare*, 1999 (with John B. Alexander); *Special Forces: A Guided Tour of U.S. Army Special Forces*, 2001; *Shadow Warriors: Inside the Special Forces*, 2002 (with Carl Stiner and Tony Koltz); *Battle Ready*, 2004 (with Tony Zinni and Koltz).

BIBLIOGRAPHY

Bishop, Chuck. "Tom Clancy's Jack Ryan: Secular Catholic Hero?" *Catholic New Times* 26, no. 16 (October 20, 2002). Essay on the Catholicism of Jack Ryan, John Kelly Clark, and other major characters in Clancy's books. Also compares the policies of fictional president John P. Ryan with actual president George W. Bush.

Cowley, Jason. "He Is the Most Popular Novelist on Earth, Whose Images of Catastrophe Animate the American Psyche." *New Statesman*, no. 130 (September 24, 2001). An essay on Clancy arguing that the main reason for his popularity is that his novels are responding to a kind of nihilism permeating American culture that is driven by the need to entertain.

Greenberg, Martin H., ed. *The Tom Clancy Companion*. Rev. ed. New York: Berkeley Books, 2005. Features an introduction by Larry Bond, Clancy's collaborator on *Red Storm Rising* and consultant for *The Hunt for Red October*; a long essay by Marc A. Cerasini,

"Tom Clancy and the Coming of the Techno-Thriller," which examines the concept of the technothriller while comparing and contrasting Clancy with other authors; an interview with Clancy by Greenberg, explaining how Clancy came to write *The Hunt for Red October* and other books; reprints of short essays by Clancy on a variety of subjects; and a concordance on military units, ships, planes, equipment, and characters in the novels.

Vinciguerra, Thomas. "Word for Word: The Clancy Effect." *The New York Times*, August 18, 2002. Quotes passages from several of Clancy's novels as examples of poor literary style and comments on the good and bad aspects of his fiction.

WALTER VAN TILBURG CLARK

Born: East Orland, Maine; August 3, 1909
Died: Reno, Nevada; November 10, 1971

PRINCIPAL LONG FICTION

The Ox-Bow Incident, 1940
The City of Trembling Leaves, 1945
The Track of the Cat, 1949
Tim Hazard, 1951

OTHER LITERARY FORMS

In addition to his three major novels, Walter Van Tilburg Clark published one short-story collection, *The Watchful Gods, and Other Stories* (1950), and an early poetry volume, *Ten Women in Gale's House, and Shorter Poems* (1932).

ACHIEVEMENTS

By the time of his death in 1971, Walter Van Tilburg Clark's reputation had been largely eclipsed by almost twenty years of inactivity since the publication of his last book. The author of but a slender corpus of work—three novels, one short-story collection, and one volume of poetry—he had suffered the particular misfortune of a talented writer who felt unable to fulfill the promise of a successful first novel. The critical and commercial popularity of *The Ox-Bow Incident* invariably led critics and reviewers to compare his next two novels with his first achievement. The disappointing reception of his second novel, *The City of Trembling Leaves*, and the failure of his third novel, *The Track of the Cat*, to match the response to his first book may have led Clark to become overly sensitive about his work. After 1951, he published no further books during his lifetime, although he left at least two novels uncompleted at his death. His first and third novels, however, were adapted to the screen and became successful motion pictures.

One critic, L. L. Lee, has written of the personal and human "tragedy" of Clark's abortive writing career. There is no denying that Clark's reluctance to continue publishing was a loss to American letters, but it may well have been that the author's greatest obstacle consisted of his own rigorous critical standards, which would not allow him to publish anything he suspected was second-rate. He was particularly aware of the need for good writers in the literature of the American West, a field dominated by pulp romances and dime-store paperbacks. In Clark's case, however, literature's loss was teaching's gain, since he enjoyed a distinguished career as a professor of creative writing during the last twenty years of his life, teaching at half a dozen different colleges and universities in the West and serving as visiting lecturer at many others. Clark is by no means the only writer who ever abandoned the craft for the academy, but his particular hesitancy to publish is still unusual, as he was a writer of genuine talent and ability.

Clark was a sensitive and demanding writer with a keen sense of craftsmanship and exacting critical standards. He had little patience with poor writing and no desire to write for a popular market, although he clearly could have done so after the success of his first novel. He also had no desire to be pegged as merely another "Western writer." He wanted above all to be a good writer who happened to write about the American West because that was what he knew and understood best. In a letter written September 1, 1959, he stated, "In part, I set about writing *The Ox-Bow Incident* as a kind of deliberate technical exercise." He was determined to take the ingredients of the conventional Western plot and "bring both the people and the situations alive again." He succeeded brilliantly in his tense melodrama of a Nevada rustling incident in 1885, a suspected murder, a posse, a chase, and the lynching of three innocent men by a cowardly and unthinking mob.

Clark's initial success with *The Ox-Bow Incident* was not an accident. The same lean, spare, carefully modulated prose marks his subsequent novels and stories. Clark's work demonstrates his mastery of several techniques. First, as an intensely masculine writer, he has an uncanny knack for capturing the language and behavior of real men. He is careful, however, not to allow artificial or melodramatic elements to intrude on his characterizations. His characters, especially in *The Ox-Bow Incident*, are direct and laconic in speech; there is nothing contrived or romanticized about their conversation or action. In this sense, especially, Clark rejects the romantic formula used by Owen Wister and others in favor of a realistic, historically accurate treatment of the late nineteenth century West. In the introduction to his master's thesis on the legend of Tristram and Isolde, Clark had argued that the past must be made alive again through literature, and he proceeded to accomplish this reanimation through his own work.

The period about which Clark wrote in both *The Ox-Bow Incident* and *The Track of the Cat* was that transitional period after the American Civil War when the West was neither frontier nor fully settled. His town of Bridger's Wells in *The Ox-Bow Incident* is scarcely more than a stagecoach stop with a saloon, a general store, a boardwalk, and a few ramshackle storefronts. The Bridges, the ranching family in *The Track of the Cat*, live in an even more remote mountain valley in the Sierra Nevada. Their nearest neighbors live in the next valley. In short, Clark's characters are either cattlemen or employees of ranchers and cattlemen.

Clark had little material to work with in the Nevada of the 1880's. His society was a raw world of men—violent, transient, and rootless. It was not yet tamed by the more permanent forms of settlement—the family, the school, and the church. As Walter Prescott Webb has pointed out, however, Clark concentrated on three aspects of his world: the spectacular mountain landscape, the harsh and dramatic weather, and the men themselves. Out of these elements, Clark shaped his Western fiction.

Perhaps Clark demonstrated his finest abilities as a writer in his depictions of the landscapes and climate of the American West—those harsh natural forces and vast stretches of land that distinguish the high plains and mountainous regions. Each of Clark's novels is set in the Nevada region, but the natural environment figures most prominently in *The Ox-Bow Incident* and *The Track of the Cat*; the harsh winter climate of the Sierra Nevada and the imposing presence of the mountains dominate both books. The natural environment functions as more than simply a backdrop or setting—it is a brooding, implacable presence, always to be reckoned with in its sudden storms and heavy, isolating snows. Moreover, it is symbolic of all the latent powers of nature that the white American has tried to subdue.

Clark's characters ignore or defy nature at their peril, since it will eventually have its revenge on them. Clark's white characters lack the wise passivity of the Native Americans, the Indians whom he so admired, with their responses to nature shaped by long adjustment to their environment. He believed that eventually white Americans in the West would come to resemble the Indian, if their culture survived, but their impulse to dominate and exploit the natural environment would first have to give way to a wise ethic of land use. As Arthur Bridges comments in *The Track of the Cat*, the American Dream-turned-nightmare is a "belly dream" of property greed and material abundance, regardless of the cost to the land itself or to the Native Americans who had formerly inhabited the land. Clark believed that, unless the white man's attitude to the land could change, natural forces would return to haunt him. In Clark's works, this stance is represented perhaps by the mythic black panther in *The Track of the Cat* or by the darkness and sudden snowstorm that panic the posse into hasty mob revenge and lynch law in *The Ox-Bow Incident*.

Any assessment of Clark's career must return finally to the question of why this talented and gifted novelist failed to fulfill his early promise as a writer. What may

Walter Van Tilburg Clark. (Library of Congress)

finally have thwarted his literary development was not his lack of ability but perhaps the limitations of his genre. He may simply have failed to find a suitable direction for his work after his third novel was published. Although he had exploited the possibilities of the conventional Western myth in his historical Nevada regionalism and local color, he could not break from the restrictions of the formula Western enough to write a really good novel of the modern American West. In fact, his attempt to accomplish this in his second novel, *The City of Trembling Leaves*, resulted in his weakest book. Rather than submit to the endless reiteration of the romantic Western myths and their trappings, Clark stopped writing. The tenacity of the Western myth proved more potent, finally, than the resources of his imagination. Clark's dilemma was that of the serious Western writer today: to find ways to reinterpret the history and materials of the West from

new perspectives—either through revisionist views of history that acknowledge the costs as well as the achievements of the winning of the West or through the incorporation of other perspectives, such as Spanish American, Native American, or feminist views of the American West.

BIOGRAPHY

The first of four children in an academically talented family, Walter Van Tilburg Clark was born in East Orland, Maine, on August 3, 1909. His parents, Walter Ernest and Euphemia Abrams Clark, were cultured, refined people who introduced their children to music and the arts. Dr. Clark often read to his children in the evenings, and his wife Euphemia, who had studied piano and composition at Columbia University before she turned to social work, encouraged her son to paint and learn to play the piano. Thus, early in life he "developed a love of reading and writing, music, and art."

Dr. Walter Ernest Clark enjoyed a distinguished career as economics professor at City College of New York, where he served as chairman of the Economics Department and was awarded the French Legion of Honor during World War I. The Clarks lived in West Nyack, New York, until 1917, when Dr. Clark resigned his position at City College in order to become president of the University of Nevada at Reno, where he served until 1933. Thus, at the age of nine, young Van Tilburg Clark moved to the West, the region that was to become the focus of his later writing. The Clarks did not live a sheltered academic life in Reno. Many of their friends were, in fact, miners and ranchers, and Clark came to know these people well. He also spent much of his time "camping and hiking in the desert hills and the Sierras." Not being native-born, he saw the landscape and character of the West afresh, with a sensitivity and receptiveness that is registered in his fiction.

In the city of Reno, Walter Van Tilburg Clark enjoyed an active and conventional adolescence. He attended public schools in the city—Orvis Ring Grammar School and Reno High School—and became an accomplished tennis player. A fictionalized portrait of these years appears in his autobiographical novel *The City of Trembling Leaves*, a bildungsroman that traces the development of the young musician Tim Hazard and his friends as they grow up in Reno during the 1920's. At that time, the city had not yet become a garish gambling and divorce center, and it retained much of its original flavor as a town of the American West. After high school graduation, Clark entered the University of Nevada in Reno in 1926, majoring in English and earning his bachelor's degree (1930) and master's degree (1931) there.

While at the university, Clark was active in theater, contributed to the campus literary magazine, and played varsity tennis and basketball. After completing his college work, he decided to remain at Reno and begin his graduate study in English. For his master's thesis he wrote "The Sword-Swinger: The Tale of Tristram Retold," a creative reinterpretation in verse of the Tristram and Isolde legend, to which he added a critical introduction. Continuing his graduate study in English, he came east in 1931 to the University of Vermont, where he served as a teaching assistant and earned a second master's degree in English in 1934. This time, he concentrated on American literature and the Greek classics, writing his master's thesis on Robinson Jeffers. As Max Westbrook has pointed out, Clark had met Jeffers at the California poet's home, Thor House, and was "immediately impressed." Echoes of Jeffers and E. A. Robinson appeared in Clark's first volume of poetry, *Ten Women in Gale's House*, published in Boston in 1932.

While in graduate school, Clark married Barbara F. Morse in Elmira, New York, on October 14, 1933. They had two children, Barbara Ann and Robert Morse. After he finished his master's study at Vermont in 1934, Clark and his family spent most of the next ten years in the small upstate New York town of Cazenovia, where he taught high school English and dramatics and coached basketball and tennis. There he wrote *The Ox-Bow Incident*, which became a best seller in 1940.

In 1940, Clark went to Indian Springs, Nevada, for a year before returning to Cazenovia. He then taught for a year in Rye, New York, in 1945, before permanently moving to the West with his family a year later. By that time, he had published two novels and had won the O. Henry Award in 1945 for one of his short stories, "The Wind and the Snow of Winter," an event that influenced him to quit teaching and devote himself to his writing. In 1946, the Clarks lived in Taos, New Mexico, before moving to a ranch in the Washoe Valley and then

finally settling in Virginia City. Clark's last published novel, *The Track of the Cat*, appeared in 1949, followed by *Tim Hazard*, the enlarged version of *The City of Trembling Leaves*. Clark then published *The Watchful Gods and Other Stories* in 1950.

After 1950, finding it difficult to sustain his writing career, Clark returned to teaching. He taught creative writing at the University of Nevada until 1953, when he resigned to protest the "autocratic" administration of the university. Following that position, he taught intermittently at a number of schools, including Reed College, the University of Montana, and San Francisco State College. He earned a reputation as a dedicated and demanding professor of creative writing at the University of Montana from 1953 to 1956 before moving to San Francisco State, where he subsequently became director of creative writing from 1956 to 1962. He was awarded an honorary D.Litt. by Colgate University in 1957. In 1962, Clark returned to the University of Nevada in Reno as writer-in-residence, but by that time his career as a writer had virtually ended. He edited the papers of the Western writer Alfred Doten and even began a biography of him, which he did not live to finish. He died of cancer on November 10, 1971, in Reno, leaving two novels incomplete, his early promise as a writer never entirely fulfilled.

ANALYSIS

In his afterword to *The Ox-Bow Incident*, Walter Prescott Webb quotes Walter Van Tilburg Clark as saying, "Though I was born in Maine . . . I am essentially a westerner, and mostly of the desert breed." Although not a westerner by birth and in fact the product of a distinctly eastern academic family, Clark absorbed enough of the history and flavor of his adopted region to consider himself a genuine Western writer. In addition to his sense of character and place, he developed what amounted to a Native American sensibility—an almost mystical reverence for the natural environment that places his novels in an authentic Western natural setting, one in which mountains, desert, and weather assume the proportions of protagonists in the human drama. This Western sensibility is evident in his first novel, *The Ox-Bow Incident*, and becomes even more pronounced in his third book, *The Track of the Cat*.

THE OX-BOW INCIDENT

The Ox-Bow Incident is by any standards a brilliant first novel, and it won recognition for Clark as a major new talent among Western writers. His novel was praised by critics as the prototype of a new kind of Western that would lend dignity and stature to the genre. Indeed, Clark had accomplished something new in reinvigorating the tired and hackneyed conventions of the Western. As Webb argues, *The Ox-Bow Incident* is a taut, relentless tragedy in five acts. It portrays all of the familiar archetypes of the Western experience—good men and bad, thieves and outlaws, cattlemen and rustlers, sheriffs and posses—yet it manages to retell the story in a new way.

Dealing with the attempt to establish law and order in a lawless land, the novel does not, however, allow justice to be served in the conventional fashion of the Western romance. Instead, in Clark's novel, a posse's attempt to take the law into its own hands results in a miscarriage of justice. After an all-night pursuit and capture, three innocent men are tried, convicted, and hanged on the basis of compelling but misleading circumstantial evidence. The posse is browbeaten into taking revenge by a sadistic and psychopathic leader, Gerald Tetley, a former Confederate officer turned cattleman who hungers for swift justice and has little use for the formalities of the law. There are no other potential leaders to speak for restraint and due process or to stand up to Tetley's domineering egotism, although the old storekeeper, Arthur Davies, tries, later blaming himself for lacking the courage to defy Tetley. These events, the report of a supposed murder, the formation of the posse, and the pursuit and capture of the supposed rustlers all occur within twenty-four hours. The novel is narrated in the first person by Art Croft, a cowhand who has wandered down from the mountains to Bridger's Wells after spending the winter with his buddy, Gil Carter, holed up in a cabin on the winter range. He is deputized into the posse against his better judgment and serves as an unwilling participant in and observer of the subsequent action.

While the ostensible theme of the novel is the weakness and culpability of the mob deputized to pursue the alleged rustlers, the abiding issue is the establishment of justice in the West. One might argue that as regions of the West passed from territory into statehood, the status of the law also changed from the near anarchy of "natural law," to the rough and ready status of common law or territorial law, to the more fixed and certain statutory law that was finally imposed. Men in a lawless region are always ready to take the law into their own hands, and Clark dramatizes the tragic consequences of lynch law, particularly for the young cattleman Donald Martin, who leaves a widow and two young children. Martin, who has the misfortune to be caught driving another man's cattle without a bill of sale, has committed no greater crime than rashness and lack of foresight.

There are obviously no heroes in this novel—only villains and victims—and everyone is tainted in some way by mob violence or moral cowardice. The mob in fact takes on a kind of collective identity that reminds one of Reinhold Niebuhr's observation about groups and nations behaving less responsibly than individuals. The common enemy is rumor and impulsiveness, and in the absence of responsible leaders, the mob is easily swayed by demagogues. In a town inflamed by rumors of rustling and murder, the forces of law and order are ironically absent, or are unable to dissuade the mob from setting forth hastily (and, as it turns out, illegally) in pursuit of the rustlers. Clark once wrote in a letter that the novel contained a veiled warning against the threat of fascism, and one might even call it a parable about the fate of justice in a democracy that degenerates into mob rule.

THE CITY OF TREMBLING LEAVES

Clark's second novel, *The City of Trembling Leaves*, is a very different kind of book, one that some critics suspect Clark had written previous to *The Ox-Bow Incident*. A rather unconvincing "portrait of the artist as a young man" in Reno, the novel tells the story of Tim Hazard, a sensitive young artist manqué who hopes to become a musician. Unfortunately, too much of the novel is preoccupied with Hazard's adolescence and high school experiences and too little with his later accomplishments. Too much of the book is about wanting to be an artist—or rather about the burden of growing up with an artistic temperament in a philistine society—and too little is about the specifics of musical training and the development of a career.

Tim Hazard does not mature into a convincing American composer—he remains too much the sensitive and troubled adolescent—nor does he evidence a strong will to succeed or triumph over adverse circumstances. In short, the protagonist is not a convincing or interesting enough character to fill a 690-page novel. The book does not compare well with Willa Cather's *The Song of the Lark* (1915), for example, which brings the heroine, Thea Kronborg, out of the provincial West and back to Chicago, and eventually to a distinguished opera career in New York. *The City of Trembling Leaves* is, in short, the kind of novel a young writer will often try once and then put aside without publishing. It merely demonstrates that Clark's true métier was the frontier West.

THE TRACK OF THE CAT

In his third novel, *The Track of the Cat*, Clark returns to Nevada frontier material in his powerful account of the Bridges family, isolated on their mountain ranch deep in the Sierra, and their attempts to stalk a panther that has been ravaging their cattle. The action takes place during a winter blizzard as the three brothers—Arthur, Curt, and Harold—set out successively to hunt down the killer mountain lion. The quest itself becomes something of a parable of the American Dream, about the discovery, settlement, and exploitation of the West. Through the Bridges family, Clark explores the question of the American's proper relationship with the land—as dreamer, exploiter, or preserver—with the black panther representing the violent and unpredictable forces of nature that oppose man's attempts to subdue the land. The novel's action shifts between the Bridgeses' ranch and the surrounding valley and rugged mountain ranges as the brothers attempt to track the cat and thus meet their fate. The thematic focus alternates between dream and reality as each of the brothers dreams his fate before he meets it.

In part 1, Arthur, the impractical dreamer, trusting too much in the goodness of the natural world, is ambushed and killed by the cat. The second part of the book shifts back to the Bridges family, whose unnatural tensions and conflicts are heightened by the suspense of waiting for Arthur's return and the confinement enforced by the storm. The father, a maudlin alcoholic, escapes from the present by heavy drinking; the mother, a cold, bitter, religious woman, tried to interfere with her youngest son Harold's engagement to Gwen Williams, who is visiting from a nearby ranch; and the sister, Grace, is a hysterical spinster. The entire family represents, as L. L. Lee suggests, the decline in the American

pioneer stock and its ideals, which were never very noble. The land seems to harden and distort the character of these people, making them ruthless and exploitative; there is none of the American Indian's reverence or understanding of the land. Instead, these people live isolated and apart from nature without roots, connections, or a sense of place. The old Piute, Joe Sam, who works with the Bridges as a farmhand, suggests the gap between the Native American and white cultures and the inability of the white to learn or benefit from the Indian.

In part 3, the longest section of the novel, Curt's dream turns to nightmare as he sets out to find his brother Arthur and becomes lost and disoriented in the storm. His arrogant self-sufficiency proves inadequate in the face of the prolonged storm, until he cannot tell whether he is tracking or being tracked by the great cat, who comes to assume in Curt's confused imagination the proportions of Joe Sam's mythological panther. After two days of hunger and exposure, Curt loses his bearings in the storm and panics, believing he is being pursued; he runs away wildly, finally plunging over a snow-covered cliff.

In part 4, Curt's frozen body is finally found the following day by Harold, the youngest brother, and Joe Sam. Harold, who combines reverence for the cat with common sense and decency to the old American Indian, finally kills the cat and puts an end to its slaughter of their herd. Presumably, he will also marry Gwen Williams and carry on the family's ranch, eventually earning his birthright to the land and becoming a true westerner. He will find a way to combine the white American's energy and enterprise with the Native American's reverence for the land and sense of the sacredness of the natural world. This introduction of serious themes to an otherwise romanticized genre perhaps marks Clark's most lasting contribution to the literature of the American West.

Andrew J. Angyal

OTHER MAJOR WORKS

SHORT FICTION: *The Watchful Gods, and Other Stories*, 1950.

POETRY: *Ten Women in Gale's House, and Shorter Poems*, 1932.

EDITED TEXT: *The Journals of Alfred Doten, 1849-1903*, 1973 (3 volumes).

BIBLIOGRAPHY

Alt, John. "*The City of Trembling Leaves:* Humanity and Eternity." *South Dakota Review* 17 (Winter, 1979-1980): 8-18. Discusses the novel, noting that although it begins with a tribute to the spiritual healing of nature, its story complicates that theme. Elaborates on the novel's focus on the growth of the character of Hazard, who realizes that his drive for rationality must be frustrated by nature itself.

Benson, Jackson J. *The Ox-Bow Man: A Biography of Walter Van Tilburg Clark*. Reno: University of Nevada Press, 2004. First full-length biography of Clark describes his life as a writer and teacher and addresses his significant role in transforming Western literature. Chapter 4 focuses on *The Ox-Bow Incident* and its relation to the Western novel in general; other chapters discuss *The City of Trembling Leaves* and *The Track of the Cat*.

Eisinger, Chester E. *Fiction of the Forties*. Chicago: University of Chicago Press, 1963. Includes an analysis of Clark's novels, describing their themes as the search for identity, desire to merge with nature, and rejection by nature. Also contains lengthy analyses of Clark's short stories "The Buck in the Hills," "Hook," and "The Watchful Gods."

Kich, Martin. *Western American Novelists*. Vol. 1. New York: Garland, 1995. Provides a brief account of Clark's career and an extensive annotated bibliography that includes commentary on reviews of virtually every significant piece of Clark's prose fiction.

Laird, Charlton, ed. *Walter Van Tilburg Clark: Critiques*. Reno: University of Nevada Press, 1983. Collection of eighteen pieces, some by Clark himself, presents discussion of Clark's life, his major published work, and his literary craftsmanship. Includes essays on the novels *The Ox-Bow Incident*, *The City of Trembling Leaves*, and *The Track of the Cat*.

Lee, L. L. *Walter Van Tilburg Clark*. Boise, Idaho: Boise State College Press, 1973. Presents biographical material and analyzes Clark's novels as well as a number of his short stories, which Lee asserts repeat the themes of the novels but with greater clarity and insight. Supplemented by a helpful bibliography.

Westbrook, Max. *Walter Van Tilburg Clark*. New York: Twayne, 1969. One of the best overall assessments of Clark's literary work available. Offers discussion of *The Ox-Bow Incident* and other novels and includes biographical information, a chronology of Clark's life, and a select bibliography.

_____. "Walter Van Tilburg Clark and the American Dream." In *A Literary History of the American West*, edited by J. Golden Taylor. Fort Worth: Texas Christian University Press, 1987. Blends biography with criticism in analyzing Clark's fiction and defining the author's place in literary history. Using examples of characters from Clark's stories and novels, Westbrook argues that the Clark "hero" is an idealistic dreamer incapable of practical action; as a result, the American Dream, or its nightmarish counterpart, becomes a real concern for Clark.

Yardley, Jonathan. "Broadening the Western's Horizons." *The Washington Post*, April 7, 2007. Provides biographical information about Clark and discusses *The Ox-Bow Incident*, concluding that the novel is "proof that the story of the West can rise above cliché and become the material of literature."

ARTHUR C. CLARKE

Born: Minehead, Somerset, England; December 16, 1917
Died: Colombo, Sri Lanka; March 19, 2008
Also known as: Arthur Charles Clarke; E. B. O'Brien; Charles Willis

PRINCIPAL LONG FICTION

Prelude to Space, 1951
The Sands of Mars, 1951
Against the Fall of Night, 1953 (revised as *The City and the Stars*, 1956)
Childhood's End, 1953
Earthlight, 1955
The Deep Range, 1957
Across the Sea of Stars, 1959
A Fall of Moondust, 1961
From the Ocean, from the Stars, 1962
Glide Path, 1963
Prelude to Mars, 1965
"The Lion of Comarre" and "Against the Fall of Night," 1968 (novellas)
2001: A Space Odyssey, 1968
Rendezvous with Rama, 1973
Imperial Earth, 1975
The Fountains of Paradise, 1979
2010: Odyssey Two, 1982
The Songs of Distant Earth, 1986
2061: Odyssey Three, 1987
Cradle, 1988 (with Gentry Lee)
Rama II, 1989 (with Lee)
Beyond the Fall of Night, 1990 (with Gregory Benford)
The Ghost from the Grand Banks, 1990
The Garden of Rama, 1991 (with Lee)
The Hammer of God, 1993
Rama Revealed, 1993 (with Lee)
Richter 10, 1996 (with Mike McQuay)
3001: The Final Odyssey, 1997
The Trigger, 1999 (with Michael Kube-McDowell)
The Light of Other Days, 2000 (with Stephen Baxter)
Time's Eye, 2004 (with Baxter)
Sunstorm, 2005 (with Baxter)
Firstborn, 2007 (with Baxter)
The Last Theorem, 2008 (with Frederik Pohl)

OTHER LITERARY FORMS

Best known for his novels, Arthur C. Clarke also wrote numerous science-fiction short stories, which are available in several collections; two of his stories, "The Star" and "A Meeting with Medusa," won major awards. Clarke is also noted as the author of scientific essays and science-related books for general readers, usually about outer space or the ocean, and he published a few loosely structured autobiographies.

ACHIEVEMENTS

Beginning in the 1950's, Arthur C. Clarke became acknowledged as a major science-fiction author, winning several Hugo and Nebula Awards for his works, and he earned the Kalinga Prize in 1961 for science writing. He garnered greater renown in 1968 as author of the novel *2001: A Space Odyssey* and as a screenwriter of the Stanley Kubrick film of the same title, which led to an Academy Award nomination; a year later, he joined newscaster Walter Cronkite as a television commentator on the Apollo 11 space mission to the Moon. From the 1970's on, his novels were best sellers, the most successful being his sequels to *2001*. In the 1980's and 1990's, Clarke hosted three documentary television series about strange phenomena, *Arthur C. Clarke's Mysterious World* (1980), *Arthur C. Clarke's World of Strange Powers* (1985), and *Arthur C. Clarke's Mysterious Universe* (1994). In 1998, he was knighted by the British government for his contributions to literature, and in 2005 his adopted home country of Sri Lanka bestowed on him its highest civil honor, Sri Lankabhimanya.

BIOGRAPHY

Arthur Charles Clarke, born December 16, 1917, first displayed his interests in science fiction and science as a child, reading pulp magazines and conducting his own experiments. By the late 1930's, he was living in London, working for the British Interplanetary Society and publishing scientific articles. During World War II, he helped develop a system for radar-assisted airplane landings, an experience he recounted fictionally in his 1963 novel *Glide Path*. In 1945, he published a now-famous article that first proposed communications satellites. After the war, he graduated from college and worked as assistant editor of *Physics Abstracts* before quitting to pursue a writing career.

In the 1950's, Clarke grew fascinated with the sea, and, in 1956, he moved to the island nation of Sri Lanka, which became his permanent residence. His 1953 marriage to Marilyn Mayfield ended in divorce in 1964. After the success of *2001*, Clarke signed a million-dollar contract to write *Rendezvous with Rama*, *Imperial Earth*, and *The Fountains of Paradise*, once announced as his final work. Clarke continued writing novels—sequels to *2001* along with *The Songs of Distant Earth*, *The Ghost from the Grand Banks*, and *The Hammer of God*—though many were disappointed by a flurry of collaborations: *Cradle*, *Rama II*, *The Garden of Rama*, and *Rama Revealed*, all cowritten with Gentry Lee; *Beyond the Fall of Night*, cowritten with Gregory Benford; *Richter 10*, cowritten with Mike McQuay; *The Trigger*, cowritten with Michael Kube-McDowell; and *The Light of Other Days*, *Time's Eye*, *Sunstorm*, and *Firstborn*, cowritten with Stephen Baxter. In these works, Clarke's participation was presumed to be minimal. A final novel, *The Last Theorem*, was begun by Clarke alone but completed by Frederik Pohl because of Clarke's declining health. Shortly after reviewing the proofs of this novel, Clarke died of heart failure and respiratory complications on March 19, 2008.

ANALYSIS

Arthur C. Clarke's fiction consistently displays tremendous scientific knowledge combined with a boundless imagination, often touching on the mystical, and flashes of ironic humor. One of Clarke's specialties was the novel that, with meticulous realism, describes near-future events, such as the first space flight (*Prelude to Space*), humans living under the sea (*The Deep Range*), lunar settlements (*Earthlight*, *A Fall of Moondust*), colonies on Mars

(*The Sands of Mars*), and efforts to raise the *Titanic* (*The Ghost from the Grand Banks*). While these novels are involving, Clarke's determination to be plausible can make them less than dramatic, and they are rarely celebrated. More noteworthy to most readers are Clarke's novels that envision incredible engineering accomplishments (*Rendezvous with Rama*, *The Fountains of Paradise*), venture far into the future (*Against the Fall of Night*, *The Songs of Distant Earth*), or depict encounters with enigmatic aliens (*Childhood's End*, *2001* and its sequels, *The Last Theorem*). Few writers can match Clarke's ability to take a broad perspective and regard vast expanses of space and time as mere episodes in an even vaster cosmic drama inaccessible to human understanding.

Arthur C. Clarke. (© Washington Post; reprinted by permission of the D.C. Public Library)

Early critics frequently complained about Clarke's undistinguished prose style and wooden characters, but he steadily improved in these areas, and if his fiction of the 1980's and 1990's brought no spectacular new visions, the writing was generally more impressive than that of the 1950's and 1960's. *The Ghost from the Grand Banks*, for example, effectively employs short chapters that jump forward and backward in time and reveal Clarke's skill in crafting superb opening and closing lines. Many have observed that the previously underdeveloped Heywood Floyd and Frank Poole evolve into realistic characters in the sequels to *2001*. Although much critical commentary on Clarke's work tends to focus on the earlier works, his later novels also merit attention.

AGAINST THE FALL OF NIGHT

Clarke's first major novel features Alvin, a restless young man, in Diaspar, a city in Earth's distant future where machines provide for all needs. Alvin quickly disrupts the placid, unchanging lives of Diaspar's nearly immortal residents with his remarkable discoveries. An underground vehicle transports him to Lys, a previously unknown civilization where people choose agrarian lifestyles aided by telepathic powers rather than machines. There, an old man's strange robot reveals the location of a spaceship, which Alvin uses to journey to a faraway planet, where he encounters a disembodied intelligence named Vanamonde. Back on Earth, Alvin and the elders of Lys deduce humanity's history: After humans worked with aliens to create pure intelligences, their first product, the Mad Mind, went insane and unleashed its destructive energies throughout the galaxy. After creating other, sane intelligences like Vanamonde, humans left the universe entirely, leaving behind a few who preferred to remain on Earth. Dispatching a robot to search for the departed humans, Alvin stays behind to solve other mysteries of human history.

Overflowing with ideas, presented with breathless haste, *Against the Fall of Night* commands attention for its evocative and imaginative portrayal of decadent future humans haunted by a misunderstood heritage, and the arrogance with which Alvin dominates and upsets their sterile existence may reflect the self-confidence of a young author who felt destined to accomplish great things. However, a dissatisfied Clarke soon took the unusual step of writing an extensive revision of the novel, published as *The City and the Stars*. While the later version offers fascinating new details about life in Diaspar, many readers preferred the youthful exuberance of the original story, and a consensus developed that the first version is superior. Thus, in continuing Alvin's story, writer Gregory Benford chose to follow the original version, republished together with Benford's sequel as *Beyond the Fall of Night* in 1990.

CHILDHOOD'S END

Considered by many to be Clarke's masterpiece, *Childhood's End* begins when Earth is peacefully taken over by the benevolent alien Overlords. Concealing themselves because they resemble devils, the Overlords govern through human intermediaries such as the secretary-general of the United Nations, whom they effortlessly rescue when he is kidnapped by rebels who oppose the Overlords. When they finally reveal their appearance fifty years later, humanity is enjoying a golden age of peace and prosperity thanks to the Overlords' wise rule and advanced technology. Streaks of rebelliousness persist, however, and a man named Jan Rodricks stows away on a starship to visit the Overlords' home world. Later, on Earth, George and Jean Greggson are upset when their son begins dreaming about other worlds and their daughter manifests telekinetic powers. An Overlord now explains the true motives behind their takeover. Certain races, such as humans, have the capacity to achieve a higher level of evolution by merging into a group mind and joining the mysterious Overmind that controls the universe; the Overmind assigns the Overlords, who paradoxically lack this potential, to supervise these races during the transitional stage. Soon, all human children have mentally united and seem like aliens to their distraught parents. While the adults, their dreams shattered, commit suicide in various ways, Rodricks returns to Earth to observe its final moments, as the children employ psychic powers to disintegrate their world and merge with the Overmind.

Perhaps perturbed by his own prophecy, Clarke adds this introductory comment: "The opinions expressed in this book are not those of the author." Certainly, *Childhood's End* stirs strong and conflicting emotions in its final portrait of Earth's children seemingly reduced to naked savages engaged in senseless activities, even while the reader is assured that they represent a glorious new stage in human evolution. If not wholly satisfactory in style and character development, the novel persuasively presents its unsettling developments and, decades after publication, continues to inspire heated discussion.

2001: A SPACE ODYSSEY

Clarke's novel *2001: A Space Odyssey* differs from the film based on it both in major details and in its overall tone, which is clear and explanatory, in contrast to Kubrick's directorial mystification. Clarke develops the character of Moon-Watcher, the ape-man of the distant past who first notices the alien monolith that teaches Moon-Watcher and his companions to use tools. Next, in the near future, Heywood Floyd visits the Moon to examine another monolith, which suddenly emits a powerful radio signal toward Saturn (not Jupiter, as in the film). The spaceship *Discovery* is sent to investigate, though the crewmen who are not placed in hibernation, David Bowman and Frank Poole, know nothing about the monolith. Driven insane by contradictory commands to cooperate with Bowman and Poole while concealing their real mission, the onboard computer HAL kills Poole in space and attempts to kill Bowman by opening the ship's air locks, exposing him to the vacuum of space. Bowman finds an emergency shelter with a spacesuit, disables HAL, and proceeds to Saturn, where another monolith waits on the surface of Saturn's moon Japetus. An alien transportation system then takes Bowman to a distant planet and a crude replica of an Earth hotel, where he is transformed into a baby with immense powers who returns to Earth and destroys its nuclear weapons.

Critics agree that *2001* stands on its own as a masterful saga of human evolution and exploration; the later sequels do not enhance its impact, however. In *2010: Odyssey Two*, Floyd returns to Jupiter (following the film version) to discover Bowman's fate, meets a ghostly Bowman (now cast more as a messenger for the aliens than as the harbinger of a new human race), and flees when Jupiter becomes a star, with its moons offered to humanity as new homes (except Europa, declared off-limits by the aliens). In *2061: Odyssey Three*, Floyd journeys to Halley's comet but accidentally lands on Europa, and in *3001: The Final Odyssey*, a revived Poole helps to disable the monoliths, now likened to out-of-control computers. Although readers may enjoy meeting old friends, the sequels to *2001* never reveal the unseen aliens or their final plans for humanity, which is perhaps as it should be.

RENDEZVOUS WITH RAMA

Clarke's first novel after *2001* begins with the discovery of a gigantic cylindrical object, clearly artificial in origin, approaching the Sun. William Norton, commanding the spaceship *Endeavour*, leads an investigation of the object, named Rama. Entering through an airlock, Norton and his crew observe a huge interior landscape divided by the Cylindrical Sea, with clusters of buildings dubbed "cities" and other inexplicable objects. As they descend to the surface, massive lights suddenly illuminate Rama, as if it were coming to life. When a crewman crosses the Cylindrical Sea in a glider and investigates strange formations, he notices the first of many "biots"—biological robots manufactured to perform functions such as observation and removal of debris. The people of Mercury, fearing Rama is hostile, launch a nuclear missile to destroy it, but another crewman disables the bomb. As the humans depart, the biots destroy themselves and the lights go out, signaling that Rama has finished its work. Rama then absorbs energy and matter from the Sun before leaving the solar system—though a scientist notes, "The Ramans do everything in threes," suggesting other alien vehicles may arrive soon.

Despite the novel's weak characterization, Clarke's unique ability to evoke the bizarre with straightforward exposition is well displayed in this story, which intrigues readers with its narrative unpredictability and unanswered questions. *Rendezvous with Rama* earned both the Hugo Award and the Nebula Award as the best science-fiction novel of 1973. Clarke later continued the story in three sequels cowritten with Gentry Lee—*Rama II*, *The Garden of Rama*, and *Rama Revealed*—describing the coming of another Raman spaceship and the astronauts who stay on board for a cosmic journey. Despite revealing new information about the Ramans and their goals, the sequels leave many mysteries unresolved, ultimately adding little to the original novel.

THE FOUNTAINS OF PARADISE

Projected as the capstone of Clarke's career, *The Fountains of Paradise* describes a future engineer, Vannevar Morgan, planning to construct an enormous "space elevator" to connect the surface of Earth to a geosynchronous satellite, providing cheap and safe transportation into space. His story is interwoven with that of another great builder, Kalidasa, the ancient king of Taprobane (an island analogous to Sri Lanka) who built the magnificent Fountains of Paradise at the mountain where Morgan wishes to build his space elevator. When the monks inhabiting the mountain abandon their home after an old prophecy is fulfilled, Morgan begins work, and soon the tower is slowly being constructed from a point between Earth and space. When scientists are stranded on the incomplete tower, Morgan pilots a transport vehicle to bring supplies, though the effort strains his weak heart and causes his death. In an epilogue set further in the future, an alien visiting Earth marvels at its "Ring City," with Morgan's tower as only one spoke in an immense wheel of satellites circling the globe, all linked to each other and to the ground.

Inspired by the history and traditions of Sri Lanka, Clarke's adopted homeland, *The Fountains of Paradise* seems one of his most personal works, blending reverence for ancient accomplishments with dreams of futuristic space exploration. Like *Rendezvous with Rama*, it earned both the Hugo Award and the Nebula Award. The concluding chapters describing Morgan's rescue may be the most gripping sequence Clarke ever wrote, but its awe-inspiring vision of a world transformed by cosmic engineering is what makes the novel memorable.

TIME ODYSSEY TRILOGY

The Time Odyssey trilogy—comprising *Time's Eye*, *Sunstorm*, and *Firstborn*, all cowritten with Stephen Baxter—stands out among Clarke's collaborations because of its relationship to *2001*; not a sequel or prequel, it is what the authors term an "orthoquel," employing the premise of *2001*—unseen aliens enigmatically manipulating human destiny—to develop an entirely different narrative. Here, the aliens' presence is represented not by monoliths but by "Eyes"—floating spheres, detached from our own reality, that observe and sometimes interact with our universe—and the aliens' purpose is unambiguously inimical: Believing that the survival of life in the cosmos depends on strict conservation of energy, they eliminate intelligent civilizations that consume too much of it.

In *Time's Eye*, aliens slice small regions of Earth from various past and present eras and assemble them as a new world, called Mir, presumably to preserve and study, in a separate universe, the species they will destroy. United Nations peacekeepers and astronauts from the year 2037, then, find themselves in a world with australopithecines, Neanderthals, the armies of Alexander the Great and Genghis Khan, and nineteenth century British soldiers accompanied by young Rudyard Kipling. One peacekeeper, a woman named Bisesa Dutt, develops a strange rapport with one immense Eye that eventually transports her back to her own world, where she arrives one day after her initial disappearance.

In *Sunstorm*, Bisesa learns that an immense burst of energy from the Sun, which had catastrophic results, was only the prelude to an even more massive sunstorm that will effectively eliminate all life on Earth. Her suspicion that this impending doom has been caused by aliens is confirmed by evidence that a gigantic planet was deliberately smashed into the Sun long ago, setting in motion disturbances that will eventually trigger the sunstorm. The only way to save humanity, as explained by the artificial intelligence Thales, is to construct a huge, ultrathin "shield" to divert some harmful radiation away from Earth. Humans work valiantly and succeed in constructing the necessary shield, which reduces the scale of the disaster so that "only" one-tenth of their race is killed.

In *Firstborn*, the thwarted Firstborn launch another attack, a "Q-bomb" aimed at Earth that will employ quantum energy to devastate the planet. Scientists on Mars, however, discover an Eye apparently trapped within an energy field by the extinct Martian race, which battled the Firstborn before being destroyed by them. Mysteriously returned to Mir, Bisesa uses an idea from Thomas Alva Edison to send a message to a surviving Martian in that world's universe, and the Martian contrives to disturb the Eye further. This inspires the Q-bomb to change course to destroy Mars instead of Earth, again saving humanity. In an epilogue, Bisesa meets a member of another race, called the Lastborn, that is desperately struggling against the Firstborn.

In some respects, the Time Odyssey trilogy seems an ideal melding of Clarke's visionary ideas and Baxter's ability to convey those ideas with more involving characters and dramatic activities than are often found in Clarke's works. Like Clarke's own continuations of

2001, however, the trilogy is ultimately disappointing because it again fails to explain its aliens fully or to conclude their story clearly, making the entire saga exciting but pointless.

THE LAST THEOREM

Clarke's final novel involves a Sri Lankan college student, Ranjit Subramanian, who dreams of rediscovering Fermat's own proof of his famous theorem. A chance encounter with a family friend brings Ranjit into the company of seagoing pirates, leading to his arrest and torture. During the ordeal, however, he somehow manages to figure out the proof, which he carries in his mind until he is released and can finally write it down and publish it. Ranjit then achieves worldwide fame and a lifetime professorship at a Sri Lankan university, where he settles down to a satisfying life of teaching and raising two children with his wife. All the while, enigmatic aliens known as the Grand Galactics, having detected signs of destructive technology on Earth, have dispatched client races to exterminate the human species. As Ranjit observes events from his privileged position, however, humanity finally seems on the verge of achieving lasting peace: An international project known as Silent Thunder peacefully stymies hostile nations by employing electromagnetic radiation to disable all their equipment, and a newly constructed space elevator will finally grant humanity easy access to other planets. A visiting Grand Galactic, perhaps impressed by all this, cancels the order to destroy humanity, though this requires first contact with Earth and an emergency landing by the aliens recruited to destroy humanity; an attempt by diehard American militarists to attack the unthreatening aliens is effortlessly repelled. New technology introduced to Earth by another client race then allows Ranjit's wife and later Ranjit himself to achieve immortality by being converted into computer programs. An epilogue set in the far future reveals that the Grand Galactics, dissatisfied with their own stewardship of the galaxy, have bequeathed all responsibility for its affairs to another species, the human race.

The Last Theorem might be regarded as a summary of Clarke's career, bringing together familiar items of careful prediction (such as a space elevator similar to that of *The Fountains of Paradise* and spaceships with solar sails as seen in his 1964 story "The Wind from the Sun")

with expansive visions of highly advanced, mysterious aliens meddling in human affairs—although some touches, like the business of converting humans into computer programs, seem more a reflection of Pohl's influence. It is also significant that, in contrast to previous works that convey a certain degree of pessimism regarding humanity's ability to prosper and endure in a staggeringly vast and often inimical cosmos, Clarke concluded his career with his most optimistic prediction, as humanity not only achieves a genuine utopia on Earth but also eventually becomes the true master of the universe. Still, *The Last Theorem* cannot be regarded as Clarke's final masterpiece, as its disparate elements do not always blend well together; in particular, the titular proof ultimately seems inconsequential, important only because it elevates an appealing protagonist to a status that makes him a better witness to key developments in humanity's future.

Gary Westfahl

OTHER MAJOR WORKS

SHORT FICTION: *Expedition to Earth*, 1953; *Reach for Tomorrow*, 1956; *Tales from the White Hart*, 1957; *The Other Side of the Sky*, 1958; *Tales of Ten Worlds*, 1962; *The Nine Billion Names of God*, 1967; *Of Time and Stars: The Worlds of Arthur C. Clarke*, 1972; *The Wind from the Sun*, 1972; *The Best of Arthur C. Clarke, 1937-1971*, 1973; *The Sentinel: Masterworks of Science Fiction and Fantasy*, 1983; *Dilemmas: The Secret*, 1989; *Tales from Planet Earth*, 1989; *More than One Universe: The Collected Stories of Arthur C. Clarke*, 1991; *The Collected Stories of Arthur C. Clarke*, 2000.

POETRY: *The Fantastic Muse*, 1992.

NONFICTION: *Interplanetary Flight*, 1950; *The Exploration of Space*, 1951 (revised 1959); *The Exploration of the Moon*, 1954; *Going into Space*, 1954; *The Coast of Coral*, 1956; *The Making of a Moon*, 1957; *The Reefs of Taprobane*, 1957; *Voice Across the Sea*, 1958; *The Challenge of the Spaceship*, 1959; *The Challenge of the Sea*, 1960; *The First Five Fathoms*, 1960; *Indian Ocean Adventure*, 1961 (with Mike Wilson); *Profiles of the Future*, 1962; *Indian Ocean Treasure*, 1964 (with Wilson); *Man and Space*, 1964 (with others); *The Treasure of the Great Reef*, 1964; *Voices from the Sky*, 1965; *The Promise of Space*, 1968; *First on the Moon*, 1970 (with others); *Into Space*, 1971 (with Robert Silverberg); *Beyond Jupiter*, 1972 (with Chesley Bonestall); *The Lost Worlds of 2001*, 1972; *Report on Planet Three*, 1972; *The View from Serendip*, 1977; *1984: Spring, a Choice of Futures*, 1984; *The Odyssey File*, 1985 (with Peter Hyams); *Arthur C. Clarke's July 20, 2019: Life in the Twenty-first Century*, 1986; *Astounding Days: A Science Fictional Autobiography*, 1989; *How the World Was One: Beyond the Global Village*, 1992; *By Space Possessed*, 1993; *The Snows of Olympus: A Garden on Mars*, 1994; *Greetings, Carbon-Based Bipeds! Collected Essays, 1934-1998*, 1999; *From Narnia to a Space Odyssey: The War of Ideas Between Arthur C. Clarke and C. S. Lewis*, 2003 (Ryder W. Miller, editor).

CHILDREN'S LITERATURE: *Islands in the Sky*, 1952; *Dolphin Island*, 1963.

EDITED TEXT: *Time Probe: The Sciences in Science Fiction*, 1966.

BIBLIOGRAPHY

Blackford, Russell. "Technological Meliorism and the Posthuman Vision: Arthur C. Clarke and the Ultimate Future of Intelligence." *New York Review of Science Fiction* 14 (November, 2001): 1, 10-12. Examines Clarke's visionary predictions in his nonfiction *Profiles of the Future* and discusses how certain ideas later reappeared in his fiction.

Hollow, John. *Against the Night, the Stars: The Science Fiction of Arthur C. Clarke*. San Diego, Calif.: Harcourt Brace Jovanovich, 1983. Presents an analysis of the major themes found in Clarke's fiction.

James, Edward. "Clarke's Utopian Vision." *Foundation: The International Review of Science Fiction* 34 (April, 2005): 26-33. Analyzes Clarke's fiction and notes that his apparently utopian futures are often undermined by assertions that humanity's destiny is in fact tied to the human tendencies toward endless dissatisfaction and questing.

McAleer, Neil. *Arthur C. Clarke: The Authorized Biography*. Chicago: Contemporary Books, 1992. Provides a definitive account of Clarke's career, written with Clarke's cooperation. Draws on extensive interviews with Clarke's friends, colleagues, and family members.

Meisenheimer, Donald K., Jr. "Machining the Man: From Neurasthenia to Psychasthenia in SF and the Genre Western." *Science-Fiction Studies* 24 (November, 1997): 441-458. Argues that although Clarke works within the tradition of Wellsian science fiction, he also makes heavy use of the elements of the genre Western as established by Owen Wister and Frederic Remington.

Olander, Joseph D., and Martin Harry Greenberg, eds. *Arthur C. Clarke*. New York: Taplinger, 1977. Collection of nine essays is a good source of textual criticism of Clarke's fiction. Examines both individual works and his science-fiction writings in general. Supplemented by a select bibliography and a biographical note.

Rabkin, Eric S. *Arthur C. Clarke*. San Bernardino, Calif.: Borgo Press, 1980. Provides a good short introduction to Clarke's most important science-fiction works, with brief descriptions of each. Includes biographical information, an annotated bibliography, and a chronology.

Reid, Robin Anne. *Arthur C. Clarke: A Critical Companion*. Westport, Conn.: Greenwood Press, 1997. General introduction to Clarke's life and work presents a brief biographical chapter, a discussion of his science fiction in general, and nine chapters devoted to individual novels. Includes bibliography and index.

Zivkovic, Zolan. "The Motif of First Contact in Arthur C. Clarke's 'A Meeting with Medusa.'" *New York Review of Science Fiction*, February/March, 2001, 1, 8-13; 10-17. Examines in detail four Clarke stories that involve humans' first contact with alien beings: "Report from Planet Three," "Crusade," "History Lesson," and "A Meeting with Medusa."

MICHELLE CLIFF

Born: Kingston, Jamaica; November 2, 1946

PRINCIPAL LONG FICTION

Abeng, 1984
No Telephone to Heaven, 1987
Free Enterprise, 1993

OTHER LITERARY FORMS

In addition to being a novelist, Michelle Cliff is a poet, essayist, short-story writer, and literary critic. Her first writing was a response to an article about Jamaica that, in her opinion, contained inaccuracies. In her poems, short stories, and essays, she portrays the "real" Jamaica and what it is like to be Jamaican. A collection of her essays, *If I Could Write This in Fire*, was published in 2008. Cliff examines oppression, lost oral history, and sexual and racial prejudice, and she addresses the importance of revising official history. Her novels treat these same issues and concerns.

ACHIEVEMENTS

Michelle Cliff is recognized as one of the most significant writers of fiction exploring the complex issues of race, color, sexual orientation, and feminism as well as the postcolonial concerns of identity and heritage for people of mixed race. She has played a critical role in revealing the "other," or unofficial, history in her novels, and in a sense has been rewriting history. Cliff also is respected as a literary critic. In 1982, she received a fellowship from the National Endowment for the Arts and a fellowship for study at MacDowell College. In 1984, she won a Massachusetts Artists Foundation award and was named an Eli Kantor Fellow.

BIOGRAPHY

Michelle Cliff, the daughter of an American father and a Jamaican mother, was born on November 2, 1946, in Kingston, Jamaica. A light-skinned Creole, she was born into a mixed-race family that valued lightness of skin and continually insisted that she pass for white. This pressure to reject her Creole and black heritage has influenced her writing. During her childhood and adolescence,

Cliff lived in Jamaica and the United States. Her family moved to the United States when she was three years old. She remained in Jamaica with other family members for some time, but she later joined the family in a Caribbean neighborhood of New York City. During the 1940's and early 1950's, Cliff often returned to Jamaica with her family for short visits; in 1956, when she was ten years old, she returned to Jamaica to attend boarding school.

After graduating from secondary school, Cliff returned to the United States and studied at Wagner College. She received a bachelor of arts degree in 1969 and then became involved in politics, including the feminist movement. She also was an active opponent of the war in Vietnam. After graduating from college, she worked in the publishing field as a reporter, researcher, and editor. She completed a master of philosophy degree in 1974 and received a doctorate from the Wartburg Institute at the University of London.

Although Cliff had been attracted to a classmate while at an all-female boarding school in Jamaica, it was during her residency in England that she realized she was lesbian. In 1976, she began a long-term relationship with American poet Adrienne Rich. That same year, Cliff began writing poetry and published her first book in that genre: *Claiming an Identity They Taught Me to Despise* (1980). From 1981 to 1983, she and Rich coedited *Sinister Wisdom*, a multicultural lesbian journal. In 1985, Cliff published another collection, *The Land of Look Behind: Prose and Poetry*.

In 1985, Cliff published her first novel, *Abeng*, which draws upon her multiracial and multicultural heritage. Her second novel, *No Telephone to Heaven*, is a sequel to *Abeng*. She began writing short stories, which were first published in *Bodies of Water* (1990). In 1993, she published her third novel, *Free Enterprise*. In 1998, she published her second collection of short stories, *The Store of a Million Items*. Cliff has had several university teaching positions as well.

ANALYSIS

Michelle Cliff writes about Jamaica and the tightly structured society of the island. She addresses problems inherent to a postcolonial culture, including prejudice, oppression, class structure, the devaluing of women, and the lost history—especially oral history—of the oppressed. Although her novels are not truly autobiographical, much of what the character Clare confronts in *Abeng* and *No Telephone to Heaven* is a reflection of her own experiences growing up in Jamaica and the United States and in living in England as a university student. Her novels display an ever-present consciousness of skin color, which is closely connected to identity, but for Cliff, the color of one's skin is both a means of identity and a means of losing identity.

Cliff's stories depict a society in which each person's place is determined by his or her skin color. This caste system is accepted simply as "the way it is." In the prejudicial thinking of her characters, skin color not only indicates certain flaws but also virtues. In *Abeng*, the character Mattie Freeman, Clare's grandmother, knows who she is. She is a Maroon, a red-skinned woman with a history that traces to Nanny, the Maroon resistor to slavery. Nanny had magical powers and spiritual insights no colonial would ever enjoy. Boy Savage, in contrast, has lost a part of his identity through his rejection of his color ancestry and his insistence on passing for white.

Language plays an important role in Cliff's novels as well. The language spoken by a character is an identifier of that character. In *Abeng*, when Clare is at her grandmother's farm with Zoe, her dark-skinned "friend," she speaks patois, which is forbidden in her middle-class existence in Kingston. For Cliff, Jamaican patois is just as viable a language as Standard English, and it is critical for readers without knowledge of patois to understand the meanings of the words. *No Telephone to Heaven* includes a glossary of patois words used in the novel.

Oral history and ethnic-specific stories, which rarely are included in the "official" accounts of the past, are integral to Cliff's novels. The novels are multilayered and create a sort of international tapestry of the history of oppressed and marginalized individuals and ethnic groups. The story of Nanny, the Maroon woman who refused to accept slavery and led her people in rebellion, is recounted or referred to in *Abeng*, *No Telephone to Heaven*, and *Free Enterprise*. In *Free Enterprise*, additional oral histories are told by minor characters.

Cliff extends this multilayering into the names she gives to her characters and to her novels. *Abeng* is an African word for conch shell. The conch shell served two purposes during the colonial period: It called slaves to the cane fields and was used by the Maroons to pass messages to one another. *Free Enterprise* refers both to the free enterprise of dealing in slaves in a capitalist market and to the enterprise of the main characters of the novel, resisters of slavery, and their freely entering into the fight.

Cliff writes her novels in a rich lyrical style reminiscent of her prose poems. Her descriptions of the Jamaican countryside are colorful and reflect the bond between the Maroons and nature. Jamaica becomes real for the reader with its mangoes, its tropical foliage, cane fields, and sun-drenched red earth.

ABENG

Abeng is the story of Clare Savage, a young girl growing up in a complex multicultural world. It is a world fraught with oppression, rejection, and denial. Her family belongs to the Jamaican middle class. Her father, James Arthur "Boy" Savage, is a light-skinned man of white-black ancestry who rejects his black heritage and insists upon passing for white. He takes pride in his white colonial ancestry, which traces back to Judge Savage, one of the most of brutal slave owners. Her mother, Kitty Savage, is a Maroon, or red-skinned, woman who is deeply attached to her color ancestry. Clare has one sister; she is younger than Clare and darker-skinned.

Boy and Kitty are an intriguing and often incomprehensible couple. They remain separate and contradictory. On Sunday mornings, the family goes to Boy's church, the John Knox Memorial Church. On Sunday evenings, they go to Kitty's church, the Tabernacle of the Almighty. They both consider Clare, the light-skinned daughter, to be Boy's child and the dark-skinned younger sister to be Kitty's child. The husband and wife have almost nothing in common and argue bitterly, which frightens Clare.

Clare spends summers in the country with Miss Mattie, her maternal grandmother. Although Miss Mattie was born after the freeing of the slaves, she had worked in the cane fields and remembers the harsh treatment by the overseers and how the cane cut her legs. She no longer cuts cane, and is now a landowner. She is not of the same social class as the light-skinned Jamaicans; she is higher on the social scale as a landowner. Known for her kindness, she lets Miss Ruthie, a market woman, live on her land and raise produce to sell. Miss Ruthie has a daughter named Zoe, who becomes Clare's playmate. Miss Ruthie constantly warns Zoe not to get too involved with Clare because they are different and cannot really be friends. Clare is a *buckra*, a white-skinned person, who is not to be trusted.

The twelve-year-old Clare does not understand why so many things are the way they are. She enjoys the country, the lifestyle, and the connection with her mother's heritage. She has no comprehension of the necessity of not breaking the rules of her society. She resents the greater freedom afforded to the boys; she does not understand why she is admonished for considering Zoe her friend and equal. Then, one day, Clare breaks every rule that governs her life as a middle-class Jamaican female. She takes Miss Mattie's gun and sets out with Zoe to hunt Cudjoe, a legendary wild boar. Climbing to his lair proves too difficult, so they abandon the hunt and go for a swim in the river. Sunbathing nude, Clare is physically attracted to her forbidden friend. They are surprised by male cane cutters and become frightened. Clare fires the gun. The bullet ricochets and kills her grandmother's bull, Old Joe.

Clare admits to killing Miss Mattie's bull, but she is given no chance to explain how and why it happened. Her parents take her to Miss Beatrice, a widow who has buried all of her children. Kitty tells her daughter that Miss Beatrice will teach her how to be a "proper lady" so she can make something of herself. However, in the presence of Miss Beatrice, Clare also learns more about prejudice, oppression, and cruelty. She witnesses Miss Beatrice's harsh treatment of the elderly Minnie Bogle, a black woman who is hired to clean the dog feces from her yard. Miss Beatrice often strikes Minnie with her cane.

Miss Beatrice brings Clare to see her sister, who is considered mad. Clare is told not to talk to her, but the independent and rebellious Clare does. She learns what happens when she says "coons" and *buckras* mix. The sister tells Clare that as a young girl, she had a baby by a black man who worked for her family. She insists that what she did was wrong, and that her family was right in sending her to a convent. The sister has spent her life trying to expiate her sin.

The novel ends with Clare dreaming of fighting with Zoe, with blood trickling down Zoe's face and her apologizing and treating the wound. Awakening, Clare goes outside and discovers she is experiencing her first menstrual cycle. Clare is leaving the world of childhood and the magic of the Jamaican countryside and her summers with Zoe. In *No Telephone to Heaven*, she will deal with her fight to find her identity as an adult.

FREE ENTERPRISE

Free Enterprise is a novel of resistance and reclamation, the story of Annie Christmas and Mary Ellen Pleasant (M. E. P.), two women with black ancestry, who are dedicated to the abolition of slavery in the United States. Cliff draws upon the many stereotypes that envelop M. E. P. in official histories to present her in the novel as a powerful and determined individual who is feared by white society. She is very dark-skinned and uses her blackness to become a successful businesswoman in San Francisco. By being what white society expects her to be, a black madam catering to rich white men, she acquires money, which she uses to fund the abolitionist movement. Annie, in contrast to M. E. P., is light-skinned and is victimized by the white society she challenges.

Free Enterprise centers on the failure of John Brown's raid on Harper's Ferry, Virginia, in 1859. Through fortuitous circumstances, M. E. P., who was present at the raid, slips away from Harper's Ferry and returns to San Francisco. She remains active in the abolitionist movement and works for the rights of black citizens after the American Civil War. Annie is denied such good fortune. She is captured and put on a confederate chain gang. She disguises herself as a man but is soon discovered to be a woman. She becomes an amusement for her captors as a collar is placed around her neck. She is forced into sexual acts with male prisoners, while the captors watch. Annie is devastated. She had left the Caribbean to avoid being the mistress of a rich white man. She is emotionally and physically "broken," and she does not have the fortitude to continue actively in the fight. She retreats to Mississippi, where she lives a hermetical life.

Cliff also examines the lack of freedom of women regardless of their skin color. The secondary story of Alice and Clover Hooper, white abolitionists, elucidates the common bond of denial of freedom that unites all women. In their upper-class society, Alice and Clover are not free to speak their minds or pursue a career. They dream of going West and freeing themselves from male domination.

Shawncey Webb

OTHER MAJOR WORKS

SHORT FICTION: *Bodies of Water*, 1990; *The Store of a Million Items*, 1998.

NONFICTION: *If I Could Write This in Fire*, 2008 (essays).

EDITED TEXT: *The Winner Names the Age: A Collection of Writing by Lillian Smith*, 1978.

MISCELLANEOUS: *Claiming an Identity They Taught Me to Despise*, 1980 (prose and poetry); *The Land of Look Behind: Prose and Poetry*, 1985; *If I Could Write This in Fire*, 2008.

BIBLIOGRAPHY

Adisa, Opal Palmer. "Journey into Speech: Writer Between Two Worlds—An Interview with Michelle Cliff." *African American Review* 28, no. 2 (1994). In this special issue on black women's culture, essays explore Cliff's work on race and oppression in Jamaica and her ideas on resistance as a form of community and the significant role of women in the history of political resistance.

Browdy de Hernandez, Jennifer. *Women Writing Resistance: Essays on Latin America and the Caribbean.* Cambridge, Mass.: South End Press, 2003. Cliff is one of eighteen women whose work—including their writing—against all forms of oppression is examined in this book. The focus is on Latin American and Caribbean women who have used literature and other creative works to resist the political regimes of the countries in which they were born.

Edmondson, Belinda. "Race, Privilege, and the Politics of (Re)Writing History: An Analysis of the Novels of Michelle Cliff" *Callaloo* 16, no. 1 (1993): 180-191. A useful study of how Cliff seeks out obscure events of history and reworks those histories to include factors of race and oppression.

Elia, Nada. *Trances, Dances, and Vociferations: Agency and Resistance in Africana Women's Narratives.* New York: Garland, 2001. Examines Cliff's use of alternative and oral history, sexual disguise, and racial passing in her work. Chapter 3 is an analysis of the character Annie Christmas from *Free Enterprise*. Includes a bibliography.

Hudson, Lynn M. *The Making of Mammy Pleasant: A Black Entrepreneur in Nineteenth-Century San Francisco.* Urbana: University of Illinois Press, 2003. Contrasts Cliff's portrayal of M. E. P. with that character's portrayal in the novels of others.

JEAN COCTEAU

Born: Maisons-Laffitte, France; July 5, 1889
Died: Milly-la-Forêt, France; October 11, 1963
Also known as: Jean Maurice Eugène Clément Cocteau

PRINCIPAL LONG FICTION

Le Potomak, 1919
Le Grand Écart, 1923 (*The Grand Écart*, 1925)
Thomas l'imposteur, 1923 (*Thomas the Impostor*, 1925)
Le Livre blanc, 1928 (*The White Paper*, 1957)
Les Enfants terribles, 1929 (*Enfants Terribles*, 1930; better known as *Children of the Game*, 1955)
Le Fantôme de Marseille, 1933
La Fin du Potomak, 1939

OTHER LITERARY FORMS

Never limited by distinctions among genres, Jean Cocteau (kawk-TOH) was an important figure in many arts. After an early and not particularly interesting "dandyistic" phase in his poetry, including *La Lampe d'Aladin* (1909; Aladdin's lamp), *Le Prince frivole* (1910; the frivolous prince), and *La Danse de Sophocle* (1912; the dance of Sophocles), he was influenced by Futurism, Dadaism, and Surrealism, and he developed a classical rigor and purity mingled with linguistic and imaginative originality. *Le Cap de Bonne-Espérance* (1919; the Cape of Good Hope), for example, glorifies pilots and flying, emphasizing sensation. *L'Ode à Picasso* (1919; ode to Picasso) seeks the wellspring of creativity in the great artist. *Vocabulaire* (1922; vocabulary) exhibits further linguistic creativity, and *Discours du grand sommeil* (1922; discourse on the great sleep) explores the experience of World War I. Later works use the suggestions of mythology, classical simplicity, and the subconscious, particularly *Plain-Chant* (1923), *L'Ange Heurtebise* (1925), *Mythologie* (1934), *Allégories* (1941), *La Crucifixion* (1946), *Clair-obscur* (1954; chiaroscuro), *Gondole des morts* (1959), and *Cérémonial espagnol du phénix* (1961).

Cocteau was a witty playwright on similar themes in *Orphée* (pr. 1926; *Orpheus*, 1933), *La Voix humaine* (pr., pb. 1930; *The Human Voice*, 1951), *La Machine infernale* (pr., pb. 1934; *The Infernal Machine*, 1936), *Les Chevaliers de la table ronde* (pr., pb. 1937; *The Knights of the Round Table*, 1955), *Les Parents terribles* (pr., pb. 1938; *Intimate Relations*, 1952), *Les Monstres sacrés* (pr., pb. 1940; *The Holy Terrors*, 1953), *La Machine à écrire* (pr., pb. 1941; *The Typewriter*, 1948), the verse drama *Renaud et Armide* (pr., pb. 1943), *L'Aigle à deux têtes* (pr., pb. 1946; *The Eagle Has Two Heads*, 1946), and *Bacchus* (pr. 1951; English translation, 1955). He was director or writer, or both, of a number of films that have become classics because of their striking visual imagery and their evocation of the archetypal and mythological. *Le Sang d'un poète* (1930; *The Blood of a Poet*, 1949), *La Belle et la bête* (1946; *Beauty and the Beast*, 1947), *Les Parents terribles* (1948; *Intimate Relations*, 1952), *Les Enfants terribles* (1950), *Orphée* (1950; *Orpheus*, 1950), and *Le Testament d'Orphée* (1959; *The Testament of Orpheus*, 1968) are considered his best. He also wrote ballet scenarios, including those for Erik Satie's *Parade* (pr. 1917), Darius Milhaud's *Le Boeuf sur le toit* (pr. 1920), and Les Six's *Les Mariés de la Tour Eiffel* (pr. 1921; *The Wedding on the Eiffel Tower*, 1937), and two musical dramas, *Antigone* (pr.

1922; English translation, 1961), with music by Arthur Honegger, and *Oedipus-Rex* (pr. 1927; English translation, 1961), with music by Igor Stravinsky.

Cocteau's nonfiction is witty and incisive and usually based on his life and role as a poet in the control of forces he does not understand. The books in this category include *Le Rappel à l'ordre* (1926; *A Call to Order*, 1926), *Lettre à Jacques Maritain* (1926; *Art and Faith*, 1948), *Opium: Journal d'une désintoxication* (1930; *Opium: Diary of a Cure*, 1932), *Essai de la critique indirecte* (1932; *The Lais Mystery: An Essay of Indirect Criticism*, 1936), *Portraits-souvenir, 1900-1914* (1935; *Paris Album*, 1956), *"La Belle et la bête": Journal d'un film* (1946; *"Beauty and the Beast": Journal of a Film*, 1950), *La Difficulté d'être* (1947; *The Difficulty of Being*, 1966), and *Poésie critique* (1960).

ACHIEVEMENTS

Twentieth century art in many areas is indebted to Jean Cocteau. His accomplishments span the artistic and literary activities of his times, the diversity unified by his vision of all art as facets of the purest form: poetry. Whether working in film, fiction, theater, drawing, or verse, he considered himself to be revealing the poet in him. Critics now generally agree that his finest achievements are in the novel and the cinema. One of the most crystalline stylists among French writers of the twentieth century, Cocteau employed brilliant imagery and extraordinary visual qualities that make his novels powerfully evocative despite their terse style. Some regard him as a dilettante interested only in stylishness and facile demonstrations of his gifts; his classical style, however, allows him to transcend the limitations of ordinary novelists and their message-oriented prose to explore the resonances of mythology and archetype in a modern context. His versatility, irony, and playfulness encouraged his contemporaries to dismiss him, and he received few honors other than his 1955 election to the Académie Française. His novels are quirky, experimental, often chaotic, but filled with intriguing imagery and wit. *Children of the Game* is almost universally agreed to be his masterpiece.

BIOGRAPHY

Jean Cocteau's background was solidly Parisian bourgeois. Georges and Eugénie Lecomte Cocteau, his

Jean Cocteau. (National Archives)

parents, were a cultivated couple who introduced Jean, his brother Paul, and his sister Marthe to the fine arts. Near their suburban home, Cocteau would recall, the children played on the grounds of a "magical" castle designed by François Mansart. When living in the city with his grandparents, Cocteau would wander through rooms that contained classical busts, vases, a painting by Eugène Delacroix, and drawings by Jean-Auguste-Dominique Ingres. The celebrated violinist Pablo de Sarasate often visited Cocteau's grandfather, who was a cellist, and they would play music together. What impressed the young Cocteau most, however, were his trips to the circus, the ice palace, and the theater, particularly the Comédie-Française. His memories of these trips, he would later come to realize, were even brighter than the real experiences. In his own productions years later, he would ask technicians to duplicate the lighting or brilliance of childhood theatrical events and be told it had been technically impossible to create such effects when he was a boy. Memory had heightened the splendor of the past, including the recollections of the castle and of

his grandparents' house; his own life began to assume mythological dimensions.

At the Petit Lycée Condorcet, Cocteau was a poor student, especially after his father killed himself in 1899 because of financial pressures. He did, however, meet the haunting Pierre Dargelos, who would become the dark "god" of *Children of the Game*. At the Grand Condorcet, Cocteau was frequently truant, exploiting his illnesses to stay home. Like many creative people, he was irritated by institutions, and he much preferred having his German governess sew doll clothes for a model theater to sitting behind a school desk. Réné Rocher, one of his best friends, often played with Cocteau's miniature theaters and, in adulthood, became a director himself.

Cocteau traveled with his mother to Venice, then began study for his *baccalauréat*. He was more interested, however, in his first love affair—with Madeleine Carlier, ten years his senior—and his deepening involvement in theater. He became a protégé of Édouard de Max, who acted opposite Sarah Bernhardt. All of these diversions contributed to Cocteau's failing the *bachot*.

De Max, however, thrust Cocteau into the public eye by organizing a reading of Cocteau's poetry by de Max, Rocher, and other prominent actors and actresses, at the Théâtre Fémina, on April 4, 1908. Several important literary critics and many of the elite of Paris attended. Cocteau's debut was a great success, and reviewers compared him to Pierre de Ronsard and Alfred de Musset. Subsequently, Cocteau met many literary notables, including Edmond Rostand, Marcel Proust, Charles-Pierre Péguy, Catulle Mendès, and Jules Lemaître. Comtesse Anna de Noailles particularly enchanted him, and he tried to write refined and sensual poetry like hers. He helped found the literary magazine *Schéhérazade*, dedicated to poetry and music, and moved into the Hôtel Biron, whose residents at the time included Auguste Rodin and his secretary, Rainer Maria Rilke.

Meeting the great impresario Sergei Diaghilev of the Ballets Russes caused Cocteau to abandon his previous enthusiasms for a while. He begged Diaghilev to let him write ballets. Diaghilev eventually said, "Étonne-moi!" ("Astonish me!"), perhaps to quiet him, but Cocteau took it as an order and a goal for the rest of his life's work. Though Diaghilev produced Cocteau's first ballet, *Le Dieu bleu* (pr. 1912), for the coronation of George V, it was not successful. Believing that the score rather than his scenario was at fault, Cocteau began to associate with composer Igor Stravinsky, even moving in with him for a while. During this period, Henri Ghéon of *La Nouvelle Revue Française* accused Cocteau of being an entirely derivative poet. Stung by the validity of the review (perhaps coauthored by André Gide), Cocteau began a search for himself as an artist. He underwent what he called a "molting" around 1914, rebelling against older writers who had influenced him, such as Rostand and the Comtesse de Noailles, and moving in the direction of poets such as Max Jacob and Guillaume Apollinaire. *Le Potomak*, with its radical mixture of prose, drawings, and verse, was completed while Cocteau was living with Gide and Stravinsky and is the first important, truly original expression of Cocteau's personality.

Cocteau's attempted enlistment at the outset of World War I was rejected because of his health. He nevertheless became an ambulance driver on the Belgian front (albeit illegally). He was discovered and ordered back to Paris immediately before the group to which he had attached himself was decimated in an attack. These experiences formed the basis for his novel and film *Thomas the Impostor*. As the war continued, Cocteau met artists Amedeo Modigliani and Pablo Picasso in Paris. The latter he introduced to Diaghilev, who put him to work on Satie's ballet *Parade*; the scenario was written by Cocteau, the costumes and set were by Picasso, and the ballet was choreographed by Léonide Massine. The ballet's atonal music and radical set and costumes caused a near riot in the theater. Apollinaire, wearing his uniform and a dressing over his wounded head, barely managed to keep the spectators from assaulting the stage. Cocteau responded in the press, vigorously attacking the musical influence of Claude Debussy, Richard Wagner, and, surprisingly, Stravinsky, and aligning himself with the radical group called Les Six (Georges Auric, Louis Durey, Arthur Honegger, Darius Milhaud, Francis Poulenc, and Germaine Tailleferre).

Raymond Radiguet was fifteen, handsome, and a poetic genius, Cocteau believed, when he met and fell in love with him in 1919. Radiguet was a major influence in moving Cocteau toward a simpler, more classical style. Cocteau's energy revived, and he produced several new works, including *The Grand Écart* and the volume of poems *Plain-Chant*. When in December, 1923, Radiguet died of typhoid, Cocteau was devastated. Diaghilev took Cocteau to Monte Carlo to help him recover, but the discovery of opium there was Cocteau's only comfort. His friends and family were forced to persuade him to enter a sanatorium in 1925, when his addiction had become serious. Jacques Maritain, the Catholic philosopher, briefly restored Cocteau's faith in religion during the cure. The faith waned, but works such as *L'Ange Heurtebise*, *Orpheus*, and *Children of the Game* followed. Patching up his friendship with Stravinsky, Cocteau wrote the libretto for the oratorio *Oedipus-Rex*.

Though Cocteau contracted typhoid in 1931, his artistic output in the 1930's was astonishing. He wrote plays, poems, songs, ballets, art criticism, and a column for the newspaper *Ce Soir*. He published a journal chronicling a trip taken in imitation of Jules Verne's *Le Tour du monde en quatre-vingt jours* (1873; *Around the World in Eighty Days*, 1873). He also became the manager of bantamweight boxer Alphonse Theo Brown. His first attempt at *poésie cinématographique* (poetry of the film), however, was probably his most important activity. He wrote and directed the film *The Blood of a Poet*, which became a classic. His abilities in the visual arts and in visual imagery expressed themselves well in cinema, and he became responsible for a number of major films, including *Beauty and the Beast*, *Intimate Relations*, *The Testament of Orpheus*, and *Les Enfants terribles*.

During the German occupation of France, Cocteau was constantly vilified by the press. His play *The Typewriter* was banned. At one point, he was beaten by a group of French Nazis for not saluting their flag. He testified in court for thief, novelist, and Resistance fighter Jean Genet in 1942, despite much advice to the contrary. Cocteau gained respect for his courage and, after the war, found himself a "grand old man" of the artistic world.

His muse, however, would not let him retire. He traveled, made recordings, and wrote plays, journals, and films. His frescoes for the city hall at Menton, the Chapel of Saint Pierre at Villefranche-sur-Mer, the Chapel of Notre Dame in London, the Church of Saint Blaise-des-Simples in Milly-la-Fôret, and the Chapel at Fréjus, No-tre-Dame-de-Jérusalem created controversy among art critics. He also designed fabrics, plates, and posters. In 1955, he was elected to the Royal Belgian Academy and to the Académie Française. In 1956, he was awarded an honorary doctorate of letters from Oxford University. He died on October 11, 1963, distressed at hearing of the death of his friend Edith Piaf earlier in the day.

ANALYSIS

Le Potomak was a crucial work in Jean Cocteau's development, as he used it to break free of former influences and find an individual voice. Highly experimental, it is, however, not of compelling interest for any other reason, consisting as it does of an exploration of the subconscious through a hodgepodge of verse, prose, and drawings, all of which reveal Cocteau's talents but mostly demonstrate rebellion rather than a mature concept of the novelistic art. Its writing was interrupted by World War I, and the influence of the war is apparent in the revised edition. Under the influence of Radiguet, Cocteau wrote *The Grand Écart* and *Thomas the Impostor*. Mythologizing memories of his childhood, Cocteau based *The Grand Écart* on a childhood visit to Venice and his recollections of boarding school. One of his recurrent images appears indistinctly in this novel in the form of the Englishman Stopwell. Like Dargelos and the Angel Heurtebise, Stopwell is an angel in the form of a tempter who brings about annihilation or metamorphosis. *Thomas the Impostor* was based largely on Cocteau's own experiences during the war. Rejected for service, he posed as an ambulance driver on the Belgian front and was "adopted" by a group of Fusiliers Marins. When discovered by a superior officer, he was arrested and taken from the front. A day later, most of his comrades were killed. Rather than portraying the war as a horror, however, the novel turns it into a ghastly joke, a reflection of humanity's chaotic mind, a cruel trick played by a Euripidean god. Being an impostor is likened to being a poet, and reality and impostorship merge only when Thomas the Impostor is shot in the Waste Land. The "Prince of Frivolity," as Cocteau was known, uses flippant, humorous, outlandish imagery that accentuates the horror. The book is clearly one of his better novels, though not nearly equal to his next.

CHILDREN OF THE GAME

Children of the Game is considered to be Cocteau's most successful novel by far. In addition to being beautifully written, it is an extraordinary evocation of adolescent hopes, fears, dreams, and obsessions; it is said to have been regarded by French teenagers as capturing their alienation from adult society in the same way that J. D. Salinger articulated teen alienation in American culture. Perhaps because Cocteau, as an artist and a man, always held himself as a kind of alien visitor to the realms of the establishment from the world of subjectivity and irrationality, his sensitivity to adolescent alienation was enhanced. *Children of the Game* is not a realistic portrayal of adolescence, however. It is sensitive, but it is so overlaid with dream imagery and mythological overtones that whatever autobiographical elements and psychological truths it might contain are submerged.

Fragments from many mythological sources are identifiable upon even a cursory reading of the work. Cocteau was fascinated with mythology and at various times in his career wrote works dealing with Antigone, Orpheus, Bacchus, and the "Beauty and the Beast" motif. Cocteau wrote *Children of the Game* very rapidly—at the rate of seventeen pages a day for three weeks—while he was undergoing treatment for opium addiction, as if he were trying to let archetypal and subconscious elements flow freely onto the page. Too careful an artist to practice automatic writing without aesthetically manipulating the result, he nevertheless refused to make later changes in the text for fear of destroying the fabric of the book. Characters in *Children of the Game* quite often suggest beings from mythology, as Cocteau imbues people and events from his own life and imagination with a supernatural or divine aura.

Dargelos, for example, whose name is taken from a real boy whom Cocteau admired in his school days, takes on the characteristics of a god. Early in the book, Paul seeks Dargelos among the snowball wars in the Cité Monthiers. Paul's love for Dargelos is described as "sexless and purposeless," and his seeking him in order to fight beside him, defend him, and prove what he can do takes on religious overtones. Paul, however, is silenced by a snowball from one of his idol's acolytes, condemning him to Dargelos's wrath. Dargelos rises up in an immense gesture, his cheeks on fire and his hair in disorder, like a statue of Dionysus. Paul feels the blow of the snowball on his chest—a dark blow, the blow of a marble fist. As Paul loses consciousness, he imagines Dargelos upon a dais, in a supernatural light. Dargelos has struck Paul in the heart, with a snowball like Thor's hammer or Zeus's thunderbolt. Dargelos, throughout the rest of the book, is hardly mentioned; his presence, however, seems to loom over all subsequent events. As Wallace Fowlie has observed, he "grows into the figure of a dark angel who haunts the dreams and thoughts of the protagonist."

Eden is evoked when Paul, his sister Elisabeth, and Gérard find themselves alone without adult supervision. In "the Room," they are free of conventional worries about food and seem innocent of evil. Their childhood seems to be prolonged. Although the situation appears to be fraught with incestuous overtones—Paul and Elisabeth sleep in the same room and bathe together—there is instead a matter-of-fact sexlessness, a lack of shame. When a ball of poison (associated with Dargelos's snowball) causes the cold, outside world of snow and death to blow into their Eden, one may see an analogy to the expulsion from Eden, the coming of mortality into Eden.

One must not, however, treat *Children of the Game* as allegory. Cocteau is weaving a fugue of implications and mythological elements. One critic has found the novel to be about the impossibility of escaping bourgeois ideology; another has found it to be the playing out of fate in the form of Eros-Thanatos. There is certainly a hint of inevitability in the sequence of events. Tragedy is suggested from the beginning, and the classical structure and sparkling sentences help convey this impression. The characters are in the grip of forces beyond their control. When Michael, the rich American Jew, is killed, it seems as if the Room reaches out to protect itself. When Dargelos gives Paul the fist-sized ball of poison, one is reminded of the marble-hard snowball and the apple that destroyed Eden. A reddish gash in the ball is reminiscent of both a wound and female genitalia, suggesting an association between mortality and the loss of innocence.

The end is destined, and nothing can hold it back. Childhood is doomed. As Cocteau himself wrote in *The Difficulty of Being:* "Childhood knows what it wants. It wants to emerge from childhood. The trouble starts when it does emerge. For youth knows what it does not want before it knows what it does want. But what it does not want is what we do want." Thus are the "holy terrors" doomed.

LA FIN DU POTOMAK

Le Fantôme de Marseille is a slight work containing associations and local color that Cocteau recalled from his running away to Marseilles at the age of fifteen. Later, in Le Picquey, in a hotel where he had stayed with Radiguet in 1923, Cocteau watched over the convalescence of a new love, actor Jean Marais, and returned to the inspiration of *Le Potomak* for his last novel. *La Fin du Potomak* is a curious mixture of fairy tales, aphorisms, riddles, and true stories recalling Cocteau's experiences after 1913. A revival of Cocteau's classicism has been seen in the work, but most often it is regarded as a mere shadow of *Le Potomak*, as if the author's creative interests had shifted away from *poésie de roman* (poetry of the novel). Brooding over the entire work is a disappointment with human nature and recurrent imagery of death, perhaps evoked by Marais's illness and the memory of Radiguet's sudden death. There is also an acceptance of the author's own death (which was many years in the future), indicated by some lines of poetry at the end: "Death, don't be clever/ . . . You see, I wait standing still/ I even offer you my hand/ . . . What does it matter? I leave behind a book/ That you will not take from me."

J. Madison Davis

OTHER MAJOR WORKS

PLAYS: *Antigone*, pr. 1922 (libretto; English translation, 1961); *Orphée*, pr. 1926 (*Orpheus*, 1933); *Oedipus-Rex*, pr. 1927 (libretto; English translation, 1961); *La Voix humaine*, pr., pb. 1930 (*The Human Voice*, 1951); *La Machine infernale*, pr., pb. 1934 (*The Infernal Machine*, 1936); *L'École des veuves*, pr., pb. 1936; *Les Chevaliers de la table ronde*, pr., pb. 1937 (*The Knights of the Round Table*, 1955); *Les Parents terribles*, pr., pb. 1938 (*Intimate Relations*, 1952); *Les Monstres sacrés*, pr., pb. 1940 (*The Holy Terrors*, 1953); *La Machine à écrire*, pr., pb. 1941 (*The Typewriter*,

1948); *Renaud et Armide*, pr., pb. 1943; *L'Aigle à deux têtes*, pr., pb. 1946 (*The Eagle Has Two Heads*, 1946); *Bacchus*, pr. 1951 (English translation, 1955); *Théâtre complet*, pb. 1957 (2 volumes); *Five Plays*, pb. 1961; *L'Impromptu du Palais-Royal*, pr., pb. 1962; *The Infernal Machine, and Other Plays*, 1964.

POETRY: *La Lampe d'Aladin*, 1909; *Le Prince frivole*, 1910; *La Danse de Sophocle*, 1912; *Le Cap de Bonne-Espérance*, 1919; *L'Ode à Picasso*, 1919; *Escales*, 1920; *Poésies, 1917-1920*, 1920; *Discours du grand sommeil*, 1922; *Vocabulaire*, 1922; *Plain-Chant*, 1923; *Poésie, 1916-1923*, 1924; *Cri écrit*, 1925; *L'Ange Heurtebise*, 1925; *Prière mutilée*, 1925; *Opéra*, 1927; *Morceaux choisis*, 1932; *Mythologie*, 1934; *Allégories*, 1941; *Léone*, 1945; *Poèmes*, 1945; *La Crucifixion*, 1946; *Anthologie poétique*, 1951; *Le Chiffre sept*, 1952; *Appogiatures*, 1953; *Clair-obscur*, 1954; *Poèmes, 1916-1955*, 1956; *Gondole des morts*, 1959; *Cérémonial espagnol du phénix*, 1961; *Le Requiem*, 1962.

SCREENPLAYS: *Le Sang d'un poète*, 1930 (*The Blood of a Poet*, 1949); *L'Éternel Retour*, 1943 (*The Eternal Return*, 1948); *Le Baron fantôme*, 1943; *L'Aigle à deux têtes*, 1946; *La Belle et la bête*, 1946 (*Beauty and the Beast*, 1947); *Ruy Blas*, 1947; *Les Parents terribles*, 1948 (*Intimate Relations*, 1952); *Les Enfants terribles*, 1950; *Orphée*, 1950 (*Orpheus*, 1950); *Le Testament d'Orphée*, 1959 (*The Testament of Orpheus*, 1968); *Thomas l'Imposteur*, 1965.

NONFICTION: *Le Coq et l'Arlequin*, 1918 (*Cock and Harlequin*, 1921); *Le Secret professionnel*, 1922; *Lettre à Jacques Maritain*, 1926 (*Art and Faith*, 1948); *Le Rappel à l'ordre*, 1926 (*A Call to Order*, 1926); *Opium: Journal d'une désintoxication*, 1930 (*Opium: Diary of a Cure*, 1932); *Essai de la critique indirecte*, 1932 (*The Lais Mystery: An Essay of Indirect Criticism*, 1936); *Portraits-souvenir, 1900-1914*, 1935 (*Paris Album*, 1956); *"La Belle et la bête": Journal d'un film*, 1946 (*"Beauty and the Beast": Journal of a Film*, 1950); *La Difficulté d'être*, 1947 (*The Difficulty of Being*, 1966); *Journal d'un inconnu*, 1952 (*The Hand of a Stranger*, 1956; also known as *Diary of an Unknown*, 1988); *The Journals of Jean Cocteau*, 1956; *Poésie critique*, 1960.

BALLET SCENARIOS: *Le Dieu bleu*, pr. 1912 (with Frédéric de Madrazo); *Parade*, pr. 1917 (music by Erik Satie, scenery by Pablo Picasso); *Le Boeuf sur le toit*, pr.

1920 (music by Darius Milhaud, scenery by Raoul Dufy); *Le Gendarme incompris*, pr. 1921 (with Raymond Radiguet; music by Francis Poulenc); *Les Mariés de la tour Eiffel*, pr. 1921 (music by Les Six; *The Wedding on the Eiffel Tower*, 1937); *Les Biches*, pr. 1924 (music by Poulenc); *Les Fâcheux*, pr. 1924 (music by Georges Auric); *Le Jeune Homme et la mort*, pr. 1946 (music by Johann Sebastian Bach); *Phèdre*, pr. 1950 (music by Auric).

TRANSLATION: *Roméo et Juliette*, 1926 (of William Shakespeare's play).

BIBLIOGRAPHY

Brown, Frederick. *An Impersonation of Angels: A Biography of Jean Cocteau*. New York: Viking Press, 1968. Study of the life and work of Cocteau focuses on his artistic milieu and his collaborators and sources of inspiration, such as poet Guillaume Apollinaire, artist Pablo Picasso, novelist André Gide, and filmmaker Jean Marais. Includes illustrations and bibliography.

Crosland, Margaret. *Jean Cocteau: A Biography*. New York: Alfred A. Knopf, 1956. Charming biography written with the help and encouragement of Cocteau himself. The goal is to relate Cocteau's work to his life and to relate the different aspects of his work to one another. Offers lively comments by fellow artists as well as discussion and interpretation of individual works by Cocteau. Includes excerpts from letters of Cocteau and numerous illustrations.

Crowson, Lydia. *The Esthetic of Jean Cocteau*. Hanover: University of New Hampshire Press, 1978. Scholarly work devotes chapters to Cocteau's milieu, the nature of the real, and the roles of myth, consciousness, and power. Includes introduction and bibliography.

Fowlie, Wallace. *Jean Cocteau: The History of a Poet's Age*. Bloomington: Indiana University Press, 1966. General study defines Cocteau's originality by comparing him with other French writers and film directors of his lifetime. Proposes a very sensible evaluation of Cocteau's real accomplishments.

Knapp, Bettina L. *Jean Cocteau*. Updated ed. Boston: Twayne, 1989. Thorough study pursues both psychological and literary views of Cocteau's work, with chapters following a chronological approach. Includes chronology, notes, bibliography, and index.

Lowe, Romana N. *The Fictional Female: Sacrificial Rituals and Spectacles of Writing in Baudelaire, Zola, and Cocteau*. New York: Peter Lang, 1997. Highlights the sacrificial victim common in nineteenth and twentieth century French texts: woman. Traces structures and images of female sacrifice in the genres of poetry, novel, and theater with close readings of the works of Charles Baudelaire, Émile Zola, and Cocteau.

Mauriès, Patrick. *Jean Cocteau*. Translated by Jane Brenton. London: Thames and Hudson, 1998. Brief but excellent biography provides information that places Cocteau's works within the context of his life. Illustrated with many photographs.

Selous, Trista. *Cocteau*. Paris: Centre Pompidou, 2003. Retrospective catalog compiled by the Centre Pompidou and the Montreal Museum offers an illustrated review of Cocteau's creative output along with seventeen essays on his life and work.

Steegmuller, Francis. *Cocteau*. Boston: D. R. Godine, 1986. Major biography discusses Cocteau's childhood, the influence of his mother, and fellow poets. Defines Cocteau as a "quick-change artist" with a propensity for constant self-invention, discarding old views and activities and assuming new roles or guises with remarkable facility. Includes illustrations, twelve informative appendixes, bibliography, and index.

Williams, James S. *Jean Cocteau*. London: Reaktion Books, 2008. Biography chronicles the development of Cocteau's aesthetic and his work as a novelist, poet, dramatist, filmmaker, and designer. Concludes that Cocteau's oeuvre is characterized by a continual self-questioning.

J. M. COETZEE

Born: Cape Town, South Africa; February 9, 1940
Also known as: John Michael Coetzee

PRINCIPAL LONG FICTION

Dusklands, 1974
In the Heart of the Country, 1977 (also known as *From the Heart of the Country*)
Waiting for the Barbarians, 1980
Life and Times of Michael K, 1983
Foe, 1986
Age of Iron, 1990
The Master of Petersburg, 1994
Disgrace, 1999
Elizabeth Costello, 2003
Slow Man, 2005
Diary of a Bad Year, 2007

OTHER LITERARY FORMS

In addition to his long fiction, J. M. Coetzee (kuht-SEE-uh) has published a number of book reviews and essays, primarily dealing with South African authors and Thomas Hardy. He has also published translations of other writers' work into Afrikaans, Dutch, French, and German. In *White Writing: On the Culture of Letters in South Africa* (1988), he surveys South African literature from its beginnings up to, but not including, World War II. Coetzee has also published two memoirs, *Boyhood: Scenes from Provincial Life* (1997) and *Youth: Scenes from Provincial Life II* (2002), both written in the third person. In these works, with characteristic restraint, he tells of his youth in the dreary suburbs and farms of Cape Town Province and of the growing awareness of contradiction that led to his becoming a writer. Coetzee continually publishes scholarly essays and speeches on literature, animal rights, censorship, and other topics. Many of these have been collected in *Inner Workings: Literary Essays, 2000-2005* (2007).

ACHIEVEMENTS

J. M. Coetzee is recognized as one of South Africa's finest writers, one whose allegorical fiction suggests that apartheid is but a particularly virulent expression of humankind's will to dominate. At the same time, like many contemporary writers, he is acutely aware of problems of language and representation, and his fiction reflects an increasing preoccupation with the complex interplay of language, imagination, and experience. It is Coetzee's distinctive achievement to fuse such philosophical concerns with probing social and psychological insights.

Coetzee has received many prestigious literary awards. His second book, *In the Heart of the Country*, won South Africa's premier literary award, the Central News Agency (CNA) Prize, in 1977. *Waiting for the Barbarians*, chosen as one of the best books of 1982 by *The New York Times*, won the CNA Prize, the Geoffrey Faber Memorial Prize, and the James Tait Black Memorial Prize; *Life and Times of Michael K* won Great Britain's Booker Prize in 1983. In 1987, Coetzee received the Jerusalem Prize for writing "that contributes to the freedom of the individual in society." He became the first person to win the Booker Prize twice, receiving the second in 1999 for *Disgrace*. In 2003, Coetzee was awarded the Nobel Prize in Literature. In 2008, he was awarded the high honor of the Order of Mapungubwe by the South African government for his literary achievements.

BIOGRAPHY

John Michael Coetzee was born on February 9, 1940, in Cape Town, South Africa. His family soon moved to the Karoo, a dreary region of semiarid plains in Cape Town Province, and he was raised there and on his grandparents' farm. His father was an unsuccessful lawyer, and his mother was a teacher. His family spoke English at home, but he studied Afrikaans, South Africa's other official language, in school. Coetzee attended the University of Cape Town, earning degrees in both mathematics and English. Soon after graduation, he moved to London. There he took a job as a computer programmer and wrote a master's thesis on the English writer Ford Madox Ford. He earned his master of arts degree from the University of Cape Town in 1963 but remained in London for two more years working with computers.

Coetzee returned to the academic world in 1965, joining the doctoral program in linguistics at the University of Texas in Austin. Significantly, he was in the United States to witness the dramatic events of the Civil Rights and anti-Vietnam War movements of the 1960's at the same time that South Africa's apartheid system and racial turmoil were drawing increased international attention. After completing his thesis on the playwright Samuel Beckett, he moved to the State University of New York at Buffalo, where he taught from 1968 to 1971 and began work on his first major work, *Dusklands*.

When Coetzee returned to South Africa in 1972, it was to teach at the University of Cape Town, his alma mater, and to take up the life of a writer. He has produced a major literary work every three or four years since his repatriation

J. M. Coetzee. (© Jerry Bauer)

and has published translations and academic essays focusing on the history of South African and Western literature and the role of the writer in society. He has traveled widely throughout the United States and England, lecturing and serving as a visiting professor of literature.

Coetzee retired from the University of Cape Town in 1984. Between 1984 and 2003, he taught at several prestigious American universities, spending some years at the University of Chicago, serving there on the Committee on Social Thought. After visiting Australia, he moved to Adelaide, South Australia, in 2002; he became an Australian citizen in 2006. He currently serves as an honorary research fellow at the University of Adelaide.

Coetzee is a vegetarian and has lectured extensively on the issue of animal rights. Married in 1963 and divorced in 1981, he had two children, a daughter, Gisela, and a son, Nicholas; his son was killed in 1989. Coetzee continues writing prolifically and by all accounts leads a reclusive and acetic lifestyle, granting few interviews.

ANALYSIS

Although contemporary South Africa is seldom mentioned or referred to explicitly in most of J. M. Coetzee's novels, the land and the concerns of that country permeate his works. One may see this indirect approach as an evasion of the censorship that was a factor for any writer in that state during the years of apartheid, but this necessary blurring of temporal and geographic actualities also endows each work with universal overtones. On one level, Coetzee's novels deal with the suffering that human beings inflict on one another, whether as agents of the state or as the victims of their own obsessions. Colonialism and its legacy form the basis for much of his fiction. Also permeating his work is the issue of the treatment of animals and the perception of difference in the rights of humans and the rights of animals, a perception that Coetzee often challenges.

DUSKLANDS

Coetzee's first major work, *Dusklands*, is composed of two novellas, *The Vietnam Project* and *The Narrative of Jacobus Coetzee*; the common thread that runs through the two seemingly unrelated pieces is the obsession of each protagonist with the personal dimension of colonization. Eugene Dawn, the narrator of *The Vietnam Project*, is a mythographer inquiring into the efficacy of American propaganda in Vietnam. His discoveries are disturbing and soul shattering to the point that Dawn is driven to kidnap his child from his estranged wife and use him as a hostage. In the course of his confrontation with the police, Dawn stabs his son, marveling at the ease with which the knife slips into the flesh. He is last seen in an insane asylum, his consciousness peopled with images of power and powerlessness.

The second novella purports to be a narrative of an eighteenth century Boer settler, translated from the Dutch by J. M. Coetzee, with an afterword by Coetzee's father. The work relates a trek undertaken ostensibly to hunt elephants but really to see what lies beyond the narrator's immediate environment. The decorous, antiquarian headings that break up the narrative—"Journey Beyond the Great River," "Sojourn Among the Great Namaqua"—contrast strangely with the horrors endured by both the narrator and the tribespeople he meets. Stricken with illness, Jacobus remains with the not-yet-colonized Namaqua, whose relations with him are at times contemptuous, at times nurturing, but never the expected ones of respectful native to European explorer. Jacobus's Hottentot servants desert him to stay with the Namaqua, and naked, unarmed, and alone, he returns to civilization after an arduous journey. He goes back to the land of the Namaqua with troops and takes his revenge on the tribespeople, who have shown him less respect than he wanted.

Throughout, the narrator hints, almost unconsciously, at what he is seeking: a sense of limits, and therefore a definition of his self. This motif is introduced in the first novella by Dawn's analysis of the hate felt by Americans toward the Vietnamese: "Our nightmare was that since whatever we reached for slipped like smoke through our fingers, we did not exist. . . . We landed on the shores of Vietnam clutching our arms and pleading for someone to stand up without flinching to these probes of reality . . . but like everything else they withered before us."

This concern with boundaries seems to stem from the physical environment of the vast African plain, into which Jacobus expands endlessly but joylessly. There are no rules, and Jacobus is worried by the possibility of "exploding to the four corners of the universe." There is an unmistakable grandeur in such a concept, one that reflects the position of the powerful in relation to the powerless, but it is a qualified grandeur. It is one that Coetzee's protagonists reject, drawing back from the spurious apotheosis of limitless being, understanding that it is not worth the dreary awareness of the void. Transcendence cannot occur when there is nothing to transcend.

In the Heart of the Country

Indeed, transcendence is the object of the quest for all of Coetzee's main characters, and what they seek is the obstinate, obdurate object that will resist them to the point that they know that they exist, and against which they may define themselves. This quest is an important factor in Coetzee's second book, *In the Heart of the Country*, a novel written in the form of a diary kept by a young woman on a sheep farm. The farm is isolated in the featureless landscape, and Magda has recourse to fantasies, terrible and bloody, of revenge on her father, who to her has always remained an "absence." Little by little, Magda peoples her life, writes variations on reasons that she wants to kill her father, imagines situations in which she becomes the servant of her father and his brown mistress, and ultimately kills him, more or less by accident, while he is making love to Anna, the wife of the servant Hendrik. The uncertainty of the act's reality lingers after the occurrence; the father really has been shot, however, and takes several days to die.

At this point, the diary takes on a more straightforward tone, as if the difficulty of disposing of the body has finally focused Magda's life. Hendrik and Anna are moved into the house, and Magda begins sleeping with Hendrik, who now seems to despise her and who treats her as if she were the servant. Eventually, worried that they will be blamed for the murder of Magda's father, Hendrik and Anna disappear in the middle of the night, and Magda is left alone in the great house.

Without money, without any visible means of support, she manages to live into an old age in which she hears voices from airplanes passing overhead. The voices say things that she takes to be comments on her condition: "Lacking all external enemies and resistances, confined within an oppressive narrowness and regularity, man at last has no choice but to turn himself into an adventure." The solipsism that is evidenced in the earlier part of the diary (and that is a function of the diary form)

is thus recalled to cast doubt on the truth of what Magda has been writing. Has all the foregoing been the product of a spinster's fevered imagination? Every event surrounding the father's murder and burial may have been so, and Magda herself wonders whether her father will come striding back into her life. Yet the one point in which Magda truly lives is the point where her father has ceased being an absence, when the weight and increasing rigidity of his corpse have lent reality to his dutiful daughter's heretofore thwarted love.

Waiting for the Barbarians

This relationship between the violent act and the affirmation of one's identity, along with the connection between hate and love, between master and slave, between the tortured and the torturer, forms the central theme of *Waiting for the Barbarians* (the title of which alludes to a poem by Constantine P. Cavafy). An unnamed, aging magistrate of a town on the far borders of "the Empire" narrates the story of an attempt by the Empire to consolidate its northern border against the depredations of "the barbarians," nomads who had previously existed peacefully—with the exception of some dubious raids—in the face of increasing expansion by the agrarian settlers. The magistrate is far more interested in comfort, his books, and his antiquarian researches into the ancient sand-buried buildings near the town than he is in the expansion of empire. He is disturbed by the arrival of the sinister Colonel Joll of the "Third Bureau," a police force given special powers for the duration of the "emergency."

At first, the magistrate merely resents the intrusion of such affairs into the somnolent world that keeps him comfortable. He is severely shaken, however, by the torture of two obviously innocuous prisoners (and the killing of one of them) by Joll. As a result, the magistrate is compelled to place himself, quiet servant of the Empire, in opposition to the civilization to which he has been dedicated.

Joll has taken out an expedition to capture barbarians, some of whom he interrogates upon his return. The magistrate cannot simply ignore what is happening, but neither can he act. When Joll leaves, the barbarians are released and they depart; they have left behind a girl who has been tortured: Her eyes have been burned and her ankles broken in order to wring information from her father. The magistrate takes her into his house and enters into a bizarre relationship with her, one that consists of washing her swollen feet and badly healed ankles; the washing progresses to the other parts of her body, but there is no straightforward sexual act. During these ministrations, both the magistrate and the girl fall asleep, a normal sleep for the girl but a heavy, drugged torpor for the man. He cannot fathom his fascination with this girl who has been so cruelly marked, but he begins to understand that perhaps it is her damaged quality that so attracts him. She is unresponsive to him, accepting his tenderness as he imagines she accepted her torture, passive, impenetrable. He decides to take her back to her people after he realizes that to her, he and Colonel Joll are interchangeable, two sides of the same empire.

After an arduous journey, the magistrate and his small party come face-to-face with the barbarians in the mountains; he gives the girl back to them, since she expresses her desire to leave him and civilization. Upon his return, he is arrested by the occupying force of the Empire on charges of collaborating with the barbarians. A new policeman has installed himself in his office, and the magistrate goes to his cell almost gladly: "I had no duty to her save what it occurred to me to feel from moment to moment: from the oppression of such freedom who would not welcome the liberation of confinement?"

He manages to escape, but he returns, knowing that he cannot survive in the open spaces. Eventually he is released: The expedition against the barbarians has been a dismal failure, the town is emptying of soldiers and civilians, and the Empire is crumbling at the edges. He assumes his former responsibilities and tries to prepare the town for approaching winter. The novel ends with the same image that has haunted the magistrate's dreams: children playing in the snow in the town square. The children are making a snowman, however, not a model of the empty town, and the faceless girl is not among them.

The Empire could be anywhere: Its geography encompasses Africa as well as Mongolia or Siberia. The townspeople are not described physically, and the description of the barbarians gives the impression that they are Mongols. Colonel Joll and the warrant officer—and their methods—evoke the Gestapo, the KGB, and, for that matter, the apartheid-era South African police. The time appears to be set in a future so distant that sand dunes have engulfed buildings of staggering antiquity. What does endure, Coetzee seems to be saying, are the sad constants of human history: the subjugation of the weak by the strong, the effects of slavery on masters as well as slaves, and the impotence of good intentions. If the magistrate has survived, it is because the Empire has considered his rebellion of no consequence.

LIFE AND TIMES OF MICHAEL K

It is difficult to present limited expectations as an affirmation of the value of life. This subject, touched on in *Waiting for the Barbarians*, is realized in *Life and Times of Michael K*, a novel set in a South Africa of the future. Coetzee had, until this novel, furnished his readers with introspective, articulate narrators who reveal their complicated thoughts in precise language. With *Life and Times of Michael K*, he departed from this pattern.

Michael K's survival is precarious from the beginning of his life; born with a deformed lip, he must be painstakingly fed with a spoon by a mother repelled by his appearance. His mother, Anna K, a domestic worker, takes him with her when she works. When he reaches school age, he is put in an institution for the handicapped, where he learns a bit of reading and writing and the skills of the unskilled: "scrubbing, bedmaking, dishwashing, basket weaving, woodwork, and digging." Eventually, at the age of fifteen, he joins the Parks and Gardens Service and becomes a gardener, a job to which he returns after an attempt at night work.

At the age of thirty-one, K receives a message to fetch his mother from the hospital. For a time, they live together in Anna's old "servant's room"—a windowless cubicle under a staircase, originally meant for air-conditioning equipment that was never installed—but a riot in the vicinity of the apartment buildings convinces them to leave. Anna, as her dropsy gets worse, harbors a confused dream of returning to the farm where she spent her childhood. She has saved some money, and K attempts to buy a railroad ticket, but a bureaucratic nightmare of reservations and permits forces them to walk, the son pushing his mother on a two-wheeled cart that he has built through persistence and ingenuity.

They travel through a disquieting landscape: At times thronged with people leaving the city, at times ominously empty, the roads are the domain of enormous army convoys, the purpose and destination of which remain unknown, but that, along with the riots in the cities, indicate an ongoing civil war in the unnamed country. Towns still exist, however, and it is in one of these that Anna and K stop; exhaustion and exposure to the cold rain have aggravated the mother's illness, and K takes her to a hospital, where, after a few days, she dies. A nurse hands K a box of ashes, tells him that these are his mother's remains, and sends him on his way. He is robbed of his money by a soldier, but he keeps his mother's ashes. He finally reaches an abandoned farm that might be the one mentioned by his mother. He decides to live there. The leaking of a windmill pump on the farm has formed an oasis in the barren land. K plants a garden and sprinkles his mother's ashes over the soil. A grandson of the departed owners of the farm appears, seeking safety from what is happening in the cities. Dimly, K realizes that if he stays, it will be as a servant to this boy; he therefore shuts off the pump so that everything will die, and he leaves.

K is subsequently interned in a work camp from which he escapes; he returns to the farm and again plants his garden. The boy is gone, and K builds himself a shelter with stones and a piece of corrugated iron. One day, he sees men approaching. From concealment, he is somehow aware that these men must be "the other side," the antagonists to the dispirited government soldiers he has known. Although their donkeys destroy half his crop, K feels sympathy with these men. He makes plans to tend his garden so that there will be many crops and they will have more to eat when they come back. Ironically, the next soldiers are government soldiers, who appear months later, and they arrest K under suspicion of being connected to the rebels. They destroy the garden, explode the pump, and burn the farmhouse. K is again interned.

Up to this point, the third-person account has been from K's point of view: a registering of random impressions by someone who has no language to impose a pattern on events, who seldom wonders how he must appear, and who periodically achieves states approaching the meditative or vegetative. The second section is a first-person narrative by the medical officer—a pharmacist in civilian life, but it seems that many old men have been called back to military service, indicating that the

civil war has spread everywhere—of K's new camp. An articulate, compassionate man, reminiscent of the magistrate in *Waiting for the Barbarians*, he is by turns annoyed and inspired by K's refusal to eat "the food of the camp." When K escapes, the medical officer convinces the aged commandant of the camp to report him dead.

K returns to the city from which he set out, and there he falls in with others who live by scavenging; he undergoes a sexual initiation among these people, who mean him no harm but by whom he is repelled. At the end of the third section, K has gained self-consciousness. His thoughts are now phrased in the first person and told to the reader: "I am a gardener." This burst of self-awareness does not cut his ties to what he has been before; the final image is an emulation of the slow, patient rhythms of the earth: "He would bend the handle of the teaspoon in a loop and tie the string to it, he would lower it down the shaft deep into the earth, and when he brought it up there would be water in the bowl of the spoon; and in that way, he would say, one can live."

THE MASTER OF PETERSBURG

For his novel *Foe*, Coetzee turned to Daniel Defoe's novel *Robinson Crusoe* (1719) for setting and source. *Foe* is told by a female narrator washed ashore on the same island as Robinson Crusoe. With his novel Coetzee "writes back" to Defoe, challenging and expanding on the assumptions and themes of the earlier novel. In a similar vein, Coetzee's *The Master of Petersburg* draws on his novelist's sensibilities and ideas about the modern world as well as his scholar's knowledge of earlier literature.

The protagonist of *The Master of Petersburg* is the Russian novelist Fyodor Dostoevski (1821-1881); the novel begins in 1869, shortly after Dostoevski has completed his own great novel, *Crime and Punishment* (1866), and the less important *The Idiot* (1868). He is avoiding debtors' prison by living in exile in Dresden, and there he has begun writing *The Possessed* (1871-1872) when he learns that his stepson Pavel has died. He travels back to St. Petersburg using a false passport and moves into the rooming house where Pavel lived. This situation, which sets the story in motion, demonstrates an essential element of the novel: the combining of fact and fiction. Dostoevski did have a stepson named Pavel, and he did live with his second wife in Dresden during the years in question. The real Pavel lived until 1900, however, and there is no evidence that he was involved in many of the activities ascribed to him in the novel. Coetzee stays true to the record where it suits him but changes the facts freely and with no warning.

The fictional Dostoevski becomes obsessed with Pavel's death and consumed by his grief and guilt over his failures as a parent. His grief is marked by sudden and dramatic changes, from sorrow to anger to lust. He begins a turbulent affair with Anna, Pavel's landlady, hoping that it will keep Pavel somehow alive, at least in memory. Soon he learns that Pavel was involved with an underground revolutionary group, The People's Vengeance, and may have died at their hands. As Dostoevski discovers the manuscripts of Pavel's short stories and struggles to understand Pavel's role as both a writer and a revolutionary, he expresses his own (and, perhaps, Coetzee's own) ideas about the writer's responsibility—not to take sides in political conflict overtly but to present accurately and dramatically the humans involved in the conflict. Dostoevski can do this only by abandoning his quest to bring Pavel back to life, by burying his own needs and feelings. *The Master of Petersburg* was published just as apartheid was ending in South Africa, and it has been read by several critics as Coetzee's explanation for what has often been perceived as his failure to write more directly against apartheid.

Coetzee has been accused of being too political in his concerns; he has also been accused of not being political enough. To accuse him of either is to miss the point of his novels. He is concerned with humanity and with what it means to be human. In *Waiting for the Barbarians*, the magistrate says of his torturers, "They came to my cell to show me the meaning of humanity, and in the space of an hour they showed me a great deal." To be human is to suffer, but the one who causes the suffering also suffers and also is human. The torturer's hatred is twisted love, a rage against the victim for not pushing back, not allowing the torturer humanity. This is the root of all evil in the world, and this is what Coetzee shows. Humanity's history is one of suffering, and the only way to escape suffering is to live outside history.

DISGRACE

Disgrace is set in postapartheid South Africa, where the shifting political landscape alters the personal lives of the characters. Protagonist David Lurie is fifty-two years old, white, divorced, and a professor at Cape Technical University. A scholar of poetry and opera, he taught modern languages before being demoted to the position of adjunct professor of communications in deference to changing priorities at the university. Lurie constantly contemplates his advancing age while continually seeking erotic satisfaction. In this, he frequently misunderstands power relationships in respect to himself and women; he also confuses his urges with romance. His attempt to have a relationship with a prostitute, Soraya, strains their professional liaison, and Soraya discontinues her services. He then initiates a relationship with one of his students, Melanie, despite the vast differences in their ages and situations. Despite Melanie's apparent reluctance, Lurie continues to pursue her, and, at one juncture, he forces himself on her in what is arguably a rape. Melanie files a harassment complaint against him with the university, and Lurie is charged before a committee of his peers. He resigns his post amid much publicity and humiliation.

Disgraced, Lurie departs for the rural Eastern Cape, where his grown daughter, Lucy, lives on a farm. Lucy runs a dog kennel and keeps a garden, selling the produce. Lurie settles in for a while, assisting Lucy and volunteering at an animal clinic, helping to euthanize many sick, old, or unwanted dogs. One day, Lurie and Lucy are approached by two men and a boy who then force their way into the house. The intruders shoot the dogs in their kennels, Lurie is knocked out and set on fire (briefly), Lucy is brutally raped, the house is ransacked, and Lurie's car is stolen. In the aftermath of these horrific crimes, Lurie implores Lucy to press charges for the rape but she refuses, rejecting the legal process. Complicating this is the figure of Petrus, a black African who once worked for Lucy and now holds title to the land adjoining hers. Petrus's relation to one of the perpetrators and his offer to protect Lucy by taking her as his third wife frustrate Lurie, who wants to see justice done. Lucy considers the offer of marriage seriously, as she has become pregnant as a result of the rape.

Lurie returns to working on an opera that he has envisioned on the life of Lord Byron. The opera, which began as a lushly imagined romance, is reduced to a song accompanied by a lone banjo. So, too, Lurie's existence becomes increasingly stripped down, his former apartment ransacked, his possessions and job lost, his youth dissipated, and his ideas of justice meaningless in a new society.

Disgrace evokes the difficulty of life in a land riddled with violence and change. A motif of dogs in the novel calls up parallels between the treatment of animals and the treatment of blacks in South Africa and also alludes to the use of dogs against blacks in the apartheid era. Further, the discussions of notions of justice and revenge that weave through the novel allude to the hearings of the Truth and Reconciliation Commission that took place after the dismantling of apartheid and the difficulty of achieving reconciliation when power structures shift.

ELIZABETH COSTELLO

The structure of Coetzee's novel *Elizabeth Costello* is unusual. The work comprises eight chapters, or "lessons," each centered on a formal address or speech. The protagonist, Elizabeth Costello, is a sixty-six-year-old Australian writer of fiction and nonfiction. Her fame and reputation were established with a novel about Marion (Molly) Bloom, wife of the fictional Leopold Bloom of James Joyce's famous novel *Ulysses* (1922).

Elizabeth Costello opens in 1995 as Costello is traveling to Pennsylvania to receive a prestigious award. There, she gives the first speech of the book, titled "What Is Realism?" Framing and interweaving the speech and all the chapters are Costello's ongoing reflections about the events at hand and her life. In each chapter, her past, her relationships with her son John, an academic, her sister Blanche, a missionary, and others are integrated into the story.

Each chapter takes as its title the subject of a speech given at an event. The second chapter, or lesson 2, "The Novel in Africa," takes place on a cruise ship, where Costello's lecture "The Future of the Novel in Africa" is overshadowed by another lecture by a man who was once her lover. Lessons 3 and 4 both have the title "The Lives of Animals," but with different subtitles: "One: The Philosophers and the Animals" and "Two: The Poets and the Animals." In the first, Costello addresses an audience at Appleton College, where her son teaches. Tensions are high between mother and son and are exacerbated by her lecture, which discusses Kafka and employs parallels between the Nazi extermination camps and the treatment of animals in contemporary society. The discussion of animal rights continues in lesson 4, which refers to a seminar Costello holds at Appleton the day after her lecture and a debate later that day.

Lesson 5, "The Humanities in Africa," presents a speech not by Costello but by her sister Blanche, who is receiving an honorary degree from a South African university. Lesson 6 takes place in Amsterdam, where Costello attends a conference titled "The Problem of Evil" and speaks to the issue, using as an example the work of a contemporary novelist who happens to be in attendance. Lesson 7, "Eros," and lesson 8, "At the Gates," find their richness in Costello's self-exploration and assessment as she grows older.

Particularly unusual in this novel is that it incorporates six lectures previously published by Coetzee—often as nonfiction. The longest, *The Lives of Animals*, was published on its own in 1999; that volume was the product of a lecture Coetzee gave as part of the Tanner Lectures on Human Values at Princeton University in 1997. The lecture was presented at Princeton with the fictional setting, given as though Costello herself was speaking—including the narration of the dinner that followed the lecture. *Elizabeth Costello* has frequently been discussed as a view into Coetzee's life, ideas, and beliefs. Such interpretation, however, may elide the skill of the author and divert attention from the ideas presented.

Jean-Pierre Metereau; Cynthia A. Bily
Updated by Adrienne I. Pilon

OTHER MAJOR WORKS

NONFICTION: *White Writing: On the Culture of Letters in South Africa*, 1988; *Doubling the Point: Essays and Interviews*, 1992 (David Attwell, editor); *Giving Offense: Essays on Censorship*, 1996; *Boyhood: Scenes from Provincial Life*, 1997; *Stranger Shores: Literary Essays, 1986-1999*, 2001; *Youth: Scenes from Provincial Life II*, 2002; *Inner Workings: Literary Essays, 2000-2005*, 2007.

TRANSLATION: *Landscape with Rowers: Poetry from the Netherlands*, 2003.

MISCELLANEOUS: *The Lives of Animals*, 1999 (with others; Amy Gutmann, editor).

BIBLIOGRAPHY

Attridge, Derek. *J. M. Coetzee and the Ethics of Reading: Literature in the Event*. Chicago: University of Chicago Press, 2004. Scholarly study discusses Coetzee's long fiction through *Elizabeth Costello*, with an emphasis on exploring ethical issues presented by the works. Asserts that the act of reading the literature presents both intellectual and ethical challenges and should move the reader to self-examination.

Attwell, David. *J. M. Coetzee: South Africa and the Politics of Writing*. Berkeley: University of California Press, 1993. Explores the relationship between imagination and the real world and argues that while Coetzee may be right that his fiction is not about history, history nevertheless lies inescapably below the surface of his fiction. Although perhaps difficult for nonspecialists, with its focus on "postmodern metafiction," this work offers a valuable review of Coetzee's intellectual sources.

Castillo, Debra A. "The Composition of the Self in Coetzee's *Waiting for the Barbarians*." *Critique* 27 (Winter, 1986): 78-90. Presents in-depth examination of the novel, noting that Coetzee carefully charts "the physical and mental topography" of a fictitious place and, in so doing, invites readers to confront "the essential nature of both history and the self in history." Offers valuable criticism and comments on Coetzee's theme of the seductress and the magistrate's relation to her, which leads to his downfall and "degradation to animality."

Gallagher, Susan VanZanten. *A Story of South Africa: J. M. Coetzee's Fiction in Context*. Cambridge, Mass.: Harvard University Press, 1991. Analyzes Coetzee's novels as postmodern allegories and thoroughly explicates their South African contexts. Although Coetzee himself rejects the label "South African writer" and tries to distance himself from politics, Gallagher argues convincingly that Coetzee's stories are essentially about South Africa.

Head, Dominic. *J. M. Coetzee*. New York: Cambridge University Press, 1998. First postapartheid study of Coetzee's first seven novels focuses on Coetzee as a postcolonial writer, influenced by and influencing both Europe and Africa. While considering theories of postmodernism and postcolonialism, concentrates on the novels themselves to bring the theoretical issues to a level that might be understood by the general reader. Includes an extensive bibliography.

Huggan, Graham, and Stephen Watson, eds. *Critical Perspectives on J. M. Coetzee*. New York: St. Martin's Press, 1996. Collection of essays examines Coetzee's importance as a national and international writer and his handling of issues such as colonialism, history, and language. Includes an introduction by Nadine Gordimer and an afterword by David Attwell.

Kossew, Sue, ed. *Critical Essays on J. M. Coetzee*. New York: G. K. Hall, 1998. Collection of scholarly essays addresses the central critical questions about Coetzee and his work: the ethical and political natures of the novels, the role of the white writer in South Africa, Coetzee's use of allegory, his use of canonical texts as jumping-off points for his own novels, and his representation of women. Includes several important essays by influential critics.

Penner, Dick. *Countries of the Mind: The Fiction of J. M. Coetzee*. New York: Greenwood Press, 1989. Valuable study explores how Coetzee's novels "replicate and subvert traditional forms" as well as address the concept of individual freedom. Explores the diversity of his works and gives useful background information on South Africa, the Afrikaners, and Coetzee's academic achievements. A useful bibliography includes sources on South African literature within their political contexts.

Poyner, Jane, ed. *J. M. Coetzee and the Idea of the Public Intellectual*. Athens: Ohio University Press, 2006. Selection of essays by prominent literary scholars addresses the issues surrounding intellectual endeavor and the ways in which Coetzee's fiction engages this topic. Includes a brief interview with Coetzee on his role as writer and intellectual.

COLETTE
Sidonie-Gabrielle Colette

Born: Saint-Sauveur-en-Puisaye, Burgundy, France;
January 28, 1873
Died: Paris, France; August 3, 1954
Also known as: Sidonie-Gabrielle Colette; Colette
Willy

PRINCIPAL LONG FICTION

Claudine à l'école, 1900 (*Claudine at School*,
1956)
Claudine à Paris, 1901 (*Claudine in Paris*,
1958)
Claudine en ménage, 1902 (*The Indulgent
Husband*, 1935; also known as *Claudine
Married*)
Claudine s'en va, 1903 (*The Innocent Wife*, 1934;
also known as *Claudine and Annie*)
La Retraite sentimentale, 1907 (*Retreat from
Love*, 1974)
L'Ingénue libertine, 1909 (*The Gentle Libertine*,
1931; also known as *The Innocent Libertine*)
La Vagabonde, 1911 (*The Vagabond*, 1954)
L'Entrave, 1913 (*Recaptured*, 1932; better
known as *The Shackle*)
Mitsou: Ou, Comment l'esprit vient aux filles,
1919 (*Mitsou: Or, How Girls Grow Wise*,
1930)
Chéri, 1920 (English translation, 1929)
Le Blé en herbe, 1923 (*The Ripening Corn*, 1931;
also known as *The Ripening Seed*)
La Fin de Chéri, 1926 (*The Last of Chéri*, 1932)
La Naissance du jour, 1928 (*A Lesson in Love*,
1932; also known as *Break of Day*)
La Seconde, 1929 (*The Other One*, 1931)
La Chatte, 1933 (*The Cat*, 1936)
Duo, 1934 (English translation, 1974; also known
as *The Married Lover*)
Le Toutounier, 1939 (English translation, 1974)
Julie de Carneilhan, 1941 (English translation,
1952)
Gigi, 1944 (English translation, 1952)
Seven by Colette, 1955 (includes short fiction)

OTHER LITERARY FORMS

Many of the works written by Colette (kaw-LEHT)
defy ready classification. Aside from creating tales that
are of such a length as to make it difficult to decide
whether to term them short novels or long short stories
(the term *nouvelle*, which Colette often used for her
work, means both "novelette" and "novella"), Colette
also frequently mixed fiction with fact in a confusing
blend. *La Maison de Claudine* (1922; *My Mother's
House*, 1953), for example, can pass for fiction; however, the book is essentially a series of sketches from
Colette's life, primarily dealing with her mother, the famous Sido. Indeed, it has been observed that almost every page of this author's very personal writing contains
something that can be traced to her life. Several of her
particular fixations, such as animals and flowers, thus
not only appear prominently in her fiction but also are
dealt with at length (and with great knowledge and sensitivity) in her full-length essays.

When a film was made of her life in 1952, Colette
told an interviewer who had not seen the production to
go and see what a wonderful life she had led; she then remarked that she wished that she had been aware of its
quality earlier. In fact, her interest in and wonder at life
can be found in all of her writings. These works include,
in addition to a number of short stories, a variety of reminiscences, adaptations of her tales for the stage and the
cinema, and virtually unclassifiable publications on life
as a music-hall performer, on cats, on writing, and on life
in general. *Œuvres complètes de Colette*, the "complete"
works of Colette (prepared under the eye of the author,
who excised a number of titles that she considered unworthy of republication), published from 1948 to 1950,
fill fifteen large volumes; these do not contain a sizable
correspondence, most of which has been published separately.

ACHIEVEMENTS

One indication of Colette's persisting appeal is the
impressive number of republications of her chief works,
including a sometimes bewildering array of retransla-

tions. In her lifetime, Colette enjoyed an enormous popularity with everyday readers and eventually was recognized by the literary establishment as a genuine talent. She was elected to the Académie Goncourt (1945) and was the first woman to serve as its president (1949); she was given the Grand Cross of the Légion d'Honneur (1953); and she was the first woman in France to be accorded a state funeral. Perhaps a more significant index of Colette's literary importance is the record of her friendships with towering figures such as Marcel Proust and André Gide, both of whom admired her work. Since her death, numerous biographical and critical studies (from writers in France, England, and America) have attested Colette's impact on French letters and on world literature.

BIOGRAPHY

For a woman who was to become something of a symbol of feminism, Sidonie-Gabrielle Colette was born into the most unlikely surroundings. Saint-Sauveur-en-Puisaye was a small village in Burgundy, and little Sidonie grew up as a country girl—she retained a strong Burgundian accent until her death. Her mother, whose tremendous influence on Colette's life cannot be overestimated, was Adèle-Sidonie Landoy Robineau-Duclos, referred to by her second daughter as "Sido," whose first husband, Jules (by whom she had two children) died in 1865. In the same year, his widow married Captain Jules-Joseph Colette, who had been invalided out of the army in 1860 and had come to Saint-Sauveur as a tax collector. Sido bore two more children, a ne'er-do-well son, Léopold, who was a great disappointment, and her last offspring, Sidonie-Gabrielle, who made her mother famous.

Nature was a source of constant delight to the young Colette, whose writings reveal her fascination with nearly every aspect of the natural world. Even when she lived in Paris, years later, she was never happy without several pets (usually cats) and plenty of flowers and plants in her apartment. Her family life was evidently reasonably happy, although

her father, who retired from government service in 1880, was somewhat shiftless. Through neglect and mismanagement, the Colette fortune was lost by 1890, forcing the family to move to a nearby village, to the home of Colette's half brother, Doctor Achille Robineau-Duclos. Oddly enough, Colette's father claimed to be writing a book and acquired several large, expensive writing books, the pages of which were discovered to be blank at his death in 1905.

The move and the change in the family finances caused Colette to leave school at age sixteen, and her formal education ended at that point, although she continued to be an enthusiastic reader for the rest of her life, two of her favorite authors being Honoré de Balzac and Marcel Proust. Little is known of her life for the four years between the end of her schooling and her meeting with Henri Gauthier-Villars (known to his Parisian friends, and later to the world, as Willy, one of his favorite pen names), who was to become her first husband. It was Willy—a successful Parisian editor and publisher—who gave her the pen name Colette and almost acciden-

Colette. (Library of Congress)

tally provided her with the stimulus for creating fiction. After hearing his wife tell of her school days, Willy suggested that she write down some of the incidents, adding some spicy touches to make them more interesting. Although Willy was a gifted editor and arranger of literary projects (it is now known that he wrote almost none of the numerous works that bear his name—his management of ghostwriters, of whom his wife became the best, amounted to a career), it took him several years to recognize the quality of the sketches that Colette had created and that were to constitute her first published work, *Claudine at School*, which enjoyed a striking popular success. Typically, this work and its three sequels were all published under Willy's name alone.

Since their marriage in 1893, Colette and Willy had lived in Paris, where Willy was a prominent figure on the literary scene. The surprising success of *Claudine at School* impelled him to force Colette to turn out three sequels, one every year. His "force" was based on his greater age (he was almost fifteen years older than she) and superior experience of the world, especially that of Paris. According to the legend (which has perhaps considerable truth in it), he used to lock her in her room for four hours at a stretch, having given her strict orders to write for the entire time. Colette later asserted that she did not really mind the enforced effort and that the recollections of her young girlhood, which formed the basis for the first volume, were a pleasant emotional return to a time of greater peace and certainty. Although the Claudine series is now regarded as inferior to her later work, there is in it the mark of a born writer.

The marriage, however, was not as successful as the series. Colette was simply too independent—and her success with the Claudine series helped her to recognize and develop this very important quality in her personality—to live in the shadow of the lively but inconsiderate Willy. They separated in 1906, and the divorce was finalized in 1910, by which time Colette was no longer the provincial girl who had to be introduced to Paris. As early as 1903, she had taken lessons in mime (her marked accent temporarily discouraged her from vocal performance), and she appeared in several stage productions; the sensuality of the productions created something of a scandal, but the work enabled her to support herself. Also, she had met Henri de Jouvenel, the aristo-

cratic editor of *Le Matin*, a leading newspaper, to which Colette contributed articles for many years.

Meanwhile, she continued writing, for herself rather than for Willy and under her permanent pen name, Colette; her novel *The Vagabond* was given serious consideration by the prize committee of the Académie Goncourt. The story of the rest of Colette's life is chiefly literary, the only striking personal note being her intimate friendships with several women (notably the Marquise de Belboeuf, nicknamed Missy) and her amicable divorce in 1924 from Jouvenel, whom she had married in 1912. Aside from her writing, Colette's other activities were chiefly mime and, later, dramatic performances (occasionally in dramatized versions of her own works). As honors were offered to her and as her reputation grew, not only in France but also in England and the United States, Colette became something of a national treasure. She was undisturbed by the Germans during World War II (in World War I, she had served as a volunteer nurse and reported on some aspects of the combat near Verdun), and she took little evident interest in politics.

In 1924, Colette had met the much younger (by some eighteen years) Maurice Goudeket. They were married in 1935 and had, all evidence indicates, a very happy life together until her death in 1954. Perhaps the greatest irony of Colette's life story was the refusal of the Catholic Church to allow her a religious funeral even though she was given a state ceremony. This refusal, which was based on her two divorces, aroused considerable resentment even outside France: Graham Greene sent a stinging open letter to the cardinal-archbishop of Paris.

The funeral was one of the largest Paris had ever seen. It was noted that by far the larger proportion of the mourners were women, evidently paying homage to the woman who had more than any other given them a voice.

ANALYSIS

Maurice Goudeket, in his memoir *Près de Colette* (1956; *Close to Colette*, 1957), provides a touching and revealing picture of Colette's last hours. The most remarkable incident is the choice of her last spoken words. Looking toward an album of insects and birds, a case of butterflies, and an open window outside which swallows were flying, Colette waved expansively and said,

"Look! Maurice, look!" Several scholars have noted that the French word *regarde* signifies more than its usual English equivalent, having the connotation of close observation and even study. Colette was never interested in abstractions, a fact that has earned her some severe critical reprimands, yet she has no equal as an observer of the tangible world.

Colette frequently complained of the difficulty of writing, saying she disliked it, which might cause one to wonder why she did so much of it. Aside from the melancholy economic fact that, especially in her earlier years, even successful books earned their authors trifling sums by today's standards, it seems clear that Colette wrote in order to make sense of her long and eventful life. She did not attempt to theorize about it, though some of her offhand remarks bear the mark of high-quality epigrams, such as her insightful observation, "A happy childhood is a bad preparation for human contacts." Instead, she rewrote her life in differing versions, countless times, mingling truth and imagination.

Colette's refusal to theorize about life was accompanied by a reluctance to judge other people and their modes of life. This detachment provided her with a sort of aesthetic distance from her subjects that helped to counter the elements of personal involvement that infuse her fiction. A work of partial autobiography, originally published as *Ces plaisirs* (1932) but better known as *Le Pur et l'impur* (1941; *The Pure and the Impure*, 1967), which includes extensive examinations of sexual practices, both "normal" and irregular, is considered by several scholars to be one of her most important works, yet in this brief volume there is no moral judgment, only understanding and sympathy. Colette is content simply to "look," to try to comprehend without condemnation.

A vital feature of Colette's writing is her use of point of view. Almost all of her stories are told in the first person, a phenomenon that has encouraged autobiographical interpretations but that also gives her texts an impressive immediacy and warmth. Thus, when the heroine of the brief tale *Chambre d'hôtel* (1940; *Chance Acquaintances*, 1952) declares, near the end of the story, that she must leave her home and says, "I went to collect the few personal belongings which, at that time, I held to be invaluable: my cat, my resolve to travel, and my solitude," one can sympathize with her, whether the voice is solely that of a character or is partly that of the author as well. The most notable example of Colette's abandonment of the first person is the novel that many critics believe to be her masterpiece, *Chéri*, which, along with its sequel, *The Last of Chéri*, is possibly the closest thing to a truly "modern" novel in her entire canon. The modernity of *Chéri* can be ascribed in part to the relatively detached tone of the narrative. All the emotion in this tragic story is felt only in relation to the characters; the author does not intrude at all.

Another aspect of *Chéri* that marks it as unusual among Colette's fictions is the fact that the central male character is the dominant figure and is painstakingly studied; though several female characters play important roles in the novel, Chéri is the basis of the story and is clearly the chief character. In most of Colette's works, the women are the outstanding figures; the male characters are often merely sketched in. Colette focuses on the problems and interests of women, particularly in their relationships with men but also in their position as human beings trying to come to terms with loneliness and failure. Again and again in her fiction, she dramatizes the failure of sexual relationships, usually placing the blame on the man but recognizing that the woman also bears responsibility in such matters. Although not a philosopher, Colette came to a number of reasonably profound and often unhappy conclusions about the battle of the sexes. One is that there is no guarantee of happiness in any liaison and that, indeed, happiness is not necessary for a meaningful life. She also concluded that a woman suffers fully only once, when her initial romance fades.

Colette has been justly praised for her sense of place. Her settings, even the interiors, are presented in great detail and precision, most often with the impress of a mood or an element of characterization. As Sir Walter Scott is credited with seeing places in human terms, so Colette tends to perceive people in concrete manifestations, frequently presenting characters in the light of their surroundings, their clothes, even their pets. Léa de Lonval, the aging courtesan in *Chéri*, is seen most often in her pink boudoir—the silks are pink, as are some of the furniture and the curtains; even the light coming in through the windows is usually pink. In the earlier novels, Colette re-creates the memories of her childhood days in the beautiful Burgundian countryside. No item is too small for her notice, from a blade of grass to a tiny insect; she invests everything with a sense of the wonder and magnificence of nature. If people in her books are often undependable and even treacherous, nature is not. So strong was Colette's affinity with natural things that she created in *The Cat* an animal character that overshadows both of the human characters. The novel is a love story, but the true passion exists between Alain and his cat, Saha, not between him and his wife, Camille. The tension of the disintegrating marriage becomes so great, and Camille's recognition of Saha's moral superiority so strong, that the jealous wife attempts to kill the animal, an act that brings the relationship of husband and wife to an end and reconfirms the bond between a man and his "pet."

CLAUDINE AT SCHOOL

The Claudine series, which comprises Colette's first four novels, though inferior to her later masterpieces, displays several of the qualities that distinguish her work and reveals themes and topics that recur throughout her long career (Claudine, a character first conceived in 1900, has obvious affinities with Gigi, the title heroine of Colette's 1944 novella). Claudine is certainly a persona of Colette herself, and much of the first novel, *Claudine at School*, is taken directly from the author's experience, from the almost extravagant descriptions of the lush countryside to the delineation of real people as characters in the plot. (Colette, years later, learned that her portrait of the immoral headmistress, Mademoiselle Sergent, had seriously distressed the model for that character, and Colette regretted her callousness.)

The opening novel in the series introduces Claudine as a lively, intelligent, fun-loving fifteen-year-old student whose life at school is enlivened by scandal, such as the "affair" between the headmistress and one of the younger instructors (a relationship that at first disturbs Claudine, since she has suffered from a powerful infatuation with the same young lady). An occasionally unnoticed quality of Colette's writing, her humorous irony, emerges in this first volume most agreeably. When Claudine discovers the "romance" between the headmistress and Mademoiselle Lanthenay (she secretly observes the two women in a passionate embrace), her first reaction is neither shock nor dismay; instead, she comments wryly to herself, "Well done! No one could say

this Headmistress bullied her subordinates!" Apart from her escapes to the calming serenity of walks in the woods, Claudine's life is chiefly centered on events at her school. Her home life is quite dull; her father hardly notices her presence, and (perhaps because Colette was in reality very close to her mother) her mother is not on the scene. One feels, despite the frivolous adventures and trivial concerns of the girls, that Colette is sincere when she has Claudine remark, at the end of the novel, "Farewell to the classroom; farewell, Mademoiselle and her girl friend. . . . I am going to leave you to make my entry into the world. . . . I shall be very much astonished if I enjoy myself there as much as I have at school."

CLAUDINE IN PARIS *and* CLAUDINE MARRIED

In *Claudine in Paris*, Claudine and her father have moved to Paris, where she is unhappy at being isolated from the countryside that she loves. In this state of near misery and surrounded by friends (one of whom was at school with her) who all seem to be engaged in some form of physical lovemaking (even her cat Fanchette is pregnant), including the gay man Marcel, Claudine is easy prey for Marcel's father, the forty-year-old roué Renaud. Instead of becoming his mistress, as she has decided, Claudine marries him (a plot turn revived effectively as the climax of *Gigi*). As might be expected, the marriage is not completely successful; in the next volume, *Claudine Married*, a triangle forms: Renaud, Claudine, and Rézi, the attractive woman with whom both of them have an intense love affair. The book ends with a rather contrived reunion of Claudine and her husband. It seems certain that the character of Renaud was partly based on Willy, though the happy ending is obviously not autobiographical.

CLAUDINE AND ANNIE

In the fourth Claudine novel, *Claudine and Annie*, Renaud and Claudine are primarily observers of and commentators on the dissolution of the marriage of Annie and Alain, largely the result of Annie's awakening to life during her husband's prolonged absence on a trip to South America. Finally, after much sentimental advice from Claudine and a series of relationships of her own, Annie (who is the primary character in the story) decides to leave. Although this volume, like the others in the series, is marred by an occasional confusion of plot and uncertainty of theme, the Claudine series hints at the profound sensitivity, engaging irony, and perceptive vision of Colette's mature work.

CHÉRI *and* THE LAST OF CHÉRI

This maturity is evident in *Chéri* and *The Last of Chéri*. The plot of the two volumes is direct and uncomplicated. Fred Peloux, nicknamed Chéri, is spoiled by his immoral and malicious mother, Charlotte, whose indulgence is encouraged by his extreme good looks. Early in his life, his mother's old friend and fellow courtesan, Léa, becomes fond of the boy and later takes him as a lover, though she is nearly twice his age. When Chéri grows to manhood, his mother arranges a marriage for him with a lovely and acceptable young lady named Edmée. Like nearly every other girl that Chéri meets, Edmée is infatuated with the young man for his beauty (it was Colette's firm conviction that men can possess beauty just as women can) as well as for his talents in making love, developed with Léa's tutelage. The first volume closes with Chéri's resolve to abandon Léa, whom he believes to be no longer an important part of his life.

In the interval between *Chéri* and *The Last of Chéri*, five years have passed, the years of World War I; Colette captures the empty, futile mood of postwar France. Chéri is in gloomy harmony with this mood. He is idle, purposeless, and without substance. Nothing in his previous experience has prepared him for the challenge of creating some meaning for his life. In this vacuum, Chéri begins to think constantly of Léa and believes that he must attempt to revive their old romance, from a time when he felt really alive. In one of the most effective recognition scenes in literature, Chéri confronts Léa and for a time does not even recognize her: "A woman was seated at a desk, writing, her back turned to him. Chéri saw a great back, thick gray hair, cut short, like his mother's, a fat, bulging neck." It takes a few moments for Chéri to realize that this aging figure is his former lover. Léa has simply decided that, since she is nearing sixty, it is time for her to settle down to a comfortable old age. She has stopped dieting and dying her hair and performing the multifarious rituals required by her beauty regimen.

When Chéri finally realizes that his old life is gone and that he is unable to build a new one to replace it, he turns to the only escape possible: suicide. It is a clever touch of Colette's that he performs this ultimate act in a sordid room surrounded by old pictures of Léa as a youthful beauty. The compact development of the plot and the sure depiction of Chéri's decline give the climax a tragic stature; indeed, throughout the two novels, every scene clearly advances the plot and the characterization. Colette never exceeded the mastery displayed in these works. Seldom have such slender materials (the two volumes together occupy only a bit more than two hundred pages) yielded such tragic power.

GIGI

When Colette published the very short novel *Gigi* in 1944, she had not written a substantial piece of fiction for several years; some had thought that she never would again. *Gigi* was therefore an especially happy surprise. In this, her last work of fiction, written when she was seventy years old, Colette produced a delightful tale with one of the few happy endings in all of her works. It is also one of her few novels to be narrated in the third person. Because the plot was based on an anecdote told to Colette many years earlier, her powers of invention were not taxed. Two wise decisions helped the novel to succeed: Colette set the story in 1899, and most of the text is in dialogue form. *Gigi* thus benefits both from a charming setting in an uncomplicated distant past and from a liveliness of presentation.

The tone of the narrative is ironic, but cheerfully so. Gigi, having just reached adolescence, is being reared by a grandmother and a great aunt, who are both retired courtesans, to follow in their "professional" footsteps. Fortunately, Gigi is too honest and skeptical to be much affected by this instruction; in the end, she outsmarts her teachers by marrying the bored and wealthy Gaston, whom they had only hoped to persuade to keep her as a mistress. The story abounds in jollity and good humor—it is no wonder that *Gigi* was very successfully adapted as a hit play and an Academy Award-winning film. There is a pleasing irony in that Colette's last story comes, at least in tone and atmosphere, full circle to the innocent ambience of her first novel, *Claudine at School*. Though Gigi's experience is told with far greater skill, she and Claudine seem sisters under the skin and even somewhat on the surface, especially in their eye for the ridiculous, their impatience with pompousness, and their sincere good intentions toward others.

The chief elements of Colette's fiction thus appear at the beginning and the end of her long career. She studied love—young love (even between adolescents, as in *The Ripening Seed*), ardent love, failed love, married love, illicit love, and also family love—as no other writer has ever studied it. W. Somerset Maugham once wrote that the truly great authors (he used Fyodor Dostoevski as an example) could see "through a stone wall," so great was their perception of life; he modestly claimed only that he could see very well what was right in front of him, hastening to add that such an accomplishment was not to be underrated. Colette "looked" at life in such minute detail and with such aesthetic integrity that one might say that now and again she penetrated the stone wall.

Fred B. McEwen

OTHER MAJOR WORKS

SHORT FICTION: *Les Vrilles de la vigne*, 1908 (*The Tendrils of the Vine*, 1983); *L'Envers du music-hall*, 1913 (*Music-Hall Sidelights*, 1957); *La Chambre éclairée*, 1920; *La Femme cachée*, 1924 (*The Other Woman*, 1971); *Bella-Vista*, 1937 (English translation, 1996); *Chambre d'hôtel*, 1940 (*Chance Acquaintances*, 1952); *Le Képi*, 1943; *Gigi, et autres nouvelles*, 1944; *La Fleur de l'âge*, 1949 (*In the Flower of the Age*, 1983); *Paysage et portraits*, 1958; *The Stories of Colette*, 1958 (also known as *The Tender Shoot, and Other Stories*); *Contes des mille et un matins*, 1970 (*The Thousand and One Mornings*, 1973); *The Collected Stories of Colette*, 1983.

PLAYS: *Chéri*, pb. 1922 (with Léopold Marchand; English adaptation, 1959); *L'Enfant et les sortilèges*, pb. 1925 (opera; music by Maurice Ravel; *The Boy and the Magic*, 1964); *Gigi*, pr., pb. 1952 (adaptation of her novel; with Anita Loos).

NONFICTION: *Les Heures longues, 1914-1917*, 1917; *Dans la foule*, 1918; *La Maison de Claudine*, 1922 (*My Mother's House*, 1953); *Le Voyage egoïste*, 1922 (*Journey for Myself: Selfish Memories*, 1971); *Sido*, 1929 (English translation, 1953); *Histoires pour Bel-Gazou*, 1930; *Ces plaisirs*, 1932 (better known as *Le Pur et l'impur*, 1941; *The Pure and the Impure*, 1967); *Paradis terrestres*, 1932; *Prisons et paradis*, 1932; *La Jumelle noire*, 1934-1938; *Mes apprentissages*, 1936 (*My Apprenticeships*, 1957); *Mes cahiers*, 1941; *Journal à*

rebours, 1941, and *De ma fenêtre*, 1942 (translated together as *Looking Backwards*, 1975); *Flore et Pomone*, 1943; *Nudité*, 1943; *Trois . . . Six . . . Neuf*, 1944; *Une Amitié inattendue: Correspondance de Colette et de Francis Jammes*, 1945; *Belles Saisons*, 1945; *L'Étoile vesper*, 1946 (*The Evening Star*, 1973); *Pour un herbier*, 1948 (*For a Flower Album*, 1959); *Le Fanal bleu*, 1949 (*The Blue Lantern*, 1963); *Places*, 1970 (in English; includes short sketches unavailable in a French collection); *Letters from Colette*, 1980.

ANIMAL VIGNETTES AND DIALOGUES: *Dialogues de bêtes*, 1904 (*Creature Conversations*, 1951); *Sept dialogues de bêtes*, 1905 (*Barks and Purrs*, 1913); *Prrou, Poucette, et quelques autres*, 1913 (*Other Creatures*, 1951); *La Paix chez les bêtes*, 1916 (revision of *Prrou, Poucette, et quelques autres*; *Cats, Dogs, and I*, 1924); *Douze dialogues de bêtes*, 1930 (*Creatures Great and Small*, 1951); *Chats*, 1936; *Splendeur des papillons*, 1937; *Chats de Colette*, 1949.

MISCELLANEOUS: *Œuvres complètes de Colette*, 1948-1950 (15 volumes); *The Works*, 1951-1964 (17 volumes).

BIBLIOGRAPHY

Crosland, Margaret. *Colette: The Difficulty of Loving.* Indianapolis: Bobbs-Merrill, 1973. Critical biography analyzes the subject's work as well as her life. Janet Flanner, long a commentator on the French scene, contributes an interesting introduction. Supplemented with a chronology and a bibliography of works by and about Colette.

Eisinger, Erica Mendelson, and Mari Ward McCarty, eds. *Colette: The Woman, the Writer.* University Park: Pennsylvania State University Press, 1981. Collection of essays is divided into sections on Colette's early development as a writer, the relationship between gender and genre in her work, and her exploration of a feminist aesthetic. Contributors draw extensively on feminist scholarship and on studies of the ways female writers use language and relate to their roles as women writers. Includes an informative introduction and an index.

Francis, Claude, and Fernande Gontier. *Creating Colette.* 2 vols. South Royalton, Vt.: Steerforth Press, 1998-1999. Worthwhile and comprehensive biography of Colette. The first volume chronicles the first forty years of her life and stresses the importance of her African ancestry and maternal family background in understanding her work. The second volume covers the years from 1912 to her death in 1954. Includes bibliographical references and index.

Holmes, Diana. *Colette*. New York: St. Martin's Press, 1991. Notes how Colette's fiction deals with female sexuality, domestic life, and the problems of working women in a man's world. Argues that Colette's stories need to be judged by female critics and asserts that the stories are open-ended and thus innovative for their time.

Kristeva, Julia. *Colette*. Translated by Jane Marie Todd. New York: Columbia University Press, 2004. Scholarly critique of Colette's life and work assumes that readers have some familiarity with the author. Kristeva, a Parisian professor of linguistics, examines Colette's life from a psychoanalytical perspective, maintaining that Colette's "writing itself appears as a substitute for erotic pleasure and the text as a fetish."

Marks, Elaine. *Colette*. New Brunswick, N.J.: Rutgers University Press, 1960. An examination, insofar as possible, of the relationship of Colette's works to her life. Begins from the premise that Colette's books totally lack analogues in philosophy and politics, asserting that they are informed by a highly personal moral admonition, summed up in the term *regarde*—look, experience, feel.

Mitchell, Yvonne. *Colette: A Taste for Life*. New York: Harcourt Brace Jovanovich, 1975. Biography makes the argument that, although some of her readers found her choice of subject matter objectionable or even depraved, Colette was instinctively deeply moral. She accepted no arbitrary hierarchies, choosing instead to be led by the life force and her five senses. Includes a chronology, a bibliography, notes, and an index—all extensive.

Richardson, Joanna. *Colette*. New York: Franklin Watts, 1984. The first full-scale biography of Colette written in English by a scholar steeped in French literature. Richardson had access to Colette's papers and cooperation from her family. Includes illustrations, notes, and bibliography.

Sarde, Michèle. *Colette: Free and Fettered*. Translated by Richard Miller. New York: William Morrow, 1980. Study of Colette's life and work is one of the most informative books on Colette available. It has not been superseded by subsequent studies and profits from a Gallic stamp and mood that non-French commentators have not yet begun to match. The research is superior to that of other biographies, and the bibliographical appendixes are thoroughly practical, including posthumous publications and the translator's additions, with considerable assistance from the Gibbard chronology, of available English translations.

Southworth, Helen. *The Intersecting Realities and Fictions of Virginia Woolf and Colette*. Columbus: Ohio State University Press, 2004. Argues that although the two authors lived in different countries, there were similarities in their lives, literary styles, and the themes of their works. Places the two subjects within the context of a group of early twentieth century artists and writers and describes Woolf's contacts with France and Colette's connections with British and American writers.

Stewart, Joan Hinde. *Colette*. New York: Twayne, 1996. Provides discussion of how Colette emerged as a writer, her apprenticeship years, the erotic nature of her novels, and her use of dialogue. Includes chronology, notes, and annotated bibliography.

Thurman, Judith. *Secrets of the Flesh: A Life of Colette*. New York: Alfred A. Knopf, 1999. Presents an admiring but nevertheless candid account of the life and times of Colette, helping to place her work in a larger context.

WILKIE COLLINS

Born: London, England; January 8, 1824
Died: London, England; September 23, 1889
Also known as: William Collins

PRINCIPAL LONG FICTION

Antonina: Or, The Fall of Rome, 1850
Basil: A Story of Modern Life, 1852
Hide and Seek, 1854
The Dead Secret, 1857
The Woman in White, 1860
No Name, 1862
Armadale, 1866
The Moonstone, 1868
Man and Wife, 1870
Poor Miss Finch: A Novel, 1872
The New Magdalen, 1873
The Law and the Lady, 1875
The Two Destinies: A Romance, 1876
My Lady's Money, 1878
The Fallen Leaves, 1879
The Haunted Hotel: A Mystery of Modern Venice,
    1879
A Rogue's Life, 1879
Jezebel's Daughter, 1880
The Black Robe, 1881
Heart and Science, 1883
I Say No, 1884
The Evil Genius: A Dramatic Story, 1886
The Guilty River, 1886
The Legacy of Cain, 1889
Blind Love, 1890 (completed by Walter Besant)

OTHER LITERARY FORMS

In addition to his novels, Wilkie Collins produced a biography of his father in 1848 as well as travel books, essays and reviews, and a number of short stories. He also wrote and adapted plays, often in collaboration with Charles Dickens.

ACHIEVEMENTS

Wilkie Collins's reputation more than a century after his death rests almost entirely on two works: *The Woman in White*, first published serially in *All the Year Round* from November 26, 1859, to August 25, 1860; and *The Moonstone*, published in 1868. Mystery author Dorothy L. Sayers called the latter work "probably the finest detective story ever written." No chronicler of crime and detective fiction can fail to include Collins's important contributions to the genre; simply for the ingenuity of his plots, Collins earned the admiration of T. S. Eliot. *The Woman in White* and *The Moonstone* have also been adapted numerous times for the stage, film, radio, and television. For an author so conscientious and industrious, however—Collins averaged one "big" novel every two years in his maturity—to be known as the author of two books would hardly be satisfactory. The relative obscurity into which most of Collins's work has fallen cannot be attributed completely to the shadow cast by his friend and sometime collaborator Charles Dickens, to his physical infirmities and his addiction to laudanum, or to the social vision that led him to write a succession of thesis novels. Indeed, the greatest mystery Collins left behind concerns the course of his literary career and subsequent reputation.

BIOGRAPHY

A pencil drawing of the author titled "Wilkie Collins by his father William Collins, R. A." survives; it shows a pretty, if serious, round face. The features beneath the end of the boy's nose are shaded, giving particular prominence to the upper face and forehead. The viewer is at once drawn to the boy's eyes; they are large, probing, mysterious—hardly the eyes of a child. Perhaps the artist-father sought to impart to his elder son some of his own austere, pious nature. William Collins (1788-1847), whose life began on the verge of one great European revolution and ended on the verge of another, was no revolutionary himself, nor was he the bohemian others of his calling imagined themselves. Instead, he was a strict Sabbatarian, an individual who overcame by talent and perseverance the disadvantages of poverty. The novelist's paternal grandfather was an art dealer, a restorer, and a storyteller who lovingly trained and cajoled his son in painting and drawing. William Collins did not begin to taste success until several years after the death of his father in 1812, but gradually commissions and patrons did come, including Sir Robert Peel. Befriended by noted artists such as Sir David Wilkie and Washington Allston, William Collins was at last elected to the Royal Academy in 1820. Two years later, he married Harriet Geddes. The names of both of their sons, born in 1824 and 1828, respectively, honored fellow artists: William Wilkie Collins and Charles Allston Collins.

Little is known of Wilkie Collins's early years, save that they appear to have been relatively tranquil. By 1833, Collins was already enrolled at Maida Hill Academy. In 1836, William Collins elected to take his family to Italy, where they remained until the late summer of 1838. The return to London required taking new lodgings at Regent's Park, and the fourteen-year-old Wilkie Collins was sent to boarding school at Highbury. By the close of 1840, he was presumably finished with school. His father's health began to fail, and the senior Collins made known his wish that Wilkie take holy orders, though the son apparently had no such inclination. The choice became university or commerce. Wilkie Collins chose business, and he became an apprentice to the tea merchants Antrobus and Company in 1841. He performed well there and was able to take a leave in order to accompany his father to Scotland the following summer. While still an apprentice, Collins began to write occasional pieces, and in August, 1843, the *Illuminated Magazine* published his first signed story, "The Last Stage Coachman." A novel about Polynesia was also written but discarded. In 1844, Collins traveled to Paris with his friend Charles Ward, and he made a second visit in 1845. While William Collins's health began to deteriorate more rapidly, his son was released from his apprenticeship and decided on the study of law. In February, 1847, William Collins died.

Wilkie Collins emulated his father's self-discipline, industry, and especially his love of art and beauty, yet if one judges by the series of self-serving religious zealots who populate Collins's fiction, one must assume that, while he respected his father's artistic sensibilities, he did not admire his pious ardor. Instead, Wilkie Collins seems in most things to have taken the example of his mother, a woman of loving good nature and humor with whom both he and his brother Charles remained close

until her death. Nevertheless, William Collins near the end of his life had asked Wilkie to write his biography, providing the opportunity for the young man's first published book, *Memoirs of the Life of William Collins, R. A.*, published in 1848 in two volumes. While the narrator tends toward self-effacement and burdens his readers with minute detail, the work is nevertheless a formidable accomplishment. His research in preparing the book led Collins into correspondence with the American writer Richard Henry Dana, Jr., and with a circle of established and rising artists, including E. M. Ward (brother of his friend Charles), Augustus Egg, John Everett Millais, Holman Hunt, and the Rossettis. At this time, Collins completed his historical novel *Antonina*, which is filled with gothic violence and adventure, a work that attracted the serious attention of John Ruskin. It was published in 1850, the same year that saw the production of Collins's first publicly staged dramatic work, *A Court Duel*, which he had adapted from the French. With the success of his play and the surprisingly positive reception of *Antonina*, Collins began to enjoy a rising reputation.

In January, 1851, Richard Bentley published Collins's account of a Cornwall hiking trip taken during the summer of 1850 as *Rambles Beyond Railways*. Two months later, Egg introduced the twenty-seven-year-old Collins to Dickens, and the initial contact resulted in Collins's taking part in Dickens's theatrical *Not So Bad as We Seem: Or, Many Sides to a Character* (pb. 1851), written by Edward Bulwer-Lytton. Until Dickens's death in 1870, he and Collins remained staunch friends, though there is some indication that there was friction between the two authors following Collins's success with *The Moonstone* and Dickens's supposed attempt to outdo his junior with his novel *The Mystery of Edwin Drood* (1870), which remained unfinished at Dickens's death.

In 1852, after having tried to sell the version of a story that would become "Mad Monkton" to Dickens, Collins published the story "A Terribly Strange Bed" (anthologized often since) in *Household Words*, a magazine edited by Dickens from 1850 to 1859. The following years saw considerable collaboration between the two authors, not the least of which were Collins's stories for the Christmas annuals such as *Mr. Wray's Cash-Box: Or,*

The Mask and the Mystery (1852), the collaboration *The Seven Poor Travellers* (1854), *The Wreck of the Golden Mary* (1856), a work often attributed to Dickens until the late twentieth century, the novel *The Dead Secret*, and numerous other stories and articles. In 1853, Collins, Dickens, and Egg traveled together in Italy and Switzerland. Four years later, Dickens produced Collins's play *The Frozen Deep*, later noting that the self-sacrifice of the central character, Richard Wardour (played by Dickens), provided the germ for *A Tale of Two Cities* (1859). Although never published as a play, *The Frozen Deep* was published in 1866 as part of a collection of short stories.

The impact each had on the writing of the other has long been a topic of controversy and speculation for critics and biographers; generally unchallenged is the influence of Collins's meticulous plotting on the work of his senior. In turn, Dickens often corrected and refined by suggestion Collins's fiction, although he never agreed with Collins's practice of including prefaces that upbraided critics and the public alike. When Collins published *Basil* (having included for Bentley's publication in book form the first of those vexing prefaces), he forwarded the volume to Dickens. After a two-week silence, there came a thoughtful, admiring reply: "I have made *Basil*'s acquaintance," wrote Dickens at the end of 1852, "with great gratification, and entertain high respect for him. I hope that I shall become intimate with many worthy descendants of his, who are yet in the limbo of creatures waiting to be born." Collins did not disappoint Dickens on that count over their years of friendship and collaboration; indeed, they became "family" when Charles Allston Collins married Dickens's daughter Kate.

Household Words faded in 1859 along with Dickens's association with the publishers Bradbury and Evans. Dickens's new periodical, *All the Year Round* (1859-1870), began auspiciously with the publication of *A Tale of Two Cities*. After the run of that novel, he needed something to keep public interest in the new magazine from abating, and Collins provided it with *The Woman in White*. This work's monumental success put Collins into that rarest literary circle: that of well-to-do authors. Its success also coincided with important personal events in Collins's life.

Collins had lived the life of a bachelor, residing with his brother and mother at least into his early thirties. Their house was often open to guests. On one such evening, the author and his brother escorted home the artist John Everett Millais through then-rural North London. Suddenly, a woman appeared to them in the moonlight, attired in flowing robes, all in white. Though distraught, she regained her composure and vanished as quickly as she had appeared. The author was most astounded and insisted he would discover the identity of the lovely creature. J. G. Millais, the painter's son, who later narrated this anecdote in a life of his father, did not reveal the lady's ultimate identity, saying, "Her subsequent history, interesting as it is, is not for these pages." The woman was Caroline Elizabeth Graves, born 1834, mother of a little girl, Harriet. Her husband, G. R. Graves, may or may not have been dead. Of him, only his name is known. Clearly, however, the liaison between Caroline Graves and Wilkie Collins was fully under way when he began to write *The Woman in White*.

From at least 1859, the couple lived together in a secret relationship known only to their closest friends, until the autumn of 1868, when for obscure reasons Caroline married the son of a distiller, John C. Clow. Collins, not one to waste time, started a new liaison with Martha Rudd. This union produced three children: Marian (1869), Harriet Constance (1871), and William Charles (1874). The children took the surname Dawson, but Collins freely admitted his paternity. By this time, too, Caroline and her daughter returned, and Harriet Graves for a time served as her mother's lover's amanuensis; Collins adopted her as his daughter. A lover of hearty food, fine champagne, and good cigars, Collins appears to have lived in private a life that would have shocked many of his readers. Still, Collins treated his "morganatic family" quite well: He provided handsomely for his natural and adopted children and for their mothers. When she died in 1895 at age sixty-one, Caroline Elizabeth Graves was interred beside the author of *The Woman in White*.

As Collins's private life began taking on its unconventional proportions in the 1860's, his public career grew more distinguished. His output for *All the Year Round* in shorter forms declined; he simply did not need the money. In March, 1861, his novel *No Name*, a didactic work about inheritance, began its run in the maga-

Wilkie Collins. (Library of Congress)

zine; it was published in volume form in December, 1862. A year later, Collins resigned his editorial assignment for Dickens's periodical and also published, with Sampson Low, Son, and Company, *My Miscellanies*, bringing together, in two volumes, work that had first appeared in the two Dickens periodicals. After about seven years of almost obsessive productivity, Collins relented, but only for a time; he began his novel *Armadale* in the spring of 1864, for serial publication in the *Cornhill Magazine* in Britain and *Harper's Monthly* in the United States. This exploration of inherited and personal guilt remains one of Collins's most adept and popular novels; it is also his longest. He wrote a dramatic version of the novel in 1866, but the play was not produced until it appeared in 1876 as *Miss Gwilt*.

In 1867, Collins and Dickens began their last collaboration, the play *No Thoroughfare* (pr., pb. 1867), an ad-venture set in the Alps and perhaps not unaffected by the two men's shared Swiss journey many years before. By this time, too, Collins began to suffer tremendously from the good living he had long enjoyed—gout of the areas around the eyes caused him excruciating pain, requiring the application of bandages for weeks at a time. To allay the ache, Collins developed a habit for laudanum, that tincture of opium that fills the darker recesses of middle-Victorian culture. It was in this period of alternating pain and bliss that Collins penned *The Moonstone*, for *All the Year Round*, beginning in January, 1868. The novel was an uncontestable triumph; Collins himself thought it wonderfully wrought.

The Moonstone had hardly begun its run, however, when Collins's mother died, and later that same year, Caroline married Clow. When the novel was finished, Collins again turned to the stage, writing *Black and White* with his friend Charles Fechter, an actor; the play successfully opened in March, 1869. At the end of the year, the serialization of *Man and Wife* began in *Harper's Weekly* and in January, 1870, in *Cassell's Magazine*. Posterity has judged *Man and Wife* more harshly than did its first readers. It was a different kind of novel from *The Moonstone*: It attacked society's growing obsession with athleticism and castigated marital laws that Collins believed to be cruel, unfair, and unrealistic. According to Collins's modern biographer Kenneth Robinson, *Man and Wife* was the turning point in Collins's career, the start of the "downhill" phase of the writer's life. The novel sold well after its serialization; Collins also wrote a four-act dramatic version that was not produced on the stage until 1873.

At the same time, Collins adapted *No Name* for the theater and, in 1871, *The Woman in White*. The stage version of *The Woman in White* opened at the Olympic Theatre in October and ran for five months before going on tour. The same year saw the beginning of a new novel in serial form, *Poor Miss Finch*, about a blind woman who falls in love with an epileptic whose cure turns him blue. When she is temporarily cured of her affliction, she finds herself in a dilemma about her blue lover, whose healthy twin also desires her love. A year later, the indefatigable Collins published *The New Magdalen* in a magazine called *Temple Bar*; the novel's heroine, a virtuous prostitute, outraged contemporary critics, but the work's dramatization in 1873 was greeted with enthusiasm.

As his work increasingly turned to exposing social hypocrisies, Collins sought, as a writer of established repute, to regulate the body of his published work. Since *Basil*, wholesale piracy of his writings had angered him and hurt his finances. By the early 1870's, he had reached agreements with the German publisher Tauchnitz and with Harper & Brothers in the United States, and, by 1875, with Chatto & Windus in Britain. Chatto & Windus not only bought all extant copyrights to Collins's work but also became his publisher for the rest of his life. This arrangement was finalized in the year after Collins, like his friend Dickens before him, had undertaken a reading tour of the United States and Canada.

The years 1875 and 1876 saw the publication of two popular but lesser novels, *The Law and the Lady* and *The Two Destinies*. The next year was marked, however, by the successful dramatization of *The Moonstone* and the beginning of Collins's friendship with Charles Reade. In 1879, Collins wrote *The Haunted Hotel* for the *Belgravia Magazine*, a ghost story fresh in invention that extends one's notions about the genre. Meanwhile, however, Collins's health became less certain and his laudanum doses became more frequent and increasingly potent. The decade took away many close friends, beginning with Dickens and, later, his brother Charles, then Augustus Egg.

In the last decade of his life, Collins became more reclusive, although not much less productive. He adapted his 1858 play *The Red Vial* into the novel *Jezebel's Daughter*. He also began, for serialization in the *Canadian Monthly*, the novel *The Black Robe*, the central figure of which is a priest plotting to encumber the wealth of a large estate. This work has been regarded as the most successful of his longer, late novels. It was followed by a more controversial novel, *Heart and Science*, a polemic against vivisection that appeared in 1883. The same year saw Collins's last theatrical work, *Rank and Riches*, an unqualified disaster that brought the leading lady to tears before the first-act curtain and that led her leading man, G. W. Anson, to berate the audience. Collins thereafter gave up writing for the stage, save a one-performance version of *The Evil Genius* in 1885; the work was

quickly recast as a novel that proved his single most lucrative publication.

Although 1884 saw the passing of Reade, his closest friend of the time, Collins continued to write steadily. *The Guilty River* made its appearance in the *Arrowsmith Christmas Annual* for 1886; in 1887, Chatto & Windus published *Little Novels*, collecting earlier stories. Two works also appeared that ended the battle Collins had long waged with critics. A young man, Harry Quilter, published an encomiastic article for the *Contemporary Review*, "A Living Story-Teller." Collins himself wrote "How I Write My Books" for the newspaper *The Globe*, an account of his work on *The Woman in White*. As his health at last began to fail precipitously in 1888, Collins completed his final serial novel, *The Legacy of Cain*. It appeared in three volumes the following year, at a time when he was finishing the writing of *Blind Love* for the *Illustrated London News*. On the evening of June 30, 1889, Collins suffered a stroke. He requested that Walter Besant, then traveling in the north, return and complete the tale.

Collins had long before befriended Dickens's physician and neighbor, Frank Beard, who did what little could be done to comfort Collins in his final days. Just past midmorning on September 23, 1889, Wilkie Collins died, Beard at his bedside. Four days following his death, Collins was buried at Kensal Green; his procession was headed by Caroline Graves, Harriet Graves, and his surviving literary, theatrical, and household friends. Despite infirmities, Collins had lived a life long and full, remaining productive, industrious, and successful throughout his career.

Analysis

At its best, Wilkie Collins's fiction is characterized by a transparent style that occasionally pleases and surprises the reader with an apt turn of word or phrase, by a genius for intricate plots, by a talent for characterization that in at least one instance must earn the epithet "Miltonic," and by an eye for detail that seems to make the story worth telling. These are the talents of an individual who learned early to look at things like a painter, to see the meaning, the emotion behind the gesture or pose—a habit of observation that constituted William Collins's finest bequest to his elder son.

NARRATIVE STYLE AND PLOTTING

The transparency of Collins's style rests on his adherence to the conventions of the popular fiction of his day. More so than contemporaries, he talks to readers, cajoles them, often protesting that the author will recede into the shadows in order that readers may judge the action for themselves. The "games"—as one critic has observed—that Collins plays with readers revolve about his mazelike plots, his "ingenuous" interruptions of the narrative, and his iterative language, symbolic names, and metaphors. Thus, at the beginning of "Mrs. Zant and the Ghost," published in *Little Novels*, the narrator begins by insisting that this tale of "supernatural influence" occurs in the daylight hours, adding, "The writer declines to follow modern examples by thrusting himself and his opinions on the public view. He returns to the shadow from which he has emerged, and leaves the opposing forces of incredulity and belief to fight the old battle over again, on the old ground." The apt word is "shadow," for certainly, this story depicts a shadow world. At its close, when the preternatural events have occurred, the reader is left to assume a happy resolution between the near victim Mrs. Zant and her earthly rescuer, Mr. Rayburn, through the mood of the man's daughter:

Arrived at the end of the journey, Lucy held fast by Mrs. Zant's hand. Tears were rising in the child's eyes. "Are we to bid her good-bye?" she said sadly to her father.

He seemed to be unwilling to trust himself to speak; he only said, "My dear, ask her yourself."

But the result justified him. Lucy was happy again.

Here, Collins's narrator has receded like Mrs. Zant's supernatural protector, leaving the reader to hope and to expect that Mrs. Zant can again find love in this world.

This kind of exchange—direct and inferred—between author and reader can go in other directions. For example, when, near the middle of *The Woman in White*, one realizes that Count Fosco has read—as it were—over one's shoulder the diary of Miss Halcolmbe, the author surely intends that one should feel violated while at the same time forced into collusion with the already attractive, formidable villain.

Because Collins's style as narrator is so frequently self-effacing, it sustains the ingenuity of his plots. These are surely most elaborate in *The Woman in White* and *The Moonstone*. In both cases, Collins elects to have one figure, party to the main actions, assemble the materials of different narratives into cohesive form. It is a method far less tedious than that of epistolary novels and provides for both mystery and suspense. Although not the ostensible theme in either work, matters of self-identity and control over one's behavior operate in the contest between virtue and vice, good and evil. Thus, Laura Fairlie's identity is obliterated in an attempt to wrest from her her large fortune; thus, Franklin Blake, heavily drugged, unconsciously removes a gem that makes him the center of elaborate investigation. In each novel, the discovery of the actual circumstances restores identity to the character. The capacity to plot allows Collins to surprise his readers profoundly: In *The Woman in White*, one is astounded to be confronted by Laura Fairlie standing in the churchyard, above her own grave. In *The Moonstone*, one is baffled when the detective, Sergeant Cuff, provides a plausible solution to the theft of the diamond that turns out to be completely incorrect.

Collins's novels of the 1860's find the author having firmly established his transparent detachment from the subjects at hand, in turn giving full scope to his meticulous sense of plot. *No Name* and *Armadale* are no less complex in their respective actions than their more widely read counterparts. It is interesting to note, however, that all of these novels explore matters of identity and motive for action; they attest to Collins's ability to relate popular tales that encompass more serious issues.

CHARACTERIZATION

Because he had a painter's eye for detail, Collins was a master of characterization, even when it appears that a character is flat. Consider, for example, this passage from "Miss Dulane and My Lord," published in *Little Novels*:

Mrs. Newsham, tall and elegant, painted and dyed, acted on the opposite principle in dressing, which confesses nothing. On exhibition before the world, this lady's disguise asserted she had reached her thirtieth year on her last birthday. Her husband was discreetly silent, and Father Time was discreetly silent; they both knew that her last birthday had happened thirty years since.

Here an incidental figure in a minor tale remains fixed, the picture of one comically out of synchronization with her own manner; before she has uttered a syllable, one dislikes her. Consider, on the other hand, the initial appearance of a woman one will grow to like and admire, Marian Halcolmbe, as she makes her way to meet Walter Hartright in *The Woman in White*:

> She turned towards me immediately. The easy elegance of every movement of her limbs and body as soon as she began to advance from the far end of the room, set me in a flutter of expectation to see her face clearly. She left the window—and I said to myself, The lady is dark. She moved forward a few steps—and I said to myself, The lady is young. She approached nearer—and I said to myself (with a sense of surprise which words fail me to express), The lady is ugly!

This passage reveals not only Collins's superb sense of pace, his ability to set a trap of astonished laughter, but also some of Hartright's incorrect assumptions about the position he has taken at Limmeridge House; for example, that the two young women he will instruct are pampered, spoiled, and not worth his serious consideration. Preeminently, it shows the grace of Marian Halcombe, a grace that overcomes her lack of physical beauty in conventional senses and points to her indefatigable intelligence and loyalty, so crucial to future events in the novel. Marian is, too, a foil for her half sister, Laura Fairlie, the victim of the main crimes in the book. While one might easily dismiss Laura Fairlie with her name—she is fair and petite and very vulnerable—she also displays a quiet resilience and determination in the face of overwhelming adversaries.

The most memorable of Collins's characters is Count Fosco in the same novel, whose name immediately suggests a bludgeon. Collins gives the job of describing Fosco to Marian Halcombe: "He looks like a man who could tame anything." In his characterization of Fosco, Collins spawned an entire race of fat villains and, occasionally, fat detectives, such as Nero Wolfe and Gideon Fell. One is not surprised that Sydney Greenstreet played both Fosco and his descendant, Caspar Gutman, in the 1948 film version of *The Woman in White* and the 1941 film version of Dashiell Hammett's *The Maltese Falcon* (1930). In one of his best speeches, Fosco reveals the nature of his hubris, his evil genius:

> Crimes cause their own detection, do they? . . . there are foolish criminals who are discovered, and wise criminals who escape. The hiding of a crime, or the detection of a crime, what is it? A trial of skill between the police on one side, and the individual on the other. When the criminal is a brutal, ignorant fool, the police in nine cases out of ten win. When the criminal is a resolute, educated, highly-intelligent man, the police in nine cases out of ten lose.

In pitting decent people against others who manipulate the law and social conventions to impose their wills, Collins frequently creates characters more interesting for their deficiencies than for their virtues. His novels pit, sensationally at times, the unsuspecting, the infirm, or the unprepossessing against darker figures who are usually operating under the scope of social acceptance. Beneath the veneer of his fiction, one finds in Collins a continuing struggle to legitimate the illegitimate, to neutralize hypocrisy, and to subvert the public certainties of his era.

Kenneth Friedenreich

OTHER MAJOR WORKS

SHORT FICTION: *Mr. Wray's Cash-Box: Or, The Mask and the Mystery*, 1852; *The Seven Poor Travellers*, 1854; *After Dark*, 1856; *The Wreck of the Golden Mary*, 1856; *The Lazy Tour of Two Idle Apprentices*, 1857 (with Charles Dickens); *The Queen of Hearts*, 1859; *The Frozen Deep*, 1866; *Miss or Mrs.?, and Other Stories*, 1873; *The Frozen Deep, and Other Stories*, 1874; *Alicia Warlock: A Mystery, and Other Stories*, 1875; *The Guilty River*, 1886; *Little Novels*, 1887; *The Yellow Tiger, and Other Tales*, 1924.

PLAYS: *The Lighthouse*, pr. 1855; *The Red Vial*, pr. 1858; *No Thoroughfare*, pr., pb. 1867 (with Charles Dickens); *The Woman in White*, pr., pb. 1871 (adaptation of his novel); *Man and Wife*, pr. 1873 (adaptation of his novel); *The New Magdalen*, pr., pb. 1873 (adaptation of his novel); *The Moonstone*, pr., pb. 1877 (adaptation of his novel).

NONFICTION: *Memoirs of the Life of William Collins, R. A.*, 1848 (2 volumes); *Rambles Beyond Railways,*

1851; *The Letters of Wilkie Collins*, 1999 (William Baker and William M. Clarke, editors); *The Public Face of Wilkie Collins: The Collected Letters*, 2005 (4 volumes; William Baker, editor).

MISCELLANEOUS: *My Miscellanies*, 1863; *The Works of Wilkie Collins*, 1900, 1970 (30 volumes).

BIBLIOGRAPHY

Bachman, Maria K., and Don Richard Cox, eds. *Reality's Dark Light: The Sensational Wilkie Collins*. Knoxville: University of Tennessee Press, 2003. Collection of fourteen essays analyzes Collins's novels, focusing on the themes and techniques that he introduced to the genre. Includes analysis of *The Moonstone* and *The Woman in White* as well as some of his lesser-known novels.

Gasson, Andrew. *Wilkie Collins: An Illustrated Guide*. New York: Oxford University Press, 1998. Well-illustrated volume provides an alphabetical guide to the characters, titles, and terms in Collins's works. Also includes a chronology, the Collins family tree, maps, and a bibliography.

Nayder, Lillian. *Wilkie Collins*. New York: Twayne, 1997. Good introductory study of the author features analysis of his novels and other works, placing them within the context of the political and cultural issues of Collins's time.

O'Neill, Philip. *Wilkie Collins: Women, Property, and Propriety*. New York: Macmillan, 1988. Seeks to move the discussion of Collins away from populist categories by using modern feminist criticism deconstructively to open up a more considered version of his thematic material. Contains a full bibliography.

Page, Norman, ed. *Wilkie Collins: The Critical Heritage*. London: Routledge & Kegan Paul, 1974. Collection reprints critical responses to Collins's works from 1850 through 1891. Includes a short bibliography.

Peters, Catherine. *The King of Inventors: A Life of Wilkie Collins*. Princeton, N.J.: Princeton University Press, 1991. Comprehensive biography draws on a newly discovered autobiography by Collins's mother and on thousands of Collins's unpublished letters. Supplemented by detailed notes and bibliography.

Pykett, Lyn. *Wilkie Collins*. New York: Oxford University Press, 2005. Traces the various debates that have arisen since 1980, when literary critics began seriously reevaluating Collins's work. The essays focus on Collins's preoccupation with the themes of social and psychological identity, class, gender, and power.

_____, ed. *Wilkie Collins*. New York: St. Martin's Press, 1998. Provides an excellent introduction to Collins for the beginning student. In addition to essays that discuss Collins's place within Victorian detective fiction and the "sensation novel," some essays analyze his individual works, including *The Woman in White*. Includes bibliographical references and an index.

Taylor, Jenny Bourne, ed. *The Cambridge Companion to Wilkie Collins*. New York: Cambridge University Press, 2006. All aspects of Collins's writing are discussed in this collection of thirteen essays. His common themes of sexuality, marriage, and religion are examined, as well as his experiences with publishing companies and the process of adapting his works for film. Includes a thorough bibliography and index.

Thoms, Peter. *The Windings of the Labyrinth: Quest and Structure in the Major Novels of Wilkie Collins*. Athens: Ohio University Press, 1992. Focuses on seven major novels, analyzing the theme of the quest in *Basil*, *Hide and Seek*, *The Dead Secret*, *The Woman in White*, *No Name*, *Armadale*, and *The Moonstone*.

IVY COMPTON-BURNETT

Born: Pinner, Middlesex, England; June 5, 1884
Died: London, England; August 27, 1969

PRINCIPAL LONG FICTION

Dolores, 1911
Pastors and Masters, 1925
Brothers and Sisters, 1929
Men and Wives, 1931
More Women than Men, 1933
A House and Its Head, 1935
Daughters and Sons, 1937
A Family and a Fortune, 1939
Parents and Children, 1941
Elders and Betters, 1944
Manservant and Maidservant, 1947 (also known
    as *Bullivant and the Lambs*, 1948)
Two Worlds and Their Ways, 1949
Darkness and Day, 1951
The Present and the Past, 1953
Mother and Son, 1955
A Father and His Fate, 1957
A Heritage and Its History, 1959
The Mighty and Their Fall, 1961
A God and His Gifts, 1963
The Last and the First, 1971

OTHER LITERARY FORMS

Ivy Compton-Burnett (KAHMP-tuhn BUHR-nuht)
is known only for her novels.

ACHIEVEMENTS

Known as a novelist's novelist, Ivy Compton-
Burnett is much appreciated by her peers. She has been
compared by her partisans to figures as various as Jane
Austen, Jean Racine, Henry James, Leo Tolstoy, George
Eliot, Anton Chekhov, the Elizabethan tragedians, William
Congreve, Oscar Wilde, George Meredith, Elizabeth
Gaskell, Harold Pinter, and the cubists. Her appeal
is to a growing circle of admirers, though her work has
enjoyed neither popular adulation nor widespread critical
attention. Her novels require slow and attentive reading
and make heavy demands on the reader, yet they do

not offer the inviting depths of works such as James
Joyce's *Ulysses* (1922) and William Faulkner's *The
Sound and the Fury* (1929). Compton-Burnett's modernism
is of a different kind: Her works present hard and
brittle surfaces, and her style reaches its purest expression
in pages of unbroken dialogue, highly stylized and
crackling with suppressed emotion. Her uncompromising
artistry won for her a small but permanent place in
twentieth century world literature.

BIOGRAPHY

Ivy Compton-Burnett always thought she would
write, even when she was quite young. She came from a
well-to-do family: Her father, James Compton Burnett
(no hyphen), was a doctor and direct descendant of the
ecclesiastical writer Bishop Gilbert Burnett. Ivy adored
her father and from him inherited a love of words and of
nature. Her mother, Katharine Rees Compton-Burnett,
was the second wife of her father: Katharine became
stepmother to five children at marriage and mother of
seven more, of whom Ivy was the eldest. Katharine
seems to have been the prototype for several of the tyrants
in Compton-Burnett's works: She was beautiful,
autocratic, indifferent to her stepchildren and distant to
her own. The real mother to the children was their nurse,
Minnie. Olive, the eldest of all the children, was bitterly
jealous of her stepmother and of Ivy for her close relationship
with their father.

Compton-Burnett's closest companions were her
two younger brothers, Guy and Noel (Jim). The three
were educated together, first by a governess and then by
a tutor, and Compton-Burnett always remained proud
that she had had a boy's education. She loved Latin and
Greek. In 1902, she entered Royal Holloway College,
London University; in 1904, she was awarded the
Founder's Scholarship; in 1906, she passed the bachelor
of arts honors examination in the classics. Her love
of the classics appears clearly in her works: Her plots,
with their recurring motifs of incest and family murder,
seem straight from Greek tragedy; her characters
often allude to Greek tragedy; her view of life as cruel
and ironic is the tragic view of the Greek dramatists,

skewed by modern experience and by her own temperament.

Compton-Burnett claimed to have written very little before her first novel, *Dolores*, was published. She discounted *Dolores* entirely in later life, uncertain which parts were hers and which were the work of her overly enthusiastic brother Noel. Between the publication of *Dolores* and *Pastors and Masters*, her second novel, is a gap of fourteen years that was filled with family turbulence. After the deaths of both her parents, Ivy became head of the household and a bit of a tyrant herself. Her four younger sisters and Minnie moved out and set up their own household, which they refused to let Ivy visit. Compton-Burnett's only remaining brother, Noel (Guy had died earlier), was killed in World War I, and the author cared for his brother's widow after she took an overdose of sleeping pills. Around the same time, Ivy's two youngest sisters committed suicide. She herself had a bout with Spanish influenza that drained her energy for some years.

In the early 1920's, Compton-Burnett settled in a flat in London with her friend Margaret Jourdain, an authority on Regency furniture, with whom she lived for thirty years. Jourdain was the more famous and remained the dominant of the pair. The two women traveled abroad together every year, where Compton-Burnett pursued her passion of collecting wildflowers. Every odd-numbered year, with only a few exceptions, she produced a novel. World War II disturbed her greatly, and she and Jourdain fled to the country to escape the bombings in London. When Jourdain died in 1951, Compton-Burnett felt betrayed by her "desertion."

In her later years, Compton-Burnett was the recipient of many honors. She was made a Commander of the Order of the British Empire in 1951 and was awarded the James Tait Black Memorial Prize in 1956. In 1960 she received an honorary doctor of letters degree from the University of Leeds, and in 1967 she was made a Dame Commander of the British Empire.

Compton-Burnett dedicated her life to her art, reading and working continually. She had little wish to reveal the details of her private life—

"I haven't been at all deedy"—and believed that all she had to offer the world could be found in her books.

ANALYSIS

Ivy Compton-Burnett has no wide range of style or subject in her twenty novels. Like Jane Austen, she limits her characters to a few well-to-do families in the country. The action takes place in the late Victorian era, though there are few indications of any time period. Scenery is almost nonexistent, and no heavy Victorian furnishings clutter the scene.

Compton-Burnett concentrates entirely on her characters, not in describing them but in having them reveal (and sometimes betray) themselves in what they do and do not say. Her novels demand more of the ear than of the eye. They have been likened to plays in their spareness of description, narration, and exposition and their concentration on talk. Dialogue indeed is the reason Compton-

Ivy Compton-Burnett. (Getty Images)

Burnett's novels draw readers and is her chief contribution to the art of the novel. Each chapter contains one event, which is discussed in detail by one family and then perhaps another, or by the masters in the house and then the servants. Although Compton-Burnett as an omniscient author does not comment on or analyze her characters or their motives, her chorus of servants, children, neighbors, and schoolmistresses do so incessantly. In this way, she achieves many points of view instead of only one.

Compton-Burnett's novels do have plots—melodramatic and sometimes implausible ones with murders, incest, infidelity, and perversions of justice. At times, she drops enough clues for the reader to know what will happen; at other times, events occur arbitrarily. Characters lost in shipwrecks often reappear; documents are stolen or concealed only to turn up later. Eavesdroppers populate her novels. Several characters, for example, coincidentally walk into rooms where they are being slandered. Although the events themselves are often too coincidental, the highly crafted conversations about them prove Compton-Burnett's talent as a writer. These witty and ironic conversations insist on the revelation of truth and on the precise use of language, making Compton-Burnett's novels memorable. Language insulates people against the primitive forces, the unmentionable deeds of which they are capable. Compton-Burnett's witty dialogue tends to anesthetize the reader's response (and the characters' as well) to horrendous crimes of passion.

In her novels, Compton-Burnett explores all the tensions of family life—between strong and weak, between generations, between classes. Power is her chief subject, with love, money, and death as constant attendants. Her main foes are complacency, tyranny, and hypocrisy. Compton-Burnett deplores sloppy thinking and dishonesty, whether with oneself or with others. Her novels clearly indicate her view of human nature. She believes that wickedness is often not punished and that is why it is prevalent. When wickedness is likely to be punished, most people, she thinks, are intelligent enough to avoid it. She also sees very few people as darkly evil; many people, when subjected to strong and sudden temptations without the risk of being found out, yield to such urges. Even her bad characters have some good in them. Although the good points of the tyrants can be recognized, their cruelty can never be forgiven. Ironically, however, their cruelty often produces good results. The victims build up bravery, loyalty, and affection as defenses against the wicked and cruel. Compton-Burnett's novels, above all, elicit concern for human suffering.

Though she does believe in economic and hereditary forces, Compton-Burnett also believes in free will. She is one of the rare novelists whose good-hearted characters are credible as well as likable. The good and innocent characters in her novels, particularly the children, are not corrupted and usually remain unharmed. They conquer by truth, affection, and, most important, by intelligence. Compton-Burnett shows the great resilience of the human spirit; her characters survive atrocities and then settle down to resume their everyday lives. In her novels, the greatest crimes are not crimes of violence but crimes against the human spirit: one person beating down, wounding, or enslaving another's spirit. Her novels do not end with a feeling of despair, however; rather, they end with a feeling of understanding. The good characters see the faults of the tyrants yet continue to love them and gallantly pick them up when they have fallen. The good characters realize that evil and good are inextricably joined.

Compton-Burnett's strengths and weaknesses as a novelist are both suggested by the fact that she has no masterpiece, no best or greatest novel. Her oeuvre has a remarkable consistency, the product of an unswerving artistic intelligence yet also evidence of a certain narrowness and rigidity. By general consensus, her strongest works are those of her middle period, including *Brothers and Sisters*, *More Women than Men*, *A Family and a Fortune*, and *Bullivant and the Lambs*.

Brothers and Sisters

Brothers and Sisters, Compton-Burnett's third novel, is distinguished by the appearance of the first of many tyrannical women in her oeuvre. Sophia Stace (who, like the later tyrants, is a tragic figure as well) wants attention and affection, but she is never willing to give in return. She never sees beyond herself or acts for anyone but herself. Her daughter Dinah succinctly comments: "Power has never been any advantage to Sophia. . . . It has her worn out, and everyone who would have served her."

Sophia's self-absorption leads to disaster. Thinking her father's instructions, which are locked in a desk, will cut her and her adopted brother out of his will, Sophia leaves them there unread, marries her adopted brother (who is really her half brother), and bears three children. Her husband dies of a heart attack after finding out the truth about his and Sophia's parentage, and Sophia reacts to his death by imprisoning herself in her home. Intending to draw attention to herself, Sophia dramatizes her grief. When her children attempt to resume life as usual, she moans that they feel no affection for her: "I don't know whether you like sitting there, having your dinner, with your mother eating nothing?" Like other Compton-Burnett tyrants, she turns mealtime into domestic inquisition.

The only one who can control Sophia, modeled on Compton-Burnett's mother Katharine, is Miss Patmore, modeled on Compton-Burnett's own nurse Minnie. The children love and respect "Patty" as a mother since their own is incapable of giving love. When Sophia herself finds out the truth, she has no feeling for what the revelation will do to her children. They meet the tragedy with characteristic wittiness to cover the pain: "Well if we are equal to this occasion, no other in our lives can find us at a loss. We may look forward to all emergencies without misgiving." The children, though they have been Sophia's victims, are able to realize after her death that she, more than anyone else, has been her own victim: "The survey of Sophia's life flashed on them, the years of ruthlessness and tragedy, power and grief. Happiness, of which she held to have had so much, had never been real to Sophia. They saw it now." Power thus eats away at the powerful while their victims rise to a higher moral plane of understanding.

Brothers and Sisters has many of the standard Compton-Burnett plot ingredients: incest, illegitimacy, domestic torture, and the family secret that becomes public knowledge. What gives the novel added strength is the subplot of Peter Bateman and his children, another example of a parent who blithely torments his children. Socially gauche, Peter's vicious stupidity inflicts painful embarrassment on his skulking son Latimer and his self-effacing daughter Tilly. He determinedly pigeonholes his children into demeaning positions.

While the bond between parents and children in the novel is a brutal one, the bond between brothers and sisters becomes a saving one. Sophia's children, Andrew, Robin, and Dinah, support one another, and they are not the only brothers and sisters in the novel to do so. There are three other sets of brothers and sisters: Edward and Judith, Julian and Sarah, and Gilbert and Caroline, all friends of the Stace children. At various points in the novel, Andrew and Dinah are engaged to Caroline and Gilbert, then to Judith and Edward, and finally Julian proposes to Dinah but is rejected. The Stace children and their friends change romantic partners as if they were merely changing partners at a dance, partly in reaction to the tragic secrets that are revealed, and partly because Compton-Burnett has little faith in marriage or in romantic love. Her marriages are matters of convenience, timing, and location; none of her husbands and wives grow together in a fulfilling relationship. The strongest love bond is always the fraternal bond.

MORE WOMEN THAN MEN

Like Compton-Burnett's first two novels, *More Women than Men* is a school novel. The schoolmistresses of Josephine Napier's girls' school function as the villagers do in Compton-Burnett's manor novels: They serve as a chorus for the main action and provide comic relief from the main tragic action (Miss Munday, the senior teacher, is particularly good at this). The schoolmistresses, however, have less freedom than the villagers: In a society where unmarried or widowed women have few options in supporting themselves, they are bound to the tyrant Josephine.

More Women than Men, like *Men and Wives* and *A House and Its Head*, the novels that immediately preceded and followed it, is a very somber work. Josephine is morally, though not legally, guilty of murder; she exposes her nephew Gabriel's wife, who is deathly ill with pneumonia, to cold blasts of air. She is also a hypocrite par excellence. When her husband Simon dies, she affects ostentatious mourning and claims, "I am not a person to take a pride in not being able to eat and sleep," yet she does exactly that. In reality, she feels little at his death. Gabriel, her morose victim, is also one of the few people who stands up to her. When she makes such claims as "I am not an ogress," Gabriel flatly replies, "Well, you are rather." His standing up to her, however, cannot prevent his wife's murder.

There are two other important elements in Josephine's complex personality: sexual repression and dominance. Indeed, *More Women than Men* is preoccupied with the psychology of sex and with gender differences. Men and women are attracted both to women and to men. Josephine, for example, many years before the book begins, has stolen Simon from Elizabeth Giffard; she disposes of Ruth Giffard so she can reclaim her nephew Gabriel's affections; she thrusts herself on Felix Bacon and, when rejected, accepts the love of Miss Rossetti, Gabriel's natural mother. For Josephine, sex is purely an expression of power.

Josephine's cruel oppression is counterbalanced by another sexually amorphous character, the comic Felix Bacon. Felix begins the novel as the gay companion of Josephine's brother, inherits a manor and a fortune in the course of the novel, and marries the intelligent young heroine Helen Keats at the end. He triumphs in that he escapes Josephine's smothering affection and is able to be master of his own world, yet he still feels a longing for the old situation. One can never break completely free from the stranglehold of the tyrant.

Gender differences are explored in many of Compton-Burnett's novels. In *Pastors and Masters*, she had already dealt with the relative merits of men and women. Emily Herrick, the novel's main character, had maintained that men are egotistical and "devious." In *More Women than Men*, Compton-Burnett raises the problem of the shoddy attention women receive. Felix, for example, wryly remarks that parents express surprise that their daughters' education should be taken seriously. "It is a good thing that they entrust it to other people . . . they don't seem to give any real thought to their being the mothers of the race." Although never an ardent supporter of feminist causes, Compton-Burnett did object to the unequal treatment women received, especially in terms of education.

A FAMILY AND A FORTUNE

A Family and a Fortune is one of Compton-Burnett's kindliest novels. Matty Seaton, the tyrant, is not like the tyrants of earlier novels: She has neither the highly dramatic and tragic sense of Sophia Stace nor the magnetizing and suffocating attraction of Josephine Napier. She wants to be needed by others and craves power, but her tyranny is limited because she is a maiden aunt (not a mother), because she is financially dependent on her sister's family, because she cannot actively move about

(she was crippled in a riding accident), and because she lives in a lodge separated from the main family in the manor. With these limitations, she becomes a study of frustrated tyranny. Compton-Burnett introduces her thus: "Her energy seemed to accumulate and to work itself out at the cost of some havoc within her." All that is left of her youthful attractiveness is her overpowering self-regard. She tries to make herself needed by cutting down others with recrimination and guilt, but all her maneuvers are transparent. She releases her frustration by browbeating her paid companion Miss Griffin, whom she even drives out into the cold one night.

While Matty's energies are loosed into negative and destructive channels, her niece Justine releases her own similar energies in positive and constructive routes. Justine is one of the best of the strong-minded, clear-seeing, female characters whom Compton-Burnett uses to balance her tyrants (Patty in *Brothers and Sisters* and Rachel in *Men and Wives* are other examples). Justine is the one who patches the leaky boat of family life with her optimistic matter-of-factness. Self-effacing and comic, she is "utterly honest" with herself, particularly about her own potential weaknesses. She busies herself about everyone's business but never lapses into tyranny and willingly yields her power when her father remarries. Though a bit officious, she brings a positive force to the family and the novel, insisting that life has meaning: "All human effort must achieve something essential, if not apparent," she explains. She is one of the few Compton-Burnett characters who is morally good and truthful, but not cynical (nor very witty). It is she who makes the ending of the novel happy—with the two brothers Edgar and Dudley once again arm in arm—happy because she insists it is.

Another remarkable character in the novel is Aubrey, Justine's fifteen-year-old retarded brother. Compton-Burnett first introduced children into her novels in *Daughters and Sons*, and they never left her novels thereafter. Children prove useful to Compton-Burnett in the contrast they make with their parents; in the choric comments they can make on the action; in the helpless victims they provide for the tyrants; and in themselves, because Compton-Burnett knows the difficult and sometimes fearful world of children. Aubrey senses his inadequacies and is always trying to reassure himself by saying how much he is like someone else in the family. His dialogue brings out real family resemblances: At times he is peevish like his grandfather, at other times he consciously (and sometimes unconsciously) imitates his uncle Dudley's clearheaded, mannered speech. Aubrey's attempts to be normal constitute some of the most moving scenes in Compton-Burnett's fiction.

One important theme of *A Family and a Fortune* is that to be "normal" is to be flawed. Matty Seaton treats her devoted companion brutally; her nephew Clement Gaveston hoards gold coins in his bedroom; and Dudley Gaveston, the generous bachelor uncle who inherits the fortune, leaves the manor in a jealous rage when his brother Edgar steals his fiancé. Dudley sums up their behavior by saying that all have their ridiculous moments.

Dudley and Edgar have the very close fraternal relationship so common in Compton-Burnett novels. They almost exclude Blanche, Edgar's first wife, from close communion, and the greatest threat in the novel is not murder or incest as in the early novels, but that the brotherly bond will be broken. At the end of the novel, however, it is clear that Edgar will return to Dudley.

BULLIVANT AND THE LAMBS

Bullivant and the Lambs has been the most popular of all Compton-Burnett's novels; some critics have named it as their favorite, and Compton-Burnett even said it was one that she particularly liked. It is less spare than the other novels, with more exposition, more sense of place (a smoking fireplace begins and ends the novel, for example), and fully drawn characters. A story of reformation, it shows strong bonds of affection among Horace Lamb, his cousin Mortimer, and his counterpart in the servants' world, Bullivant, the butler.

Horace, a penny pincher who makes his children do calisthenics to keep warm in winter, is one of Compton-Burnett's crotchety male tyrants. He often looks aside in apparent abstraction as "punishment to people for the nervous exasperation that they produced in him, and must expiate." His wife Charlotte and his cousin Mortimer plan to run away and take the children with them to save them from suffering. Horace finds a letter detailing their plans and becomes Compton-Burnett's first and only tyrant who attempts to reform. His reformation does not erase the past (his children, in particular,

point this out); in fact, it makes the children suffer more because he inevitably has lapses. The ups and downs of being nourished and then starved torture the children far more excruciatingly than would consistent oppression, yet Horace draws forth deep love from Mortimer and devoted service from Bullivant. Mortimer explains the tyrant's appeal: "Is there something in Horace that twines itself about the heart? Perhaps it is being his own worst enemy." The wise characters may be victims of the tyrants, but they also understand and pity them.

Mortimer, like Dudley Gaveston, is an example of Compton-Burnett's unmarried, rather impotent characters who attach themselves to their richer relatives in the manor. Like Dudley, Mortimer cares more about the children than their own father does. It is these dependent characters who have the strength to challenge the tyrant's ruthlessness, who speak with caustic honesty to expose the tyrant's pretentiousness. They act courageously, even though they must mortify themselves (thus Mortimer's name) and expose their own weakness in the cause of truth. The exploiter needs the exploited, and vice versa.

Bullivant and the Lambs introduces an important new element in Compton-Burnett's novels: the servants. Like the children, they can mirror their masters or can serve as a chorus discussing the action. The characters of Compton-Burnett's servants are never better than in this novel: the timid maid; the motherly, nonconformist cook; George, the workhouse boy with grandiose pretensions; and Bullivant, the wonderfully comic butler. Bullivant holds both upstairs and downstairs together with his wry wit and firm hand. He knows everything that has transpired and anticipates what will come. He is also a character of great tenderness and protectiveness, though he hides it under a mask of strict propriety. His devotion to Horace is almost that of an elder brother, though he is always careful to keep his place.

Two important themes of *Bullivant and the Lambs* are the conflict between instinct and social conventions and the pernicious effects of do-gooders' meddling. Compton-Burnett had no belief in God, but she was a great supporter of social conventions as necessary restraints on man's primitive instincts. The decent majority of men create social and moral rules; the unscrupulous minority violate them. Horace claims that civilized life consists in suppressing one's instincts, but his wife Charlotte corrects him by saying that all life consists in fulfilling them. Charlotte expresses the complexity of Compton-Burnett's vision: "There is so much truth on all the different sides of things."

Compton-Burnett first sounded the theme of meddling do-gooders in *Pastors and Masters*, in which one character remarks, "I think it's rather terrible to see it [good] being done." In *Bullivant and the Lambs*, Mortimer breaks his engagement to Magdalen because of her interference: "At any time you might act for my good. When people do that, it kills something precious between them." Like Charles Dickens in *Bleak House* (1852-1853, serial; 1853, book), Compton-Burnett believes that do-gooders are usually thinly veiled tyrants. The novel ends happily, however, with an act of goodness: The maid will teach Miss Buchanan, the illiterate shopkeeper, to read.

A God and His Gifts

After *Bullivant and the Lambs*, Compton-Burnett's novels weaken, showing signs of strain, repetition, melodrama, and lack of inventiveness. One exception to this is *A God and His Gifts*, in which the tyrant Hereward Egerton overflows with sexual and artistic energy. Through his character, Compton-Burnett reflects on the nature of the artist, which includes essential and consuming egoism as well as godlike creativity.

The most telling criticism leveled against the novels of Compton-Burnett is their sameness. The plots of her novels tend to become indistinguishable after one has read many; the speech of all her characters, no matter what their social class or background, is witty and stylized, and her characters themselves become habitual types. Such charges have a degree of validity, yet Compton-Burnett's novels must be accepted on their own terms. She was not interested in realistic dialogue; she was concerned with speech as a means of revealing human character. Her tyrants tend to be careless in their discourse, relying on clichés or using words inexactly, just as they are careless in the way they trample moral laws and people. They pretend to be open, but their speech incriminates them for lack of self-knowledge and candor. Their victims, who seek truth, always correct the tyrants' misuse of language by questioning the real meaning of the words they use.

Whatever her flaws as a novelist, Compton-Burnett was an artist of uncommon intelligence, originality, and control. Her work might best be described in a phrase from one of her own novels, *More Women than Men*: "Like agate, beautiful and bright and hard."

Ann Willardson Engar

Bibliography

Baldanza, Frank. *Ivy Compton-Burnett*. New York: Twayne, 1964. Good introductory work packs a great deal of information into a short space. Offers brief characterizations of all the novels, organized around common themes, such as home and family, and analyzes major evaluations of Compton-Burnett's work.

Burkhart, Charles. *I. Compton-Burnett*. London: Victor Gollancz, 1965. Categorizes Compton-Burnett as an eccentric novelist and offers a psychological account of this type of writer. Presents themes found in Compton-Burnett's works, such as conventions, secrets, people and power, and ethos, devoting a chapter to each. Concludes with a summary of each of the novels, ranking *Bullivant and the Lambs* as the most brilliant.

Cavaliero, Glen. "Family Fortunes: Ivy-Compton Burnett." In *The Alchemy of Laughter: Comedy in English Fiction*. New York: St. Martin's Press, 2000. Discussion of works by Compton-Burnett is part of an examination of comedy in English novels that addresses the elements of parody, irony, and satire as well as other types of humor in these books.

Gentile, Kathy Justice. *Ivy Compton-Burnett*. New York: St. Martin's Press, 1991. Very thorough study presents a shrewd feminist rereading of Compton-Burnett's work, with chapters on her "ethic of tolerance," her early novels, her treatment of mothers and martyrs, her view of civilization, her later novels, her reading of human character, and the responses of her critics. Includes notes and bibliography.

Ingman, Heather. "Ivy Compton-Burnett: Tyrants, Victims, and Camp." In *Women's Fiction Between the Wars: Mothers, Daughters, and Writing*. New York: St. Martin's Press, 1998. Chapter on Compton-Burnett is part of an examination of how six female authors depict the mother-daughter relationship in their work. Ingman asserts that Compton-Burnett's novels "provide a devastating insight into the psychopathology of Victorian family life and a critique of the patriarchal power structures underpinning it."

Kiernan, Robert E. *Frivolity Unbound: Six Masters of the Camp Novel—Thomas Love Peacock, Max Beerbohm, Ronald Firbank, E. F. Benson, P. G. Wodehouse, Ivy Compton-Burnett*. New York: Continuum, 1990. Traces the decline of Compton-Burnett's literary reputation.

Liddell, Robert. *The Novels of I. Compton-Burnett*. London: Victor Gollancz, 1955. Offers extended discussions of Compton-Burnett's works. Includes a bibliography.

Nevius, Blake. *Ivy Compton-Burnett*. New York: Columbia University Press, 1970. Provides a general account of the novelist's works, noting that they stress the conflict of passion and duty. Notes that their peculiar form, consisting almost entirely of dialogue, has led many to dismiss Compton-Burnett as an eccentric, but argues that although her characters are static, her theme of the abuse of power has continuing relevance.

Sprigge, Elizabeth. *The Life of Ivy Compton-Burnett*. New York: George Braziller, 1973. Focuses more on Compton-Burnett's life than on her works. Sprigge is extremely favorable toward her subject and accepts Compton-Burnett's claims at face value.

Spurling, Hilary. *Ivy: The Life of I. Compton-Burnett*. New York: Alfred A. Knopf, 1984. One of the most comprehensive accounts of Compton-Burnett's life available, based on exhaustive research and conversations with her friends. The novelist's severely repressed life as a child in the late Victorian era dominates the first half of the book. Discusses how her childhood experiences influenced her stories and novels, all of which are discussed at length.

MARYSE CONDÉ

Born: Point-à-Pitre, Guadeloupe, West Indies;
February 11, 1937
Also known as: Maryse Boucolon

PRINCIPAL LONG FICTION

Hérémakhonon, 1976 (English translation, 1982)
Une Saison à Rihata, 1981 (*A Season in Rihata*, 1988)
Ségou: Les Murailles de terre, 1984 (*Segu*, 1987)
Moi, Tituba, sorcière noire de Salem, 1985 (*I, Tituba, Black Witch of Salem*, 1992)
Ségou II: La Terre en miettes, 1985 (*The Children of Segu*, 1989)
La Vie scélérate, 1987 (*Tree of Life*, 1992)
Traversée de la mangrove, 1989 (*Crossing the Mangrove, 1995*)
Les Derniers Rois mages, 1992 (*The Last of the African Kings*, 1997)
La Colonie du nouveau monde, 1993
La Migration des cœurs, 1995 (*Windward Heights*, 1998)
Desirada, 1997 (English translation, 2000)
Célanire cou-coupé, 2000 (*Who Slashed Celanire's Throat? A Fantastical Tale*, 2004)
La Belle Créole, 2001
Histoire de la femme cannibale, 2003 (*The Story of the Cannibal Woman*, 2007)
Victoire, les saveurs et les mots, 2006
Les Belles Ténébreuses, 2008

OTHER LITERARY FORMS

A prolific writer, Maryse Condé (kohn-DAY) has published extensively in many genres. She has edited collections of francophone writings from former French colonies in Africa and the Caribbean, and has written plays, one of which was produced in France in 1974 and in New York in English in 1991. She has published works of literary criticism, including a book about women novelists in the French Caribbean, as well as collections of short stories, books for children, and a childhood memoir. She also has written articles for journals and other periodicals.

ACHIEVEMENTS

Maryse Condé's books have been translated into six languages. She has won numerous awards, including the grand prix de la Femme and the Prix Alain Boucheron in 1986 for *I, Tituba, Black Witch of Salem*; the Anaïs Nin Prize from the French Academy for *Tree of Life* in 1988; and the Prix Carbet de la Caraibe in 1997 for *Desirada*. She was the first woman to receive the University of Oklahoma's Puterbaugh Fellowship, and in 1999 she won a Lifetime Achievement Award from New York University's Africana Studies Program and Institute of African-American Affairs. In France, she was appointed Commander of the Order of Arts and Letters (2001), Chevalier of the Legion of Honor (2003), and Commander of the National Order of Merit (2007). The two volumes of the Segu series have been best sellers, the first being a selection of the French Le Livre du Mois (book-of-the-month club). Condé has honorary degrees from Occidental College, Lehman College of the City University of New York, and the University of the West Indies at Cave Hill in Barbados.

BIOGRAPHY

The life of Maryse Condé, and the source of many of her preoccupations as a writer, is the story of relocations from an obscure French Caribbean colony to other regions of the francophone world: Paris, West Africa, back to Paris, then back to her natal island. She has earned a living by holding academic posts in Paris, West Africa, and the United States, while acquiring increasing fame as a writer.

Née Boucolon, Maryse Condé grew up in Guadeloupe, one of the two French islands in the West Indies. Her mother was the first black female instructor of her generation, and her father had been recognized by the Legion of Honor. Despite these solid achievements, the family was socially insecure, aware of being black in a racially hierarchical colony. Intelligent and critical, the young Condé was bored in Guadeloupe and found the little island suffocating. Still, she did well as a student and was sent to a high school in Paris; she was later expelled for insubordination after she reacted strongly against attitudes she regarded as racist. She moved on to the Sorbonne (the esteemed university in Paris).

Condé escaped West Indian circles, which she saw as limiting, and made friends in the African community in Paris, where she met and fell in love with Mamadou Condé, a Guinean actor. They were married in 1959 and moved to Guinea. Soon the relationship was facing difficulties, and Condé, who had defied her family by marrying Mamadou, accepted that the marriage was a failure and left her husband, supporting herself and her children by teaching in the Ivory Coast, Guinea, Ghana, and Senegal. In 1969, she met Richard Philcox, who would translate many of her novels into English. They were married in 1982. She returned to Paris in 1970 to work at the Sorbonne on a doctorate in comparative literature, which she completed in 1976. Condé stayed at the Sorbonne as a lecturer for nearly a decade, then returned to Guadeloupe.

Condé also held prestigious academic posts in the United States until her retirement in 2002. She was professor of French at the University of California (Los Angeles and Berkeley), the University of Maryland, and Columbia University, where she also was chair of the French and Francophone Institute.

ANALYSIS

Maryse Condé's works deal with themes considered central by many contemporary authors and critics. She writes in the aftermath of decolonization, in and of a realm increasingly globalized and interconnected. In the course of the eighteenth and nineteenth centuries, France had established a worldwide empire, exporting its culture and values into the Americas, Asia, the Pacific, and especially Africa, vast areas of which came under French control. French colonialism led to the building of hospitals and roads, and to the development of industry and trade. French colonialism also had a manifest "civilizing mission" (*mission civilisatrice*), not crude land-grabs but "beneficent" incursions into less developed or fortunate regions. This mission involved the export of the fruits of a high French culture; exposure to this new culture, it was believed, would benefit all, regardless of geographical or ethnic origin. France's relationship with its colonies was often strained and sometimes bloody, but the mother country, too, imbued many of its colonized subjects with an occasionally ambiguous respect for and admiration of the art, customs, and political system of the French.

Maryse Condé. (AFP/Getty Images)

This cultural and imperialist tide, having flowed, would eventually ebb. Exhausted by the bloodletting of two world wars, France had to withdraw from nearly all of its colonial possessions, sometimes, as with Indochina (in Southeast Asia) and Algeria, in circumstances that were traumatic for colonizer and colonized alike. In former colonies as well, a more or less Gallicized elite found itself in a culturally ambivalent position: not fully French, occasionally exposed to racism or other forms of discrimination, but unable, too, to embrace unselfconsciously the indigenous culture, insofar as that culture had survived. In the case of female members of that elite, perceived gender inequalities added to the sense of a false position within the former colonies. Condé's writing is a prolonged attempt to examine her position as a colonized woman of African origin situated in a world still culturally and economically dominated by Western Europe, including France, and the anglophone United States.

HÉRÉMAKHONON

Hérémakhonon, published in Paris in 1976, is Condé's first novel. The predicament of its central character is recognizably suggested by that of her creator, Condé. Veronica has spent her childhood in Guadeloupe and, after a period as a student in Paris, wants to escape that island's respectable black bourgeoisie, which she regards as secretly afraid of its own inferiority. She travels to an unnamed West African state and, while there, seeks an authentically African past with which she will be able to identify.

However, Veronica comes to see that, despite a wish she acknowledges as sentimental, this newly independent country can no more return to a precolonial past than the Sahara can return to its condition before desertification. Furthermore, the state, which encourages its people to believe in "progress," is facing political unrest: Students who demonstrate against the leader are hauled off by the army; one of Veronica's colleagues, described as a militant member of a banned party, is arrested and maltreated; and her newfound lover is a government bureaucrat who lives in the sort of luxury that is almost obscenely beyond the reach of most of his countryfolk. Indeed, Veronica is chauffeured past mud huts to and from his villa, named Hérémakhonon (Mandingo for welcome house). His own wish to preserve the past leads to his being labeled a "reactionary" and a mystifier of the people. Unable to commit to any side, Veronica returns to Paris.

An incidental paragraph reveals the inextricable confluence of cultures brought about by France's imperial ambitions: The gardener at Hérémakhonon is a member of the Fon people, from Dahomey, a former French colony. He has fought in Indochina, was a docker at Marseilles, was a truck driver in Algeria, and talks to himself in bits of French, English, and Arabic. He reads from an old copy of Victor Hugo's 1862 novel *Les Misérables*.

I, TITUBA, BLACK WITCH OF SALEM

Condé added to her fifth novel, *I, Tituba, Black Witch of Salem*, a "Historical Note," in which she explains the novel's origins. Tituba was a historical figure, a black slave from Barbados who confessed to practicing witchcraft in Salem in 1692. It is known that she survived the hysteria and was sold about one year later. However, Condé writes, because of conscious or unconscious racism, history knows little more than this.

I, Tituba, Black Witch of Salem is the fictional autobiography of a person almost erased from history because of her race and gender. Condé imagines for her a life before and after the brief period in which her existence is carefully documented only because of the malignant fear and religious bigotry of her persecutors.

Tituba is conceived in an act of real, and symbolic, violence: the rape of a black slave by a white sailor in a ship ironically named *Christ the King*. Living in Barbados, Tituba escapes slavery by running away after her mother is hanged for resisting another rape, this time at the hands of her master. For a time, Tituba leads an idyllic existence and is taught the healing power of certain plants and how to communicate with the spirits of the dead by an old woman who lives outside society, in an isolated hut. It is Tituba's desire for John Indian, another slave, that draws her back into contact with her kind, as human chattel and the wife of another.

The couple are sold to the Reverend Samuel Parris,

who becomes minister in Salem village. There, despite the Puritan beliefs of the villagers, Tituba is obliged more than once to decline using her knowledge to harm others. She sees that her exotic background and abilities add "spice" to the lives of the repressed children she looks after, who listen with fascination and fear to her stories of diabolic possession. When the witchcraft hysteria strikes, Tituba is tortured and questioned. She confesses, falsely, to hurting children at the devil's behest, knowing such an admission is expected of her.

Finally released, Tituba's is sold again, this time to a Jew who becomes her lover. She returns to Barbados, becomes involved in a slave uprising, and is consequently hanged. Her spirit roams Barbados and foresees the eventual end of the suffering of enslaved Africans and their descendants.

In addition to its focus on racial, gender, and sexual oppression, *I, Tituba, Black Witch of Salem* is a postmodern novel that, in its repeated insistence on the possibility of communication between living and dead, raises doubts about the reliability of the narrator's perceptions. Furthermore, Condé playfully makes Nathaniel Hawthorne's Hester Prynne (the central character of *The Scarlet Letter*, 1850) appear as a character within her own work: Tituba is imprisoned with Hester in Massachusetts, and Hester teaches her about feminism.

THE LAST OF THE AFRICAN KINGS

Condé spoke of her admiration for Bruce Chatwin's *The Viceroy of Ouidah* (1980), a novel that, she believes, deals with themes very similar to those in her Segu series of novels. *The Last of the African Kings* tells the story of the once proud kings of Dahomey, exiled by the French from their West African fiefdom to Martinique, the second of the two French Caribbean islands. In this novel, the reader is once again confronted with the reworking of the connections among West Africa, the Caribbean, and the United States. The novel is another treatment of the confluence of cultures brought about by the African diaspora and its consequences.

In this novel, however, Condé asks whether the idea of an African origin should one day be forgotten. When should one let the past go and live in the American present? The king's illegitimate son, Djéré, is obsessed by his father's story and his own attempts to come to terms with his inadvertent abandonment in Martinique. Djéré reads as much as possible about African history, as does his son Justin. Neither Djéré nor Justin achieves anything in life, however; both spend their days drinking rum and immersed in the legends of the displaced royal family and its former glories.

The young Spero, Justin's son, begins his life just as entranced as his father and grandfather had been. However, Spero learns to live in his "American present," specifically in South Carolina, where he now lives, away from the failures and poverty of the French Caribbean. He has observed his father's wasted life. He soon marries Debbie, an African American and as much a prisoner of past events as anybody on her new husband's side of the family. Her obsessive focus is on the injustices meted out to African Americans and on post-Reconstruction American history. Political correctness is satirized as Spero rejects his wife's beliefs in a simple dualism of black "victim" and white "oppressor."

Spero chooses to name his coming child (a girl) not Jomo or Patrice or for any other heroes of African independence or African American enfranchisement, but instead for a blues singer he admires. He is banished from Debbie's bed when he has an affair with a white woman, and he loses his job at a black Catholic college because he insists on teaching about the European painters Edgar Degas and Pierre-Auguste Renoir rather than about painters of African origin.

M. D. Allen

OTHER MAJOR WORKS

SHORT FICTION: *Pays mêlé*, 1985 (*Land of Many Colors*, 1999).

PLAYS: *Dieu nous l'a donne*, pb. 1972; *Mort d'Oluwemi d'Ajumako*, pb. 1973; *Le Morne de Massabielle*, pr. 1974 (*The Morne of Massabielle*, 1991); *Pension les Alizes*, pr. 1988 (*The Tropical Breeze Hotel*, 1994); *An tan revolisyon: Elle court, elle court la liberté*, pr. 1989.

NONFICTION: *La Civilisation du bossale*, 1978; *Cahier d'un retour au pays natal: Césaire—Analyse critique*, 1978; *La Parole des femmes: Essai sur des romancières des Antilles de langue française*, 1979; *Entretiens avec Maryse Condé*, 1993 (*Conversations with Maryse Condé*, 1996); *Le Cœur à rire et à pleurer: Contes vrais de mon enfance*, 1998 (*Tales from the Heart: True Stories from My Childhood*, 2001).

TRANSLATIONS: *De Christophe Colomb à Fidel Castro: L'Histoire des Caraïbes*, 1975 (of Eric Williams's *From Columbus to Castro: The History of the Caribbean, 1492-1969*); *Tim, tim: Bois sec! Bloemlezing uit de Franstalige Caribsche Literatuur*, 1980 (of her edited texts *La Poésie antillaise* and *Le Roman antillaise*).

CHILDREN'S LITERATURE: *Haiti chérie*, 1987; *Victor et les barricades*, 1989; *Hugo le terrible*, 1991.

EDITED TEXTS: *Anthologie de la littérature d'expression française*, 1966; *La Poésie antillaise*, 1977; *Le Roman antillaise*, 1977; *L'Héritage de Caliban*, 1992; *Penser la créolité*, 1995 (with Madeleine Cottenet-Hage); *Nouvelles d'Amérique*, 1998 (with Lise Gauvin).

BIBLIOGRAPHY

Barbour, Sarah, and Gerise Herndon, eds. *Emerging Perspectives on Maryse Condé: A Writer of Her Own*. Trenton, N.J.: Africa World Press, 2006. A good resource for varied interpretations of Condé's writings. Includes several chapters that examine her novels and their recurrent themes.

Bruner, David K. "Maryse Condé: Creative Writer in a Political World." *L'Esprit créature* 17, no. 2 (Summer, 1977): 168-173. Discussion of the politics informing Condé's early work, including her first two plays and her first novel, *Hérémakhonon*.

Condé, Maryse, with VèVè A. Clark. "I Have Made Peace with My Island." *Callaloo* 12, no. 1 (Winter, 1989): 85-133. A wide-ranging interview that includes an account of Condé's life experiences and a discussion of how her political beliefs affect her writing.

Fulton, Dawn. *Signs of Dissent: Maryse Condé and Postcolonial Criticism*. Charlottesville: University of Virginia Press, 2008. In this first full-length biographical study of Condé in English, Fulton examines the "exceptional role" her writings have had "in shaping a dialogue between francophone studies and the English-dominated field of postcolonialism."

Hohl, Anne Mullen. "Maryse Condé." In *Multicultural Writers Since 1945: An A-Z Guide*, edited by Alba Amoia and and Bettina L. Knapp. Westport, Conn.: Greenwood Press, 2005. A readable account of Condé's life and works in this comprehensive, encyclopedic collection of postwar multicultural writers.

EVAN S. CONNELL

Born: Kansas City, Missouri; August 17, 1924
Also known as: Evan Shelby Connell, Jr.

PRINCIPAL LONG FICTION

Mrs. Bridge, 1959
The Patriot, 1960
The Diary of a Rapist, 1966
Mr. Bridge, 1969
The Connoisseur, 1974
Double Honeymoon, 1976
The Alchymist's Journal, 1991 (expanded as
    Alchymic Journals, 2006)
Deus Lo Volt! A Chronicle of the Crusades, 2000

OTHER LITERARY FORMS

Despite the critical and popular success of his novels *Mrs. Bridge* and *Mr. Bridge*, it might be argued that long fiction is not Evan S. Connell's best form; certainly, it is only one of many literary forms in which he has worked. His *Notes from a Bottle Found on the Beach at Carmel* (1963) and *Points for a Compass Rose* (1973) are haunting, sometimes cryptic prose poems, the latter of which was nominated for the National Book Award for poetry in 1974. Termed "vatic literature" by one critic, these books have been compared to T. S. Eliot's *The Waste Land* (1922), Ezra Pound's *Cantos* (1925-1970), and Albert Camus's *Carnets* (1962, 1964; *Notebooks*, 1963, 1965)—even to "an exotic, unexpurgated *Encyclopaedia Britannica*."

Connell's fascination with the odd particulars of human existence has also produced two well-received collections of essays, *A Long Desire* (1979) and *The White Lantern* (1980). Both of these books blend history, legend, and whimsy in essay form as Connell contemplates the singular obsessions of some of the great travelers, explorers, plunderers, and thinkers of world history. His growing fascination with "the Little Bighorn Fiasco" narrowed Connell's plans for a third book of essays, this time about the Old West, to a nonfiction work about General George A. Custer titled *Son of the Morning Star: Custer and the Little Bighorn* (1984). In 2004, he published *Francisco Goya*, a history of the painter's life and

times. Connell's highly praised short stories have appeared in numerous anthologies and magazines such as *Esquire* and the *Saturday Evening Post*. Several volumes of his short fiction have been published, including *The Anatomy Lesson, and Other Stories* (1957) and *Lost in Uttar Pradesh: New and Selected Stories* (2008). From 1959 to 1965, Connell was editor of *Contact*, a well-respected San Francisco literary magazine. He has also written reviews for *The New York Times*, *New York* magazine, the *San Francisco Chronicle*, *The Washington Post*, and other publications.

ACHIEVEMENTS

Evan S. Connell's first novel, *Mrs. Bridge*, was a best seller and was nominated for the National Book Award for fiction in 1960; in 1973, Connell was one of the five judges for that award. Three of his six novels (*Mrs. Bridge*, *The Diary of a Rapist*, and *Mr. Bridge*) were selected by the editors of *The New York Times Book Review* as being among the best novels of their respective years. Writers praise his mastery, but scholars have found no enigmas demanding explication. His instinct for telling details and the crisp straightforwardness of his narrative style have been widely admired.

Apart from work by Gus Blaisdell, however, little systematic study of Connell's writing exists. One of the most private of contemporary writers, Connell has never intentionally courted the public, writing only about subjects that interest him and only in ways that interest him, paying no attention to current literary fashion. While not an "experimental" writer in the usual self-conscious sense of the term, Connell freely searches among forms and styles for each of his works, and the category-defying forms of *Mrs. Bridge* and *Notes from a Bottle Found on the Beach at Carmel* made publication of both books difficult: Eight publishers rejected *Mrs. Bridge* before the Viking Press gambled on it, and even Viking might not have published *Notes from a Bottle Found on the Beach at Carmel* had it not first appeared in *Contact*, providing them printing plates that they could reuse.

Apart from the two nominations for National Book Awards, Connell's writing has earned him numerous honors, including Saxton and Guggenheim fellowships and a Rockefeller Foundation grant. One mark of his distinction is that in 1981, North Point Press reissued his two Bridge books in keeping with its commitment to reissue out-of-print contemporary classics. *Son of the Morning Star* was a best seller and garnered for Connell a National Book Critics Circle Award as well as the Los Angeles Times Book Prize for history. In 2000, Connell was the recipient of the Lannan Foundation Lifetime Achievement Award.

BIOGRAPHY

Evan Shelby Connell, Jr., was born on August 17, 1924, in Kansas City, Missouri, and graduated from Southwest High School there in 1941. He attended Dartmouth College as a premedical student but left in 1943 to enter the U.S. Navy as an aviation cadet, later noting that without World War II he might have fol-

lowed further in the footsteps of his father and grandfather, both doctors. Connell graduated from flight school in Pensacola in May, 1945, attended instructors' training school in New Orleans, and spent the remainder of his service as a flight instructor at the Glenview Naval Air Station outside Chicago. His flight experience provided him much of the background for his second novel, *The Patriot*, just as his childhood in Kansas City contributed to the Bridge books.

After the war, Connell returned to school on the G.I. Bill, studying art and English at the University of Kansas, where he began writing fiction as a student of Ray B. West. Art has remained for him "an avocation, or second occupation," and he has explained its place in his life in pragmatic terms, noting that he saw some chance of making a living as a writer, but none as a painter. Receiving his B.A. in English from the University of Kansas in 1947, Connell went on to study writing with

Evan S. Connell. (Janet Fries)

Wallace Stegner at Stanford, with Helen Hull at Columbia University in 1948-1949, and with Walter Van Tilburg Clark at San Francisco State College. He "floated" in Paris and Barcelona for two years, writing short stories that eventually began appearing in commercial magazines, a development that Connell has credited in part to Elizabeth McKee, who remained his literary agent until her death in 1997.

For many years from the 1950's onward, Connell lived in San Francisco, explaining that "it seems I've always needed a sense of landscape and topography." He at times supported his writing with what he has called "stupid jobs," working as a postal clerk and a meter reader, hauling ice, and interviewing unemployed workers for the California Department of Unemployment—the job he recalls as his worst and the one he gives to Earl Summerfield in *The Diary of a Rapist*. Connell now lives and works in Santa Fe, New Mexico.

ANALYSIS

When he was asked by interviewer Dan Tooker whether he could generalize about what he wanted to "get across" in his work, Evan S. Connell, characteristically laconic, answered, "No." He has said of his writing only "I want to exemplify." For Connell, exemplification usually consists more of brief, understated vignettes than of heavily embroidered plots and fully textured characterization. He has stated his preference for doing "very, very short things" and admits that he has "always had trouble constructing a fifteen chapter novel." A reviewer in London's *The Times Literary Supplement* once compared Connell to "a coral insect, who piles one tiny, exactly shaped fragment on top of another until by the end something solid, impressive and durable has been created," a description that accurately reflects both Connell's predominant technique and its impact. Three of his novels are literally composed of "tiny, exactly shaped fragments," as the Bridge books and *The Diary of a Rapist* consist of short chapters or diary entries, a form that has been called mosaic or pointillistic. Precision and economy characterize Connell's style, described by Gus Blaisdell as the prose equivalent of the sieve of Eratosthenes: "Everything nonessential is filtered out until only what is prime remains." The "solid, impressive, and durable" result of Connell's writing is a poetics

of obsession structured in all his novels by a dialectic of wonder and despair.

Each Connell novel presents a kind of case history of some form of obsession, ranging from Earl Summerfield's violent hatred of women to Mrs. Bridge's quiet hope for perfect conformity. His protagonists tend to define themselves in terms of single goals that they may or may not be able to perceive, much less articulate. These goals may be of tremendous import, as is true of Melvin Isaac's stubborn attempt to understand his place in a world apparently in love with war and death, or they may be of limited but intense significance, as is true of Karl Muhlbach's almost desperate love of pre-Columbian artifacts or of his infatuation with the young, beautiful, but destructive Lambeth Brett. Their particular obsessions seem to be all that separates Connell's characters from despair at the emptiness of their lives, and often their obsessions are themselves further causes of despair. Moments of exciting prospect light their lives, but those prospects usually dim, suggesting more often than not that "life is a condition of defeat."

Even after acquiring such a negative realization, Connell's characters rarely give up: Like William Shakespeare's Macbeth, but for widely differing reasons and to widely differing effects, his characters echo the cry of "tomorrow and tomorrow and tomorrow." For Walter Bridge, this thought is actually reassuring, but it stamps the narrow sameness of his life. For Muhlbach, it is the dreary, disappointed, but safe cadence that will allow him to march away from the tragedy of Lambeth Brett. For Melvin Isaacs, tomorrow is the day when his life may start to make some sense to him. For Earl Summerfield, tomorrow is an oath of vengeance, and for India Bridge, it is the day when something important might happen, but never does.

Applauding the human spirit in all its vagaries, Connell paints a world that is anything but cheerful, but one that has values even if it has no meaning. In the very different lives of Melvin Isaacs and Karl Muhlbach, Connell suggests that endurance and integrity are themselves cause for minor celebrations, and while his characters all seem to face defeat after defeat, they keep struggling to make the sound and fury of their lives signify *something*. That, Connell seems to suggest, may be enough.

Running through Connell's novels is a persistent note of frustration that often shades into despair. While Connell's novels acknowledge and sometimes celebrate the intensity, enthusiasm, and scattered triumphs that attend the many levels and ranges of human obsession, they seem to protest that life itself should be the end or object of obsession and not merely its means: Humanity should be obsessed *with* life, not only obsessed *in* it. What finally emerges most strongly from this note of frustration or despair is not a sense of fatalism or of defeat, but a sense of the author's own fierce respect for human life and his outrage at the follies—large and small—that threaten to stifle or still the human spirit. Blaisdell calls this stance of Connell "a position of untempered humanism, primitively Christian at the core . . . his outrage and indignation ameliorated by love." Indeed, some combination of outrage, indignation, and love, both for his characters and for the human traits they represent, can account for most of Connell's writing.

At a time when many novelists argue that the only interesting and promising subject of fiction is fiction itself, Connell remains committed to the belief that the novel should have some substantial connection to the powerful feelings of human experience. This is not to say that Connell's novels are conventionally "realistic," but that they strive to be true to human emotion—in the tradition of Anton Chekhov, Leo Tolstoy, and Thomas Mann. While Connell's craftsmanship in each of his novels reveals a fascination with language, his novels always point beyond themselves to human experience and beyond human experience to the wonder of life.

MRS. BRIDGE

Mrs. Bridge consists of 117 short chapters, each a brief, ironic glimpse into the life of India Bridge, bona fide Kansas City country-club matron, a woman whose first name is the only chink in the armor of her militant orthodoxy. Her greatest fear is that she and her children will—even in small ways—be perceived as different from everyone else. "Everyone else" means a small circle of socially prominent Kansas Citians. Each of Connell's vignettes captures the instinctive, self-imposed narrowness of Mrs. Bridge's life in the years between the world wars.

Mrs. Bridge cannot imagine any departure from the narrow custom of her life: She flies into an inarticulate rage because her son actually uses one of the fancy towels put out for guests and is even vaguely distressed by his penchant for coming into the house through the "servants' entrance." She teaches her children that you can judge people by their shoes and their table manners. Mrs. Bridge reads only what her friends say they are reading and diligently tries to think only as they think, yearning for a world in which every vote is unanimous. So implacable is her innocent provinciality that she discusses the outbreak of World War II in almost surreal terms: "Piggly Wiggly still delivers, thank heavens, but the service is so much slower than it used to be."

Connell's satire would become sadistic were it not for his ability to reveal the emptiness beneath the crushing boredom of Mrs. Bridge's narrowly circumscribed life. Several times she almost recognizes her own plight, but the nature of her vague dissatisfaction eludes articulation. She is always about to ask an important question, about to do something interesting, about to embark on a worthwhile project, but she never does. Her life settles into a necessary sequence of delays and interruptions, ensuring her a contentedness that is also a kind of despair; as her children grow up and she realizes that her successful lawyer husband will never cut back on his long hours at the office, she finds it harder and harder to pass the time. One morning she stays in bed, wondering if she is about to die, cheering only when she remembers that "her husband had told her to get the Lincoln waxed and polished." The measure of her tragedy is that even that task had been done the week before.

THE PATRIOT

One of Connell's longest novels, *The Patriot* is also one of the least tightly wound; the book is somewhat uneasily split between its protagonist's military and civilian experiences. This clumsiness, however, may be entirely necessary for telling the story of Melvin Isaacs, the impressively inane misfit who is Connell's patriot. The novel follows Melvin's often spectacular misadventures as he first washes out of naval flight school during World War II, then, after the war, washes himself out of a fraternity and finally out of success as an artist when he abandons abstractionism just when it is becoming most popular. Never really sure of his motivations, Melvin simply refuses to be incorporated, displaying for most of the novel an almost saintlike ingenuousness; more unconscious than conscientious, he is nevertheless an objector to the meticulous and mysterious processes that prepare young men for war. To the jingoistic exhortations of his Polonius of a father, Melvin says as he departs for flight training, "I'll do the best I can, as long as it makes some kind of sense." His problem, of course, is that most of military life and all of the war can never make sense at the basic intuitive level of Melvin's perceptions.

Melvin bumbles through his flight training, getting everything wrong, asking, "Why?" when given orders, going to sleep during relaxation class, getting his foot stuck underneath the rudder pedal on an early training flight, even accidentally managing to put a couple of rounds through his instructor's plane during gunnery practice, and finally willfully tearing his plane apart on his pro forma last flight, crash-landing it in the face of certain dismissal from the flight program. So incredible is his performance that Melvin becomes something of a legend in the ranks of naval aviators, the prototypal dumb "dilbert." If Melvin has a virtue, it is his stubborn persistence in wanting to understand what he is doing, although he is not intellectually suited for much of a quest; faced with puzzles or problems, he usually goes to sleep. He is the black chick to be pecked to death in any grouping, and yet for all his weaknesses and for all the embarrassments he suffers, Melvin instinctively protects his individuality—whatever the cost. In fact, his ingenuousness, so pure as to make him seem at times imbecilic, sheathes him in a kind of dopey but unassailable existential integrity.

Put simply, Melvin values life and freedom. Spending the last few months of the war shagging golf balls at an officers' club in Texas, Melvin learns with horror of the effects of the bombing of Hiroshima. After the war, he begins to understand the significance of his own inscrutable rebellion, seeing that he had been caught up in an insanely murderous tide that had almost made of him "a derelict raft, or a sea anemone, some sodden ruptured polyp washing senselessly to and fro in the ebb and flow of the littoral foam." As *The Patriot* ends, Melvin has identified the tide against which he had struggled: He decides that he will not report for his draft physical (this time the tide flows to Korea), and when his father, obviously excited by the prospect of a new war, tries to give Melvin and his wife the latest in civil-defense equipment

and advice, Melvin kicks him out of their house. To his father's cry of "What will you do?" Melvin simply says, "I know what I won't do," affirming once and for all his commitment to the dignity of life.

THE DIARY OF A RAPIST

Earl Summerfield, the psychopathic protagonist of Connell's third novel, *The Diary of a Rapist*, thinks that the world's decency "went up in a column of smoke above Hiroshima," and the stark evidence of his diary supports his despair. "We set the past on fire," he writes in a diary that sears the present with Earl's rage. Indeed, this novel has a frightening intensity as Connell turns his examination of obsession to the pathology of rape. He has cited as one of his influences the story of a man who had raped a Miss California on two separate occasions, driving her home after the second time. "I remember wondering what could have caused him to behave in that way unless he had fallen in love with her and was thinking that maybe once she got to know him, she would love him too," Connell explained, adding that this kind of insane romanticism struck him as a peculiarly American notion.

Each day, twenty-six-year-old Earl, a chillingly modern Bartleby the Scrivener, dazedly works at an unemployment bureau, waiting for a promotion that will never come, as anonymous as the countless unemployed he must interview. Each rattle of a bottle sliding down the trough of the office soft-drink machine times the disappearance of Earl's life. At night and on holidays he channels his hatred for his life, his job, his wife, and women in general into entries in his diary, augmenting its private horrors with a scrapbook of newspaper clippings about beatings, murders, rapes, and executions. Earl is one of those whom author Nathanael West termed "the cheated": He feels betrayed by a world that refuses to recognize his superiority, humiliated and dominated by a succession of women, adrift in a world so corrupt that only violence can purify it. He writes in his diary that he has looked for love, but has found only "strokes of revenge, back and forth, regular as a metronome."

Earl's diary begins on January 1 and continues for almost a year, during which time his alienation warps into madness, his moralism into monstrosity. His fantasies begin to displace reality, his memory fails, he suffers from vertigo and blackouts; more and more he loses control of his actions. "Have tried praying, it doesn't help," he writes. "My knees hurt and the words break between my teeth like eggshells." His general rage hardens into an obsession with one woman, a beauty-contest winner whom he first sees on Washington's Birthday, rapes on the Fourth of July, and then suicidally surrenders himself to on Christmas Day.

Ironically, through the violence and hatred of the rape, Earl finds an even sadder prospect of love: Falling in love with his victim, Mara St. John, he attempts a bizarre and terrifying courtship. Anonymously, he begins to send her presents, and he repeatedly calls her, wanting to explain how he had been so terrified with life that he fell in love with hate. He always loses control during these calls, however, and they end in his curses. Finally, he decides to give himself up to Mara on Christmas morning and calls to tell her that he will then bow down and ask to be forgiven. His chilling diary entry for December 25 reads: "In the sight of our Lord I must be one of many." The last pages of his diary bear only the dates for the rest of the month.

Connell's depiction of Earl is horrifyingly compelling, justifying Blaisdell's judgment that *The Diary of a Rapist* is "a voyage through one of the darkest nights of the soul ever encountered in literature." What is most powerful and frightening about Earl's madness is that it serves as an outlet for the sicknesses of his society. The little horrors of his scrapbook pale before the "column of smoke above Hiroshima," and Connell, too, seems to agree that "there isn't much decency left in the world."

MR. BRIDGE

Written ten years after *Mrs. Bridge*, *Mr. Bridge* displays little of the gentleness of the former work and much less humor, but is its necessary completion: To read one Bridge book without reading the other would be to miss the stunning depth of Connell's characterizations. Unlike the hapless, purposeless Mrs. Bridge, her husband, Walter, efficiently structures his life around a few severe and inflexible principles—beliefs that would cheer anyone worried that Herbert Hoover was a bit too liberal. Mr. Bridge prides himself in providing for his family's fiscal and philosophical welfare: Good, safe stocks and bonds supply the former, quotations from Abraham Lincoln the latter. In *Mrs. Bridge*, Walter Bridge appears hardworking, honest, and dour—a good man even if an unlikable one. *Mr. Bridge* does nothing to change the essentials of this picture, but the world forced through the nozzle of Walter Bridge's stern perspective becomes a far darker place than it was in *Mrs. Bridge*.

Because Mr. Bridge's life is so much more complicated than his wife's, his story takes more than one hundred pages longer to tell, continuing the pointillist format of the first book. Mr. Bridge's world is almost exclusively composed of relationships indicated by money, which means little to him in itself but provides the markers that measure his achievement in the three areas essential to his self-image: "financial security, independence, and self-respect." Mr. Bridge can imagine no hardship that will not yield to the virtue of hard work, and he finds all the concern over the Great Depression a bit puzzling. While he is not totally unaware of his limitations, Mr. Bridge rationalizes most of them into virtues, and the book's humor rises from the few occasions when doubt momentarily undermines his priggishness. What he cannot dismiss or rationalize is his troubled relationship with his eldest daughter, Ruth, whose sullen rebelliousness and flaunted sexuality arouse both consternation and pangs of desire in his otherwise tightly controlled life. It may well be, as Guy Davenport has suggested, that "in Mr. Bridge's intuitive sense that Ruth is somehow right in her rebellion is the meaning of the two novels."

The reader knows Mrs. Bridge through her failures, Mr. Bridge through his successes, and realizes that both have imprisoned themselves in sadly limited views of the world. Mr. Bridge's opinions infuriate as much as Mrs. Bridge's naïveté amuses; the two books are different yet perfectly matched. Not since Gertrude Stein's *Three Lives* (1909) have the rhythms of daily life been so marvelously represented, the repetitions of the mind made to seem so inexorable.

THE CONNOISSEUR

The Connoisseur is the strangest of Connell's novels; it seems least like a novel—being instead a compendium of information about pre-Columbian art—and the reader must infer and reconstruct its most important themes, in much the same way that Connell's connoisseur must approach pre-Columbian culture. The connoisseur is Karl Muhlbach, a middle-aged widower with two children, a New York insurance executive whose life seems without focus until he buys a small pre-Columbian figurine while on a business trip to New Mexico. Muhlbach is the protagonist of several earlier Connell short stories, most notably "Arcturus," "Otto and the Magi," and "Saint Augustine's Pigeon," and *The Connoisseur* actually has the texture and development of a short story more than of a novel.

From his initial whimsical purchase of the figurine in a Taos gift shop, Muhlbach moves steadily, if somewhat dreamily, into two worlds, one of the ancient world of pre-Columbian artisanship, the other the modern world of fanciers, collectors, auctioneers, and dealers of art. As Muhlbach becomes more expert in the details of the ancient world, he also becomes more aware of the vagaries of the contemporary status of pre-Columbian objects. He learns from experience of the trade in fake artifacts and of the exquisite uncertainties in trying to determine whether a piece is fake or authentic, and, as he encounters others obsessed by this art, he sees and then shares in the peculiar intensity of its collectors and dealers. The reader learns right along with Muhlbach; a significant portion of the novel seems to consist of direct excerpts from studies of pre-Columbian art and comments that serve as minilectures from the string of connoisseurs whom Muhlbach encounters. His immersion into this lore raises a number of questions about the psychology of collecting and of obsession, about the ethics of removing national treasures from their native countries, and about the aesthetic difference between originals and imitations. Underlying all these issues is the contrast between past and present, between the fragile permanence of centuries-old artifacts and the impermanence of Muhlbach's own life, which threatens to leave a mark no more substantial than steps in the snow.

More difficult to isolate, but more important, are the questions raised by Muhlbach's obsession itself. His relationships with his children, with his woman friend, and with the world around him become completely eclipsed by his desire for pre-Columbian art. Late in the novel, he realizes that he is so gripped by this obsession that he can no longer distinguish reality, and he has to remind himself that his children "mean more than all the world's Olmec masks." Sleepwalking through the other aspects of his life and finding meaning only in his collecting, the connoisseur muses to himself: "I suppose I should be alarmed, but as a matter of fact I'm not. This is really rather pleasant. I want more."

DOUBLE HONEYMOON

The title of Connell's sixth novel, *Double Honeymoon*, is itself doubly ironic, as it is both the title of a pornographic film that counts in the book's plot and a caustic description of the contours of that plot. This is the story of a hopeless affair between Connell's most familiar protagonist, Karl Muhlbach, and a beautiful, tragically unstable twenty-year-old girl, Lambeth Brett. Bored with his life, which he compares to a "stale chopped liver sandwich," Muhlbach convinces himself that even a fleeting relationship with the exotic Lambeth is worth enduring "a reasonable amount of nonsense." Although he recognizes that Lambeth is as "unstable as a bead of mercury," and that his own rather staid life can never really change, Muhlbach grows more and more infatuated—if not exactly with Lambeth, with the idea of her youth and the mystery of her supreme indifference to the world around her. Constrained by traditions, "condemned to worry about consequences," Muhlbach realizes that Lambeth offers him—however remotely—a last chance to break the confining "threads of half a lifetime."

Of course, Muhlbach's obsession with Lambeth frees him from nothing, offering instead piece after piece of unavoidable evidence that any relationship with her can only underscore his dissatisfaction with his life. "You're more screwed up than I am," Lambeth tells him. Even after one of Lambeth's many former lovers shows Muhlbach a pornographic film in which she is one of the brides on a "double honeymoon," Muhlbach cannot free himself from his infatuation, although he recognizes all its irony. Art, in the guise of his old stamp collection and of a show of Japanese woodcuts, offers him some distraction, but only Lambeth's suicide allows him to blend back into the sameness of his life.

Because *Double Honeymoon*, like *The Connoisseur*, dispenses with quotation marks, the reader is often uncertain whether Muhlbach is talking or thinking, the result being a dreamlike quality of the narration that perfectly suits the dreamlike, sometimes nightmarish, relationship between Muhlbach and Lambeth. What makes this story so complicated is that Lambeth is as much victim as she is victimizer: Muhlbach does offer her a stability she needs even more desperately than he needs her unpredictability, and she is drawn to him just as surely as she acts in ways that must repel him. Her "likes" and "wows" make Muhlbach think that he may need an interpreter for talking with her, and their language differences only hint at the ultimately unbridgeable chasm between their lives. Protected by the very staidness he wants to escape, Muhlbach survives while Lambeth does not, partially confirming an adage he shared with her: "Life being what it is, one dreams of revenge."

THE ALCHYMIST'S JOURNAL

In *The Alchymist's Journal*, Connell draws on his extensive readings of earlier cultures to construct an examination of pre-Renaissance scientific views through the journal entries of seven fictional alchemists. Permeating the diaries is the sense of mystery and the occult that characterized social mores in the period immediately preceding the Renaissance. The book opens with Paracelsus, a noted medieval physician and alchemist, reflecting on the relationship of chemistry and medicine. His journal is followed by those of a novitiate, a skeptic, a physician, a historian, a revolutionary, and a philosopher.

As in Connell's other works, the narrative is fragmented, but the prose is much more inventive than is typical of his earlier novels. In considering the diligence of the alchemist, Paracelsus notes that "the mind proves adroit at generating monsters, since as we draw shapes on canvas or wood and reconstruct our similitudes with marble so does the mind formulate basilisks which act against us—contriving aspects and molds of grim apprehension." Like the alchemist mixing elements, Connell is adept at mingling his prose and poetic voices, as exemplified in the words of the revolutionary contemplating the seeds of rebellion: "Time unfurls, buried images out of joint. Souls mortgaged to grievous error. Ideals pass, titles follow. Priests withdraw, casting back morality. Ash begets ash. Truth legislated from existence. Gold thickens."

DEUS LO VOLT!

Connell's *Deus Lo Volt!* parallels the school of narrative writing classified as the documentary novel. Works in this genre mold their core stories from contemporary documents of specific eras. For his chronicle of the Crusades, Connell collected a kaleidoscope of historical fragments from records, journals, and memoirs of the pre-Renaissance period from Christian and Muslim writers. He then painstakingly correlated the splinters of information from the juxtaposed records of the Dark Ages into a story without fictional embellishments. Other writers—such as Paul Metcalf, Guy Davenport, and W. G. Sebald—have also explored how stories can be told based solely on historical facts.

Connell first experimented with this style of writing in his 1991 novel *The Alchymist's Journal*, which uses the voice of Paracelsus, an actual sixteenth century physician and alchemist; in that work, seven fictional alchemists follow Paracelsus's narrative to discuss scientific issues of the period. In *Deus Lo Volt!* Connell shifts to a single narrator, Jean de Joinville (1225-1317), a crusader and memoirist who followed King Louis of France to Egypt and back. Joinville serves as historian on this journey of survival through the turbulent times of the thirteenth and early fourteenth centuries. It is a world of Christian knights and kings, Muslim caliphs and sultans, savagery, innocence, and blind belief.

Connell opens the novel with Pope Urban II's call to arms with the battle cry *Deus lo volt!*—God wills it—which initiated the First Crusade in 1095. Then the narrator conveys the reader along history's torturous course to the crusaders' final defeat in 1250. Both sides in the conflict embraced the prevailing sentiment of religious fervor and lack of compassion. The brutality of the siege of Cairo, the march of the Innocents, the savagery used by both sides to hold on to what they saw as divinely decreed as theirs show this time as an age of contradictions and conundrums.

In *Deus Lo Volt!* Connell's literary archaeology exposes two centuries of constant warring among Christians, Jews, and Muslims. As Donovan Hohn has observed, in this work Connell "excavates and shifts several cubic tons of anthropological, scientific, and historical scholarship, rescuing and recombing the brightest shards he finds. . . . He scrutinizes human behavior and human history with such forensic intensity that he attains a kind of curatorial omniscience." Thousands of Christian knights and crusaders flocked to Jerusalem; sons followed fathers and grandfathers to invade the Muslim and Jewish worlds. They sustained the unshakable conviction that heresy must be uprooted, not with words but with the sword. The novel, however, does not answer the enduring questions that remain unanswered: Why did thousands of Christians flock to Jerusalem to die? Was it the promise of Arab land and wealth? Was it the clash of conflicting religious ideologies, with neither side willing to accept the other?

Connell's extensive research and his artistry in rendering the medieval language help to make this venture into the violent world of the Crusades compelling. His portrayal of the human spirit's determination to struggle on, endlessly striving, leaves the reader wondering if the modern age is really very different from that earlier time.

Brooks Landon; William Hoffman
Updated by Modrea Mitchell-Reichert

OTHER MAJOR WORKS

SHORT FICTION: *The Anatomy Lesson, and Other Stories*, 1957; *At the Crossroads: Stories*, 1965; *Saint Augustine's Pigeon: The Selected Stories of Evan S. Connell*, 1980; *The Collected Stories of Evan S. Connell*, 1995; *Lost in Uttar Pradesh: New and Selected Stories*, 2008.

POETRY: *Notes from a Bottle Found on the Beach at Carmel*, 1963; *Points for a Compass Rose*, 1973.

NONFICTION: *A Long Desire*, 1979; *The White Lantern*, 1980; *Son of the Morning Star: Custer and the Little Bighorn*, 1984; *The Aztec Treasure House: New and Selected Essays*, 2001; *Francisco Goya*, 2004.

BIBLIOGRAPHY

Blaisdell, Gus. "After Ground Zero: The Writings of Evan S. Connell, Jr." *New Mexico Quarterly* 36 (Summer, 1966): 181-207. Provides helpful and revealing insights into Connell's earlier works. Novels discussed include *Mrs. Bridge* and *The Diary of a Rapist*.

Brooke, Allen. "Introverts and Emigres." *New Criterion* 14 (October, 1995): 58-63. Discusses primarily Connell's short fiction, arguing that the author's best stories are those that feature conventional characters.

Connell, Evan S. "Evan S. Connell." Interview by Patricia Holt. *Publishers Weekly*, November 20, 1981. Connell speaks perceptively about his efforts and aims in his writing and offers some interesting sidelights on his critical and popular reception.

_____. "Evan S. Connell, Jr." Interview by Dan Tooker and Roger Hofheins. In *Fiction: Interviews with Northern California Writers*. New York: Harcourt Brace Jovanovich, 1976. Connell is articulate in presenting his views, especially on the themes and methods of his own writing. Connell is often cited by critics as the foremost of the Northern California writers, who created a literary movement that has had considerable impact on contemporary American fiction.

_____. "Notes from a Bottle Found on the Beach at Sausalito: An Interview with Evan S. Connell." Interview by Edward Myers. *Literary Review* 35 (Fall, 1991): 60-69. In this wide-ranging interview, Connell discusses his literary influences and his interest in alchemy, the early West, and pre-Columbian art.

Gilmore, Shawn. "The 'Double Exposure' of History in Evan S. Connell's *Mrs. Bridge* and *Mr. Bridge*." *Journal of American Studies* 42 (2008): 67-87. Examines how the two novels depict the racial and social geography of pre-World War II Kansas City and the alienation of postwar suburban life.

Hohn, Donovan. "Evan S. Connell." In *American Writers: A Collection of Literary Biographies, Supplement 14*, edited by Jay Parini. New York: Charles Scribner's Sons, 2003. Provides a solid overview of Connell's writing style as it has evolved and changed from his earlier to his later works.

Landon, Brooks. "On Evan Connell." *Iowa Review* 13 (Winter, 1982): 148-154. Praises Connell's work, in particular the author's evocation of daily life in *Mrs. Bridge*. Asserts that Connell's satire reveals the emptiness of the Bridges' lives with tact and sympathy.

JOSEPH CONRAD
Jósef Teodor Konrad Nałęcz Korzeniowski

Born: Near Berdyczów, Podolia, Poland (now
  Berdychiv, Ukraine); December 3, 1857
Died: Oswalds, Bishopsbourne, England; August 3,
  1924
Also known as: Jósef Teodor Konrad Nałęcz
  Korzeniowski

PRINCIPAL LONG FICTION

Almayer's Folly: A Story of an Eastern River,
  1895
An Outcast of the Islands, 1896
The Children of the Sea: A Tale of the Forecastle,
  1897 (republished as *The Nigger of the
  Narcissus: A Tale of the Sea*, 1898)
Heart of Darkness, 1899 (serial), 1902 (book)
Lord Jim, 1900
The Inheritors, 1901 (with Ford Madox Ford)
Romance, 1903 (with Ford)
Nostromo: A Tale of the Seaboard, 1904
The Secret Agent, 1907
The Nature of a Crime, 1909 (serial), 1924
  (book; with Ford)
Under Western Eyes, 1911
Chance, 1913
Victory: An Island Tale, 1915
The Shadow-Line, 1917
The Arrow of Gold, 1919
The Rescue, 1920
The Rover, 1923
Suspense, 1925 (incomplete)

OTHER LITERARY FORMS

Joseph Conrad's many short stories were published
in seven collected editions. The majority of the stories
appeared earlier in magazine form, especially in *Blackwood's Magazine*, a periodical that Conrad referred to as
"Maga." Of the short stories, three—"Youth," "The Secret Sharer," and "An Outpost of Progress"—have been
widely anthologized and are generally recognized as
classics of the genre. Two memoirs of Conrad's years at
sea, *The Mirror of the Sea* (1906) and *Some Reminis-*

cences (1912), which is also known as *A Personal Record*, are prime sources of background information on
Conrad's sea tales. Conrad wrote three plays: *The Secret
Agent* (pb. 1921), a four-act adaptation of his novel that
enjoyed a brief success on the London stage; and two
short plays, *Laughing Anne* (pb. 1923) and *One Day
More* (pr. 1905), which had no success. His oeuvre is
rounded out by two books of essays on widely ranging
topics, *Notes on Life and Letters* (1921) and *Last Essays*
(1926); a travel book, *Joseph Conrad's Diary of His
Journey Up the Valley of the Congo in 1890* (1926); and
the aborted novel *The Sisters*, left incomplete at his death
in 1924 but published in fragment form in 1928.

ACHIEVEMENTS

In the late twentieth century, Joseph Conrad enjoyed
an extraordinary renaissance in readership and in critical
attention. Readers and critics alike have come to recognize that although one of Conrad's last novels, *The
Rover*, was published in the early 1920's, he is the most
modern of writers in both theme and technique.

Conrad is, in fact, the architect of the modern psychological novel, with its emphasis on character and character analysis. For Conrad, people in plot situations, rather
than plot situations themselves, are the primary concern.
Indeed, Conrad once professed that he was incapable of
creating "an effective lie," meaning a plot "that would
sell and be admirable." This is something of an exaggeration, but the fact remains that Conrad's novels center on
the solitary hero who, either by chance or by choice, is
somehow alienated and set apart from his fellow human
beings. This theme of isolation and alienation dominates
Conrad's novels and spans his work from the early sea
tales to the political novels to what Conrad called his "romances."

Conrad's "loners" are manifest everywhere in his
work—Jim in *Lord Jim*, Kurtz in *Heart of Darkness*,
Razumov in *Under Western Eyes*. This emphasis on the
alienated and isolated figure had a considerable impact
on the direction of the novel in the twentieth century, and
Conrad's influence may be discerned in such disparate

writers as Stephen Crane, F. Scott Fitzgerald, and T. S. Eliot.

Conrad made another contribution in shaping the modern novel: He was the forerunner (although not the originator) of two techniques that have found much favor and wide employment in the novel. Conrad was among the first of the modern novelists to employ multiple narrators, or shifting points of view, as he does in *Heart of Darkness* and *Lord Jim*. This technique enabled Conrad to make the probing analyses of characters and their motivations that are the hallmarks both of his work and of the work of so many others to follow. The reader sees both Kurtz and Jim, for example, through several pairs of eyes, some sympathetic, some not, before both tales are turned over to Charlie Marlow, who does his best to sort out the conflicting testimonies and to give the reader objective and rounded views of both men.

The extensive use of the flashback in the modern novel and, indeed, in film, is another technique that Conrad pioneered. In Conrad's case, as is the case with all writers who employ the technique, the flashback creates suspense, but it also serves another and more important function in his work, enabling him to examine more thoroughly the minds and the motivations of his characters. Having presented the crisis or the moment of action or the point of decision, Conrad then goes back in time, in an almost leisurely fashion, and retraces step-by-step the psychological pattern that led to the crisis, to the action, or to the decision.

Finally, Conrad finds a place and a role among the moderns in still another way: He is one of the great Symbolists in English literature. Conrad's use of thoroughly unconventional symbols, related in some way to the metaphysical metaphors to be found in much modern poetry, has had an inestimable influence on the modern novel.

Biography

Joseph Conrad was born Jósef Teodor Konrad Nałęcz Korzeniowski on December 3, 1857, near the rural village of Berdyczów in Poland, under Russian domination. Conrad's mother, Ewa Bobrowski, came from an affluent and influential family of landowners who had made their peace, as best they could, with their Russian overlords. Conrad's father, Apollo Korzeniowski, was a would-be poet, a dedicated patriot, and a translator of William Shakespeare into Polish who found no peace in Russian Poland. The marriage of Apollo and Ewa was frowned upon by the Bobrowskis, who felt that Ewa had married beneath herself, and Ewa's brother, Tadeusz, a prominent lawyer and member of the landed gentry, seldom missed an opportunity to remind his nephew, Jósef, that he bore the tainted Nałęcz blood.

Apollo Korzeniowski devoted all his energies and, ultimately, his life to the Polish freedom movement. As a result of his political activities, he was labeled an enemy of the state and exiled to Vologda in northern Russia. The five-year-old Jósef and his mother followed Apollo into exile. Three years later, her health ruined by the fierce Russian winters, Ewa Korzeniowski died, and Apollo, equally weakened by the ordeal, succumbed four years after his wife. There is little doubt that Conrad's own lifelong precarious physical state had its genesis in these years in exile.

From these blighted early years, two convictions were impressed in Conrad's consciousness that surfaced in his work: a continuing hatred for all things Russian and for autocratic regimes, and a strong sense of man as victim, instilled by his father's fate, and of man's essential loneliness and isolation, instilled by his own orphanage at the age of twelve. The victimization of the innocent lies at the heart of Conrad's political novels, especially *Under Western Eyes* and *The Secret Agent*, and is a major theme in *Heart of Darkness*. The alienated figure, forced to cope as best he can alone, is the essential Conrad.

With the deaths of Apollo and Ewa Korzeniowski, Conrad came under the tutelage of his concerned but somewhat demanding maternal uncle, Tadeusz Bobrowski. Bobrowski, a man of many affairs and very positive ideas and ideals, sent his young ward to St. Anne's School in Kraków for a brief term and later provided Conrad with a tutor and companion in the hope of creating a proper Polish gentleman. These few years constituted the extent of Conrad's formal education. An avid reader from his early childhood, Conrad was largely self-educated, and the wide knowledge of English, French, and Russian literature apparent in his works (especially in his critical essays) was acquired through his own efforts.

Bobrowski's hopes and plans for Conrad's becoming an accepted member of the right circles in Polish society were not to be realized. Chafing under the regimen of his oversolicitous uncle and, perhaps, convinced that there was no place for Apollo Korzienowski's son in Russian Poland, Conrad finally persuaded his reluctant uncle that his future lay elsewhere: at sea, a dream with which Conrad had been obsessed since seeing the Adriatic during a walking tour of northern Italy in 1873.

In 1874, Conrad left Poland for the port city of Marseilles, France, and the seaman's life to which he would devote the next twenty years. He carried with him his uncle's begrudging blessing and, more important, considerable financial support. The break with his native land was to be more complete than Conrad may have realized at the time, since he returned to Poland on only three occasions during the remainder of his life.

Conrad's adventures and misadventures during his four years in and about Marseilles provided the material, many years later, for the almost lyrical memoir *The Mirror of the Sea* and the novel *The Arrow of Gold*, the latter of which has been the subject of much critical dispute. With his uncle's backing, Conrad acquired, during that time, part ownership of the bark *Tremolino*, which was then employed in smuggling arms for the Spanish Pretender, Don Carlos. It was a period of much intrigue, and Conrad appears to have been at the center, enjoying it hugely.

What is not clear about the Marseilles years, unless one accepts Conrad's highly fictionalized version of the events in *The Arrow of Gold*, is how his ventures at that time all came to a disastrous end. Conrad apparently invested a considerable sum of money in a quixotic mining venture. Moreover, if the Doña Rita of *The Arrow of Gold* did, in fact, exist as Conrad describes her in the novel, then a particularly painful and hopeless love affair complicated Conrad's desperate financial straits. In any event, in February, 1878, Conrad attempted suicide and almost succeeded by placing a bullet in his chest, very near the heart.

Uncle Tadeusz made a hasty trip to Marseilles and restored some kind of order to Conrad's tangled affairs, and, on April 24, 1878, Conrad signed on to the British ship *Mavis*, bound from Marseilles to England. Conrad's career as a seaman—more particularly, as a British sea-

Joseph Conrad. (Library of Congress)

man—had begun. In the next twenty years, sailing on a variety of ships on passages that encompassed half the globe, Conrad accomplished an incredible feat. An alien from a landlocked country, bearing an unpronounceable foreign name and speaking English with a strong Slavic-French accent, Conrad rose from able seaman to master mariner in the British Merchant Service. He took great pride in being addressed as Captain Korzeniowski, just as he took great pride in his British citizenship, acquired in 1885.

Many of the ships on which Conrad sailed make appearances in his works. For example, there actually was a *Narcissus* on which Conrad sailed from Bombay to Dunkirk and a *Palestine* that became the *Judea* of "Youth"; the SS *Roi des Belges* was the counterpart of Marlow's "tinpot" steamboat in *Heart of Darkness*. In similar fashion, many of Conrad's characters are based on real-life prototypes, men whom Conrad had encountered or of whom he had heard while at sea. These include the characters Jim, MacWhirr, Almayer, Axel Heyst, and Tom Lingard; the real-life Charlie Marlow was born Jósef Korzeniowski.

In 1889, while between ships in London, Conrad began work on the strange tale of Kaspar Almayer. The work continued sporadically during Conrad's six-month tour in the Belgian Congo in 1890, a sojourn that later provided the material for his first major work, *Heart of Darkness*, and also succeeded in further undermining his already unstable health. In 1893, Conrad, then first mate of the ship *Torrens*, showed the nine completed chapters of *Almayer's Folly* to an English passenger and was encouraged to finish the book. *Almayer's Folly* was published in 1895, to be followed by *An Outcast of the Islands* in 1896, *The Nigger of the Narcissus* in 1897, *Heart of Darkness* (in serial form) in 1899, and *Lord Jim* in 1900.

Conrad enjoyed almost immediate critical acclaim, but despite the string of critical successes, he had only a modest public following. In fact, Conrad did not have a best seller until 1913, with *Chance*. Ironically, the reading public did not find Conrad until after he had written his best work. Given this limited popular success, Conrad did not feel secure enough to devote himself entirely to a writing career, and, for a six-year period, 1889 to 1895, he vacillated between the safety of a master's berth aboard ship and the uncertainty of his writing table. Even as late as 1898, when he was well established with a publisher and several reputable magazines were eager for his work, Conrad seriously considered returning to the sea.

With his marriage to Jessie George in 1894, Conrad had, in effect, returned from the sea and settled down to a life of hectic domesticity and long, agonizing hours of writing. Jessie, an unassuming, maternal woman, was the perfect mate for the often unpredictable, volatile, and ailing Conrad, and she cheerfully nursed him through his frequent attacks of malaria, gout, and deep depression. The marriage produced two sons, Borys and John, and lasted until Conrad's death.

Except for a brief trip to his native Poland in 1914, a few holidays on the Continent, and an even briefer trip to the United States in 1923, Conrad was resigned to the endless hours at his desk and content to live the life of an English gentleman in his adopted land. The Conrads were something of a nomadic family, however, moving frequently whenever Conrad tired of one of their rented dwellings. His last five years were spent at Oswalds, Bishopsbourne, near Canterbury.

After World War I, the acclaim and the recognition that he had so richly earned finally came to Conrad—an offer of knighthood (which he declined) and the friendship and the respect of many of the literary greats of the time. Essentially a very private man, Conrad, while never denying his Polish origins or renouncing his Roman Catholic faith, tried to live the quiet life of the quintessential English country squire. There was always, however, something of the foreigner about him—the monocle, the Continental-style greatcoat, the slightly Asian eyes, the click of the heels and the formal bow from the waist—which did not go unnoticed among his English friends and neighbors. Like so many of the characters in his novels, Conrad remained somehow apart and alienated from the mainstream of the life about him.

On August 3, 1924, Conrad succumbed to a massive heart attack at his home near Bishopsbourne. He is buried in the cemetery at Canterbury, in—according to the parish register of St. Thomas's Church—"that part reserved for Catholics." Even in death, Conrad, like so many of his fictional creations, found himself alone and apart.

ANALYSIS

Three themes are dominant among Joseph Conrad's sea tales, considered by most critics as his best work. The first of these themes is an unremitting sense of loyalty and duty to the ship; this quality is exemplified by Conrad's seamen who are successful in practicing their craft. In *The Mirror of the Sea*, Conrad summarizes this necessity for keeping faith, as he also does through Singleton, the exemplar of the faithful seaman in *The Nigger of the Narcissus*, in observing, "Ships are all right. It's the men in them." The note of fidelity is struck again in *A Personal Record*, when Conrad says of his years at sea, "I do not know whether I have been a good seaman, but I know I have been a very faithful one." Conversely, it is the men who break faith—Jim is the prime example—who fail and who are doomed to be set apart.

A second major theme in the sea tales, noted by virtually all of Conrad's critics, is the therapeutic value of work. To Conrad, the ancient adage "Idle hands are the devil's workshop" was not a cliché but a valid principle. The two most damning words in Conrad's lexicon are "undisciplined" and "lazy," and, again, it is the men whose hands and minds are without meaningful employment who get into difficulties, who fail, and who suffer the Conradian penalty for failure, alienation and isolation. Kurtz, in *Heart of Darkness*, is Conrad's chief exemplar here, but Jim's failure, too, partially results from the fact that he has very little to do in the way of work during the crucial passage aboard the *Patna*.

Finally, a sense of tradition, of one's place in the long continuum of men who have gone to sea, is a recurring theme in Conrad's sea tales. Marlow expresses this sense of tradition best when he speaks of the faithful seamen who band together and are bonded together in what he calls "the fellowship of the craft." The Jims, on the other hand, the captains who display cowardice, the seamen who panic under stress, all those who bring disgrace on the men who have kept faith and do keep faith, are dismissed from the fellowship and are set apart, isolated and alienated. Conrad, then, played a central role in setting the stage for the alienated, solitary figures and, ultimately, the rebels-at-arms who people the pages of the modern novel.

HEART OF DARKNESS

In *Heart of Darkness*, the first of Conrad's recognized masterpieces and one of the greatest novellas in the English language, a number of familiar Conradian themes and techniques coalesce: the author's detestation of autocratic regimes and their special manifestation, colonialism; the characteristic Conradian alien figure, isolated and apart; the therapeutic value of work; and the use of multiple points of view and of strikingly unconventional symbols.

Charlie Marlow, the ostensible narrator of the story, finds himself (as Conrad did on occasion during his sea career) without a ship and with few prospects. As a last resort, he signs on to command a river steamboat for a Belgian trading company, then seeking ivory in the Congo. In a curious way, Marlow's venture into the Congo represents a wish fulfillment, since, Marlow recalls, as a child he had placed his finger on a map of Af-

rica and said, "Someday, I will go there," "there" being the Congo. (This is "autobiography as fiction" again in that Conrad himself had once expressed such a desire and in exactly the terms Marlow employs.)

The mature Marlow, however, has few illusions about what he is undertaking. He characterizes his "command" as "a two-penny-half-penny river-steamboat with a penny whistle attached," and he is quite aware that he will be working for a company whose chief concern is turning a profit, and a large one at that. Moreover, the Company's success will come only at the expense of the innocent and helpless natives who have the misfortune of living in an area that has immense possibilities as a colony.

Marlow, like Conrad, abhors the concept of one people dominating another unless, as he says, the colonizing power is faithful to the "idea" that provides the sole rationale for colonialism—that is, the "idea" of actually bringing the benefits of civilization to the colonized. He believes that only in the British Crown Colonies is the "idea" being adhered to, and he has grave reservations about what he will find in the Congo. Despite these reservations, Marlow is hardly prepared for what awaits him.

Marlow finds in the Congo disorder bordering on lunacy, waste, intrigue, inefficiency, and the cruelest kind of exploitation. The "pilgrims of progress," as Marlow calls them, go about their aimless and pointless tasks while the steamboat he is to command sits idle in the river with a hole in its bottom. Mountains are leveled to no purpose, while equipment and supplies rust or rot in the African sun or never reach their destination. As long as the ivory flows from the heart of darkness, however, no one is overly concerned. Marlow is appalled by the hypocrisy of the situation. An entire continent is being ruthlessly ravaged and pillaged in the name of progress, when, in fact, the real motivation is sheer greed. Nor is there the slightest concern for the plight of the natives in the Company's employ. Marlow sees once proud and strong tribesmen, divorced from their natural surroundings and from all that is familiar to them, sickened and weakened, sitting passively in the shade waiting to die.

Herein is Marlow/Conrad's chief objection to colonialism. By taking people from their normal mode of life and thrusting upon them a culture that they neither want nor understand, colonialism places people in isolation and makes them aliens in their own land. The cannibals who serve as woodcutters for Marlow's steamboat have lost their muscle tone and belong back in the jungle practicing the peculiar rites that, however revolting by other standards, are natural for them. The native fireman on the steamboat—"an improved specimen," Marlow calls him—watches the water gauge on the boiler, lest the god inside become angry. He sits, his teeth filed, his head shaved in strange patterns, a voodoo charm tied to his arm, a piece of polished bone inserted through his lower lip. He represents the perfect victim of the white man's progress, and "he ought to have been clapping his hands and stamping his feet on the bank."

The evil that colonialism has wrought is not, however, confined to the natives. The whites who seek adventure or fortune in the Congo are equally uprooted from all that is natural for them, equally isolated and alienated. The doctor who gives Marlow a perfunctory examination in the Company's headquarters in Brussels asks apologetically for permission to measure Marlow's head while, at the same time, noting that the significant changes will occur "inside." To some degree or other, such changes have come to the whites whom Marlow encounters in Africa. The ship on which Marlow sails to the Congo passes a French gunboat firing aimlessly into the jungle as an object lesson to the natives. The accountant at the Central Station makes perfectly correct entries in his impeccable ledgers while just outside his window, in the grove of death, the mass of displaced natives is dying of fever and malnutrition. The Company's brick maker makes no bricks because there has been no straw for more than a year, but he remains placid and unconcerned.

Marlow's summation of what he has seen in the Congo is acerbic, withering in its emotional intensity, but it is also an accurate statement of Conrad's feelings toward this, the cruelest exercise of autocratic power. Marlow says, "It was just robbery with violence, aggravated murder on a great scale . . . and with no more moral purpose at the back of it than there is in burglars breaking into a safe." The voice is Charlie Marlow's, but the sentiments are Joseph Conrad's.

One man alone among the Company's disreputable, if not depraved, white traders appears to be an exception, a man who is faithful to the "idea" and is bringing prog-

ress and betterment to the natives in exchange for the ivory he gathers. Kurtz is by far the Company's most productive trader, and his future in Brussels seems assured. At the same time, Kurtz is both hated and feared by all the Europeans in the Company's employ. He is hated because of the unconventional (an ironic adjective) methods he has adopted, and he is feared because these methods are apparently working.

With the introduction of Kurtz into the tale, Conrad works by indirection. Neither Marlow nor the reader is allowed to see Kurtz immediately. Rather, one is exposed to Kurtz through many different viewpoints, and, in an effort to allow the reader to see Kurtz from all perspectives, Conrad brings forth other narrators to take over the story briefly: the accountant, the brick maker, the manager of the Central Station, the Russian. Penultimately, Marlow himself serves as narrator, and ultimately, Kurtz's fiancé, the Intended. In addition to the many shifting points of view that Conrad employs, it should be noted that the story, from beginning to end, is told by a dual narrator. Charlie Marlow speaks, but Marlow's unnamed crony, the fifth member of the group gathered on the fantail of the *Nellie*, is the actual narrator of the story, retelling the tale as he has heard it from Marlow. In some sense, then, it is difficult to say whether *Heart of Darkness* is Kurtz's story or Marlow's story or the anonymous narrator's story, since Marlow's tale has obviously had a significant impact on the silent listener.

Marlow is fascinated by Kurtz and what his informants tell him of Kurtz, and throughout the long journey upriver to the Inner Station, he is obsessed with meeting this remarkable man, but he is destined for a shocking disappointment. Kurtz is perhaps the extreme example among all the isolated and alienated figures to be found in Conrad's works. Philosophically and spiritually alienated from the "pilgrims of progress," he is also physically isolated. He is the only white man at the Inner Station, and, given the steamboat debacle, nothing has been heard from or of him for months. He has been alone too long, and the jungle has found him out. He is, in Marlow's words, "a hollow man" with great plans and hopes but totally lacking in the inner resources vital for survival in an alien environment. As a result, he has regressed completely to the primitive state; he has become a god to the natives, who worship him in the course of "unspeakable rites." He has taken a native woman as a consort, and the Russian trader who tried to befriend him has been relegated to fool and jester in Kurtz's jungle court. Kurtz exercises absolute power of life and death over the natives, and he punishes his enemies by placing their severed heads on poles about his hut as ornaments. The doctor in Brussels, Marlow recalls, was fearful of what physical and spiritual isolation might do to people's minds, and on Kurtz, the effect has been devastating. Kurtz is mentally unbalanced, but even worse, as Marlow says, "His soul was mad."

Marlow has confessed that he, too, has heard the appeal of "the fascination of the abomination," the strange sounds and voices emanating from the banks of the river as the steamboat makes its way to Kurtz. Meaningless and unintelligible as the sounds and voices are, they are also somehow familiar to Marlow and strike deep at some primordial instinct within him. Yet, while Kurtz is destroyed, Marlow survives, "luckily, luckily," as he observes. The difference between the two men is restraint, a recurrent term in the novel: With restraint, a man can survive in isolation. The cannibals on the steamboat have it, and Marlow is at a loss to explain the phenomenon. The manager at the Central Station also has it, largely the result of his unfailing good health, which permits him to serve, virtually unscathed, term after term in the darkness. The accountant has restraint by virtue of concentrating on his correct entries in his meticulous ledgers and, at the same time, by forfeiting his humanity and closing his mind to the chaos around him.

Chiefly, however, restraint (in Conrad's worldview) is a function of work, and Conrad's major statement of the redeeming nature of work comes in *Heart of Darkness*. Marlow confesses that, like most human beings, he does not like work per se. He does, however, respond to "what is in the work," and he recognizes its salutary effect, "the chance to find yourself." Indeed, the fact that Marlow has work to do in the Congo is his salvation. The steamboat must be salvaged; it must be raised from the bottom of the river. No supplies are available, and the boiler is in disrepair. Marlow needs rivets and sheeting to patch the gaping hole in the boat. The task seems hopeless, but Marlow attacks it enthusiastically, almost joyously, because his preoccupation with rescuing his "two-

penny, half-penny" command effectively shields him from "the fascination of the abomination." Later, during the trip upriver to the Inner Station, it is again the work of piloting the vulnerable steamboat around and through the myriad rocks and snags of the convoluted river and the intense concentration required for the work that shut Marlow's eyes and, more important, his mind to the dangers to psyche and spirit surrounding him. Marlow does not leave the Congo completely untouched; he has paid a price, both physically and mentally, for venturing into the darkness, but he does escape with his life and his sanity. As he later recognizes, he owes his escape to the steamboat, his "influential friend," as he calls it, and to the work it provided.

Symbols abound in *Heart of Darkness*, many of them conventional: the interplay of light and darkness throughout the novel, for example, carrying essentially the traditional symbolic meanings of the two terms, or the rusting and decaying equipment Marlow comes across at the Central Station, symbolizing the callous inefficiency of the Company's management. More striking, however, is Conrad's use of thoroughly unconventional symbols; dissimilar images are yoked together in a startling fashion, unique in Conrad's time. Kurtz's totally bald head, for example, is compared to a ball of ivory, and the comparison moves beyond metaphor to the realm of symbol, adumbrating the manner in which the lust for and preoccupation with ivory have turned flesh-and-blood human beings into cold, lifeless ivory figures. There are also the shrunken heads fixed as ornaments on the fence posts surrounding Kurtz's hut. These are Kurtz's "rebels," and, notably, all but one are facing inward, so that, even in death, they are compelled to worship their god. The one facing outward, however, is irretrievably damned and without hope of salvation.

LORD JIM

Similar in many ways to *Heart of Darkness*, *Lord Jim* is considered by many critics to be not only Conrad's greatest sea tale but also his greatest novel. *Lord Jim* is not a sea tale, however, in the purest sense, since most of the action of the novel takes place on land. *Lord Jim* is one of Conrad's psychological studies; Jim's mind and his motivations are searched and probed in meticulous detail in an effort to "see Jim clearly." In making this effort, Conrad employs two characteristic techniques:

shifting, multiple points of view and the extensive use of flashbacks.

The narrative begins conventionally with an unnamed third-person narrator who brings the reader to the point of Marlow's first encounter with Jim at the Board of Inquiry investigating the strange case of the pilgrim ship *Patna*. At this point, Marlow takes over the tale, recounting his meeting with Jim. Marlow's account, however, is filtered through the consciousness of the anonymous narrator, much as is the case in *Heart of Darkness*. The manipulation of the narrative voices in *Lord Jim* is much more complex, however, since Jim speaks through Marlow and Marlow through the ultimate narrator.

Again, as in *Heart of Darkness*, other narrators enter the scene briefly, and Marlow gives way to a series of speakers, each of whom is qualified to tell the reader something more about Jim. Montague Brierly, captain of the crack ship *Ossa*, is troubled by Jim's failure to meet the demands of "the fellowship of the craft" and is also troubled by his doubts about his own ability to meet those demands. The French lieutenant who boarded the abandoned *Patna* and brought it safely to port is a bit more sympathetic toward Jim's moment of cowardice but is also more rigid in his condemnation of Jim's loss of honor. At the opposite end of the scale, Chester, the preposterous seaman-at-large, dismisses Jim's canceled mate's certificate as nothing more than "a bit of ass's skin" and solicits Marlow's aid in involving Jim in Chester's lunatic scheme of extracting guano from an island that is totally inaccessible. In Chester's view, Jim is the right man for the job, since he is now good for nothing else. Through Chester as interim narrator, Marlow recognizes how desperate Jim's plight is and how equally desperate Jim is for his help.

Marlow does help by putting Jim in touch with Mr. Denver, the owner of a rice mill, and Jim thrives for a time, becoming, in essence, a surrogate son to his employer. The specter of the *Patna* affair overtakes Jim, however, in the form of the fated ship's second engineer, who comes to work at the rice mill. Through Denver, through Egström, who employs Jim briefly as a water clerk, and, finally, through the seedy Schomberg, proprietor of an equally seedy hotel in Bangkok, Marlow learns of Jim's gradual decline and his erratic flight from the *Patna* or, as Marlow puts it, his flight "from himself."

In an attempt to help Jim, Marlow turns to Stein, an extraordinary trader and shrewd judge of both butterflies and people. Stein's eminently "practical" solution is to send Jim to Patusan, virtually the ends of the earth, where the *Patna* has never been heard of and from where Jim need run no more. Marlow's visit to Patusan and to Jim is relayed, as is the bulk of the novel, through the unnamed listener among Marlow's small circle of friends gathered over their evening cigars, to whom Marlow has been addressing his tale. In the final chapters, Conrad's tour de force of narrative technique takes yet another twist. The disaster in Patusan is recounted through the medium of a lengthy letter that Marlow writes to the ultimate narrator, the narration thus coming full circle from third-person narrator, to Marlow, to a series of intermediate narrators, and finally returning to the speaking voice that began the tale.

Adding to the difficulties that Conrad's dizzying shift of narrators presents for the reader is his frequent use of time shifts in the narrative. Jim's long colloquy with Marlow in Marlow's room at the Malabar House, for example, takes the reader back in time to the events aboard the *Patna*, which occurred several months earlier. While observing the seemingly bored Brierly in the courtroom at the Board of Inquiry, Marlow abruptly moves ahead in time to Brierly's suicide, which follows a week after the end of the trial, and then ahead again some two years for the mate's detailed account of Brierly's methodical leap over the side of the *Ossa*. Marlow's letter, which Conrad employs to bring the novel to its close, represents yet another flashback. Examples of this movement back and forth in time in the novel could be multiplied.

Conrad's complex manipulation of his narrators and of the disjointed time sequence of the events of the novel have a single purpose: to give the reader a complete view of a psychologically complex figure. It is an effort, as Marlow insists several times, to "see Jim clearly." Yet, for all Conrad's (and Marlow's) efforts, Jim remains an enigma. Marlow, in fact, confesses at the end of his letter that Jim continues to be "inscrutable."

Two particular problems have plagued critics in coming to grips with Jim. Stein, on whom Marlow relies for enlightenment, pronounces Jim "a romantic," which Stein says is "very bad . . . and very good too." In attempting to resolve the problem of how a romantic may cope with reality, Stein uses the metaphor of a man falling into the sea (the overtones of Jim's leap from the *Patna* are obvious here). Stein continues, "The way is to the destructive element submit yourself, and with the exertions of your hands and feet in the water make the deep, deep sea keep you up." The trouble here is that Stein does not make clear whether it is Jim's dream of heroes and heroics that is the "destructive element" or whether it is the practical and mundane world in which he must endeavor to carry out this dream that is destructive. Does Jim immerse himself in the dream yet keep his head above "water" in the world of reality, or immerse himself in the world of reality and yet keep the dream alive directly above the surface? The critical controversy that Stein's cryptic advice has provoked continues.

Critics are also divided on the meaning of the end of the novel. When Jim presents himself to the old nakhoda, Doramin, and suffers the pistol shot that ends his life, is this the act of a man who has finally accepted that he is capable of failure and who "has mastered his destiny," or is it merely the desperate act of a man who has simply run out of options? The distinction may seem fine, since, in any case, Jim's gesture is a positive act, but it governs the reader's final judgment on whether Marlow is correct in accepting Jim as "one of us."

If Jim is not "one of us," he is clearly one of "them," them being the familiar Conradian figures, the isolated and alienated solitaries, and he is so both spiritually and physically. In abandoning the *Patna*, Jim has violated a cardinal principle of the seaman's code, placing his own safety above that of the pilgrims who have entrusted themselves to him. As Brierly puts it, "We are trusted," and he is unforgiving of Jim's dereliction, as is Marlow, although Marlow is willing to admit mitigating circumstances. To the seamen whom Jim encounters, who raise the specter of the *Patna*, Jim is a pariah who has broken the bond of "the fellowship of the craft." Jim himself is quite conscious of his alienation. When he sails aboard Marlow's ship from Bangkok, he takes no interest in the passage as a seaman would, but instead, in Marlow's words, skulks below deck, "as though he had become a stowaway."

Jim is also isolated physically. In a moving passage, Marlow speaks with great feeling of the seaman's ties with and affection for his native land, for home. Jim, however, can never go home; he has, in effect, no home, and his destiny lies everywhere and anywhere but in the village in Essex where he came into being.

On Patusan, Jim's physical isolation is complete. Except for the unspeakable Cornelius, he is the only white man for hundreds of miles. With the *Patna* safely behind him, as he supposes, Jim thrives in isolation, bringing order and security to the troubled land, and is called by the natives "Tuan Jim," "which is to say, Lord Jim." The years of unparalleled success take their toll. Jim is convinced that "nothing can touch me," and his egotism proves fatal when Gentleman Brown finds him out. Jim spends his last hours isolated, and he dies alone.

In addition to the alienated hero, another familiar Conradian motif may be observed in *Lord Jim*: Conrad's continuing insistence on the redeeming nature of work. Earlier in the novel, the unnamed narrator makes an attempt to sum up Jim, and it comes in the form of Jim's failure to accept or to appreciate the nature of the demands of life at sea. The narrator says that "the only reward [one may expect in the seafaring life] is in the perfect love of the work. This reward eluded him." Notably, throughout the novel, Jim is most vulnerable when he is without work. During his long stay in the hospital at Singapore, he is infected by the malaise of the seamen ashore who have been in the East too long and who have given up all thought of returning to the more demanding Home Service. Under this debilitating influence, Jim takes the fateful step of signing aboard the *Patna*. The ship's passage is deceptively uneventful and undemanding, and Jim has so little to do as mate that his "faculty of swift and forestalling vision," as Marlow calls it, is given free reign. Thus, in the emergency, Jim sees with his imagination rather than with his eyes. In like fashion, after the initial heroics on Patusan, the demands on Jim are minimal. In the absence of anything practical for Jim to do, except carry out his role as Tuan Jim, he is again vulnerable. Gentleman Brown is enabled, as a result, to catch Jim off guard, to find the "weak spot," "the place of decay," and Jim's idyllic but precarious world comes crashing down.

Conrad the Symbolist may also be observed in *Lord Jim*. Again, as in *Heart of Darkness*, some of the symbols are conventional. Jim's retreat from the *Patna*, for example, is always eastward toward the rising sun, and

Jim has bright blue eyes—the eyes, one assumes, of the romantic that darken in moments of stress—and wears immaculate white attire during his climactic confrontation with Gentleman Brown across the creek in Patusan.

As in *Heart of Darkness*, however, some of the symbols in *Lord Jim* are thoroughly original. In pronouncing Jim a "romantic," Stein is, in part, also pronouncing judgment on himself. Stein's romanticism, however, is mixed with a strong alloy of the practical, and he is prepared, as Jim is not, to act or to react immediately when action is called for, as is evident when he is ambushed and defends himself with skill and daring. Thus, Stein the romantic collects butterflies, while Stein the practical man collects beetles. The ring that Doramin gives his old "war-comrade" Stein as a talisman of the bond between white and native ultimately assumes symbolic import. Stein, in turn, gives the ring to Jim as his entrée to Patusan, and Jim wears it proudly during his brief days of glory. In the midst of the Gentleman Brown affair, Jim sends the ring to Doramin's son, Dain Waris, as a token of the white man's faith. In the closing scene of the novel, the ring, taken from the finger of the dead Dain Waris and placed in Doramin's lap, falls to the ground at Jim's feet. Jim glances down at it, and, as he raises his head, Doramin shoots Jim. The ring, then, paradoxically, is both a symbol of faith and of a breach of faith.

VICTORY

Victory, one of Conrad's later novels, was published in 1915. As such, it represents in one sense a Conrad who had mastered the techniques of the genre he had made his own, the novel, and in another sense a Conrad in decline as a creative artist. The early experimentation in narrative technique—the multiplicity of narrators and the complex, and sometimes confusing, manipulation of chronology—is behind Conrad. *Victory* is a linear narrative told by a single, first-person speaking voice without interruption of the forward chronological thrust of the tale. For the noncritical reader, this straightforward handling of his material on Conrad's part was a boon and may very well account for the fact that not until *Chance*, in 1913, and *Victory*, two years later, did Conrad enjoy genuine popular success.

At the same time, Conrad made forward strides in narrative technique and in command of the language in the fifteen years between *Lord Jim* and *Victory*. These

steps took him past clarity to simplicity. *Victory* is, perhaps, too straightforward a tale, freed of occasional confusion and of the varied and variable speaking voices but also lacking the richness and the range contributed by those same voices. Confined as Conrad is to one point of view, the extensive searching and probing of his characters, seen in Kurtz and Jim, are denied him. Axel Heyst is an interesting character, but he is only that. He is not, like Kurtz and Jim, a provocative, puzzling, and ultimately enigmatic figure.

The other characters in the novel are similarly unimpressive. Heyst finds the heroine, Alma, or Lena, a thoroughly intriguing young woman, but the reader is at a loss to understand the fascination, even the appeal, she seems to have for Heyst. Other than the commitment Heyst has made to Lena in rescuing her from the odious Schomberg, the tie between the two is tenuous. Many critics have noted that Conrad's women are generally lifeless, and it is true that, with the possible exception of Doña Rita in *The Arrow of Gold* (and here Conrad may have been writing from direct emotional involvement), women generally remained mysteries to him. As his greatest work attests, he was essentially a man's writer.

The three other principal characters in *Victory* are male, yet they, too, are wooden and artificial. Much has been made of "plain Mr. Jones," Ricardo, and Pedro's representing Conrad's most searching study of evil. In this construct, Jones stands for intellectual evil, Ricardo for moral (or amoral) evil, and Pedro for the evil of force. On the whole, however, they emerge as a singularly unimpressive trio of thugs. The lanky, emaciated Jones, called the "spectre," is indeed a ghostlike figure whose presence is observed but scarcely felt. Ricardo, with his bluster and swagger, is almost a comic character, and some of his lines are worthy of a nineteenth century melodrama. Pedro's chief function in the novel appears to be his availability to be bashed on the head and suffer multiple contusions. Compared to Gentleman Brown, "the show ruffian of the Australian coast" in *Lord Jim*, they are theatrical, and while they may do harm, the evil they represent pales beside that ascribed by Conrad to Brown, "akin to madness, derived from intense egoism, inflamed by resistance, tearing the soul to pieces and giving factitious vigor to the body."

Victory is a talky novel, with long passages devoted

to inconclusive conversations between Heyst and Lena. It is relevant here to contrast the lengthy exchange between Jim and Marlow in the Malabar House and the "getting to know one another" colloquies in which Heyst and Lena engage. In the former, every line is relevant and every word tells; in the latter, the emotional fencing between the two ultimately becomes tedious.

Gone, indeed, in *Victory* are the overblown passages of the earlier works, which can make even the most devout Conradian wince. Gone too, however, are the great passages, the moments of magic in which by the sheer power of words, Conrad moves, stirs, and thrills the reader. On the whole, the style in *Victory*, like the format of the novel itself, is straightforward; the prose is clear, but the interludes of splendor are sadly missing, and missed.

Whatever differences are to be found in the later works in Conrad's technical handling of the narrative and in his style, one constant remains. Heyst—like Kurtz, Jim, and so many of the figures who fill Conrad's pages—is an alien, isolated and apart, both spiritually and physically. He does differ somewhat from his counterparts, however, in that he stands alone by choice. Heyst, following the dying precept of his gifted but idealistic father—"Look-on—make no sound"—proposes to spend his life aloof and divorced from humankind; in this way, he believes, nothing can ever touch him. In general, except for his brief involvement with the unfortunate Morrison, Heyst manages to maintain his role of the amused and detached skeptic, living, as Conrad puts it, an "unattached, floating existence." He accommodates himself to all people but makes no commitments to anyone. Thus, chameleonlike, he is known under many guises; he is called, for example, "Enchanted Heyst" because of his expressed enchantment with the East and, on other occasions by would-be interpreters, "Hard Facts Heyst," "the Utopist," "the Baron," "the Spider," and "the Enemy." A final sobriquet, "the Hermit," is attached to Heyst when, with the collapse of the Tropical Belt Coal Company, he chooses to remain alone on the deserted island of Samburan. Heyst's physical isolation is now of a piece with his spiritual isolation.

The encounter with Lena changes this attitude. With his commitment to Lena, Heyst is no longer the detached observer of the world, and with the flight to Samburan,

his wanderings come to an end. Paradoxically, this commitment brings about both his spiritual salvation and his physical destruction. It is a redeemed Heyst, freed at last from the other enchantment of his life (the living presence of his dead father), who, at Lena's death, is able to assert, "Woe to the man whose heart has not learned while young to hope, to love—and to put its trust in life!" Thus, Heyst differs from Conrad's other alien spirits in that he "masters his destiny," as Jim could not and Kurtz, perhaps, would not.

In still another way, Heyst "masters his destiny" as Jim and Kurtz do not. Kurtz dies the victim of his own excesses and of the debilitating effect of the jungle; Jim places his life in the hands of Doramin. Heyst, however, governs his own fate and chooses to die with Lena, immolating himself in the purgative fire that he sets to destroy all traces of their brief idyll on Samburan, a fire that, ironically, blazes over the ruins of a defunct coal company.

Other echoes of the earlier Conrad may be seen in *Victory*. For example, albeit to a lesser degree than in *Lord Jim*, *Heart of Darkness*, *The Arrow of Gold*, and *Almayer's Folly*, *Victory* is another instance of Conrad's writing "autobiography as fiction." In the Author's Note to the novel, Conrad speaks of a real-life Heyst whom he remembers with affection but also with a sense of mystery. So too, Mr. Jones, Ricardo, and Pedro come from Conrad's store of memories, although he encountered each individually and not as the trio they compose in the book. The character of Lena is drawn from a brief encounter in a café in the south of France with a group of entertainers and with one girl in the company who particularly caught Conrad's eye. The settings of *Victory*, exotic names such as Malacca, Timor, and Sourabaya, were, of course, as familiar to the seagoing Conrad as the streets of London, and there is no reason to doubt that somewhere in the tropics, the fictional Samburan has its counterpart.

Finally, in *Victory*, Conrad the Symbolist may again be seen. Noticeably, however, in this later novel, just as Conrad's narrative technique and his style have become simplified and his ability to create vivid characters has declined, the symbols employed lack the freshness and the depth of those of the earlier novels. Conrad makes much of the portrait of the elder Heyst that dominates the sparse living room on Samburan, just as the subject of the portrait has dominated Heyst's existence. In fact, Conrad makes too much of the portrait as a symbol, calling attention to it again and again until the reader can virtually predict that each time Heyst enters the room, the portrait will be brought to his and to the reader's attention. As a symbol, then, the portrait is overdone, overt, and obvious. Similarly, the darkening storm that threatens Samburan as the events of the novel reach their climax is a bit heavy-handed and hardly worthy of Conrad at his best.

Even so, there is a brief moment of the true Conrad shortly before the climactic violence that brings about both Heyst's redemption and destruction. Conrad writes: "The thunder growled distantly with angry modulations of its tremendous voice, while the world outside shuddered incessantly around the dead stillness of the room where the framed profile of Heyst's father looked severely into space." Here the two symbols coalesce in a telling and effective manner. Regrettably, telling and effective instances such as this are rare in *Victory*. Conrad's work as a whole, however, with its stylistic and narrative innovations, testifies to the quality of his contribution to twentieth century literature.

C. F. Burgess

OTHER MAJOR WORKS

SHORT FICTION: *Tales of Unrest*, 1898; *Youth: A Narrative, and Two Other Stories*, 1902; *Typhoon, and Other Stories*, 1903; *A Set of Six*, 1908; *'Twixt Land and Sea, Tales*, 1912; *Within the Tides*, 1915; *Tales of Hearsay*, 1925; *The Sisters*, 1928; *The Complete Short Stories of Joseph Conrad*, 1933.

PLAYS: *One Day More: A Play in One Act*, pr. 1905; *The Secret Agent: A Drama in Four Acts*, pb. 1921; *Laughing Anne: A Play*, pb. 1923.

NONFICTION: *The Mirror of the Sea*, 1906; *Some Reminiscences*, 1912 (also known as *A Personal Record*); *Notes on Life and Letters*, 1921; *Joseph Conrad's Diary of His Journey Up the Valley of the Congo in 1890*, 1926; *Last Essays*, 1926; *Joseph Conrad: Life and Letters*, 1927 (Gérard Jean-Aubry, editor); *Joseph Conrad's Letters to His Wife*, 1927; *Conrad to a Friend*, 1928 (Richard Curle, editor); *Letters from Joseph Conrad, 1895-1924*, 1928 (Edward Garnett, editor); *Let-*

tres françaises de Joseph Conrad, 1929 (Jean-Aubry, editor); *Letters of Joseph Conrad to Marguerite Doradowska*, 1940 (John A. Gee and Paul J. Sturm, editors); *The Collected Letters of Joseph Conrad*, 1983-2005 (7 volumes; Frederick R. Karl and Laurence Davies, editors).

BIBLIOGRAPHY

Davis, Laura L., ed. *Conrad's Century: The Past and Future Splendour*. New York: Columbia University Press, 1998. Collection of essays provides context for Conrad's work as it examines the author's life and his times. Includes bibliographical references and index.

Gordon, John Dozier. *Joseph Conrad: The Making of a Novelist*. Cambridge, Mass.: Harvard University Press, 1940. Classic work of Conrad scholarship presents excellent discussion of the author's early novels. This volume was especially important in the revival of interest in Conrad's work in the 1940's and 1950's.

Hawthorn, Jeremy. *Sexuality and the Erotic in the Fiction of Joseph Conrad*. New York: Continuum, 2007. Although Conrad's works are usually thought to be lacking in sexuality, this book opens his writing up to new interpretations by citing passages that support erotic interpretations.

Jordan, Elaine, ed. *Joseph Conrad*. New York: St. Martin's Press, 1996. Excellent introductory study of Conrad focuses on three novels: *Heart of Darkness*, *Nostromo*, and *The Secret Agent*. Discusses the works from postcolonial feminist, Marxist, and other perspectives.

Kaplan, Carola M., Peter Mallios, and Andrea White, eds. *Conrad in the Twenty-first Century: Contemporary Approaches and Perspectives*. New York: Routledge, 2005. Collection of essays examines Conrad's depictions of postcolonialism, empire, imperialism, and modernism. Section 1 contains four essays that discuss *Heart of Darkness*, while other essays focus on *The Secret Agent*, *Nostromo*, *Under Western Eyes*, and other novels.

Karl, Frederick R. *Joseph Conrad: The Three Lives*. New York: Farrar, Straus and Giroux, 1979. This book is, and will likely remain, the definitive Conrad biography, elucidating as it does Conrad's life in Poland, on the seas, and in England. The well-documented study is also replete with generously thorough analyses of Conrad's major works as well as of his artistic development and political orientation.

_____. *A Reader's Guide to Joseph Conrad*. Rev. ed. Syracuse, N.Y.: Syracuse University Press, 1997. Useful handbook for students provides in-depth analysis of Conrad's work. Includes bibliographical references and an index.

Lothe, Jakob, Jeremy Hawthorn, and James Phelan, eds. *Joseph Conrad: Voice, Sequence, History, Genre*. Columbus: Ohio State University Press, 2008. Collection of essays examines Conrad's use of narrative in his fiction and nonfiction, focusing on the four issues listed in the subtitle. Provides several perspectives on *Heart of Darkness* and *Lord Jim*.

Meyers, Jeffrey. *Joseph Conrad: A Biography*. New York: Charles Scribner's Sons, 1991. Briskly moving, no-nonsense biography surveys the key points and themes of Conrad's major works. Very good at placing Conrad within the social and intellectual milieu of his day and offering good insights from other literary figures, such as Ford Madox Ford, who significantly influenced Conrad's literary career.

Najder, Zdzislaw. *Joseph Conrad: A Chronicle*. Translated by Halina Carroll-Najder. Rev. ed. New York: Cambridge University Press, 2007. Thorough and sympathetic biography stresses the influence of Conrad's Polish heritage on his personality and art. Draws many telling and intriguing parallels between Conrad's life and his writing.

Peters, John G. *Conrad and Impressionism*. New York: Cambridge University Press, 2001. Examines the influence of impressionism on Conrad's narrative style and other literary techniques as well as on his philosophy and political opinions. Includes a valuable bibliography.

Stape, J. H., ed. *The Cambridge Companion to Joseph Conrad*. New York: Cambridge University Press, 1996. Collection of essays addresses most of Conrad's major works, including analysis of *Lord Jim*, *Nostromo*, and *Under Western Eyes*. Other topics covered include the Conradian narrative, Conrad and imperialism, Conrad and modernism, and Conrad's literary influence.

Swisher, Clarice, ed. *Readings on Joseph Conrad*. San Diego, Calif.: Greenhaven Press, 1998. Collection features essays on Conrad's works by notable authors such as J. B. Priestley, Robert Penn Warren, and Richard Adams.

PAT CONROY

Born: Atlanta, Georgia; October 26, 1945
Also known as: Donald Patrick Conroy

PRINCIPAL LONG FICTION

The Great Santini, 1976
The Lords of Discipline, 1980
The Prince of Tides, 1986
Beach Music, 1995

OTHER LITERARY FORMS

Pat Conroy is known principally for his novels. His earliest published work, *The Boo*, is a collection of sketches about one of his college teachers; it was self-published in 1970. Two nonfiction books, *The Water Is Wide* (1972) and *My Losing Season* (2002), are autobiographical. He is also coauthor, with Suzanne Williamson Pollak, of *The Pat Conroy Cookbook: Recipes of My Life* (2004). His interest in regional cuisines of the American South is evidenced by his contributing introductory material for several cookbooks by southern chefs. Others who have included his introductory remarks in their works. Conroy cowrote the Oscar-nominated screenplay for the film *The Prince of Tides* (1991), which is based on his 1986 novel.

ACHIEVEMENTS

Pat Conroy's novels have all been best sellers, and he is part of a group of writers contributing a distinctly southern sensibility to popular novels of the late twentieth century. He is a major part of the post-Civil Rights movement generation of writers who write about their conflicted feelings toward the South. He speaks with honesty about both the bad and the good in the region. Most of his literary prizes and awards have recognized his excellence as a southern artist. These awards include the Georgia Governor's Award for Arts; the Lillian Smith Award for Fiction, given by the Southern Regional Council; the Thomas Cooper Society Library Award from the University of South Carolina; and the South Carolina Governor's Award in the Humanities for distinguished achievement. Additionally, Conroy was the first recipient of the Stanley W. Lindberg Award, given by the Georgia Center for the Book, and he won the Thomas Wolfe Prize from the University of North Carolina at Chapel Hill.

Conroy is also known for his contributions to the ongoing struggle for racial equality, and he was awarded the Georgia Commission on the Holocaust Humanitarian Award in 1996. Most of his major novels have been made into films, and in 1991, he was nominated, along with Becky Johnston, for Best Adapted Screenplay by the Academy of Motion Picture Arts and Sciences for the film *The Prince of Tides*.

BIOGRAPHY

Pat Conroy was born Donald Patrick Conroy in Atlanta, Georgia, in 1945. His father, Donald Conroy, was a U.S. Marine Corps fighter pilot, so Conroy lived in many places around the United States as a child. The details of Conroy's life are well known from his repeated autobiographical uses of them in his novels, particularly *The Great Santini* and *The Lords of Discipline*. His father, though an outstanding pilot and officer who served with distinction in three wars, was extremely volatile. His mother, Frances "Peg" Peck of Atlanta, is credited by Conroy as a source of literary inspiration. Unfortunately, she did little to protect the young Conroy and his six younger siblings from the physical and emotional abuse of their father. Apparently, she played an active part in hiding this cruelty from those outside the immedi-

ate family. The concurrent difficulties of constantly moving and dealing with his terrifying home life led Conroy to develop mental and emotional problems that are detailed in his books; his experiences growing up also contributed to his two divorces and several emotional breakdowns.

Conroy graduated from Beaufort High School in 1963 and attended The Citadel in Charleston, South Carolina, on a basketball scholarship. His love-hate relationship with this college is explored in *The Lords of Discipline* and also in *My Losing Season*, which follows his final year as a Citadel athlete. While there, he began writing his first book, *The Boo*, a tribute to Lieutenant Colonel Thomas Nugent Courvoisie. The book was self-published in 1970 and reissued when Conroy became a well-known writer. Upon graduation from college, Conroy did not seek a military commission, but worked as a teacher. His experience as an educator in a segregated and racist area of South Carolina contributed to his great concern with issues of racial justice.

Conroy has stated many times that his writing is an effort to deal with his unhappy childhood, and the pervasive presence in his books of violent fathers and miserable children bears this out. His mining of the personal lives of his troubled siblings for his novels has caused a great deal of conflict and estrangement within his family. His harsh portrayal of his father in *The Lords of Discipline* ironically led to a reconciliation between father and son, as the elder Conroy changed his behavior after the book was published and became a more reasonable and tolerable individual.

Conroy has been married three times, first to Barbara Jones, whose two daughters he adopted after their father was killed in Vietnam; Conroy and Jones have a daughter, Megan, as well. Conroy's second wife, Lenore Gurewitz Fleischer, is the mother of his fourth daughter, Susannah. His third wife is the novelist Cassandra King. He has lived primarily in Fripp Island, South Carolina.

ANALYSIS

Pat Conroy's books have four key factors in common. The first and most significant factor is his tendency to use autobiographical material. All writers write from their experiences, but Conroy is more direct than many in reproducing his dysfunctional family story over and over in different guises, so that his works of long fiction can almost be viewed as a generational saga with differing character names. Conroy is also much more frank with his readers in admitting this autobiographical focus and discussing his real family with unflinching honesty.

The reliance on personal narrative creates the second of Conroy's common factors, the presence of dysfunctional families with hidden and painful secrets. Sometimes these secrets are fairly straightforward, such as physical and emotional abuse by fathers, and sometimes they are far more complicated, such as being raped by escaped convicts. In spite of this, mothers are usually positive figures in Conroy's work, though his portrayal of them grows more nuanced in his later books.

A third factor important to Conroy's novels is their setting in the American South. His major characters are all from the South or attached to the South in some way, and their subjective view of themselves as uniquely southern is critical to the novels. Conroy self-identifies as a southern writer, and he sees the American South as distinct from other regions in the United States. He maintains a modern sensibility, however, viewing this uniqueness as both positive and negative rather than as strictly sentimental, which was a common sensibility of earlier generations.

The fourth and final factor common to Conroy's work—a concern with racial justice and the deleterious effects of racism on society—grows out of this clear-eyed modern view of the American South. Whether dealing with racism against African Americans or prejudice against Jews, Conroy brings concerns with social equality to the fore in most of his novels. His work is usually positive about the ability to overcome racial bigotry, showing a belief that humans can emerge from the bigotry and change, but only through much difficult effort.

THE GREAT SANTINI

Conroy's first novel, *The Great Santini*, establishes the pattern for all his major works. The coming-of-age tale centers on the main character, Ben Meecham, and his fractious relationship with his Marine pilot father, Bull Meecham. Bull calls himself the Great Santini as a way to boast of his prowess as both a fighter pilot and the patriarch of the Meecham clan. Bull runs both his Marine squadron and his household with an iron fist and uses frequent beatings and constant emotional bombard-

ment to keep his wife and children in line. Ben, the eldest son, is the main target of his father's rage, as he fails to live up to what Bull thinks a "man" should be. Ben's mother, Lillian, is well aware of Bull's abuses but does nothing to stop him or remove Ben from his presence. The setting and characters of this novel align neatly with Conroy's own family and his senior year of high school in Beaufort, South Carolina.

The novel takes place during one year of Ben's life, as he and the family once again attempt to get accustomed to a new town, this time Ravenel, which is in the Deep South. Ben is a basketball player who uses his athletic skills and winning personality to make new friends. Because of his love/hate relationship with his father, Ben is always seeking surrogates in the form of important older males who advise him and treat him with more dignity and respect than his own father. Coach Spinks

Pat Conroy. (AP/Wide World Photos)

serves this role, as does Toomer Smalls, who becomes Ben's mentor even though he is African American.

Ben consistently fails to meet his father's expectations and alternates between resignation and despair. When he becomes eighteen years old, he is given a flight jacket by his father, signifying his entry into the rarefied masculine world.

Toomer is mocked by racist boys in town, and a confrontation with one of them leads to violence. Ben unsuccessfully tries to intervene and protect Toomer, despite his father's admonitions. Ironically, even though Ben hates his father, he tells him he tried to help Toomer because he felt it was something he (his father) would do in the same circumstances.

Bull is on a routine flight when an engine fire in his plane forces him to choose between ejecting from the plane over a populated area or staying on board to make sure the plane crashes in a remote location. He chooses the latter, even though he knows he will die. This decision shows that Bull does have heroic qualities, despite his mostly despicable character. Learning of his father's death, Ben admits that he once prayed his father would die. Despite his anger, Ben takes up the mantle of his dead father and becomes the new head of his family, driving them away to a new town in the early morning hours, just as Bull often did. Though his conflicted feelings are never resolved, he learns to live with the disjunction and move ahead with his life, having been changed by the trials and sorrows.

THE LORDS OF DISCIPLINE

Conroy's second novel finds the protagonist, Will McClean, attending South Carolina Military Institute in Charleston. (This book is based on Conroy's own experience as a cadet at The Citadel.) Will is a surrogate for Conroy himself, and he experiences the same revulsion at the treatment of plebes, or "knobs," at the institute. The novel follows Will's senior year, with extensive flashbacks to his entire college experience. He remembers life in his violent and fractious family, with a father he could never please and an enabling mother who bribes him to stay in school even though he hates it there. He finds particular pleasure and solace in the beauty around him, a pleasure that is an integral part of the South.

As in *The Great Santini*, Will seeks father surrogates.

At the institute he becomes especially close to Colonel Berrineau, known as the Bear to cadets. The Bear assumes the role of kindly father figure to Will and enlists his help in protecting the first African American cadet at the college, Tom Pearce. Will agrees, primarily because he will do anything Colonel Berrineau asks of him, but also because he feels that racial prejudice is wrong. As the year goes on he tries to protect both Pearce and himself from the Ten, a secretive group of cadets who vow to remove Pearce from the institute. Will becomes convinced that Berrineau is involved with the Ten, but eventually realizes he has been manipulated by one of his friends. He learns the machinations of the Ten were carried out in concert with the school administration. The Bear helps Will avoid expulsion on trumped-up charges, and he manages to graduate, while Pearce stays in the corps of cadets.

In this novel, the student body of the school functions as a sort of family for Will, and they hide dark secrets that are harmful to its members. Will is also very close to the St. Croix family of Charleston, the parents of one of his roommates, and he eventually realizes that this family also has something to hide. Just like Ben in *The Great Santini*, Will grows up and assumes the burdens of true manhood, with all the sorrow and disturbing knowledge they represent.

THE PRINCE OF TIDES

This novel is Conroy's best-selling and best-known, mainly because of the well-received film adaptation directed by Barbra Streisand. Like his other novels, *The Prince of Tides* takes place in a southern town—Colleton, South Carolina. The troubled family includes Henry and Lila Wingo and their children, Luke, Tom, and Savannah. The story alternates between episodes current at the time of its publication in 1986 and the childhoods of Tom Wingo, the main character, and his siblings. Henry Wingo is, like most of Conroy's fathers, explosive and violent, and the children live in constant fear of his rages. They band together to protect each other, but each is damaged emotionally and mentally by the abuse. When the story opens, Tom must go to New York to visit with Savannah's psychiatrist, because of Savannah's recent attempted suicide.

Tom's talks with Dr. Lowenstein cause him to fall in love with her, and they also reveal the ugly secrets of his family, including that Tom, Savannah, and Lila had been raped by some escaped convicts when Tom was a teenager. Luke had rescued his family, but Lila, the mother, insisted they never speak of the matter to their father or anyone else. This traumatic experience leads to Savannah's first suicide attempt. Tom also reveals that Luke was killed when he refused to leave his home in Colleton on orders of the federal government, who wanted the land to build a weapons plant. Tom used the skills he gained as a U.S. Navy SEAL to harass the government workers to stop the plant from being built, but he eventually put himself in a situation where he was shot and killed, rather than face imprisonment. Tom especially held Lila accountable for Luke's death, because she married the man who orchestrated the land sale and profited from the deal. Eventually, Tom leaves New York and reconciles with his wife, though he feels a lingering connection to Dr. Lowenstein.

The aspect of racism against African Americans is not especially significant in this novel, a departure from Conroy's usual themes. However, the other factors common to Conroy's work are all well-represented.

Vicki A. Sanders

OTHER MAJOR WORKS

NONFICTION: *The Boo*, 1970; *The Water Is Wide*, 1972; *My Losing Season*, 2002; *The Pat Conroy Cookbook: Recipes of My Life*, 2004 (with Suzanne Williamson Pollak).

SCREENPLAY: *The Prince of Tides*, 1991 (with Becky Johnston; based on his novel)

TELEPLAY: *Unconquered*, 1989 (based on Martin Chitwood's story)

BIBLIOGRAPHY

Burkholder, Robert E. "The Uses of Myth in Pat Conroy's *The Great Santini*." *Critique* 21, no. 1 (1979): 31-37. This analysis of *The Great Santini* discusses the ways in which Conroy's treatment of the father/son relationship fits into the traditional Oedipal construct. The author also examines the various mythologies that drive the characters and the resulting effects on their actions.

Burns, Landon C. *Pat Conroy: A Critical Companion*. Westport, Conn.: Greenwood Press, 1996. This volume gives detailed information on Conroy's life and work. It analyzes general themes and motifs common to his books, and also examines each novel through *Beach Music*, including their plots, thematic issues, styles, and characters.

Malphrus, P. Ellen. "*The Prince of Tides* as Archetypal Hero Quest." *Southern Literary Journal* 39, no. 2 (Spring, 2007): 100-118. This detailed examination of the novel advances the idea that the real hero of the book is not Tom Wingo but Luke Wingo. A step-by-step comparison of how Luke fits into the archetypal hero frame elucidated by Joseph Campbell is easy to follow even for those not familiar with Campbell.

Toolan, David. "The Unfinished Boy and His Pain: Rescuing the Young Hero with Pat Conroy." *Commonweal* 118, no. 4 (February, 1991): 127-131. This brief article discusses Conroy's lapsed Catholic faith and how images and ideas from Catholicism nevertheless inform his writing. The specifically Christian and Catholic elements of his major novels are analyzed in some detail.

JAMES FENIMORE COOPER

Born: Burlington, New Jersey; September 15, 1789
Died: Cooperstown, New York; September 14, 1851
Also known as: James Cooper

PRINCIPAL LONG FICTION

Precaution: A Novel, 1820
The Spy: A Tale of the Neutral Ground, 1821
The Pilot: A Tale of the Sea, 1823
The Pioneers: Or, The Sources of the Susquehanna, 1823
Lionel Lincoln: Or, The Leaguer of Boston, 1825
The Last of the Mohicans: A Narrative of 1757, 1826
The Prairie: A Tale, 1827
The Red Rover: A Tale, 1827
The Wept of Wish-Ton-Wish: A Tale, 1829
The Water-Witch: Or, The Skimmer of the Seas, 1830
The Bravo: A Tale, 1831
The Heidenmauer: Or, The Benedictines—A Tale of the Rhine, 1832
The Headsman: Or, The Abbaye des Vignerons, 1833
The Monikens, 1835
Home as Found, 1838
Homeward Bound: Or, The Chase, 1838
Mercedes of Castile: Or, The Voyage to Cathay, 1840
The Pathfinder: Or, The Inland Sea, 1840
The Deerslayer: Or, The First War-Path, a Tale, 1841
The Two Admirals: A Tale, 1842
The Wing-and-Wing: Or, Le Feu-Follet, 1842
Le Mouchoir: An Autobiographical Romance, 1843 (also known as *Autobiography of a Pocket Handkerchief*)
Wyandotté: Or, The Hutted Knoll, 1843
Afloat and Ashore: A Sea Tale, 1844
Miles Wallingford: Sequel to "Afloat and Ashore," 1844
The Chainbearer: Or, The Littlepage Manuscripts, 1845
Satanstoe: Or, The Littlepage Manuscripts, a Tale of the Colony, 1845
The Redskins: Or, Indian and Injin, Being the Conclusion of the Littlepage Manuscripts, 1846
The Crater: Or, Vulcan's Peak, a Tale of the Pacific, 1847
Jack Tier: Or, The Florida Reef, 1848
The Oak Openings: Or, The Bee Hunter, 1848
The Sea Lions: Or, The Lost Sealers, 1849
The Ways of the Hour, 1850

OTHER LITERARY FORMS

Although James Fenimore Cooper was primarily a novelist, he also tried his hand at short stories, biographies, and a play. Among these works, only the biographies are considered significant. He also wrote accounts of his European travels, history, and essays on politics and society. Among his political writings, *The American Democrat* (1838) retains its appeal as an analysis of contemporary political and social issues and as an expression of Cooper's mature political and social thought. His *The History of the Navy of the United States of America* (1839, two volumes) is still considered a definitive work. Cooper was an active correspondent. Many of his letters and journals have been published, but large quantities of material remain in the hands of private collectors.

ACHIEVEMENTS

Though he is best known as the author of the Leatherstocking Tales, James Fenimore Cooper has come to be recognized as America's first great social historian. The Leatherstocking Tales—*The Pioneers, The Last of the Mohicans, The Prairie, The Pathfinder*, and *The Deerslayer*—are those novels in which the frontier hunter and scout Natty Bumppo is a central character. Along with *The Spy* and *The Pilot*, two novels of the American Revolution, the Leatherstocking Tales are familiar to modern readers, and critics agree that these are Cooper's best novels. Less well known are the novels he began writing during his seven-year residence in Europe, his problem and society novels. In these books, he works out and expresses a complex social and political theory and a social history of America seen within the context of the major modern developments of European civilization. Because his problem and society novels often are marred by overstatement and repetition, they are rarely read for pleasure, but they remain, as Robert Spiller argues, among the most detailed and accurate pictures available of major aspects of American society and thought in the early nineteenth century.

Cooper achieved international reputation with *The Spy,* his second novel, which was translated into most European languages soon after its publication. With this work, he also invented a popular genre, the spy novel. He is credited with having invented the Western in the Leatherstocking Tales and the sea adventure with *The Pilot,* another popular success. His ability to tell tales of romance and adventure in convincingly and often beautifully described settings won for him a devoted readership and earned a title he came eventually to resent, "The American Scott." His reputation began to decline when he turned to concerned criticism of American society. Though his goal in criticism was always amelioration through the affirmation of basic principles, Cooper's aristocratic manner and his frequent opposition to popular ideas made him increasingly unpopular with the public. The political and social atmosphere was not favorable to his opinions, and his works routinely received scathing reviews as pretentious and aristocratic, also as politically motivated and self-serving. As Spiller argues, Cooper was too much a man of principle to use consciously his public position for personal ends. His suits against the press to establish a definition of libel, his exploration of the principles of democracy in his novels and essays, and his careful and objective research in his naval histories and biographies reveal a man who passionately sought truth and justice regardless of the effect on his popularity.

Though his popularity declined after 1833, Cooper continued writing with energy. In his thirty-year writing career, he wrote more than thirty novels, the naval history, several significant social works, and many other works as well. Howard Mumford Jones credits Cooper with early American developments of the international theme, the theme of the Puritan conscience, the family saga, the utopian and dystopian novel, and the series

novel. By general agreement, Cooper stands at the headwaters of the American tradition of fiction; he contributed significantly to the themes and forms of the American novel.

BIOGRAPHY

James Cooper was born in Burlington, New Jersey, on September 15, 1789, the twelfth of thirteen children of William and Elizabeth Cooper. He added Fenimore to his name in 1826 in memory of his mother's family. Elizabeth Fenimore was an heiress whose wealth contributed to William Cooper's success in buying and developing a large tract of land on which he founded Cooperstown, New York. Cooper's father, descended from English Quakers, expressed enlightened ideas about developing wilderness lands in his *A Guide in the Wilderness* (1810). William Cooper and Cooperstown became models for Judge Temple and Templeton in *The Pioneers.* The Coopers moved to Cooperstown in 1790, and Cooper grew up there as the son of the community's developer and benefactor, a gentleman who eventually became a judge and a Federalist congressman. Cooper's conservative Enlightenment views of the frontier, of American culture, and of democracy had their roots in his Cooperstown youth.

Like many sons of the wealthy gentry, Cooper had some difficulty deciding what to do with his life. In his third year at Yale, he was dismissed for misconduct. In 1806, he began a naval career that led to a commission in the U.S. Navy in 1808, and he served on Lake Ontario, scene of *The Pathfinder.* In 1809, his father died from a blow delivered from behind by a political opponent, and Cooper came into a large inheritance. In 1811, he married Susan Augusta DeLancey, of an old and respectable Tory family, and he resigned from the Navy. For eight years he lived the life of a country gentleman, eventually fathering seven children. By 1819, however, because of the financial failures and deaths of all his brothers, which left him responsible for some of their families, Cooper found himself in financial difficulty. Cooper began writing at this time, not with the hope of making money—there was no precedent for achieving a living as an author—but in response to a challenge from his wife to write a better novel than one he happened to be reading to her. Once he had begun, Cooper found in various ways the energy and motivation to make writing his career. Susan's support and the family's continued domestic tranquillity inspired Cooper's writing and protected him from what he came to see as an increasingly hostile public.

The success of *The Spy* and of his next four novels made him secure enough in 1826 to take his family to Europe, where he hoped to educate his children and to improve the foreign income from his books. While living in Paris and London and traveling at a leisurely pace through most of Europe, Cooper involved himself in French and Polish politics and published several works. Before his return to the United States in 1833, he met Sir Walter Scott, became intimate with Marie de La Fayette, aided the sculptor Horatio Greenough in beginning his career, and cultivated his lifelong friendship with Samuel Morse. This period of travel was another turning point in his life. In *Notions of the Americans* (1828), Cooper wrote an idealized defense of American democracy that offended both his intended audiences, the Americans and the English. When he went on to publish a series of novels set in Europe (1831-1833), Cooper provided American reviewers with more reasons to see him as an apostate. Upon his return to the United States, he tended to confirm this characterization by announcing his retirement as a novelist and publishing a group of travel books, satires, and finally a primer on republican democracy, *The American Democrat*. When he returned to writing novels with *Homeward Bound* and *Home as Found* in 1838, he indicated that he had found America much decayed on his return from Europe. The promises of a democratic republic he had expressed in *Notions of the Americans* were fading before the abuse of the Constitution by demagogues and the increasing tyranny of the majority. *The American Democrat* was, in part, a call to return to the original principles of the republic.

Having resettled in Cooperstown in 1833, Cooper soon found himself embroiled in controversies over land title and libel, controversies that the press used to foster the image of Cooper as a self-styled aristocrat. He is credited with establishing important legal precedents in the libel cases he won against editors such as Thurlow Weed and Horace Greeley. By 1843, Cooper's life had become more tranquil. He had settled down to the most productive period of his life, producing sixteen novels

James Fenimore Cooper. (Library of Congress)

between 1840 and 1851; among them are many marred by obtrusive discussions of political and social issues but also several that are considered American classics, such as *The Pathfinder* and *The Deerslayer*, the last two of the Leatherstocking Tales. His last five novels show evidence of increasing interest in religious ideas. Although Cooper had been active in religious institutions all his life, and although all his novels express Christian beliefs, he was not confirmed as an Episcopalian until the last year of his life. He died at Cooperstown on September 14, 1851.

ANALYSIS

James Fenimore Cooper was a historian of America. His novels span American history, dramatizing central events from Columbus's discovery (*Mercedes of Castile*) through the French and Indian Wars and the early settlement (the Leatherstocking Tales) to the Revolution (*The Spy* and *The Pilot*) and the contemporary events of the Littlepage and Miles Wallingford novels. In some of his European novels, he examines major intellectual developments, such as the Reformation, that he thought important to American history, and in many of his novels he reviews the whole of American history, attempting to complete his particular vision of America by inventing a tradition for the new nation. Modern criticism is divided concerning the meaning and nature of Cooper's tradition. Following the lead of D. H. Lawrence, a group of myth critics have concentrated on unconscious elements in Cooper's works, while Robert Spiller and a group of social and historical critics have concentrated more on Cooper's conscious opinions.

In his *Studies in Classic American Literature* (1923), Lawrence argues that Cooper's myth of America is centered in the friendship between Natty Bumppo and the American Indian Chingachgook, and in the order of composition of the Leatherstocking Tales. Of the friendship, Lawrence says, Cooper "dreamed a new human relationship deeper than the deeps of sex. Deeper than property, deeper than fatherhood, deeper than marriage, deeper than love. . . . This is the nucleus of a new society, the clue to a new epoch." Of the order of writing, Lawrence observes says that the novels "go backwards, from old age to golden youth. That is the true myth of America. She starts old, old and wrinkled in an old skin. And there is a gradual sloughing of the old skin, towards a new youth." These insightful statements have been elaborated by critics who have looked deeply into Cooper's works but have concentrated most of their attention on the Leatherstocking Tales to find in Cooper affinities with Herman Melville, Mark Twain, and others who seem to find it necessary, like Natty Bumppo, to remain apart from social institutions to preserve their integrity. Because these critics tend to focus on mythic elements in the tales, they may be better guides to American myth than to Cooper. Although Cooper contributed images and forms to what became myths in the hands of others, his own mind seems to have been occupied more with making American society than with escaping it.

Another more traditional mythic pattern pervades all of his works, including the Leatherstocking Tales. Several critics have called attention to a key passage in *The Last of the Mohicans* when Natty describes the waterfall where the scout and his party take refuge from hostile Native Americans. The pattern of a unified flow falling into disorder and rebellion only to be gathered back again by the hand of Providence into a new order not

only is descriptive of the plot of this novel but also suggests other levels of meaning that are reflected throughout Cooper's work, for it defines Cooper's essentially Christian and Enlightenment worldview, a view that he found expressed, though with too monarchical a flavor, in Alexander Pope's *An Essay on Man* (1733-1734).

In *Home as Found*, Cooper sees the same pattern in the development of frontier settlements. They begin with a pastoral stage in which people of all kinds cooperate freely and easily to make a new land support them. The second stage is anarchic, for when freed of the demanding laws of necessity, society begins to divide as interests consolidate into factions and as families struggle for power and position. Though it appears painful and disorderly, this phase is the natural, providential reordering process toward a mature society. In the final phase, established, mutually respecting, and interdependent classes make possible a high civilization.

In *The American Democrat*, Cooper often echoes Pope's *An Essay on Man* as he explains that human life in this world is a fall into disorder where the trials exceed the pleasures; this apparent disorder, however, is a merciful preparation for a higher life to come. Many of Cooper's novels reflect this pattern; characters leave or are snatched out of their reasonably ordered world to be educated in a dangerous and seemingly disordered one, only to be returned after an educational probation into a more familiarly ordered world, there to contribute to its improvement. This pattern of order, separation, and reintegration pervades Cooper's thought and gives form to his conscious dream of America. He came to see America as moving through the anarchic and purifying phase of the Revolution toward a new society that would allow the best that is in fallen humankind to be realized. This dream is expressed, in part, in *The Pioneers*.

THE PIONEERS

The Pioneers is Cooper's first great novel, the first he composed primarily to satisfy himself. The popular success of *The Spy* increased both his freedom and his confidence, encouraging him to turn to what proved to be his richest source of material, the frontier life of New York state. This first novel in the Leatherstocking series has a complex double organization that is an experimental response to what Robert Spiller sees as Cooper's main artistic problem, the adaptation of forms developed in aristocratic civilized Europe to his democratic frontier material. On one hand, *The Pioneers* describes daily life in the new village of Templeton on Otsego Lake and is ordered within a frame of seasonal change from Christmas, 1793, until the following autumn. Behind this organization, on the other hand, stands a hidden order that gradually reveals itself as the story unfolds; central to this plot is the transfer of title of the largest portion of land in the district from Judge Marmaduke Temple to Edward Oliver Effingham. These two structures interact to underline the providential inevitability and significance of this transfer.

The seasonal ordering of events brings out the nature of the community at Templeton at this particular point in its development. Templeton is shown to be suspended between two forms of order. Representing the old order are the seventy-year-old Natty Bumppo, the Leatherstocking, and his aged Indian friend, John Mohegan, whose actual name is Chingachgook. The forest is their home and their mediator with divine law. Natty, through his contact with Chingachgook and his life in the forest, has become the best man that such a life can produce. He combines true Christian principles with the skills and knowledge of the best of American Indian civilization. Natty and the Indian live an ideal kind of life, given the material circumstances of their environment, but that environment is changing. Otsego Lake is becoming settled and civilized. Chingachgook remains because he wishes to live where his ancestors once dwelt. Natty stays with his friend. Their presence becomes a source of conflict.

The new order is represented at first by Judge Temple, but the form of that order remains somewhat obscure until the revealing of motives and identities at the end of the novel. Temple's main function in the community is moral. He is important as the owner and developer of the land. He has brought settlers to the land, helped them through troubled times, and, largely at his own expense, built the public buildings and established the institutions of Templeton. During the transition to civilization, Temple is a center of order, organization, and—most important—restraint. In part through his efforts, the legislature is enacting laws to restrain the settlers in the state. Restraint on two kinds of behavior is necessary. On one hand, there are characters such as Billy Kirby, whose wasteful use of community resources stems primarily

from the inability to understand the needs of a settled country. These individuals live in the old forest world but without the old forest values. On the other hand, there are the settlers themselves: Some, such as Richard Jones and Hiram Doolittle, tend toward cupidity, while others, such as the community's poor, are so unaccustomed to having plenty that they waste it when they have it. These attitudes are shown in the famous scenes of pigeon shooting and lake fishing, and they are pointedly contrasted with the old values practiced by Natty and Chingachgook. The settlers need restraint; Judge Temple feels in himself the desire to overharvest the plentiful natural resources of Templeton and knows at first hand the importance of restraining laws that will force the settlers to live by an approximation of the divine law by which Natty lives.

The central conflict in the seasonal ordering of the novel is between Natty, who lives by the old law, the natural law of the forest that reflects the divine law, and the settlers, who are comparatively lawless. This conflict is complicated as the new restraining civil laws come into effect and the lawless members of the community exploit and abuse those laws in order to harass Natty. Hiram Doolittle, a justice of the peace, and Richard Jones, the sheriff, become convinced that Natty is secretly mining silver on Judge Temple's land. In reality, Natty is concealing the aged and senile original white owner of this land, Major Effingham, helping to care for the old man until his grandson, Oliver Effingham, is able to move him to better circumstances. Doolittle succeeds at maneuvering the law and its institutions so that Judge Temple must fine and jail Natty for resisting an officer of the law. Natty thus becomes a victim of the very laws designed to enforce his own highest values, underlining the weakness of human nature and illustrating the cyclical pattern of anarchy, order, and repression and abuse of the law. When Doolittle's machinations are revealed and Natty is freed, he announces his intent to move west into the wilderness that is his proper home.

The conflict between the old order and the new is resolved only in part by Natty's apparent capitulation and retreat into the wilderness. Before Natty leaves, he performs a central function in the land transfer plot, a function that infuses the values of the old order into the new order. The land to which Judge Temple holds title was given to Major Effingham by a council of the Delaware chiefs at the time of the French and Indian Wars. In recognition of his qualities as a faithful and brave warrior, Effingham was adopted into the tribe as a son of Chingachgook. In this exchange, the best of Native American civilization recognized its own qualities in a superior form in Effingham, a representative of the best of European Christian civilization. This method of transfer is crucial because it amounts to a gentleman's agreement ratified by family ties; the transfer is a voluntary expression of values and seems providentially ordained. The history of the land, as it passes from the Major to his son, illustrates these same values. The Major confidently gives his son control over his estates, knowing that his son will care for them as a gentleman should. Generosity and honor, rather than greed and violence, characterize these transfers.

For the transfer to be complete, the owners must be Americanized by means of the American Revolution. This process is a purification that brings to culmination in Oliver the traditions of American democracy and European and American Indian aristocracy. The Effinghams are a Tory family. Oliver's father and Judge Temple are brothers in honor, a civilized reflection of Natty and Chingachgook. Temple is an example of Americanized aristocracy. His aristocratic family had declined in the New World, but beginning with his father, they reemerged as democratic "aristocrats," what Cooper referred to as gentlemen. A gentleman is one whose superior talents are favored by education and comparative leisure to fit him as a moral leader of the community. The gentleman differs from the Old World aristocrat in that he has no hereditary title to political power. In the ideal republic, the gentleman is recognized for his attainments by the common people, who may be expected to choose freely their political leaders from among the gentry. The Effinghams have not undergone this Americanizing process. The process is portrayed in the novel in Oliver Effingham's resentful efforts to restore his grandfather to his accustomed way of life.

Oliver labors under the mistaken idea that Temple has usurped his family's land, but as the final revelations show, the Americanized gentleman has remained faithful, holding the land in trust for the Effinghams to take once they have become American. Oliver's deprivation, the military defeat of his family, and his working in disguise for Judge Temple are lessons in humility that reveal to him the moral equality between himself and the Temples. Without such an experience, he might well consider himself above the Judge's daughter, Elizabeth, unable to marry her and unable to bring together the two parts of the estate. The other main component of Oliver's transformation comes under the tutelage of Natty and Chingachgook, who attempt to impress on Oliver, as well as on Elizabeth, their obligations to the land and to its previous owners. Through this two-pronged education, the aristocrat becomes a gentleman and the breach caused by the American Revolution is healed. This healing is manifested most clearly in the marriage of Oliver and Elizabeth. The best of the Old World is recognized by the best of New World Indians and, by means of the Revolution, is purified of its antidemocratic prejudices; the aristocrat becomes a gentleman worthy to rule in America.

The transfer of title takes place within the context of inevitable seasonal change; its rhythm of tension and crisis reflects similar events within the seasons. The transition from the old order of Native American occupation to the new order of white democratic civilization is shown, despite local tensions and conflicts, to be providentially ordered when viewed from a sufficient distance. Within the seasons as well as in the human actions, the central theme of displacement underlines and elaborates the meaning of the overall movement.

The novel is filled with displaced persons. Remarkable Pettibone is displaced as mistress of the Temple mansion by Elizabeth. Natty and Chingachgook are displaced by white civilization. Oliver is displaced by the American Revolution, Le Quoi by the French Revolution. Finally, Judge Temple is displaced as the first power in the community. Within this thematic pattern, two general kinds of resolution occur. Oliver, Chingachgook, and Le Quoi are variously restored to their proper places, though Chingachgook must die in order to rejoin his tribe. Pettibone and Temple come to accept their displacement by their superiors. Natty is unique. His displacement seems destined for repetition until Providence finally civilizes the continent and no place is left that is really his home. For him, as for Chingachgook, only death seems to offer an end to displacement.

Natty's legacy must live on, however, in those gentlemen who combine "nature and refinement," and there is some hope that in a mature American society, Natty as well as good American Indians might find a home.

Critics tend to see Natty as an idealized epic hero who is too good for any society he encounters, but this is not quite true. In each of the books in which he appears, he acts as a conserver of essential values. This role is clearest when he teaches Elizabeth the ethics of fishing for one's food and when he saves her and Oliver from a fire on the mountain. His complaints about the "wasty ways" of civilization and about the laws that ought to be unnecessary are a part of this function. Although he fails to understand the weaknesses of civilized people and their need for the civil law, he still functions to further the best interests of civilization, not only by taming the wild but also by performing a role like that of the Old Testament prophets. He constantly calls people's attention back to the first principles of civilized life. In this respect, Natty is much like Cooper.

The Pioneers is a hopeful novel, for in it Cooper reveals a confidence in a providential ordering of history that will lead to the fulfillment of his ideas of a rational republic. This novel resolves the central anarchic displacements of the native inhabitants and of the traditional European ruling class by asserting that the American republic is the fruition of these two traditions. Though far from perfect, the American experiment seems, in this novel, to be destined for a unique success.

THE LAST OF THE MOHICANS

The Last of the Mohicans is the best known of the Leatherstocking Tales, probably because it combines Cooper's most interesting characters and the relatively fast-paced adventure of *The Spy* and *The Pilot*. Set in the French and Indian Wars, this novel presents Natty and Chingachgook in their prime. Chingachgook's son, Uncas, is the last of the Mohican chiefs, the last of the line from which the Delaware nation is said to trace their origins. Although the novel moves straightforwardly through two adventures, it brings into these adventures a number of suggestive thematic elements.

The two main adventures are quests, with filial piety as their motive. Major Duncan Heyward attempts to escort Cora and Alice Munro to their father, commander of Fort William Henry on Horican Lake (Lake George).

Led astray by Magua, an American Indian who seeks revenge against Munro, the party, which comes to include a comic psalmodist, David Gamut, encounters and enlists the help of Natty and his Indian companions. This quest is fully successful. Magua joins the Hurons who are leagued with the besieging French forces at William Henry and captures the original party, which is then rescued by Natty and his friends to be delivered safely to the doomed fort. This adventure is followed by an interlude at the fort in which Heyward obtains Munro's permission to court Alice and learns, to his own secret pain, that Cora has black blood. Also in this interlude, Munro learns he will get no support from nearby British troops and realizes that he must surrender his position. Montcalm allows him to remove his men and equipment from the fort before it is destroyed, but the discontented Native Americans, provoked by Magua, break the truce and massacre the retreating and exposed people for booty and scalps. Magua precipitates the next quest by capturing Alice and Cora and taking them, along with David Gamut, north toward Canada. The second quest is the rescue mission of Natty, Chingachgook, Uncas, Heyward, and Munro. This attempt is only partly successful, for both Cora and Uncas are killed.

Cooper heightens the interest of these quests in part through a double love plot. During the first movement, Duncan and Alice come to love each other and Uncas is attracted to Cora. Though thematically important, the first couple is not very interesting. Except for the slight misunderstanding with Munro that reveals the secret of Cora's ancestry, the barriers between Heyward and Alice are physical and temporal. More complicated and puzzling is the relationship between Cora and Uncas. Whereas Alice seems to spend most of the two quests calling on her father, weeping, and fainting, Cora shows a spirit and courage that make her an interesting character and that attract the admiration of Uncas. Magua is also interested in Cora, proposing in the first capture that if she will become his wife, he will cease his persecution of the rest of the family. Magua is primarily intent on revenge against Munro, but it seems clear that his interest in Cora as a woman grows until it may even supplant his revenge motive. Near the end of the novel, Natty offers himself in exchange for Cora, but even though Natty is a much more valuable prisoner, Magua prefers to keep

Cora. When the hunted Magua's last remaining comrade kills Cora, Magua turns on him. Though there is no indication that Magua's is more than a physical passion, he seems strongly attracted to Cora, perhaps in part because of her courageous refusal to fear or to submit to him.

Critics have made much of the relationship between Cora, Uncas, and Magua, suggesting that Cooper gives Cora black blood to "sanitize" her potential relationship with Uncas and the heavenly marriage between them suggested in the final funeral service of the Indians. Cora becomes an early example of "the tragic mulatto" who has no place in the world where racial purity is highly valued. Natty insistently declares that even though he has adopted American Indian ways, he is "a man without a cross"; his blood is pure white. On the other hand, the three-part pattern that seems to dominate Cooper's historical vision might imply a real fulfillment in the Indian funeral that is intended to bring Cora and Uncas together in the next life. This incident may be as close as Cooper came to a vision of a new America such as Lawrence hints at, in which even the races are drawn together into a new unity. The division between races is a symptom of a fallen and perverse world. Natty more than once asserts that there is one God over all and, perhaps, one afterlife for all.

The first meeting of Heyward's party with Natty's party in the forest has an allegorical quality that looks forward to the best of Nathaniel Hawthorne and begins the development of the theme of evil, which—in Cooper's vision—can enjoy only a temporary triumph. Lost in the forest, misled by the false guide, Magua, this party from civilization has entered a seemingly anarchic world in which they are babes "without the knowledge of men." This meeting introduces two major themes: the conception of the wilderness as a book one must know how to read if one is to survive, and the conception of Magua and his Hurons as devils who have tempted Heyward's party into this world in order to work their destruction. Though Magua is represented in Miltonic terms as Satan, he is not so much a rebel angel as he is a product of "the colonial wars of North America." Magua's home is the "neutral territory" that the rival forces must cross in order to fight each other; he desires revenge on Munro for an imprudent act, an act that symbolizes the whites' disturbance of Magua's way of life.

As Magua asserts, Munro provided the alcohol that unbalanced him, then whipped him for succumbing to that alcohol. Magua has most of the qualities of the good men: courage, cunning, the ability to organize harmoniously talent and authority, and highly developed skills at reading the book of nature. He differs from Natty and his Native American companions, however, in that he allows himself to be governed by the evil passion of revenge rather than by unselfish rationality. Of his kind, the unselfishly rational men must be constantly suspicious. Montcalm's failure to control his Indian forces demonstrates that only the most concerted efforts can prevent great evil. The novel's end shows that ultimately only divine Providence can fully right the inevitable wrongs of this world.

Within this thematic context, a crucial event is David's response to Natty's promise to avenge his death if the Hurons dare to kill him. David will have no vengeance, only Christian forgiveness. Natty acknowledges the truth and beauty of the idea, but it is clear that his struggle is on another level. Those he fights are devils, the dark side of himself, of Chingachgook and Cora and Uncas—in fact, of all the main characters—for Magua is doubled with each of the main characters at some point in the novel. Magua comes to represent the evil in each character. In this forest world, the dark self takes shape in passionate savages who must be exterminated absolutely, like those who first capture Heyward's party. To show them pity is to endanger oneself; to neglect killing them is to open one to further jeopardy, such as the "descent into hell" to rescue the captured maidens, which is one element of the second quest. Only under the rule of civil law in civilization does human evil become a forgivable weakness rather than a metaphysical absolute.

THE PRAIRIE

Critics have noted the improbable plot of *The Prairie* while acknowledging its powerful and moving episodes. Ishmael Bush, an opponent of land ownership and of the civil law, has led onto the vast western prairie his considerable family, including a wife, seven sons, and an unspecified number of daughters; his brother-in-law, Abiram White; a well-educated and distantly related orphan, Ellen Wade; Obed Battius, a comic naturalist and doctor; and Inez Middleton, whom Abiram has kidnapped for ransom. Bush's ostensible motive is to escape the various restraining regulations of civilization and, particularly, to set up his farm far from the irksome property law. It is never made clear why he has consented to join the kidnapping or how anyone expects to collect a ransom. This expedition draws in its wake Paul Hover, a secret suitor of Ellen, and a party of soldiers led by Duncan Uncas Middleton, who seeks to recover his bride, who was snatched between the ceremony and the consummation. On the prairie, they all meet the eighty-seven-year-old Natty, who has forsaken human-made clearings in order to avoid the sound of the axe and to die in a clearing made by God. The situation is complicated by the presence of feuding American Indian bands: the bad Indians, the Hurons of the plains, are the Sioux, led by the treacherous Mahtoree; the good Indians are the Pawnee, led by the faithful Hard Heart. With these melodramatic materials, Cooper forges a moving tale that he makes significant in part by bringing into play issues of law and morality.

During the captivities and escapes that advance the novel's action, the white characters divide into two alliances that are then associated with the two Native American tribes. Both alliances are patriarchal, but their characters are significantly different. Bush is the patriarch of physical power. He lives by the "natural law" that "might makes right," establishing his dominance over his family through physical strength and his conviction of his own power and rectitude. This alliance is beset by internal danger and contradiction. The second alliance is a patriarchy of wisdom and virtue. Bound together by the faith of its members, it grows under the leadership of Natty to include Paul, Duncan, Ellen, Inez, and Dr. Battius. The conflict between these two groups is prefigured in the first confrontation between Natty and Ishmael. Ishmael is represented in the opening of the novel as being out of place on the prairie, for he is a farmer who has left the best farmland to take the route of those who, "deluded by their wishes," are "seeking for the Eldorado of the West." In one of the many great tableaux of this novel, Ishmael's group first sees Natty as a gigantic shadow cast toward them by the setting sun. He is a revelation who suggests to them the supernatural. Bush has come to the prairie in the pride of moral self-sufficiency, but Natty is an example of humble dependence on the wisdom of God. In part, through Natty's ex-

ample, Ishmael finally leads his "wild brood" back to civilization at the novel's end.

Pride on the prairie, as in the wilderness of New York, leads to the subjection of reason to passion, to precipitate actions and death, whereas humility, though it may not save one from death, leads to the control of passion, to patience and probable survival. Natty teaches this lesson repeatedly to the group of which he becomes father and leader. Ishmael and the Sioux, "the Ishmaelites of the American deserts," learn the lesson through more bitter experience. The narrator implies that both Ishmael and Mahtoree, in attempting to be laws unto themselves, are playing God. In the central dialogue of the novel, Natty tells Dr. Battius, in terms that echo *Essay on Man*, that humankind's "gifts are not equal to his wishes . . . he would mount into the heavens with all his deformities about him if he only knew the road. . . . If his power is not equal to his will, it is because the wisdom of the Lord hath set bounds to his evil workings." Mahtoree, unrestrained by the traditional laws of his tribe, seeks through demagoguery to manipulate his people to effect his selfish desire for Inez. He and his band are destroyed in consequence. Bush's lesson comes when he discovers that Natty is not actually the murderer of Bush's eldest son, Asa.

The lesson Bush learns is always present to him. When his sons learn the well-kept secret that Ishmael is assisting Abiram in a kidnapping, they become indignant and rebellious. Cooper uses this conflict to demonstrate the precariousness of arbitrary power. Bush knows that he deserted his parents when he felt strong enough, and he is aware that only his strength keeps his sons with him in the present danger from American Indians. This knowledge of instability becomes complete when he learns that Abiram has returned the blow he received from Asa by shooting the boy in the back. It is difficult to determine how fully Bush understands this revelation. He feels his dilemma, for he admits that while he suspected Natty, he had no doubt that the murderer deserved execution, but when he learned of his brother-in-law's guilt, he became unsure. The wound to his family can hardly be cured by killing another of its members. For the first time in his life, Bush feels the waste and solitude of the wilderness. He turns to his wife and to her Bible for authority. He feels the extent to which Abiram has carried out Ishmael's own desire to punish his rebellious son, and thus he himself suffers as he carries out the execution of Abiram. This bitter lesson humbles him and sends him back to settled country and the restraints of civil law.

For Natty's informal family, there are gentler lessons. Paul and Duncan learn to be humble about their youthful strength, to realize their dependence on others, and to become better bridegrooms. Battius learns a little intellectual humility from Natty's practical knowledge of the wilderness. The center of Natty's teaching is that the legitimate use of power is for service rather than for self. This lesson arises out of the relationship between Natty and Hard Heart. Natty and the faithful Pawnee chief adopt each other when it appears the Sioux will kill Hard Heart. Natty later asserts that he became Hard Heart's father only to serve him, just as he becomes the figurative father of the more civilized fugitives in order to serve them. Once their relationship is established, it endures. Natty lives the last year of his life as a respected elder of the Pawnee and dies honored in their village. Having learned their lesson on the humble use of power in God's wilderness, Paul and Duncan carry their wisdom back to the high councils of the republic, where they become respected family men, property owners, and legislators. Like the Effinghams at Otsego Lake, the Hovers and the Middletons—the latter descending from the Heywards of *The Last of the Mohicans*—infuse the wisdom of the wilderness into the social order of America.

Cooper believed he had ended his Leatherstocking Tales when he completed *The Prairie*. Probably for this reason, he brought together his themes and characters and clarified the importance of Natty Bumppo to American civilization. Most critics have agreed that Cooper was drawn toward two ideals, the ability to exist in the wilderness and the ideal of a "natural aristocracy" of social and political order. It may be, however, that the first three of the Leatherstocking Tales are intended in part to create a history of America in which the wisdom of the wilderness is transferred to the social and political structure of the republic. Natty distrusts written tradition because "mankind twist and turn the rules of the Lord to suit their own wickedness when their devilish cunning has had too much time to trifle with his commands." Natty's experience provides a fresh revelation that re-

news the best of the Christian tradition and calls people back to basic Christian principles. That revelation consists essentially of a humble recognition of human limitations, justifying Cooper's vision of a republic where rulers are chosen for wisdom and faithfulness, where the tradition is not rigidly controlled by a hereditary elite but is constantly renewed by the unfettered ascendancy of the good and wise.

Throughout his career, Cooper worked within a general understanding of human history as a disordered phase of existence between two orders and a particular vision of the contemporary United States as a disordered phase between the old aristocratic order and the new order to be dominated by the American gentleman. In the first three of the Leatherstocking Tales, Cooper reveals a desire to naturalize the aristocratic tradition through exposure to the wilderness and its prophet, the man who reads God's word in the landscape. The result of this process would be a mature natural order that, though far from divine perfection, would promise as much happiness as is possible for fallen humankind. In his later novels, Cooper gives increasing attention to the ways in which American society failed to understand and to actualize this purified tradition. He looks back often, especially in *The Deerslayer*, to the purity and goodness of those basic values. Although they are rarely read today, novels such as *Satanstoe* and *The Oak Openings* among his later works are well worth reading, as is *The Bravo* from among his problem novels. In all these works, Cooper continues to express his faith in the possibility of a high American civilization.

Terry Heller

OTHER MAJOR WORKS

NONFICTION: *Notions of the Americans*, 1828; *A Letter to His Countrymen*, 1834; *Sketches of Switzerland*, 1836; *Gleanings in Europe: England*, 1837; *Gleanings in Europe: France*, 1837; *The American Democrat*, 1838; *Chronicles of Cooperstown*, 1838; *Gleanings in Europe: Italy*, 1838; *The History of the Navy of the United States of America*, 1839 (2 volumes); *Ned Meyers: Or, A Life Before the Mast*, 1843; *Lives of Distinguished American Naval Officers*, 1845; *New York*, 1864 (wr. 1851; unfinished; reprinted as *New York: Being an Introduction to an Unpublished Manuscript, by* the Author, Entitled *"The Towns of Manhattan,"* 1930); *The Letters and Journals of James Fenimore Cooper*, 1960-1968 (6 volumes; J. F. Beard, editor).

BIBLIOGRAPHY

Barker, Martin, and Roger Sabin. *The Lasting of the Mohicans: History of an American Myth*. Jackson: University Press of Mississippi, 1995. Discusses how Cooper's novel has acquired mythic status through numerous adaptations to film and television. Argues that each adaptation provides a new interpretation of the idea of the American frontier.

Clark, Robert, ed. *James Fenimore Cooper: New Critical Essays*. Totowa, N.J.: Barnes & Noble Books, 1985. Eight essays cover different aspects of Cooper's fiction, with most contributors focusing on specific novels. Includes detailed index.

Darnell, Donald. *James Fenimore Cooper: Novelist of Manners*. Newark: University of Delaware Press, 1993. Explores the themes of manners and customs in fifteen of Cooper's novels. Includes bibliographical references and index.

Fields, W., ed. *James Fenimore Cooper: A Collection of Critical Essays*. Boston: G. K. Hall, 1979. Presents both nineteenth century reviews of Cooper's novels and essays by modern critics. Valuable as a beginning point for students of Cooper's work.

Franklin, Wayne. *James Fenimore Cooper: The Early Years*. New Haven, Conn.: Yale University Press, 2007. Well-written, informative work—the first part of a planned two-volume biography—covers Cooper's life from birth until his move to Europe in 1826. Describes his personal life as well as the events surrounding the writing and publishing of *The Last of the Mohicans*.

_____. *The New World of James Fenimore Cooper*. Chicago: University of Chicago Press, 1982. Examines Cooper's attitude toward the frontier through a close reading of five of his novels—*The Pioneers*, *The Wept of Wish-Ton-Wish*, *Wyandotté*, *The Crater*, and *The Last of the Mohicans*. Maintains that for Cooper the wilderness begins as a place of hope and promise but ends as the source of tragedy.

Long, Robert Emmet. *James Fenimore Cooper*. New York: Continuum, 1990. General study of Cooper and his fiction touches on all the major works. Bibliography lists the most important studies of Cooper up to the 1990's.

McWilliams, John P. *"The Last of the Mohicans": Civil Savagery and Savage Civility*. New York: Twayne, 1995. Provides a general introduction to Cooper's most widely read novel as well as a particular approach to it. Divided into two sections: The first explores the literary and historical context of *The Last of the Mohicans*, and the second is devoted to analysis of the style of the novel as well as what Cooper was attempting to say about race, gender, history, and imperialism.

Peck, H. Daniel, ed. *New Essays on "The Last of the Mohicans."* New York: Cambridge University Press, 1992. Collection of essays begins with an introduction that provides information about the composition, publication, and contemporary reception of the novel as well as the evolution of critical opinion concerning it. Each of the five original essays that follow places the novel in a particular context, thus providing readers with an array of interesting perspectives from which to view Cooper's masterpiece.

Person, Leland S., ed. *A Historical Guide to James Fenimore Cooper*. New York: Oxford University Press, 2007. Collection of essays includes a brief biography by Wayne Franklin and a survey of Cooper scholarship and criticism. Among the works examined are the multivolume *Gleanings in Europe*, the four novels about the Revolutionary War, and the five Leatherstocking novels. Also features an illustrated chronology of both Cooper's life and important nineteenth century historical events.

Ringe, Donald A. *James Fenimore Cooper*. Updated ed. New York: Twayne, 1988. Provides a succinct and helpful introduction to Cooper's life and work. Includes complete chronology and index.

Tawil, Ezra F. *The Making of Racial Sentiment: Slavery and the Birth of the Frontier Romance*. New York: Cambridge University Press, 2006. Examines the frontier romance, a popular genre of nineteenth century American fiction, focusing on how novels by Cooper and Harriet Beecher Stowe helped to redefine the concept of race. Two chapters concentrate on Cooper's early fiction and *The Wept of Wish-Ton-Wish*.

ROBERT COOVER

Born: Charles City, Iowa; February 4, 1932
Also known as: Robert Lowell Coover

PRINCIPAL LONG FICTION

The Origin of the Brunists, 1966
The Universal Baseball Association, Inc.,
    J. Henry Waugh, Prop., 1968
Whatever Happened to Gloomy Gus of the
    Chicago Bears?, 1975 (expanded 1987)
The Public Burning, 1977
Hair o' the Chine, 1979 (novella/screenplay)
A Political Fable, 1980 (novella)
Spanking the Maid, 1981 (novella)
Gerald's Party, 1985
Pinocchio in Venice, 1991
Briar Rose, 1996 (novella)
John's Wife, 1996
Ghost Town, 1998
The Adventures of Lucky Pierre: Directors' Cut,
    2002
Stepmother, 2004 (novella; illustrated by Michael
    Kupperman)

OTHER LITERARY FORMS

In addition to his novels and novellas, Robert Coover has published numerous, usually experimental short fictions, most of which have been collected in *Pricksongs and Descants* (1969), *In Bed One Night, and Other Brief Encounters* (1983), *A Night at the Movies: Or, You Must Remember This* (1987) and *A Child Again* (2005). His reviews and essays, while few in number, are exceptional in quality; his studies of Samuel Beckett ("The Last Quixote," in *New American Review*, 1970) and Gabriel García Márquez ("The Master's Voice," in *New American Review*, 1977) are, in addition to being important critical works in their own right, useful for the light they shed on Coover's interests and intentions in his own fiction. His plays *The Kid* (pr., pb. 1972), *Love Scene* (pb. 1972), *Rip Awake* (pr. 1972), and *A Theological Position* (pb. 1972) have been successfully staged in Paris and Los Angeles, and the New York production of *The Kid* at the American Place Theatre in November, 1972,

won for its director, Jack Gelber, an Obie Award. Coover, who finds some relief from the fiction writer's necessary isolation in the communal aspect of theater and motion-picture production, has also written, directed, and produced one film, *On a Confrontation in Iowa City* (1969), and published other screenplays, including the novella/screenplay *The Hair o' the Chine* (written some twenty years before it was published in 1979). His poetry and one translation have appeared in various "little magazines."

ACHIEVEMENTS

Robert Coover's preeminent place among innovative contemporary writers has already been firmly established by academic critics. His various honors include the William Faulkner Award for best first novel (1966), a Rockefeller Foundation grant (1969), two Guggenheim Fellowships (1971, 1974), a citation in fiction from Brandeis University (1971), an Academy of Arts and Letters award (1975), and a National Book Award nomination for *The Public Burning*. In 2000, he received the Lannan Literary Award for Fiction.

Even before its publication by the Viking Press, *The Public Burning* became a *succès de scandale* when Alfred A. Knopf, which had originally contracted for the novel, refused to publish it. The ensuing literary gossip undoubtedly fueled sales (including copies of the book club edition), though not to the extent expected, and had the unfortunate result of bringing to both the book and its author the kind of notoriety neither deserved. The short-lived paperback editions of *The Public Burning* and *The Origin of the Brunists* (the latter novel had long been out of print) seemed to confirm that, except for *The Universal Baseball Association, Inc., J. Henry Waugh, Prop.*, which has attracted a diversified readership, Coover's works appeal to a fairly specialized audience.

BIOGRAPHY

Robert Lowell Coover was born in Charles City, Iowa, on February 4, 1932. His family later moved to Indiana and then to Herrin, Illinois, where his father, Grant Marion Coover, managed the town newspaper. (Both the newspaper and a local mining disaster figure prominently in Coover's first novel.) Small-town life as the son of a newspaperman gave Coover both an interest in journalism and a desire to travel. After beginning his college education at nearby Southern Illinois University (1949-1951), he transferred to Indiana University, where he received a B.A. in 1953, at which time he enlisted in the U.S. Naval Reserve, where he attained the rank of lieutenant. While serving in Europe, he met Marie del Pilar San-Mallafre, whom he married on June 13, 1959.

Coover's serious interest in fiction dates from the period immediately prior to his marriage, and his novel writing followed the favorable response to his first published story, "Blackdamp" (1961), which he reworked and expanded into *The Origin of the Brunists*. Unable to make a living as a fiction writer, Coover left Spain, his wife's native country, and began teaching in the United States; he held positions at Bard College (1966-1967),

Robert Coover. (National Archives)

the University of Iowa (1967-1969), Columbia University (1972), Princeton University (1972-1973), and Virginia Military Institute (1976), and has served as writer-in-residence at Wisconsin State University-Superior (1968) and Washington University (1969). Since 1979, he has taught at Brown University.

Coover's attitude toward the university is similar to his attitude toward his native country. Contending that residence abroad stirs the memory and frees the imagination, Coover has, since 1953, spent more than half of his time and done most of his writing in Guatemala, Spain, and England. At a time when much of American literature no longer seems distinctly American, Coover has written plays and fiction about some of his country's most characteristic myths, traits, events, and institutions, including baseball, millenarianism, the West, Dr. Seuss, the Rosenberg spy case, and Rip Van Winkle. He lives in Providence, Rhode Island, teaches at Brown University, and continues to explore the relations between narrative possibilities and American popular culture, including film, pornography, and detective fiction.

On June 21, 1992, Coover published an article in *The New York Times Book Review* titled "The End of Books." In this article, he discusses some of his observations and conclusions drawn from an experimental course he had been teaching at Brown on hypertext. Coover borrows his definition of hypertext from a computer populist named Ted Nelson, saying that hypertext is "writing done in the nonlinear or nonsequential space made possible by the computer. Moreover, unlike print text, hypertext provides multiple paths between text segments, now often called 'lexias'"—a term borrowed from the poststructuralist critic Roland Barthes. Coover's point seems to be that computers have made possible the deconstructionist's ideal of navigation through "networks of alternate routes" of textual meaning "as opposed to print's fixed unidirectional page-turning." This argument for the death of the printed novel is different from John Barth's earlier declaration of the novel's death in his 1963 essay "The Literature of Exhaustion," because, where Barth lamented that the possibilities of the novel as a genre had been exhausted, Coover's essay opines that computer technology has made the author-controlled, printed mode of textual transmission passé. Coover argues that fictions of the future will be created for the computer so that the hypertext reader will become a cowriter and fellow traveler with the creator of the text, coinvolved with the "mapping and remapping of textual (and visual, kinetic and aural) components, not all of which are provided by what used to be called the author." In a subsequent article titled "Hyperfiction: Novels for the Computer," he offers an examination of some early forays into the hypertext genre.

ANALYSIS

In Robert Coover's work, humanity is presented not as the center of the universe, the purpose of creation, but, instead, as the center of the fictions it itself creates to explain its existence. Only when people learn the crucial difference between these opposing viewpoints will they understand their possibilities and limitations; only then will they be free to use their imaginations to live life fully and in all its perplexing variety.

Coover strongly distrusts humankind's reasoning faculty and, more particularly, the Enlightenment concept of human progress. As he explains in the prologue to *Pricksongs and Descants*, Coover finds himself in the same position that Miguel de Cervantes was in four hundred years before: at the end of one literary tradition and the beginning of another, where the culture's traditional way of perceiving the world is breaking down. Reading the classic Greek poet Ovid, Coover came to understand that humanity's basic and continual struggle is to resist these and other changes, to struggle "against giving in to the inevitability of process." Accordingly, his stories depict a constantly shifting or metamorphosing world, one in which the sheer abundance of material implies the abundance of life and where the straight linear plot of conventional realistic fiction no longer suffices. In these works, the active imagination battles the deadening influence of various systems of thought—religious, political, literary—that are, as Larry McCaffery has pointed out, ideological rather than ontological in nature. Understanding this difference brings people to the edge of the abyss, from which they then recoil, seeking safety and comfort in various rituals and explanatory systems that are necessary and, to some degree, related to the artistic process itself. These rituals and systems, however, are dangerous insofar as people allow themselves to believe in them as other than self-generated imaginative constructs.

Coover urges his readers both to live in a more direct relationship to unmediated experience and to create fictions that will relieve them of their burden of anxiety in the indeterminate world. This balance of self-conscious fiction making and unselfconscious participation in life is, however, not always achieved by Coover's characters. Even the best of them, the pattern breakers, are often guilty of the same rigidity of the imagination that typifies their antagonists, the pattern keepers. Refusing to accept their own mortality or that of their systems and beliefs, they venture forth on a spurious quest after immortality and platonic absolutes. Their terror of the void is real enough, but because their responses to it are ludicrous and absurd, the terror is rendered comically, fears turning into pratfalls, as in the misadventures of the Chaplinesque "Charlie in the House of Rue." If, as Coover believes, existence does not have an ontological status, then life necessarily becomes not the serious business his characters make it but a kind of play, to which social historian Johan Huizinga, author of *Homo Ludens: A Study of the Play Element in Culture* (1938), is the appropriate guide.

Coover is a fiction writer who distrusts fiction, not because it is "exhausted," as Barth has claimed, but because he feels that writers' various fictions—not only their stories and novels but also their histories and religions—are always in danger of being confused with reality. He parodies myths, history, literary formulas, and elements of popular culture in an effort to expose their artifice. He imposes order on his fictions, both as structure and as subject, to undermine that order effectively, to prove its arbitrariness, and thus to lay bare the indeterminacy of the world. In place of the inadequate, narrowly conceived systems that some of his characters devise or even the more expansive but eventually imprisoning fantasies of others, Coover writes what one critic has called "cubist fictions," inviting readers' participation in works that are less products than processes, revelations of the instability and uncertainty of modern existence.

The parallels between Coover's fiction and process-oriented abstract expressionist art, modern physics, and postexistentialist philosophy mark Coover as a distinctly contemporary writer. His works are often discussed as leading examples of "metafiction," a formally experimental, highly reflexive literary mode that, as critic Robert Scholes has explained, "assimilates all the perspectives of criticism into the fiction itself." While many of Coover's shorter works are clearly metafictional in nature, in the novels and novellas formal inventiveness gives way to an interest in traditional narrative, in telling a good story. What results is a tension between contemporary and traditional narrative modes that is analogous to Coover's notion of the artist-audience relationship (dramatized in his story "The Hat Act"). In Coover's view, the fiction maker is at once an anarchist and a priest: "He's the one who tears apart the old story, speaks the unspeakable, makes the ground shake, then shuffles the pieces back together into a new story." Coover's power to disturb is clearly evident in reviews of his work. More important, however, is the fact that these relationships between Coover and his readers, artist and audience, innovation and tradition, bear a striking similarity to the plight of his characters.

The Origin of the Brunists

Coover's first novel, *The Origin of the Brunists*, is not "a vicious and dirty piece of writing," as one reviewer claimed; rather, it is a work in which Coover pays his dues (as he has said) to the naturalistic novel and exhaustively details the various ways in which people imaginatively respond to the randomness and variety of their world. Briefly stated, the story concerns a mining disaster that kills ninety-seven men, the formation of a millenarian cult around the sole survivor, Giovanni Bruno, and the reactions of the townspeople, especially Justin "Tiger" Miller, editor of the local newspaper, to the Brunists. An odd assortment of immigrant Italians, Protestant Fundamentalists, a composer of folk songs, a numerologist, and a Theosophist, the Brunists are drawn together by their desire to live meaningful lives in a comprehensible, cause-and-effect world, one in which they misinterpret random events as providential signs. Many of those who do not join the cult find a sense of purpose and a release from the frustrations (often sexual) of living in a small, dying town by forming the Common Sense Committee. By accepting their roles as generally passive participants in these groups, the Brunists and their opponents gain the social approval, the feeling of power and significance, and the sense of communal purpose that make their unimaginative lives bearable.

Miller suffers from the lack of purpose and sense of frustration that afflict the others—perhaps more so because he is able to articulate these feelings to a degree that they are not. This same consciousness, however, also frees Miller from delusions concerning the truth of the fictions they accept without question. Unlike the others, who read his headline "Miracle in West Condon" literally, Miller, the ironist, distinguishes between experience on one hand and history and journalism on the other; he knows that history and journalism are not unmediated, factual accounts but imaginative constructions. The Brunists commit themselves to their version of reality and as a result become trapped within it. Miller, who is vaguely troubled by his own lack of commitment, joins the cult only to meet Bruno's attractive sister, relieve his boredom, and work up material for his paper. He does not serve the Brunists in the way his namesake, the apologist Justin, did the early Christians, for Miller only pretends to be a believer. In fact, as the movement's chronicler, he creates the cult and its members the way a novelist creates story and characters. Miller's problem, one that recurs throughout Coover's work, begins when his creation slips out of his control and takes on a life of its own, forcing its creator to assume an unwanted role: part Antichrist, part blood sacrifice.

Life, of course, does not conform to the Brunist view; yet, even though the world does not end on the date predicted and despite the fact that their vigil on the Mount of Redemption turns into a Roman circus, the Brunists survive and prosper in their delusion. Growing into a worldwide religion with its own ecclesiastical hierarchy, the Brunists find a mass audience for their apocalyptic gospel. Miller also survives, resurrected by his author and comforted by his nurse, Happy Bottom, and it is their lusty, playful, and imaginative relationship, their finding the "living space between the two," that Coover puts forth as the alternative to Brunism and the denial of life it represents.

The Universal Baseball Association, Inc., J. Henry Waugh, Prop.

Coover is not the only contemporary American author to have written a novel about baseball and myth, but unlike Philip Roth's *The Great American Novel* (1973), which is played chiefly for laughs, or Bernard Malamud's *The Natural* (1952), where the mythic parallels seem forced, *The Universal Baseball Association, Inc., J. Henry Waugh, Prop.* successfully incorporates its various elements into a unified but complex and richly ambiguous work of narrative art. More than its baseball lore, mythic resonance, theological probings, stylistic virtuosity, or wordplay, it is the novel's blend of realism and fantasy and the elaborate development of its simple main idea or conceit that mark its achievement.

The novel focuses on a fifty-six-year-old bachelor named J. Henry Waugh and the tabletop baseball game he invents: not only dice and charts, but also eight teams, players with full biographies, and fifty-five years of league records and history. Henry's fantasizing is not so much childish as necessary, given his environment, the urban equivalent of Miller's West Condon. Whereas the real world oppresses Henry with "a vague and somber sense of fatality and closed circuits," his fantasy liberates and fulfills him in several ways. For the meaningless routine of accounting, Henry substitutes the meaningful rituals of baseball and in this way finds the continuity, pastoral wholeness, and heroic purpose that his everyday existence lacks. In his Association, Henry directs and chronicles the course of history; outside it he is merely a loner, an anonymous clerk.

The advantages of his Association are not without their risks, however, for at the same time that Henry uses his imagination to enliven his moribund world, he also reduces it to the narrow confines of his league: the USA miniaturized in the UBA, with its own "closed circuits." What is needed, Henry understands, is a balance of fact and fantasy, but in his attempt to right the imbalance that characterizes his life as an accountant, Henry goes to the opposite extreme, withdrawing into his fantasized realm. When a chance throw of the dice "kills" his rookie hero, Damon Rutherford ("His own man, yet at home in the world, part of it, involved, every inch of him a participant"), Henry despairs, choosing to exert that "unjustifiable control" that destroys the necessary balance of chance (dice) and order (imagination) and transforms his useful fiction into a version of the Brunists' providential universe. No longer a free, voluntary activity (according to Huizinga, a defining characteristic of true play), the Universal Baseball Association becomes repetitive work. Although the novel concludes with an unambiguous affirmation of the play spirit, the ending is itself ironic, for

Henry, the godlike creator of his fiction (Jahweh), is no longer in control; having disappeared into the intricate mechanism of his Association, he is now controlled by it.

Henry's fate, which is very nearly Miller's in *The Origin of the Brunists*, represents for Coover the danger all writers face. As he has explained, *The Universal Baseball Association*, "as I wrote it, not necessarily as it ought to be read, is an act of exemplary writing, a book about the art of writing." In the light of Coover's belief that all people are fiction makers insofar as they create systems to explain their world, the novel serves the related purpose of pointing out to the reader how difficult—and how necessary—is the task of distinguishing the real from the imaginary if one is to avoid Henry's fate. The need to make this distinction is the explicit subject of *The Universal Baseball Association*; the difficulty of making it is implicit in Coover's method. In the novel's opening pages, for example, Coover forces the reader to share Henry's predicament in the parallel act of reading about it.

At first, the reader assumes Henry is actually at the ballpark where rookie pitcher Damon Rutherford is a few outs away from a no-hitter, but when Henry takes advantage of the seventh-inning stretch to grab a sandwich at Diskin's delicatessen, one floor below, the reader corrects his or her mistake, perhaps unconsciously, now assuming that the game is being watched on television. Even when it becomes clear that the game is being played in Henry's mind and that Henry is himself having trouble separating fact from fiction, the reader does not stop reading to consider what this means because, thanks to Coover's pacing, the reader, like Henry, is completely caught up in being "*in* there, *with* them." Once the game is over, the reader does have the opportunity to consider Henry's state of mind, but by the end of the first of the novel's eight chapters (seven for the days of creation plus one for the apocalypse), the reader again becomes lost in Coover's exuberant fantasy, as Henry, now in the guise of his imaginary hero Damon Rutherford, and local B-girl Hettie Irden (earth mother) play a ribald game of sexual baseball. Throughout the novel, the reader not only reads about Henry's dilemma but is also made to experience it.

Tiger Miller understands that it is better to undertake numerous short "projects" than to commit himself to any one, as J. Henry Waugh does. Similarly, Coover has explained that the writing of short plays or stories involves very little commitment on the author's part—at most a few weeks, after which the work is either complete or discarded—whereas a novel requires not only a greater expenditure of time and energy but a certain risk as well. The starting point for each of Coover's works is not a character or a plot but a metaphor, the "hidden complexities" of which he develops by means of some appropriate structural device, as in the play *The Kid* or the short stories "The Babysitter" and "The Elevator." At times, the demands of the metaphor exceed the limits of structural devices appropriate to these short forms, and here Coover turns to the novel; thus he transformed and expanded his two early stories "Blackdamp" and "The Second Son" into *The Origin of the Brunists* and *The Universal Baseball Association*, respectively.

The Public Burning

The composition of Coover's third novel, *The Public Burning*, followed a similar but longer and more involved course, going from play to novella to novel over a difficult ten-year period during which Coover often questioned whether the expanding work would ever be completed. One reason the novel took so long to write is that its main character, Richard Nixon, began taking real-life pratfalls in the Watergate scandal of 1973-1974, outstripping the ones that Coover had imagined for him in *The Public Burning*. A second reason lies in the nature of the work Coover chose to write: a densely textured compendium of American politics and popular culture in which literally thousands of details, quotations, names, and allusive echoes had to be painstakingly stitched together so as to suggest a communal work written by an entire nation. Against this incredible variety (or repetitive overabundance, as many reviewers complained) is the novel's tight and self-conscious structure: four parts of seven chapters each (traditionally, magical numbers), framed by a prologue and epilogue and divided by three intermezzos.

Using two alternating narrators—Vice President Nixon and the sometimes reverent, sometimes befuddled, even frantic voice of America—Coover retells the familiar story of Ethel and Julius Rosenberg, specifically the three days leading up to their execution, which Coover sardonically moves from Sing Sing Prison to Times Square. Although it is clear that Coover is distressed by the injustice done the Rosenbergs, his aim is not to vindicate them; rather, he uses their case to expose American history as American fantasy.

Originally titled "An Historical Romance," *The Public Burning* interweaves ostensible "facts," such as newspaper and magazine articles, courtroom transcripts, presidential speeches, personal letters, and obvious fantasy, including the superhero Uncle Sam and a ludicrous death-house love scene involving Nixon and Ethel Rosenberg. By creating "a mosaic of history," Coover provides the reader with a self-consciously fictive version of the Rosenberg case designed to compete with the supposedly historical view (as reiterated, for example, in Louis Nizer's *The Implosion Conspiracy*, 1973, which Coover reviewed in the February 11, 1973, issue of *The New York Times Book Review*). Coover's point is that, more often than not, human beings do not see experience directly (and therefore cannot presume to know its truth value) because they place that experience—or have it placed for them—in a context, an aesthetic frame, that determines its meaning. *The New York Times*, for example, is not shown printing "all the news that's fit to print"; rather, it selects and arranges the news on its pages ("tablets") in ways that, intentionally or not, determine the reader's ("pilgrim's") perception of what he or she assumes to be objective reality.

In sifting through the plethora of materials related to the Rosenberg case, Nixon comes very close to accepting Coover's view of history as essentially literary romance, or myth. He realizes that the Rosenberg conspiracy trial may actually be a government conspiracy against the accused (ritual scapegoats), depending chiefly on fabricated evidence, or stage props, and dress rehearsals for the prosecution; indeed, American life itself may be a kind of nationwide theatrical performance in which individuals play the roles assigned to them in the national scripts: manifest destiny, the Cold War, Westerns, and the Horatio Alger rags-to-riches plot. Nixon, however, is too much a believer in the American myths to break entirely free of them. Moreover, suffering from the same loneliness that afflicts Miller and Waugh, but being much less imaginative than they, Nixon desperately craves approval, and that requires his playing his part as it is written: "no ad-libbing," as the stage directions in

The Kid make clear. To have a role in the Great American Plot, to be a part of the recorded "History" that he carefully distinguishes from merely personal "history," is the limited goal Nixon sets for himself because he is either unwilling or unable to imagine any other projects as equally viable and fulfilling. As a result, he plays the role Coover has appropriately assigned him: chief clown in the national farce.

The Public Burning is not a piece of easy political satire of the sort Philip Roth dashed off in his Nixon book, *Our Gang* (1971); in fact, Coover's Nixon is a surprisingly sympathetic character. Nor is *The Public Burning* "a cowardly lie" that defames a nation and exonerates criminals, as one reviewer claimed. This novel, like all of Coover's major works, is a warning to the reader concerning the uses and the dangers of the imagination: Humankind must accept its role as fiction maker and its responsibility for its fictions, or it will pay the penalty for confusing its facts with its fables.

GERALD'S PARTY

After 1977, Coover continued to explore literary and "mythic" forms and to stretch generic classifications, revising or recycling a number of short fictions as "novels"—"A Working Day" (1979) as *Spanking the Maid*, "The Cat in the Hat for President" (1968) as *A Political Fable*, and "Whatever Happened to Gloomy Gus of the Chicago Bears?" (1968) as a 1987 novel of the same title—and producing an intertextual triple feature of film parodies titled *A Night at the Movies*, including previews, weekly serial episode, shorts, intermission, cartoon, travelogue, and musical interlude. All these texts manage to subvert the disclaimer that appears at the beginning of *A Night at the Movies*—"Ladies and Gentlemen May safely visit this Theatre as no Offensive Films are ever Shown Here"—but none so flagrantly as *Gerald's Party*. Harking back to Coover's two "Lucky Pierre" stories about an aging pornographer, *Gerald's Party* constitutes a full-scale narrative onslaught, a playfully sadistic attack on its clownishly masochistic reader, and a vast recycling project that reverses the centrifugal reach of *The Public Burning*, moving centripetally in on itself to form Coover's fullest and most claustrophobic exploration of a single narrative metaphor.

Considered reductively, *Gerald's Party* parodies the English parlor mystery, but the parody here serves as little more than a vehicle for Coover's Rabelaisian exploitation in which John Barth's "literature of exhaustion" meets Roland Barthes's "plural text." The result is at once exhilarating and exhausting, freely combining murder mystery, pornography, film, theater, video, sex, puns, jokes, rituals, slapstick, clichés, fairy tales, party chatter, memory, desire, and aesthetic and philosophical speculation, all in one thickly embedded, endlessly interrupted yet unstoppable, ribald whole. The narrative is at once abundant (like the food and drink), full of holes (like the one in the victim Ros's breast), clogged (like Gerald's upstairs toilet), and stuck (as Gerald becomes in one sex scene). Plots proliferate but do not progress in any conventional way. As Inspector Pardew tries to solve the murder mystery, Gerald pursues Alison; Sally Ann pursues Gerald; Jim, a doctor, attends to the dying; Steve, a plumber, fixes everything but the stopped-up toilet; Gerald's wife continues to prepare food, vacuum, and make wondrously inappropriate remarks ("I wish people wouldn't use guns in the house," she says after one guest has been fatally shot); and Gerald's mother-in-law, trying to put her grandson Mark to bed, looks on disapprovingly. These are but a few of the novel's myriad plots.

Gerald's efforts to understand what is happening, along with his inability to order the chaos, parallel the reader's. The novel in fact anticipates and thus short-circuits the reader's own efforts to understand Coover's bewildering but brilliant text, which seems to question its own purpose and seriousness and the structure of which follows that of an all-night party, including the inevitable winding down to an anticlimactic end, or death. Not surprisingly, Pardew's solution resolves little and interests the reader not at all. Moreover, the most serious and philosophical comments in the novel—the ones upon which the conventional reader would like to seize for their power to explain and control the rest of the text—seem to be nothing more than additional false clues. Clearly, here as in all of Coover's novels, stories, and plays, the reader can survive and in fact enjoy this narrative assault on his or her abilities and sensibilities only by resisting the inspector's obsession with patterns and "holistic criminalistics." Even if the reader takes a pratfall or two, Coover's parodic range and supercharged narrative energy make the ride worth the risk.

JOHN'S WIFE

John's Wife is Coover's postmodern version of small-town life in middle America, much as *Winesburg, Ohio* (1919) is Sherwood Anderson's modernist take on the subject. Coover continues and expands the modernist angst expressed in *Winesburg, Ohio* and other fin de siècle works by focusing on the clichéd sexual repression and personal alienation of the characters until the corruption of the American Dream becomes mythic parody. Coover presents a plethora of characters whose lives revolve around the most powerful man in town, a late twentieth century "mover and shaker," a builder and businessman whose power to transform the small town and the lives of the people who live in it is matched only by his amorality. John, the builder, rewards personal loyalty from those who work for him with business promotions and upward social mobility, while destroying those who get in his way, including his own father-in-law. John becomes the archetype of the late twentieth century materialist who will stop at nothing in his own rise to power. Concepts such as culture and tradition become palimpsest commodities to be bought and sold and ultimately transformed into consumer goods.

John's wife, the titular character, is seen only through the impressions of the other characters. In fact, John's wife becomes an ironic archetypal exemplar of the feminist concept of the woman as "other" in much putatively patriarchal fiction. She is the focus of desire, both sexual and artistic, for the male characters of the book, while she is the friend and confidant of most of the female characters; yet, as one character states, she is "a thereness that was not there." She seems to fade out of existence even while people are talking to her. The theme of the book seems to be that persons are born into stories made by others.

GHOST TOWN

Ghost Town is a fabulation (to use a term coined by Robert Scholes) of the trope of the American Western, first introduced in the dime novels of the late nineteenth century and then popularized by the films and television of the twentieth. *Ghost Town* transmogrifies the clichéd elements of the genre (character, plot, and setting) in the "play space" of the fiction, allowing the author's imagination to explore the ironic possibilities inherent in the form. The main character, for example, is at times both good and bad. He is the archetypal hero, innocent yet tempered by experience. He is "leathery and sunburnt and old as the hills. Yet just a kid. Won't be anything else." Instead of his riding into the town from a Beckettian nonplace, the town "glides up under his horse's hoofs from behind." Thus, in this ghost town, the hero can become the sheriff as well as a gunslinger and a train robber. The officious schoolteacher can also be the saloon chanteuse in disguise. The hackneyed plots (the hanging, the train robbery, the shoot-out, the rescue of the schoolteacher from her bondage to the train tracks) and the setting itself (the saloon, the jail, the rough-hewn church, the hideout) all become available for parody and ironic paradigmatic substitutions.

THE ADVENTURES OF LUCKY PIERRE

In *The Adventures of Lucky Pierre*, Coover takes a trip down memory lane, one that includes his earlier novel *Pinocchio in Venice*. *The Adventures of Lucky Pierre* literally wears the connection on its sleeve in the form of the man sporting a Pinocchio nose and wearing a Pierrot costume pictured on the dust jacket, and it is through *Pinocchio in Venice* that the later novel is perhaps best approached. Like so many of Coover's works, *Pinocchio in Venice* plays off and with a well-known text, in this case Carlo Collodi's *Le avventure di Pinocchio* (1883; *The Adventures of Pinocchio*, 1892), but Coover's parodies are never simple, and far from being a straightforward reimagining, his *Pinocchio* is an intertextual extravaganza, replete with allusions to and echoes of Dante's *La divina commedia* (c. 1320; *The Divine Comedy*, 1802), Homer's *Odyssey* (c. 725 B.C.E.; English translation, 1614), William Shakespeare's *King Lear* (pr. c. 1605-1606), Franz Kafka's *Das Schloss* (1926; *The Castle*, 1930), Samuel Beckett's plays, Italo Calvino's *Se una notte d'inverno un viaggiatore* (1979; *If on a Winter's Night a Traveler*, 1981), Miguel de Cervantes' *Don Quixote de la Mancha* (1605, 1615), and Thomas Mann's *Der Tod in Venedig* (1912; *Death in Venice*, 1925).

Having learned his lessons all too well (and having spent time in Hollywood working on Disney's animated version of his adventures), the reformed, well-behaved Pinocchio has become a world-renowned professor who now returns to Italy to complete his latest—and probably his last—book, *Mamma*, about the blue-haired fairy who restored the puppet to life. (In Collodi's original serialized version, the puppet is hanged; the fairy restores the puppet to life so that the narrative can go on and the story can have a happy ending suitable for children.) Coover's Pinocchio is much older but no wiser, his many academic accomplishments notwithstanding. From the moment he arrives in Venice, on the eve of carnival season, Pinocchio repeats his earlier mistakes, losing his way, his money, his nearly completed manuscript, his dignity (of course, this being a Coover novel), and eventually his humanness. That this *"gran signore"* should be brought so low is entirely appropriate, for Coover's Rabelaisian retelling of Collodi's children's classic is set during carnival season, when all that is revered is ridiculed and all that is high is brought low, including Venice, which Pinocchio's beloved Petrarch described as that "noblest of cities, sole refuge of humanity, peace, justice and liberty."

Like *Pinocchio in Venice*, *The Adventures of Lucky Pierre* is a story about growing old and about returning to the past. Like *A Night at the Movies* and *A Child Again*, it even returns to Coover's own earlier works (several Lucky Pierre stories), and, like *A Night at the Movies*, it deals with film. Indeed, *Lucky Pierre* is dedicated to three filmmaking "saints"—Buster Keaton, Luis Buñuel and Jean-Luc Godard—"who kept the light burning in this dark century." Orson Welles famously described film as "a ribbon of dream," and ever since his days as a graduate student in anthropology at the University of Chicago, Coover has been interested in Roger Caillois's concept of dream time, when a society returns to its mythical roots. In *The Public Burning*, dream time involves a ritualistic return to the American nation's roots. In *The Adventures of Lucky Pierre*, dream time involves a return to the narrative roots of film, the most intertextual of all the arts, and more specifically to pornographic film, the most formulaic and reductive of all cinematic genres.

Coover takes his title and overall structure from Herschell Gordon Lewis and David F. Friedman's 1961 "nudie cutie" film, itself a satire of Russ Meyer's porn classic *The Immortal Mr. Teas* (1959). Organized into nine "reels," Coover's novel is much more wildly intertextual than the titular reference indicates. Films such as *Fritz the Cat* (1972), *Who Framed Roger Rabbit*

(1988), *Groundhog Day* (1993), and *The Truman Show* (1998) play their parts, as do the various porn genres that Coover recycles to hilarious effect. Set in Cinecity, *The Adventures of Lucky Pierre* also recalls both the films of Federico Fellini—especially *8½* (1963)—filmed at Rome's Cinecittà and Fred Miller's soft-porn graphic-novel series *Sin City*; it also anticipates David Lynch's nour-ish, meta- and intertextual look at the Hollywood dream machine in *Mulholland Drive* (2001).

The vast but self-enclosed and self-referential world of Cinecity is in danger—from terrorists, from amateur pornographers, and from virtual reality—and only one man can save it, the Cineman of Cinecity, Lucky Pierre, also known as Wee Willie, Peter Prick, Badboy, and the Beast. He is an unlikely superhero: an aging porn star whose pants dropping is more slapstick than sexual. Formerly the stud of porn, he is now the Pierrot figure of commedia dell'arte, the naïve and lovelorn sad clown. Coover not only explores Lucky Pierre's absurdly funny existential predicament—both as a would-be hero and as someone trying desperately to escape from the closed, entropic world of Cinecity—but he also exploits the full array of film genres (in their most debased and reductive pornographic forms) and film techniques (framing, looping, wipes, dissolves, sound bridges, retakes, and so on), exploring/exploiting as well the difference between the real and the reel.

Porn here stands in for any human-made and therefore arbitrary system for ritualistically structuring and thereby giving meaning to life—the fictive systems that Coover has spent his career exploring, exploiting, and exposing. By investing pornographic films with the significance usually reserved for high art, Coover exposes not only the ritualistic quality of porn (and indeed of all art) and the basis for all human fiction making but also the ways these fictions become confining rather than liberating. Trapped in the reel world ruled by his nine muses—his female costars and directors—Lucky Pierre does attain a measure of freedom at "the end" of reel 9, otherwise devoted to a Lucky Pierre film festival. Recalling Molly Bloom's soliloquy at the end of James Joyce's *Ulysses* (1922), Cally's (Calliope's) "yes" affirms the present moment that fictions of all kinds try to disguise by turning into parts of a narrative sequence. Cally's "now," spoken in the novel's unstopped final line, echoes *The Magic Kingdom* (1985), a novel about terminally ill children written by Coover's friend Stanley Elkin, who died in 1995. The fierce energy of Elkin's novel ironically underscores the critical assessment of reviewers who have complained of the pointlessness and repetitiveness of Coover's later novels, which either work better in short bursts, as the brilliance of *A Night at the Movies* shows, or require the more compelling subject matter of Coover's first three novels.

Robert A. Morace
Updated by Gary P. Walton

OTHER MAJOR WORKS

SHORT FICTION: *Pricksongs and Descants*, 1969; *The Water Pourer*, 1972 (a deleted chapter from *The Origin of the Brunists*); *Charlie in the House of Rue*, 1980; *The Convention*, 1981; *In Bed One Night, and Other Brief Encounters*, 1983; *Aesop's Forest*, 1986; *A Night at the Movies: Or, You Must Remember This*, 1987; *The Grand Hotels (of Joseph Cornell)*, 2002 (vignettes); *A Child Again*, 2005.

PLAYS: *The Kid*, pr., pb. 1972; *Love Scene*, pb. 1972; *Rip Awake*, pr. 1972; *A Theological Position*, pb. 1972; *Bridge Hound*, pr. 1981.

SCREENPLAYS: *On a Confrontation in Iowa City*, 1969; *After Lazarus*, 1980.

BIBLIOGRAPHY

Andersen, Richard. *Robert Coover*. Boston: Twayne, 1981. Provides a very accessible introduction to Coover's production up to 1981. Combines plot summary with commentary, helping the reader to make an initial acquaintance with Coover's work. Includes select bibliography and index.

Coover, Robert. Interview by Amanda Smith. *Publishers Weekly*, December 26, 1986. Coover discusses the motivations that lie behind his experimental fiction and states that he believes that the artist finds metaphors for the world in the most vulnerable areas of human outreach; he insists that he is in pursuit of the mainstream. What many people consider experimental, Coover argues, is actually traditional in the sense that it has gone back to old forms to find its new form.

Evenson, Brian K. *Understanding Robert Coover*. Columbia: University of South Carolina Press, 2003. Comprehensive survey explains the particularly dense style of Coover's metafiction. Guides readers through Coover's postmodern fiction, which deals with mythmaking and the power of stories to shape collective community action that often turns violent.

Gordon, Lois. *Robert Coover: The Universal Fictionmaking Process*. Carbondale: Southern Illinois University Press, 1983. Provides a good introduction to Coover's work, placing it within the context of metafictional or postmodernist literature. Includes select bibliography and index.

Hume, Kathryn. "Robert Coover: The Metaphysics of Bondage." *Modern Language Review* 98, no. 4 (October, 2003): 827-841. Views Coover as "an intellectual" writer rather than essentially a writer of metafiction, and examines his "metaphysical quest" to determine which bonds are necessary to sustain human life and which need to be broken.

McCaffery, Larry. *The Metafictional Muse: The Works of Robert Coover, Donald Barthelme, and William H. Gass*. Pittsburgh, Pa.: University of Pittsburgh Press, 1982. Describes metafiction as a major current in contemporary American fiction and discusses the metafictional traits of the works of Coover and two other important contemporary American writers.

Maltby, Paul. *Dissident Postmodernists: Barthelme, Coover, Pynchon*. Philadelphia: University of Pennsylvania Press, 1991. Presents a comparative examination of the fiction of Donald Barthelme, Thomas Pynchon, and Coover. Includes bibliography and index.

Pughe, Thomas. *Comic Sense: Reading Robert Coover, Stanley Elkin, Philip Roth*. Boston: Birkhäuser, 1994. Analyzes the humor in the three writers' books. Includes bibliographical references and index.

Shaw, Jonathan Imber. "Cocktails with the Reader Victim: Style and Similitude in Robert Coover's *Gerald's Party*." *Critique* 47, no. 2 (Winter, 2006): 131-146. Uses Sigmund Freud's theory of trauma to examine the unease that *Gerald's Party* creates in Coover's reader.

ROBERT CORMIER

Born: Leominster, Massachusetts; January 17, 1925

Died: Boston, Massachusetts; November 2, 2000

Also known as: Robert Edmund Cormier; John Fitch IV

PRINCIPAL LONG FICTION

Now and at the Hour, 1960
A Little Raw on Monday Mornings, 1963
Take Me Where the Good Times Are, 1965
The Chocolate War, 1974
The Bumblebee Flies Anyway, 1983
Beyond the Chocolate War, 1985
Heroes, 1998
The Rag and Bone Shop, 2001

OTHER LITERARY FORMS

As a working journalist from 1946 to 2000, Robert Cormier prepared radio commercials and wrote columns and articles for periodicals and newspapers, including *Redbook*, *McCall's*, *The Saturday Evening Post*, *Catholic Library World*, and the *Fitchburg Sentinel*. He was a writing consultant, wire editor, associate editor, columnist, book reviewer, contributor to anthologies, and freelancer, a job list that suggests the range of his literary work. He published three novels for adults—*Now and at the Hour*, *A Little Raw on Monday Mornings*, and *Take Me Where the Good Times Are*—before writing *The Chocolate War*, the first of his thirteen young adult novels. Another young adult novel, *Fade* (1988), was his only mystical work.

Eight Plus One (1980) features Cormier's short stories. *Other Bells for Us to Ring* (1990) is his only book for children, and his young adult novel *Frenchtown Summer* (1999) uses free verse for narration. His autobiography, *I Have Words to Spend: Reflections of a Small Town Editor* (1991), is a compilation of his newspaper columns. His wife, Constance Senay Cormier, helped edit the book. Cormier left two unpublished novels, "The Rumple Country" and "In the Midst of Winter," upon his death in 2000.

ACHIEVEMENTS

Robert Cormier's many journalistic awards include the Human Interest Story of the Year Award from the Associated Press in New England (1959, 1973). His young adult books in particular have earned many accolades, including *The New York Times* Outstanding Book of the Year Award for *The Chocolate War*, *I Am the Cheese*, and *After the First Death*. In 1977, *I Am the Cheese* was named the American Library Association's (ALA) Best Book for Young Adults. Both the *School Library Journal* and the ALA listed *The Bumblebee Flies Anyway* as a best book for 1983. He also received the ALAN Award (1982) from the National Council of Teachers of English for lifetime achievement in young adult literature.

In addition to more than thirty other honors, Cormier accepted the German Catholic Book of the Year, Bishops of Germany Award for *Tunes for Bears to Dance To*, the Lewis Carroll Shelf Award for *The Chocolate War*, and an honorary doctorate from Fitchburg State College (1977). Translations of Cormier's works appear in French, Spanish, Italian, Swedish, Japanese, Danish, Hungarian, German, and other languages.

BIOGRAPHY

Robert Edmund Cormier was born in Leominster, Massachusetts, on January 17, 1925, to Lucien Joseph Cormier, a French-Canadian Catholic, and Irma Margaret Collins Cormier, an Irish Catholic. Lucien supported his wife and eight children by working in factories around Leominster. Cormier attended a local Catholic school, where one day in particular affected his view of religion: He had seen from the school that his home was burning. His teacher, however, demanded that he recite three prayers before leaving to rescue his mother and younger sibling.

In high school, Cormier wrote for the yearbook, sang in the chorus, and acted in plays. After graduation, he worked nights in a comb factory; he later used this work experience in his first novel, *Now and at the Hour*. During the day, Cormier attended Fitchburg State College (1943-1944). Professor Florence Conlon encouraged

Cormier to write. She submitted his story "The Little Things That Count" to *The Sign*, a Catholic magazine, without his knowledge, and the story won a prize. Intrigued by the possibilities of a writing career, Cormier soon dropped out of the teachers' college.

Cormier's first writing job was in journalism. He wrote commercials for radio station WTAG in Worcester, Massachusetts (1946-1948). In 1948, he married Constance Senay and took a night job at the *Worcester Telegram and Gazette*; he worked seven years at the *Telegram* before beginning a day job as a reporter (1955-1959) for the *Fitchburg Sentinel* (later the *Fitchburg-Leominster Sentinel and Enterprise*). His assignments at the *Fitchburg Sentinel* included wire editing (1959-1966) and associate editing (1966-1978). Under the pseudonym John Fitch IV, Cormier wrote the human-interest column "1177 Main Street" (1969-1978), also for the *Fitchburg Sentinel*.

On January 14, 1978, Cormier resigned from the *Fitchburg-Leominster Sentinel and Enterprise* to write fiction full time from an alcove off the dining room in his home. He contributed to such anthologies as *Celebrating Children's Books: Essays on Children's Literature in Honor of Zena Sutherland* (1981), *Sixteen: Short Stories by Outstanding Writers for Young Adults* (1984), and *Trust Your Children: Voices Against Censorship in Children's Literature* (1988). He died from a blood clot on November 2, 2000, in Boston. He was seventy-five years old.

ANALYSIS

For the plots and settings of his realistic fiction, Robert Cormier drew primarily from his own experiences as a father and family man, and from the town he knew so well. His first three novels treat somber topics and avoid idealism, common features of most of his later fiction as well. The first three novels, respectively, focus on terminal illness, a seventy-year-old resident of a home for the destitute who has dreams of escape, and a female factory worker with three children who fears an unwanted pregnancy and dreams of a decent home, sufficient food, adequate money, some enjoyment, and companionship.

Cormier's writing is concise. He deliberately avoids

Robert Cormier. (Courtesy, Delacourt Press)

long, descriptive passages. His use of literary devices such as metaphors and similes, however, helps to convey his points succinctly to the reader. Cormier's quick-paced style often appeals to young people accustomed to the rapid tempo of modern media, especially television. Cormier often claimed, however, to write about adolescents and not for adolescents.

Although Cormier wrote primarily for young people, all his books—for adults, adolescents, and children—typically transcend traditional boundaries. His fiction touches on difficult and often taboo topics, including sex, death, murder, terminal illness, vandalism, human suffering, abortion, revenge, betrayal, alcoholism, terrorism, divorce, gang action, religion, and, sometimes, mysticism.

THE CHOCOLATE WAR

Although all of his young adult books have been popular, *The Chocolate War* ranks as one of the best-selling books of all time. Cormier's memory of his son's reluctance to participate in his school's candy sale led to the theme for this controversial work. The novel is a bleak account of life in a Catholic boys' school in Boston. The protagonist is student Jerry Renault, who finds that he must defend himself after he is labeled a rebel by school headmaster Brother Leon and, later, other students.

The Chocolate War is a novel of initiation in which Jerry learns crucial lessons about society—most of them negative. Jerry soon discovers the consequences of nonconformity, of the search for self-identity and achieving one's individuality.

Ultimately, Jerry is defeated, resulting in a not-so-happy ending for the novel. Before *The Chocolate War*, young adult novels managed to end on an upbeat note; after *The Chocolate War*, the young adult novel was capable of tragedy. Publishers asked Cormier to modify the work. Cormier refused to do so and left the novel unchanged. The story's sexual references, violence, and language led some critics to advocate banning the book, and many libraries and other institutions followed the call. The novel remains on the American Library Association's (ALA) list of most frequently banned books. Even with the controversy—and perhaps because of it—*The Chocolate War*, along with another of his controversial works, *I Am the Cheese*, was adapted for film.

NOW AND AT THE HOUR

Cormier wrote *Now and at the Hour*—his first adult novel—as his father was dying from cancer. The book's title is taken from the words of a Catholic prayer ("Pray for us sinners now and at the hour of our death"). For forty-four years, the novel's main character, Alphege LeBlanc, has been a comb-factory employee, a job Cormier knew firsthand; he, too, worked in a comb factory while attending college in a town much like the one in the novel. Alphege faces both his imminent death from cancer and his fear that his life has been meaningless. Though *Now and at the Hour* remained on *Time* magazine's list of recommended readings for several weeks, the novel sold only five thousand copies. Readers found no happy endings and no magical solutions to the pain, fear, and doubts of a dying man in this first book.

BEYOND THE CHOCOLATE WAR

Beyond the Chocolate War is Cormier's only sequel. The book takes the reader back to Trinity School, the setting of *The Chocolate War*. The use of a symbolic guillo-

tine by characters in the novel foreshadows the violence that is to follow. The truth of the gang's cruelty, and a plan for revenge, gradually emerge as the story progresses. In this novel, Cormier again focuses on the vulnerability of youth and the cruelty of life.

THE BUMBLEBEE FLIES ANYWAY

Set in a hospital wing for terminally ill youths, *The Bumblebee Flies Anyway* features a variety of characters who are spending their last days alive participating in experimental medical studies. Cormier allows his characters to form friendships, some of them intimate. He also allows his protagonists—and his readers—to dare to dream. The dying adolescents dream about the impossible. Like bees who aerodynamically should not be able to fly—yet do—even with their impossibly short wings, the patients, one in particular, tries to fly under seemingly impossible circumstances. That patient, Mazzio, has a plan to fly from the roof of the hospital using the Bumblebee, a full-scale wooden replica of a red sports car. Mazzio pushes the Bumblebee to the roof's edge, hoping to depart his life in style.

THE RAG AND BONE SHOP

The Rag and Bone Shop is the story of the grisly murder of a child and the police investigation that follows. After the discovery of the bludgeoned body of the seven-year-old girl in a pile of leaves, an interrogator begins to question twelve-year-old Jason, the innocent friend of the victim and the last person to have seen her alive. As the questioning becomes more intense, the insecure young boy admits to the crime, even though he is not the killer. When the real killer confesses, Jason and the police interrogator undergo life changes. The novel explores the powers of suggestion and the seeds of evil and suspicion that exist in every community.

Anita Price Davis

OTHER MAJOR WORKS

SHORT FICTION: *Eight Plus One*, 1980.

NONFICTION: *I Have Words to Spend: Reflections of a Small Town Editor*, 1991.

YOUNG ADULT LITERATURE: *I Am the Cheese*, 1977; *After the First Death*, 1979; *Fade*, 1988; *Other Bells for Us to Ring*, 1990; *We All Fall Down*, 1991; *Tunes for Bears to Dance To*, 1992; *In the Middle of the Night*, 1995; *Tenderness*, 1997; *Frenchtown Summer*, 1999.

BIBLIOGRAPHY

Beckman, Wendy Hart. *Robert Cormier: Banned, Challenged, and Censored*. Berkeley Heights, N.J.: Enslow, 2008. An interesting look at the controversies surrounding Cormier's novels. Also includes discussion of Cormier's life as a young writer and emerging novelist of primarily young adult fiction.

Campbell, Patricia J. "A Loving Farewell to Robert Cormier." *Horn Book Magazine* 77 (March-April, 2001): 245-248. Cormier's obituary for *Horn Book Magazine*, a bimonthly periodical about literature for children and young adults. Campbell acknowledges the censorship of Cormier's works but recognizes also the honesty and "the brilliance of his writing."

_____. *Robert Cormier: Daring to Disturb the Universe*. New York: Random House, 2006. As a long-time friend of Cormier, Campbell provides an extensive study of the author. This 287-page analysis of his writing also examines the recurring themes in Cormier's writings. Also includes a comprehensive bibliography of his life and works.

JULIO CORTÁZAR

Born: Brussels, Belgium; August 26, 1914
Died: Paris, France; February 12, 1984
Also known as: Julio Denís

PRINCIPAL LONG FICTION

Los premios, 1960 (*The Winners*, 1965)
Rayuela, 1963 (*Hopscotch*, 1966)
62: Modelo para armar, 1968 (*62: A Model Kit*, 1972)
Libro de Manuel, 1973 (*A Manual for Manuel*, 1978)
El examen, 1986 (wr. 1950; *Final Exam*, 2000)

OTHER LITERARY FORMS

Early in his career, Julio Cortázar (cohr-TAH-sahr) published two volumes of poetry—*Presencia* (1938; presence), under the pseudonym Julio Denís, and *Los reyes* (1949; the kings), using his own name—both still generally unnoticed by the critics. His short fiction, however, is considered among the best in Hispanic literature. His best-known short story is perhaps "Las babas del diablo" (the devil's slobbers), the basis of the internationally acclaimed film *Blow-Up* (1966), directed by Michelangelo Antonioni. Cortázar's collection of short fiction *Bestiario* (1951; bestiary) contains fantastic and somewhat surrealistic tales dealing mainly with extraordinary circumstances in the everyday lives of ordinary characters. Their common denominator is the unexpected turn of events at each story's end; such surprise endings are a well-known trait of Cortázar's short fiction. His second collection of stories, *Final del juego* (1956; end of the game), was followed by *Las armas secretas* (1959; secret weapons), *Historias de cronopios y de famas* (1962; *Cronopios and Famas*, 1969), *Todos los fuegos el fuego* (1966; *All Fires the Fire, and Other Stories*, 1973), *Alguien que anda por ahí, y otros relatos* (1977; included in *A Change of Light, and Other Stories*, 1980), *Queremos tanto a Glenda, y otros relatos* (1980; *We Love Glenda So Much, and Other Stories*, 1983), and *Deshoras* (1982; bad timing).

Two collage books, *La vuelta al día en ochenta mundos* (1967; *Around the Day in Eighty Worlds*, 1986) and *Último round* (1969; the last round), reflect the author's life through the use of anecdotes, photographs, newspaper clippings, drawings, and other personal items. They are not, however, as engagé as are Cortázar's political essays in the collections *Viaje alrededor de una mesa* (1970; voyage around a table), which contains discussions of Marxism and capitalism; *Fantomas contra los vampiros multinacionales: Una utopía realizable* (1975; Fantomas battles the multinational vampires), a tirade in comic-strip form attacking capitalism; and *Nicaragua tan violentamente dulce* (1983; *Nicaraguan Sketches*, 1989), a collection of articles on Nicaragua and the Marxist revolution. *Un tal Lucas* (1979; *A Certain Lucas*, 1984) is a series of interlocking fictions, somewhat autobiographical in nature, that reveal the essence of a particular man's life. One of Cortázar's last works, a travelogue of sorts titled *Los autonautas de la cosmopista: O, Un viaje atemporal Paris-Marsella* (1983; *Autonauts of the Cosmoroute: A Timeless Voyage from Paris to Marseille*, 2007), is both a never-ending trip and a love song, detailing a trip with his last wife, Carol Dunlop, who predeceased him by several months. It contains descriptions, reflections, cultural parody, sometimes nostalgia, a potpourri of feelings and perceptions à la Cortázar.

In addition to the several volumes mentioned above, Cortázar published the nonfiction works *Buenos Aires Buenos Aires* (1968; English translation, 1968) and *Prosa del observatorio* (1972; with Antonio Galvez). As a professional translator, he rendered into Spanish such works as Daniel Defoe's *Robinson Crusoe* (1719), G. K. Chesterton's *The Man Who Knew Too Much* (1922), and André Gide's *L'Immoraliste* (1902; *The Immoralist*, 1930). He translated many volumes of criticism, including Lord Houghton's *Life and Letters of John Keats* (1867) and two erudite essays by Alfred Stern, *Sartre, His Philosophy and Psychoanalysis* (1953) and *Philosophie du rire et des pleurs* (1949; philosophy of laughter and tears). Himself a critic of English, French, and Spanish literature, Cortázar also published many articles, reviews, and literary essays on a variety of topics ranging from Arthur Rimbaud, John Keats, Antonin Artaud, Graham Greene, and Charles Baudelaire to contemporary Latin American writers such as Octavio Paz, Leopoldo Marechal, and Victoria Ocampo.

ACHIEVEMENTS

At a moment when fiction in Spanish enjoyed little international esteem, Julio Cortázar's multinational and multicultural orientation brought recognition of a sophistication and cosmopolitan awareness previously assumed to be lacking among Spanish-language writers. His unusual success in translation was an important ingredient in the "boom" in Latin American fiction, bringing the Spanish American novelists of his generation to unprecedented prestige and popularity in Europe and North America. His most celebrated novel, *Hopscotch*, un-

questionably had an impact on experimental and vanguard writing in Spain and Latin America, and the notion of a variable structure and reassembled plot had a number of imitators among younger writers. In addition to influencing the literature of his "native" Argentina, Cortázar has had a significant impact on the younger generation of novelists throughout the Spanish-speaking world.

BIOGRAPHY

The fact that Julio Cortázar was born in Brussels, Belgium, rather than in Argentina was something of an accident, as his Argentine parents were then abroad on business. He learned French at about the same time he learned Spanish, and this international beginning colored most of his life. His paternal great-grandparents were from the Basque area of northern Spain; his maternal origins can be traced to Germany and France. The boy and his parents remained for several years in Europe, returning to Buenos Aires when he was about four years old. While Cortázar was still a boy in Argentina, his father abandoned the family; Julio was reared by his mother and aunt. He earned degrees in elementary, secondary, and preparatory education, and from 1937 to 1944, he worked as a high school teacher in Bolívar and Chivilcoy while simultaneously beginning to write short stories in his spare time. In 1938, his first collection of poems, *Presencia*, appeared under the pseudonym Julio Denís without receiving much critical attention.

In 1944, Cortázar began to teach French literature at the University of Cuyo, but his activism against the dictatorship of Juan Perón brought his arrest, with a subsequent resignation from his post at the university. He moved to Buenos Aires in 1946, obtaining the post of manager of the Argentine Publishing Association; while working there, he earned a degree as public translator. His dramatic poem *Los reyes* was published under his own name in 1949 but, like his earlier poetry, was ignored by the critics. In 1951, Cortázar was awarded a scholarship by the French government to study in Paris, where he would reside until his death, working as a freelance translator and for the United Nations Educational, Scientific, and Cultural Organization (UNESCO). The same year he left Argentina, his short-story collection *Bestiario* was published.

In 1953, Cortázar married Aurora Bernárdez, also an

Argentinian translator, and together they visited Italy, where he translated the prose works of Edgar Allan Poe, on commission from the University of Puerto Rico, and wrote most of *Cronopios and Famas*. In 1960, he visited the United States and his first novel, *The Winners*, appeared in Argentina. Cortázar was especially impressed by New York's Greenwich Village, and his attraction to jazz appears in his later long fiction. He visited Cuba in 1963, the year *Hopscotch* was published, was fascinated by the Marxist revolution, and became a good friend of dictator Fidel Castro; an attraction to Marxism is noticeable in many of his nonfiction works. Cortázar's third novel, *62: A Model Kit*, appeared in 1968, at a time when his reputation was firmly established, thanks especially to the film *Blow-Up*, which Antonioni based on one of Cortázar's short stories. In 1973, celebrating the publication of his fourth novel, *A Manual for Manuel*, he journeyed to Argentina, visiting Chile, Ecuador, and Peru as

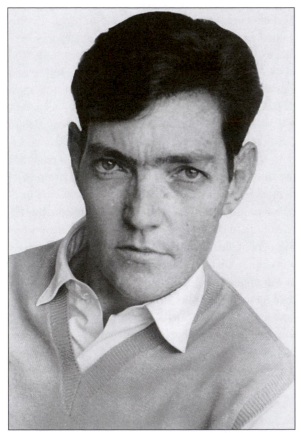

Julio Cortázar. (Library of Congress)

well. After that, his production was limited to short stories and nonfiction, and he participated in many congresses and traveled throughout Europe and the Americas. Cortázar died in France on February 12, 1984.

ANALYSIS
THE WINNERS

Julio Cortázar's first novel, *The Winners*, tells the story of a voyage aboard a rather sinister ship. This mystery cruise—the ship's destination is never revealed—is a prize awarded to the winners of a lottery, a heterogeneous group of Argentines who, as the novel begins, are gathered at the London Café in Buenos Aires. The group represents a cross section of the Argentine class structure, suggestive of the novel's implicit sociopolitical critique. From the café, the winners are transported by bus to the ship, under a shroud of secrecy. The café is taken over by the Office of Municipal Affairs, arrangers of the lottery, and all but the winners are required to leave the premises. In the café, on the bus, and boarding the ship, the winners engage in conversations as varied as their class and cultural origins, making new acquaintances and provoking a few hostile confrontations.

The ship's name, the *Malcolm*, is a clue of what is to come: The passengers are not "well come"; rather, they are regarded by the ship's crew as an imposition. Attempting to speak to the officers, they discover that the crew speaks another language; the passengers are refused the itinerary and forbidden access to the stern. Protesting their treatment, they are informed that a rare strain of typhus has infected the crew, and this news provokes a division among the passengers between those who fear contamination and those who believe that they are being deceived (and offer other answers as to what is taking place). Jorge, a young boy, falls ill, and a group of passengers (led by Gabriel Medrano, who admits to a frivolous previous life) storm the radio room hoping to cable ashore for help. A sailor shoots and kills Medrano, ending the cruise. Medrano's body is removed under mysterious circumstances while the remaining winners are transported to Buenos Aires in a hydroplane. There, the officer in charge urges them to sign a statement, allegedly to prevent rumors about the incident. Most accede, but some refuse to forget the senseless killing and to believe the official explanation.

Aside from possible allusions to the "ship of fools" theme, it is obvious that the novel is fraught with existential implications: The unknown destination of ship and passengers represents the situation of the existentially unaware, those who have not taken charge of their lives and begun to chart their course through time. The secrecy surrounding the trip is emblematic of the existentialist tenet that there is no answer to the ultimate questions, no essential meaning or absolute truth, and the epidemic on the ship is a symbol of "being-toward-death" as well as of death's ultimate inescapability. Medrano, with his previously unaware (existentially inauthentic) life, represents the individual who comes to terms with his existence and endows it with meaning by his death. On a secondary level of meaning, the political implications of life under a totalitarian regime are likewise well developed: the high-handed way in which authorities on land treat both the winners and the general public, the inability of the passengers to communicate with the crew, their not being privileged to know the itinerary or to have access to areas of command, as well as the violent retribution when they transgress the regime's rules and prohibitions. The ending is a clear allegory of censorship and news "management."

Structurally, the novel is composed of nine chapters, with passages in italics that convey the linguistic and metaphysical experiments of Persio (a passenger and amateur astronomer). His monologues provide a metaphysical, loosely structured commentary on events that some critics have found distracting—an unnecessary digression—whereas others have seen therein an adumbration of the innovative structure of *Hopscotch*. Persio's monologues, often poetic, provide a contrast with the realistic and prosaic style of the remainder of the novel; they exemplify the "automatic writing" propounded by Surrealists. Although Cortázar denied such imputations, many critics also have seen *The Winners* as an allegory of Argentinian society and the constant struggle between civilization and barbarism.

HOPSCOTCH

Hopscotch is Cortázar's best-known novel and probably his literary masterpiece; according to *The Times Literary Supplement*, it was the "first great novel of Spanish America." Critically acclaimed throughout the Spanish-speaking world, it was promptly translated into many languages, receiving well-deserved praise from critics and reviewers (the English version by Gregory Rabassa received the first National Book Award for translation).

A significant and highly innovative aspect of the novel is its "Table of Instructions," in which Cortázar informs the reader that "this book consists of many books, but two books above all." The first can be read in normal numerical order from chapter 1 to chapter 56 and is divided into two sections titled "From the Other Side" (that is, Paris) and "From This Side" (Argentina). Upon completing chapter 56, the reader may ignore the rest of the book "with a clear conscience." This, however, would be the conventional reader (*hembra*, or feminine/passive), as opposed to the more collaborative (*macho*, or masculine/active) reader, who becomes the author's accomplice in the creative act, reading the book in the hopscotch manner to which the title alludes. In this second book, the reading begins at chapter 73, following a sequence of chapters—nonconsecutive and apparently haphazard—indicated by the author at the end of each chapter in question. Upon reaching the final chapter, however, the collaborative reader is directed to return to chapter 58 (the next to the last), which in turn sends him or her back to chapter 131, the final one. Thus there is no definitive ending, but an endless movement back and forth between the last two chapters. This double (or multiple) structure is a principal basis for the novel's fame, involving two prime factors: the study of man's search for authenticity (by Oliveira, the protagonist) and a call for innovation or change in the structuring of narrative fiction, a departure from the traditional novelistic form.

Horacio Oliveira, an Argentinian intellectual living in Paris around 1950 (and thus a possible mask of the author), is involved in a search for authenticity. Some forty years old, he spends his time in continual and prolonged self-analysis and introspection. With a group of bohemian friends who call themselves the Serpent Club, he drinks, listens to jazz, and converses on philosophy, music, literature, art, and politics. Obsessed with the unconventional, Oliveira, during one of many drunken binges, strives to gain some sort of mystical vision through sexual intercourse in an alley with a destitute combination streetwalker and bag lady. Discovered by the police, he is deported to Argentina, where he encounters old friends and continues his search, first working in an emblematic circus and then in an equally symbolic insane asylum. Despite the inconclusive end described above, some suggest that he committed suicide, while others see a positive ending.

Given Oliveira's overpowering importance in the novel, the remaining characters are foils whose major and all but exclusive function is to provide a better perspective on him. The members of the Serpent Club, representing different countries and cultures, afford opportunities for comparison and contrast. They include Ossip Gregorovius, a Russian émigré and intellectual whom Oliveira suspects of having an affair with his own lover, "La Maga," an Uruguayan woman living in Paris with her infant son Rocamadour. Also prominent are a North American couple, Babs and Ronald; a Chinese named Wong; a Spaniard, Perico; and two Frenchmen, Guy and Étienne.

The Argentinian section or half of the novel presents the mirror image (the doppelgänger theme) in La Maga's counterpart, Lolita, whom Oliveira imagines to be the woman he left in Paris and whom he attempts to seduce. As a result, he fears that his friend (ironically and symbolically named Traveler), who is also his double, is attempting to kill him, a probable exteriorization of his own self-destructive urge. While talking to Lolita from a second-story window moments after the attempted seduction, Oliveira appears to fall or jump, allowing for the interpretation that he has committed suicide. Other chapters, however, suggest (without explaining how) that he survived the fall and insinuate as well that he became insane. Like the children's game of hopscotch, at once simple and complex, the novel has many possibilities, numerous variants, and a similar cluster of meanings, depending ultimately on the reader-player for its specific form and resultant action, and thus for its interpretation and elucidation. All of this places the work very much in the mainstream of experimental fiction and novelistic theory, in which the reader is incorporated as an important and essential part of the creative process.

62: A MODEL KIT

In Cortázar's next novel, *62: A Model Kit*, separated by some five years from *Hopscotch*, there are traces of chapter 62 of *Hopscotch*, and, lest the reader overlook this, the author mentions it in his introduction, stating that his intentions were "sketched out one day past in the

final paragraphs of chapter 62 of *Rayuela* [*Hopscotch*], which explains the title of this book." In that chapter, one of those termed "expendable," Morelli plans to write a book in which the characters will behave as if possessed by "foreign occupying forces, advancing in the quest of their freedom of the city; a quest superior to ourselves as individuals and one which uses us for its own ends." Even more so than *Hopscotch*, *62: A Model Kit* may be considered an antinovel. The suggestions of science fiction or fantastic narrative notwithstanding, it is an extremely difficult novel, as yet little studied and less elucidated by critics.

On one level, there is experimentation with language and polysemous signification, a semiserious meditation on connotation and denotation and the possible mystical or metaphysical meanings of their congruence. Thus, at the outset, Juan overhears a customer in a Paris restaurant order a *château saignant* (a rare steak) and deliberately confuses this with a *château sanglant* (a bloody castle), with all the obvious attendant gothic associations regarding such juxtaposition as a "coagulation" of myriad meanings and events. Such constellations are formed throughout the novel through the manipulation by several characters whose paths cross in the separate realms of the City and the Zone (reminiscent of the two cultures—Argentine and French—in *Hopscotch*). The Zone, where apparent existential authenticity is the norm, offers characters who attempt to master their fate and negate the mundane, while in the City, conformity and ritualism reign supreme and characters are engaged in compulsive searches of which they have no understanding, an atmosphere at once Kafkaesque and absurd, with occasional undertones of Aldous Huxley's *Brave New World* (1932) or George Orwell's *Nineteen Eighty-Four* (1949).

Principal characters include Juan, an Argentine interpreter and thus a hypothetical fictional double of the author; he loves Hélène, an anesthetist (who may symbolize Nirvana or *ataraxia* by reason of her profession), but she is hostile, cold, and bisexual. Juan's lover, the sensual Dane Tell, accompanies him on his travels. Celia, a young student at the Sorbonne, runs away from her family and eventually becomes Hélène's lover. The married couple, Nicole and Marrast, live in Paris and visit London; he is an artist, bored with his wife and generally plagued by ennui, seeking new means of amusement. Upon seeing an advertisement for Neurotics Anonymous, he writes an open letter suggesting that all neurotics gather at a gallery to see a certain painting, thus all but precipitating a riot because of the mob of neurotics who attend. Marrast makes the acquaintance of Austin, a neurotic young lutist whose sexual naïveté and ludicrous experiences with a prostitute, Georgette, Cortázar humorously exploits. Georgette insists that during intercourse Austin must take extreme care not to disarrange her coiffure. Marrast's wife, an illustrator of children's books, no longer loves her husband and, although she continues to live with him, draws gnomes that may reflect her feelings toward him. Two especially strange characters, Calac and Polanco, Argentines referred to as Tartars or Pampa savages, exemplify linguistic experimentation in their continual, senseless conversations in the subway before curious crowds; their speech consists almost totally of neologisms. Finally, and most difficult, *paredros* can be considered a sort of collective double of all the characters mentioned—although any one of them might be another *paredros*, and yet in other instances the *paredros* emerges alone and contemplates characters from an external vantage point, while participating at times in conversations and external events.

Throughout the novel, Cortázar drops hints that the whole is a gothic tale, that it is in fact a variant of that particular subgenre of the horror story that deals with vampires, and during a trip to Vienna, Juan and Dane visit the Basilisken Haus on Blutgasse (blood street), encountering legends that tell how one resident, the Blood Countess, Erzebet Bathori, bled and tortured girls in her castle, bathing in their blood. Juan and Dane associate these tales with what they imagine to be the intentions of another guest of the hotel, Frau Marta, regarding a young English girl, and manage to prevent the girl's seduction, although the door is left open to possible vampirism rather than lesbian sexuality. Otherwise, a parallel exists between Frau Marta and Hélène, as both are seduced young girls (perhaps a reappearance of the doppelgänger). Both may be considered mirrors or doubles of the Blood Countess. Although there is no clear resolution, the thematic connections between such incidents and the opening reflections on rare steak and bloody castles are immediately evident.

The fact that the structuring function exercised by plot in the conventional novel has here been replaced by a sort of poetic counterpoint and reiteration, with sustained or connected sequential action replaced by thematic repetition or idea rhyme, is but one of the several convincing arguments for classifying this work as an antinovel. Such noncharacters as the *paredros*, as well as the noncommunication of the dialogues of Calac and Polanco, are additional cases in point. The handling of time is another, as it is neither linear nor connected and usually rather vague as well, so that the reader wonders whether the "kit" of the title will prove upon assembly to be a working model with moving parts or more of a static jigsaw puzzle. The novel's concerns seem to be more with form, narrative theory, and literary double entendre than with such immediate, human, and accessible considerations as appear in *The Winners* and *Hopscotch*, points that probably explain its relative lack of popularity with the public, if not with critics.

A MANUAL FOR MANUEL

An excellent example of the perils of writing committed fiction appears in *A Manual for Manuel*, a novel that is more a political pamphlet than a work of art. Cortázar's purpose in writing this piece was to denounce the systematic torture of political prisoners in Latin America, with the somewhat naïve hope that his protest might curb such inhumane behavior. During a visit to Buenos Aires in 1973 upon publication of the book, he contributed the authorship rights to two Argentine organizations involved in working for the rights and release of political prisoners and to such prisoners' families. On the formal level of the novel, there is nothing new: The structure repeats that of Cortázar's earlier works, with similar patterns and characters; the language is stereotyped, with frequent instances of Marxist rhetoric.

Andrés, the protagonist (much like Oliveira in *Hopscotch*), finds himself torn between two worlds, although in this case they are not so much geographic and cultural as ideological. Faced with choosing between bourgeois comforts and Marxist commitment, he is unable to decide which path to take (and thus falls short of achieving existential authenticity). In a fashion recalling the collage technique of *La vuelta al día en ochenta mundos*, the novel mixes truth with fiction through the author's insertion of new articles detailing the horrors suffered by political prisoners within the fictional text, which likewise abounds in references to real-life guerrilla activities, societal taboos (especially homosexuality), and other sociological data.

Essentially, the plot concerns the activities of a group of revolutionaries in Paris who kidnap an important Latin American diplomat in order to obtain the release of political prisoners at home. The narration is handled from the perspective of two characters: Andrés, with his indecisiveness about joining the group, and a member of the guerrillas, usually identified only as "you know who." At the same time, there is a metaliterary level, where the business of writing a novel is interwoven with the political plotting, an implied contrast between two approaches to novelistic construction: Should the novelist proceed from a preconceived, fully elaborated plot, or should he follow the internal logic of the characters and situations rather than forcing them to conform to some prior plan? The two narrative perspectives of Andrés and "you know who" correspond to these approaches, for the guerrilla attempts to develop a logical progression that takes into account the characters and their circumstances, while taking notes on the plans and execution of the kidnapping. Andrés in effect assumes the position of the omniscient author-narrator who has a godlike overview, obtained in his case by reading the assault plans and thus coming to understand what is the plot of the novel. From his original posture of uncommittedness, Andrés moves to *engagement*, becoming an active participant in the events of Verrières as reflected in his later writing or rewriting of the novel (with the benefit of hindsight).

Mechanically, the plot hinges on the smuggling into France of twenty thousand dollars in counterfeit bills by two Argentineans who rendezvous with the guerrillas and exchange the money in various Paris banks. Although the diplomat is kidnapped, the group is apprehended by police and most of the guerrillas are deported, at which point Andrés becomes the novelist, compiling and ordering the notes taken by "you know who"—and thus (the reader is to believe) the novel is born. In addition to a somewhat tardy indication of the influence of Jean-Paul Sartre and the notion of politically committed literature, the novel exhibits a certain attenuated formal experimentation in the combination of the collage tech-

nique with metaliterary motifs and dual narration. Whether the novel falls by reason of its ideological weight or because of insufficient integration between the revolutionary plot (straight out of the novel of espionage and intrigue) with the factual material on political torture is an open question, but the result is not: *A Manual for Manuel* is the least fortunate of Julio Cortázar's novels.

Genaro J. Pérez

OTHER MAJOR WORKS

SHORT FICTION: *Bestiario*, 1951; *Final del juego*, 1956; *Las armas secretas*, 1959; *Historias de cronopios y de famas*, 1962 (*Cronopios and Famas*, 1969); *End of the Game, and Other Stories*, 1963 (also known as *Blow-Up, and Other Stories*, 1967); *Todos los fuegos el fuego*, 1966 (*All Fires the Fire, and Other Stories*, 1973); *Octaedro*, 1974 (included in *A Change of Light, and Other Stories*, 1980); *Alguien que anda por ahí, y otros relatos*, 1977 (included in *A Change of Light, and Other Stories*, 1980); *Un tal Lucas*, 1979 (*A Certain Lucas*, 1984); *A Change of Light, and Other Stories*, 1980; *Queremos tanto a Glenda, y otros relatos*, 1980 (*We Love Glenda So Much, and Other Stories*, 1983); *Deshoras*, 1982.

POETRY: *Presencia*, 1938 (as Julio Denís); *Los reyes*, 1949; *Pameos y meopas*, 1971; *Salvo el crepúsculo*, 1984.

NONFICTION: *Buenos Aires Buenos Aires*, 1968 (English translation, 1968); *Viaje alrededor de una mesa*, 1970; *Prosa del observatorio*, 1972 (with Antonio Galvez); *Fantomas contra los vampiros multinacionales: Una utopía realizable*, 1975; *Literatura en la revolución y revolución en la literatura*, 1976 (with Mario Vargas Llosa and Oscar Collazos); *Paris: The Essence of Image*, 1981; *Los autonautas de la cosmopista: O, Un viaje atemporal Paris-Marsella*, 1983 (with Carol Dunlop; *Autonauts of the Cosmoroute: A Timeless Voyage from Paris to Marseille*, 2007); *Nicaragua tan violentamente dulce*, 1983 (*Nicaraguan Sketches*, 1989); *Cartas*, 2000 (3 volumes).

TRANSLATIONS: *Robinson Crusoe*, 1945 (of Daniel Defoe's novel); *El inmoralista*, 1947 (of André Gide's *L'Immoraliste*); *El hombre que sabía demasiado*, c. 1948-1951 (of G. K. Chesterton's *The Man Who Knew Too Much*); *Vida y Cartas de John Keats*, c. 1948-1951 (of Lord Houghton's *Life and Letters of John Keats*); *Filosofía de la risa y del llanto*, 1950 (of Alfred Stern's *Philosophie du rire et des pleurs*); *La filosofía de Sartre y el psicoanálisis existentialista*, 1951 (of Stern's *Sartre, His Philosophy and Psychoanalysis*).

MISCELLANEOUS: *La vuelta al día en ochenta mundos*, 1967 (*Around the Day in Eighty Worlds*, 1986); *Último round*, 1969; *Divertimiento*, 1986.

BIBLIOGRAPHY

Alazraki, Jaime, and Ivan Ivask, eds. *The Final Island*. Norman: University of Oklahoma Press, 1978. Collection of essays, including two by Cortázar himself, addresses the role of magic or the marvelous as it works alongside what appears to be realism in Cortázar's fiction. Includes a chronology and an extensive bibliography that offers data on Cortázar's publications in several languages.

Alonso, Carlos J., ed. *Julio Cortázar: New Readings*. New York: Cambridge University Press, 1998. Collection of essays examines all of Cortázar's work from a variety of critical perspectives. Includes discussions of Cortázar's ethics of writing, Cortázar in the age of mechanical reproduction, and Cortázar and postmodernity. Supplemented by bibliographical references and index.

Bloom, Harold, ed. *Julio Cortázar*. Philadelphia: Chelsea House, 2005. One in a series of books designed for students that provide analysis of literary works and biographical information about authors. This volume features essays on the novels *Hopscotch, 62: A Model Kit*, and *A Manual for Manuel* as well as analysis of some of Cortázar's other works. Includes bibliographical references and index.

Boldy, Steven. *The Novels of Julio Cortázar*. New York: Cambridge University Press, 1980. Presents a helpful biographical sketch linked to the major developments in Cortázar's writing in an introduction and then concentrates on four Cortázar novels: *The Winners, Hopscotch, 62: A Model Kit*, and *A Manual for Manuel*. Includes notes, bibliography, and index.

Garfield, Evelyn Picon. *Julio Cortázar*. New York: Frederick Ungar, 1975. Begins and ends with personal interviews that Garfield obtained with Cortázar at his home in Provence, France. Examines the neurotic obsession of the characters in Cortázar's fiction and offers firsthand commentary by Cortázar on his methods of writing and his own experiences that helped create his work. Cortázar's philosophies, his preferences, and even his own personal nightmares are expounded upon, illuminating much of the symbolism found in his work. Includes chronology, analysis, complete bibliography, and index.

Hernandez del Castillo, Ana. *Keats, Poe, and the Shaping of Cortázar's Mythopoesis*. Amsterdam: John Benjamins, 1981. Discusses the influence of the works of John Keats and Edgar Allan Poe on Cortázar. Asserts that of the two poets, whose works Cortázar translated, Poe had the greater influence on Cortázar. Examines the role of archetypes in mythology and psychology and how they have been used in the works of all three writers. Includes an excellent index.

Peavler, Terry J. *Julio Cortázar*. Boston: Twayne, 1990. Divides Cortázar's fiction into four categories—the fantastic, the mysterious, the psychological, and the realistic—to show how Cortázar used these genres as games. Includes a chronology and a thorough bibliography.

Standish, Peter. *Understanding Julio Cortázar*. Columbia: University of South Carolina Press, 2001. Assessment of Cortázar's novels and other works is structured around metaphors of boxing. Offers a brief overview of Cortázar's life and synopses of his books and then provides a more detailed analysis of the themes in Cortázar's works, his opinions of literary genres and the creative process, and how he handled tension between his political and aesthetic goals.

Yovanovich, Gordana. *Julio Cortázar's Character Mosaic: Reading the Longer Fiction*. Toronto, Ont.: University of Toronto Press, 1991. Three chapters focus on Cortázar's four major novels and his fluctuating presentations of character as narrators, symbols, and other figures of language. Includes notes and bibliography.

DOBRICA ĆOSIĆ

Born: Velika Drenova, Kingdom of Serbs, Croats, and Slovenes (now in Serbia); December 29, 1921

PRINCIPAL LONG FICTION

Daleko je sunce, 1951 (*Far Away Is the Sun*, 1963)
Koreni, 1954
Deobe, 1961 (3 volumes)
Bajka, 1966
Vreme smrti, 1972-1979 (4 volumes; *This Land, This Time*, 1983 [includes *Into the Battle*, *A Time of Death*, *Reach to Eternity*, and *South to Destiny*])
Vreme zla, 1985-1990 (includes *Grešnik*, 1985; *Otpadnik*, 1986; and *Vernik*, 1990)
Vreme vlasti, 1996, 2007 (2 volumes)

OTHER LITERARY FORMS

Dobrica Ćosić (CHOH-seech) is primarily a novelist, but he has also written a series of books and articles on sociopolitical themes, collected in the books *Sedam dana u Budimpešti* (1957; seven days in Budapest) and *Akcija* (1965; action). These books gave Ćosić opportunities to express his views on various ideological, political, and cultural problems that have preoccupied him his entire adult life. They shed some light on his novels, but, for the most part, they reflect the other half of the author's sphere of interest. Among the other significant books that Ćosić has published in addition to his novels are *Stvarno i moguće* (1982; real and possible), *Piševi zapisi* (2000-2004, 4 volumes; writer's notes), *Kosovo* (2004), and *Prijatelji* (2005; friends). These volumes collect Ćosić's articles and notes, offering a gold mine of details about the author's thinking and experiences in his various activities, especially in his literary life.

ACHIEVEMENTS

Throughout his literary career, Dobrica Ćosić has been interested in the forces that have molded, influenced, and decided the fate of his countrymen. In particular, he has attempted to shed light on the effects of the

two world wars on his country. Having been primarily politically oriented all of is life, Ćosić found it natural to turn to historical and social themes once he discovered his artistic urge. He was one of the first post-World War II novelists in Yugoslavia to broach sensitive subject matter, not so much to describe it as to find the real moving forces behind the actors and their actions in these tragic events. From World War II, in which he participated directly, he moved back to World War I and then to the period following World War II, searching for the links between them. By tracing the rise and fall of two families in almost all of his novels, he presents a powerful saga of the Serbian society passing from a primitive stage of the late nineteenth century into the modern era. A pronounced artistic prowess adds to his works a mark of excellence, making him one of the best contemporary Serbian writers.

BIOGRAPHY

Dobrica Ćosić was born on December 29, 1921, in a village in central Serbia, Velika Drenova. His parents were farmers, and he was destined to enroll in an agricultural school. There, he was exposed to illegal Socialist literature and was accepted in the Communist Youth League in 1938, for which he was expelled from school. In World War II, he participated actively on the side of the partisans as a political commissar. After the war, he occupied several official positions, among them the office of parliamentary representative and director of the venerable Srpska Književna Zadruga (Serbian literary society). He began to publish during the war, and with the publication of his first novel, *Far Away Is the Sun*, he quickly became one of the leading young Serbian writers. His fame grew with every new novel, but so did his dissatisfaction with political developments in his country. He began to call for more freedom, became a leading dissident, and as a result was stripped of all of his posts and duties. Thereafter, he worked as a freelance writer, completing his magnum opus, *This Land, This Time*, and leading the fight for greater democratic freedom in his country. He spent his later years writing works of nonfiction as well as two trilogies, *Vreme zla* (a time of evil) and *Vreme vlasti* (a time of authority); the third volume of the latter planned trilogy remains unwritten because Ćosić has declared that he is finished with writing.

ANALYSIS

Dobrica Ćosić's entry into literature was made easier by his rich experiences in World War II. He came out of it as a proud young victor, full of hopes for a better future and ready for further sacrifices. This desire to help in building a better life for his fellow human beings undoubtedly spurred him to his first literary efforts. As he grew as a writer, however, another desire became even stronger—to seek the truth and to tell it in an artistic fashion, regardless of consequences.

FAR AWAY IS THE SUN

Ćosić's first novel, *Far Away Is the Sun*, is more than another fictional account of war experiences. Although based on true events and largely autobiographical, it is a skillfully written war novel, with fast-moving action, believable events, and well-developed characters. It had a refreshing effect after Ćosić experienced several abortive attempts at writing war fiction in the manner of Socialist Realism. The novel's refreshing quality is reflected in a much greater objectivity. To be sure, the partisan struggle is still glorified; the leading characters display, at times, the superhuman powers and the instinctive ability to separate right from wrong characteristic of Socialist Realist heroes; and the enemy is, for the most part, utterly evil. There is also, however, a willingness to admit that the heroes might sometimes be wrong after all. This attitude is best illustrated by an interesting possibility that all four parties involved in the climactic decision at the end of the novel, when the survival of the partisan unit is at stake, could be both right and wrong. By taking such an attitude, the author shows his awareness of the complexity of situations in which the warring sides often found themselves. He also seems willing to admit that, even though the correctness of the partisan cause was never in doubt, individual actions and decisions were not always above reproach.

The novel's restrained tone and its traditional realistic manner, as well as its undeniable originality, despite some similarities to Aleksandr Aleksandrovich Fadeev's *Razgrom* (1927; *The Nineteen*, 1929) and Nikolai Alekseevich Ostrovsky's *Kak zakalialas' stal'* (1932-1934; *The Making of a Hero*, 1937), make it understandable why *Far Away Is the Sun* is enduringly popular in Ćosić's homeland—almost a classic. Ćosić would surpass himself in later novels, but this work will always remain one of those whose success defies an easy explanation, especially when it is considered in the light of what it meant in the struggle against Socialist Realism.

KORENI

With *Koreni* (roots), Ćosić began a series of novels that would, when completed, offer a large canvas of the development of Serbian society in the twentieth century. The time of *Koreni* actually goes back to the last decade of the nineteenth century. The main character, a strong-willed, rebellious, and stubborn peasant, Aćim Katić, is driven by an often expressed desire to see the creation of a just democratic society among the Serbian peasants, who had been ruled by primitive impulses for centuries. For that purpose, he sends his younger son to be educated in France. When his son refuses to return to his native village upon the completion of his studies and, what is worse, joins a political party opposing his father's, the true nature of Aćim Katić comes through. Deeply hurt by his son's betrayal, he manifests through his grief and anger a frustrated will to dominate everyone and everything around him, as well as a hidden fear of defeat by both human beings and fate. He marries his sterile older son to a strong peasant woman and arranges for an offspring with the help of an equally virile neighbor. At the end of the novel, the powerfully created characters and their destinies remain in limbo, to be taken up again in later novels. The roots are revealed, but the growth is yet to come.

This stark peasant tale is told in a highly lyric and experimental style, which fits the dark, naturalistic atmosphere of the life of Serbian peasants at the beginning of the twentieth century. The rather simple realism of Ćosić's first novel gives way to a poetic realism, revealing his preoccupation not only with social and political matters but also with a search for a truly artistic idiom—a search that will be repeated from novel to novel.

DEOBE

In his ambitious novel *Deobe* (divisions), Ćosić returns to World War II, taking up again many themes from *Far Away Is the Sun:* bravery under the most trying conditions; the struggle of a small nation against an overpowering enemy; peasants bearing the brunt of that struggle, reluctant to fight away from their homes; corruption of the existing order; and the weaknesses and sins of the enemy. The basic change lies in the point of view. In the former novel, the war struggle is seen from the vantage point of the partisans; in *Deobe*, the point of view shifts to the opposing side, the Chetniks, a nationalist force fighting both the Germans and the partisans. The Chetniks are not treated favorably at all; their point of view is used mainly to discredit them. In this sense, *Deobe* is much less objective than any other of Ćosić's novels. The Chetniks are maligned, while the partisans, though barely visible in the distant background, show their moral superiority.

Ćosić's subjectivity, however, can be explained by his desire, among other things, to understand why the Chetniks committed the despicable acts ascribed to them and whether they could have behaved differently. Why do human beings commit such bestial acts of horror? (The knife, used most often in perpetrating these horrors, becomes here the symbol of bestiality.) Why is hatred so deep that it destroys reason? Can the descendants of those same people comprehend and believe many years later that such acts were, and even could be, committed by humans? Thus the purpose of the author's efforts in this novel is not the objective, or even subjective, depiction of the civil war, but rather an attempt to penetrate the way of thinking of people responsible for war. Seen from this angle, *Deobe* attains a much more universal significance than may be perceived on first reading.

Not that Ćosić offers satisfactory answers. As the war drags on and the inhumanity of the participants intensifies to an alarming degree, he becomes more philosophical about it. He is convinced that war leads to utter demoralization, total chaos, and despair. Everybody feels compelled to fight everybody else, hatred permeates everything, all are killers. The eye-for-an-eye principle becomes dominant. Even though Ćosić attributes most of these aberrations to the enemies of the partisans, a realization grows in him that more is involved than the struggle for social, political, and ideological causes and changes for the better. On one hand, war has moved inward, into the very hearts and souls of the participants. On the other, the signs of resignation and helplessness are increasingly visible, illustrated by statements such as, "It's war. . . . We are guilty because we are humans

and because we are alive." There is even a hint that war is a total mystery, beyond anyone's ability to explain it.

Descendants of the characters from *Koreni* reappear in *Deobe*, though in somewhat secondary roles. Ćosić again experiments with his style, mostly by using a film-influenced technique of numerous quick shots, many flashbacks, scant description, frugal punctuation, and a choruslike, impersonal character, a kind of Everyman on his descent into Hell. The multiple voices of the chorus symbolize the universality of the tragedy portrayed in the novel. In this sense, *Deobe* is an important step toward the mature style of Ćosić's final works, especially *This Land, This Time*.

Bajka

Bajka (the fairy tale) is more of an interlude than an organic step in Ćosić's development. His only novel not based fully on realistic events, it is nevertheless a repository of his ideas about the same problems depicted in his more realistic works. In a thinly veiled allegory about a mythical state, in the tradition of Yevgeny Zamyatin's *My* (1952, written 1920-1921; *We*, 1924), Aldous Huxley's *Brave New World* (1932), and George Orwell's *Nineteen Eighty-Four* (1949), the author attempts to visualize the future on the basis of the present developments. In this respect, *Bajka* is also an anti-utopian novel.

It is not easy to penetrate the allegorical and symbolic framework of this "fairy tale." Moreover, Ćosić's desire to modernize his expression—a process evident since *Koreni*—makes it more difficult to follow the already thin main thread. Action and plot, however, are not as important to the author as is his intention to examine in a semiessayistic, pseudophilosophical fashion the underpinnings of the events depicted in his earlier works (as well as in his later ones). Ćosić's obsession with endless strife among human beings—above all, with war as its most drastic manifestation—is the moving force in this work. The result is a complex vision of a man's endeavor to forge his own destiny, his successes and failures, and his belief, almost a fanatical faith, that the ideal of a better humanity can indeed be realized. At the end of the novel, the man is still looking at a shimmering quartz stone lying on the river bottom. That, however, does not dampen his enthusiasm and faith, for he vows to continue his search for a better future.

Bajka is, therefore, more a testimony to a human being's determination to achieve his goal of a perfect society than a criticism of the shortcomings of the present world. In this sense, the deeply humanistic views of the author attest his success in lifting his vision above the horizon of everyday concerns. The examples of Adolf Hitler and Joseph Stalin as equal partners in their efforts to dehumanize the individual, which Ćosić analyzes at length, serve as warnings of what could happen if one abandons vigilance and hope.

THIS LAND, THIS TIME

In 1972, Ćosić began what became a series of four volumes about the fate and struggle of the Serbian nation in World War I. Next to *Far Away Is the Sun*, *This Land, This Time* is the most realistic of Ćosić's works, adhering closely to the historical facts and chronological order of events that enveloped the small state of Serbia during World War I: a short prewar scene, the outbreak of the war, initial defeats and ensuing military and moral victories, the crushing though not final defeat in 1915, the superhuman retreat through the snow-covered mountains, and the rescue of the survivors on the Albanian seashore. It is not so much the subject matter, however, monumental though it may be, that lends the work epic proportions; rather, it is Ćosić's approach to the work's theme, his flair for the dramatic and his skill in shaping characters, actions, and situations, and, above all, his understanding of the little man, who carries the heaviest burden in any war.

Another aspect of this work outweighs all others, a subject that has concerned Ćosić from his very first novel: the phenomenon of war as humankind's most fateful mode of behavior and the author's philosophical attitude toward it. *This Land, This Time* offers a wide variety of opinions about war and what makes people wage war, not all of which can be attributed to the author. These opinions depend on the persons expressing them. By tracing the opinions about and characterizations of war in this work, one can find a key to Ćosić's most important concern as a writer.

For a long time, the notion of war in Ćosić's novels depended to a large degree on the social backgrounds and positions of the persons involved. The old peasant leader from *Koreni*, Aćim, expresses a conservative peasant view when he advises his grandson against deserting: "Go with people, son. One has no better road." His son Vukašin, a politician and opposition leader educated in France, has a much more sophisticated notion of war, as befits a highly educated intellectual: "War is the only time when we work for history and acquire respect through suffering and dying." For the crafty political leader of the country, war is a supreme test of statesmanship and of the stamina of the people. A high commanding officer expresses, perhaps not surprisingly, a loathing for war. He considers himself to be the greatest coward, yet it is he who continually insists that Serbia fights only for survival and, therefore, that right and justice are on its side. A young Socialist has his misgivings, believing that Serbia can be saved only through a revolution, yet even he fights on bravely, as does almost everyone else.

Other opinions on war, expressed at random as the situation dictates, indicate the degree to which the participants were forced to cope with this cataclysmic upheaval. For some, war is a great equalizer that unmasks everything and shames people more than it kills them, a terrible illness that will conquer all. As the disaster brings on more misery, suffering, and death, some people become more philosophical, seeing war as older and more eternal than humankind and as revealing essential truths about life; others, less stouthearted, seem to falter under the weight of the calamity. Peasants and city dwellers, leaders and simple soldiers alike are disappointed in their allies and in civilization in general. They believe that small nations never win a war forever and that the deck is always stacked against them. Europe is for them a criminals' hunting ground and a thieves' bazaar where politics has a field day, removing all restraints and giving the right to all means, so that murderers kill murderers. All of these opinions can be summed up in the oft-repeated phrase "War is hell."

As the agony of the Serbian army and nation unfolds in *This Land, This Time*, most, if not all, of the characters come to an agreement about the calamity that has befallen them as well as about the reasons for, and the meaning of, war. They tend to concur that war, cruel and unjust as it is, must be endured because the alternative is even worse. Death becomes unimportant as everyone's will to survive is put to the sternest test. This iron will is expressed through the commanding officer, General

Mišić. Himself of peasant stock, unpretentious and down-to-earth, he repeats time and again the reason that Serbia must fight on and endure beyond the humanly possible: "Ours is a peasant army, defending its home and children. . . . When one fights for survival, he has the right to do anything. . . . Only the sacrifices made for one's survival are not in vain." Most people accept this simple reasoning and endure more than they believe they are capable of enduring. Even the young Socialist changes his thinking and accepts his date with destiny.

It is through General Mišić that Ćosić expresses his conclusions about war. If in *Far Away Is the Sun* he condones war primarily for the sake of an idea, and in *Deobe* he has no answer for the incomprehensible cruelty of man, in *This Land, This Time* he finds the justification for war, even if in one case only: in self-defense and in the struggle for survival. He has found a perfect example for such justification in the death struggle of his small nation against seemingly insurmountable odds. He does so not out of chauvinistic impulses but rather from the position that all human beings, through their nations, have the right and obligation to defend their dignity and liberty. It must be added that it is not so much biological survival that Ćosić has in mind as it is the defense of nations and societies where liberty, justice, and human dignity prevail. He believes that in such a fateful struggle, humankind must display high moral qualities, for only then is life worth living, and only then does freedom become necessary. He believes that his nation values justice above freedom, that war is won and lost in the soul, and that the victor's bravery is not always the most important thing. Barbarism in the name of one's country and freedom is a sign of military despair.

In *This Land, This Time*, Ćosić found the answer to the question that had plagued him since he began writing—indeed, since he began thinking. While people will probably never stop warring and committing atrocities and inflicting suffering, war acquires justification for those who defend themselves against annihilation—and then only if they fight for freedom and justice at the same time. This is the final and most significant message of *This Land, This Time* and of Ćosić's entire opus. Through it, Ćosić seems to have found peace with himself.

In addition to the epic theme and the problems Ćosić tackles and solves in his magnum opus, *This Land, This Time* shows the maturity of the author's style. His control over the plot and characters, his skillful description of war scenes without glorification of heroic deeds or dwelling on gruesome aspects, and his modernistic blend of narration, dialogue, and documentary material—all contribute to a powerful impact on the reader. The logical fifth volume in the series, depicting the final triumph of Serbia in World War I—which remains unwritten—would offer support for the claim that *This Land, This Time* is the best novel in Serbian literature. Even as it is, it could be favorably compared with Leo Tolstoy's *Voyna i mir* (1865-1869; *War and Peace*, 1886) and Mikhail Sholokhov's *Tikhii Don* (1928-1940; *The Silent Don*, 1942), their many differences notwithstanding.

LATER WORKS

In his next two series of novels, Ćosić follows the development and activities of the main characters of *This Land, This Time*, especially of the Katić family. The political life in Serbia turned to the left, but the leftist characters show also signs of rebellion against the dictatorial nature of the Communist Party. In the trilogy *Vreme zla*—consisting of *Grešnik* (1985; the sinner), *Otpadnik* (1986; the apostate), and *Vernik* (1990; the believer)—some leftist characters become less convinced of the correct policy of the party; in the process, they pay the price for their idealism through persecution and even death. Ćosić mixes fact and fiction, using his personal experiences, yet his artistic skill keeps the novels from becoming political tracts. At the same time, the reader who knows of Ćosić's personal experiences arrives inevitably at the conclusion that the fate of the main character, the young socialist Bogdan Dragović, is similar to that of the author himself (fortunately without the same end result). Knowing also that the author has changed his beliefs in the party, the reader can see that the use of the fates of the sinners and apostates in *Vreme zla* serves the author as a personal catharsis. Moreover, *Vreme zla* is an example of the politically tinged belletristic literature popular after World War II.

The same can be said of Ćosić's next, and probably final, work, *Vreme vlasti*. In this work, Ćosić makes it sound almost inevitable that the sins of the past lead to the rise of authoritarianism, almost to dictatorship, as shown by the Communist Party in Yugoslavia. As is so often the case, a totalitarian society must have enemies in order to justify its existence. The enemy in this instance includes several thousand former party members who had declared allegiance to Stalin and the Soviet Union after the 1948 break between the two parties. Many of them have died interned in the infamous island of Goli Otok, and almost all of them have been psychologically maimed for life. Although the author refrains from realistic depiction of the tortures and other kinds of inhumane treatment suffered by the prisoners, the impact on the readers remains strong. It is interesting to note that Ćosić appears here personally for the first time in all of his novels. It is unfortunate that he abandoned the completion of this planned trilogy, but the zenith of his entire literary career has been achieved. That the reader willingly suspends disbelief and follows Ćosić as a real actor in the drama can be attributed to the author's artistic prowess.

Vasa D. Mihailovich

OTHER MAJOR WORKS

NONFICTION: *Sedam dana u Budimpešti*, 1957; *Akcija*, 1965; *Odgovornosti*, 1966; *Moć i strepnje*, 1971; *Stvarno i moguće*, 1982; *Srpsko pitanje: Demokratsko pitanje*, 1992; *Piščevi zapisi*, 2000-2008; *Kosovo*, 2004; *Prijatelji*, 2005; *Razgovori i životopis*, 2005.

MISCELLANEOUS: *Sabrana dela Dobrice Ćosića*, 1966 (8 volumes); *Dela Dobrice Ćosića*, 2000-2005 (25 volumes).

BIBLIOGRAPHY

Đjukić, Slavoljub. *Lovljenje vetra: Politička ispovest Dobrice Ćosića*. Belgrade: Samizdat B92, 2001. Provides a thorough presentation of Ćosić's political views as reflected in his works and in his participation in the political life of Yugoslavia in the 1990's.

Kadić, Ante. *Contemporary Serbian Literature*. The Hague: Mouton, 1964. Includes Ćosić among the authors discussed.

Lukić, Sveta. *Contemporary Yugoslav Literature: A Sociopolitical Approach*. Translated by Pola Triandis, edited by Gertrude Joch Robinson. Urbana: University of Illinois Press, 1972. Includes discussion of Ćosić's treatment of social matters from the political point of view.

Mihailović, Vasa D. "Aspects of Nationalism in Dobrica Ćosić's Novel *A Time of Death*: Chauvinism or Sincere Patriotism." *World Literature Today* 60, no. 3 (1986): 413-416. Suggests that what is sometimes criticized as chauvinism in Ćosić's magnum opus is in reality an expression of love for his country, with a healthy dose of criticism of its mistakes.

_____. "War in the Works of Dobrica Ćosić." *Serbian Studies* 3, nos. 1/2 (1984/1985): 27-34. Explains how Ćosić's views of war influence his works, all of which are concerned with war, directly or indirectly.

Miller, Nick. *The Nonconformists: Culture, Politics, and Nationalism in a Serbian Intellectual Circle, 1944-1991*. New York: Central European University Press, 2007. Discusses Serbia's national movement by examining the works of three Serbian intellectuals—Ćosić, painter Mića Popović, and literary critic Borislav Mihajlović Mihiz.

Milojković-Djurić, Jelena. "Approaches to National Identities: Ćosić's and Pirjeve's Debate on Ideological and Literary Issues." *East European Quarterly* 30, no. 1 (March 22, 1996): 63-73. Focuses on a public discussion carried out from 1961 onward by writers Ćosić and Dušan Pirjeve regarding the role of cultural collaboration among Yugoslavia's republics.

JAMES GOULD COZZENS

Born: Chicago, Illinois; August 19, 1903
Died: Stuart, Florida; August 9, 1978

PRINCIPAL LONG FICTION

Confusion, 1924
Michael Scarlett, 1925
Cock Pit, 1928
The Son of Perdition, 1929
S.S. San Pedro, 1931
The Last Adam, 1933 (also known as *A Cure of Flesh*, 1958)
Castaway, 1934
Men and Brethren, 1936
Ask Me Tomorrow, 1940
The Just and the Unjust, 1942
Guard of Honor, 1948
By Love Possessed, 1957
Morning, Noon, and Night, 1968

OTHER LITERARY FORMS

In addition to his thirteen novels, James Gould Cozzens (KUHZ-uhnz) published two collections of short stories, *Child's Play* (1958) and *Children and Others* (1964), that contain most of the twenty-seven stories he wrote between 1920 and 1950 for mass-circulation magazines such as the *Saturday Evening Post*, *Collier's*, and *Redbook*. Another collection, *A Flower in Her Hair*, was published in 1975. Cozzens also served as an associate editor for *Winged Foot*, a small in-house magazine published by the New York Athletic Club, in the period 1928-1929 and for *Fortune* magazine in 1937-1938. Matthew Bruccoli has edited a collection of some of these miscellaneous pieces, published under the title *Just Representations* (1978).

ACHIEVEMENTS

James Gould Cozzens might best be characterized as a writer's writer. His work has traditionally been praised more highly by fellow writers and editors than it has by critics or book buyers. From the beginning of his writing career, when *The Atlantic Monthly* printed an essay Cozzens wrote as a sixteen-year-old high school student,

professionals have been drawn to his taut, disciplined style, his carefully structured plots, and his complex, precise renderings of character and background detail. His first novel, written during his freshman year at Harvard University, received a favorable review from *The New York Times*. His fifth, *S.S. San Pedro*, won the Scribner's Prize for fiction. Most of his next eight novels were Book-of-the-Month Club selections.

Cozzens won the O. Henry Award for a short story in 1936, a Pulitzer Prize for *Guard of Honor* in 1948, and, in 1957, the William Dean Howells Medal, which the American Academy of Arts and Letters gives only once every five years for outstanding achievement in fiction, for *By Love Possessed*. In his speech nominating the novel for the Howells Medal, Malcolm Cowley called the work a solid achievement, written with a craftsmanship and intelligence that would be envied by all of Cozzens's fellow novelists. Literary critic Orville Prescott claimed that at least three of Cozzens's novels were among the finest ever written in America, and C. P. Snow thought Cozzens one of the country's best realistic novelists. When John Fischer reviewed *By Love Possessed* in *Harper's* in 1957, he suggested that Cozzens was one of the very few important serious novelists in the country. He claimed that the body of Cozzens's work clearly needed reevaluation, and he recommended it for a Nobel Prize. The editor who collected many of his shorter pieces, Matthew Bruccoli, has compared him favorably to another Nobel Prize winner, claiming that Cozzens's work is often so distinguished that it could make even William Faulkner's prose look amateurish by comparison.

Despite such praise, Cozzens's novels did not fare well with the book-buying public or with the country's major reviewers during his lifetime. He achieved best-sellerdom only once, when *By Love Possessed* sold 170,000 copies within the first six weeks of its publication.

Cozzens led a quiet, reclusive life, intentionally shying away from the channels of publicity through which many twentieth century authors promoted their works. He wrote slowly, spending more than twenty-five years on his last three novels alone, while doing little to keep his name before his audience or the publishing trade. More decisively, the novels themselves celebrated such a complex view of everyday human life that critics and readers alike regularly abandoned them unread, half-read, or misread. Cozzens was frequently condemned in print not for what he wrote but for what he did not write. Objections were regularly leveled against his choice of characters or his lack of social concern. The heroes of his fictions were most often professional men who lived unobtrusively in the small towns of the Atlantic seaboard. Their stories seldom showed the drama, outrage, alienation, terror, or rebellion that distinguished the characters of other mid-twentieth century writers.

The tensions that preoccupied his contemporaries seemed not to touch Cozzens very deeply; their major solutions—social reform, rugged individuality, anarchy, or despair—did not accord with his complicated worldview. For avoiding the fashionable in plot, character, and theme, he was often branded conservative, apathetic, bigoted, or reactionary—a spokesman for a traditional point of view far out of step with the realities of urban, industrial, and international America. By the time of his death, however, critics and readers alike had begun to see his intricate plots, complex ideas, and detailed psychological studies of modern men as the work not of a conservative mind but of an independent thinker who simply took a broader and deeper view than most of his contemporaries.

BIOGRAPHY

James Gould Cozzens's life was as quiet, as competently professional, and as outwardly uneventful as the lives of the prosperous executives, lawyers, ministers, and generals who inhabit his fiction. He was born in Chicago, Illinois, on August 19, 1903, to a comfortable though not wealthy businessman, Henry William Cozzens, and his wife, Bertha. The family moved east, and Cozzens grew up on Staten Island. He attended private schools in New York and, for six years, Kent School, a preparatory school in Connecticut. By the time he was sixteen, he was already showing a precocious ability for writing.

While still at Kent School, he managed to have his essay "A Democratic School" published by *The Atlantic Monthly*. A year later, he matriculated to Harvard University and spent much of his freshman year writing his first novel, *Confusion*. It was published in 1924 by B. J. Brimmer, and the success of it, he later admitted, went to his head. He immediately began a second, taking a leave of absence from school to complete it. *Michael Scarlett* was published in 1925 and received such favorable press from publications such as *The New York Times* that Cozzens gave himself over completely to writing. Instead of returning to college, he spent the next year in Cuba, planning his next fictions and earning pocket money by tutoring the children of American engineers. During the next eleven years, he published seven lengthy novels, the first three of which—*Cock Pit*, *The Son of Perdition*, and *S.S. San Pedro*—drew heavily on his experiences in the Caribbean. During 1926, he continued his wandering, spending more than a year in Europe; the

James Gould Cozzens. (Library of Congress)

trip eventually formed the basis for *Ask Me Tomorrow*. He met Bernice Baumgarten, and, on December 31, 1927, he married her. The Cozzenses settled into a quiet Connecticut suburb where Bernice could commute regularly to Manhattan for her career as a literary agent and where Cozzens could have the seclusion to continue writing full time.

The Cozzenses spent much of their next forty years single-mindedly dedicated to their professional endeavors, their careers intertwined: Bernice was Cozzens's first reader and his literary agent. In the little contact Cozzens allowed himself with the outside world, the troubled sense of duty and the gritty sense of honor that characterized many of his fictional heroes could be detected. When the Depression and a decline in his own royalties strained the family finances in the late 1930's, Cozzens took on an editorial job at *Fortune*. When patriotic idealism swept the country after the Japanese attack on Pearl Harbor in 1941, Cozzens—at age thirty-nine—volunteered to serve in the U.S. Army Air Corps and by 1945 had earned himself the rank of major. He avoided public appearances, shunned interviews, and allowed himself to be caught up in few causes. For most of his professional career, a career that spanned more than fifty years, Cozzens wrote. He died of pneumonia while vacationing in Florida on August 9, 1978.

ANALYSIS

In an often-quoted letter written to his English publishers, James Gould Cozzens defined the essence of his work, "the point of it all," as an attempt to give structure and understanding to "the immensity and the immense complexity" of human experience. This was more than a platitude for Cozzens; it was an obsession. "I wanted to show," he continued, "the peculiar effects of the interaction of innumerable individuals functioning in ways at once determined by and determining the functioning of innumerable others." Cozzens was sure that the key to understanding modern man lay neither in exploring the individual psyche nor in analyzing social institutions. Rather, he believed the key lay in exploring human interaction: the way tough-minded individuals gave shape to but were also shaped by the lives and destinies of many others. He saw society not as an organization but as an organism "with life and purposes of its own" that threat-

ened to leave little for a modern man to do in the complicated world he had created. He dissected the lives of ordinary men, probing their beliefs and decisions and weighing the outcomes of their failures and their successes.

Beginning with *S.S. San Pedro* in 1931 and ending with his last novel, *Morning, Noon, and Night*, in 1968, Cozzens singled out progressively smaller pieces of these ordinary lives and studied them more and more intensely. He was like a physicist, bent on unlocking the secrets of the social universe by examining smaller and smaller particles of matter with ever greater precision—and, like the modern physicist, Cozzens eventually resigned himself to the notion that chance and uncertainty played a disproportionately large role in the outcomes of the lives he studied. The networks of interaction, he warned, are infinitely more complex than a man can imagine. Nevertheless, novel by novel, he also groped toward an affirmation of the small but dignified role that a man could still play in the intricate world he had devised, if only he would live "rightly." This single-minded effort to define precisely how a man should live gave Cozzens's novels many of their strengths and most of their weaknesses.

Studying the outlaw, the outcast, or the superhero did not suit these purposes. Neither did studying the pawn, the downtrodden, or the disadvantaged. Cozzens would not allow himself the luxury of writing about singularly interesting characters or immediately sympathetic ones. He focused instead on those everyday beings who were influential enough to be society's leaders and flawed enough to be its victims. In *S.S. San Pedro*, he fixed his attention on Anthony Bradell, the ship's senior second officer. In *The Last Adam*, he investigated a rural country doctor. In *Men and Brethren*, he studied a series of decisions made by one minister. In *The Just and the Unjust*, Cozzens finally combined the best qualities of these early characters. His hero, Abner Coats, is a reasonable and intelligent lawyer who can understand human weakness, who can distrust the excesses of his own emotionalism, and who can use his honest realism to resist the commonplace responses of his fellow people, yet finds his commitment to living dutifully and honorably sorely strained. For Coats, living well comes to mean trying to prevail over the randomness, the meanness, and the stupidity that surround him. As Cozzens's studies of how to live well grew more intricate, it took him longer to complete each of his novels. Cozzens's next novel, *Guard of Honor*, required six years of gestation; his last two novels, *By Love Possessed* and *Morning, Noon, and Night*, took him another twenty years to write.

As Cozzens examined his protagonists more slowly, he also narrowed his focus, plotting his novels more densely and condensing their actions to briefer segments of time. The action of *The Last Adam* takes place in exactly four weeks; the action in *Men and Brethren* spans about two days. In *Guard of Honor* and *By Love Possessed*, time is compressed even further, and by *Morning, Noon, and Night*, the action is reduced to a ten-hour stretch studied in more than four hundred pages of close analysis. At the same time, Cozzens progressively reduced the scope of his novels. His earliest fictions tended to be sprawling. *Michael Scarlett* was set in Elizabethan England, while *Cock Pit*, *The Son of Perdition*, and *S.S. San Pedro* wandered over much of the Caribbean. With *The Last Adam*, however, Cozzens began to understand what could be accomplished by limiting the events he studied to a tightly structured few and by exploring in depth all their intricate consequences. By the time he published *Morning, Noon, and Night*, his control of setting was so secure that the entire novel could be plotted from a single room: the downstairs study of Henry Dodd Worthington's management consultant firm.

Novel by novel, Cozzens continued to reduce the range of characters, incidents, and locales. Each novel examined more closely the tangled implications of human choice, developing a complex vision of man that both admitted his smallness, helplessness, and isolation and celebrated the triumphs that right living still made attainable. Unlike many of his contemporaries, the more Cozzens came to understand and shape his material, the more quietly optimistic he grew. In *Michael Scarlett*, a dashing and intelligent Cambridge student, interested in poetry, dueling, brawling, and sex, and a friend of Christopher Marlowe, Thomas Nashe, Ben Jonson, John Donne, and William Shakespeare, uses his brilliance only to fashion for himself an early and violent death. Francis Ellery, the slightly autobiographical hero of *Ask Me Tomorrow*, comes to realize that his intelligence has limits, that his fate is bound up with a Europe whose complicated history and incomprehensible languages he might never understand, and that his only hope lies in continuing to survive. Gradually, Cozzens transforms the pessimism of these early efforts to affirmations of a quieter, steadier path. The heroes of his last four novels come to share a deeper appreciation for the complications in their lives and their lack of clear-cut choices, but they learn also to confront their own fears openly and to strive for competence in spite of them. These quiet professionals seemed to have a greater impact on their world than the flashy heroes of the earlier novels. General Ira Beal's overcoming of his own weaknesses in *Guard of Honor* could have a small or perhaps an immeasurably large influence on the outcome of World War II. Arthur Winner's and Henry Worthington's honest confrontations with love, corruption, and human frailty in the last two novels benefit their families, their societies, and even themselves. Cozzens had set out to study the webs of people's interactions; he concluded that their world was far more difficult than most humans would allow themselves to believe, and far more ennobling.

EARLY NOVELS

Cozzens's early novels—*Confusion, Michael Scarlett, Cock Pit, The Son of Perdition, S.S. San Pedro, The Last Adam*, and *Castaway*—mark his development from a talented apprentice to a steady professional. It took him fourteen years to turn out these seven works and thirty-four years to write his next six. The mature Cozzens was not particularly proud of the early attempts, and he eventually convinced his publisher to remove the first four from his official list of works. Among these seven novels, however, are some of his most accessible works; taken as a group, they show his steady growth toward the styles, themes, and characters that would come to dominate his mature fiction.

Most of the early novels feature a spokesperson, usually one close to Cozzens's own age, who comments on the sometimes violent, sometimes melodramatic, but always hectic action. In *Confusion*, this role is played by Cerise D'Atree, a brilliant young European woman on tour in the United States. In *Cock Pit*, Cozzens hides behind the same gender-distancing technique, creating in Ruth Micks a tough-minded intellectual who stands out from what one character in the book calls the muddled thinkers who create the novel's tensions. By *Cock Pit*,

Cozzens was also showing interest in the flawed, influential, and willful professional. Ruth's father, Lancy Micks, is a field engineer for a sugar corporation; his company and his personality have the potential to shape the lives of hundreds of Cuban peasants.

Cozzens finally combined his honest and intelligent spokesman with his willful professional in *The Son of Perdition*, an ambitious, complicated novel that studies the cross-cultural effects of American imperialism. Joel Stellow, director of the United Sugar Company's Cuban holdings, exhibits the detached, unconventional, and brilliant mind that characterizes all of Cozzens's mature heroes. Though he is defeated by the anarchical forces of the island and by the footloose decadence of a wandering, ugly-American type, Stellow is beginning to develop the appreciation for the complex patterns governing people's lives that enables Cozzens's later heroes to achieve a measure of success.

S.S. SAN PEDRO

S.S. San Pedro was the first novel Cozzens would officially admit to writing. Loosely based on the 1928 sinking of the *S.S. Vestris*, the novel focuses on another competent professional, Anthony Bradell, the ship's senior second officer. Like Stellow, Bradell finds himself all but powerless to check the intricate forces that lead to the destruction of the ship and many of its passengers. For the first of many times, Cozzens matches an ordinary, hardworking, and dedicated professional against a confluence of circumstances: the aging and largely incompetent captain, the purposeful and malicious ocean, and the enigmatic Doctor Percival, an old gentleman in black whose albatross-like presence seems to make the other passengers nervous. The face of Dr. Percival haunts Bradell's dreams, and somehow, Cozzens suggests, Percival is as responsible for the sinking as is any other single agent. By leaving this enigmatic figure unexplained, Cozzens emphasizes the role of chance and of inexplicable factors in human affairs: Even his most intelligent heroes can be confounded by complex, natural patterns that are simply too difficult to be understood.

The confined structure of *S.S. San Pedro*, with its limited crew, its closed environment, its concentrated span of time, and its focus on a single human event, appealed to the craftsman and the philosopher in Cozzens. He learned what could be achieved by limiting the archi-

tecture of a novel to a compact segment of space and time; it was a lesson he would never forget. Moreover, *S.S. San Pedro* marked his turning inward, his abandonment of the pyrotechnics of fast-paced plots and his growing interest in deciphering the interactions of personality, irrationality, meanness, luck, weakness, and fate that influence every human act and challenge even the most competent people.

If *S.S. San Pedro* ends with Bradell still puzzled by the haunting presence of Dr. Percival, it also outlines the curriculum for Cozzens's further studies. In *The Last Adam*, he focuses on an enigmatic, small-town doctor. Moving from the sprawling geography of his earlier fiction, placing his competent professional in the controlled, laboratory-like environment of a Connecticut village, carefully scrutinizing the interior landscapes of his central characters' psyches, Cozzens's *The Last Adam* lays out the themes, techniques, and interests that would occupy him for the remainder of his career. The study of Dr. George Bull is focused on one critical month in one small, cliquish town. The doctor tries to understand the deaths of two women, the outbreak of a typhoid epidemic for which he is partially responsible, the increasingly strident charges against his own professional competence, and the miraculous recovery of a paralyzed patient whose bout with typhoid leaves him better than he has ever been. Cozzens's doctor finds no clear answers to the "whys" of this complicated chain of events. Why some should live, why some should hate, why some negative act should lead to some positive result, puzzles Bull as much as it had Bradell in *S.S. San Pedro*.

CASTAWAY

If Cozzens was no closer to answers, he was at least learning how to frame questions more precisely. His next novel, *Castaway*, explores the possibility of finding answers by studying in detail an individual psyche cut off from any social network. It is Cozzens's only exploration into the territory that fascinated many of his contemporaries. He examines the isolated, alienated soul of the intelligent but frightened Mr. Lecky. For reasons Cozzens felt were not important enough to explain, the character finds himself in a deserted department store, mysteriously cut off from his fellow people, from the social connections that puzzle Cozzens's earlier characters, and from the luck, chance, or providence that guides their lives. Cozzens's Mr. Lecky simply goes mad in his isolation, transforming himself into a homicidal maniac.

The individual self, Cozzens seems to conclude, does not have the characteristics that others have so often attributed to it, no Emersonian store of answers that well up and reveal humankind's true direction. The fear that the unconnected self can generate leads instead to self-destruction.

Men and Brethren

Having ranged from the social criticism of *Cock Pit* to the expressionism of *Castaway*, Cozzens finally settled on a voice and a theme that was uniquely his own. In *Men and Brethren*, Cozzens turned back permanently to the investigations he had begun in *The Last Adam*. Focused on Earnest Cudlip, an Episcopalian minister, the novel is an intense, almost clinical study of the psychology of yet another competent professional. Cudlip has his flaws, but he has found solutions to the problems that stumped Bradell and Bull. Cudlip's sense of responsibility to others helps him maintain order in a complex world he can never fully understand. Like that of many of his predecessors, Cudlip's intelligence penetrates the shallow, emotional responses that most people allow to pass for truth, but more than any of his predecessors, he abandons an absolute faith in intellect and shows himself willing to let destiny, nature, or God guide the events that he acknowledges to be beyond his control.

Foreshadowing the techniques Cozzens uses in his last four novels, *Men and Brethren* is plotted compactly: All the events dovetail into a series of decisions that Cudlip is forced to make during a hectic two-day period. He saves a woman from committing suicide by compromising his religious beliefs and helping her secure an abortion. He helps a minister who has been dismissed from his parish for homosexuality, but the minister turns ungrateful, strikes him, and brands him a hypocrite. He helps an alcoholic parishioner out of one problem, then watches her drown herself because of another. Cozzens concludes the novel ambiguously. Cudlip is resolutely dedicated to the duty of continuing to serve his flock and his God, but he realizes that his actions will seldom change the complicated, unfathomable courses of his parishioners' lives. All he can do, Cudlip concludes, is his best.

Ask Me Tomorrow

Unable to live with that resigned conclusion, Cozzens tried to break new ground. In *Ask Me Tomorrow*, he decided to explore a different kind of professional, choosing, for the first and last time, a novelist as his protagonist. Critics regard Frances Ellery as Cozzens's most autobiographical character. Like Cozzens himself, Ellery has known early success. The author of several well-received novels, Ellery turns out to be the least sympathetic of Cozzens's professionals. Losing himself on a grand tour of Europe, unsure of his writing, unsure of his purpose, unsure of his own attractiveness, Ellery stumbles through a series of romantic encounters trying desperately to understand what they mean to him and he to them. Cozzens invests Ellery with a keener intelligence than any of his previous case studies, but he gives him, too, less strength of will. The results prove to be disastrous for the youthful writer. Ellery fails in his romantic entanglements, in the tutoring duties through which he aimed to support himself, and in his ability to find peace or meaning in the accidents that befall him. As his novelist moves through his tour without deciphering his own life's complexities, Cozzens concludes that honesty and rationality are not sufficient for a man to live rightly: He needs the aid of some other faculty.

The Just and the Unjust

For *Men and Brethren*, Cozzens spent the better part of a year researching the theology and everyday workings of Episcopalianism. For *The Last Adam*, he carefully researched rural medicine. For *The Just and the Unjust*, he enmeshed himself in the study of law and the workings of a small county courthouse. In the case of the latter, this research helped Cozzens impart the vivid, precise, realistic detail that characterizes all his fiction about professionals while also providing a clue as to what a professional needs to reach the fulfillment that Frances Ellery fails to achieve. Abner Coats, a district attorney prosecuting two men for murder, discovers the strength of will and sense of purpose that Ellery lacks. The novel advances an idea that is out of fashion: Strength of character can overcome the limitations of intelligence.

The thesis of *Men and Brethren* was a startling and ultimately unpopular solution to the questions Cozzens had been raising in his previous fictions, implying that much of the ambiguity, much of the uncertainty, and much of the doubt experienced by his earlier professionals had actually been self-imposed. By giving too much credence to their own innocent ideals or innate fears, men such as Bradell, Bull, and Ellery had shut themselves off from a human network that seldom worked by the principles they had imagined. Abner Coats offers an alternative. In the brief three-day period chronicled by the novel, he is forced to learn that his ideas bear little relationship to the world. As he prepares a case against two men who have kidnapped and murdered a drug dealer, he has to acknowledge that the law can provide no absolute judgments about right and wrong, that judges and juries behave in unpredictable or downright ignorant ways, and that even the legal system, like all human creations, is best served by compromise rather than by absolute principle. Ideals and values, Coats concludes, are simplifications, abstract, almost featureless models of the complicated forces that lie behind human motivations. Outside the courtroom, abstract principles are even less reliable guides to understanding or empathy. Often, they prevent a man such as Coats from a meaningful participation in the lives around him. *The Just and the Unjust* confused many of Cozzens's readers. When Coats learns that the county's political boss is corrupt, readers accustomed to romantic fiction expect him to refuse to compromise his principles. Instead, Coats accepts the flaws of the world, allies himself with the party boss, and tries to use his skills to achieve what good he can. This moral ambiguity provoked criticism, and in his next novel, Cozzens defensively tried to explain his conclusions more fully.

Guard of Honor

Critics have usually called *Guard of Honor* one of Cozzens's two best novels. It is a densely plotted examination of a U.S. Army Air Corps general who faces the same sort of crisis that challenges Abner Coats. During a particularly critical Thursday, Friday, and Saturday during World War II, General Ira Beal has to confront both the destructiveness of his own fears and the inadequacies of his own intelligence—lessons that many of the characters in Cozzens's longest and most complicated novel have to learn.

Set at Ocanara Army Air Corps Base in Florida in 1943, the novel presents Beal and his subordinates in a pattern of interconnected events at once profoundly complicated, apparently random, and yet frighteningly powerful in their consequences. Beal freezes at the controls of a plane and comes close to causing a midair collision. The base's black pilots begin to protest the segregationist practices of the Officers' Club. A colonel commits suicide; another assaults and wounds a black pilot who is scheduled to receive the Distinguished Flying Cross. A paratroop exercise, meant to help celebrate Beal's birthday, ends with several jumpers accidentally landing in a swamp and drowning. Beal has to deal with several episodes of impotence with his wife, while a captain and a lieutenant share an adulterous moment. These various events create a six-hundred-page web for Beal to understand and overcome. He cannot fully explain why these events are happening, how they are related, or what their consequences for his future might be. Their energy and capriciousness paralyze him with fear, yet Cozzens allows Beal to redeem himself. He finds the strength of will to face each crisis; he has the luck to have an intelligent second-in-command officer to help cover for him, the humility to accept his limitations, and, most important, the resolve to continue doing his best.

By Love Possessed

In *By Love Possessed*, Cozzens amplifies the austere, rather stoic message of *Guard of Honor*. Returning to the familiar territory of a small county courthouse, Cozzens presents a collection of competent attorneys, prosecutors, judges, and victims who are confronted with a series of interactions far more complicated than anything faced by Beal. Each struggles to understand the tangled workings of four subplots from his or her own particular point of view, and amid such ambiguities, each tries to find the right way to act. As Cozzens moves more deeply into their psyches and away from the plot, he sustains tension not by adding dramatic incidents, but by contrasting the leading characters' different philosophical assumptions.

Not much happens in this novel: For three days, Cozzens's characters chiefly talk to one another. Their discourses are so lucidly argued, however, their particular biases so honestly explored, and their interminglings of love, hate, and hurt so convincingly retold that the novel builds toward an intellectual climax as compelling as any of Cozzens's more dramatic ones. The novel juxtaposes the cool rationality of Julius Penrose, the fervid mysticism of Mrs. Pratt, the raw sexuality of Marjorie Penrose, the stifling love of Helen Detweiler, the opportunism of Jerry Brophy, the cynicism of Fred Dealy, the cowardice of Ralph Detweiler, and the despair of Noah Tuttle: all of them connected to the law firm of Winner, Tuttle, Winner, and Penrose; all of them crippled by their own unique certitudes. In the younger Winner, Cozzens develops fully the notion of remaining "of good heart" that informs *Guard of Honor*. Like Beal, Arthur Winner has learned painfully that each of the lives around him has weaknesses that affect the rest. Like Beal, Winner has to face the knowledge that his own weaknesses have added to the complications. Not intellect, not love, not good intentions, not intuition, he concludes, are enough to guide any of the characters to right choices. Early in the novel, the slow cancerous death of Winner's father teaches Winner that even the best of minds remains firmly rooted to a mortal body. Each of the four subplots explores the equally cancerous effects of depending too much on rationality or emotionalism. At the novel's end, Winner discovers a third and more reliable faculty: Like Beal, Winner learns to trust his own strength of will and strength of character.

MORNING, NOON, AND NIGHT

Still, Cozzens remained unsatisfied with the clarity of this recommendation. He was trying to understand and affirm an old abstraction and its relation to a modern setting. His last novel, *Morning, Noon, and Night*, tried to explain yet again the central thought that had informed *Guard of Honor* and *By Love Possessed*, a thought that was at once a cliché and an exciting discovery for Cozzens. Henry Dodd Worthington, founder of the nation's most successful management consulting firm and scion to landed New England gentry who for generations had amused themselves by becoming college professors, is twice a husband and once a father, and he is Cozzens's most complicated professional. Set entirely in Worthington's study, with its action concentrated in a ten-hour period of wide-ranging reminiscences, the novel centers itself on a precise definition of the strength of character advocated in Cozzens's previous novels.

By training, inheritance, temperament, and experience, Worthington is probably better equipped than any of Cozzens's previous creations to understand why complex human systems behave the way they do. As a spe-

cialist in organizational development, he has already learned that even the best human systems operate under the handicaps of inadequate ideals, reflexive emotional responses, and blind luck. Having enhanced his own fortune by capitalizing on these weaknesses in others, Worthington is ready to turn his intelligence on himself. In his late sixties, the eccentric consultant has arrived at the age where self-deception can no longer be tolerated. For ten demanding hours, he thinks through the consequences of his life's choices and comes resignedly to conclude that luck has largely determined his grandfather's career, his father's, his daughter's, his wives', and his own. Fortune and misfortune, he decides, have been the workings of chance: not skill, not intelligence, not idealism, and certainly not careful planning. His own failings as husband, father, businessman, and tawdry high school thief are enough to convince him that he is no better and no worse than other humans with whom he has shared the planet. Remembering a fool such as his grandfather, a sound businessman such as his uncle, or a failure such as his daughter convinces Worthington that neither victory nor defeat serves as a clear guide to people's hearts. A man finds peace, he concludes, not in victory but in the nobility of doing whatever he does well.

Troubled, at the novel's end, that his intense examination has led to such trivial conclusions, Worthington cheers himself with the notion that life's great truths are usually trivial. Such is the consolation offered by Cozzens's mature novels.

Philip Woodard

OTHER MAJOR WORKS

SHORT FICTION: *Child's Play*, 1958; *Children and Others*, 1964; *A Flower in Her Hair*, 1975.

NONFICTION: *Just Representations*, 1978 (Matthew Bruccoli, editor); *A Time of War: Air Force Diaries and Pentagon Memos, 1943-1945*, 1984 (Matthew Bruccoli, editor); *Selected Notebooks, 1960-1967*, 1984 (Matthew Bruccoli, editor).

BIBLIOGRAPHY

Bracher, Frederick. *The Novels of James Gould Cozzens*. 1959. Reprint. Westport, Conn.: Greenwood Press, 1972. Offers a thorough commentary on Cozzens's literary career. Of the eight novels by

Cozzens published from 1931 to 1957, Bracher argues that at least four are of "major importance by any set of standards." Defends Cozzens from attacks by critics for his lack of personal commitment, showing him to be a novelist of intellect whose strength is storytelling.

Bruccoli, Matthew J. *James Gould Cozzens: A Life Apart*. New York: Harvest/HBJ, 1983. Biography of the reclusive writer provides a highly readable and interesting account of Cozzens's career. Bruccoli, who has emerged as Cozzens's most ardent literary champion, worked with limited cooperation from Cozzens and critically examined the author's letters, diaries, and notebooks. Includes several appendixes, notes, and index.

_____, ed. *James Gould Cozzens: A Documentary Volume*. Vol. 294 in *Dictionary of Literary Biography*. Detroit, Mich.: Gale Group, 2004. Compilation of information about Cozzens includes biographical data, excerpts from Cozzens's writings, critical analyses, discussion of his critical reception, letters, notebook entries, and essays.

_____ ed. *James Gould Cozzens: New Acquist of True Experience*. Carbondale: Southern Illinois University Press, 1979. Collection of ten varied essays on Cozzens examines his work in general and in specific novels. Also included are a variety of short statements by well-known writers such as Malcolm Cowley, James Dickey, and C. P. Snow, who praise Cozzens's literary achievements. Includes a complete list of publications by Cozzens.

Hicks, Granville. *James Gould Cozzens*. Minneapolis: University of Minnesota Press, 1966. Provides an accessible introduction to Cozzens as well as some criticism of his novels from *Confusion* to *Guard of Honor* and *By Love Possessed*. Argues that the pre-tentiousness in Cozzens's early work was transformed in later novels to "competent, straightforward prose."

Kinder, John M. "The Good War's 'Raw Chunks': Norman Mailer's *The Naked and the Dead* and James Gould Cozzens's *Guard of Honor*." *Midwest Quarterly* 46, no. 2 (Winter, 2005): 187-202. Compares the two World War II novels, arguing that the books do not share the "sense of moral rectitude" about the war that is common to most other novels about the conflict. Instead, these novels do not romanticize the war or the military personnel who fought it, and they take exception to the conventional wisdom that Americans during wartime were united behind a common goal.

Michel, Pierre. *James Gould Cozzens*. Boston: Twayne, 1974. Good literary study examines Cozzens's short stories, early novels, transitional novels, and major works. Demonstrates a continuity and evolution of themes in Cozzens's fiction over the decades as well as a ripening mastery of his craft. Includes chronology and select bibliography.

Mooney, Harry John, Jr. *James Gould Cozzens: Novelist of Intellect*. Pittsburgh, Pa.: University of Pittsburgh Press, 1963. Closely examines eight of Cozzens's novels and defends the writer against some critics' negative responses to the works. Mooney views Cozzens as a deliberate and complicated artist and argues for his growing literary mastery as well as his ability to work well within the mainstream framework of the American novel.

Sterne, Richard Clark. *Dark Mirror: The Sense of Injustice in Modern European and American Literature*. New York: Fordham University Press, 1994. Contains a detailed discussion of Cozzens's novel *The Just and the Unjust*.

STEPHEN CRANE

Born: Newark, New Jersey; November 1, 1871
Died: Badenweiler, Germany; June 5, 1900

PRINCIPAL LONG FICTION

Maggie: A Girl of the Streets, 1893
The Red Badge of Courage: An Episode of the American Civil War, 1895
George's Mother, 1896
The Third Violet, 1897
The Monster, 1898 (serial), 1899 (novella; in *The Monster, and Other Stories*)
Active Service, 1899
The O'Ruddy: A Romance, 1903 (with Robert Barr)

OTHER LITERARY FORMS

Stephen Crane was an accomplished poet, short-story writer, and journalist as well as a novelist. His first collection of poems, *The Black Riders, and Other Lines*, appeared in 1895; in 1896, a collection of seven poems and a sketch was published as *A Souvenir and a Medley*; and *War Is Kind*, another collection of poetry, was published in 1899. Crane's previously uncollected poems form part of the tenth volume of *The University of Virginia Edition of the Works of Stephen Crane* (1975). *The Blood of the Martyr*, a closet drama believed to have been written in 1898, was not published until 1940. One other play, *The Ghost* (pr. 1899), written for a Christmas party at Crane's home in England by Crane and others, has not survived in its entirety. Crane's short stories and sketches, of which there are many, began appearing in 1892 and have been discovered from time to time. Some of his journalistic pieces also have literary value.

ACHIEVEMENTS

Stephen Crane's major achievement, both as a fiction writer and as a poet, was that he unflinchingly fought his way through established assumptions about the nature of life, eventually overcoming them. His perceptions were the logical end to the ideas of a long line of American Puritans and Transcendentalists who believed in the individual pursuit of truth. The great and perhaps fitting irony of that logic is that Crane repudiated the truths in which his predecessors believed.

Rejecting much that was conventional about fiction in his day—elaborate plots, numerous and usually middle-or upper-class characters, romantic settings, moralizing narrators—Crane also denied values of much greater significance: nationalism, patriotism, the greatness of individual and collective man, and the existence of supernatural powers that care, protect, and guide.

In his best fiction, as in his life, Crane squarely faced the horror of a meaningless universe by exposing the blindness and egotism of concepts that deny that meaninglessness. He was, unfortunately, unable to build a new and positive vision on the rubble of the old; he died at age twenty-eight, his accomplishments genuinely astounding.

BIOGRAPHY

Born on November 1, 1871, in the Methodist parsonage in Newark, New Jersey, Stephen Crane was the fourteenth and last child of Mary Peck Crane and Reverend Jonathan Crane, whose family dated back more than two centuries on the American continent. On the Peck side, almost every male was a minister; one became a bishop. By the time his father died in 1880, Crane had lived in several places in New York and New Jersey and had been thoroughly indoctrinated in the faith he was soon to reject. Also around this time, he wrote his first poem, "I'd Rather Have." His first short story, "Uncle Jake and the Bell Handle," was written in 1885, and the same year he enrolled in Pennington Seminary, where he stayed until 1887. Between 1888 and 1891, he attended Claverack College, Hudson River Institute, Lafayette College, and Syracuse University. He was never graduated from any of these, preferring baseball to study. In 1892, the New York *Tribune* published many of his New York City sketches and more than a dozen Sullivan County tales. Having apparently forgotten Miss Helen Trent, his first love, he fell in love with Mrs. Lily Brandon Munroe. That same year, the mechanics union took exception to his article on their annual fete, which resulted in Crane's brother Townley being fired from the *Tribune*.

In 1893, Crane published, at his own expense, an early version of *Maggie: A Girl of the Streets*. William Dean Howells introduced him to Emily Dickinson's poetry, and in the next year he met Hamlin Garland. Also in 1894, the Philadelphia *Press* published an abridged version of *The Red Badge of Courage*.

During the first half of 1895, Crane traveled in the West, where he met Willa Cather, and in Mexico for the Bachellor Syndicate; *The Black Riders, and Other Lines* was published in May; and *The Red Badge of Courage* appeared in October. By December, he was famous, having just turned twenty-four. In 1896, he published *George's Mother* and *The Little Regiment, and Other Episodes of the American Civil War* and fell in love with Cora Stewart (Howarth), whom he never married but with whom he lived for the rest of his life.

In January, 1897, on the way to report the insurgency in Cuba, Crane was shipwrecked off the Florida coast. Four months later, he was in Greece, reporting on the Greco-Turkish War. Moving back to England, he became friends with Joseph Conrad, Henry James, Harold Frederic, H. G. Wells, and others. During that year, he wrote most of his great short stories, including "The Open Boat," "The Bride Comes to Yellow Sky," and "The Blue Hotel."

Never very healthy, Crane began to weaken in 1898 as a result of malaria contracted in Cuba while he was reporting on the Spanish-American War. By 1899, Crane was back in England and living well above his means. Although he published *War Is Kind*, *Active Service*, and *The Monster, and Other Stories*, he continued to fall more deeply in debt. By 1900, he was hopelessly debt-ridden and fatally ill. Exhausted from overwork, intestinal tuberculosis, malaria, and the experiences of an intense life, Crane died at the early age of twenty-eight, leaving works that fill ten sizable volumes.

ANALYSIS

As one of the impressionist writers—Conrad called him "The Impressionist"—Stephen Crane was among the first to express in writing a new way of looking at the world. A pivotal movement in the history of ideas, impressionism grew out of scientific discoveries that showed how human physiology, particularly that of the eye, determines the way everything in the universe and

Stephen Crane. (Library of Congress)

everything outside the individual body and mind is perceived. People do not see the world as it is; the mind and the eye collaborate to interpret a chaotic universe as fundamentally unified, coherent, and explainable. The delusion is compounded when human beings agglomerate, for then they tend to create grander fabrications such as religion and history. Although Crane is also seen as one of the first American naturalistic writers, a Symbolist, an imagist, and even a nihilist, the achievements designated by these labels all derive from his impressionistic worldview.

MAGGIE

Stephen Crane's first novel, *Maggie: A Girl of the Streets*, was written before Crane had any intimate knowledge of the Bowery slums where the novel is set. It is the first American novel to portray realistically the chaos of the slums without either providing the protagonist with a "way out" or moralizing on the subject of social injustice. It obeys Aristotle's dictum that art imitates life and the more modern notion that art is simply a mirror held up to life. *Maggie* is the story of a young Irish American girl who grows up in the slums of New York. The novel seems to belong to the tradition of the bildungsroman, but its greatness lies in the irony that in this harsh environment, no one's quest is fulfilled, no one learns anything: The novel swings from chaos on the one side to complete illusion on the other.

By the time Maggie reaches physical maturity, her father and young brother have died, leaving only her mother, Mary, a marauding drunken woman, and another brother, Jimmie, a young truck driver who scratches out a place for himself in the tenements. Living with an alcoholic and a bully, Maggie is faced with a series of choices that tragically lead her to self-destruction. First, she must choose between working long hours for little pay in the sweatshops or becoming a prostitute. She chooses the former, but the chaotic reality of home and work are so harsh that she succumbs to her own illusions about Pete, the bullying neighborhood bartender, and allows herself to be seduced by him. When this happens, Mary drives Maggie out of their home. For a short time, Maggie enjoys her life, but Pete soon abandons her to chase another woman. Driven from home and now a "fallen woman," Maggie must choose between prostitution and suicide. Deciding on the life of a prostitute, Maggie survives for a time but ultimately is unable to make a living. She commits suicide by jumping into the East River.

The form of the novel is that of a classical tragedy overlaid by nihilism that prevents the final optimism of tragedy from surfacing. The tragic "mistake," what the Greeks called *hamartia*, derives from a naturalistic credo: Maggie was unlucky enough to have been born a pretty girl in an environment she was unable to escape. Although she tries to make the best of her limited choices, she is inexorably driven to make choices that lead her to ruin and death. The novel's other characters are similarly trapped by their environment. Mary drinks herself into insensibility, drives her daughter into the street, and then, when Maggie kills herself, exclaims, "I fergive her!" The irony of this line, the novel's last, is nihilistic. Classical tragedy ends on an optimistic note. Purged of sin by the sacrifice of the protagonist, humankind is given a reprieve by the gods, and life looks a little

better for everyone. In *Maggie* there is no optimism. Mary has nothing on which to base any forgiveness. It is Maggie who should forgive Mary. Jimmie is so egocentric that he cannot see that he owed his sister some help. At one point he wonders about the girls he has "ruined," but he quickly renounces any responsibility for them. Pete is a blind fool who is destroyed by his own illusions and the chaos of his environment.

For the first time in American fiction, a novel had appeared in which there clearly was no better world, no "nice" existence, no heaven on earth. There was only the world of the stinking tenements, only the chaos of sweat and alcohol and seduction, only hell. Also for the first time, everything was accomplished impressionistically. Maggie's sordid career as a prostitute would have required an earlier writer several chapters to describe. In *Maggie*, the description requires only a paragraph or two.

GEORGE'S MOTHER

George's Mother, which Crane originally called "A Woman Without Weapons," is Crane's only other Bowery novel, a companion piece to *Maggie: A Girl of the Streets*. Mrs. Keasy and her son George live in the same tenement as Mary Johnson, Maggie's mother. The story is more sentimental than that of *Maggie*, and therefore less effective. George gradually succumbs to the destructive elements of the Bowery—drink and a subsequent inability to work—in spite of the valiant efforts of his mother to forestall and warn him. As Maggie has her "dream gardens" in the air above sordid reality, so young George has dreams of great feats while he actually lives in the midst of drunkenness and squalor. As drink provides a way out of reality for George, so the Church provides his mother with her escape. In both *Maggie* and *George's Mother*, illusions simultaneously provide the only way out of reality and a way to hasten the worsening of reality.

THE RED BADGE OF COURAGE

In his most famous novel, *The Red Badge of Courage*, Crane takes his themes of illusion and reality and his impressionistic method from the Bowery to a battlefield of the Civil War, usually considered to be the Battle of Chancellorsville. A young farm boy named Henry Fleming hears tales of great battles, dreams of "Homeric" glory, and joins the Union Army. Published in 1895, the story of Henry Fleming's various trials took the literary world by storm, first in England and then in the United States. Crane became an immediate sensation, perhaps one of America's first media darlings. *The Red Badge of Courage* became a classic in its own time because it combined literary merit with a subject that captured the popular imagination. Never again did Crane reach the height of popularity that he achieved with *The Red Badge of Courage.*

Structurally, the novel is divided into two parts. In the first half, Henry's illusions disappear when he is confronted by the reality of battle. During the first skirmish, he sees vague figures before him, but they are driven away. In the next skirmish, he becomes so frightened that he runs away, becoming one of the first heroes in literature actually to desert his fellow soldiers in the field. Although Achilles had done something similar in Homer's *Iliad* (c. 750 B.C.E.; English translation, 1611), in the intervening millennia, few heroes had imitated him.

Separated from his regiment, Henry wanders through the forest behind the lines. There he experiences the kinds of illusions that predominate in all of Crane's writing. First, he convinces himself that nature is benevolent, that she does not blame him for running. Next, he finds himself in a part of the woods that he interprets as a kind of religious place—the insects are praying, and the forest has the appearance of a chapel. Comforted by this, Henry becomes satisfied with himself until he discovers a dead soldier in the very heart of the "chapel." In a beautiful passage—beautiful in the sense of conveying great emotion through minute detail—Henry sees an ant carrying a bundle across the face of the dead man. Shifting to a belief in nature as malevolent or indifferent, Henry moves back toward the front. He soon encounters a line of wounded soldiers, among whom is his friend Jim Conklin and another man called simply "the tattered man." Conklin, badly wounded, is dying. Trying to expiate his crime of desertion, Henry attempts to help Conklin but is rebuffed. After Conklin dies, the tattered man probes deeply into Henry's conscience by repeatedly asking the youth, "Where ya hit?" The tattered man himself appears to be wounded, but Henry cannot abide his questions. He deserts the tattered man as well.

When Henry tries to stop another Union soldier to ask the novel's ubiquitous question "Why?" he is clubbed on the head for causing trouble. Ironically, this wound becomes his "red badge of courage." Guided back to his regiment by a "Cheery Soldier," who performs the same function as the ancient gods and goddesses who helped wandering heroes, Henry embarks on the novel's second half. Between receiving the lump on his head and returning to his regiment, Henry's internal wanderings are over. Not until the last chapter does Henry ask questions of the universe. Most of the repudiations are complete: Heroes do not always act like heroes; no one understands the purpose of life or death; nature may be malevolent, probably indifferent, but is certainly not the benevolent, pantheistic realm of the Transcendentalists; and God, at least the traditional Christian God, is simply nowhere to be found.

In the second half of the novel, Henry becomes a "war devil," the very Homeric hero he originally wanted to be. Wilson, his young friend, who was formerly called "the loud soldier," has become a group leader, quiet, helpful, and utterly devoted to the regiment. He becomes, in short, what Henry would have become had he not run from the battle. The idea of "brotherhood," so prevalent in Crane's works, is embodied by Wilson. Henry is another kind of hero, an individual owing allegiance to no group; he leads a successful charge against the enemy with the spirit of a primitive warrior.

When the battle is over, however, all that Henry has accomplished is negated. Many critics have found the last chapter confused and muddled, for Henry's feelings range from remorse for the "sin" for which he is not responsible to pride in his valor as a great and glorious hero. Finally, he feels that "the world was a world for him," and he looks forward to "a soft and eternal peace." The beautiful lyricism of the novel's last paragraphs is, like that of many of Crane's conclusions, completely ironic. No one lives "eternally peacefully"; the world is not a world for Henry. As John Berryman says, Crane's "sole illusion was the heroic one, and not even that escaped his irony."

Thus, the novel's conclusion is not at all inconsistent. During the course of his experiences, Henry learns at first hand of the indifference of the universe, the chaos of the world, and the illusory nature of religion and patriotism and heroism, but he learns these lessons in the heat of the moment, when recognition is virtually forced on him. When the memory has an opportunity to apply itself to past experience, that experience is changed into what humanity wants it to be, not what it was. Henry, then, becomes representative of humankind. The individual memory becomes a metaphor for collective memory, history. Everything is a lie. Not even heroism can last.

THE THIRD VIOLET

Crane was only twenty-two when he began working on *The Third Violet*, and before it was published he had already written *Maggie*, *The Red Badge of Courage*, and *George's Mother*. Of the four, *The Third Violet* is by far the least successful. In Crane's attempt to portray middle-class manners, his best portraits, as well as his most admirable characters, are the simple farmer and the heiress, whereas the others, who actually fall within the middle class, are more or less insipid.

The protagonist of *The Third Violet*, Billie Hawker, is a young New York artist who returns to his family's farm for a summer vacation. While there, he falls in love with Grace Fanhall, a young heiress vacationing at a nearby resort hotel called the Hemlock Inn. The remainder of the novel recounts Hawker's anxieties as he botches repeated attempts to declare his love and win the fair maiden at the hotel, during summer picnics, in New York studios, and in mansions. Aside from portraits of Hawker's father and the heiress, the most rewarding portraits are of a little boy and his dog. A memorable scene occurs when Grace Fanhall and Billie's father ride together in a farm wagon, their disparate social standings apparently freeing them from rigid middle-class stiffness. Equally worthwhile is the scene in the New York bohemian studio where Hawker's friends "Great Grief," "Wrinkles," and Pennoyer manage to divert the landlord and concoct a meal in a manner reminiscent of the opening scenes of Giacomo Puccini's opera *La Bohème* (pr. 1896). There is even a beautiful young model named "Splutter" O'Conner, whose easy and cheerful love for Hawker provides a contrast to his own doleful courtship of Fanhall.

The reality behind the mask of convention in *The Third Violet* is never sufficiently revealed. Reality in *The Third Violet* seems to be that love would predominate if only Hawker could free himself of his inferiority com-

plex at having been born poor. While others might make great fiction from such a feeling, Crane could not.

ACTIVE SERVICE

The only great piece of fiction Crane produced from his experience of reporting the Greco-Turkish War of April and May, 1897, was "Death and the Child." By contrast, his Greek novel, *Active Service*, is lamentably bad. Following a creakingly conventional plot, *Active Service* relates the story of a boy and a girl in love: The girl's parents object; the boy pursues the girl and overcomes her parents' objections by rescuing the family from danger and by manfully escaping the snares of another woman.

Crane's protagonist, Rufus Coleman, Sunday editor of the *New York Eclipse*, is in love with Marjory Wainright, the demure and lovely daughter of a classics professor at Washurst University. Disapproving of the match on the rather solid evidence that Coleman is "a gambler and a drunkard," Professor Wainright decides to include his daughter in a student tour of Greece, a tour the professor himself is to lead. While touring ruins near Arta in Epirus, the group is trapped between the Greek and Turkish lines. Meanwhile, back in the offices of the *Eclipse*, the not so mild-mannered reporter, Coleman, is discovering that he cannot exist without Marjory. Arranging to become the *Eclipse*'s correspondent in Greece, he heads for Europe. Temporarily distracted while traveling to Greece by a beautiful British actor and dancer, Nora Black, Coleman finally arrives in Athens and discovers that the Wainright party is in danger. He jauntily sets out to rescue them and equally as jauntily succeeds. So heroic and noble is Coleman that the professor is quite won over. The novel finishes like hundreds of turn-of-the-century love adventures, with the hero and heroine sitting with the Aegean Sea in the background while they declare their love for each other in the most adolescent manner.

Indeed, Crane intended to write a parody of love adventures. The hero is too offhandedly heroic; the rival is too mean and nasty. The "other woman" wears too much perfume; the parents are too inept. The novel is banal and trite, however, because the characters lack interest, and the parody cannot sustain the reader's interest in the absence of a substantial form worthy of parody. The novel is probably bad for extraliterary reasons: Crane's poor health and finances. Crane began the book late in 1897, when he was still fairly healthy and when his finances were not yet completely chaotic. The effects of the malaria and the tuberculosis, however, were becoming increasingly debilitating and began to take their toll long before *The Third Violet* was finished in May, 1899. By then, too, his finances were depleted. Crane had the intellectual and cultural resources to write a first-rate book on this subject, but not the health and good fortune. One must agree with Crane: "May heaven help it for being so bad."

THE MONSTER

The Monster was Crane's last great work. A short book even when compared to his notably short novels, *The Monster* is often regarded as a novella rather than as a novel. Like *The Red Badge of Courage*, it is divided into twenty-four episodes, is divided in half structurally, and concerns a man caught in a straitjacket of fate. Like *Maggie*, Dr. Trescott, the hero, is led down a road that gradually leaves behind all side trails until his only choice is essentially made for him by his circumstances. Trescott is more intelligent and educated than Maggie, and he is certainly more conscious of his choices, but the most crucial difference lies in the intensity of the tragedy. Whereas *Maggie* is about the individual facing chaos without the mediating power of a civilized group, *The Monster* concerns the conflict between individual ethics and the values of the group. For Crane, small towns in America exist to mediate between the individual and chaos. Ordered society blocks out reality, providing security.

Henry Johnson, the Trescotts' black hostler, is badly burned while rescuing Jimmy, the doctor's young son, from the Trescotts' burning house. This heroic act creates Trescott's tragic dilemma: Personal ethics dictate that he care for the now horrific-looking and simple-minded Henry; public security requires that Henry be "put away" or allowed to die, for civilization does not like to see reminders of what humankind would be like without the thin veneer of order. While Trescott faces his responsibility toward Henry, he fails to reckon with the task of forcing the community to face it as well. When he does, he consciously sets himself on a collision course with that society. Unlike Henry Fleming, Trescott cannot win even a temporary victory. The community defeats him utterly.

Trescott at first tries to avoid conflict by paying Alex Williams, a local black man who lives on the outskirts of town, to care for Henry. When Henry escapes into town and, although harmless, frightens little children, the community demands that Trescott do something. Standing by his obligation to Henry, Trescott is quickly ostracized by the community. At the novel's end, Trescott recognizes that he has lost. He cannot retain his moral and ethical stance toward Henry Johnson and remain within the community. He cannot concede defeat to the community without doing irrevocable damage to his own honor. The dilemma is a classical tragic one that must be faced by each individual. Ralph Ellison called *The Monster* a metaphor for America's treatment of the black minority, but the greatness of the work lies in the fact that it is a larger metaphor for the human community's treatment of the individual.

THE O'RUDDY

The O'Ruddy is a parodic picaresque romance about English and Irish manners. Its humor belies the fact that Crane was writing on his deathbed, in great anguish and pain. Crane's only first-person novel, *The O'Ruddy* exposes the "dullness of the great mass of people, the frivolity of the gentry, the arrogance and wickedness of the court," and celebrates the notion that "real talent was usually engaged in some form of rascality." Similar to *Active Service* in that it recounts the story of an adventure-loving hero who overcomes the objections of a stuffy father and vehement mother for the hand of a somewhat demure but beautiful young lady, *The O'Ruddy* is similarly unable to sustain greatness. Although sketchy as to the date of the events, *The O'Ruddy* seems to be set in late eighteenth century England, where young Tom O'Ruddy, a poor but noble Irishman, has come to return to the earl of Westport some papers given to Tom by his father. The reader learns more than halfway through the novel that the papers give title to certain lands in Sussex. Smitten by Lady Mary, the earl's daughter, Tom eventually trades the papers for her hand in marriage. Before the novel's conclusion, in which Tom and Mary are married, there are many duels, robberies, journeys through secret passages, and portraits of literary meetings and turnings at Kensington Gardens, all of which are parodied. Crane disliked the manners of many of the English, saying at one point that western New York farmers had better manners.

The parody is occasionally amusing, but since parody must mock form as well as content to be great, the novel fails. Understandably, given Crane's illness and the reluctance of Robert Barr to finish the novel after Crane's death, there are numerous discrepancies, among which is a confusion as to whether Tom O'Ruddy can read and write. All in all, Crane's intensity is lacking in this slight novel, his freshness, his impressionistic insights, his accustomed power gone. The last words he wrote in the novel before dying are lamentably apropos of the book itself: "This is no nice thing."

Chester L. Wolford

OTHER MAJOR WORKS

SHORT FICTION: *The Little Regiment, and Other Episodes of the American Civil War*, 1896; *The Open Boat, and Other Tales of Adventure*, 1898; *The Monster, and Other Stories*, 1899; *Whilomville Stories*, 1900; *Wounds in the Rain: War Stories*, 1900; *Last Words*, 1902.

PLAYS: *The Ghost*, pr. 1899 (with Henry James; fragment); *The Blood of the Martyr*, pb. 1940 (wr. 1898?).

POETRY: *The Black Riders, and Other Lines*, 1895; *A Souvenir and a Medley*, 1896; *War Is Kind*, 1899.

NONFICTION: *The Great Battles of the World*, 1901; *The War Dispatches of Stephen Crane*, 1964.

MISCELLANEOUS: *The University of Virginia Edition of the Works of Stephen Crane*, 1969-1975 (10 volumes).

BIBLIOGRAPHY

Berryman, John. *Stephen Crane*. 1950. Reprint. New York: Cooper Square Press, 2001. Combined biography and analysis of Crane's works has been superseded as biography but continues to provide an absorbing Freudian reading of Crane's life and work. Berryman, himself a major American poet, eloquently explains the patterns of family conflict that appear in Crane's fiction. In addition, Berryman's wide-ranging interests allow him to tackle such large topics as Crane's influence on the development of the short story, a form that came to prominence only in the 1890's. Includes notes and index.

Cady, Edwin H. *Stephen Crane*. Rev. ed. Boston: Twayne, 1980. Excellent introductory volume presents a chronological account of Crane's career, with chapters on his biography, his early writing, and *The Red Badge of Courage*. Includes chronology, notes, bibliographical essay, and index.

Davis, Linda H. *Badge of Courage: The Life of Stephen Crane*. Boston: Houghton Mifflin, 1998. Describes Crane as "an explosion of color in a gray age" and depicts the author as a perpetual adolescent who was very much an enigma.

Halliburton, David. *The Color of the Sky: A Study of Stephen Crane*. New York: Cambridge University Press, 1989. Though somewhat thematically disorganized, this work's philosophical grounding and effort to look at Crane's works from unusual angles make for many provocative readings. Includes discussion of the novels *The Red Badge of Courage* and *Maggie* as well as other writings.

Johnson, Claudia D. *Understanding "The Red Badge of Courage": A Student Casebook to Issues, Sources, and Historical Documents*. Westport, Conn.: Greenwood Press, 1998. Excellent accompaniment to the novel is particularly useful for students. Provides literary analysis and a discussion of the book as an antiwar novel. Features primary and secondary source documents aimed at placing the book within the broader context of the Civil War, among which are firsthand accounts of the Battle of Chancelorsville and other battles, excerpts from memoirs, newspaper articles, and interviews.

Knapp, Bettina L. *Stephen Crane*. New York: Frederick Ungar, 1987. Provides a succinct introduction to Crane's life and career. Presents a brief biography, several chapters on his fiction, and an extensive discussion of two poetry collections. Includes a detailed chronology, a bibliography of primary and secondary sources, and an index.

Monteiro, George. *Stephen Crane's Blue Badge of Courage*. Baton Rouge: Louisiana State University Press, 2000. Demonstrates the ironic role of temperance propaganda, in which Crane was immersed as a child, in the imagery and language of his darkest and best-known work.

Robertson, Michael. *Stephen Crane: Journalism and the Making of Modern American Literature*. New York: Columbia University Press, 1997. Argues that Crane's success as a novelist inspired later journalists to think of their work as preparatory for writing fiction, and asserts that the blurring of fact and fiction in newspapers during Crane's lifetime suited his own narrative experiments.

Sorrentino, Paul, ed. *Stephen Crane Remembered.* Tuscaloosa: University of Alabama Press, 2006. Brings together nearly one hundred documents from acquaintances of the novelist and poet for a somewhat more revealing look at Crane than has previously been available.

Wertheim, Stanley. *A Stephen Crane Encyclopedia.* Westport, Conn.: Greenwood Press, 1997. Very thorough volume features articles about the full range of Crane's work, his family and its influence on him, the places he lived, his employers, the literary movement with which he is associated, and his characters.

Wertheim, Stanley, and Paul Sorrentino. *The Crane Log: A Documentary Life of Stephen Crane, 1871-1900.* New York: G. K. Hall, 1994. Attempts to counter many of the falsehoods that have bedeviled analyses of Crane's life and work by providing a documentary record of the author's life. Divided into seven chapters, beginning with the notation in Crane's father's diary of the birth of his fourteenth child, Stephen, and ending with a newspaper report of Crane's funeral, written by Wallace Stevens. Includes biographical notes on all important persons mentioned in the text.

MICHAEL CRICHTON

Born: Chicago, Illinois; October 23, 1942
Died: Los Angeles, California; November 4, 2008
Also known as: John Michael Crichton; Michael Douglas; Jeffrey Hudson; John Lange

PRINCIPAL LONG FICTION

A Case of Need, 1968 (as Jeffrey Hudson)
The Andromeda Strain, 1969
The Terminal Man, 1972
The Great Train Robbery, 1975
Eaters of the Dead, 1976
Congo, 1980
Sphere, 1987
Jurassic Park, 1990
Rising Sun, 1992
Disclosure, 1994
The Lost World, 1995
Airframe, 1996
Timeline, 1999
Prey, 2002
State of Fear, 2004
Next, 2006

OTHER LITERARY FORMS

Best known as a writer of science-fiction thrillers with compulsively page-turning plots, Michael Crichton (KRI-tuhn) also wrote nonfiction books on a variety of topics: *Five Patients: The Hospital Explained* (1970), an exposé of the inner workings of a big-city hospital; *Electronic Life: How to Think About Computers* (1983), an introduction to computer programming; *Jasper Johns* (1977), a biography-cum-portfolio of the artist; and *Travels* (1988), an autobiography-cum-travelogue. He also frequently contributed opinion pieces on scientific topics to newspapers and magazines.

Other than as a novelist, however, Crichton is best known as a screenwriter. He wrote the script for the popular science-fiction film *Westworld* (1973) as well as the script for the film adaptation of his novel *The Great Train Robbery* (1979); he also directed both of those motion pictures. He also, with the help of collaborators, worked on the screenplays for the adaptations of *Jurassic Park* (1993) and *Rising Sun* (1993). Along with his then wife, Anne-Marie Martin, he wrote the script of one of the most popular films of the 1990's, *Twister* (1996).

In addition to his work in films, Crichton created the hugely popular television series *ER*, drawing on his own experiences as a doctor. He served as an executive producer for the show, which premiered in 1994, and he wrote the first three episodes.

ACHIEVEMENTS

A doctor and research scientist, Michael Crichton began writing mystery novels under pseudonyms as a way to support himself while he was in medical school. His first novel under his own name, *The Andromeda Strain*, became an immediate best seller and was promptly made into a big-budget Hollywood film—a pattern that was to be followed by many of his subsequent novels. None of his principal works of long fiction ever failed to make the best-seller lists in the United States, and Crichton has enjoyed similar success in world markets. His immensely popular novel *Jurassic Park*, and its subsequent film version and sequels, brought to science fiction a fresh approach to one of its favorite tropes, that of modern humans encountering prehistoric species: the re-creation of extinct life-forms via reclaimed DNA (deoxyribonucleic acid). The success of *Jurassic Park* and its sequel, *The Lost World*, inspired a generation of science-fiction thriller writers to employ a similar "hard science" approach.

Crichton twice won the Edgar Award, the highest prize awarded by the Mystery Writers of America: first in 1968 for his abortion-themed novel *A Case of Need*, which he originally published under the name Jeffrey Hudson, and again in 1980 for the screenplay for *The Great Train Robbery*. The Association of American Medical Writers gave a best-book award to *Five Patients* in 1970. With other producers and writers, Crichton shared the George Foster Peabody Award for *ER* in 1995 and an Emmy for Best Drama Series the following year. In 1998, the American Academy of Science Fiction, Fantasy, and Horror Films presented him with its Life Career Award.

BIOGRAPHY

John Michael Crichton was born in Chicago, Illinois, but grew up in Long Island, New York. He had three siblings, one a younger brother named Douglas, with whom he once collaborated on a comic novel in 1971, *Dealing*.

Written under the pen name Michael Douglas, the book was an account of upper-middle-class college students who become marijuana dealers. Crichton received his undergraduate degree from Harvard University in 1964 and his M.D. from the same school in 1969. His other early academic activities included lecturing at Cambridge in England in 1965 and studying at the Salk Institute in California in the late 1960's.

To eke out a living as a student, Crichton began to write mystery novels under the pseudonyms Jeffrey Hudson and John Lange, a practice that he maintained through the early 1970's, even after he had published his first two best sellers under his own name. The fourth of these mysteries, *A Case of Need*, was one of the first pieces of American popular fiction to deal forthrightly with the issue of abortion, then illegal throughout the United States. The publication of *The Andromeda Strain* in 1969 began Crichton's long stream of best-selling popular novels, most of which drew on the genres of science fiction and the espionage thriller.

Crichton was always vocal about his political views pertaining to topics in the fields of medicine and science. In the early twenty-first century, he attracted much attention by questioning whether "global warming" was actually occurring and, if it was, whether it was being induced by human activities such as industry and the use of fossil fuels. He also publicly questioned other contemporary fears related to the environment and health, such as the purported danger posed by secondhand cigarette smoke. He raised these questions most frequently in articles in magazines and journals, op-ed pieces in newspapers and magazines, and speeches, but he addressed them most dramatically in his 2004 novel *State of Fear*. Crichton's views on such issues triggered criticism and rebuke, much of which came from the author's colleagues in the medical and scientific community, with some of it insinuating that he was a shill for big business and conservative political factions—the latter somewhat surprising in light of the passionately argued pro-choice stance of *A Case of Need*.

Crichton was married five times. Four of his marriages ended in divorce; he was married to his fifth wife at the time of his death from cancer in 2008. His fourth wife, actor and screenwriter Anne-Marie Martin, is the mother of his only child, a daughter.

Michael Crichton. (AP/Wide World Photos)

ANALYSIS

Thought of primarily as a writer of slick, exciting popular fiction, Michael Crichton has received far more praise for the sensational premises of his novels and their action-fueled plots than for his writing style, which is at best serviceable and at worst far less imaginative than his story lines. A chief importance of Crichton in popular American fiction of the late twentieth and early twenty-first century, however, is his adroit manipulation of science-fiction texts, as he boldly rewrote and reenvisioned the more far-fetched and fanciful stories of classic fantastic novels and films within a framework of straightforward "hard" science as he perceived it as a working scientist. As such, Crichton rivals Stephen King as the foremost "pop" practitioner of metafiction (fiction addressing the reading and writing of fiction) and intertextuality (text addressing other texts), trends in literature usually associated with belletristic, "highbrow" writers.

For example, as some reviewers noted when his second best seller, *The Terminal Man*, was published, the book is in many ways an update of *Frankenstein*, by Mary Wollstonecraft Shelley, who, because of this 1818 novel, is often seen as the originator of the modern science-fiction genre. In the early 1880's, electricity was still a fairly new discovery and hence a mysterious force, and so Shelley's suggestion that it might somehow revitalize

inert limbs and organs seemed not implausible. Today, however, such an idea is laughable. In *The Terminal Man*, then, Crichton rewrites Shelley's scenario: The "monster" is not a creature stitched together from cadavers but a living man beset by physical and emotional ailments whose brain has been wired so as to control his moods and impulses, thereby giving him a new life. These procedures as described may be in advance of contemporary science, but they still fall within the realm of near-future possibilities.

Likewise, in *Next*, Crichton reworks H. G. Wells's *The Island of Dr. Moreau*, that seminal science-fiction writer's exploration of the borderlands between humanity and other species. Whereas in 1896 Wells had Dr. Moreau create humanoid creatures from animals through painful operations, Crichton's characters employ more believable twenty-first century science involving DNA and gene splicing. Consciously or unconsciously, Crichton seems to have devoted much of his career to creating a vast patchwork quilt of intertextual reconstructions of classic science-fiction stories.

Crichton's dedication to "real" science is his most obvious and recurrent theme. Many reviewers and even ardent fans of his work have assumed that Crichton's principal concern is with the dangers of science run amok, as is the case with Shelley in *Frankenstein*. However, although Shelley was indeed concerned with scientific inquiry and invention going so far as to be dangerous and dehumanizing, Crichton is more specific: His fiction addresses the dangers posed by science when it is corrupted by outside influences, most commonly business, the government and military, and popular media.

THE ANDROMEDA STRAIN

The first novel published under Crichton's own name—and his first work that was not a conventional murder mystery—*The Andromeda Strain* remained until the publication of *Jurassic Park* in the 1990's Crichton's most widely read book. In it, we see at the inception of his career as a best-selling science-fiction/thriller writer the themes and techniques that he used most consistently throughout his life. The plot is simple and fast-moving: A space probe crashes in the American Southwest bearing a dangerous microscopic organism that causes the death of an entire town except for one small boy and one old man. A team of scientists must figure out how the organism attacks the human body in order to end the threat.

In his debut science-fiction work, Crichton clearly displays his spin on the Frankenstein theme: The danger is not so much science getting out of hand as it is science falling into the wrong hands. The danger is not created by the scientist-heroes but by "corrupt" scientists whose work has been co-opted by the U.S. military: The crashed probe had been part of an attempt by the military and the government to find dangerous microbes in space to use in biological warfare. The heroes are the "pure" scientists untainted by outside influence, brought in as troubleshooters—a plot device Crichton would repeat in his most popular novels, *Jurassic Park* and *The Lost World*.

To underscore the role of the military in bringing this threat literally to Earth, in the conclusion of the novel Crichton has one of his heroes run a gamut of threats that are part of a secret military base's "defense" and "security" measures, the irony lying in the fact that Earth would not be facing the danger posed by an alien microbe had the military not misused science in the cause of "national security." A further irony lies in the name given to the dangerous organism: Andromeda, an innocent princess in Greek mythology who is doomed to be sacrificed to a sea monster because of her mother's impious boast that she is more beautiful than the sea goddesses. To the Greeks, such extreme pride, hubris, was the ultimate sin, one certain to bring disaster. By alluding to this myth, Crichton seems to be commenting on the hubristic arrogance of the military leaders, who court disaster with their arrogant assumption that they can control forces for which they have little understanding or respect.

In keeping with the metafictional and intertextual tendencies of Crichton's canon, the novel's central plot is a hard-science rewrite of the plot of one of the most popular horror films of all time, George A. Romero's *Night of the Living Dead* (1968), in which hordes of cannibal undead are created by a satellite that returns from Venus carrying an alien virus. Romero was interested in horrific effect and social commentary, and the explanation of a plague from space was merely a pretext for these things; in *The Andromeda Strain*, however, Crichton takes Romero's premise and puts an ultra-realistic spin on it, with carefully thought-out accounts of how such an organism would invade and affect the human body. *The Andromeda Strain* was made into a film in 1971 and remade as a television miniseries in 2008.

JURASSIC PARK *and* THE LOST WORLD

In Crichton's most famous work, *Jurassic Park*, as well as its sequel, *The Lost World*, readers can easily detect the same ploys and techniques that Crichton used in his first best seller. As in *The Andromeda Strain*, the threat springs from science corrupted by outsiders—in this case, entrepreneurs. A multimillionaire named John Hammond sets up, off the coast of Central America, a theme park featuring live dinosaurs created from DNA retrieved from prehistoric insects that drank reptilian blood and then became preserved in amber. Hammond soon has to bring paleontologists to the island to help when his program of saurian re-creation goes awry.

Reviewers in 1990 made much of Crichton's discussion of "chaos theory," which is evoked repeatedly to explain why things went wrong in the park, and indeed *Jurassic Park* introduced this concept into mainstream American thought. The real origin of the threat posed by the revived species of dinosaurs, however, lies in Hammond's hubristic attitude: He understands next to nothing of the science he exploits and is motivated solely by avarice. His arrogance is most clearly evinced in the scenes (the most exciting scenes in the novel) in which he sends his young grandchildren out into the park, smugly assuming that he controls the ancient environment that his millions have brought back to life. In a fate worthy of a villain in myth or fairy tale, Hammond is ultimately killed and eaten by his own (re)creations. As in *The Andromeda Strain*, the virtuous "true" scientists must then clean up the mess—environmental, legal, and ethical—that he has left behind.

In wordplay typical of his metafictional and intertextual tendencies, Crichton names the two "bad" scientists who through treachery make Hammond's meddling far worse: Dennis Nedry and Lewis Dodgson. Nedry's name is an anagram of "nerdy," and his first name suggests the comic-strip brat "Dennis the Menace." Lewis Dodgson's name is an amalgamation of the first name of the pseudonym and the actual surname of the author of *Alice's Adventures in Wonderland* (1865) and *Through the Looking Glass and What Alice Found There* (1871)—Charles Lutwidge Dodgson writing as Lewis Carroll—and thus establishes parallels between Alice and the heroic paleontologists, all of whom stumble into a pocket of existence where nothing works as expected.

Further intertextual references are more obvious. As the title of the sequel clearly indicates, these two novels are Crichton's reworking of Arthur Conan Doyle's *The Lost World* (1912), which, like Crichton's books, features humans encountering dinosaurs in Latin America. Again, Crichton seeks to provide a feasible explanation for human-dinosaur coexistence. Though scientists have expressed doubts about whether extinct species could be reborn through the sorts of DNA experimentation that Hammond's lackeys employ, the process depicted in Crichton's novels at least involves state-of-the-art "hard" science and offers possibilities that are more likely than the explanation in Doyle's novel: that a large relic population of ancient reptiles could somehow survive in a remote corner of the world. None of Crichton's other books has had effects on popular culture as immense as those of *Jurassic Park* and *The Lost World*; both were made into blockbuster films, and both have inspired further sequels and imitations, adding to the American fascination with prehistoric reptiles.

Thomas Du Bose

OTHER MAJOR WORKS

SCREENPLAYS: *Westworld*, 1973; *Coma*, 1978 (adaptation of Robin Cook's novel); *The Great Train Robbery*, 1979 (adaptation of his novel); *Looker*, 1981; *Runaway*, 1984; *Jurassic Park*, 1993 (adaptation of his novel; with David Koepp); *Rising Sun*, 1993 (adaptation of his novel; with Philip Kaufman and Michael Backes); *Twister*, 1996 (with Anne-Marie Martin).

NONFICTION: *Five Patients: The Hospital Explained*, 1970; *Jasper Johns*, 1977; *Electronic Life: How to Think About Computers*, 1983; *Travels*, 1988.

BIBLIOGRAPHY

Crichton, Michael. "Ritual Abuse, Hot Air, and Missed Opportunities." *Science* 283, no. 5407 (March 5, 1999): 1461-1463. One of Crichton's best articles presents his definitive statement on the portrayal of science and scientists in popular culture, especially films.

Grazier, Kevin R., ed. *The Science of Michael Crichton: An Unauthorized Exploration into the Real Science Behind the Fictional Worlds of Michael Crichton*. Dallas: BenBella Books, 2008. Focuses on Crichton's use of science and examines the real-world validity of the various scientific elements in his novels, including cloning, nanotechnology, and time travel.

Sandalow, David B. *Michael Crichton and Global Warming*. Washington, D.C.: Brookings Institution, 2005. Excellent brief publication focuses on Crichton's novel *State of Fear* and provides one of the best analyses available regarding Crichton's controversial stance on global warming.

Trembley, Elizabeth A. *Michael Crichton: A Critical Companion*. Westport, Conn.: Greenwood Press, 1996. Presents good, detailed critical analyses of Crichton's best sellers through *The Lost World*. Includes biographical information and a chapter devoted to Crichton's literary heritage. Supplemented with bibliography and index.

A. J. CRONIN

Born: Cardross, Dumbartonshire, Scotland; July 19, 1896

Died: Glion, near Montreux, Switzerland; January 6, 1981

Also known as: Archibald Joseph Cronin

PRINCIPAL LONG FICTION

Hatter's Castle, 1931
Three Loves, 1932
The Grand Canary, 1933
The Stars Look Down, 1935
The Citadel, 1937
The Keys of the Kingdom, 1941
The Green Years, 1944
Shannon's Way, 1948
The Spanish Gardener, 1950
Beyond This Place, 1953
A Thing of Beauty, 1956 (also known as *Crusader's Tomb*)
The Northern Light, 1958
The Judas Tree, 1961
A Song of Sixpence, 1964
A Pocketful of Rye, 1969
Desmonde, 1975 (also known as *The Mistral Boy*)
Lady with Carnations, 1976
Doctor Finlay of Tannochbrae, 1978
Gracie Lindsay, 1978

OTHER LITERARY FORMS

In addition to the many novels he published, A. J. Cronin wrote one play, *Jupiter Laughs*, which was produced in Glasgow and New York City in 1940. His autobiography, *Adventures in Two Worlds* (1952), remains the best account of his formative years as well as an engaging vehicle for many of his opinions. In 1926, he also wrote two medical studies, *Report on First-Aid Conditions in British Coal Mines* and *Report on Dust Inhalation in Haematite Mines*. His journeys to investigate the conditions on which he reported became the basis of the fictional accounts of mining communities found in *The Stars Look Down* and *The Citadel*.

ACHIEVEMENTS

In the spring of 1930, a tall, sandy-haired, genial physician sold his London practice and home, moved with his family to an isolated farmhouse near Inverary, Scotland, and at the age of thirty-four wrote a novel for the first time in his life. *Hatter's Castle*, published the following year by Victor Gollancz, became an immediate success. It was the first novel to be chosen by the English Book Society for the Book-of-the-Month Club. It was later translated into many languages, dramatized, and made into a motion picture starring James Mason and Deborah Kerr (released in the United Kingdom in 1942). Before long, critics hailed A. J. Cronin as a new and important author whose writing was comparable in content and style to that of Charles Dickens, Thomas Hardy, and Honoré de Balzac.

Cronin and his wife moved to a small apartment in London and then on to a modest cottage in Sussex, where he went to work on another novel, *Three Loves*. His popularity continued to increase following *The Grand Canary* and *The Stars Look Down*, and the former physician became something of a literary lion, in demand at dinners, bazaars, and book fairs. His writing launched him on a literary career with such impetus that, once and for all, he "hung up [his] stethoscope and put away that little black bag—[his] medical days were over."

The physician-novelist is of course by no means an unfamiliar literary figure. Arthur Conan Doyle, W. Somerset Maugham, C. S. Forester, Oliver Goldsmith, and Robert Bridges, among others, had rich medical backgrounds into which they reached for ideas for their books. None of these examples, however, quite parallels the dual career of Cronin. Medicine with him was not a stopgap or a stepping-stone. He was an outstanding professional and a financial success as a physician; moreover, he was ambitious, desperately tenacious, and single-minded in his pursuit of that success. It was hard won and well deserved. His second success, in an entirely different field, was equally substantial. Twenty novels (several of which have been adapted to the cinema), a play, an autobiography, and one of the longest-running British television series represent a career that spans one-half of the twentieth century—1930 to 1978—and a life that was itself as engrossing and multifaceted as Cronin's fiction.

Perhaps just as remarkable as the extraordinary commercial success of the novels is the fact that most of them are much more than highly readable potboilers. Like Emily Brontë, Dickens, and Hardy—three writers with whom he is often compared—Cronin was a natural-born storyteller who transcended the category of "academic" fiction writer. His novels are realistic, purporting to present the actual experiences of actual people. They present life not in the vacuum of timelessness but in the timely flux of ordinary experience. They rely on a specific sense of place—interiors and exteriors—and reflect a rapid mastery of the different settings and environments to which Cronin's travels had taken him. Even in his most extreme formal experimentation—as in *The Stars Look Down*—Cronin's fiction retains accessibility and readability.

A. J. Cronin. (Popperfoto/Getty Images)

Although Cronin's popularity has somewhat waned, he was for many years one of the best-known and most controversial of British writers; through a number of books remarkable for their honesty and realism, he helped entertain and educate a generation of readers. As a writer, he was always promoting tolerance, integrity, and social justice. His favorite theme was that people should learn to be creative rather than acquisitive, altruistic rather than selfish.

BIOGRAPHY

In order to appreciate Archibald Joseph Cronin's novels fully, one must have a reasonable acquaintance with the author's life. This is not necessarily true in the case of many writers, whose private lives are less clearly reflected in their work than are those of writers such as Dickens and Maugham, to whom Cronin bears a resemblance in this matter. Throughout his career as a novelist, Cronin drew heavily on his memories of what he had actually observed. Henry James's argument that the writer of fiction should be "one upon whom nothing is lost" received an emphatic embodiment in the life of Cronin, whose experiences as a child, a medical student, and a physician are woven inextricably into the fabric of his novels.

As is the case with so many of his fictional characters, life for young Cronin was by no means idyllic. Archibald Joseph Cronin was born in Cardross (Dumbartonshire), Scotland, on July 19, 1896, the only child of a middle-class family whose fortunes were soon to decline rapidly. His mother, Jessie Montgomerie, was a Scottish Protestant woman who had defied her family—and a host of ancestors—by marrying an Irishman and turning Catholic. His father, Patrick Cronin, was a mercantile agent who until his death was able to offer his family a fairly comfortable existence. After the death of his father, however, Cronin was forced to retreat with his penniless mother to the bitter and poverty-stricken home of her parents.

To most neighbors and relatives in the small, strictly moral, and sternly Protestant town of Cardross, Jessie Montgomerie's marriage and conversion were considered a disgrace, and on young Cronin they inflicted the inevitable ridicule and persecution. On one hand there was sectarian antagonism, not far short of the kind that erupted in the late twentieth century in Northern Ireland as violence. On the other hand was the stern Protestant morality. Cronin was permanently marked by an environment that was noisy, quarrelsome, profoundly unhappy, and emotionally dramatic—a source of endless tension and grief for the growing boy and of endless material for the future novelist.

Cronin's delight in reading and learning perhaps compensated for his frustrations. Among the authors he read were Robert Louis Stevenson (an only child like himself and a firm favorite right to the end of his life), Sir Walter Scott, Guy de Maupassant, Dickens, Maugham, and Samuel Butler—whose *The Way of All Flesh* (1903) Cronin cited as his favorite book. At Cardross Village School and later at the Dumbarton Academy—where literature was his best subject—the boy became something of a prodigy, repeatedly winning prizes and discovering in himself the love for learning that would be a source of stability all his life. Both as a student and, later in life, as a physician-writer, he spent enormous stretches of time at his desk, wrestling with his work. This compulsiveness, combined with his intelligence and his eagerness, won Cronin the approbation of his uncle—a poor, kindly Catholic priest who helped secure for him his education and who later became the model for Father Chisholm in *The Keys of the Kingdom*—and of his great-grandfather, who later became the model for Alexander Gow in *The Green Years*.

Cronin's talent also meant, however, that he would suffer the emotions of premature loneliness that so often afflict unusually bright boys. He was highly regarded by his teachers, but other students—and their parents—sometimes resented his abilities. One father whose young hopeful was beaten by Cronin in an important examination became so enraged that years later *Hatter's Castle* took shape around his domineering personality. The theme—"the tragic record of a man's egotism and bitter pride"—suggests the dark and often melodramatic atmosphere of Cronin's early novels. In them, some characters are drawn with humorous realism, but for the most part humor is dimmed by gloomy memories of his own neglected childhood, and sensational scenes are shrouded in an atmosphere genuinely eerie and sinister. Inevitably, Cronin clung to the notion that between the life of the mind and the life of the senses, between a dis-

ciplined commitment to scholarship and a need to share in the common pleasures of humankind, there is an irremediable conflict.

The religious bigotry, the family's unceasing poverty, the interest in learning—this trio of forces worked at shaping the young Cronin. A shy, sensitive, lonely boy, aware of his peculiarities yet hungry for the town's acceptance, he developed, like Robert Shannon of *The Green Years*, an overt mistrust of organized religion. Until his father's death Cronin had been devout, and the question of his becoming a clergyman may have been considered, but if Cronin had entertained any such ambitions, his increasing indifference, which emerges very clearly in his novels, must have caused him to abandon such plans. Instead, he decided he would become a doctor—the only other thing for an ambitious poor boy living in Scotland to do—and in 1914 he entered Glasgow University Medical School.

Cronin had begun his medical studies when World War I took him into the Royal Navy Volunteer Reserve as a surgeon sublieutenant. Back at the university, he was struck forcefully by the contrast between his sincere idealism and the cynicism, selfishness, and muddled incompetence of many of the students and doctors he met. This conflict later found expression in his fiction, in which his idealized heroes' enthusiasm is contrasted sharply with the satiric descriptions of other doctors, civic officials, and small-town bigots. In *The Stars Look Down*, *The Citadel*, *The Green Years*, and *Shannon's Way*, for example, every aspect of the medical profession is criticized: medical schools, small-town practice, public health, fashionable clinics, and even research centers.

Having been graduated M.B., Ch.B. with honors in 1919, Cronin was appointed physician to the outpatients in Bellahouston war pensions hospital, and later medical superintendent at Lightburn Hospital, Glasgow. Two years later, he married Agnes Mary Gibson—also a medical school graduate—and entered into general practice in a mining area of South Wales from 1921 until 1924. In the latter year, he became a medical inspector of mines for Great Britain. In 1925, he took his M.D. degree with honors; a year later he prepared a report on first-aid conditions in British coal mines and another report on dust inhalation in hematite mines. After his service with the ministry of mines was completed, Cronin moved to London and built a practice in London's West End. Throughout these experiences and contacts with people of every kind, he continually thought of stories he could create. His patients and colleagues provided him with a dramatic cast of characters, a ready-made network of complex relationships, and a complete set of thunderous emotions. In all of this, he was not only an active participant but also, as the trusted doctor, an advantaged spectator.

"It has been said that the medical profession proves the best training ground for a novelist," Cronin wrote, "since there it is possible to see people with their masks off." Certainly, in his own writings, Cronin drew heavily on his experiences as a doctor. The Glasgow medical school environment; the touch-and-go associations with mental patients at a suburban asylum; the medical practice in a Welsh mining village with its calls in the night and impromptu surgery on the kitchen tables and in mine shafts; the drama, pathos, and cynical worldliness that passed under his eyes as a medical practitioner in London—all these episodes were used as material for his novels.

The richest source of material for his novels, however—especially the later ones, beginning with *The Keys of the Kingdom*—was his newfound faith. At the height of financial prosperity and great reputation, in good health and with his work flowing smoothly and abundantly, Cronin felt a deep malaise, a feeling of emptiness and "interior desolation." For years he had ignored matters of the spirit; then, almost coinciding with the end of one career and the start of a new, even more successful one, he found himself confronted with a fundamental fact of existence. He had been born a Catholic, observing the outward practice of his faith, but had gradually drifted into a position where religion was something entirely outside his inner experience. In the years after World War II, he took his wife on pilgrimages to Vienna, Italy, and France, in particular Normandy. Each trip to war-battered Europe provided experiences that further crystallized Cronin's maturing faith. The source of his renewed strength can be summed up in a few words: "No matter how we try to escape, to lose ourselves from our divine source, there is no substitute for God." This is a simple statement of sincere faith by a man whose adventures in various environments were marked by a steady development in spirit and in art.

ANALYSIS

Everything that A. J. Cronin wrote was stamped by his personality, his sincerity, his direct concern with ethical issues, his seemingly instinctive knowledge of ordinary people, and his tremendous gift for storytelling. An examination of five of his most popular novels—*Hatter's Castle, The Stars Look Down, The Citadel, The Keys of the Kingdom*, and *The Green Years*—reveals a consistent commitment to the value of the individual— the personal—and a remarkable development in narrative technique.

HATTER'S CASTLE

Hatter's Castle was in many ways a happy accident, securing for its author laudatory reviews and substantial earnings and establishing him as a writer of great promise. In its hero, readers found an outstanding personality: a hatter in Levenford, in strongly characterized surroundings, who lived through a destiny of suffering and tragedy. Readers were also treated to a return to the English novel in the grand tradition. Its themes of the rejected family, the struggle against poverty, the desire for wealth, the illusion of limitless opportunity, and the conflict between personal desire and conventional restraint were recurring ones throughout Cronin's fiction.

To develop the plot of *Hatter's Castle*, Cronin used the familiar Victorian conventions available to all aspiring writers of the time: a straightforward linear chronology unfolded through the agency of the omniscient third-person narrator, with an emphasis on melodrama and horror. Added to these conventions is one of the most familiar themes of Greek tragedy, the retribution that attends overweening pride. James Brodie is a man whose inordinate self-love and unusually strong physique have made him the most feared person in town as well as the tyrant of a trembling household. He has deluded himself into believing that his hat shop is a thriving business, that his house is a romantic castle, and that he himself is related to the aristocracy. The novel proceeds almost consecutively from its beginning, with the hero at the "peak" of his power, to his decline into futility, frustration, and finally, alienation.

Woven through the book are patterns of developing

images and symbols that serve important structural functions: They relate and unify the individual lives presented in the book; they support and embody its themes; and they are the means by which the texture of an event or feeling is conveyed. One cluster of these images grows out of the title, which refers, of course, literally to the house, and also to James Brodie himself and his career. The "castle," at once a physical structure and symbol of the Brodie family, is pictured early in the novel in terms that both symbolize the owner's pride and prophesy the dreadful environment and outcome of the story. It is a place of gloom and solitude, "more fitted for a prison than a home," "veiled, forbidding, sinister; its purpose likewise 'hidden and obscure.'" The pompous dignity of the gables greets the visitor with "cold severity." The parapet embraces the body of the house like a "manacle." Its windows are "secret, close-set eyes [which] grudgingly admitted light." Its doorway is "a thin repellent mouth." This description not only provides a haunting counterpoint to the action of *Hatter's Castle* but also establishes the essential character of Brodie well before he appears, before he is even named.

The members of the Brodie family share with the house a condition of imminent collapse. Typical of so many novelists, Cronin's device—here and elsewhere—is to put his minor characters in dire straits at the outset of the action so that they can be tested against the hardships life has to offer. This strategy he accomplishes by introducing the family members as they wait for Brodie, moving from grandmother to elder daughter, from younger daughter to mother, and each picture is presented as a miniature scene in a continuous drama of frustration. All along, the reader notes a strange absence of the usual signs of domesticity in a large country household.

The driving force of the book, however, is the portrayal of the successive disasters that Brodie brings upon himself and his family. Margaret, his feeble, downtrodden wife, is reduced to abjection and dies horribly of cancer. Mary, his elder daughter, is a lovely, gentle girl not quite able to cope with her father. She becomes pregnant, is thrown out of the house into a raging storm, and eventually marries the young doctor whom Brodie hates. Nessie, the younger daughter, is driven to insanity and suicide by Brodie's morbid determination that she shall win a scholarship and go to college. Matthew, Brodie's

weakling son, robs his mother, lies to both of his parents, and runs off with his father's mistress. By the end of the novel, therefore, any manifestations of Brodie's supposed supremacy have vanished. Not only has he lost his family, but he has lost his business and has become a drunkard. He is left shattered, with no companion but his tragic, greedy old mother, and with no hope but death.

Although *Hatter's Castle* is in many ways a conventional novel, there are ideas, themes, and techniques in it that reappear in Cronin's later, more mature work. The characters are typical of Cronin: paradoxical mixtures of good and bad, weak and strong. Possessiveness, to the point of the pathological, is used as a catalyst to introduce a conflict and action, and, as in his later novels, it is always expressly condemned. The unrequited love theme that appears so often in Cronin's writing is present in the form of Mary's plight. Also, the central idea of rebellion against social pressures anticipates the kinds of revolt that motivate so many Cronin characters, including artists, seekers, and criminals.

Perhaps a legitimate criticism of the plot is that the sheer number of misfortunes suffered by Brodie and his family seems excessive and implausible. Possibly, but it seems to be a part of Cronin's philosophy that troubles never come singly, and, certainly, all of Brodie's misfortunes can be convincingly traced to his character and actions. "Character is Fate," quotes Thomas Hardy in *The Mayor of Casterbridge* (1886), and his nemesis works unerringly through Brodie's own glaring defects. Imaginative belief in Brodie compels belief in what happens to him. As one critic observed, "The plot may creak, but Brodie lives."

THE STARS LOOK DOWN

Cronin's fourth novel, *The Stars Look Down*, surpasses its predecessors by many standards. It develops in greater depth his major preoccupations—a concern with the chaos of life, its bitterness and desolation—but keeps under restraint the tendency toward melodrama without weakening the force of his instinct for drama. Characters reflect the special types to which Cronin is attracted, but the theme of the futility of the British working class against the greed and selfishness of the moneyed overlords receives fuller treatment here.

With action ranging over much of England, the novel takes place in the period from 1903 to 1933. The story's center is the Neptune coal mine in Ryneside County. The plot moves back and forth between two families, the Fenwicks and Barrases, adding constantly to their widening circle of acquaintances. Working primarily (although not exclusively) within the minds of his characters, Cronin maintains a tightly unified texture as he changes focus from one character to another. The six main characters are rather schematically drawn: One character is paired off with another, usually to show contrasting versions of a general type. The six major characters fall into three pairs: David Fenwick and Joe Gowlan; Laura Millington and Jenny Sunley; and Arthur Barras and his father, Richard. David, Laura, and Arthur are the generally praiseworthy characters in the novel, the ones who gain the greatest share of the reader's sympathy. The "evil" ones, or those who obstruct the good characters, are Joe, Jenny, and Richard. The good are characterized by genuineness, sincerity, and a general lack of pretense; the bad, on the other hand, continually disguise their motives and present a false appearance.

If the six main characters have obvious symbolic import, so has the title of the novel. Subject to their own laws and compulsions, heeding little outside them, the stars look down on a scene of chaos and social revolution and go on looking, unperturbed. "'Did you ever look at the stars?'" asks the fat man in Robert Louis Stevenson's "The Merry Men" (1887). "'When a great battle has been lost or a dear friend is dead, when we are hipped or in high spirits, there they are, unweariedly shining overhead.' 'I see,' answered Will. 'We are in a mousetrap.'" This is the idea Cronin suggests in the title and acts out through his characters, intending to convey something of the aloofness of eternity compared to the chaos of the earth below.

Cronin conveys the atmosphere of a typical mining community by piling up factual detail on factual detail in an attempt to re-create the very look, texture, and smell of the life of the miner. Frequently, he uses the slangy, ungrammatical language of these people even in descriptive or explanatory passages when the omniscient narrator is speaking. A work on a subject as technical as coal mining is bound to have a somewhat specialized vocabulary, and a reader without firsthand knowledge of life in the pits must search for the meanings of such words as "collier," "hewer," "getter," "breaker," "pikeman," and "pikeman." To come to grips with the actualities of life in the mine, Cronin describes scenes such as the gaunt, unfriendly landscape, perpetually shrouded in grit; the silent and laconic manner of the miners; and the pervasive atmosphere of grim suffering and endurance. The town's very name—"Sleesdale," suggesting "sleazy"—is emblematic. This, then, is the backdrop to the human drama Cronin reconstructs—a drama about defeat and disappointment, about how people are victims of the greed and selfishness of others in power.

THE CITADEL

Set partly in the same atmosphere as *The Stars Look Down*—the dusky, dirty towns of the English coal-mining region—Cronin's fifth novel, *The Citadel*, is the savage and fiercely idealistic story of a young physician's struggle to achieve success in life. For many readers, doctors particularly, the novel's main interest lies in Cronin's indictment of both the unethical practices of the medical profession and the system under which the miners lived and worked. For other readers, the interest lies in the unmistakable similarity between the hero's personal philosophy and Cronin's own opinions. There is the same integrity of character, the same effort to focus public attention on social forces that are responsible for many of the ills of his patients, and the same deep concern as an individual for lessening human disaster. In the hero, these readers welcome the titillating sense of being "inside" the medical profession. Reading Cronin, they enjoy the especially comforting thought that they were being educated as well as entertained.

If there is any single clue as to Cronin's intention in *The Citadel*, it is in the title. This simultaneously tragic and romantic novel was first called "Manson, M.D.," after its hero, but it was felt that the title finally chosen was a better expression of the underlying meaning of the novel. Andrew Manson is a man who in spite of great odds tries and ultimately succeeds in freeing himself from materialistic influences. The word "citadel" stands for medical competence and medical integrity, the ideals to which Manson aspires. That this symbol is central to the plot of the novel is made clear when Chris Manson tells her husband, "Don't you remember how you used to speak of life, that it was an attack on the unknown, an assault uphill . . . as though you had to take some castle that you knew was there, but could not see, on the top?" At the end of the story, as Manson leaves Chris's grave, he sees in the sky before him a bank of clouds "bearing the shape of battlements." The reader is left to assume that Manson will once more assault the battlements, and that the conquest of them will be the greatest of all his achievements.

A large part of the novel's impressiveness stems from the way it functions throughout on a realistic level. Having grown out of Cronin's years as a physician and his experiences in Wales and London from 1921 to 1930, *The Citadel* may be read autobiographically, but with great caution. The reader may be sure that the greedy Mrs. Edward Page, the bitter Philip Denny, the incompetent but fashionable Doctors Ivory, Freedman, and Hampton, and a score of others had their living counterparts in Cronin's own experience. From a full spectrum of professional men and women, Cronin tells of the jealousies of the assistants and the scheming rivalries of their supervisors, of questionable medical practices, unsanitary conditions, hostile patients, rejected treatments, ephemeral successes and horrifying failures, and always the drudgery of endless plodding hackwork.

Significantly, these supporting characters remain stereotypes, since Cronin's main point is that, except for Denny, they ease through life, think and talk mostly of fees, and scheme to get ahead. The lazy among them learn little and continue to prescribe routine drugs and treatments. The ambitious think up tricks to entice rich patients, prompting them to believe they are sick whether or not they are. These antagonists—the nonprogressive, materialistic doctors—are mostly figures of straw, their outlines only vaguely discernible through the young doctor's self-concern. Relative to Manson's vigor and vitality, these characters appear flat and insipid.

Another striking achievement of the book is the solid underlayer of fact. Almost all of Cronin's books, including the poor ones, have this foundation, giving them a satisfying density and bulk. In *The Citadel*, the details of Manson's experiences—without the use of abstruse technical terms and too many scientific explanations—are tremendously appealing to the reader. His restoration to life of Joe Morgan's stillborn baby, his coal-pit amputation of a miner's arm in the perilous tunnel, his restoration to consciousness of hysterical Toppy Le Roy, and the shocking butchery of the operation by Dr. Ivory—all

of these scenes rouse the emotions as a means of persuading the mind. With its sober factuality, it is not difficult to understand why this novel has been enormously popular in both the United States and Great Britain.

While *The Citadel* has much to say about a society that seems unwilling to allow Manson to do his best work, commenting at length on the evil practices of other physicians, it is also an unusual love story, with Andrew and Chris Manson at the center. Chris is effectively presented as a frank, well-educated, levelheaded young woman whose instinctive enjoyment of life is the counterpart of Andrew's integrity and determination. She knows the secret of turning hardships into fun, of forgetting irritation in laughter. Hard work and poverty do not scare her. The passionate integrity her husband brings to his science she brings to human relations—above all to her husband. From him, she refuses to accept any compromise of principle, even though this course leads them for a time to obscurity and poverty. She is strongly opposed to materialism and its shabby, cheapening results. She fights as best she can against every influence that she thinks will hurt her husband either as a scientist or as a man.

If one demands purity of conception and unflagging precision of execution in a novel, then *The Citadel* is clearly disappointing. Cronin, however, surmounts these flaws as an artist to represent seriously, and at times movingly, some of the significant problems of his day. To one concerned with literary movements, part of the interest of the book lies in its representation of the many facets of its cultural and social milieu. It contains elements of Romantic optimism, of realistic appraisal, and of naturalistic pessimism. In attempting to trace in *The Citadel* the progression of his own attitudes toward life, Cronin makes a comment about human experience that frequently strikes home with compelling force.

THE KEYS OF THE KINGDOM

Perhaps Cronin's most popular novel, *The Keys of the Kingdom* emphasizes with incisiveness the problems encountered when a religious man rebels against the human-made rules, limitations, and barriers that are continually thrust between human beings and their God. Its merit lies precisely in its analysis of the conflicts between kindliness, sincere faith, and human understanding on one side and smugness, intolerance, bigotry, and assumed piety on the other. Francis Chisholm is the medium through which Cronin presents his conception of what has been called the most difficult subject in the world: religion.

In *The Keys of the Kingdom*, it is not the profession of medicine but that of the priesthood that is held up to examination. The verdict, however, is much the same as that found in *The Citadel*. The priest who serves God according to the teachings of Christ, viewing himself as the selfless shepherd and servant of humankind, accepting poverty, humility, and perhaps even martyrdom, is likely to be misunderstood, undervalued, and cruelly censored by his brethren. The more worldly priest, on the other hand, will win the power and the glory that the Church has to bestow. Cronin's priest, like Cronin's doctor, is an individualist with the courage to accept the guidance of his conscience rather than his self-interest. In the Church, as in the medical profession, such courage may put one at a disadvantage, often bringing disappointment and disillusionment. *The Keys of the Kingdom*, therefore, is an entrancing story but also an expression of personal faith.

The title for this novel comes from the words of Christ to Peter—"And I will give to thee the keys of the kingdom of heaven"—and the central theme comes from Geoffrey Chaucer's famous description of the poor parson of the town, which ends, "But Christes' lore and his apostles twelve/ He taught, but first he followed it himself." Thus the keys, according to Cronin and his mouthpiece, Francis Chisholm, are one's knowledge and use of the fundamentals of tolerance, humility, charity, and kindness. Where creeds divide, deeds of love and sympathy unite.

Like the great Victorians from whose rich tradition they spring, Cronin's characters, according to his modest moral aims, are unmistakably "good" or "bad." The reader knows as soon as they appear that Aunt Polly, Nora Bannon, Mr. Chia, Dr. Willie Tullock, and Bishop McNabb are "good." One also can be reasonably sure that these people will endure their share of misfortune. The reader can find in these characters a schooling in generous humanity. Also easily recognizable are the unsympathetic characters: Bishop Mealey, Father Kezer, Mrs. Glennie, and Monsignor Sleeth. Readers always know where they stand with Cronin.

This contrast between the "good" and the "bad" is apparent especially through the comparison of Francis Chisholm and his lifelong associate Anselm Mealey, who lacks the feeling and innate spirituality of his friend but who uses a certain veneer and his commanding appearance to get himself elevated to the bishopric. As a picture of the worldly priest, Mealey is eloquent in his sermons, popular with the women of the parish, and especially assiduous in those good works that gain him the approbation of his superiors. He attracts large donations, makes many converts, and fights the outward battles of the Church. He is even willing to capitalize on a "miracle" that proves to be no miracle at all.

Francis Chisholm, on the other hand, is the dissenter, the man who is different and therefore doomed to disappointment and failure in the eyes of the world. Through him, however, Cronin celebrates a central conviction: the significance—in possibility and promise, in striving if not in attainment—of tolerance and compassion and of encouragement for those striving to be true to their aspirations. Francis wins the priesthood the hard way: Being plain, outspoken, and unprepossessing in appearance, he never gets far in the Church. While Mealey attends to the social affairs of the Church, Francis works with the poor and lonely. While Mealey complies with all of the Church's teachings, Francis speaks his mind. Christlike yet human, Francis believes in tolerance rather than dogma, and he holds humility above pride and ambition.

It is doubtful that a book has ever been more timely. Appearing as it did when most of the world was at war, and with most writers preoccupied with that topic, a book with religion as its background was most refreshing. When religion is presented logically and unpretentiously, as in *The Keys of the Kingdom*, without mawkishness or condescension, it is sufficiently novel to make the reading public take notice. In this atmosphere and with these attributes, Cronin's most popular novel achieved its immense success.

THE GREEN YEARS

Until *The Green Years*, most of Cronin's attention had been focused on the absurdities and complications of the adult world. In *The Green Years*, however, Cronin set himself the added difficulty of working within the limited consciousness of a small child while at the same time avoiding the sentimentality of so many books about childhood written for adults. To accomplish all of this Cronin takes his hero quite seriously, and he often describes his experiences with the same gravity as Robert, the protagonist, would view them. What is more, the novel consists of a grown man's remembered experience, for the story is told in retrospect of a man who looks back to a particular period of intense meaning and insight. "Our purpose," the author says, "is to reveal [the young Robert] truthfully, to expose him in all his dreams, strivings and follies." This double focus—the boy who first experiences and the man who has not forgotten—provides for the dramatic rendering of a story told by a narrator who, with his wider, adult vision, can employ the sophisticated use of irony and symbolic imagery necessary to reveal the story's meaning.

The Green Years is a story of initiation, of a boy's quest for knowledge. The plot covers a period of ten years (1902-1912) and falls into three sections of nearly equal length as the hero progresses from innocence to perception to purpose. In the early chapters, Robert's innocence is expressed as a mixture of bewilderment and ignorance. The opening establishes with Proustian overtures the desolation that haunts him upon his arrival at his new home, Levenford, with his new "mama," Grandma Leckie: "I was inclined to trust Mama, who, until today, I had never seen before and whose worn, troubled face with faded blue eyes bore no resemblance to my mother's face." Robert's sensitivity to his new surroundings is apparent in his acute perception of details. At the dinner table, Papa says "a long, strange grace which I had never heard before." Robert has difficulty managing "the strange bare-handled knife and fork," does not like the cabbage, and finds the beef "terribly salty and stringy." He wonders why he is "such a curiosity" to all these people. The feeling of "being watched" is an experience that is repeated and a notion that reverberates throughout the novel. Suggested here is his continual need to perform for others and to be evaluated by others. Robert is the typical uncomprehending child caught in an uncomfortable situation. Lonely, imaginative, and isolated, he lacks the understanding necessary for evaluation and perspective.

Robert's gradual development into a perceptive young man functions, in large part, as a kind of organizing principle in the novel, uniting the common interest of a variety of disparate characters. These figures include Papa and Mama Leckie, Uncle Murdock, and Adam Leckie—all of whom are caught by marked shifts in their lives: illness, the death of those close to them, the breakup of careers, and the discovery of new opportunities. To compensate for this unhappy environment, Robert turns in part to nature and literature. His appreciation of nature, for example, may be attributed to his friend, Gavin Blair, in whom he discovers the companionship he craves. Like the companions of so many of Cronin's protagonists, Gavin is intelligent, gifted, and handsome. Particularly appealing to Robert is Gavin's "inner fibre, that spiritual substance for which no words suitable can be found."

While Cronin makes it clear that there is great comfort in all this, he also shows that this friendship initiates a problem that haunts Robert for much of the novel: a weakness for idealism. For Cronin, the great struggle of youth coming to maturity is the search for reality. This process involves disillusionment and pain. Robert endures a great deal of anguish each time one of his illusions is destroyed, but these disillusionments are necessary if he is to achieve intellectual and emotional independence. Once he must fight with his best friend, Gavin, to stop the taunts of his fellow classmates. At night, he is terrified by his grandmother's tales of Satan. He witnesses Gavin's death and on the same day fails the important Marshall examinations. All of this contributes to his temporary loss of faith in himself and his God.

Helping to shape Robert's purpose and philosophy is Alexander Gow, the one character with whom Robert feels secure. Robert quite naturally takes to Gow, with his apocryphal tales of the Zulu War, his eye for the ladies, his orotund views of human frailty, and his love for drink. Gow possesses "those faint ennobling virtues—never to be mean, always kind and inspiring affection." He defends Robert's right to Catholicism and to an education. Robert sees him as the reader sees him: erratic, not always dependable, yet—as one reviewer wrote—"still with an unquenchable zest for experience, an insatiable hunger for vital and beautiful things, an instinctive understanding of the human heart, especially a heart in trouble or in extreme youth."

In retrospect, *Hatter's Castle*, *The Stars Look Down*, *The Citadel*, *The Keys of the Kingdom*, and *The Green*

Years fall into a pattern, illustrating Cronin's recurring themes. Each of the five novels features a protagonist who has glimpses of values beyond the reach of his environment and who must struggle to achieve them. All five novels focus with dramatic force on the essential evil of injustice: the personal suffering that is the real reason for hating such injustice. Cronin's humanitarian sympathies, his reaction against political, social, and religious injustice in his time, led him to a philosophical position somewhat akin to Thomas Carlyle's. He believed that it is the responsibility of individuals to work, to prove their worth in whatever social stratum they happen to find themselves.

Dale Salwak

OTHER MAJOR WORKS

PLAY: *Jupiter Laughs*, pr., pb. 1940.

NONFICTION: *Report on Dust Inhalation in Haematite Mines*, 1926; *Report on First-Aid Conditions in British Coal Mines*, 1926; *Adventures in Two Worlds*, 1952 (autobiography).

BIBLIOGRAPHY

Bartlett, Arthur. "A. J. Cronin: The Writing Doctor." *Coronet* 35 (March, 1954): 165-169. Readable, entertaining article provides biographical details concerning Cronin's transition from life as a doctor to life as a writer.

Bromley, Roger. "The Boundaries of Hegemony." In *The Politics of Theory: Proceedings of the Essex Conference on the Sociology of Literature, July, 1982*, edited by Francis Barker et al. Colchester, England: University of Essex, 1983. Scholarly essay examines class structure in *The Citadel*.

Cronin, Vincent. "Recollection of a Writer." *Tablet* 235 (February 21, 1981): 175-176. One of Cronin's sons writes a moving appreciation of his father, with biographical details and a discussion of *Hatter's Castle* through *The Spanish Gardener*. States that Cronin's novels were both "indictments of social injustice" and expressions of "a deep religious faith" from which stemmed "the warm humanity which gave his novels a worldwide appeal."

Davies, Daniel Horton. *A Mirror of the Ministry in Modern Novels*. New York: Oxford University Press, 1959. Includes a perceptive discussion that compares and contrasts the portrayal of a Protestant missionary in W. Somerset Maugham's "Rain" with Cronin's depictions of clergy in *The Grand Canary* and *The Keys of the Kingdom*.

Frederick, John T. "A. J. Cronin." *College English* 3 (November, 1941): 121-129. One of the earliest important considerations of Cronin's reputation in the light of his flaws as a writer. Discusses *Hatter's Castle*, *The Grand Canary*, *The Citadel*, *The Stars Look Down*, and *The Keys of the Kingdom*. Judges Cronin's novels to suffer from a lack of humor, an absence of stylistic grace, obvious construction, and some feeble characters. On the positive side, finds that Cronin exhibits "deliberate choice of fictional material of the highest value and importance, unquestionable earnestness of purpose and—most important of all—positive evidence of capacity for self-criticism and for growth."

Fytton, Francis. "Dr. Cronin: An Essay in Victoriana." *Catholic World* 183 (August, 1956): 356-362. Important discussion covers the man behind the novels and his religious thinking since his return to the faith. Divides Cronin's works into two groups: those before *The Keys of the Kingdom* (which grow in quality) and those after (which descend in quality). Argues that "the descent exactly corresponds with the author's growth in religious conviction."

Salwak, Dale. *A. J. Cronin*. Boston: Twayne, 1985. Offers a full introduction to Cronin's life and works. After discussing his life as a doctor and his transition to that of a writer, examines each of Cronin's novels and concludes with an assessment of his career. Supplemented by chronology, notes, comprehensive bibliography, and index.

_____. *A. J. Cronin: A Reference Guide*. Boston: G. K. Hall, 1982. Annotated bibliography is an indispensable research tool for those interested in tracing the judgments passed on Cronin, the writer and the man, by his English and American readers from 1931 until his death in 1981. The annotations are descriptive, not evaluative, and are fully indexed. An introduction traces the development of Cronin's literary reputation.

MICHAEL CUNNINGHAM

Born: Cincinnati, Ohio; November 6, 1952

PRINCIPAL LONG FICTION

Golden States, 1984
A Home at the End of the World, 1990
Flesh and Blood, 1995
The Hours, 1998
Specimen Days, 2005

OTHER LITERARY FORMS

Michael Cunningham edited and wrote the introduction for *Laws for Creations* (2006), a collection of poems by Walt Whitman. Cunningham has also published short stories that have appeared in several well-known literary magazines. His story "The Destruction Artist" appeared in *A Memory, a Monologue, a Rant, and a Prayer* (2007), a collection edited by Eve Ensler and Mollie Doyle. With Susan Minot, Cunningham cowrote a screenplay adapted from Minot's novel *Evening* (1998), which subsequently became a 2007 film release. Cunningham also has written introductions or afterwords for new editions of works by such authors as Thomas Mann, Henry James, and Virginia Woolf.

ACHIEVEMENTS

In 1999, Michael Cunningham received the Pulitzer Prize for fiction and the PEN/Faulkner Award for his novel *The Hours*. He also received the Whiting Writers' Award (1995), a Guggenheim Fellowship (1993), a National Endowment for the Arts Fellowship (1988), and a Michener Fellowship from the University of Iowa (1982). His short fiction has been published widely, including in *The New Yorker*, *The Atlantic Monthly*, and *The Paris Review*. Cunningham's story "White Angel," taken from his novel *A Home at the End of the World*, was chosen for the Best American Short Stories series in 1989. Another short story, "Mister Brother," appeared in the O. Henry Awards' Prize Stories collection of 1999.

BIOGRAPHY

Michael Cunningham was born in Cincinnati, Ohio, and raised in La Cañada, Southern California. He earned his bachelor's degree in English literature from Stanford University and his master of fine arts (M.F.A.) degree from the University of Iowa. A gay man partnered for several years, Cunningham defies definition as a "gay author." While gay characters and themes are part of his novels, they do not serve as the prism through which his novels are viewed. Cunningham has taught at the Fine Arts Work Center in Provincetown, Massachusetts, and in the M.F.A. creative-writing program at Brooklyn College. He also has taught writing in formal courses and in workshops around the world.

ANALYSIS

Two of Michael Cunningham's early works, *A Home at the End of the World* and *Flesh and Blood*, focus on family, the need for community and connections, and the obligations inherent in belonging. *The Hours*, his most celebrated novel, is a well-crafted three-dimensional gem. Flawless in design, it holds up to close inspection and presents a sturdy structure, like a pyramid. Cunningham's appreciation for form helps him to reimagine Virginia Woolf's perhaps finest novel, *Mrs. Dalloway* (1925). He reconstitutes the novel into a story of three women, in three equal parts. Incidentally, *The Hours* was Woolf's working title for *Mrs. Dalloway*.

Critics wondered if Cunningham could do for Whitman with his next novel, *Specimen Days*, what he did for Woolf with *The Hours*. This question was asked and apparently answered by reviewers of *Specimen Days*, which takes its title from Whitman's autobiographical collection *Specimen Days and Collect* (1882-1883). While Lev Grossman of *Time* proclaimed Cunningham's book "one of the most luminous and penetrating novels to appear" in 2005, critic Theo Tait, writing in *New Statesman*, observed, "*Specimen Days* is as muddled, and as silly, as it sounds." *The Hours*, *Specimen Days*, and *A Home at the End of the World* have a common structure: limited perspectives and alternating chapters or novella-like sections that ultimately connect, often to the reader's surprise and amusement. The novels reveal a unity, a coming together, an underlying theme.

Michael Cunningham.

A HOME AT THE END OF THE WORLD

This work, to use the author's words, is an examination of the difference between what can be imagined and what can actually exist. *A Home at the End of the World* is the story of two men, Bobby and Jonathan, who are growing up together in Cleveland, Ohio. Their stories intermingle, and Cunningham takes turns narrating their lives, documenting their friendship, and lamenting their losses.

Jonathan is gay. His mother, Alice, is a whiz in the kitchen, and his father, Ned, operates a failing movie theater. An only surviving child, Jonathan adores his father and cherishes his mother while trying to understand his sexual feelings. His best friend and first real love is

Bobby, a man-child whose older, rebellious, idolized brother died suddenly and tragically. Bobby's family was decimated by the death; his mother was driven to suicide and his father became an empty suit who drank himself into a nightly stupor. Bobby was alone, a young drug addict confused about adulthood, about sex, and about women. He loved music, especially Van Morrison and Jimi Hendrix or any artist of the Woodstock generation. Bobby inherited his dead brother's rebel mantle and his record collection. Bobby's whole life could be summed up by the lyrics of a Crosby, Stills, Nash, and Young or Buffalo Springfield song. Too young to have participated in the culture of the 1960's, his attitude and personality are frozen in tribute to its memory.

Jonathan has an active love life, relishing his freedom and sleeping with multiple partners. Living in New York City, he rooms with Clare. Clare is an older woman, once divorced and once the lover of a female celebrity, and now childless and living off a trust fund but estranged from her family. She clings to Jonathan and they joke about having a baby. Jonathan's favorite lover is a man named Erich, a would-be actor who tends bar and makes Jonathan happy. The two men share a strictly physical intimacy and never grow together emotionally. They take from one another passion without giving comfort.

In addition to Bobby and Jonathan, Alice and Clare also are narrators in the book, though they are never the center of the story. The story always revolves around the relationship between Bobby and Jonathan, even when they are apart. Alice worries about Jonathan, knowing that he is gay and not wanting to know any particulars. She wishes Jonathan would find a love of his own, not one shared with Bobby, Clare, and their daughter Rebecca.

After Ned's death, Alice moves on with her life, still hoping for a chance at happiness. Though Jonathan swears that Rebecca is as much his daughter as she is Bobby's or Clare's, Alice tells him otherwise. She knows Clare will never leave her baby to be raised by Jonathan and Bobby, even if they love Rebecca just as much as Clare does.

Erich visits Jonathan and his family. It has been several years, and Erich looks different. He is living with AIDS. The country life, a home away from the bright lights, the noise, and congestion of the city, appeals to

Erich. After a weekend visit, he is invited back. Regular visits become an extended stay, and it becomes clear that Erich will eventually die in the country house.

Clare acts as a mother, protecting her child. She lies and leaves, severing her ties with her best friend Jonathan and with Bobby, the father of her child. This is the point in the story where what is imagined and what can be done part ways. It is a lovely thought to imagine that three adults and one child can be a family, and that the family can expand to accommodate a dying man with no loved ones to comfort him in his last days. While each character in *A Home at the End of the World* can achieve a measure of peace, that peace does not mean a shared vision.

THE HOURS

This novel resembles a trip to a carnival's house of mirrors. However, instead of seeing one's self, one sees multiple images of Woolf reflected everywhere. Carefully constructed, *The Hours* is, in an important way, like *A Home at the End of the World* in that they both utilize multiple narrators, each narrator providing a vital part of the book's larger story. *The Hours* features four women: Virginia Woolf, Laura Brown, Clarissa Vaughan, and Clarissa Dalloway. Only the first three characters are narrators. The fourth character, the protagonist of Woolf's novel, is represented, to some degree, by the other three women.

Each woman is living at a different time and in a different place from the others. The novel is set during a period of one day only. Woolf appears as she was in 1941, the year she killed herself. She is hoping to move from Richmond, England, where she is recovering her health, to London, where she longs to live and work. Brown is living just a few years later, in 1949, after the war and during a time when the American Dream, especially in sunny California, abounds. Finally, Clarissa Vaughan's story is set in late twentieth century New York City.

In the book's prologue, Woolf is nearing the end of her life. She is walking toward the river, loading her pockets with heavy rocks, and wading in to her death. She reappears in later chapters, alive once more, as she documents her troubled life and her work on *Mrs. Dalloway* in the early 1920's. She is visited by her older sister, Vanessa, and her children. Woolf is both mentally

tough and emotionally fragile, and she hopes to convince her husband, Leonard, that her recovery is going well, and that she is strong enough to move back to London.

The first chapter of *The Hours* begins with the story of Mrs. Dalloway, though she is not Woolf's Mrs. Dalloway. In *The Hours*, she is Clarissa Vaughan, who is nicknamed Mrs. Dalloway by her former lover, Richard, who is dying from AIDS. Mrs. Dalloway is organizing a dinner party in Richard's honor; he has been recognized recently for his life's work as an author and poet. The party is set for the evening, and there are many details to attend to, including buying flowers, checking with the caterer, and dealing with last-minute uninvited guests, such as the insufferable Walter. A successful writer as well, Walter is nevertheless disrespected and disliked by Richard. Another uninvited guest is the emotional Lewis, another of Richard's former lovers, who still carries a torch for him and resents Mrs. Dalloway for "stealing" Richard from him.

The third narrator of *The Hours*, Laura Brown, is also attending to party plans. It is her husband's birthday. She is baking him a cake, and it has to be perfect. His birthday is set for today, and everything must be ready when he comes home. Laura would rather be in her bedroom reading, coincidentally, Woolf's *Mrs. Dalloway*. Laura would like her life to be more satisfying, more rewarding. Her husband and her young son Richie; her house in the suburbs; and her pregnancy all leave something to be desired by her, a hole of some sort. Her personality mirrors Woolf's own.

The Hours represents time that must be filled, whether one is happy, sad, emotionally crippled, or dying of AIDS. As long as one lives and breathes, the hours stretch on and must be endured. The uncertainty of release, the waiting for deliverance, haunts those who exist only to serve time.

SPECIMEN DAYS

If the universe were repeating patterns, if spirits were immortal, if these spirits kept finding one another over and over again through the ages, then *Specimen Days* would reflect reality and not fantasy. The novel's structure is familiar: All the characters in all the stories within the novel are tied together.

Specimen Days is divided into three stories or parts. In the first part we meet Lucas, a deformed young man who has memorized Whitman's *Leaves of Grass* and spouts lines from the poet's work at times when normal conversational give-and-take would suit him better. Lucas has recently lost his older brother, Simon, in a factory accident. He was mauled by a machine. The story is set at the dawn of the Industrial Revolution. Simon was to be married to Catherine, who works long hours as a seamstress in what would today be considered a sweatshop. Lucas, Simon, and Catherine, or versions of them, meet again and again throughout the story.

There are other common threads in the novel. Whitman appears in all the stories—as himself in the first and then through surrogates in the later stories. A china bowl with strange markings appears in all three stories, as well, and is usually sold by a woman named Gaya who also appears (or her descendants appear) in all three stories. Other than by helping to tie the three stories or parts together, Gaya and the china bowl do not seem to have greater meanings.

The second part of the novel is easily the strongest of the three. This story reads like a police procedural, with boys strapping pipe bombs to their bodies and then detonating the bombs as they hug random passersby on the streets of New York. Cat is now a police profiler, talking to the sick and twisted callers who phone her to make threats. Simon, her boyfriend, is a futures trader who collects art objects and tries to soothe Cat's frayed nerves. Cat has lost a child, Luke, to cancer. She has left her first husband and she blames herself for her son's death.

It turns out the boys with bombs have been raised by a woman they call Walt. The boys are lost, claimed by Walt as orphans. The boys have no names or identities, and no families. The home they share with Walt is pasted with pages from *Leaves of Grass*. The pages cover the ceilings and are even pasted over the windows.

Cat reaches out to the last of these three boys after finding that she is his intended target. In the process of negotiating with the boy for her life, she becomes part of his underground world. She learns there are other likeminded boys in other cities, all loosely connected and united in a cause to end civilization so that it may be started anew.

The novel's third story is set in "Old New York," a theme park located where New York City once stood. Simon is an automaton who works for a company called Dangerous Adventures. He is programmed to offer tourists lifelike experiences of the real New York City. For a price, he provides a level of terror mixed with sleaziness to the men or women who purchase his time. Simon's world is controlled by monitors, drones that fly and take pictures and come complete with laser weapons. The drones are the tools of the larger company that owns Old New York, and part of their everyday routine is to destroy faulty automatons such as Simon and his friend Marcus.

Catareen is an alien, a Nadian. The Nadians resemble reptiles, complete with narrow eyeballs, flaring nostrils, and claws. The Nadians, however, are not a warrior species. They have been transported to Earth from their native planet, where the terrain is unforgiving, the sky is perpetually dim, and the air is always dank. Catareen lives in Old New York and works as a nanny to human children.

Randy L. Abbott

OTHER MAJOR WORKS

SCREENPLAYS: *A Home at the End of the World*, 2004 (based on his novel); *Evening*, 2007 (with Susan Minot; based on Minot's novel).

NONFICTION: *I Am Not This Body: Photographs*, 2001 (photographs by Barbara Ess); *Land's End: A Walk Through Provincetown*, 2002.

EDITED TEXT: *Laws for Creations*, 2006 (by Walt Whitman).

BIBLIOGRAPHY

Hughes, Mary Joe. "Michael Cunningham's *The Hours* and Postmodern Artistic Re-Presentation." *Critique* 45, no. 4 (Summer, 2004): 349-361. Examines Cunningham's retelling, or re-presentation, of an earlier postmodern novel for his own work, *The Hours*.

Johnson, Sarah Anne. *The Very Telling: Conversations with American Writers*. Hanover, N.H.: University Press of New England, 2006. Features a frank interview with Cunningham, who discusses the craft of writing and how he came to write many of his novels, including *Specimen Days* and *The Hours*. Includes a bibliography.

Peregrin, Tony. "Michael Cunningham After Hours." *Gay and Lesbian Review Worldwide* 10, no. 2

(March-April, 2003): 30-31. Discusses Cunningham's novel, *The Hours*, the screen adaptation of the novel, and plans for future projects.

Schiff, James. "Rewriting Woolf's *Mrs. Dalloway*: Homage, Sexual Identity, and the Single-Day Novel by Cunningham, Lippincott, and Lanchester." *Critique* 45, no. 4 (Summer, 2004): 363-382. A study of three novels, including Cunningham's *The Hours*, which present variations on Virginia Woolf's novel, *Mrs. Dalloway*.

Young, Tory. *Michael Cunningham's "The Hours": A Reader's Guide*. New York: Continuum, 2003. Part of the Continuum Contemporaries series, this brief guide is especially useful for beginning readers of Cunningham's best-known novel.

CYRANO DE BERGERAC

Born: Paris, France; March 6, 1619
Died: Paris, France; July 28, 1655
Also known as: Hector Savinien de Cyrano

PRINCIPAL LONG FICTION

L'Autre Monde: Ou, Les États et empires de la lune et du soleil, 1656-1662 (*Comical History of the States and Empires of the Worlds of the Moon and Sun*, 1687; also known as *Other Worlds: The Comical History of the States and Empires of the Moon and the Sun*, 1965; includes *Histoire comique des états et empires de la lune*, 1656 [*Comical History of the States and Empires of the Moon*; also known as *The Government of the World in the Moon*, 1659], and *Histoire comique des états et empires du soleil*, 1662 [*Comical History of the States and Empires of the Sun*])

OTHER LITERARY FORMS

In the course of his brief and turbulent life, Cyrano de Bergerac (SEE-rah-noh deh BEHR-zheh-rahk) tried his hand at an array of genres and acquitted himself honorably in all of them. His tragedy *La Mort d'Agrippine* (pr. 1653) compares favorably with the lesser works of Pierre Corneille. Cyrano's one comedy, *Le Pédant joué* (pb. 1954; the pedant outwitted), though never staged in his lifetime, was almost certainly the unacknowledged source of two highly effective scenes in Molière's *Les Fourberies de Scapin* (pr., pb. 1671; *The Cheats of Scapin*, 1701). *Le Pédant joué* is essentially a burlesque of the pedantry and *préciosité* that were rife in Cyrano's day—though Cyrano himself could tap a "precious" vein when he chose.

The same gift for burlesque is evident in Cyrano's satiric poem, or *mazarinade* (attack on Cardinal Mazarin), of 1649, *Le Ministre d'état flambé* (the minister of state goes up in flames), and in the best of his letters. The latter were not genuine correspondence but showpieces designed for publication. They are of several kinds: love letters full of exaggerated compliments and reproaches, set off by far-fetched figures of speech in the worst *précieux* style; elaborate and fanciful descriptions of nature; satiric attacks on real and imagined enemies; and polemic pieces on a variety of political and philosophical issues. The letters "For the Sorcerers" and "Against the Sorcerers" are especially noteworthy for their satiric power and cogency of argument; they also anticipate the attacks on superstition and intolerance in *Other Worlds*, Cyrano's most important work.

ACHIEVEMENTS

It is a great irony of literary history that Cyrano de Bergerac, a minor but talented and aggressively ambitious seventeenth century writer, at last achieved world renown in the twentieth century—as a fictional character who scarcely resembles his original. To be fair to Edmond Rostand (the playwright whose *Cyrano de Bergerac*, staged in 1897, spread Cyrano's fame), the unexpurgated manuscripts that were to reveal the full extent of his hero's boldness and malice were as yet unpublished when he wrote; yet it took a deal of willful misreading—and, of course, imaginative reworking—to make a noble Platonic lover of the dissolute and misanthropic Cyrano. Whatever his failures as a man, the real Cyrano deserves to be remembered as a competent literary craftsman and an inspired satirist. There is no denying that his libertinism had its sordid side, but its essence was simply "freethinking," a rejection of the Catholic Church's exclusive claim to truth and an espousal of the cause of scientific investigation.

In his best works, the two volumes of *Other Worlds* and the letters for and against sorcerers, Cyrano anticipates the form and some of the major themes of Voltaire's *contes philosophiques* (philosophical tales—a distinct genre). Indeed, Voltaire's *Le Micromégas* (1752; *Micromegas*, 1753), as well as Jonathan Swift's *Gulliver's Travels* (1726), owes a debt of inspiration to Cyrano. Perhaps Cyrano's greatest single achievement was his astonishing vision of cultural pluralism and toleration in an age clouded by superstition and repression.

BIOGRAPHY

For serious readers of his works, the facts of Cyrano de Bergerac's life offer an important corrective to his legend. Though his family laid claim to noble status, the only basis for that claim was their ownership of two "fiefs," or manorial properties—Mauvières and Bergerac—in the valley of the Chevreuse near Paris. The Cyranos were in fact of bourgeois origin; their son was christened Hector Savinien de Cyrano, and he himself added the title "de Bergerac" as a young man (as he occasionally assumed the pretentious given names of Alexandre or Hercule). This was deceptive on two counts, for, aside from smacking of nobility, the title suggests a Gascon origin. Rostand thus portrays his hero as born and bred in Gascony, which the real Cyrano never visited.

Cyrano was born in Paris and christened there on March 6, 1619. Some of his childhood was spent on his father's properties in the Chevreuse valley, where he acquired a love of nature and a hatred of dogmatic authority. The hatred was inspired by a country priest to whom Cyrano was sent for schooling; it was to grow into a lifelong passion, reinforced by his experiences at the Collège de Beauvais in Paris, where he completed his education. (The headmaster of the collège, Jean Grangier—a man of considerable scholarly reputation—is mercilessly satirized in Cyrano's comedy, *Le Pédant joué*, while the country priest is pilloried in *Comical History of the States and Empires of the Sun*.) Once out of school, Cyrano gave free rein to his rebellious streak and joined the circles of *libertins*, or freethinkers—and free livers—who frequented certain Paris cabarets. Among his libertine friends were several pupils of the materialist philosopher Pierre Gassendi, including the avowed atheist Claude-Emmanuel Chapelle and possibly the young Molière. Whether he studied with Gassendi himself, Cyrano was heavily influenced by his ideas, which are discussed at length in *Other Worlds*.

At about this time, Cyrano's father suffered serious financial reverses and was forced to sell his fiefs; it has been suggested that Cyrano's gambling losses may have been a factor. Whatever the reasons, relations between father and son were strained, and they continued to be so until the father's death; according to records left by his lawyers, Abel de Cyrano suspected his two sons of robbing him as he lay on his deathbed. It is worth noting as well that Cyrano includes a bitter tirade against fathers in *Other Worlds* and depicts the sons of the moon people as exercising authority over their old fathers.

His financial straits, as well as the desire to make a name for himself, inspired Cyrano to seek a commission in the Guards, a company made up almost entirely of Gascons, whose reputation for bravado was apparently well deserved. One element of the Cyrano legend that seems to bear up under inspection is his reputation for bravery in the duels for which the Guards were notorious. After being wounded in two battles, however (at the sieges of Mouzon and Arras), he gave up the military life in disgust and turned to a literary career. Frédéric Lachèvre, who produced the first accurate biography of Cyrano in 1920, has suggested that the serious illness from which Cyrano suffered during this period also influenced his decision by forcing him to withdraw from other spheres of activity. The exact nature of the disease is unknown, but several biographers have accepted Lachèvre's suggestion that it may have been syphilis. Illness and poverty combined to reinforce the misanthropic strain in Cyrano's character; during this period, he broke with and reviled many of his former friends.

Cyrano de Bergerac. (Library of Congress)

An opponent of Cardinal Mazarin at the outbreak of the Fronde in 1649, he changed sides—possibly for pay—and wrote a scathing letter, *Contre les Frondeurs* (1651; against the Frondeurs). Jacques Prévot, editor of Cyrano's complete works, suggested that one of the most violent of these ruptures may have had an erotic dimension: Charles d'Assoucy, a satiric poet, was known to be homosexual, and Cyrano seems to have shown little interest in women.

Unfortunately, Cyrano enjoyed no greater success as a writer during his lifetime than he did as a soldier. In an age of censorship, he was too bold for most publishers, and he succeeded in publishing his plays and some letters only after accepting the patronage of the duke of Arpajon, a man of limited intelligence who wished

to make a name for himself as a patron of the arts. With his support, Cyrano staged his tragedy, *La Mort d'Agrippine*, but it was closed after a few performances by a group hired to boo his "atheistic" stance (the hirelings, ironically, missed the more daring speeches and booed at a line they simply misunderstood). Shortly thereafter, Cyrano was hit on the head by a log dropped by one of the duke's servants. It seems at least as likely that this was an accident as that someone hired the servant to ambush Cyrano (for fear of facing him in a fair fight, as Rostand would have it): By this time, Cyrano's dueling days were behind him. The incident precipitated a rupture with the duke, however, and forced Cyrano to take to his bed. Fourteen months later, on July 28, 1655, he died at the age of thirty-six.

Lachèvre suggests that the primary cause of death was tertiary syphilis, but a lack of definite evidence has left this surmise in doubt. Cyrano is said to have returned to the faith on his deathbed at the urging of his relative, Mother Marguerite of Jesus, and his oldest friend, Henry Le Bret. Le Bret became Cyrano's literary executor and published a heavily expurgated version of *Other Worlds* in 1657, two years after Cyrano's death.

ANALYSIS: OTHER WORLDS

Erica Harth, in *Cyrano de Bergerac and the Polemics of Modernity* (1970), claims Cyrano de Bergerac to have been "the first of the Moderns," forerunner of a position more clearly formulated later in the seventeenth century in the great Quarrel of the Ancients and Moderns. Cyrano went beyond his contemporaries the *libertins*, Harth argues, by refusing to settle for a critique of received wisdom; the "destructive spirit" in which he attacks tradition and Church authority "is accompanied by a positive acceptance and propagation of the same scientific and philosophical ideas which, although not directly transmitted by Cyrano, were to have a profound impact on the minds of the eighteenth century *philosophes*."

Cyrano, however, was also undeniably a man of his own time, attracted to as well as repulsed by the excesses of *préciosité*, charmed as well as amused by the arcane theories of thinkers such as Tommaso Campanella, in which allegory and myth are still intertwined with rationalistic investigation. If we can trust the priest's report, Cyrano even returned to the faith in time to die "a good

Christian death," and as one critic has shown, it is impossible to deduce a consistent atheistic view even from the unexpurgated manuscripts of *Other Worlds*. However one looks at Cyrano's masterpiece, contradictions emerge. Before examining these contradictions in detail, a brief description of the work is in order.

Although *Comical History of the States and Empires of the Sun* was first published separately from *Comical History of the States and Empires of the Moon*, it seems clear that this division does not reflect any intention of the author; the two works relate voyages of similar scope by a single narrator, and the second of these voyages is said to be motivated by persecution arising from a published account of the first. Combined, the voyages form a continuous narrative—as do, for example, the two parts of Miguel de Cervantes' *Don Quixote de la Mancha* (1605, 1615)—and may be referred to without distortion by the collective title *Other Worlds*. (The French title, literally translated, is "the other world," a phrase that in French as well as English usually refers to the abode of souls after death; Cyrano probably meant it to be taken ironically, for his aim is to suggest that there are "other worlds" in the here and now as well.) This was Cyrano's only work of prose fiction, but it proved to be the most effective vehicle for his fractious talents and libertine perspective. Because of its subject, it has often been classified as a work of utopian fiction, but the genre to which it really belongs is that of the *conte philosophique*, or philosophical tale, as practiced preeminently by Voltaire one hundred years later.

A PHILOSOPHICAL TALE

The essence of the *conte philosophique* is its unique combination of satiric, even farcical, elements with serious philosophical or ideological ones. Consistency or fullness of characterization and cogency of plot tend to be sacrificed to the primary goals of ridiculing an opposing (usually dogmatic) intellectual position and of suggesting more enlightened alternatives. Because of the variety of scientific and philosophical positions, many of them incompatible, that are detailed by different characters of *Other Worlds*, it has been maintained that Cyrano—admittedly a dilettante rather than a true scholar—was himself confused about the ideas he wished to advance. While the confusion may be real, Prévot, in *Cyrano de Bergerac, romancier* (1977), has

argued for a subtler reading that qualifies the didactic intent of the work. Insofar as Cyrano has a "message," Prévot suggests, it is one of radical skepticism; Cyrano considers all doctrines, however scientific, inherently suspect, and having rid himself of one set is not at all eager to embrace another.

In addition to fitting Le Bret's description of his old friend's beliefs, this analysis would tally with Cyrano's own warnings, in the second chapter of his fragmentary treatise on physics (never completed but published in Prévot's edition of *Œuvres complètes*, 1977) against taking one's hypotheses for realities. There is, moreover, an anarchic streak in *Other Worlds*, corresponding to its satiric intent; in that respect, Cyrano is a worthy heir of Aristophanes, Lucian, and François Rabelais, from whom he may have borrowed specific motifs but whose satiric vein he made his own.

The narrator of *Other Worlds*, who speaks in the first person, is not named until the opening pages of the second volume; he is there called Drycona, an obvious anagram of Cyrano. On the strength of his anagrammatic name, many critics have assumed that the narrator speaks for the author. While at times it is hard to deny that he does, his own position fluctuates from scene to scene, enabling him to serve as a foil for a variety of interlocutors. Thus, in conversation with an avowed atheist he defends the faith, whereas in conversation with an Old Testament prophet he blasphemes. Nor is he always in opposition: He listens deferentially to speakers of the most disparate opinions. It seems best to admit, with Prévot, that Drycona is primarily a fictional creation—as are the other "real" characters who appear, such as Campanella and René Descartes.

THE VOYAGES

The narrator's first voyage is inspired by a moonlit walk with friends, who try to outdo one another in *précieux* descriptions of the full moon (an attic window on heaven, the sign outside Bacchus's tavern). His friends ridicule the narrator for suggesting that the moon may be "a world like this one, for which our world serves as a moon." On reaching home, however, the narrator finds that a book has mysteriously appeared on his desk and is lying open at the page where the author (Jerome Cardan, a sixteenth century mathematician and astrologer) describes a visit from two men who said they lived on the moon. The narrator, determined to verify his hunch, contrives a first mode of space travel: He covers himself with small flasks of dew, which the sun draws upward. He rises so quickly toward the sun, however, that he is obliged to break most of the flasks, and falls back to the earth—in Canada, at that time New France. There he is entertained by the viceroy, with whom he discusses his belief that the earth travels around the sun (still a heretical proposition in 1648); his own displacement from France to Canada is of course evidence that the earth rotates.

In a second attempt to reach the moon, he builds a flying machine, which at first crashes; while he is tending his bruises, the colonial troops outfit the machine with fireworks, transforming it into a multistage rocket. The narrator manages to jump in before it takes off and, when the last stage falls to earth, finds himself still being drawn to the moon by the beef marrow he had rubbed on his bruises. (It was a popular superstition that the waning moon "sucked up" animal marrow.) As luck would have it, he falls in the Earthly Paradise and strikes against an apple from the Tree of Life, whose juice revivifies and rejuvenates him. The prophet Elias, one of two inhabitants of the Earthly Paradise (the other is Enoch), tells him its history, but the narrator cannot resist the impulse to tell a blasphemous joke, and he is cast out of Paradise.

The rest of the moon is inhabited by a race of giants who resemble human beings but move about on all fours; indeed, they take the narrator for an animal because he walks on two feet, and they exhibit him as a kind of sideshow (an idea borrowed by Swift). He is befriended by a spirit whose native land is the sun but who has visited the earth in various ages and was once the Genius or monitory Voice of Socrates; the spirit speaks Greek with the narrator and arranges to have him brought to the royal court. There he is taken for a female of the same species as a Spaniard who has arrived before him (the Spaniard, Gonsales, was the hero of Francis Godwin's 1638 book *The Man in the Moone: Or, A Discourse of a Voyage Thither*).

In the hope of producing more "animals" of their species, the moon people have them share a bed, where they have long talks on various scientific problems. As the narrator learns the moon language (which is of two

kinds, musical notes for the upper classes and physical gestures for the lower), a controversy arises over his status: Is he a man or an animal? The moon priests consider it "a shocking impiety" to call such a "monster" a man, so he is interrogated before the Estates General. He tries to defend the principles of Aristotle's philosophy but is unanimously declared an animal when he refuses—as he was taught in school—to debate the principles themselves. A second trial, occasioned by his claim that "the moon"—that is, our earth—"is a world," leads to acknowledgment of his human status, but he is forced to recant the "heresy" of the claim itself. For the remainder of his stay, he is the guest of a moon family in which—according to custom—the son has authority over the father. In a series of conversations, the young man explains his radical materialist views of the universe; he is defending his atheism when a devil appears to snatch him away. The narrator, who tries to help his host, is thus transported back to earth (presumably because Hell is at its center). Thus ends the first volume.

The second volume opens with a clear reference to the first. Urged by a friend who shares his philosophical and scientific interests, the narrator—hereafter known as Drycona—writes an account of his moon voyage. He becomes a local celebrity but is accused of witchcraft by a malevolent country priest, who exploits the people's ignorance and persuades them to arrest the "sorcerer." Drycona escapes from prison by building a new flying machine—this one using the principle of the vacuum—in which he takes off for the sun. Once again, the machine can get him only part of the way there; it is the force of his desire, drawing him to the sun as source of life, that enables him to complete the voyage (which takes twenty-two months). The sun is divided into many regions of differing "opacity" (suggested by the then-recent discovery of sunspots); there is a rough correspondence between the intensity of light and the "enlightenment" of the inhabitants. One race—that of "spirits," such as the Genius of Socrates—can alter their outward forms as their imagination dictates.

The race of birds, who prevent abuses of power by choosing as king one of their weakest members (a dove), capture Drycona and put him on trial, as had the moon people; this time, however, the charge is simply "being a man"—belonging to a pernicious and destructive species. On the advice of a friendly bird, Drycona claims to be a monkey raised by humans, but he is convicted; he is on the point of being devoured by insects (included among the birds) when a parrot whom he had once freed on earth testifies on his behalf and obtains a pardon for him. After an encounter with a forest of talking trees, who try to convince him of their moral superiority, Drycona witnesses a battle between a Fire-Beast and an Ice-Animal (the latter is defending the trees). The battle is also observed by the philosopher Tommaso Campanella (author of *La città del sole*, 1602; *The City of the Sun*, 1880), who becomes Drycona's guide. Together, they visit the Lake of Sleep and the Streams of the Five Senses, which empty into the Rivers of Memory, Imagination, and Judgment. A couple from the Province of Lovers, on their way to the Province of Philosophers (where the soul of Socrates is to settle a dispute between them), give the two travelers a lift in a basket suspended from a giant bird. Campanella is returning to his province to greet the soul of Descartes, newly arrived (he died in 1650). The narrative of the second volume ends, unfortunately, at the moment that Drycona and Campanella meet Descartes; Cyrano's ill health during the last year of his life prevented him from finishing the manuscript.

DIMENSIONS OF THE NOVEL

A brief résumé can give only the faintest idea of the inventiveness and satiric verve of *Other Worlds*. Cyrano takes every opportunity to make minor but telling—and often cutting—observations on various aspects of the human condition. The chief defect of his masterpiece, lack of unity, is merely the excess of a virtue: the acknowledgment that there are more things in heaven and on earth than are dreamed of in any one human philosophy. Quick of wit and eye, Cyrano was ever ready to bolt off in new directions. This quality gives his narrative a certain inclusiveness and makes it consistently entertaining, despite long stretches of philosophical argument. It also, however, gives the work a chaotic quality, which seems to reflect both the temperament of the author and the intellectual ferment of his day. (This feature of *Other Worlds* has been aptly contrasted with the unity, in tone and perspective, of Swift's *Gulliver's Travels*.) Perhaps the only way to do justice to the many dimensions of *Other Worlds* is to isolate some of the most im-

portant ones and assess them individually. They are, in ascending order of importance, *préciosité*, utopianism, didacticism or popularization, and satire.

Cyrano's use of *préciosité* reveals a deep-seated ambivalence symptomatic of his relationship to his own age. The *préciosité*, or cultivation of extravagantly refined language, that flourished in seventeenth century France grew out of the court mentality fostered by centralization of the monarchy; the salons, where *préciosité* emerged, were miniature "courts" on the model of the royal one and could be stepping-stones to power for those who learned the "art of pleasing." The earliest of Cyrano's letters seem to have been undertaken as exercises in this courtly form of entertainment. That he longed for fame, and for public acceptance of his work, is clear, but it is equally clear that his wit was too sharp for his own good and that, instead of ingratiating, it often alienated his audience. This tendency was not altogether involuntary.

Cyrano was rebellious by nature and could not resist the shock value of a daring bon mot; he was also too intelligent not to see how easily *préciosité* could be turned to ridicule. Yet he had a truly lyric imagination, which lent itself to *précieux* elaboration, as in some descriptive passages of *Other Worlds*. The landscape of the Five Senses recalls Mademoiselle de Scudéry, the *précieuse par excellence*, and it is hard to deny the passage its charm, despite a hint of affectation. At his best, Cyrano manages to walk the fine line between *préciosité* and burlesque. He can indulge in witty definitions of the moon, ascribing them to Drycona's friends, and then allow his hero to deflate them by remarking that they serve only to "tickle the time, to make it go faster." Like Aristophanes, who made his characters trot out old jokes while affecting disdain for them, Cyrano usually manages to have it both ways.

In addition to its occasional *préciosité*, *Other Worlds* also contains a utopian vein, though it scarcely belongs to the utopian genre. This vein is chiefly visible in Cyrano's treatment of machines and practical inventions. The most prominent are, of course, the flying machines, which, though fanciful (and less than fully effective), are all posited on genuine physical principles—the vacuum, magnetism, evaporation. It was doubtless the sheer fluidity and daring of his imagination that enabled

Cyrano to anticipate other inventions of whose physical bases he was wholly ignorant; most striking of these inventions is the "talking book," or phonograph. There are also some radical social and political innovations in Cyrano's vision of the "other worlds" his protagonist visits: Battles on the moon can be fought only between armies of perfectly equal numbers, while the most important "battles" are debates between the scholars and wits of the two sides; in the realm of birds, the king is seen as the servant, not the master, of his people. Some of these innovations are transparent wish fulfillments to one familiar with Cyrano's life; the most pointed is the role inversion of fathers and sons, but there are humorous ones as well, such as the use of poetry for money (with value based on quality, not quantity) and the recognition, among the moon people, that a large nose is the infallible sign of a noble and witty nature.

Despite such pleasant surprises, however, Drycona encounters no ideal society: The moon people have their bigoted priests and heresy trials; the sun people, their disputes and unequal "enlightenment." The realm of the birds, which comes closest to a model state, also has the Draconian stamp that makes many utopias (Plato's Republic, Swift's land of the Houyhnhnms) so unpalatable, and Cyrano acknowledges that—as did Swift, perhaps in emulation of Cyrano—human beings may not live there. Despite a certain escapist impulse, then, the book is never more than guardedly optimistic about the realization of ideals. It may be significant that the closest thing to an ideal state of affairs in *Other Worlds* is set in our world: This is Drycona's brief but happy stay with his friends Colignac and Cussan. In a passage reminiscent of Rabelais's Abbey of Thélème (*Gargantua*, 1534; chapter 53), he describes the material comfort and intellectual stimulation of their life together:

> The innocent pleasures of which the body is capable were only the lesser share. Of all those the mind can derive from study and conversation, we lacked none; and our libraries, united like our minds, summoned all the learned into our company.

The idyll is soon threatened, and then shattered, by the malice of a priest and the ignorance of the peasants, but it offers a glimpse of the conditions Cyrano considered most likely to foster human happiness.

The prominence of learning in this vision raises the questions of whether Cyrano had a didactic or pedagogical aim in writing *Other Worlds*. It has been claimed that he was essentially a popularizer, concerned to present the new scientific theories of his contemporaries in a form accessible to the commoner. As with the utopian view, there is clearly some warrant for this interpretation; again, however, it seems less than adequate to account for the work as a whole. Drycona's abortive first flight, which lands him in Canada, is surely designed as a concrete illustration of the Copernican theory; it is appropriately followed by a discussion of the theory, and of various objections to it, in the conversation between Drycona and the viceroy. The sheer amount of space devoted to similar conversations throughout the book is an indication of their importance to Cyrano. At times, as in Drycona's long exchange with the young atheist on the moon, the plot is allowed to atrophy entirely: The focus of interest is on the ideas discussed and on the arguments for or against them. Yet Prévot has done well to point out that in each such discussion personalities are involved; there is no omniscient narrator and no completely reliable speaker.

Moreover, the universe of the book is hardly constrained by any one of the theories it sets forth, and it sometimes operates according to superstitious or supernatural beliefs: A devil can carry a man off for impiety, and the waning moon can "suck" the beef marrow Drycona uses as a salve. It seems particularly striking that on *both* of Drycona's outward voyages, the "scientific" method gets him only halfway there at most; the beef marrow gets him to the moon, while the "strength of his desire" for the source of all life draws him to the sun. The fictional data thus undercut not only specific scientific accounts but also any thoroughgoing rationalistic perspective.

This is not to suggest that the author has no clear-cut attitudes to convey: He does indeed, but his medium is satire rather than exposition. Drycona's motive in leaving the earth may be to explore the heavens, but Cyrano's purpose is to find a radically different perspective from which to observe the human world. The heliocentric theory espoused by the Church is symptomatic of human vanity, which insists that the universe was made for humans and continues, literally and figuratively, to revolve around them. Cyrano's protagonist finds himself in a position from which he is forced to reexamine virtually all of his assumptions—scientific, philosophical, religious, and social. Indeed, he is twice put on trial, not as an individual but as a representative of the human species. Yet each of the extraterrestrial societies he visits displays some of the defects of human societies, so that the lesson is one of cultural relativism, and the necessity for tolerance is made obvious, as in Voltaire's *contes philosophiques*, by the mistreatment of the sympathetic protagonist. The satire of religious abuses is particularly prominent, as befitted an age in which the Church was the chief opponent of free speech and investigation. Yet, as Prévot has shown, Cyrano's quarrel is not with God so much as with his vicars, who abuse their moral authority to indulge their own base motives.

The satiric effectiveness of *Other Worlds* is fueled by a keen sense of the comic. Cyrano's attitude toward his fellow humans was a complex one, compounded of anger, amusement, occasional admiration, and occasional hatred. It is the amusement, however, that tends to predominate. In this respect, Cyrano resembles his compatriots Rabelais and Voltaire (the first of whom he read, and the second of whom read him) more than he resembles his great English emulator, Swift. Between philosophical debates, he finds time to tell how the moon people make sundials of their teeth by pointing their noses toward the sun, how a "hypervegetarian" abstains even from vegetables that have not died a natural death, how a man from the Province of Lovers is forbidden to use hyperbole on pain of death after nearly persuading a young woman to use her own heart as a boat—because it is so "light" (fickle) and can hold so many. As well as an eloquent plea for tolerance and freedom of thought, *Other Worlds* is a consistently entertaining book, whose author clearly deserves to be remembered as an original writer of fiction, not merely as a character in a play by Rostand.

Lillian Doherty

OTHER MAJOR WORKS

PLAYS: *La Mort d'Agrippine*, pr. 1653; *Le Pédant joué*, pb. 1954.

NONFICTION: *Contre les Frondeurs*, 1651; *Lettres*, 1654 (*Satyrical Characters and Handsome Descriptions in Letters*, 1658).

MISCELLANEOUS: *Cyrano de Bergerac: Œuvres complètes*, 1977 (Jacques Prévot, editor).

BIBLIOGRAPHY

Addyman, Ishbel. *Cyrano: Adventures in Space and Time with the Legendary French Hero.* New York: Simon & Schuster, 2008. Presents a precise, balanced, and well-documented study of Cyrano. Includes notes, select bibliography, and index.

Aldington, Richard. *An Introduction to "Voyages to the Moon and the Sun."* New York: Orion, 1962. Aldington, one of England's best critics and a translator of Cyrano's fiction, discusses the legend and life of Cyrano as well as his friends and works.

Alter, Jean. "Figures of Social and Semiotic Dissent." In *A New History of French Literature*, edited by Denis Hollier et al. Cambridge, Mass.: Harvard University Press, 1994. Alter's essay includes information about Cyrano and his contemporaries. It is one of many brief, chronologically arranged essays that in their totality provide a comprehensive survey of French literature.

Campbell, Mary Baine. "A World in the Moon: Celestial Fictions of Francis Godwin and Cyrano de Bergerac." In *Wonder and Science: Imagining Worlds in Early Modern Europe.* Ithaca, N.Y.: Cornell University Press, 1999. Campbell analyzes a number of early modern texts, including fiction by Cyrano and other French and English writers, to demonstrate how people responded with awe to the new geographic and scientific discoveries of the seventeenth century.

Harth, Erica. *Cyrano de Bergerac and the Polemics of Modernity.* New York: Columbia University Press, 1970. Contains a thoughtful analysis of Cyrano's criticism of core Christian beliefs and his development of a mechanistic view of the universe in which God is not necessary, according to Cyrano.

Muratore, Mary Jo. *Mimesis and Metatextuality in the French Neo-Classical Text, Reflexive Readings of La Fontaine, Molière, Racine, Guilleragues, Madame de La Fayette, Scarron, Cyrano de Bergerac, and Perrault.* Geneva: Droz, 1994. Analyzes Cyrano as a science-fiction writer. Muratore makes good use of late twentieth century criticism. In spite of some jargon, this book can be helpful even for beginning students.

Popkin, Richard H. *The History of Scepticism from Erasmus to Descartes*. New York: Humanities Press, 1964. Provides a good description of Cyrano's originality in relation to other European freethinkers of the sixteenth and seventeenth centuries. The one weakness of Popkin's book is that he links atheists, such as Cyrano, to liberal-minded Christians, such as Desiderius Erasmus and René Descartes.

Sankey, Margaret. "From Seventeenth-Century Clandestine Manuscript to Contemporary Edition: *L'Autre Monde* of Cyrano de Bergerac." In *The Editorial Gaze: Mediating Texts in Literature and the Arts*, edited by Paul Eggert and Margaret Sankey. New York: Garland, 1998. Examines Cyrano's novel from a postmodern perspective, analyzing how his work was altered by editing and how editing changed the relationship between the book and its readers.

Van Baelen, Jacqueline. "Reality and Illusion in *L'Autre Monde:* The Narrative Voyage of Cyrano de Bergerac." *Yale French Studies* 49 (1973): 178-184. An excellent literary study, concentrating on the structure of the novel.

D

GABRIELE D'ANNUNZIO

Born: Pescara, Italy; March 12, 1863
Died: Gardone, Italy; March 1, 1938
Also known as: Gaetano Rapagnetta

PRINCIPAL LONG FICTION

Il piacere, 1889 (*The Child of Pleasure*, 1898)
Giovanni Episcopo, 1892 (*Episcopo and Company*, 1896)
L'innocente, 1892 (*The Intruder*, 1898)
Il trionfo della morte, 1894 (*The Triumph of Death*, 1896)
Le vergini della rocce, 1896 (*The Maidens of the Rocks*, 1898)
Il fuoco, 1900 (*The Flame of Life*, 1900)
Forse che si forse che no, 1910
La Leda senza cigno, 1916 (*Leda Without Swan*, 1988)

OTHER LITERARY FORMS

The literary production of Gabriele D'Annunzio (dahn-NEWNT-syoh) encompasses many other genres: short stories, poetry, autobiographical essays, political writings, and several plays, both in Italian and French. It would appear difficult as well as arbitrary, however, to draw a sharp distinction between D'Annunzio's fiction and his memoirs, for his works in both forms are eminently autobiographical. The only possible differentiation between the two genres depends on the mere change from first-person to third-person narration. Moreover, D'Annunzio's fiction and nonfiction follow a pattern of parallel development that escapes chronological schematization. Finally, to exclude memoirs would present only a partial vision of the author's work, thereby greatly reducing the understanding and appreciation of his achievements in this field.

G. Barberi Squarotti, in his book *Invito alla lettura di D'Annunzio* (1982), affirms that D'Annunzio's work should be taken in its totality, openly opposing traditional literary criticism, which has constantly chosen an anthological approach, favoring one aspect or another of his work. This constant search for a formula that could define D'Annunzio to the exclusion of relevant parts of his work, aside from being substantially reductive, has given quite unsatisfactory results. The various labels of "decadent," "nocturnal," or "sensual" ignore the essence of his writing, which consists in the very plurality of its aspects, reflecting the motifs, themes, and poetics of fifty years of European intellectual life.

When D'Annunzio wrote his first book in prose, the dominant personality in Italian narrative was Giovanni Verga, a powerful writer whose main contributions consisted of a collection of short stories and two novels, *I Malavoglia* (1881; *The House by the Medlar Tree*, 1964) and *Mastro-don Gesualdo* (1889; English translation, 1923). These works, in their style and themes, represent a clear departure from academic prose of the day. Verga derived his inspiration from the humble life of Sicilian people and created a personal language, harsh and concise, to express these realities. The new generation was deeply influenced by the innovative impact of his writing and recognized in Verga the leader of a new literary trend, the Italian *Verismo*, which, in spite of some substantial distinctions, can be equated with French naturalism.

D'Annunzio's first work in prose, *Terra vergine*, a collection of short stories, was published in 1882. Other collections followed, and finally all the short stories were included in two revised editions of *Terra vergine* (1884, 1902) and *Le novelle della Pescara* (1892, 1902; *Tales from My Native Town*, 1920). These writings, inspired by the folklore of the Abruzzi region, are clearly influenced by Verga's narrative models, but some basic innovations are already present. Beyond the *tranche de vie* (slice of life), photographically faithful to a somber and modest reality, D'Annunzio pursues the extraordinary and the exceptional. The sober representation of basic human passions is replaced by the analysis of morbid sensations, the description of natural landscapes is heightened by feelings of panic participation, and the language becomes particularly expressive in its tones of exasperated chromatism. From the beginning, it was evident that D'Annunzio was taking new steps beyond the boundaries of naturalism toward "decadentistic" excesses.

ACHIEVEMENTS

During his lifetime, Gabriele D'Annunzio, surrounded by the admiration of his contemporaries, met extraordinary success; his writings deeply affected Italian society, and most of his literary works were awaited and welcomed by an enthusiastic public. This favorable reception was followed by a period of neglect and even of open rejection. The negative judgment that fell on D'Annunzio's works should be ascribed mainly to the sharp change of perspective that characterized the 1920's intellectual debate in Italy and elsewhere in Europe. Politically, D'Annunzio's ideas, after being superficially assimilated into the fascist ideology, were harshly condemned; morally, his anticonformist lifestyle was stigmatized as decadent; aesthetically, his language, rich in lexical novelties and classical allusions, was rejected as a futile exercise in rhetoric. Now, most authoritative critics recognize D'Annunzio as the fecund interpreter of several generations of European intellectual life, whose greatest achievement remains the renewal of Italian culture.

Prior to the advent of D'Annunzio, the young Italian nation, absorbed in its political and economic struggle, was still dominated by provincial interests and the literary traditions of the past. D'Annunzio, a prodigious reader extremely receptive to the stimuli coming from abroad, renovated the literary scene, introducing new techniques and developing new themes.

D'Annunzio's vast work in prose, which registers the influence of the major European writers and follows the suggestions of the various literary movements, shows a steady evolution toward a greater freedom and richness

of expression. Moving beyond the boundaries of naturalism, through a segmented process of experimentation and assimilation, D'Annunzio reached his expressive measure in the memoirs that are now considered his highest achievement in prose.

BIOGRAPHY

Gabriele D'Annunzio's tumultuous life elicited great fascination from his contemporaries and nourished the works of his biographers with a number of romantic anecdotes. D'Annunzio himself orchestrated and publicized his "inimitable life," paying careful attention to the preservation of his legend. His correspondence (more than ten thousand letters) also maintained and renewed, with countless details, the interest in his life.

This romantic aspect of D'Annunzio's biography appears today outdated and even laughable; nevertheless, beyond the ostentatious facade there are elements of du-

Gabriele D'Annunzio. (Library of Congress)

rable truth that bring into proper perspective the man and his work. D'Annunzio's thirst for new experiences corresponds in fact to his indefatigable search for new literary solutions, and his existential adventures represent the prime source of his inspiration.

D'Annunzio was born in Pescara, a small and, at that time, somnolent little city on the coast of the Abruzzi region. His family belonged to the middle class and was wealthy enough to provide him with an excellent education. Young Gabriele did not feel a great respect for his father, nor did he show a particular attachment for his relatives, apart from a deep affection for his mother. It was not the family, but rather the Abruzzi region, with its primitive society dominated by ancestral laws, that influenced him deeply. The landscape, people, and folklore of his native land were to be a recurrent motif in D'Annunzio's works.

D'Annunzio soon left his hometown for Prato, in Tuscany, where at the renowned Liceo Cicognini he received a solid preparation in the humanities. A brilliant student and a daring young rebel, D'Annunzio excelled in all his classes, protested against the strict discipline, and led his classmates in knavish escapades. Later, the recollection of these years would give substance to some beautiful pages of his memoir prose. D'Annunzio's years in Prato culminated in 1879 with the publication of a collection of verses, *Primo vere* (early spring), which was very well received by the critics.

This first success opened the way to a brilliant literary career. In 1881, D'Annunzio was in Rome with the intention of pursuing his studies at the university, but soon he abandoned academia to embrace the elegant and worldly life of the capital. Brilliant contributor to journals and magazines, cherished guest of aristocratic and literary circles, D'Annunzio succeeded in combining an effervescent social life with unrelenting literary activity. After a romantic elopement, his marriage in 1883 to Maria Hardouin, duchess of Gallese, crowned the success of his social ambitions, and the publication of *The Child of Pleasure* (in Italian in 1889) consolidated his literary reputation. The marriage, which saw the birth of three children, was to last seven years. For the first four years, D'Annunzio seemed to accept an approximation of conventional domesticity, but in 1887, the encounter with Barbara, the wife of Count Leoni, precipitated the

end of his already precarious union with Maria. His sensual passion for "Barbarella" inspired in part the novel *The Triumph of Death* and all the verses of *Elegie romane* (1892).

Naples, where D'Annunzio moved in 1891, represents another step in his life and writings. There he collaborated with his friend, Eduardo Scarfoglio, the editor of *Il corriere di Napoli*, in which he published his novel *The Intruder* in installments. D'Annunzio's first engagement in politics dated from this time, with the publication of an article, "La bestia elettiva." In this article he attacked universal suffrage, restating Friedrich Nietzsche's theory of the inevitable supremacy of one group over another. These aristocratic ideas constantly recur in his writings, and the influence of the German philosopher is particularly evident in the works of the next decade.

While in Naples, the love affair with Barbara came to an end, and the writer became involved with Princess Maria Gravina, who left her husband to live with him *more uxorio*. Two children were born from this union, but his love for Maria did not survive a cruise to Greece in 1904. Upon his return, he separated from her to start a new love relationship, this time with the great actor Eleonora Duse. Duse, an extremely intelligent and passionate woman, brought to D'Annunzio the most enriching and stimulating love of his life. Under her influence he began his career as a dramatist and with her, in the splendid retreat of La Capponcina, his Tuscan villa, he wrote the first three books of *Le laudi* (1949), which remain the greatest accomplishment of D'Annunzio the poet. The relationship also provided him with the narrative nucleus of the novel *The Flame of Life*, published in 1900, in which he did not hesitate to portray in the aging actor Foscarina the generous and loving Eleonora. Added to his chronic unfaithfulness, this portrayal was one of the factors that prompted their separation in 1905. During the exceptionally productive years from 1895 to 1905, D'Annunzio also published the novel *The Maidens of the Rocks* and actively engaged in politics. In 1897, his name appeared on the list of right-wing candidates, and he was elected as a representative to the Italian parliament.

This first contact with political life did not mark D'Annunzio deeply, since his attendance in parliament was sporadic and his interventions capricious. His boredom with the ruling conservative party, which he described as "a group of screaming dead men," soon became open rejection. When, in 1900, the Pelloux government proposed its harsh reactionary laws, D'Annunzio, ostentatiously, moved his seat from the extreme right to the extreme left. Was this gesture dictated by his usual indulgence in theatrical effects or by genuine indignation? In D'Annunzio, it is difficult to separate the authentic from the artificial, since artifice was for him quite genuine. In an article that appeared a few days later, the writer justified his abrupt conversion by explaining that what he appreciated in the Socialist Party was its destructive potential—the same thing he admired in Nietzsche's theories. For D'Annunzio, extreme right and left seem to have coincided in a type of anarchic program aiming at the destruction of sclerotic institutions, whose only function was to protect incompetence and corruption. The following year, D'Annunzio presented himself as a candidate for the Socialist Party, but he was defeated and subsequently retired from the parliamentary arena.

After his separation from Eleonora Duse, D'Annunzio continued his amorous career with new affairs: first, Marquise Carlotti, who, once abandoned by him, found peace in a convent; then Countess Mancini, who, shattered by the impact of their turbulent and precarious relationship, collapsed into moments of despair and mental insanity. It was a sad episode, recounted by D'Annunzio in *Forse che si forse che no* (yes or no) and in *Solus ad solam*, an autobiographical writing that was published only after his death, in 1939.

Although D'Annunzio was a skillful manager of his literary success, the costly experiments with cars and planes he financed and his extravagant tastes drove him to bankruptcy. In 1909, he was obliged to sell his mansion, La Capponcina, and, being pursued by his creditors, he decided to leave Italy for France. Friends and admirers welcomed the famous writer, and he remained in France until the outbreak of World War I. During his voluntary exile, he took an active part in the social and intellectual life of Paris and published several works in French. Among them, the most prominent work is *Le Martyre de Saint Sébastien*, a theatrical text with music by Claude Debussy, which was presented in Paris in 1911.

The most magnificent adventure of D'Annunzio's life began with World War I. Upon his return to Italy in 1914, he campaigned for the intervention against Germany, and as soon as Italy entered the war, he enlisted as a volunteer. He fought first on the front line and at sea. Afterward he participated in several risky actions with the first military planes, until a plane accident cost him three months of immobility and the loss of his right eye. During this period of forced inactivity, he painfully scribbled a number of notes that were to become the nucleus of *Il notturno* (1921), one of his most valuable works in prose.

By the end of the war, D'Annunzio, quite naturally, assumed the role of the poet-prophet, voicing the feeling of frustration and discontent of the Italian people, confronted by an economic crisis and peace negotiations that did not favor Italian interests. Popular unrest reached its apex with the question of the annexation of Fiume, a city on the Dalmatian coast. D'Annunzio chose action; leading a group of volunteers in the famous Marci dei Ronchi, he occupied Fiume, where he established a temporary government. The Italian government, which was trying to avoid open conflict over this issue, first ordered D'Annunzio to leave the city, then sent the fleet with the order to bomb Fiume to force him to retreat.

Meanwhile, Benito Mussolini had assumed the leadership of the nationalist forces. In 1920, when D'Annunzio returned from his unsuccessful enterprise, there was no place left for him on the political scene. Abandoning any hope of playing an active role in the country, D'Annunzio retired to a large estate on Lake Garda, later named Il Vittoriale (the name means "pertaining to victory"), where, in semi-isolation, he spent the rest of his life. Officially, he maintained his support for the Fascist government, although he despised Adolf Hitler and had no respect for Mussolini, whom he considered a bad imitator of his own style. Mussolini, who did not trust D'Annunzio as a friend and feared him as an enemy, approved his timely retreat and bestowed honors and subventions upon him.

D'Annunzio's last years were devoted to the editing of his *Opera omnia* (1927-1936). He also gathered some of his previous writings, which he published in two volumes as *Le faville del maglio* (1924, 1928). Memories, erotic obsessions, and feelings of disillusionment fill the pages of *Le cento e cento e cento pagine del libro segreto di Gabriele D'Annunzio tentato di morire* (1935), which, apart from some privileged moments, lacks the vigor and drive of his other works. Without the fresh inspiration of a life intensely lived, literature had become for D'Annunzio an empty form. He died at Il Vittoriale in 1938 and lay in state in the uniform of an air force general.

ANALYSIS

After testing his narrative potential in short fiction, Gabriele D'Annunzio confronted the challenge of long fiction with the novel *The Child of Pleasure*, which confirmed in his prose writing a success already established in poetry. During the next twenty years, seven other novels followed, including *Leda Without Swan*, which could be better defined as a long short story.

The passage from short to long fiction presents substantial changes. Abandoning naturalistic themes and atmosphere, the writer directs his attention to the aristocratic world of the capital: Natural landscapes are substituted for elegant interiors or closed gardens; simple characters with primitive passions are replaced with sophisticated figures corroded by subtle torments. The language, highly refined, flows with an even rhythm, avoiding chromatic effects, and the prevailing subdued tones cast an aura of imperceptible melancholy on characters and events. All the subsequent novels are patterned on the same narrative structure: Little action is involved in the plot, which centers on the figure of the hero, a man of exceptional qualities who is confronted by a vulgar and base society dominated by utilitarian interests and aspirations. The narration is punctuated by digressions on artistic issues, meditations, detailed descriptions of objects and landscapes, and above all, by the minute analysis of fugitive sensations.

THE CHILD OF PLEASURE

In his first novel, *The Child of Pleasure*, D'Annunzio portrays the idle and decadent aristocratic society of Rome, totally absorbed in the pursuit of the most refined pleasures of the mind and of the senses. The autobiographical motif is evident in the projection of the author's personality onto the figure of the protagonist, Andrea Sperelli, a young aristocrat endowed with the spark of artistic genius.

A poet and a painter of great potential, Andrea wastes his intellectual energies in a futile worldly life; he finds his greatest challenges in his jousts of love. Forgetting his artistic aspirations, Andrea feels irresistibly attracted to the beautiful and sensuous Elena Muti, who responds with the same passion. The short season of their love comes to a sudden end when Elena abandons him for a rich husband. While trying to overcome his rejection with new conquests, Andrea is involved in a scandal and, in the duel that ensues, he is gravely wounded. After a long period of moral and physical prostration, love and life are revived by the apparition of Maria in the peaceful retreat where Andrea is slowly recovering. Maria, a beautiful and noble creature, endures with dignity the distress of an unhappy marriage, devoting her life to the education of her young daughter. Enticed by her sensibility and intelligence, Andrea discovers a new aspect of love, based on the communion of intellectual interests and spiritual aspirations. Maria tries to resist the growing attraction she feels for the young artist, which she confesses to her diary, but an amorous complicity has already flawed their friendship.

Upon their return to Rome, the idyll continues, until it becomes for Maria a total engagement that overcomes her last resistance. Andrea, on the contrary, is torn between conflicting sentiments and impulses. In the elegant circles of the capital, he has seen Elena, and once again he has been captivated by her charm. His feelings become troubled and confused; he slips into morbid fancies in which the images of the two women coalesce; old memories creep into new sensations, and in Maria's transports of love, Andrea savors Elena's gestures. The ambiguous situation explodes when, in a moment of total abandon, he calls Maria by the name of Elena. Maria, horrified by the brutal discovery that his thoughts are of someone else, runs away, and Andrea is left with nothing but the sad realization of his inability to love.

The novel ends with a melancholic scene that symbolizes Andrea's failure; his personal experience parallels the irreversible process of dissolution of a society whose only aspiration is the pursuit of pleasure. Maria's husband, a notorious gambler of ill repute, has lost his entire fortune at the game table. Now the creditors are auctioning his mansion. A horde of greedy merchants fights over the possession of precious furniture and artistic objects, while Andrea wanders in the empty rooms, aware of the spiritual ruin of an entire society and of his own life.

The story is told, according to traditional rules, by the omniscient author, but the protagonist acts as a center of consciousness, reflecting the outside reality through his own sensibility. Rather than seeing the events themselves, the reader knows the sentiments, sensations, and reactions that those events provoke in Andrea. As for the other characters, they seem to exist only in relation to the protagonist; when the author deems it necessary to present their feelings, he chooses an indirect approach, resorting to literary devices such as the introduction of intimate diaries or confessional letters.

In addition to being D'Annunzio's most popular novel, *The Child of Pleasure* offers a particular interest for its original interpretation of the decadent hero. Des Esseintes, the protagonist of Joris-Karl Huysmans's *À rebours* (1884; *Against the Grain*, 1922), remains the prototype of the genre, and, compared with him, Andrea Sperelli appears a superficial character. A spectator rather than an actor on the stage, Andrea lacks the tension for transgression, the turbid introspective search, the attraction to the abyss of nothingness that characterize Huysmans's hero; and the weary melancholy of *The Child of Pleasure* does not attain the disturbing depth of *Against the Grain*. Nevertheless, the two novels present a remarkable parallelism in their approach and technique. Both, in fact, restrict the parameters of the inquiry to a vision of the world filtered through the exacerbated sensibility of the hero, developing a rather tenuous plot in a rich texture of descriptions and analysis.

EPISCOPO AND COMPANY *and* THE INTRUDER

The next two novels, *Episcopo and Company* and *The Intruder*, represent a new phase of D'Annunzio's constant exploration of new motifs and techniques. In these works, the author experiments with the psychological and humanitarian themes proposed by the great Russian writers of the nineteenth century. Exploring the ambiguities of the human soul, he portrays tormented characters who are torn between guilty complexes and pretensions of innocence, wicked tendencies and aspirations to purity. In an attempt to render the inner struggle of the protagonists, the already slow rhythm of the narration is interrupted by exclamations, self-accusations, and justifications until it dissolves in tedious repetition.

The great dilemma of good and evil was not a burning issue of D'Annunzio's moral sensibility, and these sordid stories of moral degradation appear today quite monotonous and artificial.

THE TRIUMPH OF DEATH

In *The Triumph of Death*, D'Annunzio reiterates the theme of *The Child of Pleasure* in a more dramatic contest. In this novel, inspired by the author's personal experiences with Barbara Leoni, the dualism of sensuality and spiritual love becomes the conflict between lust and intellectual achievements. The protagonist, Giorgio Aurispa, is a writer who fails to realize his dream of artistic creativity because of his love for the beautiful Ippolita. The woman, a nymphomaniac afflicted with sterility, appears here as the enemy whose dangerous power hinders humankind's greatest aspirations. Giorgio, slave of his passion, is confronted by the prospect of a future of physical and intellectual impotence: Ippolita's sterility frustrates his natural desire for biological procreation; her lust destroys his creative potential. Unable to overcome his plight, Giorgio chooses suicide, plunging into a violent death with Ippolita.

THE MAIDENS OF THE ROCKS

According to Carlo Salinari, the publication of *The Maidens of the Rocks* in 1896 marks the official birth of the superman in Italian literature. The protagonist, Claudio Cantelmo, disgusted with the corruption and degradation of political institutions, pursues a dream of national renewal. Realizing that only the next generation will be ready to follow his program, Claudio leaves the capital with the firm resolution of devoting his life to the education of a son who, under his guidance, will become the superman for whom history is waiting. Following his project, he decides to choose among three sisters, descendants of a noble family, the spouse who will bear his child, the future leader of national renovation. From the beginning, Claudio realized that his program is condemned to fail. The three sisters live in a secluded world of physical and spiritual beauty outside reality and time, and the rocks surrounding their estate symbolize the barrier that separates them from the historical context. Idealistic aspirations and concrete action belong to two distinct levels of reality that Claudio cannot bridge. Renouncing every hope of active engagement, he leaves the sisters in the cloistered serenity of their retreat.

Formally, the novel repeats the narrative structure of the preceding works; ideologically, through the protagonist, D'Annunzio conveys his own political dream of aristocratic supremacy, spurning barbarian masses and greedy bourgeoisie, both responsible for the destruction of art and beauty in the world.

THE FLAME OF LIFE

If all of D'Annunzio's heroes are projections of his personality and aspirations, the autobiographical inspiration is especially vivid in *The Flame of Life*. In the love story of Foscarina, an aging actor, and Stelio Effrena, a young intellectual, D'Annunzio revives his own relationship with Eleonora Duse. Stelio is in Venice to present a program for a national theater, based on the fusion of poetry, music, and dance; the new theater, instead of being restricted to an elite audience, will be addressed to the people. The ambitious project is an attempt to rescue theater from the monopoly of the bourgeoisie, which, while despising art, pretends to control it.

In Venice, Stelio meets the famous Foscarina, who falls in love with him. At first, he thinks he loves her with equal passion; in reality, he is seduced by the art of the actor rather than by the charms of the woman. The realization of the true nature of his sentiments strikes him when, in the young and pure Donatella Arvale, he recognizes the ideal woman he has desired all of his life. The brief period of elation associated with Donatella's appearance acts as a catalyst for Stelio's awareness of himself. When she disappears, Stelio abandons himself to his involvement with Foscarina and accepts being loved rather than loving. With acute analysis, the author dissects the sentiments of the two lovers, tracing step-by-step the dissolution of their union. For Stelio, the initial passion rapidly becomes a habit and then degenerates into fatigue and boredom. For Foscarina, it turns into an obsession. Constantly afraid of being abandoned, she oppresses the young man with her neurotic and pathetic attachment; Stelio, aware of his power, plays the game with a hint of cruelty, feeling at the same time a sincere compassion for the vulnerability of the woman. The painful romance is ended by Foscarina, who accepts an acting tour overseas, leaving Stelio to his artistic dreams.

The degenerative process of the love affair is paralleled by the progressive decay of Venice and its surroundings. Wandering in the countryside, Foscarina and Stelio come across the once-splendid Venetian villas on the river Brenta, now abandoned to deterioration and oblivion. In the silent parks, mutilated statues, covered with moss, look with blind eyes at piles of manure and the cultivation of cabbages. Images of death and ruin punctuate the narration, and the city itself seems to decompose among the stagnant waters of the lagoon. The same irreversible process of dissolution seems to supersede love, art, and beauty.

FORSE CHE SI FORSE CHE NO

A noble style, compatible with aristocratic ideals and a mood of slight melancholy, prevails in all of D'Annunzio's novels published between the years 1894 and 1900. His next novel, published in 1910, presents a sharp change of perspective, theme, and style. In *Forse che si forse che no*, D'Annunzio introduces a new type of hero, a young man who embodies the hopes, risks, and excitements proposed by the rising technology. While the protagonists of the other novels were intellectuals absorbed in artistic dreams, Paolo Tarsis is a man of action; he is an airplane pilot and an exalted worshiper of speed and cars. The author's own experiences give substance to this celebration of the machine. In 1909, D'Annunzio, with the American pilot Glenn Curtis and the journalist Luigi Barzini, accomplished the first aeronautic experiment in Italy. This fact, while verifying once more the intrinsic unity of D'Annunzio's life and art, also confirms his avant-garde role in Italian literature: D'Annunzio's revolutionary concept of the hero anticipated the Futurists' celebration of the power of technology in modern society.

In the novel, the engine constitutes for Paolo the way to salvation, the means to overcome the plights of a vulgar existence oppressed by utilitarian interests and temptations of lust. With the two sisters, Isabella and Vana, D'Annunzio reenacts the drama of dual love he had already explored in *The Child of Pleasure* and *The Flame of Life*. Like Elena and Foscarina, Isabella is a sensual and possessive woman who enslaves the man in the vortex of passion; the pure and spiritual Vana belongs instead to the same category of ideal woman as Maria Ferees and Donatella Arvale. Both sisters are in love with Paolo, who is attracted to the sensitive Vana yet cannot resist Isabella's erotic seductions. This favorite theme here assumes a tragic depth. The characters are vividly drawn, and the conflict reaches unprecedented intensity, increasing the tension until tragedy explodes in the final catastrophe. Vana kills herself after revealing to Paolo Isabella's incestuous love with their brother Aldo; Isabella, after a devastating confrontation with Paolo, becomes totally insane. In the anguished scene of Isabella roaming semiconscious in the desert city, the author recalls with documentary simplicity the tragic end of his relationship with Giuseppina Mancini.

The degrading aspects of life lead Paolo to seek purification in an extreme challenge with death. Without a precise destination, he flies with his plane away from reality. After an elated flight in the purity of the sky, the plane crashes on the desert coast of Sardinia. Paolo, injured, crawls painfully to the sea to find solace in the calm waters. In front of him, the sea suggests purification and renewal; behind him, the burning wreck of the plane implies the failure of the engine ideology. The novel ends on this uncertain note, restating the ambiguous meaning of the title: "perhaps yes, perhaps no."

In this novel, D'Annunzio gives a virtuoso performance, mastering all the inspirations and techniques of his previous writings. Powerful descriptions of natural landscapes, erudite evocations, naturalistic motifs, erotic scenes, memories, subtle analysis of sensations—all merge in this prose, unified by the fluidity of the language, constantly sustained by lyric intensity.

LEDA WITHOUT SWAN

Leda Without Swan, a short novel written in 1912 and published in 1916, explores a theme already implicit in the perspective of *Forse che si forse che no*. The ivory tower of art and beauty does not offer a safe refuge from the assaults of life. The vulgar and the sublime, farce and tragedy are tightly intertwined, and it is impossible to isolate the one from the other. Thus, D'Annunzio's meditations on life and art had come to a turning point. The writer who had affirmed that "Il verso e' tutto" (the verse is everything) realized that life cannot be controlled by literature; consequently, he turned to action. D'Annunzio's decision is prefigured in his new perception of the hero-protagonist, as if in Paolo Tarsis he had unconsciously projected his own tension toward his future engagement.

Leda Without Swan was D'Annunzio's last purely fictional prose work. The war absorbed all of his energies, and when he resumed writing, he chose the more direct expression of autobiographical prose. Ettore Paratore suggests an interesting hypothesis to explain the drastic elimination of the third-person narration in D'Annunzio's prose. According to Paratore, the writer, who shared with his generation the cult of the hero, felt compelled, at first, to represent in his fictional writings a hero-protagonist with whom he could identify. After the war, D'Annunzio, who had lived his heroic hour, discarded fiction, now useless, and assumed for himself the role of the protagonist.

Thus, total disillusionment sealed the prestigious adventure of D'Annunzio's life. His art remains as a literary monument to fifty years of European culture. In its variety, D'Annunzio's work mirrors the multiform aspects of the process of renovation that characterizes the passage from the nineteenth to the twentieth century, constituting a timeless testimonial of the Italian contribution to Western literature.

Luisetta Elia Chomel

OTHER MAJOR WORKS

SHORT FICTION: *Terra vergine*, 1882, 1884, 1902; *Il libro della vergini*, 1884; *San Pantaleone*, 1886; *Le novelle della Pescara*, 1892, 1902 (*Tales from My Native Town*, 1920); *Le faville del maglio*, 1924, 1928 (2 volumes).

PLAYS: *Sogno di un mattino di primavera*, pr., pb. 1897 (*The Dream of a Spring Morning*, 1902); *La città morta*, pb. 1898 (*The Dead City*, 1900); *Sogno di un tramonto d'autunno*, pb. 1898 (*The Dream of an Autumn Sunset*, 1904); *La Gioconda*, pr., pb. 1899 (*Gioconda*, 1902); *La gloria*, pr., pb. 1899; *Francesca da Rimini*, pr. 1901 (verse play; English translation, 1902); *La figlia di Jorio*, pr., pb. 1904 (*The Daughter of Jorio*, 1907); *La fiaccola sotto il moggio*, pr., pb. 1905 (verse play); *Più che l'amore*, pr. 1906; *La nave*, pr., pb. 1908 (verse play); *Fedra*, pr., pb. 1909 (verse play); *Le Martyre de Saint Sébastien*, pr., pb. 1911 (music by Claude Debussy, choreography by Ida Rubinstein); *La Chèvrefeuille*, pr. 1913 (*The Honeysuckle*, 1915); *Parisina*, pr., pb. 1913 (music by Pietro Mascagni); *La Pisanelle: Ou, La Mort parfumée*, pr., pb. 1913 (music by Ildebrando Rizzetti and Mascagni).

POETRY: *Primo vere*, 1879, 1880; *Canto novo*, 1882, 1896; *Intermezzo di rime*, 1884, 1896; *San Pantaleone*, 1886; *Isaotta Gùttadauro ed altre poesie*, 1886, 1890; *Elegie romane*, 1892; *Poema paradisiaco—Odi navali*, 1893; *Laudi del cielo del mare della terra e degli eroi*, 1899; *Maia*, 1903; *Alcyone*, 1904 (English translation, 1977); *Elettra*, 1904; *Merope*, 1912; *Canti della guerra latina*, 1914-1918; *Asterope*, 1949; *Le laudi*, 1949 (expanded version of *Laudi del cielo del mare della terra e degli eroi*, 1899; also includes *Maia, Elettra, Alcyone, Merope,* and *Asterope*).

SCREENPLAY: *Cabiria*, 1914.

NONFICTION: *L'armata d'Italia*, 1888; *L'allegoria dell'autunno*, 1895; *Contemplazione della morte*, 1912; *Vite di uomini illustri e di uomini oscuri*, 1913; *La musica di Wagner e la genesi del "Parsifal,"* 1914; *Per la più grande Italia*, 1915; *La penultima ventura*, 1919, 1931 (2 volumes); *Il notturno*, 1921; *Il libro ascetico della giovane Itali*, 1926; *Le cento e cento e cento pagine del libro segreto di Gabriele D'Annunzio tentato di morire*, 1935; *Teneo te, Africa*, 1936; *Solus ad solam*, 1939.

MISCELLANEOUS: *Opera omnia*, 1927-1936; *Tutte le opere*, 1930-1965; *Tutte le opere*, 1931-1937; *Opera complete*, 1941-1943 (41 volumes); *Nocturne, and Five Tales of Love and Death*, 1988.

BIBLIOGRAPHY

Becker, Jared. *Nationalism and Culture: Gabriele D'Annunzio and Italy After the Reisorgimento*. New York: Peter Lang, 1994. Becker studies Italian nationalist culture before the rise of Fascism by focusing on D'Annunzio's political and literary career. He links the author to the proto-Fascist movement, tracing D'Annunzio's impact on racial thinking and the evolution of Italian imperialism. Includes a bibliography and an index.

Bonadeo, Alfredo. *D'Annunzio and the Great War*. Cranbury, N.J.: Associated University Presses, 1995. A scholarly examination of the impact of World War I on D'Annunzio; Bonadeo describes the conflict as the central experience in the writer's life and literature.

Duncan, Derek. "Choice Objects: The Bodies of Gabriele D'Annunzio." In *Reading and Writing Italian Homosexuality: A Case of Possible Difference*. Burlington, Vt.: Ashgate, 2006. Duncan explores the representation of male homosexuality in Italian literature from the 1890's through the 1990's, devoting a chapter to the work of D'Annunzio. The study demonstrates how Italian literature can further the understanding of homosexuality in Italy.

Ledeen, Michael Arthur. *D'Annunzio: The First Duce*. Rev. ed. New Brunswick, N.J.: Transaction Books, 2002. At the end of World War I, D'Annunzio helped capture Fiume (now Rieka, Slovenia) and occupied it for sixteen months. Leeden's book is a history of the occupation, which examines D'Annunzio's political activities and beliefs. Originally published in 1977 under a different title, this reprint contains a new introduction by Leeden.

Schoolfield, George C. *A Baedeker of Decadence: Charting a Literary Fashion, 1884-1927*. New Haven, Conn.: Yale University Press, 2003. Discusses thirty-two works written in more than one dozen languages that characterize the style of literary decadence. Chapter 3 focuses on the writings of D'Annunzio. Includes information about his novels *The Flame of Life, The Intruder, The Child of Pleasure,* and *The Triumph of Death*.

Valesio, Paolo. *Gabriele D'Annunzio: The Dark Flame*. New Haven, Conn.: Yale University Press, 1992. A critical examination of the philosophical and poetic thought in D'Annunzio's works. Valesio concludes that the author's writings were an answer to the philosophy of Friedrich Nietzsche and explains how D'Annunzio was interested in the interaction between sacred language and profane language.

Woodhouse, John Robert. *Gabriele D'Annunzio: Defiant Archangel*. 1998. Reprint. New York: Oxford University Press, 2001. An authoritative biography, in which Woodhouse focuses on D'Annunzio's work and life in the context of Italian culture, theater, and politics and evaluates the writer's lasting influence on Italian culture.

EDWIDGE DANTICAT

Born: Port-au-Prince, Haiti; January 19, 1969

PRINCIPAL LONG FICTION

Breath, Eyes, Memory, 1994
The Farming of Bones, 1998
The Dew Breaker, 2004

OTHER LITERARY FORMS

Edwidge Danticat has published in a wide variety of literary forms. Her early plays were produced while she was still a graduate student at Brown University, and her short-story collection *Krik? Krak!* was published in 1995. Her short stories also have been published in major periodicals and in anthologies. She has edited, written forewords to, and translated the works of other Haitian writers. She has also published novels for children and young adults, including *Anacaona, Golden Flower* (2005).

Danticat's nonfiction works include *After the Dance: A Walk Through Carnival in Jacmel, Haiti* (2002), which examines her first visit to carnival in Haiti, and *Brother, I'm Dying* (2007), an autobiographical account of her elderly uncle's emigration to Miami and his encounter with the U.S. Department of Homeland Security.

ACHIEVEMENTS

Through her award-winning writings, Edwidge Danticat has brought an awareness of Haitian culture and Haitian immigrant experience to readers in the United States. Her short fiction won a Pushcart Prize, and her first novel, *Breath, Eyes, Memory*, led to her selection as one of *Granta*'s Twenty Best Young American Novelists in 1996. The novel also was selected for Oprah Winfrey's Book Club, in 1998. Danticat's short-story collection *Krik? Krak!* was nominated for a National Book Award in 1995. *The Farming of Bones* was written with the help of a Lila Wallace-Reader's Digest Foundation grant and won an American Book Award from the Before Columbus Foundation. *The Dew Breaker* was nominated for a National Book Critics Circle Award in 2004 and a PEN/Faulkner Award in 2005.

Brother, I'm Dying won the National Book Critics Circle Award for autobiography in 2007.

Danticat also has written professionally and worked as an educator. She taught creative writing at New York University and the University of Miami, edited anthologies, and worked with filmmakers on documentaries about Haiti and Haitian art.

Danticat's writings, which have been translated into several languages, form a whole and complement one another to create a larger picture of Haitian and Haitian American experience. She is considered a leading voice for Haitian American women and has been embraced by feminists, the Haitian American community, the literary establishment, and the general reading public.

BIOGRAPHY

Edwidge Danticat was born on January 19, 1969, in Port-au-Prince, Haiti, the eldest child of André Miracin Danticat and Rose Danticat. Her father emigrated to the United States (New York) when Danticat was two years old; her mother emigrated when Danticat was four years old, leaving her and her brother, Eliab, in the care of an aunt and uncle in Haiti. The siblings joined their parents and two New York-born younger brothers in Brooklyn when Danticat was twelve years old. The members of her extended family in Haiti and the stories and traditions that she learned there were major influences on her later writing.

Danticat was raised speaking Haitian Creole, and she was educated in French while in Haiti. As a teenager in Brooklyn, she began to write in English, her third language. She majored in French literature at Barnard College and graduated from there in 1990. Danticat went on to earn a master of fine arts degree in writing from Brown in 1993. A version of her graduate thesis was published as her first novel, *Breath, Eyes, Memory*.

Danticat's second novel, *The Farming of Bones*, a rich and mature work based on the 1937 massacre of Haitians in the Dominican Republic, was published in 1998. *The Farming of Bones* was followed by work in editing, translation, and film. In 2002, Danticat published her first full-length nonfiction work, *After the*

Dance, and a novel for young adults, *Behind the Mountains* (2002). This novel, presented in the form of the diary of a teenage Haitian girl who is reunited with her family in Brooklyn after eight years' separation, is a coming-of-age story reflecting the stress of emigration on families.

Danticat moved from New York to Miami's Little Haiti and was married in 2002 to Faidherbe "Fedo" Boyer, owner of a service offering creole-language translation. She and her husband have one child, daughter Mira Boyer.

ANALYSIS

Edwidge Danticat writes fiction in a realistic style, making the lives of ordinary people central to her plots. Haitian history, culture, and politics merge with compelling storytelling and characters. She is a writer who turns historical events into art. Writing in beautifully crafted English, Danticat succeeds in portraying the poverty, madness, and violence of Haiti while honoring the country's history, traditions, and beauty. The rhythms of Africa, the lyricism of French, and the realism of English come together in Danticat's language and style. Her work connects the great literary themes of the journey, return, and reconciliation with the experiences of the contemporary Haitian American woman.

Edwidge Danticat. (© Arturo Patten)

BREATH, EYES, MEMORY

Like Danticat, the main character of *Breath, Eyes, Memory*, Sophie Caco, is raised by her aunt in Haiti and emigrates to Brooklyn to join her mother when she is twelve years old. The novel's exclusion of the male figures of Danticat's youth—an uncle, a father, and a brother—strengthens the theme of the enduring strength of Haitian women.

The novel opens as Sophie's mother sends her a plane ticket to join her in New York. On her first night in Brooklyn, Sophie discovers that her mother has nightmares that cause her to wake up screaming. Before long, Sophie learns the story of her birth: She is a child of rape. She also learns that her mother and aunt were "tested"

regularly by their own mother, who would insert her fingers into their vaginas to check for "evidence" ensuring their virginity.

Once Sophie turns age eighteen and is ready to start college, she becomes interested in Joseph, a musician who lives next door and who asks her to marry him. When her mother finds out, she begins testing Sophie's virginity weekly. Sophie learns to mentally separate herself from her physical body while the testing occurs. Finally she cannot bear the intrusion any longer and violently mutilates herself to make the testing stop. She then runs to Joseph and insists they marry immediately.

The second half of the book brings together the four generations of women in the Caco family. Sophie brings her infant daughter, Brigitte, to Haiti to visit Tante Atie and Grandmother Ifé as she attempts to reconcile the past with the present. Sophie has been traumatized by her mother's testing, and is unable to enjoy a happy sexual relationship with her husband. Meanwhile, her mother, who has been mentally unstable since being raped, becomes pregnant by her longtime Haitian American lover and contemplates an abortion. In the end, Sophie makes an uneasy peace with her past, but is too late to save her mother, who commits suicide. It is only through the journey back to Haiti for her mother's funeral that Sophie is able to face both the past and the future.

Breath, Eyes, Memory explores the pain, strength, and connection with the land that make up the psyche of the Haitian woman. The novel is dedicated to "the brave women of Haiti, grandmothers, mothers, aunts . . . on this shore and other shores. We have stumbled but we will not fall." The novel, which emphasizes the significance of oral tradition and Haitian and African stories, has been praised by critics for its deep sense of place, its imagery, and its emotional complexity.

THE FARMING OF BONES

Danticat's second novel, *The Farming of Bones*, is a historical novel based on the 1937 massacre of Haitians in the Dominican Republic. Amabelle Désir, the protagonist, was orphaned at the age of eight and is now the maid and companion to the young Dominican wife of an army colonel. Amabelle loves Sebastien, a Haitian cane-cutter. As the story opens, they are preparing to marry.

Amabelle helps deliver her employer's twins. The infant boy is light-skinned, but the tiny girl's skin is dark. The young mother says, rather ingenuously, that she hopes her daughter will not be mistaken for one of Amabelle's people, the Haitians. The scene is set for a tale of prejudice and violence. Haitians are necessary workers on the Dominican side of their common border, but they are persecuted and treated as inferiors.

Amid growing rumors of violence against Haitians, the family doctor urges Amabelle to leave the country. Amabelle convinces Sebastien to join her on a truck leaving for the border. She is delayed by complications with her employer's childbirth, and by the time she reaches the departure rendezvous, the doctor and all the departing Haitians have been arrested.

Amabelle escapes to Haiti by swimming across the same river in which her parents had drowned, but not before being badly beaten by a Dominican mob; several of her companions have been killed. She spends the rest of her life as a seamstress in Cap Haitien, ultimately accepting Sebastien's disappearance, one among so many other Haitians who were lost. The rest of the novel deals with Amabelle's endurance as she lives a hollow, posttraumatic life. Many years later she journeys back to her old town on the Dominican side of the border and meets with her old employer in a sort of reconciliation.

Witnessing, remembering, and naming are among the themes of the novel. Amabelle has been a witness to horrendous events. Many would like to suppress these memories, but Amabelle still remembers. The opening line of *The Farming of Bones* is "His name is Sebastien Onius." Sebastien's fate remains unknown, but his name must be remembered.

The Farming of Bones has been described as "haunting." It is a deeper, more mature work than Danticat's first novel, bringing a piece of Haitian history to the attention of a wider public through the fictional technique of telling one woman's story. The novel shares themes with *Breath, Eyes, Memory* as well, including the posttraumatic stress of a woman ever-connected with Haiti, the journey of reconciliation, and the connections between the old life and the new.

THE DEW BREAKER

The Dew Breaker is a series of short stories connected by one character, a Tonton Macoute, a member of the secret police-militia of Haitian dictator François Duvalier. As the book opens, the reader meets the dew breaker (so named because he attacks before dawn, before the dew breaks) through the eyes of his grown daughter. He is now a barber living in Brooklyn, a man with a terrible scar on his face and nightmares of his life in Haiti. His daughter has been told only that he got the scar in prison in Haiti, but in the opening story he reveals a part of the truth: He worked in the prison. The acts of remembering and telling are as essential to the perpetrator's story in *The Dew Breaker* as they are to those of the victims in *The Farming of Bones*.

The reader meets several characters who have been touched by the dew breaker—his tenants, neighbors, and clients in Brooklyn, and some of his victims. They are the witnesses to the dew breaker's history. The characters range from young to old, educated to uneducated, born in Haiti to born in New York, happy to unhappy, communicative to secretive. By emphasizing individual persons, focusing each chapter of the book on a character, Danticat once more makes the reader understand the complicated, multifaceted story of Haiti through the details of ordinary lives. The picture that emerges is one of interconnectedness of past and present, and the connection of life in Haiti to the many faces of the immigrant experience in New York.

The final story of the novel is the most compelling. The tale focuses on the never-named dew breaker's last act as a Tonton Macoute, his desire to break free of his violent life, and his meeting with the woman who will become his wife (and who will redeem him, as much as redemption is possible). The story is complex, as the dew breaker's actions are neither condoned nor condemned, but presented as another aspect of the reality of Haiti's history.

The Dew Breaker showcases Danticat's skills as a writer and storyteller, her graphic yet understated realism, and her grasp of the madness of life in Haiti. The language is spare and beautiful, in contrast to the ugliness of the story, and the fragmented, nonlinear structure of the novel emphasizes the secrecy and mystery of the dew breaker's life.

Susan Butterworth

OTHER MAJOR WORKS

SHORT FICTION: *Krik? Krak!*, 1995.

PLAYS: *The Creation of Adam*, pr. 1992; *Dreams Like Me*, pr. 1993; *Children of the Sea*, pr. 1997.

NONFICTION: *After the Dance: A Walk Through Carnival in Jacmel, Haiti*, 2002; *Brother, I'm Dying*, 2007.

TRANSLATION: *In the Flicker of an Eyelid*, 2002 (of Jackes Stephen Alexis's novel; with Carrol F. Coates).

CHILDREN'S/YOUNG ADULT LITERATURE: *Behind the Mountains*, 2002; *Anacaona, Golden Flower*, 2005.

EDITED TEXTS: *The Beacon Best of 2000: Great Writing by Women and Men of All Colors and Cultures*, 2000; *The Butterfly's Way: Voices from the Haitian Dyaspora in the United States*, 2001.

BIBLIOGRAPHY

Bell, Madison Smartt. "A Hidden Haitian World." *The New York Review of Books*, July 17, 2008. A leading writer about Haiti discusses Danticat's work, especially *The Farming of Bones*, in the context of other Haitian writers who are lesser known outside Haiti. In discussing the role of translation in bringing Haitian authors to a wider audience, Bell positions Danticat as an exception, a Haitian writer who writes in English.

Bennett, Ian A. B., ed. *Four Writers: Women Writing the Caribbean*. San Juan, P.R.: Sargasso, 2005. Includes an interview with Danticat titled "Haiti: History, Voice, Empowerment" and a review of *The Dew Breaker* among essays on the works of Merle Hodge, Jamaica Kincaid, and Paule Marshall.

Danticat, Edwidge. "An Interview with Edwidge Danticat." Interview by Bonnie Lyons. *Contemporary Literature* 44, no. 2 (Summer, 2003): 181-198. An extensive interview of Danticat in a respected academic journal.

Laforest, Marie-Hélène. *Diasporic Encounters: Remapping the Caribbean*. Naples, Italy: Liguori Editore, 2000. Criticism and interpretation of the works of Danticat, as well as Jamaica Kincaid and Michelle Cliff, by an authority on twentieth century Caribbean literature.

Munro, Martin. *Exile and Post-1946 Haitian Literature: Alexis, Depestre, Ollivier, Laferrière, Danticat*. Liverpool, England: Liverpool University Press, 2007. Discusses the role of writers in exile and their relationship to a Creole identity.

Wucker, Michelle. "Edwidge Danticat: A Voice for the Voiceless." *Américas* 52, no. 3 (May/June, 2000): 40-45. A brief but helpful article examining the empowerment of the oppressed—the voiceless people of the developing world—through Danticat's writings.

ALPHONSE DAUDET

Born: Nîmes, France; May 13, 1840
Died: Paris, France; December 16, 1897

PRINCIPAL LONG FICTION

Le Petit Chose, 1868 (*My Brother Jack*, 1877; also known as *The Little Good-for-Nothing*, 1878)

Aventures prodigieuses de Tartarin de Tarascon, 1872 (*The New Don Quixote*, 1875; also known as *Tartarin of Tarascon*, 1910)

Fromont jeune et Risler aîné, 1874 (*Fromont the Younger and Risler the Elder*, 1880)

Jack, 1876 (English translation, 1877)

Le Nabab, 1877 (*The Nabob*, 1878)

Le Rois en exil, 1879 (*Kings in Exile*, 1880)

Numa Roumestan, 1881 (English translation, 1882)

L'Évangéliste, 1883 (English translation, 1883; also known as *Port Salvation*, 1883)

Sapho, 1884 (*Sappho*, 1886)

Tartarin sur les Alpes, 1885 (*Tartarin on the Alps*, 1887)

L'Immortel, 1888 (*One of the Forty*, 1888)

Port-Tarascon, 1890 (*Port Tarascon*, 1890)

OTHER LITERARY FORMS

Alphonse Daudet (doh-DEH) was one of the most prolific authors of his generation, publishing works in several genres. His first effort was a volume of poems, *Les Amoureuses* (1858, 1873). Throughout his career, Daudet wrote for the theater; his best-known play is *L'Arlésienne* (1872; *The Woman from Arles*, 1930), for which Georges Bizet composed the incidental music. Other plays include *La Dernière Idole* (pr., pb. 1862, with Ernest L'Épine), *L'Oeillet blanc* (pr. 1865, with Ernest Manuell; *The Last Lily*, 1870), *Lise Tavernier* (pr. 1872; English translation, 1890), and stage adaptations of his most successful novels. Before turning to the novel, Daudet composed many short stories, sketches, and vignettes, which eventually were collected in volume form, the two most famous being *Lettres de mon moulin* (1869; *Letters from My Mill*, 1880) and *Contes*

du lundi (1873, 1876; *Monday Tales*, 1927). In addition, he contributed many critical pieces, translations, and topical commentary to newspapers and journals.

ACHIEVEMENTS

The variety and breadth of Alphonse Daudet's literary production have traditionally made it difficult to provide any single, lasting critical evaluation of his works. During his lifetime, Daudet's reputation rested especially on his novels and on his association with the French realists. His personality, particularly his talent as a conversationalist, seems also to have played a role in establishing his popularity among contemporaries. At the height of his career, Daudet overshadowed his friends Gustave Flaubert and Émile Zola, whose works posterity has judged more favorably.

Daudet's fame became international as his works were translated, attracting the attention and praise of such figures as Joseph Conrad and Henry James. Conrad, writing upon Daudet's death, expressed an ambivalence found in many critics. He suggested that the French author's weaknesses stemmed from his strengths: Daudet's tendency toward melodramatic pathos and need to "dot his *i*'s" resulted from a sincere empathy with his characters, and his limited vision, which took in only surface things, was nevertheless accurate in its observations. Conrad admired Daudet not as a great artist but for having accurately reflected humankind's destiny. The fate of Daudet's characters, Conrad suggested, is poignant, intensely interesting, and without consequence.

Like Conrad's, the praise of James, an admired and admiring personal friend of Daudet, is not without its reservations. James did not like Daudet's taste for melodramatic effects and felt that his characters were often psychologically blank. On the other hand, the American greatly esteemed his colleague's talents for narration and pictorial description, and he admired Daudet's poetic touch and sense of beauty. (These last attributes were ones to which Zola objected, as well as to Daudet's empathy with his characters.) James maintained that Daudet's chief virtue lay in his talents as a sensitive and exacting observer.

During the twentieth century, Daudet's reputation has waned, although he remains an important historical figure in the development of the realist movement. In France, his works are still read and studied, especially the short stories and early novels. Outside France, the novels are no longer regarded with much interest, having fallen victim to a taste that prefers characters with more psychological depth and eschews the overt sentimentality typical of Daudet. The short stories have retained their popularity, however, because they illustrate what has been judged the best of Daudet's talent. To paraphrase James's opinion of them, they are graceful in form, light of touch, and alert of observation.

BIOGRAPHY

Alphonse Daudet was the fifth child of Vincent Daudet and Adeline Raynaud, but only the third to survive. Childhood was not a particularly happy time for Daudet. His health was delicate, and the family was forced to live in a state of financial stress, which grew as his father's silk business gradually declined and finally collapsed. In 1849, the family was forced to move to Lyons in search of work.

Daudet's formal schooling took place in Lyons. During this period, he showed some signs of literary talent, but they were not encouraged. A fairly good student when he attended classes, the youngster often chose to explore the city instead. In the spring of 1857, Daudet was taken out of school and sent to Alès in Provence as a study assistant in a secondary school. By November, he had resigned his position and was soon in Paris with his first literary manuscript.

Daudet's older brother, Ernest, gave Daudet shelter and encouragement. In quick order, the young literary hopeful had entered the bohemian circles of the capital, had taken a mistress, and had found a publisher for his poems. Throughout his career, Daudet would draw on his own life for his fiction. His childhood and adolescence are chronicled in his first novel, as is his early life in Paris. Reminiscences of this later period and its bohemian aspects are frequent in many of his works.

The slight reception given to *Les Amoureuses* convinced Daudet that he was not a good poet. He turned to short, topical pieces for Paris journals, and in 1860 was fortunate enough to receive a sinecure as secretary to the duke of Morny, a position he held until the duke's death, five years later. Daudet had been frail since childhood, and health problems began to affect him in the early 1860's. Under doctor's orders, he spent winters in his native Provence and in Algeria and Corsica. During these southern sojourns, he became acquainted with the Provençal poet Frédéric Mistral. In 1862, Daudet's first play, *La Dernière Idole*, written with L'Épine, was successfully produced at the Théâtre de l'Odéon. Daudet began to write for the theater, concentrating on plays for the next ten years. None of his efforts, however, had the success of the first. Even *The Woman from Arles*, Daudet's most familiar play, was a failure when initially staged in 1872. During this same period, he continued to polish his style in journal articles.

In 1867, Daudet married Julie Allard, a published author in her own right; she became his lifelong collaborator. The question of plagiarism has been raised several times in conjunction with Daudet's career: The extent to which Paul Arène contributed to *Letters from My Mill*; the extent to which Allard polished her husband's works; the possible influence of Charles Dickens's novels. The modern consensus is that Daudet unquestionably developed his own ideas and turned to so-called collaborators only for criticism and advice.

Three children were eventually born to Daudet and Allard: Léon, Lucien, and Edmée. The five-year period from 1868 to 1872 was influential in Daudet's career. He wrote what were to remain the most popular of his works—*The Little Good-for-Nothing*, *Letters from My Mill*, *Tartarin of Tarascon*, *Monday Tales*, and *The Woman from Arles*—and experienced the Franco-Prussian War. As a result of his observations during the war, Daudet became attracted to the urban scene. He began to write increasingly about things outside his sphere of experience, extending his concerns to what he conceived as the serious matters of the period.

The ten years that follow the success of *Fromont the Younger and Risler the Elder* in 1874 mark the zenith of Daudet's artistic production. He formed a literary group with Flaubert, Edmond de Goncourt, Ivan Turgenev, and Zola. The maturation of his natural talent for observation was encouraged by his association with this group. His international reputation grew as he published a series of realist novels, most with the subtitle *Moeurs parisiennes* (Parisian manners). Daudet became an important enough figure in French letters that friends and admirers believed he could be elected to the French Academy. His general antipathy toward such organizations, however—and more particularly his refusal to make the traditional round of preelection courtesy calls on members of the academy—prevented Daudet's agreeing even to become a candidate. His health again became a matter of serious concern following a hemorrhage in 1879.

Starting with *L'Évangéliste* in 1883, Daudet gradually abandoned the objective stance of his previous novels in order to expound personal views on various causes—religious fanaticism, unwed cohabitation, divorce, and the shortcomings of the younger generation. The atypical bitterness and pessimism of *One of the Forty* probably reflect Daudet's reaction to his family problems and literary squabbles of the immediately preceding years. During 1886, Daudet's son, Léon, had begun to rebel against his parents' plans for his future, and a temporary rift, of unknown cause, had occurred between Daudet and Allard. In 1887, Daudet had been implicated as intellectual author of the *manifeste des cinq* (the manifesto of five), five young writers' gratuitously insulting protest against Zola's *La Terre* (1887; *Earth*, 1954). Daudet's physical problems worsened during this period as well; doctors had diagnosed locomotor ataxia, an extremely painful illness of muscles and joints that is associated with the third phase of syphilis.

During the last years of Daudet's life, his works showed a decline of his literary talents. His last plays and novels were all too often dull and didactically moralistic. In spite of the difficulties caused by his illness, the author maintained an active schedule, even journeying to England with Allard during a respite in his suffering. He died in Paris on December 16, 1897.

ANALYSIS

Alphonse Daudet's novels do not fit any single mold. Most frequently labeled as realist, their Romantic traits and emotionalism belie such an easy classification. Although Daudet was popularly re-

garded as a regional novelist of Provence, many of his novels center on Paris. Criticism has been directed paradoxically at both his excessive moralizing and his immorality, at his tendency toward pity, and at his lack of sympathy. That his novels should represent such a variety of contradictions can be traced, in great part, to Daudet's changing conception of himself as a novelist. He evolved from a satiric observer to an objective one and eventually to a subjective one. Murray Sachs, in his seminal study of Daudet, *The Career of Alphonse Daudet* (1965), argues convincingly that the French author's unsteady artistic vision was deeply rooted in self-doubt and the consequent inability to adopt any specific position.

Daudet made his novelistic debut with the semi-autobiographical *The Little Good-for-Nothing*, which has become a classic of French literature for its charm and gentle, ironic wit. It is, however, an uneven work. The transformation of the main character, Daniel

Alphonse Daudet. (Library of Congress)

Eyssette, which occurs between the two parts of the novel, is not well motivated, for example, and the structure is very loosely organized. The "oral style" of this work provides an excellent example of Daudet's ability to spin a fine tale, and the second part is of special interest for the preview it contains of the themes and types of characters that are found throughout the author's novels.

TARTARIN OF TARASCON

The satiric humor of *Tartarin of Tarascon* distinguishes it from Daudet's other novels. In this second novel, the author directs good-natured barbs at several targets: the meridional French character, men with a mania for hunting, tourists abroad, and the eternal conflict in us all between heroic ambitions and prosaic, everyday reality.

In form and style, *Tartarin of Tarascon* bears more relationship to the short stories that preceded it than to the novels that followed. Rather than a sustained narrative, it is a series of vignettes. Peaceful, home-loving Tartarin, whose fanciful imagination and penchant for talking take him one step too far, is shamed into embarking for Africa to hunt lions. On this voyage, Tartarin must pass through the clutches of individuals who take advantage of unsuspecting innocents abroad, and the sole big game he encounters is an old and domesticated lion.

The oral quality of Daudet's prose, as in his first novel, leads to a certain looseness of organization, but, at the same time, the distinctive narrative voice and its ironic asides—traditional strategies of the raconteur, which Daudet was to employ in varying degrees during his entire career—early established for Daudet a reputation for charm and wit.

The style of description Daudet employs in *Tartarin of Tarascon* is one that produces a brilliant, rapid sketch by a selective accumulation of colorful details. Description is piled upon description, creating a vivid visual panorama. A note of fantasy often creeps into descriptions, such as in the masterfully comic recounting of the sea voyage to Algiers, in which Tartarin's suffering is largely rendered through the positions assumed by his fez.

Since his creation, Tartarin has acquired the stature of a universal type. He incarnates the very spirit of Provence: talkative to the point of garrulousness and possessing an overactive imagination. Counteracting these qualities are Tartarin's innocence and naïveté. The southern French personality is a frequent theme in Daudet's works; in *Numa Roumestan*, he specifically explores the contrast between the southern and northern French mentalities.

At one point in *Tartarin of Tarascon*, the narrator invokes the spirit of Miguel de Cervantes. It is similar to *Don Quixote de la Mancha* (1605, 1615), especially in the major theme that both authors treat: the conflict between illusion and reality, idealism and pragmatism. Cervantes approached this theme by contrasting two characters; Daudet chose to combine both aspects in a single personality, which carries on a dialogue with itself. Tartarin-Quixote suggests wild adventures and is always transforming reality with his imaginative and idealistic gaze. Tartarin-Sancho never fails to provide pragmatic counterpoint. This incessant conflict between the two voices of Tartarin's personality makes it impossible for him ever to make a clear decision: Tartarin-Quixote sees a miniature baobab in his garden, while Tartarin-Sancho sees a turnip. The narrator offers an explanation for this trait. The Meridional, he claims, does not tell falsehoods, but is misled as to the reality of what he sees. The southern sun, which creates a mirage in which all things appear transformed, is at fault. The southerner is not lying, consequently, because he *believes* that he is telling the truth. He is, however, in almost constant conflict with reality.

Tartarin's seeming inability to distinguish genuine from false makes him vulnerable to confidence games. A certain Prince Gregory of Monténégro befriends Tartarin. This man seems affable and offers assistance on several occasions, until the right moment arrives when he can steal Tartarin's money and belongings. Tartarin becomes involved with a beautiful, sensuous woman whom he believes to be Moorish. In fact, she is a common prostitute from Marseilles who has connived with Prince Gregory to act the part.

Toward the end of the novel, the narrator briefly sketches images of Algeria that Tartarin could have seen had his sight not been set on imaginary lions. A similar charge of misdirection might be leveled at the author as well, both here and in other novels. Starving tribes, ravenous locusts, and colonists sipping absinthe and discussing reform are merely mentioned in passing.

Daudet creates a marvelous surface texture with his all-observing eye, but the consequences of what is described are not investigated.

In any case, the novel's end is comedy, not exposé. Nothing irremediable befalls Tartarin. He survives his predicaments, no worse for the experience. The narrator's irony allows the reader to laugh at Tartarin rather than condemn him. It is a measure of the author's benevolent and essentially comic view in this novel that Tartarin accepts as his the flea-bitten camel who had followed him back to Tarascon. Under the meridional sun, the hunter transforms the camel from a reminder of ignominious experiences into the faithful companion of heroic exploits.

FROMONT THE YOUNGER AND RISLER THE ELDER

The change in style that occurs in *Fromont the Younger and Risler the Elder* reflects two factors: new literary acquaintances among the realist authors and the effect the Franco-Prussian War had on Daudet's habits of observation. His interest was drawn to urban society, and he began to turn away from personally experienced situations in favor of documentation and observation of others. Concurrently, the authorial intrusions that had produced such an atmosphere of intimacy in his early works changed in tonality and frequency. In place of the gentle self-mockery of *The Little Good-for-Nothing* and the equally gentle satiric irony of *Tartarin of Tarascon*, the reader finds a sharper note in the author's voice, one with a moralizing edge to it. The loose, conversational style of earlier works has given way to one that uses a more formal third-person narrative. Whereas direct discourse had largely sufficed to present his characters before, with *Fromont the Younger and Risler the Elder*, Daudet turned to the device of *style indirect libre*, or free indirect discourse, which he handled effectively.

Fromont the Younger and Risler the Elder, whose popular and critical success established Daudet as an important author, traces the social rise and fall of Sidonie Chèbe and the devastating effect she exerts on the lives of the people around her. A child of her Paris environment, she rises through marriage into the comfortable bourgeoisie. Jealous, selfish, greedy, unscrupulous, and shallow, Sidonie unfailingly forces all around her to ruin while she herself manages to survive.

This novel represents a significantly more ambitious work artistically than the previous ones. The chronology is not linear, several subplots arise from the central action, and the number of characters is considerably increased. The first chapter suggests these new directions. instead of beginning Sidonie's story with her birth, as he had done in that of Daniel Eyssette, Daudet first portrays her on the day she marries the aging Risler, a partner in the Fromont manufacturing company. He then uses a lengthy flashback to explain the years preceding that moment. Using a technique often employed in the first act of a play, Daudet, in the first scene of this novel, unites all the important characters in a single moment and previews elements of the plot that are to be developed: the veiled antagonism of certain social classes toward others, the family as a social entity, disappointed marriage plans, personal rivalries and hatreds.

Daudet uses free indirect discourse to render the quality of his characters' thoughts but rarely offers a truly penetrating glimpse into his creations' innermost workings. The narrator suggests that Sidonie acts out of a sense of revenge for childhood disappointments and humiliations. In view of her childhood, this is a likely motivation; it remains, nevertheless, an exterior analysis of the situation and not one coming directly from the character herself.

The characters in *Fromont the Younger and Risler the Elder*, like those in most of Daudet's novels, tend to fall into two groups; the good, who are weak and passive, and the evil, who are strong and domineering. The two men of the novel's title, although honorable, intelligent, and well-meaning, still fall prey to Sidonie. The good woman figure, who often balances that of the temptress in Daudet's works, is here split into two characters, Claire Fromont and Désirée Delobelle. While these two women are far stronger than the men, their strength still proves insufficient against Sidonie's machinations. The goodness and weakness of these characters make them pale beside the unabashed wickedness of Sidonie.

Sidonie is one of a bevy of forceful, rapacious females who populate Daudet's fiction. Even more alluring than they are beautiful, they attract men to inevitable destruction. They impress by the shallowness of their personality. Sidonie is consistently portrayed in terms of her superficiality and fakery. When she must learn a trade, she is apprenticed in a shop that makes costume jewelry. When she attends the theater, it is not the play that interests her but the shiny glitter and false elegance, the costumes and mannerisms of the actresses. When Claire Fromont, the wife of Georges Fromont (who has inherited his family's business), has a baby, Sidonie envies not the child but the vision of young motherhood that Claire projects. Sidonie's soul is compared to a shelf of bric-a-brac—banal, vain, and cluttered, but empty and insignificant.

Sex, not love, causes the downfall of Georges Fromont and Franz Risler, the younger brother of Sidonie's husband, Risler *aîné*. The physical attraction they feel toward Sidonie allows her to seduce them. By means of the two adulterous triangles thus formed, Daudet expresses his concerns for the status of the family unit and for the individual's integrity. Sidonie's first lapse, the seduction of Georges, who is her husband's business partner, raises the question of personal integrity. Sidonie is doubly to blame, because she is unfaithful to not only her husband but also her lover's wife, who has been both friend and benefactor. Discovery of the affair causes the dual rupture of Sidonie's marriage and of her lover's family. Sidonie's selfish personal demands eventually bring the business to the verge of bankruptcy and destroy the business partnership. Her husband's professional honor is salvaged by his personal integrity, but, in the end, Sidonie manages to destroy his personal honor by seducing his younger brother Franz, who is on the verge of denouncing her infidelity. By means of the seduction, Sidonie blackmails Franz into silence. As in the first adultery, a good woman is harmed by Sidonie's actions. Franz had been on the verge of proposing to the ever-faithful and long-suffering Désirée when Sidonie stole him away.

Sidonie's first infidelity was a serious crime, but the second one is graver still, for it constitutes an attack on the family unit, of which Sidonie is a member. Two deaths result: Her husband hangs himself, and the woman who would have been her sister-in-law tries to drown herself in the Seine and eventually dies of a fever resulting from the attempt. The family is destroyed completely.

The most fully drawn character in *Fromont the Younger and Risler the Elder* is Désirée's father, Delobelle, a theatrical has-been. Like the other men in the novel, he is weak, seduced not by Sidonie but by the theater, a repository of illusion. Although never very talented, he maintains that he has "no right to renounce the theater" and spends his days in cafés frequented by theater people, always stylishly attired, waiting for an important role. Daudet condemns the falsity of Delobelle's facade by revealing the actor's means of support. Delobelle and his pretensions are financed by the industry of his wife and daughter, both of whom believe and encourage their man's pretensions, to their own detriment. They remain unhealthily closeted in their tiny apartment; Madame Delobelle is losing her eyesight from so much hard work in badly lit conditions. The family exists by selling the brightly colored, lifelike stuffed birds that Désirée creates to adorn women's hats. There is no part of this family's existence that does not depend on illusions. Even at Désirée's funeral, the mourners, primarily her father, act out their grief. Tartarin-Quixote's illusions were never depicted in so devastating a manner.

Delobelle the actor represents a negative force on the people around him, because he perpetrates illusions that destroy the elements of true value in their lives. Images of the theater surround Sidonie: For her introduction into society, Delobelle shows her how to act and talk; her country house belonged to an actress; and the last glimpse Risler *aîné* has of her is as a performer, under Delobelle's tutelage again, in a *café chantant*. Actresses not only represent persons devoid of meaningful substance but also incarnate the threat to Daudet's men of the degradation and corruption of a bohemian lifestyle. Daniel Eyssette becomes completely despicable when his actress-mistress forces him into a theatrical troupe.

An important presence in *Fromont the Younger and Risler the Elder*, as in a number of Daudet's works, is the city of Paris itself. Paris represents the unhealthy crowding together of human beings deprived of sun and natural surroundings that produces such unnatural creatures as Sidonie Chèbe. Paris signifies the rich, glittering, excitement-filled bohemian life that seduces and corrupts young provincials such as Daniel and Jacques Eyssette, the Risler brothers, and Jean Gaussin of *Sappho*, who go there seeking their fortune. Daudet's talent for description captures a changing organism whose surface, pulsating with a beautifully attractive life force, conceals a dark void capable of destroying the weak and unwary. The last scene of *Fromont the Younger and Risler the Elder* resumes the ambivalence with which Daudet typically portrayed Paris. In a potent image, a splendid early morning view of Paris is tinged with menace: Smoke from the factories replaces the river fog as the city lumbers into action.

As a purely objective realist, Daudet has weaknesses. Fantastic notes appear incongruously, such as in the episode of the Little Blue Man, who stalks the midnight chimneys of Paris to taunt Delobelle, Georges Fromont, and others that their debts are coming due. Traditionally known as a realist who nevertheless subjectively expressed great sympathy for his characters, Daudet often employed a too-direct sentimental appeal, which in his late works verges on bathos. One has only to compare Désirée Delobelle's suicide to that of Emma Bovary to see the extent to which Daudet could vary from the objectivity of the literary group in which he is most frequently classified.

SAPPHO

Sappho is probably Daudet's best-known novel. It marks several changes for the author. While the narrative voice of Daudet's works had always demonstrated a certain tendency toward moralizing observations, in *Sappho* Daudet becomes more openly didactic, a trend that typifies most of his late works. The dedication, "To my sons when they are twenty," suggests the thesis character of this work as well as Daudet's growing concern with what he considered the "lovely oblivious egotism" of the younger generation. Fortunately, the occasional moralistic asides do not detract from the exceptionally fine psychological observations the novel contains.

In contrast to the broad panoramas presented in earlier works, *Sappho* concentrates on only two characters: Jean Gaussin, a young man from Provence who has come to Paris to prepare a diplomatic career, and Fanny Legrand, a Parisian cocotte, or prostitute. The subplots are few and distract very little from the main focus; they reflect back on it, rather, reinforcing it in various ways. In both scope and form, *Sappho* is tighter and more controlled than Daudet's previous novels.

The first chapter is a forceful and immediate entry into the action. In the garden room of a bohemian residence, the two main characters converse for the first time while a costume ball swirls around them. The setting suggests what will follow. This relationship, which receives its initial impulse in a rarefied greenhouse setting, will require a special, artificial environment in which to flourish. A primordial Eve, the bohemian woman represents a threat to the young son of a distinguished family. The exotic costumes and colored lights of the ball create a phantasmagoric atmosphere that foreshadows the nightmarish quality the mature relationship will assume.

Sappho is Daudet's most complete treatment of the relationship between the sexes and the role physical passions play in it. Daudet's weak-willed men are confronted with two female personalities: the sensual, domineering woman and the sweet, passive girl. The men inevitably choose the former, succumbing to their own sensuality while at the same time regretting the loss of the comfortable, nurturing security offered by the latter.

The attraction between Jean and Fanny is founded from the beginning on lust, not love: Jean responds to "a will superior to his, to the impetuous violence of a desire." Imperceptibly, he is drawn into the relationship. Naïvely setting a time limit on the liaison, he imagines that he will simply walk away from Fanny when his career begins in earnest. The couple establishes a household, and being cared for by Fanny, as if they were married, becomes a comfortable habit for Jean.

Daudet convincingly traces the step-by-step effect of this union on Jean's psyche. The more the young man comes to know his mistress, the more he is repulsed both by her and by his own actions. Her promiscuous past, when it comes to light, disgusts him and arouses his jealousy. It also stimulates new and unsuspected sexual desires in him, which Fanny encourages by initiating the young man into new depravations of pleasure. Thus, Jean's passions are attracted by the very things that the rest of his being finds repugnant.

Jean attempts several times to escape this bondage to sexual desire. A return to the salubrious atmosphere of the family home proves futile because, in Fanny's absence, Jean's imagination acts as a powerful aphrodisiac, conjuring up feverish scenes of lovemaking. When, under the sway of his imagination, he responds to his aunt's gesture of maternal tenderness by passionately kissing her bared neck, Jean realizes the terrible extent to which his relationship with his mistress has affected his ability to control his actions and feelings. Hoping to marry a young woman with whom he has fallen in love, Jean leaves Fanny for a time but cannot resist his physical passions when he returns to see her.

The trap is finally released by Fanny herself, but Jean's victory is empty. Although he is free at last from a degrading influence on his life, he is left with a sense of ruin. He has lost the woman he loved and has been disowned by his family.

Minor characters surround Jean and Fanny like so many visions of what their own personalities and relationship might be. Their neighbors have made an honorable but extremely banal marriage of a situation like theirs. The double suicide of an acquaintance and his mistress suggests a parallel with Jean and Fanny. Particularly striking is a dinner at the home of Rosa, Fanny's employer and patroness. Present are Rosa, two other formerly infamous courtesans, and de Potter, Rosa's lover of twenty years. The heavily made-up and bejeweled women, the incongruity of their stylish spring dresses with the infirmities of their old age, and the presence of a mollycoddled pet iguana present Jean with a horror-provoking vision of what his fate could be if he remains with Fanny.

Sappho was more scandalous for its topic than for the author's execution of it. Just as the realism with which the characters are presented in this novel had become psychological, so, too, Daudet's descriptions centered less on reported detail and more on suggestive images. Rather than describe physical aspects of the couple's relationship, Daudet generally implied the tenor of their feelings through the mood of the surroundings. The direct portrayal of a lustful embrace is saved to highlight critical moments: Jean's reaction to his aunt, the provocative surprise of bare flesh as Fanny kisses him good-bye after the separation scene.

To a certain extent, Fanny Legrand is typical of Daudet's domineering, superficial females. The author has also, however, endowed her with positive attributes, such as her generosity and devotion. A dual portrait results—that of seductress and that of a woman painfully coping with approaching old age. Ageless in the first chapter, Fanny has begun to show unmistakable signs of

aging by the end of the novel. Her affair with Jean, who is much younger than she, is a last attempt to appear beautiful and desirable. The intense pain Daudet shows her suffering, after her initial outburst of anger when Jean announces his pending marriage, realistically stems as much from the loss of an object of passion as from the implied revocation of her capacity to be a sexual being. Fanny is finally able to reconcile herself to what must be when she rejects the reprieve that Jean eventually offers her. Although portrayed simplistically at times, to fit didactic aims, Fanny acquires some intriguing psychological complexity by the novel's end.

Daudet's sources of inspiration were two: the society around him and his own life. The rich, colorful texture of his descriptions of both Provence and Paris derived from a remarkable sense of observation. Daudet was particularly adept at rendering surfaces. The world and the values he depicted were primarily those of the bourgeois milieus he himself inhabited, with occasional forays into the artistic Bohemia he had frequented in his youth. The psychological nuances with which he endowed many of his characters surely came from a sensitive analysis of his own personality. Whatever his weaknesses, Daudet was always an exemplary raconteur, an author who has remained famous in his nation's literature for his extraordinary success in transferring oral storytelling techniques to the written page. Generally, Daudet's prestige has waned. Excluded from the primary ranks of his literary generation for excessive sentimentality and exaggerated characterizations, Daudet nevertheless continues to occupy a place among authors of the second rank in importance and esteem.

Joan M. West

OTHER MAJOR WORKS

SHORT FICTION: *Lettres de mon moulin*, 1869 (*Letters from My Mill*, 1880); *Contes du lundi*, 1873, 1876 (*Monday Tales*, 1927); *Les Femmes d'artistes*, 1874 (*Artists' Wives*, 1890); *La Belle Nivernaise: Histoire d'un vieux bateau et de son equipage*, 1886 (*Le Belle Nivernaise: The Story of a Boat and Her Crew, and Other Stories*, 1887); *La Fédor*, 1896 (English translation, 1899); *Le Trésor d'Arlatan*, 1897 (*Arlatan's Treasure*, 1899).

PLAYS: *La Dernière Idole*, pr., pb. 1862 (with Ernest L'Épine); *L'Oeillet blanc*, pr. 1865 (with Ernest

Manuell; *The Last Lily*, 1870); *L'Arlésienne*, pr. 1872 (*The Woman from Arles*, 1930); *Lise Tavernier*, pr. 1872 (English translation, 1890).

POETRY: *Les Amoureuses*, 1858, 1873.

NONFICTION: *Lettres à un absent, Paris, 1870-1871*, 1871 (*Letters to an Absent One*, 1900); *Souvenirs d'un homme de lettres*, 1888 (*Recollections of a Literary Man*, 1889); *Trente Ans de Paris*, 1888 (*Thirty Years of Paris and of My Literary Life*, 1888).

MISCELLANEOUS: *The Complete Works*, 1898-1900 (24 volumes).

BIBLIOGRAPHY

Daudet, Alphonse. *In the Land of Pain*. Edited and translated by Julian Barnes. New York: Alfred A. Knopf, 2003. Daudet's mind continued to think and reflect while tertiary syphilis was attacking his body, and his noted thoughts about the banal as well as the transformative aspects of pain, suffering, and attempts at treatment were published by his son as *La Doulou* (*In the Land of Pain*). Barnes's translation of the book includes a biographical introduction and extensive notes.

Daudet, Léon. *Alphonse Daudet*. Translated by Charles De Kay. Boston: Little, Brown, 1898. Reprint. Eastbourne, England: Gardners Books, 2007. A biography by Daudet's son, a journalist. Also includes the essay "My Brother and I," by Ernest Daudet.

Dobie, Grace Vera. *Alphonse Daudet*. London: Nelson, 1949. This dated literary biography remains a reliable source of facts on the writer's life from a traditional viewpoint. Provides, however, little assessment of his works.

Donaldson-Evans, Mary. *Medical Examinations: Dissecting the Doctor in French Narrative Prose, 1857-1894*. Lincoln: University of Nebraska Press, 2000. An analysis of works by Daudet and other nineteenth century French writers that examines their depictions of medicine and physicians in their writings. Donaldson-Evans argues that these writers were critical of physicians, and this criticism was often tainted by anti-Semitism.

Sachs, Murray. *The Career of Alphonse Daudet: A Critical Study*. Cambridge, Mass.: Harvard University Press, 1965. An excellent, reliable study of the author and his works. Dated but still valuable.

Vitaglione, Daniel. *The Literature of Provence: An Introduction*. Jefferson, N.C.: McFarland, 2000. An introduction to and examination of Provençal literature, focusing on the authors, including Daudet, whose lives and careers have been devoted to depicting the region. Chapter 3 features Daudet.

ROBERTSON DAVIES

Born: Thamesville, Ontario, Canada; August 28, 1913
Died: Toronto, Ontario, Canada; December 2, 1995
Also known as: William Robertson Davies; Samuel Marchbanks

PRINCIPAL LONG FICTION

Tempest-Tost, 1951
Leaven of Malice, 1954
A Mixture of Frailties, 1958
Fifth Business, 1970
The Manticore, 1972
World of Wonders, 1975
The Rebel Angels, 1981
The Deptford Trilogy, 1983 (includes *Fifth Business*, *The Manticore*, and *World of Wonders*)
What's Bred in the Bone, 1985
The Salterton Trilogy, 1986 (includes *Tempest-Tost*, *Leaven of Malice*, and *A Mixture of Frailties*)
The Lyre of Orpheus, 1988

The Cornish Trilogy, 1991 (includes *The Rebel Angels*, *What's Bred in the Bone*, and *The Lyre of Orpheus*)
Murther and Walking Spirits, 1991
The Cunning Man, 1994

OTHER LITERARY FORMS

A dramatist, journalist, and essayist as well as a novelist, Robertson Davies (DAY-veez) wrote plays such as *Fortune, My Foe* (pr. 1948), *A Jig for the Gypsy* (pr., pb. 1954), *Hunting Stuart* (pr. 1955), and dramatizations of some of his novels; histories (notably *Shakespeare's Boy Actors*, 1939); numerous newspaper commentaries and columns (often for the *Peterborough Examiner* and the *Toronto Star*); and essays of all kinds, including many for volume 6 (covering the years 1750-1880) of *The Revels History of Drama in English*. Other occasional writings by Davies are collected in *The Merry Heart: Reflections on Reading, Writing, and the World of Books* (1997). A volume of his letters, titled *"For Your Eyes Alone": Letters, 1976-1995*, was published in 1999.

ACHIEVEMENTS

Perhaps the foremost Canadian man of letters of his generation, Robertson Davies achieved virtually every literary distinction his country offers, including the Governor-General's Award for fiction and fellowship in the Royal Society of Literature. He was the first Canadian honorary member of the American Academy and Institute of Arts and Letters. Professor of English at the University of Toronto, he held the Edgar Stone Lectureship in Dramatic Literature (as its first recipient); he was also the founding master of Massey College.

BIOGRAPHY

William Robertson Davies was born on August 28, 1913, into a family of enterprising and individualistic Canadian entrepreneurs and newspaper publishers. The third child of Rupert and Florence MacKay Davies was to inherit the verbal skills and high-energy work ethic of his parents, along with their Welsh temperament. Receiving a cultural education that included frequent visits to the opera and theater, balanced with regular exposure to church music, Davies learned to love words very early

from the family habit of reading aloud. He learned to read at the age of six and promptly began consuming the classics as well as popular newspaper and magazine fare.

When his family moved to Renfrew, Ontario, young Davies was forced to attend a country grade school, where ruffians and jealous peers made his quiet, bookish life miserable. These times were to be recalled in some of his best fiction. Travel with his father, in Europe as well as throughout Canada, convinced him of the importance of a British education; after undergraduate work at Upper Canada College, Davies spent 1932 to 1938 at Queen's College and Oxford University, reading literature, drama, and history. A predilection for acting led him to the Old Vic (1938-1939), until World War II sent him back to Canada to begin a journalistic career, following his father's financial interests. By 1942 he was editor of the *Peterborough Examiner*, a man of great interests and broad education trapped by circumstance in a fairly provincial Canadian town, forced to deal daily with the pedestrian affairs of journalism. Far from fading into the woods, however, he found his creative voice and energy in the contradiction and began a fruitful writing career.

At the center of Davies' strange reconciliation of apparent opposites was his ability to live moderately, sanely, while expressing his outrageous imagination in writing. He took on the journalistic persona of Samuel Marchbanks, an outspoken man of letters, at once the antithesis and the complement of Davies the man. So successful was his ability to generate a reality for Marchbanks that for eleven years the Marchbanks columns of the *Peterborough Examiner* were syndicated in Canadian papers.

Responding to his love of theater, Davies wrote several plays as well during this period, notably *Eros at Breakfast* (pr. 1948) and *Fortune, My Foe*. He was also instrumental in founding, with Sir Tyrone Guthrie, the Shakespeare Festival in Stratford, Ontario. Although his plays were only modestly successful outside Canada, in his homeland he is highly respected for his original stage works and his adaptations of classics such as Ben Jonson's *Bartholomew Fair* (pr. 1614).

Davies underwent a major career change in 1962, when he joined the faculty of Trinity College, University of Toronto, first as a visiting professor and then, in 1967, as founding master of Massey College, a nonteaching graduate college in the University of Toronto. While his new duties meant giving up his editorship (his father died in 1967, and the business was sold), the change of career gave Davies time to begin a long and full fiction-writing career while continuing his stage and essay work. He had become disenchanted with theater as a full-bodied medium when his stage adaptation of *Leaven of Malice* failed to enjoy a long run on Broadway in 1960. He turned to the novel form as more independent of outside interference and the uncertain financial fortunes of the stage. What became *The Salterton Trilogy* demonstrated the transition in Davies' own life by concentrating on the backstage events, mostly humorous, of amateur and professional acting companies trying to put on classic and modern plays. However successful these novels were, it remained for Davies to find in his next trilogy a more suitable setting and cast of characters to inform his novels.

Davies' most interesting and, according to many critics, most long-lasting writing began with his 1970 publication of the novel *Fifth Business*, the first of the works that would become *The Deptford Trilogy*, to be continued with *The Manticore* in 1972 and concluded with *World of Wonders* in 1975. These novels combined Davies' previous experiences in rural Canada and cosmopolitan Europe, his familiarity with academic circles, and his love of the world of theater to bring to life a series of characters that would appear repeatedly in his subsequent fiction.

Davies retired from his post at Massey College in 1981, but he continued to live and write in Toronto. During the next ten years of his academic life, a second trilogy appeared, examining in depth a Canadian family so similar to his own that some early critics considered it an autobiographical series. *The Rebel Angels* (1981) and *What's Bred in the Bone* (1985) were followed by *The Lyre of Orpheus* in 1988. These works continued in fresh perspective the lives and adventures of characters very like those in the previous trilogy. Many readers of Davies' work enjoy his habit of moving his characters from peripheral to central positions in a retrospective reintroduction of their favorite narratives, so that characters sometimes serve support roles and sometimes take

Robertson Davies. (© Jerry Bauer)

center stage in exciting, humorous, and erudite stories that can be read separately, in any order, or enjoyed in their entirety.

ANALYSIS

At the core of Robertson Davies' novels is a sense of humor that reduces pompous institutional values to a refreshing individuality. Interplays of the formal with the specific—officious academia versus lovable satyr-professor, self-important charitable foundation versus reclusive forger-artist, elaborately constructed "magic" paraphernalia versus truly gifted magician, Viennese Jungian psychology versus painfully intimate self-exploration—are the pairings that make the novels come alive. The theatrical metaphors from his early work come forward whenever Davies' novels are to be described: Behind the scenes, his cast of characters perform their roles even more effectively than on the stage of their professional lives, but Davies, often in his fictive personas of Dunstan Ramsay and, in the later trilogy, Simon Darcourt, is there to unmask them and make them laugh at themselves.

Davies perceives a basic duality in human nature and exploits the tensions between the two sides to produce novelistic excitement and philosophical insight. Another way to clarify the duality of Davies' view is to make use of the central "grid" in *The Manticore*: reason versus feeling. Giving both of the main characters' human impulses their proper due, Davies finds the fissure in their marriage and wedges his humor into the gap, penetrating the surface of their union to reveal the weakness of one and the domination of the other. The "gypsy" in each individual (a subject at the center of *The Rebel Angels*) must be answered to, or else an imbalance will turn life sour. For David Staunton in *The Manticore*, reason has overpowered his ability to feel; for Parlabane in *The Rebel Angels*, feelings and emotions have made his intellectual life a hollow pretense. Davies finds and repairs the imbalances, giving to each novel a closure of reconciliation between feeling and reason. Thus, despite the intertwining of characters and incidents, providing a "perspectivist," kaleidoscopic view of both, each novel stands apart, complete, while at the same time the richness of the situations promises more.

Coupled with Davies' vast erudition and education (he has been called a "polymath" by more than one critic) is a fine sense of how the English language works; these qualities combined provide both the broad stroke and the marvelous attention to detail that make his novels successful. One unusual feature of all of his work is the very high level of education enjoyed by virtually all the characters, an intellectual mise-en-scène that allows the reader and Davies to share all kinds of sophisticated observations. The title *Rebel Angels* subtly suggests its subject, François Rabelais; *What's Bred in the Bone* echoes the "paleopsychology" of a character in *The Rebel Angels*; and the character Magnus prepares the reader for the fact that another character, Pargetter, will be called a "Magus" in a subsequent novel. The puns and plays on words are polylingual and are never spelled out (the character names Parlabane, Cruikshank, and Magnus Eisengrim are examples ready to hand); Davies does not patronize his readers. Ramsay lost his leg in World

War II; he may be David Staunton's biological father, having been in love with Leola Cruikshank Staunton (her maiden name means "crooked leg"). These few examples point to a general trend: metaphor before bald statement, reflected heat before direct blast, euphemism before naked statement. When Dr. von Haller refers to a person's age as "a psalmist's span," she makes no apologies. Full appreciation of what Davies is getting at in his work requires of the reader a fairly comprehensive cultural literacy.

The earthiness of real life is never lost among the intellectual conceits, however: A plot line of one entire novel deals with the quality of dung to improve the tonal qualities of stringed instruments. When the time is right for describing sexual aberrations or cadaverish details, Davies is ready. It is true that Ramsay's vast knowledge of arts and letters (Davies himself was famous among his colleagues for extemporaneous but highly informative lectures on obscure subjects of every kind) gives glimpses, if not insights, into such a broad range of cultures and historical periods that Davies' full canon can almost serve as a checklist of gaps in the reader's erudition. Still, as Ramsay himself points out while speaking of his own book in *World of Wonders*, Davies' novels are "readable by the educated, but not rebuffing to somebody who simply wanted a lively, spicy tale."

FIFTH BUSINESS

Dunstan Ramsay is clearly the authorial persona in the Deptford novels, as actor and audience; whether taking part in the plot directly, as in *Fifth Business*, or as observer and narrator in *World of Wonders*, or as a coincidental facilitator in *The Manticore*, Ramsay emerges as having the closest to Davies' own fine sense of the observably ridiculous, along with a forgiving spirit that makes Davies' work uplifting and lighthearted, despite its relentless examination and criticism of everything spurious and mediocre in the human spirit. Simon Darcourt, a priest and academician in the later novels, is yet another Davies persona, recognizable by his penetration into (and forgiveness of) the foibles of the rest of the characters.

Fifth Business, the first novel of what became *The Deptford Trilogy*, has been cited by many critics as the real beginning of Davies' major work, a "miracle of art." The novel marks Davies' first real "thickening" of plots and details, and a list of the subjects dealt with reads like a tally sheet of Western civilization's accomplishments to date: saints' lives, psychology, mythology, folk art, place-names and family lineages, magic arts, medieval brazen heads and other tricks of the trade, and the complex workings of nineteenth century theater. It is the autobiography of Dunstan Ramsay himself, at age seventy, looking backward at the impulses that formed his life and character, beginning with an accident in a winter snowball fight in which a passerby, Mary Dempster, was injured, causing the premature birth of her son.

The "friend/enemy" relationship between Ramsay and Boy Staunton (intended target and careless launcher, respectively) is the singular metaphor for Davies' pursuit of the dichotomy in every person: a drive for worldly success foiled by a need for spiritual or aesthetic grace. For Ramsay, the reverse is true: His life is so affected by the snowball-throwing incident that he never succumbs to merely material reward but spends his life in self-examination. In this novel, all the major characters for the next two are introduced in some form or another: David Staunton (Boy's son) is the central figure in *The Manticore*; the stunted child of Mary Dempster, now Magnus Eisengrim, centers the third novel, *World of Wonders*.

THE MANTICORE

The Manticore, an examination of Jungian psychology, serves as *dramatis personae* for all Davies' novels: The archetypes appear again and again in various disguises, from the shadow figure to the father figure to the hero, from the anima to all of its component parts. David Staunton's analyst, Dr. von Haller, a woman truly balanced between reason and feelings, helps him find the missing part of his life and represents the Davies character that appears in every novel: the grown woman, wise, often not beautiful but very attractive nevertheless, who leads the central figure past his conventional assumptions about all women into a deeper, more substantive appreciation of the Eternally Feminine.

As Staunton describes the death of his "swordsman" father, Boy Staunton (the name's significance becomes clearer as the analysis progresses), he learns to recognize all sorts of shadows in his past that have led to his celibacy, his indifference to feelings, and his essential loneliness. Ramsay was one of David's tutors, and their reunion at the novel's end, also in the presence of Magnus

Eisengrim and Liesl Naegeli, an "ogress," is another example of the sense of reconciliation and closure that each novel offers, despite the interrelationship of the trilogies themselves. The reader is treated to a full-length portrait of the major characters and then finds them, like old friends, reappearing in other places, other novels, so that the reader is in fact dwelling in the same regions as the heroes of the books. It is a reassuring and comforting realization that, once a book is finished, the characters will be back to reacquaint themselves with the reader in future volumes.

WORLD OF WONDERS

World of Wonders follows Magnus's career up to the point at which Ramsay is asked to write a fictional autobiography of Magnus as part of a large commercial enterprise that includes a film on the life of Harry Houdini, with Magnus in the title role. The central metaphor is once again a duality, the division of illusion and reality, for Magnus's real genius lies not in the tricks of the trade but in a spiritual gift, given to him at his unusual birth. Now the story of Ramsay and Boy Staunton and Mary Dempster is told from yet another perspective, that of the putative victim, enriched beyond measure by the accident of the stone-filled snowball. The stone inside the snowball, like the knives of Spanish literature, is almost alive, with a mind and a direction all its own; Boy Staunton's body will be found in the river with the stone in his mouth; at the end of *The Manticore*, Ramsay had tossed the stone down a mountain, remarking almost in passing, "I hope it didn't hit anybody." In this way Davies looks at the cause-effect duality apparently at work on the plane of reality, reflecting a larger karmic cause-effect relationship on the spiritual plane. Magnus's life and success, unforeseen at his birth, tell the listeners (they gather each night to continue the story) that human beings can neither foresee nor alter the future by conscious acts, but they affect the future nevertheless by their own facticity. That is the "world of wonders" the book's title introduces.

THE REBEL ANGELS

A special and very important motif for Davies is the mentor-protégé relationship, which appears in every novel in some form or another. *The Rebel Angels*, which begins a new trilogy, is an example. The protagonists are three professors who have been asked to oversee the distribution of a vast collection of art and manuscripts that has been left to a charitable foundation by Francis Cornish (the subject of the next novel in the trilogy, *What's Bred in the Bone*). Their contentions and agreements form the framework for a deeper discussion of the nature of human achievement. Simon Darcourt is one of the executors, the kindest and broadest in his interests; he shares the narration with his gifted student Maria Magdalena Theotoky, a young woman about to venture on the same academic, "reasoned" path as her tutors. Her Gypsy mother insists, however, on a larger image of her life, and in the reexamination of her values, Maria discovers the Rabelaisian side of herself in the person of Parlabane, a dissolute, perverted, and most warmhearted individual, a murderer and a suicide, who gives her a great gift in his dying wish.

At least three plots join and part as the book progresses, even the two narrative voices alternating as the story unfolds. Parlabane is a modern manifestation of the seventeenth century Rabelais, Maria's dissertation topic and the author of three valuable letters stolen by one of the three executors. A thoroughly unlikable character named McVarish serves as a foil to the larger, more humanitarian lives of the other professors and the idealized free-enterprise benefactor, Arthur Cornish. Cornish eventually marries Maria, but not before her idol, Clement Hollier, almost absentmindedly has his way with her on the office couch (a false start in the mentor-protégé relationship). In the process of telling four or five stories at once, Davies manages to give the reader a tour of dozens of cultural worlds, including the care and feeding of rare violins, the cataloging of art collections, the literary secrets of seventeenth century letter writers, the habits of obscure monastic cults, and the fine points of academic infighting.

WHAT'S BRED IN THE BONE

The second novel in the trilogy, *What's Bred in the Bone*, moves backward one generation, to Canada and Europe just before World War II. Francis Cornish, a member of the Cornish clan, recognizably similar to but different from the Staunton clan, is the scion of a rich Canadian entrepreneur. Brought up both Catholic and Protestant (like Davies), Francis combines a quiet talent for drawing with an uncanny ability to imitate the brushstrokes of the masters. A series of circumstances finds

him forging paintings in a German castle, painting his own personal life story into large canvases (a metaphor for Davies' own work), and spying for the British government by counting the clacks of the passing Nazi trains on their way to concentration camps. This mild form of spying is inherited from his military father, in the mold of Boy Staunton, a great diplomatic success but something of a failure as a nurturing parent and an aesthetic model.

Most valuable to scholars seeking biographical references are Davies' descriptions of Francis's childhood in rural Canada, especially his gradual, painful understanding about class differences and the sexual indiscretions of adults (a theme examined more fully in *The Manticore*). Simon Darcourt, academic-priest, has been commissioned to write a biography of Francis Cornish but has turned up some questionable material about Cornish's European experiences: He may have forged some drawings that are now in the possession of a prestigious public museum. Davies uses the device of splitting the narration (as he does in *The Rebel Angels*) between two supernatural beings, one Zadkiel, the "angel of biography," and the other the Daimon Maimas, a dark but energetic manifestation of the artistic conscience. Their otherworldly debate as Cornish's story unfolds allows Davies to investigate once again the necessity of balancing human dualities for sanity and satisfaction.

THE LYRE OF ORPHEUS

The Lyre of Orpheus finds a musical theme for Davies, a lost and incomplete musical treatment of the Arthurian legend by E. T. A. Hoffmann. The music student Hulda, indirectly under Simon Darcourt's tutelage, decides to complete the opera, and Darcourt is asked to supply a text—his choice of Sir Walter Scott's poetic rendition of the legend makes for an excellent example of how Davies winds the arts around themselves into a whole act of achievement. Here the mentor-protégé relationship is developed fully, not only between the narrator and Hulda but also between the student and a visiting composer-conductor, Gunilla, one of Davies' strong, ugly (but attractive), mature women. The "ominous" Professor Pfeiffer, called in as external examiner to Hulda's examination, provides Davies with an opportunity to lampoon all that is disagreeable about certain academics of his acquaintance.

MURTHER AND WALKING SPIRITS *and* THE CUNNING MAN

Two final novels complete Davies' oeuvre. Both are set in present-day Toronto; each story is complete and unrelated to the other, though the main character in the first is the son of a friend of characters in the second, and a third novel could have conceivably united them into a trilogy.

Murther and Walking Spirits is a technical rarity in that the point-of-view character, Conor Gilmartin, is dead before the story begins, murdered by his wife's lover. He stalks the murderer to the Toronto Film Festival, where he views all the films in the annual competition but sees a series that is uniquely his: film after film showing the story of his family, from their Welsh roots to their arrival in Canada after the American Revolution through their integration into the new society. After his "personal film festival" is over, Gilmartin has the satisfaction of watching his murderer exposed by the priest from whom he seeks absolution. The priest, a Roman Catholic on the faculty of the University of Toronto, belongs to a group of intermediaries between the physical and spiritual worlds who appear in all of Davies' novels. It is fitting, then, that his last novel, *The Cunning Man*, concerns the mysteries of faith.

The Cunning Man tells the story of Jonathan Hullah, a doctor who witnessed the death, possibly the murder, of an Anglican priest at an Easter service in 1951. As the doctor discusses the events with a journalist, he reflects on his long life. He remembers the medicine woman who saved his life when he was deathly ill as a child in a remote wilderness outpost and who inspired his love of medicine. He recalls his education and his first years in the city, when he became involved in the parish where the strange events took place. His "cunning" is the semisupernatural knowledge that enables him to participate in the real world of money-grubbing, fame-seeking people while serving as a force for good.

Thomas J. Taylor
Updated by Thomas Willard

OTHER MAJOR WORKS

SHORT FICTION: *High Spirits*, 1982.

PLAYS: *Overlaid*, pr. 1947 (one act); *At the Gates of the Righteous*, pr. 1948; *Eros at Breakfast*, pr. 1948;

Fortune, My Foe, pr. 1948; *Hope Deferred*, pr. 1948; *The Voice of the People*, pr. 1948; *Eros at Breakfast, and Other Plays*, 1949 (includes *Hope Deferred, Overlaid, At the Gates of the Righteous*, and *The Voice of the People*); *At My Heart's Core*, pr., pb. 1950; *King Phoenix*, pr. 1950; *A Masque of Aesop*, pr., pb. 1952; *A Jig for the Gypsy*, pr., pb. 1954 (broadcast and staged); *Hunting Stuart*, pr. 1955; *Love and Libel: Or, The Ogre of the Provincial World*, pr., pb. 1960 (adaptation of his novel *Leaven of Malice*); *A Masque of Mr. Punch*, pr. 1962; *Hunting Stuart, and Other Plays*, 1972 (includes *King Phoenix* and *General Confession*); *Question Time*, pr., pb. 1975.

TELEPLAY: *Fortune, My Foe*, 1953 (adaptation of his play).

NONFICTION: *Shakespeare's Boy Actors*, 1939; *Shakespeare for Younger Players: A Junior Course*, 1942; *The Diary of Samuel Marchbanks*, 1947; *The Table Talk of Samuel Marchbanks*, 1949; *Renown at Stratford: A Record of the Shakespeare Festival in Canada, 1953*, 1953 (with Tyrone Guthrie); *Twice Have the Trumpets Sounded: A Record of the Stratford Shakespearean Festival in Canada, 1954*, 1954 (with Guthrie); *Thrice the Brinded Cat Hath Mew'd: A Record of the Stratford Shakespearean Festival in Canada, 1955*, 1955 (with Guthrie); *A Voice from the Attic*, 1960; *The Personal Art: Reading to Good Purpose*, 1961; *Marchbanks' Almanack*, 1967; *Stephen Leacock: Feast of Stephen*, 1970; *One Half of Robertson Davies*, 1977; *The Enthusiasms of Robertson Davies*, 1979; *The Well-Tempered Critic*, 1981; *Reading and Writing*, 1993; *Happy Alchemy: On the Pleasures of Music and the Theatre*, 1997; *The Merry Heart: Reflections on Reading, Writing, and the World of Books*, 1997; *"For Your Eyes Alone": Letters, 1976-1995*, 1999.

BIBLIOGRAPHY

Cameron, Elspeth, ed. *Robertson Davies: An Appreciation*. New York: Broadview Press, 1991. Collection of essays presents criticism and interpretations of Davies' life and works, including many of his novels. Also includes an interview with Davies and a bibliography.

Grant, Judith Skelton. *Robertson Davies: Man of Myth*. New York: Viking Press, 1994. Authorized biography covers all but the last year of Davies' life. Provides critical commentary on Davies' novels as well as information on his dealings with publishers.

Journal of Canadian Studies 12 (February, 1977). This special issue, edited by Ralph H. Heintzman, is devoted to criticism of Davies' work. Six essays examine *The Deptford Trilogy*. Includes a valuable Davies log of writing and important events.

La Bossière, Camille R., and Linda Morra, eds. *Robertson Davies: A Mingling of Contrarieties*. Ottawa: University of Ottawa Press, 2001. Collection of essays reassesses Davies' works, including discussions of his use of masks, humor, and doubles. Some of the essays analyze the Salterton novels, *The Deptford Trilogy*, *World of Wonders*, and *What's Bred in the Bone*.

Lams, Victor J. *Robertson Davies's "Cornish Trilogy": A Reader's Guide*. New York: Peter Lang, 2008. Examines each of the three books in the trilogy—*The Rebel Angels*, *What's Bred in the Bone*, and *The Lyre of Orpheus*—addressing the plots, characters, and other elements of the works.

Lawrence, Robert G., and Samuel L. Macey, eds. *Studies in Robertson Davies' "Deptford Trilogy."* Victoria, B.C.: English Literary Studies, University of Victoria, 1980. Davies introduces this collection with a personal retrospective of the creative impulses that resulted in *The Deptford Trilogy*. The studies range from traditional historical criticism to folklore backgrounds to Jungian analysis to examinations of law. An opening article surveying *The Salterton Trilogy* brings the reader up to the Deptford novels.

Little, Dave. *Catching the Wind: The Religious Vision of Robertson Davies*. Toronto, Ont.: ECW Press, 1996. Discusses an important theme in Davies' fiction: "the search for the self as a religious journey." Includes a helpful list of biblical allusions in the novels through *Murther and Walking Spirits*.

Monk, Patricia. *The Smaller Infinity: The Jungian Self in the Novels of Robertson Davies*. Toronto, Ont.: University of Toronto Press, 1982. One of the most thorough book-length studies of Jungian influences in all of Davies' writing, but especially concentrating on *The Manticore*. Finds the archetypal constructions of the characters a more overpowering leitmotif than Davies' own autobiographical renditions; systematizes *The Deptford Trilogy*'s characters around the traditional figures of Jungian psychology.

Peterman, Michael. *Robertson Davies*. Boston: Twayne, 1986. Devote four chapters to Davies' careers in journalism and drama before discussing the Salterton novels, *The Deptford Trilogy*, and *The Rebel Angels*. Explains well the importance of Davies' Canadian birth and childhood. Includes bibliography and index.

Woodcock, George. "A Cycle Completed: The Nine Novels of Robertson Davies." *Canadian Literature* 126 (Autumn, 1990): 33-48. Provides a good overview of Davies' major literary contribution. Argues that Davies' use of "traditional" forms is "calming and comforting" in an otherwise "permissive" literary world.